*COLLEGE SERIES OF LATIN AUTHORS*

THE

# ODES AND EPODES

OF

# HORACE

EDITED, WITH INTRODUCTION AND NOTES,

BY

CLEMENT LAWRENCE SMITH
POPE PROFESSOR OF LATIN IN HARVARD UNIVERSITY



*SECOND EDITION*

GINN & COMPANY
BOSTON · NEW YORK · CHICAGO · LONDON

---



---



711.10

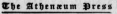

The Athenæum Press
GINN & COMPANY · PROPRIETORS · BOSTON · U.S.A.

# PREFACE.

In preparing this edition of the Odes and Epodes I have borne in mind the fact that the reading of these poems presents, at least to the American student, the first, as well as the best, opportunity for the discriminating study of Latin poetic usage in syntax and diction. Vergil and Ovid regularly precede Horace in our Latin course, but they come at a stage at which the pupil's faculties are so fully occupied in following the verses intelligently, that although these poets are undoubtedly read with pleasure by many pupils, anything beyond a rather dim appreciation of the quality and flavor of their poetry is hardly to be expected. With Horace the case is quite different. Horace is reserved for the college course, often for the second year of the course; and at that stage the student should have acquired by practice in reading and writing such mastery of Latin prose idiom that the peculiarities of poetic language ought to arouse attention and interest. It has been usual for editors of Horace to notice the more striking of these peculiarities in the places where they occur. It has seemed to me better to treat the whole subject together in the Introduction, so that the various usages may be seen in their relations to one another, while their exemplification in any particular passage can be pointed out by a simple reference in the notes. I have desired, in presenting the matter in this form, to leave the teacher free to use it in whatever way he deems best, and according to his estimate of its importance. In my own judgment it is of vital importance; for although the appreciation of poetry must in the last resort be a matter of taste and feeling, beyond the reach of categorical statement, yet an intelligent study of the poet's language and literary method is the only adequate basis for such appreciation.

In preparing this exposition I have had the benefit of a number of monographs in which certain parts of the subject are treated in a more or less thorough manner, but no previous work dealing with the whole subject is known to me. I am sensible of the imperfections which are inevitable in a first attempt of this kind, and shall welcome friendly suggestions from any quarter for its improvement. Two things ought perhaps to be said: While much, if not most, of my statement applies to other poets of the Augustan and subsequent periods, I have made it with sole reference to Horace; and in the absence of any sharp line of division between the usage of prose and of poetry I have in some cases purposely included a recognized prose construction in order to set the poetic usage in a clearer light. For constructions not explained in the Introduction occasional reference is made in the notes to grammars in current use, chiefly to Madvig's, Roby's, and Allen and Greenough's. For the last named the abbreviation 'Gr.' is used.

The text of Horace is open in a number of places to the grave suspicion, which sometimes approaches certainty, of interpolation. In the absence, however, of any general agreement among scholars in condemning definite passages, I have not thought it desirable, in an edition of this kind, to bracket verses or strophes which appear to me suspicious or spurious, or to vex college students with critical discussions where they could be avoided. The text has been constituted in accordance with the principles stated in § 39 of the Introduction. A list of the most important variants has been given in an appendix, where I have adopted, with some modifications, the convenient method of indicating the comparative weight of MS. authority used by Professor Arthur Palmer in his edition of the Satires.

In printing the poems I have adhered to the traditional arrangement, which (not without some reason) has relegated the Epodes to the position of a sort of appendix to the Odes; but I cannot do so without advising every one who wishes to become acquainted with Horace, as well as with his poetry, to follow the chronological order and read the Epodes first.

For the interpretation and illustration of the poems I have availed myself freely of the resources which have been accumulated by many generations of Horatian scholars and are accessible in the larger editions and elsewhere. This general acknowledgment covers a great number of suggestions adopted from various sources, for which particular credit could not well be given, even when the author could be determined, in a book of this kind. Especial mention ought to be made, however, of the editions of Orelli (ed.[4] by Hirschfelder) and Wickham, and particularly of the stimulating and suggestive commentary of Kiessling, from all of which I have derived much assistance. In preparing the life of the poet, I have found, next to the material collected in the Prolegomena of the Orelli edition, Sellar's *Horace and the Elegiac Poets* the most useful of the works I have consulted.

I take this opportunity also to express my obligations to my friends and colleagues: to Professors Lane, Greenough, and Morgan, from each of whom I have received useful advice and criticism in preparing the Introduction; and especially to Professor Allen, who has kindly read a large part of both Introduction and Commentary, as they were passing through the press, and aided me with many valuable suggestions.

C. L. S.

CAMBRIDGE, MASSACHUSETTS,
September 15, 1894.

---

SINCE the first edition was issued, such errors as have come to my notice have been corrected in the plates. In preparing a second edition I have carefully weighed the criticisms with which I have been favored by personal friends and friendly reviewers, with the result that a number of notes have been rewritten. The distinctive feature of this edition, however, is the series of indexes, by which I trust the usefulness of the book will be materially enhanced.

C. L. S.

CAMBRIDGE, September 20, 1902.

# INTRODUCTION.

## I. LIFE AND WRITINGS.

### Sources.

**1.** Our knowledge of the facts of Horace's life is derived in part from a biography, appended to certain manuscripts of his poems, which has been shown by conclusive evidence to be, in substance, the life of the poet which Suetonius wrote in his encyclopedic work, *De Viris Illustribus*. There are briefer lives in some of the other manuscripts, and scattered notices in the scholia. But all these sources afford — beyond a few dates and facts — little information that we do not already possess, in fuller and more authentic form, in the poet's own writings. To these we must go for an adequate understanding of his mind and character. In the Satires and Epistles, and to a less degree in the Epodes, Horace takes the reader into his confidence and speaks of his circumstances and feelings with singular frankness. The Odes, too, contain much biographical material, but it is of a kind that must be used with caution. As a poet Horace claims the freedom of his craft and frequently puts himself, for poetical effect, in situations which may perhaps reflect his mode of thought and feeling and even shadow forth his personal experiences, but must not be taken literally as autobiography.

### Birth and Early Training.

**2.** Quintus Horatius Flaccus was born on the 8th of December, B.C. 65, and died on the 27th of November, B.C. 8.

It is important to observe the significance of these dates. Horace's life began when the Romans were still living under the forms of the Republic; when it closed, the Empire was fully established. When our poet first saw the light, Cicero was planning his canvass for the consulship. His boyhood fell in the stormy decade of the 'First Triumvirate' (B.C. 60–50), which formed the prelude of the Civil War. Horace was old enough to be interested in the later victories of Caesar in Gaul, and the destruction of Crassus with his army at Carrhae in 53 may well have made a deep impression on a lad of twelve. The two decades of civil strife which followed were experiences of his youth and early manhood, and when peace came with the deaths of Antony and Cleopatra in B.C. 30, Horace was thirty-five years old. The remaining twenty-two years of his life belong to the first half of the principate of Augustus, the period of the growth and consolidation of his power under the guidance of his two great ministers, Agrippa and Maecenas, whose deaths, B.C. 12 and 8, were closely followed by that of Horace.

3. Horace's birthplace was Venusia, a colony planted for military purposes in the Samnite wars, high up on the northern slope of the Apennine range, in Apulia, near the Lucanian border. It stood on a branch of the Aufidus, in that region a swift mountain stream, among the wooded hills which culminate in the lofty peak of Mt. Voltur. There the poet's father by shrewdness and thrift had not only secured his own freedom — for he was born a slave — but had acquired a modest farm and an income which enabled him to educate his son. His occupation was that of a *coactor*, that is, a collector of money — whether of money due for taxes or for goods sold at auction, the corrupt text of the Suetonian biography leaves us in doubt. It is supposed by some that he had acted in this capacity

as a public slave, and on his manumission took the name of Horatius because Venusia belonged to the Horatian tribe. But we do not know that freedmen were ever so named; from the ordinary practice in such cases we should assume that he had belonged to a master named Horatius.

4. Horace himself was born free, that is, he was born after his father's manumission. His mother is nowhere mentioned. It may well be that he inherited from her his poetic nature; but whether because she died in his infancy — which is probable — or from lack of personal force, she appears to have had little or no influence in moulding his character. His father's influence, on the other hand, was of the utmost importance and value, as the poet himself acknowledges with warm gratitude. The elder Flaccus was a shrewd observer of men and manners. Horace was, it seems, his only son, and the child of his later years, when he had accumulated a fund of experience and practical wisdom, and when he was, moreover, in possession of a competence which enabled him to lay aside his business and give his whole attention to the training of his boy. He naturally knew nothing of ethical theories, and he relied little on precept alone. He sought to awaken his son's moral perception by teaching him to observe good and bad in the world about him, to note the consequences of virtue and of vice in the actual lives of men, and to take to heart these examples and warnings in guiding his own life and guarding his reputation. The ethical code of the Venusian freedman was of a rough-hewn sort. It was a coarse sieve, and allowed some things to pass which do not meet the test of our finer standards. He claimed, in fact, no more for his moral teaching than that it would keep his son from falling into ruinous courses during that critical period when he was not yet able to 'swim without cork.' But so far as it went it was sound and wholesome. And it was effective:

Horace's habitual self-control during the period of his life when we know him best, his dislike of passionate excess either of desire or fear, his temperance in conduct and language, his aversion to the grosser forms of vice, — these were the fruit of inherited traits, fostered and strengthened by wise training. To the same training Horace attributes his habit of critical observation of social phenomena, which led him to write satire.

## School Days at Rome.

5. Horace's mental development received no less careful attention. There was a school at Venusia, kept by one Flavius and resorted to by the sons of the local aristocracy, — 'great lads, from great centurions sprung.' But Horace's father had higher views for his son, who had already, we may suppose, given promise of exceptional ability. Anxious to provide him with the best advantages, he determined to send him to Rome, 'to receive the education which a knight or a senator gives to his sons.' But unlike a knight or a senator, the obscure freedman had no social connections which would enable him to place his son under the charge of some family or friend; and rather than entrust him to strangers or slaves, he determined to leave his farm and accompany the boy in person to the city. Here, too, he was unremitting in his watchful care. Horace has left us a pleasing picture of the devoted father, going round to all the lessons with his boy, whom he had fitted out with suitable dress and attendant slaves, so that he might hold up his head with the best of his school-fellows.

6. Horace was taken to Rome perhaps in his ninth or tenth year, and remained there possibly until he was twenty; the precise dates are not recorded. Of his teachers only one is known to us, Orbilius Pupillus, of Beneventum, an old cavalry soldier who had resumed his books when his

campaigns were over, and at the age of fifty had set up a school in the capital in the year when Cicero was consul. He was a gruff old fellow, with a caustic tongue, and his ready resort to the rod Horace remembered many years after. The course of study which Horace pursued was presumably the ordinary course of the 'grammatical' and 'rhetorical' schools of the day, which aimed, first, at a mastery of the Latin tongue, and, secondly, at the cultivation of eloquence. With these ends in view the training, — after the elements of reading, writing, and reckoning were acquired, — was largely literary, and consisted mainly in a thorough study of Latin and Greek literature. Horace read Livius Andronicus — probably his version of the Odyssey — under the rod of Orbilius, and became familiar with the other old Roman poets, for whom he did not conceive, or did not retain, a very high admiration. He also read the Iliad, as he informs us, and no doubt other Greek classics in prose and verse; and these kindled in him a genuine enthusiasm, which kept him a devoted student of Greek letters, particularly of Greek poetry, all his life.

### Athens.

**7.** With this taste developed by his studies in Rome, it was natural that Horace should be drawn into the current which at that day carried the more ambitious students to Athens, in quest of what we may call their university training in the schools of philosophy there. Horace attended the lectures of the Academic school, and the acquaintance which he shows with the doctrines of the other sects must have been acquired at this time. For speculative philosophy and the subtleties of dialectics he had little taste. The Roman, as a rule, felt the strongest attraction to philosophy on its ethical side, where it came nearest to the practical problems of life; and in Horace this ethical tendency was ingrained and was peculiarly strong. It was fostered by his father's training; it no doubt added zest, at this time, to his study of the various ethical systems of the Greeks; it was confirmed as his mind and character matured, and impressed itself strongly on all his writings, even his lyrics. In his later years he protested that his chief desire was to put aside poetry and devote the rest of his days to the study of the philosophy of life.

**8.** In his philosophical views Horace was, like most of his countrymen who interested themselves in the subject at all, eclectic; he found something to his taste in this creed and in that, but declined to enroll himself as the disciple of any school. Of his religious belief it is not possible to speak definitely,— probably it never crystallized into definite shape in his own mind. For a time he was a convert to the doctrine of Epicurus,— probably from reading Lucretius, whose poem was published in his boyhood,— and believed that there were gods, but that their serene existence was never troubled by any concern for the affairs of men. In one of his odes he professes to have been startled out of this 'crazy' creed by the actual occurrence of what the Epicureans averred to be a physical impossibility,— a clap of thunder in a clear sky. It is not likely that this experience had the importance in actual fact which it appears to have in its lyrical setting; Horace's change of view was a matter of growth. But it was real. Otherwise he would surely not have published this poem; and there is, besides, plenty of evidence elsewhere in his works that in his maturer years he recognized a divine providence and control in human affairs. Horace's ethical views, too, were strongly tinged with Epicureanism, but here, as everywhere, he went to no extreme; and, although he combats the Stoic theory and mocks at their ideal sage, he was at heart in sympathy with Stoic

principles in their substance and practical application to life, and he more than once holds up their ideal of virtue for its own sake, — though even virtue itself he will not exempt from his maxim 'nil admirari'.

9. How far Horace pursued his study of the Greek poets along with his philosophy at Athens, we are not informed; we may be sure that he gave them a large share of his attention. The broad and intimate acquaintance with Greek poetry, which is the very life-blood of his own poetic achievement, was not the acquisition of a few years; but his sojourn was long enough for the influences of the place to give a permanent bent to his literary taste. One of Horace's marked characteristics as a poet is his freedom from Alexandrinism, which dominated Roman education and Roman poetry in his youth. Alexandrine learning, filtered through his Roman teachers, furnished him with his technical outfit as a poet, with a knowledge of the forms and categories and of the history of his art, and with the common stock of illustrative material, mythological, astrological, and other. There is evidence also of his diligent study of some of the Alexandrine poets: he is indebted to them for many phrases and figures and turns of thought. This is especially apparent in his love poetry. But the same evidence shows that the Alexandrine poets who exerted this influence on his style were precisely those who, like Callimachus and Theocritus, were freest from the peculiar weakness of their school, — the sacrifice of freshness and good taste to formality and erudition. In the spirit and form of his verse Horace took as his models the older Greek poets; and his loving study of these masters we may confidently date from his residence at Athens, where the older traditions still maintained themselves.

10. The fashion of sending young men to get the finishing touches of their education at Athens had grown up with the generation into which Horace was born. Cicero, who in his

youth was eager to grasp every opportunity for the best training, did not visit Greece at all until after he had entered on the practice of his profession: Cicero's son, who was just of Horace's age, was now at Athens studying rhetoric and philosophy. There, too, Horace found a number of other young men of distinguished families, among them Valerius Messala, who traced his descent from the Valerius Poplicola who held with Brutus the first consulship of the Republic. On what terms Horace stood with these fellow-students we are left to conjecture; but his genial nature and conversational gifts, combined with tact and good sense, must have drawn many to him. His friendship with Messala and many closer intimacies, to which his poems bear witness, date no doubt from this period. There was nothing out of the way in this association of the freedman's son with the young nobles in common studies and literary interests. Aristocracy of birth has never aspired to monopolize the brain-work of the world, and youth and good fellowship are not strenuous about social distinctions. In the next stage of Horace's career he found his position very different.

### In the Army of Brutus.

**11.** In September, 44 B.C., six months after the assassination of Julius Caesar, Marcus Brutus came to Athens, and for some months, while waiting for the turn of political events, devoted himself to the schools of philosophy. His appearance created no little sensation. The Athenians, who lived largely in the traditions of their past, welcomed 'the liberator' with enthusiasm, and voted to set up his statue beside those of their own tyrannicides, Harmodius and Aristogeiton. The young Romans were flattered by the accession of so illustrious a fellow-student, whose real interest in philosophy was well known; and before the winter was

over Brutus had enlisted a number of them in his service for the coming struggle with the triumvirs. Among these recruits was the young Cicero, who had already seen some service under Pompey. The most distinguished adherent was Messala, and the least distinguished, certainly, was Horace. It argues a high estimate on Brutus' part of Horace's intelligence and capacity, that he appointed this youth of one and twenty, with neither military experience nor family influence to recommend him, to a place among his officers, and eventually gave him, as tribune, the command of a Roman legion. It was high promotion for the freedman's son, and envious tongues were not slow to direct attention to the fact.

**12.** Horace was in Brutus' army the greater part of two years (B.C. 43 and 42). He is almost entirely silent about this experience, but from our knowledge of the movements of Brutus in those two campaigns we may gather that it gave him the opportunity to visit various places in Thessaly, Macedonia, and Thrace, and many famous cities of Asia Minor, which he mentions in his poems in a way that implies personal acquaintance. He remained with Brutus to the end, and shared the victory and subsequent rout at Philippi. The suicide of his chief at once absolved him from further allegiance and was a confession that the cause for which they had fought was irretrievably lost. Horace was fain to accept the result, and while some of his friends held out and joined the standard of Sextus Pompeius, he followed the example and advice of Messala and made his submission to the victors, who pardoned, or at least did not molest him.

### Return to Rome.

**13.** It was not improbably on his homeward voyage from Greece after Philippi that Horace came near being shipwrecked on the dangerous promontory of Palinurus, on the

Lucanian coast; the critical condition of the times may have been his motive for preferring that roundabout way to the ordinary route. He returned to Rome in a depressed and bitter mood. His father was dead. His estate had been swept away in the confiscation of the territory of Venusia. The outlook was gloomy. He seems, however, to have saved some money from his two campaigns, and with this he purchased a clerkship in the Quaestors' office, which yielded him a small income and, apparently, a good deal of leisure. Under these circumstances, poor in purse and still poorer in favor, Horace began life again at the age of twenty-three. He was thoroughly cured of his aspirations for a public career. His short, but severe experience had taught him that, however strong his interest in his country's welfare, he had no taste for the practical business of war and politics; and he had had enough of running counter to the popular prejudice against humble birth in high station. On the other hand his training and his knowledge of his own powers alike pointed to literature as the career most suitable and promising for him.

### Choice of a Career.

**14.** That Horace had practiced verse-writing in the course of his literary studies might be taken for granted. He confesses that at one time, — it was probably while he was at Athens, — he undertook to write poetry in Greek; and these essays were not, it should seem, in the nature of school exercises, but serious efforts. This was by no means a new thing in Roman literature. The earliest Roman annals were written in Greek, and the same phenomenon had reappeared in the highly Hellenized culture of the Ciceronian period, when Roman writers occasionally used Greek for prose or verse, partly for the pleasure of handling a language of so much richer capacity than their own, partly to reach a wider circle of appreciative readers. But Horace did not persist in an undertaking which his good sense presently convinced him was as futile as it was unpatriotic.

**15.** At the time when Horace began his literary career, Vergil, who was five years his senior, had published some youthful verses and was beginning to be known as a sweet singer of pastoral scenes by the publication of his earliest Eclogues. The epic poet of the day was Varius Rufus, who won credit and favor by his poem on the death of Julius Caesar. He was a few years older than Vergil, who lived to rival him in epos; but that was many years later. Asinius Pollio, who as governor of Cisalpine Gaul had recently won Vergil's gratitude by timely assistance, and who was afterwards eminent as an orator and a critic and patron of literature, had at this time attained some distinction as a writer of tragedy. Various other fields were diligently cultivated by writers of less note, or less known to us. Looking over the ground Horace thought he saw a field suited to his powers in Lucilian satire, which Varro Atacinus and some others had undertaken to revive, but in Horace's opinion without success.

## The Satires.

**16.** The word *satura* appears to have meant originally a medley. It was used as the name of a variety performance on the rude stage of early times, consisting of comic songs and stories, with dance and gesticulation, to the accompaniment of the pipe. It found its way into literature as the title of a collection of what we should call 'miscellanies in verse:' Ennius (B.C. 239–169) employed it for this purpose, and his example was followed by Lucilius. The *Saturae* of Lucilius, who had been dead about sixty years when Horace began to write satire, were a series of tracts on every topic that it came into his head to discuss, — personal, social, political, philosophical, literary, philological. In form they were equally varied, — sometimes didactic, sometimes narrative, or dramatic, or epistolary; and they were written in a variety of metres. More than two thirds, however, of the thirty books were in dactylic hexameters, which Lucilius appears to have finally settled upon as most suitable for his purpose; and this metre was used exclusively by his successors. And in spite of its heterogeneous variety of subjects, there were two features which gave distinctive character to Lucilius' work. One of these was the footing of personal and familiar intercourse on which he placed himself with his reader; his tone was the tone of conversation and his words the utterance of his own mind and heart, as if on the impulse of the moment. The other was that he entered on a field which Roman literature had not yet ventured to tread, but which thenceforth became the peculiar province of *satura*, as it had been of the Old Comedy of the Greeks, — the criticism of contemporary manners and men.

**17.** By inheritance and training a critical observer of the life about him, Horace justly deemed himself fitted to take up the task of Lucilius, whom he greatly admired in everything but the roughness of his literary workmanship. The unreserved personalities in which Lucilius indulged were no longer permissible in Horace's day, and he avoided them except in a few of his earlier satires. Politics, too, were forbidden ground. In other respects he adopted the method of his master, but in a kindlier spirit and rarely with any exhibition of personal feeling. His manner is that of the accomplished man of the world in familiar conversation, easy and self-possessed, witty but never flippant, discussing with keen insight and a quick sense of humor, but with the abundant charity of a man who knows his own shortcomings, and with a ground-tone of moral earnestness, the various phases of every-day life. He laughs at vice and folly; but satire is essentially didactic, and ridicule is the weapon of a serious purpose. Horace never speaks from the platform, or with any assumption of superior virtue; he talks as one of the crowd who has stopped to reflect on their common weaknesses, and he disarms resentment by sometimes turning the laugh against himself. There are some who esteem these 'talks' (*sermones*), as he himself preferred to call them, the greatest of Horace's achievements. Certainly there are few works of classical antiquity in which literary art has brought us so near to ancient life. The satires were written from time to time in the decade following Horace's return to Rome (B.C. 41–31), and became more or less widely known before they were issued in collected form. The collection consisted of two books, of which the first was published about 35 or 34, and the second about 30, B.C.

## The Epodes.

**18.** Horace constructed the hexameter of his satires with some care, and succeeded in reconciling with the easy conversational tone a smoothness of rhythm which marked a great advance on the strong but rugged verses of his model Lucilius. But he hardly cared to claim for his satires the dignity of poetry. They are in their nature, he protests, and except for a certain recurrence of rhythm, mere prose discourse. And meanwhile he was trying his hand at poetry based on Greek models, and was in fact touched with the ambition to strike out a new path for Latin literature in this field. His first effort was to reproduce in Latin the iambic rhythm which tradition said had been forged, as a weapon of wrath, by Archilochus of Paros, — the fact being that Archilochus, who lived in the seventh century B.C., had developed and perfected the rhythm which had existed long before him. The form which Horace adopted was a couplet, the second verse of which, as a sort of refrain, was called by metrical writers *epōdus* (ἐπῳδός, adjective ; cf. ἐπᾴδειν). This term was later extended in meaning, so that Horace's collection of seventeen poems, all but one composed of epodic couplets, has come down to us under the title of Epodes (*Epodon liber*). Horace himself called them only *Iambi*, which expresses their prevailing character and is sufficiently accurate, although other metres are combined with the iambic in some instances.

**19.** The composition of the Epodes probably began as early as that of the Satires, possibly earlier, and was continued through the same period. The sixteenth of the series, which displays at once remarkable mastery of form and immaturity of thought, was written in the first years after the poet's return from Philippi ; the ninth celebrates the victory at Actium. The book was published about the same time as the second book of the Satires, B.C. 30.

**20.** Horace says truly that he reproduced the spirit as well as the rhythms of Archilochus ; in some of his epodes he has certainly used the iambus as 'a weapon of wrath.' In others again he has descended to a depth of coarseness from which his later lyrics are, for the most part, happily free. These, the survivors perhaps of a larger number of their kind, belong, we must suppose, to his earliest efforts, and tell of a dark period in his mental history, — the first years after his return from Philippi, — when life went hard with him, and he was embittered and demoralized by associations which later, under more congenial influences, he was able to throw off. The most fortunate of these influences was his acquaintance with Varius and Vergil, who inspired him with warm admiration and regard ; and it was these friends who performed for him the inestimable service of introducing him to Maecenas.

## Maecenas.

**21.** Gaius Maecenas came of noble Etruscan stock. The Cilnii, once a powerful family of Arretium, were the most distinguished of his ancestors, and Tacitus (*Ann.* VI. 11) calls him Cilnius Maecenas; but there is reason to believe that this was not his gentile name. He was born on the 13th of April in some year not far from 70 B.C., so that he was Horace's senior by a few years. From our earliest knowledge of him he appears as the trusted friend and confidential minister of the triumvir Octavian, who sent him on several occasions to negotiate with Antony, — at Brundisium in B.C. 40, at Athens in 38, at Tarentum in 37. In B.C. 36, during his absence in the war with Sextus Pompeius, and again in 31, on setting out for the final struggle with Antony, Octavian left Maecenas behind to watch over Rome and Italy with the power, if not the name, of the city prefect of regal times. This was as near as Maecenas ever came to holding public office. He studiously refrained from seeking or accepting political preferment, which would have raised him to the senatorial order, and remained all his life an untitled 'knight.' He was a man in whom the most opposite qualities appeared to be reconciled. His capacity was unquestioned, and on occasion he could display all necessary industry and vigor; but ordinarily he lived a life of almost ostentatious indolence, and was self-indulgent to the point of effeminacy. Devoid of personal ambition and apparently indifferent to politics, he was yet public-spirited and patriotic, and by sheer force of sagacity and tact he exercised for many years a powerful and a wholesome influence in shaping the policy of the government. His self-indulgence appears to have been due to his health, which was always delicate. He was subject to fever and sleeplessness, which increased as he grew older; we have the elder Pliny's word for it that in the last three years of his life he did not sleep at all. Maecenas married Terentia, a sister (by adoption) of Licinius Murena, who was executed for conspiracy against the emperor in B.C. 23. She was a beautiful woman, who counted, the gossips said, Augustus himself among her lovers; and her husband oscillated between furious jealousy and complete subjection to her fascination. He incurred the emperor's displeasure, when her brother's conspiracy was detected, by letting her draw the secret from him. These jars produced no permanent estrangement between Augustus and his minister, but there were other circumstances which inevitably caused Maecenas' influence to wane. When the rule of Augustus had become firmly established and began to take on the character of an hereditary monarchy, the members of his own family naturally came into greater prominence in his councils. Among these was Agrippa, who had married his daughter Julia. Maecenas was outside the circle and his relation with his chief could not be the same as before.

**22.** Maecenas was a man of cultivated mind and taste, with a genuine appreciation of literature and enjoyment of the conversation of men of letters. He even wrote indifferent verses himself. But he showed his love of literature in a much better way by bestowing upon it a liberal, and what was more to the purpose, a discriminating patronage. He did this in part as a measure of policy; he saw that literature might serve a useful purpose in reconciling the nation to the new order of things. It was rare good fortune for Octavian to have a minister who not only saw the wisdom of this policy, but had the taste and the tact to carry it out with success; it was something more than good fortune for Maecenas that he won the gratitude and admiration of the two greatest poets of the age, and that his name from that day to this has been a synonym for patron of letters.

**23.** Horace was introduced to Maecenas apparently in B.C. 39; but it was not till nine months after the first meeting that he was definitely admitted to his circle. It was probably in B.C. 37 that Maecenas invited him, with Vergil and Varius, to accompany him on the journey to Brundisium, which he has humorously described in the fifth Satire. The acquaintance between the two men ripened gradually into a warm attachment. Maecenas found in Horace a man after his own heart, whose society gave him great content, and whose good sense and sound moral fibre were proof alike against servility and presumption. He won Horace's gratitude by very substantial favors; he won his affection by the tact and sincerity which made it plain that these favors were the gifts of a friend and not of a mere patron, and that only friendship was exacted in return. Others were quick enough to point out the social inequality of the two men, and Horace was once more forced to hear ill-natured remarks about 'the freedman's son'; but he comforted himself with the knowledge that however it might have been on the former occasion, when he was tribune in the army of Brutus, humble birth was not a matter to be considered against personal qualities in the choice of a friend, and that the distinguished favor which he enjoyed was not purchased by any unworthy compliances on his part. The balance of obligation, in a material point of view, was enormously against him; but he was ready, and frankly avowed his readiness, to resign all these advantages rather than surrender his own independence. And Maecenas accepted him on these terms.

### The Sabine Farm.

**24.** Chief of all the benefits that came to Horace from this friendship was the gift of a farm in the Sabine hills, which he received from Maecenas about 33 B.C., not long after the publication of the first book of Satires. The precise situation of this estate has not been determined; but it lay on the banks of the Digentia (now Licenza), a cold mountain stream that flows directly south and joins the Anio about eight miles above Tibur (Tivoli). Near by was a shrine of the Sabine divinity Vacuna, which archeologists have located with considerable probability at the village of Roccagiovane, about three miles up the valley on its western slope. Behind this point, within a distance of two or three miles, there are mountain peaks rising to a height of more than 3000 feet above the sea, one of which may have been Lucretilis; though that name is more commonly supposed to have designated the whole mountain mass lying between the Digentia and the more westerly tributaries of the Anio, the highest point of which, Monte Gennaro (or Zappi) rises above 4000 feet. At the junction of the valleys, on the Anio, was the market town of Varia (Vicovaro) where Horace's five tenant-farmers carried their produce to sell. In the country-house, which Horace himself appears to have built or remodeled for his own use, he maintained an establishment of eight slaves, including presumably the *vilicus*, who had charge of the whole estate. The environment of beautiful scenery, with abundance of shade, cool streams, and pure air, — it was about 2000 feet above the sea-level — made the place exceedingly attractive to a man like Horace, who was strongly susceptible to the impressions of Nature in her various aspects. He came into possession of his Sabine villa when he was a little over thirty years old, and from that time on he spent much of his life there, glad to escape from the feverish bustle of the city to his mountain retreat, not thirty miles away, but completely secluded and restful to both mind and body. To Maecenas' generous gift he was indebted for a good deal more than the mere provision of an income which secured him against want for the rest of his days, though that too was all-important for a man of letters in that age.

### Political Views.

**25.** Through his intimacy with Maecenas Horace came to the acquaintance and notice of Octavian, towards whom his feelings, in the course of this decade, underwent a complete change. Like many of the followers of Brutus and Cassius, who had remained quiescent or hostile during the harmonious supremacy of the triumvirs, Horace saw that when it became necessary to choose between Octavian and Antony, the best hopes of the country were bound up with the success of the former. His change of heart was no doubt hastened by the influence of Maecenas, and in fact the prevailing influences at Rome set in that direction. When the contest reached its crisis at Actium, Horace's conversion was complete. He celebrated the victory and the death of Cleopatra, — with true Roman spirit he was silent about Antony, — with odes of triumph, and cordially accepted the result which placed the sole supremacy in the hands of the one man who could command peace. Towards Augustus personally, however, Horace was not inspired at this time, and probably not any time, with any warmer feeling than patriotic admiration and gratitude.

### The Odes.

**26.** When Octavian returned to Rome and celebrated his triple triumph in 29 B.C., — the year after Vergil completed his seven years' labor on the Georgics, — Horace had published his two books of Satires and the Epodes. In each of these the opening poem was addressed to Maecenas, which was equivalent to a dedication. Horace's work in satire was not pursued further, at least in the same form. He had become deeply interested in lyrical composition, and his success in the Epodes had encouraged him to try his hand at more complicated lyrical metres. He made careful studies in early Greek lyric, taking as his especial models and guides the two great poets of Lesbos, Alcaeus and Sappho (about 600 B.C.) Just when Horace began to write what we call the Odes, but which he called simply poems (*carmina*), it is not possible to say. In fact, the line of division between the Epodes and the Odes is a somewhat arbitrary one, and a few poems are found under each head that might equally well have been placed under the other. The earliest of the odes to which a date can be assigned with certainty is I. 37, written on receiving the news of the death of Cleopatra in B.C. 30. Possibly some were written before this, but probably not many. From this time on, for about seven years, Horace devoted himself with great zeal and industry, and almost to the exclusion of every other kind of literary work, to lyrical composition. His mastery of form and fine rhythmical sense had here their highest opportunity, and the result was a body of lyric which in volume and variety and in perfection of finish was never equaled in Latin literature before or after. Catullus, a generation earlier, had written lyrics which in freshness and spontaneity, and as direct and unaffected expressions of the poet's personality, Horace himself could not equal. But Catullus had written chiefly in the easier lyrical metres, — iambics, Glyconics, and particularly the Phalaecean, his favorite rhythm. He tried the Sapphic strophe in only two poems, — one of these a translation, — and the Alcaic not at all. These two, with three Asclepiad strophes which Catullus did not touch, were the rhythms that Horace developed most successfully, and, after many experiments with other forms, came to use almost exclusively. He also worked in accordance with strict metrical theories, formulated probably by the Roman philologians of the time, and not by

Horace himself, whereas Catullus had allowed himself the full liberty of his Greek models as he found them, so that his verses sometimes, to the ears of later critics, had a touch of harshness. It was not unnatural that Horace should regard his own achievement, wrought out with much study and labor, as the first adequate and successful adaptation of the Lesbian rhythms to the Latin language, in comparison with which the slighter efforts of Catullus might be deemed to have gone, in point of artistic workmanship, little beyond the point he had himself reached in his Epodes. And his claim, in this limited sense, must be allowed. But it is to be wished that he had accorded to the genius of his predecessor in lyric the same generous recognition which he gave to that of Lucilius in satire.

**27.** Horace's Odes, many of which are addressed to one or another of his friends, were privately read and circulated long before they were published in collected form. The first publication, which embraced three books, dedicated in a fitting introductory ode to Maecenas, took place, according to almost conclusive internal evidence, in B.C. 23, when Horace had reached the age of forty-two. It was the gathered fruits of the best years of his life, when his mind had attained its full maturity and his spirit had not yet lost its freshness. The collection is arranged with some reference to the chronological order of composition, but with more to variety of subject and pleasing sequence of rhythms. The odes range in quality from mere studies or versions from the Greek to products of the poet's matured skill and poems in which motive and thought are wholly Roman. Horace gave his work to the world with the undisguised assurance of its immortality and his own. It did not immediately silence his detractors; but it won its way surely, and he did not have to wait many years for a general verdict of approval from the reading public.

### The First Book of Epistles.

**28.** With this achievement Horace's ambition to make foı himself a unique place in Roman literature was satisfied, or his lyric impulse was spent; at any rate he wrote no more odes for some years. His old propensity for the study of life reasserted itself and found expression in a new series of *sermones*, as he calls them, indicating their close resemblance in subject and method, as they were identical in metre, with the Satires. In form they were Epistles, and this is the title under which they have come down to us. Some are letters in fact as well as in form, relating to personal matters,—one is a letter of introduction. Others contain some admixture of personal communication, while in many the insertion of a name is no more than a compliment or serves only to lend a certain personal interest to the discourse. It was a practice to which he had become habituated in the Odes, the influence of which on the Epistles is further apparent in a more finished rhythm and a more compact and sententious style than he had attained in the Satires. The first series of Epistles was written in the years immediately following the publication of the Odes, and was published in B.C. 20 or 19. The book, like its predecessors, was dedicated to Maecenas.

### Personal Traits.

**29.** In the epilogue of this first book of Epistles Horace has left a brief sketch of his own person and temper at the age of forty-four: 'short of stature, prematurely gray, quick to take offense, but quickly appeased.' He was stout as well as short; but in his younger days, with black hair and the low forehead which the Romans admired, and an agreeable voice and smile, he was personally far from unattractive. He enjoyed good health in his youth except that he was troubled with an affection of the eyes. But as he grew older his health began to fail, and he found it necessary to guard it carefully. In spite of the friendly reproaches of Maecenas, he spent a good part of the year away from the city, among the hills at his villa or at Tibur or Praeneste, or on the seashore at Baiae or Tarentum.

**30.** Horace never married, nor was he ever taken possession of by an overmastering passion, like his friend Tibullus and the other elegiac poets. Among all the feminine names that occur in his lighter odes only one appears to be real, — that of Cinara, of whom he speaks only after her early death. The Lydias and Lalages, and all the rest of the Greek ladies who figure in his love poems are creatures of his fancy, or of the fancy of some Greek poet before him; and if, as is no doubt to some extent true, the poems reflect the poet's own experiences, they also show how lightly these experiences touched him. Horace was not of a temperament to make a serious business of love; and his artistic delineations of it are pretty, but they have not the ring of genuineness and true passion. Something of the same sort must be said of his convivial odes. They must be taken as artistic productions, not as self-portraiture. Horace enjoyed good wine and was very sociable by disposition, and he no doubt often found himself, especially in his younger days, in boisterous company; but by his whole nature and training excess of all kinds was distasteful to him, and it is impossible not to believe that his strong self-control rarely failed to assert itself here. The odes in which he enjoins moderation in the use of wine reflect not only his rule but, we may confidently believe, his habitual practice.

## THE *CARMEN SAECULARE* AND THE FOURTH BOOK OF ODES.

**31.** In the year 17 B.C. Horace's eminence as a poet received the stamp of official recognition in his appointment to write a hymn to be sung at the Secular Games which Augustus celebrated in that year. His services as poet laureate were further called upon a few years later to celebrate in two odes the exploits of the Emperor's stepsons, Tiberius and Drusus Nero, who had gained important successes against some of the Alpine tribes. In the meantime his reawakened lyrical activity had produced other odes, and in B.C. 13, or perhaps a little later, he gathered these together and added a fourth book to the three already published. This was done, Suetonius tells us, to gratify the emperor, who wished the odes in honor of his stepsons to have a permanent place in Horace's works. The *Carmen Saeculare* was not included in this book, but has been preserved separately.

## Relations with the Court.

**32.** The fourth book of the Odes, unlike all of the poet's previous publications, was not dedicated to Maecenas, and this circumstance has given rise to the suspicion that Horace was guilty of neglecting his old friend, now that he had himself come into the sunshine of court favor, while his benefactor had withdrawn into the background, or was even under a cloud. But there is no sufficient ground for such an aspersion, and it is contradicted by what we know of Horace's character and his ideals of life. Horace had long before this time come into entire sympathy, politically, with the government of Augustus. The emperor was fully alive to the value of such an ally, and was ready to bestow upon him social favors and rewards of a more substantial sort. Both the one and the other were no doubt agreeable enough to the poet, and Horace was not the man to withhold the one favor he could bestow in return, — the service of his muse. There is nothing to show that his relations with the court went beyond this interchange of civilities. Horace had already won the prizes of life that he most valued, and court favor could add nothing that he really cared for. Nor is there any evidence of a close friendship between the poet and the emperor. The warmest expression of Horace's feeling towards Augustus is in the fifth ode of the fourth book; but it is the warmth of loyal gratitude to the author of his country's peace, and not at all of personal affection. On the other hand we are told that the emperor's advances towards a closer relation, in inviting the poet to become his private secretary, were coldly received and the appointment was declined. As to the new book of lyrics, Horace's unerring tact would forbid him to dedicate to Maecenas a work that he had published at the request of the emperor; the significant fact is that it is not dedicated to Augustus. Of his loyalty to Maecenas, which we should otherwise have no right to question, he reminds us in the eleventh ode; and of Maecenas' undiminished affection for the poet we have striking evidence in his dying message to the emperor, recorded by Suetonius: 'Horati Flacci ut mei esto memor.'

### The Literary Epistles.

**33.** Suetonius further tells us that Augustus reproached Horace not only for slighting his friendly advances, but for having left him, among so many friends addressed in his 'sermones,' conspicuous by his absence; and that Horace absolved himself from this reproach by composing the poem which now stands at the head of the second book of Epistles. It is, in form, an epistle to the emperor; in substance, a review of Latin poetry, with a defense of the modern school, of which Varius and Vergil and Horace himself were the foremost representatives, and with which the name of Augustus was destined to be permanently associated, against the disparagement of conservative critics and their indiscriminate veneration of the old Roman poets. The second poem of this collection, an epistle to a young friend and man of letters, Julius Florus, is also mainly devoted to literary matters, and is especially interesting for its many allusions to Horace's own literary career. Its general purport is that he has now come to a time of life when he must put aside poetry with other amusements of youth, and address himself to the 'rhythms and harmonies of real life.' For this reason its composition is assigned with great probability to the period immediately following the publication of the first book of the Epistles, when Horace's lyrical muse was still silent, — say B.C. 19 or 18. The epistle to Augustus, on the other hand, was probably written at least as late as B.C. 14.

**34.** These two epistles are followed in modern editions by the longest of Horace's poems (476 hexameters) and the one that approaches nearest to the character of a formal treatise. It is largely didactic, setting forth with much detail of precept and illustration, the correct principles of poetry as an art; and as early as the first century it was known under the title of *Ars Poetica* (or *De Arte Poetica liber*). It is, nevertheless, written in the form, and to a considerable extent preserves the character and tone, of an epistle, being addressed to three friends, a father and two sons, of the Piso family, and ostensibly designed for the special benefit of the elder of the two young men, who had literary aspirations. It is, moreover, for a formal treatise, very incomplete; it deals with only one branch of poetry,— the drama, — with any degree of thoroughness, touching on the rest lightly or not at all. It seems probable, therefore, that the somewhat pretentious title *Ars Poetica* did not originate with Horace himself, but was given to the poem later, when it was issued separately, either for educational purposes or as material for learned commentary. The date of its composition is in dispute. Some place it as early as the first book of the Epistles, but the better view appears to be that it was written in the last years of the poet's life.

## Death and Permanent Fame.

**35.** Of Horace's personal history in these last years we have no record. His health, as we have seen, had long been precarious, and he had not yet completed his fifty-seventh year when he died, in the latter part of November, B.C. 8. He was buried on the Esquiline, not far from the tomb of Maecenas, who had passed away only a few months before him.

**36.** The favor which Horace had won from the best minds of his own time has been confirmed by the permanent verdict of posterity. His works at once took their place among the classics of Latin literature. By the beginning of the second century, as we know definitely from Juvenal, and undoubtedly long before (see Quint. I. 8. 6), they were used as school-books, and thus became a part of the literary outfit of the educated Roman. They continued to be read to some extent through the middle ages, and since the revival of letters their popularity has been steadily maintained. Perhaps no ancient writer has won a warmer place in the personal regard of modern men, — and not only men of books, but men of affairs; for the secret of his power is not merely, or perhaps so much, in the unrivaled mastery of language and rhythm which lends such charm to his lyric poems, — still less in the force of poetical genius, in which his greatness does not pass unchallenged, but rather in the character which shines through his verses, of the keen but kindly, urbane, wise, genial observer of life.

## Scholia and Manuscripts.

**37.** Horace's poems became early the subject of learned criticism and interpretation. The oldest commentary that has come down to us is that of Pomponius Porphyrio, who is supposed to have written in the fourth century, perhaps earlier. At any rate he lived at a time when the old Roman pagan customs had not yet died out, and he had access to still older authorities which are now lost; so that his work is of great value to us. We also have a collection of scholia under the name of Helenius ACRO, a distinguished grammarian who lived perhaps a century before Porphyrio; but although Acro unquestionably wrote a commentary on Horace, the one which now bears his name is a composite production, made up at a much later date by one or more unknown writers, who quote liberally from Porphyrio.

38. If we may take the word of Jacques de Crusque (better known by his Latinized name, Cruquius), professor at Bruges in the latter part of the sixteenth century, the oldest manuscript of Horace known to exist in modern times was preserved in the monastery of St. Peter at Blankenberg (Mons Blandinius), near Ghent, and presumably perished in the fire which consumed that institution in 1566. It was one of four codices which Cruquius had borrowed from the monastery and collated for his edition of Horace, which he first published in complete form in 1578. Although, therefore, these Blandinian manuscripts are themselves lost, we have in the edition of Cruquius a considerable number of readings from them; and some of these are of a very striking character. Cruquius regarded the manuscripts as of great value; three of them he assigned to the ninth century while the other, which he called 'vetustissimus' he thought might possibly date from the seventh. We have no means of revising this estimate. Keller and Holder, to whom we are indebted for the fullest existing critical apparatus of Horace, question the accuracy and even the good faith of Cruquius, and set little value on his manuscripts. The majority of Horatian scholars, however, dissent from this view and acquit Cruquius of any worse offense than care-

lessness, while the 'Blandinius Vetustissimus' is justly held to be of exceptional importance both on account of the excellence of some of its peculiar readings and because it represents a tradition in large measure independent of the great mass of Horatian manuscripts. Cruquius also published in his edition a collection of scholia from his Blandinian manuscripts, the unknown writer or writers of which are commonly quoted as 'Commentator Cruquianus.' They are of no great value, being evidently derived, for the most part, from Acro and Porphyrio.

**39.** The extant manuscripts of Horace, about two hundred and fifty in number, range in date from the eighth or ninth to the fifteenth century. The oldest is one now in the public library at Berne, written by a Scotch or Irish monk in the latter part of the eighth or early in the ninth century. We have nearly twenty in all which appear to have been written before the end of the tenth century. All of the manuscripts (except one at Gotha, which appears to be derived from the Blandinian recension) come from a common archetype, which Keller thinks may have been written as early as the first or second century. No satisfactory classification has yet been discovered, which shall enable us to decide on disputed readings by the weight of manuscript testimony; nor is it probable that the relations of the manuscripts to one another can ever be sufficiently made out to establish such a classification. Owing to the practice in which copyists and revisers often indulged, of comparing their codex with one or more others, and borrowing readings from these at their discretion, the lines of tradition have become so confused that it is probably no longer possible to separate them. This appears in Keller's attempted classification, in which an important manuscript will be found now in one class, now in another. Keller sets up three classes, and in general accepts the united testimony of two against the remaining one. His Classes II. and III. may be said to be fairly made out, though their value is much impaired by the vacillation of individual manuscripts. The case for his Class I. is by no means so clear. The serious problems of Horatian textual criticism involve, as a rule, the choice between two (seldom three) variants, each resting on good, but not conclusive, manuscript support; and the decision cannot be reached by any balancing of authorities, but calls for the exercise of sound judgment, trained by careful study of the poet's mode of thought and habit of expression.

---

## II. LANGUAGE AND STYLE.

**40.** Saturated as Horace was with Greek literature, it was inevitable that his language and style should bear the impress of a strong Greek influence. But to this influence he by no means surrendered himself unreservedly. His sturdy Roman character stamped itself upon his writings as upon his life, and he was no more spoiled as a literary artist by Greek culture than he was as a man by aristocratic society. He was strong enough to absorb the spirit of Greek art, and make it his own. The task he set himself was not to imitate the Greek poets, but to achieve with his own language what they had achieved with theirs. He understood well the genius of his native tongue, its capacities and its limitations; and his good sense and good taste saved him from attempting to do with it some of the things which the older poets had tried, — such as the formation of unwieldy compounds, — just as he refrained from their sonorous rhetoric and extravagant use of assonance and alliteration, and from the studied prettiness of Catullus and his school. While his syntax often has a strong Greek flavor, he rarely uses a construction of which we cannot find at least the germ in the Latin idiom. If we bear in mind that Latin was a spoken language, in process of growth and decay, not hardened into the forms in which the grammarians have systematized it for us, we may well hesitate to assert that Latin idiom was ever consciously violated by Horace. His language is, in the main, the every-day language of cultivated Romans, but free from the sprinkling of Greek words and phrases with which polite conversation covered up its own poverty, and which he expressly condemns in Lucilius. Horace uses Greek words sparingly, and as a rule only of Greek things. His diction betrays no striving to avoid the commonplace. His power and charm lie rather in the skill with which he moulds common materials into exquisite forms, and in that perfect adaptation of word to thought which invests his carefully wrought phrase with all the appearance and the freshness of a happy inspiration. This 'Horati curiosa felicitas,' as Petronius has so aptly characterized it, is his supreme merit; and it is all his own.

The exposition which follows is designed to help the student to a better understanding of the poet by pointing out the most salient characteristics of his syntax, — chiefly those in which he goes beyond the limits of literary prose usage, — and to set forth some of the more striking features of his use and arrangement of words. This will serve, it is hoped, to show the student what to look for, but the largest part must still be done by himself. There are innumerable subtleties of form and setting which are beyond the reach of description. To grasp the full beauty and charm of Horace's style, we must read and read over again, read many times and learn by heart, till the poet's thought and his verse are inseparably blended in our memory.

## (A) SYNTAX.

### *The Accusative.*

**41.** The passive voice is sometimes used with its original middle force and takes an object accusative; as

*S.* II. 7. 38 **nasum supinor,** *I lay back my nose; Ep.* II. 3. 302 **purgor bilem**; *Ep.* I. 1. 50 **coronari Olympia** (after the Greek στεφανοῦσθαι, *to win a crown for oneself*); *Ep.* I. 17. 28 **quidlibet indutus.**

**42.** In descriptions of dress or personal adornment the perfect participle, with an instrumental ablative, is frequently used in the middle sense, and takes an accusative of the part of the body affected; as

*C.* I. 2. 31 **nube candentis umeros amictus,** *having thy bright shoulders wrapt in cloud; C.* II. 11. 15 **rosa odorati capillos**; *Ep.* II. 1. 110 **fronde comas vincti.**

**43.** The accusative of the 'part affected' is sometimes used with the passive voice in its proper sense, thus becoming practically an accusative of specification; as

*S.* I. 8. 37 **caput inquiner,** *I get my head befouled; S.* I. 1. 5 **iam fractus membra labore,** *with his frame all shattered by toil and hardship; S.* II. 3. 295 **mentem concussa.**

**44.** The accusative specifying the 'part affected' occurs once in Horace with an active verb: *S.* II. 7. 57 **tremis ossa pavore** (cf. *C.* I. 23. 8 et corde et genibus tremit). Its occurrence with an adjective is doubtful, the *MSS.* in *C.* III. 10. 18 being divided between *animum mitior* and *animo mitior. Cetera* with an adjective occurs thrice: *C.* IV. 2. 60 **cetera fulvus**; *Ep.* I. 10. 3, 50. Cf. § 45 *b*.

**45.** (*a*) The character of the action may be expressed by an adjective with a cognate accusative; as

*C.* III. 29. 50 **ludum insolentem ludere**; *C.* II. 17. 26 **laetum crepuit sonum.**

(*b*) The neuter plural of an adjective in this construction is equivalent to an adverb; as

*S.* I. 8. 40 **alterna loquentes** (*alternately*); *S.* I. 4. 44 **os magna sonaturum** (*in lofty strain*); *Ep.* I. 1. 101 **insanire sollemnia** (*in the ordinary way*); *S.* I. 10. 37 **haec ego ludo.**

46. The action of a verb may be characterized by an adjective or participle in apposition with the verb itself, or with the whole predicate; as *S.* I. 4. 10 **in hora saepe ducentos, ut magnum, versus dictabat** (*as a great feat*); *S.* II. 1. 53 **dente lupus, cornu taurus petit,— unde nisi intus monstratum?** *S.* II. 2. 19 **cum sale panis latrantem stomachum bene leniet,—unde putas aut qui partum?**

47. The accusative singular neuter of pronouns and of *nihil* is freely used as a cognate object with adverbial force; as

*C.* I. 32. 1 **si quid lusimus**; *S.* II. 1. 78 **nisi quid tu dissentis**; *Ep.* II. 3. 354 **si peccat idem**; *C.* I. 14. 14 **nil pictis puppibus fidit**; *S.* II. 8. 41 **nihilum nocuere lagenis.** In one instance *nihil* is modified by an adjective: *Ep.* I. 12. 15 **nil parvum sapias** (*in no small way*).

48. The accusative singular neuter of many adjectives is attached to verbs, both transitive and intransitive, with adverbial force; as

*C.* I. 22. 23 **dulce ridentem**; *S.* I. 3. 26 **cernis acutum**; *Ep.* II. 2. 9 **canet indoctum sed dulce bibenti**; *C.* II. 12. 14 **lucidum fulgentis**; *S.* I. 8. 41 **resonarint triste et acutum.**

49. The accusative singular neuter of adjectives of quantity is used adverbially with adjectives and participles; as

*C.* I. 25. 5 **multum facilis**; *Epod.* 15. 11 **dolitura multum**; *Epod.* 17. 20 **amata multum**; *S.* II. 5. 80 **nec tantum Veneris quantum studiosa culinae.** So *nihilum*: *S.* II. 3. 54 **nihilum metuenda.**

50. Horace uses **insuesco** with two accusatives (on the analogy of *doceo*) in *S.* I. 4. 105 **insuevit pater hoc me.** The use of **decipior** with an accusative in *C.* II. 13. 38 **dulci laborem decipitur sono** is to be explained on the analogy of *celor* (cf. the use of *fallo* with an accusative of the thing disguised, e. g. *S.* II. 2. 12 **studio fallente laborem**, from which *fallor laborem* would be a natural development); but see § 67. In the expression, *Ep.* II. 3. 383 **census equestrem summam**, borrowed from legal phraseology (cf. Cic. *Flacc.* 80), **censeo** is likewise treated as a verb that takes two accusatives.

51. The tendency of verbs originally intransitive to acquire a transitive use appears at a more advanced stage in poetry than in prose. The following verbs, used transitively by Horace, had a very restricted transitive use, or were not so used at all, in prose before his day:

(*a*) Verbs denoting emotion or the expression of emotion: **erubesco, fleo, gemo, ploro, pallesco, expallesco, paveo, expavesco, tremo, contremisco, horresco, fastidio, gravor**; as, *Epod.* 14. 11 **cava testudine flevit amorem**; *C.* IV. 12. 5 **Ityn flebiliter gemens**; *C.* III. 27. 27 **pontum palluit** (*turned pale at the sight of*); *C.* IV. 11. 27 **Pegasus terrenum equitem gravatus.**

(*b*) Verbs expressing haste, strife: **propero, depropero, festino, certo, pugno, milito**; as *Ep.* I. 2. 61 **poenas festinat**; *S.* II. 5. 27 **foro si res certabitur**; *Epod.* 1. 23 **libenter hoc et omne militabitur bellum.**

(*c*) Verbs of vocal expression: (1) with object denoting the form or content of the expression: **sono, crepo, balbutio, elatro**; as *C.* II. 13. 26 **sonantem plectro dura navis, dura fugae mala**; *Ep.* I. 7. 84 **sulcos et vineta crepat**; (2) with external object: **iurgo, sibilo, latro**; as *S.* II. 2. 100 **Trausius iurgatur**; *S.* I. 1. 66 **populus me sibilat**: *Epod.* 5. 57 **senem latrent canes.**

(*d*) Verbs expressing some physical act or state: (1) in a literal sense: **ceno, stillo**; *Ep.* II. 2. 168 **emptum cenat holus**; *Ep.* II. 3. 429 **stillabit ex oculis rorem**; (2) in a figurative sense: **mano, spiro**; *Ep.* I. 19. 44 **fidis manare poetica mella te solum**; *C.* IV. 13. 19 **spirabat amores**; (3) of dramatic action, the accusative denoting the character represented: **salto, moveor, edormio**; *S.* I. 5. 63 **pastorem saltaret uti Cyclopa rogabat**; *Ep.* II. 2. 125 **nunc Satyrum, nunc agrestem Cyclopa movetur** (i. e. saltat; cf. *Ep.* II. 3. 232); *S.* II. 3. 61 **Fufius ebrius Ilionam edormit**, '*slept off*' *Iliona*, i. e. actually went to sleep in his part, instead of simulating it (with the additional idea, however, that he was sleeping off a debauch, from the phrase *edormire crapulam*, which occurs in prose).

(*e*) **invideo, impero, regno** (see also § 68), **triumpho**, and **iuro** are used in the passive with a subject-nominative; as *Ep.* II. 3. 56 **ego cur invideor?** *Ep.* I. 5. 21 **haec ego procurare imperor**; *C.* III. 29. 27 **regnata Cyro Bactra**; *C.* III. 3. 43 **triumphatis Medis**; *Ep.* II. 1. 16 **iurandas aras.** In *C.* IV. 6. 14 **mentior** is used for *simulo.*

(*f*) Many intransitive verbs acquire a transitive use in composition. Such are: **adnuo** (= *concedo*), as *S.* I. 10. 45 **molle atque facetum Vergilio adnuerunt Camenae**; **adsuesco**, *S.* II. 2. 109 **pluribus adsuerit mentem** (*adsuetus* is common in prose); **circumgemo, circumtono, circumvolo, circumvolito**; **exsudo**, *S.* I, 10. 28 **cum Pedius causas exsudet** (= sudans peragat); **evagor, insisto, intono, perambulo, pererro, praefluo, remeo, subrepo, supervenio.**

**52.** There are a few instances in the Satires and Epistles of a colloquial form of expression in which an object accusative depends on a verbal idea vaguely implied in the phrase itself; as *S.* II. 7. 116 **unde mihi lapidem? unde sagittas**, *where shall I get*, etc.? *Ep.* I. 5. 12 **quo mihi fortunam, si non conceditur uti?** Here **mihi** is added **to**

**quo** (= *quorsum*) to mean 'What object can it be to me?' (as in *S.* I. 6. 24; see § 94 *p*), and **fortunam** depends on the vaguely implied idea of having or obtaining.

## *The Dative.*

**53.** The person towards whom motion is directed is sometimes expressed, as 'the person for whom' action is performed, by the dative; and this usage is extended, by a more or less conscious personification, to places and things; as

*C.* I. 28. 10 **habentque Tartara Panthoiden, iterum Orco demissum** (i. e. to Orcus as a *person*, the *place* being already expressed by **Tartara**; cf. *Il.* I. 3 ψυχὰς Ἄϊδι προΐαψεν); *C.* IV. 4. 69 **Carthagini iam non ego nuntios mittam superbos**; *C.* I. 24. 15 **num vanae redeat sanguis imagini**, *would the blood return* (i. e. be restored) *to the empty form?* *C.* III. 23. 1. **caelo si tuleris manus** (cf. Verg. *Aen.* V. 451 it clamor caelo).

**54.** The dative is used with verbs (chiefly in the perfect participle) of perception and emotion; as

*C.* II. 1. 31 **auditum Medis sonitum** (i. e. audible to them; cf. the usual construction with *videor*); *C.* I. 1. 24 **bella matribus detestata** (*hateful to*); I. 21. 4 **Latonam dilectam Iovi** (= dear to); *Ep.* II. 1. 256 **formidatam Parthis Romam**; *C.* III. 25. 3 **quibus antris audiar?**

**55.** The dative of the agent, which had its origin perhaps in these and similar uses (notably its use in the gerundive construction), is also found; as

*C.* I. 32. 5 (barbite) **Lesbio modulate civi**; *Ep.* II. 3. 427 **versus tibi factos.**

**56.** The dative is used with verbs signifying to *unite*, *mix*, *compare*; such are

**iungo, figo, socio, continuo, gemino, coeo; misceo, confundo; confero, comparo, contendo**; as *Ep.* II. 3. 1 **humano capiti cervicem equinam iungere**; *Ep.* II. 3. 13 **ut serpentes avibus geminentur, tigribus agni**; *C.* I. 1. 30 **me dis miscent superis** (i. e. set me among them; cf. stellis inserere, *C.* III. 25. 6); *S.* I. 10. 20 **verbis Graeca Latinis miscuit** (Latin being his vernacular); *S.* I. 1. 111 **neque se maiori turbae comparet.**

**57.** The dative is used with verbs signifying *difference*, *disagreement*, *contention;* such are

**differo, disto, discrepo, dissentio, dissideo, disconvenio, discordo, pugno, certo, decerto, luctor, altercor**; as *C.* IV. 9. 29 **distat inertiae virtus**; *S.* I. 4. 48 **differt sermoni**; *C.* II. 2. 18 **dissidens plebi**; *S.* I. 2. 73 **pugnantia istis.**

**58.** The dative is used with adjectives, —

(*a*) Depending on a verbal idea contained in the adjective; as *C.* I. 11. 8 **credula postero**; *C.* III. 26. 8 **foribus minacis**; *C.* II. 15. 8 **fertilibus domino pricri** (i. e. quae ferebant; cf. *C.* III. 24. 12); *S.* II. 2. 6 **acclinis falsis animus**; *S.* II. 7. 83 **sibi imperiosus.**

(*b*) With adjectives conveying the notion of fitness or likeness, or the reverse; as *C.* I. 23. 12 **tempestiva viro** (*of fit age for*); *C.* III. 11. 12 **cruda marito**; *S.* II. 2. 101 **divitias tribus amplas regibus**; *Ep.* I. 18. 5 **huic diversum vitio.** So with **idem**: *Ep.* II. 3. 467 **invitum qui servat, idem facit occidenti.**

(*c*) To express purpose or use after adjectives of capacity, skill, incapacity; as *C.* I. 12. 42 **utilem bello**; *Ep.* II. 3. 82 **natum rebus agendis**; *Ep.* II. 2. 21 **talibus officiis prope mancum**; *C.* III. 27. 61 **acuta leto saxa** (i. e. sharp enough to kill).

**59.** The dative is rarely appended to a substantive to denote purpose, service, or destiny; as

*Epod.* 2. 33 **tendit retia, turdis dolos**; *S.* II. 5. 16 **ne illi comes exterior ire recuses**; *C.* II. 1. 13 **insigne maestis praesidium reis et consulenti, Pollio, curiae**; *S.* II. 2. 107 **o magnus posthac inimicis risus!**

**60.** In the predicate after *licet esse* and the like, Horace always uses the dative; as *Ep.* I. 16. 61 **da mihi fallere, da iusto sanctoque videri**; *Ep.* II. 3. 372 **mediocribus esse poetis non homines, non di, non concessere columnae.**

## *The Genitive.*

**61.** The genitive of quality may be attached directly to the name of a definite individual or class; as

*S.* I. 1. 33 **magni formica laboris** (for 'formica, animal magni laboris'); *C.* I. 36. 13 **multi Damalis meri.** Similarly, where the omitted appellative would be in the predicate; as *S.* I. 4. 17 **di bene fecerunt, inopis me quodque pusilli finxerunt animi**; *S.* II. 8. 84 **Nasidiene, redis mutatae frontis.** Sometimes coupled with an adjective; as *S.* II. 7. 52 **ditior aut formae melioris.**

**62.** The possessive genitive in the predicate is used with greater freedom than in prose, often differing little from a partitive genitive ; as

*S.* I. 7. 35 **operum hoc tuorum est**; *C.* III. 13. 13 **fies nobilium tu quoque fontium**; *Ep.* I. 9. 13 **scribe tui gregis hunc.**

**63.** The partitive genitive is often used with adjectives where in prose the substantive and adjective would stand in agreement ; as

*C.* IV. 6. 31 **virginum primae**; *C.* I. 10. 19 **superis deorum et imis**; *S.* II. 2. 60 **natalis aliosve dierum festos**; *C.* I. 9. 14 **quem fors dierum cumque dabit.** Sometimes with an adjective and pronoun ; as *C.* I. 29. 5 **quae tibi virginum barbara serviet?** Or a pronoun and substantive, as *S.* II. 1. 61 **maiorum ne quis amicus frigore te feriat.** With **unus** (= solus) : *S.* I. 10. 42 **unus vivorum** (cf. *S.* II. 6. 57 unum mortalem). The genitive is also used with **unus,** *one, S.* I. 9. 72 **unus multorum**; elsewhere the ablative with *de* or *ex*.

**64.** The genitive (partitive or possessive), used in this way with the neuter plural of an adjective in an abstract sense, gives the latter greater prominence than if it were merely expressed as an attribute of the substantive; thus in

*C.* IV. 12. 20 **amara curarum,** there is more stress on the *bitterness* than there would be in 'amaras curas'; *C.* II. 1. 23 **cuncta terrarum**; *C.* IV. 4. 76 **acuta belli**; *S.* II. 2. 125 **contractae seria frontis.** The colorless genitive **rerum** especially is used in the Satires and Epistles to round out a phrase; as *Ep.* I. 17. 21 **vilia rerum**; *S.* II. 2. 25 **vanis rerum**; *S.* II. 8. 83 **fictis rerum.** In one instance **rerum** is used in the same way with a masculine superlative : *S.* I. 9. 4 **dulcissime rerum.**

**65.** A geographical proper name is occasionally put in the genitive (instead of in apposition) with its generic noun ; as *C.* II. 6. 10 **Galaesi flumen,** *the river Galaesus; C.* IV. 14. 50 **tellus Hiberiae.** Sometimes it is treated as an adjective : *C.* IV. 4. 38 **Metaurum flumen**; *Ep.* II. 3. 18 **flumen Rhenum.** This adjective use of substantives is sometimes extended to personal names ; as *C.* I. 15. 10 **Dardanae genti,** *the race of Dardanus; C.* IV. 5. 1 **Romulae gentis**; and even to an appellative ; as *C.* III. 12. 1 **patruae linguae.** In the same way Horace is fond of using the shorter forms of adjectives of nationality, which are commonly used as substantives in prose ; as **Marsus, Afer, Medus, Colchus,** for *Marsicus, Africus,* etc.

**66.** The wide development and vague limits of the use of the objective genitive with adjectives (and participles with adjective meaning) gave the poets freer scope in this than in most other constructions. The examples in Horace com prise —

(*a*) The objective genitive proper, depending on adjectives implying the action of a transitive verb, or their opposites; such are

**tenax, ferax, fertilis, fecundus, prosperus, prodigus, benignus, parcus, fastidiosus, bibulus, avarus, metuens, timidus, securus, incautus**; as *Epod.* 5. 22 **Hiberia venenorum ferax**; *C. S.* 29 **fertilis frugum pecorisque tellus**; *Ep.* II. 3. 164 **iuvenis prodigus aeris**; *S.* II. 3. 3 **vini somnique benignus** (cf. our expression, 'a generous liver'); *S.* II. 5. 79 **donandi parca iuventus**; *Ep.* II. 3. 28 **timidus procellae**; *Ep.* II. 2. 17 **poenae securus.**

(*b*) The genitive of reference, with adjectives denoting mastery, knowledge, skill, and their opposites; such are

**potens, prudens, sciens, sollers, consultus, divinus** (*prophetic*), **sagax, docilis, indoctus, nescius, inscius**; as *C.* I. 3. 1 **diva potens Cypri**; *Ep.* II. 3. 407 **musa lyrae sollers**; *C.* I. 34. 2 **insanientis sapientiae consultus** (after the analogy of *iuris consultus*); *C.* III. 27. 10 **imbrium divina avis**; *Ep.* II. 3. 218 **utilium sagax rerum**; *C.* IV. 6. 43 **docilis modorum**; *Ep.* II. 3. 380 **indoctus pilae discive trochive.**

(*c*) The genitive of reference, with adjectives of plenty and want; such are

**dives, opulentus, satur, lassus, inanis, egens** (cf. § 67), **pauper, exsors, liber, vacuus, purus, abstinens**; as *Ep.* II. 2. 31 **multarum divite rerum**; *Ep.* I. 7. 35 **satur altilium**; *C.* II. 6. 7 **lasso maris et viarum militiaeque** (cf. Verg. *Aen.* I. 178 fessi rerum); *C.* III. 11. 26 **inane lymphae dolium**; *Ep.* I. 17. 22 **nullius egentem**; *C.* III. 30. 11 **pauper aquae**; *Ep.* II. 3. 212 **liber laborum rusticus**; *S.* II. 2. 119 **operum vacuo**; *C.* I. 22. 1 **sceleris purus.**

NOTE. — Of these adjectives, **dives, vacuus,** and **purus** are also used by Horace with the ablative; as *Ep.* II. 3. 421 **dives agris, dives positis in faenore nummis**; *C.* IV. 15. 8 **vacuum duellis Ianum**; *S.* II. 3. 213 **purum est vitio tibi cor?** With **nudus, orbus,** and **viduus** Horace uses the ablative only; *C.* I. 14. 4 **nudum remigio latus**; *C.* IV. 2. 44 **forum litibus orbum**; *C.* I. 10. 11 **viduus pharetra Apollo.**

(*d*) The genitive of reference (specification), with other adjectives:

*S.* II. 3. 65 **integer mentis** (cf. Plaut. *Trin.* 454 satin tu sanu's mentis aut animi tui?); *S.* I. 9. 11 **cerebri felicem**; *C.* II. 2. 6 **notus animi paterni**; *S.* I. 10. 21 **seri studiorum**; *S.* II. 2. 66 **cultūs miser**; *C.* III. 5. 42 **capitis minor** (for the technical *capite deminutus*).

**67.** The analogy of adjectives of plenty and want is extended in a few cases to verbs. Horace has the genitive with **egeo, solvo, purgo, abstineo, desino, invideo**; as *S.* I. 4. 118 **dum custodis eges** (cf. *egens* § 66 *c*); *C.* III. 17. 16 **famulis operum solutis** (cf. *operum vacuo* § 66 *c*); *S.* II. 3. 27 **miror morbi purgatum te** (cf. *liber*, *purus* § 66 *c*); *C.* III. 27. 69 **abstineto irarum** (cf. *abstinens* § 66 *c*); *C.* II. 9. 18 **desine querellarum**; *S.* II. 6. 84 **neque ille sepositi ciceris nec longae invidit avenae** (cited by Quintilian IX. 3. 17 to illustrate Horace's fondness for Greek idioms). Here also belongs *C.* II. 13. 38 **laborum decipitur**, if that reading, given in some good *MSS.*, be correct; but see § 50. Horace also uses the more common prose constructions, — the ablative with **egeo, solvo, abstineo,** and the accusative and dative with **invideo.**

**68.** For a supposed instance of the genitive with **regno** see note on *C.* III. 30. 12.

## *The Ablative.*

**69.** The ablative is often used without a preposition to denote the 'place where'; as

*C.* I. 9. 10 **ventos aequore fervido deproeliantis**; *C.* II. 9. 24 **exiguis equitare campis.** Often without an adjective, as *S.* I. 5. 87 **mansuri oppidulo.**

**70.** With verbs denoting separation or motion from a place, the ablative is often used without a preposition; as

*C.* I. 1. 32 **me secernunt populo**; *S.* II. 3. 203 **abstinuit vim uxore**; *Ep.* II. 3. 379 **abstinet armis**; ib. 370 **actor causarum mediocris abest virtute diserti Messalae**; *C.* II. 20. 21 **absint funere neniae**; *C.* III. 1. 39 **decedit aerata triremi**; *Ep.* II. 3. 53 **si Graeco fonte cadent.**

**71.** The ablative is used with **haereo, religo, suspendo**; as *C.* I. 2. 9 **summa haesit ulmo**; *C.* I. 32. 8 **religarat litore navim**; *S.* I. 6. 74 **suspensi loculos tabulamque lacerto.** The ablative may be that of 'place where' (cf. *S.* I. 3. 32 in pede calceus haeret), but with *religo* and *suspendo*, at least, the feeling is probably that of (prevented) separation, as in Verg. *Aen.* VII. 106 gramineo ripae religavit *ab aggere* classem; Lucan, VII. 860 nullus *ab Emathio* religasset *litore* funem navita. With *haereo* Horace also uses the dative; as *C.* I. 32. 9 **illi semper haerentem.** (Cf. the opposite points of view that find expression in *proximus alicui* and *proximus ab aliquo.*)

**72.** The ablative of cause is used with certain verbs denoting passion or mental disturbance; such are

**ardeo, caleo, uro, pecco; furo, insanio; langueo, stupeo, torpeo;** as *C.* II. 4. 8 **arsit virgine rapta;** *C.* I. 27. 16 **ingenuo semper amore peccas;** *S.* I. 4. 28 **stupet Albius aere.** Horace has the ablative with *in*, once each, with **uro, laboro,** and **stupeo:** *Epod.* 11. 4; *C.* I. 17. 19; *S.* I. 6. 17; and **ardeo** once, perhaps, with the accusative: *C.* IV. 9. 13 **comptos arsit adulteri crinis** (cf. Verg. *Ecl.* 2. 1 Corydon ardebat Alexin); but see note on the passage.

**73.** An instrumental ablative with a verbal substantive in *-tor* occurs *C.* III. 4. 55 **truncis iaculator;** with a verbal adjective, *C.* IV. 6. 8.

**74.** The ablative of price, added to the accusative after **muto** may denote either the thing given or the thing received in exchange; as *Ep.* I. 7. 36 **nec otia divitiis muto,** i. e. give up my leisure (acc.) for wealth (abl.); *C.* I. 17. 2 **Lucretilem mutat Lycaeo Faunus,** i. e. gives up Lycaeus (abl.) for Lucretilis (acc.). (Cf. the double use of *ἀλλάσσω τί τινος.*) Similarly with **verto** the ablative is twice used to denote that into which the object is transformed: *C.* I. 35. 4 **vertere funeribus triumphos;** *Ep.* II. 3. 226 **vertere seria ludo;** (cf. Ovid *M.* X. 157 nulla alite verti dignatur). The accusative with *in* is commonly used.

**75.** The ablative after comparatives is frequent, instead of the more logical expression with *quam;* as

*C.* I. 8. 9 **olivum sanguine viperino cautius vitat** (for *quam sanguinem*); *C.* III. 1. 9 **viro vir latius ordinet** (for *quam vir*). So with *alius: Ep.* II. 1. 240 **alius Lysippo** (for *quam Lysippus*). The ablative is rarely used when the first member of the comparison is not in the nominative or the accusative; as *Ep.* I. 10. 11 **pane egeo, iam mellitis potiore placentis.**

### *The Construction* ἀπὸ κοινοῦ.

**76.** An inflected word is sometimes placed in such relation to two other words that it may be governed by either of them, and is, in some cases, necessary to both to complete their meaning. By this arrangement, called by grammarians the σχῆμα ἀπὸ κοινοῦ, a repetition of the idea, by means of a pronoun or otherwise, is avoided ; as

*C.* II. 11. 11 **quid aeternis minorem consiliis animum fatigas?** (= quid aeternis consiliis animum, illis minorem, fatigas?) ; *C.* II. 14. 15 **frustra per autumnos nocentem corporibus metuemus austrum** (where both **nocentem corporibus** and **corporibus metuemus** can hardly fail to convey to the reader the usual significance of such juxtaposition) ; *Epod.* 9. 9 **vincla quae detraxerat servis amicus perfidis.**

## *Number and Tense of the Verb.*

**77.** Horace is noticeably fond of using a singular verb where there are two or more subjects ; as

*C.* II. 13. 38 **quin et Prometheus et Pelopis parens dulci laborem decipitur sono**; *C.* II. 18. 26 **pellitur paternos in sinu ferens deos et uxor et vir sordidosque natos**; *C.* III. 16. 32 **rivus aquae silvaque . . . et segetis certa fides . . . fallit sorte beatior.**

**78.** The colloquial present with future meaning, common in old Latin, is occasionally used by Horace ; as

*C.* III. 9. 17 **quid si prisca redit Venus, diductosque iugo cogit aeneo, si flava excutitur Chloe, reiectaeque patet ianua Lydiae?** *Ep.* I. 7. 34 **hac ego si compellor imagine, cuncta resigno, . . . nec otia divitiis Arabum liberrima muto.**

**79.** The future indicative is sometimes used with a concessive force, expressing, with indifference or acquiescence, the action of some other person or persons, with which that of the speaker, or of some one in whom he is more nearly interested, is brought into contrast ; as

*C.* I. 7. 1 **laudabunt alii claram Rhodon aut Mytilenen, . . . me nec tam,** etc. ; *C.* II. 12. 10 **tuque pedestribus dices historiis proelia Caesaris, . . . me dulcis dominae musa Licymniae cantus, me voluit dicere** (Cf. Verg. *Aen.* VI. 847 *excudent alii* spirantia mollius aera, | credo equidem, vivos *ducent* de marmore voltus, | *orabunt* causas melius, . . . | *tu* regere imperio populos, Romane, memento.)

**80.** The perfect indicative is used by the Augustan poets, like the Greek 'gnomic' aorist, to express a general truth or a customary action, — the statement that such and such a thing has proved true in the past conveying the implication that it is always true (cf. *invictus*, 'unconquered,' hence by implication, *unconquerable*); as

*Ep.* I. 17. 37 **sedit qui timuit ne non succederet,** *he sits still who fears he may fail;* *C.* I. 28. 20 **nullum saeva caput Proserpina fūgit;** *Ep.* I. 7. 21 **haec seges ingratos tulit et feret omnibus annis** (i. e. produces and always will produce).

**81.** (*a*) The archaic use of the perfect infinitive with *volo*, *nolo*, etc. (see § 94) was adopted by the poets, partly for metrical convenience, often merely to give variety to their diction. Horace in particular uses this construction with great freedom, the tense being often quite without significance; as

*S.* I. 2. 28 **sunt qui nolint tetigisse;** *S.* II. 3. 187 **ne quis humasse velit Aiacem vetas** (an intentional imitation of the archaic legal form); *Ep.* II. 3. 455 **tetigisse timent fugiuntque poetam.**

(*b*) It may be doubted, however, whether the consciousness of the tense was ever entirely lost, and in many cases the idea to be expressed is distinctly that of completed action; as

*C.* III. 4. 51 **tendentes Pelion imposuisse Olympo** (i. e. aiming at the achievement of that feat); *S.* II. 8. 79 **nullos his mallem ludos spectasse** (*prefer to have seen*); *Ep.* I. 17. 5 **si quid et nos quod cures proprium fecisse loquamur;** *Ep.* II. 3. 168 **commisisse cavet quod mox mutare laboret.**

### *Conditional and Concessive Clauses.*

**82.** By a rhetorical exaggeration the pluperfect indicative is occasionally used in apodosis, instead of the pluperfect subjunctive, to indicate that the result of a condition contrary to fact was partly accomplished, or to give a vivid impression of the imminence of its accomplishment; as

*C.* III. 16. 3 **inclusam Danaen turris aenea robustaeque fores et vigilum canum tristes excubiae munierant satis, si non Acrisium Iuppiter et Venus risissent** (they had proved sufficient up to that point); *C.* II. 17. 28 **me truncus inlapsus cerebro sustulerat, nisi Faunus ictum levasset.**

**83.** In concessive clauses with *quamvis*, Horace, like the early Latin writers, uses both the indicative and the subjunctive, more commonly the former. The indicative usually expresses a conceded fact, the subjunctive an assumption; but there are some exceptions; as

*C.* III. 11. 18 **cessit . . . Cerberus, quamvis furiale centum muniant angues caput . . . saniesque manet ore** (fact); *C.* IV. 6. 7 **tibi miles impar, filius quamvis Thetidis marinae Dardanas turris quateret** (fact); *S.* II. 5. 15 **qui quamvis periurus erit** (assumption), . . . **ne tamen illi tu comes exterior . . . ire recuses.**

## *Relative Clauses.*

**84.** In relative clauses of characteristic after *sunt qui* and the like, Horace frequently uses the indicative (a construction familiar in comedy), but also the subjunctive, with no apparent distinction of meaning; as

*C.* I. 7. 5 **sunt quibus unum opus est**; *Ep.* II. 1. 63 **interdum volgus rectum videt, est ubi peccat**; *Ep.* I. 1. 78 **sunt qui viduas venentur avaras excipiantque senes**; *Ep.* II. 2. 182 **sunt qui non habeant, est qui non curat habere** (where the more definite implication of the second relative clause is due to the number, not to the mood).

**85.** In a relative clause of characteristic with causal or concessive implication, Horace commonly uses the subjunctive, but sometimes the indicative; as

*Ep.* II. 3. 302 **o ego laevus, qui purgor bilem sub verni temporis horam!** *C.* II. 13. 34 **quid mirum, ubi illis carminibus stupens demittit atras belua centiceps auris et intorti capillis Eumenidum recreantur angues?**

**86.** In temporal clauses of repeated action after a past tense, Horace has the subjunctive once (two verbs):

*S.* I. 4. 107 **cum me hortaretur parce frugaliter atque viverem uti contentus eo quod mi ipse parasset, . . . a turpi meretricis amore cum deterreret, . . . aiebat.**

Elsewhere he uses the pluperfect indicative; as

*S.* II. 1. 71 **quin ubi se a volgo et scaena in secreta remorant, . . . nugari et ludere soliti** (sc. *sunt*); *Ep.* I. 15. 34 **hic ubi fautoribus nil aut paulum abstulerat, patinas cenabat omasi**; ib. 39 **ubi omne verterat in fumum et cinerem, . . . aiebat**; *Epod.* 11. 13 *sqq.*

## *Commands and Prohibitions.*

**87.** In commands and prohibitions, Horace uses the hortatory subjunctive in the second person singular as well as in the third, and whether the injunction is addressed to a definite person or to the general reader; as

*C.* I. 11. 6 (to Leuconoe) **sapias, vina liques, et spatio brevi spem longam reseces**; *C.* II. 11. 3 **quid bellicosus Cantaber et Scythes, Hirpine Quincti, cogitet, . . . remittas quaerere, nec trepides**; *S.* I. 1. 93 **cum habeas plus, pauperiem metuas minus, et finire laborem incipias**; *S.* II. 3. 88 **ne sis patruus mihi.**

**88.** In prohibition, besides the customary forms, — *ne feceris*, *cave* (or *cave ne*) *facias*, and *noli facere* with its various equivalents (see § 94 β) — Horace uses very rarely the imperative itself; as

*C.* I. 28. 23 **ne parce**; *C.* II. 7. 20 **nec parce cadis**; *C.* III. 7. 30 **neque in vias despice.**

**89.** An emphatic *non*, standing at the head of a sentence and belonging rather to the whole sentence than to the verb, — as *C.* II. 10. 17 non, si male nunc, et olim sic erit; *Ep.* I. 3 21 non tibi parvum ingenium, non incultum est, — is sometimes used even with a hortatory subjunctive in prohibition; as

*Ep.* I. 18. 72 **non ancilla tuum iecur ulceret ulla puerve**; *S.* II. 5. 91 **cautus adito, neu desis operae neve immoderatus abundes. . . . non etiam sileas**; **Davus sis comicus**, etc.

NOTE. — *Nec* (*neque*), for *neve* (*neu*), is very common.

**90.** A command or prohibition is often expressed by the future indicative; as

*Ep.* I. 1. 87 **cras ferramenta Teanum tolletis, fabri**; *Ep.* I. 13. 2 **ut docui te saepe diuque, Augusto reddes signata volumina, Vini**; *Ep.* I. 18. 37 **arcanum neque tu scrutaberis illius umquam, commissumque teges . . . ; nec tua laudabis studia aut aliena reprendes.** (Cf. the form of modern military orders: 'You will proceed with your command to such and such a place, etc.')

## *The Infinitive.*

**91.** The so-called '*Historical Infinitive*' occurs nowhere in the Odes and only once in the Epodes (5. 84 lenire). In the Satires it is not infrequent, and three instances of its use are found in the Epistles.

**92.** The *Infinitive in Exclamation* is used twice in the Epodes (8. 1 rogare; 11. 11 valere), and four times in the Satires (I. 9. 73 surrexe; II. 4. 83 *sq.* radere, dare; II. 8. 67 torquerier). In all these examples except the first it is introduced by *-ne.* It does not occur in the Odes or Epistles.

**93.** The *Infinitive of Purpose* was an old colloquial construction, used especially after verbs of movement; as Ter. *Hec.* 345 intro iit videre, *he has gone in to see.* It is frequent in comedy, but except in the phrase *do* (or, once, *ministro*) *bibere* is not found in classical prose writers; nor did it, like most poetical constructions, obtain a footing in later prose. The Augustan poets took it up, under Greek influence, but used it sparingly. The examples in Horace are as follows:

After verbs of movement: *C.* I. 2. 8 **pecus egit altos visere montis**; *C.* I. 23. 10 **non te frangere persequor**; *C.* III. 8. 11 **amphorae fumum bibere institutae.** With **trado**: *C.* I. 26. 3 **tristitiam et metus tradam protervis in mare Creticum portare ventis.** With **sumo,** *to take* or *choose* (as a subject): *C.* I. 12. 2 **quem sumis celebrare?** *Ep.* I. 3. 7 **quis sibi res gestas Augusti scribere sumit?** With other verbs; *Ep.* I. 2. 27 **fruges consumere nati**; *Epod.* 16. 16 (see note).

**94.** The *Complementary Infinitive.* For the colorless expression of will, desire, intention, effort, power, capacity, and the like, by such verbs as *volo, nolo, cupio, possum, cogito, conor,* which take a simple infinitive to denote the action (of the same subject) to which they point, it is natural in animated discourse to substitute words more vividly expressive of the feeling or power to be indicated. Some of these found their way into classical prose. Thus Cicero, to express desire, frequently uses *studeo*, *aveo*, *concupisco*, *gestio*, and (once each) *praegestio* and *expeto*, with a complementary infinitive; for unwillingness through indifference he has *non curo*, *non laboro*, *non induco animum;* for unwillingness due to fear, *vereor* and *timeo* (not *metuo*); for anxious effort *quaero*, *laboro*. The poets, as was to be expected, carried this process much further, and permitted themselves great freedom, especially to give livelier expression to the feeling which prompts or accompanies an action. The verbs used by Horace in this construction (with the exception of those very common in prose) are as follows:

(I.) Expressions of *will*, *desire*, *intention*, *effort*.

(α) POSITIVE.

(*a*) Mere *willingness* or *approval:* **patior, dignor, probo**; as *C.* III. 9. 15 **bis patiar mori**; *Ep.* I. 19. 40 **non ego grammaticas ambire tribus et pulpita dignor**; *C. S.* 15 **Lucina probas vocari.**

(*b*) *Concern, interest:* **curo, laboro**; as *C.* II. 7. 25 **quis deproperare coronas curat?** (but *curo* is more commonly negative or with negative implication; see (*i*), below); *Ep.* I. 3. 2 **scire laboro** (see also under (*h*), below).

(*c*) *Preference, desire, passion:* **praefero, amo, studeo, quaero, iuvat, aveo, gestio, praegestio, furo**; as *Ep.* II. 2. 184 **cessare et ludere et ungui praeferat**; *C.* I. 2. 50 **hic ames dici pater atque princeps**; *C.* I. 16. 26 **mitibus mutare quaero tristia**; *Epod.* 9. 37 **capaciores adfer huc, puer scyphos, . . . curam metumque iuvat dulci Lyaeo solvere** (i.e. I feel a desire to); *C.* I. 15. 27 **furit te reperire.**

(*d*) *Delight:* **gaudeo, delector, glorior, renideo**; as *C.* III. 6. 21 **motus doceri gaudet Ionicos**; *Ep.* I. 16. 32 **vir bonus et prudens dici delector**; *Epod.* 11. 23 **gloriantis vincere**; *C.* III. 6. 12 **adiecisse praedam torquibus exiguis renidet.**

(*e*) *Demand, claim:* **posco, flagito**; as *Ep.* II. 3. 339 **ne poscat sibi fabula credi**; *S.* II. 4. 61 **flagitat refici.**

(*f*) *Purpose, resolve:* **meditor, coniuro**; as *C.* III. 8. 23 **meditantur cedere campis**; *C.* I. 15. 7 **coniurata tuas rumpere nuptias.**

(*g*) *Eagerness, haste:* **propero, festino, occupo, urgeo, trepido**; as *C.* II. 12. 28 **(oscula) rapere occupet**; *C.* II. 18. 20 **urges submovere litora**; *C.* II. 4. 23 **octavum trepidavit aetas claudere lustrum.**

(*h*) *Effort, struggle:* **peto, expeto, tendo, laboro, enitor, certo**; as *Ep.* I. 11. 29 navibus atque quadrigis petimus bene vivere; *Epod.* 11. 3 me expetit urere; *Ep.* I. 10. 20 aqua tendit rumpere plumbum; *Ep.* I. 20. 16 quis invitum servare laboret? (No clear line can be drawn between this use of **laboro**, 'anxiously try,' and that under (*b*) above, 'anxiously wish.'); *Ep.* II. 3. 236 nec sic enitar tragico differre colori; *C.* I. 1. 8 certat tollere honoribus.

(β) NEGATIVE.

(*i*) *Unconcern, reluctance:* **non curo, non magni pendo, contemno, sperno, non induco animum, indignor, invideo**; as *C.* II. 13. 39 nec curat Orion leones agitare; *S.* II. 4. 92 quem tu vidisse non magni pendes; *Ep.* I. 1. 50 quis coronari contemnat Olympia? *S.* I. 3. 2 ut numquam inducant animum cantare; *Ep.* II. 3. 90 indignatur privatis ac prope socco dignis carminibus narrari cena Thyestae; *C.* I. 37. 30 saevis Liburnis invidens deduci triumpho.

(*j*) *Neglect, inaction:* **mitto, omitto, remitto, cesso, moror, differo**; as *Epod.* 13. 7 cetera mitte loqui; *C.* II. 11. 3 remittas quaerere; *C.* IV. 4. 21 quaerere distuli.

(*k*) *Refusal, avoidance:* **recuso, denego, vito, fugio, refugio, aufero, caveo, parco**; as *Ep.* II. 3. 39 quid ferre recusent, quid valeant umeri; *C.* III. 16. 38 nec si plura velim tu dare deneges; *Ep.* I. 3. 16 ut tangere vitet; *C.* I. 9. 13 fuge quaerere; *S.* II. 7. 43 aufer me voltu terrere (= noli terrere); *Ep.* II. 3. 168 commisisse cavet quod mox mutare laboret.

(*l*) *Fear, hatred:* **vereor, timeo, metuo, formido, perhorresco, odi**; as *C.* III. 9. 11 non metuam mori; *Ep.* I. 19. 46 naribus uti formido; *C.* III. 16. 18 iure perhorrui late conspicuum tollere verticem; *Ep.* I. 16. 52 oderunt peccare boni.

(*m*) *Pain, regret:* **doleo, ploro**: *C.* IV. 4. 62 non Hydra secto corpore firmior vinci dolentem crevit in Herculem; *C.* III. 10. 4 me obicere plorares Aquilonibus.

## (II.) Expressions of *power* or *capacity*.

(*n*) *Power:* **valeo, evalesco, habeo, est** (= ἔξεστι, *it is possible*); as *C.* I. 34. 12 valet ima summis mutare; *Ep.* II. 1. 201 quae pervincere voces evaluere sonum, referunt quem nostra theatra? *Epod.* 16. 23 sic placet, an melius quis habet suadere? *S.* II. 5. 103 est gaudia prodentem voltum celare.

(*o*) *Capacity, skill, incapacity:* **scio, calleo, novi, nescio, ignoro**; as *Ep.* I. 17. 14 si sciret regibus uti (*knew how*); *C.* IV. 9. 49 callet pauperiem pati; *S.* II. 3. 24 hortos egregiasque domos mercarier

**unus cum lucro noram**; *Ep.* II. 3. 87 **descriptas servare vices operumque colores cur ego si nequeo ignoroque poeta salutor?**

(III.) Expressions of *propriety* or *necessity.*

(*p*) *Propriety, fitness, obligation:* **vincit** (=*praestat*), **quo tibi?**, **restat**; as *S.* II. 5. 73 **sed vincit longe prius ipsum expugnare caput**; *S.* I. 6. 24 **quo tibi, Tilli, sumere depositum clavum fierique tribuno?** (cf. § 52); *Ep.* I. 6. 27 **ire tamen restat Numa quo devenit** (i. e. that destiny is in store for you).

**95.** The complementary infinitive is often hardly distinguishable from a substantive object of the verb; but in some cases the distinction is important; as

*C.* I. 28. 31 **neglegis fraudem committere?** *do you treat lightly the commission of a wrong?* *C.* III. 14. 15 **nec mori per vim metuam,** *nor shall I be in fear of a violent death* (in contrast with *C.* III. 9. 11 non metuam mori, = 'I shall be willing to die'); *Ep.* I. 7. 4 **quam mihi das aegro, dabis aegrotare timenti** (*fear I am going to be ill*); *Ep.* I. 16. 60 **labra movet, metuens audiri.**

**96.** In one instance Horace uses the infinitive after a preposition: *S.* II. 5. 69 **inveniet nil sibi legatum praeter plorare.** But here the infinitive really depends on **legatum**; cf. the example with **damnatus**, § 97 *b*.

**97.** The infinitive is used by Horace with the following verbs (after the analogy of *iubeo*, *cogo*, *doceo*, *sino*, *prohibeo*), denoting influence of the subject on the action of other persons:

(*a*) Verbs signifying to *ask*, *encourage*, *advise*, *bid:* **rogo, voco, hortor, moneo, admoneo, censeo, refero**; as *S.* I. 3. 2 **cantare rogati**; *C.* II. 18. 40 **levare pauperem vocatus**; *Ep.* I. 1. 69 **Fortunae te responsare superbae . . . hortatur et aptat**; *S.* I. 6. 126 **me fessum sol acrior ire lavatum admonuit**; *Ep.* I. 2. 9 **Antenor censet belli praecidere causam**; *Ep.* I. 8. 1 **Celso gaudere et bene rem gerere, Musa, rogata refer** (i. e. 'tell him to' or 'tell him I bid him').

(*b*) Verbs signifying to *urge*, *command*, *require* (mostly passive): **impello, impero, damno, auctoro, addico**; as *C.* III. 7. 14 **ut Proetum mulier perfida impulerit Bellerophontae maturare necem**; *Ep.* I. 5. 21 **haec ego procurare imperor**; *S.* II. 3. 86 **gladiatorum dare centum damnati paria** (by the terms of a will); *S.* II. 7. 59 **uri virgis ferroque necari auctoratus** (bound by the terms of enlistment as a gladiator); *Ep.* I. 1. 14 **nullius addictus iurare in verba magistri.**

(*c*) Verbs signifying to *show, teach:* **monstro, fingo, apto**; as *S.* II. 8. 52 **inulas ego primus monstravi incoquere**; *Ep.* I. 2. 64 **fingit equum magister ire viam**; see also third example under (*a*), above.

(*d*) Verbs signifying to *permit:* **do, dono, reddo, permitto, concedo, relinquo, fero**; as *S.* II. 3. 191 **di tibi dent classem reducere**; *S.* II. 5. 60 **divinare mihi donat Apollo**; *Ep.* I. 7. 27 **reddes forte latus, . . . reddes dulce loqui, reddes ridere decorum, et inter vina fugam Cinarae maerere protervae**; *S.* II. 3. 190 **dicere permitto** (with dative); *Ep.* I. 5. 12 **quo mihi fortunam, si non conceditur uti?** *S.* I. 1. 52 **dum nobis tantundem haurire relinquas**; *Epod.* 15. 13 **non feret potiori te dare noctes.**

(*e*) Verbs signifying to *prevent:* **invideo, adimo, interpello**; *S.* I. 2. 100 **quae invideant apparere tibi rem**; *Ep.* I. 19. 9 **adimam cantare severis**; *S.* I. 6. 127 **pransus non avide, quantum interpellet inani ventre diem durare** (*prevent me from passing*).

**98.** The infinitive of indirect discourse, with or without a subject accusative, is used after the following verbs:

**induco** (of dramatic representation), **vinco** and **evinco** (*maintain, triumphantly prove*), **contendo** (*assert*), **fido, do** (*admit, grant*); as *S.* I. 2. 21 **pater ille Terenti fabula quem miserum vixisse inducit**; *S.* II. 3. 225 **vincet enim stultos ratio insanire nepotes**; ib. 250 **puerilius his ratio esse evincet amare**; *Ep.* I. 16. 37 **si clamet furem, neget esse pudicum, contendat laqueo collum pressisse paternum**; *Ep.* I. 19. 44 **fidis manare poetica mella te solum**; *S.* I. 4. 39 **dederim quibus esse poetas.**

**99.** (*a*) In indirect discourse the subject of the infinitive is sometimes omitted if it is the same as the subject of the leading verb or is readily understood from the context; as

*Ep.* I. 2. 11 **quid Paris? . . . cogi posse negat**; *Ep.* I. 9. 5 **cum rogat et prece cogit, scilicet ut tibi se laudare et tradere coner, . . . munere cum fungi propioris censet amici, quid possim videt ac novit me valdius ipso.** Sometimes both subject and verb (*esse*) are omitted; as *Ep.* I. 18. 2 **metues scurrantis speciem praebere, professus amicum.**

(*b*) In two instances, where the subject is identical with that of the leading verb, the predicate is attracted, after the Greek manner, into the nominative:

*C.* III. 27. 73 **uxor invicti Iovis esse nescis**; *Ep.* I. 7. 22 **vir bonus et sapiens dignis ait esse paratus.**

**100.** The infinitive of indirect discourse is used with the following, as verbs of feeling :

**gestio, gemo, ploro, lamentor, indignor**; as *S.* I. 4. 37 **quodcumque chartis inleverit omnis gestiet scire**; *Ep.* I. 20. 4 **paucis ostendi gemis** (see § 99 *a*) ; *Ep.* II. 1. 9 **ploravere suis non respondere favorem speratum meritis**; ib. 76 **indignor quicquam reprehendi**; ib. 224 **lamentamur non apparere labores.**

**101.** *The Infinitive with Adjectives.* This construction is confined in classical prose to a few adjectives of verbal origin, like *paratus*, and is rare in poetry before the Augustan age. In the hands of Vergil and Horace it received a rich development and was thenceforth an established feature of poetic diction. The infinitive is usually complementary in character. It is attached to participles (used adjectively) of verbs which take an infinitive, as *sciens* (cf. § 94 *o*), *doctus* and *doctior*, *meritus;* to adjectives of similar origin, as *nescius*, *indoctus*, *indocilis*, *audax*, *callidus*, *timidus;* finally, to a great number of adjectives expressing in various phases the power, will, capacity, fitness (or the reverse) to do something. The adjectives so used in Horace are as follows :

(*a*) Expressing *disposition:* **praesens** (of a goddess, implying power and readiness), **lenis** (also of a divinity, *indulgent*, *gracious*), **saevus** (*ruthless*), **impotens** (*wild*, *undisciplined*) ; **audax, fortis, contentus, cautus, timidus**; as *C.* I. 35. 2 **o diva . . . , praesens vel imo tollere de gradu mortale corpus**; *C.* I. 24. 17 (**Mercurius**) **non lenis precibus fata recludere**; *Ep.* I. 15. 30 **opprobria fingere saevus**; *C.* I. 37. 10 **quidlibet impotens sperare**; *C.* I. 3. 25 **audax omnia perpeti**; *C.* I. 37. 26 **fortis et asperas tractare serpentes**; *S.* I. 10. 59 **pedibus quid claudere senis, hoc tantum contentus**; *S.* I. 6. 51 **cautum dignos (amicos) adsumere**; *C.* III. 19. 2 **non timidus mori.**

(*b*) Expressing *capacity*, *energy*, or their opposites : **efficax, pertinax, celer, pernix, largus** (*liberal*, *generous*), **firmus** (*to be depended upon*), **impiger**; **piger, segnis** (*slow*, *reluctant*), **dolosus** (*not to be trusted*, *too fickle*) ; as *C.* IV. 12. 20 **(cadus) spes donare novas largus amaraque curarum eluere efficax**; *C.* III. 29. 50 **(Fortuna) ludum insolentem ludere pertinax**; *C.* I. 15. 18 **celerem sequi**; *Ep.* II. 3. 165 **amata relinquere pernix**; *Ep.* I. 17. 47 **fundus nec vendibilis nec pascere firmus**; *C.* IV. 14. 22 **impiger hostium vexare turmas;**

*S.* I. 4. 12 **piger scribendi ferre laborem**; *C.* III. 21. 22 **segnes nodum solvere Gratiae**; *C.* I. 35. 28 **amici ferre iugum pariter dolosi.**

(*c*) Expressing *knowledge, skill,* or the reverse: **sciens, doctus, doctior, callidus, catus, sollers, prudens, blandus** (*with charm*), **nobilis; nescius, indoctus, indocilis, durus, minor**; as *C.* III. 7. 25 **flectere equum sciens**; *C.* III. 24. 56 **ludere doctior**; *C.* I. 10. 7 **callidum quicquid placuit iocoso condere furto**; *C.* III. 12. 4 **catus cervos iaculari**; *C.* IV. 8. 9 **hic saxo, ille coloribus sollers nunc hominem ponere, nunc deum**; *Epod.* 17. 47 **in sepulcris prudens anus dissipare pulveres**; *C.* I. 12. 11 **(Orphea) blandum et auritas fidibus canoris ducere quercus**; ib. 26 **[Pollucem] superare pugnis nobilem** (the infinitive here may possibly be attributed to the idea of *nosco* contained in the adjective, like that of *doceo* in *indocilis;* cf. Sil. Ital. XII. 331 Troianos notus semper minuisse labores; but it is much more probable that *nobilem* is intended to express preëminent skill, and that the infinitive is complementary; cf. Verg. *Ecl.* 5. 2. boni calamos inflare; Lucan III. 697 eximius animam servare; and the use of *minor*, below; see also § 102); *C.* IV. 6. 18 **nescios fari** (= infantes) **pueros**; *C.* I. 1. 18 **indocilis pauperiem pati**; *S.* I. 4. 8 **durus componere versus** (implying lack of capacity; but see § 102); *S.* II. 3. 313 **certare minorem** (cf. Verg. *Ecl.* 7. 5 cantare pares.)

(*d*) Expressing *fitness, merit,* or the opposite: **idoneus, utilis, dignus, meritus, indignus, immeritus**: as *Ep.* I. 16. 12 **fons rivo dare nomen idoneus**; *Ep.* II. 3. 204 **(tibia) adspirare et adesse choris erat utilis**; *Ep.* I. 10. 48 **tortum digna sequi potius quam ducere funem** (see also (*e*), below); *Ep.* I. 3. 35 **indigni fraternum rumpere foedus** (i. e. men for whom such conduct is unbecoming); *C.* III. 2. 21 **immeritis mori.** Cf. the dative with adjectives of this class, § 58 *b* and *c*.

(*e*) With **dignus** the passive infinitive is more frequent; as *S.* I. 3. 24 **dignus notari**; and it is also found with **levis** and **cereus**; C. II. 4. 11 **leviora tolli Pergama** (*easier*); *Ep.* II. 3. 163 **(iuvenis) cereus in vitium flecti** (*like wax, as easy as wax*).

**102.** As the quality which fits one for an action is likely to be displayed in the action itself, — e.g. 'swift to pursue' passes into 'swift in pursuit,' — the infinitive with an adjective readily acquires the force of an ablative of respect. This is manifest in many of the examples given above, such as those with *saevus*, *cautus*, *pertinax*, *celer*, *impiger*, *nobilis*, *durus*. In the following examples it is the prevailing signification, the infinitive, if it is passive, being equivalent to a verbal noun in *-u*.

*C. S.* 25 **veraces cecinisse**, where the perfect (found only here in this construction) has its proper force; *S.* II. 8. 24 **ridiculus totas simul absorbere placentas**; *C.* I. 19. 8 **voltus nimium lubricus adspici** (= adspectu); *C.* IV. 2. 59 **niveus videri** (= visu).

### *The Participle.*

**103.** The participle is used, more freely than in prose, as a substantive or adjective, often retaining its verbal force; as

*Ep.* I. 17. 43 **coram rege sua de paupertate tacentes plus poscente ferent**; *C.* II. 16. 1 **otium divos rogat in patenti prensus Aegaeo**; *C.* III. 7. 19 **peccare docentis historias.**

**104.** The future participle often fulfils the function of a clause appended to its subject, with various shades of meaning: —

(*a*) Simple future fact or intention; as *C.* I. 35. 29 **serves iturum Caesarem in ultimos orbis Britannos** (i. e. qui iturus est).

(*b*) With prophetic force, — 'sure to,' 'doomed to'; as *Epod.* 15. 11 **o dolitura multum Neaera**; *C.* II. 3. 27 **versatur urna serius ocius sors exitura et nos in aeternum exsilium impositura cumbae.**

(*c*) Equivalent to a relative clause of characteristic; as *Epod.* 6. 4 **quin me remorsurum petis?** (*a dog that will bite back*); *S.* II. 8. 85 **Nasidiene, redis mutatae frontis, ut arte emendaturus fortunam** (*as one resolved*, etc.); *Epod.* 15. 3 **cum tu, magnorum numen laesura deorum, in verba iurabas mea** (with concessive implication).

(*d*) Conditional statement: *S.* II. 8. 44 **haec gravida capta est, deterior post partum carne futura** (i. e. quae quidem carne deterior esset, si post partum capta esset); *Epod.* I. 22 **non, ut adsit, auxili latura plus** (i. e. etsi non plus auxilii ferat, si adsit); *S.* I. 10. 89 **doliturus si placeant spe deterius** (*and I should be sorry if*, etc.). — Hence

(*e*) With a vague condition, like *si libeat, si opus sit*, expressed or understood, giving it the force of 'ready to,' 'able to'; as *C.* IV. 3. 20 **o mutis quoque piscibus donatura cycni, si libeat, sonum** (= 'able to give'); *C.* II. 6. 1 **Septimi, Gadis aditure mecum** (*ready to go*).

**105.** (*a*) The combination of a substantive with a participle, an adjective, or another substantive to express an abstract idea, — familiar in prose in the gerundive construction, in the ablative absolute, and in the similar use, to a limited extent, of the accusative (as *ante me consulem* = *ante meum consulatum*) — was given a much wider range by the poets; as

*C.* II. 4. 10 **postquam ademptus Hector tradidit leviora tolli Pergama Grais** (*the taking-off of Hector*); *C.* III. 6. 29 **non sine conscio marito** (*with the connivance of her husband*); *Epod.* 9. 2 **victore laetus Caesare** (*glad of Caesar's victory*).

(*b*) The ablative of this construction is sometimes equivalent to an ablative of manner or means; as

*S.* II. 1. 84 **iudice laudatus Caesare,** *commended by the verdict of Caesar; Ep.* I. 1. 94 **curatus inaequali tonsore capillos,** *my hair trimmed with a lopsided cut; Ep.* I. 16. 42 **quo multae magnaeque secantur iudice lites, quo res sponsore, et quo causae teste tenentur** (*by whose verdict, credit, testimony*).

---

## (B) ORDER AND USE OF WORDS.

**106.** In reading Latin prose the feature of the language which is at once the most difficult and the most important for us to master, is the freedom which inflexion gives of separating in expression ideas closely connected in sense, and the consequent demand that is made upon us to hold in suspense, as we proceed, a partially expressed thought, and to grasp at once the meaning of a whole group of words. For us, who speak an uninflected language, this must be an acquired habit; but it is quite indispensable: he who has not cultivated it cannot read Latin, though he may be able to translate it. For reading Latin poetry we have to carry this cultivation still farther; but it is only a higher degree of the same capacity that is required, not a new kind of capacity.

**107.** There is, in fact, no clear line of distinction between prose and verse, in respect to the order of words, although their general characteristics are plainly marked. In prose the greatest freedom of movement is accorded to the verb, which may be placed, with little reference to the position of its subject or object, wherever emphasis or the order of thought or rhetorical form may suggest. On the other hand a modifier of any kind must keep reasonably near its noun or verb, and the least liberty of all is allowed to an attribute and its substantive. These as a rule are not separated except by unemphatic words, — pronouns, particles, and the like, — as 'magna ex parte,' 'angustos se fines (habere),' 'quanto id cum periculo (fieret).' Yet Roman prose writers permit themselves occasionally a compact group like 'eodem usi consilio,' '(de) ea quam habeat gratia'; or even a longer group, especially where the inserted words themselves constitute a modifier, as 'tua in me vel nota omnibus vel ipsa novitate meorum temporum clarissima et maxima beneficia,' 'meam tuorum erga me meritorum memoriam.' But such combinations have a rhetorical flavor in prose, and are in fact sparingly used. In verse, on the other hand, they are rather the rule than the exception; the poets have studiously wrought out artistic groupings and sequences which the reader must train himself to grasp and follow, if he would appreciate the beauty of poetical expression. The forms are too varied and complex to be set forth fully, but the following examples, chiefly from Horace's lyric poems, may serve to indicate their character and point out the way to study them.

### *Grouping of Connected Words.*

**108.** The following are examples of simple groups:

(*a*) Groups of three words (very common):

| | |
|---|---|
| *C.* I. 3. 8 | animae dimidium meae |
| *C.* I. 27. 11 | quo beatus volnere |
| *C.* II. 13. 29 | sacro digna silentio |

| | |
|---|---|
| *C.* I. 35. 12 | purpurei metuunt tyranni |
| *C.* I. 5. 4 | flavam religas comam |
| *C.* III. 17. 5 | auctore ab illo |

(*b*) Groups of four words :

| | |
|---|---|
| *C. S.* 29 | fertilis frugum pecorisque tellus |
| *C.* III. 16. 17 | crescentem sequitur cura pecuniam |
| *C.* I. 7. 23 | populea fertur vinxisse corona |
| *C.* IV. 2. 3 | vitreo daturus nomina ponto |

(*c*) Groups of five words :

| | |
|---|---|
| *C.* I. 27. 1 | natis in usum laetitiae scyphis |
| *C.* I. 3. 30 | nova febrium terris incubuit cohors |
| *C.* III. 1. 10 | generosior descendat in campum petitor |
| *C.* I. 4. 15 | spem nos vetat incohare longam |
| *C.* I. 4. 9 | viridi nitidum caput impedire myrto |

(*d*) Longer groups :

| | |
|---|---|
| *C.* III, 29. 11 | beatae \| fumum et opes strepitumque Romae |
| *Ep.* I. 10. 48 | tortum digna sequi potius quam ducere funem |
| *C.* I. 27. 9 | (voltis) severi me quoque sumere \| partem Falerni? |

**109.** The arrangement within these groups presents great variety. (The arrow-head in the following examples indicates the governing word.)

*C.* I. 1. 22 — aquae lene caput sacrae

*C.* IV. 1. 4 — dulcium | mater saeva Cupidinum

*C.* III. 13. 9 — flagrantis atrox hora Caniculae

*C.* III. 8. 13 (a rare form) — cyathos amici sospitis centum

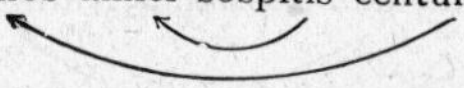

*C.* III. 1. 16 — omne capax movit urna nomen

*C.* III. 13. 6 — gelidos inficiet tibi | rubro sanguine rivos

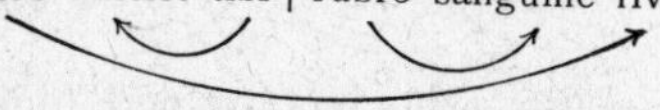

*C.* II. 3. 11 — obliquo laborat | lympha fugax trepidare rivo

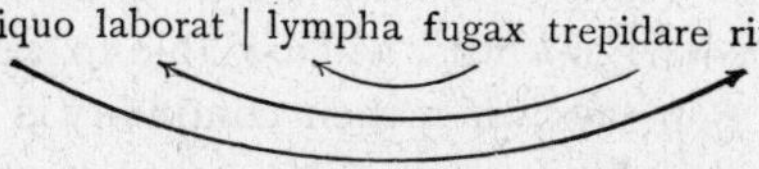

**110.** When a word within a group is closely connected in sense with a word preceding or following the group, there results an alternating or interlocked order, which occurs in great variety; as,

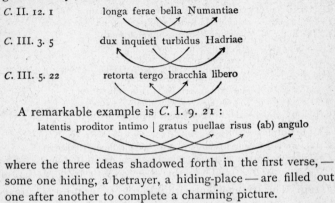

*C.* II. 12. 1 longa ferae bella Numantiae

*C.* III. 3. 5 dux inquieti turbidus Hadriae

*C.* III. 5. 22 retorta tergo bracchia libero

A remarkable example is *C.* I. 9. 21:

latentis proditor intimo | gratus puellae risus (ab) angulo

where the three ideas shadowed forth in the first verse,— some one hiding, a betrayer, a hiding-place — are filled out one after another to complete a charming picture.

**111.** Two groups are sometimes linked together by the connection of their interior words; as

*C.* III. 11. 26

inane lymphae | dolium fundo pereuntis imo

*C.* II. 5. 10

lividos | distinguet autumnus racemos | purpureo varius colore

*C.* II. 9. 13 (at non ter aevo)

functus amabilem | ploravit omnis Antilochum senex | annos

*C.* I. 22. 17 (pone me)

pigris ubi nulla campis | arbor aestiva recreatur aura

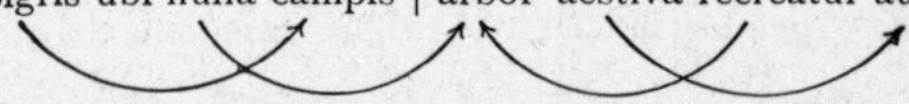

**112.** The reader who has trained himself to recognize coherent groups of words, will be able to keep his hold on the connection even when their continuity is interrupted; as

| | |
|---|---|
| *C.* III. 20. 3 | *dura* post paulo fugies *inaudax*<br>*proelia raptor* |
| *C.* IV. 7. 27 | nec *Lethaea* valet Theseus abrumpere *caro*<br>*vincula Pirithoo* |
| *C.* I. 2. 39 | *acer* et Marsi peditis *cruentum*<br>*voltus in hostem* |
| *C.* III. 4. 9 | *me fabulosae* Volture in Apulo<br>nutricis extra limen Apuliae<br>ludo fatigatumque somno<br>fronde nova *puerum palumbes*<br>texere |

where *puerum*, reviving the idea of *me*, supplies the necessary link between *fabulosae* and *palumbes*. Similarly in

| | |
|---|---|
| *C.* I. 22. 9 | namque *me* silva *lupus* in Sabina,<br>dum meam canto Lalagen et ultra<br>terminum curis vagor expeditis,<br>*fugit inermem* |

*fugit* recalls *me* through its subject *lupus*.

**113.** The poet often uses the metre to suggest the connection of separated words, by placing them at the beginning and end of a verse or other definite portion of the rhythm; as

| | |
|---|---|
| *C.* I. 1 14 | *Myrtoum* pavidus nauta secet *mare* |
| *C.* II. 3. 1 | *aequam* memento rebus in arduis<br>servare *mentem* ‖ |
| *C.* II. 6. 15 | ‖ *viridi*que certat<br>baca *Venafro* |
| *C.* III. 18. 11 | *festus* in pratis vacat otioso<br>cum bove *pagus* |

or one at the end of each half of a verse (especially in the Sapphic verse, and in the Asclepiad, where a rhyme is often produced); as

| | |
|---|---|
| *C.* I. 22. 17 | pone me *pigris* ‖ ubi nulla *campis*<br>arbor *aestiva* ‖ recreatur *aura* |
| *C.* I. 1. 9 | illum si *proprio* ‖ condidit *horreo*<br>quicquid de *Libycis* ‖ verritur *areis* |

or by giving them corresponding positions in different verses or hemistichs; as

C. II. 6. 13 — *ille* terrarum mihi praeter omnis
*angulus* ridet

C. I. 26. 2 — tradam *protervis* || in mare Creticum
portare *ventis* ||

C. I. 20. 6 — simul et *iocosa*
redderet laudes tibi Vaticani
montis *imago*

C. II. 2. 23 — quisquis *ingentis* || oculo inretorto
spectat *acervos*

C. IV. 4. 69 — Carthagini iam non ego *nuntios*
mittam *superbos* ||

This is especially common at the close of an Alcaic or Sapphic strophe; as

C. I. 16. 11 — nec *tremendo*
Iuppiter ipse ruens *tumultu*

C. I. 12. 7 — unde vocalem temere *insecutae*
Orphea *silvae*

**114.** A relative or interrogative pronoun or a particle which regularly stands at the head of a clause or phrase is often taken within the group, giving place to a more important word; as

*C.* I. 25. 17 laeta *quod* pubes hedera virenti gaudeat; *C.* I. 2. 7 omne *cum* Proteus pecus egit; *C.* I. 2. 18 vagus *et* sinistra labitur ripa; *C.* I. 37. 20 daret *ut* catenis fatale monstrum.

Sometimes two or more words precede; as

*C.* I. 18. 3 siccis omnia *nam* dura deus proposuit; *C.* III. 1. 17 destrictus ensis *cui* super impia cervice pendet; *Epod.* 16. 40 Etrusca praeter *et* volate litora; *C.* IV. 4. 42 dirus per urbis Afer *ut* Italas . . . equitavit.

## *Prepositions.*

**115.** (*a*) A preposition placed between a substantive and its modifier, often follows the substantive; as

mensis per omnis; tempus in ultimum; collibus in suis.

(*b*) Dissyllabic prepositions still in use as adverbs, — *circa*, *circum*, *citra*, *supra*, *prope*, — with *inter*, *praeter*, *sine*, are used with great freedom of position, often separated from their object, whether preceding or following it; as

haec inter; quos inter; aequalis inter; *C.* III. 27. 31 nihil astra praeter vidit et undas; *S.* I. 10. 31 natus mare citra; *S.* I. 3. 60 genus hoc inter vitae; *S.* II. 3. 40 insanos qui inter vereare insanus haberi; *C.* III. 19. 15 tris prohibet supra; *S.* I. 10. 91 discipularum inter iubeo plorare cathedras.

(*c*) In such cases Horace is fond of placing the preposition before the verb of the sentence, as if it were an unattached prefix; as

C. II. 16. 33 te greges centum Siculaeque *circum*
*mugiunt* vaccae

*C.* III. 3. 37 dum longus *inter* ‖ *saeviat* Ilion
Romamque pontus

*C.* III. 27. 51 utinam *inter errem* | nuda leones

*Ep.* I. 3. 4 freta vicinas *inter currentia* turris

*Ep.* II. 1. 43 veteres *inter ponetur*

(*d*) Conversely the prefix of a compound verb is treated as detachable in some cases:

S. I. 1. 86 cum tu argento *post* omnia *ponas*

*Ep.* II. 2. 93 quanto molimine *circum*
*spectemus*

*Ep.* II. 3. 424 si sciet *inter*
*noscere* mendacem verumque beatus amicum

(*e*) The caesura of the verse is sometimes allowed to fall between a monosyllabic prepositional prefix and the following syllable of a compound word; as

*C.* I. 37. 5 antehac nefas de‖promere Caecubum

*C.* II. 12. 25 cum flagrantia de‖torquet ad oscula

*C.* I. 16. 21 hostile aratrum ex‖ercitus insolens

## *Emphasis.*

**116.** Emphasis is secured (besides the methods usual in prose) —

(*a*) By placing in juxtaposition the two words of a group which express contrasted ideas; as

C. I. 3. 10 qui *fragilem truci* | commisit *pelago ratem*

C. IV. 4. 31 neque *imbellem feroces* | progenerant *aquilae columbam*

(*b*) By rhythmical position. The places best adapted for this purpose are the beginning of a strophe or verse (especially when the word is held in reserve and stands at the end of its sentence in this position) and the end of a verse or hemistich; as

C. III. 18. 2 per meos finis et aprica rura
*lenis* incedas, abeasque parvis
*aequus* alumnis

C. IV. 9. 25 vixere fortes ante Agamemnona
*multi*

C. II. 10. 9 *saepius* ventis agitatur *ingens*
pinus, et *celsae* || *graviore* casu
decidunt turres, feriuntque *summos*
fulgura montis

In C. II. 9 observe the emphasis on *non semper*, *tu semper*, *at non*, vss. 1, 9, 13 (under the first ictus), *usque* 4, *omnis* 6, *omnis* 14, *semper* 17, *minores* 22.

(*c*) By giving related or contrasted words prominent rhythmical positions; as

C. III. 2. 17 virtus *repulsae* || nescia *sordidae*

C. III. 11. 31 impiae sponsos potuere *duro*
perdere *ferro*

C. II. 10. 13 s p e r a t *infestis*, || m e t u i t *secundis*

(See also the examples under § 113.)

(*d*) By repetition, — either immediately, in the same clause (Epizeuxis, especially common in the Epodes); as

*Epod.* 4. 20 *hoc hoc* tribuno militum; ib. 14. 6 *deus deus* nam me vetat; C. II. 17. 10 *ibimus ibimus*, utcumque praecedes;

(*e*) or immediately, at the beginning of a new clause, sometimes with some variation of form (Anadiplosis); as

*C.* III. 5. 21 'arma
militibus sine caede' dixit
'derepta *vidi ; vidi* ego civium
retorta tergo bracchia libero'

*C.* III. 16. 15 subruit aemulos
reges *muneribus ; munera* navium
saevos inlaqueant duces

(*f*) or, after intervening words, at the beginning of a new clause or of successive clauses (Anaphora); as

*C.* III. 3. 65 *ter* si resurgat murus aeneus
auctore Phoebo, *ter* pereat meis
excisus Argivis, *ter* uxor
capta virum puerosque ploret

(*g*) The emphasis of Anaphora is usually enhanced by rhythmical position; as

*C.* II. 4. 4 serva Briseis niveo colore
*movit* Achillem
*movit* Aiacem . . .

*C.* II. 8. 13 *ridet* hoc, inquam, Venus ipsa, *rident*
simplices Nymphae

(*h*) Anaphora, however, is sometimes used without special emphasis, merely serving the purpose of a connective; as

*Epod.* 5. 17 *iubet* sepulcris caprificos erutas,
*iubet* cupressos funebris . . .
flammis aduri Colchicis

**117.** (*a*) The poet, whose appeal is to the imagination rather than to the intellect, seeks to make a more vivid impression by presenting a picture in preference to an abstract conception, and by putting forward a particular person, object, or action to represent a whole class; as

*C.* I. 1. 9 proprio condidit horreo (for amassing wealth in general); 11 findere sarculo (i. e. to till). Cf., further, 3 pulverem *Olympicum ;* 10 *Libycis* areis; 13 trabe *Cypria ;* 14 *Myrtoum* mare; 15 *Icariis* fluctibus *Africum ; C.* II. 18. 3 non trabes *Hymettiae* premunt columnas ultima recisas *Africa*, neque *Attali* ignotus heres regiam occupavi, nec *Laconicas* mihi trahunt honestae purpuras clientae. So the wind is *Eurus*, *Notus*, *Aquilo ;* wine is *Falernum*, *Caecubum*, *Sabinum ;* the

Roman legionary *Marsus* et *Apulus;* the outside barbarian *Dacus* et *Aethiops;* and so on in endless variety.

(*b*) In the same way a part may produce a more distinct impression than the whole (Synecdoche); as

*C.* I. 1. 13 *trabe* Cypria (i. e. ship); I. 8. 7 Gallica *ora* (i. e. horse); *C.* III. 2. 16 nec parcit (mors) imbellis iuventae *poplitibus* timidove *tergo; Epod.* 16. 59 *Sidonii* (i. e. Phoenicians).

## *Ellipsis.*

**118.** The common substantive of the antecedent and relative clauses is sometimes expressed only in the clause that comes second; as

*Epod.* 2. 37 malarum quas amor habet curas (in prose, malarum curarum quas amor habet); *S.* I. 4. 2 alii quorum comoedia prisca virorum est; *S.* II. 2. 59 vinum et cuius odorem olei nequeas perferre (i. e. et oleum cuius odorem nequeas perferre).

**119.** (*a*) A word or phrase belonging to two words, phrases, or clauses in common is sometimes expressed with the second only; as

*Epod.* 7. 13 furorne caecus an *rapit* vis acrior? *C.* III. 25. 2 quae nemora aut quos *agor in* specus.

(*b*) It is a favorite device of Horace to indicate this ellipsis by attaching an enclitic *-que* or *-ve* to the word, which then, as nothing precedes to which the conjunction can join it, suggests *itself* as the word to fill the omission; as

*C.* III. 1. 12 moribus hic meliorque fama (= melior moribus meliorque fama); *S.* II. 3. 139 non Pyladen ferro violare aususve sororem (= non Pyladen violare ausus aususve sororem); *C.* I. 30. 6 solutis Gratiae zonis properentque Nymphae (= properent Gratiae properentque Nymphae);

(*c*) So *sive* (*seu*) often implies a preceding *si* or *sive;* as

*S.* II. 5. 11 turdus sive aliud privum (= si(ve) turdus sive aliud); *C.* I. 3. 16 quo non arbiter Hadriae maior, tollere seu ponere volt freta (= sive tollere seu ponere).

(*d*) But *sive* (*seu*) in such a position more frequently follows an absolute statement or injunction or a description, to which it adds an alternative with a condition attached, — to be translated *or, if;* as

*C.* I. 15. 25 Sthenelus sciens pugnae, sive (= vel, si) opus est imperitare equis, non auriga piger; *S.* II. 6. 20 Matutine pater, seu Iane libentius audis (= vel Iane, si 'Iane' libentius audis).

**120.** A group of words which belongs to two or more members of a sentence in common is sometimes distributed among them, each part serving to suggest the rest; as

*Ep.* I. 3. 29 si patriae *volumus,* si nobis *vivere cari; C.* III. 21. 2 seu *tu* querellas sive *geris* iocos; *C.* II. 13. 39 nec *curat Orion* leones aut timidos *agitare* lyncas · *C.* I. 27. 11 quo *beatus* volnere, qua *pereat* sagitta.

**121.** *Suggestion by similarity.* Where two or more qualities belong to a series of objects, the poet is sometimes content to express one with each, leaving the rest to suggestion; as

*Ep.* I. 16. 50 cautus enim metuit foveam lupus, accipiterque suspectos laqueos, et opertum miluus hamum, — where the cautiousness of the animal (*cautus*) and his distrust (*suspectos*) of a masked danger (*opertum*) are to be understood of all three instances; *Epod.* 5. 37 exsecta uti medulla et aridum iecur (*the dry marrow and liver, cut out*).

**122.** *Suggestion by contrast.* Where a twofold contrast exists between two objects, it may be indicated by attributing to them single qualities which *do not match.* Each quality expressed will then suggest its opposite in the other object; as

*C.* III. 13. 6 *gelidos* inficiet tibi *rubro* sanguine rivos, — where the *clear, cold* water is contrasted with the *warm, red* blood; *C.* II. 3. 9 quo pinus *ingens albaque* populus umbram hospitalem consociare amant, — i. e. the *tall, dark* pine and the *shorter, white* poplar.

**123.** In illustrative comparisons Horace is fond of giving greater vividness to the figure by identifying the subject with it completely (with or without omission of the particle of comparison); as

*Ep.* II. 2. 97 caedimur et totidem plagis consumimus hostem, lento Samnites ad lumina prima duello (i. e. velut Samnites, etc.); *Ep.* II. 3. 475 quem vero arripuit [poeta] tenet occiditque legendo, non missura cutem nisi plena cruoris hirudo; *C.* I. 15. 29 quem *tu*, cervus uti vallis in altera visum parte lupum *graminis immemor*, *sublimi fugies mollis anhelitu; Ep.* I. 2. 42 *rusticus; Ep.* I. 10. 5 *columbi.*

## *Attributes.*

**124.** In poetical language a quality of a person or thing is often attributed to some part of it, or to some object which from close association is felt to partake of the quality, or to some action which manifests it; as

*C.* III. 1. 17 destrictus ensis cui super *impia cervice* pendet; *C.* I. 3. 40 neque patimur *iracunda* Iovem ponere *fulmina; Epod.* 10. 14 *impiam* Aiacis *ratem; C.* I. 37. 6 dum Capitolio regina *dementis ruinas* . . . parabat; *C.* III. 1. 42 purpurarum *sidere clarior usus.* In this way a quality is often suggested without being expressly attributed; as *C.* IV. 4. 57 ut ilex tonsa bipennibus nigrae feraci frondis in Algido, — where the dark foliage is that of the ilex itself.

**125.** A quality is often attributed to an object which it does not itself possess, but which is reflected upon it, as it were, from the effect it produces in others; as

*C.* I. 5. 7 *nigris* ventis (i. e. those that darken the sky); so I. 7. 15 *albus* Notus; *C.* II. 7. 21, *oblivioso* Massico (that induces forgetfulness); *C.* II. 10. 15 *informis* hiemes (marring the face of nature).

**126.** An attribute may be brought into greater prominence — (*a*) By Hendiadys; as

*Epod.* 5. 54 iram atque numen, *all-powerful wrath;*

(*b*) By means of an abstract substantive, with the person who possesses the quality and is the logical subject of the sentence appended in the form of a limiting genitive or an adjective (a Homeric device); as

*S.* II. 1. 72 ubi se a volgo et scaena in secreta remorant *virtus Scipiadae* et *mitis sapientia Laeli; C.* III. 21. 11 narratur et prisci *Catonis* saepe mero caluisse *virtus; Ep.* II. 1. 191 trahitur *regum fortuna; C.* I. 3. 36 perrupit Acheronta *Herculeus* labor;

(*c*) By a substantive in apposition; as

*C.* I. 1. 1 atavis edite *regibus* (= *regiis*); *C.* I. 4. 16 iam te premet nox *fabulae*que manes. The appositive may itself have a modifier; as *C.* I. 3. 20 *infamis scopulos* Acroceraunia.

## *Enallage.*

**127.** The singular is occasionally used for the plural, either collectively (especially with an adjective of number or quantity) or putting one object to represent its class; as

*Epod.* 2. 31 *multa cane; Ep.* II. 3. 203 (tibia) *foramine pauco; Epod.* 3. 14 (Medea) *serpente* fugit *alite; C.* I. 37. 3 ornare *pulvinar* deorum.

**128.** The poets use the plural not only of abstracts and of names of things reckoned in bulk (*amores*, *irae*, *calores*, *acumina; cruores*, *vina*, *Caecuba*, and the like), expressing occurrences of a quality, kinds of a substance, etc., as in prose, but even of substantives which designate only a single object or action; as

C. I. 2. 15 *monumenta* regis *templa*que Vestae (each a single structure); *C.* III. 27. 75 *tua* sectus orbis *nomina* ducet; *C.* III. 5. 52 populum *reditus* (sc. of Regulus to Carthage) morantem; *Epod.* 17. 3 Dianae non movenda *numina.*

**129.** The poet often uses an archaic simple verb in place of the more exact compound form in current use; as

*C.* III. 25. 16 manibus *vertere* fraxinos (for *evertere*); *C.* III. 27. 74 *mitte* singultus (for *omitte*); *C.* III. 24. 32 virtutem incolumem odimus, sublatam ex oculis *quaerimus* invidi (for *requirimus*).

## *Metonymy.*

**130.** The name of a divinity standing for his special province is particularly common; as

*Epod.* 7. 3 campis atque *Neptuno* super (i. e. on land and sea); *C.* III. 24. 13 iugera liberas fruges et *Cererem* ferunt; *C.* III. 16. 34 *Bacchus* in amphora languescit. (See Lucr. II. 652 *sqq.*)

## *Alliteration and Assonance.*

**131.** Alliteration and assonance hold a very subordinate place in the structure of Horace's poetry, but he employs them to a limited extent. Alliterative sequences that bear the stamp of conscious effort, such as

*S.* I. 6. 57 — *p*udor *p*rohibebat *p*lura *p*rofari

are extremely rare, except where correspondence of sound with sense is aimed at, as

*S.* II. 8. 78 — videre*s*
*s*tridere *s*ecreta divi*s*o*s* aure *s*u*s*urro*s*

*C.* I. 4. 13 — *p*allida mors aequo *p*ulsat *p*ede *p*au*p*erum tabernas

*C.* III. 5. 49 — quae sibi b*ar*b*ar*us
t*or*t*or* p*arar*et

Alliterative or assonant pairs, like

dulce decus, Pontica pinus, vera virtus,
maius meliusve, arcis attigit, obruit otio,

come in from time to time in a natural way; sometimes two pairs in succession, as

*C.* I. 1. 16 — *m*ercator *m*etuens, *o*tium et *o*ppidi

*C.* II. 1. 1 — *m*otum ex *M*etello *c*onsule *c*ivicum

*C.* III. 2. 1 — *a*ngustam *a*mice *p*auperiem *p*ati

But in general Horace avoids mere iteration by alternating the recurring sounds with one another or judiciously distributing them, often with reference to metrical or syntactical connection, so that the reader feels the pleasing effect with little or no consciousness of the manner in which it is produced. The following examples will illustrate his method:

*C.* I. 29. 11 — *p*ronos *r*elabi *p*osse *r*ivos

*C.* IV. 5. 24 — *c*ulpam *p*oena *p*remit *c*omes

*C.* III. 17. 8 — *lit*o*r*ibu*s* *t*enui*ss*e *L*i*r*im | *lat*e *ty*rannu*s*

*C.* IV. 2. 3 — *n*ititur *p*ennis, vitreo daturus
*n*omina *p*onto

*C.* II. 8. 15 — *s*emper *a*rdentis *a*cuens *s*agittas
*c*ote *c*ruenta

*C.* II. 6. 15 — *v*iridique certat | baca *V*enafro

*C.* II. 1. 36 — quae c*ar*et *or*a cru*or*e n*o*str*o*?

*Epod.* 16. 47 — *mel*la cava *m*anant ex *il*ice, *m*ontibus *al*tis
*l*evis cre*p*ante *l*ym*p*ha desi*l*it *p*ede

# III. VERSIFICATION AND PROSODY OF THE LYRIC POEMS.

## (A) VERSIFICATION.

NOTE.—In all the rhythms used by Horace the last syllable of the verse is *syllaba anceps*, i. e., its quantity is not considered. This is to be understood in all cases, though, for the sake of greater simplicity, it has not been indicated in the metrical schemes here given, being common to all. The sign ⏑⏑ is used to indicate two short syllables which are to be pronounced in the time of one short. In other respects the metrical notation is that adopted in the grammars in current use. 'Caesura' ( ‖ ) is used to denote the regular pause in the verse, whether it falls within a measure (caesura in the stricter sense) or between two measures (diaeresis).

### *Dactylic Verses.*

**132.** The *Hexameter* (dactylic hexameter catalectic):

–́ ⏔ | –́ ⏔ | –́ ‖ ⏔ | –́ ⏔ | –́ (–)⏑⏑ | –́ ⏑ ∧

Caesura in the second and fourth feet instead of the third, and 'feminine' caesura (*i. e.* between the short syllables of the dactyl) in the third are occasionally found, as *Epod.* 16. 31, *C.* I. 28. 15. A spondee in the fifth foot occurs four times, always in proper names: *C.* I. 28. 21 *Ōrī|ōnīs; Epod.* 13. 9 *Cȳllē|nēā;* 16. 17 *Phōcāe|ōrum;* 16. 29 *Āppēn|nīnus.* (There is only one spondiac verse in the Satires and Epistles,—*Ep.* II. 3. 467.)

**133.** The *Dactylic Tetrameter* (catalectic):

–́ ⏔ | –́ ⏔ | –́ (–)⏑⏑ | –́ ⏑ ∧

A spondee in the third foot occurs once (*C.* I. 28. 2).

**134.** The *Lesser Archilochian* verse (dactylic trimeter catalectic):

–́ ⏑ ⏑ | –́ ⏑ ⏑ | –́ ⊼

## *Iambic and Trochaic Verses.*

**135.** The *Iambic Trimeter:* *

⏒ ⏉ ⏑ ⏉ | ⏒ ‖ ⏉ ⏑ ⏉ | ⏒ ⏉ ⏑ ⏉
⏑ ⏑́⏑ ⏑ ⏑́⏑ | ⏑ ‖ ⏑́⏑ ⏑ ⏑́⏑ |
> ⏑́⏑ | > ‖ ⏑́⏑ |
(⏖ ⏉)? | | (⏖ ⏉)?

The caesura is occasionally hepthemimeral (as *Epod.* 1. 15; 4. 3; 5. 3, etc.); in two verses it falls after the prefix of a compound word: *Epod.* 1. 19 *im* ‖ *plumibus;* 11. 15 *in* ‖ *aestuet* (cf. 149, 150, 155, and see 115 *e*). Resolution is sparingly used. The apparent dactyl occurs chiefly in the first foot, seldom in the third; the tribrach oftenest in the second and third, rarely in the first or fourth; and both of these substitutions are always so made that the ictus coincides with a word-accent (in two cases with a secondary accent only: *Epod.* 17. 12 *hómicidam;* 74 *ínimicis*), usually falling on the antepenult of a trisyllabic word. The anapaest occurs in the first foot only twice: *Epod.* 2. 35 *pavidum,* 65 *positos* (which are perhaps to be read by syncope as spondees; see 183); and apparently three times in the fifth: *Epod.* 2. 35 *laqueo,* 5. 79 *inferius,* 11. 23 *mulierculam;* but see 180, 181.

**136.** The *Pure Iambic Trimeter:*

⏑ ⏉ ⏑ ⏉ | ⏑ ‖ ⏉ ⏑ ⏉ | ⏑ ⏉ ⏑ ⏉

A hepthemimeral caesura occurs once (*Epod.* 16. 4).

**137.** The *Iambic Dimeter:*

⏒ ⏉ ⏑ ⏉ | ⏒ ⏉ ⏑ ⏉
> ⏑́⏑ ⏑ ⏑́⏑ |

---

* The metrical scheme is here given, to avoid confusion, in the form presented in the Greek and Latin grammars in common use. Iambic rhythm may also be represented, in accordance with our modern system of musical notation, thus: ⏒ ⁞ — ⏑ — ⏒ | — ⏑ etc.; and it will be necessary to adopt this method for those rhythms which are used in composite and logaoedic verse, where, though technically iambic, they are essentially trochaic in character.

Resolution occurs in only four verses (*Epod.* 2. 62; 3. 8; 5. 48; 15. 24) and under the same restrictions as in the trimeter (135). The scheme may also be written thus:

⏓ ⁝ –́ ⏑ – ⏓ | –́ ⏑ – ∧

**138.** The *Iambic Trimeter Catalectic:*

⏓ ⁝ –́ ⏑ – ⏓ ‖ –́ ⏑ – ⏑ | ⏑́⏑ – ∧
(⏑ ⏑)?

Resolution occurs once, — *C.* II. 18. 34 *regumque pueris,* — unless we are to read by synizesis, *p$\widehat{ue}$ris* (see 180).

**139.** The *Nine-Syllable Alcaic* (two trochaic dipodies, with anacrusis):

⏓ ⁝ –́ ⏑ | –́ > | –́ ⏑ | –́ ⏑

The second trochee is always irrational.

**140.** The *Euripidean* verse (pure trochaic dimeter catalectic):

–́ ⏑ – ⏑ | –́ ⏑ – ∧

## *Composite Verses.*

**141.** In several of the epodic distichs used by Horace, one of the verses is made up of two distinct *cola*, one dactylic and the other iambic or trochaic. Such a verse is usually 'asynartete,' that is, its two *cola* are not welded together (as, for example, the two halves of a hexameter are), but the end of the first *colon* is treated in all respects as the end of a verse, having *syllaba anceps*, and admitting hiatus before a following vowel. Whether the dactyl was read in trochaic time (cyclic dactyl) is uncertain. It is not improbable that there was a change of time in the middle of the verse.

**142.** The *Greater Archilochian* verse, composed of a dactylic tetrameter acatalectic and a trochaic tripody:

–́ ⏕ | –́ ⏕ | –́ ‖ ⏕ | –́ ⏑ ⏑ | –́ ⏑ | –́ ⏑ | –́ ⏑

In the ten verses which Horace has left us in this measure

(*C.* I. 4) there is always caesura after the third ictus, and the first *colon* ends with a short final syllable, without hiatus.

**143.** The *Elegiambus*, composed of a lesser Archilochian (134) — which is identical with the second *colon* of the elegiac pentameter — and an iambic dimeter (137):

⏗ ⏑⏑ | ⏗ ⏑⏑ | ⏗ ∧ ‖ ⏒ : ⏗ ⏑ ⏗ ⏒ | ⏗ ⏑ ⏗ ∧

**144.** The *Iambelegus*, composed of the same *cola* as 143, but in reverse order:

⏒ : ⏗ ⏑ ⏗ ⏒ | ⏗ ⏑ ⏗ ∧ ‖ ⏗ ⏑⏑ | ⏗ ⏑⏑ | ⏗ ∧̄

No resolution occurs in the iambic *cola*, and no substitution in the dactylic, of either 143 or 144.

## *Logaoedic Verses.*

**145.** Most of the Odes are composed in logaoedic rhythms, made up of trochaic, with an admixture of dactylic, elements. The combination of dactyl and trochee produces a succession of syllables identical with the *choriamb* (— ⏑ ⏑ —), especially where the trochee is syncopated (‿⏑ ⏑ | ⌞́) and the measure thus formed is repeated (as in 149 and 150, below). For this reason the rhythms were regarded by late Roman metrical writers as choriambic, and some of the verses (147–150, and sometimes 152) are still so called. Their choriambic character is only apparent; but it is nevertheless important to observe this measure, — which may, for convenience be called the 'choriambic measure' — as its repetition constitutes the characteristic feature of some of the verses now to be explained. Thus, in 149 the rhythm proceeds through the choriambic measure (‿⏑ ⏑ | ⌞) precisely as in 148; it then goes back, as it were, to the beginning of that measure and repeats it, but without syncopation (‿⏑ ⏑ | ⌞ ‖ ‿⏑ ⏑ | — ⏑), and continues with trochaic movement to the close of the verse, as in 147. In the same way, 150 is developed from 149, and 152 from 151.

**146.** In his logaoedics Horace observes the following rules, prescribed in the metrical theories of his time, but unknown to the Greek lyric poets and to Catullus:

(*a*). Two choriambic measures in the same verse are separated by caesura.

(*b*). An irrational spondee takes the place of a trochee before the first dactyl; thus, – > | –⏑ ⏑ |, not – ⏑ | –⏑ ⏑ |.

Horace's logaoedic verses are as follows:

**147.** The *Glyconic* (second Glyconic catalectic):

–́ > | –́⏑ ⏑ | –́ ⏑ | –́ ∧

Horace appears to have admitted a trochee before the first dactyl (cf. 146 *b*) in *C.* I. 15. 36; but see note.

**148.** The *Pherecratic* (second Pherecratic, to be read as a doubly catalectic tetrapody):

–́ > | –́⏑ ⏑ | ⊔́ | –́ ∧

**149.** The *Lesser Asclepiad:*

–́ > | –́⏑ ⏑ | ⊔́ ‖ –́⏑ ⏑ | –́ ⏑ | –́ ∧

Caesura is neglected in *C.* IV. 8. 17; but the text here is in doubt. Caesura falls after the prefix of a compound word in II. 12. 25 *de‖torquet* (cf. 135, 150, 155, and see 115 *e*).

**150.** The *Greater Asclepiad:*

–́ > | –́⏑ ⏑ | ⊔́ ‖ –́⏑ ⏑ | ⊔́ ‖ –́⏑ ⏑ | –́ ⏑ | –́ ∧

Caesura falls after a prefix in *C.* I. 18. 16 *per‖lucidior* (cf. 135, 149, 155, and see 115 *e*).

**151.** The *Lesser Sapphic:*

–́ ⏑ | –́ > | –́ ‖ ⏑⏑ | –́ ⏑ | –́ ⏑

In the hands of Sappho and Alcaeus, and of Catullus, this verse had a much freer movement. The quantity of the fourth syllable was not fixed, and there was no regular caesura. In Horace the fourth syllable is invariably long (see 146 *b*) and caesura in the dactyl is strictly observed, usually falling after the long syllable; 'feminine' caesura (–⏑ ‖ ⏑) is frequent in the *Carmen Saeculare* and in Book IV., rare in the earlier books.

**152.** The *Greater Sapphic:*

–́ ⏑ | –́ > | –́ ‖ ⏑⏑ | ⊔́ ‖ –́⏑ ⏑ | –́ ⏑ | –́ ⏑
(or, perhaps, ‖ –́⏑ ⏑ | –́ ⏑ | ⊔́ | –́ ∧)

**153.** The *Adonic:*

–́⏑ ⏑ | –́ ⏑ (or, perhaps, –́⏑ ⏑ | ⊔́ | –́ ∧)

**154.** The *Aristophanic:*

–́⏑ ⏑ | –́ ⏑ | –́ ⏑ (or, perhaps, –́⏑ ⏑ | –́ ⏑ | ⊔́ | –́ ∧)

**155.** The *Greater* (*eleven-syllable*) *Alcaic:*

⏒ : –́ ⏑ | –́ > ‖ –́⏑ ⏑ | –́ ⏑ | –́ ∧

In Alcaeus the fifth syllable, like the anacrusis, is of variable quantity, and there is no fixed caesura. In Horace the anacrusis is usually, and in Book IV. always, long; caesura is neglected in only two instances (*C.* I. 37. 14, IV. 14. 17); in three it falls after a prefix, — *C.* I. 16. 21 *ex‖ercitus;* 37. 5 *de‖promere;* II. 17. 21 *in‖credibili* (cf. 135, 149, 150, and see 115 *e*).

**156.** The *Lesser* (*ten-syllable*) *Alcaic:*

–́⏑ ⏑ | –́⏑ ⏑ | –́ ⏑ | –́ ⏑

## *Strophes and Systems.*

**157.** In the Epodes, with the exception of the seventeenth, which consists of 81 iambic trimeters, every poem has an even number of verses, the unit of versification being a strophe of two verses, — the epodic distich from which the book derives its name (§ 18). In the Odes the number of verses is in all cases a multiple of four, with the exception of *C.* IV. 8, which contains 34 verses. In view of this striking fact, and in spite of *C.* IV. 8, — the text of which is open to grave suspicion on grounds quite independent of its metrical structure, — Meineke laid down the canon that Horace's odes were composed in tetrastichs, or strophes of four verses, and that accordingly where an ode is apparently written in distichs or monostichs, these were designed to be grouped together to form tetrastichs. This theory rests on a much narrower basis of induction than appears at first sight; for of Horace's 104 odes only 18 are written in distichs, and in monostichs only 7. Horace may have desired to make these few odes conform to the rule imposed on the great majority by their metrical structure, but that is a different thing from saying that the unit of versification was the tetrastich. In a number of the odes the distichs are of the same character, — in two odes identical (see 162), — with those used in the Epodes, where they cannot be grouped in twos. It is true that the text of *C.* IV. 8 is probably corrupt, but it is by no means clear that a reduction to 32 or to 28 verses is the way to heal it. It is true, further, that in *C.* III. 9, which is a dialogue, two distichs at a time are assigned to each speaker, — one would be rather short for the purpose; but in *C.* I. 1, on the other hand, a division into tetrastichs is curiously at cross purposes with the course of thought, while the significant manner in which the first two and the last two verses are set off by their content from the rest of the poem points to a probable grouping of such monostichs in twos, if they have any strophic character at all. In the remaining monostichic odes (I. 11, 18, III. 30, IV. 10) — leaving out of account III. 12 which has only four verses — the connection of thought gives no suggestion of an arrangement by strophes.

The lyric metres used by Horace are as follows :

**158.** The *Iambic Trimeter* (see 135). *Epode* 17.

**159.** The *Iambic Strophe:* an iambic trimeter (135) coupled with an iambic dimeter (137) :—

⏒ –́ ⏑ –́ | ⏒ ‖ –́ ⏑ –́ | ⏒ –́ ⏑ –́
⏒ –́ ⏑ –́ | ⏒ –́ ⏑ –́

For substitutions see 135, 137. *Epodes* 1–10.

**160.** The *First Pythiambic Strophe:* a dactylic hexameter (132) coupled with an iambic dimeter (137) : —

–́ ⏕ | –́ ⏕ | –́ ‖ ⏕ | –́ ⏕ | –́ ⏑⏑ | –́ ⏑ Λ
⏒ –́ ⏑ –́ | ⏒ –́ ⏑ –́

*Epodes* 14, 15.

**161.** The *Second Pythiambic Strophe:* a dactylic hexameter (132) coupled with a pure iambic trimeter (136) :—

–́ ⏕ | –́ ⏕ | –́ ‖ ⏕ | –́ ⏕ | –́ (⏕) | – ⏑ Λ
⏑ –́ ⏑ –́ | ⏑ ‖ –́ ⏑ –́ | ⏑ –́ ⏑ –́

*Epode* 16.

**162.** The *Alcmanian Strophe;* a dactylic hexameter (132) coupled with a dactylic tetrameter (133) :—

–́ ⏕ | –́ ⏕ | –́ ‖ ⏕ | –́ ⏕ | –́ (⏕) | –́ ⏑ Λ
–́ ⏕ | –́ ⏕ | –́ (⏕) | –́ ⏑ Λ

*C.* I. 7, 28 ; *Epod.* 12.

**163.** The *First Archilochian Strophe:* a dactylic hexameter (132) coupled with a lesser Archilochian verse (134):—

–́ ⏕ | –́ ⏕ | –́ ‖ ⏕ | –́ ⏕ | –́ ⏑⏑ | –́ ⏑ Λ
–́ ⏑⏑ | –́ ⏑⏑ | –́ Λ̄

*C.* IV. 7.

**164.** The *Second Archilochian Strophe:* a dactylic hexameter (132) coupled with an iambelegus (144):—

–́ ⏕ | –́ ⏕ | –́ ‖ ⏕ | –́ ⏕ | –́ ⏑⏑ | –́ ⏑ ∧
⏓ ⋮ –́ ⏑ –́ ⏓ | –́ ⏑ –́ ∧ | –́ ⏑⏑ | –́ ⏑⏑ | –́ ⊼

*Epod.* 13.

**165.** The *Third Archilochian Strophe:* an iambic trimeter (135) coupled with an elegiambus (143):—

⏓ –́ ⏑ –́ | ⏓ ‖ –́ ⏑ –́ | ⏓ –́ ⏑ –́
–́ ⏑⏑ | –́ ⏑⏑ | –́ ∧ | ⏓ ⋮ –́ ⏑ –́ ⏓ | –́ ⏑ –́ ∧

*Epod.* 11. (For vs. 23, see, 135, 181.)

**166.** The *Fourth Archilochian Strophe:* a greater Archilochian verse (142) coupled with an iambic trimeter catalectic (138):—

–́ ⏕ | –́ ⏕ | –́ ‖ ⏕ | –́ ⏑⏑ | –́ ⏑ | –́ ⏑ | –́ ⏑
⏓ ⋮ –́ ⏑ –́ ⏓ ‖ –́ ⏑ –́ ⏑ | ⌞́ –́ ∧

*C.* I. 4.

**167.** The *Trochaic Strophe:* a Euripidean verse (140) coupled with an iambic trimeter catalectic (138):—

–́ ⏑ –́ ⏑ | –́ ⏑ –́ ∧
⏓ ⋮ –́ ⏑ –́ ⏓ ‖ –́ ⏑ –́ ⏑ | ⌞́ –́ ∧

*C.* II. 18. (For vs. 34, see 138).

**168.** The *Ionic System*, consisting of pure *Ionici a minore* (⏑⏑ – –) in series of ten. There is usually diaeresis at the end of each foot.

⏑⏑ –́ – | ⏑⏑ –́ – | ⏑⏑ –́ – | ⏑⏑ –́ – |
⏑⏑ –́ – | ⏑⏑ –́ – | ⏑⏑ –́ – | ⏑⏑ –́ – |
⏑⏑ –́ – | ⏑⏑ –́ –

*C.* III. 12.

**169.** The *Lesser Asclepiad Metre:* a series of lesser Asclepiad verses (149; see also 157):—

–́ > | –́⏑ ⏑ | ⌞́ ‖ –́⏑ ⏑ | –́ ⏑ | –́ ∧

*C.* I. 1; III. 30; IV. 8.

**170.** The *Greater Asclepiad Metre:* a series of greater Asclepiad verses (150; see also 157):—

–́ > | –́⏑ ⏑ | ⊔́ ‖ –́⏑ ⏑ | ⊔́ ‖ –́⏑ ⏑ | –́ ⏑ | –́ ∧

*C.* I. 11, 18; IV. 10.

**171.** The *First Asclepiad Strophe:* a Glyconic (147) coupled with a lesser Asclepiad (149):—

–́ > | –́⏑ ⏑ | –́ ⏑ | –́ ∧
–́ > | –́⏑ ⏑ | ⊔́ ‖ –́⏑ ⏑ | –́ ⏑ | –́ ∧

*C.* I. 3, 13, 19, 36; III. 9, 15, 19, 24, 25, 28; IV. 1, 3. Elision at the end of the Glyconic occurs *C.* IV. 1. 35.

**172.** The *Second Asclepiad Strophe:* three lesser Asclepiads (149) and a Glyconic (147):—

–́ > | –́⏑ ⏑ | ⊔́ ‖ –́⏑ ⏑ | –́ ⏑ | –́ ∧
–́ > | –́⏑ ⏑ | ⊔́ ‖ –́⏑ ⏑ | –́ ⏑ | –́ ∧
–́ > | –́⏑ ⏑ | ⊔́ ‖ –́⏑ ⏑ | –́ ⏑ | –́ ∧
–́ > | –́⏑ ⏑ | –́ ⏑ | –́ ∧

*C.* I. 6, 15, 24, 33; II. 12; III. 10, 16; IV. 5, 12.

**173.** The *Third Asclepiad Strophe:* two lesser Asclepiads (149), a Pherecratic (148), and a Glyconic (147):—

–́ > | –́⏑ ⏑ | ⊔́ ‖ –́⏑ ⏑ | –́ ⏑ | –́ ∧
–́ > | –́⏑ ⏑ | ⊔́ ‖ –́⏑ ⏑ | –́ ⏑ | –́ ∧
–́ > | –́⏑ ⏑ | ⊔́ | –́ ∧
–́ > | –́⏑ ⏑ | –́ ⏑ | –́ ∧

*C.* I. 5, 14, 21, 23; III. 7, 13; IV. 13.

**174** (*a*). The *Sapphic Strophe:* three lesser Sapphic verses (151) and an Adonic (153):—

–́ ⏑ | –́ > | –́ ‖ ⏖ | –́ ⏑ | –́ ⏑
–́ ⏑ | –́ > | –́ ‖ ⏖ | –́ ⏑ | –́ ⏑
–́ ⏑ | –́ > | –́ ‖ ⏖ | –́ ⏑ | –́ >
–́⏑ ⏑ | –́ ⏑

Next to the Alcaic (176) the metre most used by Horace: *C.* I. 2, 10, 12, 20, 22, 25, 30, 32, 38; II. 2, 4, 6, 8, 10, 16; III. 8, 11, 14, 18, 20, 22, 27; IV. 2, 6, 11; *C. S.*

(*b*). For the 'feminine' caesura, see 151. Sappho appears to have treated the third Sapphic and the Adonic as one continuous verse. Horace does not follow this practice absolutely, but he has hiatus between the two verses in only four cases (*C.* I. 2. 47; 12. 7, 31; 22. 15) in a total of 206 strophes; and in all but 12 instances a spondee (by synapheia) precedes the dactyl of the Adonic. He makes the two verses continuous in *C.* I. 2. 19, 25. 11, II. 16. 7; and he allows elision at the end of the third verse in IV. 2. 23 and *C. S.* 47. Elision at the end of the second verse occurs in II. 2. 18, 16. 34, IV. 2. 22.

**175.** The *Greater Sapphic Strophe:* an Aristophanic verse (154) coupled with a greater Sapphic (152):—

–́⏑ ⏑ | –́ ⏑ | –́ ⏑
–́ ⏑ | –́ > | –́ ‖ ⏑⏑ | ⊔́ ‖ –́⏑ ⏑ | –́ ⏑ | –́ ⏑

*C.* I. 8.

**176** (*a*). The *Alcaic Strophe:* two greater Alcaic verses (155), a nine-syllable Alcaic (139), and a lesser Alcaic (156):—

⏒ : –́ ⏑ | –́ > ‖ –́⏑ ⏑ | –́ ⏑ | –́ ∧
⏒ : –́ ⏑ | –́ > ‖ –́⏑ ⏑ | –́ ⏑ | –́ ∧
⏒ : –́ ⏑ | –́ > | –́ ⏑ | –́ ⏑
–́⏑ ⏑ | –́⏑ ⏑ | –́ ⏑ | –́ ⏑

The metre most frequently used by Horace: *C.* I. 9, 16, 17, 26, 27, 29, 31, 34, 35, 37; II. 1, 3, 5, 7, 9, 11, 13, 14, 15, 17, 19, 20; III. 1–6, 17, 21, 23, 26, 29; IV. 4, 9, 14, 15.

(*b*). Elision at the end of the third verse occurs II. 3. 27; III. 29. 35.

## (B) PROSODY.

**177.** A final syllable ending in a short vowel is not lengthened in Horace before a word beginning with two consonants.

**178.** The prosody of certain proper names is unsettled: *C.* III. 30. 13 *Ītalos*, but II. 7. 4 *Ĭtalo;* I. 28. 20 *Prōserpina*, II. 13. 21 *Prŏserpinae;* I. 28. 21 *Ōrionis*, *Epod.* 15. 7 *Ŏrion; C. S.* 1 *Dĭana*, ib. 70 *Dīana.* Cf. also *Epod.* 2. 42 *Apŭli*, 3. 16 *Apūliae.*

Horace has *-ĕrunt* in the third person plural of the perfect indicative active, *Epod.* 9. 17 *vertĕrunt.* It occurs also *S.* I. 10. 45 *adnuĕrunt* and *Ep.* I. 4. 7 *dedĕrunt* (cf. *C.* III. 6. 7 *dedērunt*); but nowhere in the Odes.

**179.** The final syllable of the third person singular, present or perfect, indicative is long in a few instances under the ictus, as in old Latin (see Allen's *Remnants of Early Latin*, *Introd.* 52 ff.):

| | |
|---|---|
| *C.* I. 3. 36 | pérrupít Acherónta Hérculeús labór |
| *C.* I. 13. 6 | cérta séde manē̍t ‖ úmor et ín genás |
| *C.* II. 6. 14 | ángulús ridḗt ‖ ubi nón Hymétto |
| *C.* II. 13. 16 | caéca timē̍t aliúnde fáta |
| *C.* III. 16. 26 | quám si quícquid arā̍t ‖ ímpiger Ápulús |
| *C.* III. 24. 5 | sí fīgít adamántinós |

Once in arsis, before the caesura:

| | |
|---|---|
| *C.* III. 5. 17 | si nón perírēt ‖ immiserabilis |

Horace practiced this license in the Satires also, but in his latest writings, the Epistles and the fourth book of the Odes, he abstained from it altogether.

**180.** SYNIZESIS: *C.* II. 7. 5 *Pompei;* apparently also, *Epod.* 2. 35 *laqueo* (see 135); and perhaps *C.* II. 18. 34 *pueris* (see 138). Under this head also are usually classed *C.* I. 35. 17 *anteit* and 37. 5 *antehac;* but the *e* of *ante* was probably elided, and the words pronounced *ant'it*, *ant'hac.*

**181.** SYNAERESIS: *C.* III. 4. 41 *consilium;* III. 6. 6 *principium* (in both cases the consonantal *i* lengthens the preceding syllable, and its own syllable is elided at the caesura); *Epod.* 12. 7 *vietis;* perhaps also *Epod.* 5. 79 *inferius*, and 11. 23 *mulierculam* (see 135).

**182.** DIALYSIS: *C.* I. 23. 4, *Epod.* 13. 2 *siluae.*

**183.** SYNCOPE: *C.* I. 36. 8 *puertiae;* II. 2. 2 *lamnae;* III. 20. 1 *periclo;* IV. 13. 20 *surpuerat; Epod.* 9. 1 *repostum;* 9. 9, 17. 72 *vincla;* perhaps also *Epod.* 2. 35 *pav(i)dum*, 65 *pos(i)tum* (see 135). Syncopated verb forms like *natarunt, complesti, intrarit, promorat* are of frequent occurrence.

**184.** ELISION. In his earliest Epodes Horace appears to have studiously avoided elision. In Epode 16 the hexameters are altogether free from it, and it occurs but three times in the iambics. There is no case in Epode 13, and only one in Epode 12. Later he was less strict, but confined it chiefly to short final syllables, and avoided harsh combinations. Monosyllables are never elided, except the pronouns *me* and *te*, and (once) the adverb *iam* (*Epod.* 17. 1).

**185.** HIATUS occurs after the interjections *a* and *o*, which, for obvious reasons, are never elided, and in the following undisputed cases: *Epod.* 5. 100 *Esquilinae alites;* 13. 3 *Threicio Aquilone: C.* I. 28. 24 *capiti inhumato.* The following are doubtful: *C.* II. 20. 13 *Daedaleo* ‖ *ocior*; III. 14. 11 *male ominatis* (see notes). For hiatus between the *cola* of 'asynartete' verses, see 141.

# Q. HORATI FLACCI

# CARMINA

## LIBER PRIMVS

### I.

Maecenas atavis edite regibus,
o et praesidium et dulce decus meum :

I. This is Horace's prologue, as III. 30 is his epilogue, to the first edition of his Odes (Intr. 27); and the two poems thus set apart from the rest are written in a metre reserved for them alone. In addressing the prologue to Maecenas the poet dedicates the volume to him. After a brief tribute to his patron he puts forward a modest assertion of the claim of literature, and of lyric poetry in particular, to a place among the varied objects of human pursuit and ambition, which, after all, he implies, have no defense, as against one another, but the overmastering force of individual bent and taste; and he closes with an expression of his own aspiration to win for himself a place among the poets of the lyre. — Metre, 169 (page lxxxiii).

1. **Maecenas** : Intr. 21 ff. — **atavis** : here used, like *avus*, in a general sense, but indicating remoter ancestors, — *forefathers*. — **regibus** : in apposition with **atavis** ; Intr. 126 *c*. The compliment is not an extravagant one, as *rex* suggested to a Roman a much less exalted monarch than 'king' does to us. For similar allusions to Maecenas' ancestry, cf. III. 29. 1, *S.* I. 6. 1 *sqq.*, Prop. IV. 8. 1 *Maecenas eques Etrusco de sanguine regum*.

2. **o et** : for the hiatus, see Intr. 185.—**praesidium, decus** : cf. II. 17. 4 *mearum grande decus columenque rerum*. In each of these places the poet acknowledges both sides of his obligation to his patron, for substantial support and protection, and for the distinction which the friendship of so eminent a man confers. Horace elsewhere (*S.* II. 6. 32) confesses how sweet this distinction was to him ; but **dulce** here, with double application, expresses also his affection for Maecenas ; cf. *dulcis amice*, *Ep.* I. 7. 12.

Sunt quos curriculo pulverem Olympicum
collegisse iuvat metaque fervidis
evitata rotis palmaque nobilis
terrarum dominos evehit ad deos ;
hunc, si mobilium turba Quiritium
certat tergeminis tollere honoribus ;
illum, si proprio condidit horreo

3–6. The ruling passion of the Greek is athletic contests, and a victory at the national games is the summit of his aspirations. For Horace's method in this and the following descriptions, see Intr. 117.

3. **sunt quos . . . iuvat,** *some men delight.* For the mood, see Intr. 84. — **curriculo** (from *curriculus*), *with the chariot.* — **Olympicum** : *i.e.* at Olympia, in the great national games held there every four years.

4. **collegisse,** *to whirl ;* lit., 'to gather' (in a cloud); cf. *pulvis collectus turbine, S.* I. 4. 31. For the tense, see Intr. 81. The meaning is, to be in the chariot race in full career. To make the picture more telling, the two most critical points of the race, the turning-post and the finish, are included (vss. 4, 5).— **meta evitata** (sc. *iuvat*), *to clear the goal:* Intr. 105. The Greek *hippodromos*, like the Roman circus, was divided longitudinally by a low wall, round which the racing chariots were driven several times. At each end of this wall was a column or turning-post (**meta**). To turn this as closely as possible, without striking either it or other chariots, called for the utmost skill and, being attended with considerable danger, was the most exhilarating part of the race.

5. **palmaque** : for *quosque palma ;* cf. *C. S.* 26. The victor at Olympia was crowned with olive, and a palm branch was placed in his hand (Paus. VIII. 48. 2). The latter practice was borrowed by the Romans (Liv. X. 47. 3), and hence the palm became to them the especial symbol of victory.

6. **dominos** : in apposition with **deos.** — **evehit ad deos,** *exalts them to gods ;* expressing the pride and exultation of victory; cf. IV. 2. 17 ; Cic. *Flacc.* 31 *hoc* (to win at Olympia) *est apud Graecos prope maius et gloriosius quam Romae triumphasse.*

7–10. The highest objects of Roman endeavor, political preferment and wealth. Cf. *Ep.* I. 1. 42 *quae maxima credis esse mala, exiguum censum turpemque repulsam.*

7. **hunc** : *sc. iuvat,* the force of which, from vs. 4, is still felt, *evehit ad deos* 6 being only a more specific expression of the same idea. — **mobilium** : in disparagement ; Horace had no respect for office-seeking for the mere purpose of self-advancement. Cf. *S.* I. 6.

8. **tergeminis honoribus** : instrumental abl. The reference is to the three curule offices, the curule aedileship, praetorship, and consulship. — **tollere** : Intr. 94 *h.*

9. **illum** : see vs. 7 n. The great landowner is put forward as a type of successful but unsatisfied craving for wealth. — **proprio** : *i.e.* not acting merely as agent for

quicquid de Libycis verritur areis.
Gaudentem patrios findere sarculo
agros Attalicis condicionibus
numquam demoveas, ut trabe Cypria
Myrtoum pavidus nauta secet mare;
luctantem Icariis fluctibus Africum
mercator metuens otium et oppidi

another or for the government. — **horreo**: Intr. 69.

10. **quicquid,** *all the grain that,* suggesting unbounded desire; cf. III. 16. 26. — **Libycis**: before the conquest of Egypt Africa was the largest source of the city's grain supply, and expressions like this appear to have become proverbial; cf. *S.* II. 3. 87. — **verritur areis**: the *area* was a circular space, enclosed with a low wall and paved with concrete, on which the heads of grain, usually without the straw, were trampled out by cattle (*tritura*). A common way of winnowing was by tossing in the wind with a shovel (*ventilatio*) till the chaff was blown away. The grain was then swept together and removed.

11. **gaudentem,** etc.: from national characteristics the poet proceeds to individual tastes, which he presents in a series of contrasted sketches; and first the rustic who finds his happiness in keeping up the old farm. — **patrios**: indicating his lack of enterprise; he has added nothing to the fields his fathers tilled before him. Cf. 12. 43, and the picture of contentment in *Epod.* 2. 3; for the opposite spirit, II. 18. 23, *S.* II. 6. 8, Juv. 14. 140 *sqq.* — **findere**: Intr. 94 *d.* — **sarculo**: suggesting the small scale on which he farms; he works with his own hands. The *sarculum* was a hoe used for loosening the soil between the rows of growing grain (*sarritio*).

12. **Attalicis condicionibus,** *terms that an Attalus might offer.* The Attali, kings of Pergamon, in Asia Minor, were famous for their patronage of literature and for the munificence with which they adorned their capital with works of art. The Romans received a vivid and lasting impression of their splendor when the treasures of Attalus III., the last of the line, who died B.C. 133, bequeathing his kingdom to the Roman people, were brought to Rome.

13. **demoveas ut,** *tempt away to.* — **Cypria**: Cyprus produced within its own borders all kinds of material required for shipbuilding (Am. Marc. XIV. 8. 14). For the epithets **Cypria, Myrtoum,** etc., see Intr. 117, and cf. 35. 7 *sq.*

15. **luctantem,** etc.: in contrast with the farmer, the restless trader cannot endure the dullness of country life, though in the storm he may sigh for peace and long for the quiet rural scenes of his childhood. — **fluctibus**: dative; Intr. 57. — **Africum,** *the Sou'wester* (blowing from Africa).

16. **mercator**: not 'merchant' in our sense, but *trader,* who sails with his wares in his own ship. — **metuens**: with an accusative, because the fear is temporary; with the genitive it would express a per-

laudat rura sui: mox reficit ratis
quassas, indocilis pauperiem pati.
Est qui nec veteris pocula Massici
nec partem solido demere de die
spernit, nunc viridi membra sub arbuto
stratus, nunc ad aquae lene caput sacrae.
Multos castra iuvant et lituo tubae
permixtus sonitus bellaque matribus

manent trait, as *S.* II. 2. 110.— **otium,** *peace and quiet;* cf. II. 16. 1 *sqq.* — **oppidi rura**: every town had its *ager*, or adjacent country district under its jurisdiction (cf. *ager Romanus*, *ager Tusculanus*, etc.).

17. **laudat**: *sc.* as happy or conferring happiness (εὐδαιμονίζει), a sense in which Horace often uses the word; cf. *S.* I. 1. 9, *Ep.* I. 11. 6. — **sui,** *his native.* — **mox**: the asyndeton suggests the promptness with which his natural disposition asserts itself when the danger is past.

18. **pauperiem**: *i.e.* moderate circumstances, such as those of the farmer, not actual want (*inopia*, *egestas*). Horace calls his father, who was a man of some means, *macro pauper agello* (*S.* I. 6. 71). — **pati**: Intr. 101 *c*.

19–22. Between the restless enterprise of the trader and the excitement of war and the chase, the poet sets a quiet picture of leisurely enjoyment.

19. **est qui**: the singular suggests that this character is met with only now and then. — **Massici** (*sc. vini*): a much esteemed wine produced on the slopes of Mt. Massicus, on the border between Latium and Campania. See Intr. 117.

20. **solido die**: *i.e.* one (that would otherwise be) devoted wholly to business or serious work (cf. Sen. *Ep.* 83. 3 *hodiernus dies solidus est; nemo ex illo quicquam mihi eripuit*). The Roman 'day,' in this sense, lasted from early dawn to about the middle of the afternoon, *octavam circiter horam* (*Ep.* I. 7. 47).— **demere**: see Intr. 94 *i*.

21. **(nec) spernit**: *i.e.* does not deem it beneath his dignity, as, according to the old Roman notions, it was. For the mood, see Intr. 84. — **membra**: Intr. 41. — **arbuto**: a handsome flowering shrub or tree, common in Greece and Italy, with evergreen leaves something like those of our laurel, and fruit resembling the strawberry, — hence called the 'strawberry tree.' See Sibthorp's *Flora Graeca*, tab. 373.

22. **ad aquae caput**: *i.e.* by the side of some spring. — **lene, sacrae**: the epithets are interchanged: the stream is gentle, and the spring is sacred (as the haunt of a naiad). Cf. Intr. 124.

23. **lituo**: for *litui sonitu*, an economy of phrase common in prose and verse. The *lituus* was a long, straight brass trumpet, curved slightly at the larger end; it was used by the cavalry. — **tubae**: the trumpet of the infantry, straight throughout.

24. **matribus**: Intr. 54.

detestata. Manet sub Iove frigido
venator tenerae coniugis immemor,
seu visa est catulis cerva fidelibus,
seu rupit teretis Marsus aper plagas.
Me doctarum hederae praemia frontium
dis miscent superis; me gelidum nemus
Nympharumque leves cum Satyris chori
secernunt populo, si neque tibias

25. **manet**, *spends the night*, as in *S.* I. 5. 37; cf. *S.* II. 3. 234. — **Iove**, *the open sky*. The poets use the name of *Iuppiter*, with certain cognate forms from the root *DI, DIV* (cf. *sub divo*, III. 2. 5, *sub divum*, I. 18. 13, *sub diu*, Lucr. IV. 211), for the sky or the air, in which the god of heaven manifests his presence and power in the various phases of sunshine and rain, heat and cold, storm and lightning. Cf. Ennius *ap.* Varr. *L. L.* V. 65 *ístic est is Iúpiter quem díco, quem Graecí vocant | áerem, qui véntus est et núbes, imber póstea, | átque ex imbre frígus, ventus póst fit, aer dénuo.*

26. **tenerae coniugis**: *i.e.* of her anxiety for his safety, the contrast, as in *matribus detestata* 24, bringing out in stronger relief the hardihood of the man.

27. **seu . . . seu**: in either case the game will be lost unless pursued at once.

28. **Marsus**: Intr. 117. — **plagas**: used to bar the openings in the thicket (cf. *Epod.* 2. 31 *sq.*). The boar has escaped into the open country.

29. **me**: the emphatic position (Intr. 116 *b*) marks the transition to his own taste and ambition. In contrast with such pursuits as those last described, Horace finds his own greatest happiness far away from the busy world, in the presence of nature, where his poetic fancy sees the light-footed denizens of the woods and hears strains of divine music. — **doctarum**: *of men of letters*. *Doctus* denotes accomplishment in any art (cf. *docte Trebati*, *S.* II. 1. 78; *docte Cati*, *S.* II. 4. 88). In literature it is a connoisseur as well as a writer (*e.g.*, *S.* I. 10. 87). Here its meaning is limited by **hederae**, the ivy wreath which was the especial prerogative (**praemia**) of the poet, as being sacred to Bacchus, who was one of the patron gods of poets (cf. *Ep.* II. 2. 78, I. 19. 4). — **praemia**: here rather the emblem (cf. *S.* I. 5. 35, Verg. *E.* 7. 25) of the recognized poet than a prize of victory. For the plurals, see Intr. 128.

30. **dis miscent superis**: cf. vs. 6; but here the feeling expressed is ecstatic delight.

32. **si neque**, etc.: the favor of the muse is an essential condition. — **tibias**, *pipes*. The *tibia* (αὐλός) was a straight, flute-like instrument, but with mouth-piece at the end, like the clarinet; in some varieties the outer end was curved and flaring. The plural is used because two were commonly played together. (See Howard, *Harv. Studies* IV. p. 1.) The *tibia* as well as the lyre was associated with lyric

Euterpe cohibet nec Polyhymnia
Lesboum refugit tendere barbiton.
Quod si me lyricis vatibus inseris,
sublimi feriam sidera vertice.

## II.

Iam satis terris nivis atque dirae
grandinis misit pater, et rubente

poetry; cf. I. 12. 1 *sq.* III. 4. 1. — **neque cohibet** : *i.e.* plays freely.

33. **Euterpe, Polyhymnia**: see note on *Clio*, 12. 2.

34. **Lesboum tendere barbiton** : *i.e.* to inspire him as she had inspired Alcaeus and Sappho; see Intr. 26. — **tendere,** *to tune;* lit., to stretch or tighten (the chords). For the mood see Intr. 94 *k*.

35. **quod si,** *and if.* The ode closes as it began, with two verses of personal address to Maecenas. These two couplets are rather sharply divided from the rest of the poem, giving the impression that the intervening verses may have been originally written without reference to their present purpose, though they are admirably adapted to it. — **lyricis vatibus** : *i.e.* those of Greece, of whom there were nine recognized by the critics as classic. Horace's hope is that his achievement in Latin lyric may be regarded by his patron as making him worthy to be added to this noble company. — **inseris** : cf. II. 5. 21. For the tense, see Intr. 78; for its use with a future in the apodosis, cf. III. 24. 5.

36. **sublimi** : proleptic. — **feriam sidera** : expressing pride of achievement, like vs. 6. The extravagant phrase is legitimate enough, involving, as it does, a compliment to Maecenas' literary judgment, and there is a touch of humor in it.

II. The first place in the volume after the dedication is very properly given to an ode in honor of the emperor. It is the poet's declaration of allegiance to the second Caesar. There are no certain indications of its date; the two great inundations of the Tiber in B.C. 27 and 22 (Dio Cassius LIII. 20. 1; LIV. 1. 1) were too late to be treated by Horace as visitations of divine wrath for the killing of Julius Caesar (B.C. 44). But as an appeal to rescue the country from ruin (vs. 25), the ode could not have been composed after the settlement of January 27, when Octavian as first citizen (*princeps*) received, with the new title *Augustus*, a renewal of the *imperium* for ten years, and his friends, at least, regarded the fortunes of the state as established on a firm basis. It was probably written in the period of uncertainty which preceded this settlement, *i.e.* between the return and triumph of Octavian in August, 29, and the end of 28. The portents which form the subject of the opening strophes need not be supposed to have all occurred at one time; they may have extended through a number of years. Beginning with an impressive account of these signs of the wrath of heaven at the Romans for shedding the blood of their countrymen, the

dextera sacras iaculatus arcis
 terruit urbem,
terruit gentis, grave ne rediret
saeculum Pyrrhae nova monstra questae,
omne cum Proteus pecus egit altos
 visere montis,
piscium et summa genus haesit ulmo,
nota quae sedes fuerat columbis,

poet points out the need of a divine mediator, and then leads on skilfully to the suggestion that the messenger of heaven is already among them, fulfilling his appointed task. — Metre, 174.

1. **satis,** etc.: for the repetition of the *is* sound, see Intr. 131. It suggests to the ear the fierce persistency of the storm. — **terris**: dative; Intr. 53. — **dirae,** *portentous,* applying to **nivis** as well as to **grandinis**; Intr. 119. *a.* A heavy fall of snow or a severe hail-storm was rare enough at Rome to be accounted a *monstrum,* or sign of divine displeasure.

2. **pater,** *the Father* (of gods and men; cf. 12. 13 *sqq.*), Jupiter; here as the god who wields the elements; cf. 1. 25 n. — **rubente**: from the glow of the red-hot thunderbolt.

3. **iaculatus**: here with an accusative of the thing aimed at; cf. *cervos iaculari,* III. 12. 4. — **arcis**: the twin summits of the Capitoline hill, on one of which was the *Capitolium,* the great temple of Jupiter, Juno, and Minerva (hence **sacras**), while the other was the *Arx* proper.

5. **terruit**: Intr. 116 *g.* — **gentis** (sc. *humanas*), *all mankind;* cf. 3. 28, II. 13. 20. — **ne**: after the idea of fear implied in **terruit.** For its position and that of **cum,** **et,** and **quae,** below, see Intr. 114.

6. **saeculum Pyrrhae**: *i.e.* the Deluge (Ovid, *M.* I. 260 *sqq.*). Pyrrha, daughter of Epimetheus and Pandora, was the wife of Deucalion, the Noah of Greek mythology. Many people believed that the earth would one day be overwhelmed in a second flood (cf. Sen. *N. Q.* III. 27. 1 *cum fatalis dies diluvii venerit*); and the dreadful prodigy of Jove hurling his bolts at his own greatest temple was to the superstitious a warning that the time was at hand.— **nova,** *strange.*— **monstra,** *marvels;* lit., 'signs' (cf. *moneo*); see note on *dirae* 1.

7. **omne cum,** etc.: it is a favorite device of Horace to break the continuity of an enumeration of persons or events by dwelling on some subject in the series and letting the reader's mind rest for a moment on a picture. Better examples than this are 12. 27 *sqq.,* III. 4 60 *sqq.* — **Proteus**: the keeper of Neptune's sea-calves (seals), endowed with the gift of prophecy and the power of assuming various forms (hence our word 'protean'); cf. *Odys.* IV. 455 *sqq.* Verg. *G.* IV. 405 *sqq.*— **egit,** *drove.*

8. **visere**: see Intr. 93.

9. **piscium genus,** *the finny tribe.* — **ulmo**: Intr. 71.

et superiecto pavidae natarunt
    aequore dammae.
Vidimus flavum Tiberim retortis
litore Etrusco violenter undis
ire deiectum monumenta regis
    templaque Vestae,
Iliae dum se nimium querenti
iactat ultorem, vagus et sinistra

11. **superiecto,** *the overwhelming.*

13. **vidimus**: the poet returns from his digression to the prodigies which his own generation has witnessed. — **flavum**: a standing epithet of the Tiber, owing to its permanent muddy color; cf. 8. 8, II. 3. 18; Verg. *A.* VII. 31 (*Tiberinus*) *multa flavus harena.* — **retortis**: *sc.* from the opposite shore, here called *litus Etruscum.* This term usually designates the seacoast from the Tiber northward, and many take it in that sense here, relying on the ancient theory that the inundations of the Tiber were caused by strong southwest winds blocking the discharge of its waters into the sea (cf. Dio XXXIX. 61). But Horace is not here accounting for the river's conduct, — he does that in the next strophe; his words are descriptive, and they would imply, if **litore Etrusco** meant the seashore, a visible reversal of the stream, which was no part of the ancient theory, and which elsewhere (29. 12) he uses as a type of the impossible. In reality the Tiber, in time of flood, flows with a strong current down its winding channel through the city, and when its tumultuous waters poured over the left bank into the low ground between the Palatine and Capitoline hills, they may well have had the appearance of being 'hurled away' from the curving shore opposite. *Litus* is used of the shore of the Tiber by Verg. *A.* VIII. 83. Conversely *ripa* is sometimes used of the seashore, as II. 18. 22, III. 27. 24.

15. **deiectum**: supine. The river is here the river-god, coming in wrath to destroy; cf. *sub Iove,* 1. 25 n. — **monumenta regis**: the Regia, or 'palace' of Numa, used under the Commonwealth as the official residence of the pontifex maximus. *Monumentum* ('memorial'; cf. *moneo*) is often used of a building.

16. **templa Vestae**: the round temple, near the Regia, in which the sacred fire was kept. These two buildings, with the Atrium Vestae or 'House of the Vestals,' formed an enclosed group adjoining the eastern end of the old Forum, at the foot of the Palatine. The flood is represented as threatening the most venerable monuments of the city and its holiest shrine. The visitation of divine wrath on a holy place was the punishment for its desecration (cf. 12. 59), — in this case by the murder of the pontifex maximus, Caesar. For the plurals **monumenta, templa,** see Intr. 128.

17. **Iliae**: mother of Romulus and Remus. According to the older tradition, which Horace fol

labitur ripa Iove non probante u-
xorius amnis.
Audiet civis acuisse ferrum,
quo graves Persae melius perirent,
audiet pugnas vitio parentum
rara iuventus.
Quem vocet divum populus ruentis
imperi rebus ? Prece qua fatigent

**lows**, she was the daughter of Aeneas and therefore sister of Iulus, the mythical ancestor of the Julian family. After the birth of the twins she was thrown into the Tiber, but received by the river-god as his wife. He is here represented as enraged at the wrong done her family in the murder of Julius Caesar.—**dum**: introducing, as mere attendant circumstance, the cause or occasion of the main action; cf. 6. 9 and see Roby 1665.

18. **sinistra**: *i.e.* the eastern. The banks of a river are designated as 'right' or 'left' in reference to the personified river himself as he moves in his course.

19. **ripa**: here *over* the bank, in contrast with *Epod.* 2. 25. The ablative in both places is that of 'the way by which.' — **non probante**: *i.e.* he had not appointed the river to this office nor ordained such extreme retribution. — **u-xorius**: see Intr. 174 *b*.

21. **audiet**, etc.: after setting forth the signs of divine wrath the poet proceeds to the cause of it, — unnatural civil strife; and this he presents more effectively by carrying his reader forward to a time when it will be dispassionately judged by a generation which feels only its disastrous effects. — **civis**: the emphasis (Intr. 116 *b*) and the usual meaning of '**fellow-citizens**' attaching to the word indicate that they are preparing for a struggle against one another, as if we should speak, *e.g.*, of '*brothers* drawing their daggers.'

22. **Persae**: *i.e.* the oriental peoples, called by Horace indifferently *Medi*, *Persae*, and *Parthi*, at this time under the sway of the Parthian kings, but formerly subject to the Medes and Persians successively, whose names were thus permanently impressed upon them. — **perirent**: imperfect subjunctive of softened assertion in past time, with apodosis implied in **melius**; cf. *falleret*, IV. 6. 16 n; Gr. 311 *a*.

23. **pugnas**: *i.e.* not only of preparations for war (**acuisse ferrum**) but of actual conflict.

24. **rara**, *thinned*. — **iuventus**: *i.e.* a younger generation.

25. **divum**: implying that no mere human help would avail. — **ruentis**: the figure is taken from a building; cf. II. 1. 32 *Hesperiae sonitum ruinae*.

26. **rebus**: dative, because **vocet**, with **divum**, expresses a call for favor or help. — **prece qua**, *with what* (new) *prayer*, in contrast with the ordinary ritual (**carmina**). — **prece**: the singular is rare, and is used by Horace only in the ablative. — **qua**: Intr. 114.

virgines sanctae minus audientem
carmina Vestam?
Cui dabit partis scelus expiandi
Iuppiter? Tandem venias precamur,
nube candentis umeros amictus,
augur Apollo;
sive tu mavis, Erycina ridens,
quam Iocus circum volat et Cupido;
sive neglectum genus et nepotes
respicis, auctor,

27. **virgines sanctae**: the Vestals. — **minus**: here merely a softened negative (like *parum*) with no definite comparative force; cf. Plaut. *Cas.* 998 *monebo, si quidem meministi minus.* According to Ovid (*F.* III. 699 *sqq.*) Vesta was offended by the wrong done her in the murder of her priest, Caesar.

28. **carmina**, *their litanies.* These were old formulas (the proper meaning of *carmen*) cast in rythmical form in order to be better held in memory at a time when the art of writing was not in common use.

29. **partis**, *office;* properly 'rôle.' — **scelus expiandi**, *of purging away our sin*, sc. by casting out the spirit of strife and leading the people to worthy achievements. For **scelus**, cf. 35. 33. For answer to his question the poet appeals in succession to three divinities who might be supposed to have a special interest in the welfare of Rome: Apollo, who had recently rendered such signal assistance in the critical struggle at Actium (cf. Verg. *A.* VIII. 704, Prop. V. 6. 27.) and was adopted by the emperor as his patron god; Venus, as mother of Aeneas, the divine ancestress of the race (*Aeneadum genetrix*, Lucr. I. 1) and of the Julian family in particular; and Mars, the father of Romulus, and hence *auctor generis* (36).

30. **tandem**: implying that our prayers have long been in vain. — **venias**: Intr. 87.

31. **umeros**: Intr. 42.

32. **augur**: as the god of prophecy; cf. Verg. *A.* IV. 376.

33. **sive tu mavis** = *vel tu (venias) si mavis;* Intr. 119 *d.* — **Erycina**, *Lady of Eryx*, *i.e.* Venus. The epithet is appropriate here, as her temple at Eryx, in Sicily, was ascribed to Aeneas (Verg. *A.* V. 759). There was also a temple of Venus Erycina at Rome near the Colline gate. — **ridens**: after the Homeric φιλομμειδής; with **Iocus** (*Mirth*) and **Cupido** it makes up a picture in bright contrast to the grim scene next presented.

34. **circum**: see Intr. 115 *c.*

35. **sive respicis**: see 33 n. — **neglectum**: cf. *tandem*, 30 n. — **genus et nepotes**: expressing the same idea in two aspects, — collectively and individually.

36. **auctor**: Mars is appealed to, not as the god of war, as the

heu nimis longo satiate ludo,
quem iuvat clamor galeaeque leves
acer et Marsi peditis cruentum
voltus in hostem;

sive mutata iuvenem figura
ales in terris imitaris almae
filius Maiae, patiens vocari
Caesaris ultor,

serus in caelum redeas diuque
laetus intersis populo Quirini,
neve te nostris vitiis iniquum
ocior aura

next strophe shows, but as the father of the race.

37. **ludo**: the nature of the sport is explained in the picture that follows, which, as a specimen of Horace's skill in graphic portrayal may be compared with II. 1. 17 *sqq*. See also note on vs. 7.

38. **leves**: notice the quantity of the penult.

39. **acer voltus**, *the fierce look*—**Marsi**: see Intr. 117. The Marsian troops were among the bravest in the Roman army; cf. II. 20. 18, Verg. *G.* II. 167, and the proverb 'No triumph over the Marsi, nor without them' (Appian *B. C.* I. 46). If the reading **Mauri** be adopted, **peditis** will mean 'unhorsed.'—**cruentum**: the epithet places the scene in the midst of a hot fight at close quarters.

41. **sive**: see 33 n; the apodosis begins with **serus** 45 and extends to the close of the ode.—**mutata**: *sc.* from that of a god; cf. **ales**.—**iuvenem**: here the poet gives the first intimation of the thought to which he has been gradually leading us. He indicates who the *iuvenis* is in vs. 44, but reserves the full revelation of his personality to the very end of the poem. Octavian was at this time about thirty-five years old.

42. **ales filius**: in agreement with the subject of **imitaris**.—**in terris imitaris**, *dwellest on earth under the form of*.

43. **Maiae**: daughter of the titan Atlas, and mother of Mercury.—**vocari**: Intr. 94 *a*.

44. **Caesaris ultor**: the punishment of his uncle's assassins was avowed by Octavian as one of the chief objects of his career.

47. **iniquum**, *estranged*. *Aequus* and *iniquus* are regular expressions for the favorable or adverse disposition of a divinity towards men; cf. 28. 28, II. 4. 15.

48. **ocior aura**: keeping in mind the character of the god as *ales* (42). Observe how, while the language of the last two strophes applies equally well to the god and the man, the human side is gradually brought out more distinctly till fully revealed in the name itself at the end.

tollat; hic magnos potius triumphos,
hic ames dici pater atque princeps,
neu sinas Medos equitare inultos
te duce, Caesar.

## III.

Sic te diva potens Cypri,
sic fratres Helenae, lucida sidera,

49. **triumphos**: in allusion probably to the three triumphs which Octavian celebrated on his return from the East in August, B.C. 29.

50. **ames**: see Intr. 94 *c* and 119 *a*. For the combination of an object accusative with a complementary infinitive, cf. 1. 19 *sqq*. — **pater**: here a general expression of reverence, habitually applied to a god (as *Bacche pater*, 18. 6, *Iane pater*, *Ep*. I. 16. 59), and often to a man, as in the phrases *pater patriae*, *pater senatus*, *pater urbis*, etc., and also absolutely (cf. *S*. II. 1. 12, *Ep*. I. 6. 54, 7. 37). The formal title of *pater patriae* was not conferred upon Augustus till many years later, B.C. 2. — **princeps**: apparently abbreviated originally from *princeps senatus* (the title given to the senator of highest dignity, who was placed first on the roll by the censors), and used even under the Republic in the sense of *princeps civitatis*, since the 'first senator' would usually be in fact 'first citizen.' Octavian became *princeps senatus* in B.C. 28, and from that time on he cherished the title in its shorter form and wider signification as best expressing the character in which he wished to appear to his fellow-citizens. It thus came to be the usual term to designate the civil power of the ruler, *imperator* expressing his military power; cf. Tac. *Ann*. I. 1. 3 *cuncta discordiis civilibus fessa nomine principis sub imperium accepit*.

51. **Medos**: see 22 n. — **equitare**, *to ride on their raids*.

52. **te duce**, *so long as thou art, etc*. — **Caesar**: the name by which Octavian (as we call him, to avoid ambiguity) was known to his contemporaries from the time of his adoption by Julius Caesar (in his will, B.C. 44), his full name being C. Julius Caesar Octavianus. In B.C. 27 the title *Augustus* was added, but he was still usually called simply *Caesar*, as in III. 14.3, *Ep*. II. 1. 4 etc.; and this name is used by Horace for Julius Caesar in only two places, vs. 44, above, and *S*. I. 9. 18.

III. The third place in the series of odes is given to Vergil, and bears witness to Horace's warm regard for the friend to whom he owed his introduction to Maecenas (*S*. I. 5. 40 *sqq*., I. 6. 55; Intr. 20). The occasion is a proposed visit of Vergil to Athens, and in wishing him a safe voyage Horace indulges in some rather extravagant reflections on the temerity of man in braving the dangers of the sea, which is only an instance of the daring

ventorumque regat pater,
obstrictis aliis praeter Iapyga,
navis, quae tibi creditum
debes Vergilium, finibus Atticis

spirit with which in all things he overleaps the bounds that Providence has established. The poem bears the marks of an early effort and, like many of the odes of this book, was probably worked out on a Greek model. Of the voyage referred to nothing further is known. It could not have been the voyage of B.C. 19, on the return from which Vergil died, as there is convincing evidence that these books were published before that time. — Metre, 171.

1. **sic**, *so ; i.e.* on condition that (you grant my prayer) ; cf. *Ep.* I. 7. 69 *sic ignovisse putato me tibi, si cenas hodie mecum.* The prayer begins in vs. 6, and the words **sic . . . Iapyga** are parenthetical, introducing the prayer by an expression of good will to the ship, which is here the power appealed to ; cf. *S.* II. 3. 300 ; Verg. *E.* 9. 30 *sic tua Cyrneas fugiant examina taxos, | sic cytiso pastae distendant ubera vaccae, | incipe* ; Prop. V. 3. 67. The clause with *sic* sometimes follows the prayer, as I. 28. 23 *sqq.* In the present instance the appeal is not quite logical, since the fortunes of the ship and the voyager are bound up together. — **diva potens Cypri**: *i.e.* Venus, Ἀφροδίτη πελαγία or ποντία (*Venus marina ;* cf. III. 26. 5 and 9 ; IV. 11. 15), whose worship, as a protectress of seafaring men, was widely disseminated by the Phoenician traders. — **Cypri** : objective gen. after **potens** (Intr. 66 *b*), expressing here the worshippers over whom the goddess' control is exercised. The phrase is sometimes used to denote the special province of the divinity, as 5. 15 *potenti maris deo* (*i.e.* Neptune); 6. 10 *imbellis lyrae musa potens ; C. S.* 1 *silvarum potens Diana.*

2. **fratres Helenae**: Castor and Pollux, whose constellation (Gemini) was believed to have a quieting influence on the sea ; cf. 12. 27 *sqq.*, IV. 8. 31 *sq.* Sailors also told of twin lights, which they attributed to these gods, appearing on the yards of their ships in the darkness of the storm, heralds of good weather (Plin. *N. H.* II. 101).

3. **ventorum pater** : Aeolus. — **regat**, *guide.*

4. **obstrictis aliis** : cf. Verg. *A.* I. 52 *sqq.* — **Iapyga** : so named by the Greeks as blowing from the southeastern extremity of Italy, which they called Iapygia, across the Ionian sea ; hence favorable in the present instance. It is the same as the Latin Favonius.

5. **creditum debes** : a figure borrowed from commercial life : the ship has received Vergil as a *depositum*, and accordingly is bound to give him up (**reddas**) in unimpaired condition, at the time and place stipulated. **Vergilium**, standing in the accusative with **reddas**, in the place where the amount of the *depositum* is usually put, and before the caesura of the verse (Intr. 116 *b*) expresses emphatically the greatness of the ship's responsibility.

6. **finibus** : best taken as dative, but with **reddas** only, and not ἀπὸ κοινοῦ, see last note.

reddas incolumem precor
 et serves animae dimidium meae.
Illi robur et aes triplex
 circa pectus erat, qui fragilem truci
commisit pelago ratem
 primus, nec timuit praecipitem Africum
decertantem Aquilonibus
 nec tristis Hyadas nec rabiem Noti,
quo non arbiter Hadriae
 maior, tollere seu ponere volt freta.
Quem mortis timuit gradum,
 qui siccis oculis monstra natantia,

7. **reddas,** *deliver him*. The prefix *red-* denotes the reversal of the operation of giving, so far as it affects the recipient, — the *giving up* of what was received, not necessarily restoring it to the first giver; so here and *Ep*. I. 13. 2 *Augusto reddes volumina;* cf. also the regular expression for delivering a letter, *epistulam reddere*. From this it is a short step to the meaning 'to pay' *sc*. what is due (*debitum* = 'withheld').

8. **animae dimidium**: cf. II. 17. 5. The conception is borrowed from an old Greek definition of friendship, μία ψυχὴ δύο σώματα ἐνοικοῦσα (Diog. Laert. V. 1. 20); cf. Cic. *Lael*. 92 *cum amicitiae vis sit in eo ut unus quasi animus fiat ex pluribus*.

9. **illi,** etc., *his heart was cased in*, etc., *i.e.* was impenetrable to all impressions of fear. The figure is taken from the heavy armor of the soldier, but it is only a figure, and **pectus** is the heart; cf. IV. 4. 34.

10. **erat**: Intr. 77. — **fragilem truci**: Intr. 116 *a*.

12. **primus**: Intr. 116 *b*. — **praecipitem**: as coming in sudden squalls (*creber procellis*, Verg. *A*. I. 85; *protervus*, *Epod*. 16. 22). — **Africum**: see 1. 15 n.

13. **Aquilonibus,** *with the blasts of Boreas;* see Intr. 57. Aquilo blew from between north and north-east, and his name was derived by some from the resemblance of his violent onset to the swoop of an eagle (Fest. *ap*. Paul. p. 22).

14. **tristis**: as bringing wet and gloomy weather; cf. *tristis Orion*, *Epod*, 10. 10; *pluvias Hyadas*, Verg. *A*. III. 516. — **Noti**: the Greek name corresponding to Auster, the South Wind.

15. **quo non arbiter maior** (sc. *est*), *than whom no mightier master sways;* cf. III. 3. 4.

16. **seu**: see Intr. 119 *c*. — **ponere,** *to allay;* cf. 40 n.

17. **quem** (= *qualem;* cf. *Ep*. I. 15. 1 *sq*.) **mortis gradum,** *what form of death's approach*. For this conception of death cf. vs. 33 and III. 2. 14; Tib. I. 10. 4.

18. **siccis oculis**: *i.e.* without being moved to tears. The argument is *a fortiori:* the man who

qui vidit mare turbidum et
infamis scopulos Acroceraunia?
Nequiquam deus abscidit
prudens Oceano dissociabili
terras, si tamen impiae
non tangenda rates transiliunt vada.
Audax omnia perpeti
gens humana ruit per vetitum nefas.

could contemplate these things without profound emotion would of course not be daunted by mere physical danger. The thought in this strophe is not, as in the preceding, of the storm with its perils, which might attract a man of adventurous spirit, but of the awful grandeur of the sea itself, the tremendous force of its waves, and the portentous shapes that people its waters. The man who gazes with indifference on these manifestations of a power immeasurably above all human strength is lacking, not in fear, but in reverence (*pietas*), and will brave the displeasure of Heaven in other ways. This thought is developed in the remainder of the ode.

20. **infamis**: from the frequency of shipwrecks there. — **scopulos**: Intr. 126 *c*. — **Acroceraunia**: a long narrow promontory forming the northwestern extremity of Epirus and enclosing the gulf of Oricum. It had to be passed on the voyage to Athens.

21. **deus prudens,** *divine providence.* The divine power that rules the world is often expressed by the word *deus* without further definition (cf. 18. 3, 34. 13, III. 16. 43, 29. 30, *Epod.* 13. 7, *Ep.* I. 11. 22, 16. 78), giving evidence of the persistence of a dim conception of a supreme being through the multifarious development of Roman polytheism. See Preller-Jordan, *Röm. Myth.*, I. 48. As a personality, however, this supreme ruler was no other than Jupiter; incomparably more powerful than all other beings in the universe (cf. 12. 13 *sqq.*) but not the one God. — **abscidit,** *set apart . . . from;* cf. Ov. *M.* I. 22 *nam caelo terras et terris abscidit undas.*

22. **prudens**: *sc.* for man's best good. — **Oceano**: Intr. 70. — **dissociabili,** *incompatible;* cf. Tac. *Agr.* 3 *res olim dissociabiles, principatum ac libertatem.* The separation of land and water was necessary to make human life possible.

23. **impiae**: Intr. 124.

24. **non tangenda,** *which they ought not to touch.* — **transiliunt,** *course over;* suggesting entire freedom from scruple or caution.

25. **audax perpeti**: Intr. 101 *a.* — **omnia**: 'everything' (without exception), hence *anything;* more forcible than *quidlibet* (cf. *Ep.* II. 3. 10 *quidlibet audendi*) or *quidvis* (III. 24. 43, *Ep.* I. 15. 17); cf. *holus omne*, *Ep.* I. 5. 2.

26. **ruit**: cf. *transiliunt* 24 n. — **per vetitum nefas**: *i.e.* not only through sin, but in the face of an express prohibition.

Audax Iapeti genus
ignem fraude mala gentibus intulit.
Post ignem aetheria domo
subductum macies et nova febrium
terris incubuit cohors,
semotique prius tarda necessitas
leti corripuit gradum.
Expertus vacuum Daedalus aera
pennis non homini datis;
perrupit Acheronta Herculeus labor.
Nil mortalibus ardui est;
caelum ipsum petimus stultitia, neque

27. **audax**: the anaphora (Intr. 116 *f*) indicates that the cases now cited are instances of the impious audacity just described. — **Iapeti genus**: Prometheus.

28. **ignem**, etc.: in the separation of the four elements from chaos (cf. 21 n), fire, the subtlest of all, rose to the highest place, in the ethereal spaces (**aetheria domo** 29) above the air (Ov. *M.* I. 26 *sq.*) From there it was obtained for man surreptitiously and in defiance of the will of Zeus by Prometheus, who brought down a portion concealed in a reed (Hes. *Op.* 50.) — **mala**, *wicked;* cf. *malos fures*, *S.* I. 1. 77 and the legal form *dolus malus*. — **gentibus**: cf. *gentis*, 2. 5 n.

29. **post ignem subductum**: Intr. 105 *a*.

30. **macies**, etc.: according to the same myth (Hes. *l.l.*) disease came among mankind with the first woman, Pandora, whom Zeus sent with her fatal box (or vase) in resentment for the theft of fire. — **nova**: cf. 2. 6 n.

31. **incubuit**, *settled upon;* cf. Verg, *A.* I. 89 *ponto nox incubat atra;* Lucr. VI. 1143 (*mortifer aestus*) *incubuit populo*. — **cohors**, *troop;* properly 'retinue.'

32. **semotique**, etc.: *i.e.* death formerly, though inevitable (**necessitas**), was far off and came with slow pace; cf. Tib. II. 3. 38 *hinc cruor, hinc caedes, mors propiorque venit*. **prius** modifies the whole description, more particularly **semoti** and **tarda** (Intr. 76).

34. Daedalus invaded still another element not designed for such use. For the story, see Verg. *A.* VI. 14, Ov. *M.* VIII. 183. — **vacuum**, *unsubstantial.*

35. **non datis**: *i.e.* designedly withheld (litotes).

36. Hercules invaded even the realms of death. — **perrupit**, *broke into.* For the prosody, see Intr. 179. — **Herculeus labor**: Intr. 126 *b*.

37. **nil ardui est** (to be pronounced *arduist*), *no path is steep.* Strictly, however, **est** is predicative ('there is'). — **mortalibus**: dat. of reference.

38. **stultitia**: in attempting the impossible; **scelus**: in transgressing the bounds set by divine will.

per nostrum patimur scelus
iracunda Iovem ponere fulmina.

## IV.

Solvitur acris hiems grata vice veris et Favoni,
trahuntque siccas machinae carinas,
ac neque iam stabulis gaudet pecus aut arator igni,
nec prata canis albicant pruinis.

40. **iracunda**: Intr. 124. — **ponere**: equivalent to *deponere*, as often in prose and poetry; cf. Intr. 129.

IV. L. Sestius, who is thought to have been a son of the P. Sestius defended by Cicero in a speech now extant, had been an enthusiastic partisan of Brutus, under whom he served as quaestor. Horace's acquaintance with him very likely dated from that time. On his return to Rome, Sestius was wealthy enough to be independent, but in spite of his undisguised fidelity to the memory of his former chief, he accepted the new order of things, and in B.C. 23 became consul (suffectus) on the retirement of Augustus from the consulship in July, — a fact that may have determined the place of this ode in the collection, which was probably published in that year.

The ode is a highly artistic production, with an elaborate metre and a carefully balanced strophic symmetry. The main motive, expressed in the two middle couplets (vss. 9–12) grows naturally out of the description of spring which precedes (vss. 1–8) and is again enforced by the thought presented in the concluding verses (13–20). 'The cramping fetters of winter are bursting under the warm breath of spring, and man and nature are full of fresh, glad life. The season invites to enjoyment; and life is too short and death too sure for us to count on many such opportunities.' The poem is similar in construction to I. 7; in sentiment, to IV. 7. — Metre, 166.

1. **solvitur**, *is breaking up*. The hard and fast condition of the ground produced by winter is attributed to the season itself, just as death is 'pale' (vs. 13 n) etc. For the literal application of the word, see vs. 10. — **Favoni**: the West Wind (Ζέφυρος), which began to blow, according to the Italian Farmer's Almanac, about February 10, and was accounted a harbinger of spring (*veris praenuntius, Zephyrus*, Lucr. V. 737). The season for navigation opened about a month later. Notice the alliteration in this verse (Intr. 131).

2. **trahunt**: the technical term is *deducere;* here the direction in which the ships are drawn is indicated by **siccas**. — **machinae**: simply rope and tackle and rollers (*phalangae*); cf. Caes. *B.C.* II. 10. 7.

3. **neque iam gaudet**: marking the contrast between winter, which made the warm stable and

Iam Cytherea choros ducit Venus imminente luna,
  iunctaeque Nymphis Gratiae decentes
alterno terram quatiunt pede, dum gravis Cyclopum
  Volcanus ardens visit officinas.
Nunc decet aut viridi nitidum caput impedire myrto,
  aut flore terrae quem ferunt solutae;
nunc et in umbrosis Fauno decet immolare lucis,
  seu poscat agna sive malit haedo.

the cosy fireside so attractive, and the spring, which has robbed them of their charm.

5. The awakening of the regenerative power of nature and the renewal of life and beauty in the spring of the year are typified in mythology by the renewed activity of Venus. Cf. the fine invocation to Venus in Lucr. I. 6, *te, dea, te fugiunt venti, te nubila caeli | adventumque tuum, tibi suavis daedala tellus | summittit flores, tibi rident aequora ponti, | placatumque nitet diffuso lumine caelum; | nam simul ac species patefactast verna diei*, etc.; and the picture in V. 737 *sqq.* — **Cytherea**: *i.e.* in Cythera; cf. *Delius et Patareus Apollo*, III. 4. 64 n. — **choros ducit**, etc.: cf. the picture in the Homeric hymn to Apollo 194, *αὐτὰρ ἐυπλόκαμοι Χάριτες καὶ ἐύφρονες Ὧραι | Ἁρμονίη θ' Ἥβη τε Διὸς θυγάτηρ τ' Ἀφροδίτη | ὀρχεῦντ' ἀλλήλων ἐπὶ καρπῷ χεῖρας ἔχουσαι.* — **imminente luna**: the scene is laid in the solitude of the night, when the gods love best to visit the earth (*sub nocte silenti, cum superis terrena placent*, Stat. *Silv.* I. 1. 94).

6. **iunctae**: *sc.* with their arms, forming a row or ring (*ἐπὶ καρπῷ χεῖρας ἔχουσαι*).—**decentes**, *comely*.

7. **alterno terram**: the spondees imitate the measured tread of the dance. — **dum gravis**, etc.: a contrasted picture with heavy strokes, to set off the lighter lines of the preceding picture. — **gravis**, *ponderous*. — **Cyclopum officinas**: popularly located under the 'Volcanic' islands north of Sicily; cf. Verg. *A.* VIII. 416. The Cyclopes were three sons of Uranus and Gaea, who forged the thunderbolts of Zeus (Hes. *Theog.* 139), a conception of them quite distinct from that of the Odyssey, where they are represented as living the rude life of shepherds.

8. **ardens**: as the god of fire, working assiduously at the forge.— **visit**: cf. the description in Verg. *A.* VIII. 423 *sqq.* The conception of the gods visiting from time to time their favorite haunts or the scenes of their activity is a familiar one in classical mythology; cf. 17. 1 *sqq.*, III. 28. 14 *sq.*, Verg. *A.* IV. 144. (According to many MSS. the verb here is **urit**, *fires*.)

9. **nitidum**: *sc.* with ointment. — **impedire**: poetical for *cingere*. Perfumes and garlands were regular concomitants of a feast; cf. II. 3. 13 n. — **myrto**: *i.e.* with a garland of its leaves; see II. 15. 6 n.

10. **flore**: the singular is used collectively; Intr. 127. — **solutae**: cf. *solvitur*, 1 n.

11. **nunc et** (*too*) etc.: another form of feasting; the victim will furnish forth the banquet.

Pallida mors aequo pulsat pede pauperum tabernas
regumque turris. O beate Sesti,
vitae summa brevis spem nos vetat incohare longam.
Iam te premet nox fabulaeque manes
et domus exilis Plutonia; quo simul mearis,
nec regna vini sortiere talis
nec tenerum Lycidan mirabere, quo calet iuventus
nunc omnis et mox virgines tepebunt.

12. **seu poscat,** etc.: economy of phrase for *vel agnā, si* (*agnā immolari*) *poscat, vel haedo, si malit,* or the like; cf. 2. 33 n. For the ablatives, which are instrumental, cf. Cic. *Leg.* II. 29 *quibus hostiis immolandum cuique deo.*

13. **pallida**: the paleness which accompanies death is ascribed as a physical characteristic to the personified figure of the destroyer; Intr. 125. — **aequo,** *impartial;* Intr. 124. — **pulsat pede**: for the practice cf. Plaut. *Most.* 453 *pultando pedibus paene confregi hasce foris.* For the repetition of the *p*-sound, see Intr. 131.

14. **regum,** *princes.* The word is constantly used for a man of wealth, and particularly for the patron of a person in humble circumstances; cf. *Ep.* I. 7. 37. — **turris**: *i.e.* lofty houses. — **beate,** *favored;* usually referring to riches.

15. **summa,** *span;* properly the 'sum' of the days (or whatever portion of time we may take as a unit) allotted to us; cf. IV. 7. 17. — **brevis, longam**: the contrast is enhanced by rhythmical position; Intr. 116 *c.*

16. **te premet,** *will close round you;* cf. Verg. *A.* VI. 827 *concordes animae dum nocte premuntur.* — **fabulae** (in apposition with **manes**; Intr. 126 *c*), *phantom;* lit. talk, mere talk, empty names. Cf. *Epod.* 11. 8. *per urbem fabula quanta fui;* Pers. 5. 152 *cinis et manes et fabula fies.*

17. **domus Plutonia**: here the whole lower world. — **exilis**: in contrast with the comforts with which Sestius is now surrounded. — **simul**: without *ac*, as often.

18. **regna vini**: at a drinking bout (*comissatio*) it was usual to select by lot a *magister convivii,* who presided with arbitrary power over the festivities, regulating the strength of the wine, the amount drunk, etc., in accordance with certain stringent rules. For the manner of choosing this *arbiter bibendi,* see II. 7. 25 n. For the plural **regna,** see Intr. 128.—**talis**: like dice, except that the faces were of different shapes, and there were only four faces (1, 3, 4, 6) on which the *talus* could stand.

19. **Lycidan**: the name, like all of Horace's Greek names, is fictitious, and stands for any handsome lad; Intr. 117 *a.*— **mirabere,** *feast your eyes upon. Miror* expresses a fascinated gaze, as III. 25. 14, 29. 11; *Ep.* I. 6. 18 *Tyrios mirare colores.* — **quo**: Intr. 72. — **calet,** *are enamoured.*

20. **mox**: *i.e.* when he is a little older — **tepebunt**: denoting a milder degree of warmth than **calet,** — the first step from indifference to interest.

## V.

Quis multa gracilis te puer in rosa
perfusus liquidis urget odoribus
grato, Pyrrha, sub antro?
Cui flavam religas comam,
simplex munditiis? Heu quotiens fidem
mutatosque deos flebit et aspera
nigris aequora ventis
emirabitur insolens,

V. To a coquette. The poet writes in the character of one who has himself been led on to shipwreck under her spell, and retains a lively recollection of her wiles. — Metre, 173.

1. **multa rosa**: Intr. 127. The singular here suggests quantity rather than number. — **in**: *i.e.* wearing them; cf. *Ep.* II. 3. 228 *regali conspectus in auro nuper et ostro;* Cic. *Fin.* II. 65 *potantem in rosa.* The roses were worn in a great garland round the head and shoulders. — **gracilis puer,** *slip of a boy;* in disparagement, as *S.* I. 5. 69 *gracili sic tamque pusillo.* There is nothing disparaging in **puer** itself; see 9. 16 n.

2. **perfusus liquidis odoribus,** *bathed in perfume.*— **urget,** *courts.*

3. **Pyrrha**: Πυῤῥά (cf. πῦρ), maid with the auburn hair (**flavam comam** 4), much admired by the Romans; cf. II. 4. 14, III. 9. 19, IV. 4. 4; Verg. *A.* IV. 698 (of Dido).— **sub**: for *in*, but directing the thought more specifically to the shelter afforded by the grotto; cf. II. 1. 39, III. 29. 14 *sub lare, Epod.* 9. 3 *sub alta domo.*— **antro**: such grottos or bowers, natural or artificial, were common in Roman country places, serving the purpose of our summer-house. The youth and maid are making holiday together in the manner suggested in 1. 19 *sqq.* Hence the roses and perfume (see 4. 9 n).

4. **cui,** *for whose eyes?*—**religas**: *i.e.* in a knot at the back of the head, the simplest mode of wearing the hair; cf. II. 11. 23; Ov. *M.* VIII. 319 *crinis erat simplex, nodum collectus in unum.*

5. **simplex munditiis,** *in unadorned neatness.* The girl adopts a very effective simplicity of dress. — **fidem**: here broken faith, as the context shows. *Fides* is sufficiently elastic to take on this meaning; cf. 18. 16 *arcani fides prodiga,* III. 24. 59 *periura fides.*

6. **mutatos deos**: *sc.* in their disposition towards him, — the loss of their favor; see Intr. 105 *a.* — **flebit**: Intr. 51 *a.* — **aspera** etc.: *i.e.* when she is tired of him and seeks a quarrel to get rid of him. The metaphor prepares the way for the figure with which the ode closes.

7. **nigris**: Intr. 125; cf. *Epod.* 10. 5 *niger Eurus.*

8. **emirabitur**: the **e-** is intensive, as in *ediscere, elaborare, edurus,* etc. The word first occurs in Horace. — **insolens,** *innocent soul.*

qui nunc te fruitur credulus aurea,
qui semper vacuam, semper amabilem
sperat, nescius aurae
fallacis. Miseri quibus

intemptata nites: me tabula sacer
votiva paries indicat uvida
suspendisse potenti
vestimenta maris deo.

The word is here used in its primitive sense of 'unaccustomed to,' 'unfamiliar with' something. Horace also uses it objectively, as II. 3. 3 *insolenti laetitia*, *unusual* or *excessive joy*; and in this sense it was sometimes applied to a person, as Ter. *And.* 907 *quid tu Athenas insolens*, (*i.e.* seldom seen, 'a stranger')? Finally it is used of a person who holds himself aloof, is reserved, unsympathetic, haughty, arrogant, — its commonest meaning, as 16. 21, II. 4. 2, etc.

9. **credulus aurea**: the juxtaposition of the two epithets (Intr. 116 *a*) is as expressive as a separate clause (*credens te auream esse*). — **aurea**, *all gold*; denoting supreme excellence; cf. IV. 2. 23 *mores aureos*, II. 10. 5 *auream mediocritatem*, Verg. *A.* X. 16 *Venus aurea* (χρυσέης Ἀφροδίτης, *Il.* III. 64), and our 'golden rule,' 'silence is golden,' etc.

10. **vacuam**, *fancy-free*; cf. 6. 19.

11. **nescius aurae**: returning to the figure introduced in vs. 6; but *aura* in the sense of fickle favor had almost ceased to be figurative; cf. *popularis aurae*, III. 2. 20.

13. **nites**: of outward beauty; cf. *S.* II. 1. 64 *nitidus per ora* (*i.e.* in public) *cederet, introrsum turpis*. — **tabula sacer**, etc.: alluding to the custom, not yet extinct, by which the shipwrecked mariner commemorated his escape and his gratitude by depositing in the temple of the divinity to whom he attributed his safety a picture (**tabula**) of the occurrence, together with his clothes, the sole possessions which he saved with his life. Cf. Vergil's description of the sacred olive-tree of Faunus at Laurentum (*A.* XII. 766), *nautis olim venerabile lignum,* | *servati ex undis ubi figere dona solebant* | *Laurenti divo et votas suspendere vestes.*

14. **votiva**: the sailor in his peril would vow the offering; cf. *votas vestes*, Verg. *l.l.*, — **paries**: that of the temple, on which the picture was hung.

16. **maris**: with **potenti**; cf. *Cypri*, 3. 1 n. — **deo**: Neptune.

## VI.

Scriberis Vario fortis et hostium
victor Maeonii carminis alite,
quam rem cumque ferox navibus aut equis
miles te duce gesserit.

VI. To Marcus Agrippa; an apology. It would seem that Agrippa had intimated a desire that Horace should write an ode in his honor. Horace protests in half playful strain that the subject is beyond his humble powers, a theme fit for epic verse, and by weaving in a good deal of complimentary allusion really grants the favor he professes to withhold. For similar instances of his skill in declining such requests, cf. *S.* II. 1. 12 *sqq.*, *Ep.* II. 1. 250 *sqq.*—Metre, 172.

1. **scribēris**: the emphasis (Intr. 116 *b*) is that of assurance, and the ground of the assurance naturally follows at once, — 'Your achievements will not lack a historian; there's Varius, etc.,' — drawing **Vario** away from its syntactical connection. *Scribere* with a personal object (cf. vs. 13 *quis Martem scripserit*) or with a personal subject in the passive is rare; and the real subject here is not merely *tu*, understood, but *tu* **fortis et hostium victor,** *i.e.* your prowess and success; see Intr. 105 *a*. — **Vario . . . alite**: ablative absolute, but with a force approaching that of the examples in Intr. 105 *b*. The thought is, 'Your fame is safe in the fact that Varius is an epic poet.' (Some editors change unnecessarily to *aliti*, making **Vario** dat. of the agent.)

2. **Maeonii**: *i.e.* Homeric. According to one of many conflicting traditions Homer was born at Smyrna in Lydia (Maeonia). When this ode was written Varius was looked upon as the epic poet of the age, and even after the publication of the Aeneid in B.C. 19 Horace couples his name with that of Vergil on equal terms (*Ep.* II. 1. 247, 3. 55); see Intr. 15. — **alite**: for poet or 'singer'; cf. IV. 2. 25 *Dircaeum cycnum* (of Pindar), and II. 20.

3. **quam rem cumque**, etc.: *i.e.* whatever exploit the army or navy has achieved under your command will be an occasion for Varius to record your praises in his expected epic. The construction is similar to our own use of the general relative clause, when it is equivalent to a general condition, summing up all cases that may have occurred: 'If in any case the soldier, etc. (*i.e.* in every case where the soldier, etc.), your prowess will be recorded.' Cf. *Ep.* I. 2. 14 *quicquid delirant reges, plectuntur Achivi.* — **cumque**: treated by Horace as a detachable suffix; cf. 7. 25, 9. 14, 16. 2, etc. — **navibus**: alluding especially to the naval victories of Naulochus, B.C. 36, and Actium, B.C. 31. — **equis**: *i.e.* (in contrast with **navibus**), on land. Agrippa commanded in Gaul in B.C. 39 and 38, and gained some successes on the Rhine and elsewhere.

5. **nos**: Intr. 116 *b*. — **neque haec dicere nec**: *i.e.* I no more attempt these themes than I

Nos, Agrippa, neque haec dicere nec gravem
Pelidae stomachum cedere nescii
nec cursus duplicis per mare Vlixei
nec saevam Pelopis domum

conamur, tenues grandia, dum pudor
imbellisque lyrae musa potens vetat
laudes egregii Caesaris et tuas
culpa deterere ingeni.

should, etc.; cf. III. 5. 27 *sqq*. By classing Agrippa's exploits with those of the heroes of Greek epos and tragedy, ostensibly to excuse himself, he pays the highest possible compliment to the Roman general. — **gravem Pelidae stomachum**: the subject of the Iliad, — μῆνιν . . . Πηληιάδεω Ἀχιλῆος οὐλομένην, *Il*. I. 1. — **dicere**, *to sing*; a common use of the word, especially where the theme of song is given; cf. 12. 25, 21. 1 *sq*., II. 13. 30, I. 32. 3, III. 4. 1, IV. 12. 9, etc.

6. **stomachum**, *spleen*; cf. *S*. II. 7. 44. The word has a colloquial flavor, and is used in playful irony of so dignified a subject; so also **duplex** (7), *wily*, for the Homeric πολύτροπος, πολύμητις. — **cedere**: see Intr. 101 *c*.

7. **cursus**, etc.: the theme of the Odyssey. — **Vlixei**: genitive; cf. *Achillei*, 15. 34, *Epod*. 17. 14. The name of Ὀδυσσεύς invariably used by Latin writers is *Vlixes*, from a dialectic (Doric) form, Οὐλίξης. The genitive *Vlixei*, from a parallel form *Vlixeus*, which however does not occur (cf. *Perses* and *Perseus*), is quadrisyllabic here and *Epod*. 16. 60, 17. 16; but necessarily trisyllabic in hexameter (*Ep*. I. 6. 63, 7. 40).

8. **saevam Pelopis domum**, *Pelops' savage line*, — the subject of many of the most famous Greek tragedies, among them the *Agamemnon* of Aeschylus, the *Electra* of Sophocles, and the *Orestes*, *Electra*, and *Iphigenia* of Euripides, still extant. Varius himself had written a *Thyestes*. The story of the family was a series of murders, from Pelops himself, who slew his father-in-law Oenomaus, to Orestes, who killed his mother Clytemnestra.

9. **tenues grandia** (agreeing with **nos** and **haec** respectively), *grand themes for slender powers*; Intr. 116 *a*. — **dum**: see 2. 17 n.

10. **imbellis**: indicating the nature of his unfitness to deal with Agrippa's exploits. — **lyrae**: cf. *Cypri*, 3. 1 n. — **musa**: see note on *Clio*, 12. 2. — **vetat**: Intr. 77.

11. **egregii Caesaris**: cf. III. 25. 4, and see 2. 52 n. The poet dexterously introduces the fact that Agrippa was associated with Augustus in his greatest achievements.

12. **culpa ingeni**: cf. *Ep*. II. 1. 229 *sqq*., where Horace expresses himself at length on this subject. — **deterere**, *to belittle*. — **ingeni**: substantives with stems in *-io-* have only the shorter form of the genitive in Horace.

Quis Martem tunica tectum adamantina
digne scripserit aut pulvere Troico
nigrum Merionen aut ope Palladis
Tydiden superis parem?

Nos convivia, nos proelia virginum
sectis in iuvenes unguibus acrium
cantamus vacui, sive quid urimur,
non praeter solitum leves.

## VII.

Laudabunt alii claram Rhodon aut Mytilenen
aut Epheson bimarisve Corinthi

13–16. Scenes from the Iliad. It is implied, of course, that Agrippa's prowess is to be ranked with that of the god and the heroes mentioned.

13. **tunica tectum adamantina**: a paraphrase of χαλκοχίτων, a stock epithet of the Homeric warrior. *Adamas* (ἀδάμας, *unyielding;* cf. δαμάω) is not a specific metal, but a poetic term for the hardest iron or brass.

14. **digne scripserit**: the more accurate Latin use of the future perfect, the question having reference not so much to the action itself as to its quality, which can be submitted to judgment only after the action is completed.

15. **Merionen**: charioteer of Idomeneus of Crete (*Il.* XIII. 528); cf. 15. 26, IV. 9. 20 n.—**ope Palladis** etc.: alluding to the combat (*Il.* V. 334 *sqq.*) in which Diomed, with the aid of Athena, wounds Venus and Mars and drives them from the field.

18. **sectis,** *but . . . pared;* not really dangerous.—**in iuvenes acrium**: cf. *acer in hostem*, 2. 39.

19. **vacui**: see 5. 10 n.—**sive**: Intr. 119 *d.*—**quid**, *at all.*

20. **non praeter solitum**, *as usual.*

VII. This ode is similar in plan to Ode 4, the main motive being an exhortation to forget the troubles and enjoy the pleasures of life, with an introduction and a conclusion designed to enforce this counsel. The introduction commends the beauty of a place (as in Ode 4 of a season) that invites to enjoyment, and the conclusion supports the counsel given by an example. The parts are not so skilfully fitted together, however, as in Ode 4, so that some critics, as early as the second century, have thought that we really have here two odes (vss. 1–14 and 15–32); and this division appears in some manuscripts. It is possible that vss. 1–14 were originally written independently, but there is no sufficient reason to doubt that Horace finally composed the ode in its present form, on the plan indicated above.

moenia vel Baccho Thebas vel Apolline Delphos
insignis aut Thessala Tempe.
Sunt quibus unum opus est intactae Palladis urbem
carmine perpetuo celebrare et
undique decerptam fronti praeponere olivam ;

L. Munatius Plancus, to whom the ode is addressed, was a man of advanced years and great prominence in the state. He had been one of Caesar's lieutenants in Gaul and in B.C. 43, while holding the chief command in that country, founded the colony of Lugdunum (Lyons). He was consul in 42, and for many years after that was the trusted friend and agent of Antony in the East. The latter's relations with Cleopatra however, finally drove him (or gave him an excuse) to go over to Octavian just before the decisive struggle at Actium. His course made him, justly or unjustly, many bitter enemies, who have painted him as an unscrupulous trimmer. If so, it was a master stroke to make in the senate in B.C. 27 the proposal by which the title of Augustus was conferred upon Octavian; and for this he received his reward in the censorship in B.C. 22. Horace's tribute implies nothing as to his character, being little more than a formal compliment. — Metre, 162.

1. **laudabunt** : Intr. 79. For the meaning, see I. 17 n. — **claram**, *renowned* (cf. *Rhodum nobilem*, Cat. 4. 8), applying to the first three cities named (connected by **aut . . . aut**). All three were noted for beauty of situation and delightful climate. Rhodes was also famous for its commerce and for its school of rhetoric which exerted no small influence on Roman oratory, counting Cicero among its pupils. Mytilene was the capital of Lesbos, the city of Alcaeus and Sappho. Ephesus was the capital of the province of Asia.

2. **bimaris** : from its position on the Isthmus. The word, formed on the model of the Greek διθάλασσος, occurs first here, but was afterwards much used by Ovid. — **Corinthi moenia** : at this time in ruins. The city was destroyed by the Romans in B.C. 146, and the colony of freedmen established there by Julius Caesar had not as yet attained any great degree of prosperity.

3. **Baccho, Apolline** : abl. of cause, with **insignis**.

4. **Tempe** (Τέμπη, acc. pl. neut., like γένη) : the beautiful defile through which the Peneus makes its way between Olympus and Ossa to the sea.

5. **quibus unum opus est** : *i.e.* who devote themselves wholly to this one theme. — **intactae**, *the Virgin*, Ἀθήνη Παρθένος. — **urbem** : Athens.

7. **undique decerptam** etc.: *i.e.* to seek distinction by writing on every possible topic in Attic history and legend. The same figure is used by Lucretius, I. 928: *iuvatque novos decerpere flores | insignemque meo capiti petere inde coronam, | unde prius nulli velarint tempora musae.* — **fronti praeponere** : *i.e.* in a garland. — **olivam**, *an olive twig*. The olive, the gift of Athena to Athens, grew in great abundance in Attica and was closely associated with the fame of that country.

plurimus in Iunonis honorem
aptum dicet equis Argos ditisque Mycenas.
Me nec tam patiens Lacedaemon
nec tam Larisae percussit campus opimae
quam domus Albuneae resonantis
et praeceps Anio ac Tiburni lucus et uda
mobilibus pomaria rivis.
Albus ut obscuro deterget nubila caelo

8. **plurimus,** *a great many;* cf. Verg. *A.* II. 369 *plurima mortis imago;* Juv. 3. 232 *plurimus hic aeger moritur vigilando;* Lucan III. 707 *multus sua volnera puppi adfixit moriens.* — **in Iunonis honorem,** etc: cf. *Il.* IV. 51, where Hera says: ἦ τοι ἐμοὶ τρεῖς μὲν πολὺ φίλταταί εἰσι πόληες, | Ἄργος τε Σπάρτη τε καὶ εὐρυάγυια Μυκήνη.

9. **aptum equis Argos**=Ἄργος ἱππόβοτον (*Il.* II. 287). — **dicet:** cf. 6. 5 n. — **ditis Mycenas:** cf. πολυχρύσοιο Μυκήνης, *Il.* VII. 180. The city was already in ruins in Horace's time.

10. **me:** cf. 1. 29 n. The enumeration of Greek cities is continued into this sentence, and makes the connection with what follows. — **patiens,** *hardy.* — **Lacedaemon:** the third of the favorite cities of Juno. Cf. vs. 8 n. All these were insignificant at this time, and interesting to Horace and his readers, as they are to us, from their historical or traditional associations.

11. **Larisae:** in Thessaly, in the fertile valley of the Peneus. — **percussit:** *sc.* with admiration. — **opimae:** cf. Λάρισαν ἐριβώλακα, *Il.* II. 841.

12. **domus,** etc: *i.e.* Tibur (Tivoli) and its beautiful surroundings. — **domus Albuneae:** *i.e.* the grotto sacred to this sibyl, which was resorted to as an oracle in early times from all parts of Italy. See Verg. *A.* VII. 82 *sqq.* — **resonantis,** from the neighboring cataract.

13. **praeceps Anio:** after passing through the town, which stands on the edge of the Sabine hills, commanding a fine view of the Campagna, the river descends to the plain in a series of beautiful waterfalls. — **Tiburni:** the mythical eponymous founder of Tibur. Tradition made him a grandson of the Argive prophet Amphiaraus, banished with his brothers Catillus and Coras; cf. II. 6. 5 *Tibur Argeo positum colono,* I. 18. 2, where the town is called *moenia Catili,* and Verg. *A.* VII. 670 *sqq.* — **lucus,** *the sacred grove;* the regular meaning of *lucus* in distinction from *nemus.* Cf. *Ep.* I. 6. 32. — **uda:** *i.e.* irrigated; cf. III. 29. 6.

14. **mobilibus rivis:** the streams that flow into the Anio, with their frequent waterfalls. — **pomaria:** cf. Propert. V. 7. 81 *pomosis Anio incubat arvis.*

15. Here begins the second and main part of the ode, for which the preceding praise of Tibur paves the way. — **albus,** *bright;* cf. III. 27. 19; Intr. 125. It belongs with **saepe** and the predicate: *as the South Wind is often bright and wipes away,* etc. Notus was ordinarily

saepe Notus neque parturit imbris
perpetuos, sic tu sapiens finire memento
tristitiam vitaeque labores
molli, Plance, mero, seu te fulgentia signis
castra tenent seu densa tenebit
Tiburis umbra tui. Teucer Salamina patremque
cum fugeret, tamen uda Lyaeo

a stormy wind (cf. 3. 14 *rabiem Noti*), but sometimes brought clear weather, in which case he was called by the Greeks *Λευκόνοτος*.

16. **parturit,** *is pregnant with, breeds*.

17. **perpetuos**: cf. *primus*, 3. 12 n. — **sapiens**: equivalent to an adverb with **finire.** — **finire,** *to seek relief from;* lit. to set limits to, so that they shall not be *perpetua*. Cf. III. 4. 39; *Ep*. II. 3. 406 *ludusque repertus et longorum operum finis*. — **memento**: a common form of command or advice, softening the direct injunction; cf. II. 3. 1, III. 29. 32, *S*. II. 5. 52, *Ep*. I. 8. 16, etc.

18. **labores,** *troubles*.

19. **molli**: referring at once to the mellowness of the wine (from age) and to its soothing influence. — **fulgentia**: the eagle of the legion and the silver disks on the standards of the cohorts were kept highly polished.

20. **tenent . . . tenebit**: the natural inference from this change of tense,— that Plancus was at the time in camp,— places the date of the ode at least as early as B.C. 30, as there is no evidence and no probability that Plancus was engaged in military operations after that year.

21. **tui**: according to Porphyrio Plancus was a native of Tibur. He must at least have had a villa there. — **Teucer**: the example which the poet quotes to enforce his counsel is that of a man who, with hardships and struggles staring him in the face, refused to let them gain complete possession of his mind, and devoted to enjoyment the few hours that were left before the inevitable time of their coming. It is idle to search for any special resemblance to his case in that of Plancus. Teucer, the son of Telamon and brother of Ajax, on returning home to Salamis after the Trojan war, was repulsed and driven into banishment by his father, who had sent the brothers to the war with the strict injunction that neither should return without the other. Teucer sailed with his companions to Cyprus and there founded a city, to which he gave the name of his native Salamis; cf. Verg. *A*. I. 619. The story was familiar to Horace's contemporaries from a popular play of Pacuvius.

22. **cum fugeret,** *when going into exile from;* cf. *S*. I. 6. 13 *Tarquinius regno pulsus fugit*, and the Greek *φεύγειν*. The time indicated is apparently the night before he sailed away from Salamis. — **uda Lyaeo,** *moist from wine*, *i.e.* from drinking; cf. Tibul. I. 2. 3 *multo perfusum tempora Baccho*. Lyaeus ('the Releaser'; as if from λύω), a surname of Bacchus, stands here for his province, as *Baccho* in the example quoted; Intr. 130.

tempora populea fertur vinxisse corona,
sic tristis adfatus amicos :
'Quo nos cumque feret melior fortuna parente,
ibimus, o socii comitesque !
Nil desperandum Teucro duce et auspice Teucro ;
certus enim promisit Apollo
ambiguam tellure nova Salamina futuram.
O fortes peioraque passi
mecum saepe viri, nunc vino pellite curas ;
cras ingens iterabimus aequor.'

23. **pōpulea** : the poplar was sacred to Hercules, the great traveller of heroic times (*vagus Hercules*, III. 3. 9), under whose protection Teucer at this juncture would naturally place himself. — **corona** : cf. 4. 9 n.

25. **cumque**: cf. 6. 3 n. — **melior**, *kinder*. — **parente** : represented, in the tragedy of Pacuvius, as harsh and stern (Cic. *de Or.* II. 193).

27. **Teucro**: the use of his own name instead of *me*, — the name by which he is known to them, with the associations attached to it in their minds, — is an appeal to their confidence in him. — **duce et auspice** : an expression borrowed from the institutions of the Commonwealth, under which all military operations in the province of a consul were done under his *auspicia*, though not necessarily under his immediate personal direction (*ductus*). Cf. Suet. *Aug.* 21 *domuit autem partim ductu partim auspiciis suis Cantabriam*, etc. The phrase here, however, expresses something more than complete leadership, **auspice** being used with reference to the prophecy which he proceeds to quote.

28. **certus**, *unerring*.

29. **ambiguam** : *i.e.* one that will rival the original Salamis so that the name will no longer serve, without further definition, to indicate which of the two is meant. — **futuram** : *sc. esse.*

30. **o fortes peioraque passi** : cf. Verg. *A.* I. 198 *o passi graviora.*

31. **nunc** : *i.e.* while you may ; in contrast with **cras** ; cf. 9. 18 and 21.

32. **iterabimus** : having just completed one voyage (from Troy) ; cf. *Odys.* XII. 293 ἠῶθεν δ' ἀναβάντες ἐνήσομεν εὐρέι πόντῳ.

VIII. A spirited sketch of a young athlete in love. The name Lydia, sometimes Lyde (Λύδη), as III. 11 and 28, occurs frequently in amatory poetry, and is here appropriate with its suggestion of oriental effeminacy. Sybaris, after the name of a town in Magna Graecia proverbial for its luxury, is equally suitable for the lover in his present state. The poet expresses his amazement at the transformation which has been wrought, in a volley of questions which do not wait for an answer, adjuring Lydia to tell how she has worked such a spell upon the

## VIII.

Lydia, dic, per omnis
te deos oro, Sybarin cur properes amando
perdere, cur apricum
oderit campum, patiens pulveris atque solis.
Cur neque militaris
inter aequalis equitat, Gallica nec lupatis
temperat ora frenis?
Cur timet flavum Tiberim tangere? Cur olivum

youth. The questions are at first indirect, depending on *dic*, but afterwards proceed more quietly in the direct form. The ode is no doubt formed on a Greek model, — Horace's only experiment in this difficult metre, — but is worked out as usual with Roman details. — Metre, 175.

1. **per omnis te deos oro**: this interlocked order (Intr. 110) is a favorite one in adjurations; cf. Ter. *And.* 538 *per te deos oro;* 834 *per ego te deos oro.* Here **te** brings out the emphasis on **omnes** and **deos** by separating them.

2. **cur properes amando**: *i.e.* why he is hastening to his ruin under her spell; not asking why she does so, but adjuring her to explain the marvelous result. What has she done to him to change him so utterly? — **amando**: used in a neutral sense, neither active nor passive, like an abstract noun; cf. Verg. *E.* 8. 71 *cantando rumpitur anguis;* Lucr. I. 312 *anulus in digito subter tenuatur habendo.*

4. **campum**: *sc. Martium*, a portion of which, on the bank of the river, was set apart for athletic exercises. The usual time was early in the afternoon, before the hottest part of the day. See *S.* I. 6. 125 *sqq.* — **patiens,** *he who can bear;* cf. *metuens*, I. 16 n.

5. **neque . . . nec**: *i.e.* neither in the common exercises nor alone. — **militaris aequalis,** *the soldierly young fellows of his own age.*

6. **equitat**: an exercise which Augustus made more fashionable by the institution (or restoration) of the Game of Troy (*lusus Troiae*, Suet *Aug.* 43; Verg. *A.* V. 545); cf. III. 7. 25 *sq.*, 12. 3, 24. 54 *sq.* — **Gallica**: *i.e.* of the Gallic steed. Gaul supplied the Romans with their best horses. — **lupatis**: cf. Verg. *G.* III. 208.

7. **temperat,** *govern.*

8. **timet tangere**: humorous exaggeration to express the extreme distaste which the youth has conceived for what was once his favorite exercise. For the infinitive see Intr. 94 *l.* — **flavum**: see 2. 13 n. — **Tiberim**: swimming in the warm climate of Rome was naturally a very attractive form of exercise. Cf. III. 7. 27; 12. 3; *S.* II. 1. 8; Cic. *Cael.* 36 *ad Tiberim, eo loco quo omnis iuventus natandi causa venit.* — **olivum**: with which the body was anointed before swimming (cf. III. 12. 3) and the exercises of the palaestra, such as those that follow. Cf. Sat. I. 6. 123.

sanguine viperino
cautius vitat neque iam livida gestat armis
bracchia, saepe disco,
saepe trans finem iaculo nobilis expedito?
Quid latet, ut marinae
filium dicunt Thetidis sub lacrimosa Troiae
funera, ne virilis
cultus in caedem et Lycias proriperet catervas?

9. **sanguine viperino**: regarded as poisonous; cf. *Epod.* 3. 6. For the abl. see Intr. 75.

10. **cautius vitat**: cf. *timet tangere*, 8 n. — **neque iam**, *and no longer*. — **livida**: *e.g.* from carrying the discus, from occasional bruises, perhaps from blows with the boxing glove (*caestus*, called *arma* Verg. *A.* V. 412). — **gestat**: seldom used except of things separate from the body, but cf. *non obtusa pectora gestamus*, Verg. *A.* I. 567. — **armis**: *sc. campestribus* (*Ep.* II. 3. 379); *i.e.* the discus, javelin, and other implements used in the sports on the Campus.

11. **disco**: a heavy disc of stone or metal. The exercise was similar to our 'throwing the hammer' and 'putting the shot.' See the cut of Myron's famous *discobolus* in Baumeister II., p. 1003. Apparently the javelin was also used in this way, among others.

12. **trans finem expedito**, *for having put . . . clear beyond the farthest mark* ('broken the record'), like Ulysses among the Phaeacians, *Od.* VIII. 192: ὁ δ (λᾶας) ὑπέρπτατο σήματα πάντων. For the construction see Intr. 105 *a.* — **nobilis**, *he who is famous;* concessive, like *patiens* 4 n.

13. **ut dicunt**: the story that Thetis, foreseeing the fate of her son if he should join the expedition against Troy, placed him, disguised in girl's clothes at the court of Lycomedes, king of Scyros, where he was discovered by the shrewdness of Ulysses, is not alluded to in Homer, but occurs in later Greek literature. Cf. Ovid *M.* XIII. 162, and Stat. *Achil.* I. 207 *sqq.*, where it is worked out in detail.

14. **filium**: Achilles. — **sub**, *on the eve of;* see III. 7. 30 n.

16. **cultus**, *dress.* — **Lycias catervas**: the most important allies of the Trojans.

IX. In contrast with Ode 4, the scene is here laid in mid-winter, when the forbidding aspect of nature invests the warm fireside with a special charm. The ode is modeled upon a drinking song of Alcaeus, a part of which is preserved (*Fr.* 34):

*Ὕει μὲν ὁ Ζεύς, ἐκ δ' ὀράνω μέγας*
*χείμων, πεπάγασιν δ' ὑδάτων ῥόαι.*
. . . . . . . . . . . .

*κάββαλλε τὸν χείμων', ἐπὶ μὲν τίθεις*
*πῦρ, ἐν δὲ κίρναις οἶνον ἀφειδέως*
*μέλιχρον, αὐτὰρ ἀμφὶ κόρσᾳ*
*μάλθακον ἀμφι⟨τίθη⟩ γνόφαλλον·*

but the details of the picture are, as in the preceding ode, Italian. 'Thaliarchus' (θαλίαρχος = *magister convivii;* cf. 4. 18 n) is in all probability not an assumed name

## IX.

Vides ut alta stet nive candidum
Soracte, nec iam sustineant onus
silvae laborantes, geluque
flumina constiterint acuto.

Dissolve frigus ligna super foco
large reponens, atque benignius
deprome quadrimum Sabina,
o Thaliarche, merum diota.

for one of Horace's friends, but with the whole setting of the ode existed only in the poet's fancy. The poem is one of Horace's early studies of his Greek masters, and may be counted among the most successful. — Metre, 176.

1. **ut**, *how*. — **stet**: of the mountain towering up against the sky; more picturesque than *sit*. Cf. Verg. *A*. VI. 471 *stet Marpesia cautes*. — **alta**: cf. *Epod*. 6. 7.

2. **Soracte**: on the western side of the Tiber valley, rising to a height of about 2000 feet. It was in sight from the city, about 25 miles to the north, but the scene, so far as it is definitely conceived at all, must here be imagined at some country place.

3. **laborantes**, *struggling*, *sc*. to hold their own against the weight of snow.

4. **constiterint**: *i.e.* are frozen entirely over: cf. Ov. *Tr*. V. 10. 1 *ut sumus in Ponto, ter frigore constitit Hister*. Such extreme cold and heavy snow as here described did not occur in middle Italy once in a lifetime. The picture is borrowed from the Greek original; cf. πεπάγασιν δ' ὑδάτων ῥόαι in the fragment quoted above.

5. **dissolve**: cf. *solvitur*, 4. 1 n. — **super**, *upon*; cf. *super Pindo*, 12. 6. In this sense *super* usually takes the accusative in prose, and with the ablative is more commonly equivalent to *de*, as III. 8. 17, *C. S.* 18. — **foco**: in country houses a low square platform of stone or brick in the middle of the atrium. The fire of logs was built on the top of it, and the smoke made its way out through the roof. On one side was the altar of the Lares. It was the centre of household worship and work, and around it the family would gather evenings, with such guests as they had with them; cf. *Epod*. 2. 65 *sq*., *S*. II. 6. 65 *sqq*.

6. **reponens**, *replenishing*. The word properly means to make good the loss of what has been consumed, which carries with it, however, the notion of an adequate supply. Cf. *epulae repostae*, Verg. *G*. III. 527. — **benignius**, *more generously*.

7. **deprome**, *draw*. — **Sabina**: *i.e.* containing Sabine wine (Intr. 124). It was a plain wine (cf. 20. 1), but in this case somewhat mellowed by age (**quadrimum**).

8. **Thaliarche**: see intr. note. — **diota**, *flagon*; the amphora or

Permitte divis cetera; qui simul
stravere ventos aequore fervido
deproeliantis, nec cupressi
nec veteres agitantur orni.

Quid sit futurum cras fuge quaerere, et
quem fors dierum cumque dabit lucro
adpone, nec dulcis amores
sperne puer neque tu choreas,

donec virenti canities abest
morosa. Nunc et campus et areae

two-handled (lit. 'two-eared') jar in which the wine was kept in the *cella vinaria*, and from which it was poured (**deprome**) into the mixing-bowl (*cratera*) on the table.

9. **cetera,** *all else, sc.* than enjoyment of the present moment; cf. III. 29. 33 *sq.* — **qui simul,** *the moment they.* See 4. 17 n.

10. **stravere,** *have laid.* — **aequore**: Intr. 69.

11. **deproeliantis**: *sc.* with one another; cf. 3. 12 *sq.* The prefix is intensive, as in *deamo, demiror, depereo,* etc. — **nec cupressi**: *i.e.* the warring winds give place to absolute calm. The meaning of the whole strophe is that the gods, and they alone, can make the storm cease; we must bide their time, and not waste such opportunities for enjoyment as the present affords in fretting over what is beyond our control. This thought Horace proceeds to work out with details which are obviously his own, and not taken from Alcaeus. For **cupressi** see II. 14. 23 n.

13. **fuge quaerere**: Intr. 94 *k*.

14. **quem . . . cumque,** *each day that.* — **fors**: here personified and equivalent to *Fortuna.* The goddess was worshipped under the name of *Fors Fortuna;* cf. Ter. *Phor.* 841; Cic. *Leg.* II. 28. — **dierum**: Intr. 63. — **lucro adpone,** *set down as gain;* lit. insert it in that category, on that side of the balance-sheet.

15. **nec sperne**: see Intr. 88 and 89 note. — **amores**: the plural of repeated instances; see Intr. 128.

16. **puer,** *while you are young.* The word is frequently used for early manhood (cf. III. 2. 2, IV. 4. 28, *S.* II. 1. 60), as *puella* is often a young woman. — **neque tu**: the insertion of the pronoun with the second verb points the exhortation with special emphasis at the person addressed, — 'However it may be with others, don't *you,* at any rate, etc.' Cf. *Ep.* I. 2. 63 *hunc frenis, hunc tu compesce catena.*

17. **virenti**: *sc. tibi.*

18. **morosa,** *fretful,* easily irritated, and hence incapable of enjoyment. — **nunc**: repeating with emphasis the idea of **donec virenti,** etc. — **campus**: see 8. 4 n; **areae,** *the squares,* open spaces about public buildings; both especially attractive for saunterers in a city where the streets were very narrow.

lenesque sub noctem susurri
composita repetantur hora;
nunc et latentis proditor intimo
gratus puellae risus ab angulo
pignusque dereptum lacertis
aut digito male pertinaci.

## X.

Mercuri, facunde nepos Atlantis,
qui feros cultus hominum recentum

19. **sub noctem,** *at nightfall;* cf. 8. 14 n.

20. **composita,** *appointed* (by agreement).—**repetantur,** *be claimed. Repetere,* 'to demand what is due' (cf. **composita hora**), corresponds to *reddere* (3. 7 n.), as *petere* to *dare;* cf. the technical phrases for demanding and making restitution, *res repetere, res reddere.*

21. **nunc et:** the anaphora (Intr. 116 *h*) carries over from the preceding sentence (with a slight zeugma) the idea of **repetantur.**—**latentis,** etc.: the arrangement is highly artistic, each word in this verse expressing a partial notion, to be completed by the word holding the corresponding position in the next verse; see Intr. 110.

23. **pignus:** *i.e.* a bracelet or a ring, as the following words show.—**lacertis:** dative.

24. **male pertinaci,** *not very obstinate. Male,* like a negative quantity in mathematics, diminishes the force of an adjective which expresses a positive or desirable quality, as here and in *male sanos, Ep.* I. 19. 3, *male parentem, Ep.* I. 20. 15; but strengthens one that expresses a negative quality or a defect, as *male dispari,* 17. 25, *male laxus, S.* I. 3. 31, *rauci male, S.* I. 4. 66.

X. A hymn to Mercury, after Alcaeus. The first lines of the original were perhaps (*Fr.* 5):—

*Χαῖρε Κυλλάνας ὂ μέδεις, σὲ γάρ μοι*
*θῦμος ὔμνην, τὸν κορύφαις ἐν αὔταις*
*Μαῖα γέννατο Κρονίδᾳ μίγεισα.*

Accordingly Mercury appears here with the finer attributes of the Greek Hermes, with whom he was identified at a very early period, rather than as the god of trade, which was the character under which he was most widely worshipped in the Roman world; and his attributes of cunning and deception, which he necessarily bore as the patron of traders in an age when trade had not even advanced so far as to regard honesty as the best policy, are lightly touched upon and presented in the more agreeable aspect of the harmless practical joke.—Metre, 174.

1. **facunde:** as the *nuntius deorum* (vs. 5), Ἑρμῆς λόγιος.—**nepos Atlantis:** as *filius Maiae* (2. 43 n).

2. **feros cultus,** etc., *the savage life of early man.*

voce formasti catus et decorae
more palaestrae,
te canam, magni Iovis et deorum
nuntium curvaeque lyrae parentem,
callidum quicquid placuit iocoso
condere furto.

Te boves olim nisi reddidisses
per dolum amotas puerum minaci
voce dum terret, viduus pharetra
risit Apollo.

3. **voce,** *by language, i.e.* by teaching them articulate speech, the first step in civilization which raised man above the level of the brute. Cf. *S.* I. 3. 99 *sqq.*, where the poet's Epicurean view of man's progress is the same, except that it excludes the intervention of any god. — **formasti,** *didst mould, i.e.* reduce to symmetry and order. — **catus**: *i.e.* in foreseeing the efficacy of such means. The word has an antique flavor, an instance of the rule which Horace lays down *Ep.* II. 2. 115.

4. **more,** *the practice; i.e.* by the institution of it.—**palaestrae**: here the exercise, not the place; hence **decorae.** Physical training was regarded by the Greeks as an essential factor of education.

6. **nuntium**: as Ἑρμῆς διάκτορος. In this capacity he appears frequently in Greek and Latin literature, *e.g. Odys.* V. 29, Verg. *A.* I. 297, IV. 222 *sqq.* — **lyrae parentem**: according to the myth, which is substantially the same as given in the Homeric *Hymn to Hermes* 22 *sqq.*, this feat and the one recounted in the next strophe occurred on the day the god was born. The lively infant caught a tortoise and with the shell constructed the first tetrachord.

7. **iocoso**: *i.e.* in fun, with no malice.

8. **condere,** *to hide.* For the mood see Intr. 101 *c.*

9. **te**: cf. vss. 5, 13, and 17. The emphatic repetition of the personal pronoun of the second person (Intr. 116 *f*) is particularly characteristic of hymns and eulogies; cf. 35. 5–21, IV. 14. 33–51. — **nisi reddidisses**: the apodosis is implied in **minaci voce,** which must have stated what would happen if the cattle were not brought back. The pluperf. subj. is here used in indirect discourse to represent the future perf. indic. used by Apollo: *nisi boves reddideris.*

10. **puerum minaci**: Intr. 116 *a.*

11. **dum terret**: *i.e.* before the threat was out of his mouth he found his quiver gone.

12. **risit**: emphatic (Intr. 116 *b*), indicating the complete success of his joke: even his victim was left in good humor and joined in the laugh. The two brothers at once became fast friends; Mercury gave Apollo his lyre, and received from the latter the magic rod (*virga* 18 n.).

Quin et Atridas duce te superbos
Ilio dives Priamus relicto
Thessalosque ignis et iniqua Troiae
castra fefellit.

Tu pias laetis animas reponis
sedibus virgaque levem coerces
aurea turbam, superis deorum
gratus et imis.

13–20. The poet now returns to Mercury's office as *nuntius deorum* in their dealings with men, recalling a signal example of his success in that capacity and closing with a reference to his high function of conductor of the shades of the righteous to Elysium (Ἑρμῆς ψυχοπομπός).

13. **quin et** : the story is introduced as merely a more marked example of the god's success in concealment, and hence suggested by the preceding. But it serves to make the transition to the subject of his beneficent activity in behalf of mankind, and to the more serious thought with which the ode very properly closes. The story is from *Il.* XXIV. 159 *sqq.*

14. **Ilio** : here and elsewhere in Horace (III. 19. 4, IV. 4. 53, *Epod.* 10. 13), neuter in the ablative. He uses a feminine nominative and accusative, *Ilios, Ilion* (IV. 9. 18, *Epod.* 14. 14). — **Ilio relicto** : and so placing himself at the mercy of his enemies. — **dives** : and hence a prize they would have been most eager to capture, had they known of his presence.

15. **Thessalos** : *i.e.* those of Achilles' men, the Myrmidons, from Phthia, in Thessaly. Cf. II. 4. 10. — **ignis** : suggesting the danger of detection. — **Troiae** : dative.

16. **fefellit,** *passed unobserved.*

17. **tu** : cf. *te* 9 n. — **laetis . . . reponis sedibus,** *dost bring safely to the homes of bliss. Re-ponere,* in the sense of 'put away' (cf. *tellure repostos,* Verg. *A.* VI. 655) gives to *sedes* here the meaning of *permanent* abode. For the case of **sedibus** see Intr. 69.

18. **virga aurea** : cf. *Hymn to Herm.* 529: ὄλβου καὶ πλούτου δώσω περικαλλέα ῥάβδον, | χρυσείην, τριπέτηλον, ἀκήριον ἥ σε φυλάξει, | πάντας ἐπικραίνουσ' οἴμους ἐπέων τε καὶ ἔργων | τῶν ἀγαθῶν. The *caduceus,* with its two intertwining serpents, symbolical of peace and commerce, was of later origin. — **levem coerces turbam,** *keepest together the unsubstantial throng,* as a shepherd his flock; cf. 24. 16 *sqq.; Odys.* XXIV. 1 *sqq.*

19. **deorum** : Intr. 63.

20. **imis** : for the more usual *inferis.*

## XI.

Tu ne quaesieris (scire nefas) quem mihi, quem tibi
finem di dederint, Leuconoe, nec Babylonios
temptaris numeros. Vt melius quicquid erit pati,
seu pluris hiemes seu tribuit Iuppiter ultimam
quae nunc oppositis debilitat pumicibus mare
Tyrrhenum. Sapias, vina liques, et spatio brevi
spem longam reseces. Dum loquimur fugerit invida
aetas ; carpe diem, quam minimum credula postero.

XI. The superstition of the Romans made them an easy prey to the soothsayers and astrologers (cf. *S.* I. 6. 114) who flocked to the city after the conquest of the East. Leuconoe,— a name chosen apparently for its pleasing sound and its metrical value,— represents in the poet's fancy a young person whose attachment to him leads her to resort to the fortune-tellers, to learn what she can of his future and of her own. Horace meets this folly with his usual Epicurean maxims,— a repetition, substantially, of 9. 13 *sqq.* The ode is no doubt, like the two others written in this metre (I. 18., IV. 10), a free imitation or paraphrase of a Greek original. — Metre, 170.

1. **scire nefas,** *it is not vouchsafed us to know.* Cf. III. 29. 29 *sq.* — **quem finem** etc.: *i.e.* when is our appointed time to die.

2. **nec**: for *neve* (Intr. 89 note). The clause defines more particularly the kind of inquiry against which his warning (**ne quaesieris**) is directed. — **Babylonios numeros** : the calculations of the Chaldean astrologers.

3. **temptaris,** *meddle with.* — **ut,** *how much.*

4. **hiemes** : *i.e.* years, but used as in modern poetry, to give the desired color to the thought, — the same background as in Ode 9. — **tribuit,** *has assigned, i.e.* at our birth, the question which the astrologers professed to solve. For its position see Intr. 119 *a.* — **ultimam** : agreeing with the antecedent of **quae** (*sc. hanc*), *as the last.*

5. **debilitat,** *breaks ;* lit. 'cripples.' — **pumicibus** : instrumental abl. The word is here used of the rocks eaten away and hollowed out by the action of the waves ; cf. Plin. *N. H.* XXXVI. 154 *appellantur quidem ita* (*sc. pumices*) *erosa saxa ;* Verg. *A.* V. 213 *columba | cui domus et dulces latebroso in pumice nidi.*

6. **Tyrrhenum** : see Intr. 117. — **sapias,** etc.: Intr. 87. — **liques,** *strain.* The wine as it came from the amphora contained a good deal of sediment, which was removed by pouring it through a coarse linen *saccus* or a colander (*colum*). — **spatio brevi** (abl. abs.), *since our time is short, sc.* for the realization of far-reaching plans and hopes.

7. **spem longam** : cf. 4. 15. — **reseces,** *prune down.* — **fugerit,** *will be gone.* — **invida** : personify

# XII.

Quem virum aut heroa lyra vel acri
tibia sumis celebrare, Clio,

ing **aetas,** to express more vividly the inexorable promptness of its departure.

8. **diem,** *the passing day*, **carpe** implying a transitory character in its object; cf. Mart. VII. 47. 11 *fugitiva gaudia carpe.* — **credula**: cf. 5. 9; it expresses more than *credens* (= *fidens*), and alludes to her foolish faith in the astrologers. — **postero** (*sc. diei*): Intr. 58 *a.*

XII. This ode, like Ode 2, was written to glorify the mission of Caesar Augustus, as the heaven-sent ruler of the world. For the form, Horace has worked upon a suggestion which he found in Pindar's second Olympian ode, the opening verses of which he has closely imitated: —

Ἀναξιφόρμιγγες ὕμνοι,
τίνα θεόν, τίν' ἥρωα, τίνα δ' ἄνδρα
κελαδήσομεν;

As in this ode Pindar approaches the praise of the victor Thero through the long story of the fortunes and sorrows of his ancestors, so Horace presents Augustus as the culmination of the long line of benefactors, — gods, heroes, and men, — to whose activity or suffering mankind is most indebted for its progress. The tone of the ode, in keeping with Augustus' professed view of his mission, is serious and free from any note of triumph. It presents him as the bearer of a great responsibility, the successor, not of the great warriors and powerful monarchs of the past, but of the men who died for their country or who served her without exalting themselves. See notes on vss. 35 and 41–44.

The allusion to Marcellus (vs. 45 *sq.*) shows that the ode could not have been written much before his marriage with Julia, the daughter of Augustus (B.C. 25), nor later than 23, the date of his death. — Metre, 174.

1. **quem virum . . . heroa . . . deum**: these three classes are taken up in reverse order, — *dei* in vss. 13–24, *heroes* in vss. 25–33, *viri* in 34–48. — **heroa,** *demigod.* — **lyra vel tibia**: cf. III. 4. 1–4. Either instrument from its traditional use would be suitable for the present purpose: the Greek rhapsodist sang the exploits of his heroes to the notes of the lyre; the tibia was said to have been used to accompany the songs which the Romans in early times, according to Cato (Cic. *Tusc.* IV. 3), sang at banquets in praise of their ancestors. — **acri,** *shrill,* a highly appropriate and expressive epithet according to Quintilian (VIII. 2. 9).

2. **sumis,** *dost thou take, i.e.* as a subject. Cf. *Ep.* II. 3. 38 *sumite materiam vestris, qui scribitis, aequam | viribus.* The present implies that the muse has already determined to sing; the poet feels her inspiration, and asks what is the theme. The future, which is found in a few MSS., would be suitable if it were an invitation to sing. — **celebrare**: Intr. 93. — **Clio**: possibly addressed here in the character, which she gradually acquired, of muse of history. But

quem deum? Cuius recinet iocosa
nomen imago
aut in umbrosis Heliconis oris
aut super Pindo gelidove in Haemo?
Vnde vocalem temere insecutae
Orphea silvae,
arte materna rapidos morantem
fluminum lapsus celerisque ventos,
blandum et auritas fidibus canoris
ducere quercus.

the special attributes of the muses which have come down to us are not sharply defined in Horace, whose muse is sometimes Euterpe or Polyhymnia (1. 33), or Clio, as here, or Melpomene (cf. 24. 3, III. 30. 16, IV. 3. 1), or Calliope (III. 4. 2); often simply *musa*, as II. 1. 37, 12. 13, III. 3. 70, etc.; or *mea musa*, 17. 14; sometimes with a qualifying phrase, as 6. 10 *imbellis lyrae musa potens; S.* II. 6. 17 *musa pedestris; Ep.* II. 3. 407 *musa lyrae sollers;* cf. II. 1. 9 *musa tragoediae.*

3. **iocosa**, *merry*, personifying Echo, as if she mocked people in jest. Cf. Ov. *M.* III. 356 *sqq.*, where Echo is represented as a nymph.

4. **imago**: used in prose also for the Greek ἠχώ; cf. Varro, *R. R.* III. 16. 12 *ubi non resonent imagines.*

5. **Heliconis**: a mountain in Boeotia, on the borders of which, at Ascra, there existed from very early times a μουσεῖον, devoted to the worship of the muses, and under their protection to the promotion of literature. Hesiod was the most famous leader of this school or guild, and ancient copies of his works with the Homeric and doubtless other poems were preserved there. The mountain in consequence, and particularly the springs of Aganippe and Hippocrene, had come to be regarded as a favorite haunt of the muses.

6. **super**: cf. 9. 5 n. — **Pindo**: the mountain range between Thessaly and Epirus, also regarded as a seat of the muses; cf. Verg. *E.* 10. 11. — **Haemo**: tradition made the Heliconian school of song an offshoot from an older school which had been established at Libethrum, in Pieria, on the slopes of Olympus, by a tribe or guild of Thracians whose leader, Orpheus, was the son of the muse Calliope and the Thracian king Oeagrus. Hence the name *Pieris* for muse.

7. **unde**: *i.e.* from Haemus. — **temere**: *i.e.* spell-bound, not of their own will and intent; they could not choose but follow.

9. **arte materna**: *i.e.* music. See note on *Haemo*, 6.

11. **blandum**, *with charm.* — **et**: Intr. 114. — **auritas** (proleptic), *to lend ears to . . . and.*

12. **ducere**: for the mood see Intr. 101 *c*.

Quid prius dicam solitis parentis
laudibus, qui res hominum ac deorum,
qui mare et terras variisque mundum
temperat horis?

Vnde nil maius generatur ipso,
nec viget quicquam simile aut secundum;
proximos illi tamen occupavit
Pallas honores.

13. **quid prius,** etc.: it being prescribed by ancient tradition to begin heroic songs with the glory of Jove (**solitis laudibus**). Cf. Pind. *Nem.* 2. 1 *ὁθένπερ καὶ Ὁμηρίδαι ῥαπτῶν ἐπέων ταπόλλ᾽ ἀοιδοὶ ἄρχονται, Διὸς ἐκ προοιμίου.* The form *ἐκ Διὸς ἀρχώμεσθα* is found in Aratus (*Phaen.* 1) and Theocritus (17. 1); cf. Verg. *E.* 3. 60 *ab Iove principium.* — **parentis**: *sc.* of gods and men, as is indicated in the following clause; cf. II. 19. 21, and see I. 2. 2 n.

14. **laudibus**: Intr. 75.

15. **mundum,** *the firmament. Mundus* strictly includes the earth (**mare ac terras**), but as we naturally think of the latter more in its connection with our own lives than its place in the universe, *mundus* comes to mean the sky and the heavenly bodies.

16. **temperat,** *governs.* — **horis,** *seasons;* cf. *hora Caniculae,* III. 13. 9; *sub verni temporis horam, Ep.* II. 3. 302.

17. **unde** = *ex quo,* referring to *parentis* 13; cf. *S.* I. 6. 12. *Valeri genus, unde superbus Tarquinius regno pulsus fugit.* The use of *unde* with a personal antecedent is not infrequent in prose, as Sal. *Iug.* 14. 22 *tibi, unde minime decuit, vita erepta est.* — **nil,** *no one;* but stronger than *nemo;* cf. *S.* I. 3. 18. — **generatur**: the present expresses what is true at all times, so that the meaning is that Jove is eternally supreme. The statement includes all gods and men, Jove being here thought of as the parent of all (cf. *parentis,* 13 n.)

18. **nec viget,** etc.: *i.e.* no living being can compare with Jove in power and glory (**viget**). The relative construction is abandoned, and *ei* must be supplied with **simile.** — **quicquam**: cf. *nil,* 17 n. — **aut secundum; proximos tamen**: *i.e.* though Pallas, as compared with the common throng of gods, is *nearest* to Jove, she cannot be called *next* to him: she is separated from him by a long interval. Cf. Cic. *Brut.* 173 *duobus summis, Crasso et Antonio, L. Philippus proximus accedebat, sed longo tamen intervallo proximus; itaque eum . . . neque secundum neque tertium dixerim; neque enim in quadrigis eum secundum nominaverim . . . qui vix e carceribus exierit cum palmam iam primus acceperit;* Verg. *A.* V. 320.

19. **occupavit,** *holds.*

20. **Pallas**: as goddess of wisdom exalted above all other gods but Jove himself. Cf. Hesiod, *Theog.* 896 *ἶσον ἔχουσαν πατρὶ μένος καὶ ἐπίφρονα βουλήν.*

Proeliis audax neque te silebo
Liber, et saevis inimica virgo
beluis, nec te, metuende certa
Phoebe sagitta.

Dicam et Alciden puerosque Ledae,
hunc equis, illum superare pugnis
nobilem ; quorum simul alba nautis
stella refulsit,

defluit saxis agitatus umor,

21. **proeliis audax**: Horace not infrequently begins an address with a descriptive phrase in agreement with the name of the person addressed, which is inserted in the sentence later, as II. 7. 1, *Ep.* I. 1. 1. Bacchus was endowed with a greater variety of attributes and epithets (cf. Ov. *M.* IV. 11 *sqq.*) than any other god. His prowess in war was displayed in the battle of the Giants (II. 19. 21 *sqq.*), and his triumphal Indian journey, according to one form of the myth, was a military expedition. The poet naturally mentions this, one of his nobler qualities, in a list of gods and heroes who have contributed to the welfare of mankind. So Diana is here not simply the goddess of the chase, but the destroyer of monsters (**saevis beluis**), and Apollo is joined with her as the god of the bow; see vs. 23 n. Hercules and the Dioscuri are well known benefactors of the race.

22. **et**: connecting the description of Diana with **proeliis audax Liber**. The idea of **neque te silebo** (= *te quoque memorabo; non silere* being a mere rhetorical variation (litotes) for *dicere* or *memorare;* cf. IV. 9. 31) is repeated with **virgo**, which is vocative.

23. **metuende sagitta**: see vs. 21 n. The allusion is to Apollo's destruction of the python (Ov. *M.* I. 438 *sqq*). — **certa**, *unerring*.

25. **dicam**: see 6. 5 n. — **et**, *too*. — **Alciden**: Hercules, whose reputed father, Amphitryon, was the son of Alceus. His services, like those of the Roman heroes who follow, are not enlarged upon, being well known. — **pueros Ledae**: Castor and Pollux.

26. **hunc**, etc.: cf. *S.* II. 1. 26 *Castor gaudet equis, ovo prognatus eodem | pugnis; Il.* III. 237 Κάστορα θ᾽ ἱππόδαμον καὶ πὺξ ἀγαθὸν Πολυδεύκεα. — **superare nobilem**: see Intr. 101 *c*. — **pugnis**: from *pugnus*.

27. **quorum simul**: cf. *qui simul*, 9. 9 n, and the whole description there. — **alba**, *bright*.

28. **stella**: cf. 3. 2 n. — **refulsit**, *has flashed* (out of the darkness) *upon*.

29. **defluit**, etc.: Horace here introduces one of his graphic pictures (cf. 2. 7 n), to break the monotony of his long catalogue of benefactors. In this passage and in IV. 8. 31 he reproduces a description of Theocritus, 22. 17 ἀλλ᾽ ἔμπας ὑμεῖς (*sc.* Διόσκουροι) γε καὶ ἐκ βυθοῦ ἕλκετε νᾶας | αὐτοῖσιν ναύταισιν διομένοις θανέεσθαι · | αἶψα

concidunt venti fugiuntque nubes,
et minax, quod sic voluere, ponto
unda recumbit.

Romulum post hos prius an quietum
Pompili regnum memorem an superbos
Tarquini fascis dubito, an Catonis
nobile letum.

δ' ἀπολήγοντ' ἄνεμοι, λιπαρὰ δὲ γαλήνα | ἂμ' πέλαγος· νεφέλαι δὲ διέδραμον ἄλλυδις ἄλλαι.

31. **voluere,** *have willed.* Such parenthetical clauses, referring the events described to the will of some deity, are not uncommon; cf. *Il.* I. 5 Διὸς δ' ἐτελείετο βουλή.

32. **recumbit,** *subsides;* lit. 'lies down,' having been **minax,** *i.e.* towering aloft as it approached.

33. **Romulum,** etc.: from the demigods who have befriended mankind, Horace proceeds to the founders and builders of the great empire which is destined to bring the whole earth under its beneficent sway. The number of these is so large as to be embarrassing, and the poet is in doubt where to begin.

34. **Pompili**: *sc. Numae.* Roman tradition assigned almost equal merit to Romulus and Numa for their very different services in establishing the state. Cf. Liv. I. 21. 6 *duo deinceps reges, alius alia via, ille bello hic pace, civitatem auxerunt.* — **superbos Tarquini fascis,** *the haughty power of the Tarquin.* The epithet belongs logically to **Tarquini** (Intr. 124), and hence the reference must be to Tarquin the Proud, whose contributions to Rome's greatness, through the subjection of neighboring tribes, were very considerable, and whose memory, in spite of the bitter hatred which he incurred in his struggle with the people, was at least respected. Cf. Cic. *Phil.* 3, 9 *Tarquinius . . . non crudelis, non impius, sed superbus habitus est; . . . nihil humile de Tarquinio, nihil sordidum accepimus.*

35. **Catonis,** etc.: it is noteworthy that Horace, coming now to the time of the Commonwealth, passes over the greatest warriors and statesmen, and selects only typical instances of the Roman *virtus* which courted poverty or death for the public good.

36. **nobile letum**: Cato's contemporaries were entirely convinced of his disinterestedness and his sincerity in carrying his Stoic principles into political life, and his dramatic suicide at Utica, after Caesar's victory at Thapsus, in B.C. 46, invested him with something of the halo of a saint, whose lofty character and motives were a safe subject of eulogy even in an ode in honor of the heir and successor of Caesar. Horace's admiration for him, which appears here and in II. 1. 24, dated no doubt from the time when he joined the army of Brutus. Vergil's tribute is still higher: he makes Cato another Minos, judging the dead (*secretosque pios, his dantem iura Catonem, A.* VIII. 670).

Regulum et Scauros animaeque magnae
prodigum Paullum superante Poeno
gratus insigni referam camena
Fabriciumque.

37. **Regulum**: the poet's second example of a *nobile letum*. M. Atilius Regulus, in his second consulship, B.C. 256, during the first Punic war, successfully invaded Africa, but the next year he was defeated and captured by the Carthaginians. The story of his mission to Rome with a Carthaginian embassy to arrange ransom for the prisoners, his advice to the senate to leave the latter to their fate, and his voluntary return to captivity and death, is told in III. 5. 13 *sqq*. — **Scauros**: M. Aemilius Scaurus and his son. The latter was involved in the panic of the Roman cavalry under Catulus in the disastrous battle on the Adige (B.C. 101), when they were so effectively routed by the Cimbri that they abandoned their general and fled incontinently to the city. Young Scaurus was met by a stern message from his father that his dead body brought home from the battle-field would have been more welcome than his return alive after so disgraceful a repulse, and thereupon put an end to his own life. Val. Max. V. 8. 4.

38. **prodigum,** *that squanderer*. The touch of censure implied in the word only heightens the effect of the eulogy. L. Aemilius Paullus, consul in B.C. 216 with Terentius Varro, fell in the battle of Cannae, which his colleague had brought on against his advice. As the story is told by Livy (XXII. 49. 6) Paullus could have escaped without personal dishonor, but chose to die with his men rather than return from such a disastrous defeat.

39. **gratus** : *i.e.* for the sacrifice which such splendid devotion to duty and country has cost. — **insigni camena,** *with no ordinary song*. The Camenae (earlier form, *Casmenae*; cf. *carmen* = *casmen*), originally nymphs in whose songs the magical or prophetic knowledge of the spirits of the woods found expression, enjoy a wider province in the Augustan and later poets, who identify them with the Greek muses (cf. II. 16. 38 *Graiae Camenae*; *C. S.* 62), and use the singular, as here, concretely for 'song' (cf. *Ep.* I. 1. 1).

40. **Fabriciumque** : by including one of the group of great men next described in his *grata relatio* Horace virtually includes them all.

41–44. The three worthies named in this strophe too are selected not so much for the greatness of their achievements as for the lesson which their example conveys. They stand for the highest type of citizenship in the best days of the Commonwealth,— men whose training for public service was hard work at home, and whose eminence in the state did not affect the simplicity of their lives and their indifference to riches. C. Fabricius Luscinus and M'. Curius Dentatus were prominent in the wars against the Samnites and Pyrrhus, and tradition loved to tell of the futile efforts of the latter to move them either with flattery or with gold (Val. Max. IV. 3. 5 *sq.*, Cic. *C. M.* 55, *Rep.* III. 6). M. Furius Camillus, the conqueror of Veii (B.C. 396) and deliverer of Rome

Hunc et intonsis Curium capillis
utilem bello tulit et Camillum
saeva paupertas et avitus apto
cum lare fundus.

Crescit occulto velut arbor aevo
fama Marcelli; micat inter omnis

from the Gauls (390), was the most eminent Roman of his time.

41. **intonsis capillis**: this characteristic of earlier and simpler times was made familiar to every Roman by the public statues. Cf. Varro *R. R.* II. 11. 10 *olim tonsores non fuisse adsignificant antiquorum statuae, quod pleraeque habent capillum et barbam magnam*. There were no barbers in Rome, according to Varro (cf. Plin. *N. H.* VII. 211), till B.C. 300, which was in the lifetime of Curius, and it was a long time after that date that the fashion of trimming the hair short and shaving off the beard became general. Hence *intonsus*, *barbatus*, etc., are used to connote ancient times and simple manners. Cf. *intonsi Catonis*, II. 15. 11; *barbato regi*, Juv. 4. 103.

42. **utilem**: applying to all three men. — **bello**: dative; Intr. 58 *c*.

43. **saeva paupertas**: cf. III. 6. 33–44, where the poet points more sharply the contrast between the severe training which made the sturdy manhood of early times, and the degeneracy of his own day when poverty was a reproach (III. 24. 42). — **avitus**: *i.e.* not purchased or enlarged by him, implying his abstinence from the pursuit of wealth; cf. *patrios agros* I. 11 n. — **apto**, *to match*; not a great country-house such as a man of his station would now have.

44. **lare**, *a dwelling*. The word itself excludes the idea of a large house.

45. **crescit**, *is growing*. The present prepares the reader for the transition which the poet now makes to his own times. This he does by selecting as his last example of the great men of old, M. Claudius Marcellus, the conquerer of Syracuse (B.C. 212) and the first Roman general who fought Hannibal with success. He was killed in a skirmish in his 5th consulship, B.C. 208. The mention of this famous warrior could not fail to carry with it to Horace's readers an allusion to Marcellus, the nephew and son-in-law of Augustus, whose untimely death Vergil commemorates in the Aeneid (VI. 860); and the poet manages, without expressly naming this young man, who had performed no achievement as yet worth mentioning, to intimate that he has a great career before him. — **occulto aevo**, *which does not show its age*; descriptive ablative. Since the time of the great Marcellus no member of that family had attained any special eminence; his fame, which would have been enhanced by distinguished descendants, appeared to be at a standstill; but like a tree, which appears the same from year to year, it is really growing. The compliment to the young Marcellus is obvious.

46. **inter omnis**: sc. *duces*, or the like; 'in the whole galaxy,' as we should say, of great men.

Iulium sidus velut inter ignis
luna minores.

Gentis humanae pater atque custos,
orte Saturno, tibi cura magni
Caesaris fatis data : tu secundo
Caesare regnes.

Ille seu Parthos Latio imminentis
egerit iusto domitos triumpho
sive subiectos Orientis orae
Seras et Indos,

te minor latum reget aequus orbem ;
tu gravi curru quaties Olympum,
tu parum castis inimica mittes
fulmina lucis.

47. **Iulium sidus**: *i.e.* the Julian house. The figure paves the way for the comparison that follows, which is from Sappho (*Fr.* 3). Some see in it an allusion to the comet that appeared after Caesar's death (Plin. *N. H.* II. 94, Suet. *Iul.* 88); but the poet wishes us to think here of Augustus, and refers only indirectly to Julius Caesar. — **inter ignis**, etc.: cf. *Epod.* 15. 2.

49. **gentis humanae**, etc.: the ode closes with a solemn appeal to Jupiter, the father of all mankind, to accept the predestined ruler of the race as his vicegerent on earth.

51. **secundo Caesare**, *with Caesar next to thee.* There is no allusion to verse 18, the point of view here being entirely different. The other gods have their special provinces and do not come under consideration at all here, where the government of the earth is the topic in mind.

53. **ille seu**, etc.: *i.e.* he, on his part, whatever triumphs may be in store for him, will ever own his dependence on thee. — **Parthos**: see 2. 22 n. — **Latio**: used like *Roma* for the Roman state; cf. 35. 10 with III. 3. 44.

54. **egerit**, *shall lead;* lit. 'shall have driven,' a more exact expression than *ducere* (which is also used), since the prisoners preceded the victor's car in the triumphal procession. — **iusto**, *well earned. Iustus triumphus* is a technical phrase, expressing compliance with certain well understood conditions relating to the rank of the general and the extent and importance of his victory.

55. **subiectos Orientis orae**, *who dwell beneath the borders of the eastern sky.* **Orientis** is a substantive, like *Occidentis*, *Epod.* 1. 13.

56. **Sērăs** (Σῆρας) **et Indos**: vague names to convey the impression of unlimited future conquests ; cf. IV. 15. 21 *sqq.*, *C. S.* 53 *sqq.*

57. **te minor**, *as subordinate to*

## XIII.

Cum tu, Lydia, Telephi
cervicem roseam, cerea Telephi
laudas bracchia, vae meum
fervens difficili bile tumet iecur.
Tum nec mens mihi nec color
certa sede manet, umor et in genas
furtim labitur, arguens
quam lentis penitus macerer ignibus.
Vror, seu tibi candidos
turparunt umeros immodicae mero

*thee;* cf. III. 6. 5 *dis te minorem quod geris, imperas.* For **te, tu, tu**, see 10. 9 n; Intr. 116 *f.* — **aequus**, *with justice.*

58. **tu gravi**, etc.: *i.e.* thou wilt maintain thy supreme authority by the usual manifestations of thy power and of thy wrath.

59. **parum castis**, *polluted.* — **inimica fulmina**: cf. 3. 40 n, and see Intr. 124.

60. **lucis**: dat.; cf. *terris*, 2. 1; Intr. 53. Lightning as a sign of the divine will held a prominent place in Roman divination, and it was regarded as of momentous significance if a sacred grove or temple (cf. 2. 16 n.) was struck. Preller-Jordan *Röm. Myth.* I. 192.

XIII. The jealous lover's appeal. — Metre, 171.

2. **cerea**: *i.e.* smooth and free from blemishes, like a waxen image. — **Telephi**: repeated with bitterness, in imitation of her maddening iteration of the name. Cf. *S.* I. 6. 45 *sq.*

3. **vae**, *ugh!*

4. **difficili**, *uncomfortable.* — **iecur**: regarded as the seat of the passions, especially of anger (cf. *S.* I. 9. 66 *meum iecur urere bilis*) and love (cf. IV. 1. 12).

5. **nec mens**, etc.: *i.e.* I lose control of my feelings and my color comes and goes. For this use of *mens* cf. Cat. 61. 33 *mentem amore revinciens.*

6. **manēt**: Intr. 179. — **umor**, *the tear.*

7. **furtim**, etc.: *i.e.* to my surprise, making me aware of the depth of my feeling.

8. **quam**: with **penitus**. — **lentis**, *persistent, lingering.* — **macerer**, *I am wasting away.*

9. **uror**, etc.: *i.e.* I am enraged by the sight of these unseemly marks of the intimacy which you have allowed him.

10. **turparunt**: *i.e.* have left them 'black and blue.' Cf. 17. 25 *sqq.;* Prop. III. 7. 19 *quin etiam, si me ulterius provexerit ira, | ostendes matri bracchia laesa tuae.* — **immodicae**, (*carried to excess*), *indecent.* — **mero**, *over your cups.* The abl. expresses the cause of **immodicae**.

**rix**ae, sive puer furens
    impressit memorem dente labris notam.
Non, si me satis audias,
    speres perpetuum dulcia barbare
laedentem oscula, quae Venus
    quinta parte sui nectaris imbuit.
Felices ter et amplius,
    quos inrupta tenet copula nec malis
divolsus querimoniis
    suprema citius solvet amor die.

11. **sive,** etc.: the passionate youth has been as violent in his caresses as in his anger.

14. **perpetuum,** *constant.*

16. **quinta parte**: *i.e.* a generous share. Others explain the phrase as indicating the degree of sweetness, referring to a fancy found in the Greek lyric poets that honey was *ἔνατον μέρος τῆς ἀμβροσίας* or *τῆς ἀθανασίας δέκατον μέρος* (Athen. II. 8, Schol. on Pind. *Pyth*. 9. 16); but this would imply that the substance with which Venus bathed Lydia's lips was something else than nectar. It has also been conjectured that *quinta pars* was used, like *quinta essentia* in mediaeval Latin, for *ἡ πέμπτη οὐσία*, the name given by the Pythagorean philosophers to the ether, the subtlest of the five elements. This would be very appropriate here (*quintessence*), but there is no evidence and little probability that the phrase was used in this sense. — **sui,** *her own.*

17. **ter et amplius**: cf. Verg. *A*. I. 94 *terque quaterque beati.*

18. **inrupta,** *that nothing can sever.* The word is found only here and is used, like *invictus, indomitus,* etc., with the force of an adjective in *-ilis*. — **nec malis,** etc., *and whom no estrangement, begotten of hateful reproaches,* etc.; an amplification of the preceding clause.

19. **divolsus amor**: see Intr. 105 *a.*

20. **suprema,** *the last* (*sc.* of life). — **solvet**: with reference to *copula*, 18. — **die**: Intr. 75.

XIV. Quintilian (VIII. 6. 44) cites this ode as an example of that species of allegory (*inversio*) which *aliud verbis aliud sensu ostendit*, and adds this explanation: *navem pro re publica, fluctus et tempestates pro bellis civilibus, portum pro pace atque concordia dicit.* The figure of the 'ship of state' Horace found already employed by Greek writers (as Theognis 671, Plato *Rep*. VI. 488), and among others by Alcaeus in an ode (*Fr*. 18) beginning

Ἀσυνέτημι τῶν ἀνέμων στάσιν·
τὸ μὲν γὰρ ἔνθεν κῦμα κυλίνδεται,
    τὸ δ᾽ ἔνθεν· ἄμμες δ᾽ ἀν τὸ μέσσον
        νᾶϊ φορήμεθα σὺν μελαίνᾳ,
χείμωνι μοχθεῦντες μεγάλῳ μάλα·
πὲρ μὲν γὰρ ἄντλος ἰστοπέδαν ἔχει,
    λαῖφος δὲ πᾶν ζάδηλον ἤδη
        καὶ λάκιδες μέγαλαι κὰτ᾽ αὖτο·
χόλαισι δ᾽ ἄγκυραι.

## XIV.

O navis, referent in mare te novi
fluctus! O quid agis? Fortiter occupa
portum! Nonne vides ut
nudum remigio latus
et malus celeri saucius Africo
antemnaeque gemant ac sine funibus
vix durare carinae
possint imperiosius

Horace's treatment, however, is essentially different. In the Greek poet the ship is merely the metaphor under which he pictures to his fellow-citizens their political situation; in the present ode, as in Longfellow's famous poem, she is the personified Commonwealth, the ideal object of patriotic devotion which we usually express by 'our country.' There is no direct evidence to show when the ode was written, but it probably belongs to the period of uncertainty between the battle of Actium and the settlement of the year 27. The ship is still at sea, sailing now in the quieter waters near the shore, but so shattered and torn that she cannot possibly live through another storm. Her only safety lies in making without delay a secure harbor. The plain meaning of this is that the state is in too exhausted a condition to endure another civil contest; what is needed above all else is peace, — the very sentiment to which Octavian appealed and on which he established his power. — Metre, 173.

1. **in mare**, *out to sea*. The ship is imagined as sailing along, according to the ancient practice, within a safe distance of the shore; cf. II. 10. 1–4. — **novi fluctus**: *i.e.* another storm coming up, (another civil conflict).

2. **fortiter occupa**, *be active now, and gain*.

3. **nonne vides**, *seest thou not?* But **vides** is vague enough in its meaning to express the perception of sounds (**gemant**, 6); cf. *S.* II. 8. 77 *videres stridere susurros;* Verg. *A.* IV. 490 *mugire videbis | sub pedibus terram et descendere montibus ornos.* — **ut**: cf. 9. 1 n.

4. **nudum remigio** (*sc. sit*), *is stripped of its oars* (broken off by the violence of the storm). See Intr. 66 *c*, note.

5. **mālus**: to be taken with **gemant**.

6. **gemant**, *creak*, — not by rubbing against one another, but each for itself; they have all been strained by the force of the storm. — **funibus**: used for undergirding the ship (cf. *N. T. Acts* 27. 17), to keep the planks from springing apart under the strain of a rough sea.

7. **durare**, *hold out against*. — **carinae**, *the hull*. For the plural see Intr. 128.

8. **imperiosius**, *in his sterner mood*, personifying **aequor**.

aequor? Non tibi sunt integra lintea,
non di, quos iterum pressa voces malo.
Quamvis Pontica pinus,
silvae filia nobilis,
iactes et genus et nomen inutile,
nil pictis timidus navita puppibus
fidit. Tu nisi ventis
debes ludibrium, cave.
Nuper sollicitum quae mihi taedium,
nunc desiderium curaque non levis,
interfusa nitentis
vites aequora Cycladas.

10. **non di**: *i.e.* the images of gods, which were carried in the stern (cf. Verg. *A.* X. 171 *aurato fulgebat Apolline puppis*; Pers. 6. 30), have been dashed overboard in the storm.—**iterum pressa malo**, *when again in distress.*

11. **Pontica**: the woods of Pontus and Bithynia were famous for their excellent ship-timber. Cf. Cat. 4. 9 *Ponticum sinum,* | *ubi iste post phaselus antea fuit* | *comata silva.*

12. **silvae filia**: cf. Mart. XIV. 90. 1 *silvae filia Maurae* (of a table).

13. **iactes**: observe that this is the emphatic word of the verse, and **inutile** is only thrown in incidentally: *boast as thou wilt of thy worthless pedigree and name.*—**genus et nomen**: carrying out the fancy expressed in **filia**.

14. **pictis**: the after part of a ship was often richly decorated; cf. Seneca, *Ep.* 76. 13.

15. **tu**: cf. 9. 16 n, 11. 1.

16. **debes**, *art bound to furnish* (*sc.* by fate), *art doomed to be* (so that no effort can save thee).—**ludibrium**, *food for laughter.*—**cave**: used absolutely (as in *Epod.* 6. 11), but the caution is expressed more fully below (vss. 19, 20).

17. **nuper sollicitum**, etc., *whom I but lately looked upon with apprehension and disgust; i.e.* disgust at the turn things had taken, and apprehension of worse results that might ensue. The allusion is to the time following the defeat of the republican army at Philippi, when Horace, whose whole heart was in the lost cause, could see in the triumph of its enemies nothing but the utter rottenness of politics; cf. *Epodes* 7 and 16.—**quae**: *sc. eras.*

18. **nunc desiderium**, etc., *now my heart's desire and deep solicitude.* Cf. Cic. *Fam.* XIV. 2. 2 (to Terentia) *mea lux, meum desiderium*; Cat. 2. 5; Verg. *A.* I. 678 *puer, mea maxima cura.*

19. **nitentis**, *glistening;* alluding to their marble-quarries. Cf. III. 28. 14 *fulgentis Cycladas;* Verg. *A.* III. 126 *niveam Parum.*

20. **Cycladas**: object of **interfusa.** The sea in the neighbor-

## XV.

Pastor cum traheret per freta navibus
Idaeis Helenen perfidus hospitam,
ingrato celeres obruit otio
  ventos ut caneret fera
Nereus fata : ‘ Mala ducis avi domum
quam multo repetet Graecia milite,
coniurata tuas rumpere nuptias
  et regnum Priami vetus.

hood of these islands, like the rest of the Aegean (cf. II. 16. 2, III. 29. 63, etc.), was subject to sudden and dangerous storms. The mention of these particular waters has no significance in the allegory (Intr. 117 *a*).

XV. The motive of this ode, according to Porphyrio, was borrowed from an ode of Bacchylides, in which Cassandra was represented as foretelling the events of the Trojan war. If so, Horace has improved upon his model by transferring the scene to the ship of Paris on his homeward voyage with Helen, and substituting for the Trojan prophetess the sea-god Nereus; for Paris is thus confronted with the disastrous consequences of his crime in the very hour of his triumph. — Metre, 172.

1. **pastor** : Paris, who was exposed in his infancy and brought up among the shepherds on Mt. Ida. So *Phrygius pastor*, Verg. *A*. VII. 363. — **traheret,** *was carrying off.*

2. **Idaeis** : *i.e.* built of wood from Mt. Ida. — **perfidus hospitam** : Intr. 116 *a*. No treachery could be more heinous than that of the man who used the sacred rights of hospitality to plot against his host.

3. **ingrato,** *unwelcome* (*sc.* to the winds). — **obruit,** *smothered.*

4. **caneret,** *foretell ;* frequently used in this sense, oracles and prophecies being in metrical form. Cf. *C. S.* 25 ; Verg. *A*. II. 124.

5. **Nereus** : eldest of the sons of Pontus, father of Thetis and the other Nereids; always called in Homer the ‘old man of the sea’ (*e.g. Il*. I. 556 *ἁλίοιο γέροντος*), and never by name. Cf. Hes. *Theog.* 233 Νηρέα δ' ἀψευδέα καὶ ἀληθέα . . . καλέουσι γέροντα | οὕνεκα νημερτής τε καὶ ἤπιος. — **malā avi** : for *malis auspiciis ;* cf. *mala alite*, *Epod*. 10. 1 ; *bona alite*, Cat. 61. 20. — **dūcis** (sc. *eam*) **domum,** *thou art bringing home a bride.*

6. **multo milite** : Intr. 127.

7. **coniurata** : referring probably not to the oath by which Tyndareus bound the suitors of Helen before her marriage, but to the league of the assembled chiefs at Aulis, alluded to in Verg. *A*. IV. 425 *non ego cum Danais Troianam exscindere gentem | Aulide iuravi.* — **rumpere,** *to break up.* For the mood, see Intr. 94 *f*.

Heu heu, quantus equis, quantus adest viris
sudor! Quanta moves funera Dardanae
genti! Iam galeam Pallas et aegida
currusque et rabiem parat.

Nequiquam Veneris praesidio ferox
pectes caesariem grataque feminis
imbelli cithara carmina divides;
nequiquam thalamo gravis

hastas et calami spicula Cnosii
vitabis strepitumque et celerem sequi

9. **heu heu,** *ah me!* The sympathy of the god is called forth by the actual vision which he has as a seer of the events foretold. The following scenes are all taken from the Iliad. — **quantus equis,** etc.: cf. *Il.* II. 388 *ἱδρώσει μέν τευ τελαμών . . . ἱδρώσει δέ τευ ἵππος.*

10. **quanta moves funera,** *what a train of disaster . . . thou art starting.* For the plural, see Intr. 128 and cf. 8. 15. — **Dardanae**: Intr. 65.

11. **iam,** *even now.* — **Pallas,** etc.: cf. *Il.* V. 719 *sqq.* — **aegida**: sometimes represented as the shield of Zeus, more commonly as the corselet of Athena (*Il.* V. 738). As such it appears in numerous statues of that goddess, — a coat of mail, with the head of the gorgon Medusa in the middle, as described by Verg. *A.* VIII. 435: *aegidaque horriferam, turbatae Palladis arma, | certatim squamis serpentum auroque polibant | conexosque anguis, ipsamque in pectore divae | Gorgona, desecto vertentem lumina collo.*

12. **currus**: Intr. 128. — **et rabiem**: added with powerful effect to complete the inventory of her outfit for battle; cf. *Il.* IV. 447 *σύν ῥ' ἔβαλον ῥινούς σὺν δ' ἔγχεα καὶ μένε' ἀνδρῶν.*

13. **nequiquam** etc.: cf. the taunt of Hector, *Il.* III. 54 *οὐκ ἄν τοι χραίσμῃ κίθαρις τά τε δῶρ' Ἀφροδίτης | ἥ τε κόμη τό τε εἶδος, ὅτ' ἐν κονίῃσι μιγείης.* — **ferox,** *emboldened.* The phrase suggests a scornful contrast with genuine courage.

14. **grata feminis**: contemptuous, like **imbelli cithara** and **thalamo,** below.

15. **imbelli cithara**: cf. *imbellis lyrae,* 6. 10. — **divides,** *wilt sing to the accompaniment of.* The word, which is nowhere else used in this sense, is apparently intended to express the effect of the instrumental accompaniment in marking the parts or measures of the air. Others, however, suppose that Horace had in mind the division into strophes by interludes on the lute.

16. **thalamo**: see Intr. 69. and cf. *Il.* III. 380 *τὸν δ'* (*sc.* Paris) *ἐξήρπαξ' Ἀφροδίτη | κὰδ δ' εἷσ' ἐν θαλάμῳ εὐώδεϊ, κηώεντι.*

17. **Cnosii**: Intr. 117 *a.* The Cretans were famous archers, and Cnosus was one of their principal towns; cf. Verg. *A.* V. 306 *Cnosia spicula.*

Aiacem : tamen, heu, serus adulteros
crinis pulvere collines.
Non Laertiaden, exitium tuae
gentis, non Pylium Nestora respicis?
Vrgent impavidi te Salaminius
Teucer, te Sthenelus sciens
pugnae, sive opus est imperitare equis,
non auriga piger. Merionen quoque
nosces. Ecce furit te reperire atrox
Tydides, melior patre,
quem tu, cervus uti vallis in altera
visum parte lupum graminis immemor
sublimi fugies mollis anhelitu,
non hoc pollicitus tuae.

18. **vitabis,** *wilt thou stay . . . out of the way of.*— **sequi** : Intr. 101 *b.*

19. **Aiacem** : the son of Oileus ('Οιλῆος ταχὺς Αἴας, *Il.* II. 527). — **serus,** *though long deferred the day will come when.* Cf. III. 11. 28 *sera fata.* For the adjective used to express time, cf. 2. 45, *Ep.* II. 1. 161. —**adulteros crinis**: Intr. 124.

21. **Laertiaden** : Ulysses. — **exitium tuae gentis** : to the shrewdness of Ulysses, culminating in the seizure of the Palladium, the success of the Greeks was held to be chiefly due. Cf. *Ep.* I. 2. 18 *Vlixen, qui, domitor Troiae,* etc., a free translation of the opening lines of the Odyssey.

22. **non respicis,** *seest thou not behind thee?* cf. Verg. *A.* VIII. 697 *necdum geminos a tergo respicit anguis.* The god in his vision sees the dangers of the battle-field already close upon the unconscious Paris.

24. **Teucer** : see 7. 21 n. — **Sthenelus** : charioteer of Diomed.

25. **sive** : Intr. 119 *d.*

26. **Merionen** : see 6. 15 n.

27. **reperire** : Intr. 94 *c.*

28. **Tydides** : cf. 6. 15 n. — **melior patre** : *i.e.* as a warrior; suggested by the saying of Sthenelus, *Il.* IV. 405 ἡμεῖς τοι πατέρων μέγ' ἀμείνονες εὐχόμεθ' εἶναι.

29. **cervus uti,** etc.: *sc. fugit,* of which **lupum** is the object. — **in altera parte,** (on the other side of), *across; i.e.* without waiting for him to come near.

30. **visum,** *at the sight of.*— **graminis immemor** : a further touch to indicate the fright of the stag.

31. **sublimi anhelitu,** *panting with head high in air.* This description properly belongs to the stag : the comparison and its subject are purposely confused ; Intr. 123. — **mollis,** *faint heart.*

32. **non hoc,** etc.: *i.e.* something very different from this (litotes). With this final touch of scorn the god dismisses Paris, and closes his prophecy with the fate of Troy itself. — **tuae**: cf. *tuo,* 25. 7.

Iracunda diem proferet Ilio
matronisque Phrygum classis Achillei:
post certas hiemes uret Achaicus
  ignis Iliacas domos.'

## XVI.

O matre pulchra filia pulchrior,
quem criminosis cumque voles modum

33. **iracunda classis**: see Intr. 105 *a*. The followers of Achilles, who shared the inactivity of their chief, are regarded as sharing the wrath to which it was due. — **diem proferet**, *will put off the day*, *i.e.* the day of doom, already foreshadowed in vss. 8 and 21.

34. **matronisque Phrygum**: not strictly necessary after the comprehensive **Ilio**, but added to lend a touch of pathos to the otherwise colorless statement, by recalling the class of persons on whom the calamity will bring the most intense suffering; cf. I. 24, 35. 11 n.— **Phrygum**: for Trojan, as in II. 9. 16; cf. Verg. *A*. I. 182, etc. — **Achillei**: for the form, cf. *Vlixei*, 6. 7 n.

35. **post certas hiemes**, *when the predestined number of winters is past*, *i.e.* in the fullness of time. Observe the asyndeton and the emphatic position of these words. The preceding sentence is not concessive, but the two together sum up, in its successive stages, the course of the war which is to come. Translated into prose the thought is: For a time internal dissension will paralyze the Greek and the doom of Troy will be withheld; when the appointed hour is come, he will burn the city. For **hiemes** cf 11. 4 n.

36. **Iliacas**: this reading of all the MSS. has been questioned for two reasons: (1) because of **Ilio** in 33, and (2) on account of the trochee **īgnĭs**, which violates a rule elsewhere strictly observed by Horace (see Intr. 146 *b*, 147). The second objection may be explained on the supposition that in this, which is probably one of his early odes, Horace followed his Greek models, and allowed himself a liberty which he subsequently refrained from using. The first objection has some weight, but no substitute for **Iliacas** is offered by any authority. Conjectures such as *Pergameas*, *Dardanias*, *barbaricas* have been adopted by various editors.

XVI. The inscription in the manuscripts, *Palinodia*, indicates the nature of this ode, in which the poet represents himself as having given vent to his anger against his mistress in some verses which he now begs her to destroy and forget. The fact that he calls the offending verses *iambi*, his own name for the Epodes (*Ep*. I. 19. 23, II. 2. 59), gives some color to the supposition that here for once Horace is dealing with a definite experience of his own. But the humorous extravagance

pones iambis, sive flamma
sive mari libet Hadriano.

Non Dindymene, non adytis quatit
mentem sacerdotum incola Pythius,
non Liber aeque, non acuta
sic geminant Corybantes aera

with which he urges the lady to calm her mind and dilates on the dreadful effects of anger is hardly to be taken as the expression of genuine repentance. In any case the ode cannot be connected with any of the extant Epodes.— Metre, 176.

2. **criminosis**, *abusive*. — **cumque**: cf. 6. 3 n. — **modum pones**, *you shall put an end to*. The context gives the future a half-concessive, half-hortatory force; Intr. 79, 90.

3. **iambis**: a rapid rhythm (cf. vs. 24 and *Ep*. II. 3. 251 *iambus, pes citus*) well adapted for invective, a use to which it was said to have been turned by its reputed inventor Archilochus (*Ep*. II. 3. 79 *Archilochum proprio rabies armavit iambo*; see Intr. 18).

4. **mari Hadriano**: Intr. 117 *a*. The language is purposely exaggerated, as if we should say, 'You may fling them into the middle of the Atlantic.'

5. **non**, etc.: the poet proceeds to discourse with humorous irony on the overmastering force of anger, which unbalances the intellect of man and drives him irresistibly upon a course of slaughter and destruction. It is first compared with the religious frenzy exhibited in the worship of certain divinities. — **Dindymene**: *i.e.* Cybele, identified with Rhea, the mother of Zeus. Dindymus was a mountain in Phrygia, near Pessinus, one of the principal seats of the worship of Cybele, whose rites were celebrated with the wildest orgies, the priests in their frenzy often slashing themselves with knives. Cf. Catullus 63.— **adytis**, *in the sanctuary*, in contrast with the mountains and woods where Cybele and Bacchus exercise their power. For the abl. see Intr. 69.

6. **incola Pythius**, *he that dwelleth in Pytho*, *i.e.* Apollo, Pytho being the ancient name of Delphi. The frenzy of the priestess of Apollo (the Cumaean sibyl), when possessed by the oracular spirit of the god, is described by Vergil, *A*. VI. 46 *sqq*.

7. **Liber**: alluding to the orgiastic rites practiced by the bacchanals, under the overpowering inspiration, as they claimed, of the god. Cf. II. 19. 5 *sqq*. — **aeque**, *as much*, completing the predicate, **non aeque mentem sacerdotum quatit**, which is distributed, in Horace's favorite manner, among the three subjects; Intr. 120. The place of *ac*, which would naturally follow **aeque**, is supplied by **ut**, vs. 9, the change being due to the intervening **sic**, vs. 8. — **acuta**, *shrill*.

8. **sic**, *with such effect*, *sc.* in exciting the mind. — **geminant**, *clash together*; lit. put together in pairs. Cf. Stat. *Theb*. VIII. 221 *gemina aera sonant*. — **Corybantes**: priests of Cybele. — **aera**: *i.e.* cymbals, used by the Corybantes in their rites.

tristes ut irae, quas neque Noricus
deterret ensis nec mare naufragum
nec saevus ignis nec tremendo
Iuppiter ipse ruens tumultu.

Fertur Prometheus, addere principi
limo coactus particulam undique
desectam, et insani leonis
vim stomacho adposuisse nostro.

9. **tristes ut irae,** *as unhappy anger has.* The predicate to be supplied, however, is *mentem quatiunt* or the like, expressing the general sense of the preceding strophe, which is implied even in **sic,** on which **ut** grammatically depends. — **irae** : Intr. 128. — **Noricus** : Intr. 117. The iron foundries in Noricum are alluded to by Ovid, *M.* XIV. 712 *durior et ferro quod Noricus excoquit ignis.*

10. **deterret** : *i.e.* from pursuing its course of vengeance. — **ensis, mare, ignis** : stock examples of obstacles ; cf. *S.* I. 1. 38 : *cum te neque fervidus aestus | demoveat lucro, neque hiems ignis mare ferrum, | nil obstet tibi.*

12. **Iuppiter** : cf. *Iove*, 1. 25 n. — **ruens,** *descending. i.e.* in thunder and lightning.

13. **fertur,** *we are told that.* — **Prometheus** : the myth of the creation of man and the other animals from clay and water by Prometheus, though unknown to Homer and Hesiod, was very old (cf. Plato, *Protag.* 320 D). In its present form, however, it is not found in any other author now extant, though the notion of man being endowed with the qualities of various other animals, — the cunning of the fox, the timidity of the hare, etc., — occurs very early. — **principi,** *first, original,* that of which the first man was created.

14. **particulam**: that a material portion is meant, and not a portion of the soul (as *S.* II. 2. 79), is shown by **desectam**. The idea seems to be that each of the animals had been created by mixing with the clay out of which it was shaped a certain material which gave it its peculiar disposition, but that when he came to the creation of man, Prometheus was obliged, in order to obtain the requisite amount, to take from each of the animals which he had already created (**undique**) a portion of its predisposing substance.

16. **stomacho**: *i.e.* to the organ which is the seat of our passion (cf. 6. 6 n) was added, among other elements (**et**), a particle taken from the lion, bringing with it the violence of his rage.

17. **irae** : repeated from vs. 9. — **Thyesten** : son of Pelops and brother of Atreus, whose vengeance took the monstrous form of a supper at which Thyestes was induced to eat unawares the flesh of his own son. — **exitio,** etc.: this part of the myth has not come down to us. It was probably familiar to Horace and his readers from the *Thyestes* of Varius, recently published.

Irae Thyesten exitio gravi
stravere et altis urbibus ultimae
stetere causae cur perirent
funditus imprimeretque muris
hostile aratrum exercitus insolens.
Compesce mentem! Me quoque pectoris
temptavit in dulci iuventa
fervor et in celeres iambos
misit furentem: nunc ego mitibus
mutare quaero tristia, dum mihi
fias recantatis amica
opprobriis animumque reddas.

18. **altis**: a frequent poetical epithet of cities, denoting lofty walls and buildings, and hence implying power and splendor; cf. IV. 6. 3; Verg. *A.* I. 7 *altae moenia Romae.*—**urbibus**: virtually dative of possessor (see note on **stetere**), anticipating the subject of the interrogative clause.—**ultimae**, *primary*, the last reached in tracing backwards the series of results; cf. Cat. 4. 15 *ultima ex origine.*

19. **stetere**: more expressive than *fuere*, implying the persistent efficacy of the cause.

20. **imprimeretque muris**, etc.: amplification of **funditus**, to illustrate how far the victor is carried in his rage. To drive a plow over the ruins of a city as the Romans did in the case of Carthage (Mommsen *Hist.* III. p. 54), was to proclaim its absolute and final effacement.

21. **hostile aratrum**: Intr. 124.—**insolens**: cf. 5. 8 n. For the caesura of this verse, see Intr. 155.

22. **compesce mentem**: the moral of his discourse, which was therefore meant as a warning to the lady, and not an apology for his own indulgence in anger. That, he goes on to say (**me quoque**, etc.), is a thing of the past.

23. **temptavit**, *attacked* (as a disease); cf. *Ep.* I. 6. 28 *si latus aut renes morbo temptantur acuto.*—**dulci**: not an idle epithet. The **fervor pectoris** was one phase of the strong passions and quick impulses that made life so sweet at that time.

24. **celeres iambos**: see vs. 3 n.

25. **mitibus . . . tristia**, *kind feelings . . . bitterness.* For the use of the neuter plural cf. *ima summis*, 34. 12 n; for the construction see Intr. 74, and cf. 17. 1 *sq.*

26. **mutare**: Intr. 94 *c.*

27. **recantatis**, *now that I have retracted;* the verb being here used as a translation of παλινῳδεῖν.—**amica**, *friendly.*

28. **animum reddas**, *give me back your heart.* Cf. 19. 4.

## XVII.

Velox amoenum saepe Lucretilem
mutat Lycaeo Faunus et igneam
defendit aestatem capellis
usque meis pluviosque ventos.

Impune tutum per nemus arbutos
quaerunt latentis et thyma deviae
olentis uxores mariti,
nec viridis metuunt colubras

XVII. On the attractions of his Sabine farm, with an invitation to a fair friend, whom he calls Tyndaris, to visit him there and enjoy with him the quiet country pleasures which it affords. — Metre, 176.

1. **Lucretilem**: Intr. 24.

2. **mutat**: see Intr. 74 and cf. 16. 25. — **Lycaeo**: a mountain range near the southern border of Arcadia. — **Faunus**: an old Italian divinity, still worshipped in the country, sometimes as a benevolent god of woods and pastures (cf. III. 18), sometimes as a prophetic spirit who secluded himself in the forest, from which his loud voice occasionally resounded, filling all who heard it with terror and foreboding (Cic. *Div.* I. 101., *D. N.* II. 6, III. 15; cf. Liv. II. 7. 2). The Arcadian Pan, the son of Hermes, with whom Faunus was identified in literature, was also a spirit of the hills and woods, who punished men that disturbed his midday sleep (Theocr. 1. 15) by frightening them out of their senses with demoniacal cries (hence the expression 'panic fear'); but in general he was a merry spirit, always accompanied by dancing and singing nymphs, to whom he played on his marvelous pipe, while the shepherds down in the valley listened in spell-bound silence or terror (Mart. IX. 61. 12).

3. **defendit**, *wards off*. — **aestatem**: *i.e.* heat. — **capellis**: dative; cf. Verg. *E.* 7. 47 *solstitium pecori defendite.* Gr. 229 *c.*

5. **impune**, *with impunity;* referring to **deviae**, which implies a neglect of the precautions ordinarily necessary to keep them from harm. — **arbutos**: see 1. 21 n.

6. **quaerunt deviae**, *stray . . . in search of.* — **latentis**: *i.e.* easily escaping notice among the other trees and bushes.

7. **olentis uxores mariti**, *the wives of the unfragrant spouse.* — **mariti**: *sc. gregis;* a common way of designating the male animal. Cf. Verg. *E.* 7. 7 *vir gregis ipse caper;* Theocr. 8. 49 ὦ τράγε, τᾶν λευκᾶν αἰγῶν ἄνερ.

9. **Martialis**: *i.e.* sacred to Mars; cf. *Martius lupus*, Verg. *Aen.* IX. 566, and the story of the birth of Romulus and Remus. — **haediliae** (*sc. metuunt*), *the kids.* The word does not occur elsewhere, but this interpretation of it as a diminutive form from *haedus*

nec Martialis haediliae lupos,
utcumque dulci, Tyndari, fistula
valles et Vsticae cubantis
levia personuere saxa.

Di me tuentur, dis pietas mea
et musa cordi est. Hic tibi copia
manabit ad plenum benigno
ruris honorum opulenta cornu;

hic in reducta valle Caniculae
vitabis aestus et fide Teia

is supported by the parallel form *porcilia*, from *porcus*. The old hypothesis, that *Haedilia* was the name of a place in the neighborhood, rejected by Bentley, is still maintained by some editors.

10. **utcumque**: always temporal in Horace. With the perfect definite, here and IV. 4. 35, it introduces a determining circumstance, like *simul* (*e.g.* 9. 9). — **fistula**, *with his pipe*. *Fistula* is the Latin name for the Greek σύριγξ, Pan's pipe. Cf. Tib. II. 5. 31 *fistula, cui semper decrescit harundinis ordo; | nam calamus cera iungitur usque minor;* and Verg. *E.* 3. 25.

11. **Vsticae**: said by Porphyrio to be a hill or mountain of gentle slope (**cubantis**) in the neighborhood of the Sabine farm.

12. **personuere**, *have rung;* perfect, because the strains of the *fistula*, once heard, are an assurance of the presence of the god, inspiring the animals with the feeling of security described. The music is not thought of as continuing.

14. **musa**: see note on *Clio*, 12. 2. — **copia**: not personified as in *C. S.* 60 and *Ep.* I. 12. 29, where *Plenty* is the goddess who showers blessings from her overflowing horn. Here, as in the oldest Greek conception of the 'horn of plenty' (the horn of Amalthea, the nurse of Zeus, taken by Hercules from the river-god Acheloos), **copia** is the contents of the horn, which was represented as in the possession of various divinities, Demeter, Dionysus, Fortuna (Tyche), Autumnus, etc.

15. **benigno**: cf. 9. 6 n.

16. **honorum**, *the glories*, *i.e.* fruits, vegetables, flowers; cf. *S.* II. 5. 12 *dulcia poma | et quoscumque feret cultus tibi fundus h o n o r e s*. For the case, see Intr. 66 *c*.

17. **Caniculae**, *the Dog-star;* properly the constellation of the Lesser Dog, which the Greeks called Προκύων (cf. III. 29. 17 n) as rising before the (Greater) Dog; but the name was popularly applied to Sirius, the chief star of the Greater Dog, whose rising, July 26, heralded the hot season. Cf. III. 13. 9, *S.* II. 5. 39.

18. **aestus**: Intr. 128. — **fide Teia**: *i.e.* in love songs, such as those of Anacreon, who was a

dices laborantis in uno
Penelopen vitreamque Circen:
hic innocentis pocula Lesbii
duces sub umbra, nec Semeleius
cum Marte confundet Thyoneus
proelia, nec metues protervum
suspecta Cyrum, ne male dispari
incontinentis iniciat manus
et scindat haerentem coronam
crinibus immeritamque vestem.

native of Teos (*Epod.* 14. 10); cf. *Lesboum barbiton*, 1. 34 n. The ablative is instrumental and means 'to the accompaniment of.'

19. **dices**: cf. *dicere*, 6. 5 n. — **laborantis** (*sc. amore*), *heart-sick;* cf. *ambitione laborat*, *S.* I. 4. 26. — **in**: an extension of its use in the sense of 'in the case of'; see Intr. 72 and cf. Verg. *A.* II. 540 *at non Achilles | talis in hoste fuit Priamo; Epod.* 11. 4; Cat. 64. 98 *in flavo hospite suspirantem;* translate *for.* — **uno**: Ulysses.

20. **vitream**, *crystal*, suggesting a brilliant, dazzling beauty; cf. 19. 5 *Glycerae nitor splendentis Pario marmore purius* and III. 13. 1 *splendidior vitro.* The Romans, though they used glass very little for their windows, on account of its expensiveness, were very skilful in working it for artistic purposes — vases, ornaments, imitations of precious stones, etc. The epithet is perhaps applied to her as a sea-goddess; cf. IV. 2. 3 *vitreo ponto* and *Epod.* 13. 16 *mater caerula* (Thetis). — **Circen**: *Odys.* X. 274 *sqq.*

21. **innocentis**: *i.e.* not intoxicating, as explained in the next clause. — **Lesbii**: one of the sweeter Greek wines.

22. **duces**, *you shall quaff.* For the tense, cf. 16. 3 n. — **nec Semeleius**, etc.: *i.e.* nor will there be any quarrelling over the cups, as there is in the companies where she meets his rival. — **Semeleius**, *the son of Semele;* cf. Cat. 61. 225 *Telemacho Penelopeo.*

23. **confundet proelia**: a variation of the ordinary *committere proelia*, to express a disorderly squabble. — **Thyoneus**: a name of Bacchus meaning 'son of the raving one,' (Θυώνη; cf. θύω). The latter name was very early applied to Semele; cf. Hom. *Hym. to Dionys.* (34) 21 σὺν μητρὶ Σεμέλῃ ἥνπερ καλέουσι Θυώνην.

25. **suspecta**: because of his jealousy. — **male**, *very;* see 9. 24 n.

26. **incontinentis manus**: cf. 13. 9 n, and see Intr. 124.

27. **coronam**: cf. 4. 10 n.

28. **crinibus**: probably dative, as *S.* I. 10. 49 *haerentem capiti multa cum laude coronam;* but see Intr. 71. — **immeritam**: *i.e.* having done nothing to deserve such treatment.

## XVIII.

Nullam, Vare, sacra vite prius severis arborem
circa mite solum Tiburis et moenia Catili.
Siccis omnia nam dura deus proposuit neque
mordaces aliter diffugiunt sollicitudines.
Quis post vina gravem militiam aut pauperiem crepat?

XVIII. On the blessings of wine when used with moderation, and the folly and sin of intemperance. The ode appears to be a translation, with a few touches to give it a local setting, of a poem of Alcaeus, in the same metre, of which the first verse is preserved (*Fr.* 44):

Μηδὲν ἄλλο φυτεύσῃς πρότερον δένδριον ἀμπέλω.

The Varus addressed is probably the literary critic, Quintilius Varus, whose death is mourned in Ode 24. — Metre, 170.

1. **sacra**: *sc.* to Bacchus. The word sets the tone of the ode at the outset: wine is not for the mere pleasure of our palate; it is a divine gift, the abuse of which will be punished as sin. — **severis**, *plant;* cf. Caecilius *ap.* Cic. *C. M.* 24 *serit arbores quae saeclo prosint alteri.* — **arborem**: cf. δένδριον, intr. note, and Plin. *N. H.* XIV. 9 *vites iure apud priscos magnitudine quoque inter arbores numerabantur.*

2. **circa**, *about;* used in different senses, as the English word may be, with its two objects: with **solum**, equivalent to 'here and there in,' with **moenia**, 'in the neighborhood of.' — **mite**, *mellow, i.e.* light and crumbling, yielding readily to the plough. Such soil was suitable for the vine (Verg. *G.* II. 226 *sqq.*). — **Tiburis**: it would seem that Varus had a country place there. — **moenia Catili**: see 7. 13 n. With the name of Catillus (Verg. *A.* VII. 672) Horace has allowed himself a Homeric license; cf. Ἀχιλλεύς, Ἀχιλεύς, *e.g. Il.* I. 148, 199.

3. **siccis**: *i.e.* those who abstain; cf. IV. 5. 39, *Ep.* I. 19. 9. — **omnia dura**, *only the hard side of life;* **dura** has a predicate force, expressing the aspect under which everything is presented. — **nam**: Intr. 114. — **deus**: cf. 3. 21 n.

4. **aliter**, *in any other way;* used illogically, as if the preceding statement had been put in the converse form: all things are softened to those who drink wine.

5. **gravem militiam**, *the hardships of a soldier's life.* This topic would hardly have occurred to Horace, who had seen nothing of war for a dozen years; it is no doubt taken from the ode of Alcaeus; cf. 32. 5 *sqq.* — **crepat**, *prattles;* cf. *Ep.* I. 7. 84 *sulcos et vineta crepat mera.* The word simply means rattling on, as men do when their tongue is loosened by wine, about subjects fit or unfit (*Ep.* I. 7. 72), and is to be understood in this sense in the next verse. The censure is directed against the depressing topics of conversation, and not specially against the manner of talking.

Quis non te potius, Bacche pater, teque, decens Venus?
Ac ne quis modici transiliat munera Liberi,
Centaurea monet cum Lapithis rixa super mero
debellata, monet Sithoniis non levis Euhius,
cum fas atque nefas exiguo fine libidinum
discernunt avidi. Non ego te, candide Bassareu,
invitum quatiam nec variis obsita frondibus

6. **te potius,** etc.: *i.e.* of the brighter side of life,—its joys and solaces, rather than of its troubles. —**Bacche, Venus**: cf. 19. 2 n, 32. 9.—**pater**: a title of reverence (cf. 2. 50 n) suited to the character of benefactor, in which Bacchus is here invoked; cf. III. 3. 13, *Ep.* II. 1. 5 *Liber pater*.—**decens**: cf. 4. 6 n.

7. **ac,** *and yet*, qualifying the preceding recommendation of wine. For this use of *ac* cf. *S.* II. 2. 118, *Ep.* II. 1. 208.—**ne quis transiliat,** *against a reckless use of*.—**munera Liberi**: not simply wine, but wine as Liber designed it, for the good of mankind. The condition imposed in his design is expressed in **modici**. With **munera** thus limited the poet uses **transiliat,** *go beyond*, with the implication of recklessness, as in 3. 42.

8. **Centaurea,** *of the Centaurs*. At the wedding of Pirithous, king of the Lapithae, with Hippodamia, Eurytion, one of the Centaurs, who were present as guests, attempted in his drunkenness to carry off the bride. The battle that ensued became a famous subject in literature (cf. *Odys.* XXI. 295, Ov. *M.* XII. 210) and in art (as in the metopes of the Parthenon and in the pediment of the temple at Olympia).—**monet,** *there is warning in*.—**super**: cf. 9. 5 n.

9. **debellata**: the contest ended in the extirpation of the Centaurs (*Il.* I. 267), a result which, in the form of the myth which Horace follows, took place then and there (**super mero**).—**Sithoniis**; a Thracian tribe, used here for the Thracians in general.—**non levis,** *the severity of*; Intr. 105 *a*. The allusion is to the bloody quarrels over their wine for which they were notorious (cf. I. 27. 1 *sq.*), and which are here represented as punishments inflicted by the god.—**Euhius**: a name of Bacchus, formed from εὐοῖ (cf. II. 19. 5), the cry of the bacchantes.

10. **exiguo,** *faint*, scarcely perceptible, instead of the broad and distinct line that separates right and wrong in the mind of one whose moral perceptions are unclouded.—**fine libidinum,** *the line which appetite draws;* cf. III. 24. 44 *virtutis viam* (the path that virtue prescribes); *S.* I. 1. 50 *naturae finis* (the limits that nature sets).

11. **avidi,** *in their strong craving*. —**non ego te**: this is the usual order where *non* and *ego* are both emphatic; cf. 23. 9, II. 7. 26, 17. 9, *S.* I. 1. 103, etc.—**candide,** *radiant;* of the ever youthful beauty of the god (cf. *candide Bacche*, Ov. *F.* III. 772; *candida Dido*, Verg. *A.* V. 571), in accordance with the ordinary Greek conception, yet not inconsistent with the more serious character attributed to him here.—**Bassareu**: a name of Bacchus said to be de-

sub divum rapiam. Saeva tene cum Berecyntio
cornu tympana, quae subsequitur caecus amor sui
et tollens vacuum plus nimio gloria verticem
arcanique fides prodiga, perlucidior vitro.

## XIX.

Mater saeva Cupidinum
Thebanaeque iubet me Semelae puer

rived from βασσάρα, a fox-skin, worn by the Thracian bacchantes, hence called Βασσαρίδες. Under this name he was represented with a beard and the features of mature age (Macrob. *Sat.* I. 18. 9).

12. **quatiam,** *rouse.* — **variis obsita frondibus,** *the mysteries enveloped in divers leaves* (especially grape and ivy); alluding to the caskets containing mysterious symbols carried in bacchanalian processions. See the vivid description in Catullus, 64. 254 *sqq.* Under the figure of respect for these mysteries the poet professes his own resolution to conform to the will of the god, and again deprecates intemperate indulgence.

13. **sub divum,** *to light;* cf. *sub Iove* I. 25 n. — **saeva,** *barbarous.* — **Berecyntio cornu**: named from Berecyntus, one of the mountains in Phrygia on which the orgies of Cybele were celebrated, and therefore belonging, like the **tympana** (vs. 14), *tambourines* (cf. Cat. 63. 21), to the worship of that goddess; but the orgies of the two divinities were always more or less confused with one another. See III. 19. 19 n.

14. **quae subsequitur**: keeping up the figure, the qualities that follow being personified in the bacchanals who march behind this wild music.

15. **tollens verticem**: cf. I. 36. — **plus nimio,** *all too high;* a colloquial expression (cf. Cic. *Att.* X. 8 A. 1 *quia te nimio plus diligo*), in Horace always used of censurable excess (33. 1, *Ep.* I. 10. 30). — **gloria,** *vainglory, vanity,* as in *Ep.* I. 18. 22 *gloria quem supra viris et vestit et ungit.*

16. **arcanique fides prodiga**: see 5. 5 n. — **perlucidior**: *i.e.* with no more power of concealment, a familiar result of intoxication; cf. the practice of the Germans described by Tacitus, *Ger.* 22. For the peculiar caesura of this verse, see Intr. 150. — **vitro**: see note on *vitream,* 17. 20.

XIX. The poet will have us believe that he has once again had to surrender to the charms of a fair girl, when he thought his days of love were over long ago. — Metre, 171.

1. **Cupidinum**: the original conception of Eros as the one son of Aphrodite was later enlarged by poets and artists, who represented numberless Loves, all in the shape of pretty winged boys, in attendance on Aphrodite, and sometimes on Bacchus. See Preller-Robert, *Gr. Myth.* I. p. 507.

2. **Semelae puer**: cf. *Semeleius,* 17. 22. Here, in contrast

et lasciva Licentia
finitis animum reddere amoribus.
Vrit me Glycerae nitor
splendentis Pario marmore purius;
urit grata protervitas
et voltus nimium lubricus adspici.
In me tota ruens Venus
Cyprum deseruit, nec patitur Scythas
et versis animosum equis
Parthum dicere nec quae nihil attinent.
Hic vivum mihi caespitem, hic
verbenas, pueri, ponite turaque
bimi cum patera meri:
mactata veniet lenior hostia.

with the last ode, he is the youthful Bacchus (**puer**), the companion of Venus. Cf. 32. 9.

4. **animum reddere**: cf. 16. 28 n.

5. **nitor**, *the beauty*. Cf. *nites*, 5. 13.

6. **splendentis purius**, *who shines with purer lustre*. — **Pario**: from Paros, one of the *nitentes Cyclades* (14. 20), preferred for sculpture on account of its fineness and purity.

8. **et voltus**, etc., *and her too dazzling face*.— **lubricus adspici**: *i.e.* on which one's glance can no more rest steadily than one's foot upon a slippery surface. For the infinitive, see Intr. 102.

9. **tota**, *with all her force*. — **ruens**: cf. 16. 12.

10. **Cyprum**: cf. 3. 1, 30. 2.— **Scythas, Parthum**: subjects of national importance that engage the public attention. Cf. 26. 5 n.

11. **animosum**: in contrast with **versis equis** (Intr. 116 *a*), which ordinarily indicates fear or cowardice. The allusion is to the favorite stratagem of the Parthian cavalry, of turning suddenly while in full retreat and sending a shower of arrows in the face of the pursuing enemy; cf. Verg. *G.* III. 31.

12. **quae nihil attinent**, *any such irrelevant subject*; a delicious touch of feminine assumption.

13. **hic . . . hic**: Intr. 116 *g*. The case calls for immediate attention; a sacrifice must be instituted on the spot. — **vivum caespitem**: often used for a temporary altar; cf. III. 8. 4.

14. **verbenas**, *green sprigs* (of certain sacred trees and plants, here probably myrtle). — **pueri**: *i.e.* slaves (not necessarily young); the usual term in addressing them; cf. 38. 1.

15. **patera**: a saucer-shaped vessel with a handle, used especially for libations. — **meri**: in its literal sense, only unmixed wine being permitted for this purpose.

16. **veniet lenior**: in contrast

# XX.

Vile potabis modicis Sabinum
cantharis, Graeca quod ego ipse testa
conditum levi, datus in theatro
cum tibi plausus,
care Maecenas eques, ut paterni
fluminis ripae simul et iocosa

with *tota ruens*, 9. — **hostia**: victims were sometimes sacrificed to Venus (Plaut. *Poen.* 449 *sqq.*, Tac. *H.* II. 3), but her sacrifices were commonly bloodless.

XX. To Maecenas, in anticipation of a visit from him, perhaps at the poet's country place (Intr. 24). The ode lacks the usual finish of Horace's lyric works, and if genuine, — which some even of the more conservative editors doubt, — must be regarded as a hasty and informal production, preserved only for the sake of the allusion in vss. 3 *sqq.* The abrupt beginning may be explained on the supposition that the poem is an answer to a note from Maecenas, announcing his intended visit. — Metre, 174.

1. **vile**, *plain*, in contrast with the fine and costly brands mentioned in the last strophe. — **modicis**, *modest*, referring not so much to the size of the cups as to the quality of their contents. Cf. *S.* II. 6. 70 *modicis* (sc. *poculis*) *uvescit laetius*, where it is contrasted with *acria pocula; S.* I. 5. 2 *hospitio modico; Ep.* I. 5. 2 *modica cenare patella.* — **Sabinum** (sc. *vinum*): the wine of the district; cf. 9. 7 n. According to *Ep.* I. 14. 23, it could not have been produced on his own place.

2. **cantharis**, *bowls.* The *cantharus* was a large cup with handles, said to have been named for its inventor. — **Graeca testa**: *i.e.* a jar which, having contained Greek wine, would improve the flavor of the Sabine put into it. For the case of **testa** see Intr. 69. — **ipse**, *with my own hands.*

3. **conditum levi**, *stored and sealed.* The cork of the amphora was smeared with pitch to make it air-tight; cf. III. 8. 10. — **datus**: sc. *est.* — **theatro**: probably that of Pompey, the only permanent theatre existing in Rome at the time. It stood in the Campus Martius, about a thousand feet from the river.

4. **cum**, *at the time when.* See Intr. 114. — **plausus**: the occasion, as appears from II. 17. 22 *sqq.*, was the first public appearance of Maecenas after a serious illness, probably in B.C. 30. The date of this ode must be set some years later.

5. **care**: cf. *dilecte Maecenas*, II. 20. 7. — **eques**: Intr. 21. — **paterni fluminis**: the Tiber, as rising in Etruria (*amnis Tuscus, S.* II. 2. 32), the home of Maecenas' ancestors.

6. **ripae**: the plural for one side of the river only, as *Aen.* VI. 305. See Intr. 128. — **iocosa imago**: cf. 12. 3 n.

redderet laudes tibi Vaticani
montis imago.

Caecubum et prelo domitam Caleno
tu bibes uvam: mea nec Falernae
temperant vites neque Formiani
pocula colles.

## XXI.

Dianam tenerae dicite virgines,
intonsum, pueri, dicite Cynthium,
Latonamque supremo
dilectam penitus Iovi.

7. **redderet,** *repeated.* — **Vaticani montis:** here used for the whole range of hills along the west bank of the Tiber, rising to a height of over 250 feet above the river. The part opposite the theatre of Pompey was called *Ianiculum*. Echoes from the steep slopes of this hill were no doubt familiar to the Romans, but Horace's introduction of them here is purely ornamental. The applause in the theatre, could not possibly have been so reëchoed. The short *i* of *Vaticanus* is peculiar to Horace.

9. **Caecubum,** etc.: fine wines of Latium and Campania respectively, standing for rich wines in general (Intr. 117 *a*). — **domitam,** *crushed.*

10. **tu bibes:** *sc.* at home; not the simple future, like *potabis*, vs. 1, but with a concessive-hortatory force, brought out by the antithesis of **tu** and **mea**; see Intr. 79. — **Falernae . . . Formiani:** again a choice Campanian and a choice Latin wine, from the same districts respectively as the Calenian and the Caecuban. They therefore repeat, with variation of form, the same general idea.

11. **temperant,** *flavor;* lit. 'mix' (in due proportion), as *Epod.* 17. 80; hence 'determine the quality of.' Observe that the subject is not the wine but the vines and the hills.

XXI. An ode in honor of Apollo and Diana, — especially the former as the patron god of Augustus, — in the form of an address to a chorus of boys and girls employed in some festival of these divinities. It may be compared with the latter part of IV. 6 (vss. 31 *sqq.*) addressed to the chorus that sang the *Carmen Saeculare*, and with Catullus 34. — Metre, 173.

1. **Dīanam:** Intr. 178. — **dicite:** cf. 6. 5 n.

2. **intonsum:** as possessed of eternal youth, Apollo was represented with a beardless face (*lēvis*, IV. 6. 28) and long golden locks (ἀκερσεκόμης, *Il.* XX. 39; ὁ χρυσοκόμας, Pind. *Ol.* 7. 58). Cf. Tib. I. 4. 37 *solis aeterna est Phoebo Bacchoque iuventa,* | *nam decet in*

Vos laetam fluviis et nemorum coma
quaecumque aut gelido prominet Algido
nigris aut Erymanthi
silvis aut viridis Gragi;

vos Tempe totidem tollite laudibus
natalemque, mares, Delon Apollinis
insignemque pharetra
fraternaque umerum lyra.

*tonsus crinis utrumque deum*, and II. 5. 121. — **Cynthium**: Apollo; so named from the hill Cynthus, in Delos, where Apollo and Diana were born. The latter is for the same reason often called *Cynthia*, as III. 28. 12.

3. **Latonam**: to be included in the hymn as the mother of the twin deities.

5. **vos**: sc. *dicite;* addressed to the girls, as *mares*, 10, shows. — **fluviis**, etc.: cf. Verg. *A.* I. 498 *qualis in Eurotae ripis aut per iuga Cynthi | exercet Diana choros*, etc. — **coma**, *the tresses*, *i.e.* the foliage, as in IV. 7. 2.

6. **prominet**, *tower aloft.* — **Algido**: the range of hills between Tusculum and the Via Latina, north of the Alban mount, being the northern member of the semicircular range that encloses that extinct volcano. The whole range, which was thickly wooded and cool in comparison with the surrounding plain (hence the name *Algidus* and the epithet **gelido**; cf. *nivali* III. 23. 9), was regarded as a favorite haunt of Diana (*quae tenet Algidum*, *C. S.* 69), and at its southern extremity, near Aricia, there was a famous grove and altar of the goddess (*Diana Nemorensis;* cf. *Ep.* II. 3. 16). For the case see Intr. 69.

7. **nigris**: referring rather to the color of the leaves than to the thickness of the foliage. See note on **viridis**, 8. — **aut**: Intr. 114. — **Erymanthi**: a mountain on the north-western borders of Arcadia, a famous hunting ground of Artemis (*Odys.* VI. 103).

8. **silvis**, *in the forests*, of which the *nemora* (open woods and glades) are a part. — **viridis**: the lighter color of deciduous trees in contrast with the dark evergreens (**nigris**) of Erymanthus; cf. IV. 12. 11 *nigri colles Arcadiae;* though not belonging grammatically to **silvis**, it supplants the epithet **nigris**, and *silvis* alone is understood with **Gragi**. — **Gragi**: a mountain range (Κράγος; cf. *Agrigentum* for Ἀκράγας) on the western coast of Lycia, the seat of some of the oldest legends of Latona and her children.

9. **Tempe**: see 7. 4 n. Here Apollo was purified after slaying the Python, and here an altar marked the spot where he plucked the laurel branch with which he returned to establish his oracle at Delphi.

10. **natalem Delon**: see note on *Cynthium*, 2.

12. **fraterna**: as a present from Mercury; cf. 10. 12 n. — **umerum**: object of **tollite**; cf. III. 28. 9 *cantabimus Neptunum et Nereidum comas.* Some editors take it as

Hic bellum lacrimosum, hic miseram famem
pestemque a populo et principe Caesare in
Persas atque Britannos
vestra motus aget prece.

## XXII.

Integer vitae scelerisque purus
non eget Mauris iaculis neque arcu
nec venenatis gravida sagittis,
Fusce, pharetra,
sive per Syrtis iter aestuosas
sive facturus per inhospitalem
Caucasum vel quae loca fabulosus
lambit Hydaspes.

an accusative of specification with **insignem**, which would then stand for *eum qui insignis est* (cf. *laetam*, 5); but it is very doubtful whether Horace ever used a masculine accusative, in this construction, with an *adjective*; see Intr. 44.

13. **hic**, etc.: an extension of his functions as ἀλεξίκακος, or defender against plague; cf. Preller-Robert, *Gr. Mythol.* I., p. 276.

14. **principe**: see 2. 50 n.

15. **Persas**: see 2. 22 n. — **Britannos**: cf. III. 5. 3, where they are coupled, as here, with the Parthians as not yet vanquished foes of Rome.

XXII. Aristius Fuscus, to whom this ode is addressed, was a man who dearly loved his joke, as appears from the part he took in Horace's famous encounter with the bore, *S.* I. 9. 61 *sqq.*; and Horace was in thorough sympathy with him (*paene gemelli, fraternis animis*, *Ep.* I. 10. 1 *sqq.*; cf. also *S.* I. 10. 83). Fuscus therefore could not have been misled by the high moral tone in which this ode opens, only to be puzzled by the somewhat flippant anticlimax at the end. No one who has learned to know Horace in the Satires could for a moment suppose that he would seriously propound the extravagant sentiment in the first two strophes, much less that he would seriously point to himself as an example of such lofty virtue. The incident of the third strophe was probably real, and our ode has no higher purpose than to tell his friend the story with a mock-serious moral attached. — Metre, 174.

1. **vitae**: Intr. 66 *d*. — **sceleris**: Intr. 66 *c*.

2. **Mauris**: Intr. 117 *a*.

3. **gravida**, *stuffed*.

5. **Syrtis**: here not (as in *Epod.* 9. 31) the dangerous waters

Namque me silva lupus in Sabina,
dum meam canto Lalagen et ultra
terminum curis vagor expeditis,
fugit inermem,

quale portentum neque militaris
Daunias latis alit aesculetis
nec Iubae tellus generat, leonum
arida nutrix.

Pone me pigris ubi nulla campis
arbor aestiva recreatur aura,

of that name, but the adjacent coast of Libya, east of the province of Africa; a district infested with wild beasts and poisonous serpents (Plin. *N. H.* V. 26.) — **iter facturus** (sc. *est*): Intr. 120. — **aestuosas**, *sweltering*; cf. *aestuosae Calabriae*, 31. 5.

7. **fabulosus**, *storied*, *i.e.* rich in legends.

9. **me silva lupus**: observe the skilful arrangement. The first three words set before us the scene and the two characters in the little drama; then follow, in their actual order, the poet's light-hearted unconcern before the encounter, the quick *dénoûment*, and the impression left behind by the retreating monster. See, further, Intr. 112.

10. **Lalagen**: the name (λαλαγή, 'prattle') is paraphrased in *dulce loquentem*, vs. 24. The accusative of the theme of song is usual after *cantare*; cf. 6. 17 *sqq.*

11. **terminum**: apparently that of his own farm. He had strolled away deeper into the forest. — **curis expeditis**: for the usual *curis expeditus*, as if the cares were fettered to the man instead of the man by the cares. Cf. *Epod.* 13. 5 *obducta solvatur fronte senectus*; Cat. 31. 7 *o quid solutis est beatius curis?*

12. **fugit inermem**: Intr. 116 *a*.

13. **quale portentum**: *i.e. tale portentum* (nom., in apposition with **lupus**) *quale* (acc.). — **militaris**: *i.e.* producing good soldiers; cf. III. 5. 9.

14. **Daunias**: Apulia, so named from a mythical king Daunus (III. 30. 11 n, IV. 14. 26), who ruled over the northern part of the country. In the Aeneid he is the father of Turnus (X. 616); elsewhere the father-in-law of the exiled Diomed. In form the word is a Greek feminine adjective, like Ἰλιάς, Ἀμβρακιάς, etc. That Apulia was infested with wolves appears also from 33. 7 *sq.*

15. **Iubae tellus**: Mauretania. The younger Juba, here referred to, had lived in Rome in Horace's time, having come there as a captive after the battle of Thapsus, in which his father fought against Caesar. He was made king of Mauretania by Augustus in B.C. 25.

17. **pone**: equivalent to a condition. — **pigris**, *sluggish*, with no quickening power for vegetation. — **nulla arbor recreatur**: *i.e.* there is no summer breeze and hence no tree or shrub (cf. 18. 1 n).

quod latus mundi nebulae malusque
Iuppiter urget;
pone sub curru nimium propinqui
solis, in terra domibus negata:
dulce ridentem Lalagen amabo,
dulce loquentem.

## XXIII.

Vitas inuleo me similis, Chloe,
quaerenti pavidam montibus aviis
matrem non sine vano
aurarum et siluae metu;
nam seu mobilibus vepris inhorruit
ad ventum foliis, seu virides rubum
dimovere lacertae,
et corde et genibus tremit.

19. **quod latus**, etc.: cf. *quale portentum*, 13 n. — **latus mundi**: in accordance with the Roman conception of the earth as a flat surface; cf. Tac. *Agr.* 12. The far North is the 'side' referred to. — **malus**, *unkind*.

20. **Iuppiter**: cf. I. 25 n. — **urget**, *broods over*.

21. **sub curru**, etc.: *i.e.* in the far South. — **nimium propinqui** *where he is all too near*.

23. **dulce**: Intr. 48.

XXIII. The comparison which forms the substance of this pretty ode is found in a fragment of Anacreon (52):

*Ἀγανῶς οἷά τε νεβρὸν νεοθηλέα*
*γαλαθηνόν, ὅστ' ἐν ὕλῃ κεροέσσης*
*ἀπολειφθεὶς ὑπὸ μητρὸς ἐπτοήθη·*

and we probably have here another of Horace's early studies. The name Chloe (χλόη, 'a young shoot') is perhaps chosen to suit the character portrayed. — Metre, 173.

2. **quaerenti**: *i.e.* having strayed away or been left behind, and suddenly found herself alone. — **pavidam**, *timid*, enhancing the impression of the timorous nature of the fawn. — **aviis**, *lonely*.

3. **non sine**: a favorite litotes with Horace; cf. 25. 16, III. 4. 20, etc.

4. **siluae**: see Intr. 182.

5. **seu**, *if*. — **vepris . . . ad ventum**: Bentley's reading for *veris . . . adventus* of the MSS., which is interpreted by those who retain it to mean the blowing of Favonius (see 4. 1 n). — **inhorruit**, *rustles*.

6. **ad ventum**, *in the wind*; lit., when the wind blows, **ad** denoting the occasion of the action, as in *ad haec*, *ad famam*, etc.

Atqui non ego te tigris ut aspera
Gaetulusve leo frangere persequor;
tandem desine matrem
tempestiva sequi viro.

## XXIV.

Quis desiderio sit pudor aut modus
tam cari capitis? Praecipe lugubris
cantus, Melpomene, cui liquidam pater
vocem cum cithara dedit.

7. **dimovere**: *i.e.* in gliding through it.

10. **Gaetulus**: cf. III. 20. 2 and see Intr. 117 *a.* — **frangere,** *to crush you;* suggested, perhaps, by the Homeric simile, *Il.* XI. 113 *ὡς δὲ λέων ἐλάφοιο ταχείης νήπια τέκνα | ῥηιδίως συνέαξε λαβὼν κρατεροῖσιν ὀδοῦσιν.* For the infinitive see Intr. 93.

12. **tempestiva viro**: cf. Verg. *A.* VII. 53 *iam matura viro, iam plenis nubilis annis.* Intr. 58 *b.*

XXIV. To Vergil, on the death of their common friend, Quintilius Varus, in B.C. 24. Quintilius, so far as we know, was not an author himself; but as an accomplished critic he had a high reputation among the writers of the day, who often submitted their compositions to his friendly judgment. (*Ep.* II. 3. 438.) Vergil's affection for him is sufficiently attested by the present ode. He was the friend of the poet's maturer years — he is not mentioned in the Eclogues — and his death was at once a personal bereavement and the loss of an invaluable literary adviser. Horace apparently stood on no such intimate terms with him; otherwise he could hardly have failed to mention him among the literary friends whose good opinion he valued, in *S.* I. 10. 81 *sqq.* But Horace's relations with him were nevertheless, — perhaps not till later than the period of the Satires, — so friendly that he addressed to him the eighteenth ode of this book. — Metre, 172.

1. **quis desiderio,** etc.: *i.e.* who can feel ashamed of mourning, or can control his grief. The case of **desiderio** is determined by **modus**; the dative would hardly be used with **pudor** alone.

2. **tam cari capitis,** *for one so dear.* For this use of *caput,* in the sense of 'person,' cf. *Epod.* 5. 74; Verg. *A.* IV. 354 *puer Ascanius capitisque iniuria cari.* — **praecipe**: *i.e.* start the strain, so that the poet may sing with her voice to guide and sustain him.

3. **Melpomene**: the muse of tragedy; but see 12. 2 n. — **liquidam**: *i.e.* clear and smoothly flowing. — **pater**: *i.e.* Jupiter. The muses were daughters of Zeus and Mnemosyne (Hes. *Theog.* 52).

Ergo Quintilium perpetuus sopor
urget! Cui Pudor et Iustitiae soror,
incorrupta Fides, nudaque Veritas
quando ullum inveniet parem?

Multis ille bonis flebilis occidit,
nulli flebilior quam tibi, Vergili;
tu frustra pius heu non ita creditum
poscis Quintilium deos.

Quid si Threicio blandius Orpheo
auditam moderere arboribus fidem?
Num vanae redeat sanguis imagini,
quam virga semel horrida,

5. **ergo,** *and so;* an expression of reluctant conviction and resignation; cf. *S.* II. 5. 101 *ergo nunc Dama sodalis nusquam est.*

6. **urget,** *holds in its embrace;* cf. *premet,* 4. 16 n. — **cui**: dative with **parem,** vs. 8. — **Pudor,** etc.: personified not simply as qualities of the man, but in the abstract, as in *C. S.* 57 *sq.* Judged by the standard of these personified virtues Quintilius was a rare type of man, — unassuming, absolutely just, sincere, and candid. — **soror**: *i.e.* the constant companion, implying that *Iustitia* also dwelt with Quintilius. Cf. Cic. *Off.* I. 23 *fundamentum autem iustitiae est fides, id est dictorum conventorumque constantia et veritas.*

7. **incorrupta Fides**; the epithet is included in the personification. See note on *fidem* 5. 5, and cf. *rara Fides,* 35. 21, *vitiosa Cura,* II. 16. 21, *Pudor priscus, C. S.* 57.

9. **ille flebilis occidit,** *his death was cause for tears.* See II. 14. 6 n.

11. **frustra pius,** *with vain piety;* cf. Cat. 76. 26 *o di reddite mi hoc pro pietate mea,* and see note on *poscit,* 31. 1. — **non ita creditum**: sc. *illis a te.* The meaning is that Vergil, in his anxiety for his sick friend, had piously commended him to the keeping of the gods, but **non ita,** — not that they should never give him back.

13. **quid si,** etc.: the thought gently suggested in *frustra,* vs. 11, is now further developed, and forms the transition from the sympathetic tone with which the poem opens to the exhortation to firmness with which it closes. — **Threicio,** etc.: see 12. 7 *sqq.* — **blandius**: cf. 12. 11 n.

14. **arboribus**: Intr. 54.

15. **vanae imagini,** *to the empty form.* The ancient conception of the dead in the underworld was very similar to the modern idea of ghosts, — not disembodied spirits, but disembodied forms, which were intangible, but retained, along with the spirit, enough of their material quality to be seen and heard, — *tenuis sine corpore vitas, cava sub imagine formae* (Verg. *A.* VI. 292 *sq.*) For the dative see Intr. 53. —

non lenis precibus fata recludere,
nigro compulerit Mercurius gregi?
Durum: sed levius fit patientia
quicquid corrigere est nefas.

## XXV.

Parcius iunctas quatiunt fenestras
iactibus crebris iuvenes protervi,
nec tibi somnos adimunt, amatque
ianua limen,
quae prius multum facilis movebat

**sanguis**: cf. *Odys.* XI. 98, 153, etc., where the dead are revived by drinking blood.

16. **virga**: cf. 10. 18 n.—**semel**, *once* (for all); implying, as often, that the act is decisive and final.

17. **precibus**: with **recludere**, better taken as ablative of cause: because of (*i.e.* in answer to) our prayers. *Recludere* with the dative means to open to those who are to enter, as II. 18, 33, III. 2. 21. —**fata recludere**, *to open the doors of fate*, *i.e.* the doors of the tomb, which fate has closed forever on the departed; cf. Prop. V. 11. 2 *panditur ad nullas ianua nigra preces.* For the infinitive see Intr. 101 *a*.

18. **nigro gregi**: *i.e.* the endless procession passing into the darkness of the underworld. *Niger* is sometimes used like *ater* (see 28. 13 n) as an epithet of death and of things connected with death; cf. IV. 2. 23, IV. 12. 26; Tib. I. 3. 4 *abstineas avidas, mors modo nigra manus; | abstineas mors atra, precor.*—**compulerit**, *has gathered to.*

19. **levius fit patientia**: cf. 11. 3. According to Donatus, Vergil himself was in the habit of commending patience as the most useful of human virtues.

20. **est nefas**, *Heaven forbids us.*

XXV. In this ode Horace portrays, with his usual light touch but with powerful effect, the career of a courtesan,—her short-lived triumph, her waning power, and her inevitable doom of a despised and neglected old age, in which the passions she has fostered remain to torture her.—Metre, 174.

1. **iunctas**, *closed;* cf. the phrase *iungere flumen* (*e.g.* Liv. XXI. 47. 2) for bridging a river. The word is here used with reference to the two wooden shutters with which alone the window-aperture was closed (cf. *bifores fenestras*, Ov. *Pont.* III. 3. 5).

2. **iactibus**: *i.e.* of stones and the like, the windows being as a rule above the ground floor, which was occupied by shops. Cf. III. 7. 29 *domum claude, neque in vias despice.*

3. **amat**: *i.e.* cleaves to, seldom parts from; cf. Verg. *A.* V. 163 *litus ama et laeva stringat sine palmula cautes.*—**-que**: cf. 27. 16 n.

5. **multum**: Intr. 49.

cardines; audis minus et minus iam
'Me tuo longas pereunte noctis,
Lydia, dormis?'

Invicem moechos anus arrogantis
flebis in solo levis angiportu,
Thracio bacchante magis sub inter-
lunia vento,

cum tibi flagrans amor et libido,
quae solet matres furiare equorum,
saeviet circa iecur ulcerosum,
non sine questu,

laeta quod pubes hedera virenti
gaudeat pulla magis atque myrto,
aridas frondis hiemis sodali
dedicet Euro.

7. **me tuo**, etc.: words of a serenade. Hence the plural **noctis**: the lover complains of her persistent indifference. — **tuo**, *your lover;* cf. *tuae*, 15. 32.— **pereunte**, *languishing.*

9. **invicem**, *your turn will come, and;* the arrogance will be on the other side. — **moechos**: no longer the *protervi iuvenes* (vs. 2), the bold admirers and the sighing lovers of the days of your pride; even the most vulgar sort of game will be beyond your reach.

10. **in solo levis angiportu**, *neglected in your lonely alley.* The window and door mentioned above open on an alley which runs along the side and rear of the tenement (*insula*), separating it from other buildings (whence its name). For **levis** cf. *Ep.* II. 3. 423 *levi pro paupere.*

11. **Thracio vento**: Boreas (Aquilo) whose home was in Thrace; cf. *Threicio Aquilone*, *Epod.* 13. 3. — **bacchante magis**, *pursues his wilder revels.* The expression accords with his character as *Thracius;* cf. 18. 9 n. — **sub**: cf. 8. 14. The cold and darkness out of doors enhance the impression of the loneliness of the wretched creature waiting within. — **inter-lunia**: Intr. 174 *b.*

14. **matres equorum**: a paraphrase similar to that of 17. 7. For the force of the comparison cf. Verg. *G.* III. 266.

15. **circa**, *through;* cf. 18. 2 n.— **iecur**: cf. 13. 4 n. Here it is the seat of sensual passion. — **ulcerosum**, *inflamed;* cf. *Ep.* I. 18. 72.

16. **non sine**: cf. 23. 3 n.

17. **virenti . . . pulla**, *fresh . . . dark green;* both epithets applying to each of the two substantives (Intr. 121), and contrasted with **aridas**.

18. **magis** (sc. *quam aridis fron*

## XXVI.

Musis amicus tristitiam et metus
tradam protervis in mare Creticum
portare ventis, quis sub Arcto
rex gelidae metuatur orae,
quid Tiridaten terreat, unice

*dibus*): see Intr. 119 *a*. — **atque**: Intr. 114.

19. **hiemis sodali**: cf. Verg. *G.* II. 339 *hibernis parcebant flatibus Euri*, and, for the expression, 28. 21 and IV. 12. 1.

20. **dedicet**, *consigns*. Cf. 26. 2.

XXVI. In honor of L. Aelius Lamia, one of the two sons of the intimate friend and devoted adherent of Cicero of the same name. (See Cic. *Fam.* XI. 16. 2, *Sest.* 29.) Horace enjoyed the friendship of both brothers. He alludes to the death of one, Quintus, in *Ep.* I. 14. 6. Lucius, whose name is 'enshrined' in this ode, and in 36. 7 and III. 17, is described by Velleius (II. 116. 3) as *vir antiquissimi moris, et priscam gravitatem semper humanitate temperans*. He was consul A.D. 3, and his death *vivida senectute* in A.D. 33 is recorded by Tacitus (*Ann.* VI. 27. 2). He must therefore have been much younger than Horace.

The date of this ode is fixed with considerable certainty by the allusions in vss. 3 *sqq.*, as B.C. 30; that it was one of the earliest odes is implied in *fidibus novis*, vs. 10. — Metre, 176.

1. **amicus**: here used in the sense of *gratus* or *acceptus* (*C.S.* 62), as in *dis amicum carmen*, IV. 6. 41. Cf. II. 17. 2, III. 4. 25 n, and, for the opposite, *dis inimice senex*, *S.* II. 3. 123.

2. **in mare Creticum**: see Intr. 117 *a* and cf. 16. 4.

3. **portare**: Intr. 93. — **quis metuatur**, etc.: depending on **securus, 6.** **quis** is better taken as nominative singular; cf. *quis pudor*, 24. 1. The form *quīs* (= *quibus*) occurs in the Satires and Epodes, but in the Odes this would be the only instance. — **sub Arcto**: *i.e.* in the far north; cf. *subiectos Orientis orae*, 12. 55 n.

4. **rex**: apparently Cotiso, king of the Dacians, whose threatened incursion alarmed the Romans about the time of the war of Actium. He was finally defeated by Crassus; cf. III. 8. 18 n.

5. **Tiridaten**: king of Parthia at the time of the battle of Actium, having headed a successful revolt against Phraates a few years before. In the next year (B.C. 30) the contest was renewed and Tiridates was forced to take refuge in Syria. These verses must have been written before January, B.C. 29, when the news of his flight reached Rome. Subsequently Tiridates succeeded in regaining the throne, and held it till about B.C. 27, when Phraates, with the aid of the Asiatic Scythians, among whom he had taken refuge, finally defeated him and drove him into permanent exile under the protection of Augustus. — **unice securus**, *perfectly unconcerned.*

securus. O quae fontibus integris
gaudes, apricos necte flores,
necte meo Lamiae coronam,
Pimplea dulcis. Nil sine te mei
prosunt honores. Hunc fidibus novis,
hunc Lesbio sacrare plectro
teque tuasque decet sorores.

## XXVII.

Natis in usum laetitiae scyphis
pugnare Thracum est: tollite barbarum
morem, verecundumque Bacchum
sanguineis prohibete rixis.

6. **fontibus integris**: such as Aganippe, Hippocrene, and others less famous; cf. note on *Heliconis*, 12. 5. There is reason to believe that in the oldest Greek conception of them the muses were inspired, spring-haunting nymphs (Preller-Robert, *Gr. Myth.* I. 486). **integris**, however, is no doubt intended, like *novis* 10, to convey the idea of fresh, unhackneyed poetry, and is perhaps a reminiscence of Lucr. I. 927.

7. **apricos**, *sunny; i.e.* the bright, gaily-colored ones which seem to carry with them the sunshine in which they bloom; cf. Intr. 124.—**necte flores, necte**, etc.: a graceful way of saying *necte floribus coronam.* The meaning is not 'make Lamia a poet,' but 'distinguish him in song.' Of course, the ode itself, commending him to the muses as worthy, serves that end.

9. **Pimplea**, *nymph of Pimplea.* The latter was a spring in Pieria, on the slope of Olympus, sacred to the muses; see note on *Haemo* 12. 6.—**mei**: *i.e.* those that I confer, the possessive pronoun here representing the subjective genitive. More commonly it retains its possessive force, as 6. 11 *laudes tuas.*

10. **fidibus novis**: *i.e.* in a new kind of poetry, explained by **Lesbio plectro** in the next verse; cf. *Lesboum barbiton*, 1. 34 n.

11. **sacrare**, *to enshrine, to immortalize;* to set his name in verse, as an offering is placed in a a temple to be preserved forever.—**plectro**: a small stick of ivory or other substance for striking the strings of the lyre (πλῆκτρον; cf. πλήσσω). The player held it in one hand, playing with the fingers of the other.

XXVII. A convivial scene, dramatically portrayed, though there is but one speaker. The poet finds his friends in hot dispute over their wine; offense has been given, and from angry words they have come to the verge of blows,

Vino et lucernis Medus acinaces
immane quantum discrepat: impium
lenite clamorem, sodales,
et cubito remanete presso.

Voltis severi me quoque sumere
partem Falerni? Dicat Opuntiae

when he checks them with the sharp rebuke with which the poem opens. They laugh, and for answer put a goblet into his hand. Having thus secured their attention, he proceeds to play a little comedy before them with one of the younger members of the party, in watching which they forget at once their quarrel and his reproof.

Though the wine is Falerian, the Greek origin of the sketch is hardly disguised. Porphyrio says that the poem was taken in substance from Anacreon, referring perhaps to this fragment (63):

*Ἄγε δηὖτε μηκέθ' οὕτω*
*πατάγῳ τε κἀλαλήτῳ*
*Σκυθικὴν πόσιν παρ' οἴνῳ*
*μελετῶμεν, ἀλλὰ καλοῖς*
*ὑποπίνοντες ἐν ὕμνοις.*

—Metre, 176.

1. **natis**: *i.e.* designed from the very beginning of their existence. —**in usum laetitiae,** *to promote joy and gladness*—**scyphis**: a large, two-handled cup of wood, earthenware, or metal. Its size would make it a very effective weapon.

2. **Thracum est**: Thracian drunkenness was proverbial; cf. 18. 9 n. —**tollite,** *away with!*

3. **verecundum,** *modest.* The epithet (cf. *modici*, 18. 7 n.) is used to indicate the quality which the god approves in his worshippers.

4. **prohibete,** *keep ... free from;* cf. *Ep.* I. 1. 31 *corpus prohibere cheragra.* For the sense cf. 17. 22 *sqq.*

5. **vino et lucernis**: Intr. 57. —**Medus**: cf. 2. 22 n. —**acinaces**: a short sword or dagger worn at the belt in front of the right thigh. Such a weapon would never be seen at a Roman convivium. Horace found it no doubt in his Greek original, and retained it to continue the idea of *barbarum morem*, 2.

6. **immane quantum discrepat,** *is a monstrous anomaly amid,* etc. The phrase **immane quantum** (like *nescio quis* = *aliquis*) has lost its interrogative character, and hence takes the indicative; cf. Liv. II. 1. 11 *id mirum quantum profuit ad concordiam.* —**impium** renewing the thought already suggested in *verecundum Bacchum*, 3.

8. **cubito presso**: *i.e.* on the cushions of the couches. The Greeks as well as the Romans reclined at table.

9. **severi,** *strong.* There were two kinds of Falernian wine, one harsh and tart (*austerum*, *αὐστηρός*), the other sweet (*γλυκάζων*); Athen. I. 26 c.

10. **Falerni**: the only strictly Italian feature which Horace has added to the poem. —**dicat,** *must tell us; i.e.* that we may drink her health. There was nothing extraordinary in the demand: on being asked to take a cup with the rest, he calls for a toast. —**Opuntiae**: from Opus in Locris, near the Euboean gulf.

frater Megillae quo beatus
volnere, qua pereat sagitta.

Cessat voluntas? Non alia bibam
mercede. Quae te cumque domat Venus,
non erubescendis adurit
ignibus, ingenuoque semper

amore peccas. Quicquid habes, age
depone tutis auribus. — A miser,
quanta laborabas Charybdi,
digne puer meliore flamma!

11. **frater Megillae**: a humorous variation on such honorary designations as *filius Thetidis*, 8. 14, *nepos Veneris*, Verg. *A*. IV. 163, etc.; substituted for the lad's own name, it implies, of course, that his chief recommendation to the present company is his handsome sister. — **beatus pereat**: Intr. 120.

12. **pereat**: of love, as in 25. 7, and frequently in the poets.

13. **cessat voluntas**, *does inclination falter?*

14. **mercede**, *terms*. — **cumque**: cf. 6. 3 n. — **Venus**, *love*, in a personal sense; cf. Verg. *E*. 3. 68 *parta meae Veneri sunt munera*.

15. **non**: with **erubescendis**, for which see Intr. 51 *a*.

16. **ingenuo semper**, etc., *your weakness is never for a lowborn love*. — **-que**: Horace often uses *-que* or *et* after a clause containing a negative, when the latter is closely connected with a particular word, so that the clause as a whole is felt to be affirmative; cf. 28. 34, II. 20. 4, III. 30. 6, *Epod*. 15. 14.

17. **amore**: used of a person, like *Venus*, 14. For the case, see Intr. 72. — **quicquid habes**, etc.: he urges the lad to whisper the name in his ear, if he will not tell it to all.

18. **auribus**: Intr. 69. — **a miser**: his exclamation on hearing (or pretending to hear) the name. His expectation of an *ingenuus amor* is disappointed.

19. **laborabas**, *you are struggling*; cf. 9. 3 n. The imperfect is in keeping with the humorous outburst of horror and pity. It refers to the time, just before, when he was urging the lad to confess, all unconscious of the dreadful fact now revealed; cf. Ter. *Phor*. 857 *oh, tu quoque aderas?* — **Charybdi**: expressing the insatiable rapacity of the woman; cf. Cic. *Phil*. 2. 67 *quae Charybdis tam vorax?* The comparison of this class of persons to all sorts of monsters, Chimaeras, Hydras, Scylla, Sphinx, etc., appears to have been not uncommon (Athenaeus, XIII. 558 a).

20. **flamma**: returning to the figure of vss. 15 *sq*.

21. **solvere . . . poterit**: cf. *beatus pereat*, 11 n. — **Thessalis**: Thessaly was notorious for magic and necromancy; cf. *Epod*. 5. 45, *Ep*. II. 2. 209.

Quae saga, quis te solvere Thessalis
magus venenis, quis poterit deus?
Vix inligatum te triformi
Pegasus expediet Chimaera.

## XXVIII.

Te maris et terrae numeroque carentis harenae
mensorem cohibent, Archyta,

22. **venenis**, *drugs*, used to produce magical influences on the mind; cf. *S.* I. 8. 19 *carminibus quae versant atque venenis* | *humanos animos; Epod.* 5. 87. — **deus**: observe the climax, **saga, magus, deus**.

23. **inligatum**: *i.e.* in the coils and limbs of the monster. — **triformi**: in front a lion, behind a dragon, in the middle a goat; cf. Lucr. V. 905; *Il.* VI. 181.

24. **Pegasus**: the meaning is: even with the aid of the winged horse on which Bellerophon rode when he destroyed the original Chimaera you will not escape. — **Chimaera**: cf. *Charybdi*, 19 n.

XXVIII. This ode, like the last, is a dramatic presentation, the details of which, however, are obscure. Whether the poem is a dialogue or a monologue; if the former, how it is to be divided; who the speaker or speakers are, — these are questions which have always puzzled scholars and on which they are not yet agreed. The effort, however, to arrange the ode as a dialogue may be said to have failed. According to Porphyrio, the ode is a monologue in the mouth of Archytas, whose shipwrecked body lies on the seashore. In the opening verses he apostrophizes himself, contrasting his former world-embracing range of thought with his present low estate, and reflecting on the vanity of all human achievement in the presence of the universal destroyer. He then appeals to a passing sailor for the three handfuls of dust which constituted due burial. The first part of this interpretation is difficult to accept. The language of vss. 1–20 is hardly natural in the mouth of Archytas, and the view is much more probable which attributes the monologue to a shipwrecked man whose body has been cast ashore close to the tomb of Archytas, the sight of which suggests the reflections of the opening lines. — Metre, 162.

1. **numero carentis**, *countless*. — **harenae**: referring perhaps to a discussion of the subject in the lost works of Archytas.

2. **cohibent**, *holds*, *confines*. — **Archyta**: a statesman and general of Tarentum (about 400–360 B.C.), and a philosopher of such eminence that his instruction and friendship were sought by Plato. As a Pythagorean, Archytas directed his studies to the solution, by mathematical methods, of the problems of the physical universe.

pulveris exigui prope litus parva Matinum
munera, nec quicquam tibi prodest
aerias temptasse domos animoque rotundum
percurrisse polum morituro.
Occidit et Pelopis genitor, conviva deorum,
Tithonusque remotus in auras,
et Iovis arcanis Minos admissus, habentque

3. **pulveris exigui parva munera,** *the poor boon of a handful of dust; i.e.* the 'few feet of earth' which enclose his bones, called **munera,** the last offering of affection or pity, to enhance the idea of his present helpless dependence. We have here the familiar contrast between man's unbounded ambition and the 'narrow house' to which death consigns him. Cf. Juvenal 10. 168 *sqq.* For the plural **munera** see Intr. 128. (Those who accept Porphyrio's interpretation of the ode are obliged to assume that the body of Archytas lies unburied on the shore (see vss. 23 *sqq.*), and to take **munera . . . cohibent** as meaning 'the gift, etc., holds you here,' *i.e.* is all that prevents you from entering the lower world.) — **litus Matinum**: the shore of the Adriatic near Matinus, which was apparently a mountain (cf. *Matina cacumina, Epod.* 16. 28), and has been placed by geographers on the southern side of the promontory of Garganus, where there is a modern village named Matinata. We are safe in supposing that it was within the region familiar to Horace in his boyhood, and that he had seen the tomb or mound near the shore which tradition assigned to Archytas. For the form **Matinum** see Intr. 65.

5. **aerias domos,** *the mansions of the air,* the spaces where the heavenly bodies (which the Pythagoreans regarded as divinities) dwell. — **temptasse,** *to have explored,* with the idea of boldness in venturing into the region; cf. III. 4. 30 *insanientem navita Bosporum | temptabo.* — **animoque**: Intr. 119 *a.*

6. **morituro**: expressing in a word the reason of **nec quicquam prodest.** For the meaning see Intr. 104 *b.*

7. **occidit et,** *fallen too is.* The main thought is presented first; cf. III. 8. 18, 21. — **Pelopis genitor**: Tantalus, a favorite of Jove until his head was turned by the honor, and his impiety consigned him to the punishment which made his name proverbial. — **conviva deorum,** *though he was a guest,* etc. In like manner **remotus in auras** and **Iovis arcanis admissus** are concessive.

8. **Tithonus**: brother of Priam and husband of Aurora, at whose request he was endowed with immortality, but not with eternal youth (*Hom. Hymn in Ven.* 218 *sqq*). He consequently shrunk away (*longa minuit senectus,* II. 16. 30) until he became a mere voice, like a cicada.— **remotus,** *translated.*— **in auras**: *i.e.* to heaven; cf. *aerias domos,* 5 n.

9. **Iovis arcanis**: the famous laws of Minos were represented by tradition as a revelation from his father, Zeus.

Tartara Panthoiden iterum Orco
demissum, quamvis clipeo Troiana refixo
tempora testatus nihil ultra
nervos atque cutem morti concesserat atrae,
iudice te non sordidus auctor
naturae verique. Sed omnis una manet nox
et calcanda semel via leti.
Dant alios Furiae torvo spectacula Marti,
exitio est avidum mare nautis;
mixta senum ac iuvenum densentur funera; nullum
saeva caput Proserpina fugit.

10. **Tartara**: for the lower world in general. — **Panthoiden**: properly Euphorbus (Πανθοΐδης Εὔφορβος, *Il.* XVI. 808), a Trojan hero, killed in battle by Menelaus (*Il.* XVII. 9 *sqq.*); but the patronymic is here used ironically for Pythagoras. The story was told that the latter, in accordance with his doctrine of metempsychosis, asserted that his own soul had previously inhabited, among others, the body of Euphorbus, and to prove his assertion offered to identify the shield he had carried, which was dedicated among many others in the temple of Hera at Argos. The shield he pointed out, on being taken down (**clipeo refixo**), was found to be inscribed with the name of Euphorbus. — **Orco**: Intr. 53.

11. **quamvis**, etc.: *i.e.* although, since he proved his previous existence in Trojan times, he had in fact given up nothing, etc.

13. **concesserat**: Intr. 83. — **atrae**, *sable;* a standing epithet of death and of things associated with death; cf. *S.* II. 1. 58 *mors atris circumvolat alis;* II. 3. 16, 13. 34, 14. 17, etc.

14. **auctor**, *interpreter, expounder.*

15. **sed omnis**: cutting short the list of examples with a comprehensive statement. — **una**: *i.e.* the same for all.

16. **semel**: *i.e.* there is no return; cf. 24. 16 n. — **via leti**: *i.e.* the one that death opens to man (cf. *fine libidinum* 18. 10 n); a different conception from that of 3. 17, where see note.

17. **alios**, *some*, although there is no second *alius*, a special class of persons (*nautae*) being substituted. — **Furiae**: as inflaming the passions which lead men to fight with one another. — **torvo**, *grim;* his expression as he watches the show. — **spectacula**: a striking comparison, representing war as a sort of gladiatorial contest for the entertainment of Mars; cf. 2. 37 *sqq.*

18. **exitio est**: Gr. 233 *a.*

19. **mixta**, *without distinction.* — **funera**, *the funeral trains.* — **nullum**: emphatic (Intr. 116 *b*), summing up (like *sed omnis*, 15) the fact which the foregoing examples illustrate.

20. **caput**: alluding to the fancy that Proserpina doomed her vic-

Me quoque devexi rapidus comes Orionis
Illyricis Notus obruit undis.
At tu, nauta, vagae ne parce malignus harenae
ossibus et capiti inhumato
particulam dare: sic, quodcumque minabitur Eurus
fluctibus Hesperiis, Venusinae
plectantur silvae te sospite, multaque merces
unde potest tibi defluat aequo
ab Iove Neptunoque sacri custode Tarenti.
Neglegis immeritis nocituram

tim to death by clipping a lock of hair, as the priest did from the head of the victim before the altar; cf. Eurip. *Alc.* 74; Verg. *A.* IV. 698 *nondum illi flavom Proserpina vertice crinem | abstulerat Stygio-que caput damnaverat Orco.* — **Prōserpina**: see Intr. 178. — **fūgit,** *shuns, i.e.* omits, in performing the function referred to. For the tense see Intr. 80.

21. **devexi,** *setting.* The time was early in November, a season of storms, which were attributed as usual to the influence of the constellation; cf. III. 27. 17; *Epod.* 15. 7; Verg. *A.* VII. 719. — **comes**: cf. *veris comites animae,* IV. 12. 1. — **Orionis**: for the prosody and rhythm see Intr. 178, 132.

22. **Illyricis undis**: *i.e.* in the Adriatic. See Intr. 117.— **Notus**: cf. 3. 14 n.

23. **at tu,** etc.: see intr. note. — **vagae**: *i.e.* of no value, and hence a thing it would be niggardly (**malignus**) to withhold. — **ne parce**: Intr. 88.

24. **capiti inhumato**: for the hiatus see Intr. 185.

25. **dare**: Intr. 94 *k.* — **sic**: cf. 3. 1 n. — **quodcumque,** etc.: for the construction cf. *quam rem cumque* 6. 3 n.

26. **fluctibus Hesperiis**: that wash the shores of Italy (*Hesperia,* III. 6. 8 n); here those of the Adriatic (cf. vs. 22).— **Venusinae silvae**: about forty miles inland, but exposed by their elevated situation on the spurs of the Apennines to the fury of the eastern winds.

27. **plectantur,** *suffer the loss.* — **multa merces,** *abundant recompense.*

28. **unde potest** (sc. *defluere*): anticipating **ab Iove Neptunoque.** He can offer no reward from any earthly source. For *unde* with a personal antecedent cf. 12. 17 n.— **aequo,** *approving;* cf. 2. 47 n. Jove would reward him as the god of hospitality and the protector of strangers.

29. **sacri**: *sc.* to Neptune as its patron divinity (**custode**). The mythical founder of Tarentum was Taras (gen. *Tarantos*), a son of Neptune. The sailor is thought of as belonging to Tarentum, and therefore as an object of Neptune's care.

30. **neglegis,** *will you lightly . . . ?* cf. Cat. 30. 5 *facta impia . . . quae tu neglegis,* and see Intr. 95. The sailor has turned away as if not disposed to grant the request. For the tense see Intr. 78.— **nocituram**: Intr. 104 *b.*

postmodo te natis fraudem committere? Fors et
debita iura vicesque superbae
te maneant ipsum: precibus non linquar inultis,
teque piacula nulla resolvent.
Quamquam festinas, non est mora longa: licebit
iniecto ter pulvere curras.

## XXIX.

Icci, beatis nunc Arabum invides

31. **postmodo**: with **nocituram**. — **te natis**, *your children*.— **fraudem**, *a wrong*. To refuse burial was to rob the dead of his just due (cf. *debita iura*, 32). — **fors et**, *may be, as likely as not;* a phrase used where the speaker regards his conjecture as altogether probable, and not a mere guess; cf. Verg. *A*. II. 139, XI. 50, Prop. II. 9. 1, where it is used with the indicative.

32. **debita iura**, etc.: *i.e.* your turn may come to need the service which you now withhold, and to have your righteous demand refused with the same scornful indifference.— **debita iura**, *rights withheld*, referring to the right of the dead to burial. — **vices superbae**, *pitiless retribution*. For the epithet see Intr. 124.

33. **precibus inultis**: *i.e.* without being avenged for the wrong you do me in denying my prayer. — **linquar** (sc. *a te*): *i.e.* in the predicament I am now in; cf. *S*. I. 9. 73 *me sub cultro linquit*, and see Intr. 129.

35. **quamquam festinas**, *you are in haste, I know, but*. — **non est mora longa**: the indicative is similar to that in the phrase *longum est* ('it would be tedious'); Gr. 311 *c*.

36. **iniecto ter pulvere**: to meet the requirements of the gods of the dead, the solemn form of burial in accordance with certain prescribed rules was sufficient; cf. Antigone's burial of her brother, Soph. *Ant*. 429 *sqq*. The number *three* constantly occurs in solemn rites; cf. *C. S*. 23, *Ep*. I. 1. 37; Verg. *A*. VI. 229.

XXIX. Iccius, to whom this ode and *Ep*. I. 12 are addressed, was a man in whom a taste for philosophy was combined with a restless and discontented spirit, which led him to join, with a view to bettering his circumstances, the expedition of Aelius Gallus into Arabia in B.C. 24. Horace banters his friend good-humoredly on his high hopes, and his desertion of philosophy for the pursuit of wealth. The expedition was a disastrous failure, and Iccius was disappointed. In *Ep*. I. 12 (written B.C. 20) we find him in Sicily, the agent in charge of Agrippa's estates there, — a sufficiently good place, it would seem, — but still discontented with his condition.— Metre, 176.

1. **Icci**, *What, Iccius!*— **nunc**: in contrast with his former devotion to philosophy and high thinking. — **invides**, *you are coveting?*

gazis et acrem militiam paras
non ante devictis Sabaeae
regibus horribilique Medo
nectis catenas? Quae tibi virginum
sponso necato barbara serviet?
Puer quis ex aula capillis
ad cyathum statuetur unctis,
doctus sagittas tendere Sericas
arcu paterno? Quis neget arduis
pronos relabi posse rivos
montibus et Tiberim reverti,

2. **gazis**: appropriate here, as an oriental (Persian) word. — **acrem militiam**, *a vigorous campaign.*

3. **Sabaeae**, *of Sheba*, the western portion of southern Arabia, famous for its wealth in spices and gold and precious stones (Plin. *N. H.* VI. 161; *O. T. Kings* I. 10.

4. **Medo**: see 2. 22 n. There is no probability that any operations against the Parthians were actually contemplated in connection with this expedition, but no doubt at Rome the most extravagant expectations were entertained in regard to it.

5. **nectis catenas**: implying full assurance of victory. — **quae virginum**: Intr. 63.

6. **sponso necato**: *sc.* by Iccius, who thereby obtains the *sponsa* as his prize; cf. the picture of the young Roman warrior in battle, III. 2. 6 *sqq.*

7. **puer ex aula**, *royal page;* see Madv. 298. 2.

8. **ad cyathum statuetur**: *i.e.* will be appointed to serve you and your guests with wine, dipping it from the *cratera* with the ladle-like *cyathus* and pouring it into the goblets.

9. **doctus**, etc.: the lad whom Iccius is to bring home from the palace of some Arab king, is a captive from the far East, where he had been trained for no such menial service. The possession of such a rare slave as a cup-bearer was a fashionable luxury of the day (*S.* II. 8. 14 *sq.;* cf. Juv. 5. 56), but naturally a very costly one, and marks Iccius as a great nabob. — **tendere**, *to speed;* lit. to direct towards a goal; cf. Verg. *A.* V. 508 *pariterque oculos telumque tetendit;* IX. 606 *spicula tendere cornu;* V. 489. For the mood see Intr. 101 *c.* — **Sericas**: see 12. 56 n. This epithet, in connection with **paterno**, serves to indicate the nationality of the boy (Intr. 124).

11. **pronos**: *i.e.* according to their nature, to which the supposed reversal of their course would do violence; and this is the point of the comparison.

12. **montibus**, *up the mountains;* abl. of the way by which. Others regard it as dat. (Intr. 53); but in that case **arduis** would be an idle epithet. — **reverti**, *reverse his course.*

cum tu coemptos undique nobilis
libros Panaeti Socraticam et domum
mutare loricis Hiberis,
pollicitus meliora, tendis?

## XXX.

O Venus, regina Cnidi Paphique,
sperne dilectam Cypron et vocantis
ture te multo Glycerae decoram
transfer in aedem.

Fervidus tecum puer et solutis

13. **coemptos undique,** *after buying up from every quarter,* indicating the zeal with which Iccius had pursued the studies he now abandons. — **nobilis**: better taken as accusative plural; that he could sacrifice such books shows the completeness of his apostasy.

14. **Panaeti**: a Stoic philosopher of Rhodes, who came to Rome about 156 B.C. and lived for many years on terms of great intimacy with Scipio Aemilianus and Laelius. — **domum,** *school* (cf. *lare, Ep.* I. 1. 13); *i.e.* the disciples of Socrates who recorded the teachings of their master, especially Plato, Xenophon and Aeschines. The authors here, of course, by a familiar figure of speech, stand for their works.

15. **mutare**: *i.e.* to sell; Intr. 74. — **Hiberis**: Intr. 65. Spanish steel was famous in ancient as in modern times (Plin. *N.H.* XXXIV. 144, 149).

16. **tendis,** *are bent upon.*

XXX. A hymn to Venus, imploring the goddess to bestow her favor on Glycera. In all probability a study from the Greek. — Metre, 174.

1. **regina Cnidi Paphique**: cf. 3. 1; Pind. *Fr.* 99 δέσποινα Κύπρου. Cnidus was a city in Caria, where Venus had three temples. In one of these was the famous statue of the goddess by Praxiteles, of which the Venus of the Vatican is a copy. Paphos, in Cyprus, was a very old seat of the worship of Venus (*Odys.* VIII. 363) at the spot where she was said to have come ashore on rising out of the sea; cf. Verg. *A.* I. 415. Her rites are described by Tac. *Hist.* II. 3.

2. **sperne,** *slight, forsake;* cf. *deseruit,* 19. 10.

4. **aedem**: here a private chapel (*sacrarium*) in the girl's own lodgings. The meaning is 'Be ever present to answer her prayers,' which of course were for the enhancement and perpetuation of her own charms.

5. **puer**: Cupid.—**solutis zonis**: cf. Sen. *Ben.* I. 3. 2 *tres Gratiae, sorores, manibus implexis, ridentes et virgines, solutaque ac pellucida veste.*

Gratiae zonis properentque Nymphae
et parum comis sine te Iuventas
Mercuriusque.

## XXXI.

Quid dedicatum poscit Apollinem
vates? Quid orat de patera novum
fundens liquorem? Non opimae
Sardiniae segetes feracis,
non aestuosae grata Calabriae

6. **Gratiae, Nymphae**: cf. 4. 6. — **properentque**: Intr. 119 *b*.

7. **parum comis**: *i.e.* headstrong and impatient, the unsoftened temper that belongs to the confidence of youth. The description is no doubt Horace's own; only a Roman could treat Iuventas in the retinue of Venus as a personified abstraction. — **Iuventas**: Ἥβη; cf. *Hom. Hymn. in Apol.* quoted at 4. 5 n.

8. **Mercurius**: the worship of Hermes was associated, in many places in Greece, with that of Aphrodite (Preller-Robert, *Gr. Myth.* I. 387). In Horace's mind, however, it is perhaps as the *facundus deus* (cf. 10. 1) that he has a place in her retinue.

XXXI. The poet's prayer. The dedication of the temple of Apollo on the Palatine, October 9, B.C. 28, was an event of great interest in Roman literary circles; for with the temple was united a public library (cf. *Ep.* I. 3. 17, II. 1. 216 *sq.*). Horace records his reflections on the occasion in this fine ode, in which, against a background of the various forms of wealth which the multitude crave, he formulates his own simple prayer for the few needs of a happy life. The closing verses of Epode 1 were written in a somewhat similar strain. — Metre, 176.

1. **dedicatum**, *enshrined*. For this use of the word, applied to the divinity instead of the shrine, cf. Cic. *D. N.* II. 61, Ov. *F.* VI. 637. — **poscit**: notice the tense, which is to be taken strictly: 'what *does* (not what *shall*) he demand.' As to the word itself, we must remember that the Roman idea of the relation between gods and men was that of mutual obligation. On the erection of a splendid temple the people would feel that they could *claim* some boon of the god in return; cf. 24. 12, III. 29. 59 n.

2. **patera**: see 19. 15 n. — **novum liquorem**: *i.e.* wine of the vintage just gathered. The time was late autumn.

4. **Sardiniae**: one of the great sources of the grain supply of Rome. — **segetes**, *grain lands*. For this use of *seges*, cf. *Ep.* II. 2. 161, Verg. *G.* I. 47.

5. **aestuosae**: cf. 22. 5 n. — **grata**: *i.e.* a pleasing sight. — **Calabriae**: an excellent grazing country, except in the hot season when the

armenta, non aurum aut ebur Indicum,
non rura quae Liris quieta
mordet aqua taciturnus amnis.

Premant Calena falce quibus dedit
Fortuna vitem, dives et aureis
mercator exsiccet culillis
vina Syra reparata merce,

dis carus ipsis, quippe ter et quater
anno revisens aequor Atlanticum
impune: me pascunt olivae,
me cichorea levesque malvae.

flocks were driven over into the mountains of Lucania and Sabinum; cf. *Epod.* 1. 27 *sq.*

6. **ebur**: very costly; cf. Plin. *N. H.* VIII. 31 *dentibus* (tusks) *ingens pretium.* It was used for household decorations.

8. **mordet**: cf. *lambit*, 22. 8. — **taciturnus**: cf. *loquaces lymphae*, III. 13. 15.

9. **premant Calena**, etc.: with a change of form the poet continues the catalogue of objects of desire which he does not covet.—**premant**, *prune;* lit. keep back, check luxuriant growth; cf. Verg. *G.* I. 157 *ruris opaci falce premes umbras.* — **Calena falce**: cf. 20. 9 n; Intr. 124. — **quibus dedit**: sc. *eam premere* (Intr. 97 *d*); *i.e.* 'to whom Fortune has given the control of rich vineyards,' which those of Cales here typify (Intr. 117 *a*).

11. **mercator**: see 1. 16 n. — **exsiccet**, *drain.* — **culillis**: properly a kind of earthenware cup used by the pontifices and vestals in religious rites. Here and *Ep.* II. 3. 434 the name is used for drinking cups of a richer sort.

12. **Syrā**: *i.e.* brought from the ports of Syria, especially Antioch, which had become the chief emporium for the merchandise of Arabia and the far East. — **reparata**, *purchased.* From its meaning, 'to get' (cf. 17 n.) *parare* with the prefix *re-* (see 3. 7 n.) denotes 'to get *back*' in return for something given. The construction is similar to that of *mutare* in 17. 2. The two pictures of this strophe are designed to go together, — the vine grower living quietly at home in oriental luxury, the more restless trader roving the seas according to his bent (cf. 1. 17) and enjoying the best that life affords. The impression of such enviable happiness is further heightened by the exclamation that follows, in order to point the contrast with the poet's own simple fare and simple wants.

13. **quippe revisens**: equivalent to *quippe qui revisat*, the reason for saying **dis carus**.

14. **anno**: *i.e.* between the opening of navigation in the spring (cf. 4. 2) and its close at the approach of winter.

15. **impune**: Intr. 116 *b.* — **me pascunt**, *my fare is;* cf. 1. 29 n.

16. **leves**: *i.e.* easily digested; cf.

Frui paratis et valido mihi,
Latoe, dones et, precor, integra
cum mente nec turpem senectam
degere nec cithara carentem.

## XXXII.

Poscimur. Si quid vacui sub umbra
lusimus tecum, quod et hunc in annum
vivat et pluris, age dic Latinum,
barbite, carmen,

*Epod.* 2. 57 *gravi malvae salubres corpori.*

17. **paratis,** *what I possess;* cf. *Ep.* II. 2. 196 *plura parare labores.* — **et valido,** etc.: the construction is as follows: **et . . . et** connect the two infinitives **frui, degere,** which depend upon **dones** (Intr. 97 *d*), while **nec . . . nec,** which are subordinate to the second **et,** connect **turpem** and **cithara carentem; precor** is parenthetical. For this use of **et . . . nec . . . nec** cf. Cic. *C. M.* 7 *moderati et nec difficiles nec inhumani senes.* For the purport of the prayer cf. Juv. 10. 356 *orandum est ut sit mens sana in corpore sano.* — **valido mihi,** *that I in good health may.*

18. **Latoe:** formed after the Greek Λατῷος, from Λάτω (Attic Λήτω), Latona; cf. 21. 3. For the form cf. *Semeleius,* 17. 22 n. — **integra cum mente:** thought of in closer connection with old age, as **valido** with bodily comfort (**frui paratis**); health and strength may fail with years, but the failure of the mental faculties makes a **turpem senectam.**

20. **cithara carentem:** *i.e.* robbed of the poetic gift.

XXXII. The poet to his lyre. The ode appears to be a prelude to another or to other compositions (as IV. 6 is to the *Carmen Saeculare*), but to which, it would be fruitless to inquire. The lyre is addressed as the lyre of Alcaeus, on which the poet has already played lighter strains (*lusimus sub umbra*) not without success. As the song he now calls for is characterized in no other way than as *Latinum carmen,* it is probable that the 'lighter strains' are his studies from the Greek, many of which are preserved, especially in this book, and this ode preludes his undertaking in compliance with the demand of his friends (*poscimur*), more serious and original lyric composition on strictly Roman subjects, — such odes as I. 2, etc., and the majority of those in the following books. — Metre, 174.

1. **poscimur** (sc. *carmen*): the construction is the passive of that of 24. 12 and 31. 1; cf. Ov. *M.* V. 333 *poscimur, Aonides; F.* IV. 721 *Parilia poscor.* — **si quid,** etc., *if ever . . . I have sung with thee in lighter mood some strain that,* etc.; cf. IV. 9. 9; *S.* I. 10. 37

Lesbio primum modulate civi,
qui ferox bello tamen inter arma,
sive iactatam religarat udo
litore navim,

Liberum et Musas Veneremque et illi
semper haerentem puerum canebat
et Lycum nigris oculis nigroque
crine decorum.

O decus Phoebi et dapibus supremi
grata testudo Iovis, o laborum
dulce lenimen, mihi cumque salve
rite vocanti!

*haec ego ludo.* — **sub umbra**: cf. 5. 3 n.

2. **hunc in annum,** *this year;* cf. such phrases as *in praesens, in tempus,* etc.

3. **dic**: see 6. 5 n.

5. **Lesbio civi**: Alcaeus (Intr. 26); **civi,** to recall his prominence in the political struggles of his time; cf. 2. 21 n. For the case see Intr. 55. — **primum modulate**: *i.e.* not the lyre in general, but as used by Alcaeus, the great master of the type of lyric poetry which Horace aspired to write.

6. **inter arma, sive,** etc.: *i.e.* in the midst of war or in exile (danger and excitement or adversity and discouragement).

7. **sive**: Intr. 119 *d.*

8. **litore**: Intr. 71.

10. **puerum**: cf. 30. 5 n.

11. **Lycum**: a favorite boy. — **nigris . . . nigro**: notice the variation of prosody. The same description occurs *Ep.* II. 3. 37.

13. **dapibus**: probably dative, though we say *at.*—**supremi Iovis**: cf. 21. 3.

14. **testudo**: see 10. 6 n. — **laborum,** *in trouble.*

15. **mihi salve,** *accept my greeting, i.e.* hear my call. — **mihi** is ethical dat. with **salve** (which in form is a command; cf. *iubeo te salvere,* etc.), expressing technically the person who is interested in having the command fulfilled, *i.e.* the person from whom the greeting proceeds; cf. Verg. *A.* XI. 97 *salve aeternum mihi, maxime Palla, aeternumque vale.* — **cumque vocanti,** *whenever I call. Cumque* does not occur elsewhere except as a suffix to a relative pronoun or adverb. It is supposed by some to be an archaic form, corresponding to *quandoque* = *quandocumque* (IV. 1. 17 n), *quique* = *quicumque* (*e.g.* Plaut. *Men.* 571); or it may be a bold use of the detachable suffix *cumque* (='ever'), the relative notion to which it belongs being implied in the participle, so that **mihi cumque vocanti**=*mihi quandocumque vocabo;* cf. *quippe revisens* = *quippe qui revisat,* 31. 13 n.

## XXXIII.

Albi, ne doleas plus nimio memor
immitis Glycerae, neu miserabilis
decantes elegos, cur tibi iunior
  laesa praeniteat fide.

Insignem tenui fronte Lycorida
Cyri torret amor, Cyrus in asperam
declinat Pholoen; sed prius Apulis
  iungentur capreae lupis

quam turpi Pholoe peccet adultero.

XXXIII. To the elegiac poet Albius Tibullus, who, at least in his later years (he died in the same year with Vergil, B.C. 19), was on friendly terms with Horace. The latter does not mention him in the Satires, but *Ep.* I. 4 is addressed to him, and shows, as does the present ode, a certain degree of intimacy between the two men. The character of Tibullus here represented is quite in keeping with his portrayal of himself in his elegies, but the name Glycera does not occur in any of his extant poems. — Metre, 172.

1. **ne doleas**: Intr. 87. — **plus nimio**, *overmuch;* see 18. 15 n; to be taken with **doleas**.

3. **decantes**, *keep droning;* cf. *Ep.* I. 1. 62 *puerorum nenia Curiis et decantata Camillis.* — **elegos**: poems in elegiac verse, the unit of which is a couplet consisting of a dactylic hexameter and a 'pentameter' (*versibus impariter iunctis, Ep.* II. 3. 75). It became in the Alexandrine period the verse of sentimental love, and in this use was successfully cultivated by Tibullus and other Augustan poets. — **cur**, etc.: cf. *Ep.* I. 8. 9 *irascar amicis, cur me funesto properent arcere veterno;* Cic. *Att.* III. 13. 2 *me saepe accusas cur hunc meum casum tam graviter feram.* This use of *cur* (*quor, qua re*) is probably a survival of an original relative use after *causa* and the like; cf. 16. 19 *causae cur perirent* and our 'the reason why.' — **iunior**: Tibullus was born about 55 B.C., and may have been 30 when this ode was written.

4. **laesa fide**, *her plighted faith is broken and.* — **praeniteat**, *outshines* (sc. *ei*, 'in her eyes'; cf. 5. 13 *quibus nites*).

5. **tenui fronte**: a low forehead was greatly admired by the Romans; cf. *Ep.* I. 7. 26; Mart. IV. 42. 9. — **Lycorida, Cyri**: these and the following are probably fictitious persons as well as names.

6. **Cyri** (objective gen.) **torret amor**: cf. III. 19. 28. — **asperam**, *waspish.*

7. **declinat**: *sc.* from Lycoris.

8. **lupis**: Intr. 56.

9. **turpi**, *ugly*, in contrast with the pretty Lycoris; cf. *imparis formas*, 10. — **peccet**, cf. 27. 16 n; Intr. 72. — **adultero**, *paramour.*

Sic visum Veneri, cui placet imparis
formas atque animos sub iuga aenea
saevo mittere cum ioco.

Ipsum me melior cum peteret Venus,
grata detinuit compede Myrtale
libertina, fretis acrior Hadriae
curvantis Calabros sinus.

## XXXIV.

Parcus deorum cultor et infrequens,
insanientis dum sapientiae
consultus erro, nunc retrorsum
vela dare atque iterare cursus

10. **sic visum,** *such is the will of.* Cf. 12. 31 n; Verg. *A.* II. 428 *dis aliter visum.*

11. **aenea**: *i.e.* that cannot be broken; there is no escape for her victims. Cf. III. 9. 18.

12. **saevo ioco,** *with grim humor.*

13. **melior Venus**: *i.e.* a woman of higher social position than a *libertina.* For *Venus* cf. 27. 14 n.

14. **grata detinuit compede,** *I lingered, a willing captive, in the fetters of;* cf. IV. 11. 23 *sq.* *Compede* also occurs *Epod.* 4. 4, *Ep.* I. 3. 3; the plural *compedibus* only *Ep.* I. 16. 77. The singular is not found in any author before Horace. — **Myrtale**: a common name of *libertinae.*

15. **fretis acrior Hadriae**: concessive; a further reason why he should have followed the dictates of his good sense. Cf. III. 9. 23.

16. **curvantis,** *when it hollows out; i.e.* in time of storm, the force of which changes the outline of a sandy shore like that of Calabria; cf. Verg. *A.* III. 533 *portus ab Euroo fluctu curvatus in arcum.* — **sinus,** *bays.* The acc. expresses the effect of the action (Lane's Gr. 1135).

XXXIV. For the occasion and subject of this ode see Intr. 8, and cf. *S.* I. 5. 101 *sqq.;* Lucr. VI. 400 *denique cur numquam caelo iacit undique puro | Iuppiter in terras fulmen sonitusque profundit?* The place of the ode in the collection was no doubt determined by the closing sentence, which prepares the reader for the more elaborate portrayal of the attributes of Fortuna in the next ode. — Metre, 176.

1. **parcus et infrequens**: *i.e.* coming seldom to the altar and bringing scanty offerings, at that. The time referred to is past (*I who was,* etc.), as is indicated by the contrasted *nunc,* 3.

2. **insanientis sapientiae**: oxymoron.

3. **consultus,** *an adept in;* see Intr. 66 *b.* — **erro,** *I strayed from the truth.* Gr. 276 *e.*

4. **iterare,** *to traverse again;* cf. 7. 32. — **cursus**: see Intr. 128.

cogor relictos. Namque Diespiter,
igni corusco nubila dividens
plerumque, per purum tonantis
egit equos volucremque currum,
quo bruta tellus et vaga flumina,
quo Styx et invisi horrida Taenari
sedes Atlanteusque finis
concutitur. Valet ima summis

5. **Diespiter**: see 1. 25 n.

6. **nubila dividens plerumque,** *who commonly cleaves the clouds.* For the emphasis on **plerumque** see Intr. 116 *b*, and cf. 3. 12, 31. 2.

7. **per purum,** *across the clear sky.* — **tonantis egit equos,** etc.: the phenomenon described is that of thunder rumbling overhead and passing away in the distance. The two epithets are not to be taken strictly with their substantives, but are designed to give an impression of the whole phenomenon, — the god in his car, with flying steeds, thundering across the sky; see Intr. 121.

9. **quo,** *that car by which;* passing from the special incident to a general description.—**bruta,** *heavy, sluggish* (cf. *terram inertem,* III. 4. 45); in contrast with **vaga.**

10. **invisi,** *repulsive;* a frequent epithet of things connected with death; cf. II. 14. 23 *invisas cupressos;* Verg. *A.* VIII. 245 *regna pallida, dis invisa;* Sen. *Herc. Fur.* 664 *Ditis invisi domus.* — **Taenari**: the southern point of the Peloponnesus (Cape Matapan), where, under a temple of Poseidon, tradition placed one of the entrances of the lower world (cf. Verg. *G.* IV. 467 *Taenarias fauces, alta ostia Ditis*); here used, like *Avernus,* for the lower world itself. For the case see Intr. 65.

11. **Atlanteus finis**: the end of the earth, where Atlas supports the sky on his shoulders; cf. *τερμόνων Ἀτλαντικῶν εἴσω,* Eurip. *Hippol.* 3.

12. **valet,** etc.: the power of the supreme god is also manifested in the astonishing vicissitudes of fortune in human experience. — **ima summis mutare,** *to reverse high and low.* The neuter of the adjectives is used abstractly, comprehending both persons and things (cf. *Ep.* I. 9. 4 *legentis honesta Neronis;* II. 2. 178 *metit Orcus grandia cum parvis*). The plural is that of repeated occurrence. The ambiguity in the construction of the cases with *mutare* (Intr. 74) here has its natural application, both objects having the same relation to the subject, who neither gives nor receives, but puts each in place of the other. For the mood see Intr. 94 *n.*

13. **insignem,** etc.: repeating in detail the idea just expressed collectively, by indicating the visible effect on each of the two classes mentioned. The presentation is also made more vivid by **insignem,** which brings a person before us, though the abstract recurs in **obscura.** Horace had in mind Hes. *Op.* 6 *ῥεῖα δ' ἀρίζηλον μινύθει καὶ ἄδηλον ἀέξει . . . Ζεὺς ὑψιβρεμέτης.* — **deus**: see 3. 21 n.

mutare et insignem attenuat deus,
obscura promens; hinc apicem rapax
Fortuna cum stridore acuto
sustulit, hic posuisse gaudet.

## XXXV.

O diva, gratum quae regis Antium,
praesens vel imo tollere de gradu

14. **hinc apicem**, etc.: in a moment Fortuna makes or unmakes kings. Fortuna is here obviously the minister of Jove, the *μοῖρα Διός* of Homer (*Il.* XV. 117); cf. Pind. *Ol.* 12. 1 *παῖ Ζηνὸς, Τύχα*, and Paus. VII. 26. 8 *ἐγὼ μὲν οὖν Πινδάρου πείθομαι τῇ ᾠδῇ, Μοιρῶν τε εἶναι μίαν τὴν Τύχην καὶ ὑπὲρ τὰς ἀδελφάς τι ἰσχύειν.* — **apicem**, *the crown, i.e.* kingly power.— **rapax**: not an epithet of Fortuna, but expressing, in place of an adverb, the zest with which she performs this part of her function. The same idea is expressed in the other case by **gaudet**, 16.

15. **stridore**: *sc.* of her wings; cf. III. 29. 53, and Vergil's *stridentibus alis* (*A.* I. 397).

16. **sustulit**: the perfect here expresses the quick completion of the action, and in **posuisse** also the tense appears to retain its proper force; but see Intr. 80, 81.

XXXV. A hymn to Fortuna. The powerful goddess, whose sway is owned alike on sea and land, in every nation and in every calling, whose favor is sought by peasant and king, is implored to preserve Caesar in his contemplated expedition to far-off Britain, and the throng of young Romans who were preparing to invade the East. These allusions show that the ode was written B.C. 27, when Augustus set out from the city *ὡς καὶ ἐς τὴν Βρεττανίαν στρατεύσων*, or in 26, when, though detained in Spain, he still cherished the project until diverted from it by risings there and in the Alps (Dio Cass. LIII. 22. 5, 25. 2). The expedition of Aelius Gallus into Arabia (see intr. note to Ode 29) was in preparation at this time. — Metre, 176.

1. **diva quae regis**: cf. *diva potens Cypri*, 3. 1; *Venus, regina Cnidi Paphique*, 30. 1. The designation of a divinity by a favorite haunt or a famous sanctuary, either with or (as here) instead of the proper name, is common in Greek hymns. — **gratum**: cf. Cic. *Att.* IV. 8A. 1 (speaking of Antium) *nihil quietius, nihil alsius, nihil amoenius.* — **Antium**: the seat of a renowned temple and oracle, which continued to exist to the latest pagan times. There were here two images, *Fortunae Antiates* (see Baumeister, fig. 606 f.), regarded as sisters (*veridicae sorores*, Mart. V. 1. 3), by certain motions of which oracular responses were conveyed. See Preller-Jordan, *Röm. Myth.* II. 192. They were probably consulted in regard to the military expeditions now on foot.

2. **praesens**: equivalent to *po-*

mortale corpus vel superbos
vertere funeribus triumphos:
te pauper ambit sollicita prece
ruris colonus, te dominam aequoris
quicumque Bithyna lacessit
Carpathium pelagus carina;

te Dacus asper, te profugi Scythae
urbesque gentesque et Latium ferox
regumque matres barbarorum et
purpurei metuunt tyranni,

*tens*, because by the 'presence' of a divinity we mean only the manifestation of his power. — **imo gradu**: cf. our 'lowest round of the ladder.'

3. **mortale corpus**, *our perishable clay; i.e.* man in his most helpless state, stripped of all outward show and resources; cf. Liv. XXII. 22. 7 *transfugam nihil aliud quam unum vile atque infame corpus esse ratus.*

4. **vertere**, *to turn . . . into.* It has here the meaning and construction of *mutare* (Intr. 74). — **funeribus triumphos**: both in a literal sense, — the conqueror's march to the Capitol and the march to the grave. The Romans could recall in their own history at least one conspicuous example of each of these vicissitudes of fortune, — the rise of Servius Tullius from slavery to the throne, and the pathetic case of Aemilius Paullus, the conqueror of Macedonia, who lost his two sons at the very time of his triumph (Liv. XLV. 41).

5. **te**: see 10. 9 n. — **ambit**, *courts*, as the Roman candidate courted the favor of the voter (hence *ambitio, ambitus*). — **sollicita**: Intr. 124.

6. **colonus**: a type of humble circumstances, as in II. 14. 12. But the farmer was regarded as especially dependent on the favor of Fortuna (cf. III. 1. 29 *sqq.*); like the mariner, he was at the mercy of the elements. In certain figures of Fortuna (see Baumeister, fig. 605) the goddess is represented with a rudder in one hand (**dominam aequoris**), and in the other a horn of plenty (cf. 17. 14 n). — **te**: sc. *ambit*, the subject of which is the antecedent implied in **quicumque.**

7. **quicumque**, etc.: *i.e.* any mariner; see Intr. 117 *a*, and cf. 1. 13 *sq.* — **Bithyna**: cf. *Pontica*, 14. 11 n. — **lacessit**, *braves;* lit. challenges.

9. **te Dacus**, etc.: **te** carries with it the idea of **ambit** 5, but the strict meaning of the word is lost, as the reader proceeds, in the vaguer notion of a helpless dependence; and without distinctly marking the transition, the poet introduces the idea of fear (**metuunt**), which is only another aspect of the same feeling. — **Dacus**: cf. 26. 4 n. — **profugi**, *nomad;* cf. III. 24. 10.

10. **urbesque**, etc.: *i.e.* collectively, as organized bodies, the cases hitherto presented being those of individual **men**; **the**

iniurioso ne pede proruas
stantem columnam, neu populus frequens
ad arma cessantis ad arma
concitet imperiumque frangat.

Te semper anteit saeva Necessitas,
clavos trabalis et cuneos manu
gestans aena, nec severus
uncus abest liquidumque plumbum.

strongest community is helpless against the power of the goddess. — **Latium**: the Roman state, as in 12. 53.—**ferox,** *dauntless* (against all other adversaries); cf. *Roma ferox*, III. 3. 44.

11. **regumque matres**: the introduction of the more poignant anxieties of woman adds a touch of pathos, as in III. 2. 7; cf. **15.** 34 n. — **barbarorum**: *i.e.* in the East. Under the system of polygamy which prevailed there, the succession of a prince to the throne was often due to the influence or intrigues of his mother, who therefore obtained an importance which she did not ordinarily have elsewhere. The nearest approach to it in Roman history was the case of Livia, the mother of Tiberius.

12. **purpurei** (for *purpurati*), *in scarlet robes*.—**tyranni**: in the proper sense of the word, men who have seized the supreme power (**imperium**), and whose position is therefore the more precarious. This thought is developed in the next strophe into a picture in which the portrayal of the goddess's power is brought to a climax. See also 2. 7 n.

13. **iniurioso,** *irreverent* (from the point of view of the *tyrannus*), not respecting his just rights (*iura*); cf. *Epod.* 17. 34 n; Intr. 124.

14. **stantem columnam**: figurative, meaning their established power and dignity.

15. **ad arma**: the repetition has the effect of introducing the actual cry into the verse. Cf. Liv. XXI. 49. 10. — **cessantis**: *i.e.* the cooler heads, whose adhesion to the rebellion would mean the fall of the monarch.

17. **anteit**: Intr. 180. Necessity walking before Fortuna with the symbols of her power, as the lictors with the fasces before the Roman magistrate, declares the fixedness of her decrees.

18. **clavos trabalis,** etc.: devices employed in building to secure firmness and durability, here symbols of immutability. *Clavus* in this figurative sense was not uncommon; cf. Cic. *Verr.* II. 5. 53 *ut hoc beneficium, quemadmodum dicitur, trabali clavo figeret.* — **cuneos**: used to tighten imperfect joints. — **manu aena**: cf. our 'iron grasp.' The characteristic of Necessitas is transferred to her hand. Intr. 124.

19. **severus,** *rigid, unyielding.*

20. **uncus, plumbum**: the iron clamp by which two blocks of stone were held together, and the lead, poured in hot, by which the iron was firmly fixed in the stone (Vitruv. II. 8). Such clamps may be seen in the walls of the Parthenon to this day.

Te Spes et albo rara Fides colit
velata panno, nec comitem abnegat,
utcumque mutata potentis
veste domos inimica linquis;
at volgus infidum et meretrix retro
periura cedit, diffugiunt cadis
cum faece siccatis amici
ferre iugum pariter dolosi.

21. **te Spes et . . . Fides**: in this and the following strophe we have a different conception of Fortuna from the one portrayed above, illustrating the confusion which existed in the Roman mind on the subject. Except in the single word **inimica**, 24, we have no longer the inexorable goddess, dealing out good and evil to men, which was perhaps the character of the Fortunae Antiates, but a more abstract conception of a changeable divinity, a sort of genius (cf. *Ep.* II. 2. 187 *sqq.*), attending as well as determining the lives of men, — of a state or city, of a class, or even of a family or an individual. Such a conception was *Fortuna Populi Romani*, *Fortuna Muliebris*, *Fortuna Caesaris*, etc. (Preller-Jordan *Röm. Myth.* II. 182). This divinity typifies misfortune as well as good fortune, — wears white or black (**mutata veste**); and to her cling Hope and Fidelity, — the hope that never dies in the heart, and the rare fidelity that can stand the test of adversity. — **albo**: typical of purity; cf. 'unsullied faith.'—**rara**, *rare;* with the same accessory notion of excellence as in English. For the neutral meaning of *fides*, see 5. 5 n, and for the personification, 24. 7 n.

22. **velata panno**: from the custom of the priests in the worship of Fides, as instituted by Numa, who (Liv. I. 21. 4) '*ad id sacrarium flamines bigis curru arcuato vehi iussit, manuque ad digitos usque involuta rem divinam facere, significantes fidem tutandam, sedemque eius etiam in dextris sacratam esse.*' The cloth by which the priest veils his hand is here transferred to the figure of the goddess. — **comitem** (sc. *se*), *her companionship;* cf. Ovid. *A. A.* I. 127 *siqua comitem negabat; S.* II. 8. 2 *quaerenti convivam* (sc. *te*).—**abnegat**: with **Spes** as well as **Fides** as its subject.

23. **mutata veste**: *i.e.* putting on mourning. — **potentis domos**, *the home of power* (Intr. 124). This home the once prosperous man must now leave and go out into the world with his changed fortune; but hope still attends him, and a few faithful friends.

24. **linquis**: Intr. 129.

25. **at volgus**, etc.: but the great majority of those who were the devoted friends of his prosperity will not share with him the burden of adversity.— **retro cedit**, *fall back*, refuse to follow.

27. **cum faece**, *dregs and all.*

28. **ferre iugum pariter**: to bear, as in true friendship, an equal share of the hardships, as well as the pleasures, of life; cf.

Serves iturum Caesarem in ultimos
orbis Britannos et iuvenum recens
examen Eois timendum
partibus oceanoque rubro.

Eheu cicatricum et sceleris pudet
fratrumque. Quid nos dura refugimus
aetas? Quid intactum nefasti
liquimus? Vnde manum iuventus

metu deorum continuit? Quibus
pepercit aris? O utinam nova
incude diffingas retusum in
Massagetas Arabasque ferrum.

Theocr. 12. 15 ἀλλήλους δ' ἐφίλησαν ἴσῳ ζυγῷ. For the construction of **ferre** see Intr. 101 *b*.

29. **serves**: the poet returns to the first conception of Fortuna.—**ultimos orbis**, *at the ends of the earth.*

30. **recens**: *i.e.* newly recruited.

31. **Eois partibus**: a general designation prefixed to the more definite one,—*the parts of the East towards*, etc.; cf. Verg. *A.* VIII. 686 *victor ab Aurorae populis et litore rubro.*

32. **oceano rubro**: for *mare Erythraeum*, the part of the Indian ocean adjoining Arabia. **partibus** and **oceano** are dative with **timendum**, the places standing for their inhabitants.

33. **eheu**, *ah me.*—**cicatricum**, etc.: each cause of shame suggests and explains the next: we are ashamed of our scars,—they remind us of our guilt,—guilt against our brothers.—**sceleris**: see 2. 29 n.

34. **dura**, *hardened.*—**refūgimus**, *shrunk from*, *i.e.* not dared to do.

35. **intactum**, *untried, unattempted;* cf. *S.* I. 10. 66, and Sall. *Iug.* 66. 1 *nihil intactum pati.*—**nefasti**: better taken as genitive.

36. **unde**, *from what.*

38. **o**: Intr. 185.—**nova**: because of the feeling that things were doomed to a certain career in the making, as men at their birth; cf. 27. 1. The sword is to be broken up and forged anew (**diffingas**) under altogether new influences.

39. **in** (with **diffingas**): *i.e.* for use against. The desire to wash out the stain of civil war in the blood of the enemy was no doubt a genuine feeling on the part of Horace's contemporaries, and not merely a happy fancy of the poet; cf. the feeling of the soldiers of Germanicus after their mutiny in A.D. 14 (Tac. *Ann.* I. 49. 5): *truces etiam tum animos cupido involat eundi in hostem, piaculum furoris; nec aliter posse placari commilitonum manes quam si pectoribus impiis honesta volnera accepissent.*

40. **Massagetas**: a powerful Scythian people, east of the Caspian sea.

## XXXVI.

Et ture et fidibus iuvat
placare et vituli sanguine debito
custodes Numidae deos,
qui nunc Hesperia sospes ab ultima
caris multa sodalibus,
nulli plura tamen dividit oscula
quam dulci Lamiae, memor
actae non alio rege puertiae
mutataeque simul togae.

XXXVI. A welcome to Numida on his safe return from the 'far West,' — possibly as one of the *iuvenes nuper sospites* (III. 14. 9) in the train of Augustus, B.C. 24. Numida, whose *nomen* is variously given as Plotius or Pomponius, was a much younger man than Horace, being of the same age with their common friend Lamia (see intr. note to Ode 26); and we may therefore suppose that the sacrifice and banquet with which his return was celebrated were instituted by Lamia, at whose request Horace wrote this ode for the occasion. — Metre, 171.

1. **et ture et fidibus**: both indispensable accompaniments of a sacrifice. During the progress of the rites, amid the absolute silence of the spectators, a *fidicen* (or more commonly a *tibicen*) played a solemn strain to make more sure that no ill-omened sound should reach the ears of the priest; and no sacrifice was acceptable unless the smoke of the victim was fragrant with incense. — **iuvat**, *we will gladly;* expressing here, as in *Epod.* 9. 37, disposition to do the thing rather than, as more commonly, satisfaction or pleasure in doing it; see Intr. 94 *c*.

2. **placare**, *gratify*.—**sanguine**: *i.e.* the life. Only the entrails of the victim were consumed on the altar; the flesh furnished forth the banquet which followed. — **debito**: because the sacrifice had been vowed on Numida's departure, probably by Lamia; cf. *obligatam dapem*, II. 7. 17.

3. **custodes deos**: cf. 28. 29, and see Intr. 126 *c*.

4. **Hesperia ultima**: probably Spain is meant.

6. **plura**, *a larger share*.— **dividit**, *bestows*.

8. **non alio**, *under the very same* (litotes).— **rege**, *leader* (in games); *i.e.* they had been playmates; cf. *Ep.* I. 1. 59; Allen's *Early Latin Remn.* 213 n. Others conjecture that *rex* here is equivalent to *rector* in *rectores imperatoriae iuventae* (Burrus and Seneca), Tac. *Ann.* XIII. 2. 2, which would make the sentence mean they had been schoolfellows. — **puertiae**: Intr. 183.

9. **mutatae togae**: from the *toga praetexta* of boyhood to the *toga virilis*. The change was made at about the age of sixteen and

Cressa ne careat pulchra dies nota,
neu promptae modus amphorae
neu morem in Salium sit requies pedum,
neu multi Damalis meri
Bassum Threicia vincat amystide,
neu desint epulis rosae
neu vivax apium neu breve lilium.
Omnes in Damalin putris
deponent oculos, nec Damalis novo

was of course a memorable event in a man's life.

10. **Cressa**: *i.e.* white, made with *creta*, which was commonly supposed to stand for *Creta* (= *Cressa*) *terra*, though in fact no chalk was obtained from Crete. The meaning is, 'that the day may be a bright one in our memory'; from the practice of recording especially happy days with a white mark, and unhappy with black; cf. Cat. 107. 6 *o lucem candidiore nota*. Another method, which Pliny (*N. H.* VII. 131) attributes to the Thracians, of determining the color of one's life by depositing in an urn at the end of each day a stone, white or black as the day had been happy or the reverse, had also passed into a proverb; cf. Cat. 68. 148 *quem lapide illa diem candidiore notat;* Pers. 2. 1 *hunc, Macrine, diem numera meliore lapillo;* cf. also *S.* II. 3. 246. — **ne careat**: better taken as a final clause, expressing the purpose of the action urged in the following verses.

11. **promptae** (proleptic), *broached;* lit. 'brought out,' *sc.* from the *apotheca;* cf. III. 21. 8.— **amphorae**: dative; cf. 24. 1. — The repetition of **neu** in the following verses, answering to that of *et* in vss. 1, 2, gives the impression of lively anticipation and thoughts crowding for utterance.

12. **Salium**: for the usual *Saliarem;* cf. Intr. 65. The Salii were a college of twelve priests, instituted by Numa to keep the sacred shield (*ancile*) which he received from heaven. To baffle any attempt to steal it, he caused eleven others to be made exactly like it, and with these twelve the Salii, at their annual festival in March, dressed in a motley costume, half military and half sacerdotal, moved through the streets and about the altars of the gods, singing and dancing.

13. **neu**, etc.: *i.e.* Bassus, who it would seem was ordinarily a moderate drinker, must on this occasion keep it up with the best of them. — **multi meri**: *i.e.* a generous drinker. For the construction see Intr. 61.

14. **Bassum**: otherwise unknown. — **Threicia**: cf. 27. 2 n. — **amystide**, *bumper;* from ἄμυστιν (or ἀμυστὶ) πίνειν, to drink without closing the lips (μύω).

15. **rosae**, etc.: for the use of flowers at feasts, see II. 3. 13 n.

16. **breve**, *short-lived* (as in II. 3. 13); in contrast with **vivax**.

17. **putris**, *languishing*.

18. **deponent**, *will rest*. — **nec**, *but . . . not*.

divelletur adultero,
lascivis hederis ambitiosior.

## XXXVII.

Nunc est bibendum, nunc pede libero
pulsanda tellus, nunc Saliaribus
ornare pulvinar deorum
tempus erat dapibus, sodales.

19. **adultero**: see 33. 9 n.

20. **lascivis**: a part of the comparison: twining (her arms) round him with no more restraint than the ivy round the tree. — **ambitiosior**: in a literal sense; cf. *Epod.* 15. 5 *artius atque hedera procera adstringitur ilex lentis adhaerens bracchiis*; Cat. 61. 33, 106.

XXXVII. On the good news from Egypt, September, B.C. 30. A year had elapsed since the victory at Actium, when Marcus Cicero, son of the orator, consul suffectus, published at Rome the glad tidings that Alexandria had fallen on the first of August, Antony and Cleopatra were dead, and the war was over. Of Antony the poet is silent, conforming in this to the national feeling, which never permitted a triumph to be celebrated except over a foreign foe. The ode is devoted wholly to Cleopatra, who is presented in two strikingly dissimilar scenes. The burst of exultant joy with which the poem opens is modeled upon an ode of Alcaeus on the death of the Lesbian tyrant Myrsilus, beginning (*Fr.* 20):

*Νῦν χρὴ μεθύσθην καί τινα πρὸς βίαν πώνην, ἐπειδὴ κάτθανε Μύρσιλος.*

In this strain the poet portrays the Egyptian queen in her furious onslaught on Italy and her ignominious flight. Then with sudden transition (vs. 21), his aversion and abhorrence give place to admiration as he contemplates the last scene, where she resolutely carries out her determination to die rather than be taken captive to Rome; and the ode, which began as a song of triumph over the fallen foe, fittingly closes with a warm tribute to her courage and lofty spirit. — Metre, 176.

1. **libero**, *unshackled*; *i.e.* no longer restrained by anxieties for the danger which had threatened the state; Intr. 124.

2. **Saliaribus**: *i.e.* such as are provided for the Salii (see 36. 12 n), who, with the pontifices (cf. II. 14. 28), were proverbial for the sumptuousness of their banquets; cf. Cic. *Att.* V. 9. 1 *cum epulati essemus Saliarem in modum*.

3. **ornare pulvinar**, etc.: *i.e.* to celebrate a *lectisternium*, in which the images of the gods were placed in pairs on rich couches, and banquets served to them for several days in succession; cf. Liv. V. 13. 6, XXII. 10. 9. A banquet for the priests was, as usual, an appendage of the ceremony. For the number of **pulvinar** see Intr. 127.

4. **tempus erat**, *would be the*

Antehac nefas depromere Caecubum
cellis avitis, dum Capitolio
regina dementis ruinas
funus et imperio parabat

contaminato cum grege turpium
morbo virorum, quidlibet impotens
sperare fortunaque dulci
ebria. Sed minuit furorem

vix una sospes navis ab ignibus,
mentemque lymphatam Mareotico

*time*, *sc.* for the priests; Gr. 311 *c*, with Rem.

5. **antehac**: Intr. 180. — **Caecubum**: see 20. 9 n. The Caecuban was a wine of the richer sort, which would be especially reserved for such occasions as this; cf. *Epod.* 9. 1 *repostum Caecubum ad festas dapes*; III. 28. 2 *sq.*

6. **cellis avitis**: *i.e.* made in our fathers' time. The wine was not brought directly from the *cella vinaria*, where it was fermented in large *dolia*, but from the *apotheca* in the upper part of the house (hence **de-promere**; cf. *descende*, III. 21. 7), where it was kept in sealed *amphorae*; cf. III. 8. 10 *sqq.* — **Capitolio**: see III. 30. 8 n.

7. **regina**, *a queen*; suggesting a worse prospect than the traditional *bête noire* of the Romans, subjection to a king; cf. Prop. IV. 11. 47 *quid nunc Tarquinii fractas iuvat esse secures, | si mulier patienda fuit?* — **dementis ruinas**: Intr. 124. The most extravagant reports of the designs of Cleopatra were believed at Rome, and her absolute power over Antony, as well as her previous influence over Julius Caesar, gave real cause for anxiety.

8. **funus et**: Intr. 114. — **parabat**: the imperfect gives **dum** the sense of 'so long as'; Gr. 276 *e*, N.

9. **contaminato grege**: *i.e.* eunuchs (cf. *Epod.* 9. 13), a class of persons who often rose to high positions under oriental kings.

10. **morbo**: *i.e.* unnatural lust. — **virorum**: used (rather than *hominum*) with a touch of irony, to enhance the force of **turpium**; they have debased their *manhood.* — **impotens** (sc. *sui*), *wild enough to.* See Intr. 101 *a*.

12. **minuit**: sc. *ei*.

13. **vix una sospes**, *the bare escape of a single*; Intr. 105 *a*. So it was probably reported at Rome in the first news of the battle, and Horace had not yet learned the actual fact, that she took all of her sixty ships safely out of the fight. It was Antony's fleet that was burned.

14. **lymphatam**, *unbalanced*, rendered 'flighty'; the word is apparently derived from *Lymphae*, water-nymphs (see *S.* I. 5. 97 n), at the sight of whom in the water, according to the popular belief, the unfortunate beholder was bereft of his senses (νυμφόληπτος).

redegit in veros timores
Caesar, ab Italia volantem
remis adurgens, accipiter velut
mollis columbas aut leporem citus
venator in campis nivalis
Haemoniae, daret ut catenis
fatale monstrum. Quae generosius
perire quaerens nec muliebriter
expavit ensem nec latentis
classe cita reparavit oras ;

See Preller-Jordan, *Röm. Myth.*, II. 127, and cf. 'panic fear' (see 17. 2 n) and 'lunatic.' — **Mareotico**: sc. *vino:* a sweet, fragrant wine produced at Marea, near Alexandria.

15. **veros timores**: in contrast with the fanciful hopes with which she had come to the conflict.

16. **ab Italia**, *away from Italy;* having been turned back from her journey thither. — **volantem**: sc. *eam.*

17. **remis adurgens,** etc.: a poetical exaggeration, based perhaps on misinformation (see vs. 13 n). Cleopatra was pursued by nothing more than the fear of Octavian, who did not go to Egypt till the next year. — **accipiter velut,** etc.: cf. *Il.* XXII. 138 *ἠύτε κίρκος ὄρεσφιν, ἐλαφρότατος πετεηνῶν, | ῥηιδίως οἴμησε μετὰ τρήρωνα πέλειαν*; Verg. *A.* XI. 721; Ov. *M.* V. 605 *sq.*

19. **nivalis**: *i.e.* in winter, the time for hunting hares; cf. *S.* I. 2. 105 *sq.*

20. **Haemoniae**: poetic name for Thessaly. — **daret ut**: Intr. 114. The clause depends on **adurgens** 17, which takes its time from **redegit** 15.

21. **fatale,** *deadly.* — **monstrum**: as a strange being in woman's shape. — **quae**: a construction according to the sense, which would not permit *quod;* cf. Cic. *Fam.* I. 9. 15 *illa furia* (*i.e.* Clodius) *muliebrium religionum, qui non pluris fecerat Bonam Deam quam tres sorores, impunitatem est adsecutus.* The idea of the frantic queen, which dominates in the preceding sentence at the expense of the strict grammatical construction, is understood here as there. See notes on *minuit* 12 and *volantem* 16. From this point she is consistently treated as the grammatical subject to the end. — **generosius,** *a nobler death, sc.* than that of a captive in chains, which would be the death of a slave.

22. **perire**: Intr. 94 *c.* — **nec muliebriter expavit,** *showed no womanish terror of;* alluding perhaps to the story (Plut. *Ant.* 79) that Cleopatra at the sight of Proculeius, whom Octavian had sent to take her prisoner, seized a dagger and was barely prevented from stabbing herself. For **expavit** see Intr. 51 *a.*

23. **nec latentis,** etc.: *i.e.* she did not seek safety in flight and

ausa et iacentem visere regiam
voltu sereno, fortis et asperas
tractare serpentes, ut atrum
corpore combiberet venenum,

deliberata morte ferocior,
saevis Liburnis scilicet invidens
privata deduci superbo
non humilis mulier triumpho.

concealment. There can be here no allusion to the story (Plut. *Ant.* 69) that Cleopatra attempted to have her fleet transported across the isthmus of Suez with a view to escape to some place on the coast of the Red Sea. Horace wrote in the belief that this fleet had been all but annihilated at Actium (see vs. 13 n), and the fleet he has in mind is one that might have been prepared, in the year that had since intervened, especially for flight. — **latentis,** *some unknown.*

24. **reparavit,** *gained;* lit. got as a recompense for (the loss of her own); cf. *reparata* 31. 12 n.

25. **et,** *even.* So in the next verse. — **iacentem,** *prostrate, i.e.* humbled, stripped of its splendor and prestige as a *domus potens* (35. 23); cf. Cic. *Or.* 224 *depressam, caecam, iacentem domum pluris quam te et fortunas tuas aestimasti.* — **visere,** *to gaze upon.*

26. **asperas,** *irritable,* violent if touched; cf. III. 2. 10.

27. **tractare,** *to handle.* For the mood see Intr. 101 *a.* — **atrum:** *i.e.* deadly; see 28. 13 n.

28. **corpore,** *into* (lit. *with*) *her body.* — **combiberet,** *absorb.* The manner of Cleopatra's death is not free from doubt (Dio Cass. LI. 14. 1); the report which Horace follows, that she died from the bite of an asp, was the one generally believed at Rome; cf. Verg. *A.* VIII. 697, Prop. IV. 11. 53.

29. **deliberata morte ferocior,** *her courage rising with her resolution to die.*

30. **Liburnis:** fast-sailing craft, small and low-built, modeled on those of the Liburnian pirates. They had won great renown at Actium (cf. *Epod.* 1. 1) where they proved more than a match for Antony's immense, but unwieldy ships. — **invidens:** personifying **Liburnis** (cf. also **saevis**). She begrudged them the honor of bringing her to Rome in triumph. It is said that Cleopatra repeatedly expressed her determination not to be led in triumph (οὐ θριαμβεύσομαι).

31. **privata:** *i.e.* no longer a queen. — **deduci:** Intr. 94 *i.* — **superbo:** cf. 35. 3.

32. **triumpho:** ablative. The triumph is thought of as proceeding all the way from Alexandria to the Capitol.

## XXXVIII.

Persicos odi, puer, apparatus ;
displicent nexae philyra coronae ;
mitte sectari rosa quo locorum
sera moretur.

Simplici myrto nihil adlabores
sedulus curo; neque te ministrum
dedecet myrtus neque me sub arta
vite bibentem.

XXXVIII. The first book closes in a quiet tone with an ode which is singularly simple in form as it is in spirit. The poet in the country, reclining under the deep shade of his vine, with a single slave to fill his cup, each of the two wearing a simple wreath of myrtle, — such is the picture with which Horace has chosen to leave his readers at the close of the first book. — Metre, 174.

1. **Persicos odi**, etc.: a general expression of dislike for all such elaborate furnishings of a feast, called out by seeing the garland which the slave in his zeal is constructing for him.—**Persicos**: the Persians were proverbial among the Greeks for their luxury and the splendor of their banquets. — **puer**: cf. *pueri*, 19, 14 n.

2. **nexae philyra**: *i.e.* elaborately constructed of choice flowers, which the *philyra* served to hold together (*coronae sutiles*). — **coronae**: cf. 4. 9.

3. **sectari**: Intr. 94 *j*. — **quo locorum**: Intr. 63.

4. **moretur**, *lingers;* as if the rest had in reality gone away.

5. **myrto**: see II. 15. 6 n. A simple chaplet would be made by twining the sprigs together (*corona plectilis*).—**nihil**, *not . . . at all*, the negative belonging with **curo**, as in the familiar idiom with *nego*, *nolo*, etc. — **adlabores**, *try to embellish*. *Adlaborare* (= *cum labore addere*) is found only in Horace.

6. **sedulus**: with **adlabores**.— **ministrum**, *as you wait;* corresponding to **bibentem** 12.

7. **arta**: of the foliage.

# LIBER SECVNDVS

## I.

Motum ex Metello consule civicum
bellique causas et vitia et modos

I. C. Asinius Pollio, who holds the place of honor in this book, was a man whose prominence in the community and services to literature fully entitled him to that distinction. Eleven years older than Horace, Pollio had been a friend and correspondent of Cicero, had fought under Caesar at Pharsalus, and had subsequently held important commands, first under the Dictator and then under Antony. He was governor of Transpadane Gaul in B.C. 43–41, and consul, B.C. 40. The next year he won a triumph over the Parthini, a Dalmatian tribe. With these laurels he withdrew from politics and his public life thenceforth was confined to the senate and the courts, in which he was accounted one of the foremost orators of the day. He declined to accompany Octavian to Actium, pleading his friendship for Antony. By his great ability and energy and a courage of opinion that was tempered with excellent discretion, he maintained a position of independence which Augustus found it prudent to respect. In literature Pollio already had a recognized position both as an author and as a friend of authors. He had written tragedies (*S.* I. 10. 42) and other poetry. Vergil was indebted to him for substantial aid at a very critical time. From the spoils of his Dalmatian campaign he established a library of Greek and Latin works, with busts of authors, and threw it open to the people, — the first public library in Rome.

It is not certain when he undertook the history of the civil war which Horace heralds in the present ode, nor how far down he actually brought his account; but it certainly included Pharsalus and Thapsus, and probably Philippi. As it was Pollio who introduced the practice of reading new compositions to a company of friends invited for the purpose (*recitatio*), — a practice which thenceforth became a marked feature of literary life at Rome,— we may infer that Horace had heard portions of the work which he so enthusiastically extols. — Metre, 176.

1. **motum**: more comprehensive than *bellum*, and embracing the whole disturbance of the normal order of the state. The actual war did not begin for ten years after the date named. — **ex Metello consule**: *i.e.* beginning with the year 60 B.C., when Q. Caecilius Metellus and L. Afranius were consuls. For the construction see Intr. 105 *a*. — **civicum**: an archaic form for *civile*, preserved in the technical phrase *civica corona*, but otherwise only in poetry. So *hosticus* for *hostilis*, III. 2. 6.

2. **belli**: limiting the three fol-

ludumque Fortunae gravisque
principum amicitias et arma
nondum expiatis uncta cruoribus,
periculosae plenum opus aleae,
tractas et incedis per ignis
suppositos cineri doloso.

Paulum severae musa tragoediae
desit theatris; mox ubi publicas
res ordinaris, grande munus
Cecropio repetes coturno,

lowing nouns (connected by **et**). — **vitia** : faults committed in conducting the war, *blunders;* **modos** : methods of carrying it on, *measures.*

3. **ludum** : Fortuna is here thought of, not as the stern goddess of fate of I. 35, but as delighting, like Mars in I. 2. 37, 28. 17, in the exercise of her power; cf. III. 29. 49 *sq.* No vicissitudes of fortune could be more striking than those of the three great political leaders, who for a time had the Roman world at their feet, and then one after another came to a violent end. — **gravis**, *momentous* (*sc.* to the state).

4. **principum**, *leaders ; i.e.* Caesar, Pompey, and Crassus. The genitive limits both of the following substantives. — **amicitias**: *i.e.* the so-called 'first triumvirate,' which (unlike the second) was merely a personal alliance of the three political chiefs, invested with no legal authority. — **arma** : *i.e.* those which they (in this case only Caesar and Pompey) took up against one another.

5. **nondum expiatis**: cf. I. 2. 29. — **uncta**, *smeared ;* stronger than the more usual *tincta.* — **cruoribus** : Intr. 128.

6. **plenum aleae** : because so many persons still living are affected by the story of events in which either they themselves or their kinsmen took part. — **opus** : in apposition with the whole sentence (**tractas** with its objects) ; cf. *grande certamen*, III. 20. 7.

7. **per**, *over ;* cf. *per mare*, I. 6. 7. — **ignis**, etc.: *i.e.* the smouldering passions of the civil war, which burned for a long period after peace was restored on the surface.

9. **paulum**, etc.: *i.e.* the theatre must do without tragedy for a time ; an extravagant compliment to Pollio, whose tragedies, however, it would appear from this, were actually performed on the stage, and not written merely for the *recitatio.* — **musa tragoediae** : equivalent in effect to Tragedy (personified) ; see note on *Clio*, I. 12. 2.

10. **desit** : denoting a lack of something needed ; stronger than *absit*, which would denote mere absence ; cf. Cic. *Brut.* 276 *hoc unum illi, si nihil utilitatis habebat, afuit ; si opus erat, defuit.* — **pub-**

insigne maestis praesidium reis
et consulenti, Pollio, curiae,
cui laurus aeternos honores
Delmatico peperit triumpho.

Iam nunc minaci murmure cornuum
perstringis auris, iam litui strepunt,
iam fulgor armorum fugacis
terret equos equitumque voltus.

**licas res** (with emphasis on **publicas**), *public events, the history of the state;* in contrast with the remoter interests that form the ordinary subjects of tragedy.

11. **ordinaris,** *have set in order,* brought out of the confusion of inaccurate and contradictory reports. The expression is a somewhat extravagant substitute for *ordine narraveris,* the usual phrase for giving a complete and connected account of an occurrence. — **munus,** *calling, function.*

12. **Cecropio:** *i.e.* Attic; cf. IV. 12. 6. The greatest writers and, according to tradition, the inventor (cf. *Ep.* II. 3. 275 *sqq.*) of tragedy, were Athenians. — **repetes,** *return to.* — **coturno,** *with the buskin, i.e.* wearing it. The high shoe worn by the tragic actor to give him a more imposing appearance, and used by the poets as the symbol of tragedy (*e.g.* *Ep.* II. 3. 80), is here assigned to the author, as the *soccus* of comedy to Plautus in *Ep.* II. 1. 174; cf. Milton *L'Allegro* 132 'If Jonson's learnèd sock be on.'

13. **insigne,** etc.: with the exception of the political prosecution of one C. Cato with which Pollio, after the usual manner of aspiring politicians at Rome, began his career, all his orations of which we have any notice were for the defense. — **praesidium,** *safeguard, reliance;* cf. I. 1. 2 n.

14. **curiae:** for the senate itself, as we say 'the House.' For its case and that of **reis,** see Intr. 59.

17. **iam nunc:** *i.e.* in lively anticipation. Although Horace had probably heard portions of the work, he here makes himself the spokesman of the general public, to express the great expectations with which they awaited its appearance. The scene in this strophe is the cavalry fight in the battle of Pharsalus. For the word-painting cf. Intr. 131. — **cornuum . . . litui:** both used by cavalry. The *cornu* had the shape of a semicircle or even a larger arc. For the *lituus,* see I. 1. 23 n.

19. **fugacis:** proleptic.

20. **equitumque voltus:** *i.e.* 'and paints terror on the faces of the riders.' The vivid picture instead of the plain fact (*equites terret*) is quite in Horace's manner; but it was no doubt suggested by the actual circumstances. The battle was decided by the rout of Pompey's inexperienced cavalry, who were terrified by the blows which the Gallic and German troopers, by Caesar's order, *aimed at their faces;* cf. Plut. *Caes.* 45, Florus IV. 2. 50 (*vox Caesaris*) *cruenta, sed docta et ad victoriam efficax, 'miles, faciem feri!'*

Audire magnos iam videor duces
non indecoro pulvere sordidos
et cuncta terrarum subacta
praeter atrocem animum Catonis.

Iuno et deorum quisquis amicior
Afris inulta cesserat impotens
tellure victorum nepotes
rettulit inferias Iugurthae.

21. **audire**: to hear with my own ears, not merely read. The word is placed first for emphasis and to continue the thought of the preceding strophe: I am transported to the presence of the events themselves instead of reading of them as cold facts. This distinction, with disregard of the precise meaning of *audire* (as in III, 10. 5; cf. *vides* I. 14. 3), is carried on to the second half of the strophe: I learn of the subjection of the world as a living fact accomplished before my eyes. — **magnos duces**: *i.e.* their voices (in battle, as the next verse shows). He means Caesar and Pompey themselves.

23. **cuncta terrarum**: Intr. 64.

24. **atrocem**, *stern*.— **Catonis**: see I. 12. 36 n.

25–40. The mention of Cato suggests the battle of Thapsus, in which the poet sees the impressive fact that just there, on the very soil where Rome had gained her most signal victories, she was doomed to witness a costly sacrifice of her own sons. This leads him on to some general reflections on the enormous outpouring of Roman blood in the civil war, till he suddenly checks himself and recalls his muse from the pursuit of so mournful a theme to her own proper sphere of love and mirth.

25. **Iuno**: the patron-goddess of Carthage; cf. Verg. *A.* I. 15 *sqq.* — **et deorum quisquis**, etc., *and every* (*other*) *divinity who, though disposed to be friendly to the Africans, had retired from the land, powerless to avenge it.* It was the common belief that the gods of a doomed city abandoned it before its fall; cf. Verg. *A.* II. 351 *excessere omnes adytis arisque relictis | di;* Silius Ital. II. 365 *et iam damnata cessit Karthagine Mavors.* It is said that in the third Punic war Scipio instituted certain rites to transfer Juno from Carthage to Rome (Serv. on Verg. *A.* XII. 841). — **deorum**: Intr. 63. — **quisquis**, *whoever else*. *Alius* is usually omitted in such phrases; cf. Liv. IX. 18. 13 *mirabiliores quam Alexander aut quisquam rex.*

26. **impotens**: here in its literal sense, which is unusual; cf. I. 37. 10. The helplessness is of course not general, but only relates to one object, implied in **inulta**.

27. **victorum**: *sc.* in the Jugurthine war. That this war was more prominent in Horace's mind than the greater, though more remote, Punic wars, was perhaps due to the recent publication of Sallust's monograph on the subject.— **nepotes**: among the slain at Thapsus there may well have been actual grandsons of those

Quis non Latino sanguine pinguior
campus sepulcris impia proelia
testatur auditumque Medis
Hesperiae sonitum ruinae?

Qui gurges aut quae flumina lugubris
ignara belli? Quod mare Dauniae
non decoloravere caedes?
Quae caret ora cruore nostro?

Sed ne relictis, musa procax, iocis
Ceae retractes munera neniae;

who fought in the Jugurthine war; the Pompeian commander himself, Metellus Scipio, was the grandson of Metellus Numidicus, who had earned his surname by victory over Jugurtha.

28. **rettulit,** *have offered up* (by way of atonement); see I. 3. 7 n. For the number, see Intr. 77.

29. **quis non,** etc.: two questions compressed into one: What plain is not more fertile, and does not bear witness, etc.?—**pinguior:** cf. Verg. *G.* I. 491 *nec fuit indignum superis bis sanguine nostro | Emathiam et latos Haemi pinguescere campos.*

30. **impia:** as fought by 'brothers' (cf. I. 35. 34) against one another.

31. **Medis:** see I. 2. 22 n; for the case, Intr. 54. It was a sore aggravation of the calamity to think of the glee with which the great enemy of the empire watched the Romans cutting one another's throats. Cf. *Il.* I. 255 *sqq.*

32. **Hesperiae:** here an adjective (=*Italae*); see III. 6. 8 n.—**ruinae,** *the downfall;* cf. I. 2. 25 n.

33. **gurges,** *flood,* open waters, in contrast with running streams. In the following questions we have another contrasted pair, sea and shore. It is noteworthy how skilfully the poet, without monotony, keeps the reader's attention fixed through two strophes on the one thought that holds for the moment his own fancy,—the battle ground of the civil war, stretching from one end of the empire to the other. Allowing for poetic license, the picture is a true one; cf. Flor. IV. 2. 3 *sqq.*

34. **Dauniae:** see I. 22. 14 n; here used as a special type to represent the Roman soldier in general; cf. III. 5. 9 and see Intr. 117 *a.*

35. **decoloravere,** *deeply dyed.* The **de-** is here intensive as in *dealbare, denigrare;* cf. I. 9. 11 n.

36. For the assonance see Intr. 131.

37. **sed ne,** etc.: cf. I. 6. 10 and 17 *sqq.* (with intr. note); III. 3. 69.

38. **Ceae retractes,** etc., *take up again the function of the Cean dirge, i.e.* undertake the service in poetry once performed by Simonides of Ceos, whose elegies (θρῆνοι; cf. *lacrimis Simonideis,* Cat. 38. 8; here *neniae*), — for example those in honor of the warriors who fell at Marathon and at Thermopylae, — were the best of their class.

mecum Dionaeo sub antro
quaere modos leviore plectro.

## II.

Nullus argento color est avaris
abdito terris, inimice lamnae
Crispe Sallusti, nisi temperato
splendeat usu.

39. **Dionaeo**: *i.e.* of Venus, daughter of Dione. Venus herself was sometimes called Dione; cf. *Dionaei Caesaris* (as descendant of Venus), Verg. *E.* 9. 47; Ov. *F.* II. 461. — **sub antro**: cf. I. 5. 3 n.

40. **leviore plectro**: *i.e.* of a lighter strain (descriptive abl.); cf. IV. 2. 33 n; Ov. *M.* X. 150 *cecini plectro graviore gigantas* | ... *nunc opus est leviore lyra.* For the *plectrum* see I. 26. 11 n.

II. C. Sallustius Crispus was the grandnephew and adopted son of the historian Sallust, and at the death of the latter, B.C. 34, inherited his enormous wealth. Like Maecenas, he abstained from the usual pursuit of political honors, but under the affectation of indolence and lack of ambition exercised an influence beyond that of the most powerful senators; and by his intelligence and sagacity he won a place in the secret counsels of Augustus second only to that of Maecenas himself. He maintained his influence to the end of Augustus' life and through the first years of Tiberius, and died at an advanced age A.D. 20 (Tac. *Ann.* III. 30). In regard to his style of living Tacitus calls him *diversus a veterum instituto per cultum et munditias, copiaque et adfluentia luxu propior.* Horace's testimony in this ode, on the contrary, distinctly credits Sallustius with moderation and liberality in the use of his wealth. The poem was probably written in B.C. 27, when the restoration of Phraates was still fresh in the public mind. — Metre, 174.

1. **color,** *lustre;* cf. Plin. *N. H.* XXXIII. 58 *color in argento clarior est* (sc. *quam in auro*), *magisque diei similis.* — **avaris**: the disposition of the miser is attributed to the earth, in which he hoards his money; Intr. 124.

2. **abdito terris**: cf. *S.* I. 1. 41 *quid iuvat immensum te argenti pondus et auri* | *furtim defossa timidum deponere terra?* **terris** may be either abl. (Intr. 69) or dative (Intr. 53; cf. Verg. *A.* II. 553 *lateri abdidit ensem*). — **inimice**: apodosis to the condition **nisi temperato,** etc., — (who wouldst be) *a foe . . . unless,* etc. — **lamnae**: probably a colloquial expression, used here in disparagement for money as mere metal, — *bullion.* For the form see Intr. 183.

3. **Crispe Sallusti**: such inversion of the *nomen* and *cognomen* (with omission of the *praenomen*) appears to have been common in colloquial language from early times. It is frequent in Cicero's letters, and is much affected by Tacitus.

Vivet extento Proculeius aevo,
notus in fratres animi paterni;
illum aget penna metuente solvi
fama superstes.

Latius regnes avidum domando
spiritum quam si Libyam remotis
Gadibus iungas et uterque Poenus
serviat uni.

Crescit indulgens sibi dirus hydrops,
nec sitim pellit, nisi causa morbi

5. **vivet**: *i.e.* in fame, as indicated in the following verses. — **extento aevo**, *a prolonged life* (*sc.* beyond its natural limits). — **Proculeius**: C. Proculeius Varro Murena, brother of Terentia, the wife of Maecenas. Like Maecenas and Sallustius he remained in the equestrian order, but Augustus held him in such high esteem and confidence (see I. 37. 22 n) that he at one time thought of him as a husband for his daughter Julia (Tac. *Ann.* IV. 40. 8).

6. **in**, *towards*. — **animi paterni**: he divided his own property in equal shares with his two brothers, who had lost theirs in the civil war. For the case see Intr. 66 *d*.

7. **aget**, *will waft*. — **penna**, *wing*; cf. Verg. *A.* IX. 473 *pinnata Fama*. — **metuente**: *i.e.* that refuses (Intr. 94 *l*); not implying that there is any danger of it (cf. Intr. 95).

9. **regnes**: the indefinite second person subjunctive in apodosis, the protasis being expressed in **domando**. For the thought cf. *O. T. Prov.* 16. 32 'He that ruleth his spirit (is better) than he that taketh a city.'

11. **iungas**: *i.e.* under your sway, as explained by the following clause, which repeats the same idea in another form. — **uterque Poenus**: *i.e.* the Carthaginians of Africa and those of Spain, where there was a *Carthago nova* with other Punic colonies.

12. **uni**: sc. *tibi* (implied in **iungas**).

13. **crescit**, *is aggravated*; Intr. 116 *b*. The subject is still, in thought, the *avidus spiritus*, but it is merged, in Horace's favorite manner, in the figure which he employs to describe its nature; cf. *Ep.* II. 2. 28 *sqq.*, and see Intr. 123. — **indulgens sibi**, *by self-indulgence*; joined loosely to **hydrops**, which is in a manner personified and confused with the *hydropicus*, the disease with the patient.

14. **nec sitim pellit**, etc.: *i.e.* covetousness is not cured by gratifying it, but rather increased; the only cure is to root out the desire. The patient is sick; if you give him to drink he will only want more; you must make him well, and then his thirst will cease. The comparison was not uncommon; cf. Polyb. XIII. 2. 2, Ov. *F.* I. 215, Stob. *Flor.* X. 46; Cic. *Cat.* 1. 31.

fugerit venis et aquosus albo
corpore languor.

Redditum Cyri solio Phraaten
dissidens plebi numero beatorum
eximit Virtus populumque falsis
dedocet uti

vocibus, regnum et diadema tutum
deferens uni propriamque laurum,
quisquis ingentis oculo inretorto
spectat acervos.

15. **venis, corpore** : Intr. 70. — **aquosus** : *i.e.* due to the water settling under the skin. — **albo** : the unhealthy whiteness of disease.

17–24. This subjection of the desires, and not the gratification even of the very highest of human wishes, constitutes true happiness and true power; cf. IV. 9. 45 *sqq.*

17. **Cyri solio** : the throne of Parthia is properly so called, because the Arsacidae succeeded to the power of the Persian kings (see I. 2. 22 n), which in the popular estimate was the summit of earthly happiness; cf. III. 9. 4. — **Phraaten** : see I. 26. 5 n.

18. **plebi** : *i.e.* from the popular judgment; cf. III. 14. 1 n. For the case see Intr. 57.— **beatorum** : for the synapheia see Intr. 174 *b.*

19. **Virtus,** etc.: cf. *S.* I. 3. 41 *vellem . . . isti | errori nomen Virtus posuisset honestum.* He means virtue as set forth by its expounders, the philosophers, especially the Stoics, whose doctrine on the present subject falls in with Horace's own views, so that he even employs, though only in a figurative sense, their favorite paradox that the wise man alone is king, in which elsewhere (*S.* I. 3. 124 *sqq.*) he finds rich material for his satire. See Intr. 8 (end).— **falsis,** *wrong;* the opposite of *vera vocabula rerum*, Sal. *Cat.* 52. 11.

21. **tutum** : intimating the defect in the earthly crown, as exemplified in the recent experience of Phraates.

22. **propriam,** *which shall not be taken away from him;* cf. *Ep.* II. 2. 171 *sqq.; S.* II. 6. 4 *nil amplius oro, | Maia nate, nisi ut propria haec mihi munera faxis;* Lucilius 664 L. *cúm sciam nihil ésse in vita próprium mortalí datum;* and see note on *tutum*, above.

23. **quisquis,** *whoever he be, that,* — whether peasant or king. — **oculo inretorto spectat** : *i.e.* merely glances at them as he passes by, but does not keep rolling his eyes back to see them as long as possible; gives them no further thought; cf. *respicio* and 'regard.'

24. **acervos** : *sc.* of money; cf. *S.* I. 1. 44.

## III.

Aequam memento rebus in arduis
servare mentem, non secus in bonis
ab insolenti temperatam
laetitia, moriture Delli,
seu maestus omni tempore vixeris,
seu te in remoto gramine per dies

III. Although Horace puts at the head of this ode his favorite maxim of the golden mean (II. 10, *S.* I. 1. 106 *sqq.*), he devotes the main part of it to only one side of that doctrine. The warning against over-confident joy in prosperity is left as a mere parenthetical remark in the first strophe, and the poet proceeds to teach at length the maxim, *sapiens finire memento tristitiam vitaeque labores* (I. 7. 17). 'There is nothing to be gained by brooding over the troubles of life; death will come all the same, and the brief time given us for enjoyment will be irrecoverably spent.' Q. Dellius, to whom the ode is addressed, had attained a questionable reputation in the recent political struggles, and had been wittily dubbed by Messala *desultor bellorum civilium* from the happy faculty he had displayed of jumping at the right moment and always lighting on his feet in the successful party (Sen. *Suas.* 1. 7). He was now among the more intimate friends of Augustus, and being a man of literary tastes and a writer, — he prepared a history of Antony's Parthian campaign, in which he had himself commanded part of the forces, — he was no doubt brought into more or less familiar relations with Horace in the circle of Maecenas. — Metre, 176.

1. **aequam,** *unruffled.* — **arduis:** in prose, *adversis* (cf. 10. 13 n); 'when the way is steep.'

2. **servare:** (not *parare*, as in *Ep.* I. 18. 112) implying that he has the *aequus animus* now, and putting the *res arduae* into the future, — 'when hardship comes.' — **non secus:** sc. *memento servare.*

3. **insolenti,** *extravagant;* see I. 5. 8 n.

4. **moriture:** Intr. 104 *b.* It is the apodosis of the two conditional clauses which follow: 'since you will die just the same whether . . . or . . .' It expresses the reason for the preceding injunction (cf. I. 28. 6 n), but has more special reference to the first part, which continues to be the text through the rest of the ode; see intr. note.

6. **remoto gramine,** *some grassy nook;* cf. I. 1. 21 *sq.*, *Epod.* II. 23 *sq.* — **per dies festos:** in contrast with **omni tempore.** The alternative is '*always* melancholy, or *sometimes* (on proper occasions) seeking relaxation.' **per** is distributive: on those days as they come round; cf. *per autumnos*, 14. 15.

festos reclinatum bearis
interiore nota Falerni.

Quo pinus ingens albaque populus
umbram hospitalem consociare amant
ramis? Quid obliquo laborat
lympha fugax trepidare rivo?

Huc vina et unguenta et nimium brevis
flores amoenae ferre iube rosae,
dum res et aetas et sororum
fila trium patiuntur atra.

Cedes coemptis saltibus et domo

8. **interiore**: *i.e.* older. The jars farther back in the *apotheca* would be those which had been left undisturbed the longest. — **nota**, *brand;* properly the stamp or inscription on the amphora, or on a tag attached to it, recording the name and date (consuls of the year) of the vintage; hence used in general for quality of wine; cf. *S.* I. 10. 24. — **Falerni**: cf. I. 20. 10 n.

9. **quo**, *what does it mean that;* lit. *what* (is all this beauty) *for?* — **ingens albaque**: Intr. 122.

10. **hospitalem**, *inviting*.—**consociare**: Intr. 94 *c*. The object **umbram** expresses the result of the action, as if it were *consociando facere;* cf. *sinus*, I. 33. 16 n.

11. **quid**, *why*, in the same sense as *quo* 9. — **obliquo**, *zigzag*, *winding*, always oblique in reference to the direct course. — **laborat trepidare**, *struggle and bustle;* cf. *Ep.* I. 10. 21 (*aqua*) *per pronum trepidat cum murmure rivum*. For the construction see Intr. 94 *h*.

12. **rivo**: ablative of the 'way by which.'

13. **huc**, etc.: the poet proceeds as if the answer to the preceding question were obvious.— **vina . . . unguenta . . . flores**: the three essentials of a Roman *convivium*. The ointment was for the hair, the flowers for garlands; cf. 7. 21 *sqq*., I. 4. 9. — **et . . . et**: repeated in vs. 15. — **brevis**: cf. *breve lilium*, I. 36. 16 n.

15. **res**, *circumstances*.— **aetas**: cf. I. 9. 16 *sq*.—**sororum**: the Fates, Clotho, Lachesis and Atropos, of whom the first spun (κλώθω) the thread of life, the second determined (λαγχάνω) its length, the third, 'the Inexorable' (ἀ+τρέπω) cut it off.

16. **atra**: cf. I. 28. 13 n. Although the thread is the symbol of life, the whole conception relates to death; the purpose of the allegory is to represent not the giving of life, but the ending of it.

17. **coemptis saltibus**: extensive mountain pastures, formed by buying up (**co-**) a number of contiguous tracts from small owners. Great incomes were derived from the flocks and herds raised on such pastures. — **domo**: in the

villaque flavus quam Tiberis lavit,
cedes et exstructis in altum
divitiis potietur heres.

Divesne prisco natus ab Inacho
nil interest an pauper et infima
de gente sub divo moreris,
victima nil miserantis Orci.

Omnes eodem cogimur, omnium
versatur urna serius ocius
sors exitura et nos in aeternum
exsilium impositura cumbae.

city; cf. Mart. IV. 64. 25 *hoc rus, seu potius domus vocanda est.*

18. **villa,** *country-seat.* A villa on the Tiber was especially desirable, and the banks of the river were thronged with them (Plin. *N. H.* III. 54).—**flavus** : see I. 2. 13 n.—**lavit** : in the Odes and Epodes Horace uses the forms of *lavere* only; in the Satires and Epistles those of *lavare* as well.

19. **cedes** : Intr. 116 *f.*—**exstructis in altum** : cf. *ingentis acervos,* 2. 23.

21. **dives natus ab,** *a wealthy descendant of.*—**Inacho** : first (mythical) king of Argos, here typical of very ancient as well as illustrious ancestry; Intr. 117 *a.*

23. **sub divo moreris,** *you linger in the light of day, i.e.* live, but suggesting that our life is but a brief sojourn on earth. For **divo** cf. I. 18. 13 n. The subject is no longer Dellius, but the indefinite 'you.'

24. **victima,** etc.: *i.e.* 'since you are a victim (all the same),' etc.; cf. *moriture,* 4 n.—**nil miserantis,** *pitiless;* cf. 14. 6.

25. **omnes . . . omnium** : Intr. 116 *g.* **omnium** (limiting **sors**) would more naturally have been *cuiusque.*

26. **urna** : another conception of the allotment of death to the individual. Necessity (cf. III. 1. 14 *sqq.*) holds in her capacious urn a **sors** (a small piece of wood or similar material, with distinguishing marks) for every man; the urn is continually shaken (**versatur**), and when a lot flies out the man is doomed to die. For this method of determining by lot cf. *Il.* VII. 175 *sqq.*—**serius ocius** : between two words or phrases which are opposite in meaning and together form a complete idea the conjunction is commonly omitted, as *comminus eminus, a tergo a fronte, velit nolit,* etc.

27. **exitura, impositura** : Intr. 104 *b.*—**in,** *for;* cf. I. 7. 8.—**aeternum** : Intr. 176 *b.*

28. **exsilium** : the suggestion in *moreris,* that life is only a temporary sojourn and not a home, is abandoned again, and the poet recurs to the thought of the preceding strophe, *cedes,* etc.—**cumbae** : Charon's; cf. Verg. *A.* VI. 303.

## IV.

Ne sit ancillae tibi amor pudori,
Xanthia Phoceu, prius insolentem
serva Briseis niveo colore
movit Achillem ;
movit Aiacem Telamone natum
forma captivae dominum Tecmessae ;
arsit Atrides medio in triumpho
virgine rapta,

IV. To 'Xanthias of Phocis,' on his having fallen in love with his maid-servant. Whether Xanthias here stands for a real person or is a mere creature of fancy it is impossible to say with certainty, in spite of the allusion to the poet's own age at the close. The air of reality that pervades the poem and the quality of the humor certainly give the impression that Horace is here chaffing, under an assumed name, one of his own acquaintances; but it is quite possible that his only aim was to give an impression of reality to a situation wholly fictitious. He points out with mock gravity that there is illustrious precedent for being enamoured of a slave girl, and further comforts his friend with the assurance that one so noble and so disinterested must be a princess in disguise at least. — Metre, 174.

1. **ne sit tibi pudori,** *you needn't be ashamed of.* The clause is perhaps best taken as a parenthetical clause of purpose (Gr. 317 *c*), explaining the poet's motive in citing the following examples; cf. IV. 9. 1 *sqq.* Others take it as hortatory.

2. **Xanthia Phoceu** : cf. *Opuntiae Megillae*, I. 27. 10. — **prius** : *i.e.* before you. — **insolentem,** *haughty* (see I. 5. 8 n), and hence likely to hold himself high above a **serva** ; see Intr. 116 *a*.

3. **Briseis** : see *Il.* I. 346 *sqq.*, IX. 342 *sq.* — **niveo colore** : cf. III. 27. 25 ; I. 19. 5 *Glycerae nitor, splendentis Pario purius marmore.* The ablative is instrumental.

4. **movit,** *touched.* For the anaphora, with change of rhythm, cf. I. 2. 5; Intr. 116 *g*.

6. **captivae dominum** : cf. *insolentem serva*, vs. 2 n. — **Tecmessae** : the daughter of a Phrygian king whom Ajax slew in single combat in one of his raids during the siege of Troy ; Soph. *Aiax* 210, 487 *sqq.*

7. **arsit** : *sc.* with love. — **Atrides** : Agamemnon. — **medio in triumpho** : with **arsit**, suggesting much the same contrast as *insolentem* 2.

8. **virgine** : Cassandra, who at the fall of Troy became the prize of Agamemnon. For the case see Intr. 72. — **rapta** : by Ajax, the son of Oileus, from the altar of Athena; cf. Verg. *A.* II. 403 *sqq.*, I. 39 *sqq.*

barbarae postquam cecidere turmae
Thessalo victore et ademptus Hector
tradidit fessis leviora tolli
    Pergama Grais.

Nescias an te generum beati
Phyllidis flavae decorent parentes;
regium certe genus et penatis
    maeret iniquos.

Crede non illam tibi de scelesta
plebe dilectam, neque sic fidelem,
sic lucro aversam potuisse nasci
    matre pudenda.

9. **barbarae**, etc.: an amplification of **triumpho**, to relieve the monotony of the list of examples; see I. 2. 7 n. — **barbarae**: (from the Greek point of view), those of the Trojans and their allies; cf. *Ep.* I. 2. 7 *Graecia barbariae lento collisa duello.* — **cecidere turmae**: the allusion is probably to the time when Achilles came out to battle with his Myrmidons (**Thessalo**) after the death of Patroclus, routed the Trojans with great slaughter, and finally killed Hector (*Il.* XX.–XXII.).

10. **Thessalo**: used collectively; cf. *Poeno*, I. 12. 38. — **ademptus Hector**, *the loss of Hector*; Intr. 105 *a*. Cf. *Il.* XXIV. 243 ῥηίτεροι γὰρ μᾶλλον Ἀχαιοῖσιν δὴ ἔσεσθε | κείνου τεθνηῶτος ἐναιρέμεν.

11. **tradidit**, *delivered . . . into the hands of*; in what sense, is defined by **leviora tolli** (= 'an easier prey'). — **tolli**: for the infinitive see Intr. 101 *e*.

13. **nescias an**, etc.: continuing in the same vein, the poet plays on the well known fact that children of good families were sometimes kidnapped and sold into slavery. — **nescias an**, *very likely*, — *you can't tell*; with the usual affirmative implication of *nescio an*. The meaning is: You must look up her parents, and no doubt it will turn out that you will make a distinguished match with your Phyllis. — **beati**, *rich*, *well to do*; cf. I. 4. 14 n.

14. **flavae**: see note on *Pyrrha*, I. 5. 3. — **te decorent**, *will be an honor to you*.

15. **regium genus et penatis**, etc., *she mourns* (*the loss of*) *royal ancestry*, — *i.e.* she is no longer accounted their descendant, a slave being *filius nullius*, — *and the unkindness of household gods* (Intr. 105 *a*). The two objects of **maeret** correspond accurately to *fidem mutatosque deos*, objects of *flebit*, I. 5. 5.

17. **crede**, *rest assured*. — **non illam**: cf. *non ego*, I. 18. 11 n. — **tibi**: cf. *Iovi*, I. 21. 4; Intr. 54. — **de plebe**: sc. *esse*.

19. **aversam**: the strong expression betrays the irony. — **potuisse**: emphatic; Intr. 116 *b*.

Bracchia et voltum teretisque suras
integer laudo: fuge suspicari
cuius octavum trepidavit aetas
claudere lustrum.

## V.

Nondum subacta ferre iugum valet
cervice, nondum munia comparis
aequare, nec tauri ruentis
in venerem tolerare pondus.
Circa virentis est animus tuae
campos iuvencae, nunc fluviis gravem
solantis aestum, nunc in udo
ludere cum vitulis salicto

21. **teretis,** *shapely, well turned.*

22. **integer,** *dispassionately;* cf. III. 7. 22. — **suspicari**: sc. *eum* (*one*). For the mood see Intr. 94 *k*.

23. **cuius,** etc.: Horace was 40 in B.C. 25. — **trepidavit claudere,** *has fluttered to the verge of;* Intr. 94 *g*.

V. Counsel and encouragement to an impatient lover. 'She is too young still, — a frolicsome heifer, an unripe grape. Wait patiently: by and by she will come to you of herself.' As it is Horace's practice to name the person he addresses, the ode is regarded by some as a soliloquy, like III. 12. — Metre, 176.

1. **nondum valet**: the subject (*iuvenca tua*) is postponed to the beginning of the positive description, vs. 5, and there expressed in a modified form, **animus tuae iuvencae**; cf. I. 37. 14 *mentemque* (*eius*) . . . *redegit*, . . . *ab Italia volantem remis adurgens.* This vagueness and the absence of any direct intimation in the whole description that a young girl is the real subject, — quite in contrast with III. 11. 9 *sqq.*, — shows that though the offensive form of the comparison was tolerable to Roman taste, the poet is not insensible to its grossness, and uses some skill to keep it from coming in too close contact with the subject; see vs. 9 n. — **ferre**: Intr. 94 *n*.

2. **munia comparis aequare**: equivalent to *ferre iugum pariter*, I. 35. 28. Her strength (**valet**) 'is not equal to' the task of a yoke-fellow.

5. **circa**: cf. I. 18. 2 n.

8. **ludere**: Intr. 94 *c*. — **cum vitulis**: *i.e.* (stripped of the imagery) she has still the feelings of a child, and loves best to play with other children.

9. **tolle**: cf. I. 27. 2 n. The new figure enforces the exhortation

praegestientis. Tolle cupidinem
immitis uvae; iam tibi lividos
distinguet autumnus racemos
purpureo varius colore.

Iam te sequetur; currit enim ferox
aetas, et illi quos tibi dempserit
adponet annos; iam proterva
fronte petet Lalage maritum,

dilecta quantum non Pholoe fugax,
non Chloris, albo sic umero nitens
ut pura nocturno renidet
luna mari, Cnidiusve Gyges,

quem si puellarum insereres choro,

to patience, and serves the further purpose of throwing the former comparison somewhat into the background, as we approach the name and person of Lalage.

10. **lividos**: the color of the half-ripe grapes,—a leaden blue spreading over the green; cf. Prop. V. 2. 13 *variat liventibus uva racemis*.

11. **distinguet**, *will tint*.

12. **purpureo colore** (with **distinguet**): denoting a further stage of ripening; cf. Ov. *M.* III. 484 *ut variis solet uva racemis | ducere purpureum nondum matura colorem*. Apparently a deep wine color that precedes dead ripeness (which is expressed by *niger*) is intended.—**varius**: as clothing the face of nature in many hues. For the order of words in this sentence see Intr. 111.

13. **ferox**, *headstrong;* cf. *invida aetas*, I. 11. 7.

14. **quos tibi dempserit annos**: *i.e.* the time you 'lose' by waiting will bring her to maturity. **annos** is used in a pregnant sense, the years of our life with all they bring or take away. In this sense the years that bring us to the prime of life are thought of as coming, those after our prime as passing away; cf. *Ep.* II. 3. 175 *multa ferunt anni venientes commoda secum, | multa recedentes adimunt; Ep.* II. 2. 55 *singula de nobis anni praedantur euntes.*

16. **fronte**: index of the feelings, as the cheek with us; cf. *frontis urbanae*, *Ep.* I. 9. 11.—**maritum**, *a mate.*

17. **dilecta quantum non**, *a greater favorite than.* **dilecta** takes its time from **petet**. — **fugax**, *capricious.*

18. **albo**, etc.: descriptive of Chloris.

19. **pura**, *unclouded;* cf. I. 34. 7.

20. **mari**: Intr. 69.— **Cnidius Gyges**: cf. *Xanthia Phoceu*, 4. 2 n.

21. **quem si**, etc.: cf. I. 2. 7 n. The poet has in mind here the story of Achilles at the court of Lycomedes; see I. 8. 13 n.—**choro**, *a bevy.*

mire sagacis falleret hospites
discrimen obscurum solutis
crinibus ambiguoque voltu.

## VI.

Septimi, Gadis aditure mecum et
Cantabrum indoctum iuga ferre nostra et
barbaras Syrtis, ubi Maura semper
aestuat unda:

22. **mire,** etc., *it's astonishing how keen-sighted strangers would fail to detect.* For **fallerët** cf. I. 10. 16.

23. **obscurum,** *disguised* (*as it is*).—**solutis,** *flowing;* cf. III. 4. 62.

VI. Of the trusty friend to whom the poet here confides his longings for a quiet old age nothing further is known with certainty. It is probable, however, that he is the same Septimius to whom Horace gave a letter of introduction to Tiberius (*Ep.* I. 9), in which he commends him as '*fortem bonumque,*' and also identical with the friend mentioned by Augustus in a letter to the poet which Suetonius has preserved: '*tui qualem habeam memoriam poteris ex Septimio quoque nostro audire.*' The ode was probably written in B.C. 27 or 26, when the recently conquered Cantabrians rebelled, and Augustus went to Spain to conduct the war against them in person. That it was not among the earliest odes is shown by the last verse: Horace would not have called himself *vates* unless he had felt sure that his friends at least already recognized his success in lyric poetry. Some years later he expresses (*Ep.* I. 7. 44) the same preference for the two resorts whose attractiveness he here extols.—Metre, 174.

1. **Gadis**: *i.e.* to the end of the world; cf. 2. 11.—**aditure**: see Intr. 104 *e.*—**et . . . et**: the conjunctions serve to bridge over the pauses between the verses, with an effect similar to that of elision (Intr. 174 *b*).

2. **Cantabrum**: cf. *Thessalo,* 4. 10 n. The Cantabrians were first reduced by Statilius Taurus B.C. 29, and after successive rebellions finally subdued by Agrippa B.C. 19.—**iuga**: Intr. 128.—**ferre**: Intr. 101 *c.*

3. **barbaras,** *wild.* The epithet shows that by **Syrtis** is probably meant here, as in I. 22. 5 and Verg. *A.* IV. 41 *inhospita Syrtis,* the coast rather than the adjacent waters. The thought, however, is not of travelling there but of the dangerous voyage thither. The three objects of **aditure** indicate by special examples the fatigues and dangers expressed in general terms by *maris et viarum militiaeque,* 7 *sq.*—**Maura**: most of the Roman poets betray a certain vagueness in their geographical notions; cf. Verg. *G.* I. 490 *sqq.*

Tibur Argeo positum colono
sit meae sedes utinam senectae,
sit modus lasso maris et viarum
militiaeque.

Vnde si Parcae prohibent iniquae
dulce pellitis ovibus Galaesi
flumen et regnata petam Laconi
rura Phalantho.

Ille terrarum mihi praeter omnis
angulus ridet, ubi non Hymetto
mella decedunt viridique certat
baca Venafro;

5. **Argeo** (=Ἀργείῳ): in prose, *Argivo*.—**positum**: for *conditum*; cf. Verg. *A.* IV. 212 *urbem posuit.* —**colono**, *settler*, as in Verg. *A.* I. 12 *Tyrii tenuere coloni.* For the story see I. 7. 13 n; for the case, Intr. 55.

6. **senectae**: better taken as dative; see note on *lasso*, 7.

7. **modus**: equivalent to *finis*; cf. Tac. *Ann.* II. 14. 6 *si taedio viarum ac maris finem cupiant, hac acie parari* (an imitation apparently of this passage).—**lasso**, *when I am weary* (future); agreeing in case with *mihi* (*seni*), implied in *meae senectae*, 6.—**maris et viarum**: *i.e.* travelling by sea and land. For the case see Intr. 66 *c*.

9. **unde si**, *and if from there*; cf. I. 12. 7.—**prohibent**, *exclude*; cf. I. 27. 4.—**iniquae**, *unkind*; cf. 4. 16, I. 2. 47 n.

10. **pellitis**, *skin-clad*, covered with skins to protect the fine wool; cf. Varro *R. R.* II. 2. 18 *ovibus pellitis, quae propter lanae bonitatem, ut sunt Tarentinae et Atticae, pellibus integuntur.*—**Galaesi**: a few miles from Tarentum; cf. Verg. *G.* IV. 125 *sub Oebaliae* (*i.e. Tarentinae*) *memini me turribus arcis | qua niger umectat flaventia culta Galaesus*, etc. For the case see Intr. 65.

11. **regnata**: Intr. 51 *e*.

12. **Phalantho**: the leader of a body of Lacedaemonian immigrants who colonized Tarentum after the second Messenian war, about 700 B.C. For the case see Intr. 55.

13. **omnis**: sc. (*alios*) *angulos terrarum*. See note on *quisquis*, 1. 25.

14. **angulus**, *corner*; of a retired spot, out of the current; cf. *angulus iste* (the poet's farm), *Ep.* I. 14. 23; *angulus hic mundi*, Prop. V. 9. 65.—**ridet**, *has a charm*. For the prosody see Intr. 179.—**Hymetto**: for *Hymettio* (*melli*); cf. *Venafro*, 16, *Aulon*, 18, *Formiani colles*, I. 20. 11. Hymettus is a mountain near Athens, famous for its honey.

15. **decedunt**, *yield precedence.* The *mella* and *baca* are personified, like *Aulon* in the next strophe.—**viridi**: as being filled with olive groves.

16. **baca**: *i.e.* the olive, with

ver ubi longum tepidasque praebet
Iuppiter brumas et amicus Aulon
fertili Baccho minimum Falernis
invidet uvis.

Ille te mecum locus et beatae
postulant arces, ibi tu calentem
debita sparges lacrima favillam
vatis amici.

reference, however, to the quality of the oil it yields; cf. *S.* II. 4. 69 *pressa Venafranae quod baca remisit olivae.* — **Venafro**: an old Samnite town on the eastern slope of the hills between the lower Liris and the upper Volturnus, now Venafro; famous for the excellence of its olive oil; cf. *S.* II. 8. 45; Varro *R. R.* I. 2. 6 *quod vinum* (*conferam*) *Falerno, quod oleum Venafro?* For the case see Intr. 57.

18. **amicus,** *favored of;* cf. *dilectus* in the quotation from Statius below, and see I. 26. 1 n.—**Aulon**: '*locus contra Tarentinam regionem*' (Porphyrio); whether a mountain (as Acro says) or not is uncertain. Cf. Mart. XIII. 125 *nobilis et lanis et felix vitibus Aulon | det pretiosa tibi vellera, vina mihi.*

19. **fertili**: the quality conferred by the god is attributed to him; cf. *modici Liberi,* I. 18. 7, and Intr. 125. — **Falernis uvis**: cf. I. 20. 10 n, and Varro's words, 17 n.

20. **invidet**: see note on *decedunt* 15. This passage has been imitated by Statius *Silv.* II. 2. 4 *qua Bromio dilectus ager collesque per altos | uritur et prelis non invidet uva Falernis.*

21. **et beatae arces,** *those favored heights;* nearer definition of **locus**. For **arces** cf. I. 2. 3.

22. **postulant,** *call for;* a sort of personification, as in our expression 'an *inviting* place.' — **ibi tu,** etc.: *i.e.* there we will live till death shall part us, taking *me* away, — a delicate expression of the sincerity of his affection: he wishes to be spared the pain of losing his friend. — **calentem favillam**: *i.e.* my ashes, when you gather them warm from the pyre and put them in the urn.

23. **debita**: *sc.* to me as your friend.

VII. The poet's greeting to his old friend and comrade in arms, Pompeius Varus, on his return to Rome after long years of absence. Of Pompeius nothing is known beyond what is indicated in the ode itself,— that he had made the campaign of Philippi with Horace, and afterwards persisted in the struggle against the triumvirs, serving presumably under Sex. Pompeius (Intr. 12). The mention of *ciboria* (vs. 22 n) has been conjectured to be an allusion to his having served also under Antony, but that point as well as the time of his return must remain undetermined, except that the latter, on the general evidence of the date of the odes, must be placed after the end of the war of Actium. — Metre, 176.

## VII.

O saepe mecum tempus in ultimum
deducte Bruto militiae duce,
quis te redonavit Quiritem
dis patriis Italoque caelo,
Pompei, meorum prime sodalium,
cum quo morantem saepe diem mero
fregi coronatus nitentis
malobathro Syrio capillos?

1. **saepe**: Horace's service under Brutus extended through the greater part of the two years 43 and 42, B.C. — **tempus ultimum,** *extreme peril;* lit. 'the last extremity,' like *extremae res* (*e.g.* Caes. *B. G.* II. 25. 5); cf. Cat. 64. 150 *potius quam tibi supremo in tempore deessem.*

2. **deducte . . . duce**: regarded by some as a reflection on Brutus; but the play on words is probably not intentional; cf. *fregi . . . fracta,* vss. 7, 11; *adduxere . . . ducere,* IV. 12. 13 *sq.*

3. **quis**: not necessarily implying that Pompeius owed his restoration to the favor or mediation of any particular person. The question refers not to permission to come home, which Pompeius had under the general amnesty after Actium, but to the circumstances which brought him or enabled him to come. The question is an expression of surprise, and **quis** may have for answer a god as well as a man; cf. vss. 13 and 17. — **redonavit**: stronger than *reddidit.* The word is found only in Horace. — **Quiritem,** *a citizen,* in double contrast with his former condition; no longer a soldier nor an outlaw and exile. The singular is archaic and is used only by the poets.

4. **dis patriis**: *i.e.* to the home of your fathers; cf. III. 27. 49 *liqui patrios penatis.* — **Italo**: for the prosody see Intr. 178.

5. **Pompei**: dissyllabic; Intr. 180. — **prime,** *first;* probably in the sense of *earliest.*

7. **fregi**: with reference to **morantem,** which indicates a persistent monotony that yields to the treatment named; the monotonous day is '*broken*' as we speak of 'breaking up' a cold or 'killing' time. The idea is not of 'making shorter,' but of destroying; cf. Cic. *de Or.* I. 265 *nunc et Scaevola paulum requiescet dum se calor frangat;* Verg. *A.* IV. 569 *rumpe moras;* Lucan, I. 204 *moras solvit belli.* — **coronatus**: see 3. 13 n.

8. **malobathro**: a Greek word corrupted from the Indian name, *tamalapattram* (= 'leaf of the tamala'), — of the fragrant leaf of the laurus cassia; here used for the *oil* of cassia. — **Syrio**: cf. *Syra merce,* I. 31. 12 n. — **capillos**: Intr. 42. With the whole description cf. Tib. III. 6. 63 *iam dudum Syrio madefactus tempora nardo | debueram sertis implicuisse comas.*

Tecum Philippos et celerem fugam
sensi, relicta non bene parmula,
cum fracta virtus et minaces
turpe solum tetigere mento.

Sed me per hostis Mercurius celer
denso paventem sustulit aere;
te rursus in bellum resorbens
unda fretis tulit aestuosis.

9. **Philippos,** etc.: *i.e.* the battle and the flight; not a case of hendiadys.

10. **sensi,** *I experienced.* — **relicta parmula**: whether Horace is here recalling a literal fact or merely employs the familiar Greek phrase in a figurative sense, it is difficult to say; but the latter is much more probable. The Greek ideal of 'returning with one's shield or on it' was foreign to the more business-like Roman, and belonged to war on a smaller scale, with simpler organization, and where personal prowess counted for more. It is true that as tribune Horace would have immediate charge of his men in battle, and might have occasion to use a shield (cf. Ennius *Ann.* 450 *sqq.* M), but it was no part of his duty to expose himself to personal danger. That, however, would not prevent him from using the stock phrase, — which is at least as near the reality as vss. 13 *sq.*, — especially as he found in each of his great models in Greek lyric, Archilochus, (*Fr.* 6), Alcaeus (Herod. V. 95), and apparently Anacreon (*Fr.* 28), a similar confession of the loss of his shield in battle. — **non bene**: not a confession of cowardice, as some too seriously take it; the phrase is entirely colorless and not only says nothing that is not already implied in **relicta parmula,** but rather breaks the force of that confession, as a man disarms criticism by anticipating it with a frank avowal that he does not defend his conduct. The diminutive **parmula** is in keeping with this deprecatory tone.

11. **fracta** (sc. *est*) **virtus,** etc.: *i.e.* when brave men went down in the crash, and braggarts (**minaces**) were humbled to the dust.

12. **turpe**: Intr. 125. — **solum tetigere mento**: *i.e.* in prostrating themselves before the victors; cf. Caesar's description of his prisoners at Pharsalus, *B. C.* III. 98. 2 *passis palmis proiecti ad terram flentes ab eo salutem petiverunt.*

13. **sed me,** etc., *but* (at this point we were separated;) *I*, etc. — **Mercurius**: Horace in effect calls his safe escape to Italy, through what were doubtless very real dangers (cf. **paventem**), 'providential'; cf. III. 4. 26, 28; Intr. 13. Mercury as διάκτορος conducted him as he did Priam unseen through the Greek camp (I. 10. 13 *sqq*). See, however, 17. 29 n.

14. **denso aere**: ἠέρι πολλῇ, as Aphrodite rescued Paris, *Il.* III. 381. The device occurs frequently in Homer, and was borrowed by the Latin poets, as Verg. *A.* I. 411, etc.

16. **unda**: **the surging sea of**

Ergo obligatam redde Iovi dapem,
longaque fessum militia latus
depone sub lauru mea, nec
parce cadis tibi destinatis.

Oblivioso levia Massico
ciboria exple, funde capacibus
unguenta de conchis. Quis udo
deproperare apio coronas

curatve myrto? Quem Venus arbitrum

public life (cf. *mersor civilibus undis*, *Ep*. I. 1. 16). When Pompeius seemed to be so near the shore (of peaceful private life) that like Horace he would actually gain a footing, the receding wave drew him back (**resorbens**) and carried him once more out to sea. — **fretis** : instrumental ablative.

17. **ergo** : *i.e.* since in spite of all this you are safely home at last; referring back to vs. 3. — **obligatam** (sc. *votis;* cf. 8. 5), *pledged;* cf. *debito*, I. 36. 2 n. — **Iovi** : as the universal source of help and blessing (*Iuppiter Opitulus*, *Conservator*, *Custos*), and particularly as protector of strangers; cf. I. 28. 28 n. — **dapem** : here in its proper sense of a sacrificial feast; see, further, note on *sanguine*, I. 36. 2.

18. **latus** : often used, as here, in a wider sense, for the whole body or person, or for any part of it, in reference to external contact or influence; cf. III. 10. 20; 27. 26; *S*. I. 3. 59 *nulli malo latus obdit apertum;* II. 6. 34 *aliena negotia centum circa saliunt latus;* Mart. VI. 76. 1 *sacri lateris custos* (*i.e.* the emperor's body-guard).

19. **lauru** : a favorite shade-tree on account of its thick foliage; cf. 15. 9 n.—**nec parce**: Intr. 88, 89 N.

20. **cadis** : Intr. 128. — **tibi destinatis** : *i.e.* as the event has proved; the wine was set apart for keeping high holiday (cf. *Epod*. 9. 1) and Pompeius' unexpected return has brought the fitting occasion.

21. **oblivioso** : cf. Tib. II. 1. 46 *securo mero;* Intr. 125. — **Massico** : see I. 1. 19 n.

22. **ciboria** : cups of polished metal (**levia**) shaped, according to Porphyrio, like the leaves of the Egyptian bean after which they were named.—**exple,** *fill high*. The chiastic asyndeton (**exple, funde**) marks the poet's eagerness, as he hastens forward, in imagination, to the enjoyment of the feast.

23. **conchis** : shell-shaped vessels for ointment.— **quis**: sc. *puer;* cf. 11. 18, I. 38. 1.

24. **deproperare**: a compressed expression for *propere conficere* or the like; cf. III. 24. 62. For the prefix **de-** see 1. 35 n, I. 9. 11 n. For the infinitive see Intr. 94 *b*. — **apio** : cf. I. 36. 16.

25. **curat,** *will see to*. — **-ve** : Intr. 119 *b*. — **Venus** : *i.e.* the *iactus Veneris*, the highest throw of the *tali*, in which the faces turned up were all different. — **arbitrum bibendi** : see I. 4. 18 n.

dicet bibendi? Non ego sanius
bacchabor Edonis; recepto
dulce mihi furere est amico.

## VIII.

Vlla si iuris tibi peierati
poena, Barine, nocuisset umquam,
dente si nigro fieres vel uno
turpior ungui,
crederem; sed tu simul obligasti
perfidum votis caput, enitescis
pulchrior multo, iuvenumque prodis
publica cura.

27. **Edonis**: a Thracian tribe; cf. I. 27. 2 n.—**recepto,** *found again.*

VIII. Barine, 'the Maid of Barium,' is a heartless coquette. The poet declines her professions of devotion with ironical compliments on the impunity and success with which she plays her perfidious game. — Metre, 174.

1. **ulla . . . umquam, uno . . . ungui**: the alliteration (Intr. 131) aids the emphasis. — **iuris peierati**: formed from *peierare* after the analogy of *ius iurandum* from *iurare*, the perfect being naturally used, especially with **poena,** to express the accomplished fact which the punishment should follow. The phrase is not found elsewhere.

2. **poena nocuisset**: strictly either *poena fuisset* or *ius peieratum nocuisset* would have expressed the idea sufficiently. The more pregnant expression marks the poet's earnestness, which takes two points for the emphasis to rest on.

3. **dente, ungui**: abl. of measure of difference. The predicate **fieres turpior** is divided (Intr. 120), and with it the two adjectives **uno nigro,** both of which belong with each substantive (Intr. 121). — **si fieres**: *i.e.* if ever.

5. **simul**: see I. 4. 17 n. — **obligasti**: cf. 7. 17 n. There the victim (implied in *dapem*) was pledged, to be forfeited in case the prayer for a safe return was granted; here the **caput** is put in pawn, to be offered up to the vengeance of the gods if Barine should break her oath.

6. **perfidum**: Intr. 124. The perjury was committed in the very act of swearing. — **votis,** *imprecations*, prayers to the gods to shower curses on her head should she prove false; cf. Hannibal's oath, Liv. XXI. 45. 8.

7. **prodis**: *sc.* into the streets.

8. **cura**: cf. I. 14. 18 n.

9. **expedit,** *it pays* (with emphasis). — **opertos,** *buried.*

10. **fallere**: by swearing falsely by them; cf. Prop. II. 20. 15 *ossa*

Expedit matris cineres opertos
fallere et toto taciturna noctis
signa cum caelo gelidaque divos
morte carentis.

Ridet hoc, inquam, Venus ipsa, rident
simplices Nymphae ferus et Cupido,
semper ardentis acuens sagittas
cote cruenta.

Adde quod pubes tibi crescit omnis,
servitus crescit nova, nec priores
impiae tectum dominae relinquunt,
saepe minati.

Te suis matres metuunt iuvencis,
te senes parci miseraeque nuper
virgines nuptae, tua ne retardet
aura maritos.

*tibi iuro per matris et ossa parentis;* | *si fallo cinis heu sit mihi uterque gravis.* For the assonance of this verse and the next see Intr. 131.

13. **ridet . . . rident**: Intr. 116*g*. —**Venus ipsa**: who has lovers especially under her protection.

14. **Nymphae**: to whose nature (**simplices**) such duplicity is utterly foreign. They are in the retinue of Venus here as in I. 4. 6, 30. 6.—**Cupido**: with his arrow fresh from the bleeding hearts. All the powers of love feel Barine's fascination, and can only smile when she defies their authority.

15. **ardentis**, *burning*. The attribute properly belongs to Cupid (Intr. 124).

16. **cruenta**: from the arrow-tip. Observe how, by a skilful disposition of epithets (**ferus, cruenta, ardentis**), the picture (cf. I. 2. 7 n) is made more full and graphic.

17. **adde quod**, etc.: further reason for *expedit* 9.

18. **servitus crescit nova**: explaining the somewhat vague **tibi crescit. servitus nova** is used concretely: *a new set of slaves.*

19. **impiae**: recalling the main theme, her ready perjury, and indicating the reason of **minati.**

21. **te . . . te . . . tua**: in mock eulogy; cf. I. 10. 9 n.—**iuvencis**: *i.e.* their sons; cf. 5. 6.

22. **parci**: such a person would be *impotens, procax, magnifica, sumptuosa, nobilis* (Ter. *Heaut.* 227) at the expense of her lovers.

23. **virgines**: used by the poets, like *puella*, of young wives.

24. **aura**: see I. 5. 11 n. The metaphor is here used more consciously,—'the breeze that draws to you'; cf. Cic. *Sest.* 101 *quem neque honoris aura potuit umquam de suo cursu demovere.*

## IX.

Non semper imbres nubibus hispidos
manant in agros aut mare Caspium
vexant inaequales procellae
usque, nec Armeniis in oris,

amice Valgi, stat glacies iners
mensis per omnis aut Aquilonibus
querceta Gargani laborant
et foliis viduantur orni:

IX. To C. Valgius Rufus, begging him to dry his tears for the loss of his favorite slave-boy Mystes, and turn from his incessant elegies to sing the triumphs of Augustus. Valgius was one of the group of Horace's literary friends named in *S.* I. 10. 81 *sqq.*, a writer of elegies and epigrams and perhaps of epic (*Paneg. Messal.* 180), as well as of works in prose. He was consul B.C. 12, and therefore probably considerably younger than Horace. The ode was written between B.C. 27, when Octavian received the title of Augustus (cf. vs. 19), and 23, the year of publication of these books. The allusions in vss. 20 *sqq.* do not fix the date more definitely. They refer to triumphs of diplomacy only, brought about by internal dissensions in oriental monarchies, especially Armenia and Parthia, which led one or other of the rival princes to appeal to Rome (cf. I. 26. 5 n); but of the details we are not accurately informed. The allusion in vs. 23 may be to a Scythian embassy which came to Augustus when he was in Tarraco, B.C. 26 or 25. — Metre, 176.

1. **non semper**, etc.: for the arrangement of words in this ode see Intr. 116 *b*.— **imbres, procellae, glacies, Aquilonibus**: the gloomy aspects of nature, types of human tears and grief, do not last always. The examples are grouped by **non . . . nec** in two pairs, each connected by **aut**: brief showers or squalls, protracted cold or storm. In the last example **et** merely connects the two kinds of trees named, and is subordinate to **aut**. — **nubibus**: Intr. 70. — **hispidos**, *squalid*, as they appear at the end of the winter, after long neglect and exposure to the rain; in contrast with their trim and cheerful aspect when under cultivation. The epithet is therefore necessary for the present comparison.

2. **Caspium**: Intr. 117 *a*. The Caspian was described as *atrox, saevum, sine portibus, procellis undique expositum* (Mela III. 38).

3. **inaequales**, *fitful*.

4. **Armeniis**: cf. *Caspium*, 2 n. It is clear that Armenia was much in the thoughts of the Romans when Horace wrote this ode. See also vs. 20 n.

5. **stat**: more expressive than (*e.g.*) *manet*; cf. I. 9. 1 n.

7. **Gargani**: exposed by its situation, with the sea on three

tu semper urges flebilibus modis
Mysten ademptum, nec tibi Vespero
surgente decedunt amores
nec rapidum fugiente solem.

At non ter aevo functus amabilem
ploravit omnis Antilochum senex
annos, nec impubem parentes
Troilon aut Phrygiae sorores

flevere semper: desine mollium
tandem querellarum, et potius nova
cantemus Augusti tropaea
Caesaris et rigidum Niphaten

sides of it, to the fury of the winds.— **laborant** : see I. 9. 3 n.

9. **urges,** *pursue, dwell upon.*

10. **Mysten ademptum** : Intr. 105 *a.* — **Vespero** : the planet Venus.

11. **surgente** : *i.e.* in the evening. The planet was said to 'rise' when it began to be visible as evening star. — **decedunt,** *abate.* — **amores** : the plural (Intr. 128) is used with reference to the repeated expression of his love.

12. **rapidum**: apparently a standing epithet of the sun (cf. Verg. *G.* I. 92, 424), which appears to have been used originally of his fierce, consuming heat (*rapio*); cf. Verg. *G.* IV. 263 *rapidus ignis,* 425 *rapidus Sirius, E.* 2. 10 *rapido aestu;* but here it perhaps refers to the rapidity with which he seems to move at his rising. — **fugiente solem** : *i.e.* at dawn, when Venus is morning star (Lucifer); rising before the sun, she is visible while he is still below the horizon, but vanishes as he advances.

13. **ter aevo functus senex** : *i.e.* Nestor; *aevum* here, like *aetas hominum* in Cic. *C. M.* 31 (*tertiam iam aetatem hominum vivebat*) is the ordinary or average life of man; cf. 2. 5. The phrase is a reproduction of the familiar description, *Il.* I. 250 τῷ δ' ἤδη δύο μὲν γενεαὶ μερόπων ἀνθρώπων | ἐφθίαθ' . . . μετὰ δὲ τριτάτοισιν ἄνασσεν· cf. *Odys.* III. 245.

14. **Antilochum**: son of Nestor, one of the most charming characters in the Iliad. He was killed in battle, while defending his father, by Memnon.

16. **Troilon** : a stock instance of premature death; cf. Cic. *Tusc.* I. 93. He was slain by Achilles; cf. Verg. *A.* I. 474 *sqq.* The examples of Antilochus and Troilus, both cut off in their youth, are cited as parallel to that of Mystes. — **Phrygiae** : cf. *Phrygum,* I. 15. 34 n.

17. **desine querellarum** : see Intr. 67. — **mollium,** *tender,* with a suggestion of unmanliness.

19. **tropaea**: probably referring to the Roman victories in Spain in 26 or 25; see Ode 6, intr. note.

20. **rigidum** : *sc.* with snow and

Medumque flumen gentibus additum
victis minores volvere vertices,
intraque praescriptum Gelonos
exiguis equitare campis.

## X.

Rectius vives, Licini, neque altum
semper urgendo neque, dum procellas
cautus horrescis, nimium premendo
litus iniquum.

ice. — **Niphaten**: a mountain in the interior of Armenia, mentioned also by Vergil, *G.* III. 30. Later poets supposed it to be a river (Luc. III. 245, Sil. XIII. 765, Juv. 6. 409, etc.).

21. **Medum flumen**: the Euphrates; cf. *Scythicum amnem* (the Tanais), III. 4. 36; *amnis Tusci* (the Tiber) *S.* II. 2. 32. For the form of the adjective see Intr. 65.

22. **minores**: indicating humbled pride; cf. Verg. *A.* VIII. 726 *Euphrates ibat iam mollior undis.* — **volvere**: for the acc. with inf. joined with the simple acc. of the object cf. Prop. IV. 2. 7 *et cecini Curios fratres et Horatia pila* | . . . *Hannibalemque lares Romana sede fugantes,* | *anseris et tutum voce fuisse Iovem.*

23. **praescriptum**: *sc.* by conditions of peace imposed upon them. — **Gelonos**: a Scythian tribe; here used for the Scythians in general; cf. *Sithoniis*, I. 18. 9 n.

24. **equitare**: cf. I. 2. 51 n. — **campis**: Intr. 69.

X. Licinius Murena, to whom this ode is addressed, was probably the son of Cicero's client of that name, but was adopted by Terentius Varro, the father of Proculeius and Terentia (see 2. 5 n). He reduced the Salassi in 25 B.C., and established in their territory the colony now called Aosta. In 23 he was the colleague of Augustus in the consulship, an evidence of high esteem on the part of the emperor; but in the same year he was convicted of complicity in the conspiracy of Fannius Caepio and executed. The present ode is one of the most finished of Horace's poems, and consists, like much of his best work, of a chain of pithy epigrammatic *sententiae* on the conduct of life, presenting in various forms and under various figures his favorite doctrine of the golden mean, with its corollary, μηδὲν ἄγαν, or, as he expresses it in *Ep.* I. 6, *nil admirari*, — the *aequam memento servare mentem* of Ode 3. — Metre, 174.

1. **rectius**: not used in a moral sense, but with reference to the practical ordering of one's life. — **altum urgendo**, *by pressing out to sea.* The 'voyage of life' is a favorite figure with Horace; cf. vs. 23 *sq.*, I. 34. 3 *sq.*, III. 29. 57 *sqq.*, *Ep.* II. 2. 200 *sqq.*, etc.

3. **premendo**, *hugging.*

Auream quisquis mediocritatem
diligit, tutus caret obsoleti
sordibus tecti, caret invidenda
sobrius aula.

Saepius ventis agitatur ingens
pinus et celsae graviore casu
decidunt turres feriuntque summos
fulgura montis.

Sperat infestis, metuit secundis
alteram sortem bene praeparatum
pectus. Informis hiemes reducit
Iuppiter, idem

submovet ; non, si male nunc, et olim

4. **iniquum**, *unfriendly*, on account of its rocks and shoals.

5. **auream** : see I. 5. 9 n. — **mediocritatem** : a translation of ἡ μεσότης. Cf. Cic. *de Off.* I. 89 *mediocritatem illam quae est inter nimium et parum*.

6. **diligit**, *cherishes*.— **tutus caret**, *is secure from*. — **obsoleti**, etc.: *i.e.* not merely poverty, but the slovenly poverty of the sluggard. The man who aims at *mediocritas* is *sure* to rise above this low state, because his aim is not too high to attain, nor will he be in danger of falling down to it, because he does not climb so high as to risk a fall. On the other hand, his temperateness (**sobrius**) will save him from ever becoming the mark of envy as the lord of a palace.

7. **caret** : Intr. 116 *h*.

9–12. The suggestion in **invidenda** is developed in three striking illustrations of the danger of rising too high. For the position of the emphatic words see Intr. 116 *b*.

13. **sperat**, etc.: the wise man will observe the same moderation in dealing with the conditions of his life which are beyond his control, refraining from both extremes of despair in adversity and overconfidence in prosperity.—**infestis** (for the more commonplace *adversis*), **secundis** : neut. pl., with abstract force ; cf. I. 34. 12 n. They are best taken as dative ; cf. Sal. *Cat.* 40. 2 *requirere coepit quem exitum tantis malis sperarent ; ib.* 2 (*illos videt*) *miseriis remedium mortem exspectare*.

14. **alteram**, *a reversal of ;* lit. 'the other' (not 'another,' *aliam*).

15. **informis** : Intr. 125 ; cf. Verg. *G.* III. 354 *sed iacet aggeribus niveis informis et alto | terra gelu late*.— **reducit**, *brings round*. Compounds of *re-* are frequently used in this sense of the movement of the heavenly bodies and the seasons ; cf. III. 8. 9, IV. 2. 58.

17. **non si**, etc.: the position of **non** shows that it belongs to the whole sentence, and denies, not

sic erit; quondam cithara tacentem
suscitat musam neque semper arcum
tendit Apollo.

Rebus angustis animosus atque
fortis appare; sapienter idem
contrahes vento nimium secundo
turgida vela.

## XI.

Quid bellicosus Cantaber et Scythes,
Hirpine Quincti, cogitet Hadria
divisus obiecto, remittas
quaerere nec trepides in usum

the apodosis, — which may perhaps prove to be true, — but the validity of the inference; equivalent to 'it doesn't follow that, if, etc.' — **male** (sc. *est*), *things go ill.* — **et,** *also.* — **olim,** *by and by;* see IV. 4. 5 n.

18. **quondam**: usually restricted to the past or (rarely) to the future; here general, *sometimes.* — **tacentem**: music is silent in times of pestilence, which Apollo sends with his arrows; cf. *Il.* I. 44 *sqq.* The same god who brings disease and suffering brings songs and gladness.

22. **sapienter,** *if you are wise.* — **idem,** *yet you.*

23. **contrahes,** etc.: closing with the metaphor with which he began. — **nimium**: with **secundo.**

XI. Of Quinctius Hirpinus nothing is definitely known, not even whether he is the 'optimus Quinctius' to whom *Ep.* I. 16 was written. In the present verses the poet represents himself as talking to his friend on one of his favorite themes, the folly of taking too much thought for the morrow. We may suppose the two to be walking together in the country or in a park, with the streets not far away. The allusions in the first strophe assign the ode to the years 27–25 B.C. — Metre, 176.

1. **Cantaber**: see 6. 2 n. — **Scythes**: the allusion is probably to some disturbance that occasioned the Scythian embassy to Augustus at Tarraco; see Ode 9, intr. note (end).

2. **Hirpine Quincti**: see 2. 3 n. — **Hadria divisus**: a ground for security, added only in the case of the Scythians, because there was nothing to be feared from the Cantabrians but stubborn resistance. On the other hand, a successful incursion of a barbarian horde into Moesia or Pannonia would expose Italy itself to the danger of invasion.

3. **obiecto,** *the barrier of.* — **remittas quaerere**: Intr. 87, 94 *j.*

4. **nec**: Intr. 89 N. — **trepides,** *fret yourself;* cf. III. 29. 32. — **in,**

poscentis aevi pauca. Fugit retro
levis iuventas et decor, arida
pellente lascivos amores
canitie facilemque somnum.

Non semper idem floribus est honor
vernis, neque uno luna rubens nitet
voltu. Quid aeternis minorem
consiliis animum fatigas?

Cur non sub alta vel platano vel hac
pinu iacentes sic temere et rosa
canos odorati capillos,
dum licet, Assyriaque nardo

('in reference to'), *about.* — **usum aevi,** *the use of a life, i.e.* the way to live it. For the thought cf. I. 9. 13 *sqq.*, 11. 1 *sqq.*

5. **pauca**: Intr. 116 *b.* — **fugit,** etc.: reason for the advice just given; cf. I. 11. 7.

6. **lēvis,** *smooth-cheeked,* as in IV. 6. 28 (of Apollo).

8. **facilem**: *i.e.* that comes readily; cf. III. 21. 4 and III. 1. 21 n.

9. **non semper,** etc.: reminders that everything is transitory are all about us; cf. IV. 7. 7 *sqq.* — **semper idem**: *i.e.* changeless, imperishable; it fades away. — **honor,** *beauty.*

10. **neque uno,** etc.: *i.e.* it waxes or wanes and changes its hue (**rubens**).

11. **aeternis**: *i.e.* reaching out into the unlimited future: cf. *spem longam,* I. 4. 15, 11. 7. — **minorem,** *which is unequal to them,* unable to cope with them.

12. **consiliis**: with both **minorem** and **fatigas**; Intr. 76.

13. **alta, hac**: to be taken together with each substantive; Intr. 121. — **platano**: the oriental plane tree (sycamore), with leaves more jagged and of a darker green, but otherwise closely resembling our occidental species (buttonwood). Its stately form and heavy foliage made it a favorite shade tree; cf. 15. 4.

14. **sic temere,** *just as we are, offhand;* the Homeric μὰψ οὕτω (*e.g. Il.* II. 120); cf. Verg. *A.* IX. 329 *tris iuxta famulos temere inter tela iacentis.* **temere** has its proper meaning of *sine consilio,* without premeditation. — **rosa, nardo**: see 3. 13 n. For the singular **rosa** see Intr. 127.

15. **canos**: Horace at least began to grow gray early (Intr. 29). The word adds significance to **dum licet.** — **odorati**: *i.e.* 'wreathed with fragrant,' etc. — **capillos**: Intr. 42.

16. **dum licet**: cf. 3. 15 *sq.* — **Assyria**: really Arabian or Indian, but imported from Syria, with which Assyria is often confused by the poets; cf. 7. 8, I. 31. 12 n; Tib. I. 3. 7 *Assyrios odores.* — **nardo**: here fem.; elsewhere in Horace (*Epod.* 5. 59, 13. 9) neuter.

potamus uncti? Dissipat Euhius
curas edacis. Quis puer ocius
restinguet ardentis Falerni
pocula praetereunte lympha?
Quis devium scortum eliciet domo
Lyden? Eburna dic age cum lyra
maturet, in comptum Lacaenae
more comam religata nodum.

## XII.

Nolis longa ferae bella Numantiae
nec durum Hannibalem nec Siculum mare

17. **potamus**: the present in a hortatory question, common in colloquial language, especially with *quin* (as Liv. I. 57. 7 *quin conscendimus equos*), and frequent in comedy. See Intr. 78. — **Euhius**: see I. 18. 9 n.

18. **edacis**: cf. *mordaces sollicitudines*, I. 18. 4. — **quis puer**: cf. 7. 23. — **ocius**, *quickly*.

19. **restinguet**: *i.e.* dilute its strength. The word is chosen with reference to **ardentis** (*fiery*), for which cf. Juv. 10. 27 *lato Setinum ardebit in auro.* — **Falerni**: cf. I. 27. 9 n.

21. **devium**: *i.e.* living apart, not consorting with the common herd; cf. I. 17. 6, III. 25. 12.

22. **eburna**: *i.e.* decorated with ivory, as in *S.* II. 6. 103 *eburnos lectos.* — **age**: with **dic**, as III. 4. 1, *S.* II. 7. 92.

23. **maturet**: sc. *venire*; cf. *deproperare*, 7. 24 n. — **in comptum nodum**: cf. Ov. *M.* VIII. 319 *crinis erat simplex, nodum collectus in unum.* The toilet of the music girl was to be neat but simple, in keeping with the whole spirit of the occasion, which was a protest against elaborate preparation for enjoyment; and she was not to keep them waiting. — **Lacaenae more**: cf. Prop. IV. 14. 28 (of the Spartan women) *est neque odoratae cura molesta comae.*

24. **comam religata**: Intr. 41.

XII. In this ode, as in I. 6, Horace declines to undertake epic themes with his *imbellis lyra*, and tells Maecenas that his own prose will serve better to record the achievements of Augustus. He then turns to a fit subject for his lyre, the beauty and accomplishments of Licymnia, who is undoubtedly Terentia, Maecenas' wife (Intr. 21). From the last strophes it would appear that the ode was written during their honeymoon. In the assumed name Horace has followed the usual practice of the Latin poets, selecting a Greek name metrically equivalent (◡ – ◡ ◡) to Terentia, as Catullus' Lesbia (for Clodia), Tibullus' Delia (for Plania), etc. (Apuleius, *Apol.* 10). — Metre, 172.

Poeno purpureum sanguine mollibus
aptari citharae modis,
nec saevos Lapithas et nimium mero
Hylaeum domitosque Herculea manu
Telluris iuvenes, unde periculum
fulgens contremuit domus

Saturni veteris; tuque pedestribus
dices historiis proelia Caesaris,

1. **nolis** (standing emphatically at the head of the sentence), *you surely would not have*, etc.—**longa**: the siege of Numantia lasted from 141 to 133 B.C.—**ferae**: the Numantines after their long and stubborn resistance finally set fire to their city, and in large numbers put themselves to death rather than surrender.

2. **nec**: carrying on the negative in **nolis**; see Madv. 458 *c*, Obs. 2.—**Siculum mare**: the scene of the most important battles of the first Punic war.

3. **mollibus,** etc.: *i.e.* to have such themes presented in a form so unsuitable and inadequate; cf. I. 6. 9 *sqq.*

5. **nec saevos,** etc.: the same objection applies to mythological subjects. These are grouped together by **et** and **-que,** subordinate to **nec**; cf. *et*, 9. 8, and note on 9. 1.—**Lapithas**: see I. 18. 8 n.—**nimium,** *elated, insolent;* cf. Tac. *Hist.* IV. 23 *rebus secundis nimii.*

6. **Hylaeum**: one of the Centaurs; cf. Verg. *G.* II. 457 *et magno Hylaeum Lapithis cratere minantem.*—**domitosque,** etc.: in their battle with the Giants (**Telluris iuvenes,** γηγενεῖς) the gods were assisted by Hercules. Gaea had made her sons proof against the weapons of the gods, so that they could be conquered only with mortal aid; see Preller-Robert, *Gr. Myth.* I. p. 73.—**Herculea manu**: cf. I. 3. 36.

7. **unde** (for *a quibus;* cf. I. 12. 17 n) **periculum**: cf. *aliunde fata*, 13. 16; *metu insidiarum a meis*, Cic. *Rep.* VI. 14; Madv. 298 *b*. 2. Usually a participle, *ortum*, or the like, would be inserted.

8. **fulgens domus**: cf. III. 3. 33 *lucidae sedes* (sc. *deorum*).—**contremuit**: Intr. 51 *a*.

9. **Saturni**: *i.e.* of the gods, who were Saturn's descendants.—**tuque**: a third subject, which was more than once suggested to him (see *S.* II. 1. 10 *sqq.*), Horace puts away with a compliment to Maecenas. Hence the change to an affirmative conjunction, and the emphasis on **tu.**—**pedestribus,** *prose.* The word, so far as appears, was first used by Horace in this sense (*S.* II. 6. 17 *musa pedestri*) in imitation of the Greek πεζὸς λόγος. With a similar figure he calls his hexameters *sermones repentis per humum* in contrast with the lofty style in which the exploits of Augustus should be sung (*Ep.* II. 1. 250 *sq.*). Whether Maecenas actually wrote or proposed to write such a work as is here suggested we do not know. See Plin. *N. H.* VII. 148.

10. **dices**: for the force of the future see Intr. 79.

Maecenas, melius ductaque per vias
regum colla minacium.

Me dulcis dominae Musa Licymniae
cantus, me voluit dicere lucidum
fulgentis oculos, et bene mutuis
fidum pectus amoribus;

quam nec ferre pedem dedecuit choris
nec certare ioco nec dare bracchia
ludentem nitidis virginibus sacro
Dianae celebris die.

Num tu quae tenuit dives Achaemenes

11. **per vias**: *sc.* of Rome, in the triumphal procession.

12. **regum colla**: instead of *reges*, because they were led by the neck; cf. Prop. II. 1. 33 (*canerem*) *regum auratis circumdata colla catenis* (also referring to the triumphs of Augustus).—**minacium**: cf. 7. 11 n, IV. 3. 8. The epithet sets off by contrast their present humbled state; cf. *Ep.* II. 1. 191 *mox trahitur manibus regum fortuna retortis.*

13. **dulcis**: accusative.—**dominae,** *my lady*. Married ladies were regularly addressed by this title.

14. **lucidum fulgentis**: Intr. 48.

15. **bene fidum**: like 'bien fidèle'; cf. *bene sano, S.* I. 3. 61, *bene firmum*, Enn. *Ann.* I. 105 M; and the opposite, *male fida*, Verg. *A.* II. 23. Cf. I. 9. 24 n.

17. **quam nec dedecuit,** *who could with perfect grace, i.e.* keeping within the bounds of what was becoming and womanly.—**ferre,** *move;* cf. Verg. *G.* I. 11 *ferte simul Faunique pedem Dryadesque puellae.*—**dedecuit**: cf. I. 38. 7. The perfect has its proper force, referring to the time when Maecenas became fascinated with her charms.—**choris**: dances at home or in private companies, which at this time were permissible for women within certain limits; cf. III. 6. 21.

18. **certare ioco**: *i.e.* in conversation; cf. Sall. *Cat.* 25. 5 (of Sempronia) *posse versus facere, iocum movere, sermone uti vel modesto vel molli vel procaci.*—**dare bracchia**: graceful movements of the arms were carefully studied in training for the dance.

19. **ludentem**: *i.e.* dancing, as in Verg. *E.* 6. 27 *tum vero in numerum Faunosque ferasque videres | ludere.*—**nitidis,** *spruce,* in holiday attire.—**virginibus**: dative with **dare.**

20. **Dianae celebris die**: for *die quo Diana celebris est, i.e.* when her temple is thronged (August 13); cf. Tib. IV. 4. 23 *Phoebe fave, . . . iam celeber, iam laetus eris.* Terentia as *virgo ingenua* could take part in this public religious dance.

21. **Achaemenes**: mythical founder of the Persian dynasty (Herod. I. 125, VII. 11); cf. III. 9. 4.

aut pinguis Phrygiae Mygdonias opes
permutare velis crine Licymniae,
plenas aut Arabum domos,
cum flagrantia detorquet ad oscula
cervicem, aut facili saevitia negat
quae poscente magis gaudeat eripi,
interdum rapere occupet?

## XIII.

Ille et nefasto te posuit die,

22. **Mygdonias**: *i.e.* of Midas, the mythical Phrygian king, whose touch turned all things to gold. Mygdonia was a district of Macedonia, which was associated with the legends of Midas and the Bryges, who were supposed to have migrated from that region into Asia Minor (Herod. VIII. 138, VII. 73). Another legend, however, told of a Phrygian king Mygdon (*Il.* III. 186).

23. **permutare**: see Intr. 74.

24. **Arabum**: see I. 29. 3 n.

25. **flagrantia**, *passionate*.—**detorquet cervicem**: *i.e.* turns away (**de-**) so as to expose her neck to the kiss. For the caesura of this verse see Intr. 149.

26. **negat**: sc. *ea* (*oscula*), the antecedent of **quae.**

27. **quae gaudeat, occupet**: subjunctive to express the reason for calling her *saevitia* '*facilis*.'—**poscente**: see Intr. 75, 103.

28. **rapere occupet**, *snatches them first herself*; cf. Liv. I. 30. 8 *cum bellum utrimque summa ope pararent, occupat Tullus in agrum Sabinum transire.* Intr. 94 *g*.

XIII. On the first of March B.C. 30 Horace had a narrow escape from the fall of a tree on his farm, an incident which he mentions repeatedly (17. 27, III. 4. 27, III. 8. 7) and makes the subject of the present ode. After roundly abusing the tree for so nearly causing his death, he proceeds to reflect on man's incapacity to foresee the fate which is closest at hand, and then on the great dead whom he would have met in the lower world,—a thought suggested perhaps by the famous passage in Plato's Apology of Socrates, but worked out in the form of a tribute to the power of lyric song. For the date of the accident see III. 8, intr. note.—Metre, 176.

1. **ille**: repeated with savage emphasis in the poet's outburst of wrath, which softens into reproach in **te . . . te**, vs. 11; cf. Tennyson's *The Fleet* 1 'You, you, if you should fail to understand, What England is and what her all-in-all, On you will come the curse of all the land.'—**nefasto die**: properly a day on which *nefas est praetori, apud quem lege agitur, fari tria verba 'do dico addico'* (Fest. p. 165). There was the same superstition about beginning anything

quicumque primum, et sacrilega manu
produxit, arbos, in nepotum
perniciem opprobriumque pagi;

illum et parentis crediderim sui
fregisse cervicem et penetralia
sparsisse nocturno cruore
hospitis; ille venena Colcha

et quicquid usquam concipitur nefas
tractavit, agro qui statuit meo
te triste lignum, te caducum
in domini caput immerentis.

Quid quisque vitet, numquam homini satis
cautum est in horas. Navita Bosporum

on such a day that many people nowadays feel in regard to Friday. — **posuit**, *planted*.

2. **quicumque**: sc. *posuit*. — **primum**: belonging in sense with **posuit**, although placed in the relative clause. Translate, *whoever it was in the first place*.

3. **produxit**, *reared*. — **in**, *to the*; expressing the purpose or destiny of both acts. — **nepotum**, *posterity*.

4. **pagi**, *the countryside*.

5. **et . . . et**, *both . . . and*, corresponding to **et . . . et** in the first strophe. 'He was capable of both of the two heinous forms of *impietas* named.' — **sui**: emphatic.

6. **fregisse cervicem** (sc. *laqueo*), *strangled*; cf. *Epod.* 3. 2, Sall. *Cat.* 55. 5 *laqueo gulam fregere*. — **penetralia**, *his very hearthstone*; properly the shrine of the household gods, under whose protection the life of the guest was sacred.

7. **nocturno**, *at dead of night*.

8. **Colcha**: *i.e.* such as Medea concocted; cf. *Epod.* 17. 35. For the form, see Intr. 65.

9. **quicquid**: here used adjectively as in *S.* II. 1. 60 *quisquis color*; cf. Verg. *A.* X. 493 *quisquis honos tumuli, quicquid solamen humandi est*.

10. **tractavit**, *dabbled in*. There is at most a very slight zeugma, **nefas** being the class of things to which **venena** are assigned.

11. **te . . . te**: cf. *ille*, vs. 1 n. — **triste lignum**, *dismal log*. — **caducum**, *ready to fall*; to be taken with **statuit**, as if this result was contemplated in 'setting up' the tree.

13. **quid vitet**: representing the 'question of doubt' (*quid vitem?*) of the man who is on the lookout for danger. — **homini**, *man* (in the abstract); the fact is stated as characteristic of the race.

14. **cautum est**, *is . . . on his guard*. Grammatically the subject is the clause **quid vitet**, and the perfect has its proper force ('has been provided against'). **homini** is ethical dative; cf. *tibi cautum volo* Plaut. *Pers.* 369. — **in horas**: formed after the analogy of *in dies*

Poenus perhorrescit neque ultra
caeca timet aliunde fata;
miles sagittas et celerem fugam
Parthi, catenas Parthus et Italum
robur: sed improvisa leti
vis rapuit rapietque gentis.
Quam paene furvae regna Proserpinae
et iudicantem vidimus Aeacum
sedesque discriptas piorum et
Aeoliis fidibus querentem
Sappho puellis de popularibus,
et te sonantem plenius aureo,
Alcaee, plectro dura navis,
dura fugae mala, dura belli.

—**Bosporum Poenus**: Intr. 117 *a*. The Thracian Bosporus is meant; cf. III. 4. 30.

15. **perhorrescit**: transitive, as often in Cicero. — **ultra**: with **timet**; when the danger of the sea is past, he *feels no further fear*.

16. **caeca**: here in a passive sense, *hidden*. — **timet**: for the prosody, see Intr. 179. — **aliunde fata**: cf. *unde periculum*, 12. 7 n.

17. **miles**: the Roman legionary, whose massive array (cf. *robur*, 19) was ill adapted to meet the stratagem referred to. — **sagittas**, etc.: *i.e.* the arrows of the Parthian in full flight; see I. 19. 11 n.

18. **catenas et Italum robur**: he is afraid to face *the solid strength of Italy*, and runs away to save himself from *chains*.

21. **furvae**, *dusky*, as queen of the lower world. The word was originally used (Gell. I. 18. 4) in the sense of *ater*, on which see I. 28. 13 n. — **regna**: Intr. 128. — **Prŏserpinae**: Intr. 178.

22. **iudicantem**, *sitting in judgment*. — **Aeacum**: son of Zeus and Aegina, and grandfather of Achilles; in his lifetime renowned for his righteousness, and after his death made a judge in the lower world.

23. **discriptas**, *allotted*.

24. **Aeoliis**: the dialect of Lesbos.—**querentem**: because of their coldness.

25. **Sappho**: Greek accusative (Σαπφώ). See Intr. 26.

26. **sonantem**: Intr. 51 *c*. — **plenius**, *in richer strain*, *sc*. than the love songs of Sappho. — **aureo**: implying his preëminence in song; cf. I. 5. 9 n, II. 1. 40; Quintil. X. 1. 63 *Alcaeus in parte operis aureo plectro merito donatur, qua tyrannos insectatus multum etiam moribus confert*.

27. **plectro**: see I. 26. 11 n. — **dura**, etc.: cf. I. 32. 6 *sqq*. Intr. 116 *g*. — **navis**, *of the sea*.

28. **fugae**, *of exile*; cf. *fugeret*, I. 7. 22 n.

Vtrumque sacro digna silentio
mirantur umbrae dicere; sed magis
pugnas et exactos tyrannos
densum umeris bibit aure volgus.

Quid mirum, ubi illis carminibus stupens
demittit atras belua centiceps
auris et intorti capillis
Eumenidum recreantur angues?

Quin et Prometheus et Pelopis parens

29. **utrumque**: emphatic; in contrast with **sed magis**, etc. — **sacro silentio**: *i.e.* profound silence, such as was enjoined during the performance of a religious ceremony. See I. 36. 1 n; III. 1. 2. For the ablative, which influences both **digna** and **mirantur**, see Intr. 76.

30. **mirantur**, *listen in wonder*. — **dicere**: depending on the notion of *hearing* contained in **mirantur**. The present infinitive here, as often, expresses a direct perception of the words spoken (not indirect through report); cf. Cic. *Mur.* 58 *saepe hoc maiores natu dicere audivi* ('I have heard them say,' not 'that they said'). For the meaning see I. 6. 5 n.

31. **pugnas**, etc.: the themes sung by Alcaeus.—**exactos tyrannos**: Intr. 105 *a*.

32. **densum** (= *stipatum*) **umeris**: in their eagerness to get near the singer.—**bibit aure**: cf. Prop. IV. 6. 8 *suspensis auribus ista bibam*; Verg. *A.* IV. 359 *vocemque his auribus hausi*.

33. **quid mirum**: *sc.* that the happy shades in Elysium should be entranced, when (**ubi**) even the monsters of the lower world are charmed, and the wicked in Tartarus forget their torments. For the construction of the verbs see Intr. 85.

34. **demittit**: as a watch-dog he keeps his ears usually pricked up. — **atras**: see I. 28. 13 n.—**belua**: Cerberus. — **centiceps**: like the Hydra, Cerberus was pictured with an indefinite number of heads. Hesiod (*Theog.* 312) describes him as κύνα πεντηκοντακάρηνον. In the Latin poets he usually has three, as in 19. 31; cf. Verg. *A.* VI. 417.

36. **recreantur**, *are relieved* (as in III. 24. 16), *i.e.* by the softening influence of the music on the temper of the Furies. — **angues**: masculine, as it more commonly is in prose; in poetry the feminine is more frequent.

37. **quin et**, *nay even*; passing to the stronger case of the soothing of pain. For similar descriptions of the power of music in the lower world; cf. III. 11. 15 *sqq.*, Verg. *G.* IV. 481. — **Prometheus**: usually represented as having been released from the under-world. Horace alone of extant authors (here, 18. 35, and *Epod.* 17. 67) represents him as still suffering in Tartarus. — **Pelopis parens**: see I. 28. 7 n, and cf. *Epod.* 17. 65.

dulci laborem decipitur sono,
nec curat Orion leones
aut timidos agitare lyncas.

## XIV.

Eheu fugaces, Postume, Postume,
labuntur anni, nec pietas moram
rugis et instanti senectae
adferet indomitaeque morti;
non si trecenis quotquot eunt dies,

38. **laborem,** *suffering*. For the case see Intr. 50. (For the genitive *laborum*, which has the support of some good manuscripts, and is perhaps right, see Intr. 67.) — **decipitur:** *i.e.* loses the sense of it, under the spell of the music; cf. *S.* II. 2. 12 *molliter austerum studio fallente laborem*.

39. **curat agitare:** Intr. 120. For the construction, see Intr. 94 *i*. — **Orion:** a mighty hunter, killed by Diana. He is devoted to his favorite pursuit even in Hades. (*Odys.* XI. 572); cf. Verg. *A*. VI. 653 *quae gratia currum | armorumque fuit vivis, quae cura nitentis | pascere equos, eadem sequitur tellure repostos*.

40. **lyncas:** more commonly feminine.

XIV. Whether the Postumus of this ode is a friend of the poet or merely a convenient name we can only guess. In him Horace addresses a man of wealth, surrounded by all the comforts that can contribute to the enjoyment of life, but perhaps a trifle overcareful in the use of his means. Horace preaches to him on one of his favorite themes, the swift flight of time and the inevitable approach of death, but the moral which he is fond of drawing, that not possession, but enjoyment, is the end to be sought, is here rather implied than distinctly expressed. — Metre, 176.

2. **labuntur,** *glide by*.

3. **rugis, senectae, morti:** notice the climax.

4. **indomitae,** *inexorable*. Death is here personified, the Ἀΐδης ἀμείλιχος ἠδ' ἀδάμαστος of *Il.* IX. 158.

5. **non si,** *no, not if*. The apodosis is contained in **non,** which repeats **nec adferet.** — **trecenis tauris:** three hecatombs; an intentional hyperbole to make the assertion as strong as possible; cf. vs. 26. Such enormous sacrifices, however, were not unknown, as, for example, after the battle of Lake Trasimenus; see Liv. XXII. 10. 7. — **quotquot eunt dies,** *every day that goes by;* a paraphrase for *quotidie*. For **eunt** (more expressive than *sunt*) cf. IV. 5. 7 *gratior it dies; Ep.* II 2. 55 *anni euntes*.

amice, places inlacrimabilem
Plutona tauris, qui ter amplum
Geryonen Tityonque tristi
compescit unda, scilicet omnibus,
quicumque terrae munere vescimur,
enaviganda, sive reges
sive inopes erimus coloni.
Frustra cruento Marte carebimus
fractisque rauci fluctibus Hadriae,
frustra per autumnos nocentem
corporibus metuemus Austrum.

6. **places**: conative. — **inlacrimabilem**: 'inaccessible to tears,' either in an active sense, 'incapable of weeping,' *tearless*, as here, or passively, 'incapable of being wept for,' as IV. 9. 26; cf. *flebilis*, IV. 2. 21 (active) and I. 24. 9 (passive).

7. **ter amplum**, *threefold huge;* referring both to his triple form (*forma tricorporis umbrae*, Verg. *A.* VI. 289) and supernatural size.

8. **Geryonen**: a gigantic monster of the island of Erythia, in the far West, killed by Hercules, who had been sent to take his cattle; Verg. *A.* VIII. 201 *sqq.* — **Tityon**: a giant, son of Gaea, killed by Apollo and Diana for insulting Latona. His body lay in the underworld *porrectus novem per iugera terrae* (Tib. I. 3. 75), with a vulture ever feeding on his liver; cf. Verg. *A.* VI. 595 *sqq.*

9. **compescit**, *confines.* — **unda**: the Styx. — **scilicet omnibus**, *yes, all of us;* passing from the particular examples of the irresistible power of Hades to the general fact; cf. *sed omnis*, I. 28. 15,

10. **quicumque**, etc.: a paraphrase for 'all mankind,' formed after the Homeric *οἳ ἀρούρης καρπὸν ἔδουσιν*, *Il.* VI. 142. — **munere**, *bounty.* The plural is more usual; cf. IV. 9. 48, 10. 1, 15. 26.

11. **enaviganda**: not found in this sense before Horace. *Enavigare* (= *traicere navigando*) is like *evadere* (= *traicere vadendo*), *e.g.* *angustias evadit*, Liv. XXI. 32. 13. — **reges**: see I. 4. 14 n.

12. **inopes coloni**: cf. I. 35. 6 n. — **erimus**: *i.e.* when our time shall have come.

13. **frustra**, etc.: no precautions are of any use; cf. 13. 13 *sqq.* — **carebimus**, *keep away from;* cf. 10. 6.

14. **fractis**, *breaking; sc.* on the rocks or the beach, (breakers). — **Hadriae**: Intr. 117 *a.*

15. **frustra**: Intr. 116 *g.* — **per autumnos**: a very hot and unhealthy season at Rome; cf. III. 23. 8; *S.* II. 6. 18 *plumbeus Auster autumnusque gravis; Ep.* I. 7. 1 *sqq.*

16. **corporibus**: Intr. 76. — **Austrum**: the hot south wind (Sirocco) prevailing especially in August and September.

17. **ater**: see I. 28. 13 n. — **flumine**, *current.* — **languido**: cf.

Visendus ater flumine languido
Cocytos errans et Danai genus
infame damnatusque longi
Sisyphus Aeolides laboris.

Linquenda tellus et domus et placens
uxor, neque harum quas colis arborum
te praeter invisas cupressos
ulla brevem dominum sequetur.

Absumet heres Caecuba dignior
servata centum clavibus et mero
tinguet pavimentum superbo,
pontificum potiore cenis.

Verg. *G.* IV. 478 *limus niger et deformis harundo | Cocyti tardaque palus inamabilis unda.*

18. **errans,** *meandering.* — **Danai genus**: see III. 11. 25 n.

20. **Sisyphus**: mythical founder of Corinth, of extraordinary cunning and wickedness; killed by Theseus and condemned to roll to the top of a hill a stone, which always slipped from his hands and rolled down again; *Odys.* XI. 593 *sqq.* — **laboris**: Gr. 220.

21. **linquenda,** etc.: for a similar picture cf. Lucr. III. 894 *iam iam non domus accipiet te laeta, neque uxor | optima nec dulces occurrent oscula nati | praeripere et tacita pectus dulcedine tangent.* — **placens,** *sweet;* cf. III. 7. 23.

23. **invisas,** *detested;* see I. 34. 10 n.— **cupressos**: a tall evergreen common in southern Europe, in growth like a cedar, in shape not unlike a Lombardy poplar. Cypress was associated with death from the custom of placing it before the house of mourning and around the funeral pyre, and was regarded as sacred to Pluto.

24. **brevem,** *short-lived,* like *breve lilium,* I. 36. 16; but here, with **dominum,** contrasting his brief ownership with the longer lives of the trees.

25. **Caecuba**: see I. 20. 9 n; for the number, Intr. 128. — **dignior**: because knowing better how to use the wine. In this single ironical expression is contained the only intimation of the moral which Horace usually draws from his discourses on the shortness of life and the gloominess of death, — that we must make the most of the brief space that is given us for enjoyment; cf. I. 4, I. 9. 13 *sqq.*, I. 11, II. 3, II. 11.

26. **centum**: cf. *trecenis,* vs. 5 n.

27. **tinguet,** etc.: implying reckless extravagance; cf. Cic. *Phil.* 2. 105 *natabant pavimenta vino, madebant parietes.*— **superbo**: attributing to the wine a consciousness of its excellence and a feeling of humiliation under such unworthy treatment.

28. **pontificum cenis**: see I. 37. 2 n. For the case of **cenis** see Intr. 75.

## XV.

Iam pauca aratro iugera regiae
moles relinquent; undique latius
extenta visentur Lucrino
stagna lacu, platanusque caelebs
evincet ulmos; tum violaria et
myrtus et omnis copia narium
spargent olivetis odorem
fertilibus domino priori;

XV. A protest against the growing extravagance of the day, which spends immense sums in building luxurious palaces and turns useful land into pleasure grounds, in contrast with the spirit of the fathers, who were poor for themselves and rich only for the state. The ode is singular in containing no personal allusion whatever. — Metre, 176.

1. **iam,** *soon.* — **regiae** (here for *regales*), *regal.*

2. **moles,** *piles;* cf. III. 29. 10.

3. **visentur,** *will meet our gaze;* cf. I. 37. 25. — **Lucrino lacu**: a sheet of salt water near Baiae, separated from the gulf of Pozzuoli by a natural dike about a mile long. By strengthening this dike and opening a passage through it into Lucrinus and thence into Lake Avernus, Agrippa formed the Portus Iulius (cf. *Ep.* II. 3. 63) in 37 B.C.

4. **stagna,** *ponds,* artificially constructed both for ornament and as fish preserves. — **platanus**: cf. II. 13 n. — **caelebs**: the familiar figure of the vine 'wedded' to the tree on which it twines; cf. *Epod.* 2. 9 *adulta vitium propagine | altas maritat populos;* Cat. 62. 54 (*vitis*) *ulmo coniuncta marito.* The denser shade of the platanus unfits it for this service. The meaning is that shady lawns will take the place of vineyards.

5. **evincet,** *will crowd out;* cf. Plin. *N. H.* XVIII. 185 *faba evincit herbas.* — **ulmos**: the unexpressed epithet, *maritatas* or the like, is suggested by **caelebs**; cf. Intr. 122. Elms and poplars were the trees chiefly used for training vines upon. — **tum**: *i.e.* when the state of things prophesied in the preceding lines has come to pass. — **violaria,** etc.: *i.e.* flower beds and ornamental shrubs will supplant the olive orchards.

6. **myrtus**: a bushy shrub, with small, lustrous, dark-green leaves, and pinkish white flowers, not unlike the apple blossom. — **omnis copia narium,** *all the wealth of the nostrils,* a somewhat contemptuous expression for 'every variety of fragrant flower.'

7. **olivetis**: ablative; Intr. 69.

8. **fertilibus,** *which bore fruit.* — **domino**: Intr. 58 *a.*—With this whole passage cf. Quint. VIII. 3. 8 *sterilem platanum tonsasque myrtos quam maritam ulmum et uberes oleas praeoptaverim?*

tum spissa ramis laurea fervidos
excludet ictus. Non ita Romuli
praescriptum et intonsi Catonis
auspiciis veterumque norma.

Privatus illis census erat brevis,
commune magnum ; nulla decempedis
metata privatis opacam
porticus excipiebat Arcton,

nec fortuitum spernere caespitem
leges sinebant, oppida publico

9. **laurea** (sc. *arbor*): for *laurus;* the bay, an evergreen, bush-like tree, growing often to a height of sixty feet, with rich, dark-green foliage, small yellowish blossoms, and a dark-purple berry.

10. **ictus** (sc. *solis*, suggested by **fervidos**), *rays;* cf. Lucr. I. 147 *lucida tela diei*, and our word 'sun-stroke.'

11. **praescriptum** : sc. *est.* — **intonsi**: see I. 12. 41 n.—**Catonis**: the Censor, prominent in his day for his uncompromising hostility to all corrupting innovations, and to posterity a typical Roman of the olden time.

12. **auspiciis** : *i.e.* while those men guided the state. The *auspicia* could be taken only by those highest in authority; cf. I. 7. 27 n. — **veterum norma** : the old Roman maxims on the requirements of good citizenship, which he proceeds to set forth.

13. **census** : properly the man's list of possessions returned to the Censor ; hence **brevis**.

14. **commune**: neuter used substantively, equivalent to *res publica, the common wealth.* — **nulla decempedis**, etc. : *i.e.* no private portico on a great scale, the latter being indicated by the unit of measurement (**decempedis**). For the indirect use of the epithet **privatis**, cf. Intr. 124.

15. **opacam** : as the side on which the shadows fall. Strictly the epithet belongs to the portico itself.

16. **excipiebat**, *lay open to ;* cf. Juv. 7. 183 *algentem rapiat cenatio solem*, of a winter dining-room. — **Arcton**, *the North.*

17. **fortuītum**, *the chance, i.e.* the first that presented itself; in contrast with **novo**.— **caespitem**: for building private altars (cf. I. 19. 13 n), where marble and other costly material had now begun to be used.

18. **leges** : probably referring to the rules of Roman ritual, which strictly prescribed the use of certain traditional forms and materials. What Horace points out is that under those old laws even the sod under our feet had its honorable use, for which no man could reject it as common and cheap. — **oppida** : *sc.* with public buildings, etc. — **publico**, *of the people in common*, who spent their means for this end instead of for their personal luxury.

sumptu iubentes et deorum
templa novo decorare saxo.

## XVI.

Otium divos rogat in patenti
prensus Aegaeo, simul atra nubes
condidit lunam neque certa fulgent
sidera nautis ;
otium bello furiosa Thrace,
otium Medi pharetra decori,

19. **iubentes decorare**: divided between the two objects, and so uniting **publico sumptu** and **novo saxo**, both of which belong to **oppida** as well as to **templa**; Intr. 120, 121.

20. **novo**: see I. 2. 6 n.— **saxo**: *i.e.* marble, which in Horace's day was brought in great variety from different parts of the empire for the decoration of private houses as well as of public buildings; cf. 18. 3 *sq.*

XVI. To Pompeius Grosphus, a Roman knight, the owner of extensive estates in Sicily, in the neighborhood of those which Iccius managed for Agrippa. See I. 29 (intr. note) and *Ep.* I. 12. 22 *sq.*, where Grosphus is recommended to Iccius as a man who would not take advantage of his friendship to ask improper favors. The subject of the ode is peace of mind, which is never overtaken by those who restlessly pursue it, but dwells with those who take home to themselves the truth that no man's lot can be entirely perfect, and who find their happiness in the contented enjoyment of the blessings they have. — Metre, 174.

1. **otium**, *peace*, in its widest sense, freedom from care, anxiety and passion. The subjects of **rogat** are types of men restless by nature and fond of excitement: even they pray for peace. For the first instance cf. I. 1. 15.— **patenti**, *open*, *i.e.* not near any island where he could take refuge in a harbor.

2. **prensus**: *sc.* by a storm. The nautical term was *deprensus* (Schol. on Verg. *G.* IV. 421); see Intr. 129. For the use of the participle see Intr. 103. — **Aegaeo**: Intr. 117 *a.* — **simul**: see I. 4. 17 n. — **atra**, etc.: see I. 2. 7 n. The picture is of the inky darkness of a stormy night, when the mariner without a compass was peculiarly helpless.

3. **certa**, *sure* (*sc.* as guides to the mariner), such as the Great and Little Bear (Cic. *Arat.* 37 *sqq.*); cf. Tib. I. 9. 10 *ducunt instabiles sidera certa rates.*

5. **otium**: Intr. 116 *g.* — **bello furiosa**: concessive; they are warriors at heart, and love fighting with a passion that amounts to frenzy.— **Thrace**: the country for the people; cf. IV. 14. 49.

6. **Medi**: see I. 2. 22 n.— **pharetra**: associated in the Roman

Grosphe, non gemmis neque purpura ve-
nale neque auro.

Non enim gazae neque consularis
submovet lictor miseros tumultus
mentis et curas laqueata circum
tecta volantis.

Vivitur parvo bene cui paternum
splendet in mensa tenui salinum
nec levis somnos timor aut cupido
sordidus aufert.

mind with their dashing cavalry (cf. I. 19. 11 n, II. 13. 17), and suggesting the restless and adventurous spirit of the raider (I. 2. 51).

7. **non**, etc., *peace, which no . . . can buy.* — **purpura** : used (as in English) for purple robes, tapestries, etc., which are named with precious stones and gold as the costliest things that a man could offer. — **ve-nale** : Intr. 174 *b.*

8. **neque** : the only instance in which Horace has admitted elision in the Adonic verse.

9. **non gazae neque . . . lictor** : *i.e.* no wealth nor power.

10. **submovet tumultus** : a figure borrowed from the progress of the magistrate through the streets, the lictors making the disorderly crowd give way to let him pass undisturbed. **submovet** is the technical term for this, and there is a zeugma with **gazae.**

11. **curas . . . volantis** : included in the figure : another annoying crowd against which the consul's power is helpless.— **laqueata tecta,** *panelled ceilings, i.e.* those of rich and splendid houses. Such a ceiling in its simplest form was made by inserting cross-pieces between the joists which supported the floor above, thus dividing the whole space into square or oblong panels (*lacunaria*), which could be decorated at pleasure. This simple device was imitated in stucco and elaborated with panels of divers shapes, richly ornamented with gold and ivory (cf. 18. 1 *sq.*) and various tints.

13. **vivitur** : sc. *ab eo*, the antecedent of **cui.**— **parvo** : abl. neut., as in *S.* II. 2. 1. — **cui,** etc., *on whose modest board*, etc.; *i.e.* who lives in the *aurea mediocritas* of 10. 5, above the slovenly neglect of indigence, but free from the worry of wealth. For the suggestion of contentment in **paternum** see I. 1. 11 n.

14. **splendet,** etc.: in his plain table service only one vessel, and that the smallest, is of silver ; but it is an heirloom, ever kept bright, and it gives a certain tone of elegance to his humble board. — **salinum** : cf. Plin. *N. H.* XXXIII. 153 (*Fabricius*) *bellicosos imperatores plus quam pateram et salinum habere ex argento vetabat.*

15. **nec,** *and whose . . . no.* **cui** is understood here in substantially the same construction as above.— **timor aut cupido** : accompani-

Quid brevi fortes iaculamur aevo
multa? Quid terras alio calentis
sole mutamus? Patriae quis exsul
se quoque fugit?

Scandit aeratas vitiosa navis
Cura nec turmas equitum relinquit,
ocior cervis et agente nimbos
ocior Euro.

Laetus in praesens animus quod ultra est
oderit curare, et amara lento
temperet risu: nihil est ab omni
parte beatum.

ments of wealth, fear of losing what one has, and greed for more. *Cupido*, always masculine in Horace, is usually feminine in other authors, except as the name of the god.

17. **brevi aevo**: to be taken with **iaculamur**, but **brevi**, contrasted by its position with **fortes**, suggests the folly of our confident projects; cf. I. 4. 15.

18. **multa**: the emphatic word of the sentence (Intr. 116 *b*); cf. 11. 5 *poscentis aevi pauca*. — **terras alio calentis sole**: *i.e.* foreign countries; cf. Verg. *G.* II. 512 *alio patriam quaerunt sub sole iacentem*. The omitted ablative after **mutamus** (*patriā* or *nostrā*) is implied in this description, and the next sentence assumes that it is already understood. For the construction see Intr. 74.

19. **patriae**, *from his country*; cf. *exsul mundi*, Ov. *M.* VI. 189.

20. **se quoque fugit**: cf. Sen. *Ep.* 28. 2 *quaeris quare te fuga ista non adiuvet? Tecum fugis*; Lucr. III. 1053 *sqq.* For the tense of **fugit** see Intr. 80.

21. **scandit**, etc.: amplification of the preceding: a man cannot run away from his own discontent, though he take the swiftest ship or the fastest horse; cf. III. 1. 37 *sqq.*; *Ep.* I. 11. 27 *sqq.*; Lucr. II. 48 *sqq.* That Horace himself had his periods of restless discontent, he confesses *S.* II. 7. 111 *sqq.*, *Ep.* I. 8. 3 *sqq.* — **aeratas**, *brass-bound*.—**vitiosa**, *morbid*; included in the personification; cf. I. 24. 7 n.

22. **relinquit**, *falls behind*; cf. *deseruit*, III. 2. 32.

23. **ocior**: Intr. 116 *b*.

25. **laetus in praesens**: to be taken with the predicate, in the same sense as III. 8. 27 *dona praesentis cape laetus horae*. — **quod ultra est**: *i.e.* the future; cf. I. 9. 13.

26. **oderit**: stronger than *nolit*; Intr. 94 *l*. — **lento risu**, *with a quiet smile*.

27. **nihil**, etc.: reason for the preceding; the wise man will cheerfully accept the disagreeable along with the good, and not run away from it in a futile chase after unalloyed happiness.

29. **abstulit**, etc.: two contrasted examples of the drawbacks

Abstulit clarum cita mors Achillem,
longa Tithonum minuit senectus,
et mihi forsan tibi quod negarit
porriget hora.

Te greges centum Siculaeque circum
mugiunt vaccae, tibi tollit hinnitum
apta quadrigis equa, te bis Afro
murice tinctae

vestiunt lanae : mihi parva rura et
spiritum Graiae tenuem Camenae
Parca non mendax dedit et malignum
spernere volgus.

attending the most coveted blessings: a brilliant career, cut short by an untimely death; eternal life, an infinitely prolonged bodily decay.

30. **Tithonum** : see I. 28. 8 n. — **minuit**: perfect.

31. **et mihi**, etc.: a slight shifting of the point of view, suggested by the two examples just cited, each of whom possessed what the other lacked. But the underlying thought remains unaltered. On the basis of the truth '*nihil ab omni parte beatum*' the poet boldly compares his own humble lot with that of his wealthy friend, and points out that he may perhaps be more happy in some respects than one who, according to ordinary standards, was in every way more fortunate.

32. **hora**, *the hour; i.e.* any given hour in which our fortunes may be compared.

33. **greges Siculaeque vaccae**: equivalent to *greges Siculrarum vaccarum* (hendiadys).— **centum**: for an indefinitely large number; cf. 14. 26, III. 11. 17. — **circum** : Intr. 115 *c*.

34. **tollit** : cf. *risum tollant*, *Ep.* II. 3. 381, and our phrase '*lift up* their voice.'— **hinnitum** : for the synapheia, see Intr. 174 *b*.

35. **apta**, *fit for;* implying a fine breed and a high market value. — **quadrigis**: *i.e.* for the chariot race. — **equa** : mares were preferred for this purpose; cf. Verg. *G.* I. 59. — **bis tinctae** : a translation of the technical term *dibapha* (δί-βαφα, 'twice dipped'); cf. Plin. *N. H.* IX. 137. — **Afro** : *i.e.* from the island of Girba, in the Syrtis Minor.

37. **mihi parva rura**, etc.: cf. 18. 1 *sqq.* and Bacchylides *Fr.* 28 οὐ βοῶν πάρεστι σώματ', οὔτε χρυσός, οὔτε πορφύρεοι τάπητες, ἀλλὰ θυμὸς εὐμενής, | μοῦσά τε γλυκεῖα καὶ Βοιωτίοισιν ἐν σκύφοισιν οἶνος ἡδύς.

38. **spiritum**, *inspiration*, as in IV. 6. 29; cf. *spiro*, IV. 3. 24. — **Graiae Camenae**: cf. I. 12. 39 n and note on *lyricis vatibus*, I. 1. 35. — **tenuem**, *fine, delicate.*

39. **Parca** : Intr. 127. — **non mendax** : a permanent attribute; cf. *C. S.* 25; Pers. 5. 48 *Parca tenax veri.*

40. **spernere**, *a contempt for*

## XVII.

Cur me querellis exanimas tuis?
Nec dis amicum est nec mihi te prius
obire, Maecenas, mearum
grande decus columenque rerum.
A, te meae si partem animae rapit
maturior vis, quid moror altera,
nec carus aeque nec superstes
integer? Ille dies utramque

(Intr. 97 *d*); *i.e.* a capacity to hold himself above their envy (*invidia maior*, 20. 4). — **volgus**: the unrefined 'rabble' of readers and critics who were incapable of appreciating the finer spirit of Greek poetry (cf. III. 1. 1), and pursued Horace with ridicule and detraction (*S.* I. 10. 78 *sqq.*), due partly to envy of his social advancement, until his success was established beyond cavil (IV. 3. 16).

XVII. Maecenas was a confirmed invalid, suffering constantly from fever and insomnia (Intr. 21; Plin. *N. H.* VII. 172); and at the same time he had a passionate attachment to life (Sen. *Ep.* 101. 10) which made his frequent sicknesses occasions of gloomy forebodings. Horace here consoles him with the assurance of his devotion, which will not permit death to separate them, with appeals to astrology (to which Maecenas was addicted), and by recalling their common escape from imminent death, for which thank-offerings were still due. This allusion shows that the ode was written not long after B.C. 30 (see Ode 13, intr. note). — Metre, 176.

1. **exanimas**, *kill; i.e.* torment, by suggesting such distressing thoughts; cf. *Epod.* 14. 5 *occidis saepe rogando;* Ter. *Andr.* 660 *quor me enicas?*

2. **amicum est** (equivalent to *placet*), *it is the pleasure of;* cf. *Il.* IX. 23 οὕτω που Διὶ μέλλει ὑπερμενέι φίλον εἶναι. In point of fact Horace survived his patron only a few months (Intr. 35).

4. **decus columenque**: see I. 1. 2 n.

5. **partem animae**: cf. I. 3. 8 n. — **rapit . . . moror**: for the tense see Intr. 78.

6. **vis**: used properly of premature death; cf. 13. 20 (where it is joined, as here, with *rapere*) and Cic. *C. M.* 71 *vitam adulescentibus vis aufert, senibus maturitas.* — **altera**: sc. *pars.*

7. **carus**: sc. *mihi*, as the con text implies; cf. *Ep.* I. 3. 29 *si patriae volumus, si nobis vivere cari.* — **aeque**: *sc.* as before. — — **superstes**: to be taken with **carus** as well as with **integer**; Intr. 119 *a*.

8. **integer**: repeating the thought of *te meae partem animae* 5. — **utramque** (sc. *nostrum;* cf. vs. 21 n), *of both of us. Vtriusque*

ducet ruinam. Non ego perfidum
dixi sacramentum : ibimus, ibimus,
utcumque praecedes, supremum
carpere iter comites parati.

Me nec Chimaerae spiritus igneae
nec, si resurgat, centimanus Gyas
divellet umquam ; sic potenti
Iustitiae placitumque Parcis.

Seu Libra seu me Scorpios adspicit

***nostrum*** would be more usual, but **utramque** is quite in accord with the Latin mode of thought, which conceives of two *ruinae* in this case : cf. IV. 14. 19.

9. **ducet ruinam** : a phrase suggested in its literal use by the appearance of a falling building, where one part gives way and 'draws' the rest after it ; cf. Verg. *A.* II. 465 *elapsa repente* (*turris*) *ruinam cum sonitu trahit.* — **non ego** : see I. 18. 11 n. **non** qualifies **perfidum** only, on which cf. 8. 6 n.

10. **dixi**, *pronounced;* the technical term ; cf. Caes. *B. C.* I. 86. 3 *neu quis invitus sacramentum dicere cogatur.* — **sacramentum**: the soldier's oath, by which he bound himself to follow wherever his general might lead : cf. Liv. XXII. 38. 3. — **ibimus, ibimus** : Intr. 116 *d.*

11. **utcumque** : cf. I. 17. 10 n.

13. **Chimaerae** : see I. 27. 23 n. — **igneae** : properly an attribute of **spiritus** ; Intr. 124.

14. **si resurgat** : *i.e.* from Tartarus. — **Gyas** : son of Uranus and Gaea, brother of Briareus (Hes. *Theog.* 149).

15. **sic**, etc.: *i.e.* such is the just and immutable decree of heaven.

16. **Iustitiae** : here not the personified virtue of I. 24. 6, but the powerful goddess Δίκη, daughter of Themis and sister of the Fates (Hes. *Theog.* 902), whose authority she shares. — **placitumque** : Intr. 119 *b.*

17. **seu . . . seu**, *if . . . or if;* cf. I. 23. 5 *sq.* The meaning is : If our destinies are governed by the stars, there is a marvelous agreement in the influences that rule our two lives. Horace had no faith in astrology (see I. 11), but he adopts its language to express more emphatically to his patron, who did believe in it, his confidence that their friendship was not to be severed by death. — **adspicit** : cf. IV. 3. 1. *sqq.* The astrologers held that a man's destiny was determined by the constellations and planets which looked down upon him at his birth. These constituted, grouped as they were at that moment, his 'nativity' (**natalis hora**), each member (**pars**) of which exerted its own influence, good or ill, but only so far as it was not counteracted by some other member. Libra and Jupiter were held to be salutary in their influence ; the others here mentioned, baleful. The present **adspicit** expresses the continuing influence of the constellation.

formidulosus, pars violentior
natalis horae, seu tyrannus
Hesperiae Capricornus undae,

utrumque nostrum incredibili modo
consentit astrum : te Iovis impio
tutela Saturno refulgens
eripuit volucrisque fati

tardavit alas, cum populus frequens
laetum theatris ter crepuit sonum ;
me truncus inlapsus cerebro
sustulerat, nisi Faunus ictum

18. **pars violentior**: referring to any of the three constellations. It means the influence which tends to bring violence and danger into his life.

19. **tyrannus**, etc.: cf. I. 3. 15 n. Certain constellations were held to have a dominant influence in certain parts of the earth; cf. Manil. IV. 791 *tu, Capricorne, regis quidquid sub sole cadente | est positum gelidamque Helicen quod tangit ab illo, | Hispanas gentes et quot fert Gallia dives.*

21. **nostrum**: gen. pl., substantive; cf. note on *utramque*, 8. For the caesura of the verse see Intr. 155.

22. **consentit**: *i.e.* (as appears from what follows) the *pars violentior* has in both cases been thwarted just before the fulfilment of its fatal influence. This whole passage has been imitated by Persius, 5. 45 *sqq.*—**Iovis tutela**: Intr. 126 *b.* — **impio**: the character of the Kronos of Greek mythology, with whom Saturn was identified.

23. **refulgens**: cf. I. 12. 28 n.

24. **volucris**: better taken with **alas**; cf. III. 29. 53 *si celeris quatit pennas* (of Fortuna). — **fati**: *i.e.* of death. This conception of the approach of death is similar to that of I. 3. 32.

25. **cum populus**, etc.: see I. 20. 4 n.

26. **theatris**: Intr. 69, 128. — **ter**: apparently the usual number, like our three cheers; cf. Prop. IV. 10. 4 *Camenae . . . manibus faustos ter crepuere sonos;* cf. also I. 28. 36 n. — **sonum**: see Intr. 45 *a*, and cf. Prop. *l. c.*

27. **truncus**, etc.: see Ode 13, intr. note. — **inlapsus cerebro sustulerat**: Intr. 82.

28. **Faunus**: as the accident took place on his farm, he naturally attributes his escape to the god of the woods and fields (cf. I. 17. 1 *sqq.*, III. 18) who had moreover a natural interest in poets, as the *protégés* of his father Mercury (see vs. 29 n). Cf., however, III. 8. 7.

29. **levasset**, *had averted.* — **Mercurialium virorum**: Horace here appropriates the name familiarly applied to successful business men (cf. *S.* II. 3. 25) for poets, who also stand under the protection of Mercury as the god of

dextra levasset, Mercurialium
custos virorum. Reddere victimas
aedemque votivam memento ;
nos humilem feriemus agnam.

## XVIII.

Non ebur neque aureum
mea renidet in domo lacunar,
non trabes Hymettiae
premunt columnas ultima recisas
Africa, neque Attali
ignotus heres regiam occupavi,

eloquence and the inventor of the lyre (I. 10. 1, 6). Cf. 7. 13 *sq.*

30. **reddere,** *pay* (see I. 3. 7 n), *sc.* to Jove.

XVIII. The poet illustrates his favorite maxim of the *aurea mediocritas* by contrasting his own happy lot, in which small means are united with character, talent, and a contented spirit, with the folly and blindness of those whose grasping ambition and love of show set at defiance the bounds of nature and of right. He gives the ode a slightly dramatic character by singling out one of this class for reproach, but he names no name, and probably had no particular person in mind. The reference to his own position in life will remind the reader of I. 31 and II. 16. 33 *sqq.*, and is similar to the fragment of Bacchylides quoted at 16. 37 n. Cf. also Tib. I. 1, Prop. IV. 2. 9 *sqq.* — Metre, 167.

1. **ebur** : used, like the gold, in decorating the ceiling. In prose it would be *neque eburneum neque*, etc.

2. **lacunar**: cf. *laqueata tecta*, 16. 11 n.

3. **trabes Hymettiae**: *i.e.* architraves of marble from Mt. Hymettus in Attica (6. 14 n), which was of a light bluish tint.

4. **premunt,** *rest upon.* — **columnas** : the reference is to the atrium, which being the public room of the house, was decorated with the greatest splendor ; cf. III. 1. 45 *sq.* The columns supported the roof, around the *impluvium.* — **ultima,** *far ;* cf. 20. 18. — **recisas,** *quarried.*

5. **Africa** : the yellow Numidian marble (*giallo antico*) is meant. The Romans were fond of combining marbles of various colors in their buildings, and the innumerable fragments of these dug up at the present day bear striking testimony to the former magnificence of the city. — **neque,** etc. : *i.e.* nor have I unexpectedly come into possession of enormous wealth, — a proverbial result of which is extravagant expenditure. — **Attali,** *of an Attalus.* See I. 1. 12 n.

6. **ignotus heres**: the inherit-

nec Laconicas mihi
trahunt honestae purpuras clientae ;
at fides et ingeni
benigna vena est, pauperemque dives
me petit : nihil supra
deos lacesso nec potentem amicum
largiora flagito,
satis beatus unicis Sabinis.
Truditur dies die
novaeque pergunt interire lunae :

ance of great fortunes by insignificant persons unconnected by kindred with the testator, — often adventurers who had ingratiated themselves by flattery and baser means, — was a familiar feature of Roman life in Horace's day. See *S.* II. 5, intr. note.

7. **Laconicas**: the purple-fish (*murex*) was found especially at Gythium on the Sinus Laconicus and on the coast of Cythera.

8. **trahunt,** *spin;* standing here, however, for the whole process of manufacture. — **honestae,** *respectable, well-born.* Horace says, in effect, that he is not a powerful patron whose dependents are not merely slaves and freedmen, but well-to-do families, who court his favor with rich presents; cf. Cic. *Verr.* II. 4. 59. — **purpuras,** *purple stuffs;* cf. III. 1. 42.

10. **benigna,** *generous.* — **vena**: cf. *divite vena, Ep.* II. 3. 409. The figure is probably taken from the underground water-course (*vena aquae ;* cf. Hirt. *B. G.* VIII. 43. 4, *venae fontis intercisae sunt*) rather than veins of metal; cf. Ovid, *Tr.* III. 14. 33 *ingenium fregere meum mala, cuius et ante | fons infecundus parvaque vena fuit.* — **est**: sc. *mihi.* — **pauperemque dives,** *poor as* I *am, the rich man ;* Intr. 116 *a.* **dives** is used collectively (Intr. 127). A number of rich men were among Horace's friends.

11. **me petit**: *i.e.* is attracted to me, seeks my society.

12. **lacesso,** *I importune,* with two accusatives, as a verb of asking. — **amicum**: Maecenas, as vs. 14 shows.

14. **beatus**: in its participial sense, *made rich ;* cf. *Epod.* I. 31 *satis superque me benignitas tua | ditavit.* — **unicis,** *my one,* the only one I possess; cf. *unicus filius.* — **Sabinis,** *Sabine farm ;* Intr. 24. An estate in a given territory is sometimes designated by the plural of the name of the people, — *Sabini* for *fundus Sabinus ;* cf. III. 4. 22; Plin. *Ep.* V. 6. 1 *Tuscos meos.*

15. **truditur dies die,** *day crowds upon day ;* cf. *Epod.* 17. 25.

16. **novae lunae**: not in the narrower technical sense, but as new phenomena coming with each successive month; cf. Cat. 5. 4 *soles occidere et redire possunt.* — **pergunt**: *sc.* as they always have done; the order of nature goes on, keeping the lesson ever before us. Cf. IV. 7. 7 *sqq.* — **interire**: *i.e.* to wane.

tu secanda marmora
  locas sub ipsum funus, et sepulcri
immemor struis domos,
  marisque Bais obstrepentis urges
submovere litora,
  parum locuples continente ripa.
Quid quod usque proximos
  revellis agri terminos et ultra
limites clientium
  salis avarus? Pellitur paternos

17. **secanda marmora**: *sc.* into slabs for pavements and walls; Plin. *N. H.* XXXVI. 50.

18. **locas,** *are giving contracts for;* the technical term. The corresponding word for the contractor's part was *redimere* (cf. III. 1. 35). The work to be done is expressed by the gerundive construction with either verb. — **sub**: see I. 8. 14 n. — **sepulcri**: the 'house' to which you must soon inevitably remove, in contrast with earthly houses (**domos**); see 29 n.

20. **Bais**: the favorite watering-place of Rome at this time (*Ep.* I. 1. 83, 15. 2 *sqq.*), situated on the gulf of Pozzuoli, about ten miles west of Naples. The word is dative after **ob-strepentis**. — **urges submovere litora,** *you press on the work of pushing out the shore,* for the purpose of building a house close upon the water; cf. III. 1. 33 *sqq.*, and Martial's description (X. 30) of the country-house of Apollinaris at Formiae. Horace, however, represents the rich builder as fretting within the narrow bounds of the shore, which he pushes away (**submovere**) as an obstacle in his path.

22. **continente ripa,** *while the shore confines you;* cf. Caes. *B. G.* I. 2. 3 *undique loci natura Helvetii continentur.* For **ripa** see I. 2. 14 n.

23. **quid quod**: a phrase frequently used by the orators in passing to a stronger point; in this case it is from the folly to the wickedness of the rich man. **quid,** without suggesting any particular verb, calls attention to the fact expressed by the *quod*-clause. — **usque,** *one after another.* **usque proximos** is equivalent to *proximum quemque,* the one which on each occasion is nearest.

24. **revellis**: stronger than the usual term *exarare* or *movere,* expressing, like *salis* 26, the man's unscrupulous violence. — **agri terminos,** *landmarks, boundary stones.* Such a stone was sacred, and a curse was pronounced on one who should remove it.

25. **clientium**: the wickedness was aggravated when the man he wronged was his own client, whom it was his sacred duty to protect against aggression. The laws of the Twelve Tables took cognizance of this crime in the clause: PATRONVS SI CLIENTI FRAVDEM FECERIT, SACER ESTO.

26. **salis,** *stride;* see note on *revellis,* 24, and on *transiliunt,* I 3. 24.—**pellitur**: Intr. 77.—**pater**

in sinu ferens deos
  et uxor et vir sordidosque natos.
Nulla certior tamen
  rapacis Orci fine destinata
aula divitem manet
  erum. Quid ultra tendis? Aequa tellus
pauperi recluditur
  regumque pueris, nec satelles Orci
callidum Promethea
  revexit auro captus. Hic superbum

**nos deos**: *i.e.* the little images of their household gods, their only remaining possessions; cf. Juv. 8. 110. The acquisition of the *angulus proximus qui nunc denormat agellum* (*S.* II. 6. 8) was usually a slower and safer process than in the poet's graphic picture, but was effected no less surely by gradually involving the poor neighbor in debts which in the end drove him from his farm utterly impoverished.

28. **sordidos**, *ragged;* indicating the poverty of the parents.

29. **nulla**, etc.: a fuller expression of the suggestion in vs. 18: the rich lord builds palace upon palace, but there is none he can count on so surely as the palace of Death. The construction is: *nulla aula divitem erum certior manet* (*aulā*) *rapacis Orci fine destinatā* (for *quam aula r. O. f. destinata;* Intr. 75).

30. **Orci fine**: the limit which Orcus (Pluto) sets, *i.e.* death, the limit of life (*mors ultima linea rerum est*, *Ep.* I. 16. 79); cf. *fine libidinum*, I. 18. 10 n. The ablative is instrumental. Some editors take **fine** as feminine (as in *Epod.* 17. 36; elsewhere in Horace it is masculine), and (with **destinata**) as ablative after **certior.** In either case **fine** is similar to *modus*, 6. 7. — **destinata**: sc. *ei*.

32. **ultra**: *i.e.* beyond the *finis Orci;* why do you make plans that reach far out beyond your brief span of life? cf. I. 4. 15, 11. 7, II. 11. 11 *sq.*, 16. 17. — **aequa tellus**: cf. *aequo pede* and the whole passage, I. 4. 13 n.

34. **pueris**: for the prosody see Intr. 138. — **satelles Orci**: Charon.

36. **revexit captus**, *was enticed . . . to ferry back;* cf. *hunc capit argenti splendor*, *S.* I. 4. 28. The story of such an attempt does not occur elsewhere; see 13. 37 n. — **hic**: Orcus. The meaning is: Death, the great leveler, comes to all alike, — tears the rich man inexorably away from his luxurious life, and relieves the poor man of his heavy burden.

37. **Tantalum**: see I. 28. 7 n. — **Tantali genus**: Pelops and his powerful line; see I. 6. 8 n.

38. **levare**: depending both on **vocatus** (see Intr. 97 *a* and cf. Lucr. V. 945 *at sedare sitim fluvii fontesque vocabant*), and on **audit,** which from the context acquires the meaning of *exoratur;* Intr. 76. —**functum laboribus**: equivalent

Tantalum atque Tantali
  genus coercet, hic levare functum
pauperem laboribus
  vocatus atque non vocatus audit.

## XIX.

Bacchum in remotis carmina rupibus
vidi docentem (credite posteri)
  Nymphasque discentis et auris
    capripedum Satyrorum acutas.

to *defunctum laboribus*, III. 24. 15 (cf. Intr. 129); but the phrase is used here, on the analogy of (*de*)*functus vita* (cf. 9. 13), to denote the close of a life that is all toil, and is equivalent to *functum vita laboriosa*; cf. IV. 15. 29.

40. **non vocatus audit**: oxymoron. — **audit**, *gives ear*.

XIX. A hymn to Bacchus. The main part of the poem, which is devoted, like I. 10, to the attributes and achievements of the god, is introduced by two strophes in the spirit of the dithyramb (cf. IV. 2. 10 n). The poet represents himself as having come unexpectedly, while strolling in the woods, upon the god himself, in whose overpowering presence he feels a touch of the frenzy of the bacchanal; and when the first tumultuous emotions have subsided his mind is left in a fit state of exaltation to sing the praises of the god. — Metre, 176.

1. **in remotis rupibus**: the gods when they visited the earth always sought solitary places, far away from the paths of men; cf. note on *imminente luna*, I. 4. 5. The haunts of Bacchus were in the hills and woods, hence the epithets ὄρειος, ὀρειφοίτης frequently applied to him. — **carmina docentem**: the dithyrambic hymns were attributed to the inspiration of Bacchus himself (cf. III. 25), who is here represented as training the nymphs and satyrs, as Apollo inspires and trains the muses (cf. 10. 18).

2. **credite posteri**: parenthetical, asserting the truth of the story against its inherent improbability, which will tell against it with greater force when the narrator's personal authority is no longer felt; cf. *Epod.* 9. 11. The appeal shows that the poet is not here telling of a vision, but represents himself as having actually seen the god.

3. **Nymphas . . . Satyrorum**: both always represented as musical; cf. I. 1. 31; Lucr. IV. 580 *sqq.* — **auris Satyrorum**: a poetical variation of *Satyros audientis* (parallel to **nymphas discentis**); cf. *umerum*, I. 21. 12 n, and Intr. 126 *b*.

4. **capripedum**: so also in Lucretius (*l. c.*) and in some of the later Greek poets. The attribute is borrowed from Pan and the Panisci. The Satyr was generally

Euhoe, recenti mens trepidat metu
plenoque Bacchi pectore turbidum
laetatur; euhoe, parce Liber,
parce gravi metuende thyrso!

Fas pervicacis est mihi Thyiadas
vinique fontem lactis et uberes
cantare rivos atque truncis
lapsa cavis iterare mella;

fas et beatae coniugis additum
stellis honorem tectaque Penthei

represented with pointed ears, conspicuous against his bald head, a tuft of hair on his neck, and a tail; in other respects his figure was human.

5. **euhoe**: the cry of the bacchantes (εὐοῖ) in their orgies (cf. I. 18. 9); here interjected and repeated to express vividly the poet's complete possession by the divine enthusiasm. — **recenti**: *i.e.* not yet quieted. — **metu**: the sight of a god was always a strain on human nerves (χαλεποὶ δὲ θεοὶ φαίνεσθαι ἐναργεῖς, *Il.* XX. 131); cf. Verg. *A.* IV. 279 *sqq.*

6. **pleno Bacchi**: cf. III. 25. 1 *sq.* — **turbidum**: Intr. 48.

7. **parce**: *sc.* from the full force of his inspiration, which would drive the poet to frenzy; cf. Verg. *A.* VI. 77 *sqq.*

8. **gravi**, *dread*, because its touch brought on madness.—**metuende**: cf. I. 12. 23.

9. **fas**, *vouchsafed;* cf. I. 24. 20. He feels the assurance of this in the revelation with which the god has favored him. — **pervicacis**, *untiring*, *persevering*, *i.e.* in their fanatical orgies, which were kept up day and night. — **Thyiadas**: θυιάδες (cf. θύω, 'rave') was another name for the maenads (μαινάδες; cf. μαίνομαι) or Bacchae (βάκχαι), the women who took part in the orgies of the god.

10. **vini fontem**, etc.: these miracles, effected by the stroke of the thyrsus, are described in Eurip. *Bacch.* 704 *sqq.;* cf. also 141 ὁ δ' ἔξαρχος Βρόμιος εὐοῖ. ῥεῖ δὲ γάλακτι πέδον, ῥεῖ δ' οἴνῳ, ῥεῖ δὲ μελισσᾶν νέκταρι. — **et**: Intr. 114.

11. **truncis lapsa**: Intr. 70. Cf. *Epod.* 16. 47; Verg. *E.* 4. 30.

12. **iterare**: to go over in words, equivalent to *narrare;* cf. Plaut. *As.* 567 *tua malefacta iterari multa et vero possunt.*

13. **fas**: Intr. 116 *h.* — **et**, *too.* — **beatae**, *blessed*, *i.e.* by being received into heaven.— **coniugis**: Ariadne.

14. **honorem**: *i.e.* the golden crown, her wedding present from Bacchus, which the god, on receiving her into heaven, placed among the stars (the 'Northern Crown'); cf. Ov. *M.* VIII. 176 *sqq.*, *F.* III. 459 *sqq.* For the form of expression cf. *umerum*, I. 21. 12 n. — **Penthei**: grandson of Cadmus and his successor as king of Thebes. For resist

disiecta non leni ruina
Thracis et exitium Lycurgi.

Tu flectis amnis, tu mare barbarum,
tu separatis uvidus in iugis
nodo coerces viperino
Bistonidum sine fraude crinis.

Tu, cum parentis regna per arduum
cohors Gigantum scanderet impia,
Rhoetum retorsisti leonis
unguibus horribilique mala,

ing the worship of Bacchus he was torn to pieces by his own mother Agave and other women, who in their frenzy mistook him for a wild beast, and his house was destroyed; Ov. *M.* III. 513 *sqq.* For the form cf. *Vlixei*, I. 6. 7 n.

16. **Lycurgi**: a king of the Edoni (7. 27 n) who attempted to suppress the bacchanalian orgies and the cultivation of the vine. He was driven mad by Bacchus, and after killing his own wife and son was himself devoured by panthers (Hygin. *Fab.* 132). There are, however, other versions of his punishment, as *Il.* VI. 130 *sqq.*; and later writers (as Nonnus, *Dionys.* XX. 149 *sqq.*) make him an Arab prince.

17. **tu**: see I. 10. 9 n. — **flectis**, *dost subdue to thy will* (cf. IV. 1. 6); alluding to the miracles of his Indian expedition, and particularly to his crossing the Hydaspes without wetting the feet of his panthers, and reducing the rebellious river to obedience (Nonn. *Dionys.* XXIII. 125 *sqq.*, XXIV. 7 *sqq.*). That he exercised a similar power over the waters of the Indian ocean (**mare barbarum**) is implied by Seneca, who calls him *Lycurgi domitor et rubri maris* (*Herc. Fur.* 903).

18. **separatis**: cf. *remotis*, 1 n. — **uvidus**: sc. *vino*; see IV. 5. 39 n.

19. **nodo viperino**: *i.e.* with a snake instead of a ribbon; cf. Cat. 64. 258 (*bacchantes*) *pars sese tortis serpentibus incingebant.*

20. **Bistonidum**: *i.e.* Thracian bacchantes, the Bistones being a Thracian tribe; cf. *Sithoniis*, I. 18. 9 n. — **fraude**, *harm* (*sc.* to them); an archaic use of the word, borrowed from certain legal formulas; cf. Liv. I. 24. 5 *rex respondit: quod sine fraude mea populique Romani Quiritium fiat, facio.*

21. **tu, cum,** etc.: according to one form of the tradition, Bacchus as well as Hercules was summoned to the aid of the gods in their battle with the giants; see 12. 6 n. — **parentis**, *thy father* (Jove). — **regna**: Intr. 128. — **per arduum**, *up the steep path to.*

22. **impia**: as attacking the gods.

23. **Rhoetum**: one of the Giants; cf. III. 4. 55. — **leonis**, etc.: this feature of the story is not found elsewhere, but in his adventure with the pirates Bacchus turned himself into a lion to frighten his captors; *Hom. Hymn. in Dionys.* (7). 44.

quamquam choreis aptior et iocis
ludoque dictus non sat idoneus
  pugnae ferebaris; sed idem
    pacis eras mediusque belli.

Te vidit insons Cerberus aureo
cornu decorum, leniter atterens
  caudam, et recedentis trilingui
    ore pedes tetigitque crura.

26. **dictus**: a present passive participle, if the language possessed one, would here be in place, to express what was true up to and during the time of **ferebaris**. The perfect, however, is in keeping with the feeling of the language, which tends to express the cause as preceding the effect in time as well as logically.

27. **idem,** etc.: *i.e.* thou wast (as the event proved) quite as well qualified for war as for peace. **idem** is predicate; (**medius**) **pacis** and **medius belli** belong to the subject. For the position of **-que,** showing that **medius** is to be understood with **pacis,** and hence excluding the meaning 'half-way between peace and war,' see Intr. 119 *b*. The use of the genitive with **medius** for *in media pace*, etc., is poetical, and is not found elsewhere. It is used in a different sense in *Ep.* I. 18. 9.

29. **te vidit,** etc.: the hymn concludes, like I. 10, with the visit of the god to the lower world, where he went to bring away his mother Semele and take her to heaven. — **insons**: to be closely connected with **vidit.**

30. **cornu**: apparently not here attributed to Bacchus as the symbol of strength and courage (cf. III. 21. 18 n), as it often is (*e.g.* Tib. II. 1. 3, Prop. IV. 17. 19), but the drinking horn with which he is sometimes represented in vase-paintings, the *κέρας, βεβυσμένον ἡδέος οἴνου, χρύσεον εὐποίητον*, which he carried in his left hand (the thyrsus in his right) as he marched at the head of his army to India (Nonn. XIV. 240). With the wine from this he quiets Cerberus. — **atterens,** *wagging*.

31. **recedentis**: genitive. The first part of the strophe referred to the *entrance* of Bacchus into Hades. — **trilingui ore**: equivalent to *linguis triplicis oris*. There is no good reason to suppose that Horace intended to present a conception of Cerberus different from the prevailing one; it was necessary to mention the tongue, and it was obviously desirable here to keep the number of heads so far as possible in the background, as the picture of a fawning dog with three heads is at best a difficult one to manage. Where it suits his purpose (13. 34) he makes the monster hundred-headed.

32. **tetigit**: *i.e.* licked. — **-que**: see Intr. 119 *b*.

## XX.

Non usitata nec tenui ferar
penna biformis per liquidum aethera
vates, neque in terris morabor
longius, invidiaque maior
urbis relinquam. Non ego pauperum
sanguis parentum, non ego quem vocas,
dilecte Maecenas, obibo,
nec Stygia cohibebor unda.

XX. The poet foretells his own immortality in the form of an allegory based on the familiar fancy of the Greeks that the souls of poets after death passed into swans and in this form continued to exercise their gift of song (Plat. *Rep*. X. 620 A). Such outspoken appreciation of his own merits, though foreign to our habits, was not offensive to Roman taste, and perhaps the same is true of the extremely realistic description of the transformation, though some editors have doubted this and would strike out the third strophe as at least unworthy of a man of Horace's taste. Its realism certainly goes beyond the passage of Euripides (*Fr*. 911) by which perhaps it was suggested:

*Χρύσεαι δή μοι πτέρυγες περὶ νώτῳ*
*καὶ τὰ Σειρήνων πτερόεντα πέδιλ'*
*ἁρμόζεται,*
*βάσομαί τ' εἰς αἰθέρα πολὺν ἀερθείς,*
*Ζηνὶ προσμίξων.*

The ode is not improbably the result of Horace's first attempt to write an epilogue for the three books, and was relegated to its present subordinate position when he had composed the much superior poem which now worthily fills that place. — Metre, 176.

1. **non usitata**: signifying that his fame rests on a new kind of poetry (cf. III. 30. 13); **nec tenui**: *i.e.* strong, signifying that his fame is secure.

2. **biformis**: *i.e.* first a man and then a bird. Others, however, following Porphyrio, understand it to refer to Horace's achievements in two departments of poetry (*quod et lyrica scribat et hexametros*).

4. **-que**: see I. 27. 16 n; the negatives in vs. 1. belong to the adjectives, and **neque morabor** conveys an affirmative idea (= *discedam*). — **maior**, *raised above, superior to*; the result of success which can no longer be questioned.

5. **urbis**: more picturesque than *terram*; cf. I. 35. 10, III. 4. 46.— **non ego**: cf. I. 18. 11 n; Intr. 116*g*. —**pauperum sanguis parentum**: a fact of which Horace was never ashamed even in his younger days (cf. *S*. I. 6. 71 *sqq*.), and which he brings into prominence here as adding lustre to his fame, because it shows that he owed his success solely to his own merits.

6. **quem vocas** (sc. *ad te*), *whom you invite*, *i.e.* admit to your

Iam iam residunt cruribus asperae
pelles et album mutor in alitem
superne nascunturque leves
per digitos umerosque plumae.

Iam Daedaleo notior Icaro
visam gementis litora Bospori
Syrtisque Gaetulas canorus
ales Hyperboreosque campos.

society; the converse of *me petit*, 18. 11 n; cf. *revocas*, *S.* I. 6. 61. The present expresses customary action. This appears to be the most probable explanation, but the expression is vague, and the suggestion of Bücheler (Rhein. Mus. XXXVII. p. 238) that *vocare* is the technical word for the relation of patron to client (*is qui cluet*) is plausible. In either case Horace's clear purpose is to recall, in contrast with his present position (**invidia maior**) and prospective immortality, his humble origin and the envy and detraction to which as the friend of Maecenas he was subjected in the earlier part of his career (Intr. 23).

9. **residunt**, *is settling*, owing to the limbs growing slimmer. — **cruribus**: Intr. 69. — **asperae**: with **residunt**.

10. **pelles**: Intr. 128. — **album alitem**: see intr. note.

11. **supernĕ**: referring especially to **album**. The *-e* is short also in Lucr. VI. 544 and 597. — **lēves**: in contrast with **asperae**; Intr. 116 *b*.

13. **Daedaleo Icaro**: cf. *Semeleius Thyoneus*, I. 17. 22 n. The adjective here virtually includes the father in the comparison, which would have been a more fortunate one if the mention of the son could have been omitted altogether; the reader can hardly help remembering the unhappy end of his flight. — **notior**: for the reading *ocior*, which has the support of some good manuscripts, see Intr. 185.

14. **visam**, etc.: signifying that his poems will be read and sung in the remotest parts of the earth. — **gementis Bospori**: cf. *rauci Hadriae*, 14. 14.

15. **Gaetulas**: for 'African'; cf. Intr. 117 *b*.

16. **Hyperboreos campos**: originally a mythical happyland situated 'beyond Boreas' (*ultra Aquilonem gens felix, si credimus, quos Hyperboreos appellavere*, Plin. *N. H.* IV. 89), and hence not exposed to his cold blasts, a paradise of innocence and peace. The myth was variously located by different authors, but mostly, in accordance with the name, in the far North, so that *hyperboreus* came to be a poetical term for 'northern,' as here; cf. Verg. *G.* IV. 517 *hyperboreas glacies*; III. 381.

17. **me Colchus**, etc.: the converse of the same idea: 'I shall visit the remotest lands (13–16), and their peoples shall learn to know me (17–20).' Observe further that the nations named represent two classes, the barbarians beyond

Me Colchus et qui dissimulat metum
Marsae cohortis Dacus et ultimi
noscent Geloni, me peritus
discet Hiber Rhodanique potor.

Absint inani funere neniae
luctusque turpes et querimoniae;
compesce clamorem ac sepulcri
mitte supervacuos honores.

the frontier and the peoples who have already come under the influence of Roman civilization; and the verbs (**noscent, discet**) are chosen with reference to this distinction.— **dissimulat metum**: *i.e.* is afraid, in spite of his bold front.

18. **Marsae**: cf. I. 2. 39 n. — **Dacus**: see I. 26. 4 n. — **ultimi**: see 18. 4 n.

19. **Geloni**: see 9. 23 n.— **peritus**, *accomplished*. That literature was already cultivated at this time in Spain is shown by the number of poets and prose writers whom that country began to produce in the next generation. The Senecas, Quintilian, Lucan, and Martial were the most prominent.

20. **Rhodani potor**: the Gaul. The importance of a great river to the communities through which it flows makes the phrase an appropriate one; cf. 9. 21 *sq*.

21. **absint**, etc.: cf. the epitaph of Ennius (Cic. *Tusc.* I. 34): *Nemo me lacrumis decoret nec funera fletu | faxit! Cur? Volito vivus per ora virum.* — **inani**: because there will be no body to burn.—**funere**: Intr. 70.—**neniae**: formal *dirges*, chanted usually by women hired for the purpose (*praeficae*); cf. 1. 38.

22. **luctus**: plural, of various forms of mourning.— **turpes**, *unseemly*, such as tearing the hair or face, beating the breast, etc.; Intr. 125. This, too, was done by hired mourners. — **querimoniae**: of friends and relations.

23. **compesce**: addressed to Maecenas, as the chief mourner. — **clamorem**: the *clamor supremus* (Ov. *Tr.* III. 3. 43) or wail of sorrow raised by those present at a deathbed when life was extinct.

24. **supervacuos**: because his fame was secure without any material monument; cf. III. 30. 1. Horace always uses this form instead of the Ciceronian *supervacaneus*.

# LIBER TERTIVS

## I.

Odi profanum volgus et arceo.
Favete linguis ! Carmina non prius
audita Musarum sacerdos
virginibus puerisque canto.

**The six** odes with which this book opens are marked by certain characteristics which unite them together as a group and give them a unique and conspicuous place in the collection. In contrast with Horace's usual method of arrangement, they are all in the same metre; they are addressed, not to any individual, but to all patriotic Romans; they are furnished with a common introduction, which sets the key for a discourse of unusual dignity and earnestness; and throughout them all, with whatever license of poetic digression and embellishment, the thought pursues one main theme, — the moral qualities that are indispensable alike to the happiness of the individual and to the strength of the state. For these reasons some critics, ancient and modern, have regarded them, not as separate odes, but as parts of a single poem, and have sought, with much ingenuity, to trace a connection of thought between the close of each and the opening of the next. In this, it must be said, they have not been completely successful: the odes bear the appearance of having been written separately; but they were probably all written about the same time,— the internal evidence points to the period immediately following the political settlement of B.C. 27, when Octavian, with the title of 'Augustus,' was definitely invested with the principate, and Horace's mind was full of visions of the coming regeneration of the state. And there can be no question that Horace designedly arranged the odes, as we find them, in a lyrical sequence, as poems with a common subject and purpose, and gave them here a position worthy of their dignity and importance. Not less certain is the design of the first strophe, in which, with almost startling impressiveness, he steps forward as the priest of the Muses, and, warning off the 'uninitiate herd,' makes his appeal, with solemn earnestness, to those who have ears to hear, and especially to the young, whose hearts are not yet hardened by the vices he is about to attack. Clearly, this is an introduction to the whole series, and does not belong to the first ode alone.

I. After the opening strophe, the poet sets forth the futility of seeking happiness in wealth and power. First, he raises his hearers to a higher point of view, from

Regum timendorum in proprios greges,
reges in ipsos imperium est Iovis,
clari Giganteo triumpho,
cuncta supercilio moventis.
Est ut viro vir latius ordinet

which the human distinctions we make so much of are seen in truer perspective: kings sink to the level of their meanest subjects before the supreme might of Jove; riches, high birth, fame, influence count for nothing against the inexorable allotment of death. Wealth cannot buy, nor power create, the peace of mind which belongs to him alone who has learned contentment.—Metre 176.

1. **profanum volgus**: *i.e.* all the uninitiated, whose mere presence would defile the holy rite which the bard is (figuratively) about to perform (cf. Verg. *A.* VI. 258). They typify the ignorant multitude, whose stolid minds are incapable of receiving his teaching.

2. **favete linguis**: addressed to those who remain. It means properly 'Speak only words of good omen' (cf. 14. 11), but practically (like εὐφημεῖτε) 'Keep reverent silence' (cf. *sacro silentio*, II. 13. 29 n), since laymen could not be sure what words might have an unlucky significance. Cf. Aristoph. *Thesmoph.* 39 εὔφημος πᾶς ἔστω λαός, στόμα συγκλῄσας.—**non prius audita**: the poems belong to the class called gnomic, for which the Greeks (*e.g.* Theognis) commonly used the elegiac metre. In his use of the Alcaic for this purpose, as well as in his manner of dealing with his subject, Horace might fairly lay claim to originality.

3. **Musarum sacerdos**: *i.e.* the inspired mouthpiece of their teachings. For Horace's view of the office of the poet as instructor of youth (**virginibus puerisque**) see *Ep.* II. 1. 126 *sqq.*

5. **regum**, etc.: sc. *imperium est;* but **timendorum** is virtually part of the predicate. The whole clause is in the nature of a concession: 'Dreadful is the might of kings to their own subjects, who tremble as cattle before them; but' etc.—**in**: with the accusative expressing the object on which power or influence is exercised; cf. Plaut. *Men.* 1030 *si quid imperist in te mihi;* Tac. *Ann.* III. 24. 2 *valida divo Augusto in rem publicam fortuna.*—**greges**: not to be confused with the Homeric figure of kings as 'shepherds of the people'; the thought here is quite the reverse, being complementary to that of **timendorum**.

7. **Giganteo triumpho**: cf. II. 1. 16. The unapproachable superiority of Jove's physical power is summed up in this allusion: To him whose arm has subdued the portentous strength of the Giants, what are the puny kings of men?

8. **cuncta**, etc.: the figure is Homeric (*Il.* I. 528 *sqq.*); cf. Cat. 64. 204 *sqq.*; Verg. *A.* IX. 106.

9. **est**, *it is true;* a meaning given to it by its emphatic position, making the sentence concessive,—just as we say 'He *was* (no doubt) at fault, but etc.,' and the like. The apodosis begins with *aequa lege*, 14. For the construction of **est ut**, see Gr. 332 *a* 3.—**viro vir**: Intr. 75. The juxtaposition was a favorite one; cf.

arbusta sulcis, hic generosior
descendat in Campum petitor,
moribus hic meliorque fama
contendat, illi turba clientium
sit maior : aequa lege Necessitas
sortitur insignis et imos,
omne capax movet urna nomen.
Destrictus ensis cui super impia
cervice pendet, non Siculae dapes
dulcem elaborabunt saporem,
non avium citharaeque cantus

Verg. *A.* XI. 632 *implicuere inter se acies legitque virum vir;* Liv. XXII. 14. 14, etc.—**latius ordinet**, etc.: *i.e.* is a more extensive landowner.

10. **arbusta** : *i.e.* vineyards, in which the vines were trained on trees planted at regular intervals (**ordinet sulcis**); cf. II. 15. 4 n.

11. **descendat** : *sc.* from the hills, where the houses of the better class were situated.—**Campum**: sc. *Martium*, where the elections were held. Observe that the thought here is concerned with the distinctions among men, and not with the political contest, which is introduced only as the scene in which these distinctions are conspicuously displayed.

12. **meliorque**: Intr. 119 *b*.

13. **turba clientium** : in his *atrium* at the *salutatio*, or morning reception, when the clients were expected to call and pay their respects to their patron, or in public, when they escorted him on his way to or from the Forum or the Campus.

14. **aequa** : see I. 4. 13 n, II. 18. 32 ; expressing the main point of contrast with what precedes, it naturally comes to the front in its own clause.—**Necessitas** : personified, as in I. 35. 17, where she appears as the minister who executes the decrees of Destiny; here and in 24. 6, with special reference to the decree of death to man.

15. **sortitur**, *dooms*.—**insignis**: cf. I. 34. 13.

16. **urna** : see II. 3. 26 n.

17. **destrictus ensis**, etc.: *i.e.* this ever-impending presence of death hangs over the godless man like the sword of Damocles, and robs him of all enjoyments in the midst of luxury. The well-known story of Damocles is told by Cicero, *Tusc.* V. 61.—**cui** : Intr. 114.—**super** : cf. I. 9. 5 n.—**impia** : Intr. 124.

18. **Siculae** : *i.e.* such as those served to Damocles. The high living of the Sicilian Greeks was proverbial.

19. **elaborabunt**: implying that his natural appetite is gone. For the prefix, cf. I. 5. 8 n.

20. **avium citharaeque**: artificial devices to induce sleep; cf. *Ep.* I. 2. 31. Aviaries were kept in many wealthy establishments

somnum reducent; somnus agrestium
lenis virorum non humilis domos
fastidit umbrosamque ripam,
non zephyris agitata tempe.

Desiderantem quod satis est neque
tumultuosum sollicitat mare
nec saevus Arcturi cadentis
impetus aut orientis Haedi,

non verberatae grandine vineae
fundusque mendax, arbore nunc aquas

Maecenas, who suffered from insomnia, resorted to the device of soft music played at a distance (Sen. *de Prov.* 3. 10).

21. **reducent**: implying that it has deserted him; cf. *reponi*, 5. 30. Sleep is half personified here, as in the next sentence.— **agrestium virorum**: limiting **domos**, although felt also ἀπὸ κοινοῦ with **somnus** (Intr. 76). The words are drawn away from their grammatical connection towards the head of the sentence for more emphatic contrast with the preceding. Cf. *Epod.* 2. 25 *sqq.* This brings us to the other side of the poet's subject, the contented man, whose happier lot he sets forth in the next two strophes; cf. Verg. *G.* II. 458 *sqq.*

24. **tempe**: see I. 7. 4 n; here it is an appellative, as it had already come to be used by the Greeks (*e.g.* Theocr. 1. 67); cf. Cic. *ad Att.* IV. 15. 5, Verg. *G.* II. 469.

25. **desiderantem**, etc.: cf. *Ep.* I. 2. 46 *sqq.* The man who bounds his desires by his wants is free from the harassing anxieties of avarice, as exemplified in the trader (25–28) and the great landowner (29–32). Vss 27, 28 might also refer to the latter (see Verg. *G.* I. 204 *sq.*), but **non** (29) clearly divides the two instances.

27. **Arcturi cadentis**: near the end of October; **cadentis** for *occidentis*, as in *Epod.* 10. 10; Intr. 129.

28. **impetus**: with reference to the violent storms which accompanied (and were supposed to be caused by) the setting of the constellation.— **orientis Haedi**: in the middle of October; also regarded as a source of storms; cf. *nimbosis Haedis*, Ov. *Tr.* I. 11. 13.

29. **verberatae vineae**: Intr. 105 *a*. Cf. *Ep.* I. 8. 4 *sq.*

30. **fundusque mendax**: the exasperated cry of the disappointed planter, whose abuse of the farm, as if it were a living thing, is thoroughly human. Cf. *Ep.* I. 7. 87. Personification, of the farm, with which the farmer's life was so closely bound up, was very common, as it was very natural; cf. Cic. *de Sen.* 51.— **arbore**: the personification is still kept up: the tree, speaking for itself and its fellows, is always offering some excuse for their shortcomings. **arbore** may stand for the vine (see

culpante, nunc torrentia agros
sidera, nunc hiemes iniquas.
Contracta pisces aequora sentiunt
iactis in altum molibus ; huc frequens
caementa demittit redemptor
cum famulis dominusque terrae
fastidiosus : sed timor et minae
scandunt eodem quo dominus, neque
decedit aerata triremi et
post equitem sedet atra Cura.

I. 18. 1 n), but as this has just been mentioned, the poet no doubt has in mind here simply fruit-bearing trees, and in particular the olive. — **aquas** : *i.e.* excess of wet weather.

31. **torrentia**, etc.: *i.e.* drouth, attributed, like all other meteorological conditions, to the influence of certain constellations. Cf. 29. 17 *sqq*.

33. **contracta,** etc.: cf. II. 18. 20 *sqq.;* III. 24. 3 *sq.* — **pisces sentiunt** : *i.e.* they find their realm encroached upon by creatures of another element. The hyperbole has been condemned as extravagant by rod-and-line critics, but it adds a telling stroke to the picture of wealth making its elaborate and costly provision for a life of pleasure: even the bounds which nature has set offer no check to these ambitious projects.

34. **molibus** : of stone, to serve as foundations for the house. — **huc** : *i.e. in altum.* — **frequens** : singular for plural ; cf. Plin. *N. H.* IX. 180 *ibi frequens hic piscis*, and the corresponding use of *rarus*, IV. 1. 34. The use is similar to that of *multus* (I. 5. 1), *plurimus* (I. 7. 8 n), etc.

35. **caementa**: broken stones (cf. *caedo*) of irregular size and shape, used to fill the spaces between the larger blocks. — **redemptor** : here *builder ;* see II. 18. 18 n.

36. **famulis** : *i.e.* his workmen, who would naturally be slaves. — **dominus** : he too is present, hurrying on the work, — showing his impatient eagerness to realize his dream of pleasure. — **terrae**: with **fastidiosus** ; Intr. 66 *a*.

37. **timor et minae** : hendiadys; the menaces are those which he sees in the object of his fear. The thought is the same as that expressed by the sword of Damocles, above.

38. **scandunt eodem** : he cannot take refuge from them in his lofty sea-castle.

39. **aerata**, etc.: see II. 16. 21 n, where the whole thought is the same as here. — **triremi** : usually a war vessel, here the large private yacht of the rich man ; cf. *Ep.* I. 1. 93 *quem ducit priva triremis.* For the case, see Intr. 70.

40. **atra** : in II. 16. 21, *vitiosa ;* but the uppermost thought here is that of death (see I. 28. 13 n).

41. **quod si,** *now if;* summing up the preceding considerations;

Quod si dolentem nec Phrygius lapis
nec purpurarum sidere clarior
delenit usus nec Falerna
vitis Achaemeniumque costum,
cur invidendis postibus et novo
sublime ritu moliar atrium?
Cur valle permutem Sabina
divitias operosiores?

## II.

Angustam amice pauperiem pati

cf. I. 1. 35.—**dolentem**: sc. *me.* —**Phrygius lapis**: one of the rich marbles (see II. 18. 5 n) used by the Romans in their more splendid edifices. It was mottled with red. For this and the following epithets, see Intr. 117 *a*.

42. **purpurarum**: *i.e.* scarlet robes and tapestries; cf. II. 18. 8 n.—**clarior usus**: Intr. 124. Cf. Verg. *G.* II. 466 *nec casia liquidi corrumpitur usus olivi.*

43. **Falerna vitis**: cf. I. 20. 10 and 11 nn.

44. **Achaemenium**: *i.e.* costly oriental; cf. *Attalicis condicionibus* I. 1. 12. For Achaemenes, see II. 12. 21 n.—**costum**: see II. 3. 13 n.

45. **invidendis**: cf. II. 10. 7.—**novo ritu**, *in the modern style*, some features of which are indicated,—the handsome marble portal and the great height of the atrium (**sublime**). With the establishment of peace and security under Augustus came a great flow of capital to the city and a great impetus to the building of ornate private houses as well as public edifices. We have here grammatically an ablative of manner combined with one of characteristic; but **novo ritu** is practically a qualifying adjunct of **sublime**, which is parallel with **invidendis postibus**.

46. **moliar**, *build;* suggesting a massive, laborious structure; cf. II. 15. 2; III. 29. 10.—**atrium**: see note on *columnas*, II. 18. 4.

47. **valle Sabina**: Intr. 24. For the construction, see Intr. 74.

II. In the first ode, the poet's aim was mainly negative,—to strip of their glamour the two most coveted objects of human endeavor, honor and, more particularly, riches; to show that the possession of them is but vanity and vexation of spirit. In the present ode, he assumes a positive attitude and proposes a more excellent way. In the cultivation of character and, in particular, of the sterling Roman virtues of manliness and loyalty (*virtus* and *fides*), he points out to the young Roman the worthy object of a nobler ambition, and one that brings its own sure reward.—Metre, 176.

1. **angustam**, etc.: he takes up the thought where he left it in the preceding ode: For this life of contented poverty, let the young

robustus acri militia puer
condiscat, et Parthos ferocis
vexet eques metuendus hasta,
vitamque sub divo et trepidis agat
in rebus ; illum ex moenibus hosticis
matrona bellantis tyranni
prospiciens et adulta virgo
suspiret, eheu, ne rudis agminum
sponsus lacessat regius asperum
tactu leonem, quem cruenta
per medias rapit ira caedes.
Dulce et decorum est pro patria mori :

Roman train himself in the hardships and perils of warfare, where his ambition is to be a terror to our foes, and his glory to die, if need be, for his country. Cf. IV. 9. 49 *sqq.* — **amice**, *cheerfully*, *gladly*, as something to be welcomed. Cf. *clementer ferre*, *molliter ferre* in Cicero, and our 'take kindly.' For the alliteration in this verse, see Intr. 131.

2. **robustus**, *grown sturdy*, *i.e.* through the sturdiness he has acquired. — **militia**: with **robustus**. — **puer**: see I. 9. 16 n.

3. **condiscat**: subjunctive of wish. — **ferocis**, *bold;* said with a touch of depreciation: our lad shall humble their pride.

4. **eques**, *as a*, etc.

5. **sub divo**: see I. 1. 25 n.

6. **illum**: notice the emphasis, — 'my aspiration for *him* is,' etc. The scene which follows is modeled upon *Il.* XXII. 25 *sqq.*, where Priam and Hecuba, watching Achilles from the walls, entreat Hector not to expose himself to a combat with him. — **hosticis**: cf. *civicum*, II. 1. 1 n.

7. **tyranni**: the king whose city is besieged by the Romans. The queen and princess, like the women in the Iliad (III. 141 *sqq.*, XXII. 460 *sqq.*), watch the battle from the ramparts.

9. **eheu**: expressing the woman's sigh; but what follows is not a quotation of her words. — **ne**, etc.: depending on the notion of fear conveyed by **suspiret**. — **agminum**, *of battalions*, *i.e.* of warfare in general.

10. **sponsus regius**: the son of some neighboring king, betrothed to the princess. — **asperum tactu**: see I. 37. 26 n.

11. **leonem**: the young Roman warrior. — **cruenta ira**: see Intr. 124.

13. **dulce**, etc.: the connection of thought is this: 'And if such heroic conduct should cost him his life, it is a joyful and glorious privilege; for death comes to every man, whether he face it or flee from it.' Cf. Cic. *Phil.* 14. 31 *o fortunata mors, quae naturae debita pro patria est potissimum reddita!*

mors et fugacem persequitur virum
nec parcit imbellis iuventae
poplitibus timidoque tergo.

Virtus repulsae nescia sordidae
intaminatis fulget honoribus,
nec sumit aut ponit securis
arbitrio popularis aurae;

virtus recludens immeritis mori
caelum negata temptat iter via,
coetusque volgaris et udam
spernit humum fugiente penna.

14. **et,** *as well.* — **persequitur:** the prefix denotes the persistency of the pursuit, — death is ever at his heels, no matter how fast he may run away (cf. vs. 32), and despatches him at last with a wound in the back. Horace had doubtless read in his Simonides (*Fr.* 65) *ὁ δ' αὖ θάνατος κίχε καὶ τὸν φυγόμαχον.*

15. **imbellis,** *faint-hearted.*

16. **poplitibus,** etc.: cf. Liv. XXII. 48. 4 *aversam adoriuntur Romanam aciem, tergaque ferientes ac poplites caedentes stragem ingentem . . . fecerunt.*

17. **virtus,** *true manhood,* the character of the ideal man (*vir*). The clauses that follow are not designed to describe the attitude of the man of character towards political honors, but to express the inherent nobility of character itself, and the figures borrowed from the political arena are used to mark the superiority of the power which character confers over the coveted prizes of political life: The success of character is sure, with no risk of humiliating defeat; its 'honors' are unsullied by any base practices used in winning them; its power is permanent, and not held for a brief space by the favor of the fickle populace. The same figure is used still more boldly in IV. 9. 39. — **repulsae:** the technical term for defeat as a candidate for office.

18. **fulget**: cf. 16. 31 *fulgentem imperio.* — **honoribus**: cf. I. 1. 8 n.

20. **aurae**: see I. 5. 11 n.

21. **virtus**: Intr. 116 *g.* — **recludens,** etc.: it is manhood, in its highest development, that, at the end of his earthly career, exalts the hero to heaven and makes him a god. The third ode is an expansion and illustration of this text. — **mori**: Intr. 101 *d.*

22. **negata**: *sc.* as a rule, — not open to common men; cf. *indocili collo,* 3. 14.—**temptat iter**: the conception is here shifted a little; *virtus,* which in vs. 21 is the power that opens heaven to the hero, is now merged in the personality of the hero himself, as the immortal part of him which rises above earth and death, and finds a way to heaven.

23. **udam**: referring to the rain and fogs of the lower air, and sug-

Est et fideli tuta silentio
merces. Vetabo qui Cereris sacrum
volgarit arcanae sub isdem
sit trabibus fragilemque mecum
solvat phaselon : saepe Diespiter
neglectus incesto addidit integrum ;
raro antecedentem scelestum
deseruit pede Poena claudo.

gesting by contrast the fine, pure quality of the *aether* above, the abode of the gods.

25. **est et,** etc.: another maxim from Simonides (*Fr.* 66), ἔστι καὶ σιγᾶς ἀκίνδυνον γέρας, which is said to have been adopted by Augustus (Plutarch *Moral.* 207 D). The virtue of loyalty is coupled with *virtus*, as its complement in those whose lot or whose gifts do not call them to great achievement. There can be no doubt that Horace had Maecenas here chiefly in mind; cf. Prop. IV. 8. 33 *Caesaris et famae vestigia iuncta tenebis ; | Maecenatis erunt vera tropaea fides.* Being merely a negative virtue, the importance of loyalty is best appreciated by contemplating its opposite, the wicked betrayal of trust, on which the poet accordingly dwells, expressing in a vivid way his abhorrence of it, and the certainty that sooner or later it will be overtaken by the just retribution of heaven. Cf. I. 18. 11 *sqq.*

26. **Cereris sacrum** : *i.e.* the Eleusinian mysteries, used simply as an illustration; Intr. 117 *a.*

27. **arcanae,** *mystic.* Intr. 125.

28. **sit**: the subjunctive without *ne* after *veto* is suggested, perhaps, by the familiar form of prohibition, *cave sis.* — **trabibus** : *i.e.* roof. — **fragilem**: suggesting the opportunity offered to the deity to inflict the merited punishment.

29. **phaselon,** *yacht,* as in Catullus 4; a long, narrow, fast-sailing craft of Egyptian origin, named from its resemblance in shape to the kidney bean (φάσηλος). — **Diespiter** : see I. 1. 25 n, 34. 5.

30. **neglectus** : cf. 6. 7. The neglect might consist either of failure to recognize his supremacy by due worship and sacrifice (cf. I. 34. 1) or of indifference to his commandments; more commonly the two would go together. — **incesto,** *impure,* polluted by sin, and hence offensive to the god; cf. I. 12. 59. — **addidit,** *involves . . . with ; sc.* in the same punishment, such as the fall of the building or the capsizing of the boat. For the tense, see Intr. 80. — **integrum,** *the holy man ;* in meaning (from *in* and root of *tango*) it is the opposite of **incesto.**

31. **raro**: with **deseruit.**—**antecedentem** : *i.e.* though punishment does not instantly follow the crime; implying (with **pede claudo**) a feeling of security in the offender.

32. **deseruit**: *i.e.* is left behind and gives up the pursuit; cf. II. 16. 22. — **pede claudo** : concessive, whether taken as ablative absolute or ablative of characteristic.

## III.

Iustum et tenacem propositi virum
non civium ardor prava iubentium,
non voltus instantis tyranni
mente quatit solida, neque Auster,
dux inquieti turbidus Hadriae,
nec fulminantis magna manus Iovis :

III. The poet now reverts to the praise of strong manhood, and develops the thought embodied in the strophes on *virtus* in the preceding ode, the transition from which is so natural that the two odes have been regarded as one, and are so written in some good manuscripts. What was there said of manly character in the abstract is here restated with concrete illustrations. In the fine climax of the first two strophes we see the man of upright character and resolute will stemming the tide of popular passion, braving the threats of power, facing calmly the most violent convulsions of nature. This is the quality, the poet exclaims, which carried the great benefactors of our race through their trials and enabled them to attain heaven at last, — a Hercules, a Pollux, a Bacchus, a Romulus. The last illustration tempts him away from his subject, and he follows his fancy in describing the scene in heaven, when the gods in council consented to admit the founder of Rome to their company. This long description, which occupies the greater part of the ode, is at the end treated playfully by the poet as an unwarranted digression, for which he rebukes his muse ; but it is quite in keeping with the patriotic purpose of these odes, and it serves, like the episode of Regulus in the fifth, to break the monotony of his long moral discourse. The use of the title *Augustus* in vs. 11 shows that the poem was not written before B.C. 27. — Metre, 176.

1. **iustum et tenacem propositi,** *upright and steadfast, i.e.* steadfast in the right; for of course the *propositum* of a *iustus vir* must itself be *iustum*. The quality described (*hac arte*, 9) is *constantia*, one of the cardinal Roman virtues, based on rectitude,—the man who first makes sure the course of action he proposes is right, and then consistently adheres to it.

2. **civium ardor** : Horace may have had in mind the conduct of Socrates at the trial of the nine generals (Xen. *Mem.* I. 1. 18).

3. **tyranni** : the word implies irresponsible, and hence arbitrary power. It is possible that Socrates (under the Thirty Tyrants) was the model for this part of the picture also.

4. **mente** : ablative of respect. —**neque Auster,** etc.: *i.e.* if right impels him, he will go undaunted through storm and flood. What is *audacia* in I. 3. 9 *sqq.* is here *fortitudo.*

5. **dux Hadriae** : cf. I. 3. 15 *arbiter Hadriae;* II. 17. 19. — **turbidus,** *boisterous.*

si fractus inlabatur orbis,
impavidum ferient ruinae.
Hac arte Pollux et vagus Hercules
enisus arcis attigit igneas,
quos inter Augustus recumbens
purpureo bibet ore nectar;
hac te merentem, Bacche pater, tuae
vexere tigres indocili iugum

7. **fractus,** *should break and.*—**orbis**: here used in a wider sense (= *mundus*), the sphere of the heavens; cf. vs. 53, where *mundus* (like our 'world') is used for the earth only.

9. **hac arte**: see vs. 1 n.—**Pollux**: suggesting also his inseparable twin brother; cf. 29. 64; Verg. *G.* III. 89; Prop. IV. 22. 26.—**vagus**: in reference to the long journeys which his labors entailed.

10. **enisus**: in its literal sense of struggling out of difficulties and hindrances to a position where one is free from them. Cf. Tac. *Ann.* I. 70. 6 *Vitellius in editiora enisus eodem agmen subduxit.* — **arcis**, *heights*; cf. *aetherias arcis*, Ov. *Tr.* V. 3. 19. — **igneas**: in reference to the stars (called *ignes*, I. 12. 47). Cf. Cic. *Somn. Scip.* 15 *sqq.* '*iustitiam cole et pietatem . . .; ea vita via est in caelum et in hunc coetum eorum qui iam vixerunt et corpore relaxati illum incolunt locum quem vides'—erat autem is splendidissimo candore inter flammas circulus . . . 'Nonne aspicis quae in templa veneris? Novem tibi orbibus vel potius globis conexa sunt omnia, quorum unus caelestis est extimus . . . in quo sunt infixi illi qui volvuntur stellarum cursus sempiterni.*

11. **quos inter**, etc.: *i.e.* like Pollux and Hercules, the great benefactor of the world in our day will be received, when his work is done, among the gods. Cf. Verg. *G.* I. 24, 503 and *Ep.* II. 1. 5 *sqq.*, where Horace makes the same comparison, writing at a time when the worship of Augustus was already an accomplished fact. However extravagant the compliment may seem to us, and however perfunctory it may have been on Horace's part, there was nothing in it repugnant to Roman religious notions. See the curious discussion of the subject in Tacitus, *Ann.* IV. 38. 4 *sqq.*—**recumbens**: *i.e.* at a banquet: cf. *Ep.* I. 5. 1.

12. **purpureo ore**, *with rosy lips;* the hue of eternal youth, the *lumen iuventae purpureum* (Verg. *A.* I. 590) proper to a god. Cf. Verg. *A.* II. 593.

13. **hac . . . hac**: ablatives of cause (unlike *hac arte*, 9), the first with **merentem**, the second with *merens* (with **Quirinus**), suggested by the anaphora.—**Bacche pater**: cf. I. 18. 6 n.

14. **vexere**: *sc. in caelum*, as the anaphora and **merentem** sufficiently imply. — **tigres**: so, too, Vergil (*A.* VI. 805) and Ovid (*Ars Amat.* I. 550, *Am.* I. 2. 48); in Greek poetry and art Bacchus is drawn by panthers. His control of wild beasts typifies his civilizing influence. — **indocili**: cf. *negata*, 2. 22 n.

collo trahentes; hac Quirinus
Martis equis Acheronta fugit,
gratum elocuta consiliantibus
Iunone divis: 'Ilion, Ilion
fatalis incestusque iudex
et mulier peregrina vertit
in pulverem, ex quo destituit deos
mercede pacta Laomedon mihi
castaeque damnatum Minervae
cum populo et duce fraudulento.

16. **equis**: *i.e.* in his chariot (though the abl. is instrumental); cf. *conscendit equos Gradivus*, Ov. *Met.* XIV. 820, where the apotheosis of Romulus is described. See also Liv. I. 16.

17. **gratum** (with **divis**): implying that all the rest were ready to welcome the hero. The poet's object is obviously to show how Rome now enjoys the unanimous favor of the gods, divided as they had been in feeling towards Rome's mother city. Juno voices the sentiments of those who had hated the Trojans. Her speech is thoroughly natural: in yielding all that was desired, she is at great pains to show that she yields nothing at all. Her righteous enmity was against Troy and its perjured people, — her rekindled wrath breaks out in a savage repetition of the name, **Ilion, Ilion**; but Troy has perished, and her vengeance is satisfied. Let the remnants of the accursed race live and prosper, — if only in exile; let them extend their sway over the farthest lands and people, — but they must not rebuild Troy. That she dwells at such length and recurs again to this condition, which saves her dignity and her consistency, is sufficiently explained by the poet's desire to make the scene true to life. Cf. her speech in Verg. *A.* XII. 823 *sqq.*

19. **fatalis**: *i.e.* an instrument in the hands of fate; referring to **iudex** only.—**incestus**: cf. 2. 30 n. His sin was in giving his verdict for a bribe in dealing with the gods.—**iudex et mulier**: Paris and Helen. The goddess in her lofty scorn cannot take their names on her lips; so again below, vss. 25 *sq.*

20. **vertit**: cf. Verg. *A.* I. 20; Intr. 129.

21. **ex quo**, *ever since;* defining the time of **damnatum**. — **deos**: Poseidon and Apollo, who served him for a year, one building the walls of the city, the other keeping his flocks, according to *Il.* XXI. 446 *sqq.* According to another myth, which Horace appears to have in mind in vs. 66, Apollo built the wall; cf. Verg. *G.* III. 36 *Troiae Cynthius auctor.*

23. **damnatum**, *forfeited*, given over to our vengeance. See Roby 1199.—**Minervae**: against whom, with Juno, the judgment of Paris had gone.

24. **duce**: Laomedon, at the time; but the doom actually fell on his son Priam.

Iam nec Lacaenae splendet adulterae
famosus hospes nec Priami domus
periura pugnacis Achivos
Hectoreis opibus refringit,

nostrisque ductum seditionibus
bellum resedit: protinus et gravis
iras et invisum nepotem,
Troica quem peperit sacerdos,

Marti redonabo; illum ego lucidas
inire sedes, discere nectaris
sucos et adscribi quietis
ordinibus patiar deorum.

25. **adulterae**: dative; cf. *quibus nites*, I. 5. 12.

26. **famosus**, *notorious* (*sc.* as a *hospes*). — **nec**, *no longer* (from the influence of **iam**, which belongs to both clauses).

28. **opibus**: here equivalent to *viribus;* cf. IV. 4. 60. — **refringit**, *shatters;* more commonly used in prose of breaking down an obstacle; here, of presenting so firm a resistance that the assailing force is shattered upon it. Cf. the use of *debilitat*, I. 11. 5, and Prop. IV. 3. 44 *Teutonicas Roma refringit opes*.

29. **ductum**, *prolonged*.

30. **resedit**: a very expressive word: the 'storm of war' has given way to a calm. — **protinus**: rather logical than temporal in meaning,—she is completely satisfied and waits for nothing further.

31. **nepotem**: Romulus, as son of her son Mars; **invisum**, for the reason given in the next verse; she will not make him suffer for the sins of his race, but she cannot love him.

32. **Troica**: see I. 2. 17 n. — **sacerdos**: as a Vestal.

33. **redonabo**: see II. 7. 3 n. The word is here employed, however, in the sense of 'giving up' rather than 'giving back' (cf. I. 3. 7 n), and is made to serve for both objects, **iras** and **nepotem**: she will give up, in favor of Mars, her displeasure, and she will give up to him her grandson, whom she might withhold. — **illum**: emphatic; against *him* she harbors no resentment. — **lucidas**: see vs. 10 n.

34. **discere**, *to taste;* lit. to become acquainted with (an object previously unknown), as in II. 20. 20. — **nectaris**: genitive of nearer definition; Gr. 214 *f*.

35. **sucos**: Intr. 128. — **et**: connecting the second and third infinitives, as expressing what took place after Romulus had entered heaven, more closely with one another than with the first, which expresses the entrance itself. Cf. *Ep.* I. 7. 53 and 55. — **adscribi ordinibus**: both words are borrowed from the Roman political and military systems. — **quietis**: their normal condition. In contrast with *seditionibus*, above, it expresses the

Dum longus inter saeviat Ilion
Romamque pontus, qualibet exsules
in parte regnanto beati;
dum Priami Paridisque busto
insultet armentum et catulos ferae
celent inultae, stet Capitolium
fulgens triumphatisque possit
Roma ferox dare iura Medis;
horrenda late nomen in ultimas
extendat oras, qua medius liquor
secernit Europen ab Afro,
qua tumidus rigat arva Nilus.

goddess' desire for peace. The beautiful rhythm enhances the impression of serene existence which the words convey.

37. **inter saeviat**: Intr. 115 *c*.

38. **exsules**, *in exile;* limiting the concession in **qualibet**.

39. **regnanto**: concessive; cf. *occupato*, 29. 44 n.

40. **busto**: ablative of place (Intr. 69) with **insultet** (used absolutely; cf. Verg. *A*. XI. 599 *fremit aequore toto insultans*) and **celet**. When these lines were written, Vergil had not yet published the Aeneid and fixed for all time the legend of the death of Priam (*iacet ingens litore truncus | avolsumque umeris caput et sine nomine corpus, A*. II. 557); so that there was no preconceived notion in the minds of Horace's readers (as there is in ours) to deter him from introducing a crumbling tomb of the Trojan king to complete his picture of desolation and to make a more striking contrast with the splendor of the Capitol.

42. **stet Capitolium**: see 30. 8 n.

43. **fulgens**: in reference to its gilded roof; cf. Verg. *A*. VIII. 347 *Capitolia . . . | aurea nunc, olim silvestribus horrida dumis*. — **triumphatis**, *to lead in triumph and;* Intr. 51 *e*. — **possit**, *have the power to;* the event had not yet justified prophecy in going any further than this.

44. **dare iura**: the act of an absolute sovereign; cf. Liv. I. 8. 1 (of Romulus) *vocata ad concilium multitudine, quae coalescere in populi unius corpus nulla re praeterquam legibus poterat, iura dedit*. — **Medis**: see I. 2. 22 n.

45. **horrenda**, *spreading terror*. —**late**: with **horrenda**.—**nomen**: *i.e.* her political power; cf. *Latinum nomen*, IV. 15. 13.

46. **qua . . . qua**, *where, on the one side, . . . where, on the other;* so *qua parte . . . qua*, below (55 *sq*.). — **medius liquor**: the straits of Gibraltar.

47. **Afro**: the name of the inhabitant standing for the country. The plural is more common in this use; cf. IV. 4. 63; Intr. 127.

48. **tumidus rigat**: referring

Aurum inrepertum et sic melius situm,
cum terra celat, spernere fortior
quam cogere humanos in usus
omne sacrum rapiente dextra,

quicumque mundo terminus obstitit,
hunc tanget armis, visere gestiens
qua parte debacchentur ignes,
qua nebulae pluviique rores.

Sed bellicosis fata Quiritibus
hac lege dico, ne nimium pii
rebusque fidentes avitae
tecta velint reparare Troiae.

to its annual inundation, on which the fertility of Egypt depends.

49. **aurum**, etc.: at this point the goddess, catching for a moment the inspiration of her theme, changes from assent to prophecy (*tanget*, 54, after *stet*, *possit*, *extendat;* cf. also *fata dico*, 57), and she warms with admiration for the moral fortitude of the Roman, which will enable him to triumph over all obstacles. As prophecy, this refers to the best times of the commonwealth; to Horace's readers it was designed to convey a lesson, to point out the condition of future success. — **inrepertum**: *i.e.* not sought for, though known to exist.

50. **spernere**: Intr. 101 *a*, 102. — **fortior**, *showing her courage more in*.

51. **cogere**, *gathering* (*it*). — **humanos in usus** (with **rapiente**), etc.: describing the opposite disposition, — one that shrinks from nothing in the mad race for riches. **humanos** is in contrast with **sacrum**.

52. **omne**: *i.e.* all without distinction, any and every; cf. I. 3. 25 n.

53. **mundo**: see note on *orbis*, 7. — **obstitit**: perf. definite (from *obsisto*) expressing a present state (= *obstat*); cf. *constiterint*, I. 9. 4.

54. **visere**: cf. I. 37. 25 n, II. 15. 3.

55. **qua parte**, etc.: cf. I. 22. 17 *sqq*. nn. — **debacchentur**, *revel unrestrained*, *i.e.* have full sway, with no counteracting forces to moderate them, as in the temperate zone. For this intensive force of *de-*, cf. I. 9. 11 n, and *Ep*. I. 3. 14 *desaevit*. The subjunctive indicates that these clauses are part of the wish (**gestiens**).

56. **pluvii rores**: although *ros* is used by the poets for water in general (*e.g.* 4. 61), the phrase is here a singularly happy one to express the persistent 'drizzle' which is so prominent a feature of the weather in some parts of northern Europe during a considerable portion of the year.

57. **sed**: the goddess closes with an emphatic reiteration of the terms of her concession. — **fata**: see vs. 49 n.

58. **hac lege dico**: implying that she had some control over

Troiae renascens alite lugubri
fortuna tristi clade iterabitur,
ducente victricis catervas
coniuge me Iovis et sorore.

Ter si resurgat murus aeneus
auctore Phoebo, ter pereat meis
excisus Argivis, ter uxor
capta virum puerosque ploret.'

Non hoc iocosae conveniet lyrae:
quo, musa, tendis? Desine pervicax
referre sermones deorum et
magna modis tenuare parvis.

their destiny. *Fatum* (from *fari*) is originally nothing but the expressed will (*quod semel dictum est, C. S.* 26) of Jove or of some other divinity; cf. *fato divom*, Verg. *A.* VII. 50, and see Preller-Jordan, *Röm. Myth.* II. 194. — **ne . . . velint**: in apposition with **lege**. — **pii**: here of devotion to ancestors (**avitae**).

59. **fidentes**: also modified by **nimium**. The expression implies that in entertaining such a desire they would *consciously* incur danger (cf. I. 3. 25), — that of undertaking to undo what the gods had done.

61. **Troiae**: Intr. 116 *e*. — **renascens**, etc.: sc. *si renascetur*. The protasis, already implied in the preceding strophe, is again suggested by **renascens**, which is itself, however, a part of the conclusion. — **alite lugubri**: cf. *mala avi*, I. 15. 5 n.

62. **fortuna**, *the career*.

64. **coniuge et sorore**: cf. Verg. *A.* I. 47. Intr. 116 *b*.

65. **ter**, etc.: cf. Verg. *G.* I. 281, 283. Intr. 116 *b* and *f*. — **aeneus auctore Phoebo**: of the very strongest material and with a divine architect. For Phoebus, see above, 21 n. — **meis**: see I. 7. 8 n.

67. **Argivis**: Intr. 55.

69. **non hoc**, etc.: the poet breaks off as if suddenly conscious that he is trespassing with his playful lyre on epic ground. Cf. II. 1. 37 *sqq*. The tone in which he rebukes his headstrong muse is hardly in keeping with his character as *Musarum sacerdos*, and indicates that the ode was originally written independently.—**conveniet**: the future is natural, just as we say 'this will never do,' and the like.

72. **tenuare**: cf. I. 6. 12 n. — **parvis**, *petty*; cf. 25. 17; IV. 2. 27 *sqq*.

## IV.

Descende caelo et dic age tibia
regina longum Calliope melos,
seu voce nunc mavis acuta,
seu fidibus citharave Phoebi.

Auditis, an me ludit amabilis
insania? Audire et videor pios
errare per lucos, amoenae
quos et aquae subeunt et aurae.

IV. With a fresh invocation and a renewed declaration of his loyalty to the service of the Muses, the poet proceeds in this ode to inculcate the supremacy of mind over brute force, of strength tempered with wisdom over ungoverned violence. This gentle wisdom is the gift of the Muses to men. This is their gift to Caesar, — this, and not merely diversion and refreshment, — when he leads his veterans home from war. The victory of Jove over the Titans and Giants, which Horace cites as an illustration of his precepts, could not fail to be understood by his readers as typical of the victory of Augustus, the champion of order and culture, over the turbulent forces of anarchy and civil strife. — Metre, 176.

1. **descende caelo**: the Muses were conceived as dwelling in heaven (Ὀλύμπια δώματ' ἔχουσαι, *Il.* II. 484), though having, like other divinities, their favorite haunts on earth. — **caelo**: Intr. 70. — **dic age**: cf. I. 32. 3, II. 11. 22. For the meaning of **dic**, see I. 6. 5 n. — **tibia**, etc.: see I. 1. 32, 34; 12. 1 n. For the case, see note on *fide Teia*, I. 17. 18.

2. **regina**: expressing the poet's homage; cf. III. 30. 14 *sqq.*, IV. 3. The title, like ἄνασσα and δέσποινα in Greek, was a common form of honorary address to a goddess; cf. III. 26. 11. — **longum**: he prays for, not a brief or fitful, but a long-sustained inspiration. — **Calliope**: see note on *Clio*, I. 12. 2.

3. **seu**: see I. 4. 12 n. — **voce**: *i.e.* without instrumental accompaniment.

4. **fidibus citharave**: on a Greek vase preserved in Munich are figures of the nine muses, of whom two are playing on the *lyra* and the *cithara* respectively (Baumeister, p. 1544), and two on *tibiae*, while one is apparently singing (cf. **voce**) from a scroll. — **Phoebi**: as being its inventor. The lyre (**fidibus**) was invented by Mercury; cf. I. 10. 6.

5. **auditis**: sc. *melos;* the divine melody that fills his soul comes with such vividness that at first he doubts whether it is not real music.

6. **audire et videor** (sc. *mihi*): see Intr. 119 *a*, and cf. II. 1. 21.— **pios**, *holy;* hallowed by the presence of the Muses and undefiled by the contact of the crowd; cf. I. 1. 30 *sqq.*

7. **amoenae**: Intr. 114.

8. **quos subeunt**, *'neath which course.*

Me fabulosae Volture in Apulo
nutricis extra limen Apuliae
ludo fatigatumque somno
fronde nova puerum palumbes
texere, mirum quod foret omnibus,
quicumque celsae nidum Acherontiae
saltusque Bantinos et arvum
pingue tenent humilis Forenti,

9. **me**: the emphasis here marks the connection with what precedes, not by way of contrast (as in I. 1. 29, 7. 10, etc.), but of explanation. That he could hear the divine strains, inaudible to others, was in keeping with his constant experience of the muses' favor. In recalling his marvelous preservation in childhood, — the incident may very well have been a real one, though given to us with poetical embellishment, — Horace had in mind, perhaps, the stories told of the infancy of some of the Greek poets, — as of Stesichorus, on whose lips a nightingale was said to have alighted and sung; of Pindar, whose lips, in his sleep, were bathed with honey by the bees. — **fabulosae**: with **palumbes**, a connection indicated by their being joined with **me** and **puerum** respectively (Intr. 112). For the meaning, cf. I. 22. 7 n; they are the doves 'of story,' the birds of Venus, which draw her car and carry ambrosia to Jove (*Odys.* XII. 63).

10. **Apuliae**: the text is almost certainly wrong here, and no satisfactory correction has been proposed. Apart from the improbability of the substantive following so closely upon its adjective, the double change of prosody from **Āpŭlo** to **Ăpūliae** has a very suspicious look, and the second form finds poor support in the uncertain *Ăpūlicum* of 24. 4. Some other word, in all probability, originally stood at the end of verse 10, and has been displaced and lost by the blunder of a copyist whose eye was caught by the word **Apulo** above it. See Crit. App.

11. **fatigatum**, *overcome*. For the position of **-que**, see Intr. 119 *b*. For the *fatigatum* to be supplied with **ludo**, a somewhat different translation will be necessary.

12. **nova**, *fresh; i.e.* green, plucked for the purpose.

13. **mirum quod foret omnibus**, *a marvel to all*; characteristic relative clause; cf. *Epod.* 2. 28 n. The subject of **mirum foret** is (through **quod**) the preceding sentence, but it is expanded in the interrogative clauses which follow in the next strophe, *ut tuto*, etc.

14. **quicunque**, etc.: *i.e.* all within a range of a dozen or fifteen miles, — implying that many witnesses could be called to confirm the story. The places are briefly characterized, Acherontia as perched on a hill, Bantia among the mountain pastures, Forentum in fertile lowland. They have left their names to the modern Acerenza, Banzi, and Forenza.

ut tuto ab atris corpore viperis
dormirem et ursis, ut premerer sacra
lauroque conlataque myrto,
non sine dis animosus infans.

Vester, Camenae, vester in arduos
tollor Sabinos, seu mihi frigidum
Praeneste seu Tibur supinum
seu liquidae placuere Baiae.

Vestris amicum fontibus et choris
non me Philippis versa acies retro,
devota non exstinxit arbor,
nec Sicula Palinurus unda.

17. **ut**: with *mirum*, 13; see note above, and cf. *Epod.* 16. 53. — **atris,** *deadly;* see I. 28. 13 n, and cf. Verg. *G.* I. 129 *ille malum virus serpentibus addidit atris.*

18. **premerer,** *I was covered all over;* cf. *Epod.* 1. 33. — **sacra**: to Phoebus, as the myrtle was to Venus. Both **sacra** and **conlata** are to be taken with each of the substantives; see Intr. 121.

19. **-que . . . -que**: cf. I. 26. 12. — **conlata**: *i.e.* not at haphazard, but showing design.

20. **non sine dis**: in reference to **animosus**; the child's courage came from no human inspiration. Cf. *Il.* V. 185 *οὐχ ὅ γ' ἄνευθε θεοῦ τάδε μαίνεται, ἀλλά τις ἄγχι | ἕστηκ' ἀθανάτων.*

21. **vester . . . vester . . . tollor,** *yours I am, . . . yours, when I climb.* The emphatic **vester** expresses both their choice of him and his surrender to them. Theirs he is always and everywhere; under their protection he has escaped from imminent peril in the past, with them he will cheerfully face any dangers in the future.

22. **Sabinos**: see II. 18. 14 n; it may mean here, however, merely the country. — **frigidum**: from its high situation (*altum Praeneste,* Verg. *A.* VII. 682).

23. **supinum**: cf. Juv. 3. 192 *proni Tiburis.* Both Praeneste and Tibur were favorite resorts of Horace; cf. I. 7. 11 *sqq.*, II. 6. 5 *sqq.*, *Ep.* I. 2. 2, 7. 45.

24. **liquidae**: probably referring to the atmosphere. — **placuere,** *attract.* — **Baiae**: see II. 18. 20 n; for Horace's visits to it, cf. *Ep.* I. 15. 2 *sqq.*

25. **vestris**: Intr. 116 *g.* — **amicum,** *welcome;* see I. 26. 1 n. — **fontibus**: cf. I. 26. 6 n.

26. **Philippis**: cf. II. 7. 9; Intr. 12. — **versa acies**: Intr. 105 *a.*

27. **arbor**: cf. II. 13; 17. 27.

28. **Palinurus**: a promontory of Lucania, named, according to Vergil, after the pilot of Aeneas (*A.* VI. 381). The natural inference from the allusion is, that Horace had had a narrow escape from shipwreck off this point; but we know nothing of the circumstances. See, however, Intr. 13.

Vtcumque mecum vos eritis, libens
insanientem navita Bosporum
temptabo et urentis harenas
litoris Assyrii viator ;

visam Britannos hospitibus feros
et laetum equino sanguine Concanum,
visam pharetratos Gelonos
et Scythicum inviolatus amnem.

Vos Caesarem altum, militia simul
fessas cohortis abdidit oppidis,
finire quaerentem labores
Pierio recreatis antro.

29. **utcumque**: see I. 17. 10 n.

30. **Bosporum**: cf. II. 13. 14.

32. **litoris Assyrii**: used vaguely of the far East, — the shore of the Persian gulf or Indian ocean; cf. II. 11. 16 n. — **viator**, *a wayfarer;* in contrast with **navita.**

33. **hospitibus feros**: Horace probably means that they sacrificed them, as they did their captives (Tac. *Ann.* XIV. 30). Human sacrifices were a part of their druidical rites, according to Tacitus.

34. **Concanum**: one of the Cantabrian tribes (see II. 6. 2 n). The practice here attributed to them was a Scythian custom; cf. Verg. *G.* III. 461 *Gelonus cum . . . lac concretum cum sanguine potat equino.*

35. **Gelonos**: see II. 9. 23 n.

36. **Scythicum amnem**: the Tanais (Don); cf. *Medum flumen,* II. 9. 21.

37. **vos**: continuing the emphasis in *vester* and *vestris,* above. The anaphora keeps prominent the main idea of the ode, the intellectual activity inspired and fostered by the Muses, — here as affording refreshment after the physical fatigue of war; in the next strophe as subduing the fierce passions engendered by strife, and restoring the calm control of reason. — **altum,** *august;* cf. *S.* II. 5. 62; Verg. *A.* X. 875 *altus Apollo.*

38. **abdidit**: aptly expressing the disappearance from public view of the formidable army of 120,000 men which threatened the peace of Italy when the victor returned after Actium.

39. **finire quaerentem**: implying a distaste for war and a longing for peace. For the inf., see Intr. 94 *c.*

40. **Pierio antro**: *i.e.* by literary study or conversation in some quiet retreat. Grottos, however, were actually used for entertainments; cf. Tac. *Ann.* IV. 59. Donatus (*Vita Verg.* 27) tells us that, on his way home from the East in B.C. 29, Octavian spent some time at Atella, in Campania, to recuperate, and there listened during four days to the Georgics, then just finished, which were read to him by Vergil and Maecenas. His taste for literature is attested by Suetonius (*Aug.* 84. 85). For

Vos lene consilium et datis et dato
gaudetis, almae. Scimus ut impios
Titanas immanemque turbam
fulmine sustulerit caduco

qui terram inertem, qui mare temperat
ventosum et urbis regnaque tristia
divosque mortalisque turmas
imperio regit unus aequo.

Magnum illa terrorem intulerat Iovi
fidens iuventus horrida bracchiis,
fratresque tendentes opaco
Pelion imposuisse Olympo.

**Pierio,** see I. 12. 6 n. Cf. also *Dionaeo antro*, II. 1. 39.

41. **vos** : see 37 n. — **lene consilium** : in allusion to the moderate policy pursued by Augustus after his victory. For the synaeresis in **consilium,** see Intr. 181.

42. **gaudetis** : implying that their teaching is accepted, with beneficent results; otherwise they would have no cause to rejoice. This thinly veiled commendation of Augustus continues to be the underlying thought of what follows, where the poet cites in support of his thesis a well-known (**scimus**) example. — **ut** : cf. vs. 17.

43. **Titanas,** etc. : Horace is not careful to distinguish the Titans from the Giants. — **immanem** : alluding to the monstrous shapes of the Giants. On the great altar at Pergamon, which Horace possibly had seen (Intr. 12), they are represented in a variety of grotesque forms, in which the human figure is combined with that of other animals (Baumeister, p. 1252). — **-que** : epexegetical, *and all the.*

44. **caduco,** *descending;* καταιβάτης κεραυνός, Aesch. *Prom.* 359.

45. **qui,** etc.: the triple contrast, suggesting the manifold variety of detail in the universe which Jove controls, conveys a livelier impression of his power; **inertem** (cf. II. 9. 5, and *bruta tellus et vaga flumina*, I. 34. 9) is contrasted with **ventosum; urbis** (where life is fullest and richest) with **regna tristia**, the abode of the dead; **divos** (the immortals) with **mortalis turmas** (the ranks of mortal men). The objects of **temperat** are **terram** and **mare,** which stand for inanimate nature; with the remaining objects, which represent sentient beings, **regit** is used.

49. **terrorem** : cf. II. 12. 7.

50. **fidens** : best taken absolutely. — **iuventus** : the Hecatoncheires or hundred-handed (**horrida bracchiis**) sons of Uranus and Gaea. In the ordinary form of the myth in Greek writers these three brothers take the side of Zeus.

51. **fratres** : the Aloidae, Otus and Ephialtes; *Odys.* XI. 308, Verg. *A.* VI. 582.

Sed quid Typhoeus et validus Mimas,
aut quid minaci Porphyrion statu,
quid Rhoetus evolsisque truncis
Enceladus iaculator audax

contra sonantem Palladis aegida
possent ruentes? Hinc avidus stetit
Volcanus, hinc matrona Iuno et
numquam umeris positurus arcum,

qui rore puro Castaliae lavit
crinis solutos, qui Lyciae tenet

52. **Pelion,** etc.: cf. *Odys.* XI. 315 *Ὄσσαν ἐπ' Οὐλύμπῳ μέμασαν θέμεν, αὐτὰρ ἐπ' Ὄσσῃ | Πήλιον εἰνοσίφυλλον, ἵν' οὔρανος ἀμβατὸς εἴη·* Verg. *G.* I. 280; Prop. II. 1. 19.—**imposuisse** : Intr. 81 *b.*

53. **Typhoeus,** etc.: Horace's picture of the Gigantomachia is conceived on a less portentous scale than in some forms of the myth, in which the combatants hurl mountains and islands at one another. Here, as in II. 19. 21 *sqq.*, we must imagine an assault on Olympus, and the gods fighting side by side like Homeric warriors. — **Typhoeus** : the youngest of the sons of Gaea, and the strongest and most terrible of them, sent by his mother to take vengeance on the gods for their destruction of the Giants (or, in Hesiod, of the Titans). Here he is not distinguished from the rest of the Giants. — **Mimas** : a Giant.

54. **Porphyrion** : *βασιλεὺς Γιγάντων*, Pind. *Pyth.* 8. 17.— **statu,** *posture.*

55. **Rhoetus** : see II. 19. 23.— **truncis**: instrumental abl. with the verbal idea in **iaculator**; Intr. 73.

56. **Enceladus** : imprisoned under Etna; Verg. *A.* III. 578.

57. **contra,** etc.: to be taken with **possent,** though understood also with **ruentes.** — **sonantem** : from being shaken by the goddess herself, to inspire terror. In Homer the crash of thunder is associated with the shaking of the aegis by Zeus (*Il.* XVII. 595). — **aegida** : see I. 15. 11 n.

58. **hinc . . . hinc** : *i.e.* ranged on either side of Pallas, who is the central figure; the goddess of wisdom is the foremost champion. — **avidus** : sc. *pugnae;* so Tac. *Ann.* I. 51. 1 *avidas legiones.*

60. **numquam positurus** : *i.e.* forever armed and prepared; see Intr. 104 *a*, and cf. *ponere*, I. 3. 40. In the following strophe the poet allows us to pause and contemplate the beautiful god, as a relief from the stern conflict and the grave thoughts it suggests. Cf. I. 12. 29 n.

61. **Castaliae**: a spring on Parnassus.—**lavit crinis**: cf. IV. 6. 26. For **lavit,** see II. 3. 18 n.

62. **solutos** : cf. I. 21. 2 n. — **tenet** : *sc.* under his sway; cf. 26. 9 (=I. 3. 1), *C. S.* 69; here, however, used more with reference to the abode of the god (cf. vs. 16). Horace follows the legend which made

dumeta natalemque silvam,
Delius et Patareus Apollo.

Vis consili expers mole ruit sua:
vim temperatam di quoque provehunt
in maius; idem odere viris
omne nefas animo moventis.

Testis mearum centimanus Gyas
sententiarum, notus et integrae
temptator Orion Dianae,
virginea domitus sagitta.

Iniecta monstris Terra dolet suis,
maeretque partus fulmine luridum
missos ad Orcum; nec peredit
impositam celer ignis Aetnen,

Apollo spend the six winter months at Patara, in Lycia, where he had a famous temple and oracle, and the summer in Delos (Serv. on *Aen.* IV. 143). The reference to these two places is repeated chiastically in the epithets of vs. 64.

63. **natalem**: see I. 21. 2 n.

65. **vis,** etc.: this strophe at once sums up the moral of the story,—the ineffectiveness of force without intelligence, — and advances the thought a step farther: divine favor promotes force that is under control; divine wrath overtakes the strength that pursues its selfish ends unrestrained by any controlling principle; and with illustrations of this truth the poem closes.

68. **omne**: cf. 3. 52 n.

69. **testis**: sc. *est;* cf. *scimus*, 42. — **Gyas**: see II. 17. 14 n and vs. 50 n, above.

70. **notus**: another appeal to the reader's knowledge, as in 42. — **integrae**: cf. *intactae Palladis*, I. 7. 5.

71. **temptator,** *assailant;* the word is found only here in classical literature. — **Orion**: here classed among the Giants; by others he is made a son of Poseidon. See II. 13. 39 n.

72. **virginea**: cf. *Hectoreis opibus*, 3. 28.

73. **monstris suis**: *i.e.* the Giants. — **Terra**: cf. *Telluris*, II. 12. 7; both for Γαῖα or Γῆ, who was the mother of both Titans and Giants. In some representations of the battle of the Giants she appears rising from the ground, pleading for her offspring; see Baumeister, figg. 637, 1420. — **dolet, maeret**: the first of the pain of lying upon them (**iniecta**), the second of her grief for their calamity.

74. **partus**: more particularly the Titans, who were hurled into Tartarus (Verg. *A.* VI. 580), though Tityus, the example given

incontinentis nec Tityi iecur
reliquit ales, nequitiae additus
custos; amatorem trecentae
Pirithoum cohibent catenae.

## V.

Caelo tonantem credidimus Iovem
regnare: praesens divus habebitur
Augustus adiectis Britannis
imperio gravibusque Persis.

below, was a Giant (*Odys.* XI. 576). — **luridum Orcum**: cf. *furvae Proserpinae*, II. 13. 21.

75. **nec peredit**: *i.e.* the imprisoned Giant has found no release; his punishment is eternal. For the tense, see Intr. 80.

76. **impositam**: *sc.* on one of the Giants. Enceladus, Typhoeus, and Briareus are consigned by various myths to this fate. — **celer**, *swift consuming*.

77. **incontinentis**: his offense was offering violence to Latona.— **nec**: Intr. 114. — **iecur**: the punishment was aimed at what was regarded as the seat of the passion; cf. IV. 1. 12.

78. **ales**: a vulture (Verg. *A.* VI. 597). — **additus custos**, *set to keep watch upon*.

79. **trecentae**: used simply to express a very large number; cf. II. 14. 5, 26; *S.* I. 5. 12.

80. **Pirithoum**: king of the Lapithae and friend of Theseus, who accompanied him to the lower world on his impious enterprise of carrying off Proserpina. Both were chained to a rock there, and Hercules, who succeeded in releasing Theseus, was obliged to leave Pirithous to his doom. Cf. IV. 7. 27.

V. From the contemplation of Jove triumphantly maintaining his supremacy in heaven the poet leads our thoughts down to earth again, where Augustus has a divine mission to fulfill in restoring the old Roman valor and the glory of Roman arms. Courage and patriotism in the soldier have sunk to a low ebb, — the legitimate result of relaxation of the stern discipline of earlier times, which is finely portrayed in the story of Regulus. — Metre, 176.

1. **caelo**: with **regnare**; Intr. 69. — **credidimus**: Intr. 80.

2. **praesens**, *on earth*. Augustus is placed in the same relation to Jove as in I. 12. 57 *sqq.*

3. **adiectis**: equivalent to *cum adiecerit*.—**Britannis**: see introd. note to I. 35.

4. **gravibus Persis**: see I. 2. 22 n. In passages like this Horace no doubt voiced the general feeling that Augustus should justify his leadership by completing the conquests of Julius Caesar, and, above all, should retrieve the repeated disasters which the Romans had suffered at the hands of the Parthians. The recollection of these disasters leads naturally to the reflections that follow.

Milesne Crassi coniuge barbara
turpis maritus vixit et hostium
(pro curia inversique mores !)
consenuit socerorum in armis,

sub rege Medo Marsus et Apulus,
anciliorum et nominis et togae
oblitus aeternaeque Vestae,
incolumi Iove et urbe Roma?

Hoc caverat mens provida Reguli
dissentientis condicionibus
foedis et exemplo trahenti
perniciem veniens in aevum,

5. **milesne Crassi**: the defeat at Carrhae, B.C. 53, left thousands of Romans in the hands of the Parthians, and subsequent events brought them no prospect of release. They took service in the Parthian armies and even fought against the Romans. — **coniuge barbara**: abl. of cause with **turpis**; Intr. 105 *a*.

6. **vixit**: in close connection with **turpis maritus**: 'Has he consented to *live* at the cost of such humiliation?'

7. **curia**: the symbol of Roman law and sovereignty. — **mores**, *discipline*.

8. **socerorum**, *whose daughter he has wedded;* dwelling with scorn on the odious relation already expressed in **coniuge barbara** and **maritus**.

9. **sub rege**: a hateful suggestion, even without **Medo**. — **Marsus et Apulus**: the best types of the Roman soldier; cf. I. 2. 39 n, II. 20. 18, I. 22. 13.

10. **anciliorum**, etc.: the twelve sacred shields in the keeping of the Salii (see I. 36. 12 n), closely associated, therefore, with the foundation of the city, and, like the fire of Vesta, with its permanence. — **nominis**: the evidence of his birthright. — **togae**: the badge of his citizenship.

12. **Iove**: *i.e.* his temple, the Capitol.

13. **hoc**: emphatic: *It was just this that.* — **Reguli**: consul B.C. 256, in the first Punic war. In that year the Romans successfully invaded Africa, and in the following year Regulus, who was left in command there, was defeated and taken prisoner with a part of his army. According to the story which Horace here follows, he was subsequently sent by the Carthaginians to Rome to negotiate for an exchange of prisoners, under oath to return to Carthage if the negotiations should fail.

14. **dissentientis**, *when he refused his assent.* On reaching Rome Regulus persuaded the senate to reject the overtures which he brought. — **condicionibus**: dative; Intr. 57.

15. **exemplo**, *a precedent.* —

si non periret immiserabilis
captiva pubes. 'Signa ego Punicis
adfixa delubris et arma
militibus sine caede' dixit
'derepta vidi; vidi ego civium
retorta tergo bracchia libero
portasque non clausas et arva
Marte coli populata nostro.

Auro repensus scilicet acrior
miles redibit. Flagitio additis
damnum. Neque amissos colores
lana refert medicata fuco,

nec vera virtus, cum semel excidit,

**trahenti**, *that would entail;* equivalent to *quod traheret*, and containing the apodosis of the conditional clause of the next strophe.

17. **perirēt**: Intr. 179.

18. **ego . . . vidi; vidi ego**: Intr. 116 *e*. He urges his appeal with the force of personal experience; he has seen with his own eyes the humiliation of captivity.

19. **adfixa**: as thank offerings of victory. Cf. IV. 15. 6 *sq*.

20. **sine caede**: implying that they should have shed their blood rather than submit to the indignity.

21. **civium**: emphatic, to mark by contrast the depth of their degradation. It may be translated: *I have seen* CITIZENS, *with their arms pinioned*, etc.

22. **tergo**: Intr. 69. — **libero**, *their freeman's;* repeating the thought of **civium**.

23. **portas** (sc. *Carthaginis*), etc.: *i.e.* as if there were no war; a humiliating proof of the complete failure of the Roman invasion.

24. **Marte**: Intr. 130.

25. **auro repensus**: instead of being left to the fate which his cowardice has brought upon him. The phrase, however, suggests more than this, — the degradation of the warrior who has had a price set upon him, like a slave, and has resorted to this base substitute for valor as a means of safety. — **scilicet**: indicating the irony of the sentence.

26. **flagitio**: the dishonor the state has suffered through the conduct of these prisoners; **damnum**: the breaking down of discipline which will result from their ransom.

27. **neque . . . nec**: *i.e.* the second is no more possible than the first; cf. I. 6. 5 n. — **colores**: Intr. 128. The natural color of the wool is meant.

28. **refert**, *renews, shows again.*

29. **virtus**: cf. 2. 17 n. — **semel excidit**: the phrase itself suggests what is next explicitly stated, — cowardice is not a temporary weakness; the loss of courage is instant and final, as of a jewel. Cf. I. 24. 16 n.

curat reponi deterioribus.
Si pugnat extricata densis
cerva plagis, erit ille fortis
qui perfidis se credidit hostibus,
et Marte Poenos proteret altero
qui lora restrictis lacertis
sensit iners timuitque mortem.
Hic, unde vitam sumeret inscius,
pacem duello miscuit. O pudor!
O magna Carthago, probrosis
altior Italiae ruinis!'
Fertur pudicae coniugis osculum
parvosque natos ut capitis minor
ab se removisse et virilem
torvus humi posuisse voltum,

30. **reponi**: Intr. 94 *i.*—**deterioribus**: the same persons that are understood with **excidit**; the word characterizes them as they are left when this virtue of courage has gone out of them. For the case, see Intr. 53, and cf. Liv. II. 43. 8 *si animus hosti redisset.*

33. **perfidis**: in reference to the proverbial *Punica fides;* cf. IV. 4. 49 n.—**se credidit**: in contrast with **perfidis**; Intr. 116 *a.*

34. **Marte**: cf. 24 n.—**altero**, *some other;* the war in which they were taken prisoners being regarded as ended. *Alter* is used to denote any other person or thing that is brought into comparison with the one in hand, so that these two alone are for the time under consideration; cf. 24. 22; *S.* I. 1. 40 *ne sit te ditior alter* ('thy neighbor'); Madv. 496.

35. **restrictis**: cf. *retorta,* 22.

36. **iners**, *tamely.*

37. **unde sumeret**: representing a question of doubt, *unde sumam?* The question is, in effect, 'to what he should owe his life,' *sc.* to his sword and his valor, and not to the compassion of the enemy.

38. **pacem**, etc.: *i.e.* confused the two, treated the enemy as if they were friends.

40. **ruinis**: instrumental abl. with the comparative,—higher by that much, *exalted upon,* etc.; cf. Liv. I. 30. 1 *Roma interim crescit Albae ruinis.*

41. **fertur**, *men say.* The word prepares us for something surprising; cf. I. 7. 23.

42. **capitis minor**: for *capite deminutus.* In the word *caput* were summed up a Roman's personal and political rights. As a prisoner, Regulus was technically a slave, and unfit, in his own eyes, for the caress of a Roman matron

donec labantis consilio patres
firmaret auctor numquam alias dato,
interque maerentis amicos
egregius properaret exsul.

Atqui sciebat quae sibi barbarus
tortor pararet: non aliter tamen
dimovit obstantis propinquos
et populum reditus morantem

quam si clientum longa negotia
diiudicata lite relinqueret,
tendens Venafranos in agros
aut Lacedaemonium Tarentum.

or her children. This humility of the man is the background against which the poet paints in effective contrast his moral heroism (**patres firmaret**) and his splendid victory of self-sacrifice (**egregius exsul**). For the genitive see Intr. 66 *d*.

46. **auctor,** *by his influence.*— **alias,** *before or since.*

48. **properaret**: his alacrity (cf. also *dimovit obstantis*, 51) and cheerfulness (53 *sqq.*), now that his patriotic purpose is achieved, are set forth in contrast with the sternness of his attitude (43 *sq.*) as long as there was any chance of a dishonorable release from martyrdom.

49. **sciebat**: observe the tense; he knew all the while.

50. **tortor**: Roman tradition told of the most exquisite tortures especially devised for Regulus by the Carthaginians (cf. Cic. *Off.* I. 39, III. 100; Gell. VII. 4); but they rest on no historical evidence. Polybius, our oldest authority, knows nothing of them, nor, indeed, of any embassy of Regulus.

52. **reditus**: Intr. 128; the plural is here preferred for the sake of euphony, as in *Epod.* 16. 35 for the metre.

54. **lite**: either one in which he had acted as arbitrator between his clients, or one in which some of the latter were engaged in court, where, as *patronus*, he was bound to aid them with counsel and influence. — **relinqueret**: for purposes of comparison Regulus is transported in imagination to the present, — 'than (he would), if (living in our day) he were leaving, etc.' The places named as holiday retreats had no such character in the time of Regulus.

55. **Venafranos agros**: see II. 6. 16 n.

56. **Lacedaemonium Tarentum**: see II. 6. 12 n, 13 *sqq.*; *Ep.* I. 7. 45. The quiet picture in this closing strophe, softening without weakening the tragic suggestion of vs. 49, in which the stern moral earnestness of the ode reaches its climax, is one of Horace's happiest touches.

## VI.

Delicta maiorum immeritus lues,
Romane, donec templa refeceris
aedisque labentis deorum et
foeda nigro simulacra fumo.
Dis te minorem quod geris, imperas:
hinc omne principium, huc refer exitum.
Di multa neglecti dederunt
Hesperiae mala luctuosae.

**VI.** This ode, like the preceding, deals with the degeneracy of the times, but in a broader way. The decline of the old Roman spirit is but part of a wide-spread corruption which has contaminated even the sanctity of family life and thus poisoned the springs of national strength. This corruption with its train of disasters has come in through the neglect of religion, and until religion is restored to its due honor, the sins of the fathers must continue to be visited on the children. But of this restoration the poet is not sanguine. From his own picture of the simple life of Rome's heroic age he turns away in despair, and sees in the deterioration of each succeeding generation an augury of the same downward course in the future. The ode is the least cheerful of the six, and its pessimistic close, so ill adapted to conclude the series, is of itself sufficient proof that the poems were not written on a single plan, but composed independently, and afterwards arranged, perhaps with some adaptations, in a group. The present ode is assigned with much probability to the year 28 B.C., when Augustus, in his sixth consulship, instituted many vigorous reforms, and began the restoration of eighty-two temples which had fallen into decay (*Mon. Ancyr.* 4. 17). — Metre, 176.

1. **immeritus**: in close connection with **lues,** not implying innocence in general: 'Thou shalt bear the guilt of sins thou hast not committed.'

2. **Romane**: used collectively, as in Verg. *A.* VI. 851 *tu regere imperio populos, Romane, memento.* Cf. *S.* I. 4. 85. — **templa, aedis**: here used as practically synonymous.

4. **foeda fumo**: some of the temples had suffered from fire.

5. **dis te minorem,** etc.: Horace here utters not a philosophical principle, but what was in the profound conviction of probably the great majority of his countrymen a historical fact. Cf. Polyb. VI. 56. 7 *καί μοι δοκεῖ τὸ παρὰ τοῖς ἄλλοις ἀνθρώποις ὀνειδιζόμενον, τοῦτο συνέχειν τὰ Ῥωμαίων πράγματα· λέγω δὲ τὴν δεισιδαιμονίαν*; Cic. *D. N.* III. 5 *nostrae civitatis, quae numquam profecto sine summa placatione deorum immortalium tanta esse potuisset.*

6. **principium**: sc. *est;* cf. *hinc illae lacrimae, Ep.* I. 19. 41, and

Iam bis Monaeses et Pacori manus
non auspicatos contudit impetus
nostros et adiecisse praedam
torquibus exiguis renidet.

similar phrases. For the synaeresis see Intr. 181.—**exitum**: sc. *omnem*.

7. **di neglecti**: Intr. 105; but here **di** is still consciously the subject.

8. **Hesperiae**: *i.e.* Italy, 'the Land of the West,' in contrast with the countries he has in mind and is about to name. Cf. II. 1. 32. In I. 36. 4 it is used apparently for Spain, of a man returning thence to Italy.—**luctuosae**: proleptic.

9. **iam bis**: referring to the invasion of Crassus in B.C. 53, which ended in the memorable disaster at Carrhae (cf. 5. 5 n), and the expedition of Antony with an army of 100,000 men into Media Atropatene in B.C. 36, from which he was forced to retreat with ignominy, and at the cost of enormous loss and suffering to his troops (Merivale, Ch. XXVIII). Some editors think the first of the two disasters referred to was the defeat of Decidius Saxa in B.C. 40 by the Parthians under the renegade T. Labienus; but the defeat of Saxa, though severe, was only a temporary reverse in a war in which the Romans were, on the whole, brilliantly successful, and their general, Ventidius, earned a triumph. It was a war, moreover, in which the Romans were repelling an invasion of the Parthians, and cannot therefore be included under *non auspicati impetus*.—**Monaeses**: a powerful Parthian noble who went over to the Romans in B.C. 37 and was received with great honor by Antony, but subsequently became reconciled with Phraates and returned to his allegiance. He is not known to have commanded the Parthians in any of the campaigns here referred to.—**Pacori manus**: cf. *Porsenae manus*, *Epod.* 16. 4. Pacorus, son of the Parthian king Orodes, commanded his father's troops in the invasion of Syria and Asia Minor in B.C. 40, and in the succeeding campaigns until he was defeated and killed by Ventidius, B.C. 38. Horace uses the names of Monaeses and Pacorus as conspicuous Parthian leaders, with little thought, and very likely with no accurate knowledge of their individual achievements.

10. **non auspicatos**: the expedition of Crassus was notorious in this respect; cf. Cic. *Div.* I. 29, II. 84; Val. Max. I. 6. 11; Merivale, Ch. XI. No similar particulars are recorded of Antony's expedition; but Horace refers, in both cases, rather to the wickedness (*impietas*) of the Roman people as a nation, in neglecting the gods and fighting brother against brother (cf. I. 35. 33 *sqq.*, and *impia proelia*, II. 1. 30), thus inevitably incurring the displeasure of Heaven on all their undertakings.—**contudit**: Intr. 77.

11. **adiecisse**: Intr. 94 *d*, 81 *b*.

12. **torquibus**: used as decorations for bravery or distinguished service. Among the Persians they could only be worn by those on whom the king had conferred them (Xen. *Cyrop.* VIII. 2. 8).—**exiguis**: *i.e.* in comparison with the ample booty obtained from the Romans.—**renidet**, *beams with joy.*

Paene occupatam seditionibus
delevit urbem Dacus et Aethiops,
hic classe formidatus, ille
missilibus melior sagittis.

Fecunda culpae saecula nuptias
primum inquinavere et genus et domos;
hoc fonte derivata clades
in patriam populumque fluxit.

Motus doceri gaudet Ionicos
matura virgo et fingitur artibus,
iam nunc et incestos amores
de tenero meditatur ungui;

13. **paene**: with **delevit**. This strophe carries the thought a step farther: the Romans had not only failed in their aggressive enterprises, they were so carried away by the passions of civil strife that they almost put the city itself at the mercy of the barbarian.

14. **Dacus et Aethiops**: auxiliaries who fought at Actium, the former in the army of Antony (see also I. 26. 4 n), the latter in the fleet of Cleopatra. They stand for the barbarian allies of Antony, whose approach the citizens had regarded with genuine, though no doubt exaggerated, alarm. Cf. Verg. *G.* II. 497.

17. **fecunda**, etc.: the poet proceeds to show *how* the neglect of religion and consequent looseness of living saps the strength of the nation. — **culpae**, *vice;* here, as often, with special reference to unchastity.

18. **inquinavere**: cf. *Epod.* 16. 64. — **genus**, *the stock;* cf. IV. 4. 29 *sqq.* — **domos**: *i.e.* the sanctity of domestic life and discipline; cf. IV. 4. 25 *sqq.*

19. **hoc fonte**, etc.: *i.e.* corruption in the family makes the state unsound at the core, and so robs it of the strength to resist the forces that tend to destroy it. This thesis he illustrates by the contrasted pictures of the next six strophes.

21. **motus**, *dances*, especially of a mimetic character; cf. *movetur*, *Ep.* II. 2. 125. The Ionic was a voluptuous kind of dance, which was often provided for the amusement of the guests at a dinner party (Athen. XIV. 27), the dancers being usually professionals; cf. *Anth. Pal.* V. 129 (quoted vs. 24 n).

22. **matura**: it would be innocent in a child. — **artibus**: instrumental abl.; instead of developing in a healthy and natural way, she is trained to pose on all occasions and manage her personal charms as weapons of skill.

23. **iam nunc**: *i.e.* even before marriage; in contrast with *mox*, 25. — **et**: Intr. 114.

24. **de tenero ungui**, *to her finger-tips;* cf. Apul. *Met.* X. 22 *ex unguiculis perpruriscens mulier*

mox iuniores quaerit adulteros
inter mariti vina, neque eligit
cui donet impermissa raptim
gaudia luminibus remotis,

sed iussa coram non sine conscio
surgit marito, seu vocat institor
seu navis Hispanae magister,
dedecorum pretiosus emptor.

Non his iuventus orta parentibus
infecit aequor sanguine Punico,

(an imitation of Plaut. *Stich.* 761). The phrase is a translation of the Greek *ἐξ (ἁπαλῶν) ὀνύχων*, used to express intensity of feeling (*e.g.* of impassioned movements in dancing, *τὴν ἀπὸ τῆς ’Ασίης ὀρχηστρίδα, τὴν κακοτέχνοις | σχήμασιν ἐξ ἁπαλῶν κινυμένην ὀνύχων, | αἰνέω, οὐχ ὅτι πάντα παθαίνεται, οὐδ’ ὅτι βάλλει | τὰς ἁπαλὰς ἁπαλῶς ὧδε καὶ ὧδε χέρας*, *Anth. Pal.* V. 129; of a mother's love for her young children, *ὡς ἂν ἔνδοθεν καὶ τὸ δὴ λεγόμενον ἐξ ὀνύχων ἀγαπῶσαι τὰ τέκνα*, Plut. *Mor.* 3 C), apparently with reference to the extreme sensitiveness of the nerves under the finger-nails. It appears also to have been used in the sense of 'from earliest childhood,' and possibly that is the sense in which Cicero understood it, *ad. Fam.* I. 6. 2, *qui mihi a teneris, ut Graeci dicunt, unguiculis es cognitus.* This interpretation is excluded here by **matura**, above. — **meditatur**, *is filled with thoughts of.*

26. **inter mariti vina**: *i.e.* among the guests at his table. — **neque eligit**, etc.: *i.e.* it is not merely a case of censurable flirtation with some favored admirer, allowing him a stolen kiss or the like. — **impermissa**, which occurs here for the first time, was coined or chosen to express a mild form of wrong-doing: the offense in the supposed case is purposely softened to set off the unspeakable baseness of her actual conduct. Observe the contrast in particulars: **eligit** with **vocat institor**, etc.; **donet** with **emptor**; **impermissa** with **dedecorum**; **raptim** with **iussa coram**; and **luminibus remotis** with **conscio marito.**

29. **coram**, *bluntly*, without any affectation of delicacy. — **conscio marito**: Intr. 105 *a*.

30. **institor**, *pedlar;* a despised class, but having plenty of ready money and access, in pursuit of their trade, to the women of the household. Cf. *Epod.* 17. 20.

31. **magister**, *the skipper:* another coarse character and, as a sailor, a great spendthrift on shore.

33. **non his**, etc.: from this climax of iniquity the poet turns to the Romans of earlier times, and draws a companion picture of wholesome discipline and pure living.

34. **infecit aequor**: in the first Punic war, which was waged mainly by sea.

Pyrrhumque et ingentem cecidit
Antiochum Hannibalemque dirum,

sed rusticorum mascula militum
proles, Sabellis docta ligonibus
versare glaebas et severae
matris ad arbitrium recisos

portare fustis, sol ubi montium
mutaret umbras et iuga demeret
bobus fatigatis, amicum
tempus agens abeunte curru.

Damnosa quid non imminuit dies?
Aetas parentum, peior avis, tulit
nos nequiores, mox daturos
progeniem vitiosiorem.

35. **ingentem**: a poetical variation of his surname, *Magnus* (see Cic. *pro Deiot.* 36); cf. Verg. *A.* XI. 124 *fama ingens, ingentior armis vir.* The word in this sense is found also in Sallust and in later prose writers.—**cecīdit,** *overthrew.*

36. **dirum**: cf. *dirus Afer*, IV. 4. 42.

38. **Sabellis**: Intr. 124. The epithet places the scene among the Sabines, who were proverbial for their strictness and purity of manners; *quo genere nullum quondam incorruptius fuit*, Liv. I. 18. 4.

41. **sol ubi,** etc.: even when the day's work was done, and the tired ox was allowed to rest, they must deny themselves the repose which the quiet evening hour made so tempting, and go forth again to cut and carry firewood for their mother. Horace dwells on the description of evening in his favorite way (cf. I. 12. 29 n, III. 4. 60 n), but here no stroke is superfluous.

42. **mutaret**: *i.e.* lengthened. As the sun descends lower, the change in the shadows becomes more rapid and hence more noticeable. Cf. Verg. *E.* 2. 67 *et sol crescentis decedens duplicat umbras.* The subjunctive looks like that of repeated action (**docta** = *adsueta*); but as Horace elsewhere uses the indicative with *ubi* in such clauses (see Intr. 86) it is probably to be explained as due to its close dependence on the infinitive (Gr. 342).

43. **amicum,** *welcome;* cf. I. 26. 1 n.

44. **agens,** *bringing on;* cf. Verg. *E.* 8. 17 *praeque diem veniens age, Lucifer, almum.*

45. **imminuit**: perfect. — **dies,** *time.*

46. **aetas,** etc.: the course of deterioration through four generations is skilfully expressed in three verses. — **peior avis**: Intr. 75.

47. **daturos**: Intr. 104 *b.*

## VII.

Quid fles, Asterie, quem tibi candidi
primo restituent vere Favonii
Thyna merce beatum,
constantis iuvenem fide,
Gygen? Ille Notis actus ad Oricum
post insana Caprae sidera frigidas
noctis non sine multis
insomnis lacrimis agit.

Atqui sollicitae nuntius hospitae,
suspirare Chloen et miseram tuis

VII. The unbroken vein of serious thought which runs through the preceding group of odes is fittingly relieved by a poem of more than usual lightness and grace, an idyl, as it has been called, of a young trader's love. He lies storm-bound in a foreign port, fretting at wind and wave, while the forlorn maid sits weeping at home, with no message to tell her why he tarries. The poet comforts her with the assurance that her lover is neither lost nor untrue; the spring winds will bring him back to her; meanwhile let her keep well her own troth. — Metre, 173.

1. **fles**: the object is *eum* (*one*) understood, with which **iuvenem** and **Gygen** are successively in apposition. — **Asterie**: Ἀστερίη, 'fair as a star'; cf. 9. 21, *sidere pulchrior*. — **candidi**, *fair*; cf. I. 5. 7 n, 7. 15 n.

2. **Favonii**: see I. 4. 1 n.

3. **Thyna merce**: cf. *Bithyna negotia*, *Ep.* I. 6. 33. *Thyni* and *Bithyni* were once separate peoples, but in Horace's day they had long ceased to be distinguished, and the shorter adjective was used as a poetical substitute for the other. Cf. Cat. 31. 5 *Thyniam atque Bithynos*. — **beatum**, *enriched*.

4. **fide**: contracted form of the genitive, used also by Caesar and Sallust (Gell. IX. 14. 25); cf. *S.* I. 3. 95 *fide* (dative).

5. **Notis**: see I. 7. 15 n. — **Oricum**: on the coast of Epirus, sheltered by the Acroceraunian headland.

6. **post Caprae sidera**: *i.e.* after the setting of that constellation, which occurred about the middle of December and was a sign of storm. For the expression cf. *post vina*, I. 18. 5. — **insana**: *i.e.* causing furious storms; cf. *stella vesani leonis*, 29. 19; Intr. 124.

7. **non sine**: cf. I. 23. 3 n.

9. **atqui**, *and yet* (he could easily console himself). — **sollicitae**: cf. *amore sollicitus*, *S.* II. 3. 252.

10. **Chloen**: the *hospita* of vs. 9, the wife of his host. — **tuis ignibus**: *i.e.* with the passion which is rightfully yours, — the passion inspired by Gyges. The

dicens ignibus uri,
temptat mille vafer modis.
Vt Proetum mulier perfida credulum
falsis impulerit criminibus nimis
casto Bellerophontae
maturare necem refert;
narrat paene datum Pelea Tartaro,
Magnessam Hippolyten dum fugit abstinens,
et peccare docentis
fallax historias movet.

expression is the poet's and not that of the *nuntius*.

12. **temptat**: sc. *eum*. — **mille vafer modis**, *with a thousand wiles*.

13. **ut**, etc.: stock tales of the fury of a woman scorned, 'cum stimulos odio pudor admovet' (Juv. 10. 329). — **Proetum**: king of Tiryns. The story of Bellerophon is told *Il*. VI. 152 *sqq*. — **mulier**: Anteia, in the Homeric account; according to others, Stheneboea, the name which Juvenal (*l. c.*) gives. — **perfida credulum**: Intr. 116 *a*.

15. **Bellerophontae**: Horace uses the Homeric form (Βελλεροφόντης) here and 12. 3, but has the accusative *Bellerophontem* IV. 11. 28.

16. **maturare necem**: *i.e.* to put him to death before his time. For the infinitive see Intr. 97 *b*. — **refert, narrat**: chiastic; cf. Intr. 116 *e*.

17. **datum Tartaro**: cf. *morti dedit*, *S*. II. 3. 197; both are variations on the old formal phrase much affected by the poets, *leto dare*: cf. Enn. *Telephus* 88 (Müll.) *quorum liberi leto dati sunt in bello*; Verg. *A*. V. 806; Juv. 10. 119. The construction of **paene datum Pelea** is that of Intr. 105 *a* (= 'the narrow escape of Peleus'), not indirect discourse; hence the indicative in vs. 18. The adventure is thought of as already well known to the reader. — **Pelea**: while a guest at the house of Acastus, king of Iolcus, Peleus, so the story ran, was obliged to repel the advances of his hostess, with the same result as in the case of Bellerophon. Acastus decoyed him into the wilderness and there left him alone unarmed, hoping the Centaurs would destroy him. The gods, however, protected him, and Hephaestus gave him a sword which was a sufficient defense against the Centaurs. According to another account he was found by Chiron, who received him kindly and sheltered him in his cave. Subsequently he made war on Acastus and captured Iolcus.

18. **Magnessam**: *i.e.* from the Thessalian Magnesia; to distinguish her from the more famous Hippolyte, the Amazon wife of Theseus.

19. **docentis**: Intr. 103.

20. **movet**, *rehearses*; lit. 'sets a-going' (cf. I. 15. 10 n). Vergil has *movere cantūs*, *A*. VII. 641.

Frustra: nam scopulis surdior Icari
voces audit adhuc integer. At tibi
ne vicinus Enipeus
plus iusto placeat cave,
quamvis non alius flectere equum sciens
aeque conspicitur gramine Martio,
nec quisquam citus aeque
Tusco denatat alveo.
Prima nocte domum claude, neque in vias
sub cantu querulae despice tibiae,
et te saepe vocanti
duram difficilis mane.

21. **frustra**: cf. 13. 6, where *nam* follows, as here. — **scopulis surdior**: *i.e.* no more moved than they are by the waves that dash upon them; cf. *Epod.* 17. 54. **surdior**, with **audit**, forms a very effective oxymoron. — **Icari**: the island; cf. I. 1. 15.

22. **integer**: cf. II. 4. 22.—**tibi**, *on your part.* See Intr. 116 *b*.

23. **Enipeus**: the name is borrowed from a river-god of Thessaly; cf. *Hebri*, 12. 2.

25. **quamvis**: Intr. 83. — **flectere equum**: cf. I. 8. 6 n, III. 12. 3. For the mood see Intr. 101 *c*.

26. **aeque . . . aeque** (with **sciens** and **citus**, respectively): Intr. 116 *b*. — **gramine Martio**: Intr. 69. Cf. *per gramina Martii campi*, IV. 1. 39, and see I. 8. 4 n.

28. **Tusco alveo**: *i.e.* the Tiber; cf. I. 20. 5 n. — **denatat**: found only here. For this form of exercise see I. 8. 8 n. The poet dwells on the athletic prowess of the youth, knowing well its power to captivate a girl's heart. Cf. 12. 3 *sq.*

29. **neque**: Intr. 89 N.

30. **sub cantu**, *while he is playing*, *i.e.* serenading you. *Sub*, in this use, means, with the ablative, 'during (the continuance of)'; with the accusative, 'just before' or 'just after.' Cf. *sub luce* and *sub lucem*. — **despice**: in a literal sense.

31. **vocanti** (sc. *illi*): equivalent to a concessive clause.

32. **duram**, *unfeeling*: **difficilis**, *stubborn.*

## VIII.

Martiis caelebs quid agam Kalendis,
quid velint flores et acerra turis
plena miraris, positusque carbo in
caespite vivo,
docte sermones utriusque linguae?
Voveram dulcis epulas et album

VIII. An ode for the anniversary of the poet's escape from death by the fall of a tree, recorded in II. 13. The form is dramatic. The poet is busily engaged with his servants in preparations for a sacrifice, when Maecenas appears. In answer to his expression of surprise, Horace explains the significance of the day to him, and begs his friend to join him in his quiet festival of thanksgiving.

The date of the ode, and consequently of the event in the poet's life which it commemorates, is fixed with great probability by the allusions of the last three strophes. Maecenas, presumably in the absence of Octavian (Intr. 21), is in charge of affairs. The campaigns of M. Crassus against the Dacians and other tribes of the Danube frontier (vss. 18, 23) were fought in the years immediately following the battle of Actium, B.C. 30–28. The news of the struggle between Phraates and Tiridates in Parthia reached Rome in January B.C. 29; and in the summer of the same year Octavian returned to Italy. Our ode was therefore composed in the spring of B.C. 29, and the date of the fall of the tree is March 1, B.C. 30. For it is clear that it is the *first* anniversary which is here celebrated. — Metre, 174.

1. **Martiis Kalendis**: called by Juvenal (9. 53) *femineae kalendae*, being the day of the Matronalia, when the married women of Rome made their offerings to Juno Lucina on the Esquiline (Ov. *Fast.* III. 245 *sqq.*). The day was also kept as a family festival: the mother received presents from her husband and children, and like the men at the Saturnalia waited on her slaves at table; hence called by Martial (V. 84. 10) the women's Saturnalia. Why an unmarried man should be found celebrating that day, was a puzzle which Maecenas, with all his learning, as the poet playfully says, could not solve.

2. **velint**, *mean*. — **flores**: these were a part of the offering to Juno (Ovid. *l. l.*).

4. **caespite**: see I. 19. 13 n.

5. **docte**: Maecenas is so addressed again *Ep.* I. 19. 1. — **sermones**: *i.e.* the literature. For the case cf. 9. 10. — **utriusque**: the two which to a Roman contained all literature and learning, Greek and Latin. The expression appears to have been not uncommon, *e.g.* Plin. *N. H.* XII. 11.; cf. Stat. *Silv.* V. 3. 90 *gemina lingua*, Plut. *Lucull.* 1 ἤσκητο λέγειν ἱκανῶς ἑκατέραν γλῶτταν.

6. **epulas**: the regular accompaniment of a sacrifice; cf. I. 36. 2. — **album**: the prescribed color for a victim to the gods above.

Libero caprum prope funeratus
  arboris ictu.
Hic dies, anno redeunte festus,
corticem adstrictum pice demovebit
amphorae fumum bibere institutae
  consule Tullo.
Sume, Maecenas, cyathos amici
sospitis centum, et vigiles lucernas
perfer in lucem; procul omnis esto
  clamor et ira.

7. **Libero**: patron god (with Apollo) of poets; cf. *Ep.* II. 2. 78; Juv. 7. 64. In II. 17. 28 Horace attributes his escape to Faunus.— **caprum**: cf. Verg. *G.* II. 380 *Baccho caper omnibus aris | caeditur*, for no other reason, he says, than because it eats the grape-vines.

9. **anno redeunte festus,** *a festival as the year comes round;* cf. *S.* II. 2. 83 *sive diem festum rediens advexerit annus.* In both cases *annus* is strictly a part or season of the year, as in 23. 8, *Epod.* 2. 29.

10. **adstrictum pice**: showing that the wine had been carefully put up for long keeping. Cf. I. 20. 3 n.

11. **amphorae**: dative. — **fumum bibere**: to hasten the mellowing of the wine. The store room (*apotheca*) was purposely placed in a part of the house where the smoke could reach it. For the infinitive see Intr. 93.— **institutae,** *set.*

12. **Tullo**: probably L. Volcatius Tullus, consul B.C. 33 with Octavian, so that the wine would now be four years old. There was, however, another consul of this name in B.C. 66, who may be the one referred to here. In that case the jar would be only a year older than the *pia testa* of 21. 1 *sqq.*

13. **sume**: cf. I. 27. 9. — **cyathos**: see I. 29. 8 n. — **amici**: a Greek form of expression, by which the cups are said to be his to whose health they are drunk; cf. 19, 9 *sqq.* and Antiph. *ap.* Athen. X. 21 ἔγχει, παιδίον, | κυάθους θεῶν τε καὶ θεαινῶν μυρίους. The meaning here is somewhat modified, however, by **sospitis,** which shows that present safety is more prominent in the poet's mind than future welfare as a motive for drinking (cf. II. 7. 26 *sqq.*). We may translate: *for the preservation of your friend.* See Intr. 105 *a.*

14. **centum**: used vaguely, like μυρίους above, for a very large number; cf. II. 14. 26.

15. **perfer,** *stay with;* lit. 'endure to the end.' The real object is implied in **vigiles,** as if it were *vigilias sub lucernis perfer.* This the invalid Maecenas would not be disposed to do in any ordinary drinking party; hence the assurance that follows, **procul** etc., though these words seem to imply that there are to be other guests present.

Mitte civilis super urbe curas :
occidit Daci Cotisonis agmen,
Medus infestus sibi luctuosis
dissidet armis,
servit Hispanae vetus hostis orae
Cantaber sera domitus catena,
iam Scythae laxo meditantur arcu
cedere campis.
Neglegens ne qua populus laboret,
parce privatus nimium cavere et
dona praesentis cape laetus horae ;
linque severa.

17. **super** : see I. 9. 5 n.

18. **occidit** : emphatic, as in I. 28. 7 and IV. 4. 70. — **Cotisonis agmen** : see introd. note, and I. 26. 4 n.

19. **Medus** : see I. 2. 22 n ; Intr. 127. — **sibi** : with **infestus** ; but its force cannot help being felt with **luctuosis** also. Intr. 76. — **luctuosis** : cf. 6. 8, where it is also used in reference to civil strife.

20. **dissidet** : used absolutely ; cf. *dissideat miles*, Tac. *Ann.* I. 46. 1.

21. **servit** : cf. *occidit*, 17 n, and for the meaning, II. 2. 12. — **Hispanae orae** : the mountainous district along the bay of Biscay. For **orae** cf. I. 12. 55, 26. 4. The genitive with *hostis* in this relation is rare.

22. **sera** : because he was **vetus hostis**. Livy remarks (XXVIII. 12. 12) that of all the continental provinces of the Romans, Spain was the first in which they gained a footing, the last to be completely subdued, and that not till his own day. — **domitus** : referring perhaps to their reduction by Statilius Taurus B.C. 29; see II. 6. 2 n.

23. **Scythae** : the marauding raids of these tribes had been checked by the operations of Crassus, but not yet entirely suppressed (cf. II. 9. 23 *sq.*) ; and this is all that Horace asserts (**meditantur cedere**). — **laxo**, *unstrung*.

24. **cedere** : Intr. 94 *f.* — **campis** : those south of the Danube which were exposed to their raids.

25. **neglegens**, etc. : after stating these good reasons, Horace returns to the exhortation begun in 17. **neglegens, privatus,** and **laetus** are all a part of the exhortation, the first two repeating the idea of *mitte civilis curas*, 17. — **ne** : after the idea of fear or anxiety implied in **neglegens** (here = *securus*) ; cf. *terruit ne*, I. 2. 5 n.

26. **privatus** : *i.e.* for the moment. Cf. *S.* II. 1. 71 *sqq.* — **nimium cavere**, *borrow trouble*. **cavere** is used absolutely as in *S.* II. 7. 68 ; for the mood, see Intr. 94 *k*.

27. **dona**, etc. : cf. I. 9. 13 *sqq.*, 11. 8, II. 16. 25 *sqq.*, III. 29. 41 *sqq.*

## IX.

Donec gratus eram tibi
nec quisquam potior bracchia candidae
cervici iuvenis dabat,
Persarum vigui rege beatior.
Donec non alia magis
arsisti neque erat Lydia post Chloen,
multi Lydia nominis,
Romana vigui clarior Ilia.
Me nunc Thressa Chloe regit,
dulcis docta modos et citharae sciens,

IX. A lyrical idyl, portraying with exquisite skill a lovers' quarrel and reconciliation. The brief dialogue tells the whole story. Lydia's lover has wounded her by too marked attentions to Chloe, and her resentment has sent him off in a passion. Both are sorry and proud. He makes the first overtures towards a reconciliation in terms of tender regret, mixed with reproach; she replies in the same strain, with no sign of yielding. He then tries to break her down by a show of indifference, but she answers him with equal defiance. Finally he virtually confesses his fault and offers to make amends, and she, while asserting her woman's privilege of the last word in the quarrel, consents and owns that she loves him after all. This is the only ode of Horace in dialogue form. — Metre, 171.

1. **eram**: cf. *parabat*, I. 37. 8 n.

2. **potior**, *favored rival*.

3. **dabat**: the simple form for the compound (*circumdabat*) is poetical; cf. Intr. 129.

4. **Persarum rege**: see II. 2 17 n.

5. **donec**, etc.: in this and in the second pair of strophes Horace observes the rule of amoebean verse which requires that the second speaker shall match the verses of the first, and, if possible, produce something better and stronger. Cf. Verg. *Ecl.* 3 and 7.— **aliā**: cf. *virgine*, II. 4. 8; Intr. 72.

6. **arsisti**: the perfect, for variety, matching the imperfect of vs. 1, but with the same force. Roby 1667. — **post**, *second to*.

7. **multi Lydia nominis**, *a Lydia of great renown;* her name was on everybody's lips as the fortunate object of his choice; cf. **clarior.** This verse belongs with the preceding, the name being repeated as in I. 13. 1, 2.

8. **Romana**: as the mother of the Roman race. She was a Trojan woman according to the tradition which Horace follows; see 3. 32 n.

9. **Thressa Chloe**: for this designation and that in 14, cf. I. 27. 10 *sq*. The names are chosen for their pleasing sound.

10. **modos**: for the case cf. *sermones*, 8. 5.

pro qua non metuam mori,
si parcent animae fata superstiti.
Me torret face mutua
Thurini Calais filius Ornyti,
pro quo bis patiar mori,
si parcent puero fata superstiti.
Quid si prisca redit Venus,
diductosque iugo cogit aeneo,
si flava excutitur Chloe,
reiectaeque patet ianua Lydiae?
Quamquam sidere pulchrior
ille est, tu levior cortice et improbo
iracundior Hadria,
tecum vivere amem, tecum obeam libens.

## X.

Extremum Tanain si biberes, Lyce,
saevo nupta viro, me tamen asperas

11. **mori**: Intr. 94 *l*.

12. **animae**, *my love*. — **superstiti**, *and let her live*; proleptic.

15. **mori**: Intr. 94 *a*.

16. **puero**: see I. 9. 16 n. — **superstiti**: cf. vs. 12 n.

17. **prisca**: poetical for *pristina*. — **redit**: for the present in this and the following verses, see Intr. 78.

18. **iugo aeneo**: cf. I. 33. 11 n.

19. **flava**: see I. 5. 3 n. — **excutitur**: *sc.* from her control of me (*regit*, 9); cf. Verg. *A*. V. 679 *excussaque pectore Iuno est*.

20. **Lydiae**: dative, as **reiectae** shows. **ianua patet** is not altogether metaphorical; see 15. 9 n.

21. **sidere pulchrior**: cf. 19. 26 *puro similem Vespero*; *Il*. VI. 401 ἀλίγκιον ἀστέρι καλῷ (of Astyanax).

22. **levior**: *i.e.* less steadfast, more fickle. — **improbo**, *horrid*.

23. **iracundior Hadria**: cf. I. 33. 15.

24. **vivere**: Intr. 94 *c*.

X. A serenade, of the kind called παρακλαυσίθυρον, in which the lover pleads before the barred door of his mistress' house (cf. I. 25. 7 *sq*.). In accordance with Horace's usual practice in verses of this kind the names are Greek, but the setting is Roman. Lyce is of Etruscan origin, and the mistress of a wealthy mansion.

porrectum ante foris obicere incolis
plorares Aquilonibus.
Audis quo strepitu ianua, quo nemus
inter pulchra satum tecta remugiat
ventis, et positas ut glaciet nivis
puro numine Iuppiter?
Ingratam Veneri pone superbiam,
ne currente retro funis eat rota:
non te Penelopen difficilem procis
Tyrrhenus genuit parens.

Her infatuated lover plies her in turn with reproaches for her cruelty, with warning and sarcasm, with appeals to pity, and finally with the impotent threat that he will leave her for good. — Metre, 172.

1. **extremum**, *the far off;* cf. *ultima*, II. 18. 4 n. — **si biberes**: *i.e.* if you lived on its banks, among the Sarmatians, where 'peccare nefas, aut pretium est mori' (24. 24). For the form of expression, cf. II. 20. 20 n, IV. 15. 21.

2. **saevo viro**: in contrast with the actual fact (vs. 15). — **asperas**, *pitiless.*

3. **porrectum**: implying that he has waited long. — **obicere**: Intr. 94 *m;* cf. Plaut. *Aul.* 308 *aquam hércle plorat, quóm lavat, profúndere* (of a miser). — **incolis**, *that are at home there.*

5. **nemus**, etc.: cf. *Ep.* I. 10. 22 *inter varias nutritur silva columnas.* In the wealthier Roman houses the second court (*peristylium*) was expanded into a garden, with space even for large trees.

7. **ventis**: causal ablative. — **ut**: see I. 9. 1 n; Intr. 114. The question depends on the general idea of perception in **audis**, the specific meaning of which is lost at this distance. Cf. I. 14. 3 n, II. 1. 21 n. — **glaciet**, etc.: *i.e.* the night is clear (**puro**) and so cold that the light coating of snow on the ground (**positas**), which had softened in the sunshine, is frozen hard.

8. **puro numine**, *in cloudless majesty;* cf. I. 34. 7 n. — **Iuppiter**: see I. 1. 25 n.

10. **ne**, etc.: *i.e.* your high flight in virtue is beyond your powers, and will end in a sudden and violent fall. The figure is that of a windlass, with which a man is raising a weight that proves too heavy, and the handle breaks or slips from his grasp. — **retro**: with **currente**, and then, by inference, with **eat**.

11. **non te**: cf. *non ego* I. 18. 11 n. — **difficilem**: cf. 7. 32.

12. **Tyrrhenus**, etc.: in contrast with the supposition in vs. 1. The Etruscans reached a high point of civilization, which was on the decline when the Romans came in contact with them, and had left traditions of luxury and effeminacy with their accompanying vices. See Momm. *Hist.* Bk. II. Ch. IV.

O quamvis neque te munera nec preces
nec tinctus viola pallor amantium
nec vir Pieria paelice saucius
curvat, supplicibus tuis
parcas, nec rigida mollior aesculo
nec Mauris animum mitior anguibus:
non hoc semper erit liminis aut aquae
caelestis patiens latus.

## XI.

Mercuri, nam te docilis magistro
movit Amphion lapides canendo,
tuque testudo, resonare septem
callida nervis,

13. **quamvis**: Intr. 83.

14. **tinctus viola pallor**: cf. Verg. *E.* 2. 47 *pallentis violas.* The tint was a pale yellow (wan).

15. **vir saucius**: Intr. 105 *a.*—**Pieria**: cf. *Thressa,* 9. 9.—**paelice**: causal abl., as in I. 14. 5.—**saucius**: of love, as Verg. *A.* IV. 1.

16. **curvat**: a fresh word, for the 'faded metaphor' *flectit.* — **supplicibus**, *worshippers; i.e.* if no personal consideration moves you, spare us in pure mercy (like a goddess). There is an undertone of irony in this and the next words.

17. **rigida**: continuing the figure in **curvat**.

18. **Mauris anguibus**: said to be particularly savage on account of the heat; Sall. *Iug.* 89. 5. Cf. Lucan's description of the snakes of the Libyan desert, *B. C.* IX. 630 *sqq.*—**animum**: Intr. 44.

19. **non hoc**, etc.: the comic effect of this final touch is obvious. —**liminis**: cf. *Epod.* 11. 22.—**aquae caelestis**: cf. *Ep.* II. 1. 135. The reference to rain (cf. vs. 8) shows that he has in mind other occasions besides the present.

20. **latus**: cf. II. 7. 18 n.

XI. The theme of this ode is the beautiful story of Hypermnestra and Lynceus, which is presented in a setting that adds not a little to its charm. The poet begins as if with no definite theme in mind. He calls on his lyre, and on Mercury, who gave the lyre its magic power, to play a strain to which even Lyde shall listen,—Lyde, the shy young girl, playful as a colt and with as little thought of love. He appeals to the past achievements of the lyre, how, in the hands of Orpheus, it charmed the woods and streams and wild beasts, yes, even the monsters of the underworld, and Ixion and Tityos in their torment, and the Danaids,—let Lyde hear

nec loquax olim neque grata, nunc et
divitum mensis et amica templis,
dic modos Lyde quibus obstinatas
adplicet auris,

quae velut latis equa trima campis
ludit exsultim metuitque tangi,
nuptiarum expers et adhuc protervo
cruda marito.

the tale of the Danaids. Thus he comes upon his theme naturally, as it were, and without design. He shows his skill further in disposing of the disagreeable part of the story first, the crime and the subsequent punishment of the wicked sisters; and against this dark background he paints the bright picture of the one who was found faithful. His taste is shown no less in leaving off at the point where the heroic girl is left to face death as the consequence of her devoted courage and womanly pity. Ovid has treated the same subject in the *Heroides* (14), following the lines laid down by Horace, so that the two poems afford an excellent opportunity of comparing the two poets, and the lyric with the elegiac treatment.—Metre, 174.

1. **Mercuri**: although his appeal is to the lyre, he invokes Mercury first, because the lyre is his handiwork (I. 10. 6 n), and without his inspiration it is a voiceless shell. — **nam**: introducing the reason for addressing the god,— a Homeric form of expression, *e.g.* *Odys.* I. 337; cf. Verg. *A.* I. 65 *Aeole, namque tibi, etc.* The reason is given, after Horace's manner, in the form of a particular example standing for the general fact. — **te magistro**: abl. absolute, but containing the main thought: it was thy teaching and his willingness to learn of thee that gave Amphion his (well-known) power. **docilis** is more than *doctus*, enforcing the idea of dependence.

2. **movit**, etc.: the stones were said to have moved into their places in the wall under the spell of his music; see *Ep.* II. 3. 394 *sqq.*

3. **resonare**: Intr. 101 *c.*

4. **nervis**: ablative.

5. **nec loquax neque grata**, *without voice or charm.* — **olim**: *i.e.* when a mere shell. — **et**: often placed at the end of the verse in Horace, but always, except here and IV. 13. 6, coalescing by elision with the preceding word.

6. **mensis**: the use of the lyre at banquets dates from Homeric times; cf. *e.g.* the story of the Phaeacians. — **amica**: cf. 4. 25 n and Intr. 119 *a.* — **templis**: *i.e.* in religious ceremonies; cf. I. 36. 1 n. Porphyrio says: 'Fidicines hodieque Romae sacrificiis adhiberi videmus.'

7. **dic modos**: cf. I. 32. 3.

9. **trima**: the time prescribed for breaking in a colt was in its fourth year (Verg. *G.* III. 190).

10. **ludit**, etc.: see Intr. 123. — **exsultim**, *bounding over.* The word is found here only. — **tangi**: Intr. 94 *l.*

12. **cruda**: the same figure as in II. 5. 10.

Tu potes tigris comitesque silvas
ducere et rivos celeris morari;
cessit immanis tibi blandienti
ianitor aulae

Cerberus, quamvis furiale centum
muniant angues caput eius atque
spiritus taeter saniesque manet
ore trilingui;

quin et Ixion Tityosque voltu
risit invito; stetit urna paulum
sicca, dum grato Danai puellas
carmine mulces.

13. **tu**: the lyre. The poet is recalling the feats of Orpheus; cf. I. 12. 7 *sqq.* — **comites,** *in thy train.* — **-que**: Intr. 119 *b.*

15. **cessit,** etc.: for the descent of Orpheus to the lower world in quest of Eurydice, see Ovid, *M.* X. 8 *sqq.*, Verg. *G.* IV. 457 *sqq.* — **immanis**: used of Cerberus also in Verg. *A.* VI. 418 *recubans immanis in antro.* Some join it here with **aulae**; cf. *fera regia Ditis,* Ov. *M.* IV. 438.—**blandienti**: cf. I. 12. 11, 24. 13.

16. **ianitor aulae**: better taken as expressing a single idea ('palace-doorkeeper'), modified by **immanis.** For **aulae,** cf. II. 18. 31.

17. **Cerberus,** etc.: see I. 2. 7 n. The repulsive picture of the monster serves to enhance the impression of the power of music. But some critics have doubted whether Horace wrote the strophe, which certainly has a prosaic flavor. They object particularly to the unpoetical pronoun **eius,** which Vergil nowhere uses. Horace has it, however, IV. 8. 18, as well as in the Satires, and it occurs two or three times in Ovid. — **quamvis**: Intr. 83.—**furiale,** *fury-like;* cf. II. 13. 35 *sq.* — **centum**: see 8. 14 n.

18. **angues**: conceived as growing like hair about his neck; cf. Verg. *A.* VI. 419 *horrere videns iam colla colubris.*

20. **ore trilingui**: cf. II. 19. 31 n.

21. **quin et**: cf. II. 13. 37 n.— **Ixion**: cf. Verg. *G.* IV. 484 *Ixionii cantu rota constitit orbis.*—**Tityos**: see 4. 77, II. 14. 8 n.

22. **risit**: Intr. 77.—**invito**: *i.e.* in spite of their torture. — **urna**: used collectively, — the one in which each carried water to the *dolium;* Intr. 127.

25. **audiat Lyde,** etc.: Horace's readers were familiar with the myth of the Danaids, — how the Argive king accepted the overtures of his brother Aegyptus for a reconciliation, and married the latter's sons to his fifty daughters, but instructed the brides to murder their husbands on the wedding night,— and with the doom of the wicked

Audiat Lyde scelus atque notas
virginum poenas et inane lymphae
dolium fundo pereuntis imo,
  seraque fata

quae manent culpas etiam sub Orco.
Impiae (nam quid potuere maius?),
impiae sponsos potuere duro
  perdere ferro.

Vna de multis face nuptiali
digna periurum fuit in parentem
splendide mendax et in omne virgo
  nobilis aevum;

damsels to pour water into a bottomless cistern till they filled it; they were reminded of the story whenever they went to the library of the temple of Apollo on the Palatine (I. 31), where the statues of Danaus and his daughters lined the portico, alternating with the marble columns (Ov. *Tr.* III. 1. 61 *sq.*, Prop. III. 29. 3 *sq.*). Horace could therefore pass lightly over these outlines and use them as an introduction to the golden deed of the one interesting Danaid. — **notas**: modifying **scelus** as well as **poenas**; Intr. 119 *a*.

26. **lymphae**: with **inane**; Intr. 66 *c*. For the order of words here, see Intr. 111.

27. **fundo**: instrumental abl. (the way by which). — **pereuntis**, *going to waste*.

28. **sera**, etc.: *i.e.* the doom (punishment), long delayed, which overtakes the guilty person at last, even though he go free all his life.

29. **sub**: cf. 5. 9. Orcus is the person (not the place), as in II. 18. 30.

30. **impiae . . . impiae**: the parenthetical clause supplies the requisite pause to make the repetition more effective (Intr. 116 *g*); cf. *surge*, 37 *sq*. *Pietas*, as a human obligation, commonly denotes that of blood-relationship, but is sometimes extended to marriage and other obligations that were regarded as having a sacred character. Cf. Ov. *M.* XIII. 301 *pia coniunx*. So Hypermnestra, Ov. *Her.* 14. 129, calls her punishment *pretium pietatis iniquum*.

31. **potuere**: in a moral sense, —*they had the heart;* different from its use in 30, where it denotes simple possibility, — 'What wickedness *could* be greater?' — **duro**, *pitiless;* cf. the Homeric νηλέι χαλκῷ.

33. **una**, *only one*.

35. **splendide mendax**: a fine oxymoron. Cf. Tac. *H.* IV. 50 *servus egregio mendacio se Pisonem esse respondit, ac statim obtruncatur;* Soph. *Ant.* 74 ὅσια πανουργήσασα. **mendax** implies that Danaus had bound his daughters by a promise or oath to commit the deed.

'Surge' quae dixit iuveni marito,
'surge, ne longus tibi somnus, unde
non times, detur; socerum et scelestas
falle sorores,

quae, velut nanctae vitulos leaenae,
singulos eheu lacerant. Ego illis
mollior nec te feriam neque intra
claustra tenebo:

me pater saevis oneret catenis,
quod viro clemens misero peperci;
me vel extremos Numidarum in agros
classe releget.

I pedes quo te rapiunt et aurae,
dum favet nox et Venus, i secundo
omine et nostri memorem sepulcro
scalpe querellam.'

37. **quae,** *she.*

38. **surge**: *sc.* from sleep, suggesting the figurative expression for death that follows. — **longus**: as in II. 14. 19 and IV. 9. 27, for 'eternal.' In all of these cases *longus* gets its expressive force from the substantive (*labor, somnus, nox*), which denotes a familiar experience of limited duration. — **unde**: for *inde unde*, 'from a quarter from which.'

40. **falle,** *elude;* cf. I. 10. 16 n, *Ep.* I. 5. 31. — **sorores**: sc. *tuas;* cf. Ov. *Her.* 14. 123 *si qua piae, Lynceu, tibi cura sororis.* First cousins were called *fratres* and *sorores* (*patrueles*).

42. **singulos lacerant**: a confusion of the figure with the reality (Intr. 123), **singulos** referring to the men, **lacerant** to the lions. — **eheu**: in her account of the affair in Ov. *Her.* 14. 35, she is made to say, *circum me gemitus morientum audire videbar; | et tamen audibam, quodque verebar erat.*

43. **intra claustra**: *i.e.* where others would kill you.

44. **tenebo**: for *retinebo;* Intr. 129.

45. **me**: Intr. 116 *b, g;* not continuing the emphasis of **ego**, but contrasted with **te**. The two sentences of this strophe are virtually concessive clauses added to the expression of her determination in 42–44: 'I will not compass your death, let my father do his worst to me.'

47. **extremos**: see 10. 1 n.

49. **pedes et aurae**: *i.e.* to the coast, and then across the sea; cf. *Epod.* 16. 21 *sq.*

50. **Venus**: who, as inspirer of Hypermnestra's act, has given him the opportunity to escape.

51. **nostri**, *of me*, as in 27. 14 and Juv. 3. 318; cf. 28. 9 n. — **sepulcro**: Intr. 69.

## XII.

Miserarum est neque amori dare ludum neque dulci
mala vino lavere, aut exanimari metuentis
patruae verbera linguae.

2 Tibi qualum Cythereae puer ales, tibi telas
operosaeque Minervae studium aufert, Neobule,
Liparaei nitor Hebri,

3 simul unctos Tiberinis umeros lavit in undis,
eques ipso melior Bellerophonte, neque pugno
neque segni pede victus;

XII. This ode is a study in pure Ionics, based apparently on an ode of Alcaeus, beginning ἔμε δείλαν, ἔμε πασᾶν κακοτάτων πεδέχοισαν (*Fr.* 59). Alcaeus wrote a number of poems in this metre, but Horace seems to have found the task of naturalizing it in Latin too difficult, or the effect unsatisfactory; at least, this is the only example he has left us. In form it is a monologue, the complaint of a love-sick girl, who frets against the restraints under which she is brought up, and sighs for the freedom of a young man. The names are Greek, but the local coloring is, as usual, wholly Roman. — Metre, 168.

1. **ludum**, *free play;* cf. Plaut. *Bacch.* 1083 *nimis nolo ei desidiae dare ludum.* — **lavere**: *i.e.* wash them away. For the form, see II. 3. 18 n. — **aut**, *or else; or, if they do;* cf. 24. 24; Tac. *Ann.* III. 73. 1 *huc adrogantiae venerat, ut sedem sibi atque exercitui postularet, aut bellum inexplicabile minitaretur.* — **metuentis**: accusative; the force of the genitive **miserarum** has faded, at this distance, into a vague idea of necessity, so that *eas* is felt to be understood as the subject of **exanimari**. — **patruae**: not necessarily of an actual uncle. The word *patruus*, like *noverca* (see *Epod.* 5. 9 n), had become proverbial for severity untempered by parental affection or sympathy; cf. *S.* II. 3. 88 *ne sis patruus mihi.* For the form, see Intr. 65. — **verbera**, *the lashings.*

2. **tibi qualum (aufert)**, *steals away your wool-basket.* The verb here, though used figuratively, has its literal (physical) meaning; with its other subject, **nitor Hebri**, it is purely metaphorical. — **operosae**: applied to Minerva (in contrast with Venus) as patroness of the various handicrafts, particularly of spinning and weaving (Ἀθηνᾶ Ἐργάνη). — **Minervae**: objective gen. — **Neobule**: a name borrowed from Archilochus, for its pleasing sound and metrical value; cf. *Leuconoe*, I. 11. — **Liparaei Hebri**: cf. I. 27. 10, II. 4. 2, III. 9. 9, 14. The name *Hebrus* is taken from the river in Thrace; cf. 7. 23 n. — **nitor**: cf. I. 19. 5.

3. **simul**: see I. 4. 17 n. —

4 catus idem per apertum fugientis agitato
grege cervos iaculari et celer arto latitantem
fruticeto excipere aprum.

## XIII.

O fons Bandusiae, splendidior vitro,
dulci digne mero non sine floribus,
cras donaberis haedo,
cui frons turgida cornibus

**unctos**: for the exercise that preceded the bath. On this whole passage see I. 8. 5 *sqq*., III. 7. 25 *sqq*., with notes. — **eques**: a construction according to sense (as if *Hebrus*, instead of **nitor Hebri** had been the subject of the main verb) justified by the intervention of the dependent clause with *Hebrus* understood as its subject. —**Bellerophontē**: from the form *Bellerophontes*; cf. 7. 15 n. — **segni**: with both **pugno** and **pede**; Intr. 119 *a*. The ablatives are better taken as causal.

4. **fruticeto**: Intr. 69. — **excipere**: *i.e.* to attack him when he is driven out, and kill him before he can escape. For the infinitives see Intr. 101 *b* and *c*.

XIII. To the spring of Bandusia. Where the spring was which Horace has immortalized under this name, cannot be determined. There is evidence, dating from the beginning of the twelfth century, of the existence of a 'fons Bandusinus' near Venusia, and this tradition, in itself of no great value, — for it was very common in the middle ages for a classical name to be attached to a place without the least reference to truth, — receives some support from the name itself, which, being probably a corruption of the Greek Πανδοσία, is one we should expect to find in the neighborhood of Venusia, rather than in the Sabine district where Horace had his farm. There was on Horace's farm a spring which we know he admired and valued highly (cf. *S*. II. 6. 2, *Ep*. I. 16, 12 *sqq*.), and which would fit in all respects our poem; but we do not know that it was called Bandusia or had any name at all. Some have imagined that Horace, on coming into possession of his new home, revived there a name familiar and dear to him in the place of his birth. Fortunately our ignorance need not mar our enjoyment of the poem, which would lose none of its exquisite beauty if we were obliged to relegate the spring entirely to the realm of fancy. — Metre, 173.

1. **Bandusiae**: apparently the name of the place, not of the nymph of the spring. — **splendidior vitro**, *brighter than crystal*. Ovid applies the same phrase to Galatea (*M*. XIII. 791). The brightness, of course, implies the transparency of the water, as of the glass. Cf. *splendor aquai*,

primis et venerem et proelia destinat;
frustra: nam gelidos inficiet tibi
rubro sanguine rivos,
lascivi suboles gregis.

Te flagrantis atrox hora Caniculae
nescit tangere, tu frigus amabile
fessis vomere tauris
praebes et pecori vago.

Fies nobilium tu quoque fontium,
me dicente cavis impositam ilicem
saxis unde loquaces
lymphae desiliunt tuae.

Lucr. IV. 211. For **vitro**, cf. I. 17. 20 n.

2. **mero**: poured into the water as a libation to the divinity of the spring. That the poet will make these slighter offerings of wine and flowers, along with the greater sacrifice promised in the next verse, goes without saying. The regular time for making such offerings was the festival of the Fontanalia (or Fontinalia), October 13. — **non sine**: cf. I. 23. 3 n. — **floribus**: cf. Varro *L. L.* VI. 22 (*Fontanalibus*) *et in fontes coronas iaciunt et puteos coronant.* That they also sacrificed animals appears from the present passage and from the *Acta Fratr. Arv.* (A.D. 183), where a sacrifice of two wethers is recorded. It is not necessary, however, to suppose that this ode was written on the eve of the Fontanalia. Cf. Martial VI. 47.

5. **destinat,** *foretokens.*

6. **frustra**: **nam,** etc.: cf. 7. 21 n. — **gelidos, rubro**: see Intr. 122.

9. **te . . . tu**: cf. I. 10. 9 n; Intr. 116 *g.* — **hora,** *season;* cf. Ep. II. 3. 302 *sub verni temporis horam.* The whole phrase means the furious heat of the dog-days; see I. 17. 17 n.

10. **tangere,** *come nigh.* For the mood see Intr. 94 *o.* — **frigus,** etc.: *i.e.* during the mid-day rest.

12. **vago**: answering to **fessis vomere**; the aimless movement of the grazing flock is contrasted with the steady-going ox at his work.

13. **nobilium,** *famous; i.e.* such as Hippocrene, Castalia, Arethusa, etc. The poet has kept his word. — **fontium**: Intr. 62.

14. **cavis,** etc.: with consummate skill Horace has painted the whole scene for us in these few finishing strokes. — **impositam,** *that stands upon;* cf. IV. 14. 12.

15. **loquaces**: with **desiliunt.** The fine effect of this passage is due in large measure to the succession of liquids and expressive vowel sounds; Intr. 131.

## XIV.

Herculis ritu modo dictus, o plebs,
morte venalem petiisse laurum
Caesar Hispana repetit penatis
victor ab ora.
Vnico gaudens mulier marito
prodeat, iustis operata sacris,
et soror clari ducis et decorae
supplice vitta

XIV. Early in the year B.C. 24 Augustus returned to Rome after an absence of nearly three years in the West, where he had reduced the Cantabrians to temporary submission and settled the affairs of Gaul. During the Cantabrian campaign he had lain sick at Tarraco for many months, — a period of grave anxiety for all thoughtful and peace-loving Romans, in view of the disorders that would inevitably follow his death. There was no doubt genuine rejoicing among the great mass of the people over his recovery and safe return. As he had declined the honor of a triumph for success achieved largely by his lieutenants, a public thanksgiving (*supplicatio*) would naturally be decreed. In anticipation of such a thanksgiving Horace wrote the present ode. He pictures the outward manifestations of gratitude and rejoicing, in which the women may be expected to take a prominent part; and then proceeds with his own preparations for celebrating the day in a light-hearted strain, in which, however, we are not permitted to forget the significance of the occasion. — Metre, 174.

1. **Herculis ritu,** *like Hercules;* referring both to the dangerous enterprise and the victorious return. — **modo** (with **dictus**): *i.e.* at the time of his illness. — **dictus,** *he who was said.* — **o plebs,** *O ye people.* The word had lost its earlier meaning of a political class, and signified, like *populus*, the mass of the citizens in distinction from their rulers; cf. II. 2. 18.

2. **venalem,** *whose price is.* — **petiisse,** *to have gone in quest of.*

3. **Hispana ora**: cf. 8. 21 n.

5. **unico gaudens,** *whose whole joy is in;* cf. *unicis Sabinis*, II. 18. 14 n. *Vnicus*, from its use with *filius*, *filia*, etc., had come to connote a concentration of interest and affection on a single object, who is one's 'all.' — **mulier**: Livia. She was a woman of great ability and force of character, tempered with good sense and tact, which enabled her to keep the affection of her husband to the end. Her private life was above reproach (*sanctitate domus priscum ad morem*, Tac. *Ann.* V. 1. 5).

6. **prodeat**: on a day of thanksgiving, besides the institution of public sacrifices, the temples, which were closed to the laity on ordinary occasions, were thrown open and were thronged with crowds of

virginum matres iuvenumque nuper
sospitum; vos, o pueri et puellae
non virum expertae, male ominatis
parcite verbis.

Hic dies vere mihi festus atras
eximet curas: ego nec tumultum
nec mori per vim metuam tenente
Caesare terras.

people of every age and class, who passed through the streets from shrine to shrine, crowned with wreaths and singing hymns. — **iustis,** *due; i.e.* those prescribed by the ritual. — **operata**: *i.e.* at home, before setting out to take part in the public thanksgiving. — **sacris**: the other reading, *iustis divis* (*scilicet quod Caesari victoriam et reditum merenti dederint,* Porphyrio), would be more appropriate if **operata** referred to the public ceremonies of the day. But **operata,** which implies an actual sacrifice (‘*operationes*’ *enim sacrificia dixerunt,* Porph.), cannot well apply to the mere presence of Livia and the women at the public ceremonies, in which they would take no active part; and if it could, it ought to be *operatura,* as Bentley pointed out.

7. **soror**: Octavia.

8. **supplice**: in distinction from the plain one worn ordinarily by free-born ladies. The ‘thanksgiving fillet’ would seem to have been a wreath of olive twined with a woolen ribbon. — **vitta**: abl. with **decorae,** as in II. 16. 6.

9. **virginum matres,** etc.: *i.e.* mothers with their sons and daughters (or daughters-in-law) about them, the former just home from the wars (**nuper sospitum**). Some join **nuper sospitum** with **virginum** also, but this is a strained interpretation and confuses the picture.

10. **vos**: the younger children, who would especially need this caution. This is indicated by the word **pueri** (in contrast with **iuvenes,** above) and more explicitly in the phrase attached to **puellae.** Cf. the very similar expression for ‘boys and girls,’ *Ep.* II. 1. 132 *castis cum pueris ignara puella mariti.*

11. **non virum expertae**: the MS. reading, *iam virum expertae,* would make the whole phrase a bungling and needless repetition of **virginum iuvenumque,** above. — **male ominatis,** etc.: equivalent to *favete linguis,* III. 1. 2 n. If the text is correct, the hiatus (Intr. 185) is due to the feeling that the two words belong together as a compound.

12. **parcite**: *abstain from;* cf. *Epod.* 17. 6 *parce vocibus sacris.*

13. **vere mihi festus**: used predicatively: cf. 8. 9 n. — **atras curas**: those caused by the precarious state of Caesar's health. Cf. III. 1. 40 n.

14. **tumultum,** *insurrection;* a war in the city or in Italy (cf. Cic. *Phil.* 8. 2 *sqq.*). He is thinking of personal danger.

15. **mori**: Intr. 95. — **tenente**: *sc.* as ruler; cf. 17. 8, *S.* I. 7. 18.

I, pete unguentum, puer, et coronas
et cadum Marsi memorem duelli,
Spartacum si qua potuit vagantem
fallere testa.

Dic et argutae properet Neaerae
murreum nodo cohibere crinem;
si per invisum mora ianitorem
fiet, abito.

Lenit albescens animos capillus
litium et rixae cupidos protervae;
non ego hoc ferrem calidus iuventa
consule Planco.

17. **unguentum, coronas, cadum**: cf. II. 3. 13 n. — **puer**: see I. 19. 14 n.

18. **Marsi duelli**: the Social War, B.C. 90, 89. The Marsi were among the bravest of the *socii;* cf. I. 2. 39 n. — **memorem**: *i.e.* stored at that time. Cf. Juv. 5. 31 *calcatamque tenet bellis socialibus uvam* (*dives*).

19. **Spartacum**: the Servile War occurred B.C. 73–71. — **vagantem**: *i.e.* marauding.

20. **fallere**: cf. 11. 40 n.

21. **argutae**, *sweet-voiced;* cf. *argutae Thaliae*, IV. 6. 25. — **properet**: Gr. 339. — **Neaerae**: a music girl.

22. **murreum**, *chestnut;* it is defined by Porphyrio as (*color*) *medius inter flavum et nigrum*. — **nodo cohibere**: instead of a more elaborate coiffure, which would keep him waiting; cf. II. 11. 23 n.

23. **ianitorem**: the *ostiarius* of the house where Neaera lodged.

24. **abito**: the second form of the imperative (2d person), referring to a point of future time removed by an interval from the present.

25. **albescens**: Horace was only forty-one, but his hair turned gray early (Intr. 29).

27. **non ego**: cf. I. 18. 11 n. — **ferrem**: Gr. 308 *a*. — **calidus iuventa**: in contrast with the actual fact implied in **albescens**, etc.

28. **consule Planco**: the year was that of Philippi. The reminiscence, like those of vss. 18 and 19, is not without design. To his playful reminder of the unpleasant experiences of civil war and insurrection, from which the rule of Augustus had afforded a happy escape, Horace adds an intimation of his own change from a hot partisan to a lover of peace and quiet.

XV. Horace here portrays the same type of character that he attacks with more severity in I. 25, IV. 13, and some of the Epodes, — that of the woman of faded beauty who still tries to play the part of a young girl. — Metre, 171.

1. **pauperis**: a reason why she should stay at home and work; cf. vs. 13.

2. **fige**: more forcible than *pone*

## XV.

Vxor pauperis Ibyci,
tandem nequitiae fige modum tuae
famosisque laboribus;
maturo propior desine funeri
inter ludere virgines
et stellis nebulam spargere candidis.
Non, si quid Pholoen satis,
et te, Chlori, decet: filia rectius
expugnat iuvenum domos,
pulso Thyias uti concita tympano.
illam cogit amor Nothi
lascivae similem ludere capreae:
te lanae prope nobilem
tonsae Luceriam, non citharae decent
nec flos purpureus rosae
nec poti vetulam faece tenus cadi.

(I. 16. 2), implying (with **tandem**) permanency: 'put an end to it once for all.'

3. **laboribus**: sarcastic; 'everybody knows (**famosis**) that at your years such capers are hard work.'

4. **maturo**, *the full time of*; it could not be called untimely if it should occur in the near future. — **propior**, *getting near* (*as you are*).

5. **inter ludere**: Intr. 115 *c*. For this use of **ludere**, cf. II. 12. 19 n.

6. **stellis**, etc.: her presence is like a shadow on the bright company.

7. **non, si**: cf. II. 10. 17 n. — **Pholoen** (sc. *decet*): her daughter. — **satis**, *well*.

9. **expugnat**: not a mere figure of speech; cf. Sen. *N. Q.* IV. *Praef.* 6 *dicebat adulationibus nos non claudere ostium, sed aperire, et quidem sic ut amicae opponi solet, quae si impulit, grata est, si effregit, gratior*.

10. **pulso**, *by the beating of*; Intr. 105 *a*. — **Thyias**: see II. 19. 9 n. — **tympano**: see I. 18. 13 n.

12. **lascivae**, etc.: scornful characterization of the mother's conduct. — **similem**: the adjective for the adverb, as in I. 23. 1.

13. **prope tonsae Luceriam**: Intr. 115 *b*. Apulian wool was the best in the Roman market (Plin. *N. H.* VIII. 190). As it was this that gave the town its distinction (**nobilem**) the epithet suggests the excellence of the wool.

14. **citharae**, etc.: the description is that of a music girl at a banquet.

16. **poti**: passive. — **vetulam**: reserved for this place to point and

## XVI.

Inclusam Danaen turris aenea
robustaeque fores et vigilum canum
tristes excubiae munierant satis
nocturnis ab adulteris,
si non Acrisium, virginis abditae
custodem pavidum, Iuppiter et Venus
risissent : fore enim tutum iter et patens
converso in pretium deo.
Aurum per medios ire satellites

emphasize the incongruity between her age and the scene which these words suggest.

XVI. Reflections on the power and the impotence of riches. Gold is a mighty weapon: it can bring to nought the counsels of kings; it can break through walls of rock; it can destroy princely houses, take cities, subvert thrones; but it cannot confer happiness. Wealth brings trouble and danger, and it cannot keep pace with growing desire; contentment is better than great possessions. Heaven can vouchsafe no richer boon than moderate means with a contented spirit. The ode is addressed to Maecenas, and is very similar in sentiment to II. 2 and 16, and III. 1. — Metre, 172.

1. **Danaen**: Horace, with mild irony, treats the highly poetical myth of Jupiter descending to Danae in a golden shower as the testimony of mythology to the power of gold. — **aenea**: cf. 3. 65 n.

2. **robustae**, *oaken;* cf. I. 3. 9.

3. **tristes**, *grim.* — **munierant**: see Intr. 82. The indicative expresses what had been the fact until the occurrence of the event indicated in the protasis; the precautions had been sufficient (and would have continued to be) if the power of gold had not been brought to bear against them. Cf. Tac. *Ann.* IV. 9. 1 (of the speech of Tiberius to the senate on the death of his son) *magno ea fletu ei mox precationibus faustis audita; ac, si modum orationi posuisset, misericordia sui gloriaque animos audientium impleverat.*

4. **adulteris**: cf. I. 33. 9 n.

6. **pavidum**: Acrisius had been told by an oracle that his daughter's son would slay him.

7. **fore enim**, etc.: the construction shows that the thought is quoted, and the context shows it is that of the two divinities.

8. **pretium**, *a bribe.* — **deo**: dative.

9. **per medios**: *i.e.* not secretly, by outwitting them, but right under their eyes; it paralyzes and disarms them. This idea of the power of gold is kept up in the metaphors that follow (**perrumpere, concidit, diffidit, subruit**). — **ire**: Intr. 94 *c.* — **satellites**, *royal guards.*

et perrumpere amat saxa potentius
ictu fulmineo ; concidit auguris
Argivi domus, ob lucrum
demersa exitio ; diffidit urbium
portas vir Macedo et subruit aemulos
reges muneribus ; munera navium
saevos inlaqueant duces.

Crescentem sequitur cura pecuniam
maiorumque fames ; iure perhorrui

10. **saxa** : *i.e.* those of the wall of a city or stronghold, as in *Ep.* II. 3. 395.

11. **ictu** : Intr. 75. — **concidit . . . diffidit** : Intr. 116 *b*, *c* ; cf. I. 28. 7. — **auguris Argivi** : Amphiaraus, the prophet-hero of Argos, brother-in-law of king Adrastus. When the latter was organizing the expedition of the 'Seven against Thebes,' Amphiaraus, who foresaw its disastrous end and his own death, was betrayed into the necessity of joining it by his wife Eriphȳle, who had been bribed by Polynices with the golden necklace of Harmonia. The consequences were the death of Amphiaraus, the murder of Eriphyle in revenge by their son Alcmaeon, and the madness of the latter under his mother's curse.

13. **diffĭdit**, *clove asunder.*

14. **vir Macedo** : Philip, the father of Alexander. His success in accomplishing his purposes by bribery was proverbial, so that the mention of his name is unnecessary ; cf. Cic. *ad Att.* I. 16. 12 *Philippus omnia castella expugnari posse dicebat in quae modo asellus onustus auro posset ascendere.* A Delphic oracle was quoted, advising him to fight 'with silver spears'; and it was said *ὅτι τὰς πόλεις αἱρεῖ τῶν Ἑλλήνων οὐ Φίλιππος, ἀλλὰ τὸ Φιλίππου χρυσίον.* (Plut. *Aem. Paul.* 12). — **subruit**, *undermined.*

15. **muneribus; munera**: Intr. 116 *e*. — **navium duces** : these words would recall to Horace's readers a conspicuous example of their own time, Menodorus, the freedman admiral of Sextus Pompeius, who deserted to Octavian, then back to Pompey, and finally to Octavian again.

16. **saevos**, *stern ; i.e.* for all their sternness.

17. **crescentem**, etc.: the preceding reflections on the power of wealth convey no suggestion of its desirability as a possession ; on the contrary, its wonderful power is always a power for evil, and the suggestion of danger to the possessor is not far removed ; just as in these days we might speak with admiration of electricity as a mighty force, which, however, we should shrink from handling. This underlying thought now comes to the surface. — **cura** : here simply the worry of managing great wealth.

18. **maiorum**: neuter.—**fames**: cf. *Ep.* I. 18. 23 *argenti sitis importuna famesque*, Verg. *A.* III. 57 *auri sacra fames ;* and, for the

late conspicuum tollere verticem,
Maecenas, equitum decus.
Quanto quisque sibi plura negaverit,
ab dis plura feret. Nil cupientium
nudus castra peto et transfuga divitum
partis linquere gestio,
contemptae dominus splendidior rei,
quam si quicquid arat impiger Apulus
occultare meis dicerer horreis,
magnas inter opes inops.

thought, II. 2. 13 *sqq.*; Juv. 14. 139 *crescit amor nummi quantum ipsa pecunia crevit.*

19. **late conspicuum**: proleptic. The wise man will shrink from the dangerous prominence which great wealth gives. — **tollere**: Intr. 94 *l.* — **verticem**: an appropriate word with **tollere**; cf. I. 1. 36, 18. 15.

20. **equitum**: Maecenas is himself a shining example of the wisdom of moderation; Intr. 21.

21. **quanto**, etc.: in this paradoxical sentence **plura** gets its meaning in each case from the context; in the first clause it means those things which we have in mind when we speak of 'denying ourselves,' that is, in general, luxuries; in the second clause it means the gifts of the gods, that is, those enjoyments and satisfactions that come to us, not of our own seeking, but as the fruits of a well-trained mind and character. In particular, Horace means that self-denial develops a contented spirit, which is the only condition of happiness, and his teaching here, as in II. 2. 17 *sqq.*, falls in with that of the Stoics; see Cic. *Paradoxa* 6.

22. **nil cupientium**, *of the contented.* The figure of the two camps is not intended to conform in all respects to Horace's actual circumstances, but to express vividly his strong conviction of the superiority of contentment over riches. The figure is, as often, confused with the reality; see Intr. 123.

23. **nudus peto**, *I leave all and set out for*; *i.e.* I surrender all that I possess, in exchange for the more precious treasure of contentment. — **transfuga**, etc.: *i.e.* I am (like) a soldier in the camp of the rich whose heart is in the other camp, so that he holds cheap the luxuries about him.

25. **contemptae**, *insignificant* (*sc.* in the eyes of the wealthy); cf. Cic. *Parad.* 6. 47 *meam pecuniam contemnis, et recte; est enim ad volgi opinionem mediocris, ad tuam nulla, ad meam modica.* — **splendidior**: *sc.* in the eyes of the wise; cf. II. 2. 21 *sqq.*

26. **quicquid**, etc.: cf. I. 1. 10 n. — **arāt**: here used for the whole work of production by the farmer; cf. the use of *trahunt*, II. 18. 8 n. For the prosody, see Intr. 179. — **impiger Apulus**: cf. *pernicis*

Purae rivus aquae silvaque iugerum
paucorum et segetis certa fides meae
fulgentem imperio fertilis Africae
fallit sorte beatior.

Quamquam nec Calabrae mella ferunt apes,
nec Laestrygonia Bacchus in amphora
languescit mihi, nec pinguia Gallicis
crescunt vellera pascuis,

*Apuli*, *Epod*. 2. 42. The soil of the Apulian lowlands was excellent for tillage as well as for pasture (Strabo VI. 3. 9).

27. **occultare**: a fresh word, for the more usual *condere* (cf. I. 1. 9). — **meis**: emphatic; Intr. 116 *b*.

28. **magnas**, etc., *being* (*really*), etc.; expressing the actual fact in contrast with what people say (**dicerer**).

29. **rivus aquae silvaque**: cf. Horace's description of his farm, *Ep*. I. 16. 5 *sqq*.; also I. 22. 9 *sqq*., *Ep*. I. 14. 1 *sqq*.

30. **segetis certa fides**: in contrast with *fundus mendax*, III. 1. 30 n, and *spem mentita seges*, *Ep*. I. 7. 87. **segetis** is possessive genitive; cf. Cic. *ad Fam*. XVI. 17. 1 *ager etiam fidelis dici potest*. The poet, 'desiderans quod satis est,' can always count on his crops yielding enough for his needs; it is only the man who is intent on growing rich that is worried by the uncertainties of farming.

31. **fulgentem imperio**: the man holding for the time the splendid position of proconsul. The proconsulships of Asia and Africa were the highest positions of dignity and power attainable by a Roman citizen; they were assigned by lot each year to the two senior consulars. Others take the words as an extravagant expression for great landed possessions in Africa; but the examples cited in support of this view (vs. 41, below, and II. 2. 9 *sqq*.) refer to regal power. Horace has already used the great landowners for comparison (vss. 26 *sq*.); he now uses exalted station and outward splendor, as he does in II. 2. 17. The epithet **fertilis** contributes to the picture, suggesting the great resources of the province, which give it its importance and prominence.

32. **fallit sorte beatior**: literally 'being happier in lot (than he), escapes his notice,' *i.e. is a happier lot than his, though he does not suspect it*. The construction is formed after the Greek idiom (λανθάνει ὀλβιώτερον ὄν, the Latin language, however, providing no equivalent for ὄν).

33. **quamquam**, etc.: with these typical forms of wealth cf. I. 31. 5 *sqq*., *Epod*. 1. 25 *sqq*.; Intr. 117 *a*. — **Calabrae apes**: cf. II. 6. 14.

34. **Laestrygonia**: *i.e.* Formian; see 17. 1 n, and cf. *Sabina*, I. 9. 7 n. For the wine, see I. 20. 10 n. — **Bacchus**: Intr. 130.

35. **languescit**, *is mellowing;* cf. *languidiora vina*, 21. 8. — **Gallicis**: *i.e.* of Cisalpine Gaul, where white wool of a fine quality was grown (Plin. *N. H.* VIII. 190).

36. **pascuis**: Intr. 69.

importuna tamen pauperies abest,
nec, si plura velim, tu dare deneges.
Contracto melius parva cupidine
vectigalia porrigam
quam si Mygdoniis regnum Alyattei
campis continuem. Multa petentibus
desunt multa; bene est cui deus obtulit
parca quod satis est manu.

37. **importuna,** *pinching.*

38. **nec si,** etc.: cf. *Epod.* 1. 31. — **dare:** Intr. 94 *k.*

39. **contracto,** etc.: cf. II. 2. 9 *sqq.* — **melius porrigam:** suggested by **si plura velim.** The sense is: If I *should* find my income too small for my expenses, a better way to enlarge it will be to cut down my desires till they come within it; the other way, seeking for more, never brings satisfaction; desire is never satisfied by feeding it. Horace is here preaching on a Stoic text; cf. Cic. *Parad.* 6. 49 *O di immortales! non intellegunt homines quam magnum vectigal sit parsimonia.* — **cupidine:** see II. 16. 15 n.

40. **vectigalia,** *income;* properly, public revenues, but sometimes used of private income, especially for purposes of comparison, as here and *S.* II. 2. 100; cf. also Cic. *l.c.*

41. **Mygdoniis:** *i.e.* Phrygian; see II. 12. 22 n. — **Alyattei:** king of Lydia, father of Croesus. For the form, cf. *Vlixei,* I. 6. 7 n.

42. **campis:** dative; Intr. 56. — **continuem,** *unite; sc.* under my sway, so as to enjoy the entire revenues of both countries. The word is often used of buying up large tracts of land, *e.g.* Liv. XXXIV. 4. 9 *quid legem Liciniam excitavit de quingentis iugeribus nisi ingens cupido agros continuandi?* — **multa petentibus,** etc.: the converse of *quanto quisque . . . feret,* 21 *sq.*

43. **bene est** (sc. *ei*), *blessed is the man.*

XVII. To. L. Aelius Lamia, in regard to whom see I. 26, introd. note. The ode, it would seem, is addressed to him simply as a compliment, the substance of it being a light sketch in the spirit of I. 9, very likely a study from the Greek, which it would be idle to attempt to connect with Lamia's personality. The scene is laid in the country, near the seashore. 'A great storm is brewing; you must stay indoors to-morrow, and your servants can do no work. Make ready to enjoy with them the holiday thus provided for you.' — Metre, 176.

1. **ab Lamo:** equivalent to *Lamo orte,* the idea of descent being implied in **nobilis.** Lamus was the mythical founder of the city of the Laestrygones (Λάμου αἰπὺ πτολίεθρον | Τηλέπυλον Λαιστρυγονίην, *Odys.* X. 81), which was identified with Formiae: cf. Cic. *ad Att.* II. 13. 2 *si vero in hanc* Τηλέπυλον *veneris* Λαιστρυγονίην, *Formias dico.* That the Lamiae, one of the oldest and wealthiest families of Formiae, should place

# XVII.

Aeli vetusto nobilis ab Lamo,
(quando et priores hinc Lamias ferunt
denominatos et nepotum
per memores genus omne fastos,
auctore ab illo ducis originem
qui Formiarum moenia dicitur
princeps et innantem Maricae
litoribus tenuisse Lirim

this name at the head of their pedigree, was inevitable. At this time they had little political distinction to boast of, and were therefore all the more likely to make much of the antiquity of their family. The father of our Lamia, when he went into politics as a supporter of Cicero, was still only a knight, though a distinguished one; in B.C. 44 Cicero supported him for the praetorship, with what success is unknown. (See Cic. *ad Fam.* XI. 16. 1, 17. 1.) His son, Horace's friend, was the first of the family who held the consulship, but that was at least twenty-five years after the date of this ode. We may therefore take this allusion to his pedigree as serious (not humorous, as some take it), and attribute it to the same motive as in the case of Maecenas (I. 1. 1, III. 29. 1, *S.* I. 6. 1, etc.), who likewise was without political distinction. A century later, when the Lamiae had become *nobiles* by the attainment of high curule office, we find them named as types of high nobility (Juv. 4. 154, 6. 385), a further evidence of the antiquity of their ancestry, as their *nobilitas* was even then not over three generations old.

2. **quando, etc.**; the four verses beginning here are with some reason suspected of being interpolated. If they are genuine, the whole genealogical dissertation, **quando — late tyrannus,** is parenthetical, and consists of a protasis, **quando — fastos,** introducing (and giving the reason of) a main statement, **auctore — tyrannus.** — **priores**: *i.e.* the earliest of the name; 'earlier' than the great body of descendants (**genus omne**) whose names are in the records. — **hinc,** *after him;* cf. *unde,* I. 12. 17 n.

4. **fastos**: here used of family records.

5. **auctore**: sc. *generis;* cf. I. 2. 36. It is in apposition with **illo,** which is used substantively. — **ducis**: if *ducit* is read, **genus** is its subject, and the *whole* parenthetical clause depends on **quando.**

7. **innantem,** *that floods;* referring to the marshes and inlets which prevail on that part of the coast. — **Maricae,** *Marica's.* She was an old Italian divinity, variously identified with Aphrodite and Circe, whose grove was at the mouth of the Liris, ten miles from Formiae.

8. **tenuisse**: cf. 14. 15 n.

late tyrannus,) cras foliis nemus
multis et alga litus inutili
demissa tempestas ab Euro
sternet, aquae nisi fallit augur
annosa cornix; dum potes, aridum
compone lignum; cras genium mero
curabis et porco bimenstri
cum famulis operum solutis.

9. **late tyrannus**: the Homeric εὐρὺ κρείων; cf. *late regem*, Verg. *A*. I. 21. For the construction see Mdv. 301 *c*. Obs. 2. — **nemus**: *i.e.* the ground under the trees. For this construction with *sterno*, cf. IV. 14. 32, where, as here, the simple verb is used for *consterno* (Intr. 129).

10. **inutili**; its worthlessness was proverbial; cf. *vilior alga*, *S*. II. 5. 8, Verg. *E*. 7. 42.

11. **Euro**: cf. *Epod*. 16. 54.

12. **aquae augur**: after the Greek ὑετόμαντις (cf. Euphorion, *Fr*. 65 ὑετόμαντις ὅτε κρώξειε κορώνη). Vergil describes its action when 'calling rain,' *G*. I. 388 *tum cornix plena pluviam vocat improba voce | et sola in sicca secum spatiatur harena*. Cf. 27. 10, Lucr. V. 1083. — **fallit**: used absolutely, as in *Epod*. 16. 45 *numquam fallentis olivae*.

13. **annosa**: it was supposed to live to an extraordinary age, — through nine generations of men, according to Hesiod (Plut. *Moral*. 415 C); cf. IV. 13. 25. — **dum potes**: *i.e.* today, before the storm wets it.

14. **compone**, *get in a store*. — **genium**: a man's *genius* was conceived to be an attendant spirit, divine but not immortal, inseparably associated with his life in all its phases of enjoyment or depression, 'naturae deus humanae, mortalis in unum | quodque caput, voltu mutabilis, albus et ater' (*Ep*. II. 2. 187); and on its varying moods depended his happiness or unhappiness. The conception was not unlike that of the soul in the parable of the rich man, Luke 12. 16 *sqq*. ('I will say to my soul, Soul, thou hast much goods laid up for many years; take thine ease, eat, drink, and be merry.') Hence, to deny one's self reasonable comforts was to 'cheat one's genius' (Ter. *Ph*. 44); and to take a holiday or otherwise give one's self up to enjoyment was *piare* (*Ep*. II. 1. 144) or *placare* (*Ep*. II. 3. 210) *genium*, or, more commonly, *indulgere genio*. Horace here substitutes *curare*, a word often used for bodily comfort (*curare corpus*, *curare cutem*, etc.). — **mero**: cf. Pers. 2. 3 *funde merum genio*; *Ep*. II. 1. 144; Tib. II. 2. 8.

15. **curabis**: Intr. 90. — **porco**: an offering to the Lares (cf. 23. 4, *S*. II. 3. 164), whose worship was associated with every act of family life. The flesh of the victim would furnish forth the simple feast; see I. 36. 2 n.

16. **operum**: Intr. 67.

## XVIII.

Faune, nympharum fugientum amator,
per meos finis et aprica rura
lenis incedas, abeasque parvis
aequus alumnis,
si tener pleno cadit haedus anno,
larga nec desunt Veneris sodali
vina craterae, vetus ara multo
fumat odore.

Ludit herboso pecus omne campo,

XVIII. A hymn to Faunus. The first half is a prayer for the favor of the god, which has been merited by constant and liberal offerings. In the second half his benign influence is set forth in a description of his festival on the 5th of December. This appears to have been a festival peculiar to the country, for in Rome his great day was the *Lupercalia*, on the 15th of February. For the attributes of Faunus, see I. 17. 2 n. — Metre, 174.

1. **nympharum**, etc.: this is a characteristic that belongs strictly to Pan and the Satyrs; cf. Stat. *Silv.* II. 2. 100 *sqq.*, Mart. IX. 61. 13.

3. **lenis**, *in mercy.* — **incedas**: the mere presence of the god was believed to carry with it some influence, blessing or blight, according to his mood; cf. I. 17. 5 *sqq.* — **abeasque aequus**, *and carry away a kindly feeling; i.e.* may the god be pleased with all he sees, to the very end, and go away with a desire to bless.

4. **alumnis**, *younglings* of the herd and flock, as in 23. 7.

5. **si**, etc.: a modest form of statement common in prayers, introducing the ground on which the appeal is based; cf. *S.* II. 6. 6 *sqq.*, and see note on *poscit*, I. 31. 1. — **tener haedus**: one of the *parvi alumni;* cf. I. 4. 12. — **pleno anno**: *i.e.* at the close of it, on the recurrence of the festival in December. — **cadit**: as a victim; cf. Verg. *A.* I. 334.

6. **Veneris sodali**: an epithet of the mixing-bowl not found elsewhere. It merely expresses the familiar association of 'love and wine.'

7. **craterae**: dative. When the bowl was filled, a libation would be made to the god first; but the main use of the wine, as of the kid, was to contribute to a spirited celebration of the god's day. — **vetus**: suggesting the antiquity of the festival. Notice the asyndeton, which is continued through the rest of the ode. — **multo odore**: for *multo ture* (cf. I. 30. 3); so *colores* for flowers, Prop. I. 2. 9 *aspice quos summittat humus formosa colores.*

9. **ludit**, etc.: the appeal to the god has merged insensibly into a description of the festival, which

cum tibi nonae redeunt Decembres;
festus in pratis vacat otioso
cum bove pagus;
inter audacis lupus errat agnos,
spargit agrestis tibi silva frondis,
gaudet invisam pepulisse fossor
ter pede terram.

now continues, bridging over the change in grammatical construction. The scene is a grassy meadow, — green even in December in the Italian climate, — where the whole countryside is gathered about the old altar. The sacrifice is followed, as usual, by feasting, after which the people stroll about the fields and woods, or amuse themselves with dancing and other merrymaking. Cattle and flocks peacefully grazing form the border of the picture. — **campo**: Intr. 69.

10. **tibi**, *thy;* dative of reference. — **redeunt**: cf. 8. 9 n.

11. **festus vacat**, *is making holiday.* — **otioso**, *freed from toil.* Both man and beast are enjoying a day of rest.

12. **pagus**: a few MSS. have *pardus*, a substitution evidently due to some lively monk, who remembered Isaiah 11. 6 *habitabit lupus cum agno et pardus cum haedo accubabit.*

13. **inter**: Intr. 115 *b*. — **audacis**: *i.e.* they are not afraid of him, for they feel to-day the presence of Faunus, who was also *Lupercus* (interpreted as '*qui lupum arcet*'); and he is cowed by the same presence.

14. **spargit**, etc.: cf. *Epod.* 11. 5 *December silvis honorem* (= *frondis*) *decutit.* The point here is that the woods of themselves strew the ground with leaves in honor of the god, referring to the common practice of strewing the ground with boughs on festal or solemn occasions; cf. Verg. *E.* 5. 40 *spargite humum foliis* (in honor of Daphnis). — **agrestis**: *i.e.* natural, artless.

15. **invisam**: because of the incessant hard work he is condemned to spend upon it. — **pepulisse**: Intr. 94 *d*, 81 *a*. For the expression cf. I. 37. 2 *pulsanda tellus*, I. 4. 7 *terram quatiunt pede*, IV. 1. 28. — **fossor**: the lowest grade of farm-laborer, the typical clown (Cat. 22. 10, Pers. 5. 122). He was employed especially in working the soil in orchards and vineyards; cf. Verg. *G.* II. 264. On large estates he was usually a slave in fetters (cf. Ov. *Tr.* IV. 1. 5 *hoc est cur cantet vinctus quoque compede fossor,* | *indocili numero cum grave mollit opus*); but in our present picture we must imagine him a free laborer for hire, a *farm-hand,* or perhaps the *pauper colonus* himself (cf. I. 1. 11 n, 35. 5).

16. **ter**: *i.e.* in a dance with triple beat (*tripudium*); cf. IV. 1. 28.

## XIX.

Quantum distet ab Inacho
Codrus, pro patria non timidus mori,
narras et genus Aeaci
et pugnata sacro bella sub Ilio:
quo Chium pretio cadum
mercemur, quis aquam temperet ignibus,
quo praebente domum et quota
Paelignis caream frigoribus, taces.

XIX. This ode portrays, in a lively dramatic form which reminds us of I. 27, a symposium. There are two distinct scenes, one occupying the first eight verses, and the other the remainder of the poem. How these are to be combined, Horace has by no means made clear. Perhaps the most probable explanation is this: On a sunny winter afternoon a company of literary friends sit together in some garden or elsewhere out of doors, and one of their number has been discoursing at great length on subjects which the poet begins to think are very ancient history. The sun is sinking low, the air grows chill, the cold evening is coming on. Suddenly the poet 'takes the floor,' and interrupts the learned discourse with a demand that the company consider a question of much nearer concern, — where, when, and how they can prepare to spend a merry evening. Then, as if carried away by his imagination, but really with the purpose of carrying his hearers with him, he plays the *magister bibendi* before them, with spirited dramatic action, as if the symposium had already begun, — a performance for which the serious and quiet picture in the opening verses supplies a fitting background. There is a similar anticipation of a scene of revelry in II. 7. 21 *sqq.*; cf. also III. 14. 17 *sqq.* The whole bears the impress of a Greek origin, and the only Roman name in the poem is to be explained, so far as we can see, as merely a passing compliment. — Metre, 171.

1. **quantum distet**: *i.e.* in time. — **Inacho**: see II. 3. 21 n.

2. **Codrus**: the last king of Athens; said to have deliberately sacrificed his life in battle, like the Roman Decii, to ensure victory to his countrymen (Cic. *Tusc.* I. 116). — **mori**: Intr. 101 *a.*

3. **genus Aeaci**: Telamon and Peleus and their descendants, Ajax, Teucer, Achilles, Neoptolemus, etc.

4. **pugnata bella**: so also *Ep.* I. 16. 25. — **sacro Ilio**: after the Homeric Ἴλιος ἱρή (*e.g. Il.* IV. 46). For the gender, see I. 10. 14 n.

5. **quo**, etc.: the contemplated symposium is one towards which each guest contributes his share. — **Chium cadum**: cf. *Sabina diota*, I. 9. 7 n; III. 16. 34. The Chian was a choice Greek wine.

6. **aquam**: to mix with the wine.

7. **quo praebente**, etc.: *i.e.* at whose house and when? — **quota**: sc. *hora*; cf. *S.* II. 6. 44.

8. **Paelignis**: *i.e.* such as pre-

Da lunae propere novae,
da noctis mediae, da, puer, auguris
Murenae. Tribus aut novem
miscentur cyathis pocula commodis.
Qui Musas amat imparis,
ternos ter cyathos attonitus petet
vates; tris prohibet supra
rixarum metuens tangere Gratia
nudis iuncta sororibus.

vails in that mountainous region; cf. *Sithonia nive*, 26. 10.

9. **da,** *fill up*. The object to be supplied is *cyathos* (*vini*), which the cup-bearer was to pour into the guests' goblets. Cf. *sume cyathos*, 8. 13, addressed to the guest. The genitives that follow depend on this *cyathos* understood; see 8. 13 n. — **lunae novae**, etc.: three general toasts to begin the evening with, Horace having in mind no doubt the Greek practice of beginning a drinking bout with three libations. From the first we may infer that the time of the supposed revel was the new moon, or perhaps the first day of the month, which in Greek continued to be called *νουμηνία* (= *nova luna*) after the lunar month had been abandoned; **noctis mediae** implies that that hour was to be included in their programme; **auguris Murenae** is best explained as a toast in honor of Murena's accession to the college of augurs. Whether this was the Licinius Murena of II. 10 is uncertain. We do not know that Licinius Murena was ever augur, but he may have been; and we know of no other Murena who was a friend of Horace.

10. **da**: Intr. 116 *h*. — **puer**: see I. 19. 14 n; but we may perhaps imagine an actual boy here; cf. I. 29. 7 n.

11. **tribus aut novem cyathis**: expressing, not the quantity of wine in the cups, but the *proportion* of wine in the mixture. The Romans were in the habit of reckoning fractions by twelfths (*unciae*), and the cyathus, which as a measure was one twelfth of a sextarius, served as the *uncia* in mixing wine. *Tres cyathi*, then, meant $\frac{3}{12}$ wine (+ $\frac{9}{12}$ water); and *novem cyathi* = $\frac{9}{12}$ wine (+ $\frac{3}{12}$ water). — **aut**: the *magister* offers a choice between these alternatives only.

12. **commodis,** *at your pleasure;* proleptic, and having the force of an adverb with *miscentur*. For the meaning cf. IV. 8. 1.

13. **qui**, etc.: the bard himself, who seeks a strong inspiration, will name the number of the Muses as his choice, that is, he will take the stronger mixture; but he who fears the effect of too great exhilaration will choose the number of the gentle Graces (see 21. 22 n). — **imparis**: in reference to their number, nine.

14. **attonitus,** *rapt*. — **petet,** *will call for*.

15. **tris supra**: Intr. 115 *b*.

16. **rixarum metuens**: cf. *patiens pulveris*, I. 8. 4 n; III. 24. 22.

Insanire iuvat: cur Berecyntiae
cessant flamina tibiae?
Cur pendet tacita fistula cum lyra?
Parcentis ego dexteras
odi: sparge rosas; audiat invidus
dementem strepitum Lycus
et vicina seni non habilis Lyco.
Spissa te nitidum coma,
puro te similem, Telephe, Vespero
tempestiva petit Rhode;
me lentus Glycerae torret amor meae.

— **Gratia iuncta sororibus**: *i.e.* the three Graces (in their traditional posture); cf. *Gratia cum Nymphis geminisque sororibus*, IV. 7. 5 n.

18. **insanire iuvat**: cf. *dulce mihi furere*, II. 7. 28. — **Berecyntiae**: see I. 18. 13 n.

19. **tibiae**: see I. 1. 32 n. The Phrygian pipes were distinguished by the fact that one of the pair had a curved end which gave it a deeper tone; cf. Cat. 63. 22 *tibicen ubi canit Phryx curvo grave calamo.* Hence it was sometimes called a horn, as in I. 18. 13; cf. Ov. *F.* IV. 181 *inflexo Berecyntia tibia cornu.* See Howard, *Harv. Studies*, IV. p. 35.

20. **pendet**: *sc.* on the wall. — **fistula**: see I. 17. 10 n.

21. **dexteras**, *a hand.*

22. **sparge**: emphatic, implying a generous supply of the flowers, which in winter were more costly than usual. — **invidus**, *with envy*; proleptic.

23. **dementem**: cf. *dementis ruinas*, I. 37. 7, Intr. 124. — **Lycus**: the old fellow who lives near by with a young wife (apparently) who does not care for him, is introduced as a foil to set off the hilarity of the revelers, and at the same time leads to the suggestion of the *amica*, whose presence completes the poet's picture.

24. **vicina**, *our fair neighbor.* — **non habilis**: *i.e.* too young, — or rather, he is too old for her.

25. **spissa**: as far as possible from baldness. — **te . . . te**: corresponding to **Lycus . . . Lyco.** — **nitidum**, *who look so spruce*; here of the general effect of the person's make-up, as in II. 12. 19 and *S.* II. 1. 64 (not, as in I. 4. 9 and *nitentis capillos*, II. 7. 7, with special reference to the oil put on the hair).

26. **puro**: *i.e.* shining through a clear atmosphere; cf. *pura luna*, II. 5. 19; III. 10. 8. For the comparison, cf. 9. 21. — **Telephe**: one of the guests, addressed by name, as in I. 27. 10, to give a touch of personal interest to the scene.

27. **tempestiva**, *who* IS *suitable*: in contrast with **non habilis**, 24, and, as there, with more reference to the man than to the woman.

28. **lentus torret**: see I. 13 8 n.

## XX.

Non vides quanto moveas periclo,
Pyrrhe, Gaetulae catulos leaenae?
Dura post paulo fugies inaudax
proelia raptor,
cum per obstantis iuvenum catervas
ibit insignem repetens Nearchum:
grande certamen, tibi praeda cedat,
maior an illa.
Interim, dum tu celeres sagittas
promis, haec dentis acuit timendos,

XX. The subject of this ode is the attempt of a youth, who is called Pyrrhus, to win away the handsome boy Nearchus from the (unnamed) girl who claims him as her lover. The treatment is highly figurative, so much so that the reader needs to guard against losing sight of the actual story in the graphic metaphors. Pyrrhus is likened to the bold hunter who is preparing to carry off the lion's whelps; the girl to the she-lion who watches over them. Then, with a sudden shifting of the scene, the poet pictures the beautiful boy, complacently watching the impending contest. The Greek origin of the composition is apparent.—Metre, 174.

1. **moveas**, *disturb.*

2. **Gaetulae**: cf. I. 23. 10 n.

3. **post paulo**: the usual order, *paulo post* is avoided on account of its prosaic rhythm; so in the corresponding place in the hexameter, *Sat.* I. 2. 120, *Ep.* I. 6. 43. *Post paulo,* however, occurs also in prose.—**inaudax raptor**: the contrast (Intr. 116 *a*), amounts to an oxymoron: a robber and afraid! **inaudax** is not found elsewhere.

5. **iuvenum catervas**: these stand, in the metaphor, for the hunter's attendants,—the lioness will not be daunted by them; but the metaphor is for the moment put out of sight by the introduction of the boy in his proper person (**Nearchum**): the *iuvenes* are Pyrrhus' companions; the girl will rush boldly among them to recover the boy. The figure and the reality are here blended (Intr. 123), and after vs. 10 the figure is dropped entirely.

6. **insignem**, *peerless;* lit. 'conspicuous' (among all the rest); there is none like him.

7. **grande certamen**: in apposition with the action expressed or implied in the preceding verses, in which all the elements of a contest are set before us. Cf. *opus*, II. 1. 6 n.—**tibi praeda cedat**, *whether the prey* (Nearchus) *shall fall to you* (*i.e.* as the prize of victory); cf. Verg. *A.* XII. 183 *cesserit Ausonio si fors victoria Turno.*

8. **maior**: *i.e.* victorious.—**illa**: sc. *sit.*

arbiter pugnae posuisse nudo
sub pede palmam
fertur et leni recreare vento
sparsum odoratis umerum capillis,
qualis aut Nireus fuit aut aquosa
raptus ab Ida.

## XXI.

O nata mecum consule Manlio,

11. **posuisse,** *has placed;* present perfect.—**nudo**: simply a stroke to make the picture more graphic.

13. **fertur,** *I am told;* cf. 5.41 n. —**leni recreare,** etc.: as he stands there, the breeze blows his long locks about his bare shoulders.

15. **qualis,** *as fair as.* — **Nireus**: Νιρεύς, ὃς κάλλιστος ἀνὴρ ὑπὸ Ἴλιον ἦλθεν | τῶν ἄλλων Δαναῶν μετ' ἀμύμονα Πηλείωνα, *Il.* II. 673. Cf. *Epod.* 15. 22. — **aquosa**: *i.e.* rich in springs (πολυπίδακος Ἴδης, *Il.* XIV. 157).

16. **raptus**: Ganymede, son of Laomedon, ὃς δὴ κάλλιστος γένετο θνητῶν ἀνθρώπων (*Il.* XX. 233), carried off by the eagle of Jove to become cup-bearer to the gods. For this use of the participle, see Intr. 103.

XXI. M. Valerius Messala Corvinus, in whose honor this ode is written, had studied with Horace at Athens and fought with him at Philippi. He afterwards served with distinction under the triumvirs, — under Antony, as long as he could do so with self-respect, and then under Octavian, on whose side he fought at Actium. He was consul in the year of that battle, and afterwards earned a triumph (B.C. 27) by his successes against the Aquitanians. From this time on he abstained as much as possible from participation in public affairs, and devoted himself especially to practice in the courts, where his eloquence, which, when he was still very young, had won Cicero's commendation (*ad Brut.* I. 15. 1, B.C. 43), gave him great eminence (*S.* I. 10. 29). He was distinguished also by wealth and high social position, and by a nobility of character which shone through his presence and address (*quodammodo praeferens in dicendo nobilitatem suam*, Quint. X. 1. 113). He was devoted to literature, and gathered about him a circle of writers, the most famous of whom was Tibullus. The subject of the ode is the praise of wine. The poet stands before the *amphorae* in the *apotheca*, selecting one to be opened on the occasion of a visit from Messala, and gives utterance to his reflections on the potencies for good or ill with which the jar has stood charged this many a year. — Metre, 176.

1. **nata mecum**: *i.e.* filled and stored the year I was born. — **consule Manlio**: L. Manlius Torquatus, cos. B.C. 65. Cf. *Epod.* 13. 6 *tu vina Torquato move consule pressa meo.*

seu tu querellas sive geris iocos
seu rixam et insanos amores
seu facilem, pia testa, somnum,
quocumque lectum nomine Massicum
servas, moveri digna bono die,
descende, Corvino iubente
promere languidiora vina.
Non ille, quamquam Socraticis madet
sermonibus, te negleget horridus:
narratur et prisci Catonis
saepe mero caluisse virtus.
Tu lene tormentum ingenio admoves

2. **tu . . . geris**: Intr. 120. — **querellas**, *sighs*. It means doleful utterance of any sort, in opposition to the gayety expressed by **iocos**. — **geris**: *i.e.* potentially, to be brought to pass when the jar is opened.

3. **rixam et insanos amores**: cf. I. 13. 9 *sqq.*, 17. 25 *sqq.*

4. **facilem**: cf. II. 11. 8 n; III. 1. 20 *sqq.* — **pia**, *faithful;* as conscientiously keeping its charge. — **testa**: cf. I. 20. 2, III. 14. 20.

5. **quocumque nomine**, *on whatever account* (*i.e.* for whatever end); breaking off the unfinished list with a single comprehensive phrase, which we should introduce by 'in short'; cf. I. 28. 15 n. — **lectum Massicum**, *Massic vintage*. **lectum**, referring properly to the grapes ('gathered') is here used for the whole process of producing wine; cf. *arat*, 16. 26 n. For **Massicum**, see I. 1. 19 n.

6. **moveri**: *sc.* from its place in the *apotheca;* cf. *Epod.* 13. 6. For the inf., see Intr. 101 *e*. — **bono die**: the choicest wines were reserved for choice occasions (cf. I. 37. 5 n). The compliment to Corvinus is obvious.

7. **descende**: from the storeroom, in the upper part of the house; see 8. 11 n.

8. **promere**: depending on **iubente**. — **languidiora**: a quality acquired by long keeping; cf. *languescit*, 16. 35 n. The wine here would be perhaps forty years old.

9. **non ille**: cf. *non ego*, I. 18. 11 n. — **madet**, *is steeped; i.e.* is a philosopher through and through.

10. **negleget horridus**, *be so rude as to slight.*

11. **et**, *even*. — **prisci Catonis virtus**, *excellent old Cato;* see Intr. 126 *b*, and cf. Juv. 4. 81 *venit et Crispi iucunda senectus* ('cheerful old Crispus'). Horace is speaking of the elder Cato ('the Censor'); cf. *priscis Catonibus*, *Ep.* II. 2. 117. Cicero also represents him as fond of *modica convivia* (*de Sen.* 44 *sqq.*).

13. **tu**: see I. 10. 9 n. — **tormentum**, *spur* (literally, 'rack'); it stimulates the mind to give out its thoughts, as the rack draws

plerumque duro; tu sapientium
curas et arcanum iocoso
consilium retegis Lyaeo;
tu spem reducis mentibus anxiis
virisque et addis cornua pauperi,
post te neque iratos trementi
regum apices neque militum arma.
Te Liber et, si laeta aderit, Venus
segnesque nodum solvere Gratiae
vivaeque producent lucernae
dum rediens fugat astra Phoebus.

confession from the criminal. Cf. *Ep.* II. 3. 434 *reges dicuntur multis urgere culullis | et torquere mero quem perspexisse laborant.*

14. **plerumque duro**: *i.e.* not susceptible to ordinary influences; cf. Silius XI. 285 *Bacchi munera duram | laxarunt mentem.* For **plerumque**, cf. I. 34. 6 n. — **sapientium**: limiting **curas** only.

15. **curas**, *grave thoughts.*

16. **iocoso Lyaeo**, *with the merry 'Releaser'; i.e.* with wine, amid merriment. See I. 7. 22 n. There is nothing inconsistent in saying the wine-jar does these things 'with wine': the jar is personified.

18. **viris**: object of **addis**, for the position of which see Intr. 119 *a.* — **cornua**: the emblem of confidence and independence, like our 'holding up one's head'; cf. Ov. *Am.* III. 11. 3, 6 *scilicet adserui iam me, fugique catenas, | . . . venerunt capiti cornua sera meo,* and *A. A.* I. 239 *tum pauper cornua sumit* (an imitation of the present passage).

19. **post te**: cf. *post vina,* I. 18. 5; III. 7. 6. — **iratos apices**: Intr. 124. — **trementi**: transitive; Intr. 51 *a.*

20. **apices**: see I. 34. 14 n.

21. **te**: *i.e.* thy ministrations; very much as in vs. 19. — **Liber**: here the god himself; the favoring divinities whom the *cadus* serves will bless its work.

22. **nodum**: formed by the twining of their arms round one another; cf. 19. 17. — **solvere**: Intr. 101 *b.* — **Gratiae**: they stand for the charm of social converse, sparkling with wit, but ruled by courtesy, with nothing excessive or unseemly to mar its perfect enjoyment. Cf. 19. 16.

23. **vivae**: cf. *vigiles,* 8. 14. — **producent**: cf. *S.* I. 5. 70 *prorsus iucunde cenam producimus illam.* — **lucernae**: the personality of the divinities is, after all, half merged in the things they typify, — wine, love, gracious intercourse, — to which the lights are added as a fourth influence in prolonging the enjoyment.

## XXII.

Montium custos nemorumque virgo,
quae laborantis utero puellas
ter vocata audis adimisque leto,
diva triformis,
imminens villae tua pinus esto,
quam per exactos ego laetus annos
verris obliquum meditantis ictum
sanguine donem.

XXII. A dedicatory poem, in which Horace consecrates the towering pine that stands by his country house to Diana, and vows an annual sacrifice. The invocation to the goddess has much in common with Catullus' hymn (*c.* 34), especially with these verses (9–16):

> Montium domina ut fores
> silvarumque virentium
> saltuumque reconditorum
> amniumque sonantum.
> Tu Lucina dolentibus
> Iuno dicta puerperis,
> tu potens Trivia et notho es
> dicta lumine Luna.

— Metre, 174.

1. **custos**: so Neptune is *sacri custos Tarenti*, I. 28. 29; cf. Suet. *Dom.* 5 *novam excitavit aedem in Capitolio Custodi Iovi.*— **nemorum** (sc. *custos*): cf. I. 21. 5 *sqq.* In *C.S.* 1 she is *silvarum potens;* in Verg. *A.* XI. 557, *nemorum cultrix.* According to Servius (on *Georg.* III. 332) 'omnis quercus Iovi est consecrata, et omnis lucus Dianae.'

2. **quae laborantis**, etc.: cf. *C. S.* 13 *sqq.* Diana, in this capacity, was sometimes identified with Iuno Lucina; cf. Cat. *l.l.;* Cic. *D. N.* II. 68. — **puellas**: *i.e.* young women, at their first childbirth.

3. **ter**: see I. 28. 36 n. — **vocata**: cf. Ter. *Ad.* 487. — **adimis leto**: the opposite of *dare leto;* see 7. 17 n.

4. **triformis**: properly an epithet of Hecate, with whom Diana, owing to their many common attributes, was more or less confused; cf. Verg. *A.* IV. 511 *tergeminamque Hecaten, tria virginis ora Dianae.* The significance of the triple figure of Hecate has been variously explained in ancient and modern times; see Preller-Robert, *Gr. Myth.* I. 324.

5. **imminens villae**: a large tree, therefore, as we might suppose. — **tua**: predicate.

6. **quam donem**, *one on which I may bestow;* descriptive relative clause, defining the purport of **tua esto**. — **per exactos annos**, *on the completion of each year; i.e.* at each anniversary of the dedication. Cf. *pleno anno*, 18. 5 n, and, for the distributive force of **per**, II. 3. 6 n. — **laetus**: corresponding to the *lubens* of votive inscriptions; cf. Allen's *Early Remnants*, 69 n, 70, 111. 3, 113.

7. **obliquum ictum**: a reminiscence of the wild-boar hunt in the Odyssey, where the boar wounds Ulysses, λικριφὶς ἀΐξας (XIX. 451); so Ovid *M.* VIII. 344 *obliquo latrantes dissipat ictu.*—**meditantis**,

## XXIII.

Caelo supinas si tuleris manus
nascente luna, rustica Phidyle,
si ture placaris et horna
fruge Laris avidaque porca,
nec pestilentem sentiet Africum
fecunda vitis nec sterilem seges
robiginem aut dulces alumni
pomifero grave tempus anno.

*practicing*. The description, as in 13. 4 *sq.* and IV. 2. 57 *sqq.*, is a substitute for a more prosaic statement of the age of the victim,—a young boar whose tusks are just growing.

8. **donem**: the tree, by its dedication, becomes a sanctuary of the goddess, and, as such, the offering may be said to be bestowed upon it.

XXIII. A pure life and devout spirit needs no costly sacrifice to win the favor of heaven. To set forth this truth the poet represents himself as talking with a country woman,—a farmer's wife,—whose pious soul is troubled at the meagreness of the offerings which her narrow means allow her to make, and comforting her with the assurance that her prayers will be answered.—Metre, 176.

1. **caelo**: Intr. 53.—**supinas**: *i.e.* with the palms upward. This was the attitude assumed in prayer to the gods above; cf. Verg. *A.* III. 176; Liv. XXVI. 9. 7 (*matronae*) *nixae genibus, supinas manus ad caelum ac deos tendentes, orantesque.*—**si . . . si**: Intr. 116 *h.*

2. **nascente luna**: *i.e.* at the new moon. The offering was usually made, however, at least in the city, at the beginning of the calendar month; cf. Prop. V. 3. 53 *raris adsueta kalendis* | *vix aperit clausos una puella Lares.* See 19. 9 n.—**Phidyle**: Φειδύλη ('thrifty'; cf. φείδομαι); the name is apparently chosen to suit the character.

3. **ture**: cf. Tib. I. 3. 34 *reddere menstrua tura Lari.*—**horna fruge**: a bunch or wreath of the new grain. Cf. Tib. I. 10. 20 *stabat in exigua ligneus aede deus.* | *Hic placatus erat seu quis libaverat uvam* | *seu dederat sanctae spicea serta comae.* For **horna** (a poetical word) cf. *horna vina*, *Epod*, 2. 47.

4. **porca**: cf. 17. 15 n, *S.* II. 3. 165.

5. **nec**, etc.: for the position of the subjects in this strophe, see Intr. 116 *b.*—**pestilentem Africum**: the Sirocco; see II. 14. 15, 16 nn.

6. **fecunda**, *full-clustered.*—**sterilem**: Intr. 125.

7. **robiginem**: the seriousness of this evil to the Italian farmer may be inferred from the fact that Robigo (or Robigus) was worshipped as a god, and a day (*Robigalia*, April 25) set apart for a formal service of propitiation; see Ovid *Fast.* IV. 901 *sqq.*—**alumni**: see 18. 4 n.

8. **pomifero anno**: *i.e.* autumn;

Nam quae nivali pascitur Algido
devota quercus inter et ilices
aut crescit Albanis in herbis
victima pontificum securis

cervice tinguet: te nihil attinet
temptare multa caede bidentium
parvos coronantem marino
rore deos fragilique myrto.

cf. *annus hibernus*, *Epod.* 2. 29, and see 8. 9 n. — **grave**, *oppressive, sickly;* cf. Liv. III. 6. 2 *grave tempus et forte annus pestilens erat urbi agrisque, nec hominibus magis quam pecori;* see also II. 14. 15 n; *S.* II. 6. 18 *sq.*, Juv. 4. 56 *letifero autumno.*

9. **nivali Algido**: cf. *gelido Algido*, I. 21. 6 n. Here and on the Alban mount the college of pontiffs possessed pastures, in which victims were raised for the great public sacrifices. For the case of **Algido**, see Intr. 69.

10. **devota . . . victima**: Intr. 120.—**inter**: Intr. 115 *b.*

13. **tinguet**: Intr. 79.—**te nihil attinet**, *you have no occasion, it is not for you.*

14. **temptare**, *to beset.*—**bidentium**: a technical word for animals full-grown for sacrifice (about two years old). They were so named from the two prominent incisors which displace the two front milk teeth on the lower jaw of the sheep at about that age (Hyginus *ap.* Gell. XVI. 6. 14; Serv. on *Aen.* IV. 57).

15. **parvos**: the position brings out the incongruity of *multa caedes* with the small effigies which she decks with her simple garlands. The Lares were small figures of wood or bronze, or of more precious metal if the means of the family permitted; cf. Tib. I. 10. 20 (quoted above); Petron. 29 *Lares argentei;* Juv. 8. 110. The typical form was that of a youth in a sleeveless tunic, girded high (*succinctus*, Pers. 5. 31), holding a drinking-horn aloft in his right hand and a bowl in his left. See Baumeister, pp. 77, 811. Their altar was the hearth, on (or beside) which they stood; cf. *Epod.* 2. 66 n, and Plaut. *Aul.* 1 *sqq.*—**coronantem**, *whom you crown.* This service was enjoined oftener than once a month; cf. Cato, *R. R.* 143. 2 (*vilica*) *kalendis idibus nonis, festus dies cum erit, coronam in focum indat, per eosdemque dies Lari familiari pro copia supplicet;* Plaut. *Aul.* 23 *huic fília unast; éa mihi cotídie | aut túre aut vino aut áliqui semper súpplicat; | dat míhi coronas;* Juv. 9. 137 *o parvi nostrique Lares, quos ture minuto | aut farre et tenui soleo exorare corona.* — **marino rore**: in this order in Plin. XI. 38 and Col. IX. 4. 6. It is an aromatic shrub (rosemary), which was used in worship by people who could not afford incense.

16. **deos**: object of both **temptare** and **coronantem**; Intr. 76. — **fragili**, *brittle;* referring to the twigs used in the garland.—**myrto**: see I. 4. 9 n, and cf. I. 38. 5.

Immunis aram si tetigit manus,
non sumptuosa blandior hostia,
mollivit aversos Penatis
farre pio et saliente mica.

17. **immunis**, *guiltless, blameless.* In this sense it is not found elsewhere, except with a genitive, as *immunes caedis manus*, Ov. *Her.* 14. 8. Many editors, therefore, reject this interpretation and render the word 'bringing no gift,' citing IV. 12. 23 and *Ep.* I. 14. 33. But in neither of these places does *immunis* mean simply 'bringing no gift': in IV. 12. 23 it means 'exempt from the obligation to contribute' (ἀσύμβολος); in *Ep.* I. 14. 33, 'without being required to make presents.' In both cases it has its fundamental meaning, '*qui vacat a muneribus quae alii praestare debent*' (Forcellini). From this meaning Orelli deduced its use here: the hand that comes to the altar '*immunis*,' comes, not from any obligation to make an offering in atonement for sin, but purely as an expression of gratitude and piety, or to deprecate some undeserved calamity; **immunis** is then *immunis piaculi*, rather than *immunis sceleris.* At any rate, the meaning 'guiltless' appears to be required (as well as suggested) by the context. Innocence in the worshipper is the point on which the whole sentence turns. Under the other interpretation it is, no doubt, possible to get in this essential idea of innocence by restricting the application of the strophe to Phidyle, instead of taking it as the enunciation of a general truth; but this gives it only a subordinate place: the main thought is then 'bringing no gift' (for **immunis** is the emphatic word). And this, as a description of Phidyle, is in conflict both with vss. 3, 4, and with the last verse; for the *mola salsa* was regarded as an offering; cf. Plin. N. H. *Praef.* 11 *dis lacte rustici multaeque gentes et mola tantum salsa litant qui non habent tura.* But the language of the strophe is obscure, and its meaning much disputed.

18. **sumptuosa hostia**: instrumental abl. with the comparative, as in *altior ruinis*, 5. 40. The verse is commonly understood in a parenthetical and conditional sense, — 'it would gain nothing in persuasiveness by a costly offering.' But perhaps it is less harsh to take it as more direct, — 'without the aid of a costly victim to make it more persuasive.' This, of course, is only possible if we take **immunis** as 'guiltless.'

19. **mollivit**: Intr. 80. — **aversos**, *unwilling;* not 'hostile' (*adversos*), still less 'offended' (*iratos*), but needing to be melted to pity; cf. *Epod.* 10. 18. — **Penatis**: here not distinguished from the Lares; cf. Ov. *Tr.* I. 3. 43 *illa etiam ante Lares passis adstrata capillis* | *contigit extinctos ore tremente focos,* | *multaque in adversos effudit verba Penates.*

20. **farre**, etc.: a poetical paraphrase for *mola salsa* (cf. *fruges salsae*, Verg. *A.* II. 133), the mixture of crushed spelt and salt which was used in connection with all sacrifices; here it accompanies simple prayer. The ablatives are instrumental.—**saliente**: *i.e.* when thrown on the fire.

## XXIV.

Intactis opulentior
thesauris Arabum et divitis Indiae
caementis licet occupes
Tyrrhenum omne tuis et mare Apulicum,
si figit adamantinos
summis verticibus dira Necessitas
clavos, non animum metu,
non mortis laqueis expedies caput.

XXIV. In this ode Horace inveighs against the vice and corruption of the age with more than his wonted vigor. The root of the evil is the insatiable greed for wealth, which is deterred by no danger and scruples at no crime. Here is a chance for immortal fame! Who will seize it by mastering unbridled license, and putting it under the control of law? In place of futile complaints let us have punishment. But even laws will avail little against the evil, unless supported by a thoroughgoing reform in public sentiment. The ode is referred with some probability to the year 28 B.C. for the same reason that the sixth ode is assigned to that year (see introd. note to 6); but it may well have been earlier. It comes nearer than most of the odes of its class to the spirit of the sixteenth Epode. — Metre, 171.

1. **intactis**, etc.: the first sentence (vss. 1–8) consists of a concessive clause with **licet** (vss. 1–4), depending on a conditional sentence (vss. 5–8). — **intactis**: *i.e.* not yet reached by Roman conquest and plundered, as, for example, those of the rich provinces of Asia had been.

2. **thesauris Arabum**: cf. *Arabum gazis*, I. 29. 1. For the abl., see Intr. 75. — **divitis Indiae**: from very early times a thriving trade had been carried on between India and western Asia. The articles that found their way to Rome were for the most part of a very costly sort,— especially ivory, precious stones, silks, and fine cotton goods, — which naturally gave rise to a popular impression of great wealth in the land from which they came.

3. **caementis**: see 1. 33 *sqq.* nn.

4. **Tyrrhēnum**, etc.: *i.e.* though you line the whole coast of Italy with your seaside villas. — **Ăpūlicum**: see Crit. App. and cf. 4. 10 n.

5. **figīt**: Intr. 179.

6. **summis verticibus**: *i.e.* those of your palaces. The rich man in his luxurious mansions is as helpless in the face of his doom as the poorest beggar in his hut. The same thought is put in another way in II. 18. 18 *sqq.* and 29 *sqq.;* but there, as here, the figure is suggested by the building operations of the rich man himself. **verticibus** is probably ablative (Intr. 69). — **Necessitas**: cf. I. 35. 17 n.

7. **clavos**: the driving of the

Campestres melius Scythae,
quorum plaustra vagas rite trahunt domos,
vivunt et rigidi Getae,
immetata quibus iugera liberas
fruges et Cererem ferunt,
nec cultura placet longior annua,
defunctumque laboribus
aequali recreat sorte vicarius.
Illic matre carentibus
privignis mulier temperat innocens,

nail signifies unalterable doom (see I. 35. 18 n), here the doom of death, from which he can find no escape in his palaces, any more than in the speed of horses or triremes (1. 38 *sqq.*).

8. **mortis laqueis**: cf. *O T. Psalms* 18. 5.

9. **campestres,** *of the steppes;* put first to bring this feature of nomad life, which is expanded in the next verse, into clearer contrast with the palace-building Romans. For the epithet, cf. *profugi Scythae*, I. 35. 9; IV. 14. 42.

10. **quorum**: better taken with **domos.** — **vagas,** *from place to place;* proleptic.— **rite,** *such is their custom; i.e.* it is not exceptional, but the regular thing among them.

11. **rigidi,** *rigorous;* cf. *Ep.* I. 1. 17; II. 1. 25 *rigidis Sabinis.* — **Getae**: they occupied the plains between the Transylvanian Alps and the Danube (Wallachia).

12. **immetata**: not divided up for individual ownership.—**liberas**: *i.e.* common to all.

13. **Cererem**: Intr. 130.

14. **annua**: ablative. Horace here ascribes to the Getae the custom which Caesar records of the Suevi, *B. G.* IV. 1. In contrast with the avarice of Roman land-owners, these simple communities raise only as much produce each year as is needed for their own sustenance, and the work of tillage can be done by a limited number of persons, whose places are taken (**vicarius**) at the end of the year by another squad on the same terms.

15. **defunctum laboribus**: cf. *functum laboribus*, II. 18. 38.

16. **aequali sorte**: abl. of manner.

17. **illic,** etc.: here begins the exposition of the thought in *melius vivunt* (9, 11): simple habits of life are conducive to virtuous living. Like Tacitus in the *Germania*, Horace invests his barbarians with something of the halo of a golden age, to emphasize the contrast with the vices of Rome. The whole force of the comparison, as in 6. 17 *sqq.*, is directed against the women, their husbands and sons being reserved for treatment later in the ode. — **matre carentibus,** *motherless* (*orbis*); a favorite form of paraphrase with Horace; cf. 26. 10 n, I. 28. 1 n.

18. **temperat,** *treats with forbearance;* cf. Cic. *Verr.* II. 2. 4 *superatis hostibus temperavit.* For the proverbial severity of a *no-*

nec dotata regit virum
coniunx, nec nitido fidit adultero ;
dos est magna parentium
virtus et metuens alterius viri
certo foedere castitas,
et peccare nefas aut pretium est mori.
O quisquis volet impias
caedis et rabiem tollere civicam,
si quaeret pater urbium
subscribi statuis, indomitam audeat

*verca*, see note on *patruae*, 12. 1.— **innocens**, *keeping herself blameless;* a part of the predicate.

19. **nec dotata**, etc., *no wife with great dowry*, etc.; *i.e.* there exists no such phenomenon at all among them. — **regit virum**: cf. Plaut. *Men.* 766 *ita ístaec solént quae virós subservíre | sibí postulánt dote frétae, feróces ; Aul.* 532 *sqq.;* Martial. VIII. 12. If a marriage was dissolved at the instance of the husband, he was obliged to surrender the dowry, or the greater part of it, — a rule that gave to wealthy married women a large measure of independence.

20. **nitido**: cf. 19. 25 n and *S.* II. 1. 64. — **fidit**: *i.e.* for aid and comfort against her husband. With this verb **dotata** is not understood as part of the subject; rather **fidit adultero** is parallel to **dotata regit.**

21. **magna**: with **dos.** — **parentium virtus**: as a guaranty of pure blood and a wholesome moral training.

22. **metuens**, *that shrinks from;* cf. 19. 16 n, and *metuit tangi*, 11. 10. It stands in contrast with *fidit*, above, as **dos**, etc., with *dotata*. — **alterius**: see 5. 34 n.

23. **certo foedere**: a loosely attached descriptive ablative, characterizing the *castitas* as an obligation mutually binding and never violated.

24. **nefas**: sc. *est*, parallel with *est* in vs. 21, *illic* being understood with both. — **aut**: see 12. 1 n. It follows the idea of prohibition in **nefas.** — **pretium**: cf. Juv. 13. 105 *ille crucem sceleris pretium tulit, hic diadema.*

25. **quisquis volet . . . si quaeret**: not different in sense from *si quis volet . . . et quaeret.* If any one wishes to secure immortal fame by putting away civil strife and bloodshed from the state, let him strike at the root of the evil in the rampant licentiousness of the times. — **impias**: see II. 1. 30 n.

26. **civicam**: see II. 1. 1 n.

27. **si quaeret**, etc.: *i.e.* if he seeks to have his name inscribed on the pedestals of statues in numerous cities, with the title 'Pater Vrbis' or the like. *Pater* was a common term of honor for a public benefactor, as *pater patriae, pater senatus*, etc. (see II. 1. 50 n); and possibly Horace intended the word in this general sense here, so that **urbium** should be taken

refrenare licentiam,
clarus post genitis, — quatenus, heu nefas!
virtutem incolumem odimus,
sublatam ex oculis quaerimus invidi.
Quid tristes querimoniae,
si non supplicio culpa reciditur,
quid leges sine moribus
vanae proficiunt, si neque fervidis
pars inclusa caloribus
mundi nec Boreae finitimum latus

with **statuis**; but cf. Stat. *Silv.* III. 4. 48 *pater inclitus ùrbis* (of Domitian); CIL. III. 2907 PARENS · COLONIAE, XI. 3083 PATR · PATRIAE · ET · MUNICIP (both of Augustus).

28. **subscribi**: Intr. 94 *c*.

29. **refrenare licentiam**: cf. IV. 15. 9 *sqq*.

30. **clarus**: sc. *futurus* (*and he will be*). — **post genitis**: a paraphrase for *posteris* not found elsewhere. — **quatenus**, *in as much as* (so also *S*. I. 1. 64); an archaic use of the word (Festus, p. 258) revived by the Augustan poets, from whom it was received into later prose (*e.g.* Vell. II. 68. 4; Tac. *Ann.* III. 16. 5). It here introduces the reason of **post genitis**: the true benefactors of their race are not appreciated in their lifetime; cf. *Ep.* II. 1. 5–14. — **heu nefas**: cf. IV. 6. 17.

31. **incolumem**, *in the living*.

32. **quaerimus**: for *requirimus* (Intr. 129), in the sense of *desideramus*, *we mourn*. — **invidi**: this belongs with both verbs: the spirit which stones the prophets and that which builds their tombs are one and the same. The glory of the dead is used to disparage the living. Cf. *Ep.* II. 1. 88 *sq*.

33. **quid**, etc.: the reformer's work must be unpopular, because no gentle measures will do; he must attack the evil with pains and penalties. — **tristes**, *dismal*.

34. **reciditur**: cf. *S*. I. 3. 122 *et magnis parva* (sc. *delicta*) *mineris* | *falce recisurum simili te*. The metaphor of pruning, keeping back (**re-**) luxuriant growth, is appropriate here; cf. *refrenare*, above.

35. **sine moribus vanae**, *which are*, etc. These words express the general truth exemplified in the clauses that follow. In English we should be more likely to state it in a separate sentence: 'Laws with no moral sentiment behind them are futile; what good do they do (for example) if the passion for wealth has so completely taken the place of right principles in a man's mind that no hardship or peril can deter him from the pursuit of his object?' With **leges sine moribus**, cf. IV. 5. 22 *mos et lex*; Tac. *Ger.* 19 *plus ibi boni mores valent quam alibi bonae leges*.

37. **pars**: as in 3. 55. — **inclusa**, *intrenched*; in the same sense as *domibus negata*, I. 22. 22.

38. **latus**: sc. *mundi*; cf. I. 22. 19.

durataeque solo nives
mercatorem abigunt, horrida callidi
vincunt aequora navitae,
magnum pauperies opprobrium iubet
quidvis et facere et pati,
virtutisque viam deserit arduae?
Vel nos in Capitolium,
quo clamor vocat et turba faventium,
vel nos in mare proximum
gemmas et lapides aurum et inutile,

39. **duratae,** *frozen hard, never melting.* — **solo**: Intr. 69.

40. **mercatorem**: a favorite type with Horace of restless activity: cf. I. 1. 16, *S.* I. 1. 6, *Ep.* I. 1. 45. — **horrida callidi**: Intr. 116 *a.* For the asyndeton in this sentence, cf. 18. 9 *sqq.*

42. **magnum opprobrium,** *as a great,* etc.; cf. *S.* II. 3. 91 *sq.* — **pauperies**: see I. 1. 18 n.—**iubet,** etc.: cf. *Ep.* I. 1. 46 *per mare pauperiem fugiens, per saxa, per ignis.*

43. **quidvis**: any and everything, without distinction (of right or wrong); cf. *omne,* 3. 52 n. — **et facere et pati**: cf. Livy II. 12. 9 *et facere et pati fortia Romanum est.*

44. **virtutis viam**: *i.e.* the path which Virtue prescribes, and which leads to her, as in Hes. *Op.* 289 τῆς δ' ἀρετῆς ἱδρῶτα θεοὶ προπάροιθεν ἔθηκαν | ἀθάνατοι· μακρὸς δὲ καὶ ὄρθιος οἶμος ἐς αὐτήν. — **deserit**: *deserere,* depending on **iubet,** which Bentley wished to read, would be more strictly consistent; but the personification of **pauperies** with **iubet** is no more than a figure of speech; here it becomes vivid, and **pauperies,** before a mere abstraction, is invested with the qualities and actions of the *pauper.* The same thing occurs in *paupertas impulit audax ut versus facerem, Ep.* II. 2. 51. Cf. also *indulgens sibi hydrops,* II. 2. 13 n, and *virtus temptat iter,* III. 2. 21. — **arduae**: Intr. 124.

45. In an access of poetic fervor, which may remind us of *Epode* 16, Horace calls for a general sacrifice of the costly luxuries which are the source of so much evil: no change of heart is genuine which does not engender a contempt for these things. — **in Capitolium**: *i.e.* as an offering to Jove; see 30. 8 n. The reader will supply the missing verb for himself before reaching **mittamus,** so that the adaptation of the latter to the second proposition does no violence to the sense.

46. **clamor et turba**: *i.e.* a shouting crowd; Intr. 126 *a.*—**vocat**: *i.e.* such a reception awaits us. Horace imagines a procession of rich citizens marching to the Capitol, each carrying his valuables, with applauding throngs lining the way, as in a triumph.

48. **gemmas et lapides**: it is not clear that these stood for distinct classes of precious stones.

summi materiem mali,
mittamus, scelerum si bene paenitet.
Eradenda cupidinis
pravi sunt elementa et tenerae nimis
mentes asperioribus
formandae studiis. Nescit equo rudis
haerere ingenuus puer
venarique timet, ludere doctior,
seu Graeco iubeas trocho,
seu malis vetita legibus alea,

we know, for example, that pearls were called by both names. The mention of the two is simply for greater fullness of expression, — *jewels and precious stones.*—**aurum et**: Intr. 114. — **inutile,** *good for nothing;* with something more than a merely negative force.

49. **materiem**: cf. Sal. *Cat.* 10 *primo pecuniae, deinde imperi cupido crevit; ea quasi materies omnium malorum fuere,* where *quasi* shows that Sallust was still conscious of the metaphor in *materies* (the 'stuff' of which these evils are made).

50. **bene**: *i.e.* sincerely.

51. **eradenda,** etc.: coming down to a more practical view of the problem, Horace urges that contempt for luxury be inculcated by a healthier moral and physical training of youth; cf. 2. 1 *sqq.*, 6. 37 *sqq.*

52. **elementa,** *the germs.* — **tenerae nimis**: *i.e.* those which are now *over-indulged* must (instead) be moulded, etc.

54. **studiis,** *training.* — **equo**: Intr. 71. — **rudis**: reinforcing **nescit** and opposed to **doctior**: 'Put him in the saddle, he is awkward and doesn't know how to keep his seat; tell him to play, he will show his proficiency, whether it be with, etc.'

55. **haerere**: Intr. 94 *o.* — **ingenuus**: it might be excusable in a slave or freedman.

56. **venari**: Intr. 94 *l.*—**ludere**: Intr. 101 *c.*

57. **seu . . . seu**: for the use of these conjunctions, see I. 4. 12 n. — **Graeco,** for the contrast between the traditional Roman forms of exercise, such as hunting and riding (*Romanis sollemne viris opus*, *Ep.* I. 18. 49), which were valued as good training for a soldier (hence called *militia*), and the athletic sports imported from Greece, cf. *S.* II. 2. 9 *sqq.* The *trochus* is named with the *pila* and *discus*, *Ep.* II. 3. 379 *sq.*, among the '*arma*' of the Campus (see I. 8. 10 n). — **iubeas, malis**: sc. *eum ludere.* For the construction of the ablatives, cf. *S.* I. 5. 49 *pilā ludere.*

58. **vetita legibus**: Cicero mentions a condemnation for gambling in his time (*Phil.* 2. 56) and elsewhere classes *aleatores* with '*omnes impuri impudicique*' (*in Cat.* 2. 23); but in Horace's day the law was obviously much neglected. Ovid speaks of treatises written to teach the game (*Tr.* II. 471 *sqq.*).

cum periura patris fides
consortem socium fallat et hospites,
indignoque pecuniam
heredi properet. Scilicet improbae
crescunt divitiae: tamen
curtae nescio quid semper abest rei.

## XXV.

Quo me, Bacche, rapis tui
plenum? Quae nemora aut quos agor in specus
velox mente nova? Quibus
antris egregii Caesaris audiar

59. **cum fallat, properet**: the *cum*-clause here defines the character of the situation by an added picture; see Hale's *Cum-Constructions*, p. 191. In English we should rather begin a new sentence, *Meanwhile, etc.* — **periura fides**: see I. 5. 5 n.

60. **consortem socium**, *his partner*. In mercantile language *sors* is capital.—**hospites**: cf. *perfidus hospitam*, I. 15. 2 n.

61. **pecuniam properet**: cf. *deproperare coronas*, II. 7. 24 n.

62. **scilicet**, *yes;* introducing the poet's reflections on the picture he has just drawn: Wealth goes right on growing, in spite of morality and honor and everything else (**improbae**), but it is forever doomed to fail to satisfy its possessor; 'semper avarus eget' (*Ep.* I. 2. 56). — **improbae**, *graceless.*

64. **curtae**: proleptic, expressing the aspect which the property (**rei**) presents to its covetous owner.

XXV. This short ode is a tribute to Augustus, whose glory is heralded none the less effectively because it is mentioned only incidentally, as it were, in a poem which purports to be merely the prelude to a greater work. The ode is cast in dithyrambic form: the poet represents himself as hurried away by the irresistible power of Bacchus to the wilds, haunted of nymph and maenad, where, under the joyous inspiration of the god himself, he shall rise to the level of his lofty theme. Whether the ode was called forth by some particular occasion does not appear. — Metre, 171.

1. **tui plenum**: cf. *pleno Bacchi pectore*, II. 19. 6.

2. **agor in**: Intr. 119 *a*.

3. **velox mente nova**: he feels like a changed being, moved by swift impulses. These are characteristic of orgiastic possession; cf. Cat. 63. 19 *mora tarda mente cedat*, and the whole picture there portrayed.

4. **antris**: dative (Intr. 54), — 'What caves shall hear me?' He is not thinking of an audience in the caves.— **egregii**: see I. 6. 11 n. — **audiar**: future; a question of fact, like *quo rapis*, *etc.*, above.

aeternum meditans decus
stellis inserere et consilio Iovis?
Dicam insigne, recens, adhuc
indictum ore alio. Non secus in iugis
exsomnis stupet Euhias,
Hebrum prospiciens et nive candidam
Thracen ac pede barbaro
lustratam Rhodopen, ut mihi devio
ripas et vacuum nemus
mirari libet. O Naiadum potens
Baccharumque valentium
proceras manibus vertere fraxinos,

5. **aeternum**: proleptic.—**meditans**, *essaying in song*. The word is used not only of silent composition, but of bursts of song, as **audiar** shows (cf. Verg. *E*. 6. 82 *omnia quae Phoebo quondam meditante beatus | audiit Eurotas*); yet enough of the idea of contemplation is still present to attach an infinitive to, and **inserere** is rather complementary (Intr. 94 *f*) than infinitive of purpose.

6. **stellis inserere**, etc.: *i.e.* to extol to heaven. For **stellis**, cf. *arcis attigit igneas*, 3. 10 n.

7. **dicam**: the subject of my song will be, etc.; see I. 6. 5 n.—**insigne**: cf. I. 12. 39 *insigni camena*.—**recens**, *fresh*; not hackneyed.

8. **indictum**, etc.: cf. *Ep*. I. 19. 32 *non alio dictum prius ore*.—**non secus**, etc.: the picture is that of a Thracian bacchante who has come upon a height (**iugis**) where a view of the whole valley of the Hebrus, with Rhodope beyond, bursts upon her, and stands gazing in rapture at the beautiful scene.

9. **exsomnis**: because in the full flush of her frenzy; every nerve is alive. Sleep comes with the reaction from this excitement (cf. Cat. 63. 35 *sq*.).

11. **pede barbaro lustratam**: *i.e.* inhabited by a foreign people; she has strayed far away into a strange land.

12. **ut**: with **non secus**, instead of the usual *ac*, which would be harsh after **ac** in vs. 11; cf. Plaut. *Aul*. 22 *paritér moratum ut páter avosque huiŭs fuit;* Plin. *Ep*. I. 20. 1 *cui nihil aeque in causis agendis ut brevitas placet.*

13. **ripas**: used absolutely, as in I. 23 and IV. 2. 31.—**vacuum**, *untenanted;* repeating the idea implied in **devio**. Intr. 119 *a*.

14. **mirari**: see I. 4. 19 n.—**Naiadum potens**: cf. II. 19. 3.

15. **valentium**, etc.: the allusion is to the destruction of Pentheus by the bacchantes, who tore up by the roots the tree in which he sat (Eurip. *Bacch*. 1109). It is mentioned to recall the superhuman power which the inspiration of Bacchus confers.

16. **vertere**: for *evertere;* Intr. 129. For the mood, see Intr. 94 *n*

nil parvum aut humili modo,
nil mortale loquar. Dulce periculum est,
O Lenaee, sequi deum
cingentem viridi tempora pampino.

## XXVI.

Vixi puellis nuper idoneus
et militavi non sine gloria :
nunc arma defunctumque bello
barbiton hic paries habebit,
laevum marinae qui Veneris latus
custodit. Hic, hic ponite lucida

17. **nil,** etc.: my song shall be elevated both in matter and manner. — **parvum** : cf. 3. 72.

18. **mortale**: *i.e.* of mere human inspiration. — **dulce,** *fascinating*. — **periculum** : because the near presence of the god is overpowering. The same mingling of joy and fear is expressed II. 29. 5 *sqq.*

19. **Lenaee**: supposed to mean 'god of the wine-press' (ληνός). — **deum,** *a god.*

20. **cingentem,** etc.: repeated in the suspected verse, IV. 8. 33, with the necessary change of **cingentem** to *ornatus*. Here, however, it is more natural to take **cingentem** with the subject of **sequi,** understood, — the poet.

XXVI. Our poet will have no more of love. He has acquitted himself in that field not without glory; now he will hang up his arms in Venus' shrine, for he has no longer any taste for her service. Only at the very end he lets a little word escape him which betrays the humorous aspect of the situation : it is Chloe's hard heart that is at the bottom of it all. — Metre, 176.

1. **vixi** : the perfect definite, implying 'it is all over now.' — **puellis idoneus** : *i.e.* capable of making himself agreeable to them. — **nuper,** *till lately.*

2. **militavi** : the figure is a common one ; cf. IV. 1. 2; Ov. *Am.* I. 9. 1 *militat omnis amans et habet sua castra Cupido.*

4. **hic paries,** etc. : *i.e.* the side of the shrine on the right (as you looked at it) of the image of the goddess. It was customary to dedicate implements or other tokens of completed service ; cf. *Ep.* I. 1. 4 *Veranius* (a gladiator) *armis | Herculis ad postem fixis ; S.* I. 5. 65, where a former slave is asked *donasset iamne catenam | ex voto Laribus.*

5. **laevum** : there appears to be no special significance in the choice of this side. — **marinae** : as being sea-born and exercising power over the sea ; cf. I. 3. 1 n; IV. 11. 15.

6. **hic, hic** : Intr. 116 *d.* — **ponite** : addressed to the slaves who carry the articles referred to ; cf.

funalia et vectis et arcus
oppositis foribus minacis.
O quae beatam diva tenes Cyprum et
Memphin carentem Sithonia nive,
regina, sublimi flagello
tange Chloen semel arrogantem.

## XXVII.

Impios parrae recinentis omen

I. 19. 14. — **lucida**: expressing not their present condition, but their essential property.

7. **funalia**: used for going about at night, since the streets were not lighted. See Juv. 3. 282 *sqq.* — **vectis**: to pry open doors where admittance was refused: cf. Ter. *Eun.* 773 *primum aedis expugnabo. . . . In medium huc agmen cum vecti, Donax!* — **arcus**: unless this is the name of some implement for forcing doors, the text is probably corrupt. If we could imagine the lover going about armed with bow and arrows on such an expedition, it would still be difficult to see why he should threaten barred doors with them.

8. **foribus**: Intr. 58 *a*.

9. **quae tenes Cyprum**: cf. I. 3. 1, 30. 2, and for this use of *teneo*, III. 4. 62 n. — **beatam**: Cyprus was an island of great and varied resources; cf. I. 1. 13 n.

10. **Memphin**: Herodotus (II. 112) mentions a sanctuary ξείνης Ἀφροδίτης there.— **carentem**, etc.: a poetical paraphrase for 'where it never snows'; cf. *matre carentibus*, 24. 17 n. — **Sithonia**: see I. 18. 9 n, and cf. Verg. *E.* 10. 66; Intr. 117.

11. **regina**: cf. I. 30. 1. — **sublimi**, *uplifted*.

12. **semel**, *just once*; cf. I. 24. 16 n.

XXVII. The story of Europa. The myth is treated on a plan similar to that of the eleventh ode. As a setting for his picture Horace has here, as there, constructed a situation: his imaginary friend Galatea is about to set out on a journey to the East; he reluctantly bids her farewell, with a prayer for good omens and friendly words of warning against the treachery of the sea, through all of which runs an undercurrent of unspoken protest at her incurring such risk; he thinks of her on the sea at night, with nothing but the waves about her and the stars overhead, and this recalls the lonely ride of Europa on the back of the bull. In dealing with the subject, as in the case of Hypermnestra, he disposes of the familiar features of the story briefly (vss. 25–32, 73–76), or by allusion, and selects for lyrical treatment a single scene, — the remorse and despair of Europa when she is left alone on the shore of Crete. — Metre, 174.

1. **impios**: emphatic. The sense is, 'May all bad omens be spent in confounding the wicked: I will

ducat et praegnans canis aut ab agro
rava decurrens lupa Lanuvino
fetaque volpes;
rumpat et serpens iter institutum,
si per obliquum similis sagittae
terruit mannos: ego cui timebo
providus auspex,
antequam stantis repetat paludes
imbrium divina avis imminentum,

guard her whose safety I have at heart by calling up a good sign to anticipate and counteract whatever there may be of evil import.' With the idea, which we have here and in vss. 21 *sqq.*, of diverting (rather than averting) ill by directing its force elsewhere, cf. the prayers in I. 28. 25 *sqq.* and *Epod.* 5. 53 *sqq.* — **parrae**: this bird is mentioned also by Plautus (*Asin.* 260) as an ominous fowl, and by Festus (p. 197) as classed with both *oscines* and *alites* (see vs. 11 n); but it has not been identified. For this reason the precise meaning of **recinentis** cannot be determined, but it probably expresses a droning repetition of the note; cf. *Ep.* I. 1. 55.

2. **ducat,** *attend . . . on their way.* — **agro Lanuvino**: Lanuvium was situated on a height, to the right of the Appian Way, beyond Aricia. Horace has in mind a journey to Greece or Asia, by the Appian Way to Brundisium and thence by sea; cf. vss. 19 *sq.* The uncertainties of so long a journey would invest such omens as are here mentioned with unspeakable terror in the mind of the average Roman, who was a very superstitious person.

3. **rava**: cf. *Epod.* 16. 33 *ravos leones.*

5. **rumpat** (sc. *impiis*): not simply 'interrupt' by frightening the horses, but *break off*, as **institutum** shows. The superstitious traveller would feel it necessary to go back and begin the journey anew, after due expiatory offerings.

6. **per obliquum**: modifying the idea of darting implied in **similis sagittae**, though grammatically attached to **terruit.**

7. **mannos,** *ponies;* the Celtic name of a Gallic breed of horses, small in size, fashionable for driving; cf. *Epod.* 4. 14, *Ep.* I. 7. 77. — **ego**: the emphasis falls on this word because the person contrasted with **impios** is not definitely expressed, but appears only as one in whom the poet is interested; as if we should say 'May all evil signs go to plague the wicked; for *my* friends I will pray, etc.' — **cui**: suggesting its antecedent in the same case. The future **timebo** makes the reference indefinite; but of course he means Galatea.

9. **stantis,** *stagnant.*

10. **divina,** *prophetic;* with the objective genitive, as *Ep.* II. 3. 218 *divina futuri;* Intr. 66 *b.* — **avis**: the crow (*cornix*); cf. 17. 12 n.

oscinem corvum prece suscitabo
  solis ab ortu.

Sis licet felix, ubicumque mavis,
et memor nostri, Galatea, vivas,
teque nec laevus vetet ire picus
  nec vaga cornix.

Sed vides quanto trepidet tumultu
pronus Orion? Ego quid sit ater

11. **oscinem**: an augural term, used of birds whose notes were observed in divination, in distinction from those called *alites* (cf. 3. 61) or *praepetes* (Verg. *A.* III. 361), whose flight was regarded as significant. All the birds mentioned in this ode, together with the owl (*noctua*) are mentioned by Festus (*l. l.*) as belonging to the first class; the vulture and the eagle are examples of the second (cf. Liv. I. 7. 1; Tac. *Ann.* II. 17. 2).

12. **solis ab ortu**: a favorable quarter; see below, vs. 15 n.

13. **sis licet**, etc.: after this general introduction, he addresses Galatea directly with parting words of good will and friendly warning. — **sis**: optative subjunctive, to which **licet** is joined paratactically to intimate that he interposes no objection (as 'providus auspex') to her going. For this use of **licet**, cf. Plaut. *Rud.* 139 *meá quidem hercle caúsa salvos sís licet*; Ovid *M.* III. 405 *sic amet ipse licet, sic non potiatur amato.* It is akin to *per me licet.*

14. **memor nostri**: apparently a formula of parting; cf. Juv. 3. 318, *vale nostri memor.* For *nostri*, cf. 28. 9 n.

15. **laevus**, *ill-boding.* There is a confusion in the use of this word, owing to the fact that, whereas from its application to the left hand there naturally grew up about it the meaning of 'awkward, untoward, unlucky,' — the opposite of *dexter* (cf. *dextro tempore*, *S.* II. 1. 18, with *tempore laevo*, *S.* II. 4. 4), — in Roman augury it came to have just the opposite meaning, because, as the *auspex* sat facing south, the east, which was the favorable quarter (see above, vs. 12 n) was on his left. The same is true of *sinister.* The Roman poets constantly use both words in the sense of 'inauspicious,' either following the common as opposed to technical usage or, perhaps, under the influence of their Greek models; for in Greek divination δεξιὸς ὄρνις was a lucky sign, and ἀριστερός unlucky.

16. **cornix**: see vs. 10 n, and cf. Verg. *E.* 9. 14 *nisi me | ante sinistra cava monuisset ab ilice cornix.*

17. **trepidet**: to the poet's vivid imagination, the constellation itself seems to tremble with the excitement of the storm which it brings.

18. **pronus Orion**: equivalent to *devexus Orion*, I. 28. 21 n. — — **ater**: *i.e.* in the darkness of the storm (cf. II. 16. 2 n), but with the implication which attaches to the word; see I. 28. 13 n.

Hadriae novi sinus et quid albus
peccet Iapyx.
Hostium uxores puerique caecos
sentiant motus orientis Austri et
aequoris nigri fremitum et trementis
verbere ripas.
Sic et Europe niveum doloso
credidit tauro latus et scatentem
beluis pontum mediasque fraudes
palluit audax.
Nuper in pratis studiosa florum et
debitae Nymphis opifex coronae,
nocte sublustri nihil astra praeter
vidit et undas.

19. **Hadriae sinus**: called *Ionius sinus*, *Epod.* 10. 19. — **novi**: Horace had probably crossed it on his way to Greece (Intr. 7).— **albus**: cf. *candidi Favonii*, 7. 1, *albus Notus*, I. 7. 15, and see Intr. 125. It stands here in contrast with **ater**; Intr. 116 *c*.

20. **peccet**, *plays tricks*; he is fair, but not to be trusted. — **Iapyx**: see I. 3. 4 n.

21. **hostium**: cf. Verg. *G.* III. 513 *di meliora piis erroremque hostibus illum!* and see vs. 1 n, above. — **uxores puerique**: those who are dear to the enemy, not one (Galatea) who is dear to us.— **caecos motus**: *i.e.* squalls, coming without warning; cf. *caeca fata*, II. 13. 16.

22. **sentiant**: cf. II. 7. 9 *Philippos et celerem fugam | sensi.*— **orientis**: unusual for *surgentis*, *e.g.* Verg. *A.* III. 481 *surgentis Austros.*

23. **aequoris**, etc.: observe the resonance of these verses, due mainly to the persistent *r*-sounds; Intr. 131. — **nigri**: cf. *ater*, vs. 18 n.

24. **verbere**: *sc.* of the surf. — **ripas**: see I. 2. 14 n.

25. **sic**: *i.e.* with the same readiness that you show to venture upon the sea. Horace represents Europa as having *voluntarily* taken her ride through the water; see vs. 42 n. — **et**, *too.* — **Europe**: the story is told by Ovid, *M.* II. 836 *sqq.*, *Fast.* V. 605 *sqq.* — **doloso credidit**: cf. *perfidis se credidit*, 5. 33; Intr. 116 *a*.

26. **latus**: cf. II. 7. 18. — **scatentem beluis**: cf. I. 3. 18 n.

27. **medias**, *all about her;* she had come *in medias fraudes.* — **fraudes**, *dangers;* lit. 'pitfalls.' For the accusatives, see Intr. 51 *a*.

28. **palluit audax**, *braved with blanched cheek.* The oxymoron is the result of the substitution for some colorless word like *vidit* (cf. I. 3. 19) of one that paints the danger on her face.

29. **nuper**: emphatic, in con-

Quae simul centum tetigit potentem
oppidis Creten, 'Pater, — o relictum
filiae nomen, pietasque' dixit
'victa furore!

Vnde quo veni? Levis una mors est
virginum culpae. Vigilansne ploro
turpe commissum, an vitiis carentem
ludit imago

vana, quae porta fugiens eburna
somnium ducit? Meliusne fluctus

trast with her present situation (**nocte sublustri**, etc.); cf. *plerumque* I. 34. 7.

30. **debitae**: *i.e.* vowed.

31. **praeter**: Intr. 115 *b*.

33. **quae simul**, etc.: Horace follows a form of the myth, according to which the bull disappears, on landing in Crete, and Europa is left alone awhile till Jupiter returns in his proper shape to claim her as his bride. It is here that, with the reaction from the excitement of the ride, remorse sets in. — **simul**: see I. 4. 17 n. — **centum oppidis**: after the Homeric Κρήτην ἑκατόμπολιν (*Il.* II. 649); cf. *Epod.* 9. 29.

34. **pater**: the word which comes first to her lips in her distress instantly reminds her that she has recklessly thrown away a father's love and protection, and she breaks off with bitter self-reproach, **o relictum**, etc. For the nominatives in exclamation, **nomen pietasque**, cf. Cic. *Phil.* 14. 31 (quoted 2. 13 n) and *Ep.* II. 3. 301. The accusative is usual.

35. **filiae**: defining genitive; Gr. 214 *f*.

36. **furore**, *mad folly*.

37. **unde quo**: not in reference to place, but contrasting her present situation with that of yesterday. — **una mors**: cf. Prop. V. 4. 17 *et satis una malae potuit mors esse puellae, | quae voluit flammas fallere, Vesta, tuas?*

38. **virginum**, *a maiden's;* the plural (used generically) makes it less direct, and so more natural. She feels now, in her defenseless situation, the full force and consequence of having broken through the restraints of filial duty and maidenly reserve, under the impulse of a temporary fascination (**furore**, 36). — **culpae**: dative; for the meaning, see 6. 17 n. — **vigilans**: emphatic; she cannot believe her senses; it must be all a dream.

40. **ludit imago**: cf. Verg. *A.* I. 407 *quid natum totiens crudelis tu quoque falsis | ludis imaginibus?*

41. **porta eburna**: cf. Verg. *A.* VI. 893 *sunt geminae somni portae, quarum altera fertur | cornea, qua veris facilis datur exitus umbris, | altera candenti perfecta nitens elephanto, | sed falsa ad caelum mittunt insomnia manes* (an imitation of *Odys.* XIX. 562 *sqq.*).

42. **meliusne**, etc.: a taunt at herself and her foolish choice in

ire per longos fuit, an recentis
carpere flores?

Si quis infamem mihi nunc iuvencum
dedat iratae, lacerare ferro et
frangere enitar modo multum amati
cornua monstri.

Impudens liqui patrios penatis,
impudens Orcum moror. O deorum
si quis haec audis, utinam inter errem
nuda leones!

Antequam turpis macies decentis
occupet malas teneraeque sucus

leaving the unexciting but safe amusements of childhood for a dangerous pleasure. — **fluctus longos**: cf. *longus pontus*, 3. 37.

45. **nunc**: emphatic; in contrast with the time when she wreathed his horns with flowers.

46. **lacerare**: with **cornua**, as vs. 71 shows.

47. **enitar**, *I'd try with all my might;* an expression of rage, tempered by consciousness of physical weakness. — **modo**: cf. 14. 1. — **multum**: Intr. 49.

49. **impudens**, etc.: in the swift fluctuations of her feelings, rage is succeeded by shame, mingled with fear of what may happen to her,—starvation, slavery,—and a desire, gradually shaping itself into a purpose, to end her life. It is as shameful for her now to live as it was to leave her home. Oh, if the lions would devour her! Yes, that would be better than starving slowly and losing all her beauty. But why wait to starve? The thought of her absent father spurs her to action. 'Let your own hand do it, ere you, a king's daughter, become the concubine of a foreign lord and the hated slave of his wife.'

50. **Orcum moror**, *I put off death* (lit., 'keep him waiting'); *i.e.* I ought to die, but shamelessly hold back.

51. **si quis**: here equivalent to *quisquis;* cf. *Ep.* I. 18. 57. — **inter**: Intr. 115 *c.* — **errem**: *i.e.* come upon them by chance; she has not yet reached the thought of taking her own life.

52. **nuda**, *defenseless.*

53. **antequam**, etc.: this is not mere vanity, but the outcropping of a deep-seated feeling of the ancients, based on the belief that one entered the underworld in the form in which he left life; see the descriptions in *Aeneid* VI., and cf. Stat. *Silv.* II. 1. 154 (on the death of a favorite boy) *gratum est, Fata, tamen quod non mors lenta iacentis | exedit puerile decus, manesque subivit | integer et nullo temeratus corpora damno, | qualis erat.*—**turpis**, *unsightly;* cf. *turpes luctus*, II. 20. 22 n.—**decentis**: cf. I. 4. 6 n.

54. **tenerae praedae**: a paraphrase for *mihi*, with the added suggestion of youthfulness (**tene-**

defluat praedae, speciosa quaero
pascere tigris.
Vilis Europe, pater urget absens,
quid mori cessas? Potes hac ab orno
pendulum zona bene te secuta
laedere collum;
sive te rupes et acuta leto
saxa delectant, age te procellae
crede veloci, nisi erile mavis
carpere pensum
regius sanguis, dominaeque tradi
barbarae paelex.' Aderat querenti
perfidum ridens Venus et remisso
filius arcu;

**rae**). — **sucus defluat**: cf. Ter. *Eun.* 318 CH. *Color vérus, corpus sólidum et suci plénum.* PA. *Anni?* CH. *Anni? Sédecim.* We express it otherwise: 'the bloom fades,' or the like.

55. **speciosa,** (*still*) *fair to see;* not a strong word, like *pulcher*, but merely deprecating the ugliness of emaciation.

56. **pascere**: Intr. 94 *c*.

57. **vilis,** etc.: the thought of her father spurs her resolution. The words are not a quotation of what she imagines he would say, but she knows well what his stern sentence would be, and under its influence urges herself on to put an end to her shame. — **vilis**: and hence, as a princess, unfit to live.

59. **bene te secuta,** *which, luckily, you have brought with you.* The bitter irony of these words is enhanced by the double meaning given to them by the significance of the girdle as the emblem of maidenhood.

60. **laedere,** *bruise;* used, in the same spirit of bitter mockery, for the harsher *elidere.* As her resolution assumes fixed shape ('deliberata morte ferocior') she can jest with death; cf. **te delectant** and **te crede,** below.

61. **sive**: Intr. 119 *d*. — **leto**: dative with **acuta**; Intr. 58 *c*.

62. **saxa**: those at the bottom of the cliffs (**rupes**). — **procellae,** *the gale* (that blows over the cliffs).

63. **erile**: apportioned by a mistress (*era*), *a slave's.*

64. **carpere pensum**: here of spinning an assigned portion of wool; cf. the picture in Prop. IV. 6. 15 *tristis erat domus, et tristes sua pensa ministrae | carpebant, medio nebat et ipsa loco;* Cat. 64. 310.

65. **tradi**: *i.e.* to be put at her mercy; cf. II. 4. 11 n.

66. **paelex**: and hence the especial object of her cruelty.

67. **perfidum**: see Intr. 48. — **remisso,** *unstrung;* his work was done.

mox, ubi lusit satis, 'Abstineto'
dixit 'irarum calidaeque rixae,
cum tibi invisus laceranda reddet
cornua taurus.

Vxor invicti Iovis esse nescis.
Mitte singultus, bene ferre magnam
disce fortunam: tua sectus orbis
nomina ducet.'

## XXVIII.

Festo quid potius die
Neptuni faciam? Prome reconditum,

69. **lusit**: sc. *Venus*. — **abstineto**: the second form of the imperative, here referring to a designated point of future time (**cum reddet**).

70. **irarum, rixae**: Intr. 67.

71. **invisus laceranda**, etc.: in mocking allusion to vss. 45 *sqq*.

73. **uxor esse**: for *te uxorem esse*; Intr. 99 *b*. — **invicti**: suggesting, perhaps, the necessity of submission.

74. **mitte**: Intr. 129.

75. **sectus orbis**, *a hemisphere*. Horace follows those geographers who divided the world into two parts, Europe and Asia; cf. Varro *L. L.* V. 31 *ut omnis natura in caelum et terram divisa est, sic caeli regionibus terra in Asiam et Europam*; Plin. *N. H.* III. 5 (*Europam*) *plerique merito non tertiam portionem fecere, verum aequam, in duas partes . . . universo orbe diviso.*

76. **nomina**: Intr. 128.—**ducet**, *will take*; lit. 'will draw' (*sc.* from you, implied in **tua**); cf. *S.* II. 1. 66 *duxit ab oppressa meritum Carthagine nomen.*

XXVIII. An ode for Neptune's day. This festival, the *Neptunalia*, occurred on the twenty-third of July, and was celebrated by the people in the open air, picnic fashion, on the banks of the Tiber or the seashore, with arbors (*umbrae*) to shelter them from the midsummer sun. Such, however, is not the celebration contemplated in the ode. It is past noon, and the poet, feeling in the mood for a carouse, bethinks himself that it is a holiday. 'Why not, then? Come, Lyde, bring down a jar of that fine old Caecuban, and we will celebrate the day together.' Horace speaks, apparently, in the person of a country poet, and the thrifty Lyde keeps his house. We cannot define the picture more exactly, and it is not probable that Horace did so. — Metre, 171.

1. **potius**: *sc.* than that which has occurred to me. The answer to the question is implied in the order which he gives; cf. II. 3. 9–16.

2. **reconditum**, *hoarded*; cf. *repostum Caecubum*, *Epod.* 9. 1 n. For the force of **re-**, cf. I. 10. 17 n.

Lyde, strenua Caecubum,
munitaeque adhibe vim sapientiae.
Inclinare meridiem
sentis et, veluti stet volucris dies,
parcis deripere horreo
cessantem Bibuli consulis amphoram.
Nos cantabimus invicem
Neptunum et viridis Nereidum comas;
tu curva recines lyra
Latonam et celeris spicula Cynthiae;

3. **strenua**: best taken, in an adverbial sense, with **prome.**—**Caecubum**: see I. 20. 9 n, 37. 5 n.

4. **munitae,** (*your*) *well-entrenched; i.e.* which you steadily maintain, against all temptations and distractions.—**adhibe vim,** *give a shock to.* The meaning is 'Be frivolous for once'; cf. *dulce est desipere in loco,* IV. 12. 28.

5. **inclinare meridiem**: as the whole vault of heaven was supposed to revolve with the sun ('vertitur interea caelum,' Verg. *A.* II. 250; cf. Lucr. V. 510), it was natural to think of it as erect or vertical when the sun is overhead, and to speak of the day (the bright hemisphere) or midday declining, as well as the sun itself; cf. Juv. 3. 316 *sol inclinat;* Tac. *Ann.* XII. 39. 2 *inclinabat dies.*

6. **stet,** *stood still.*—**et**: used here to connect contrasted statements (= *et tamen*); cf. Juv. 13. 91 *hic putat esse deos et peierat.*

7. **deripere,** *to bring down in haste;* the **de-** as in *Epod.* 5. 46 *lunamque caelo deripit;* cf. *descende,* 21. 7 n. For the infinitive, see Intr. 94 *k.*—**horreo**: here for the *apotheca vinaria;* see 8. 11 n, and, for the case, Intr. 70.

8. **cessantem**: simply reinforcing the idea already expressed in **parcis deripere.**—**Bibuli**: M. Calpurnius Bibulus, consul with Julius Caesar, B.C. 59. See II. 3. 8 n, and cf. III. 21. 1.

9. **nos,** *I.* Horace uses the plural of the personal pronoun in this sense only where the speaker (usually himself) is placed in direct contrast with some other person or persons, as here and I. 6. 5 and 17, *Epod.* 1. 5, *S.* I. 4. 41, 6. 18, *Ep.* I. 15. 25, 17. 5; or in such personal relation as is implied in the phrases *nostri memor* (III. 11. 51, 27. 14), *meminit nostri* (*Ep.* I. 3. 12), *studio nostri* (*Ep.* I. 13. 4), *noris nos* (*S.* I. 9. 7).—**invicem**: in reference to the subjects, not the singers.

10. **viridis**: the colors of the sea are attributed to the divinities that dwell there; cf. *caerula mater* (Thetis), *Epod.* 13. 16; Ov. *M.* XIII. 960 *hanc ego* (Glaucus) *tum primum viridem ferrugine barbam* | . . . *et caerula bracchia vidi.*

11. **curva lyra**: cf. I. 10. 6.—**recines,** *shall sing in response.* There is a specimen of this sort of amoebean song in Verg. *E.* 3. 60 *sqq.* For the future, see Intr. 90.

12. **Latonam,** etc.: notice the parallelism to vs. 10; in each case

summo carmine quae Cnidon
fulgentisque tenet Cycladas, et Paphum
iunctis visit oloribus;
dicetur merita Nox quoque nenia.

## XXIX.

Tyrrhena regum progenies, tibi
non ante verso lene merum cado
cum flore, Maecenas, rosarum et
pressa tuis balanus capillis

one object of the verb is a divinity, the other some attribute of a divinity (**comas, spicula**). Cf. I. 21. 5–8 and 9–12. — **Cynthiae**: see I. 21. 2 n.

13. **summo,** *at the close of;* so Juv. 1. 5 *summi libri.* Cf. *Ep.* I. 1. 1 *summa dicende camena.* — **quae,** etc.: see I. 30. 1, III. 26. 9. The verb to be supplied (*cantabitur* or the like) is readily suggested by **carmine** and the preceding verbs.

14. **fulgentis**. see I. 14. 19 n. —**tenet**: cf. 4. 62 n. — **Cycladas**: Naxos in particular was devoted to the worship of Aphrodite. There is evidence also of her worship in Delos and Ceos, and it was, no doubt, widespread among all the islands in the range of Phoenician commerce.

15. **iunctis oloribus**: cf. IV. 1. 10, and, for the construction, *Martis equis,* 3. 16 n. — **visit**: see I. 4. 8 n.

16. **dicetur**: see I. 6. 5 n. — **Nox**: implying, like 19. 10, that the symposium is to be prolonged into the night. — **nenia**: here not a dirge, as in II. 1. 38, but a song of slow measure, sung low, a good-night song.

XXIX. The last place in the collection before the epilogue, which the poet reserves for himself and his muse alone, is given to Maecenas, — an arrangement which Horace afterwards repeated in the first book of the Epistles. An invitation to his patron to visit him in the country, presumably on his Sabine farm, is made the occasion of a discourse on Horace's favorite maxim, 'Carpe diem.' 'Here, in the middle of the dog days, you are cooping yourself up in the hot city, worried with cares of state and harrassing your soul over Scythians and Chinese. There may be too much of this. A wise providence has hidden the future from us. Only the past is securely ours; the present is for us to control and use; all else is beyond our power. Fortune is fickle: welcome what she brings, but let not our happiness wait on her favor.' The ode purports to have been written in July, and the allusions to the responsibilities of Maecenas point to B.C. 26 or 25, the two summers which Augustus spent in the West (see intr. note to Ode 14), as the probable date. — Metre, 176.

iamdudum apud me est: eripe te morae,
ne semper udum Tibur et Aefulae
declive contempleris arvum et
Telegoni iuga parricidae.

Fastidiosam desere copiam et
molem propinquam nubibus arduis;
omitte mirari beatae
fumum et opes strepitumque Romae.

1. **Tyrrhena**, etc.: see I. 1. 1 n.

2. **verso**, *broached;* lit. 'tipped,' in pouring the wine into the *cratera*. Cf. *S.* II. 8. 39. As the *cadus* contained about five gallons, it would ordinarily hold out for more than one occasion.—**lene**: coupled with *generosum*, *Ep.* I. 15. 18 *sqq.;* cf. *languidiora vina*, 21. 8 n.

3. **flore**, etc.: see II. 3. 13 n.

4. **pressa tuis capillis**: cf. II. 7. 20, and, for a burlesque on this sort of compliment, see Juv. 4. 68. — **balanus**: properly the nut, called 'ben nut' (*myrobalanus*, Plin. *N. H.* XII. 100), growing in Arabia and Egypt; here the fragrant oil pressed from the nut.

5. **iamdudum**, etc.: *i.e.* I have long been waiting for you; this then is a second and more urgent invitation. — **morae**, *procrastination*, which holds him, as it were, captive.

6. **ne semper contempleris**, *so as not to go on gazing forever at; i.e.* only looking at these beautiful places in the distance, and never coming to them. See vs. 10 n.—**udum Tibur**: so Ovid *F.* IV. 71 *moenia Tiburis udi;* cf. I. 7. 13 *sq.* — **Aefulae**: an old Latin hill-town (cf. **declive**) probably between Praeneste and Tibur. It was garrisoned on the approach of Hannibal by the *Via Latina* in B.C. 211 (Liv. XXVI. 9. 9).

8. **Telegoni**: son of Ulysses and Circe. Sent by the latter in search of his father, he came to Ithaca, where he was obliged to plunder the country for provisions. He was set upon by Ulysses and Telemachus, and in the contest that ensued unwittingly slew his father (Hygin. *Fab.* 127). — **iuga**: those of Tusculum, of which Telegonus was the reputed founder; cf. *Epod.* 1. 29 n.

9. **fastidiosam**, *cloying;* Intr. 125.

10. **molem**, *massive structure, pile;* cf. II. 15. 2. The splendid mansion which Maecenas built in his park on the Esquiline (see *S.* I. 8. 7 n) was furnished with a lofty tower, afterwards known as *turris Maecenatiana*, from which Nero is said to have watched the great fire (Suet. *Nero* 38). This 'alta domus' (*Epod.* 9. 3) commanded a view of the whole city and of the neighboring country as far as the Tusculan and Sabine hills (cf. vss. 6 *sqq.*).

11. **mirari**: cf. 25. 14, and see I. 4. 19 n; for the mood, Intr. 94 *j.* —**beatae**: see I. 4. 14 n, III. 26. 9.

12. **fumum**, etc.: a graphic composite picture, combining the striking features of the scene,—the splendid houses and temples (evidences of wealth) looming up in the smoky atmosphere, with

Plerumque gratae divitibus vices,
mundaeque parvo sub lare pauperum
cenae sine aulaeis et ostro
sollicitam explicuere frontem.

Iam clarus occultum Andromedae pater
ostendit ignem, iam Procyon furit
et stella vesani Leonis,
sole dies referente siccos;

the ceaseless roar of the distant streets. — **opes**, *splendor*. — **strepitum**: cf. *Ep.* II. 2. 79 *inter strepitus nocturnos atque diurnos* (sc. *urbis*).

13. **gratae** (sc. *sunt*), etc.: cf. Lucr. III. 1057 *haud ita vitam agerent ut nunc plerumque videmus | quid sibi quisque velit nescire et quaerere semper | commutare locum, quasi onus deponere possit; | exit saepe foras magnis ex aedibus ille, | esse domi quem pertaesumst, subitoque revertit | . . . currit agens mannos ad villam praecipitanter*, etc. — **vices**, *change*. The thought in this verse is simply of the *fastidiosa copia*, of change for the sake of change; it grows out of what he has been saying. But close to this lies the thought of the cares that go with riches, and this brings him to the second point in his plea and the main theme of the ode,— the cares, not of riches (**divitibus** belongs to **gratae** only, and not to **explicuere frontem**), but those of which Maecenas permits himself to be the victim.

14. **mundae**, *of simple elegance*. Horace himself defines this word (*S.* II. 2. 65) as the happy mean between pretentious show and slovenliness. Cf. *Ep.* II. 2. 199 *pauperies immunda domus prŏcul absit*. — **sub**: see I. 5. 3 n. — **lare**: cf. I. 12. 44 n; we may render it here by *roof*, which conveys for us the same idea of home shelter. — **pauperum**: *a poor man's;* cf. *virginum*, 27. 38 n. For the meaning, see I. 1. 18 n.

15. **aulaeis**: a canopy suspended over the *triclinium* in fashionable houses, ostensibly to catch the dust from the ceiling; see *S.* II. 8. 54, Verg. *A.* I. 697. — **ostro**: in the *aulaea* and in the upholstery of the couches.

16. **explicuere**: Intr. 80.

17. **iam**, etc.: this description of the dog days, — a time for rest, — paves the way to his protest against Maecenas' persistent devotion to public business. The constellations used to mark the hot season are Cassiopea, represented by Cepheus (on earth an Ethiopian king, husband of Cassiopea and father of Andromeda), rising July 9; **Procyon** ('quod sidus apud Romanos non habet nomen,' Plin. *N. H.* XVIII. 268), rising July 15, eleven days before the Dog Star (see I. 17. 17 n); and the Lion, whose brightest star, which we call Regulus ('regia in pectore leonis stella,' Plin. *N. H.* XVIII. 271), rises July 30, according to Pliny. — **clarus**: with **ostendit**; cf. *strenua*, 28. 3 n. — **occultum**: sc. *antea;* cf. *quietos*, vs. 40.

18. **furit, vesani**: cf. *Ep.* I. 10. 16 *rabiem Canis et momenta Leonis,*

iam pastor umbras cum grege languido
rivumque fessus quaerit et horridi
dumeta Silvani, caretque
ripa vagis taciturna ventis:
tu civitatem quis deceat status
curas et urbi sollicitus times
quid Seres et regnata Cyro
Bactra parent Tanaisque discors.

Prudens futuri temporis exitum
caliginosa nocte premit deus,
ridetque si mortalis ultra
fas trepidat. Quod adest memento
componere aequus: cetera fluminis

*cum semel accepit solem furibundus acutum.*

19. **stella**: probably not used loosely for 'constellation' (as in Verg. *G.* I. 222), but for the conspicuous star Regulus (see vs. 17 n).

20. **siccos**, *of drouth.*

21. **iam**: referring to the time of year, when the scene he paints may be witnessed any day.

22. **rivum**: cf. II. 5. 6 *iuvencae . . . fluviis gravem solantis aestum.*—**fessus**, *wearily;* cf. *clarus*, 17 n.—**horridi**: an attribute borrowed from the **dumeta** which he inhabits.

23. **Silvani**: see *Epod.* 2. 22 n.

24. **taciturna**: a part of the predicate; it is silent because there is no motion in the air.

25. **tu civitatem**: cf. II. 9. 9. The reference is perhaps to the recent settlement of the government, B.C. 27, many details of which had no doubt still to be worked out.

26. **urbi**: with **times**.

27. **Seres**: cf. I. 12. 56 n. There is a touch of irony in the mention of these remote peoples; the city cannot be in imminent peril.—**regnata Cyro**: a part of his empire; cf. II. 2. 17 n. For the construction, cf. *regnata Phalantho*, II. 6. 11, and see Intr. 51 *e*, 55.

28. **Bactra**: the remotest dependency of Parthia. — **Tanais**: *i.e.* the Scythians; cf. IV. 15. 24. The river stands for the country through which it flows; cf. II. 9. 21 *Medumque flumen gentibus additum victis;* II. 20. 20 n. — **discors**: another reason for feeling secure at Rome.

29. **prudens deus**: cf. I. 3. 21 n. — **temporis**: Intr. 76.

30. **nocte premit**: cf. I. 4. 16.

31. **ultra fas**: cf. *scire nefas*, I. 11. 1.

32. **trepidat**: see II. 11. 4 n. — **memento**: see I. 7. 17 n.

33. **componere aequus**: both words, in contrast with **trepidat**, express coolness and deliberation. — **cetera**: *i.e.* the future, for the past does not here come into consideration.

ritu feruntur, nunc medio alveo
cum pace delabentis Etruscum
in mare, nunc lapides adesos
stirpisque raptas et pecus et domos
volventis una, non sine montium
clamore vicinaeque silvae,
cum fera diluvies quietos
inritat amnis. Ille potens sui
laetusque deget, cui licet in diem
dixisse 'Vixi; cras vel atra
nube polum pater occupato,

34. **ritu**: as in 14. 1; cf. *S.* II. 3. 268 *tempestatis prope ritu mobilia.* — **medio alveo**: rivers capable of producing such floods as are described in the next strophe are often, especially in mountainous countries, at other times quiet brooks, gliding along the middle of a broad channel. Cf. IV. 7. 3.

35. **cum pace**, *peaceably* (not 'peacefully'), expressing the disposition of the stream; cf. **inritat**, 41. The same personification appears in **clamore** and **fera diluvies**.—**Etruscum**: Intr. 117*a*, 176*b*.

36. **adesos**: from long lying in the channel.

37. **raptas**: with all three substantives.

38. **una**, *along.*

41. **potens sui**, *independent*, not subject to any other control; with especial reference, however, to the control of the passions. The man who is always taking thought for the morrow is the slave of desire and hence of fear; 'nam qui cupiet, metuet quoque; porro | qui metuens vivet, liber mihi non erit umquam' (*Ep.* I. 16. 65).

42. **in diem**, *day by day;* cf. *S.* II. 6. 47. *Quotidie* would be less suitable, because the idea is of one day added each time to the series of days.

43. **dixisse**: Intr. 81 *b.* — **vixi**: in a pregnant sense. The man who can say, at the close of each day, 'I have lived' is one who has got out of that day's life the satisfaction and enjoyment it could yield, in contrast with the man who neglects these in his anxiety to provide the means to 'live' in the future. Cf. Martial II. 90. 3 *vivere quod propero pauper nec inutilis annis,* | *da veniam: properat vivere nemo satis;* | *differat hoc patrios optat qui vincere census;* I. 15. 11 *non est, crede mihi, sapientis dicere 'vivam'; sera nimis vita est crastina; vive hodie.* The view of life here inculcated is the same as in I. 9. 13 *sqq.*

44. **pater**: cf. I. 2. 2 n. — **occupato**: the longer form of the imperative (3d pers.) is here used with concessive force.

45. **sole**: here for sunshine, as Verg. *A.* IX. 461 *iam sole infuso* (of the dawn); cf. its use for 'day,' IV. 2. 46. — **puro**: see 10. 8 n. —

vel sole puro : non tamen inritum
quodcumque retro est efficiet, neque
diffinget infectumque reddet
quod fugiens semel hora vexit.'

Fortuna, saevo laeta negotio et
ludum insolentem ludere pertinax,
transmutat incertos honores,
nunc mihi, nunc alii benigna.

Laudo manentem : si celeris quatit
pennas, resigno quae dedit et mea

**inritum, diffinget, infectum** : the distinction may be illustrated in this way: a deed of gift (for example) may be rendered *void* (**inritum**) before going into effect, by a subsequent deed, superseding it, or it may be modified by *recasting* (**diffinget**), or it may be destroyed and put out of existence (**infectum**); but if the gift has been received *and enjoyed*, then no power can do any of these things. So it is with the 'dona praesentis horae' (8. 27).

46. **retro** : *i.e.* past; with the same thought of a *current* of events as in **hora vexit.**

47. **diffinget** : cf. I. 35. 39.

48. **semel** : cf. I. 24. 16 n, *C. S.* 26. — **vexit** : sc. *secum ;* cf. Verg. *G.* I. 461 *quid vesper serus vehat.* There is nothing in **fugiens** (*fleeting*, that which comes but does not stay ; cf. 30. 5) to require us to take **vexit** in the sense of *avexit.* It is simply the experience, the enjoyment of 'the passing hour.'

50. **ludum** : as war is the *ludus* of Mars, I. 2. 37 ; cf. II. 1. 3. For **ludum ludere,** see Intr. 45 *a.* — **insolentem,** *heartless ;* see I. 5. 8 n. — **ludere** : Intr. 101 *b.*

51. **transmutat honores** : cf. I. 34. 14 *sqq.*

54. **pennas** : a regular attribute of Fortuna ; cf. I. 34. 15 n. — **resigno,** *I surrender.* In this sense the word is found in classical literature only here and *Ep.* I. 7. 34, but it must have been common in ordinary speech, as is evidenced by the corresponding use of its modern derivatives. It was a commercial word, having no reference to the breaking of seals (as it has in *Ep.* I. 7. 9 *testamenta resignat*), but probably derived from the use of *signare* instead of *scribere* (cf. Paul. *ex* Fest. 284), for making an entry in the account book ; *resignare* would then be to make an entry *opposite* (on the credit side), balancing the former and thus cancelling the claim for which it stood ; just as *rescribere* was used in the sense of *repay, e.g. S.* II. 3. 76, Ter. *Ph.* 922 *argentum rursum iube rescribi.* In fact Festus says : '*resignare*' *antiqui pro* '*rescribere*' *ponebant ut adhuc* '*subsignare*' *dicimus pro* '*subscribere*' (p. 281). — **mea,** *my own* (Intr. 116 *b*) ; in contrast with the uncertain tenure of all other so called possessions.

virtute me involvo probamque
pauperiem sine dote quaero.
Non est meum, si mugiat Africis
malus procellis, ad miseras preces
decurrere et votis pacisci,
ne Cypriae Tyriaeque merces
addant avaro divitias mari:
tunc me biremis praesidio scaphae
tutum per Aegaeos tumultus
aura feret geminusque Pollux.

55. **me involvo**: as with a cloak, — his one remaining possession. The metaphor is borrowed from Plato, in whose ideal state αἱ γυναῖκες ἀρετὴν ἀντὶ ἱματίων ἀμφιέσονται (*Rep.* V. 457 A).

56. **quaero**: *sc.* as a bride, as is shown by **sine dote**, following **probam**, by which **pauperies** was at once personified.

57. **meum**, *my way;* a colloquial expression; cf. Plaut. *Trin.* 631 *néque meumst neque fácere didici;* ib. 123 CA. *Quid féci?* ME. *Quod homo néquam.* CA. *Non istúc meumst?* — **mugiat Africis**, etc.: cf. I. 14. 5.

59. **votis pacisci**: a cynical, but not untruthful designation of the transaction; see I. 31. 1 n.

60. **Cypriae Tyriaeque**: Intr. 117 *a*.

61. **avaro**: cf. *avidum mare*, I. 28. 18.

62. **tunc**, *in such a case.* — **biremis**: here not 'bireme,' but *two-oared*, merely indicating, however, the size of the boat, — small enough to be rowed with two oars (*duorum scalmorum navicula*, Cic. *de Or.* I. 174). — **scaphae**: the boat carried or towed by a ship, like our life-boat or dory; cf. Petron. 101 *quomodo possumus egredi navi? . . . quin potius . . . per funem lapsi descendimus in scapham?* It could be rigged with a sail, as here (**aura feret**). The meaning in these two strophes is the same as in the preceding: the ship and its rich freight are the gifts of Fortune; if the heavy-laden vessel is about to founder in the storm of adversity, he will not moan over his loss, but will take to the life-boat and cheerfully sail away: the essentials of happiness make a light and safe cargo.

63. **Aegaeos tumultus**: cf. II. 16. 2.

64. **aura**, etc.: *i.e.* the breeze (in contrast to **Africis procellis**) granted by the twin divinities, — the recompense of a more genuine piety. — **geminus Pollux**: for Castor and Pollux; so Ov. *A. A.* I. 746 *geminus Castor*, probably in the same sense. It was common to use one name for both, 'quia ambo licenter et Polluces et Castores vocantur' (Serv. on Verg. *G.* III. 89). Their temple at Rome was commonly known as *aedes Castoris* (Suet. *Iul.* 10) or *Castorum* (Plin. *N. H.* X. 121). For their protection of mariners, see I. 3. 2 n.

# XXX.

Exegi monumentum aere perennius
regalique situ pyramidum altius,
quod non imber edax, non Aquilo impotens
possit diruere aut innumerabilis

XXX. This ode was written as an epilogue, as I. 1 is the prologue, of the three books (see introd. note to I. 1). Each poem is carefully adapted in spirit and tone to the place it occupies. When Horace sat down to arrange his odes for publication, he was already well assured of his success as a lyric poet by the approbation of the limited but competent circle of readers who were acquainted with his work; and as the goodly collection grew under his hand, he might well feel a pardonable pride in his achievement. It meant for him, what his earlier successes might not have meant, lasting fame. He had completed the first considerable body of lyric poetry ever published in Latin; its place was assured, as its quality was unique, in the literature of Rome, — the literature of the eternal city, the metropolis of the world. It is not surprising that the closing poem is a song of triumph; and if it is characterized by a candor which our modern poets do not permit themselves, we must make allowance for difference of time and custom. That it did not offend the taste of Horace's countrymen, we may infer from the fact that he was imitated by other poets (cf. Propert. IV. 1. 35 and 57 *sqq.;* Ovid *Am.* I. 15. 41 *sq.*, *M.* XV. 871 *sqq.;* Phaedr. IV. *Epil.* 5 *sq.*; Martial VIII. 3. 5 *sqq.*); and, knowing Horace, we may feel sure he had Greek precedent to fall back upon, if need be, as well as the example of Ennius in the well known epitaph (see II. 20. 21 n). — Metre, 169.

1. **exegi**, *I have completed;* so Ovid *M.* XV. 871 *iamque opus exegi, quod nec Iovis ira nec ignis | nec poterit ferrum nec edax abolere vetustas.* — **monumentum**: Horace's work was literally a *monumentum* in the wider sense of that word (cf. *moneo*), but he here calls it figuratively a *monument*, in our narrower sense, for the purpose of comparison. — **aere**: a common material for memorials, especially statues and inscribed tablets.

2. **regali**: *i.e.* magnificent; cf. II. 15. 1 n. — **situ pyramidum**: for 'the crumbling pyramids' (cf. Intr. 126 *b*), an intimation, like **edax** and **impotens** below, of the destructive forces to which material monuments are subject. Translate, '*the crumbling magnificence of*,' etc., or the like. For this use of *situs* cf. Mart. VIII. 3. 5 *et cum rupta situ Messalae saxa iacebunt, | altaque cum Licini marmora pulvis erunt, | me tamen ora legent.* — **altius**: the highest of them, the great pyramid of Ghizeh, was about 480 feet, — higher than any other monument known to the Romans.

3. **quod**, *one that;* descriptive relative clause. — **impotens**: cf. I. 37. 10 n, *Epod.* 16. 62. For the

annorum series et fuga temporum.
Non omnis moriar, multaque pars mei
vitabit Libitinam ; usque ego postera
crescam laude recens ; dum Capitolium
scandet cum tacita virgine pontifex,
dicar, qua violens obstrepit Aufidus

conjunctions in this clause, cf. II. 9. 1 n.

5. **fuga** : cf. *fugaces anni*, II. 14. 1 ; *fugiens hora*, III. 29. 48.

6. **non omnis**, etc.: cf. Ov. *Am*. I. 15. 41 *ergo etiam cum me supremus adederit ignis,* | *vivam, parsque mei multa superstes erit.*— **-que** : cf. I. 27. 16 n.

7. **Libitinam** : *i.e.* the funeral pyre and the tomb; cf. *S*. II. 6. 19. By an edict of Servius Tullius a fee was to be paid, on the occasion of every death, at the temple of Venus Libitina, and there also the requisite implements for the funeral were to be obtained. Hence Libitina became synonymous with death, as *Ep*. II. 1. 49, but usually with more suggestion of the funeral rites than of death in the abstract; so that this clause is not a mere repetition of **non omnis moriar.**—**usque** : lit. 'on and on,' denoting an indefinite series of repetitions ; cf. *Ep*. I. 10. 24; Cat. 5. 9. It modifies **crescam** (and hence the whole clause), but with nearer reference to **postera,** which does not mean 'of posterity,' but simply 'later.' The 'later praise' will be in every case greater than that which preceded it.

8. **recens,** *ever fresh*.— **dum Capitolium,** etc. : cf. 3. 42. The one thing unchangeable beyond all else to a Roman was his religious institutions, the head and centre of which was the worship of Jove, with Juno and Minerva, in their ancient temple on the Tarpeian hill (**Capitolium**). With this Horace joins, in the graphic sketch which he uses to express his meaning, the priestesses of Vesta whose worship was equally significant of perpetuity; cf. 5. 11 *sq*. What procession is referred to we do not definitely know; but it must have been a stated—perhaps monthly—observance, sufficiently designated to Horace's readers by the features he mentions.

9. **virgine, pontifex** : these are taken by some to mean the chief Vestal (*Virgo Maxima*) and the Pontifex Maximus ; but more probably they are used collectively (Intr. 127) for the Vestal virgins and the pontifices. The former marched in reverent silence (**tacita**), amid the hymns and chants which must have formed part of the ceremony. This clause is best taken with what follows, as the preceding statement is already provided with the notion of perpetuity in **usque.** Horace couches his prophecy in three utterances which are progressive in point of definiteness : the first is vague,—'I shall not wholly die'; the second explains this,—'my fame will survive and increase from age to age'; and finally he names the achievement for which men will praise him (**dicar — deduxisse modos**).

10. **dicar,** etc. : in accordance

et qua pauper aquae Daunus agrestium
regnavit populorum ex humili potens,
princeps Aeolium carmen ad Italos

with the Latin preference for the personal construction (cf. *videor mihi* and the like), for 'It will be said that I.' We may translate, *I shall be named as one who.* — **qua**, etc.: best taken with **dicar**, and expressing the pride with which his birth-place will cherish his fame; but his motive in inserting this reference is much the same as in IV. 9. 2 *longe sonantem natus ad Aufidum*, and *S.* II. 1. 34. It grows, like the mention of other personal characteristics in *Ep.* I. 20. 20 *sqq.*, out of the poet's desire to be to his readers something more than a mere name. — **violens**: it is a mountain torrent in the part where Horace knew it best; cf. IV. 14. 25–28, *S.* I. 1. 58. — **obstrepit**: here used absolutely, but without losing the force of **ob-**, — 'fills one's ears with its roar'; cf. Liv. XXI. 56. 9 *nihil sensere, obstrepente pluvia.*'

11. **pauper aquae**: cf. *Epod.* 3. 16 *siticulosae Apuliae.* For the genitive see Intr. 66 *c.* — **Daunus**: see I. 22. 14 n. — **agrestium**: even in Horace's time Apulia was still a farming and grazing country, with comparatively few towns; cf. 16. 26 n.

12. **populorum**, *tribes.* The genitive is commonly explained as an imitation of the Greek genitive after ἄρχω, βασιλεύω, and the like. But as no instance of this construction in Latin is cited until about two centuries after Horace wrote, and then only in a few provincial writers, who have the genitive with *dominor*, and as no such violent departure from the Latin idiom is found elsewhere in Horace, it may be questioned whether this ready explanation is open to us. For **populorum potens**, on the other hand, we have a perfect parallel in 25. 14 *Naiadum potens;* and for the position of **regnavit**, in that of *musa*, II. 12. 13, of *te*, IV. 1. 19, of *equitavit*, IV. 4. 43, and many similar examples. — **ex humili potens**: this has been taken in agreement with the subject of **dicar**, as Horace speaks of *potentes vates*, IV. 8. 26, and contrasts, on occasion, his lowly birth with his subsequent eminence (II. 20. 5, *Ep.* I. 20. 20); but to use the term *potens* of himself, would have been, as Bentley rightly held, an unnecessarily offensive assumption. It is moreover out of place if applied to Horace, and disturbs the course of thought, which is centred on the one distinction which Horace felt to be forever his, — that of being the first to master the problem of Latin lyric verse. Grammatically also it goes more naturally with **Daunus**, who did, in fact, according to the legend, rise from the condition of a refugee from Illyricum to be king of his adopted country (Festus, p. 69). For the construction, cf. Cic. *de Part. Or.* 57 *nihil est tam miserabile quam ex beato miser.* The whole clause then may be rendered: *where poor in water Daunus reigned, o'er rustic tribes a lord from low estate*, or the like.

13. **princeps**: a little more than *primus ;* he was not merely first, but a leader, a pioneer. — **Aeolium carmen**: cf. I. 1. 34, 35 nn, II. 13. 24, IV. 3. 12. — **Ita-**

deduxisse modos. Sume superbiam
quaesitam meritis et mihi Delphica
lauro cinge volens, Melpomene, comam.

**los**: here for 'Latin'; cf. *Italiae ruinis*, 5. 39, *res Italas* (= *res Romanas*) *Ep.* II. 1. 2. Since Roman citizenship had been extended to all Italians, as the Latin language spread throughout the peninsula, the more comprehensive term came naturally to be used in place of the narrower one.

14. **deduxisse**, *composed;* cf. *S.* II. 1. 4 *mille die versus deduci posse;* Ov. *M.* I. 4, *perpetuum deducite carmen.* The figure is from spinning; cf. *Ep.* II. 1. 225 *tenui deducta poemata filo.* — **modos**, *rhythm;* the inherent musical quality of the language, its structure in reference to the various elements of rhythm, in much of which it differed from the Greek. To succeed in writing lyric poetry, he had to make it conform to these conditions. — **sume superbiam**: cf. *pone superbiam*, 10. 9. The muse is addressed as the divinity who has given him the power to achieve success (cf. IV. 3. 17 *sqq.*), and who therefore may be called upon both to take pride in his achievement and to crown him with the laurel of victory. The self-gratulation of the poem is skilfully softened by this recognition in the closing verses of dependence on an inspiration not the poet's own.

15. **quaesitam meritis**, *well earned.* — **Delphica**: cf. IV. 2. 9 *laurea Apollinari.* — **volens**, *graciously;* a set formula in prayers, usually with *propitius;* cf. *C. S.* 49 n; Liv. I. 16. 3 *precibus exposcunt uti volens propitius suam semper sospitet progeniem.*

16. **Melpomene**: see I. 12. 2 n, IV. 3. 1.

## LIBER QVARTVS

### I.

Intermissa, Venus, diu
 rursus bella moves? Parce precor, precor.
Non sum qualis eram bonae
 sub regno Cinarae. Desine, dulcium
mater saeva Cupidinum,
 circa lustra decem flectere mollibus

For the facts relating to the composition and publication of the fourth book of the Odes, and the significance of its lack of a dedication, see Intr. 31, 32.

I. As if to show that he is still young at heart, as befits the lyric poet, Horace opens the new volume with an ode on love at fifty, and himself poses for the picture, as usual. He protests that he has no longer either fitness or inclination for the merry service of Venus, but the stealthy tear and the tongue-tied silence betray the unexpected passion. To offset the picture by a contrast, he pays a passing tribute to the gifts and accomplishments of his young friend Paullus Fabius Maximus. — Metre, 171.

1. **intermissa**: with **bella**. The word comes naturally to the front in a sentence the real purport of which is that the poet after a silence of many years has resumed his lyre; for the proper province of the lyre is the emotions, and above all others love; cf. I. 6. 10 and 17 *sqq.*, II. 1. 37 *sqq.*

2. **bella**: for the figure, cf. vs. 16 and III. 26. 2 *sq.* — **moves**: cf. I. 15. 10 n; Verg. *G.* I. 509 *hinc movet Euphrates, illinc Germania bellum.* — **parce**: cf. II. 19. 7 *sq.* — **precor**: Intr. 116 *d.*

4. **regno**, *sway*; cf. *regit*, III. 9. 9. — **Cinarae**: alluded to elsewhere in terms which show that she was a real person, and that this was probably her real name. She was presumably a freedwoman, and had the characteristic faults of her class and condition of life, but she had a good heart and a genuine attachment for the poet; cf. *Ep.* I. 14. 33 *quem scis immunem* (*empty-handed*) *Cinarae placuisse rapaci.* She was now dead (cf. 13. 22 *sq.*), and there is a touch of tenderness in Horace's allusion to her (**bonae**). See Intr. 30.

5. **mater**, etc.: a reminiscence of I. 19; but the phrase is expanded by the insertion of the epithet **dulcium**, in designed contrast with **saeva**, expressing the 'bitter-sweet' of love.

6. **circa lustra decem**: for the omission of the pronoun (*me*) cf.

iam durum imperiis; abi
quo blandae iuvenum te revocant preces.
Tempestivius in domum
Paulli purpureis ales oloribus
comissabere Maximi,
si torrere iecur quaeris idoneum.
Namque et nobilis et decens
et pro sollicitis non tacitus reis
et centum puer artium
late signa feret militiae tuae,

Ov. *M.* I. 20 (*pugnabant*) | *mollia cum duris, sine pondere* (sc. *corporibus*) *habentia pondus*. Horace was fifty in B.C. 15. For **lustra**, cf. II. 4. 23 *sq.*—**flectere**: see II. 19. 17 n, and cf. III. 7. 25, *Ep.* II. 3. 163. The present is here conative, as **durum** shows.

7. **imperiis**: better taken as dative with **durum**, which, in contrast with **mollibus**, expresses a species of incapacity (*hardened, unresponsive*); see Intr. 58 *c*, and cf. Cic. *Arch.* 19 *durior ad haec studia*, and *S.* I. 4. 8 *durus componere versus*, where *durus* denotes another kind of incapacity (Intr. 101 *c*).

8. **revocant**: the prefix implies that they may rightfully claim her presence; cf. *repetantur*, I. 9. 20 n.

9. **tempestivius**: in reference to the age of Paullus; cf. III. 19. 27 n.

10. **Paulli Maximi**: cos. B.C. 11, and hence probably about twenty years younger than Horace (*i.e.* approaching thirty at this time), and of about the same age as Ovid, who was his intimate friend (*Pont.* I. 2, II. 3). He belonged to one of the noblest families in Rome, and enjoyed the close confidence of Augustus, whose cousin he had married. His death in A.D. 14 preceded that of the emperor by a few months (*Tac. Ann.* I. 5. 2). — **purpureis**: the hue of divine beauty; cf. III. 3. 12 n. — **ales**, *on the wings of*, but referring to her chariot drawn by swans; cf. III. 28. 15, and for the ablative **oloribus**, cf. *Martis equis*, III. 3. 16 n.

11. **comissabere**, *carry thy revels*.

12. **torrere**: see Intr. 94 *c*. — **iecur**: cf. I. 13. 4 n.

13. **et . . . et . . .**: notice the cumulative force of the fivefold repetition, and cf. vs. 29 n. — **decens**: cf. I. 4. 6 n.

14. **pro sollicitis**, etc.: cf. II. 1. 13; Ov. *Pont.* I. 2. 118 (*vox tua*), | *auxilio trepidis quae solet esse reis*.—**non tacitus**: for the litotes, cf. I. 12. 21, IV. 9. 31.

15. **centum**: cf. II. 14. 26. — **puer**, *a lad*; see I. 9. 16 n. — **artium**, *accomplishments*.

16. **signa**, etc.: cf. *bella*, vs. 2 n. The grouping of words in this verse is at variance with Horace's usual manner, which would give us *late militiae* || *signa feret tuae* (cf. vss. 10, 12, 14, 22, 30, 32,

et quandoque potentior
　largi muneribus riserit aemuli,
Albanos prope te lacus
　ponet marmoream sub trabe citrea.
Illic plurima naribus
　duces tura, lyraque et Berecyntia
delectabere tibia
　mixtis carminibus non sine fistula;
illic bis pueri die
　numen cum teneris virginibus tuum

34, 40; Intr. 113); and that is perhaps what he really wrote.

17. **quandoque**, *whenever*, but looking forward to only one occurrence, as in 2. 34. — **potentior**: *sc.* by the force of personal charm.

18. **largi**, *lavish*. — **muneribus**: better taken with **potentior**; see Intr. 75. — **riserit**: *sc.* in triumph.

19. **Albanos lacus**: the principal ones were Albanus and Nemorensis (Nemi), both near the Appian road. It is not known that Fabius had a country-seat in the neighborhood, and the ceremonial proposed is on a scale hardly in keeping with the idea of a private chapel. The poet appears to have in mind a public shrine, a new centre of the worship of Venus.

20. **ponet**, *set up*; see 8. 8 n. — **marmoream**, *in marble*; cf. *S.* II. 3. 183 *aeneus ut stes*. — **trabe**: used collectively (= *trabibus*, III. 2. 28; Intr. 127), and meaning the inside finish of the roof. — **citrea**, *of African cedar*. This tree grew to a great size on the slopes of Mt. Atlas, and was highly prized for its durability and the beauty of its veining and color. The Romans used it especially for the circular tops of dining tables (*orbes*), some of which were handed down through generations and brought enormous prices; see Plin. *N. H.* XIII. 91 *sqq.* It was known to the Greeks (θύον or θύα) from early times, and is mentioned by Theophrastus (Plin. *N. H.* XIII. 101) as the material of the timber work of ancient temples.

21. **plurima**, *abundance of*.

22. **tura**: cf. I. 19. 14, 30. 3. — **lyra, tibia**: instrumental ablative with **delectabere**. — **Berecyntia**: *i.e.* Phrygian; see I. 18. 13 n, III. 19. 19 n.

24. **mixtis carminibus** (*strains*): abl. abs. expressing manner; *i.e.* by a concert of those instruments, with the *fistula*, as in III. 19. 18 *sqq.* The recurrence of the final ā is perhaps intended to make the description more realistic. — **non sine**: see I. 23. 3 n. — **fistula**: see I. 17. 10 n.

25. **illic**: Intr. 116 *h*. — **bis die**: morning and evening. — **pueri cum virginibus**: for the employment of choirs of children in religious ceremonies, cf. I. 21 and intr. note to *C. S.* (p. 331).

laudantes pede candido
in morem Salium ter quatient humum.
Me nec femina nec puer
iam nec spes animi credula mutui
nec certare iuvat mero
nec vincire novis tempora floribus.
Sed cur heu, Ligurine, cur
manat rara meas lacrima per genas?
Cur facunda parum decoro
inter verba cadit lingua silentio?
Nocturnis ego somniis
iam captum teneo, iam volucrem sequor
te per gramina Martii
campi, te per aquas, dure, volubilis.

27. **laudantes**: a hymn is to accompany the dance. — **candido**: more graphic than *nudo*.

28. **morem Salium**: see I. 36. 12 n. — **ter**: see III. 18. 16 n. — **quatient humum**: cf. I. 4. 7, 37. 2.

29. **nec . . . nec**, etc.: corresponding to the fivefold repetition of *et*, vs. 13 n.

30. **animi mutui**: *i.e.* that my love would be returned; cf. III. 9. 13 *face mutua*. For **animi**, cf. I. 16. 28 n. For **credula mutui**, cf. *credulus aurea*, I. 5. 9 n.

31. **certare, vincire**: complementary infinitives joined with substantives as subjects of **iuvat**; cf. *ames dici*, I. 2. 50 n. — **mero**: *i.e.* in a drinking contest; cf. I. 36. 13 *sq.*

32. **novis**: *i.e.* those of spring. — **floribus**: cf. I. 4. 9 n, 5. 1 n.

33. **sed cur**, etc.: with this unexpected break-down of his renunciation of love, cf. III. 26. 11 *sq.* — **Ligurine**: the same name as in the tenth ode.

34. **rara**: *i.e.* a single one, that is on his cheek before he knows it; the same idea as in I. 13. 6. The opposite is *plurima lacrima*, *Ep.* I. 17. 59.

35. **cur**, etc.: cf. I. 8. 3 *sqq.*; Intr. 116 *f.* — **facunda**: with **lingua**. — **parum**: with **decoro**. For the metre of this verse, see Intr. 171.

36. **cadit lingua**: cf. Cat. 51. 7 *nam simul te, Lesbia, adspexi, . . . lingua sed torpet* (after Sappho *Fr.* 2 ὡς γὰρ εὔιδον βροχέως σε, φώνας | οὐδὲν ἔτ' εἴκει· | ἀλλὰ καμ μέν γλῶσσα ἔαγε).

38. **iam . . . iam** = *nunc . . . nunc*.

40. **aquas**: *sc.* of the Tiber; cf. III. 7. 26 *sqq.* — **volubilis**: cf. *Ep.* I. 2. 43 (*amnis*) *labitur et labetur in omne volubilis aevum.*

## II.

Pindarum quisquis studet aemulari,
Iulle, ceratis ope Daedalea

II. In B.C. 16 the disturbed condition of the whole German frontier reached a crisis in the humiliating defeat of M. Lollius, the emperor's legate on the Rhine, in his effort to repel an incursion of the Sygambri and other German tribes, who had actually crossed the river and invaded Gaul. Augustus proceeded at once to the province, taking with him his step-son Tiberius; and although the Germans withdrew on the news of his approach, and gave hostages for their future good behaviour, he was occupied for three years in settling the affairs of the western provinces, and did not return to Rome until July 4, B.C. 13. It was during this interval (in B.C. 15) that he planned and carried out, through his two step-sons, the brilliant campaign against the restless Alpine tribes which is celebrated in Odes 4 and 14. The present ode was written during his absence, and most probably in the winter of B.C. 16–15; for it contains no mention of the Alpine victories, beside which the overawing of the Sygambri and their allies was an insignificant achievement. The occasion appears to have been a suggestion from Jullus Antonius that Horace should celebrate the exploits of Augustus, — not particularly those just reported, — in Pindaric odes. The poet replies with a fine eulogy of Pindar, and a warning: 'The man who ventures on such a flight is foredoomed to suffer a great fall. My gift is of a very different and much humbler sort. Yet we shall sing our song of Caesar, — you, with your more sonorous lyre, and I, too, if I shall compose anything worth the while, — when we join with the people in rejoicing and thanksgiving over his triumphant return.'

Jullus Antonius was a son of the triumvir Antonius and Fulvia, born B.C. 44. He was brought up by his stepmother, Octavia, and married her daughter Marcella; and he was treated with equal generosity by Augustus, who raised him to the highest offices of state, — the consulship in B.C. 10. He requited these benefits with the basest betrayal of confidence, and was put to death in B.C. 2 for adultery with the emperor's daughter Julia. He was evidently a man of literary tastes, and is said to have written an epic, *Diomedea*, in twelve books, and some works in prose. — Metre, 174.

1. **Pindarum**: a poem such as Horace was invited to write would have been in the manner of Pindar, the great lyric poet of Thebes (B.C. 522–448) and the classical model for odes of personal victory and triumph. — **aemulari**, *to emulate*, *i.e.* to compose successfully in his style, but with no idea of rivalry.

2. **Iulle**: an old *cognomen* of the Julian *gens*, used as a *praenomen;* cf. *Paullus* (*Fabius*) *Maximus*, I. 10. Like *Paullus* it was sometimes written with a single *l*. It was the name of the mythical ancestor of the family, from which

nititur pennis, vitreo daturus
nomina ponto.
Monte decurrens velut amnis, imbres
quem super notas aluere ripas,
fervet immensusque ruit profundo
Pindarus ore,
laurea donandus Apollinari,
seu per audacis nova dithyrambos
verba devolvit numerisque fertur
lege solutis,

their gentile name *Iulius* is formed, as *vilicus* from *villa*, *milia* from *mille*, etc. (Lachm. on Lucr. I. 313). Vergil, it appears, set the fashion of writing it as a trisyllable, with one *l*. — **ceratis**, *wax-jointed.* — **ope Daedalea**, *by the hand of a Daedalus* (the adjective here having its proper general force, unlike *Herculeus* I. 3. 36); *i.e.* such as Daedalus made for his son Icarus, with the result that the boy fell into the sea which thenceforth bore his name.

3. **nititur**, *soars;* cf. Verg. *A.* IV. 252 *paribus nitens Cyllenius alis.* — **vitreo**, *crystal;* cf. Verg. *A.* VII. 760 *vitrea te Fucinus unda,* | *te liquidi flevere lacus*, and see III. 13. 1 n, I. 17. 20 n. — **daturus**: Intr. 104 *b*.

4. **nomina**: cf. III. 27. 76 n.

5. **monte**: Intr. 70. — **velut, quem**: Intr. 114. — **amnis**: the comparison is a common one; cf. *S.* I. 10. 62 *rapido ferventius amni ingenium;* Cic. *Acad.* II. 119 *veniet flumen orationis aureum fundens Aristoteles.*

6. **notas**: cf. I. 2. 10.

7. **fervet immensusque ruit**, *rushes along with measureless, seething flood.* For the confusion of the poet with the river in the comparison, see Intr. 123. — **profundo ore**, *deep-mouthed*, *i.e.* gifted with deep and rich utterance, the 'beatissima rerum verborumque copia' which Quintilian (X. 1. 61) ascribes to him. For the expression cf. Ov. *Pont.* IV. 16. 5 *magni Rabirius oris;* *S.* I. 4. 43 *os magna sonaturum* (a requisite endowment of a genuine poet). **os** has nothing to do with the mouth of the river, where the phenomenon described in vs. 7 is seldom witnessed.

9. **laurea Apollinari**: cf. III. 30. 15. — **donandus**: the adjective use of the gerundive, expressing fitness or desert, is exceptionally frequent in this book; cf. *audiendum* 45, *laudande* 47, *loquenda* 4. 68, *socianda* 9. 4, *dicenda* 9. 21, etc.

10. **seu**, etc.: a series of hypothetical clauses with **donandus** as their common apodosis (cf. *moriture, seu*, etc., II. 3. 4 n), conveying the general meaning that Pindar was successful in whatever kind of poetry he undertook. — **nova**: *i.e.* newly coined, referring particularly to new compounds. — **dithyrambos**: originally a species

seu deos regesve canit, deorum
sanguinem, per quos cecidere iusta
morte Centauri, cecidit tremendae
flamma Chimaerae,

sive quos Elea domum reducit
palma caelestis pugilemve equumve
dicit et centum potiore signis
munere donat,

flebili sponsae iuvenemve raptum
plorat et viris animumque moresque

of choral song which grew up in connection with the worship of Dionysus and partook of the wild and tumultuous character of its origin. In its artistic form, which it owed to Arion (600 B.C.), it still retained, as the impassioned expression of strong enthusiasm, its earlier characteristics of unusual freedom of language (**audacis**) and disregard of strict metrical symmetry (**numeris lege solutis**).

11. **verba devolvit . . . fertur**: the figure of the river is still kept up.

13. **deos canit**: in his Hymns and Paeans.—**reges**: *i.e.* heroes (**deorum sanguinem**), as in *S.* I. 10. 42. The examples given are Theseus and Perithous (cf. I. 18. 8), and Bellerophon. The reference is to Pindar's Encomia.

15. **cecidit**: Intr. 116 *g*.

16. **flamma Chimaerae**: for 'the fiery Chimaera'; Intr. 126 *b*.

17. **sive quos**, etc.: *i.e.* in his Odes of Victory (Ἐπινίκια), still extant, in honor of those who won prizes at the great national games (Olympian, Pythian, Nemean, Isthmian). The Olympian festival (**Elēa**) is put forward to represent all four, as boxing and racing (vs. 18) stand for the various contests provided on each occasion (Intr. 117).

18. **palma**: see I. 1. 5 n.—**caelestis** (predicative acc. with **quos**): cf. *evehit ad deos*, I. 1. 6 n.—**pugilemve equumve**: in partitive apposition with **quos**. Cf. 3. 4, and (with this whole passage) *Ep.* II. 3. 83 *musa dedit fidibus divos puerosque deorum | et pugilem victorem et equum certamine primum . . . referre.* The steed is mentioned instead of his master,—here (with **quos**) at some sacrifice of logical connection,—as the real winner of the race.

19. **dicit**: see I. 6. 5 n.—**signis**, *statues*.

20. **munere**, *a boon;* cf. Ode 8, in which this thought is developed at length.

21. **flebili sponsae**, etc.: in his Eulogies (Θρῆνοι). This completes Horace's partial review of Pindar's work in lyric poetry.—**flebili**: here in an active sense; cf. I. 24. 9 and see II. 14. 6 n.—**-ve**: Intr. 114.—**raptum**: more forcible than *ereptum:* Intr. 129.

22. For the elision of **-que** at the end of this and the next verse see Intr. 174 *b*.

aureos educit in astra nigroque
invidet Orco.

Multa Dircaeum levat aura cycnum,
tendit, Antoni, quotiens in altos
nubium tractus : ego apis Matinae
more modoque

grata carpentis thyma per laborem
plurimum circa nemus uvidique
Tiburis ripas operosa parvus
carmina fingo.

23. **aureos**: proleptic, like *aeternum*, III. 25. 5. For the meaning, see I. 5. 9 n. — **educit**, etc.: *i.e.* exalts them in men's estimation and makes them immortal. — **in astra**: cf. *stellis inserere*, III. 25. 6 n. — **nigro**: cf. I. 24. 18 n.

24. **invidet** (*i.e.* rescues from) **Orco**: cf. 8. 28 *sq.*

25. Reverting to the subject of the opening verses and the figure of the first strophe, Horace concludes this introductory portion of the ode with a contrast between the strong poetic impulse which sustained Pindar in his lofty flight and his own humbler gift of artistic workmanship. — **multa aura**, *a full, strong breeze.* — **Dircaeum**: *i.e.* Theban, from the famous spring and brook Dirce, near the city. — **cycnum**: a stock metaphor, especially in Alexandrine literature; see II. 20, intr. note. For the prosody, cf. 3. 20 n.

27. **apis**, etc.: a frequent simile; cf. *Ep.* I. 3. 21, 19. 44; Plat. *Ion* 534 A λέγουσι γὰρ πρὸς ἡμᾶς οἱ ποιηταί, ὅτι . . . τὰ μέλη ἡμῖν φέρουσιν ὥσπερ αἱ μέλιτται; Arist. *Birds* 749. — **Matinae**: *i.e.* of my native Apulia; cf. I. 28. 3 n.

28. **more modoque**: one of those (often alliterative) phrases, common in all languages, in which two words, presenting slightly different aspects of the same thing, readily coalesce to form a fuller expression of a single idea; cf. 'might and main,' 'hearth and home,' 'safe and sound,' etc.; Intr. 131.

29. **per laborem**: more expressive than *labore*, **per** (= 'in the course of') suggesting prolonged toil; cf. the phrases *per otium*, *per ludum et iocum*, *per iram* (*aliquid facere*).

30. **plurimum**: with **laborem**. — **circa nemus**, etc.: Horace's own favorite haunts; but the details still apply to the bee; the comparison and its subject are purposely blended (Intr. 123).

31. **Tiburis**: limiting both **nemus** and **ripas**; Intr. 119 *a*. — **ripas**: *sc.* of the Anio and the brooks implied in **uvidi**; cf. I. 7. 14, III. 29. 6, IV. 3. 10. For this absolute use of *ripa*, cf. III. 25. 13. — **operosa parvus**: still keeping before our minds the 'little toiler' to whom he is comparing himself.

33. **concines**: standing first, with the emphasis of assurance (cf. I. 6. 1 n), to correct the im-

Concines maiore poeta plectro
Caesarem, quandoque trahet ferocis
per sacrum clivum merita decorus
fronde Sygambros ;
quo nihil maius meliusve terris
fata donavere bonique divi
nec dabunt, quamvis redeant in aurum
tempora priscum.

pression given by the preceding strophes, that the praises of Augustus would not be sung. There is no antithesis between Horace and Antonius as to which should be the singer, — that would require *tu* to be expressed. There is a contrast between their methods of work, but it is subordinate to the main thought, which is contained in the two emphatic words, **concines** and **Caesarem** (Intr. 116 *b*); see intr. note. — **maiore plectro** (descriptive abl.; cf. II. 1. 40 n): as we might speak of a painter 'wielding a larger brush,' in contrast to a miniature painter. It means, therefore, not a greater poet, but one who works with a freer and bolder stroke, neglecting nicety of finish, — a description that might well apply to Antonius, whose training was in epic. For the *plectrum*, see I. 26. 11 n.

34. **quandoque**: see I. 17 n. — **trahet**: in contrast with **ferocis** (Intr. 116 *a*); an appropriate verb, as implying their unwillingness to go (cf. *Ep.* II. 1. 191); but in fact the prisoners preceded the victor's car; see I. 12. 54 n.

35. **per**, *down;* cf. *Epod.* 7. 8 n. — **sacrum clivum**: that part of the Sacra Via from the summit of the Velia down to the Forum. The name occurs only here and twice in Martial (I. 70. 5, IV. 78. 7).

36. **fronde**: the laurel wreath worn by the *triumphator.* — **Sygambros**: a German tribe, dwelling on the south of the Lippe. Their warlike spirit (cf. **ferocis**, 34; *caede gaudentes*, 14. 51) gave them the lead among their countrymen at this time, and their feat of routing a Roman army invested them in Roman eyes with exaggerated importance. They were subsequently removed to the left bank of the Rhine, and furnished auxiliaries to the Roman armies.

37. **nihil**: cf. *nil*, I. 12. 17 n; *Ep.* II. 1. 17 *nil oriturum alias, nil ortum tale fatentes* (*sc.* as Augustus). — **maius meliusve**: Intr. 131. Cf. Cic. *Acad.* I. 7 *nec ullum . . . maius aut melius a dis datum munus homini.*

38. **boni**, *kind;* cf. 5. 1.

39. **nec dabunt**: in such phrases the same verb is usually repeated, as II. 13. 20 *rapuit rapietque*, *Ep.* I. 2. 43 *labitur et labetur*, *C. S.* 2 *colendi semper et culti*, *Ep.* II. 1. 17 (above), etc.; but the variation here is softened by the separation of the words. — **quamvis**, etc.: *i.e.* though the golden age (*tempus aureum*, *Epod.* 16. 64, 65 n) should return. — **redeant**: *i.e.* change back into; cf. Ov. *M.* XIV. 766 (*deus*) *in iuvenem rediit.*

40. **tempora**, *the world;* literally 'the generations,' as in *Ep.*

Concines laetosque dies et urbis
publicum ludum super impetrato
fortis Augusti reditu forumque
  litibus orbum.

Tum meae, si quid loquar audiendum,
vocis accedet bona pars, et 'O sol
pulcher, o laudande!' canam, recepto
  Caesare felix.

Teque dum procedis, 'Io Triumphe!'
non semel dicemus 'Io Triumphe!'
civitas omnis, dabimusque divis
  tura benignis.

II. 1. 130. — **priscum**: cf. *Epod.* 2. 2 n.

41. **concines**: Intr. 116 *h.* — **laetos dies**: a variation on *festos dies*.

42. **ludum**: for the more usual *ludos.* — **super**: with the abl. (see I. 9. 5 n), expressing the subject of rejoicing, as in III. 8. 17 *super urbe curas*, the subject of anxiety. — **impetrato**, *vouchsafed to our prayers;* cf. vs. 54 n.

43. **fortis**: cf. *S.* II. 1. 16. — **forum litibus orbum**: the third paraphrase in this strophe for a technical term (*iustitium*). For **litibus**, see Intr. 66 *c*, N. It is clear that when this ode was written, the return of Augustus in the near future, though no definite time had been set (cf. *quandoque*, vs. 34), was confidently anticipated, so that the manner of his reception was talked over by those in authority. His return was delayed long beyond their or his own expectation, as appears from 5. 3 *sq.*, and his entry into the city was then made, by his own choice, unannounced and by night; the triumph which Horace and his friends anticipated never came off. The *publicus ludus*, however, took place.

45. **loquar**: less common than *dico* for poetical utterance, but cf. 15. 1. — **audiendum**: cf. *donandus*, vs. 9 n, and *laudande*, vs. 47.

46. **bona pars**, *a liberal measure.* — **sol**: *i.e.* day, the sun of each new day being, for poetical purposes, another sun; cf. *C. S.* 10, *Epod.* 2. 41 n.

47. **recepto Caesare**: see Intr. 105.

49. **teque . . . dicemus**, *and on thy name . . . shall we call.* The cry of the soldiers and people, as the triumphant pageant advanced, **io triumphe**, was regarded as a shout of greeting to the personified Triumphus, **triumphe** being vocative; cf. *Epod.* 9. 21 *Io Triumphe, tu moraris aureos | currus et intactas boves? | Io Triumphe, nec Iugurthino parem | bello reportasti ducem*, etc.

50. **non semel**: *i.e.* again and again (litotes).

51. **civitas**: in apposition with

Te decem tauri totidemque vaccae,
me tener solvet vitulus, relicta
matre qui largis iuvenescit herbis
in mea vota,
fronte curvatos imitatus ignis
tertium lunae referentis ortum,
qua notam duxit niveus videri,
cetera fulvus.

the subject of **dicemus**; cf. *aetas*, I. 35. 35.

52. **tura**: cf. I. 22 n. Incense was burned on temporary altars on the streets as the procession passed.

53. **te**: emphatic, in anticipation of the comparison to be drawn between the two sacrifices. Each must make an offering according to his substance. Cf. II. 17. 30 *sqq.*

54. **solvet**: *sc.* from the obligation of our vows, which the granting of our prayers has made binding.—**relicta matre**: *i.e.* weaned. The detailed description which follows is in Horace's favorite manner; see I. 2. 7 n. It serves here to heighten the contrast between the rich Antonius, who can send victims by the score to the altar, and the owner of a modest farm, who knows well every creature in his small herd, and to whom the sacrifice is therefore more of a personal matter; and it furnishes the ode, at the same time, with a pleasing close, drawing the reader's mind away from the stirring picture just described, to rest, in parting, on a quiet rural scene. Cf. the close of III. 5.

55. **iuvenescit**: bear in mind that *iuventus* is not precisely 'youth,' in our sense, but the prime of life.

56. **in**: *i.e.* with them in view, for their fulfilment.

57. **curvatos**: *i.e.* crescent. — **ignis**: cf. I. 12. 47.

58. **tertium referentis ortum**: *i.e.* on the third evening after the new moon. Cf. III. 29. 20, and see note on *reducit*, II. 10. 15.

59. **qua** (*i.e. in fronte*): qualifying **niveus**, which, to correspond with **fulvus**, is put as a characteristic of the animal, and not merely of the spot. — **duxit**, *has got, has taken on;* cf. Ov. *M.* III. 484 *ut variis solet uva racemis | ducere purpureum nondum matura colorem.* — **niveus videri**: Intr. 102.

60. **cetera**: Intr. 44.

## III.

Quem tu, Melpomene, semel
  nascentem placido lumine videris,
illum non labor Isthmius
  clarabit pugilem, non equus impiger
curru ducet Achaico
  victorem, neque res bellica Deliis

III. The steady growth of Horace's reputation, culminating in the official recognition of his eminence in his appointment to write the Secular Hymn in B.C. 17, had the usual effect of success in silencing to a considerable degree the small critics, of whose attacks he complains occasionally in his earlier writings. He could now speak without either vanity or false modesty of the attainment of what in presenting to the public his first collection of odes he had held up as the summit of his aspiration. He speaks of it in the present poem in a spirit rather of gratitude than of boasting. His muse is here, at least, no mere creature of fancy or literary convention; she is to him 'a power, not himself,' but above him and working in him; and to her he renders all the praise for what he has done. There is a reminiscence of I. 1 in the contrast between the meditative life of the poet, seeking his inspiration in the seclusion of grove and stream, and the exciting pursuit of the great prizes of physical prowess, athletic victory for the Greek, triumph in war for the Roman. — Metre, 171.

1. **Melpomene**: cf. III. 30. 16, I. 12. 2 n. — **semel**: cf. I. 24. 16 n, *C. S.* 26.

2. **nascentem**, etc.: an idea borrowed originally perhaps from the Chaldean astrologers (see note on *adspicit*, II. 17. 17), but Horace found it in his Greek poets; cf. Hes. *Theog.* 81 *ὅντινα τιμήσωσι Διὸς κοῦραι μεγάλοιο* (*i.e.* the Muses) | *γεινόμενόν τ' ἐσίδωσι διοτρεφέων βασιλήων,* | *τῷ μὲν ἐπὶ γλώσσῃ γλυκερὴν χείουσιν ἐέρσην,* | *τοῦ δ' ἔπε' ἐκ στόματος ῥεῖ μείλιχα.*

3. **labor**: for the Greek *πόνος, κάματος*, often applied by Pindar to these struggles. — **Isthmius**: cf. *Olympico*, I. 1. 3 n; *Elea*, IV. 2. 17 n; Intr. 117.

4. **pugilem, equus**: see 2. 18 n.

5. **ducet**, *draw; sc.* in the race. — **Achaico**: *i.e.* Greek (in contrast with the Roman type of triumph next presented).

6. **victorem**, *to victory;* proleptic, like **pugilem**. — **res bellica**: a paraphrase for *bellum* (like *res ludicra*, *Ep.* II. 1. 180, for the drama), but more comprehensive, — the business of war with all its vicissitudes, *the fortunes of war*. — **Deliis**: *i.e.* of laurel, so called as sacred to Apollo; cf. *Delphica lauro*, III. 30. 15; *laurea Apollinari*, IV. 2. 9. For the practice, cf. Ov. *Tr.* IV. 2. 51 *tempora Phoebea lauro cingetur, 'Io' que* | *miles 'Io' magna voce 'Triumphe' canet.*

8. **quod regum**, etc.: in accordance with the Roman traditional

ornatum foliis ducem,
quod regum tumidas contuderit minas,
ostendet Capitolio ;
sed quae Tibur aquae fertile praefluunt
et spissae nemorum comae
fingent Aeolio carmine nobilem.
Romae, principis urbium,
dignatur suboles inter amabilis
vatum ponere me choros,
et iam dente minus mordeor invido.
O testudinis aureae
dulcem quae strepitum, Pieri, temperas,
o mutis quoque piscibus
donatura cycni, si libeat, sonum,

idea that their mission was to extend the blessings of peace and good government ; cf. *C. S.* 51 n. — **contuderit,** *crushed to earth ;* carrying out the figure in **tumidas.** — **minas** : cf. II. 12. 11 *ductaque per vias | regum colla minacium.*

9. **Capitolio** : Intr. 69. The triumphal pageant culminated in a sacrifice to Jupiter by the *triumphator* on the Capitol.

10. **sed quae Tibur,** etc.: cf. I. 1. 29 n. The environs of Tibur are put as a type of beautiful natural scenery in general (Intr. 117), but serve at the same time to prepare us for the transition to Horace's own case (cf. 2. 30 *sq.*). — **aquae** : cf. I. 7. 13 *sq.* — **praefluunt** : for the more common *praeterfluunt,* as in 14. 26.

11. **comae**: cf. I. 21. 5 n.

12. **Aeolio carmine** : see III. 30. 13 n.

13. The enunciation of the foregoing general truth has paved the way for Horace's own experience, which illustrates it. — **Romae**: the city is personified. — **principis,** *queen ;* cf. *Ep.* I. 7. 44 *regia Roma.*

14. **dignatur ponere me,** *deems me worthy a place.* — **suboles,** *the children, i.e.* the Roman nation. — **inter vatum choros** : cf. I. 1. 35 n.

16. **iam minus,** *less and less.* — **dente invido**: Intr. 124 ; cf. Cic. *Balb.* 57 *more hominum invident, . . . non illo inimico, sed hoc malo dente carpunt; Epod.* 6. 15 n.

17. **testudinis**: cf. I. 10. 6 n.— **aureae**: cf. I. 5. 9 n; *aureo plectro,* II. 13. 26 n ; Pind. *Pyth.* 1. 1 *χρυσέα φόρμιγξ,* Ἀπόλλωνος καὶ *ἰοπλοκάμων σύνδικον* Μοισᾶν *κτέανον.*

18. **Pieri** : see note on *Haemo,* I. 12. 6. — **temperas,** *dost modulate.*

19. **quoque,** *even,* as in *Ep.* II. 2. 36 ; an uncommon use of the word.

20. **donatura** : Intr. 104 *e.* — **cycni** : with the penult short ; in 2. 25 it is long.

totum muneris hoc tui est,
  quod monstror digito praetereuntium
Romanae fidicen lyrae ;
  quod spiro et placeo, si placeo, tuum est.

## IV.

Qualem ministrum fulminis alitem,

21. **muneris**: cf. 2. 20 n; 10. 1. — **tui est**: to be read *tuist;* see I. 3. 37 n.

22. **monstror**, etc.: a sort of public recognition often alluded to by Greek and Roman writers, in itself of ambiguous significance (cf. Ov. *Am.* III. 6. 77) and needing the specification of vs. 23; cf. Lucian, *Herod.* 2 εἴ πού γε φανείη μόνον, ἐδείκνυτο ἂν τῷ δακτύλῳ, Οὗτος ἐκεῖνος Ἡρόδοτός ἐστιν . . . ὁ τὰς νίκας ἡμῶν ὑμνήσας.

23. **Romanae fidicen lyrae**, *as minstrel*, etc.; cf. *Ep.* I. 19. 32 *hunc* (sc. *Alcaeum*) *ego Latinus volgavi fidicen.* The title contains the same meaning as *Aeolium carmen ad Italos deduxisse modos*, III. 30. 13; the claim there made is now publicly recognized.

24. **quod spiro**, etc.: *i.e.* my inspiration (*spiritus*, II. 16. 38, IV. 6. 29) and such success as I win. The clause is the subject of **est**. — **tuum est** (see vs. 21 n): *i.e.* is thy achievement, not mine; the praise belongs to thee.

IV. In the spring of B.C. 15, while Augustus was in Gaul (see intr. note to Ode 2), Drusus, the younger of his step-sons, then twenty-three years old, led an army up the Adige and defeated the united forces of the Raetians and Vindelicians near Tridentum (Trent). The professed object of the expedition was to put a stop to the predatory raids of the mountain tribes into the Po valley. To complete the work, Drusus crossed the Brenner pass and attacked the Breuni and Genauni in the valley of the Inn, while his brother Tiberius invaded the country from the west, coming from Gaul by way of the Rhine and Lake Constance. By this combined movement, the Romans crushed out all resistance. They scoured the valleys of eastern Switzerland and the Tyrol, driving the mountaineers from their strongholds, and doing the work of subjugation so thoroughly, that this whole mountain region (the Raetian Alps), with the country of the Vindelicians, extending northward to the Danube, was added to the empire (as the province of Raetia) by this single campaign.

The celebration of this brilliant exploit, the glory of which the emperor shared with the young conquerors, was a kind of task for which Horace had often declared his unfitness (*e.g.* in *S.* II. 1. 12 *sqq.*, and, only recently, in Ode 2); and he undertook it, Suetonius says, in deference to the express wish of Augustus. The present ode is concerned only with the first victory of Drusus, in the Tridentine Alps ; and we must suppose that Horace wrote it soon

cui rex deorum regnum in avis vagas
permisit expertus fidelem
Iuppiter in Ganymede flavo,
olim iuventas et patrius vigor
nido laborum propulit inscium,
vernique iam nimbis remotis
insolitos docuere nisus

**after that** event, before the news of the equally brilliant and much more important successes of the two brothers later in the season had reached Rome. These form the subject of Ode 14, written subsequently. Following the example of Pindar, Horace devotes the smaller part of his ode to the exploit it celebrates, and takes his main theme from the heroic age of Rome. Nothing could have been invented more suitable to his purpose than the dramatic episode of the fight on the Metaurus (B.C. 207), in which the most conspicuous part was played by a Nero, and the other chief actor was a Livius. The transition from the praises of Drusus to the glorification of his ancestors is skilfully effected by an analysis of his excellence, in which the honors are evenly divided between heredity and good home training, for the latter of which he was indebted to Augustus. — Metre, 176.

1–16. The subject of the ode is introduced by an elaborate simile in two parts, the first designed to picture to us the impetuous valor of the young hero, the other the terror his appearance inspired in the enemy.

1. **ministrum fulminis**: appositional attribute (κεραυνοφόρος) of **alitem** (Intr. 126 *c*). So in Ovid *M.* XII. 560 the eagle is *volucris quae fulmina curvis ferre solet pedibus*, and in Verg. *A*. V. 255, *Iovis armiger*.

2. **rex . . . regnum . . .**: notice the antithesis: the king of heaven has made his servant a king. — **regnum permisit**: cf. *S.* I. 3. 123. — **in**: cf. III. 1. 5 n.

3. **expertus** (sc. *eum*) **fidelem**, *having proved his loyalty*; cf. *comitem abnegat*, I. 35. 22 n.

4. **in**, *in the case of*. — **Ganymede**: see III. 20. 16 n. — **flavo**, *fair-haired* (ξανθός); see note on *Pyrrha* I. 5. 3.

5. **olim**, *one day*. Originally an adverbial form of *olle* (*ille*), meaning 'at that time' (*i.e.* not at this time), *olim* came to be applied in a vague way to any action not present, whether past ('once,' 'once upon a time'), — its commoner use, — or future, as *S.* II. 5. 27 *si res certabitur olim* ('sometime,' 'ever'); and hence, by an easy step, to an action cited as the type of a class and which may therefore occur at any time, either with the present tense, as *S.* I. 1. 25 *pueris olim dant crustula blandi doctores* ('sometimes'), or with the 'gnomic' perfect, as here. Cf. the use of *ille* itself with such a perfect, Verg. *A*. XI. 809.

6. **nido**: Intr. 70. — **laborum**, *toil and struggle*; cf. 3. 3 n; for the case, Intr. 66 *b*. — **propulit**, etc.: Intr. 80.

7. **verni**: *i.e.* soft, gentle. Hor-

venti paventem, mox in ovilia
demisit hostem vividus impetus,
nunc in reluctantis dracones
egit amor dapis atque pugnae ;

qualemve laetis caprea pascuis
intenta fulvae matris ab ubere
iam lacte depulsum leonem
dente novo peritura vidit :

ace's ornithology is at fault here, as the young eagles are not sufficiently grown to fly till late summer or autumn. — **iam . . . mox . . . nunc** : marking three stages in the growth of the eaglet's strength and courage, — his first timid ventures in flying, his attack upon an unresisting prey, and finally his entering with zest into a fight with a dangerous foe.—**nimbis,** *storm-clouds* (of winter).

11. **dracones,** *snakes.* The Greek name is perhaps a reminiscence of the description in *Il.* XII. 200 *sqq.* (cf. Verg. *A.* XI. 751 *sqq.*).

13. **qualemve** : while the case shows that Drusus is compared to the lion, the design of this comparison is to bring out the other side of the picture, and therefore the roe is made more prominent. The student should use his ingenuity to render accurately these shades of meaning in good English. — **laetis,** *glad, i.e.* luxuriant ; the word in this connection had almost ceased to be metaphorical ('*laetas segetes*' *etiam rustici dicunt* Cic. de *Or.* III. 155). — **pascuis intenta** : the point to be brought out is the helpless surprise of the victim.

14. **fulvae** : a common epithet of the lion, as Verg. *A.* II. 722, IV. 159, VIII. 552, etc. — **matris ab ubere,** etc. : a difficult passage, and not improbably corrupt, as **iam** seems hardly in keeping with the point of the comparison, which would rather require *vix* or *nuper.* Some editors have taken refuge in an interpretation which refers **fulvae matris ab ubere** (depending on a verbal idea contained in **pascuis intenta,** which is held to imply the direction of the attention *away from* something else) to the roe and **lacte depulsum** to the lion. But, to say nothing of the feebleness of applying the same description to the two contrasted animals, it is not probable that Horace gratuitously weakened his comparison by representing the enemies of Drusus as inexperienced and *naturally* timid. Some have taken **ubere** as an adjective, and this would be appropriate enough, as implying that the lion, though young, was richly nurtured by a vigorous mother ; but as *ab ubere depulsus,* as well as (*a*) *lacte depulsus,* is a technical phrase (*e.g.* Verg. *G.* III. 187, *E.* 7. 15), this explanation appears to be excluded. If the text is correct, we shall have to take **lacte depulsum** as used to express a single idea (*weaned*), to which **matris ab ubere** is attached to give an additional detail to the picture.

16. **peritura** : Intr. 104 *b.* With **vidit** it has something of the same

videre Raetis bella sub Alpibus
Drusum gerentem Vindelici (quibus
mos unde deductus per omne
tempus Amazonia securi

force as Vergil's *sensit medios delapsus in hostem* (*A.* II. 377), *i.e.* the roe becomes aware of the lion's presence and of its own doom at the same moment; cf. also Ov. *M.* IX. 545 *superata fateri cogor.*

17. **videre**: the epanastrophe in the absence of *talem*, marks the beginning of the apodosis. — — **Raetis**: for *Raeticis* (Intr. 65). The epithet is sufficient, in Horace's suggestive manner, to indicate the participation of the Raetians in the conflict. The Vindelici were evidently more prominent in people's minds at Rome, probably because they were more aggressive, having advanced beyond their own borders, and were a new enemy, while the strongholds and the raids of the Raetians were a familiar story. — **bella**: Intr. 128.

18. **Drusum**: younger son of Ti. Claudius Nero and Livia, but born after his mother's marriage to Augustus. Of singularly winning nature, he was a favorite with Augustus and with the people, who hoped he would be the emperor's successor. But he died in his thirtieth year (B.C. 9), from the effects of a fall from his horse, while engaged in his third campaign in Germany. He was the father of the equally popular Germanicus and of the emperor Claudius. — **quibus**, *their;* cf. *tibi*, III. 18. 10 n. The interrogative is **unde**, and the gist of the question is contained, as often, in the dependent word (**deductus**), — *whence the custom was derived which arms,* etc.; cf. *S.* I. 6. 12 *Valeri, unde Tarquinius pulsus fugit.* This ill-timed digression could be removed from the text without detriment to the metre, and one would gladly blot it out as unworthy of Horace's taste, were it not even more difficult to believe it the work of a forger. If Horace wrote it, we may suppose his object was, in introducing the battle-axe of the Vindelici, to make use of the anticipated astonishment of the reader at finding this Amazonian weapon in the hands of Alpine barbarians, to give his narrative something of the rush of the unstemmed torrent of Pindaric utterance which he describes in Ode 2, — as if the course of thought were: 'whose right hand wields the Amazonian battle-axe, — Where, you will exclaim, did they get that custom, after a thousand years? But I cannot stop for the question now; I must hurry on; there are some things it is not given us to know in this world.' Unfortunately the last expression has the appearance of sarcasm, as if Horace had interrupted his fine tribute to the prince and the emperor to ridicule some antiquarian who had attempted to solve the question; and some have supposed he was guilty even of this breach of good manners.

19. **per omne tempus**: *i.e.* from the remotest antiquity to the present day; modifying **deductus**.

20. **securi**: for the shape of it see Baumeister *Denkmäler* I. pp. 60, 63.

dextras obarmet, quaerere distuli,
nec scire fas est omnia), sed diu
lateque victrices catervae
consiliis iuvenis revictae
sensere quid mens rite, quid indoles
nutrita faustis sub penetralibus
posset, quid Augusti paternus
in pueros animus Nerones.

Fortes creantur fortibus et bonis;
est in iuvencis, est in equis patrum
virtus, neque imbellem feroces
progenerant aquilae columbam:

21. **obarmet**: found only here in Latin literature of the classical period. The prefix has the same force as in *obsero, obduro*, etc. — **quaerere**: Intr. 94*j*.

22. **nec scire**, etc.: *i.e.* there are some things Heaven does not intend us to know; cf. III. 29. 29 *sqq.*—**sed**: resuming the narrative after the digression.—**diu lateque victrices**: probably referring to a raid which preceded the battle with Drusus.

24. **consiliis**, *strategy*. — **revictae**, *beaten in their turn*, **re-** expressing the reversal of the tide of victory.

25. **sensere**: emphatic (Intr. 116*b*); they learned by *experience* (in their own persons); cf. II. 7. 10. — **quid posset**: Intr. 47. This and the two following strophes are the poet's tribute of praise to Augustus for his contribution to the result achieved, before proceeding to his main theme, in which Augustus has no part. — **mens . . . indoles**, *mind . . . character.*— **rite nutrita**: for the order see Intr. 120. The words **rite**, **faustis**, and **penetralibus**, with their religious associations, lend a suggestion of sacredness to the home life to which they refer.

26. **sub penetralibus**: cf. *sub lare*, III. 29. 14 n.

27. **paternus in pueros animus**: cf. II. 2. 6 n.

28. **Nerones**: Drusus and his elder brother Tiberius (Claudius Nero), afterwards emperor. As their father died soon after the divorce of their mother and her marriage to Octavian (B.C. 38), they were brought up in the house of the latter. For **pueros**, see I. 9. 16 n.

29. **fortes**, etc.: this strophe is to a certain degree concessive: heredity is all-essential, but training is no less so. Hence the emphasis on **est** (Intr. 116*g*), — *there is* (undoubtedly). — **fortibus et bonis** (ablative): a frequent formula of commendation; cf. *Ep.* I. 9. 13 *scribe tui gregis hunc et fortem crede bonumque;* Cic. *Fam.* V. 19. 1 *quod omnes fortes ac boni viri facere debent.*

31. **virtus**, *excellence*. — **imbellem feroces**: Intr. 116*a*.

doctrina sed vim promovet insitam,
rectique cultus pectora roborant;
utcumque defecere mores,
indecorant bene nata culpae.

Quid debeas, o Roma, Neronibus,
testis Metaurum flumen et Hasdrubal
devictus et pulcher fugatis
ille dies Latio tenebris,

qui primus alma risit adorea,

33. **doctrina sed**: Intr. 114. For the emphatic positions of the important words in this strophe, see Intr. 116*b*. For the sentiment cf. Cic. *Arch.* 15 *ego idem contendo, cum ad naturam eximiam atque inlustrem accesserit ratio quaedam conformatioque doctrinae, tum illud nescio quid praeclarum ac singulare solere exsistere; Tusc.* II. 13.

34. **recti**: adjective; cf. *Ep.* II. 2. 122 *sano cultu.* — **cultus pectora**: plurals of repeated occurrence. For **pectora** (the moral nature), cf. I. 3. 9 n.

35. **utcumque**, *the moment;* see I. 17. 10 n. — **defecere mores**, *discipline breaks down.*

36. **bene nata**, *a noble nature.* For this use of the neuter plural, cf. I. 34. 12 n.

37. Here Horace reaches his main theme, the glorious ancestry of Drusus. In the twelfth year of the second Punic war, when Hannibal was at Canusium, awaiting the arrival of his brother Hasdrubal, who had crossed the Alps with a large army, the consul Claudius Nero, who faced Hannibal in Apulia, intercepted a despatch which put him in possession of Hasdrubal's plans. By a rapid and secret march, with 7000 picked men, he joined his colleague Livius at Sena Gallica, and the two consuls with their united forces met and destroyed Hasdrubal's army at the river Metaurus. Nero then hastily returned to his own camp. The whole episode, which was the turning point of the war and of Hannibal's career, occupied scarcely a fortnight, and the first news which Hannibal received of Nero's absence and his own disaster came in the ghastly form of his brother's head, which the brutal Roman tossed over the lines. Horace had perhaps recently read the account of this episode in Livy's twenty-seventh book (ch. 43 *sqq.*), which was published about this time. — **quid debeas**: depending on **testis** (sc. *est*).

38. **Metaurum flumen**: Intr. 65. — **Hasdrubal devictus**: Intr. 105*a*.

39. **pulcher dies**: cf. *sol pulcher*, 2. 46.—**fugatis tenebris**: abl. (Intr. 105*a*), the cause of **pulcher.**

41. **adorea**, *victory* (more strictly, 'military glory'); an old word (cf. Plaut. *Amph.* 193) apparently revived by Horace and frequently used by later writers. Originally an adjective from *ador* (spelt), how it came to have this meaning is uncertain.

dirus per urbis Afer ut Italas
 ceu flamma per taedas vel Eurus
  per Siculas equitavit undas.
Post hoc secundis usque laboribus
Romana pubes crevit, et impio
 vastata Poenorum tumultu
  fana deos habuere rectos,
dixitque tandem perfidus Hannibal:
'Cervi, luporum praeda rapacium,
 sectamur ultro quos opimus
  fallere et effugere est triumphus.

42. **dirus Afer**: cf. III. 6. 36. — **per**: *i.e.* from one to another. — **ut**, *since* (temporal); cf. *Epod.* 7. 19; *S.* II. 2. 128; Cic. *Brut.* 19 *ut illos de re publica libros edidisti, nihil a te sane postea accepimus.* For the position, see Intr. 114.

43. **ceu**: found here only in Horace. — **flamma**: sc. *it* (zeugma). **Eurus**, however, is thought as 'riding' over the sea in Eurip. *Phoen.* 209 περιῤῥύτων ὑπὲρ ἀκαρπίστων πεδίων Σικελίας Ζεφύρου πνοαῖς ἱππεύσαντος, a passage which Horace may have had in mind here.

45. **usque**, *more and more;* cf. III. 30. 7 n. — **laboribus**: cf. 3. 3 n.

46. **pubes**: cf. III. 5. 18, *Epod.* 16. 7. — **crevit**, *waxed stronger.*

47. **tumultu**, *riot.* *Tumultus*, in a military sense, denoted a war within or upon the Roman borders (Cic. *Phil.* 8. 2 *sq.*), such as the Social and Servile wars. The Hannibalic war took this form, and the word is accordingly applied to it in disparagement.

48. **rectos**, *upright, erect.*

49. **dixitque tandem**, etc.: this speech, if we make due allowance for poetical embellishment, does not misrepresent the effect of the disaster on Hannibal; cf. Liv. XXVII. 51. 12 *Hannibal, tanto simul publico familiarique ictus luctu, agnoscere se fortunam Carthaginis fertur dixisse.* — **perfidus**: a stock epithet, born of unreasoning prejudice and hatred; cf. Livy's portrait of Hannibal, XXI. 4. 9, *inhumana crudelitas, perfidia plus quam Punica, nihil veri, nihil sancti, nullus deum metus, nullum ius iurandum, nulla religio.*

50. **cervi**: Intr. 123. — **praeda**: *i.e.* naturally, usually; cf. *negata*, III. 2. 22 n.

51. **ultro**, *actually.* *Vltro*, which commonly characterizes an action as gratuitous or voluntary (going *beyond* what the situation calls for or permits), is often applied to conduct which reverses the natural relation of two parties, as when an assailant demands redress of his victim, an evil-liver denounces vice, or the like, or when, as here, the weak attacks the strong. — **opimus triumphus**: after the analogy of *spolia opima.*

52. **fallere**: cf. I. 10. 16, III. 11. 40 n. — **effugere est triumphus**: oxymoron.

Gens quae cremato fortis ab Ilio
iactata Tuscis aequoribus sacra
natosque maturosque patres
pertulit Ausonias ad urbis,

duris ut ilex tonsa bipennibus
nigrae feraci frondis in Algido,
per damna, per caedis, ab ipso
ducit opes animumque ferro.

Non hydra secto corpore firmior
vinci dolentem crevit in Herculem,
monstrumve submisere Colchi
maius Echioniaeve Thebae.

53. **gens quae**, etc.: Horace had read the Aeneid when he wrote this strophe; cf. III. 3. 40 n. — **cremato ab**, *from the ashes of*, *i.e.* from utter ruin. With this idea **fortis** is contrasted by its position.

54. **iactata**, etc. (with **gens**): *i.e.* through the utmost hardships. — **sacra**: *i.e.* the images of the gods and their belongings, — the *effigies sacrae divom Phrygiaeque penates* (Verg. *A.* III. 148).

56. **pertulit**: the prefix expresses perseverance to the end; cf. *perficiunt*, vs. 73, and *persequitur*, III. 2. 14 n.

57. **duris ut**, etc.: Intr. 114, 123.

58. **nigrae frondis**: that of the ilex itself (Intr. 124); cf. Verg. *E.* 6. 54 *ilice sub nigra*. For the case, see Intr. 66 *a*. — **Algido**: see I. 21. 6 n, III. 23. 9 *sq.*; Intr. 117.

59. **per**: *i.e.* in the course of, right through it all; cf. 2. 29 n.

60. **ducit**, *draws*.

61. **non**: with **firmior** and **maius**. — **hydra**: this simile Horace might have found in Livy, but in the mouth of Pyrrhus instead of Hannibal; see Flor. *Epit.* I. 18. 19 *cum Pyrrhus 'video me' inquit 'plane procreatum Herculis semine, cui quasi ab angue Lernaeo tot caesa hostium capita quasi de sanguine suo renascuntur.'* The comparison more probably originated with Pyrrhus' minister, Cineas (Plut. *Pyrrh.* 19).

62. **vinci dolentem**: Intr. 94 *m*.

63. **monstrum**, *wonder*. The allusion is to the crops of armed men that sprang from the dragon's teeth sown by Jason (**Colchi**) and Cadmus (**Thebae**), — vastly more formidable than the dragon itself. So the Roman legions seemed to spring from the very soil. — **submisere**: cf. Lucr. I. 7 *tellus submittit flores*. — **Colchi**: cf. *Afro* III. 3. 47 n.

64. **Echioniae**: Echion was one of the five survivors of the fight which Cadmus precipitated among the earth-born warriors. He married Agave, daughter of Cadmus, and became the father of Pentheus.

Merses profundo, pulchrior evenit ;
luctere, multa proruet integrum
cum laude victorem geretque
proelia coniugibus loquenda.

Carthagini iam non ego nuntios
mittam superbos ; occidit, occidit
spes omnis et fortuna nostri
nominis Hasdrubale interempto.'

Nil Claudiae non perficient manus,
quas et benigno numine Iuppiter
defendit et curae sagaces
expediunt per acuta belli.

65. **merses :** sc. *eam*, the *gens* of vs. 53, but under the figure of a marvelous being (**monstrum**) as in the preceding strophe. There is perhaps an allusion in this verse to the first Punic war, which was largely a naval contest. For the mood of **merses** and **luctere**, see Intr. 87. They here do service as conditional clauses. — **profundo :** Intr. 69. — **evenit :** here used in the very rare literal sense ; cf. *pereuntis*, III. 11. 27.

66. **proruet . . . geret :** the future, expressing what *will prove* true (in every case), when the trial is made, is here coupled with a present (**evenit**) of general statement. — **integrum,** *unscathed* (*sc.* in the previous contest).

67. **laude,** *credit, éclat ;* cf. *S.* I. 10. 49 ; Cat. 64. 112 *inde pedem sospes multa cum laude reflexit.* — **victorem :** *i.e.* the antagonist who has just overthrown him. Cf. Hannibal's comment on the Romans under Marcellus, Liv. XXVII. 14. 1, *seu vicit, ferociter instat victis ; seu victus est, instaurat cum victoribus certamen.*

68. **coniugibus loquenda :** *i.e.* memorable, the theme of many a fireside talk. For the gerundive, see 2. 9 n.

69. **Carthagini :** Intr. 53. — **iam non,** *no more.*

70. **occidit :** Intr. 116 *d.*

72. **Hasdrubale interempto :** there is a climax of pathos in these closing words, in which the depressing sense of personal bereavement, which underlies the despair pictured in the preceding verses, comes to the surface.

73–76. The ode closes with a brief epilogue, summing up the merits of the Claudii, which have been illustrated in the ancient and the modern instance given.

75. **curae sagaces :** their own wisdom, in contrast with the divine protection just spoken of.

76. **expediunt :** cf. Verg. *A.* II. 632 *flammam inter et hostes expedior.* — **acuta,** *crises.* — **belli :** Intr. 64.

## V.

Divis orte bonis, optume Romulae
custos gentis, abes iam nimium diu;
maturum reditum pollicitus patrum
sancto concilio, redi.

Lucem redde tuae, dux bone, patriae;
instar veris enim voltus ubi tuus
adfulsit populo, gratior it dies
et soles melius nitent.

Vt mater iuvenem, quem Notus invido

V. The occasion of this ode was the unexpectedly prolonged absence of the emperor in the western provinces in B.C. 16–13 (see intr. note to Ode 2). The avowed, and no doubt the main object of his western journey was the settlement of the affairs of that part of the empire; but it was whispered in the capital that the real cause of his departure was the hostility of those whom he had offended by his measures of reform. Possibly it was the poet's sense of the injustice of these people that stirred him to the exceptional warmth which characterizes this ode. But however that may be, the malcontents were a small body; the great majority of the citizens recognized their indebtedness to Augustus as the restorer of peace and security and the champion of good morals, and their dependence on his single life for the continuance of these blessings. The feeling of gratitude and devotion to which Horace here gives expression was one that was widespread and growing. — Metre, 172.

1. **divis bonis**: abl. abs. of attendant circumstances,—'when the gods were in kindly mood' (*sc.* towards mankind); equivalent to 'whose birth was blest of Heaven,' or the like. Cf. *S.* I. 5. 97 *Gnatia* (a town where water was scarce) *Lymphis* (= *Nymphis*) *iratis exstructa*. — **Romulae**: Intr. 65.

2. **custos**: cf. 15. 17 *custode rerum Caesare*.

4. **sancto**, *august;* cf. Enn. *Ann.* 298 M. *indu foro lato sanctoque senatu;* Verg. *A.* I. 426.

5. **lucem**: sc. *tuam* ('the light of thy countenance'), as the next verse shows. — **tuae**, *thy own;* Intr. 116 *c*. — **dux bone**: see vs. 37 n.

6. **instar**: commonly used of size or quantity, rarely, as here, of quality.

7. **it dies**: cf. II. 14. 5 *quotquot eunt dies*.

8. **soles**: *i.e.* the sun of each successive day; cf. 2. 41 n.

9. **Notus, Carpathii**: Intr. 117; I. 3. 14, 7. 15 n. — **invido**: reflecting the mother's feeling; the obstructing winds seem to her to blow from pure spite.

flatu Carpathii trans maris aequora
cunctantem spatio longius annuo
dulci distinet a domo,

votis ominibusque et precibus vocat,
curvo nec faciem litore demovet,
sic desideriis icta fidelibus
quaerit patria Caesarem.

Tutus bos etenim rura perambulat,
nutrit rura Ceres almaque Faustitas,
pacatum volitant per mare navitae,
culpari metuit fides,

11. **spatio longius annuo**: his business has detained him beyond the close of navigation in November, so that he has to stay all winter; cf. III. 7. 1 *sqq*.

13. **votis**, etc.: cf. Liv. *Praef.* 13 *cum bonis potius ominibus votisque et precationibus deorum dearumque . . . libentius inciperemus*.—**vocat**: expressing literally the action of the mother as she stands gazing at the shore, but used with the preceding instrumental ablatives in the wider sense of seeking to bring him back, by making vows for his safety, by looking for favorable omens, and by prayers.

14. **curvo**: a standing epithet of the shore, as *Epod.* 10. 21, Verg. *A*. III. 223, Ov. *M*. XI. 352, etc.

15. **desideriis**: plural of repeated occurrence. — **icta**, *smitten*.

16. **quaerit**: for *requirit;* cf. III. 24. 32 and see Intr. 129.

17. **tutus bos**, etc.: the emphasis, enhanced by asyndeton, is on **tutus** (cf. I. 17. 5 *impune tutum per nemus*, etc.), **nutrit**, and **pacatum**; Intr. 116 *b*. — **etenim**: introducing the reason why the country cannot bear to have Augustus long absent, — namely, the blessings which his presence and care confer. — **perambulat**: *i.e.* in grazing.

18. **rura**: the repetition (after the emphatic **nutrit**) is without emphasis; it serves merely to continue the discourse (Intr. 116 *h*) and to keep the reader's mind on the country, the improvement of which was an important consideration in the emperor's policy. **rura** is here used for *arva*, as in *Epod.* 2. 3, and in a comprehensive sense, to include both the land and the crops (implied in **Ceres**) that grow on it. — **alma**: a standing epithet of a goddess; cf. 15. 31 *almae Veneris*, I. 2. 42 *almae Maiae*, Verg. *G*. I. 7 *alma Ceres*, etc. — **Faustitas**: a personification that does not occur elsewhere in literature, but was probably not invented by Horace. It is (with **alma**) the same as *Fausta Felicitas* (Fertility), a divinity to whom annual offerings were made on the Capitol.

19. **pacatum**: by the suppression of piracy, with special reference to Sextus Pompey; see *Epod.* 4. 19 n, and cf. *Mon. Anc*. 5. 1 *mare pacavi a praedonibus;* Suet. *Aug*. 98 *forte Puteolanum sinum*

nullis polluitur casta domus stupris,
mos et lex maculosum edomuit nefas,
laudantur simili prole puerperae,
culpam poena premit comes.

Quis Parthum paveat, quis gelidum Scythen,
quis Germania quos horrida parturit
fetus, incolumi Caesare? Quis ferae
bellum curet Hiberiae?

Condit quisque diem collibus in suis

*praetervehenti vectores nautaeque de navi Alexandrina . . . fausta omina et eximias laudes congesserant, 'per illum se vivere, per illum navigare, libertate atque fortunis per illum frui.'*—**volitant**, *flit to and fro;* implying a light and rapid movement, unhindered by fear. The figure has reference quite as much to the oars as to the sails; cf. Cat. 4. 4 *sive palmulis opus foret volare sive linteo,* and, conversely, Verg. *A.* I. 301 *remigio alarum.*

20. **culpari metuit**: *i.e.* shrinks from even the suspicion of unfair dealing. For **metuit**, cf. II. 2. 7, and see Intr. 94 *l.*

21. **casta**: proleptic.

22. **mos et lex**: *i.e.* law, with a healthy moral sentiment in the community to support it; cf. III. 24. 35 n. The allusion is to the *lex Iulia de adulteriis*, passed by Augustus B.C. 18.—**edomuit**: the prefix denotes thoroughness; cf. I. 5. 8 n.

23. **simili prole**: instrumental ablative. For the meaning of **simili**, cf. Cat. 61. 217 *sit suo similis patri | Manlio et facile omnibus | noscitetur ab insciis | et pudicitiam suae | matris indicet ore.*

24. **premit comes**: as in *S.* II. 7. 115 (*Cura*) *comes atra premit sequiturque fugacem;* cf. III. 2. 31 *sq.*

25. **Parthum**: see 15. 6 n.—**Scythen**: cf. 14. 42, III. 8. 23 n.

26. **Germania quos**, etc.: see intr. note to Ode 2.—**parturit**: cf. I. 7. 16 n.

27. **fetus**, *spawn.* The whole description represents them as something not quite human, the monstrous brood of an uncouth mother-land.

28. **bellum Hiberiae**: Horace has in mind particularly the stubborn struggle of the Cantabrians for their independence; cf. II. 6. 2 n.

29. **condit**, *brings to a close, i.e.* spends the whole (quietly, without interruption): cf. Verg. *G.* I. 458 *at si, cum referetque diem condetque relatum, | lucidus orbis erit; E.* 9. 51 *saepe ego longos | cantando puerum memini me condere soles.*—**collibus**: more graphic than *agris* (Intr. 117); the poet selects vine-dressing, as one of the lighter occupations of the farmer, for his picture of contented country life; cf. *Epod.* 2. 9 *sqq.*—**suis**: emphatic (Intr. 116 *b*). Secure possession of property was one of the blessings of the reign of Augustus (Vell. II. 89. 4), and a country population of small farmers who

et vitem viduas ducit ad arbores ;
hinc ad vina redit laetus et alteris
te mensis adhibet deum ;

te multa prece, te prosequitur mero
defuso pateris, et Laribus tuum
miscet numen, uti Graecia Castoris
et magni memor Herculis.

owned the land they tilled was always regarded by wise statesmen as the most solid foundation of Roman power.

30. **viduas**, *unwedded;* a common meaning of the word. For the figure, see note on *caelebs*, II. 15. 4.—**ducit**: here apparently for *maritat* (cf. *Epod.* 2. 10), though the subject of *duco* in this sense is regularly the bridegroom.

31. **redit**: sc. *domum.*—**alteris mensis**: for *mensa secunda*, when the guests sat over their wine. The poet skips the more substantial (and prosaic) part of the evening meal.

32. **adhibet**, *invites;* cf. Verg. *A.* V. 62 *adhibete Penates epulis.* The allusion, which is expanded in the following strophe, is to the libations made to Augustus—they were even enjoined by the Senate (Dio LI. 19. 7)—at public and private banquets. To that extent, as an invisible presence at the feast, he was put on a par with the gods (**deum**), particularly with the Lares, for whom a portion of the meal was always set aside. Cf. Ov. *F.* II. 633 *et libate dapes ut, grati pignus honoris,* | *nutriat incinctos missa patella Lares;* | *iamque ubi suadebit placidos nox umida somnos,* | *larga precaturi sumite vina manu,* | *et 'Bene vos, bene te, patriae pater, optime Caesar'* | *dicite suffuso ter bona verba mero.*

33. **te prosequitur,** *thy name he hails.* The verb retains its proper sense of 'accompanies' (*sc.* the thought of thee, the mention of thy name).—**prece**, *with blessings;* cf. vs. 37. For the number, see I. 2. 26 n.

34. **defuso**, *with the pouring out of;* Intr. 105 *a.*—**Laribus**: dative; Intr. 56.

35. **uti Graecia**, etc.: cf. *Ep.* II. 1. 1–17, where Horace points out that the Romans paid to Augustus in his lifetime the honors which Greece rendered her benefactors only after their death.—**Castoris**: sc. *numen*, whereas **Herculis** is in closer relation with **memor**; the result in the reader's mind is a dependence of the two proper names ἀπὸ κοινοῦ on both **numen** and **memor**; Intr. 76, 120.

37. **o utinam**: cf. I. 35. 38; Intr. 185. This prayer for long life to Augustus is conceived in the same spirit as that of I. 2. 45 *sqq.*, the essence of it being that his country's happiness is bound up with his life. Similar is the fine tribute of *Ep.* I. 16. 25 *sqq.*—**dux bone**: repeated from vs. 5. The word **dux** conveys a much warmer expression of personal allegiance than the formal *princeps;* cf. Walt Whitman's *My Captain.*—**ferias**: *i.e.* peace, regarded as an interval of repose

'Longas o utinam, dux bone, ferias
praestes Hesperiae!' dicimus integro
sicci mane die, dicimus uvidi,
cum sol Oceano subest.

## VI.

Dive, quem proles Niobea magnae

and enjoyment between the wars which preceded and those which must (it is implied) follow this happy age.

38. **integro die**, *when the day is whole*, *i.e.* when the whole day is before us.

39. **sicci**: cf. I. 18. 3, *Ep.* I. 19. 9.—**dicimus**: Intr. 116 *h*.—**uvidi**: cf. II. 19. 18, *S.* II. 6. 70 *seu quis capit acria fortis | pocula, seu modicis uvescit laetius*.

VI. Horace's authorship of the hymn sung at the secular festival of B.C. 17 was deemed by the authorities worthy of mention on the pillars of marble and bronze erected to commemorate the occasion (see intr. note to *C. S.*), and the interesting line, CARMEN COMPOSVIT·Q·HORATIVS·FLACCVS, is among the fragments of the inscription recently discovered. But Horace chose also to record his distinction in his own way, in a '*monumentum aere perennius*.' It takes the form of a prelude to the hymn. Invoking the aid of the two divinities to whom the hymn is mainly addressed, and chiefly the minstrel Apollo, he calls upon the lads and maidens of the chorus to heed well his instructions, reminding the maidens in particular of the satisfaction they will have all their lives long in recalling their part in the memorable pageant, and closes with the seemingly incidental mention of his own name. — Metre, 174.

1. **dive**: Apollo. The invocation, interrupted by the long digression on Achilles, which recounts the invaluable service of the god to Rome, is resumed in vs. 25, and the actual prayer is contained in vs. 27. The verses extolling the prowess of Apollo and those relating to Diana (33 *sq.*, 38–40) look like 'chips from the workshop' in which the Secular Hymn was constructed. — **quem vindicem**, *whose vengeance*; Intr. 105 *a*.—**proles Niobea**: seven sons and seven daughters, slain by the arrows of Apollo and Diana to punish their mother Niobe for sneering at Latona as the mother of only two children (*Il.* XXIV. 602 *sqq.*, Ov. *M.* VI. 155 *sqq.*). The story is the subject of a famous sculptured group now preserved in Florence (see Baumeister, III. pp. 1673 ff.). A similar (probably not the same) group, regarded as the work of either Scopas or Praxiteles (Plin. *N. H.* XXXVI. 28), existed in Rome in Horace's time, in a temple of Apollo built by C. Sosius. — **magnae**: *i.e.* boastful; so in Greek μεγάλη γλῶσσα (Soph. *Antig.* 127), ἔπος μέγα (Theogn. 159), etc.; cf. Ovid *M.* VI. 150 *nec tamen ad*

vindicem linguae Tityosque raptor
sensit et Troiae prope victor altae
  Phthius Achilles,
ceteris maior, tibi miles impar,
filius quamvis Thetidis marinae
Dardanas turris quateret tremenda
  cuspide pugnax,
(ille, mordaci velut icta ferro
pinus aut impulsa cupressus Euro,
procidit late posuitque collum in
  pulvere Teucro;

*monita est* (*Niobe*) *verbis minoribus uti*.

2. **raptor**: indicating the crime (see III. 4. 77 n) that drew down Apollo's vengeance on him, and so taking the place of **magnae linguae** with **sensit.**

3. **sensit**: cf. 4. 25 n. — **prope victor**: according to the prophecy put into the mouth of the dying Hector (*Il.* XXII. 359) Achilles was slain by Paris, with the aid of Apollo, in the very gate of the city: ἤματι τῷ ὅτε κέν σε Πάρις καὶ Φοῖβος Ἀπόλλων | ἐσθλὸν ἐόντ' ὀλέσωσιν ἐνὶ Σκαιῇσι πύλῃσιν. — **altae**, *towering;* the Homeric Ἴλιος αἰπεινή (*Il.* XIII. 773); cf. also I. 16. 18 n.

4. **Phthius**: from Phthia, in the southern part of Thessaly, the land of the Myrmidons (*Il.* II. 683).

5. For the positions of the two pairs of contrasted words, cf. II. 10. 13; Intr. 116 *c*.

6. **filius Thetidis**: in apposition with the subject, enforcing the concession, — 'although he *was* the son of Thetis and,' etc.

7. **Dardanas**: Intr. 65.—**turris quateret**: a hyperbole like *Lernam tremefecerit arcu* (*Hercules*), Verg. *A.* VI. 803. For the mood, see Intr. 83.—**tremenda cuspide**: modifying both **quateret** and **pugnax** (Intr. 76); for the latter, cf. Liv. XXII. 37. 8 *pugnaces missili telo gentes;* Intr. 73. The spear of Achilles is described in *Il.* XVI. 141 as βριθὺ μέγα στιβαρόν· τὸ μὲν οὐ δύνατ' ἄλλος Ἀχαιῶν | πάλλειν, ἀλλά μιν οἶος ἐπίστατο πῆλαι Ἀχιλλεύς.

9–24. These strophes are parenthetical, and are introduced to enforce the indebtedness of the Romans to Apollo by a graphic picture of the ruthless fury with which Achilles would have exterminated the whole Trojan race, had the god not cut short his career and joined with Venus in entreating Jove to spare a remnant of the doomed people. — **ille . . . ille**: both emphatic (Intr. 116 *b*), but in different ways: the first is *even he* (mighty as he was); the second, *he* would not (as others did).

11. **procidit late**: see Intr. 123. Cf., however, *Odys.* XXIV.

ille non inclusus equo Minervae
sacra mentito male feriatos
Troas et laetam Priami choreis
falleret aulam,
sed palam captis gravis, heu nefas heu,
nescios fari pueros Achivis
ureret flammis, etiam latentem
matris in alvo,
ni tuis victus Venerisque gratae
vocibus divum pater adnuisset
rebus Aeneae potiore ductos
alite muros ;)

39 σὺ δ' (Ἀχιλλεῦ) ἐν στροφάλιγγι κονίης (pulvere) κεῖσο μέγας μεγαλωστί, and, for the whole comparison, Cat. 64. 105 *sqq.*

12. **Teucro**: Intr. 65. This name of the Trojans is unknown to Homer, but was familiar to the Romans, when this ode was written, from the Aeneid.

13. **Minervae**: gen. with **sacra,** as *Iunonis sacra, S.* I. 3. 11.

14. **sacra**: for the plural, cf. Cat. 63. 9 *typanum, tubam Cybelles, tua, mater, initia;* Intr. 128.—**mentito**: see Intr. 51 *e*, and cf. Mart. III. 43. 1 *mentiris iuvenem tinctis, Laetine, capillis.*—**male feriatos**, *keeping untimely holiday.* For the whole story, see Verg. *A.* II.

16. **falleret**, *steal upon*, come upon them unawares; cf. I. 10. 16, III. 11. 40. The impf. subj. is that of softened assertion in past time, with a vaguely implied apodosis, 'if he had lived,' 'if he had been present,' or the like. This construction is naturally continued in **ureret ni pater adnuisset,** which is *urat ni pater adnuerit* transferred to past time. Cf. *S.* I. 3. 5 *si peteret, non quicquam proficeret; si collibuisset, citaret;* Gr. 311 *a*, 307 *f.*

17. **palam captis**: in contrast with the secrecy implied in **mentito** and **falleret.** It contains a distinct assertion: *he would have captured them in open fight, and,* etc.—**gravis**, *with merciless hand.*—**heu . . . heu**: a sigh of horror at the enormity to be described; cf. I. 15. 9.—**nefas**: exclamatory, as in III. 24. 30.

18. **nescios fari**: a paraphrase for *infantes*, and a reminiscence of the Homeric νήπια τέκνα; see Intr. 101 *c*.

19. **latentem**: more graphic than the plural, on the principle of Intr. 117.

21. **ni**: not found elsewhere in the Odes.

22. **divum pater**: cf. I. 2. 2, 12. 13 *sqq.*—**adnuisset**: Intr. 51 *f.*

23. **potiore alite**: cf. *mala avi*, I. 15. 5 n.—**ductos**, *built;* a natural word for construction that proceeds in a line; cf. *ducere fossam, vallum*, etc.

doctor argutae fidicen Thaliae,
Phoebe, qui Xantho lavis amne crinis,
Dauniae defende decus Camenae,
levis Agyieu.

Spiritum Phoebus mihi, Phoebus artem
carminis nomenque dedit poetae.
Virginum primae puerique claris
patribus orti,

Deliae tutela deae, fugacis
lyncas et cervos cohibentis arcu,

25. **doctor**, etc.: after propitiating the god by recounting his beneficent deeds, the poet now addresses him in the character (*Apollo Musagetes*) in which he wishes him to respond to the present appeal. The meaning of the strophe (even if we cannot accept the reading *Argivae* for **argutae**) is: Inspirer of the Greek lyrists, support now the Daunian poet. — **argutae**: see III. 14. 21, and cf. *Odys.* XXIV. 62 μοῦσα λίγεια. — **fidicen**: serving as an attributive to **doctor**; Intr. 126 *c*. — **Thaliae**: Intr. 117; see also note on *Clio*, I. 12. 2.

26. **Xantho**: in Lycia. — **lavis crinis**: cf. III. 4. 61 n.

27. **Dauniae**: for 'Italian,' as in II. 1. 34 (Intr. 117 *b*); but the word is chosen with special reference to Horace himself; see I. 22. 14 n, and cf. III. 30. 10 *sqq.* — **Camenae**: see I. 12. 39 n.

28. **lēvis**: *i.e.* beardless, youthful; see I. 21. 2 n, II. 11. 6 n. — **Agyieu**: an epithet of Apollo as guardian of the streets (ἀγυιαί).

29. From his prayer to the god the poet now turns to address the chorus, and begins, as in II. 19. 9, by declaring his commission. — **spiritum**: see II. 16. 38 n. — **artem**: *i.e.* technical knowledge and skill, contrasted in the chiastic order with **spiritum**. The main emphasis, however, is on **Phoebus**. Intr. 116 *c*, *g*.

30. **carminis**: limiting **artem** only. — **poetae**: Gr. 214 *f*. The word occurs but twice in the Odes. Horace's favorite word is *vates*; cf. vs. 44, 3. 15, I. 1. 35, II. 6. 24, etc.

31. **virginum primae**, etc.: see intr. note to *C. S.* (p. 331).

33. **Deliae deae**: Diana (Artemis) was regarded by the Greeks as the special protectress of chaste youth and maidenhood (Preller-Robert, *Gr. Myth.* I. 320); cf. Cat. 34. 1 *Dianae sumus in fide* | *puellae et pueri integri*. This gives the poet an opportunity to bring in the goddess, who could have no place in the preceding invocation, and he dwells on some of her attributes, in this and the next strophe, so that she may not be left with a bare mention alongside of the elaborate praises of her brother. — **tutela**: here in a passive sense, — *wards*; cf. II. 17. 23, where it is active. — **fugacis cohibentis**, *who stays . . . in their flight*.

34. **lyncas et cervos**: perhaps suggested by Diana's words in

Lesbium servate pedem meique
pollicis ictum,
rite Latonae puerum canentes,
rite crescentem face Noctilucam,
prosperam frugum celeremque pronos
volvere mensis.

Nupta iam dices 'Ego dis amicum,
saeculo festas referente luces,
reddidi carmen docilis modorum
vatis Horati.'

Callim. *Hymn. in Dian.* 16 ὁππότε μηκέτι λύγκας | μήτ' ἐλάφους βάλλοιμι.

35. **Lesbium pedem** : *i.e.* the Sapphic metre; cf. *Lesboum barbiton*, I. 1. 34 n.

36. **pollicis ictum** : *sc.* on the lyre. Horace represents himself as training the chorus (χοροδιδάσκαλος); but this is to be taken, as Porphyrio understood it ('suaviter hoc dicitur, quasi ipse lyram percutiat'), as a poetic fiction. In view of Horace's disposition and of the silence of the inscription, we cannot suppose that he actually directed the performance.

37. **rite,** etc. : *i.e.* singing the Secular Hymn, the main theme of which is briefly given in this strophe. **rite** has reference to ceremonial form. — **Latonae puerum** : cf. I. 21. 3 n.

38. **crescentem,** *expanding;* the participle had not hardened into an adjective denoting shape, like our 'crescent'; cf. 2. 57. — **face** : so Cicero calls the sun *Phoebi fax* in the poem on his consulship (*Div.* I. 18). — **Noctilucam** : an epithet of Luna, who appears to have had, under this name, a temple on the Palatine which was illuminated at night (Varro *L. L.* V. 68).

39. **prosperam frugum** : Intr. 66 *a.* — **celerem volvere** : Intr. 101 *b.* Cf. Cat. 34. 17 *tu cursu, dea, menstruo | metiens iter annuum | rustica agricolae bonis | tecta frugibus exples.*

41. **iam** (with **nupta**): *i.e.* even after marriage (many years hence). This appeal is addressed to the girls only, in whose lives such participation in a public function must be a rare and memorable occurrence. — **dices** : the chorus of girls is addressed in the singular, after the practice of the Greek drama; but the words suggested would of course be spoken by each girl for herself. — **amicum** : cf. I. 26. 1 n.

42. **saeculo** : see intr. note to *C. S.* (p. 328).—**referente**: cf. III. 29. 20, II. 10. 15 n. — **luces** : *i.e. dies;* cf. II. 19, 15. 25. The festival lasted three days.

43. **reddidi,** *rendered;* cf. II. 34 *condisce modos, amanda voce quos reddas.* Like the English word, *reddo* conveys the idea of giving out what has been put into one (cf. I. 3. 7 n). So, also, *chorda sonum reddit*, *Ep.* II. 3. 348. — **docilis modorum** : Intr. 66 *b.*

## VII.

Diffugere nives, redeunt iam gramina campis
arboribusque comae ;
mutat terra vices et decrescentia ripas
flumina praetereunt ;
Gratia cum Nymphis geminisque sororibus audet
ducere nuda choros.
Immortalia ne speres, monet annus et almum
quae rapit hora diem :

VII. The ingredients which go to make up this ode are the same as those of I. 4, — the coming of spring, the uncertainty of life and sureness of death, the wisdom of enjoying while we may. The materials, however, are here managed somewhat differently and with a freer hand. The rapid renewal of the seasons is made to remind us that the years are passing swiftly away, with no renewal for us; and the studied symmetry of the earlier ode, in which these two motives are nicely balanced on the lesson they inculcate, is abandoned for a more natural sequence of thought. Torquatus, for whom the ode was written, was an advocate of some distinction, and was on terms of familiar acquaintance with the poet, as appears from *Ep.* I. 5, which is addressed to him. — Metre, 163.

1. **campis, arboribus**: Intr. 53.

2. **comae**: cf. I. 21. 5 n, IV. 3. 11.

3. **mutat terra vices**: summing up what has been partially expressed in the first couplet. **terra** is the face of the earth, and is further limited, by **flumina** following, to the dry land. **mutat** is intransitive, as often in Livy, with **vices** as cognate object; cf. Verg. *G.* I. 418 *ubi tempestas et caeli mobilis umor* | *mutavere vices.* For the meaning of **vices**, cf. I. 4. 1, III. 29. 13. — **decrescentia**: after the winter floods, due to melting snows on the mountains (cf. 12. 3 *sq.*).

4. **praetereunt**, *flow by* (instead of *over*).

5. **Gratia cum geminis sororibus**: *i.e.* the three Graces (Aglaia, Euphrosyne, Thalia; Hes. *Theog.* 909); cf. III. 19. 16 n. For the scene cf. I. 4. 6, where Venus, instead of the Graces, leads the dance.

7. **immortalia**, *immortality;* cf. *ima*, I. 34. 12 n. — **ne speres, monet**: cf. I. 18. 7, 8 nn. — **annus**, etc.: *i.e.* (1) the swift panorama of the seasons (set forth in detail in vss. 9–12), which the revolving year keeps ever before our eyes, and (2) the rapid flight of time as we experience it in our daily concerns. — **almum**: as the time of life-giving sunshine; cf. *alme Sol*, *C. S.* 9.

8. **rapit hora**: cf. III. 29. 48 *quod fugiens semel hora vexit.* It is the passage, not of the years, but of the hours, that brings home to us the rapid flight of time.

frigora mitescunt Zephyris, ver proterit aestas,
interitura simul
pomifer autumnus fruges effuderit, et mox
bruma recurrit iners.
Damna tamen celeres reparant caelestia lunae:
nos ubi decidimus
quo pater Aeneas, quo Tullus dives et Ancus,
pulvis et umbra sumus.
Quis scit an adiciant hodiernae crastina summae
tempora di superi?
Cuncta manus avidas fugient heredis, amico
quae dederis animo.

9. **Zephyris**: see note on *Favoni*, I. 4. 1. — **proterit**, *tramples down;* of the devastating effect of the scorching heat on the bloom of spring; cf. Ov. *M.* II. 791 (*Invidia*) *quacumque ingreditur, florentia proterit arva* | *exuritque herbas.*

10. **interitura**: Intr. 104 *b.*

11. **pomifer**: cf. III. 23. 8 n, *Epod.* 2. 17. As in the latter passage, autumn is personified. — **effuderit**: as from a horn of plenty; cf. I. 17. 14 *sqq.*

12. **iners**: in contrast with nature's activity in other seasons.

13. **damna caelestia**: *i.e.* those of the seasons, as just described, having their origin in the air and sky (*caelum*), in contrast with us men of earth. — **celeres lunae**: *i.e.* the rapid succession of the months (cf. *soles*, 5. 8 n). The moon, however, is put as a representative of the whole celestial system (Intr. 117). Cf. *Cat.* 5. 4 *soles occidere et redire possunt:* | *nobis cum semel occidit brevis lux,* | *nox est perpetua una dormienda.*

14. **decidimus**: cf. *Ep.* II. 1. 36 *scriptor abhinc annos centum qui decidit.*

15. **quo pater Aeneas**, etc.: sc. *deciderunt.* Cf. *Ep.* I. 6. 27 *ire tamen restat Numa quo devenit et Ancus;* Lucr. III. 1025 *lumina sis oculis etiam bonus Ancus reliquit* (quoted from Ennius). — **pater**: cf. I. 2. 50 n, Verg. *A.* II. 2, etc. — **Tullus dives**: cf. Liv. I. 31. 1 *cum in magna gloria magnisque opibus regnum Tulli ac tota res Romana esset.*

16. **pulvis**: in the tomb; **umbra**: in the underworld.

17. **quis scit**, etc.: cf. I. 9. 13 *sqq.*, *Ep.* I. 4. 12 *sqq.* — **hodiernae summae** (sc. *temporum*; see I. 4. 15 n): the sum that has accumulated thus far.

19. **cuncta**, etc.: cf. II. 3. 20, 14. 25 *sqq.* and *Ep.* I. 5. 13 (also addressed to Torquatus). This attitude towards the heir is eminently natural in a childless old fellow like Horace. — **amico dederis animo**: suggested no doubt by such expressions as *Il.* IX. 705 τεταρπόμενοι φίλον ἦτορ | σίτου καὶ

Cum semel occideris et de te splendida Minos
fecerit arbitria,
non, Torquate, genus, non te facundia, non te
restituet pietas.
Infernis neque enim tenebris Diana pudicum
liberat Hippolytum,
nec Lethaea valet Theseus abrumpere caro
vincula Pirithoo.

*οἴνοιο.* But the habit of thought which marks off the emotions and appetites as a distinct portion of our nature (cf. *aeger animi*, etc.) easily takes the further step of attributing to the *animus* a quasi-separate existence and personality; cf. Plaut. *Trin.* 305 *quí homo cum animo inde áb ineunte aetáte depugnát suo,* | . . . *si ánimus hominem pépulit, actumst, ánimo servit, nón sibi ;* | *sín ipse animum pépulit, vivit, víctor victorúm cluet.* The conception of this personality, as we have it here, however, as a sort of *numen*, to be kept contented and in good humor with us (**amico**), is more commonly expressed by *genius* (see III. 17. 14 n).

21. **semel**: cf. I. 24 16 n. — **splendida**, *stately;* Intr. 124. The splendor is that of his court. — **Minos**: cf. I. 28. 9; Verg. *A.* VI. 432 *sqq.*

23. **genus**: Torquatus belonged to the Manlian gens, among the oldest of the Roman noble houses. — **facundia**: there is an appropriateness in confronting the orator with the judgment-seat of Minos as a type of the inexorable doom of death. Notice that in the varying metrical accent on **nón . . . non té . . . nón te,** the stress here falls on **te.**

24. **pietas**: cf. II. 14. 2.

25–28. Birth, eloquence, piety must fail where a goddess' love and a hero's strength have been baffled.

26. **Hippolytum**: son of Theseus, beloved of Diana, and the victim of the fury of his stepmother, Phaedra, whose advances he had repulsed. Horace follows Euripides (*Hippol.* 1436 *sqq.*), and does not accept the Roman form of the myth (cf. Verg. *A.* VII. 761 *sqq.* and Ov. *M.* XV. 533 *sqq.*), according to which Hippolytus was restored to life and was the divinity worshipped in the grove of Diana at Aricia under the name of Virbius.

27. **abrumpere**: Intr. 94 *n.*

28. **Pirithoo**: see III. 4. 80 n.

VIII. In this ode, written for C. Marcius Censorinus (consul B.C. 8), a man of amiable disposition and literary tastes, Horace takes as his theme the value of poetry as a vehicle of enduring fame, and not only, as in III. 30, asserts its superiority over material monuments, but claims for it the power to confer actual immortality, and even divinity. The ode appears to have been sent as a present to Censorinus, perhaps at the season of the Saturnalia, — a circumstance that gives occasion for a preliminary comparison between poems and material works of art, as gifts to a friend. — Metre 169.

## VIII.

Donarem pateras grataque commodus,
Censorine, meis aera sodalibus,
donarem tripodas, praemia fortium
Graiorum, neque tu pessima munerum
ferres, divite me scilicet artium
quas aut Parrhasius protulit aut Scopas,
hic saxo, liquidis ille coloribus
sollers nunc hominem ponere, nunc deum.
Sed non haec mihi vis, non tibi talium

1. **pateras**: see I. 19. 15 n. — **commodus**: with **donarem**, as in *Ep.* II. 1. 227 (*ut nos*) *commodus ultro arcessas*, and its opposite in *Ep.* I. 18. 75 (*ne te*) *incommodus angat.* Here, from its close connection with **grata**, it has the meaning of 'anticipating their tastes.'

2. **aera**: the same kind of a plural as our equivalent, *bronzes* (Intr. 128), but referring here particularly to the bronze vessels (λέβητες) which, like bowls and tripods, were often given as prizes (**praemia**) in the Greek national games. The three are mentioned together in Pind. *Isth.* I. 18 ἐν τ' ἀέθλοισι θίγον πλείστων ἀγώνων καὶ τριπόδεσσιν ἐκόσμησαν δόμον καὶ λεβήτεσσιν φιάλαισί τε χρυσοῦ (cf. *Il.* XXIII. 259, 264, 267, 270). Specimens of these 'antiques,' often elaborately wrought, had been brought to Rome in great numbers, and were highly prized.

3. **donarem**: Intr. 116 *h.* — **fortium**, *gallant;* as winners in the games.

5. **ferres**: for *auferres* (cf. Intr. 129), as often with *pretium*, *palmam*, etc.; cf. vs. 22, III. 16. 22; *Ep.* I. 17. 43 *tacentes plus poscente ferent.* — **divite me**: expressing the condition of **donarem**, and introduced by **scilicet**, *I mean, of course.* — **artium**: used concretely, *works of art;* cf. *Ep.* I. 6. 17; Intr. 66 *c.*

6. **Parrhasius**: of Ephesus, a famous painter at Athens in the time of Socrates. He was a contemporary and rival of Zeuxis, according to the well-known story of the painting of the grapes and the curtain. — **protulit**, *created;* cf. *Ep.* II. 3. 58, 130; Tib. I. 10. 1 *quis fuit horrendos primus qui protulit enses?* — **Scopas**: of Paros, the most eminent sculptor of his time (first half of 4th century B.C.). Many of his works were in Rome in Horace's day; cf. note on *proles Niobea*, 6. 1.

7. **liquidis**: suggesting by contrast the hardness of the stone.

8. **ponere**: apparently a technical word for representing an object, either in sculpture or painting: cf. I. 20, *Ep.* II. 3. 34. For the mood, see Intr. 101 *c.*

9. **non haec mihi vis**, *this is not in my power* (*i.e.* to make such presents). For this use of **vis** cf. *Epod.* 5. 94.

res est aut animus deliciarum egens :
gaudes carminibus ; carmina possumus
donare et pretium dicere muneri.
Non incisa notis marmora publicis,
per quae spiritus et vita redit bonis
post mortem ducibus, non celeres fugae
reiectaeque retrorsum Hannibalis minae,
non incendia Carthaginis impiae

10. **res, animus** : the meaning is that to make such presents to a man of means like Censorinus, even if Horace had the power to do it, would be merely giving him what he already had or could easily get, and did not really care for; whereas a poem, which Horace could give, was something he liked and could not buy. **res** is for *res familiaris*, as *Ep*. I. 1. 80, II. 1. 106, and often. — **deliciarum**, *bric-a-brac*. For the case, see Intr. 66 *c*.

11. For the arrangement of words in this verse, in which each of the three ideas expressed is in contrast with something that precedes, see Intr. 116 *b* and *e*.

12. **pretium dicere** : for the usual *pretium statuere*, *pretium ponere*, etc., and taking, like these, a dative of the thing assessed (**muneri**); cf. *S*. II. 3. 23 *callidus huic signo* (sc. *pretium*) *ponebam milia centum*.

13. Horace here begins his *pretii dictio*, which continues to the end of the ode. — **incisa** : with instrumental abl., as in Liv. VI. 29. 9 *tabula his ferme incisa litteris* (Gr. 225 *d*), instead of *incisae marmoribus notae*, or the more common prose construction, *in marmoribus;* but Horace is comparing with poetry, not the inscriptions, but the statues with their inscriptions. — **notis** : *i.e.* letters ; cf. Ov. *Tr*. III. 3. 71 *quosque legat versus oculo properante viator* | *grandibus in tituli marmore caede notis*. — **marmora** : *i.e.* statues, as the relative clause shows. — **publicis** : set up by authority of the state (*i.e.* by order of the senate).

14. **spiritus et vita** : the same thing under two aspects (notice the number of **redit**); cf. 9. 10 *sq*. and 2. 28 n. For the thought, cf. Verg. *A*. VI. 847 *excudent alii spirantia mollius aera, ... vivos ducent de marmore voltus*.

15. **ducibus** : Intr. 53. — **non celeres fugae**, etc.: *i.e.* the dramatic close of Hannibal's enterprise and (if we accept vs. 17) the burning of the great city which had well-nigh conquered Rome, were events so impressive and of such momentous import, that they would of themselves, without any written record, carry the name of Africanus down through the ages; but these brilliant memories cannot equal the glory conferred by poetry. — **fugae** : from the field of Zama (B.C. 202). For the number, see Intr. 128.

16. **reiectae minae** : *i.e.* the reduction of Carthage to the attitude of submission to which he had threatened to reduce Rome; cf. 3. 8.

17. For the grounds for believing this verse and other parts of

eius, qui domita nomen ab Africa
lucratus rediit, clarius indicant
laudes quam Calabrae Pierides; neque
si chartae sileant quod bene feceris,
mercedem tuleris. Quid foret Iliae
Mavortisque puer, si taciturnitas
obstaret meritis invida Romuli?
Ereptum Stygiis fluctibus Aeacum
virtus et favor et lingua potentium

the ode spurious, see Crit. App. — **impiae**: see note on *perfidus*, 4. 49.

18. **eius**: cf. III. 11. 17 n. — **qui domita nomen**, etc.: cf. *S.* II. 1. 66 *qui duxit ab oppressa meritum Carthagine nomen*. **ab Africa** modifies ἀπὸ κοινοῦ both **nomen lucratus** and **rediit**; Intr. 76.

19. **lucratus**, *enriched by*, *richer by;* an allusion perhaps to the indignant reply of Scipio to those who impugned his honesty in the management of his brother's Asiatic campaign, — that his surname was the only profit he brought home from Africa; '*nam cum Africam totam potestati vestrae subiecerim, nihil ex ea quod meum diceretur praeter cognomen rettuli*' (Val. Max. III. 7. 1 d).

20. **Calabrae Pierides**: *i.e.* the poetry of Ennius, a native of Rudiae, in Calabria, whose historical epic, *Annales*, included the second Punic war. He was, moreover, a close friend and admirer of Scipio, and wrote one or more separate poems in his honor. For **Pierides**, see note on *Haemo*, I. 12. 6.

21. **chartae**, *books*, *literature*. The word had come to be used for literary works, as in 9. 31, or even for definite portions of such works, as Cat. 1. 6 *omne aevum tribus explicare chartis* (*i.e.* in three volumes). — **sileant**: used transitively, as in 9. 31.

22. **tuleris**: the future perfect (Gr. 281 Rem.) carries the reader forward to the final result of the whole transaction: you will have done a good deed without having received your just reward for it. — **Iliae Mavortisque puer**: cf. 6. 37, I. 12. 25, and see I. 2. 17 n. *Mavors* is an old name of Mars, preserved in the ritual and adopted by the earlier poets.

23. **taciturnitas invida**: cf. 9. 33 *lividas obliviones*. We need not think here of envious detractors, but only of the spite with which we readily endow whatever stands between us and what we regard as our just due. Cf. 5. 9 n.

25. **Aeacum**: see II. 13. 22 n. He was celebrated in particular by Pindar (*Isth.* 8. 23, etc.).

26. **virtus**, *the genius;* properly their excellence (*sc.* as poets); cf. *Ep.* II. 3. 370 *actor causarum mediocris abest virtute diserti Messalae*. Some editors, however, understand by **virtus** the merit of Aeacus himself. — **potentium**: as having power to grant or withhold immortality.

vatum divitibus consecrat insulis.
Dignum laude virum Musa vetat mori;
caelo Musa beat. Sic Iovis interest
optatis epulis impiger Hercules,
clarum Tyndaridae sidus ab infimis
quassas eripiunt aequoribus ratis,
ornatus viridi tempora pampino
Liber vota bonos ducit ad exitus.

27. **divitibus insulis**: see *Epod.* 16. 42 n; for the case, Intr. 69. — **consecrat**, *hallows*, *i.e.* makes immortal; cf. *sacrare*, I. 26. 11 n. For the number, see Intr. 77.

29. **caelo beat**: *i.e.* deifies, — a step beyond the mere conferring of immortality (as in the case of Aeacus) expressed by vs. 28. — **sic**: *i.e.* through the power of poetry. The claim appears to involve a confusion between a purely subjective immortality in the memory and worship of mankind, — immortality of fame, — and a real, objective existence and activity after death (cf. Tac. *A.* IV. 38. 5 *optimos quippe mortalium altissima cupere: sic Herculem et Liberum apud Graecos, Quirinum apud nos deum numero additos; . . . cetera principibus statim adesse: unum insatiabiliter parandum, prosperam sui memoriam*); but it is not necessarily a denial of the latter. Granted that Romulus, Hercules, and the rest have been translated to heaven, they still cannot dispense with the aid of the poets, who have made their glory known to men; for without this they would not be worshipped, and so, in effect, would not be gods at all, but, like the rest of the dead, mere 'pulvis et umbra.' Cf. Ov. *Pont.* IV. 8. 55 *di quoque carminibus, si fas est dicere, fiunt,* | *tantaque maiestas ore canentis eget.* — **interest epulis**, etc.: in each of the three cases a particular privilege or function is put for the general fact that they are gods; Intr. 117 *a.*

30. **optatis**: as the object of his ambition; cf. *Ep.* II. 3. 412 *optatam cursu contingere metam.*

31. **clarum sidus**: in apposition with **Tyndaridae**; cf. I. 3. 2 n. — **ab infimis aequoribus**, *from* (going to) *the bottom of the sea.*

32. **quassas ratis**: cf. I. 1. 17.

33. **viridi tempora pampino**: repeated from III. 25. 20.

34. **vota**, etc.: so Vergil expresses the deification of Daphnis, *E.* 5. 79 *ut Baccho Cererique, tibi sic vota quotannis* | *agricolae facient; damnabis* (= *bonos duces ad exitus*) *tu quoque votis.*

IX. M. Lollius (cos. B.C. 21), to whom this ode is addressed, was a trusted lieutenant of the emperor, who employed him on various important missions. He organized, as first propraetor, the province of Galatia, and in B.C. 18 was made governor of Belgian Gaul, where, two years later, he suffered a humiliating defeat at the hands of the Sygambri (see intr. note to Ode 2). This reverse, however, in no wise lowered him in the esteem of his friends, — among whom we must reckon Horace, —

## IX.

Ne forte credas interitura quae
longe sonantem natus ad Aufidum
non ante volgatas per artis
verba loquor socianda chordis:
non, si priores Maeonius tenet
sedes Homerus, Pindaricae latent

nor of Augustus himself, who many years later (B.C. 1) gave him the most important of the imperial provinces, Syria, together with the confidential post of companion and adviser to his grandson, Gaius Caesar, who was sent at that time on a mission to Armenia. But the conduct of Lollius in the East, according to common report, was either a complete reversal of his previous career, or else, as Velleius charges (II. 97), his true character was at last unmasked; he was accused, it was said, of receiving bribes right and left from the potentates who had favors to ask of the young Caesar; and his sudden death, shortly after this came out, was attributed to suicide. He was succeeded by C. Censorinus, to whom the preceding ode is addressed.

It is singular that Horace should have placed on record, in one of his finest odes, his zealous testimony to the strict integrity of a man who died with such a reputation. But the evidence against Lollius is not free from doubt; Velleius, the chief witness, was a servile adherent of Tiberius, who was a personal enemy of Lollius. At any rate we may accept Horace's tribute, not only as the estimate in which Lollius was held when the ode was written,—probably not long after the disaster of B.C. 16, to which vs. 36 appears to allude,—but as good evidence that up to that time his conduct had deserved the praise so lavishly bestowed.—Metre, 176.

1. **ne credas**: expressing the purpose of introducing the examples in the second and following strophes; cf. II. 4. 1 n.

2. **longe sonantem**: cf. 14. 25 *sqq.*, III. 30. 10; Intr. 3.—**natus ad Aufidum**: *i.e.* a mere provincial; see also III. 30. 10 n.

3. **non ante volgatas**: a more moderate statement of his claim than in III. 30. 13 *sq.*; cf. Intr. 26.

4. **verba socianda chordis**: a paraphrase for 'lyric poetry.'—**loquor**: of poetical utterance, as in III. 25. 18, IV. 2. 45, etc.

5. **non si**: see II. 10. 17 n. The argument which begins here and extends through vs. 28 is very similar to that of Ode 8, with this difference, however, that Horace is here concerned to maintain the power of *lyric* poetry to confer permanent fame, and therefore begins by showing that lyric, though it yields precedence in dignity to epos, is no less enduring (vss. 5–12).—**Maeonius**: cf. I. 6. 2 n.

6. **Pindaricae (camenae)**: see 2. 1–25 nn.—**(non) latent**, *is not lost to sight.*

Ceaeque et Alcaei minaces
Stesichorique graves camenae,
nec, si quid olim lusit Anacreon,
delevit aetas ; spirat adhuc amor
vivuntque commissi calores
Aeoliae fidibus puellae.
Non sola comptos arsit adulteri
crinis et aurum vestibus inlitum
mirata regalisque cultus
et comites Helene Lacaena,

7. **Ceae**: see II. 1. 38 n. — **Alcaei**: see Intr. 26. — **minaces**: alluding to his invectives against the tyrants of Lesbos; see I. 32. 5 n, and cf. II. 13. 30 *sqq.*

8. **Stesichori**: a poet of Himera, in Sicily, contemporary with Alcaeus and Sappho, distinguished especially for perfecting the choral ode. His subjects were chiefly the heroic myths usually treated in epic poetry (hence **graves**); Quintilian (X. 1. 62) describes him as *maxima bella et clarissimos canentem duces et epici carminis onera lyra sustinentem ; reddit enim personis in agendo simul loquendoque debitam dignitatem.* See also *Epod.* 17. 42 n. — **camenae**: here of Greek poetry, as (conversely) *Pierides*, 8. 20, of Italian. Cf. *Graiae camenae*, II. 16. 38 n.

9. **nec si**, etc.: *i.e.* and not only lyrics on serious themes (such as those just mentioned), but even those written in lighter strain survive. — **olim**, *in his day;* see 4. 5 n. — **lusit**: cf. I. 32. 1 n; Cat. 50. 4 *scribens versiculos uterque nostrum | ludebat numero modo hoc modo illoc, | reddens mutua per iocum atque vinum.* It is used here, as often, of love poetry; cf. Ov. *Am.* III. 1. 27 *quod tenerae cantent lusit tua musa puellae;* Cat. 68. 17. — **Anacreon**: born in the island of Teos (cf. *Epod.* 14. 10), but a resident of various Greek cities in succession; for a time at the brilliant court of Polycrates, tyrant of Samos (B.C. 533–522), afterwards at Athens with Hipparchus. He was a courtier and man of pleasure, and a poet of love and gayety. (The collection of lyrics that bear his name are imitations, of a much later date.)

10. **spirat vivuntque; amor . . . calores**: each pair expresses one thing under two aspects; cf. *spiritus et vita*, 8. 14 n. For the use of the verbs, see Intr. 121.

11. **commissi fidibus** (with both **amor** and **calores**): cf. *S.* II. 1. 30 *ille* (*Lucilius*) *velut fidis arcana sodalibus olim | credebat libris . . . quo fit ut omnis | votiva pateat veluti descripta tabella | vita senis;* so the warm passion of Sappho still lives and breathes before us in her poems.

12. **Aeoliae puellae** (genitive, limiting **fidibus**): see Intr. 26 and II. 13. 24 *sq.*

13–28. The argument here is for poetry in general, although

primusve Teucer tela Cydonio
direxit arcu ; non semel Ilios
vexata ; non pugnavit ingens
Idomeneus Sthenelusve solus
dicenda Musis proelia ; non ferox
Hector vel acer Deiphobus gravis
excepit ictus pro pudicis
coniugibus puerisque primus.
Vixere fortes ante Agamemnona

the examples are drawn from epic only (Homer). The verses should be read with careful observance of the emphasis, which is helped by rhythmical position (**non sóla** 13, **primúsve** 17, **nón semel** 18, **só-lus** 20, **prímus** 24, **múlti** and **ómnes** 26) and anaphora (**non**); see Intr. 116 *b* and *f*.

13. **comptos crinis**: apparently the object ἀπὸ κοινοῦ of both **arsit** (Intr. 72) and **mirata**; but the former is gradually lost sight of as the sentence proceeds, and does not apply at all to **comites**. For this characterization of Paris, cf. I. 15. 14.

14. **inlitum**: lit. 'smeared on,' implying extravagant and showy embroidery, in oriental style (*picturatas auri subtegmine vestis*, Verg. *A*. III. 483).

15. **mirata**, *fascinated by*; cf. I. 4. 19 n, *Epod*. 3. 10, *Ep*. I. 6. 1. — **cultus**, *state*.

16. **Helene Lacaena**: cf. Verg. *A*. II. 601 *Tyndaridis Lacaenae*, I. 650 *Argivae Helenae*. The addition of the epithet is after the epic manner; cf. Vergil's *Troius Aeneas*, *Sidonia Dido*, etc.

17. **Teucer**: see I. 7. 21 n. He figures in the Iliad as the best bowman among the Greeks (*Il*. XIII. 313).—**Cydonio**: *i.e.* Cretan; see I. 15. 17 n. Cydonia was a town on the northern coast of Crete.

18. **Ilios**, *a Troy; i.e.* the siege (**vexata**) of Troy was not the only great siege that ever took place. For the form, see I. 10. 14 n.

20. **Idomeneus**: leader of the Cretans in the Trojan war. — **Sthenelus**: see I. 15. 24 n.

21. **dicenda Musis proelia**: cf. 4. 68 n. For **proelia**, as the object of **pugnavit**, see Intr. 51 *b*. — **non ferox**, etc.: two instances from the side of the defenders of the city.

22. **vel**: rarely used in subordination to a negative, as here, though *-ve* is common. — **Deiphobus**: brother of Hector, and one of the bravest of the Trojans. For his subsequent fate, see Verg. *A*. VI. 494 *sqq*.

25. **vixere**: standing first with the same emphasis that *fuere* would have in this position, — an emphasis corresponding to that of the preceding negatives. The series of particular negations is here cut short, and the fact implied in all of them, — that there have been in the world's history many Helens, many Teucers, many Troys, — is summed up in a general affirmative statement, which serves to introduce the application of the whole

multi; sed omnes inlacrimabiles
urgentur ignotique longa
nocte, carent quia vate sacro.

Paulum sepultae distat inertiae
celata virtus. Non ego te meis
chartis inornatum silebo
totve tuos patiar labores

impune, Lolli, carpere lividas
obliviones. Est animus tibi
rerumque prudens et secundis
temporibus dubiisque rectus,

matter to the question in hand, the value of the poet. — **ante Agamemnona**: *i.e.* before the Trojan war, in which all these heroes distinguished themselves.

26. **inlacrimabiles**: not simply 'unwept,' but *beyond the reach of tears*, or the like; see II. 14. 6 n, and cf. *flebilis*, I. 24. 9.

27. **urgentur nocte**: cf. I. 24. 5 *Quintilium perpetuus sopor urget;* I. 4. 16 *iam te premet nox.*

28. **quia**: Intr. 114. — **sacro**: because inspired (cf. 3. 24, 6. 29), and singled out for the service of the Muses (III. 1. 3), and enjoying their favor and protection (III. 4. 21 *sqq.*). Cf. Cic. *pro Arch.* 18.

29. **paulum**, etc.: the moral of the whole discourse, forming the transition to the tribute to Lollius: The sluggard dies, and his frailties are buried with him and forgotten; the hero is in no better case if his merits are not made known to men. — **inertiae, virtus**: abstract for concrete, as in III. 2. 17, 21; 4. 67; *Ep.* II. 1. 88. For the case of **inertiae**, see Intr. 57.

30. **non ego te**: cf. I. 18. 11 n.

31. **chartis silebo**: cf. 8. 21 n. — **inornatum**: proleptic.

32. **labores**: *i.e.* arduous exertions; cf. 4. 6. The word falls short of expressing achievement, and is appropriate in the defense of a man whose merits are under the cloud of temporary defeat (see intr. note).

33. **impune**, *unhindered.* — **carpere**, *to prey upon.* The word aptly expresses the wearing and disintegrating effect of time. — **lividas obliviones**: cf. 8. 23 n; Intr. 128.

34. **animus**, *a soul.*

35. **rerum prudens**: of the wisdom of experience (the opposite of *rerum inscitia*, *Ep.* I. 3. 33), in contrast with native gifts; cf. Verg. *G.* I. 416 *ingenium aut rerum prudentia.*

36. **dubiis**, *critical;* a variation on *adversis;* cf. II. 10. 13, Tac. *Ann.* I. 64. 6 *secundarum ambiguarumque rerum sciens.* — **rectus**, *steadfast;* properly 'erect' (cf. the literal use in 4. 48), 'not losing its balance.'

37. **vindex**, etc.: *i.e.* at once a champion and an example of strict integrity. This is the one idea which Horace dwells upon through this and the next strophe, — the strength of Lollius' charac-

vindex avarae fraudis et abstinens
ducentis ad se cuncta pecuniae,
consulque non unius anni,
sed quotiens bonus atque fidus
iudex honestum praetulit utili,
reiecit alto dona nocentium
voltu, per obstantis catervas
explicuit sua victor arma.
Non possidentem multa vocaveris
recte beatum; rectius occupat
nomen beati, qui deorum
muneribus sapienter uti

ter, which not only loathes venality and punishes it in others, but can itself resist temptation. For the use of **vindex, consul, iudex** with **animus**, cf. Verg. *A*. IX. 205 *animus lucis contemptor;* Liv. I. 56. 8 *liberator ille populi Romani animus* (of Brutus). — **avarae**: *i.e.* prompted by greed. — **abstinens pecuniae**: see Intr. 66 *c*.

38. **ducentis**: *sc.* by its fascination. — **cuncta**, *all the world*, with the usual reservation in favor of a 'saving remnant.'

39. **consul**, etc.: in a purely figurative sense: incorruptible character has an intrinsic strength that exalts it above common men at all times when its power is displayed (**quotiens**, etc); its eminence is not temporary and accidental, like that of a politician raised to office for a few months. Cf. III. 2. 17 n, where the same figure is employed. It was suggested, no doubt, by the ideal sage of the Stoics, who unites in himself all perfections.

41. **iudex**, *as a judge*. — **honestum utili**, *virtue to expediency*. — **praetulit**: in the manner indicated in the next clause.

42. **reiecit**: for the asyndeton here and in the next verse, cf. 5. 17–24, 8. 29–33, III. 18. 9–16. — **dona**, *bribes*.

43. **catervas**: sc. *nocentium*, who are compared to a swarm of foes through whom a brave warrior has to force his way to escape capture or the loss of his arms.

44. **explicuit**: *i.e.* has brought safely (out of the entanglement), has shaken them off, with his weapons intact. Cf. *expediunt*, 4. 76.

45. **non possidentem**, etc.: the poet's approval of the principles he has ascribed to his friend, not only as right, but as the true foundation of happiness. Cf. *Ep*. I. 16. 20 *neve putes alium sapiente bonoque beatum*. — **possidentem**: Intr. 103. — **vocaveris**: cf. *scripserit*, I. 6. 14 n. The subject is indefinite.

46. **recte beatum, rectius beati**: Intr. 116 *g*. — **rectius occupat**, *takes with a better claim*.

47. **beati**: defining gen., the regular construction in such phrases; cf. *nomen poetae*, 6. 30 n.

duramque callet pauperiem pati
peiusque leto flagitium timet,
non ille pro caris amicis
aut patria timidus perire.

## X.

O crudelis adhuc et Veneris muneribus potens,
insperata tuae cum veniet pluma superbiae
et quae nunc umeris involitant deciderint comae,
nunc et qui color est puniceae flore prior rosae

49. **pauperiem pati**: cf. I. 1. 18 n. For the inf., see Intr. 94 *o*.

50. **peius**: colloquial for *magis*, with expressions of fear and aversion; cf. *Ep*. I. 17. 30 *cane peius et angui vitabit chlamydem;* Cic. *Fam*. VII. 2. 3 *oderam multo peius hunc quam illum ipsum Clodium*. So *male* = *valde*, as Ter. *Heaut*. 531 *timui male;* Plaut. *Rud*. 920 *nimis id genus odi ego male malacum*. With a verb expressing favorable feeling, *deterius* is used with weakening effect (= *minus*) in *S*. I. 10. 89 *si placeant spe deterius nostra* (cf. I. 9. 24 n).

51. **non ille**: the pronoun serves to bring the subject into renewed prominence and single him out from the mass of mankind; cf. *neque tu*, I. 9. 16 n; Verg. *A*. I. 3.

52. **timidus perire**: Intr. 101 *a*.

**X.** The graver themes which preponderate in this book are here interrupted by four odes in lighter strain, dealing with love and social enjoyment. The first of them is constructed in the same form as I. 11, and, like that ode, is a warning: 'Beauty fades. Be not too disdainful, proud boy, of the admirers who now court your favor: the time will quickly come when you will sigh in vain for the homage which you now hold so lightly.' Horace found his theme already treated in his Greek models; cf. *Anth. Pal*. XII. 35, 186. For the passionate admiration of the Greeks for youthful beauty, cf. Cat. 63. 64 *sqq*. — Metre, 170.

1. **Veneris muneribus**: cf. *Il*. III. 54 τά τε δῶρ᾽ Ἀφροδίτης, ἥ τε κόμη τό τε εἶδος; I. 18. 7 *munera Liberi*.

2. **insperata**: *i.e.* before you have begun to think of it; to be taken with **veniet**. — **tuae superbiae**: poetical for *tibi superbo*: see Intr. 126 *b*, and, for the case, Intr. 53. — **pluma**, *down*, precisely as we use the word; but it is not found elsewhere in this sense.

3. **umeris involitant**: cf. III. 20. 14, and, for the custom of boys wearing their hair long, like girls, II. 5. 21 *sqq*. — **deciderint**: *i.e.* when shorn. The occasion was attended with some formality; cf. Juv. 3. 186 *crinem hic deponit amati; plena domus libis*.

4. **nunc**: Intr. 114. — **color**: *i.e.* the cheeks (cf. **in faciem verterit**). — **puniceae**, *red, red;* cf. III. 15. 15, where *purpureus* is used. The

mutatus, Ligurine, in faciem verterit hispidam,
dices 'Heu,' quotiens te speculo videris alterum,
'quae mens est hodie, cur eadem non puero fuit,
vel cur his animis incolumes non redeunt genae?'

## XI.

Est mihi nonum superantis annum
plenus Albani cadus; est in horto,
Phylli, nectendis apium coronis;
  est hederae vis
multa, qua crinis religata fulges;
ridet argento domus; ara castis

latter was a darker (cf. II. 5. 12 n), *puniceus* a clearer red (scarlet).

5. **Ligurine**: cf. I. 33.—**verterit**: intransitive.

6. **speculo**: instrumental abl. The *speculum* was commonly of bronze or silver; see Baumeister, III. pp. 1691 *sqq.* — **alterum**: *i.e.* changed beyond recognition. Cf. III. 5. 34 n.

7. **puero**: sc. *mihi.*

8. **animis**: Intr. 53.

XI. An ode in honor of Maecenas' birthday. The poet represents himself, in the midst of preparations for a festival, welcoming his fair neighbor Phyllis, and explaining to her the nature of the celebration which he has invited her to share. The scene, which is similar to that of III. 28, is in the country. We need not trouble ourselves to locate it more definitely. The ode is chiefly interesting for its quiet testimony to Horace's continued affection for his old friend Maecenas, who is mentioned here only in this book (see Intr. 32). — Metre, 174.

2. **Albani**: accounted one of the three or four best wines known to the Romans; cf. *S.* II. 8. 16.

3. **nectendis coronis**: dative of purpose or service (cf. Intr. 59), a construction surviving in prose chiefly in legal phrases (Gr. 299 *b*); cf. Liv. IV. 43. 10 *non ducem scribendo exercitui esse.* — **apium**: cf. I. 36. 16, II. 7. 24.

4. **vis multa**, *a plentiful supply. Vis*, in this apparently colloquial use, is often found in Cicero, as *Verr.* II. 4. 103 *magna vis eboris; Tusc.* V. 91.

5. **qua**: with **fulges** only. — **crinis religata**: cf. II. 11. 24; Intr. 42.—**fulges**: a stronger word than *nites*, I. 5. 13; so we speak of 'brilliant' or 'dazzling' beauty. It is probably from *fulgeo*, but may be future, from an old form *fulgo*, which Vergil has, *A.* VI. 826.

6. **ridet**: *i.e.* is bright and cheerful. The plate has been cleaned and polished for the occasion; cf. Juv. 14. 59 *hospite venturo cessabit nemo tuorum;* | '*Verre pavimentum, nitidas ostende columnas,* | . . . *hic*

vincta verbenis avet immolato
spargier agno;
cuncta festinat manus, huc et illuc
cursitant mixtae pueris puellae;
sordidum flammae trepidant rotantes
vertice fumum.

Vt tamen noris quibus advoceris
gaudiis, Idus tibi sunt agendae,
qui dies mensem Veneris marinae
findit Aprilem,

*leve argentum, vasa aspera tergeat alter'; Ep.* I. 5. 7 *iamdudum splendet focus et tibi munda supellex;* ib. 23 *ne non et cantharus et lanx ostendat tibi te. Rideo* in this sense was a favorite word with Lucretius, as I. 8 *rident aequora ponti;* III. 22 (*divum sedes*) *large diffuso lumine rident.* Catullus uses it even of odors, 64. 284 *domus iucundo risit odore.* — **ara vincta verbenis**: cf. I. 19. 13, 14 nn.

7. **immolato agno** = *immolatione* (*caede*) *agni* (Intr. 105 *a*); cf. Verg. *A.* IV. 21 *sparsos fraterna caede Penates.*

8. **spargier**: archaic pres. inf., found here only in the lyric poems, but eight times in the Satires and Epistles.

9. **manus**: *i.e. familia.*

10. **pueris**: see I. 19. 14 n; for the case, Intr. 56. — **puellae**: *i.e. ancillae,* as its connection with **pueris** shows. It is very seldom used in this sense.

11. **sordidum**, *sooty.* — **trepidant**: cf. III. 27. 17 n. Even the fire on the hearth seems to share in the general flutter of eager expectation pictured above in **avet, festinat, cursitant.** — **rotantes vertice**, *whirling round.*

13. **ut noris**: the purpose of the following explanation, **Idus,** etc.; cf. 9. 1 n; *Ep.* I. 12. 25 *ne tamen ignores quo sit Romana loco res, Cantaber,* etc.; *S.* II. 1. 80. — **advoceris**: here in the sense of *adhiberis,* and with the same construction; cf. 5. 32 *te mensis adhibet.*

15. **mensem Veneris**: there were various explanations of this. Horace has in mind the one according to which *Aprilis,* like Ἀφροδίτη, derived its name from ἀφρός, *sea-foam,* being the month in which the goddess rose out of the sea (hence **marinae**; see III. 26. 5 n). The month was no doubt sacred to her because of her activity at that season of the year; see I. 4. 5 n, and cf. Ov. *F.* IV. 1 *sqq.*

16. **findit**: according to the supposed derivation of *Idus* from *iduare,* an old word of Etruscan origin, meaning 'to divide' (Macrob. *Sat.* I. 15. 17).

17. **sollemnis**: the same as *festus* in III. 8. 9. — **sanctior**: the difference between *sollemnis dies* and *sanctus dies* is much the same as between 'holiday' and 'holy day.' Cf. Tib. IV. 5. 1 *qui mihi te,*

iure sollemnis mihi sanctiorque
paene natali proprio, quod ex hac
luce Maecenas meus adfluentis
ordinat annos.

Telephum, quem tu petis, occupavit
non tuae sortis iuvenem puella
dives et lasciva, tenetque grata
compede vinctum.

Terret ambustus Phaethon avaras
spes, et exemplum grave praebet ales
Pegasus terrenum equitem gravatus
Bellerophontem,

*Cerinthe, dies dedit, hic mihi sanctus | atque inter festos semper habendus erit.*

18. **paene**: cf. *prope*, 14. 20 n.

19. **luce**: cf. 6. 42 n. — **adfluentis**, *gathering;* lit. 'flowing to' him. The word contains no suggestion of old age or decline, like our 'advancing' years, but rather of an increased store of what the years bring; see II. 5. 14 n.

20. **ordinat**, *reckons*. The literal meaning is, that he makes out the series of his years with the Ides of April for the starting point (**ex hac luce**) of each, and not *e.g.* the Kalends of January, as it would be in the case of the calendar year.

21. **Telephum**: the same name is used in I. 13. 1 and III. 19. 26. — **petis**: as in I. 33. 13, III. 19. 27, and often. — **occupavit**: with its usual sense of anticipation: 'has got possession of him before you.'

22. **non tuae sortis**: *i.e.* above your station in life.

23. **dives**: so that you cannot hope to compete with her. The warning carries with it the soothing intimation that her failure to win casts no reflection on her personal attractions; the contest was unequal from the outset. Observe the chiastic arrangement of the attributes of **iuvenem** and **puella**. — **tenet grata compede**: cf. I. 33. 14.

25. **terret**: for the position, cf. *monet*, I. 18. 8. — **ambustus Phaethon**: Intr. 105 *a*.

26. **grave**: there is only mock seriousness, of course, in the present application of it. — **ales**: cf. I. 2. 42, III. 12. 2.

27. **terrenum**: hence unfit to consort with a creature of the air (**ales**), and teaching by his fate the lesson **ut disparem vites**, as well as the sin of unlawful ambition (**ultra quam licet sperare nefas**). It was said that Bellerophon, after his victory over the Chimaera (cf. I. 27. 24), attempted to fly to heaven on Pegasus, with the result here indicated. — **gravatus**: Intr. 51 *a*.

28. **Bellerophontem**: see III. 7. 15 n.

semper ut te digna sequare et ultra
quam licet sperare nefas putando
disparem vites. Age iam, meorum
finis amorum,
(non enim posthac alia calebo
femina,) condisce modos, amanda
voce quos reddas; minuentur atrae
carmine curae.

## XII.

Iam veris comites, quae mare temperant,
impellunt animae lintea Thraciae;
iam nec prata rigent nec fluvii strepunt
hiberna nive turgidi.

29. **ut sequare**, etc.: depending loosely on the notion of instruction contained in **exemplum**; cf. Ter. *Heaut.* 51 *exémplum statuite ín me, ut adulescénťuli* | *vobís placere stú-deant potius quám sibi*, and the use of an indirect question with *exemplar proposuit*, *Ep.* I. 2. 17.—**digna**: cf. *ima summis*, I. 34. 12 n.

30. **putando**: approaching the use of the present participle; Gr. 301 (footnote).

31. **age iam**, etc.: the conclusion of the plea: 'Better content yourself, then, with me; and come, let us enjoy the day together.'

32. **finis**: cf. Prop. I. 12. 19 *mi neque amare aliam neque ab hac desistere fas est;* | *Cynthia prima fuit, Cynthia finis erit.*—**amorum**: cf. I. 27. 17 n.

33. **alia calebo**: cf. *quo calet*, I. 4. 19 n; Intr. 72.

34. **condisce**: *i.e.* 'let me teach you.'

35. **reddas**: see 6. 43 n.—**atrae curae**: cf. III. 1. 40 n, 14. 13.

XII. We have in this ode the same elements as in I. 4 and IV. 7. It opens with a picture of spring. The increasing warmth brings thirst, and on this the poet hinges an invitation to his friend to join him in a carouse, to which each shall contribute an equitable share. The reminder of the shortness of life, so prominent in the two odes named, is brought in here also, but only as a momentary thought (vs. 26). Of the friend addressed, Vergilius, we know with certainty nothing beyond what the lines reveal. That it was the author of the Aeneid is not impossible, if we suppose that Horace published some years after Vergil's death a poem which he had written in his lifetime, and that two allusions (vss. 15 and 25) which appear to contradict what we know of Vergil had their explanations in circumstances unknown to us; but it is highly improbable. The Vergilius of this ode we may conjecture was

Nidum ponit, Ityn flebiliter gemens,
infelix avis et Cecropiae domus
aeternum opprobrium, quod male barbaras
regum est ulta libidines.

Dicunt in tenero gramine pinguium
custodes ovium carmina fistula

a younger friend of Horace, who was trying to better his fortunes by attaching himself to one and another of the great men of the day, or possibly a man who was brought into close relations with noble patrons by his professional work. In one manuscript he is called *medicus Neronum*, which is worthless as testimony, but contains a suggestion. (The 13th poem of Catullus, in which a similar invitation is given, may well be read with this ode, by way of comparing the two poets.) — Metre, 172.

1. **veris comites**: cf. 7. 9, I. 4. 1 n, *Ep*. I. 7. 13. For **comites**, cf. I. 25. 19 *hiemis sodali*, *Euro*. — **temperant**, *calm*.

2. **impellunt lintea**: *i.e.* navigation is already open; cf. I. 4. 2.— **Thraciae**: a literary epithet, as applied to the *Zephyri*, of Homeric origin; cf. *Il*. IX. 5 Βορέης καὶ Ζέφυρος, τώ τε Θρῄκηθεν ἄητον. It is more commonly applied to Boreas (Aquilo); cf. I. 25. 11 n, *Epod*. 13. 3.

3. **prata**: cf. I. 4. 4.—**nec fluvii**, etc.: cf. 7. 3 *sq*.

5. **Ityn**: son of the Thracian king Tereus and Procne, daughter of Pandion, king of Athens. His mother killed him, and served up his flesh to his own father in revenge (**male ulta**) for the outrage the latter had committed on her sister Philomela. When Tereus discovered the crime, and pursued the two sisters, all three were changed into birds. (See Ov. *M*. VI. 424 *sqq*.) There is a confusion of names in the myth. According to the form adopted by Roman writers, Procne was turned into a swallow, and Philomela into a nightingale (*e.g.* Verg. *G*. IV. 15, Ov. *F*. II. 853 *sqq*.). For the case of **Ityn**, see Intr. 51 *a*. — **flebiliter gemens**: properly descriptive of the nightingale's plaintive note, and it is possible that Horace so intends it, following the other form of the myth and the example of the Greek poets, in whom the nightingale is associated with the spring (cf. *Odys*. XIX. 518; Sappho *Fr*. 19 ἦρος ἄγγελος, ἱμερόφωνος ἀηδών); but the swallow was proverbially, among both Greeks and Romans, the sign of spring, and is probably intended by **avis infelix** here. Cf. *Ep*. I. 7. 12 *te, dulcis amice, reviset | cum Zephyris et hirundine prima*.

6. **Cecropiae domus**: the Attic dynasty of which Cecrops was the founder.

7. **male**: in reference not to the act of vengeance, but to the manner of it. — **barbaras**: Intr. 124.

8. **regum**: the plural generalizes, and defines the conduct of Tereus as characteristic of his class, so that it is substantially equivalent to *regias*; cf. *virginum*, III. 27. 38 n.

9. **dicunt carmina**: cf. *C. S*. 8, and see I. 6. 5 n.

10. **fistula**: see I. 17. 10 n; and for the case, I. 17. 18 n.

delectantque deum cui pecus et nigri
colles Arcadiae placent.

Adduxere sitim tempora, Vergili;
sed pressum Calibus ducere Liberum
si gestis, iuvenum nobilium cliens,
nardo vina merebere.

Nardi parvus onyx eliciet cadum,
qui nunc Sulpiciis accubat horreis,
spes donare novas largus amaraque
curarum eluere efficax.

11. **deum**: *i.e.* Faunus, here, as in I. 17. 1 *sqq.*, identified with Pan. — **nigri colles**: cf. *nigris Erymanthi silvis*, I. 21. 7 n.

14. **pressum Calibus**: cf. I. 20. 9 n. — **ducere**: cf. I. 17. 22 n. — **Liberum**: Intr. 130.

15. **iuvenum nobilium**: the word **iuvenum** appears to indicate definite persons, but we have no means of knowing who they were. — **cliens**: *i.e.* accustomed to be invited to their tables, where he was not required to contribute anything, — the same thought that is expressed in vs. 24.

16. **nardo**: see II. 11. 16 n. — **vina**: Intr. 128. The plural here obviously refers to a single jar. — **merebere**: equivalent to a mild command; cf. Intr. 90.

17. **nardi**: Intr. 116 *h.* — **parvus**: the nard was very costly; cf. *N. T. Mark* 14. 3 *sqq.* — **onyx**: usually denoting, when masculine, a box to hold ointment, originally one made of alabaster (cf. Plin. *N. H.* XXXVI. 60 *hunc aliqui lapidem* (*onychem*) '*alabastriten*' *vocant, quem cavant et ad vasa unguentaria, quoniam optime servare incorrupta dicatur*), but later an ointment box of any material. — **eliciet**: a personification of the *cadus* similar to that of III. 21. 1 *sqq.*

18. **Sulpiciis**: cf. Intr. 65; but this was the regular usage in the case of gentile and other personal names that were originally adjectives; cf. *Claudiae manus*, 4. 73; *lex Cornelia*, *Iulius* (*mensis*), *Colonia Agrippina*, *historia Augusta*, etc. The *horrea Sulpicia* stood at the foot of the Aventine, where the hill borders on the river, among numerous other buildings of the kind, which gave to the district the name of 'the Warehouses' (*Horrea*). It was built by the Galba family (hence also called *Galbiana*), and existed in Porphyrio's day (4th century or earlier), 'vino et oleo et similibus aliis referta.' The poet's wine is stored there. — **accubat**, *reclines*, the *cadus* having no base; see Baumeister III. *fig.* 2335.

19. **spes donare**: cf. III. 21. 17. For the infinitive, see Intr. 101 *b.* — **amara curarum**: Intr. 64.

20. **eluere**: cf. III. 12. 1 *mala vino lavere.* For the mood, see Intr. 101 *b.*

21. **properas**: here expressing not haste in coming, but haste

Ad quae si properas gaudia, cum tua
velox merce veni ; non ego te meis
immunem meditor tinguere poculis,
plena dives ut in domo.
Verum pone moras et studium lucri,
nigrorumque memor, dum licet, ignium
misce stultitiam consiliis brevem :
dulce est desipere in loco.

## XIII.

Audivere, Lyce, di mea vota, di
audivere, Lyce : fis anus ; et tamen
vis formosa videri,
ludisque et bibis impudens

(eagerness) to come; cf. *S.* I. 9. 40 *et propero* (I am in a hurry to go) *quo scis.* — **gaudia** : cf. 11. 14.

22. **merce** : *i.e.* the nard.

23. **immunem,** *scot-free, i.e.* without paying your contribution; in Greek, ἀσύμβολον, which Terence has in Phor. 339 *asymbolum venire* (sc. *ad cenam*). — **tinguere** : colloquial, like *siccus* and *uvidus* (5. 39), *irriguus* (*S.* II. 1. 9).

24. **plena domo** : cf. II. 12. 24.

25. **verum,** *but really* (breaking off the banter); the word occurs here only in the lyric poems. — **moras** : the plural (Intr. 128), of delay persisted in for one reason after another. — **studium lucri** : see intr. note.

26. **nigrorum** : see I. 24. 18 n.

27. **consiliis,** *with your wisdom.* Cf. III. 28. 4, and for the case, see Intr. 56.

28. **dulce est desipere**: a Greek idea; cf. Sen. *Dial.* IX. 17. 10 *sive Graeco poetae credimus, 'aliquando et insanire iucundum est'*; Menander IV. 196 M. οὐ πανταχοῦ τὸ φρόνιμον ἁρμόττει παρόν, καὶ συμμανῆναι δ' ἔνια δεῖ. — **in loco** : cf. *Ep.* I. 7. 57 *et properare loco et cessare;* Ter. *Ad.* 216 *pecúniam in locó neglegere máximum interdúmst lucrum.*

XIII. The Lyce who figures in this ode as a fading beauty may very well have been the same in the poet's fancy as the Lyce of III. 10, where her coldness and arrogance were well suited to call out the imprecations on her lover's part, the fulfillment of which he here recognizes with malicious glee. The subject is the same as that of III. 15 and I. 25.—Metre, 173.

1. **audivere,** etc.: the repetition (Intr. 116 *g*) is that of taunting exultation. — **vota** : cf. II. 8. 6 n.

4. **ludis**: cf. III. 15. 5, II. 12. 19 n.

et cantu tremulo pota Cupidinem
lentum sollicitas. Ille virentis et
doctae psallere Chiae
pulchris excubat in genis;
importunus enim transvolat aridas
quercus et refugit te quia luridi
dentes, te quia rugae
turpant et capitis nives;
nec Coae referunt iam tibi purpurae
nec cari lapides tempora quae semel
notis condita fastis
inclusit volucris dies.

5. **tremulo**: the effect of wine on a voice made unsteady by age.

6. **lentum**, *torpid, unresponsive;* different from *lentus amor*, III. 19. 28. The same difference exists between *S.* I. 9. 64 *vellere coepi et pressare manu lentissima bracchia* and *Epod.* 15. 6 *lentis adhaerens bracchiis.* — **virentis**: cf. I. 9. 17.

7. **psallere**: Intr. 101 *c.*—**Chiae**: a name like *Delia*, *Lesbia*, etc. It occurs in several inscriptions as a freedwoman's name.

8. **excubat**, *keeps watch; i.e.* lurks there, ready to attack those who come within bowshot.

9. **importunus**, *the unmannerly boy.* — **aridas**: in contrast with *virentis*, 6; cf. I. 25. 17, 19.

10. **quercus**: a type of long life. — **te quia . . . te quia**: the ἀπὸ κοινοῦ construction (Intr. 76) is helped out by the anaphora, **te** in vs. 10 being felt to be the object of **refugit**, while in vs. 11, where its repetition with **quia** serves to continue the dependent clause with another subject (Intr. 116 *h*), it is felt to be a part of that clause and the object of **turpant.**

12. **capitis nives**: cf. Lowell's 'Singer with the crown of snow.' The metaphor, so familiar to us, appears not to occur in classical literature before Horace (though Catullus, according to some texts, wrote *niveo vertice*, 64. 309). Quintilian (VIII. 6. 17) condemns it as harsh and founded on too remote a likeness, coupling in his censure this passage with a verse of the poet Furius which Horace himself ridicules, *S.* II. 5. 41.

13. **Coae**: the silk stuffs manufactured in the island of Cos were notorious for their fine, semi-transparent texture, which made them a favorite material with the class of which Lyce is a type.

15. **notis condita fastis inclusit**: Intr. 76. The meaning is that she cannot get back her past years or disguise the fact that they are past, because they are, as it were, securely stored away and locked up in the calendar, where they are known to all men. For the part attributed to the **volucris dies** in the flight of time, cf. *rapit hora diem*, 7. 8 n.

Quo fugit venus, heu, quove color, decens
quo motus? Quid habes illius, illius,
quae spirabat amores,
quae me surpuerat mihi,
felix post Cinaram notaque et artium
gratarum facies? Sed Cinarae brevis
annos fata dederunt,
servatura diu parem
cornicis vetulae temporibus Lycen,
possent ut iuvenes visere fervidi
multo non sine risu
dilapsam in cineres facem.

18. **illius, illius**: Intr. 116 *d.* The genitive is partitive, limiting **quid.**

19. **spirabat amores**: Intr. 51 *d* (2); cf. Prop. I. 3. 7 (of the sleeping Cynthia) *visa mihi mollem spirare quietem.*

20. **surpuerat**: colloquial syncopation of *surripuerat*; cf. *surpite*, *S.* II. 3. 283, and see Intr. 183. For the thought, cf. Cat. 51. 3 *qui sedens adversus identidem te | spectat et audit | dulce ridentem, misero quod omnis eripit sensus mihi.*

21. **felix post,** *favored above all but.* For **post,** cf. III. 9. 6 n. — **Cinaram**: see I. 4 n. — **nota**: she was one of the noted beauties of the day. — **artium gratarum,** *of winning graces*; descriptive genitive. Some, however, make **et** = *etiam*, and join the genitive with **nota,** as in II. 2. 6.

22. **facies**: here not the face, but her whole appearance, — *a vision, a figure*; cf. Ter. *Eun.* 296 *o fáciem pulcram! déleo omnis dehinc ex animo múlieres.*

24. **servatura**: Intr. 104 *a.* — **parem**: proleptic, — *to equal, to attain.*

25. **vetulae,** *poor old*; colloquial (cf. vs. 20 n) and disparaging; cf. the more dignified *annosa cornix*, III. 17. 13 n. — **temporibus,** *the years* (we require in English a definite measure of time to form such a plural).

26. **possent ut,** etc., *to give . . . a chance to behold.* The point of the sarcasm is that Lyce is a woman who will subject her fading charms to the ridicule of the **iuvenes fervidi,**—hence the fates have selected *her* as the instrument of their purpose.

28. **dilapsam in cineres,** *crumbled to ashes.* **in** expresses the result of the change, as in *portus curvatus in arcum* (Verg. *A.* III. 533) and the like.

## XIV.

Quae cura patrum quaeve Quiritium
plenis honorum muneribus tuas,
Auguste, virtutes in aevum
per titulos memoresque fastos
aeternet, o qua sol habitabilis
inlustrat oras maxime principum?
Quem legis expertes Latinae
Vindelici didicere nuper
quid Marte posses. Milite nam tuo
Drusus Genaunos, implacidum genus,
Breunosque velocis et arcis
Alpibus impositas tremendis

XIV. For the subject and occasion of this ode, see intr. note to Ode 4. Tiberius, who was barely alluded to in that ode, naturally receives the larger share of attention here, but the achievements of both brothers are treated as merely incidental to the praises of Augustus. His transcendent merits are extolled in the opening strophes, and, after disposing of its proper subject, the poem resolves itself into a song of praise to the great ruler before whose power all nations bow. — Metre, 176.

1. **patrum . . . -ve Quiritium**: a paraphrase for the formal *senatus populusque Romanus.*

2. **plenis,** *adequate.*—**honorum**: defining *muneribus*; cf. I. 28. 3.

3. **in aevum**: cf. III. 11. 35 *in omne aevum.* Here the idea of *omne* is supplied by **aeternet.**

4. **per titulos**: *i.e.* by statues, altars, trophies (see vs. 10 n), and other monuments inscribed with his achievements.—**memores fastos**: cf. III. 17. 4.

5. **o qua,** etc.: cf. Ter. *Phor.* 853 *o ómnium quantúmst qui vivont hómo hominum ornatíssume.* — **qua sol,** etc.: *i.e.* in the whole habitable world.

6. **principum**: see I. 2. 50 n; but as there was no other *princeps* in this sense, the word must be used here vaguely for rulers in general, under whatever title.

7. **quem didicere quid posses**: such anticipation, in the main clause, of the subject of a dependent question occurs in Horace only here and in vs. 17 *spectandus . . . quantis,* etc. It is frequent in comedy, as Ter. *Eun.* 657 *ego illum nescio qui fuerit* (cf. 'I know thee who thou art'). — **legis expertes Latinae**: *i.e.* not yet subjugated.

9. **quid posses**: cf. *quid posset,* 4. 25; Intr. 47. — **Marte**: cf. III. 5. 24, 34; Intr. 130. — **milite tuo**: referring to the operations of *both* brothers (vss. 10–16).

10. **Genaunos . . . Breunosque**: it is not clear whether Hor-

deiecit acer plus vice simplici;
maior Neronum mox grave proelium
commisit immanisque Raetos
auspiciis pepulit secundis,
spectandus in certamine Martio,
devota morti pectora liberae
quantis fatigaret ruinis,
indomitas prope qualis undas

ace regarded these two tribes of the Inn valley as a part of the Vindelician nation, which included at least four tribes (Plin. *N. H.* III. 136), or as their allies, naming the Vindelici in vs. 8 and 4. 18, as he does the Sygambri in vs. 51 and 2. 36, because of their controlling influence in the confederacy. The inscription on a trophy erected a few miles from Nice to commemorate Augustus' conquest of the Alpine tribes (CIL. V. 7817; Plin. *l. l.*) is equally ambiguous. — **implacidum genus,** *a merciless breed;* cf. *immanis,* 15 n. *Implacidus* occurs here first in extant Latin literature.

11. **velocis,** *agile; i.e.* in their warfare. — **arcis,** etc.: cf. *Ep.* II. 1. 252.

13. **deiecit,** *hurled down;* applying equally well to the barbarians (cf. *Ep.* II. 2. 30) and their stronghold (cf. Verg. *A.* XII. 655 *deiecturum arcis*).—**plus vice simplici**: *i.e.* making them suffer greater loss than they had inflicted. For **vice,** cf. I. 28. 32 n. The ablative is modal, **plus** being used as a simple adverb without influence on the case, as often in prose.

14. **maior Neronum**: see 4. 28 n. His name, *Tĭbĕrĭus,* is excluded by its prosody. He was at this time in his twenty-seventh year. — **proelium**: according to Dio (LIV. 22. 4) he fought several pitched battles.

15. **immanis**: Strabo (IV. 6. 8) describes the cruelty of the Alpine barbarians towards the prisoners captured in their raids as similar to that attributed to Achilles in 6. 18–20.

17. **spectandus,** etc.: the passive of the personal construction exemplified in vs. 7, where see note. For the use of the gerundive, cf. *donandus,* 2. 9 n. For the neglect of caesura in this verse, see Intr. 155.

18. **devota**: Intr. 103. — **pectora**: cf. 4. 34 n. — **liberae,** *a freeman's* (cf. III. 5. 22): they were determined to die rather than surrender; a difficult foe, therefore, to conquer.

19. **quantis**: Intr. 114.—**ruinis:** cf. Liv. V. 43. 3 *strage et ruina fudere Gallos.* The plural expresses repeated occurrence, — *crushing blows,* or the like. Horace here and in the following comparison has in mind the Roman pursuit of the barbarians into their native valleys.

20. **indomitas**: parallel to *devota morti liberae,* 18 n. — **prope** (with **qualis**) = 'I had almost said.' It adds to the effect of the description, as a mark of the narrator's carefulness of statement. Cf. 11. 18, *S.* II. 3. 268.

exercet Auster Pleiadum choro
scindente nubis, impiger hostium
vexare turmas et frementem
mittere equum medios per ignis.

Sic tauriformis volvitur Aufidus,
qui regna Dauni praefluit Apuli,
cum saevit horrendamque cultis
diluviem meditatur agris,

ut barbarorum Claudius agmina
ferrata vasto diruit impetu,
primosque et extremos metendo
stravit humum, sine clade victor,

21. **Auster**: cf. III. 3. 4 *sq.* — **Pleiadum choro**: cf. Prop. IV. 5. 36 *Pleiadum spisso cur coit igne chorus.* They were harbingers of storm as they approached their setting in November; cf. Prop. III. 16. 51 *non haec* (*fulmina*) *Pleiades faciunt neque aquosus Orion.*

22. **scindente nubis**: the picture is of a black night with driving clouds, through the rifts of which the stars are now and then visible. — **impiger vexare**: Intr. 101 *b.*

24. **medios per ignis**: a stock phrase for extreme peril; cf. *S.* II. 3. 56 *sq.*, *Ep.* I. 1. 46 *per mare pauperiem fugiens, per saxa, per ignis.* It seems inapt here, however, and possibly is used literally, in allusion to a definite incident known to Horace and his readers, but not to us, — a fight in a burning village, perhaps.

25. **sic . . . ut**: a rare inversion (in an affirmative sentence) of the usual form of comparison, giving up the main clause to the illustration, and remitting the subject illustrated to the relative clause; cf. Mart. IV. 13. 3 (of a wedding) *tam bene rara suo miscentur cinnama nardo,* | *Massica Theseis tam bene vina favis.* — **tauriformis**: such compounds are extremely rare in Horace. A river god was sometimes represented in the form of a bull with human face (see Baumeister, I. *fig.* 604, II. *figg.* 1136 *sq.*), suggested by the rush and roar of the stream. Cf. Verg. *G.* IV. 371 *gemina auratus taurino cornua voltu Eridanus.* — **Aufidus**: cf. III. 30. 10 n; Intr. 3.

26. **regna Dauni**: see I. 22. 14 n. — **praefluit**: see 3. 10 n.

29. **Claudius**: *i.e.* Tiberius; cf. vs. 14 n; *Ep.* I. 3. 2. — **agmina ferrata**, *mailed ranks.* The fact is not mentioned elsewhere, but Tacitus (*Ann.* III. 43. 3) mentions Gallic troops, thirty-five years later, '*quibus more gentico continuum ferri tegimen; cruppellarios vocant.*'

30. **diruit**: as if they were a fortress or a wall; cf. Tacitus' account of the *cruppellarii* in battle (*Ann.* III. 46. 6): *paulum morae attulere ferrati, restantibus laminis*

te copias, te consilium et tuos
praebente divos. Nam tibi, quo die
portus Alexandrea supplex
et vacuam patefecit aulam,
Fortuna lustro prospera tertio
belli secundos reddidit exitus,
laudemque et optatum peractis
imperiis decus adrogavit.
Te Cantaber non ante domabilis
Medusque et Indus, te profugus Scythes

*adversum pila et gladios; sed miles correptis securibus, ut si murum perrumperet, caedere tegmina et corpora.*

31. **metendo**: cf. Verg. *A.* X. 513 *proxima quaeque metit gladio.* For this use of the gerund, cf. 11. 30 n.

32. **stravit humum**: *sc.* with them; cf. III. 17. 9 n.—**sine clade victor**: so also Velleius (I. 95): *Raetos Vindelicosque . . . maiore cum periculo quam damno Romani exercitus, plurimo cum eorum sanguine perdomuerunt.*

33. **te, te, tuos,** etc.: see I. 10. 9 n.—**tuos divos**: *i.e.* the favor of the gods towards Augustus, as revealed in the auspices, was communicated to Tiberius and Drusus, who were simply his *legati;* see I. 7. 27 n.

34. **nam**: referring to **tuos divos,** and introducing the evidence of divine favor.—**quo die**: the 1st of August. The capitulation of Alexandria on that day in B.C. 30 was the end of the civil war, and the senate subsequently (B.C. 8) commemorated the event by changing the former name of the month, *Sextilis,* to *Augustus,* in honor of the emperor.

35. **portus**: there were three of them.

36. **vacuam**: having been deserted by Cleopatra, who had shut herself up in her mausoleum.

37. **lustro tertio**: *i.e.* at the expiration of fifteen years (from that day). We need not suppose that the coincidence of date was exact, but it must have been near enough to be striking.

38. **reddidit,** *granted* (as something due, something striven for and earned); cf. Cat. 76. 26 *o di, reddite mi hoc pro pietate mea.*

39. **optatum**: cf. 8. 30 n.—**peractis imperiis**: *i.e.* on the deeds done in pursuance of thy orders.

40. **adrogavit,** *bestowed;* cf. *Ep.* II. 1. 35 *scire velim chartis pretium quotus adroget annus.*

41. **Cantaber**: see II. 6. 2 n.

42. **Medus**: see I. 2. 22 n, and IV. 15. 6 n.—**Indus, Scythes**: cf. *C. S.* 55, Suet. *Aug.* 21; *Mon. Anc.* 5. 50 *ad me ex India regum legationes saepe missae sunt, numquam antea visae apud quemquam Romanorum ducem; nostram amicitiam petierunt per legatos Bastarnae Scythaeque.*—**profugus**: cf. I. 35. 9 n.

miratur, o tutela praesens
Italiae dominaeque Romae;
te fontium qui celat origines
Nilusque et Hister, te rapidus Tigris,
te beluosus qui remotis
obstrepit Oceanus Britannis,
te non paventis funera Galliae
duraeque tellus audit Hiberiae,
te caede gaudentes Sygambri
compositis venerantur armis.

43. **tutela**: here in an active sense; cf. 6. 33 n. — **praesens**: cf. III. 5. 2, I. 35. 2 n.

44. **dominae**, *imperial;* cf. 3. 13.

45. **qui celat origines Nilus**: *i.e.* the Nile to its very source, standing for both the Egyptians and the Ethiopians. The source of the Nile was to the ancients much like what the north pole is to us; cf. Lucan X. 189 (Caesar speaks) *nihil est quod noscere malim | quam fluvii causas per saecula tanta latentis | ignotumque caput; spes sit mihi certa videndi | Niliacos fontes, bellum civile relinquam;* 268 *quae tibi noscendi Nilum, Romane, cupido est | et Phariis Persisque fuit Macetumque tyrannis,* etc.

46. **Hister**: standing for the Dacians; see I. 26. 4 n.—**rapidus**: the name *Tigris* was said to mean 'arrow' (Varro *L. L.* V. 100). — **Tigris**: standing for the Armenians. For this use of the rivers to designate the peoples who dwell on their banks, cf. *Tanais,* III. 29. 28 n, and see II. 20. 20 n.

47. **beluosus**: not found elsewhere in classical Latin; cf. I. 3. 18, III. 27. 26. The ocean, however, was peopled, by common report, with creatures of monstrous form, not seen in Mediterranean waters: cf. Tac. *Ann.* II. 24. 6 (of Germanicus' soldiers, driven out into the North Sea in a storm) *ut quisque ex longinquo revenerat, miracula narrabant, . . . inauditas volucres, monstra maris, ambiguas hominum et beluarum formas, visa sive ex metu credita.*

48. **obstrepit Britannis**: cf. II. 18. 20 n.—**Oceanus**: standing, in this context, for the Britons, some of whose chiefs had sent envoys to Augustus to seek the alliance and protection of Rome (Strabo IV. 5. 3).

49. **non paventis funera**: Intr. 51 *a.* This well-known characteristic of the Gauls (cf. Lucan I. 459 *quos ille timorum maximus haud urguet, leti metus*) was attributed to the teachings of the Druids; cf. Caes. *B. G.* VI. 14. 5 *imprimis hoc volunt persuadere, non interire animas, . . . atque hoc maxime ad virtutem excitari putant, metu mortis neglecto.* — **funera**: Intr. 128. — **Galliae**: like **Hiberiae**, gen. with **tellus**; Intr. 65, 119 *a.*

50. **audit**, *heeds.*

51. **caede gaudentes**, *bloodthirsty;* cf. *ferocis,* 2. 34. — **Sygambri**: see intr. note to Ode 2.

## XV.

Phoebus volentem proelia me loqui
victas et urbis increpuit lyra,
ne parva Tyrrhenum per aequor
vela darem. Tua, Caesar, aetas

XV. This ode, in honor of Augustus, which fittingly closes the volume, is a companion-piece to Ode 14 (just as the similar tribute in Ode 5 was coupled with the praises of Drusus in Ode 4); and as early as the fourth century it was an open question whether the two were not written by Horace as one ode. Porphyrio held that they were, and they so appear in a few of our codices. But although both odes are devoted to the praises of Augustus, the subject is here treated in a different aspect. In Ode 14 Augustus is the invincible champion of Roman safety and supremacy against all nations; here he is the bulwark of peace and prosperity at home, the restorer of good morals and of good old customs, and of that old-time discipline which made Rome great. The ode was probably written not long after the return of Augustus from Gaul in B.C. 13.—Metre, 176.

1. **Phoebus**, etc.: the fancy was suggested to Horace, perhaps, by Verg. *E.* 6. 3 *cum canerem reges et proelia, Cynthius aurem | vellit et admonuit.*—**volentem**, etc.: cf. *Ep.* II. 1. 250 (written about the same time) *nec sermones ego mallem | repentis per humum quam res componere gestas | . . . si quantum cuperem possem quoque*, where, however, he is protesting his unfitness to write epic poetry; here, as in Ode 2, he has in mind lyric treatment (**loqui lyra**) of warlike themes; cf. I. 6. 5 *sqq.*, II. 1. 37 *sqq.*—**proelia**: Intr. 116 *b.*—**loqui**: cf. 2. 45 n.

2. **increpuit ne**, *cried out at me, not to.* Porphyrio explains this correctly: *non 'lyra increpuit,' sed 'volentem me proelia lyra loqui,' id est, lyrico carmine.* Most modern editors take **lyra** with **increpuit**, quoting Ov. *A. A.* II. 493 *haec ego cum canerem, subito manifestus Apollo | movit inauratae pollice fila lyrae.* But there the striking of the lyre is simply to attract the poet's attention to what the god is about to say, and there is no suggestion of 'rebuking with the lyre.' The only reason for this explanation of the text is the position of **increpuit**; but cf. vs. 15, *porrecta;* II. 6. 11 *regnata petam Laconi rura Phalantho;* IV. 1. 19 *Albanos prope te lacus ponet; Epod.* 6. 16 *inultus ut flebo puer.*

3. **parva**: of lyric, in comparison with more stately verse; cf. III. 3. 72, IV. 2. 31, *Ep.* II. 1. 257 *parvum carmen.*—**Tyrrhenum**: Intr. 117 *a.*

4. **vela darem**: a metaphor often used of poetical enterprise; cf. Prop. IV. 9. 3 *quid me scribendi tam vastum mittis in aequor? | non sunt apta meae grandia vela rati;* Verg. *G.* II. 41; Ov. *Tr.* II. 329.—**tua aetas**: put forward, in contrast with the forbidden **proelia**, etc., as a theme affording abundant scope for his lyre, in the varied blessings which he proceeds to recount.

fruges et agris rettulit uberes
et signa nostro restituit Iovi
derepta Parthorum superbis
postibus et vacuum duellis
Ianum Quirini clausit et ordinem
rectum evaganti frena licentiae
iniecit emovitque culpas
et veteres revocavit artis,

5. **fruges agris rettulit**: *sc.* after the decay of agriculture due to the civil wars. — **et . . . et . . . etc.**: the polysyndeton, continuing the enumeration without pause through three strophes, gives the impression of a throng of benefits pressing for utterance. This is succeeded through two more strophes (vss. 17–24) by an enumeration of averted evils, which are brought out with individual distinctness by the anaphora of **non** (Intr. 116 *f*). Cf. 1. 13 and 29 nn.

6. **signa**: those captured from Crassus at Carrhae (see III. 5. 5 n) and Antony (III. 6. 9 n). In B.C. 20 Augustus, then in the East, organized an expedition against the Parthians, and King Phraates, who was just then in too much trouble at home to fight the Romans, purchased a peace by surrendering, among other things, the famous standards. This demonstration of the power of Rome, without the shedding of a drop of blood, Horace naturally includes in his enumeration of the triumphs of peace.—**nostro**, *our own;* Intr. 116 *b*.—**Iovi**: cf. III. 5. 12 n. It appears from this passage that the standards were first deposited in the Capitol, and they remained there during Horace's lifetime. They were afterwards transferred to the temple of Mars Ultor (*Mon. Anc.* 5. 40), but this temple was not dedicated till B.C. 2.

7. **derepta**: hardly accurate, as denoting eagerness or indignation in the act, but well expressing the feelings of the Romans.

8. **postibus**: *sc.* of their temples; cf. *Ep.* I. 18. 57 *sub duce* (*i.e. Augusto*) *qui templis Parthorum signa refigit.*—**duellis**: Intr. 66 *c*, N.

9. **Ianum Quirini**: the famous temple of Janus, not far from the Curia, on the north side of the Forum. Horace purposely varies from the official and prosaic designation, *Ianus Quirinus*, which he evidently understood to mean 'Gateway of Quirinus' (Intr. 65); cf. Ov. *M.* XIV. 836 *colle Quirini* (= *Quirinali*). Tradition ascribed to Numa both the temple itself and the injunction to close it only in time of peace (Liv. I. 19. 2).—**clausit**: for the first time in more than 200 years. It was closed three times under Augustus (*Mon. Anc.* 2. 42), — B.C. 29, 25, and a third date, not definitely known, but later than the composition of this ode. — **ordinem evaganti**: Intr. 51 *f*. The figure is military.

10. **frena licentiae iniecit**: cf. III. 24. 29.

12. **artis**, *virtues*, as the context shows; cf. III. 3. 9 n.

13. **nomen**: cf. III. 3. 45. — **Italae**: cf. II. 13. 18, III. 30. 13 n.

per quas Latinum nomen et Italae
crevere vires famaque et imperi
porrecta maiestas ad ortus
solis ab Hesperio cubili.

Custode rerum Caesare non furor
civilis aut vis exiget otium,
non ira, quae procudit ensis
et miseras inimicat urbis.

Non qui profundum Danuvium bibunt
edicta rumpent Iulia, non Getae,
non Seres infidive Persae,
non Tanain prope flumen orti.

14. **imperi**: for the position, see Intr. 119 *a*.

15. **porrecta**: sc. *est*. With **maiestas** it means 'made widely known and felt.' — **ortus solis**: poetical for *orientem* (*solem*). The plural is that of repeated occurrence (Intr. 128), *i.e.* not the places (regions of the East) where the sun rises, but the part of the earth (the East) where it rises day by day; cf. 5. 8 n. With the whole phrase, cf. Sall. *Cat.* 36. 4 *cum ad occasus ab ortu solis omnia domita armis parerent.*

17. **custode,** etc.: cf. 5. 2, III. 14. 15 *sq.* — **furor civilis,** *political madness* (= *civium ardor prava iubentium*, III. 3. 2); distinct from **ira,** below; cf. I. 37. 12, III. 27. 36.

18. **exiget**: used in this literal sense, with rare exceptions, only of persons (cf. II. 13. 31), and therefore in keeping with the half personification which runs through the whole sentence.

19. **ira, quae,** etc.: cf. I. 16. 18 *sqq.*

20. **miseras**: proleptic. — **inimicat**: called by Porphyrio a *fictum verbum*, *i.e.* coined by Horace.

21. **qui Danuvium bibunt**: cf. II. 20. 20 n. The frontier of the empire was firmly established on the Danube by Augustus before he died, and remained so for centuries; but at this time the conquest of the tribes on the south bank was only half accomplished, and their submission had not lost, to Horace's readers, the impressiveness of novelty.

22. **edicta Iulia**: a general expression for the orders issued by Augustus and the terms imposed by him. — **rumpent**: the future is in keeping with the fact, stated above: the nations named will be reduced to obedience and made to keep the peace. — **Getae**: see III. 24. 11 n.

23. **Seres**: cf. I. 12. 56 n. — **infidi**: cf. *Ep.* II. 1. 112 *Parthis mendacior*, and see note on *perfidus*, 4. 49. — **Persae**: see I. 2. 22 n.

24. **Tanain prope orti**: cf. vs. 21 n, and see III. 29. 28 n.

Nosque et profestis lucibus et sacris
inter iocosi munera Liberi,
cum prole matronisque nostris
rite deos prius adprecati,

virtute functos more patrum duces
Lydis remixto carmine tibiis
Troiamque et Anchisen et almae
progeniem Veneris canemus.

25. **nos**: in contrast with the foreigners. The close of the ode is similar to that of Ode 5. — **et profestis et sacris**: *i.e.* every day alike. The picture is of cheerful every-day life, not merely of occasional enjoyment on holidays (cf. vs. 27 n). — **lucibus**: cf. 6. 42 n, 11. 19.

26. **iocosi**: cf. III. 21. 15 n. — **munera Liberi**: cf. 10. 1 n.

27. **cum prole**, etc.: *i.e.* each in his own family circle.

28. **adprecati**: a rare word, found only here in classical Latin.

29. **virtute functos**, *whose good work is done.* For the form of expression, see note on *functum laboribus*, II. 18. 38. — **more patrum**: with **canemus**. The custom was recorded by the elder Cato; cf. Cic. *Tusc.* IV. 3 *in Originibus dixit Cato morem apud maiores hunc epularum fuisse, ut deinceps qui accubarent canerent ad tibiam clarorum virorum laudes atque virtutes.*

30. **Lydis**: said by Donatus (on Ter. *Ad.*, *Praef.*) to have been suited to grave themes.—**remixto**: another rare word, used also *Ep.* II. 3. 151, but not found elsewhere before Seneca. The **re-** lends to the action a suggestion of iteration or persistence, as in *respergo.* — **tibiis**: here ablative, the instrument being secondary to the song.

31. **-que**: introducing a distinct topic (cf. *famaque* 14, *nosque* 25), — the Julian line, which stands preëminent among the great throng of Roman worthies, and is a subject that takes us back to Troy and the divine founders of the Roman race. — **Anchisen et progeniem Veneris**: *i.e.* Anchises and Venus and their offspring, — different from *C. S.* 50 *Anchisae Venerisque sanguis* (*i.e.* Augustus). The theme of song is to be the whole Julian house; but the interest, of course, centres in the one great figure who represented the house to Horace and his readers. The compliment to Augustus is indirect, but no less obvious than if he had been mentioned by name; cf. *Iulium sidus*, I. 12. 47 n. — **almae**: cf. Lucr. I. 2 *alma Venus*, and see 5. 18 n.

# CARMEN SAECVLARE.

## INTRODUCTORY NOTE.

In the summer of B.C. 17 Augustus instituted a remarkable festival, — one that, in the words of the herald who proclaimed the coming event, no living man had ever seen or would ever see again. The Quindecimviri, who had charge of the Sibylline Books, had produced an oracle which called for the celebration of the *ludi saeculares*.

The origin of this long forgotten festival was obscure. It appears to have grown out of the *ludi Terentini*, a religious observance associated with the oldest traditions of the Valerian family, and with a place in the Campus Martius called Terentum (or Tarentum), where there were hot springs and other evidences of volcanic influence. It was on the banks of the river, at the great bend below the Ponte Sant' Angelo. The healing properties of these springs were said to have been first revealed to Valesius the Sabine, who commemorated his gratitude for the miraculous healing of his three children by the institution of sacrifices, with other ceremonies and entertainments, on three successive nights, at the ancient subterranean altar of Dis and Proserpina, which under the guidance of an oracle he had discovered on this spot. (See Val. Max. II. 4. 5.)

Tradition ascribed the first celebration of the *ludi Terentini* as a public institution to the consul Valerius Poplicola, in the first year of the Commonwealth, and mentioned subsequent celebrations by other Valerii. The first celebration known to history occurred about the middle of the third century B.C. It was instituted under instructions from the Sibylline Books, which had been consulted in consequence of certain alarming portents; and the oracle gave further directions that the celebration should be renewed every hundred years (Varro *ap.* Censor. 17. 7). It was at this time, then, according to Varro, that the *ludi Terentini* became *ludi saeculares.*

A *saeculum* was the longest span of human life. It was an idea borrowed from the Etruscans, in whose system, we are told, the life of a city or a state was measured in *saecula*, as a man's life is measured in years. The first *saeculum* was the life of that one of the children born at the time of founding the city who survived all his fellows; the second *saeculum* began at his death, and was measured in the same way; and so on. This system, which of course never existed except in theory, left the length of the *saeculum* a variable quantity, and when the Romans came to fix it arbitrarily, there was a conflict of views and of practice. Varro's notion of a *saeculum* was 100 years (*L. L.* VI. 11); and according to Livy (*Perioch.* XLIX) a celebration of the *ludi Terentini* at the beginning of the third Punic war occurred a hundred years after the last preceding celebration. The Quindecimviri under Augustus, on the other hand, found in their Sibylline oracle (vs. 2), — which, whatever its origin, was composed apparently as early as the Social war, — 110 years as the length of the *saeculum* (cf. *C. S.* 21). As the accounts of celebrations in the past were imperfect and contradictory, it is evident that there was room for wide divergence of opinion as to the proper year for celebrating the jubilee. The Quindecimviri found or constructed in their records a series of four dates, at intervals of 110 years, at which the festival had been, or ought to have been, observed; and the celebration of B.C. 17

was set down as the fifth. The emperor Claudius, taking 100 years as his *saeculum* and the foundation of the city as his starting-point, celebrated the festival in A.D. 47 (A.V.C. 800); so that some people who witnessed the pageant under Augustus did live to see it again, after all. Domitian chose the year 88; for what reason, is not clear. The ninth centennial of the city was celebrated by Antoninus Pius. Subsequent celebrations are recorded for A.D. 204 (2 × 110 years from B.C. 17), 247 (A.V.C. 1000), 259, and 298.

Vergil's fourth eclogue shows that certainly as early as B.C. 40, when the poem was written, and probably much earlier, a Sibylline oracle was current, which foretold the near approach of a regeneration of the world and the advent of a new Golden Age. It was perhaps this prophecy and the expectations and aspirations roused by it that suggested to Augustus and his advisers the policy of signalizing his reign as a new era of peace and happiness by celebrating the *ludi saeculares* with a magnificence that would at once please and impress the people. The main outlines of the celebration were prescribed by the oracle, which has been preserved (Zosimus II. 5), and the details were worked out by Ateius Capito, the most learned expert of the time in pontifical law. Everything was done to make the occasion memorable, and a lasting record was provided by the erection of two pillars, one of marble and one of bronze, inscribed with a full account of the celebration. These monuments, which must have stood many centuries, were finally destroyed and their material turned to other uses; but in 1890 some fragments of the marble pillar were exhumed in the neighborhood of Terentum, and a considerable portion of the inscription was thus recovered.* It

* The inscription was edited, with a commentary, by Mommsen in the *Monumenti Antichi della Reale Accademia dei Lincei*, Vol. I., p. 618 (1891). The article has also been printed separately.

originally consisted of 168 lines, and contained full particulars of all the preparations for the festival and of the celebration itself, including the text of decrees, formulas of prayer, and minute details of the ritual.

The celebration was preceded by a '*distributio suffimentorum*' and a '*frugum acceptio.*' For three days (May 26–28) citizens who presented themselves, with their wives and children, at certain designated places on the Capitoline and Palatine, were supplied by the magistrates with pitch-pine, sulphur, and bitumen (*suffimenta*) for purposes of purification. During the following three days the magistrates received from the citizens offerings of wheat, barley, and beans (*fruges*), which were used in part to remunerate the musicians and actors in the scenic performances. The celebration proper began in the night before June 1, and was continued without interruption through three nights and three days. The addition of the three days, in which the gods of heaven were joined in the honors of the festival, was a signal departure from the old *ludi Terentini*, which were devoted wholly to the gods of the underworld. The ceremonies were all conducted by Augustus in person, partly with the assistance of Agrippa. They took place by night 'in campo ad Tiberim,' *i.e.* at Terentum; by day, at the appropriate temples.

The sacrifices of the first night were whole burnt offerings (*hostiae prodigivae*), nine she-lambs and nine she-goats, to the Fates (*Moerae;* cf. *C. S.* 25 *sqq.*). On the second night the Ilithyiae (cf. *C. S.* 13 *sqq.*) were propitiated with oblations of consecrated cakes; and on the third a pregnant sow was sacrificed to Mother Earth (*Terra mater;* cf. *C. S.* 29 *sqq.*). The sacrifices of the first night were followed by scenic entertainments, which were given, as in the days of Plautus, on a temporary stage, with no seats provided for the audience (IN SCAENA QVOI THEATRVM

ADIECTVM NON FVIT, NVLLIS POSITIS SEDILIBVS). These '*ludi Latini scaenici*' were kept up without interruption through the three nights and days, but after the first night they were given IN THEATRO LIGNEO QVOD ERAT CONSTITVTVM SECVNDVM TIBERIM. The *ludi scaenici* of the third day were followed by *ludi circenses* in a temporary circus near the same place, and the people were further entertained by a series of scenic performances and other shows not prescribed by the oracle (*ludi honorarii*), which lasted seven days after the close of the festival proper (June 4–11). The religious ceremonies of the first night were supplemented by *sellisternia* in honor of Juno and Diana (*i.e. Lucinae duae*, according to Mommsen), conducted by 110 matrons; and these were repeated on the following days.

On the first *day* of the festival (June 1) Augustus and Agrippa each sacrificed a white bull to Jupiter, and on the second day each a white cow to Juno Regina, on the Capitol; and after the latter sacrifice and its accompanying prayers, Augustus (probably) led the 110 matrons in a special prayer to Juno. On the third day the chief ceremonies were on the Palatine at the temple of Apollo (cf. I. 31, intr. note), where Augustus and Agrippa made an offering of consecrated cakes to Apollo and Diana. 'And on the completion of the sacrifice,' the inscription goes on, '27 boys who had been summoned for this service, sons of fathers and mothers still living (*patrimi et matrimi*), and as many girls, sang a hymn; and in the same way on the Capitol. The hymn was composed by Q. Horatius Flaccus.'

It is clear from these words that Horace's hymn was first sung on the Palatine, and that it was also sung on the Capitol. Mommsen supposes that it was sung in solemn procession from the Palatine to the Capitol and back, the middle strophes, where the sacrifice of white cattle by

Augustus (vs. 49) evidently refers to the offerings of the first and second days, being sung on the Capitol itself. There was in all probability a procession, but the inscription does not connect the hymn with it in any way. In the hymn, not only Jupiter and Juno are invoked, but all the divinities who were honored in the whole festival; and Jupiter is appealed to, not in the middle strophes alone, but in the closing verses, where the chorus confidently claims the favor of 'Jove and all the gods.' There seems to be no good reason to depart from the plain meaning of the words of the inscription, that the ceremonies of the Palatine in their main features, including the singing of the hymn, were repeated on the Capitol; for the words EODEMQUE MODO IN CAPITOLIO do not appear to refer to the hymn alone. The explanation is perhaps to be found in the fact that the ceremonies of this third day were evidently the crowning event of the whole festival; and that while Augustus was desirous of exalting his patron god Apollo to the position of patron god of Rome, he may not, or his religious advisers may not, have felt at liberty to exclude the old gods of the Roman state from the honors of the day.

Horace adopted for his hymn the Sapphic strophe (Intr. 174). A striking feature of the poem is the very large proportion of feminine caesuras. It was rendered, we must assume, with instrumental accompaniment, and was made, for those who heard it, a beautiful and impressive performance. The number of the chorus, 27 of each sex, was prescribed by the ritual, as we may infer from Liv. XXVII. 37. 7 and XXXI. 12. 9, where choirs of 27 maidens are mentioned as singing hymns especially composed for ceremonies of propitiation. In every case, however, the number is stated not as 'twenty-seven,' but as 'thrice nine,' which probably had some religious significance connected with the number three, but may have been used as a subdivision for musical purposes. The division of the chorus into two main groups (boys and girls) was prescribed by the oracle (χωρὶς δὲ κόραι χορὸν αὐταὶ ἔχοιεν | καὶ χωρὶς παίδων ἄρσην στάχυς, vs. 20). The distribution of the various parts of the hymn between the two half-choirs, or among smaller groups, was probably a complicated matter ; at any rate, it cannot now be determined. The only indications in the hymn itself are in the ninth strophe (vss. 33–36), which was apparently divided between the two half-choirs, and in the first two and the last, which were probably sung by the full choir. Beyond this neither poem nor inscription gives any light.

---

Phoebe silvarumque potens Diana,
lucidum caeli decus, o colendi
semper et culti, date quae precamur
  tempore sacro,
quo Sibyllini monuere versus

1. **Phoebe, Diana**: although the hymn belongs in a sense to the whole festival and invokes in turn all the gods who were worshipped in the various ceremonies, it was first sung at the rites in honor of Apollo and Diana, before their temple on the Palatine, and these two deities are given a corresponding preëminence in it. This arrangement was determined by the policy of Augustus to raise the Palatine Apollo to the position of especial guardian of the Roman state. — **silvarum potens**: cf. *nemorum* (*custos*), III. 22. 1 n, and for this use of *potens*, I. 3. 1 n. — **Dĭana**: cf. vs. 70, and see Intr. 178.

2. **decus**: referring to both divinities (as Sol and Luna; cf. vss. 9, 36). — **colendi et culti**: *i.e.* who shall be worshipped in the future, as in the past; a comprehensive phrase, perhaps borrowed from the ritual, like our 'As it was in the beginning, is now, and ever shall be.' For the tenses, cf. *tulit et feret*, *Ep*. I. 7. 21 (Intr. 80).

5. **quo**: with **dicere**, vs. 8. — **versus**: they were Greek hexameters. The old Sibylline books, which King Tarquin was said to have purchased of the Sibyl, were burnt up in the fire which destroyed the Capitol in B.C. 83, but a new collection of oracles had since been gathered from various sources.

virgines lectas puerosque castos
dis quibus septem placuere colles
dicere carmen.

Alme Sol, curru nitido diem qui
promis et celas, aliusque et idem
nasceris, possis nihil urbe Roma
visere maius.

Rite maturos aperire partus
lenis, Ilithyia, tuere matres,
sive tu Lucina probas vocari
seu Genitalis.

6. **lectas, castos**: both attributes belong to the whole chorus; Intr. 121. For **lectas,** cf. IV. 6. 31, and see introd. note.

7. **dis**: referring to the gods in general. — **placuere**: used here, as in III. 4. 24, like the perfect of an inceptive verb; Rome has won (and now enjoys, is established in) their favor.

8. **dicere carmen**: cf. *dic melos*, III. 4. 1 n.

9. **alme**: cf. *almum diem* IV. 7. 7 n. — **Sol**: so also in the oracle, vs. 16 Φοῖβος Ἀπόλλων, | ὅστε καὶ Ἠέλιος κικλήσκεται. — **diem celas**: *i.e.* by taking the day with him, as it were, when he 'hides' his chariot (under the earth); a poetical expression of the fact that night, as well as day, is due to the sun; cf. III. 6. 44.

10. **alius et idem**: *i.e.* through all change forever the same. It introduces the following prayer, as if he had said 'In thy everlasting course mayest thou,' etc.

12. **visere**: cf. I. 37. 25, II. 15. 3.

13. **aperire**: see Intr. 101 *a*, 102.

14. **lenis**: a part of the prayer. — **Ilithyia**: goddess of the labor of childbirth. In Homer she is sometimes one (*Odys.* XIX. 188), usually more in number, as *Il.* XI. 270, where the Εἰλείθυιαι are daughters of Hera. See Preller-Robert, *Gr. Myth.* I. 511. In the ceremonies of the second night the offerings were made DEIS [I]LITHYIS, but the prayer began ILITHYIA VTI TIBI, etc.; so that they do not appear to have been regarded as distinct divinities, but as one; as a 'diva triformis,' perhaps, but not distinctly identified with Diana. Here, however, this identity (cf. III. 22. 2 *sq.*) is silently assumed, furnishing, as it does, an excellent justification of the prominence which the policy of Augustus required to be given to Diana.

15. **sive tu**, etc. = *vel Lucina, si tu Lucina probas vocari, vel,* etc.; cf. I. 2. 33 n. It was supposed to be pleasing to the gods to be addressed by many titles, and the choice of names was also a pious precaution against giving offense to a divinity, especially one whose personality was so elusive as in this case. Cf. Cat. 34. 21 *sis quocumque tibi placet | sancta nomine*, and Callim. *Hymn. in*

Diva, producas subolem patrumque
prosperes decreta super iugandis
feminis prolisque novae feraci
lege marita,
certus undenos deciens per annos
orbis ut cantus referatque ludos,
ter die claro totiensque grata
nocte frequentis.
Vosque veraces cecinisse, Parcae,

*Dian.* 7, where Artemis prays Zeus for πολυωνυμίη. — **Lucina**: see III. 22. 2 n. — **vocari**: Intr. 94 *a.*

16. **Genitalis**: not found elsewhere as a title of this goddess; perhaps intended as the Latin equivalent of Γενετυλλίς, which was an epithet of Aphrodite, and was also used in the plural, like Εἰλείθυιαι, to denote attendant divinities who presided over childbirth (Preller-Robert I. 377, with n. 4).

17. **producas,** *rear;* cf. II. 13. 3. For the mood, see Intr. 87. — **patrum decreta,** etc.: the measure referred to was really a law (*lex Iulia de maritandis ordinibus*), passed by the votes of the *comitia*, with the approval of the senate, which was very reluctantly given; but it was the policy of Augustus to govern through the senate, which became, from now on, the law-making body of the empire, although the *comitia* continued to be held some years longer. The law was passed in B.C. 18. It discouraged celibacy by penalties, and encouraged marriage and the raising of children by relaxing somewhat the strictness of the conditions of legal marriage and by conferring on fathers of three or more children certain privileges and immunities. See Merivale, Ch. XXXIII.

18. **super**: see I. 9. 5 n. Its use with the gerundive is very rare.

19. **prolis**: Intr. 66 *a.*

20. **marita**: see Intr. 65, and cf. Prop. V. 11. 33 *facibus maritis.*

21. **certus,** etc.: the two emphatic words of the strophe are the first and last (Intr. 116 *b*), the rest being a poetical paraphrase for the *saeculum* and the festival (see intr. note). The goddess is implored to propagate the race, that the repetition of the jubilee, age after age, may be assured (**certus**), and that each festival may be celebrated by great throngs of citizens. — **per**: *i.e.* extending through; the prepositional phrase here taking the place of a defining genitive (Madv. 298. 2).

22. **orbis,** *cycle.* — **ut**: Intr. 114. — **referatque**: Intr. 119 *b.*

25. **cecinisse**: see I. 15. 4 n, and, for the construction, Intr. 102. — **Parcae**: the Μοῖραι of the oracle and the inscription, who were worshipped on the first night. They were usually represented as three aged sisters, forever spinning the thread of destiny; see Cat. 64. 305 *sqq.* Originally goddesses of childbirth, their functions had special reference, on the one hand, to

quod semel dictum est stabilisque rerum
terminus servet, bona iam peractis
iungite fata.

Fertilis frugum pecorisque Tellus
spicea donet Cererem corona;
nutriant fetus et aquae salubres
et Iovis aurae.

Condito mitis placidusque telo
supplices audi pueros, Apollo;
siderum regina bicornis audi,
Luna, puellas.

the individual (see II. 3. 15 n); but in a wider sense they were regarded as developing the general course of human events in accordance with the righteous decrees of an omnipotent power. Cf. Hes. *Theog.* 904, where they are the daughters of Zeus and Themis.

26. **quod semel dictum est**: a paraphrase for *fatum*; cf. III. 3. 58 n. It refers to the whole course of Roman destiny, past and to come. For **semel**, see I. 24. 16 n. — **stabilisque**: for *quodque stabilis* (cf. I. 1. 5 n), in which *quod* (unlike the first **quod**) is the object of its verb. — **rerum terminus**: a figurative expression for immutable destiny; cf. Verg. *A.* IV. 614 *et sic fata Iovis poscunt, hic terminus haeret.*

27. **servet**: optative subjunctive, hardly consistent with **semel dictum est**; but the inconsistency is no greater than we usually fall into when we grapple with the problem of free will and fate. It anticipates the prayer that follows (**bona**, etc.), which is also superfluous, if we insist on strict logical consistency.

29. **fertilis frugum pecorisque**: a part of the prayer. For the genitives, see Intr. 66 *a*. With **pecoris**, *fecundus* would be more usual, but cf. *S.* II. 4. 31 *mare fertile testae*, Liv. V. 34. 2 (*Gallia*) *frugum hominumque fertilis.* — **Tellus**: worshipped as *Terra Mater* on the third night.

30. **spicea**, etc.: a prayer for abundant harvests. The figure is based on the practice of making an offering of first fruits to Ceres in the shape of a wreath of ripe ears of grain; cf. Tib. I. 1. 15 *flava Ceres, tibi sit nostro de rure corona | spicea, quae templi pendeat ante foris;* II. 1. 4 *spicis tempora cinge, Ceres.*

31. **fetus**: of the *fruges* only, continuing the thought of vs. 30. —**salubres, Iovis**: Intr. 121. For **Iovis**, see I. 1. 25 n.

33–36. After invoking in turn the powers to whom the nocturnal rites of the festival were dedicated, the chorus closes this part of the hymn with an interlude, addressed to Apollo and Diana, which, however, is not disconnected in thought with the preceding: Apollo spares man and beast from pestilence (cf. I. 21. 13 *sqq.*), Diana (as Luna)

Roma si vestrum est opus Iliaeque
litus Etruscum tenuere turmae,
iussa pars mutare laris et urbem
sospite cursu,
cui per ardentem sine fraude Troiam
castus Aeneas patriae superstes
liberum munivit iter, daturus
plura relictis,
di, probos mores docili iuventae,
di, senectuti placidae quietem,
Romulae genti date remque prolemque
et decus omne;

gives increase to the crops (cf. IV. 6. 38 *sqq.*).

33. **condito telo**: see II. 10. 18 n. This is the attitude in which he was represented in the Palatine temple; see Baumeister p. 99.

35. **siderum regina**: cf. I. 12. 47 *sq.*, *Epod.* 15. 1 *sq.* — **bicornis**: in reference to the two points of the crescent; cf. IV. 2. 57 *sqq.*

37. **Roma**, etc.: here begins an invocation to the great gods of the Roman state, the gods of the Capitol, and more particularly Jupiter and Juno, who were honored on the first and second days of the festival (see vss. 49 *sq.*). — **si**: cf. III. 18. 5 n. Here the appeal is to the interest of the gods in their own handiwork. — **Iliae**: Intr. 65.

38. **litus Etruscum**: here for the coast generally about the mouth of the Tiber. — **tenuere**, *gained;* cf. Liv. I. 37. 4 *montes Sabini petebant, et pauci tenuere.*

39. **iussa pars**: *i.e.* if they were a remnant under divine protection (**sospite**) and guidance. In this dependent clause, and especially in **iussa** (Intr. 116 *b*), lies the gist of the whole condition, which is concerned, not with the well-known fact of the migration of the Trojans to Italy, but with its explanation. — **laris**, *their homes.*

40. **cursu**: with **mutare.**

41. **sine fraude**: cf. II. 19. 20 n.

42. **castus**: in contrast with the wickedness of the rest, which had brought down the wrath of the gods upon them; cf. III. 3. 18 *sqq.* It is equivalent to Vergil's constant epithet, *pius.* — **patriae**: dative; cf. *mihi*, *Epod.* 5. 101.

43. **daturus**: Intr. 104 *b*.

44. **plura relictis**: *i.e.* a greater city than Troy.

45. **probos mores**, etc.: in keeping with the policy of Augustus, which this jubilee was meant to emphasize, the blessings of peace are made most prominent in this prayer. — **docili, placidae**: both proleptic and a part of the prayer; intimating a fit state of mind on the part of the citizens as a requisite condition of receiving the blessing.

47. **Romulae**: Intr. 65.—**rem**, *wealth.*—**prolemque**: Intr. 174 *b*.

quaeque vos bobus veneratur albis
clarus Anchisae Venerisque sanguis,
impetret, bellante prior, iacentem
lenis in hostem.

Iam mari terraque manus potentis
Medus Albanasque timet securis,
iam Scythae responsa petunt, superbi
nuper, et Indi.

49. **quae veneratur**: for this use of *veneror* with the construction of a verb of asking, cf. *S.* II. 6. 8 *si veneror stultus nihil horum.* — **bobus albis**: the sacrifices of the first and second days, as the inscription records. The tenor of the prayer to each of the two deities was in the main as follows: *Iuppiter optime maxime* (or *Iuno regina*) . . . *te quaeso precorque uti imperium maiestatemque populi Romani Quiritium duelli domique auxis, utique semper Latinum nomen tuearis, incolumitatem sempiternam victoriam valetudinem populo Romano Quiritibus tribuas, faveasque populo Romano Quiritibus legionibusque populi Romani Quiritium, remque publicam populi Romani Quiritium salvam serves, uti sis volens propitius populo Romano Quiritibus XVrum collegio mihi domo familiae.*

50. **sanguis**: *i.e.* descendant; cf. II. 20. 6, III. 27. 65, IV. 2. 14. This paraphrase for Augustus, instead of the use of his name, is more in keeping with the proprieties of the occasion, and also served, like **Romulae genti,** to keep up the main thought of the whole sentence, — the connection between Rome's present and future and her divinely ordered beginnings.

51. **bellante prior,** etc.: cf. Vergil's famous *parcere subiectis et debellare superbos* (*A*. VI. 853). The thought is here the same: *tu regere imperio populos, Romane, memento, . . . pacique imponere morem.* Victory is the stepping-stone to peace and order (see vs. 45 n). This is set forth more fully in the next two strophes: in the first, victory; in the second, the advent of peace and her attendant blessings.

53. **iam**, etc.: from this point on the chorus abandons the attitude of supplication to the gods and assumes that of confidence in their favor; cf. *Ep.* II. 1. 134 *poscit opem chorus et praesentia numina sentit.*

54. **Medus, Scythae, Indi**: cf. IV. 14. 42 n. — **Albanas**: for 'Roman,' with the same suggestion as above (see vs. 50 n).

55. **responsa petunt**: a phrase implying recognized superiority in the power appealed to, being applied commonly to the consultation of an oracle or to an embassy coming to the senate with a definite request or a question to be settled.

57. **Fides,** etc.: most, if not all, of these personified abstractions were deified and worshipped by the Romans. For **Fides,** see I. 35. 22 n. Augustus erected an altar to **Pax** on the Campus Mar-

Iam Fides et Pax et Honor Pudorque
priscus et neglecta redire Virtus
audet, adparetque beata pleno
  Copia cornu.

Augur et fulgente decorus arcu
Phoebus acceptusque novem Camenis,
qui salutari levat arte fessos
  corporis artus,

si Palatinas videt aequus aras,
remque Romanam Latiumque felix
alterum in lustrum meliusque semper
  prorogat aevum;

tius, and instituted stated sacrifices. **Honos** (*Good Repute*) had a temple in connection with **Virtus** (*Manly Worth*). For **Pudor priscus**, cf. I. 24. 6 and 7 n. For **Copia**, cf. *Ep.* I. 12. 28 *aurea fruges | Italiae pleno defundit Copia cornu*, and I. 17. 14 n.

59. **audet**: Intr. 77.

61. **augur Phoebus**: cf. I. 2. 32. — **et**: Intr. 114. — **fulgente**: in Homer his bow is silver (as *Il.* I. 37, 49); in the other poets sometimes golden (*e.g.* Pind. *Ol.* 14. 10). Here the bow is simply ornamental (cf. **decorus** and vs. 33 n); Apollo is relied upon as the prophet-god who foresees the happy future, and who promotes it as patron of arts and letters and as god of healing. These are his chief functions, for which the poet finds a place here; they could not well be brought in at the outset (vs. 9), in the form which the invocation there took.

62. **acceptus Camenis**: cf. II. 10. 18. For **Camenis**, see I. 12. 39 n.

63. **qui**, etc.: cf. I. 21. 13 *sqq.*, and see Preller-Robert, *Gr. Myth.* I. 277. — **fessos**, *enfeebled* (*sc.* by sickness); a poetical use of the word adopted by later prose writers; cf. Cat. 64. 188 *non tamen ante mihi languescent lumina morte, | nec prius a fesso secedent corpore sensus*, etc.; Tac. *Ann.* II. 71. 1 *fesso corpore, ubi finis* (*i.e. mors*) *aderat*.

64. **corporis artus**, *our frame*; cf. Lucr. III. 128 *est igitur calor ac ventus vitalis in ipso | corpore, qui nobis moribundos deserit artus*.

65. **si**: the conditional form implies no doubt of the truth of the proposition, but puts it, with full confidence, as the basis of the conviction expressed in the conclusion; cf. vs. 37, and III. 18. 5 n. — **aequus**: cf. I. 2. 47 n. — **aras**: Intr. 128.

66. **remque**, etc.: a reminiscence, perhaps, of Enn. *Ann.* 477 M. *audire est operae pretium, procedere recte | qui rem Romanam Latiumque augescere voltis*. — **felix**: proleptic, with **Latium**.

67. **alterum**: see III. 5. 34 n. The idea is 'from *lustrum* to *lu*

quaeque Aventinum tenet Algidumque
quindecim Diana preces virorum
curat et votis puerorum amicas
adplicat auris.

Haec Iovem sentire deosque cunctos
spem bonam certamque domum reporto,
doctus et Phoebi chorus et Dianae
dicere laudes.

*strum.*' The word is chosen probably with reference to the successive periods of five years for which Augustus received the *imperium*. — **semper**: see note on *usque*, III. 30. 7.

69. **Aventinum**: the seat of the chief temple of Diana in Rome, built originally, under Servius Tullius, as a common shrine of all the Latin communities. — **tenet**: cf. III. 4. 62 n. — **Algidum**: see I. 21. 6 n.

70. **quindecim virorum**: a board, originally of two members (*IIviri sacris faciundis*), charged with the safe-keeping and interpretation of the Sibylline books, and with the conduct of certain religious ceremonies. The number was increased to ten, then to fifteen, with corresponding change of name. At this time, however, there were actually 21 members, with Agrippa as *magister conlegi*. No prayers offered by them on this occasion are mentioned, but they took a leading part in all the ceremonies, and prescribed the forms of prayer. — **Diana**: cf. vs. 1 n.

71. **votis adplicat auris**: cf. *S.* I. 1. 22 *votis ut praebeat aurem*. — **puerorum**, *children*; cf. *Ep.* I. 7. 7 *pueris pater et matercula pallet*. In old Latin the singular also was used of either sex; cf. Naev. *Bell. Pun.* 30 M. *Cereris puer*, *Proserpina*.

72. **curat, adplicat**: emphatic; Intr. 116 *b*.

73. **haec sentire** (depending on **spem**), *that this is the mind of*; referring to what has been said in the last three strophes. Apollo and Diana, who have assumed as their special charge the welfare of Rome, have done so with the full consent and good will of all the gods.

74. **reporto**: the chorus speaks in the singular number, as in the Greek drama; cf. *dices*, IV. 6. 41 n.

75. **doctus**, etc.: cf. IV. 6. 43. **Phoebi et Dianae**: with **laudes**.

76. **dicere**: see I. 6. 5 n.

## Q. HORATI FLACCI

# EPODON

## LIBER

### I.

Ibis Liburnis inter alta navium,
amice, propugnacula,

For a general account of the Epodes and the significance of the name, see Intr. 18–20.

I. This epode, which serves as a virtual dedication of the collection to Maecenas, is characterized by a much warmer expression of feeling than any of the other dedicatory poems, belonging as it does to a period when the poet's place in his patron's regard was assured, but the impulse of affection and gratitude had not yet lost its freshness. The occasion was the proposed departure of Maecenas, in the spring of B.C. 31, for the seat of war. Octavian, before setting out for the campaign of Actium, summoned all the most influential senators and knights to join him at Brundisium; and Maecenas naturally went with the rest. In this poem Horace begs to be allowed to go to the war with him, pleading the unhappiness and anxiety he would suffer if separated from his friend, while deprecating the suspicion of any selfish motive. Maecenas, it seems most probable, did not actually cross the sea, but returned to take charge of Rome and Italy during the absence of his chief (Dio LI. 3. 5, Vell. II. 88. 2), — though some scholars, in spite of these authorities, hold that he was present at the battle; and some think, mainly on supposed evidence in Epode 9, that Horace was with him. But the indications of that poem are very slight, and have little weight against the absence of any positive testimony and the silence of Horace himself. — Metre, 159.

1. **ibis**: the emphasis may be compared with that of *C.* I. 7. 26, II. 17. 10, *Ep.* II. 2. 39. In these instances, however, the emphasis is that of assurance; here it is that of reluctant conviction: 'You are really going!' The tone is half interrogative. Cf. Tibullus' appeal to Messala under the same circumstances: *Ibitis Aegaeas sine me, Messala, per undas*, I. 3. 1. — **Liburnis**: see *C.* I. 37. 30 n. The abl. is instrumental, though we render it with *in;* cf. Liv. XXVIII. 9. 10 *quadrigis urbem ineuntem*. — **alta**: in contrast with the light Liburnian biremes; suggesting the peril Maecenas will incur.

2. **propugnacula**, *battlements*.

paratus omne Caesaris periculum
subire, Maecenas, tuo.
Quid nos, quibus te vita si superstite
iucunda, si contra, gravis?
utrumne iussi persequemur otium,
non dulce, ni tecum simul,
an hunc laborem, mente laturi decet
qua ferre non mollis viros?
Feremus, et te vel per Alpium iuga
inhospitalem et Caucasum,

The ships of Antonius were not only of enormous size, but were furnished with towers (*turritis puppibus*, Verg. *A.* VIII. 693), so that their bulwarks looked like the walls of a fortress (Florus II. 21. 5)

4. **subire tuo** (sc. *periculo*): a choice paraphrase for 'to share,' corresponding with the expression in vs. 15 for sharing toil.

5. **si**: sc. *vivitur;* cf. vs. 8 n. The unusual insertion of *si* with the abl. abs. is explained by the fact that **te** (observe its position) is in thought the subject of two abl abs. constructions, expressing alternative events. Expressed fully, his meaning is: *quibus vita si te superstite vivitur, iucunda; si mortuo, gravis*, or in more condensed form, *quibus te vita — si superstite, iucunda; si mortuo, gravis*. This natural conception of the thought is fixed by the euphemistic substitution of **si contra** (in which **si** is indispensable) for *si mortuo*. — **superstite**: here simply in the sense of continuing to live, unlike *C.* II. 17. 7, III. 9. 12, 16.

7. **utrumne**: the enclitic *-ne*, though frequently attached to an emphatic word after *utrum*, is not found attached to *utrum* itself in any writer before Horace, who uses it here and twice elsewhere, *S.* II. 3. 251, 6. 73. Cf. also *uterne*, *S.* II. 2. 107; *quantane*, *S.* II. 3. 317; *quone*, ibid. 295. None of these forms occur in the Odes. *Vtrumne* is used by later prose writers. See Hand *Turs.* IV. p. 80. —**iussi**, *obediently*. Maecenas, then, it seems, had once refused Horace's request to be allowed to go. — **persequemur**, *consign myself to.* Cf. Cic. *de Off.* III. 1. *a re publica forensibusque negotiis prohibiti, otium persequimur*.

8. **ni**: sc. *persequimur* or the like. Cf. vs. 5 n.

9. **laborem** takes its construction from **otium** 7, but by a slight zeugma, on account of the different character of the object, the verbal notion suggested to the mind is not that of *persequor*, but rather of *suscipio*, *fero*, or the like, and first takes definite shape in **laturi**; hence the answer, **feremus** 11. — **mente laturi**, etc.: *i.e. ea mente* (*eum*) *laturi*, *qua decet*, etc.

10. **non mollis**: cf. *non amicos*, 11. 21, *non auspicatos*, *C.* III. 6. 10.

12. **inhospitalem Caucasum**: cf. *C.* I. 22. 6.

vel Occidentis usque ad ultimum sinum
forti sequemur pectore.
Roges tuum labore quid iuvem meo,
imbellis ac firmus parum?
Comes minore sum futurus in metu,
qui maior absentis habet,
ut adsidens implumibus pullis avis
serpentium adlapsus timet
magis relictis, non, ut adsit, auxili
latura plus praesentibus.
Libenter hoc et omne militabitur
bellum in tuae spem gratiae,
non ut iuvencis inligata pluribus
aratra nitantur meis

13. **sinum**, *nook;* suggesting remoteness, — places off the line of ordinary travel and traffic. Cf. Verg. *G.* II. 122 *India, extremi sinus orbis.*

15. **roges**: for *si roges;* Gr. 310 *b.* — **tuum . . . meo**: parallel with *Caesaris . . . tuo,* vss. 3 *sq.;* but *labore* (not *laborem*) is required here by the metre, and standing before the hepthemimeral caesura gives a balance to the verse like that of 2. 19.

16. **firmus parum**: referring to his health and strength.

18. **maior habet**, *takes stronger possession of.*

19. **adsidens**, *brooding.* Its meaning is determined by the dative **pullis**, which, however, is not so closely connected with it, — since the bird is supposed to be absent from the nest, — as with **timet**, *fears for.* See Intr. 76.

21. **relictis**, *when she has left them.* — **non latura**, *though she would not afford.* For the conditional force of the fut. part., see Intr. 104 *d.* — **ut adsit**, *even if she were there.* Gr. 266 *c.*

22. **praesentibus**: added (after **adsit**) for contrast with **relictis.** The Latin is fond of expressing both sides of a mutual relation; cf. Plaut. *Most.* 1075 *adsum praesens praesenti tibi;* Verg. *A.* IV. 83 *illum absens absentem auditque videtque;* Sat. II. 6. 81. But the repetition is not strictly tautological. Here the meaning is: 'without any thought that if she were there, they would find safety in her presence.'

23. **militabitur bellum**: cf. *pugnata bella, C.* III. 19. 4, and see Intr. 51 *b.*

25. **non ut**, etc.: *i.e.* not with an eye to the increase of my possessions (**pluribus** and **meis** contain the main ideas; Intr. 116 *b*) in farm-lands or pastures, or the acquisition of splendid villas.

26. **nitantur**: the straining of the oxen, here poetically transferred to the plough, suggests a rich, heavy soil.

pecusve Calabris ante sidus fervidum
Lucana mutet pascuis,
neque ut superni villa candens Tusculi
Circaea tangat moenia.
Satis superque me benignitas tua
ditavit; haud paravero
quod aut avarus ut Chremes terra premam,
discinctus aut perdam nepos.

## II.

Beatus ille qui procul negotiis,
ut prisca gens mortalium,

27. **pecusve,** etc.: sc. *mihi*, suggested by **meis** 26. — **Calabris,** etc.: cf. *C.* I. 31. 5 n.

28. **mutet**: for the cases, see Intr. 74.

29. **superni**: the lofty situation of Tusculum, commanding a magnificent view over the Campagna, together with the beauty of the surrounding scenery and its nearness to the capital (15 miles distant), made it a favorite resort for wealthy Romans, whose villas covered the slope below the town (in the neighborhood of the present Frascati), as those of their successors do now. Besides Cicero's famous *Tusculanum*, Lucullus, Hortensius, Cato, and Julius Caesar had villas in the neighborhood. Some of these country houses were probably of marble, and their brilliant whiteness (**candens**), against the darker background of the hills or even of the walls of the town itself (**tangat moenia**), made them conspicuous for miles around.

30. **Circaea**: as having been founded, according to tradition, by Telegonus, the son of Circe. Cf. *C.* III. 29. 8 n.

31. **satis superque**: cf. 17. 19; and, for the sentiment, *C.* II. 18. 12. — **benignitas**: cf. *benignius*, *C.* I. 9. 6 n., and *malignus*, I. 28. 23 n.

32. **paravero**: fut. perf., because he is thinking of what he would do with riches *after* they had been acquired. The indicative is emphatic: not 'I would not' (*haud paraverim*), but 'I shall not.'

33. **Chremes**: presumably a typical miser in some well-known comedy, not now extant. There is a Chremes in four of Terence's plays, but he is in no case a miser.

34. **nepos**: like **avarus** in the preceding verse, in apposition with the subject of the verb. In many MSS. an *ut* is inserted before **nepos**, as in 2. 5 before *miles*.

II. The banker's dream of the delights of country life. The humorous surprise to which the reader is treated at the end of this really charming picture is thoroughly characteristic of Horace, who gives us some of his most

paterna rura bobus exercet suis,
solutus omni faenore,
neque excitatur classico miles truci,
neque horret iratum mare,
forumque vitat et superba civium
potentiorum limina.
Ergo aut adulta vitium propagine
altas maritat populos,
aut in reducta valle mugientium
prospectat errantis greges,
inutilisve falce ramos amputans
feliciores inserit,

poetic passages while protesting that he has no gift for the higher flights of poetry (*e.g. C.* II. 1, III. 3, *S.* II. 1. 12 *sqq.*). For a genuine account of Horace's enjoyment of country life, see *S.* II. 6. — Metre, 159.

2. **prisca gens**: the Golden Age

3. **paterna**: see *C.* I. 1. 11 n. The ideal farmer is owner of the farm he tills, but unspoiled by ambition or avarice.

4. **faenore**, *money-lending*.

5. **neque excitatur**, etc.: cf. Verg. *G.* II. 539 *necdum etiam audierant inflari classica.* The farmer's quiet life is contrasted with the excitement of war, the dangers of the sea (vs. 6), and the worries and annoyances of the city (vss. 7 *sq.*), as in *S.* I. 1. 4 *sqq.* Cf. Verg. *G.* II. 501 *sq.* and the whole passage (vss. 495–540). — **miles**: cf. *nepos*, 1. 34 n.

7. **forum**: *i.e.* lawsuits and other legal business, in which one might be involved as suitor or defendant, advocate, bondsman, etc., and money transactions. — **superba**, etc.: *i.e.* the humiliation of paying court to the great, alluding particularly to the morning call (*salutatio*).

9. **ergo**, *and so; i.e.* with his mind free from such cares and annoyances. — **adulta**: after three years' growth in the *seminarium*.

10. **maritat**: cf. *platanus caelebs*, *C.* II. 15. 4 n, IV. 5. 30. The figure appears to have passed early into current speech; cf. Cato, *R. R.* 32 *arbores facito ut bene maritae sint.* — **populos**: these, with the elm, were regarded as the most suitable, on account of the thinness of their foliage. Their branches were trimmed to form a series of stages (*tabulata*, Verg. *G.* II. 361), over which the vine was trained.

11. **in reducta valle**: cf. *C.* I. 17. 17. It is to be taken with **errantis**. — **mugientium**: cf. Verg. *G.* I. 272 *balantum* (sheep); III. 541 *natantum* (fishes).

13. **ramos**: *sc.* of fruit-trees.

14. **feliciores**, *more fruitful*, its original meaning (cf. *fē-cundus*, *fē-tus*, *fē-mina*). '*Felices arbores* Cato dixit quae fructum ferunt, *infelices* quae non ferunt' (Fest. *ap.* Paul. p. 92). — **inserit**: *i.e* grafts; cf. *insitiva*, vs. 19 n.

aut pressa puris mella condit amphoris,
aut tondet infirmas ovis;
vel, cum decorum mitibus pomis caput
autumnus agris extulit,
ut gaudet insitiva decerpens pira,
certantem et uvam purpurae,
qua muneretur te, Priape, et te, pater
Silvane, tutor finium.
Libet iacere modo sub antiqua ilice,
modo in tenaci gramine;
labuntur altis interim ripis aquae,
queruntur in silvis aves,

15. **pressa**: *sc.* from the comb. Verg. *G.* IV. 140 *spumantia cogere pressis | mella favis.* — **amphoris**: Intr. 69.

16. **infirmas**: a standing epithet; cf. Ov. *Ib.* 43 *pecore infirmo.*

17. **decorum**, *graced.* Autumn is personified; cf. *C.* IV. 7. 11. — **mitibus**: *i.e.* ripe; cf. *immitis uvae*, *C.* II. 5. 10.

18. **agris**: Intr. 69. — **extulit**, *has lifted up.*

19. **ut gaudet**, *how happy he is.* For the participle **decerpens**, which here approaches the meaning of the infinitive, with *gaudeo* (Intr. 94 *d*), cf. *Ep.* II. 2. 106 *ridentur mala qui componunt carmina, verum | gaudent scribentes.* — **insitiva**: cf. vs. 14. The better varieties can be propagated only by grafting.

20. **et**: Intr. 114. — **purpurae**: see *C.* II. 5. 12 n, and, for the case, Intr. 57.

21. **qua**: relating to **pira** as well as **uvam** (Gr. 198 *a*). — **Priape**: a genius of fertility, whose statue, commonly of wood, was set up in gardens and orchards, 'half god and half scarecrow.' See *S.* I. 8. 2 n. — **pater**: cf. *C.* I. 2. 50 n.

22. **Silvane**: a very old Italian divinity, whose attributes bear the stamp of a time when the farmer was a pioneer, and the forest covered a large part of the land. The 'god of the woods' was felt to be very near to his life in all its interests, was the protector of his home, of his fields and flocks (*arvorum pecorisque deo*, Verg. *A.* VIII. 601; cf. *Ep.* II. 1. 143), and of his borders (**custos finium**). His statue was common in groves and gardens. See Preller-Jordan, *Röm. Myth.* I. 392.

23. **iacere**, etc.: cf. *C.* I. 1. 21, Verg. *E.* 1. 1.

24. **tenaci**: *i.e.* growing thick and luxuriant, with matted roots, in contrast with the sparse grass of a light soil, which can be easily pulled up.

25. **altis**: the scene is in summer or autumn, when the water in the streams is low. — **interim**: as he lies there. — **ripis**: cf. *C.* I. 2. 19 n; here *by* or *between* their banks, as in Lucr. II. 362 *summis labentia ripis.*

frondesque lymphis obstrepunt manantibus,
somnos quod invitet levis.
At cum tonantis annus hibernus Iovis
imbris nivisque comparat,
aut trudit acris hinc et hinc multa cane
apros in obstantis plagas,
aut amite levi rara tendit retia,
turdis edacibus dolos,
pavidumque leporem et advenam laqueo gruem
iucunda captat praemia.
Quis non malarum quas amor curas habet
haec inter obliviscitur?
Quod si pudica mulier in partem iuvet
domum atque dulcis liberos,

26. **queruntur,** *warble;* cf. Ov. *Am.* III. 1. 4 *et latere ex omni dulce queruntur aves.*

27. **frondesque,** etc.: *i.e.* the rustling of the leaves mingles with the plashing of the water. Cf. Prop. V. 4. 4 *multaque nativis obstrepit arbor aquis.* If the MSS. reading, *fontesque,* be retained, **lymphis** is instrumental abl., and **obstrepunt** is used absolutely (as in *C.* III. 30. 10) in the sense of striking upon the ear. In either case **obstrepunt** has as direct object a cognate acc., understood as the antecedent of **quod,** *a sound that.*

28. **levis**: cf. *C.* II. 16. 15.

29. **tonantis**: here not merely a stock epithet (cf. *C.* III. 5. 1), but helping to indicate the character of the season. — **annus,** *time* (of year); cf. *C.* III. 23. 8 n, and *frigidus annus,* Verg. *A.* VI. 311. — **Iovis**: see *C.* I. 1. 25 n, *C. S.* 32.

31. **trudit**: of close pursuit. Cf. the metaphorical use, *C.* II. 18. 15, *Ep.* I. 5. 17. — **hinc et hinc,** *on every side;* cf. 5. 97. It is a poetical variation (but adopted in later prose) of *hinc* (*et*) *illinc;* cf. *C.* IV. 11. 9 *huc et illuc.* — **multa cane**: Intr. 127.

32. **plagas**: cf. *C.* I. 1. 28 n.

33. **amite**: according to Porphyrio, this name was given in his day to *furculae quibus retia in venatione vel in aucupio suspenduntur;* but the epithet **lēvi** seems to show that Horace had here in mind the poles (Intr. 127) of the clap-net. See Rich, *Dict. s. v.* — **rara,** *wide-meshed* (as compared with fishing-nets).

34. **turdis**: Intr. 59. Cf. Mart. III. 58. 26 *sed tendit avidis rete subdolum turdis.*

35. **pavidum, laqueo**: Intr. 135. — **advenam**: *i.e.* migratory.

37. **malarum quas . . . curas**: Intr. 118.

39. **quod si**: the apodosis begins at vs. 49. — **in partem**: strictly, equivalent to *partim* (cf. *in universum,* etc.); but the expression

Sabina qualis aut perusta solibus
pernicis uxor Apuli,
sacrum vetustis exstruat lignis focum
lassi sub adventum viri,
claudensque textis cratibus laetum pecus
distenta siccet ubera,
et horna dulci vina promens dolio
dapes inemptas adparet :
non me Lucrina iuverint conchylia
magisve rhombus aut scari,
si quos Eois intonata fluctibus
hiems ad hoc vertat mare ;

is a condensed one for 'shares his lot in caring for,' etc.

41. **Sabina** : cf. *C.* III. 6. 38 n; Stat. *Silv.* V. 1. 122 *sqq.*, where this description is imitated.—**perusta,** *tanned.*— **solibus**: the plural expresses the repetition of the exposure, as in Lucr. V. 251 *perusta solibus adsiduis ;* cf. *C.* IV. 5. 8 n.

42. **pernicis Apuli** : cf. *C.* III. 16. 26.

43. **sacrum,** etc.: preparations to welcome her husband home to his evening repast, — pleasing details of the picture of housewifely devotion. The clauses stand in a sort of apposition with **in partem iuvet** ; hence the asyndeton. — **sacrum**: *sc.* to the Lares ; cf. *C.* III. 23. 15 n.—**vetustis,** *well seasoned.*

44. **sub** : cf. *C.* III. 7. 30 n.

45. **textis cratibus** : *i.e.* in a fold made of these. — **laetum,** *lusty ;* so Verg. *G.* II. 144 *armenta laeta.* Cf. *C.* IV. 4. 13 n.

47. **dulci** : Intr. 124. — **dolio** : the vessel in which the new wine was fermented, before bottling, which the country people commonly did not wait for (cf. **horna**).

48. **inemptas**: *i.e.* costing nothing. Cf. Verg. *G.* IV. 133 ; Mart. IV. 66. 5 *saltus aprum, campus leporem tibi misit inemptum.*

49. **Lucrina conchylia**: probably oysters, rather than the *Lucrina peloris* (*S.* II. 4. 32), a large bivalve, which, at a later period at least, was regarded as much inferior to the Lucrine oyster. Cf. Mart. VI. 11. 5 *tu Lucrina voras, me pascit aquosa peloris ;* III. 60. 3 *sq.* — **iuverint magis** : Intr. 120.

50. **scari** : called by Ennius (*Heduphagetica* 7) *cerebrum Iovis paene supremi.*

51. **si quos** : sc. *scaros.* The scar was found chiefly in the eastern part of the Mediterranean, but was also caught in the neighborhood of Sicily, and in larger numbers after a storm, by which it was thought the fish were driven to those seas.—**intonata,** *thundering down upon.* Cf. vs. 29 ; Intr. 51 *f.*

53. **Afra avis,** *the guinea-fowl,* imported from Numidia ; a new delicacy in Horace's day (Varro *R. R.* III. 9. 18).

54. **attagen**: a species of grouse,

non Afra avis descendat in ventrem meum,
non attagen Ionicus
iucundior quam lecta de pinguissimis
oliva ramis arborum,
aut herba lapathi prata amantis et gravi
malvae salubres corpori,
vel agna festis caesa Terminalibus,
vel haedus ereptus lupo.
Has inter epulas ut iuvat pastas ovis
videre properantis domum,
videre fessos vomerem inversum boves
collo trahentis languido,
positosque vernas, ditis examen domus,
circum renidentis Laris.

brought from Asia Minor (**Ionicus**), 'quondam existimatus inter raras aves' (Plin. *N. H.* X. 133).

55. **pinguissimis**: Intr. 124.

57. **herba lapathi**: used in the *promulsis* of the more elaborate city dinner; cf. *S.* II. 4. 29. — **gravi**: from torpid digestion.

58. **malvae**: cf. *C.* I. 31. 16.— **salubres corpori**: cf. Mart. X. 48. 7.

59. **vel agna**, etc.: the farmer's ordinary diet was vegetables with salt meat; and fresh meat was a rare treat, indulged in only on occasions of public or private festivity (cf. *S.* II. 2. 116 *sqq.*), unless offered by some unexpected chance, as here (vs. 60).—**Terminalibus**: the festival of Terminus, on the 23d of February. The victim sacrificed was either a lamb or a suckling pig. See Ov. *F.* II. 655 *sqq.*

60. **haedus**, etc.: cf. Mart. X. 48. 14 *haedus inhumani raptus ab ore lupi.* The wolf was supposed to have good taste in selecting his victim; cf. Plutarch, *Symp.* II. 9 τὰ λυκόβρωτα πρόβατα λέγεται τὸ κρέας γλυκύτατον παρέχειν.

61. **has inter**, etc.: the description closes with a picture of the rest and simple enjoyment of the evening hour. Cf. the opening lines of Gray's Elegy.

63. **videre**: Intr. 116 *h*.

65. **positosque vernas**, *the home-born slaves* (in contrast with the costly imported slaves of wealthy houses) *seated* (on stools or on the ground) around the hearth (*focus Larium, quo familia convenit*, Plin. *N.H.* XXVIII. 267) in the atrium (*C.* I. 9. 5 n). Cf. *S.* II. 6. 66 *sq.* These slaves were seldom sold, if the master could afford to keep them, and, like the 'man-servants and maid-servants' of patriarchal times, formed a conspicuous part of the wealth of a rich household. Cf. Tib. II. 1. 23 *turbaque vernarum, saturi bona signa coloni.* For the prosody of **positos**, see Intr. 135.

66. **renidentis**: an added touch

Haec ubi locutus faenerator Alfius,
iam iam futurus rusticus,
omnem redegit Idibus pecuniam;
quaerit Kalendis ponere.

## III.

Parentis olim si quis impia manu
senile guttur fregerit,

to the cheerfulness of the scene. The wooden figures of the Lares (see *C.* III. 23. 15 n), blackened with smoke, were cleansed from time to time, especially on any festive occasion, and rubbed with oil and wax to make them shine in the firelight. Cf. Juv. 12. 87 *graciles ubi parva coronas | accipiunt fragili simulacra nitentia cera.*

67. **locutus**: sc. *est.* — **Alfius**: a well-known *faenerator* of this name, probably of Cicero's time, is mentioned by Columella, I. 7. 2. The device of introducing a familiar character of a past generation as the type of a class is one Horace often adopted in his Satires.

68. **iam iam futurus**: cf. Tac. *Ann.* I. 47. 5 *ut iam iamque iturus, legit comites, conquisivit impedimenta, adornavit naves.*

69. **redegit**: the creditor could call in his loans at will, on giving his debtors due notice. Settlements were generally made on the Kalends, Nones, or Ides. Cf. *S.* I. 3. 87.

70. **quaerit**, etc.: the full force of the surprise is reserved for the very last verse, and is enhanced by the dry way in which this brief concluding item of the story is given, without comment. Notice the tense of **quaerit**, which brings the story close to us: it was only last week that Alfius called in his money; he will invest it again next week, if he can. — **ponere**: cf. *Ep.* II. 3. 421 *positis in faenore nummis.* For the mood, see Intr. 94 *c*.

III. A humorous diatribe against garlic, to which the poet attributes some acute sufferings that followed a dinner with Maecenas. The garlic, it would seem, was among the ingredients of a dish of herbs, such as the one of which Cicero once partook at an augural banquet ('nam dum volunt isti lauti terra nata . . . in honorem adducere, fungos, helvellas, herbas omnis ita condiunt ut nihil possit esse suavius,' *ad Fam.* VII. 26. 2) with similar results. Horace treats it as a practical joke on the part of Maecenas. — Metre, 159.

1. **olim,** *ever.* Cf. *C.* IV. 4. 5 n.

2. **guttur fregerit**: see *C.* II. 13. 6 n.

3. **edit**: pres. subj.; an old form retained in colloquial use; cf. *S.* II. 8. 90; Plaut. *Trin.* 339 *dé mendico mále meretur qui éi dat quod edit áut bibat.* — **cicutis**: the poison given to condemned criminals at Athens, made famous by the case of Socrates. Horace proposes garlic as a more efficient substitute. The plural of *cicuta* occurs also in *Ep.* II. 2. 53. — **nocentius,** *more poisonous;* cf. *her-*

edit cicutis alium nocentius.
O dura messorum ilia!
Quid hoc veneni saevit in praecordiis?
Num viperinus his cruor
incoctus herbis me fefellit, an malas
Canidia tractavit dapes?
Vt Argonautas praeter omnis candidum
Medea mirata est ducem,
ignota tauris inligaturum iuga
perunxit hoc Iasonem;
hoc delibutis ulta donis paelicem
serpente fugit alite.
Nec tantus umquam siderum insedit vapor
siticulosae Apuliae,

*bas nocentis*, *S.* I. 8. 22, with *Epod.* 5. 21 *sq.*

4. **o dura**, etc.: cf. Verg. *E.* 2. 10 *Thestylis et rapido fessis messoribus aestu* | *alia serpullumque herbas contundit olentis.*

5. **veneni**: Intr. 63.

6. **viperinus cruor**: see *C.* I. 8. 9 n.

7. **fefellit**: cf. *C.* III. 16. 32 n. — **malas**, *baneful;* cf. *S.* II. 1. 56 *mala cicuta;* Verg. *A.* II. 471 *coluber mala gramina pastus.*

8. **Canidia**: see intr. note to Epode 5. — **tractavit**: cf. *C.* II. 13. 10.

9. **ut Argonautas**, etc.: from the mention of Canidia his mind passes naturally to the queen of sorceresses, and he asserts with humorous assurance that this stuff which he has eaten is no other than the powerful drug which Medea used to protect Jason and destroy Glauce. — **ut**: temporal. — **praeter omnis**: with **mirata est**. — **candidum**: see *C.* I. 18. 11 n.

10. **mirata est**: cf. *C.* IV. 9 15 n.

11. **tauris**: the fire-breathing oxen which Jason was required to yoke, to plough the land for sowing the dragon's teeth. For the case, see Intr. 76.

13. **hoc**: Intr. 116 *g.* The main statement is in the participle **delibutis**; cf. *ulta*, 5. 63, *deductus*, *C.* IV. 4. 19. — **donis**: a robe and crown, which burst into flames and burned the wearer to death.—**paelicem**: Glauce (Creusa), daughter of the Corinthian king Creon, whom Jason was about to marry, abandoning Medea. See 5. 61 *sqq.*

14. **serpente**: *i.e.* in a chariot drawn by them. Cf. *C.* III. 3. 16 *Martis equis Acheronta fugit.* For the singular, see Intr. 127.

15. **siderum**: see 16. 61, *C.* III. 29. 17 *sqq.*—**vapor**, *heat;* cf. Lucr. I. 663 *ignis uti lumen iacit atque vaporem.*

16. **siticulosae**: cf. 2. 41 *sq.*, *C* III. 30. 11, *S.* I. 5. 77 *sqq.*, 88 *sq.*

nec munus umeris efficacis Herculis
inarsit aestuosius.
At si quid umquam tale concupiveris,
iocose Maecenas, precor
manum puella savio opponat tuo,
extrema et in sponda cubet.

## IV.

Lupis et agnis quanta sortito obtigit,
tecum mihi discordia est,

17. **munus**: the robe which the centaur Nessus, when mortally wounded by the poisoned arrow of Hercules, gave to Deianira, who sent the fatal gift to her husband on hearing of his love for Iole (Ov. *M.* IX. 101 *sqq.*); cf. 17. 31 *sq.*

18. **inarsit** (with **umeris**), *seared.*

19. **at**: in imitation of imprecations, where it expresses strong emotion, as Ter. *And.* 666 *at tibi di dignum fáctis exitiúm duint*, Cat. 3. 13 *at vobis male sit, malae tenebrae | Orci.* Verg. *A.* II. 535. — **concupiveris**, *crave.*

IV. The proscriptions and confiscations of the civil wars, which brought ruin to so many families, brought sudden wealth to others, and the rich upstart was a familiar figure in the society of the day. The vulgar striving of this personage for social recognition and political distinction call out more than once the expression of Horace's scorn, and in *S.* I. 6 he sets forth at length his view of the matter, illustrating it by a frank discussion of his own case. The present epode is an attack on one of these parvenus, the bitterness of which, in strong contrast with the good-natured tone of the satire, leaves little doubt that the poet is here not merely dealing with a social type, but assailing a real person, and probably one who had crossed his own path. But we are not informed who the person was. The inscription in some MSS., 'ad Sextum Menam, Pompei libertum' (see *C.* III. 16. 15 n) is based on a highly improbable guess; and there is not much more to be said for the inscription in other (and even in some of the same) MSS., which names one Vedius Rufus (perhaps the man described by Cicero, *ad Att.* VI. 1. 25) as the object of the attack. It is to be observed that what excites the poet's 'liberrima indignatio' is not the servile origin of the man, but his arrogant presumption in pushing himself into notoriety and usurping, in virtue of his ill-gotten wealth, the distinctions which belong to merit. — Metre, 159.

1. **lupis et agnis**: immemorial types of irreconcilable hostility; cf. *Il.* XXII. 263. Ovid makes a similar use of them, *Ib.* 43 *pax erit haec nobis, donec mihi vita manebit, | cum pecore infirmo* (cf.

Hibericis peruste funibus latus
    et crura dura compede.
Licet superbus ambules pecunia,
    fortuna non mutat genus.
Videsne, Sacram metiente te viam
    cum bis trium ulnarum toga,
ut ora vertat huc et huc euntium
    liberrima indignatio?
'Sectus flagellis hic triumviralibus
    praeconis ad fastidium

2. 16 n) *quae solet esse lupis.* — **sortito:** *i.e.* by nature; properly an impersonal abl. abs. (Gr. 255 *c*). For this use of the word, referring to the original allotment in the constitution of nature, cf. *S.* II. 6. 93 *terrestria quando | mortalis animas vivunt sortita.*

3. **Hibericis:** *i.e.* made of Spanish *spartum*, a rush of exceedingly tough fibre, of which ropes, as well as coarse articles of clothing, were made.—**peruste,** *tanned.* Cf. *Ep.* I. 16. 47 *loris non ureris.* — **funibus:** used for flogging slaves. —**latus,** *hide;* see *C.* II. 7. 18 n.

4. **crura:** also taken with **peruste** (*galled*); cf. *Ep.* I. 10. 43. For the two accusatives, see Intr. 43 — **compede:** worn only by the lowest class of slaves in the country, but by them even while they were at work.

5. **ambules,** *walk abroad;* cf. *S.* I. 4. 66

6. **fortuna:** *i.e.* wealth.

7. **Sacram viam:** the favorite promenade of Rome. Cf. 7. 8 n, *S.* I 9. 1. — **metiente te,** *as you stride along;* cf. Plaut. *Pseud.* 1049 *quin hínc metimur grádibus militáriis?*

8. **cum:** *i.e* wearing. Cf. Cic. *Brut.* 56 *cum . . . sacrificium publicum cum laena faceret.* — **bis trium ulnarum:** *sc.* in breadth. The *ulna* was about half a yard. The effect would be conspicuous in the ample folds which fell from the shoulders, draped with elaborate care; cf. *S.* II. 3. 183 *latus ut in Circo spatiere.*

9. **ora vertat:** *i.e.* they flush with indignation. Cf. *S.* II. 8. 35 *vertere pallor tum parochi faciem.* —**huc et huc,** *up and down;* to be taken with **euntium.** Cf. *hinc et hinc,* 2. 31 n. In prose, *huc* (*et*) *illuc* is used.

10. **liberrima,** *outspoken* (in the words that follow). Cf. *liber amicus, S.* I. 4. 132; *multa cum libertate notabant,* ib. 5.

11. **sectus:** a vivid variation on the usual *caesus;* cf. Tib. I. 9. 22 *verbere terga seca;* Juv. 10. 316. — **triumviralibus:** *i.e.* by order of the *triumviri capitales,* police commissioners charged with the execution of criminals and the preservation of order. In exercising the latter function they had power to inflict summary punishment on slaves and other low characters.

12. **praeconis:** who stood by while the flogging was administered, and proclaimed the offense.

arat Falerni mille fundi iugera
et Appiam mannis terit
sedilibusque magnus in primis eques
Othone contempto sedet.
Quid attinet tot ora navium gravi
rostrata duci pondere
contra latrones atque servilem manum,
hoc, hoc tribuno militum?'

13. **arat**: *i.e.* has under cultivation, owns. — **Falerni**: the *ager Falernus* was a rich wine-growing district on the Campanian side of Mt. Massicus. — **fundi**, *farm-land.*

14. **Appiam**: sc. *viam.*—**mannis**, *ponies*, fashionable for driving. The reference may be, however, to his journeys to his estates in Campania. Cf. *C.* III. 27. 7 n. — **terit**: cf. Mart. XI. 13. 1 *quisquis Flaminiam teris viator.*

15. **sedilibus primis**: the fourteen rows of seats in the theatre immediately behind the orchestra, which was occupied by the senators. These front rows, under a law passed by L. Roscius Otho, tribune of the plebs, B.C. 67, were reserved for the equestrian order. — **magnus**: ironical; cf. *S.* I. 6. 72 *magni | quo pueri magnis e centurionibus orti.*

16. **contempto**: the law in his case defeats its own object, which was to exclude just such persons as he from the seats in question.

17. **ora rostrata**, *beaked fronts*, a fanciful expression for the usual term *rostra.* — **navium**: used generically; cf. *virginum, C.* III. 27. 38 n. — **gravi pondere**, *ponderous.* The freshness of these allusions gives the impression that the construction of the ships referred to was in progress or recently completed when the epode was written. This would assign it to the year 37 or 36, when Octavian, after his disastrous defeat by Sextus Pompeius in 38, was engaged in building a new fleet of larger and stouter vessels.

19. **latrones**, etc.: the pirates and runaway slaves in the service of Sextus. Of the latter class Augustus asserts that he captured and returned to their masters about thirty thousand (*Mon. Anc.* 5. 1).

20. **hoc, hoc**: Intr. 116 *d.*—**tribuno militum**: cf. the case of Tillius, *S.* I. 6. 24 *sqq.*, and also 45 *sqq.*, where Horace admits the justice of the objection in his own case.

V. The clairvoyants and mediums of the present day had their counterpart in the professors of necromancy and magic who plied their trade with abundance of patronage and profit among a people so superstitious as the Romans. In this epode Horace exposes the practices of these persons in their worst form, where absurdity was carried to the point of crime. Four old hags, who have enticed a boy away from his home, suddenly seize him and drag him into their house, where he is to be subjected to a lingering death, buried in the ground up to his chin, with food

## V.

'At o deorum quicquid in caelo regit
terras et humanum genus,
quid iste fert tumultus, et quid omnium
voltus in unum me truces?

in sight, that they may make a philter out of his marrow and liver. That children actually were made away with in the manner described, or at least that this was firmly believed, is shown by an epitaph (CIL. VI. 19747) on a boy, Iucundus, who had been so stolen: IN QVARTVM · SVRGENS · COMPRENSVS · DEPRIMOR · ANNVM | CVM POSSEM · MATRI · DVLCIS · ET · ESSE PATRI | ERIPVIT · ME · SAGA · MANVS CRVDELIS · VBIQVE | CVM · MANET IN · TERRIS · ET · NOCIT · ARTE SVA | VOS · VESTROS · NATOS · CONCVSTODITE PARENTES | NI · DOLOR · IN TOTO · PECTORE · FIXSVS · EAT. The leader of the unlovely quartet is Canidia, whom Horace has made a conspicuous figure in his earlier writings. Her real name, the scholiasts profess to know, was Gratidia, her birthplace Naples, and her trade the manufacture of perfumes. Tradition further asserts that Horace had been her lover, that the bitter lampoons which he has left us in this and the seventeenth epode were the outcome of a lover's quarrel, and that these are none other than the *celeres iambi* which he recants in *C.* I. 16. All this is highly improbable, and may be safely dismissed as an ill-contrived hypothesis to connect together the *data* of the poems. The earliest published poem in which Canidia is mentioned is perhaps *S.* I. 8, where her magic performances are ridiculed, but without a trace of bitterness. Equally devoid of personal feeling are the verses (*S.* II. 1. 48, 8. 95, *Epod.* 3. 8) where Horace makes a passing allusion to her as a poisoner. If she was a real person,—which seems, on the whole, probable,—we may safely assume that she was an *unguentaria;* as such she would be resorted to by the ignorant and superstitious for love potions and other nostrums known to the quackery of the day, and, unless her reputation belied her, she was also ready, like her famous successor, Locusta, to concoct more harmful drugs. She was a notorious character, whom Horace felt at liberty to use as a type of her class, in holding up their practices to ridicule.—Metre, 159.

1. **at**: expressing sudden emotion; cf. its use in imprecations (see 3. 19 n). The words are those of the boy, who has been seized by the women and dragged into the atrium of the house.—**deorum quicquid**: cf. Liv. XXIII. 9. 3 *iurantes per quicquid deorum est; S.* I. 6. 1 *Lydorum quicquid.*—**in caelo**: simply used to round out the phrase, like 'all the fish in the sea,' etc. A distinction between the gods of heaven and those of the underworld is not to be thought of in the mind of the frightened boy.

3. **fert**, *means;* lit. 'brings,' *i.e.* what will it lead to?—**quid**: sc. *ferunt.*

4. **voltus in me truces**: cf. *acer ... voltus in hostem, C.* I. 2. 39.

Per liberos te, si vocata partubus
Lucina veris adfuit,
per hoc inane purpurae decus precor,
per improbaturum haec Iovem,
quid ut noverca me intueris aut uti
petita ferro belua?'
Vt haec trementi questus ore constitit
insignibus raptis puer,
impube corpus quale posset impia
mollire Thracum pectora,
Canidia, brevibus implicata viperis
crinis et incomptum caput,
iubet sepulcris caprificos erutas,
iubet cupressos funebris

5. **te:** Canidia.—**si vocata,** etc.: see 17. 50 n. The allusion in both places assumes that the poet's readers are familiar with the story.

6. **Lucina:** cf. *C. S.* 15, *C.* III. 22. 2 n.—**veris:** the poet's own malice breaks through the fiction in this insinuation, which is quite out of character in the mouth of the child.

7. **inane:** as not having secured him the respect which it ought.—**purpurae decus:** the purple border of his toga, which was a mark at once of tender years and of gentle breeding.

8. **improbaturum:** a mild term, but sufficient when applied to the deity, whose mere *displeasure* is to be dreaded.

9. **ut noverca:** cf. Sen. *Contr.* IV. 6 *hic tuus est; quid alterum novercalibus oculis intueris?* and see note on *patruae, C.* III. 12. 1.

12. **insignibus:** his *praetexta* and the *bulla* or locket which he wore on his breast, suspended from his neck.

13. **impube corpus:** in apposition with **puer.** Even if the ordinary symbols of youth and innocence had failed to affect them, the sight of his tender body might have touched the heart of a savage.

15. **brevibus,** etc.: Canidia's make-up is that of a fury, which she is called in *S.* I. 8. 45. Cf. Lucan's description of Erichtho, VI. 654 *sqq.*

16. **crinis, caput:** Intr. 42.

17. **sepulcris:** Intr. 70.—**caprificos:** the wild fig-tree grew on walls and tombs, and, sending its roots into their cracks and joints, sometimes split them apart,—a type of the destructive forces which mock the elaborate efforts of man to immortalize his memory. Cf. Mart. X. 2. 9 *marmora Messalae findit caprificus;* Juv. 10. 144 *sq.* Here it is chosen from its association with the tomb and death.

18. **cupressos:** also associated

et uncta turpis ova ranae sanguine
  plumamque nocturnae strigis
herbasque quas Iolcos atque Hiberia
  mittit venenorum ferax,
et ossa ab ore rapta ieiunae canis
  flammis aduri Colchicis.
At expedita Sagana, per totam domum
  spargens Avernalis aquas,
horret capillis ut marinus asperis
  echinus aut currens aper.

with the tomb, but here branches used at some funeral (**funebris**) are meant. See *C.* II. 14. 23 n.

19. **uncta,** *smeared.* Cf. *C.* II. 1. 5.—**ranae**: sc. *rubetae*, a poisonous frog; cf. Plin. *N. H.* VIII. 110 *ranae rubetae, quarum et in terra et in humore vita, plurimis refertae medicaminibus deponere ea cotidie ac resumere pastu dicuntur, venena tantum semper sibi reservantes.* Cf. Juv. 1. 69.

20. **strigis**: limiting both **ova** and **plumam.** The *strix* was a bugbear of the nursery, described as a screeching, owl-like bird which carried off unguarded babies from their cradles (Ov. *F.* VI. 131 *sqq.*). Pliny was unable to identify it (*N. H.* XI. 232), and it was probably nothing but a mythical distortion of the screech-owl itself, which from its appearance and habits was naturally regarded as a bird of ill omen (*funebris et maxime abominatus, . . . noctis monstrum . . . ; itaque in urbibus aut omnino in luce visus dirum ostentum est*, Plin. *N. H.* X. 34).

21. **Iolcos**: cf. vs. 45 and *C.* I. 27. 21 n. — **Hiberia**: under the Caucasus range, adjacent to Colchis.

22. **venenorum**: Intr. 66*a*.

23. **ieiunae**: in order to impart to the potion the craving of baffled appetite.

24. **Colchicis**: *i.e.* kindled with certain forms and spells which were supposed to give them magic potency; cf. *C.* II. 13. 8 n. With this whole witch's outfit, cf. Prop. IV. 6. 27 *illum turgentis ranae portenta rubetae | et lecta exsectis anguibus ossa trahunt | et strigis inventae per busta iacentia plumae | cinctaque funesto lanea vitta toro.*

25. **expedita**: *i.e.* with her skirt tucked up (cf. *succincta*, *S.* I. 8. 23) so as not to impede her brisk movements. — **Sagăna**: Canidia's companion in *S.* I. 8, where it is implied that there were two sisters of this name.

26. **spargens,** etc.: the usual form of purification (*lustratio*) in sacrifices to the gods below, funeral rites, etc.; cf. Verg. *A.* IV. 635, VI. 229 *sq.* —**Avernalis**: cf. Verg. *A.* IV. 512. Lake Avernus was supposed to be connected with the underworld.

28. **currens**: not added in reference to **capillis asperis,**—as if his bristles were erect only when he runs,—but as part of the picture which Sagana rushing about the house suggests.

Abacta nulla Veia conscientia
ligonibus duris humum
exhauriebat ingemens laboribus,
quo posset infossus puer
longo die bis terque mutatae dapis
inemori spectaculo,
cum promineret ore quantum exstant aqua
suspensa mento corpora,
exsecta uti medulla et aridum iecur
amoris esset poculum,
interminato cum semel fixae cibo
intabuissent pupulae.

29. **Veia**: the third witch, who digs in the *impluvium* the hole in which the boy is to be buried.

30. **ligonibus**: Intr. 128. — **duris**: the epithet hints at the laboriousness of her task, the hardness of the tool implying a difficult substance to dig into, as the earth in the *impluvium* was. Cf. **ingemens laboribus**, below.

31. **exhauriebat**: properly used of removing the earth after digging it loose with the hoe (Caes. *B. G.* V. 42. 3 *gladiis caespites circumcidere, manibus sagulisque terram exhaurire cogebantur*); here it stands for both operations. — **ingemens**: cf. Verg. *G.* I. 45 *depresso incipiat iam tum mihi taurus aratro | ingemere.*

32. **quo**: adverb (lit. 'into which') with **infossus**; cf. Caes. *B.G.* VII. 73. 9 (*taleae*) *in terram infodiebantur.*

33. **longo**: *sc.* to the boy, in his torture. — **bis terque**, *again and again*; cf. *Ep.* II. 3. 440 *bis terque expertum frustra.* — **mutatae**: to tempt his appetite by variety.

34. **inemori**, *pine to death at;* found only here. The prefix has the same force as in *ingemere*, 31 *indormire*, *S.* I. 1. 71, etc., and the simpler form *immori*, *Ep.* I. 7. 85. Cf. also *intabuissent*, 40 n. The poor boy's passionate craving for food was to be conveyed, through his vital parts, into the philter, and endow the latter with the power of exciting insatiable desire.

36. **suspensa mento**: a fanciful paraphrase for *natantia.*

37. **exsecta, aridum**: see Intr. 121. — **medulla**: the innermost part of the body and the hardest to reach; cf. its figurative use, *Ep.* I. 10, 28, Cat. 64. 93 *imis exarsit tota medullis*, etc.; hence imagined to be the most potent medium of magic influence. — **iecur**: the seat of the passions; cf. I. 13. 4.

39. **semel**: with **cum**, and applying to the whole clause. — **fixae**, *fastened upon.* — **cibo**: dative with both **fixae** (Intr. 56) and **intabuissent** (cf. Sen. *de Cons. ad Polyb.* 5. 2 *quid iuvat dolori intabescere?*); Intr. 76.

41. **defuisse**: implying more than *afuisse*, — that she belonged

Non defuisse masculae libidinis
Ariminensem Foliam
et otiosa credidit Neapolis
et omne vicinum oppidum,
quae sidera excantata voce Thessala
lunamque caelo deripit.
Hic inresectum saeva dente livido
Canidia rodens pollicem
quid dixit aut quid tacuit? 'O rebus meis
non infideles arbitrae,

in the company, and would have been missed if absent. — **libidinis**: Intr. 61.

42. **Foliam**: apparently a notorious character at Naples. There is no little art in the way she is introduced: by basing her presence only on hearsay, and attempting no details of her part in the orgy, the poet gives the impression that the evidence as to the others was explicit and trustworthy.

43. **otiosa**: and hence gossipy (*otium serendis rumoribus natum*, Curt. VIII. 9. 1); a characteristic, according to the Roman standard, of the Greeks (*gens lingua magis strenua quam factis*, Livy VIII. 22. 8). Cf. *NT. Acts*, 17. 21: 'Now all the Athenians and the strangers sojourning there spent their time in nothing else but either to tell or to hear some new thing.' Naples in particular was proverbial for its idle life; cf. Ovid *M.* XV. 711 *in otia natam Parthenopen.* The shores of the bay, too (**omne vicinum oppidum**), were lined with villas, the resort of people of leisure, and no doubt hotbeds of gossip.

45. **sidera**: cf. 17. 4. *sq.*, and Tib. I. 2. 43 *hanc* (*sagam*) *ego de caelo ducentem sidera vidi.* —**Thessala**: *i.e.* magic; cf. *Colchicis* 24 n, and see *C.* I. 27. 21 n.

46. **lunam**: cf. 17. 78, and Verg. *E.* 8. 69 *carmina vel caelo possunt deducere lunam.*—**deripit**: present of customary action, not historical.

47. **hic**, *then;* but it refers not so much to the time as to the circumstances and surroundings of the act,—the stage of preparation described in what precedes. Cf. Verg. *A.* I. 728 *hic regina gravem gemmis auroque poposcit | implevitque mero pateram.* — **inresectum**: cf. *S.* I. 8. 26 *scalpere terram unguibus . . . coeperunt.* For the prefix **re-** cf. *C.* III. 24. 34 n.

48. **rodens**: in her violent agitation.

49. **tacuit**: *i.e.* 'thought,' since *tacere* with an object means to refrain from saying *what one knows or thinks.* The words that follow are to be regarded as partly spoken or muttered, and partly expressing the thoughts which passed through her mind, but were not spoken aloud. — **rebus meis**, *my cause, my fortunes* (cf. *C.* IV. 6. 23), in contrast with **hostilis domos** 53; dat. after **adeste** (cf. *tuis rebus adero*, Cic. *ad Fam.* VI. 14. 3), with which **arbitrae** is joined as predicate nominative.

50. **non infideles**: *i.e.* true to

Nox et Diana, quae silentium regis,
arcana cum fiunt sacra,
nunc, nunc adeste, nunc in hostilis domos
iram atque numen vertite.
Formidolosis dum latent silvis ferae
dulci sopore languidae,
senem, quod omnes rideant, adulterum
latrent Suburanae canes,
nardo peruntum quale non perfectius
meae laborarint manus.

the obligation of secrecy which her trust imposed upon them. — **arbitrae**: equivalent, under the circumstances, to *consciae*. See next note.

51. **Nox et Diana**: cf. Ov. *M.* VII. 192 (of Medea) '*Nox*,' *ait arcanis fidissima*, . . . | *tuque triceps Hecate*, *quae coeptis conscia nostris* | *adiutrixque venis cantusque artisque magorum*, and see *C.* III. 22. 4 n. — **silentium**: essential for magic rites.

53. **nunc, nunc**: Intr. 116 *d.* — **hostilis**: not those of her rivals (which would require *inimicas*), but those of 'the enemy' in general — a common clause in ancient prayers. Cf. *C.* III. 27. 21 n.

54. **iram atque numen**, *your all-powerful wrath.* Intr. 126 *a.*

55–60. Though she has already made preparations for concocting a more potent drug, she is not without hope that an ointment previously applied, though thus far ineffective, may still do its work.

57. **senem**: named Varus in vs. 73, an old fop. There is no evidence to show whether Horace had a real person in mind. — **quod omnes rideant**, *amid general laughter.* The laughter is at the foppery of the old man; cf. Plaut. *Cas.* 222 *sénectan aetate únguentatus pér vias, ignáve, incedis?*

58. **latrent**: transitive as in *Ep.* I. 2. 66; Intr. 51 *c* (2). She hopes to hear the barking of the dogs as an indication of his approach; cf. Verg. *E.* 8. 107. — **Suburanae**: *i.e.* those of the neighborhood. The Subura, the slums of Rome, was in the hollow, east of the forums, between the Esquiline and the Quirinal and Viminal hills. It was the most densely settled and the busiest and noisiest (*clamosa* Mart. XII. 18. 2) part of the city, full of small shops, eating-houses, and low resorts. Cf. Pers. 5. 32 *sq.* Here was the house of Canidia.

59. **nardo**: see *C.* II. 11. 16 n. — **quale non**: *quo non* would be more usual. With **quale** the other term of the comparison (*tali*) is understood: 'of a sort, of which . . . none more perfect (than this)'; cf. *S.* I. 5. 41 (*Varius Vergiliusque*) *animae qualis neque candidiores terra tulit.*

61. **quid accidit**: as the stillness remains unbroken, she tries to think what unforeseen circumstance has counteracted her drugs. — **minus**: here equivalent to *pa-*

Quid accidit? Cur dira barbarae minus
venena Medeae valent,
quibus superbam fugit ulta paelicem,
magni Creontis filiam,
cum palla, tabo munus imbutum, novam
incendio nuptam abstulit?
Atqui nec herba nec latens in asperis
radix fefellit me locis.
Indormit unctis omnium cubilibus
oblivione paelicum?
A, a, solutus ambulat veneficae
scientioris carmine.
Non usitatis, Vare, potionibus,
o multa fleturum caput,

*rum*, expressing simply failure to come up to her expectations; cf. Cic. *Div.* I. 24 *at non numquam ea quae praedicta sunt minus eveniunt;* Plaut. *Cas.* 918 *monebo, si qui meministi minus.*

62. **Medeae**: *i.e.* identical in their composition with those Medea used on the occasion referred to. Cf. Tib. I. 2. 51 (of a *saga*): *sola tenere malas Medeae dicitur herbas.*

63. **quibus**: with **ulta** which here contains the main statement, like *delibutis*, 3. 13. — **superbam**: as a triumphant rival.— **paelicem**: cf. 3. 13 n.

65. **tabo imbutum**, *plague-tainted; tabum* here in the sense of *tabes*, as in Ov. *M.* XV. 627 *pallidaque exsangui squalebant corpora tabo.*

66. **abstulit**: cf. *C.* II. 16. 29, *S.* I. 9. 31.

67. **nec fefellit**: *i.e.* I have found and gathered every one (of those required by Medea's recipe).

69. **indormit**, etc.: as there are still no signs of his approach, she casts about for the cause of her failure. Her first thought is that her spells have proved ineffective: 'Can it be that he is going to sleep over (and in spite of) the magic drugs with which I have anointed his bed?' For **indormit**, cf. *inemori*, 34 n.

71. **a, a**: Intr. 185. Her second thought flashes upon her as the true explanation, — 'Some rival has done this!' — and at once puts her in a fury that spurs her on to redoubled efforts. — **solutus**: cf. *C.* I. 27. 21. — **ambulat**: cf. 4. 5 n.

72. **carmine**, *spell;* cf. 17. 4 n.

73. **non usitatis**: cf. *C.* II. 20. 1. The meaning is: I will brew a potion of no ordinary power, that will bring you swiftly back to me.

74. **multa fleturum**, *doomed to shed many a tear;* cf. *flebit*, *S.* II. 1. 46, and see Intr. 45 *b*, 104 *b*. — **caput**: cf. *C.* I. 24. 2.

ad me recurres, nec vocata mens tua
Marsis redibit vocibus:
maius parabo, maius infundam tibi
fastidienti poculum,
priusque caelum sidet inferius mari,
tellure porrecta super,
quam non amore sic meo flagres uti
bitumen atris ignibus.'
Sub haec puer iam non, ut ante, mollibus
lenire verbis impias,
sed dubius unde rumperet silentium,
misit Thyesteas preces:

75. **nec vocata**, etc.: *i.e.* and the incantations which will draw your heart back to me will not be of the Marsic sort. Others, following Porphyrio, interpret thus: 'And your heart (when I once get control of it) will not return (to those who now control it) at the call of Marsic spells.' But the contrast of the emphatic **Marsis** (Intr. 116 *b*) with **maius** 77 makes the former more probable. For **mens** in this sense, cf. *C.* I. 13. 5 n.

76. **Marsis vocibus**: here used disparagingly for the simple spells of the Italian countryside. The Marsi were especially noted for snake-charming and magic cures (Gell. XVI. 11. 1); cf. 17. 29 n.

77. **maius**: *i.e.* in quality, more powerful. — **infundam**, *administer;* stronger than *dabo;* cf. Cic. *Phil.* 11. 13 *at hic nuper sororis filio infudit venenum, non dedit.*

79. **inferius**: for the prosody see Intr. 135.

81. **uti bitumen**, etc.: a comparison drawn from her own occupations. Cf. Verg. *E.* 8. 82.

82. **atris**: here used of the actual color of the flames, and not like *nigris*, *C.* IV. 12. 26.

83. **sub haec**, *hereupon;* cf. *S.* II. 8. 43, and see *C.* III. 7. 30 n.

84. **lenire**: Intr. 91.

85. **dubius**, etc.: *i.e.* with varied emotions pressing for utterance. — **unde**, etc.: *i.e.* what he should say first, **unde** being used as with a 'word of beginning,' which **rumperet silentium** is in effect; cf. Cornif. *ad Herenn.* I. 14 *inde incipiemus narrare, unde necesse erit.*

86. **Thyesteas preces**: familiar to Romans from the *Thyestes* of Ennius. Cf. Cic. *in Pis.* 43 *Thyestea est ista exsecratio poetae volgi animos, non sapientium moventis.* The curse is quoted *l.l.* and *Tusc.* I. 107. Varius also, and, subsequently, Seneca, wrote a *Thyestes.* For **preces** in this sense, cf. *S.* II. 6. 30; Caes. *B. G.* VI. 31. 5 *omnibus precibus detestatus Ambiorigem.* For an actual instance of such dying imprecations, see Tac. *Ann.* VI. 24. 3.

87. **venena**, etc.: an obscure and undoubtedly corrupt passage for which no satisfactory expla

'Venena magnum fas nefasque non valent
convertere humanam vicem.
Diris agam vos; dira detestatio
nulla expiatur victima.
Quin ubi perire iussus exspiravero,
nocturnus occurram furor,
petamque voltus umbra curvis unguibus,
quae vis deorum est manium,
et inquietis adsidens praecordiis
pavore somnos auferam.
Vos turba vicatim hinc et hinc saxis petens
contundet obscaenas anus;
post insepulta membra different lupi
et Esquilinae alites;

nation or emendation has been suggested. See Crit. App. The general meaning appears to be this: Sorcery (**venena**) has no power to reverse, after the manner of men (**humanam vicem**), the great law of righteousness and sin; *i.e.* your drugs may influence mortal minds, as you claim; if you incur the sin of taking my innocent life, they cannot save you from the vengeance of heaven, which will give effect to my dying imprecations; and when these have been pronounced, repentance will come too late (**nulla expiatur victima**). For **fas nefasque convertere**, cf. Verg. *G.* I. 505 *fas versum atque nefas;* Ov. *M.* VI. 585 *fasque nefasque | confusura ruit;* for **humanam vicem**, *Sardanapali vicem in meo lectulo mori*, Cic. *ad Att.* X. 8. 7, is quoted. For the infin. **convertere**, see Intr. 94*n.*

89. **diris,** *curses,* as in Tac. *l. l.* **dira detestatio** is a more solemn expression for the same thing.

90. **nulla,** etc.: such was the current belief. Cf. *C.* I. 28. 34; Plin. *N.H.* XXVIII. 19 *defigi quidem diris precationibus nemo non metuit.*

92. **furor**: here used as a masculine form for *furia, an avenging spirit.*

93. **umbra**: cf. Verg. *A.* IV. 386 *omnibus umbra locis adero; dabis, improbe, poenas.*

94. **quae vis**: *i.e.* the power to return to earth and torment their murderers; cf. Val. Flacc. III. 384 *sqq.*—**deorum manium**: the (sanctified) spirits of the righteous. Cf. Liv. III. 58. 11 *manesque Verginiae . . . per tot domos ad petendas poenas vagati, nullo relicto sonte, tandem quieverunt.*

95. **inquietis**: proleptic.—**adsidens**: as a nightmare.

97. **hinc et hinc**: cf. 2. 31 n.

98. **obscaenas,** *uncanny, gruesome;* the cause of the popular aversion; cf. Verg. *G.* I. 470.

99. **post**: adverb.

100. **Esquilinae**: those that

neque hoc parentes, heu mihi superstites,
effugerit spectaculum.'

## VI.

Quid immerentis hospites vexas canis
ignavus adversum lupos?
Quin huc inanis, si potes, vertis minas
et me remorsurum petis?

haunted the hill when it was the Potters' Field of Rome. Cf. *S.* I. 8. 8 *sqq.* For the hiatus, see Intr. 185.

101. **neque hoc effugerit** (fut. pf.): *i.e.* and it will not pass by without their having seen it. — **heu mihi superstites**: the boy forgets for the moment his own horrible situation in pity for the unhappy lot of his parents, doomed to suffer an affliction from which in the regular course of nature they should be spared. The double pathos of this reversal of the order of nature impressed the ancients, whose vague and cheerless notions of future life afforded them no consolation for bereavement or untimely death, with a force which we cannot well appreciate. With admirable art the poet breaks off at this point, having carried us, along with the tender thoughts of the boy, past the repulsive scene about to be enacted, and leaving us with the picture of the bereaved parents consoled by the punishment of the murderers of their child. He illustrates here in narrative the precepts which he gives for the stage, *Ep.* II. 3. 182 *sqq.*

VI. A challenge, addressed to a scurrilous poet, who is taunted with prudently confining his abuse to those who were powerless to respond. The person addressed is unknown to us. The character attributed to him corresponds with the account given by Tacitus (*Ann.* I. 72. 4.) of Cassius Severus, who was banished by Augustus under the law of treason, — the first instance in which that law was applied to restrict liberty of speech. Cassius, however, belonged to a younger generation than Horace, and the inscription '*ad Cassium Severum*,' found in some manuscripts, can be no more than a guess. Equally conjectural is the inscription *ad Mevium* (cf. Epode 10), and the suggestions of Bibaculus, Anser, and others have no evidence to rest on. — Metre, 159.

1. **hospites**, *passers by, wayfarers*; frequently used in this sense (like *viator*, *e.g.* Mart. XI. 13. 1) in epitaphs in which the reader is directly addressed. Cf. Allen's *Remnants of Early Latin*, 137, 138. — **canis**: *i.e.* one set to watch the flocks; cf. vs. 6.

3. **inanis**: *i.e.* all bark and no bite. — **si potes**, *if you dare*; cf. *C.* III. 11. 31 n.

4. **remorsurum**: Intr. 104 *c.*

5. **Molossus aut Lacon**: without *canis*; cf. our 'Newfoundland,' 'Skye,' etc. These superior breeds are mentioned together by Vergil, *G.* III. 405. The **Molos-**

Nam qualis aut Molossus aut fulvus Lacon,
amica vis pastoribus,
agam per altas aure sublata nivis
quaecumque praecedet fera.
Tu cum timenda voce complesti nemus,
proiectum odoraris cibum.
Cave, cave: namque in malos asperrimus
parata tollo cornua,
qualis Lycambae spretus infido gener
aut acer hostis Bupalo, —
an, si quis atro dente me petiverit,
inultus ut flebo puer?

sian as house-dog occurs *S.* II. 6. 114.

6. **vis**: cf. Lucr. VI. 1222 *fida canum vis;* Verg. *A.* IV. 132 *odora canum vis.*

7. **sublata**: *i.e., arrecta.*

9. **complesti**: Intr. 183.

10. **proiectum**, *flung to you*, with a suggestion of contempt in the action, *proicere* meaning usually 'to throw away.' The ordinary word in this connection is *obicere.* But see Crit. App. — **odoraris cibum**: *i.e.* you are ready to be bribed to hold your tongue; you are seeking blackmail.

11. **cave, cave**: Intr. 116 *d.*

12. **parata**: Intr. 124. — **tollo cornua**: a metaphorical expression, not inconsistent with what precedes, because the figure of the two dogs has been abandoned, and Horace begins in vs. 11. to speak in his own person. Cf. *S.* I. 4. 34.

13. **Lycambae**: attacked with such bitterness by the poet Archilochus, to whom he had first promised and then refused (**infido**) his daughter Neobule, that both father and daughter were driven to suicide. Cf. *Ep.* I. 19. 25, 30 *sq.* The dative depends on the general notion of hostile attack, derived from *tollo cornua* 12. — **spretus**: Intr. 103. — **gener**, *as a son-in-law.*

14. **hostis**: the poet Hipponax. His resentment against Bupalus was roused by a joke of the latter, who, with another sculptor, named Athenis, had made a likeness of the poet's features, which are said to have been uncommonly homely, and exhibited it for the entertainment of their friends (Plin. *N. H.* XXXVI. 12).

15. **an**, etc.: with this conclusion, cf. 17. 76 *sqq.* — **atro dente**: *i.e.* with malicious abuse. *Ater* seems to be used as in *versibus atris, Ep.* I. 19. 30; cf. the similar use of *niger, S.* I. 4. 85, 91, 100. The tooth is figuratively the weapon of envy and malice; cf. *C.* IV. 3. 16; Ov. *Tr.* IV. 10. 123 *nec . . . livor iniquo | ullum de nostris dente momordit opus;* Mart. V. 28. 7 (*homo malignus*) *robiginosis cuncta dentibus rodit.*

16. **flebo**: the order is comparable to that of *S.* II. 1. 60 *dives, inops, Romae, seu fors ita*

## VII.

Quo, quo scelesti ruitis? aut cur dexteris
  aptantur enses conditi?
Parumne campis atque Neptuno super
  fusum est Latini sanguinis, —
non ut superbas invidae Carthaginis
  Romanus arcis ureret,
intactus aut Britannus ut descenderet
  Sacra catenatus via,

*iusserit exsul,* | *quisquis erit vitae scribam color*, where as here the hyperbaton gives the impression of strong feeling that cannot wait for orderly utterance.

VII. On the threatened renewal of civil war. The occasion cannot be determined with certainty, but it was probably the outbreak of hostilities between the triumvirs and Sextus Pompeius in the spring of B.C. 38, owing to their failure to carry out the stipulations of the treaty made at Misenum the preceding August. The treaty had been hailed with delight by the people, as affording them a prospect of peace at last, after a dozen years of civil dissension and bloodshed; and the rude shattering of their hopes within a twelvemonth might well awaken the gloomy feeling which Horace expresses, — that the curse of fraternal strife had been fastened upon the nation by the crime with which its career had begun. A poem in this spirit could hardly have come from Horace at a later date. It is cast in dramatic form, the poet throwing himself in front of the combatants, as it were, to make his appeal. — Metre, 159.

1. **quo, quo**: Intr. 116 *d.* — **scelesti**: cf. *C.* I. 2. 29, 35. 33 *sqq.*, II. 1. 5. — **ruitis**: cf. *C.* I. 3. 26. — **cur dexteris**, etc.: *i.e.* why do you grasp the hilt of your sheathed swords?

2. **conditi**: *sc.* in the scabbard. Cf. '*put up* your sword.'

3. **campis**: Intr. 69. — **Neptuno**: Intr. 130. — **super**: Intr. 115*b*. For the meaning cf. *C.* I. 9. 5 n.

5. **non ut**: added as if the fact implied in the preceding question had been stated affirmatively, — 'blood enough has been shed, and not (as of old) to destroy a powerful rival, nor to win new conquests, but, etc.' — **invidae**: cf. Sal. *Cat.* 10. 1 *Carthago aemula imperi Romani.* — **Carthaginis**, *a Carthage.*

6. **arcis**: Intr. 128.

7. **intactus**: cf. *C.* III. 24. 1 n. The epithet is here substantially, though not literally, accurate, as the raids of Julius Caesar into Britain had made no permanent impression, and the Romans had no foothold in the island. With this allusion cf. *C.* III. 5. 3, and see intr. note to *C.* I. 35.

8. **Sacra via**: the street leading from the Velia, with a gentle descent (**descenderet**) to the Fo-

sed ut secundum vota Parthorum sua
urbs haec periret dextera.
neque hic lupis mos nec fuit leonibus,
numquam nisi in dispar feris.
Furorne caecus an rapit vis acrior
an culpa? Responsum date!
Tacent, et albus ora pallor inficit,
mentesque perculsae stupent.
Sic est: acerba fata Romanos agunt
scelusque fraternae necis,
ut immerentis fluxit in terram Remi
sacer nepotibus cruor.

rum; a favorite promenade of Rome at this time (cf. 4. 7, *S.* I. 9. 1) and the most brilliant portion of the route of the triumphal procession, which passed from the Campus Martius through the Velabrum and the Circus Maximus, along the foot of the Palatine to the Velia, and thence down the *Sacra via* (cf. *C.* IV. 2. 35 n), and through the Forum to the foot of the *clivus Capitolinus.* — **catenatus**: *i.e.* as a prisoner before the triumphal car.

9. **secundum**, etc.: cf. *C.* II. 1. 31 n; *Il.* I. 255 ἦ κεν γηθήσαι Πρίαμος Πριάμοιό τε παῖδες | ἄλλοι τε Τρῶες μέγα κεν κεχαροίατο θυμῷ, | εἰ σφῶιν τάδε πάντα πυθοίατο μαρναμένοιιν. The feeling is the complement of that referred to in 5. 53, *C.* III. 27. 1 n. — **Parthorum**: the successors of Carthage as the most powerful rival of Rome. — **sua**: emphatic; Intr. 116 *c.* For the thought, cf. 16. 2.

11. **hic mos**: *i.e.* seeking to destroy their own kind. For the arrangement of words in this verse, see Intr. 120; for the tense of **fuit**, Intr. 80.

12. **dispar**: used substantively for *dispar animal* or the like. — **feris**: here in its adjective use.

13. **an rapit**: Intr. 119 *a.* — **vis acrior**: *sc.* than your own strength; some irresistible force (meaning that of fate). Cf. *maturior vis, C.* II. 17. 6, where, as here, *vis* is used vaguely of a force above human control.

14. **culpa**, *guilt* (of fratricide; cf. *C.* I. 35. 33.), which pursues you like a curse, and goads you on to new wickedness.

15. **tacent**, etc.: he pauses a moment for a reply, and then turns, as it were, to the bystanders. — **albus**, *ghastly;* cf. 10. 16 n.

16. **perculsae**, *with dismay; sc.* at the thought that they are swept on by some mighty force.

17. **acerba fata**: the *vis acrior* of vs. 13, as **scelus**, etc. repeats *culpa*, 14. — **agunt**: cf. 5. 89 *diris agam vos.*

19. **ut**: cf. *C.* IV. 4. 42 n.

20. **sacer**, *a curse to.* Cf. 16. 9.

## VIII.

Rogare longo putidam te saeculo
viris quid enervet meas,
cum sit tibi dens ater et rugis vetus
frontem senectus exaret,
hietque turpis inter aridas natis
podex velut crudae bovis!
Sed incitat me pectus et mammae putres,
equina quales ubera,
venterque mollis et femur tumentibus
exile suris additum.
Esto beata, funus atque imagines
ducant triumphales tuum,
nec sit marita quae rotundioribus
onusta bacis ambulet.

VIII. An affected taste for literature combined with gross sensuality is the subject satirized, with a degree of coarseness to which Horace rarely descends, in this epode. The person attacked is represented as a woman of wealth and noble family, and the portrait appears to have been drawn from life. — Metre, 159.

1. **rogare te**: the inf. expresses indignation (Intr. 92), the ground of which is given in **putidam**, etc. — **longo saeculo**: hyperbole for *longa aetate*.

3. **dens**: used collectively; Intr. 127. — **ater**: cf. *C.* II. 8. 3. — **vetus**, *extreme*.

7. **sed**, etc.: ironical.

11. **esto**, *you may be*, concessive. The apodosis begins in vs. 17. — **beata**, *rich*. — **atque**: Intr. 114. Its position makes **funus**, another and a somewhat brutal suggestion of her age (cf. *C.* III. 15. 4), more prominent. — **imagines**: the masks which, worn by dummies dressed in the costume of the ancestors they represented, preceded (**ducant**) the bier in the funeral procession.

12. **triumphales**: *i.e.* of ancestors who had triumphed. This would be indicated by the insignia worn with the mask, and would be a mark of the highest nobility.

13. **nec**: Intr. 89 N. — **marita**: for *matrona*. Cf. Ov. *F.* II. 139 *hic castas duce se iubet esse maritas*. — **rotundioribus**: *i.e.* more perfect in shape; cf. Plin. *N. H.* IX. 112 *dos omnis* (sc. *unionibus*) *in candore, magnitudine, orbe, levore, pondere*.

14. **bacis**, *pearls*. — **ambulet**: cf. 4. 5 n.

15. **quid quod**: continuing the concessive sentence in another

Quid quod libelli Stoici inter sericos
iacere pulvillos amant?
Inlitterati num minus nervi rigent?
minusve languet fascinum,
quod ut superbo provoces ab inguine,
ore adlaborandum est tibi?

## IX.

Quando repostum Caecubum ad festas dapes
victore laetus Caesare
tecum sub alta (sic Iovi gratum) domo,
beate Maecenas, bibam,
sonante mixtum tibiis carmen lyra,
hac Dorium, illis barbarum,
ut nuper, actus cum freto Neptunius
dux fugit ustis navibus,

form. Cf. *C.* II. 18. 23 n. — **sericos**, *silken;* cf. *punico*, 9. 27 n.

16. **iacere amant**: *i.e.* are always lying there; Intr. 94 *c*.

IX. To Maecenas, on the arrival at Rome of the first tidings of victory from Actium. The poet calls on his patron (who, according to the best evidence, was in Rome at this time; see intr. note to Epode 1) to institute a thanksgiving banquet for the great victory, as he had done a few years before, on the defeat of Sextus Pompeius. Meantime he pursues his own reflections on the contest and its glorious issue, and bids his slave bring larger cups and wine, which 'artehac nefas depromere,' but in which they may now wash away their anxieties for Caesar's fortunes. The epode was written in September, B.C. 31, nearly a year before *C.* I. 37, which celebrates the death of Cleopatra. — Metre, 159.

1. **repostum**: Intr. 183. — **Caecubum**: see *C.* I. 20. 9 n, 37. 5. — **dapes**: cf. *C.* II. 7. 17 n.

2. **victore Caesare**: Intr. 105 *a*.

3. **alta**: see *C.* III. 29. 10 n. — **Iovi**: see *C.* II. 7. 17 n.

4. **beate**: cf. *C.* I. 4. 14 n.

5. **tibiis**: cf. *lituo*, *C.* I. 1. 23 n. — **carmen**, *melody*. See Intr. 51 *c*.

6. **hac**, etc.: a construction according to the sense, as if the preceding words had been *carmen sonantibus mixtim tibiis lyraque*, or the like. — **Dorium**: spirited, but serious, adapted to warlike themes; **barbarum**: *i.e.* Phrygian (cf. *C.* III. 19. 18, IV. 1. 22, Cat. 63. 22), a more lively style, suited to revels and orgies (cf. Cat. 64. 264).

7. **nuper**: in B.C. 36, after the

minatus urbi vincla quae detraxerat
servis amicus perfidis?
Romanus eheu (posteri negabitis)
emancipatus feminae
fert vallum et arma, miles et spadonibus
servire rugosis potest,
interque signa turpe militaria
sol adspicit conopium.
Ad hoc frementis verterunt bis mille equos
Galli canentes Caesarem,
hostiliumque navium portu latent
puppes sinistrorsum citae.

battle of Naulochus. — **actus**: cf. *C.* III. 7. 5. — **freto**: sc. *Siculo.* For the case see Intr. 70. — **Neptunius dux**: Sextus Pompeius; a mocking recognition of his claim to be the son of Neptune.

9. **vincla**: Intr. 183.

10. **servis**: cf. 4. 19 n. For the case, Intr. 76. — **perfidis**: as having run away from their masters, and now fighting against them.

11. **Romanus,** *a son of Rome;* referring to the soldiers of Antonius; see Intr. 127. — **posteri negabitis**: cf. *credite posteri, C.* II. 19. 2 n.

12. **emancipatus,** *in bondage to.*

13. **fert,** etc.: *i.e.* marches in the ranks, serves as a soldier; enhancing the humiliation of his subjection to a woman. In the same way **miles,** in the next clause, is contrasted with **spadonibus.** Cf. *C.* III. 5. 9. — **et**: Intr. 114.

14. **potest**: cf. *C.* III. 11. 31 n.

15. **turpe** (with **conopium**), *a disgraceful sight.*

16. **sol adspicit**: implying a sense of shame that the Roman soldiery should be seen in the light of day in such effeminate company. — **conopium**: cf. Prop. IV. 11. 45 *foedaque Tarpeio conopia tendere saxo* (*ausa*). The scorn concentrated upon this foreign word is pointed not only at the foreign abomination itself, but at the outrage to Roman tradition and sentiment in allowing a woman to exercise authority in camp; cf. Tac. *Ann.* III. 33. 2 *haud enim frustra placitum olim ne feminae in socios aut gentes externas traherentur; inesse mulierum comitatui quae ... Romanum agmen ad similitudinem barbari incessus convertant.*

17. **vertĕrunt**: Intr. 178.

18. **Galli**: Galatians, under the younger Deiotarus, who deserted to Octavian before the battle. — **canentes Caesarem**: cf. Verg. *A.* VII. 698 *ibant aequati numero, regemque canebant.*

19. **hostiliumque,** etc.: an obscure passage, not explained by any account of the battle that has come down to us. It seems clear, however, that Horace is speaking of a defection in the naval forces of Antonius, corresponding to that

Io Triumphe, tu moraris aureos
currus et intactas boves?
Io Triumphe, nec Iugurthino parem
bello reportasti ducem,
neque Africanum, cui super Carthaginem
virtus sepulcrum condidit.
Terra marique victus hostis punico
lugubre mutavit sagum;

just referred to in his land army; and we may suppose that the first account that reached Rome not only reported such a defection, but described the manœuvre by which it was accomplished. What this manœuvre was we cannot determine. **sinistrorsum** is very likely a nautical term, and with **citae** means 'with a swift movement to port.' By this movement, it would seem, the ships were reported to have abandoned the fleet and taken refuge in the harbor from which they had sailed out to battle.

21. **io Triumphe**: cf. *C.* IV. 2. 49 n. — **tu moraris**: equivalent to an exhortation to make haste; cf. the colloquial use of *cessare*, as Ter. *And.* 343 *cessas adloqui?* *C.* III. 27. 58. — **aureos currus**, *the gilded car*, in which Caesar shall ride to the Capitol. Intr. 128.

22. **intactas** (sc. *iugo*): an essential requirement in sacrificial animals. — **boves**: with the sacrifice of which on the Capitol the ceremonies of the triumph closed.

23. **nec Iugurthino**, etc.: *i.e.* a greater than Marius is awaiting his triumph, — a greater than Africanus (Minor). The mention of the Jugurthine war, rather than the repulse of the Germanic invasion by Marius in B.C. 102 and 101, a far greater achievement, may have been due to the recent appearance of Sallust's *Iugurtha*. — **parem**: sc. *huic quem nunc reportaturus es*.

24. **reportasti**: more commonly used of the spoils of war, of glory, or even of the triumph itself (Plin. *N. H. Praef.* 30); sometimes, as here, of the triumphant general; cf. Cic. *post Red.* 28 *non reducti sumus in patriam, . . . sed equis insignibus et curru aurato reportati.*

25. **neque Africanum**: sc. *huic parem reportasti.* — **super**: in a figurative sense. Cf. *C.* III. 5. 39 *o magna Carthago, probrosis | altior Italiae ruinis!*

26. **sepulcrum**: here (with **virtus condidit**) thought of as the monument rather than as the place of burial.

27. **hostis**: Antonius. — **punico**: used like *Tyrius* (*e.g.* *S.* II. 4. 84 *Tyrias vestis*) for *purple*. *Puniceus* is the commoner form in this sense; cf. *C.* IV. 10. 4 n. A purple or white cloak was usually worn by a general going into battle. Cf. Val. Max. I. 6. 11. (of Crassus at Carrhae) *pullum* (the color of mourning) *ei traditum est paludamentum, cum in proelium exeuntibus album aut purpureum dari soleat.* For the case see Intr. 74.

28. **lugubre**, *sombre;* the change was like putting on mourning. — **sagum**: a plain soldier's mantle in place of the general's cloak

aut ille centum nobilem Cretam urbibus,
ventis iturus non suis,
exercitatas aut petit Syrtis Noto,
aut fertur incerto mari.
Capaciores adfer huc, puer, scyphos
et Chia vina aut Lesbia,
vel quod fluentem nauseam coerceat
metire nobis Caecubum.
Curam metumque Caesaris rerum iuvat
dulci Lyaeo solvere.

(more properly called *paludamentum*); see vs. 27 n. This change of dress Horace probably assumes as a matter of course; he could hardly have received any authentic report to that effect. The same was told of Pompey after Pharsalus (Caes. *B. C.* III. 96. 3): *equum nactus detractis insignibus imperatoriis decumana porta se ex castris eiecit*).

29. **ille . . . petit**: Intr. 120. — **centum**, etc.: cf. *C.* III. 27. 33 n. — **nobilem**, *famous*. Cf. *C.* I. 8. 12, 12. 27.

30. **iturus**: Intr. 104 *b*. — **non suis**: *i.e.* not favorable.

31. **exercitatas**: cf. *C.* IV. 14. 20 *undas exercet Auster*. — **Syrtis**: see *C.* I. 22. 5 n; II. 6. 3 n.

32. **incerto**: *i.e.* in which he has lost his bearings; Intr. 124.

33. **puer**: see *C.* I. 19. 14 n. — **scyphos**: see *C.* I. 27. 1 n.

34. **Chia . . . Lesbia**: sweet and mild Greek wines, likely to be drunk in excess, with the result mentioned (no doubt with less offense to Roman taste than to ours) in the next verse. The effect was counteracted by drinking the harsher Italian wines along with the Greek (see *S.* II. 8. 15), and sometimes the two were mixed (*S.* I. 10. 24). — **aut**, *or* (else); one of the two.

36. **metire**: *sc.* with *cyathi*. See *C.* III. 19. 11 n.

37. **curam solvere**: cf. *curis expeditis*, I. 22. 11 n. — **rerum**: objective genitive; cf. Verg. *A.* II. 413 *ereptae virginis ira*.

38. **Lyaeo**: cf. *C.* III. 21. 16 n. — **solvere**: Intr. 94 *c*.

X. Bavius and Mevius, two poets of the old school, made themselves so offensive by their criticism and detraction to the literary circle to which Horace belonged, that their names have become inseparably associated with those of their betters whom they decried, and have thus escaped the oblivion which speedily overtook their works. The milder tempered Vergil confines his expression of dislike to a single verse, *E.* 3. 90 *qui Bavium non odit amet tua carmina, Mevi*. Horace, in this epode, makes a voyage of Mevius to Greece the occasion of a vituperative personal attack, in which he gives free rein to his hatred and contempt, and which acquires additional force by contrast with the good wishes usually spoken on such an occasion. — Metre, 159.

## X.

Mala soluta navis exit alite,
ferens olentem Mevium:
ut horridis utrumque verberes latus,
Auster, memento fluctibus;
niger rudentis Eurus inverso mari
fractosque remos differat;
insurgat Aquilo, quantus altis montibus
frangit trementis ilices,
nec sidus atra nocte amicum adpareat,
qua tristis Orion cadit,
quietiore nec feratur aequore
quam Graia victorum manus,
cum Pallas usto vertit iram ab Ilio
in impiam Aiacis ratem.
O quantus instat navitis sudor tuis
tibique pallor luteus

1. **mala alite**: cf. *mala avi*, *C.* I. 15. 5 n; to be taken with **soluta**, for which cf. *C.* III. 2. 29.

3. **ut verberes**: optative subj. (Gr. 267 *b*), **memento** being parenthetical.—**latus**: *sc.* of the ship.

4. **Auster**, etc.: all the winds unfavorable to a voyage to Greece are called upon to concentrate their fury on the ill-fated ship.

5. **niger**: cf. *C.* I. 5. 7n.—**Eurus**: cf. *C.* I. 28. 25.—**inverso mari**: cf. Verg. *A.* I. 84 *incubuere mari, totumque a sedibus imis* | *una Eurusque Notusque ruunt* (*upheave*).

6. **differat**: cf. 5. 99.

7. **quantus**, *as powerful as when.*—**montibus**: Intr. 69.

10. **tristis**: cf. *C.* I. 3. 14.—**Orion**: see *C.* I. 28. 21 n; Intr. 178.—**cadit**: cf. *C.* III. 1. 27 n.

12. **Graia victorum manus**: cf. Cat. 31. 13 *Lydiae lacus undae.* The shifting of the attribute is similar to that of Intr. 124.

13. **cum Pallas**, etc.: for the story see *Odys.* IV. 499 *sqq.*, Verg. *A.* I. 39 *sqq.*—**Ilio**: see *C.* I. 10. 14 n.

14. **impiam**: Intr. 124. Ajax had dragged Cassandra from the altar of Pallas; cf. Verg. *A.* II. 403 *sqq.*

15. **quantus instat**, etc.: cf. *C.* I. 15. 9.

16. **lūteus**: expressing the greenish yellow hue of paleness in dark complexions, such as are common in southern Europe; cf. Tib. I. 8. 52 *nimius luto corpora tingit amor;* Cat. 64. 100 *magis fulgore expalluit auri; C.* III. 10. 14 n.

et illa non virilis eiulatio
preces et aversum ad Iovem,
Ionius udo cum remugiens sinus
Noto carinam ruperit.
Opima quod si praeda curvo litore
porrecta mergos iuverit,
libidinosus immolabitur caper
et agna Tempestatibus.

## XI.

Petti, nihil me sicut antea iuvat
scribere versiculos amore percussum gravi,

17. **illa**: insinuating that it was habitual with him. — **non virilis**: cf. Cic. *Tusc.* II. 55 *ingemescere non numquam viro concessum est, idque raro; eiulatus ne mulieri quidem.*

18. **et**: Intr. 114. — **aversum**: cf. *C.* III. 23. 19 n.

19. **Iŏnius sinus**: the same as *Hadriae sinus*, *C.* III. 27. 19. The adjective should not be confused with *Iōnicus*, 2. 54, *C.* III. 6. 21. — **udo**: *i.e.* rainy.

20. **Noto**: ablative with **remugiens**; cf. *ventis*, *C.* III. 10. 7.

21. **opima praeda**, *a rich treat.* — **quod si**: introducing the conclusion as in *C.* I. 1. 35. Intr. 114. The savage bitterness of this closing malediction is not softened, but rather enhanced by a cynical observance of the proprieties of language in abstaining from any direct mention of death and suppressing the real subject of the sentence, — either *tu* (if *iuveris* had been used) or *corpus tuum*, which is implied, however, in **porrecta** (cf. *C.* III. 10. 3).

22. **mergos**: among the most voracious of birds, but Horace is wrong in thinking they eat carrion.

23. **immolabitur**: even the usual thank-offering for a friend's safe return from sea is to have its counterpart on the luckless end of this voyage.

24. **agna Tempestatibus**: cf. Verg. *A.* V. 772.

XI. The poet professes to have lost all interest in writing verses, being once more a victim of love, after a long respite. Of Pettius, to whom the piece is addressed, we know no more than what here appears, — that he was the friend to whom Horace confided his feelings in his last love-affair, the description of which occupies the greater part of the poem. The names Inachia and Lyciscus are of course fictitious. — Metre, 165.

1. **nihil**: Intr. 47.

2. **versiculos**: the diminutive conveys mild disparagement. — **amore**: not consciously personified in this verse, though the thought takes that turn in the next (**qui me**, etc.); hence the simple

amore qui me praeter omnis expetit
mollibus in pueris aut in puellis urere.
Hic tertius December, ex quo destiti
Inachia furere, silvis honorem decutit.
Heu me, per urbem (nam pudet tanti mali)
fabula quanta fui! Conviviorum et paenitet,
in quis amantem languor et silentium
arguit et latere petitus imo spiritus!
'Contrane lucrum nil valere candidum
pauperis ingenium!' querebar adplorans tibi,
simul calentis inverecundus deus
fervidiore mero arcana promorat loco.
'Quod si meis inaestuet praecordiis
libera bilis, ut haec ingrata ventis dividat

ablative. — **gravi**: an attribute in accordance with the conception of love implied in **percussum**, with which it may well be rendered adverbially, *sorely smitten*.

3. **amore**: for this use of anaphora, cf. *arva*, 16. 42 n; *aere*, ib. 65.

4. **in**: cf. *C.* I. 17. 19 n.—**urere**: Intr. 94 *h*.

5. **hic tertius**, etc., *this December, which is smiting*, etc., *is the third since*, etc.—**December**: used in the same way *Ep.* I. 20. 27.

6. **Inachiā**: Intr. 72. — **honorem**, *their glory*, *i.e.* their foliage; cf. *C.* I. 17. 16; Verg. *G.* II. 404 *frigidus et silvis Aquilo decussit honorem*.

7. **nam**, etc.: excusing the exclamation **heu me**.

8. **fabula**, *food for gossip*; cf. *Ep.* I. 13. 9, and the use of *risus*, *S.* II. 2. 107 *o magnus posthac inimicis risus*. — **quanta**, **et**: Intr. 114.—**paenitet**, *I dislike*; historical present.

9. **quīs**: see *C.* I. 26. 3 n. — **amantem** (sc. *me*) **arguit**: cf. *C.* I. 13. 7; *Ep.* I. 19. 6 *laudibus arguitur vini vinosus Homerus*. — **languor**, *listlessness*.

11. **contrane**, etc., *to think that, etc.* For the construction, see Intr. 92. — **candidum**: cf. *S.* I. 5. 41.

12. **adplorans**: accompanying (**ad-**) my lament with tears.

13. **simul**: see *C.* I. 4. 17 n. — **inverecundus**: cf. *verecundum Bacchum*, *C.* I. 27. 3 n. Here the epithet indicates the actual effect of the wine, breaking down the restraints of modesty.

14. **mero**: abl. with **calentis**. — **arcana**: sc. *mea*; **calentis** agrees with the implied possessive genitive, as in *mea ipsius* and similar phrases. — **promorat**: Intr. 86, 183. — **loco**: from their place, *i.e.* the place where they are kept (as secrets),—his own knowledge.

15. **quod si**, etc.: continuing the quotation of his words to Pettius on former occasions.

16. **libera bilis**: cf. *liberrima*

fomenta volnus nil malum levantia,
desinet imparibus certare submotus pudor.'
Vbi haec severus te palam laudaveram,
iussus abire domum ferebar incerto pede
ad non amicos heu mihi postis et heu
limina dura, quibus lumbos et infregi latus.
Nunc gloriantis quamlibet mulierculam
vincere mollitia amor Lycisci me tenet;
unde expedire non amicorum queant
libera consilia nec contumeliae graves,
sed alius ardor aut puellae candidae
aut teretis pueri longam renodantis comam.

*indignatio*, 4. 10 n. For **bilis**, cf. *C.* I. 13. 4 n. — **ut**: expressing result: if my wrath could burn so hotly as to burst forth and scatter to the winds the 'poultices' with which I now vainly try to nurse my sore, etc. — **ingrata**, *thankless, unprofitable.* Cf. Lucr. III. 937 *commoda perfluxere atque ingrata interiere.* — **ventis**: cf. *C.* I. 26. 2 *tradam ventis.*

17. **fomenta**: *i.e.* the *querellae* (cf. *querebar*, 12) with which he tried to console himself and keep alive his hopes.

18. **desinet submotus pudor**: poetical for *desinam submoto pudore* (Intr. 105 *a*). **pudor** is the false pride which keeps him from giving up the contest. — **imparibus**: cf. vs. 11 *sq.*, and see Intr. 57.

19. **haec laudaveram**, *had uttered these praiseworthy sentiments;* lit., had commended this course (as the one I should pursue). For the construction, cf. *promorat*, vs. 14, and see Intr. 86. — **severus**: in contrast with his subsequent conduct. — **te palam**: for *coram te*; cf. Ov. *Trist.* V. 10. 39 *meque palam de me tuto mala saepe loquuntur.*

20. **iussus**: *sc.* by Pettius, urging him to carry out his sensible resolution. — **ferebar**: observe the tense. — **incerto**, *irresolute.* Intr. 124. Cf. Tib. II. 6. 14.

21. **non amicos**: cf. 1. 10 n. **heu . . . heu**: to be taken, not with **non amicos** and **dura**, but with the whole sentence, a sigh over the collapse of his brave purpose. — **postis**: for the door itself, where he was not admitted.

22. **dura**: in a literal sense, explained by the words that follow; cf. *C.* III. 10. 2 *sqq.* — **infregi**: Intr. 119 *a*.

24. **vincere**: Intr. 94 *d*.

25. **expedire**: cf. *C.* I. 27. 24.

26. **libera**, *frank.* Cf. vs. 16. — **contumeliae**: *sc.* of Lyciscus.

27. **puellae**: objective genitive with **ardor** (= *amor*); cf. the use of *ardere* with the accusative, Intr. 72.

28. **teretis**: cf. *C.* II. 4. 21 n. — **renodantis**: equivalent to *nodo solventis*, **re-** having the same force as in *refigere, recludere*, etc.;

## XII.

Quid tibi vis, mulier nigris dignissima barris?
Munera cur mihi quidve tabellas
mittis, nec firmo iuveni neque naris obesae?
Namque sagacius unus odoror,
polypus an gravis hirsutis cubet hircus in alis,
quam canis acer ubi lateat sus.
Qui sudor vietis et quam malus undique membris
crescit odor, cum pene soluto
indomitam properat rabiem sedare, neque illi
iam manet umida creta colorque
stercore fucatus crocodili, iamque subando
tenta cubilia tectaque rumpit!

cf. Val. *Flacc.* V. 380 (*Dianam*) *renodatam pharetris*. For the practice of boys wearing their hair long, cf. *C.* II. 5. 23 *sq.*, III. 20. 14, IV. 10. 3. The knot was presumably for convenience on undress occasions, or to make the hair wavy when it was let down.

XII. A coarse lampoon on a woman whose advances had become repulsive. — Metre, 162.

2. **tabellas**, *notes*.

3. **naris obesae**: *i.e.* with a dull sense of smell; in contrast with **sagacius**, 4.

4. **unus**: common with the superlative, but seldom used, as here, to add force to the comparative; cf. Verg. *A.* I. 15 *quam Iuno fertur terris magis omnibus unam | posthabita coluisse Samo.*

5. **pōlypus**: an offensive tumor that grew in the nose; hence we must supply from **cubet in alis** some such general idea as *adsit.* In the quantity of the o, Horace here and *S.* I. 3. 40 follows the Doric form πώλυπος. — **gravis**, *reeking*. — **cubet hircus**: an extravagant figure, but based on a common colloquial use of the word *hircus* in this sense.

7. **qui**: exclamatory. The poet here drops the form of address and turns to the reader. — **vietis**: Intr. 181. For the position of **vietis** and **membris**, see Intr. 120.

10. **umida**: *sc.* with perspiration. — **creta**: *i.e.* a cosmetic made of it.

11. **stercore crocodili**: cf. Plin. *N. H.* XXVIII. 108 (of the smaller species of crocodile) *in terra tantum odoratissimisque floribus vivit; ob id intestina eius diligenter exquiruntur, iucundo nidore farta; 'crocodileam' vocant; . . . inlita quoque ex oleo cyprino molestias in facie enascentis tollit, ex aqua vero morbos omnis quorum natura serpit in facie, nitoremque reddit.* **color**, then, is rouge made from *crocodilea.*

12. **tecta**, *the canopy.*

Vel mea cum saevis agitat fastidia verbis:
'Inachia langues minus ac me;
Inachiam ter nocte potes, mihi semper ad unum
mollis opus. Pereat male quae te
Lesbia quaerenti taurum monstravit inertem,
cum mihi Cous adesset Amyntas,
cuius in indomito constantior inguine nervus
quam nova collibus arbor inhaeret.
Muricibus Tyriis iteratae vellera lanae
cui properabantur? Tibi nempe,
ne foret aequalis inter conviva, magis quem
diligeret mulier sua quam te.
O ego non felix, quam tu fugis ut pavet acris
agna lupos capreaeque leones.'

13. **vel cum**: the ellipsis after **vel** is to be supplied from the general sense of the preceding sentence,—*quam odiosa est* or the like.

14. **Inachiā**: Intr. 72.—**minus ac**: cf. 15. 5 *artius atque*. This use of *atque* or *ac* for *quam* after a comparative occurs repeatedly in the Satires, in these two places in the Epodes, in the later poems not at all.

17. **Lesbia**: an *ancilla* or *lena*. For the order, see Intr. 118.

18. **Cous Amyntas**: a made-up name, like *Cnidius Gyges*, *C.* II. 5. 20, *Thressa Chloe*, III. 9. 9, etc.

20. **nova**: *i.e.* young.

21. **iteratae**: cf. *bis Afro murice tinctae*, *C.* II. 16. 35 n.

22. **cui**: Intr. 114. Here the pronoun itself gains emphasis (Intr. 116 *b*).— **properabantur**: transitive as in *C.* III. 24. 62.

23. **ne foret**, etc.: *i.e.* that this might be inferred from the fact that he had received such a costly present from her.— **magis quem**. the construction is **quem magis diligeret mulier sua** (=*amica*) **quam te** *tua deligeret*.

25. **o ego**: Intr. 185. For the case, cf. *C.* III. 27. 34 n.—**pavet**: Intr. 51 *a*.

26. **agna lupos**: cf. 4. 1 n.—**capreae leones**: cf. *C.* IV. 4. 13 *sqq*.

XIII. A light piece, constructed of the same materials as *C.* I. 9, and probably, like that ode, a study from the Greek. A stormy day, keeping the poet and his friends indoors, gives them at once the inclination and excuse for 'taking a portion from the solid day' to enjoy a jar of old wine together. Horace's usual maxims on the enjoyment of life are here illustrated by a story of Chiron and Achilles, as in *C.* I. 7 by that of Teucer.—Metre, 164.

1. **contraxit**: *i.e.* has drawn it closer about the earth; referring to the heavy storm clouds, in con-

# XIII.

Horrida tempestas caelum contraxit, et imbres
nivesque deducunt Iovem; nunc mare, nunc siluae
Threicio Aquilone sonant: rapiamus, amici,
occasionem de die, dumque virent genua
et decet, obducta solvatur fronte senectus.
Tu vina Torquato move consule pressa meo.
Cetera mitte loqui; deus haec fortasse benigna
reducet in sedem vice. Nunc et Achaemenio

trast with the open expanse of the clear sky.

2. **deducunt Iovem**: the descent of Jupiter (see I. 1. 25 n) to Earth in showers was an old conception of primitive physical speculation, and became a commonplace in later Greek and in Latin literature. Cf. Verg. *E.* 7. 60 *Iuppiter et laeto descendet plurimus imbri; G.* II. 325 *tum pater omnipotens fecundis imbribus aether | coniugis in gremium laetae descendit.* — **siluae**: Intr. 182.

3. **Threicio Aquilone**: cf. *Thracio vento*, I. 25. 11 n, and see Intr. 185. — **amici**: see note on vs. 6.

4. **de die**: the meaning simply is, that the day brings with it this opportunity, and will carry it away out of our reach if we do not promptly lay hands on it; cf. *C.* III. 8. 27. — **dum virent genua**: *i.e.* while our physical powers are in full vigor; a part (where the weakness of age is conspicuous) standing for the whole body; Intr. 117 *b*.

5. **decet**: cf. *C.* III. 15. 8.—**obducta**, *clouded*.—**solvatur fronte**: cf. *curis expeditis*, I. 22. 11 n. — **senectus**: here for the qualities commonly associated with that time of life; cf. Cic. *C. M.* 65 *morosi et anxii et iracundi et difficiles senes.* For the contrast with **virent**, cf. *C.* I. 9. 17 *sqq.*

6. **tu**: the poet here turns to one of the company, and investing him with the office of master of ceremonies, addresses him in this representative capacity through the rest of the ode, as in *C.* I. 9. The abruptness of the address, without any name, is a little awkward, and has led some editors to suspect *amici*, vs. 3 (see Crit. App.), or to explain it as *nos amici* (nom.), meaning the poet and a single companion. — **Torquato**: see *C.* III. 21. 1 n. — **move**: cf. (*testa*) *moveri digna bono die*, ibid. 6.—**pressa**: cf. *C.* IV. 12. 14.— **meo**: *i.e.* in the year of the poet's birth.

7. **cetera**: cf. *C.* I. 9. 9 n. Here, however, it appears from what follows that Horace had something definite in mind, — perhaps the unsatisfactory state of political affairs. — **mitte**, *forbear*. — **loqui**: Intr. 94 *j*. — **deus**, *Heaven*; see *C.* I. 3. 21 n.—**benigna vice**, *with generous reparation*; cf. *C.* IV. 14. 13 *plus vice simplici.* The allusion is probably to the losses which Horace and his friends had suffered in the civil war.

8. **sedem** (sc. *suam*): *i.e.* their

perfundi nardo iuvat et fide Cyllenea
levare diris pectora sollicitudinibus,
nobilis ut grandi cecinit centaurus alumno:
'Invicte, mortalis dea nate puer Thetide,
te manet Assaraci tellus, quam frigida parvi
findunt Scamandri flumina lubricus et Simois,
unde tibi reditum certo subtemine Parcae
rupere, nec mater domum caerula te revehet.
Illic omne malum vino cantuque levato,
deformis aegrimoniae dulcibus adloquiis.'

proper place or condition. Cf. the wish of Augustus, in Suet. *Aug.* 28: *ita mihi salvam ac sospitem rem publicam sistere in sua sede liceat . . . ut optimi status auctor dicar.*—**Achaemenio**: see *C.* III. 1. 44 n.

9. **nardo**: see *C.* II. 3. 13 n.—**Cyllenea**: as having been invented by Mercury (cf. *C.* I. 10. 6), who was born on Mt. Cyllene in Arcadia. For the metre, see Intr. 132.

10. **levare**, etc.: cf. *C.* IV. 11. 35 *minuentur atrae carmine curae.*—**diris**, *ill-boding.*

11. **grandi**, *tall;* cf. Juv. 7. 210 *metuens virgae iam grandis Achilles.*—**cecinit**: implying an oracular character in his utterance. Cf. *C.* I. 15. 4 n.—**centaurus**: Chiron.—**alumno**: Achilles.

12. **invicte**: used substantively, as in Verg. *A.* VI. 365 *eripe me his, invicte, malis.*—**mortalis dea**: Intr. 116 *a.*

13. **Assaraci**: king of Troy, brother of Ganymede, great-grandfather of Aeneas.—**parvi**: probably more accurate than the Homeric μέγας πόταμος (*Il.* XX. 73).

14. **findunt**, *cleave;* poetical for 'flow through.'—**flumina**, *streams.* For the plural (a reminiscence perhaps of the Homeric ῥέεθρα), see Intr. 128.—**lubricus**: *i.e.* flowing with a smooth, swift current.—**et**: Intr. 114.

15. **unde**: used attributively with **reditum**; cf. *unde periculum*, *C.* II. 12. 7 n.—**certo subtemine**: *i.e.* by an immutable decree; cf. *C. S.* 25 n, Verg. *A.* X. 814 *sq.*, Gray, *The Bard*, 48 *sqq.* The ablative is better taken as instrumental.

16. **rupere**: cf. 16. 35 *reditus abscindere.*—**nec mater**, etc.: cf. Tib. I. 7. 1 *Parcae fatalia nentes | stamina, non ulli dissoluenda deo.*—**caerula**: as a sea-goddess; cf. Ov. *Her.* 9. 14 *Nereus caerulus*, and see *C.* III. 28. 10 n.

17. **illic**, etc.: the envoys sent by Agamemnon find him engaged with the lyre, *Il.* IX. 186.—**levato**: cf. *abstineto*, III. 27. 69 n; the time is implied in **illic**.

18. **deformis**: Intr. 125.—**adloquiis**, *solace;* in apposition with **vino cantuque**.

XIV. In reply to Maecenas's urgent expostulation at the poet's indolence and delay in completing some poetry (apparently the book of Epodes), Horace protests that he is in love and can't help him-

## XIV.

Mollis inertia cur tantam diffuderit imis
oblivionem sensibus,
pocula Lethaeos ut si ducentia somnos
arente fauce traxerim,
candide Maecenas, occidis saepe rogando:
deus, deus nam me vetat
inceptos, olim promissum carmen, iambos
ad umbilicum adducere.

self, quotes the example of Anacreon, and turns upon his patron with an *argumentum ad hominem:* 'You are in love yourself, and you may thank your stars your plight is not so bad as mine.' The tone of familiarity with which he addresses Maecenas is very noticeable. — Metre, 160.

1. **mollis inertia**, etc.: indirect question, containing the gist of Maecenas's reproaches. — **cur**: Intr. 114. — **imis**: *i.e.* to their very centre; it pervades them through and through.

2. **sensibus**: dative, as with *divido* (*e.g.* II. 16), *distribuo*, etc.

3. **Lethaeos somnos**: the sleep of utter forgetfulness. Cf. Verg. *A.* VI. 714 *Lethaei ad fluminis undam | securos latices et longa oblivia potant.* — **ut si**, etc.: illustrating, not so much the degree of forgetfulness, as the completeness (**imis sensibus**) with which it has possessed him. — **ducentia**: cf. *Ep.* I. 2. 31 *ad strepitum citharae cessatum ducere somnum;* Ovid *M.* II. 735 (of Mercury's wand) *qua somnos ducit et arcet.* — **somnos**: Intr. 128.

4. **arente fauce**: *i.e.* eagerly and copiously; cf. Ov. *M.* XV. 330 *parum moderato gutture traxit.*

5. **candide**: referring to Maecenas's character in general (cf. *candidum ingenium*, II. 11), though called out by his frank reproof on this occasion, as *iocose Maecenas*, 3. 20; cf. *Ep.* I. 4. 1 *Albi, nostrorum sermonum candide iudex*, I. 6. 67 *si quid novisti rectius istis, candidus imperti.* — **occidis**: an extravagance of colloquial language; cf. Plaut. *Pseud.* 931 *occidis me quom istuc rogitas; C.* II. 17. 1 n.

6. **deus, deus**: made emphatic (Intr. 116 *d*, 114) because it sums up his whole plea: 'a superior power controls me and I am not responsible.' The god is of course Love.

7. **inceptos**, etc.: for the order, cf. *Ep.* II. 1. 234 *acceptos regale nomisma Philippos*, Verg. *E.* 2. 3 *inter densas umbrosa cacumina fagos.* Intr. 109. — **olim promissum**: *i.e.* for which the public has long been waiting; cf. *Ep.* II. 3. 45 *promissi carminis auctor.* — **carmen**: apparently used here not of a single poem, but generically (*verse*), like *nomisma*, quoted above. — **iambos**: probably the whole collection of epodes, which Horace designates by this name *Ep.* I. 19. 23, II. 2. 59; see Intr. 18.

8. **ad umbilicum adducere**,

Non aliter Samio dicunt arsisse Bathyllo
Anacreonta Teium,
qui persaepe cava testudine flevit amorem
non elaboratum ad pedem.
Vreris ipse miser; quod si non pulchrior ignis
accendit obsessam Ilion,
gaude sorte tua: me libertina nec uno
contenta Phryne macerat.

*to bring to the end of the scroll, i.e.* to finish. The *umbilici* of a Roman book were the ends (often ornamented) of the stick or reed on which the long strip of papyrus was rolled, and there is some reason to believe the name was also applied to the stick itself. In reading, the scroll was held horizontally, the left hand gradually rolling up the part already read, while the part in the right was gradually unrolled. The pages followed one another laterally from left to right, the last being next to the stick.

9. **non aliter**: more commonly used in returning to the main theme *after* an illustration, as Verg. *A.* I. 399, Ov. *M.* VIII. 473, etc.; cf. *C.* IV. 14. 25 n. — **Bathyllo**: a favorite boy. For the case see Intr. 72.

11. **testudine**: see *C.* I. 10. 6 n. — **flevit amorem**: *i.e.* gave expression to it in woful chants. The corresponding word for light and cheerful strains is *ludere*, as *si quid olim lusit Anacreon*, *C.* IV. 9. 9 n; cf. *C.* I. 32. 1 n. For the construction see Intr. 51 *a*.

12. **non elaboratum**: this criticism is not very well understood, as none of Anacreon's verses on Bathyllus are preserved. But apparently it is intended to enforce Horace's plea by pointing out that Anacreon, in similar circumstances, could not bring his mind to the proper tension for composing polished verses. For the litotes, cf. 1. 10 n.

13. **ureris**: cf. *C.* I. 19. 5. — **ipse**: no need for me to tell *you* how it is. — **quod si**: here, as in *C.* III. 1. 41, introducing a supposition assumed to be true, like *si quidem*. — **ignis**, *flame* (cf. *C.* I. 27. 20 n), with a play on the double meaning of the word: if the 'flame' that warms you is as beautiful as the one (Helen) that fired Ilion, etc. The scholiasts profess to know that the 'flame' referred to was Terentia, who subsequently became Maecenas's wife; see *C.* II. 12 intr. note.

15. **nec**: adding to **libertina** another characteristic, that carries the disparagement still farther, — *and not . . . either*.

16. **macerat**: see *C.* I. 13. 8 n. He comes back at the end to the idea (**mollis**) with which he began.

XV. In the character of a slighted lover, Horace heaps angry reproaches on the faithless Neaera, recalls her ardent vows of eternal devotion, tells her she will find he is man enough to resent her perfidy, and turns away with a parting shaft over the shoulders of his unknown rival, whom he warns

## XV.

Nox erat et caelo fulgebat luna sereno
inter minora sidera,
cum tu, magnorum numen laesura deorum,
in verba iurabas mea,
artius atque hedera procera adstringitur ilex
lentis adhaerens bracchiis,
dum pecori lupus et nautis infestus Orion
turbaret hibernum mare
intonsosque agitaret Apollinis aura capillos,
fore hunc amorem mutuum.
O dolitura mea multum virtute Neaera!
nam si quid in Flacco viri est,

of her treachery, which must inevitably bring upon him a like fate, and then the man over whom he is now enjoying his short-lived triumph will have his turn to laugh. The subject is similar to that of *C.* I. 5, but there is a marked contrast in the tone of the two poems. The greater vehemence of the epode is no doubt due to the fact that Horace was not only younger but was dealing with a fresh experience. — Metre, 160.

2. **inter**, etc.: cf. *C.* I. 12. 47.

3. **laesura**: Intr. 104 *c*.

4. **in verba mea**: *i.e.* repeating after me the oath as I dictated it. The expression, originally applied to the *sacramentum*, or military oath administered by the consul to his soldiers, came to be used for an oath of allegiance in general (cf. Tac. *Ann.* I. 7. 3 *consules primi in verba Tiberii Caesaris iuravere*), or figuratively of other kinds of devotion, as *Ep.* I. 1. 14.

5. **artius**, etc.: cf. *C.* I. 36. 20.— **atque**: see 12. 14 n.

7. **dum pecori lupus**: left without a verb by a change of the sentence from the form in which it was first conceived, *dum pecori lupus et nautis Orion infestus esset;* into this the description of Orion as *turbator hiberni maris*, coming in as an after-thought, was, instead of being simply added, incorporated in such a way as to supersede *esset*. For the comparison, see 4. 1 n. — **Orion**: see *C.* I. 28. 21 n and Intr. 178.

9. **intonsos**, etc.: another paraphrase for 'forever,' for the god's long locks were the mark of his eternal youth; see *C.* I. 21. 2 n.

10. **hunc**: *i.e.* 'my.' — **mutuum**, *returned*, as in *animi mutui*, *C.* IV. 1. 30.

11. **dolitura**: Intr. 104 *b*. — **virtute**, *spirit;* see *C.* III. 2. 17 n. The consciousness of the fundamental meaning of the word appears in **si quid viri**, 12.

12. **Flacco**: there is a touch of self-respect in the use of the name. Cf. *Teucro*, I. 7. 27 n.

non feret adsiduas potiori te dare noctis,
et quaeret iratus parem ;
nec semel offensi cedet constantia formae,
si certus intrarit dolor.
Et tu, quicumque es felicior atque meo nunc
superbus incedis malo,
sis pecore et multa dives tellure licebit
tibique Pactolus fluat,
nec te Pythagorae fallant arcana renati,
formaque vincas Nirea,
heu heu, translatos alio maerebis amores ;
ast ego vicissim risero.

13. **potiori**: see *C.* III. 9. 2 n.

14. **et**: see note on *-que*, *C.* I. 27. 16. — **parem**: *i.e.* one who will reciprocate his feelings.

15. **offensi**: sc. *Flacci*, limiting **constantia**; cf. *calentis*, 11. 13, 14 n. — **formae**, *to beauty*. Cf. Ov. *Am.* III. 11. 37 *nequitiam fugio, fugientem forma reducit.*

16. **certus**, *confirmed.* This verse betrays his weakness in spite of his brave words: the door to a reconciliation is not yet absolutely closed; cf. 11. 15 *sqq.*

17. **et tu . . . felicior**, etc.: cf. Tib. I. 2. 87; 5. 69 *at tu, qui potior nunc es, mea fata timeto.*

18. **superbus incedis malo**: cf. 4. 5.

19. **sis pecore**, etc.: no wealth, no wisdom, no beauty can save you from the inevitable result of her caprice. — **sis licebit**: conformed to the time of **maerebis**, 23.

20. **tibi fluat**: *i.e.* you enjoy the benefit of it; cf. *tibi tollit, C.* II. 16. 34. — **Pactolus**: in Lydia, famous for the gold found in its sands.

21. **nec te fallant**: *i.e.* you have the capacity to comprehend them. — **arcana**, *the mysteries, i.e.* his abstruse philosophical speculations. — **renati**: see *C.* I. 28. 10 n.

22. **Nirea**: see *C.* III. 20 15. n.

23. **heu heu**: here expressing scornful pity.

24. **ast**: a quaint form, in colloquial use as late as Cicero, who sometimes used it in his letters (*e.g. ad Att.* I. 16. 17). It was much affected by Vergil, but Horace used it only in his earliest writings (here and twice in the first book of the Satires). — **risero**: expressing stronger assurance than the simple future; cf. Ter. *Heaut.* 85 *crede inquam mihi: aut consolando aut consiliis aut re iuvero.*

XVI. This epode, the best of Horace's political poems, is probably the earliest also. It belongs to the first years after his return from Philippi, before his introduction to Maecenas, — the period of *sollicitum taedium* (*C.* I. 14. 17), when he was still the mourner for

## XVI.

Altera iam teritur bellis civilibus aetas,
suis et ipsa Roma viribus ruit.
Quam neque finitimi valuerunt perdere Marsi
minacis aut Etrusca Porsenae manus,
aemula nec virtus Capuae nec Spartacus acer
novisque rebus infidelis Allobrox,

a lost cause, and could see no hope for his country in any of the contending factions, and no prospect but the wasting away of her strength in civil strife that could end only in her falling a prey to some foreign invader. The verses are full of a genuine feeling which we miss in the odes that deal with matters of state; they glow with youthful enthusiasm and a patriotic fervor which has not yet yielded to the seductive charm of personal friendship or been cooled into political wisdom. In form, as well as in poetic sentiment, the epode is among the most perfect pieces that Horace has left us. — Metre, 161; see also 184.

1. **altera**, *a second;* looking back to the times of Marius and Sulla. — **teritur**, *is wasting away.* — **aetas**, *generation.*

2. **suis ipsa**: in prose, *suis ipsius.*

3. **quam**, *her whom.* In his list of the dangerous enemies whom Rome had withstood, Horace follows the order of distance rather than of time. — **neque**, etc.: notice the variety in the use of conjunctions.—**perdere**: Intr. 94 *n.* — **Marsi**: see *C.* III. 14. 18 n, I. 2. 39 n.

4. **aut**: Intr. 114. — **Etrusca**, etc.: cf. 10. 12 n. — **Porsenae**: king of Clusium, who took up the cause of the banished Tarquins, forced the city to surrender, and imposed terms of peace, which did not, however, include the restoration of the kings. Cf. Tac. *Hist.* III. 72 (referring to the burning of the Capitol in A.D. 69 in much the same spirit in which Horace writes here) *nullo externo hoste, propitiis si per mores nostros liceret deis, sedem Iovis optimi Maximi, . . . quam non Porsenna dedita urbe neque Galli capta temerare potuissent, furore principum exscindi.*

5. **Capuae**: cf. Cic. *Leg. Agr.* 2. 87 *quo in oppido maiores nostri nullam omnino rem publicam esse voluerunt; qui tres solum urbes in terris omnibus, Karthaginem, Corinthum, Capuam, statuerunt posse imperii gravitatem ac nomen sustinere.* This jealousy of the Romans was aroused by the conduct of the Capuans after the battle of Cannae, when they joined Hannibal and openly aspired (**aemula**) to supplant Rome in the hegemony of Italy. — **Spartacus**: see *C.* III. 14. 19 n.

6. **novis rebus**, *in times of treason;* referring to the Catilinarian conspiracy, when the Allobrogian envoys were tampered with by the conspirators, but thought it for their own interest to betray them. The tribe itself, however, which occupied the district between the

nec fera caerulea domuit Germania pube
 parentibusque abominatus Hannibal,
impia perdemus devoti sanguinis aetas,
 ferisque rursus occupabitur solum.
Barbarus heu cineres insistet victor et urbem
 eques sonante verberabit ungula,
quaeque carent ventis et solibus ossa Quirini
 (nefas videre) dissipabit insolens.

Rhone and the Isère, soon after revolted, and was reduced by C. Pomptinus, B.C. 54. Cf. Cic. *in Cat.* 3. 4 *sqq.*, Sal. *Cat.* 40 *sqq.* Their treachery at such a critical time seems to have exaggerated their importance in the eyes of the Romans, as in the case of Capua.

7. **caerulea,** *blue-eyed,* a noted characteristic of the German; cf. Juv. 13. 164 *caerula quis stupuit Germani lumina?* Tac. *Ger.* 4 (*omnibus*) *truces et caerulei oculi, rutilae comae, magna corpora.* — **Germania**: referring to the great invasion of the Cimbri and Teutones, who were defeated and destroyed, the latter at Aquae Sextiae in B.C. 102, the former at Vercellae in 101, by Marius, — probably the greatest peril to which Rome had been exposed since the destruction of the city by the Gauls.

8. **parentibus abominatus**: cf. *matribus detestata, C.* I. 1. 24. Intr. 54.

9. **impia aetas**: in apposition with the subject of **perdemus.** Cf. *C.* I. 35. 34. — **devoti sanguinis,** *with a curse in our blood.* Cf. 7. 20.

10. **feris**: Intr. 55. — **rursus**: as in the times before Romulus. How this is to be brought about is indicated in the next two couplets.

11. **barbarus**: such as the Parthian (I. 12. 53), the Dacian (III. 6. 14), the German, etc. — **cineres**: *sc.* of the burned city. — **insistet,** *will set his foot upon;* with acc. as in Ter. *Eun.* 294 *quam insistam viam, incertus sum.*

12. **eques** (with **barbarus**), *on horse.* — **sonante**: in fancy the poet hears the clatter of the hoofs breaking the stillness of the deserted street.

13. **carent,** *are sheltered from;* in contrast with the profanation to which they are to be exposed. — **solibus**: cf. 2. 41 n, *C.* IV. 2. 46 n. — **ossa Quirini**: according to Varro, as quoted by Porphyrio, Romulus was buried behind the Rostra; it would appear that the story of his apotheosis (Liv. I. 16) was by no means generally accepted at this time.

14. **nefas** (sc. *est*) **videre**: cf. *scire nefas,* I. 11. 1; the act of desecration is a sin so abominable that one would turn away or cover his eyes to avoid the pollution of even beholding it. For the omission of *est,* cf. *C.* I. 11. 1, 37. 5, III. 24. 24; Verg. *A.* VIII. 173 *quae differre nefas.* — **insolens**: cf. *C.* I. 16. 21.

15. **forte**: here equivalent to *forsitan,* the clause being virtually a condition, *si forte quaeritis,* etc.

Forte quid expediat communiter aut melior pars
    malis carere quaeritis laboribus.
Nulla sit hac potior sententia: Phocaeorum
    velut profugit exsecrata civitas
agros atque laris patrios habitandaque fana
    apris reliquit et rapacibus lupis,
ire pedes quocumque ferent, quocumque per undas
    Notus vocabit aut protervus Africus.
Sic placet, an melius quis habet suadere? Secunda
    ratem occupare quid moramur alite?

— **quid expediat,** *what it is best to do.* — **communiter**: equivalent to *omnes.* — **pars** (sc. *vestrum*): in apposition with the subject of **quaeritis**; cf. *aetas*, vs. 9 n.

16. **carere,** *to be rid of.* Best taken as infinitive of purpose (Intr. 93); cf. Verg. *E.* 4. 54 *quantum sat erit tua dicere facta;* Lucr. III. 1030 *iter dedit legionibus ire per altum.* If we read *quod expediat* (see Crit. App.), **carere** is complementary infinitive with **quaeritis**; Intr. 94 *c.*

17. **sit,** . . . *perhaps . . . is;* potential subjunctive. — **sententia**: the technical term for a proposition brought forward in a deliberative body. The poet in fancy addresses his countrymen of kindred spirit (**melior pars**) sitting in council. The actual proposition begins with **ire,** 21, which is in apposition with **hac** (sc. *sententia*). — **Phocaeorum**: the inhabitants of Phocaea, a powerful Athenian colony in Ionia, itself the mother city of Massilia and other important colonies in the West. According to Herodotus (I. 164 *sq.*), they left their city in a body to escape subjection to the Persians, and sailed away to Aleria, in Corsica. A part of them, however, subsequently returned. For the metre, see Intr. 132.

18. **velut**: Intr. 114. — **profūgit**: here transitive; a poetical usage in Horace's time. — **exsecrata**: used absolutely, — having sworn (with imprecations) *sc.* that they would not return; *under a curse.* 'They pronounced powerful curses on any of their number who should desert the enterprise; and, in addition to this, they dropped into the sea a lump of iron, and swore never to return to Phocaea till this iron should reappear' (Herod. *l.l.*).

19. **patrios**: suggesting, like **fana**, the most hallowed associations. — **habitanda,** etc.: a typical picture of utter desolation; cf. vs. 10 and *C.* III. 3. 40.

21. **pedes,** etc.: *i.e.* by land, in contrast with **per undas**; cf. *C.* III. 11, 49 n.

22. **vocabit,** *shall invite us.* Cf. Cat. 4. 19 *laeva sive dextera | vocaret aura.* — **protervus**: cf. *C.* I. 26. 2, and *praecipitem Africum,* I. 3. 12 n.

23. **sic placet,** *is such your pleasure?* keeping up the figure of a deliberative assembly. — **suadere**: Intr. 94 *n.* — **secunda alite**: cf. 10. 1 n.

Sed iuremus in haec : 'Simul imis saxa renarint
vadis levata, ne redire sit nefas ;
neu conversa domum pigeat dare lintea quando
Padus Matina laverit cacumina,
in mare seu celsus procurrerit Appenninus,
novaque monstra iunxerit libidine
mirus amor, iuvet ut tigris subsidere cervis
adulteretur et columba miluo,
credula nec ravos timeant armenta leones,
ametque salsa levis hircus aequora.'
Haec et quae poterunt reditus abscindere dulcis
eamus omnis exsecrata civitas,
aut pars indocili melior grege ; mollis et exspes
inominata perprimat cubilia.

25. **in haec** (sc. *verba*): cf. 15. 4 n. — **saxa**: for the mass of iron in the oath of the Phocaeans, which Horace evidently had in mind, as **renarint** shows. Setting out with this, the poet proposes a series of impossible contingencies to bind them more firmly to their hard resolve. For other examples of the use of this favorite figure (σχῆμα ἀδυνάτου), cf. *C.* I. 29. 10 *sqq.*, 33. 7 *sq.*; *Il.* I. 234 *sqq.*; Verg. *E.* 1. 59 *sqq.*, 8. 27 *sqq.*

26. **vadis**: Intr. 70.

28. **Matina**: see *C.* I. 28. 3 n.

29. **procurrerit**: cf. Ov. *F.* IV. 419 *terra tribus scopulis vastum procurrit in aequor.* The Apennines are an interior range. The figure is the converse of the preceding. For the metre, see Intr. 132.

30. **monstra**, *unnatural creatures;* proleptic: the **mirus amor** turns them into **monstra**.

31. **tigris**, etc.: the picture of these monstrous unions is heightened by the reversal of the natures of the animals: the tiger becomes submissive, the deer bold. The dove, moreover, was a type of conjugal fidelity; cf. Prop. III. 7. 27 *exemplo iunctae tibi sint in amore columbae;* Plin. *N. H.* X. 104.

32. **et**: Intr. 114. — **miluo**: dative. Intr. 56.

33. **credula**, *confiding, trustful;* proleptic. — **ravos**: cf. III. 27. 3.

34. **lēvis**: like a sea animal; proleptic.

35. **haec**: cognate object of **exsecrata**. — **quae**, *whatever else;* cf. *quisquis*, *C.* II. 1. 25 n; I. 19. 12. — **reditus**: see *C.* III. 5. 52 n; Intr. 128.

36. **exsecrata civitas**: repeated from 18. For the construction of **civitas**, cf. *aetas*, 9 n.

37. **pars melior**: cf. vs. 15. — **indocili grege**: the kind of people who are too dull or too deep in their ruts to take new ideas; with too little energy (**mollis**) for action and enterprise, and too little spirit to hope (**exspes**).

38. **inominata**, *ill-starred;* found here only.

Vos, quibus est virtus, muliebrem tollite luctum,
  Etrusca praeter et volate litora.
Nos manet Oceanus circumvagus ; arva beata
  petamus, arva divites et insulas,
reddit ubi Cererem tellus inarata quotannis
  et imputata floret usque vinea,
germinat et numquam fallentis termes olivae
  suamque pulla ficus ornat arborem,

39. **muliebrem** : in contrast (Intr. 116 *a*) with **virtus,** for which see 15. 11 n. — **tollite**: cf. *C.* I. 27. 2 n.

40. **Etrusca,** etc.: the usual route of voyagers to the West. — **praeter**: Intr. 115 *b*. — **et**: Intr. 114.

41. **nos**: the change of person (cf. *vos*, 39) implies that his appeal has been successful ; they are now with him, and he turns from exhortation to consolation, pointing to the greater recompense in store for those who make the sacrifice he demands. — **circumvagus**: a word probably of Horace's own coining, expressing the ever-changing movements of the sea, and a happy variation on the Homeric ἀψόρροος, which Ovid (*M.* I. 30) more literally renders *circumfluus*, an epithet properly applicable to a river, which the ocean was in Homeric geography (cf. *Il.* XX. 7). That the ocean, however, surrounded the habitable lands was also taught by Roman geographers; see Plin. *N. H.* II. 166 *sq*.

42. **arva** : repeated to form the connection with **divites insulas,** etc.; cf. *aere*, 65; *amore* 11. 3; Intr. 116 *h*. The epithet **beata** is not repeated, and is unnecessary in such close connection with **divites insulas,** with which **arva** is joined in hendiadys. — **et**: Intr. 114. — **insulas**: the 'Isles of the Blest' (μακάρων νῆσοι) of Hesiod (*Op.* 170 *sqq*.), — the Elysian plain of Homer (*Odys.* IV. 563 *sqq*.) — were the mythical abode, situated in the ocean towards the setting sun, of departed heroes. Later mythology transferred Elysium to the underworld, while the 'Insulae Fortunatae' came to be recognized in ancient geography and were placed off the coast of Africa, on the basis of reports of traders, who claimed to have seen islands in those seas (probably the Madeiras); see Plin. *N.H.* IV. 119, VI. 202. It is said that Sertorius at one time thought of abandoning the contest with the aristocracy and setting sail with his followers in search of the 'Happy Isles' (Plutarch, *Sert.* 8) ; and it is not unlikely that the same scheme actually suggested itself to Horace and his friends after Philippi.

43. **Cererem** : Intr. 130.

45. **numquam fallentis** : cf. *fundus mendax*, *C.* III. 1. 30. It implies exemption from care, as **inarata** and **imputata,** above, from toil.

46. **suam**: emphatic (Intr. 116 *b*); the finer varieties of the fig, as of the pear (cf. 2. 19 n) can be propagated only by grafting. Cf. Verg. *G.* II. 81 *sq.* (of the grafted tree)

mella cava manant ex ilice, montibus altis
levis crepante lympha desilit pede.
Illic iniussae veniunt ad mulctra capellae,
refertque tenta grex amicus ubera,
nec vespertinus circum gemit ursus ovile,
neque intumescit alta viperis humus ;
61 nulla nocent pecori contagia, nullius astri
gregem aestuosa torret impotentia.
53 Pluraque felices mirabimur, ut neque largis
aquosus Eurus arva radat imbribus,

*exsilit ad caelum ramis felicibus arbos | miraturque novas frondes et non sua poma.* — **pulla** : *i.e.* fully ripe.

47. **mella**, etc.: for the skilful construction of this and the next verse see Intr. 131. — **montibus**: Intr. 70.

48. **levis**, etc.: the beauty of this verse, which has caught up some of the music of the brook itself, was remarked by Porphyrio. It is not, however, a merely ornamental addition to the description. A natural supply of water for man and beast in contrast with a parched country like Apulia, or with the artificial supply of the city, is a necessary part of the picture; cf. *Ep.* I. 10. 20 *sq.* — **pede**: a bold extension of the metaphor in **desilit**. Cf. Lucr. V. 272 *qua via secta semel liquido pede detulit undas.*

49. **illic**, etc.: the flocks and herds need no keeper to drive them or to guard them from danger. Cf. *C.* I. 17. 5 *sqq.*

50. **refert**, *brings home.* — **tenta** = *distenta*, 2. 46; Intr. 129. — **amicus**: corresponding to **iniussae**, 49.

51. **vespertinus**: with adverbial force; cf. *Ep.* I. 6. 20 *navus mane forum, vespertinus pete tectum.* — **circum gemit**: Intr. 115 *c.*

52. **intumescit**: the action of the vipers is attributed to the ground, as where we say 'the place was swarming with ants' or the like. — **alta**: proleptic, with **intumescit**.

61, 62. This couplet is found in all the MSS. after vs. 60, where it is obviously out of place and interrupts the course of thought, which (from vs. 57 to the close of the poem) is of the immunity of the Happy Isles from corrupting human and moral influences. It must have stood originally somewhere before vs. 57, and has been misplaced in copying (see Crit. App.).

61. **nullius**: Intr. 116 *b.* — **astri**: such as those mentioned, *C.* III. 29. 17 *sqq.*

62. **aestuosa impotentia**, *furious heat*, causing pestilence. Cf. Virg. *G.* III. 478 *sqq.* For **impotentia**, cf. *impotens*, *C.* I. 37. 10 n, III. 30. 3; and for this application of it, III. 29. 18 *sq.*

53. **ut**, *how*, after **mirabimur**, as in *C.* III. 4. 17 after *mirum foret.* — **neque**, etc.: the climate is temperate, free from extremes of storm and drouth.

54. **aquosus**: cf. *udo Noto*, 10.

pinguia nec siccis urantur semina glaebis,
utrumque rege temperante caelitum.
Non huc Argoo contendit remige pinus,
neque impudica Colchis intulit pedem;
non huc Sidonii torserunt cornua nautae,
laboriosa nec cohors Ulixei:
Iuppiter illa piae secrevit litora genti,
ut inquinavit aere tempus aureum;
aere, dehinc ferro duravit saecula, quorum
piis secunda vate me datur fuga.

19 n, *pluvias Hyadas*, Verg. *A*. III. 516; Intr. 125. — **Eurus**: cf. *C*. III. 17. 11. — **radat**: *i.e.* floods them and washes away the crops.

55. **siccis**: proleptic. — **glaebis**: Intr. 69.

56. **utrumque**: *i.e.* both excess of rain and drouth. — **rege**: Jupiter; see *C*. I. 1. 25 n.

57. **non huc**, etc.: no man, not even the boldest navigator, has ever trodden the shores of this paradise; it has remained uncontaminated by the degeneracy which (largely through the corrupting influence of commerce) has spread over the rest of the world, — a bit of the Golden Age, set apart by Jove for his elect. — **Argoo**: cf. *Etrusca*, 4, and see 10. 12 n. — **remige**: used collectively (Intr. 127) and impersonally, like a body of troops, in the instrumental ablative (Madv. 254 Obs. 3). — **pinus**: for the ship; cf. *C*. I. 14. 11 *Pontica pinus;* Cat. 64. 1 *Peliaco quondam prognatae vertice pinus | dicuntur liquidas Neptuni nasse per undas.*

58. **Colchis**: Medea.

59. **Sidonii**: for the Phoenician traders in general. Intr. 117 *b*. — **torserunt cornua**: *i.e.* directed their course; a paraphrase for the commonplace *vela dare*. The action expressed is that of swinging the yards into position.

60. **laboriosa**: the epithet belonging properly to Ulysses (πολύτλας, πολυτλήμων), is here transferred to his men. Cf. 17. 16, and see Intr. 124.

63. **piae genti**, *for a righteous people*, meaning the nation which the poet and his companions should found; cf. *piis*, 66.

64. **inquinavit**, *alloyed*.

65. **aere**: with **duravit**; for the anaphora, cf. *arva* 42 n. — **quorum**, *from which;* objective genitive. The present is then with Horace, as with Hesiod, the age of iron. In Hesiod, however (*Op*. 109 *sqq*.), the iron age is the fifth, there being a silver age between the gold and the bronze, and a fourth, — the age of the heroes, not named after any metal, — preceding that of iron. The legend appears in various forms in other poets; see Mayor on Juv. 13. 30.

66. **vate me**, *according to my prophecy*.

## XVII.

Iam iam efficaci do manus scientiae,
supplex et oro regna per Proserpinae,
per et Dianae non movenda numina,
per atque libros carminum valentium
refixa caelo devocare sidera,
Canidia, parce vocibus tandem sacris
citumque retro solve, solve turbinem.

XVII. Horace's muse fairly runs riot in this burlesque, in which he makes his final attack on Canidia. He represents himself as one of her victims, reduced to submission at last by her powerful art; and in his humble recantation and piteous appeal for mercy, as well as in Canidia's stern reply, he manages to reiterate, with telling irony, all his old charges against her. Our poet tempted fate in thus giving loose rein to his fancy; for this poem, sifted through learned brains, has come out a confession that he had been a veritable lover of the witch. See intr. note to Epode 5. — Metre, 158.

1. **iam iam**: Intr. 116 *d*. — **do manus**, *surrender*, as a vanquished soldier who throws down his arms and holds out his hands to be bound.

2. **et, et, atque**: Intr. 114. — **per**: Intr. 115 *a*.

3. **Dianae**: see 5. 51 n. She is here more distinctly identified with Hecate; cf. *S.* I. 8. 33. — **non movenda**: equivalent, according to Porphyrio, who is followed by modern editors, to *non lacessenda*, 'not to be provoked' (cf. III. 20. 1); but there is reason to think that Horace uses the phrase in the sense of *inexorable*, a standing attribute of the powers of the lower world; cf. *C.* II. 3. 24, 14. 6, 18. 34 *sqq.*, etc. This use of *moveo* is common in such connection; cf. vs. 8, *C.* I. 21. 16, Verg. *G.* IV. 505 *quo fletu manis, quae numina voce moveret?* — **numina**: Intr. 128.

4. **libros**: conjuring books, containing instructions and magic formulas. — **carminum**: cf. 5. 72 n.

5. **refixa**: proleptic, — *dislodge and*. Cf. Verg. *A.* V. 527 *caelo ceu saepe refixa | transcurrunt crinemque volantia sidera ducunt.* — **devocare**: Intr. 94 *n*.

6. **parce**: cf. III. 14. 12 n. — **vocibus sacris**: a respectful expression, in accordance with the claims of sorcery, for the gibberish that accompanied the whirling of the *turbo*; see Lucian (quoted below).

7. **citum**: best taken as a participle (proleptic) with **retro**, *whirl backward and untwist*; cf. 9. 20. — **solve, solve** (Intr. 116 *d*): in reference to the binding constraint which the whirling of the *turbo* was supposed to exert on the heart of the person sought to be influenced. Cf. Prop. IV. 6. 26 *staminea rhombi ducitur ille rota*; Ov. *Am.* I. 8. 7. — **turbinem**: the Latin name for the magic rhomb (ῥόμβος), which was not, it seems, a real wheel

Movit nepotem Telephus Nereium,
in quem superbus ordinarat agmina
Mysorum et in quem tela acuta torserat.
Luxere matres Iliae addictum feris
alitibus atque canibus homicidam Hectorem,
postquam relictis moenibus rex procidit
heu pervicacis ad pedes Achillei.
Saetosa duris exuere pellibus
laboriosi remiges Ulixei

but a small lozenge-shaped board (hence the name) attached by one end to a cord and whirled round to make a loud buzzing sound. It is so defined by Hesychius: *ξυλήριον, οὗ ἐξῆπται σχοινίον, καὶ ἐν ταῖς τελεταῖς δινεῖται ἵνα ῥοιζῇ.* The use of it to charm back a lover is described by Lucian, *Dial. Meretr.* 4. 5. *εἶτα (ἡ γραῦς) ἐκ τοῦ κόλπου προκομίσασα ῥόμβον ἐπιστρέφει, ἐπῳδήν τινα λέγουσα ἐπιτρόχῳ τῇ γλώττῃ, βαρβαρικὰ καὶ φρικώδη ὀνόματα.* It is used in mystic rites among uncivilized peoples at the present day, and in Greece was no doubt a survival from ancestral barbarism. See Andrew Lang's *Custom and Myth*, pp. 29 *sqq.*

8. **nepotem**: Achilles, whose mother Thetis was the daughter of Nereus. — **Telephus**: king of Mysia and son-in-law of Priam. He resisted the Greeks in their invasion of the Troad, and was wounded by Achilles. Having been told by an oracle that he could be healed only by the rust of the spear which had made the wound, he was obliged to throw himself on the compassion of his enemy.

11. **luxere**, etc.: *i.e.* Achilles was moved by pity to grant even his bitterest enemy honorable burial. *Lugere* is the term for formal mourning; cf. Liv. II. 7. 4 *matronae annum ut parentem eum luxerunt.* The reference is to the affecting scene in the *Iliad*, XXIV. 719 *sqq.*, on Priam's return from the Greek camp with Hector's body. — **Iliae**: Intr. 65. — **addictum**, etc.: by Achilles, as a consolation to Patroclus; cf. *Il.* XXIII. 179 *χαῖρέ μοι, ὦ Πάτροκλε, καὶ εἰν Ἀΐδαο δόμοισιν, . . . Ἕκτορα δ' οὔ τι | δώσω Πριαμίδην πυρὶ δαπτέμεν, ἀλλὰ κύνεσσιν.*

12. **homicidam**: cf. *Ἕκτορος ἀνδροφόνοιο*, *Il.* XXIV. 724, and Andromache's proud words, *ib.* 737 *sqq.*

14. **heu**: the pathos lies in the humiliation of the powerful monarch, who placed himself at the mercy of his enemy (**relictis moenibus**; cf. *Ilio relicto, C.* I. 10. 14 n) and threw himself at his feet. — **pervicacis**: implying that the appeal might well have seemed hopeless.—**Achillei**: see *C.* I. 6. 7 n.

15. **saetosa**: when they were changed into swine. The story is told *Odys.* X. 135 *sqq.* — **pellibus**: ablative; see Gr. 225 *d.*

16. **laboriosi**, *much afflicted;* better taken here (in spite of 16. 60) with **Vlixei**, being the Latin equivalent of the Homeric *πολύτλας, πολυτλήμων.*

volente Circa membra ; tunc mens et sonus
relapsus atque notus in voltus honor.
Dedi satis superque poenarum tibi,
amata nautis multum et institoribus.
Fugit iuventas et verecundus color,
reliquit ossa pelle amicta lurida,
tuis capillus albus est odoribus ;
nullum a labore me reclinat otium,
urget diem nox et dies noctem, neque est
levare tenta spiritu praecordia.
Ergo negatum vincor ut credam miser,
Sabella pectus increpare carmina
caputque Marsa dissilire nenia.
Quid amplius vis ? O mare et terra, ardeo

17. **sonus** : *i.e.* voice.

18. **honor,** *grace,* in contrast with the brutish form from which they emerged ; cf. 11. 6, *C.* II. 11. 9.

20. **amata,** etc. : a mock compliment, in which the poet's irony for the first time breaks through its disguise. — **multum** : Intr. 49. — **institoribus**: see *C.* III. 6. 30 n.

21. **fūgit** : see Intr. 77 ; both **iuventas** and **color** here combine to form one idea, — the sensitive complexion of healthy youth.

22. **reliquit,** *has left behind.* — **ossa,** etc. : cf. our 'nothing but skin and bones,' and Plaut. *Capt.* 135 *ossa atque pellis sum miser macritudine.*

23. **albus,** *bleached.*—**odoribus:** *i.e.* magic ointments ; cf. 5. 59.

24. **a labore reclinat** : cf. the opposite expression, *in aliquid incumbere.* — **labore,** *distress* — **otium** : cf. *C.* II. 16. 1 n.

25. **urget,** etc. : cf. *truditur dies die, C.* II. 18. 15. — **neque,** *but . . . not.* — **est levare** : Intr. 94 *n.*

26. **tenta spiritu,** *heaving.* — **praecordia** : here used for the lungs ; translate *breast.*

27. **negatum** (sc. *a me*): Intr. 103. The clauses in the next two verses are in apposition with it.

28. **Sabella** : cf. *S.* I. 9. 29 *sqq.* The Sabines, like the Marsi and Paeligni (vs. 60), were noted for their practice of magic. — **pectus:** cf. *C.* I. 3. 10 n. — **increpare,** *do assail.*

29. **Marsa** : cf. 5. 76 n. — **dissilire,** *splits* (with pain). This effect was believed to be produced, in a literal sense, on snakes ; cf. Verg. *E.* 8. 71, Lucil. 512 *Marsus colubras disrumpit cantu.*—**nenia:** *i.e.* an incantation. The name suggests a slow crooning chant ; cf. *C.* III. 28. 16 n.

30. **o mare et terra**: a common exclamation in every-day life, either in distress or in joy. Cf. Ter. *Ad.* 790 *o caélum, o terra, o mária Neptuni!* Plaut. *Trin.* 1070 *mare terra caélum, di vostrám fidem!*

quantum neque atro delibutus Hercules
Nessi cruore nec Sicana fervida
virens in Aetna flamma: tu, donec cinis
iniuriosis aridus ventis ferar,
cales venenis officina Colchicis.
Quae finis aut quod me manet stipendium?
Effare! Iussas cum fide poenas luam,
paratus expiare seu poposceris
centum iuvencis, sive mendaci lyra
voles, sonare 'Tu pudica, tu proba
perambulabis astra sidus aureum.'
Infamis Helenae Castor offensus vicem
fraterque magni Castoris, victi prece

31. **atro**: cf. *C.* I. 37. 27 n.

32. **Nessi cruore**: see 3. 17 n. —**Sicana**: better taken with **flamma**; fervidā, with **Aetnā**.

33. **virens**, *that burns undimmed.* — **cinis**, *cinder.*

34. **iniuriosis**, *ruthless;* cf. *C.* I. 35. 13 n. — **ventis**: dative, the winds being personified; Intr. 55.

35. **cales**, *are hot;* cf. *calet uno scribendi studio*, *Ep.* II. 1. 108. Here a humorous turn is given to the figure by the extravagance of **officina**, *a very laboratory*. Cf. Plaut. *Truc.* 586 *tun . . . quae sis stabulum flagiti?* — **Colchicis**: see *C.* II. 13. 8 n.

36. **quae finis**: see *C.* II. 18. 30 n. — **me manet**: *i.e.* will be exacted of me, as your vanquished enemy.

37. **poenas luam**, *will do penance.*

38. **seu**, etc.: for the construction, cf. I. 4. 12 n.

39. **centum iuvencis**: a hecatomb. — **mendaci**: another touch of irony, lurking in the intentional ambiguity of the epithet, which can be applied to what follows, as well as to what he has previously said of her in his verse.

40. **sonare**: cf. *C.* II. 13. 26 n. —**tu pudica**, etc.: cf. Cat. 42. 24.

41. **perambulabis**, *you will stroll among;* a word in humorous contrast with the dignity of the splendid destiny promised; cf. *C.* IV. 5. 17. — **aureum**: cf. Verg. *A.* II. 488 *aurea sidera.*

42. **infamis**, etc.: the poet appeals once more to precedent, the famous case of Stesichorus (see *C.* IV. 9. 8 n), who, having become suddenly blind, was made aware that it was a penalty, inflicted (according to the version which Horace follows) by Castor and Pollux, for the aspersions (in his Ἰλίου πέρσις) on the character of their sister Helen; whereupon he promptly recanted (*Fr.* 44): Οὐκ ἔστ' ἔτυμος λόγος οὗτος· | οὐδ' ἔβας ἐν νηυσὶν ἐυσσέλμοις, | οὐδ' ἵκεο πέργαμα Τροίας· and his sight was restored. — **Helenae vicem**: cf. Plaut. *Most.* 1145 *ut tú meam timeás vicem;* Liv. XXXIV. 32. 6 *ne nostram vicem irascaris.*

adempta vati reddidere lumina:
et tu (potes nam) solve me dementia,
o nec paternis obsoleta sordibus,
nec in sepulcris pauperum prudens anus
novendialis dissipare pulveres!
Tibi hospitale pectus et purae manus,
tuusque venter Pactumeius, et tuo
cruore rubros obstetrix pannos lavit,
utcumque fortis exsilis puerpera.
Quid obseratis auribus fundis preces?
Non saxa nudis surdiora navitis
Neptunus alto tundit hibernus salo.
Inultus ut tu riseris Cotyttia

44. **vati**: Intr. 76.

45. **potes nam**: a form of appeal, at once flattering and persuasive, often inserted in prayers; cf. *C.* III. 11. 1 *sq.*, *S.* II. 3. 283, 284, *Odys.* V. 25. For the position of **nam**, see Intr. 114.

46. **o nec**, etc.: in imitation of Stesichorus he boldly proclaims false what all the world knows to be true, and true what all know to be false. — **paternis**, etc.: *i.e.* a low-born creature, brought up in squalid poverty. Cf. *C.* II. 10. 6 n.

47. **sepulcris pauperum**: *e.g.* on the Esquiline, where she is represented as performing her magic rites in *S.* I. 8. The bodies of the poor were often buried (not burnt), and would usually be unprotected; cf. *S.* I. 8. 8 *sq.*

48. **novendialis**: *i.e.* just buried, the last rites at the tomb being completed on the ninth day after death. — **dissipare**: Intr. 101 *c.* — **pulveres**: Intr. 128.

49. **hospitale**, etc.: probably referring to the story told in Epode 5.

50. **tuus . . . tuo**: Intr. 116 *g.* — **venter**, *own child;* cf. Liv. I. 34. 3. — **Pactumeius**: apparently a child Canidia tried to palm off on her lover as her own.

51. **lăvit**: see *C.* II. 3. 18 n.

52. **fortis exsilis**: another mock compliment, implying that the whole performance was a sham. Cf. 5. 5 *sq.*

53–81. Canidia's reply.

54. **non saxa**, etc.: *i.e.* they are not more deaf, when Neptune, etc. — **nudis**: *i.e.* stripped of all they possessed, implying that they have been shipwrecked. — **surdiora**: cf. *C.* III. 7. 21.

55. **Neptunus**: cf. *Ep.* I. 11. 10, where, as here, the personality of the god is not entirely merged in his element (Intr. 130), as it is *e.g.* in 7. 3. — **hibernus**: cf. 2. 29; Stat. *Theb.* III. 26 *hiberni Iovis.*

56. **inultus ut tu**, etc., *What, let you go unwhipped for having divulged and ridiculed;* for the construction see Lane's Gr. 1566, 1568. — **Cotyttia**: properly the grossly sensual orgies of the Thracian

volgata, sacrum liberi Cupidinis,
et Esquilini pontifex venefici
impune ut urbem nomine impleris meo?
Quid proderit ditasse Paelignas anus
velociusve miscuisse toxicum?
Sed tardiora fata te votis manent:
ingrata misero vita ducenda est in hoc,
novis ut usque suppetas doloribus.
Optat quietem Pelopis infidi pater,
egens benignae Tantalus semper dapis,
optat Prometheus obligatus aliti,

goddess Cotytto, which had been introduced into Athens and so became known at Rome, though they had not become prevalent there at this time. Canidia is represented as pursuing her questionable practices under this high-sounding but unsavory name. Where Horace had exposed these orgies does not appear; there can be no allusion to any of his extant poems.

58. **Esquilini**: *i.e.* such as is practiced there; cf. *venenis Colchicis*, 35. — **pontifex**: the meaning is obscure; either she taunts him with being an adept in sorcery himself, or with assuming authority over a matter in which he had no right to meddle; cf. *curiosus*, 77. The latter is substantially the explanation of Porphyrio.

59. **ut urbem**, etc.: referring to *S.* I. 8.

60. **quid proderit**, etc.: *i.e.* what was the use of my learning sorcery, at great expense, and surpassing my teachers in skill, if I fail to apply it at a time like this, when you have so wronged and insulted me? — **Paelignas**: see vs. 28 n.

61. **velocius**: *i.e.* in its effects. We speak of a 'slow poison,' 'a rapid fever,' 'galloping consumption.'

62. **sed tardiora**, etc., *but* (no *velox toxicum* is in store for you) *a more lingering*, etc. — **fata**: cf. *C.* III. 11. 28; Intr. 128. — **votis** (sc. *tuis*): cf. 70 *sqq.*; Intr. 75.

63. **in hoc** (acc.): directing attention emphatically to her savage purpose in prolonging his life; cf. *ad hoc*, *S.* II. 1. 36.

64. **novis**: *i.e.* new kinds of. Cf. *C.* II. 15. 20. — **ut usque suppetas**, *that you may be always on hand as a subject for*.

65. **optat quietem**: cf. *otium rogat*, *C.* II. 16. 1, and note the different form of anaphora (Intr. 116 *g*) in the two places. — **infidi**: as having cheated his charioteer, Myrtilus, by whose aid he had won Hippodamia, out of his promised reward, and thrown him into the sea; cf. *periuri Pelopis*, Cat. 64. 346. — **pater**: see *C.* I. 28. 7 n.

66. **benignae**, *generous;* spread in profusion before him. Cf. *benignius C.* I. 9. 6 n. — **dapis**: Intr. 66 *c*.

67. **obligatus**: in a literal sense,

optat supremo conlocare Sisyphus
in monte saxum : sed vetant leges Iovis.
Voles modo altis desilire turribus,
modo ense pectus Norico recludere,
frustraque vincla gutturi nectes tuo
fastidiosa tristis aegrimonia.
Vectabor umeris tunc ego inimicis eques,
meaeque terra cedet insolentiae.
An quae movere cereas imagines,
ut ipse nosti curiosus, et polo
deripere lunam vocibus possim meis,
possim crematos excitare mortuos
desiderique temperare pocula,
plorem artis in te nil agentis exitus?

bound upon (so as to be exposed to).

68. **supremo**: poetical for *summo*. Cf. *clamore supremos | implerunt montis*, Verg. *G.* IV. 460. — **Sisyphus**: see *C.* II. 14. 20 n.

70. **turribus**: Intr. 70.

71. **ense Norico**: cf. *C.* I. 16. 9 n. — **pectus recludere**: cf. Verg. *A.* X. 601 *pectus mucrone recludit;* Juv. 4. 110 *iugulos aperire*.

72. **vincla**, *a rope*. Intr. 128, 183. — **gutturi nectes**: cf. *C.* I. 29. 5; *Ep.* I. 19. 31 *nec sponsae laqueum nectit*.

73. **fastidiosa**: in an active sense, as in *C.* III. 29. 9.

74. **vectabor**, etc.: she will finally compel him to acknowledge her mastery in the most humiliating manner. Cf. the scene in Plaut. *Asin.* 698 *sqq.* — **inimicis**, *of my foe*, *i.e.* the poet; Intr. 124.

75. **meae insolentiae**: in prose, *mihi insolenti;* cf. *tuae superbiae*, *C.* IV. 10. 2 n. — **cedet**: *i.e.* will give way under my feet (as I rise into the air).

76. **an**, etc.: cf. 6. 15 *sq.* — **movere**, *make move* (as if they were alive). — **cereas imagines**: cf. *S.* I. 8. 30 *sqq.*, Verg. *E.* 8. 80 *sq.*

77. **ut ipse**, etc.: alluding to his account in *S.* I. 8. In this charge of eavesdropping he puts into her own mouth an unconscious indirect confession of the accuracy of his report.

78. **deripere lunam**: cf. vs. 5 and 5. 46 n. — **vocibus**: cf. vs. 6 n.

79. **possim**: Intr. 116 *h.* — **excitare** (*to call up*) **mortuos**: cf. *S.* I. 8. 29, 41.

80. **desideri pocula**: cf. *amoris poculum*, 5. 38, and the description of one there given. — **temperare**, *brew;* cf. *C.* I. 20. 11 n.

81. **te**: better taken as ablative, *in your case*, in contrast with all others. — **nil agentis**: proleptic: (*proving*) *ineffective*. — **exitus**: here (with **plorem**) virtually equivalent to 'failure.'

# CRITICAL APPENDIX.

FOR a detailed account of the manuscripts, and a copious *apparatus criticus* of the Odes and Epodes, the student is referred to the first volume (by Otto Keller; 2d ed., 1899) of the larger edition of Keller and Holder, with Keller's *Epilegomena*. For the convenience of those to whom these works are not readily accessible a selection of the more important and interesting variants from the text of this edition is here given. Sources are indicated as follows:

M° denotes the unanimous testimony of the MSS.
M, clear preponderance of manuscript testimony.
M, good manuscript support.
m, slight " "
B, the four Blandinian MSS.
Bv, the *Blandinius vetustissimus*.
(Where B or Bv is added, M°, M, etc. refer to *existing* manuscripts only.)

In addition to the MS. tradition of the poems themselves, reference is sometimes made to evidence found in the *commentary* of Porphyrio (Porph.), or in other Latin grammarians and commentators (gr.).

In citing these various authorities discrepancies of spelling are disregarded.

Conjectures are usually credited to their authors.

## THE ODES.

### BOOK I.

I. 35 **inseris** M *inseres* M

II. 39 **Marsi** Tanaquil Faber *Mauri* M°

III. 19 **turbidum** M B *turgidum* M 37 **ardui** M B *arduum* M

IV. 8 **visit** M *urit* M.

VI. 2 **alite** M° *aliti* Passerat 7 **duplicis** M *duplices* M B gr.

VII. 2 **Epheson** M gr. *Ephesum* M 5 **urbem** M *arcis* m 9 **dicet** M *dicit* M 17 **perpetuos** M *perpetuo* M

VIII. 2 **properes** M *properas* m gr. 6, 7 **equitat, temperat** m *equitet, temperet* M

XII. 2 **sumis** M *sumes* M B^v 3 **recinet** (or *retinet*) M B^v *recinit* M 31 **quod** M *quia* M B 41 **intonsis** Quint. IX. 3. 18 *incomptis* M° 57 **latum** M *laetum* M

XIII. 2 **cerea** M° *lactea* gr. 6 **manet** M *manent* M

XV. 20 **crinis** M B^v *cultus* M 22 **gentis** M *genti* M B^v 24 **te** M B^v *et* M 36 **Iliacas** M° *Pergameas* edition of 1500 *Dardanias, barbaricas* (see note)

XVI. 8 **sic** M *si* m Bentley

XVII. 9 **haediliae** M *haedilia* M *haeduleae* Bentley (but see Bücheler's explanation in note) 14 **hic** m *hinc* M

XVIII. 5 **crepat** M B^v *increpat* M

XIX. 2 **iubet** M *iubent* M **Semelae** M *Semeles* m 12 **attinent** M *attinet* m

XX. 5 **care** M *clare* m 10 **tu** M° *tum* Porph. on *S.* II. 2. 48 **bibes** M *bibis* m

XXI. 5 **coma** M *comam* M B

XXII. 11 **expeditis** M B *expeditus* m

XXIII. 1 **vitas** m *vitat* M gr. **inuleo** M B *hin(n)uleo* m 5 **vepris . . . ad ventum** Bentley et al. *veris adventus* M°

XXV. 20 **Euro** Ald. ed. of 1501 *Hebro* M°

XXVI. 9 **Pimplea** Lambinus et al. *Piplea* M° *Pimplei* N. Heinsius.

XXVIII. 3 **litus** M *latum* M 15 **nox** M *mors* M 31 **fors et** (or *forset*) M B *forsit* m *forsan* M

XXXI. 9 **Calena** M° *Calenam* (Porph.?) Bentley 10 **et** M *ut* M

XXXII. 1 **poscimur** M gr. *poscimus* M gr. 15 **mihi cumque** M° *medicumque* Lachmann *metuumque* E. Rosenberg.

XXXV. 17 **saeva** M *serva* M B

## Book II.

II. 5 **vivet** M *vivit* m 7 **aget** M *agit* M Porph.

III. 18 **lavit** M *lavat* M 28 **exsilium** M *exitium* M

V. 13 **currit** M *curret* M

VI. 18 **amicus** M° *amictus* N. Heinsius 19 **fertili** M *fertilis* m gr.

X. 18 **cithara** M *citharae* M

XI. 23 **in comptum** M *incomptum* M 24 **comam** M *comas* M *comae* M (*in comptum . . . comae* M *in comptum . . . comas* m *incomptum . . . comam* M *incomptum . . . comas* M)

XII. 25 **cum** M *dum* M 28 **occupet** M *occupat* m

XIII. 16 **timet** M° *timetve* Lachmann 23 **discriptas** M *descriptas* M *discretas* M 38 **laborem** M Porph. *laborum* M B

XVII. 14 **Gyas** Lambinus *gigas* M°

XVIII. 8 **clientae** M *clientiae* M *clientes* M

XX. 3 **terris** M *terra* M 13 **notior** M *ocior* M *tutior* Bentley.

## BOOK III.

I. 39 **triremi et** m *triremi* M

II. 27 **volgarit** M *volgavit* M

III. 12 **bibet** M *bibit* M 34 **discere** M *ducere* M

IV. 9 **Apulo** M° *avio* O. Keller 10 **nutricis** M *altricis* M **limen Apuliae** M Porph. *limina Pulliae* M For *Pulliae* (which Kiessling and Hertz, following a hint in Porphyrio, retain as the name of Horace's nurse) various conjectures have been proposed: *sedulae* (Bentl.), *villulae, pergulae, patriae, Dauniae,* etc. 38 **abdidit** M *addidit* M *reddidit* m 43 **turbam** M *turmam* M 47 **turmas** M B *turbas* M (43, 47 **turbam . . . turmas** M *turbam . . . turbas* M *turmam . . . turbas* M) 69 **Gyas** Lambinus *gigas* M° (cf. II. 17. 14) 78 **reliquit** M *relinquit* M

V. 15 **trahenti** Canter *trahentis* M° 17 **periret** M° *perirent* Glareanus *perires* Lachmann 37 **inscius** M *aptius* m *anxius* Jani 51 **propinquos** M *amicos* M

VI. 10 **non auspicatos** M *inauspicatos* M 22 **artibus** M *artubus* M Porph. 27 **impermissa** M *intermissa* M

VII. 4 **fide** m *fidei* M 15 **Bellerophontae** M *Bellerophonti* m 20 **movet** M *monet* M

VIII. 5 **sermones** M gr. *sermonis* M 27 **cape** M *rape* M

IX. 5 **alia** M *aliam* m 21 **quamquam** M *quamvis* M

X. 6 **satum** M Bv *situm* M 18 **animum** M *animo* M

XI. 52 **scalpe** M B *sculpe* m

XII. 4 **arto** M Bv *alto* M

XIV. 6 **sacris** M *divis* M Porph. 7 **clari** M *cari* M 11 **non** Bentley *iam* M° **male ominatis** M Bv *male nominatis* M *male inominatis* Bentley

XV. 2 **fige** M *pone* M 16 **vetulam** M *vetula* M

XVII. 4 **fastos** M *fastus* M 5 **ducis** M° *ducit* D. Heinsius

XVIII. 12 **pagus** M *pardus* M

XIX. 1 **distet** M *distat* M 27 **Rhode** M *Chloe* M

XX. 3 **paulo** M B *paulum* M 8 **illa** Peerlkamp *illi* M°

XXI. 5 **nomine** M *numine* M 10 **negleget** M *neglegit* M

XXIII. 19 **mollivit** M *mollibit* M

XXIV. 4 **Tyrrhenum** Mº **Apulicum** M *Ponticum* M *Punicum* m *publicum* M Bᵛ (*terrenum . . . publicum* Lachmann) 60 **hospites** M B *hospitem* M

XXV. 6 **consilio** M *concilio* M

XXVII. 5 **rumpat** M *rumpit* M 15 **vetet** M B *vetat* m 48 **monstri** M *tauri* M 55 **defluat** M *defluit* M 71 **reddet** M *reddit* M

XXIX. 2 **verso** M *versum* M 34 **alveo** M *aequore* M

## Book IV.

I. 9 **domum** M *domo* M 18 **largi** M *largis* M 20 **citrea** M Bᵛ *Cypria* M 22, 23 **lyra, Berecyntia, tibia** m Bᵛ *lyrae, Berecyntiae, tibiae* M

II. 2 **Iulle** M *Iule* M (The former is found as *praenomen* of this Antonius CIL. 12010; see Mommsen in *Hermes* XXIV. 155) 7 **fervet** M *fervit* M 33, 41 **concines** Mº *concinet* Lachmann 49 **teque dum procedis** M Bᵛ *tuque* m *procedit* m

IV. 7 **verni** M *vernis* M 17 **Raetis** N. Heinsius, Bentley, m *Raeti* M 18 **Vindelici** M *et Vindelici* m 36 **indecorant** M Porph. *dedecorant* M 65 **merses** M *mersus* M **evenit** M *exiet* m 66 **proruet** M *proruit* m 73 **perficient** M *perficiunt* Bᵛ m

VI. 21 **victus** Mº *flexus* Bᵛ 25 **argutae** M *Argivae* m

VII. 15 **pater** M Bᵛ *pius* M **Tullus dives** M *dives Tullus* M 17 **quis scit** M *qui scit* m *qui scis* m **summae** M *vitae* M Bᵛ

VIII. 1 **commodus** M *commodis* M 12 **muneri** M B *muneris* m 15 **celeres fugae** M *celeris fuga* M

The text of this ode is suspected for several reasons: (1) It is the only ode in which the number of verses is not a multiple of four (see Intr. 157). (2) Verse 17 is open to suspicion, (a) because caesura is neglected; (b) because Carthage was not burned by the Scipio who defeated Hannibal and whose praises were sung by Ennius, but by the younger Africanus (Scipio Aemilianus), many years after Ennius' death. The first of the two objections to vs. 17 is not conclusive; for Horace sometimes neglects caesura, though nowhere else in Asclepiad verse. The historical difficulty is more serious; for although it is possible to understand the words in a sense consistent with the historical fact (see note on vs. 15), their more obvious and natural meaning would expose Horace to the imputation of gross ignorance. There is no sufficient ground for rejecting any other verse, and no just ground for suspicion except in the case of vs. 33, which is a repetition, with only a necessary change in the first word, of III. 25. 20. The attempt has been made, however, to bring the ode into conformity with Meineke's canon in various ways. Vss. 17 and 33 are bracketed by Kiessling; 17 and 28 by Nauck; 15 *non*–19 *rediit*, 28, and 33 by Meineke, etc.

IX. 31 **silebo** M *sileri* M 52 **perire** M BV *peribit* M

X. 5 **Ligurine** m *Ligurinum* M 6 **speculo** M *in speculo* M

XIII. 14 **cari** M *clari* M

XIV. 4 **fastos** M *fastus* M (cf. III. 17. 4) 28 **meditatur** M Porph. gr. *minitatur* M B 35 **Alexandrea** M *Alexandria* m 49 **paventis** M *paventes* M

XV. 15 **ortus** M *ortum* m 18 **exiget** M Porph. *exigit* m *eximet* M

## Carmen Saecvlare.

5 **quo** m *quos* M *quod* M B 26 **dictum est** M *dictum* M 27 **servet** M B *servat* m 46 **senectuti** M *senectutis* M 51 **impetret** M B *imperet* M 57 **Honor** M *Honos* M 65 **aras** M B *arcis* M 68 **prorogat** M *proroget* M 71, 72 **curat, adplicat** M B *curet, adplicet* m

## THE EPODES.

I. 5 **si** M *sit* Aldine ed. of 1478 10 **qua** M *quem* M 15 **labore** Glareanus *laborem* Mo 21 **ut adsit** M Porph. *ut sit* M *uti sit* m 26 **meis** M *mea* m 28 **pascuis** M B *pascua* M 34 **nepos** M *ut nepos* M

II. 18 **agris** M *arvis* M 25 **ripis** M *rivis* M B 27 **frondesque** Markland *fontesque* Mo 65 **positosque** M *postosque* m

IV. 8 **trium** C. Barth *ter* Mo

V. 1 **regit** M B *regis* M 3 **et** M B *aut* M 15 **implicata** M *inligata* M Porph. 18 **cupressos** M *cupressus* M 21 **atque** M *aut* M 28 **currens** Mo *Laurens* N. Heinsius 37 **exsecta** M B *exsucta* m 55 **formidolosis** M B *formidolosae* M **dum** M *cum* M 60 **laborarint** M BV *laborarunt* M 63 **superbam** M B *superba* M 65 **imbutum** M *infectum* M 87 **magnum** Mo Porph. *magica* Bentley *maga non* M. Haupt *maga num . . ., num valent* C. W. Nauck 88 **convertere humanam vicem** Mo *non vertere humanas vices* Bentley *convertere humana vice* Madvig *convertere humana invicem* O. Keller

VI. 2 **adversum** M *adversus* M 3, 4 **vertis, petis** M *verte, pete* M B^v 10 **proiectum** M *porrectum* m (a XV. century MSS. in the Harvard library)

VII. 12 **numquam** Aldine ed. of 1490 *umquam* M° 13 **caecus** M *caecos* m 15 **albus ora pallor** M *ora pallor albus* M

IX. 1 **repostum** M *repositum* M 17 **ad hoc** Bentley *ad hunc* (or *adhunc*) M *adhuc* m *at huc* m *at hinc* Cuningham 25 **Africanum** M *Africano* M *Africani* Madvig

X. 19, 20 **sinus Noto** M *sinu Notus* M B 22 **iuverit** M *iuveris* m

XI. 2 **percussum** M gr. *perculsum* M 9 **languor** M *et languor* m

XIII. 3 **amici** M *amice* Bentley *amico* Kiessling

XV. 15 **offensi** Gogavius, Bentley *offensae* M

XVI. 14 **videre** M *videri* M B 15 **quid** M *quod* m *forte* (*quod expediat!*) Rutgers 33 **ravos** M B *flavos* M *saevos* m 51 **ovile** M *ovili* M B 61, 62 after 60 M°, and by some editors so retained; by others variously placed, after 48, 50, 52, or 56 61 **astri** M *Austri* M 65 **aere** M *aerea* M

XVII. 5 **refixa** M *defixa* M 11 **luxere** M *unxere* M B 17 **Circa** M *Circe* M 18 **relapsus** M *relatus* M 33 **virens** M *urens* m *furens* m 36 **quae** M *qui* m 40 **sonare** M *sonari* m 42 **vicem** m *vice* M 57 **sacrum** M *sacra* M 60 **proderit** M *proderat* M 64 **doloribus** M *laboribus* M 67 **aliti** M B *alite* M 72 **nectes** M *innectes* M 80 **pocula** M *poculum* M 81 **exitus** M *exitum* M

# INDEXES.

---

Note. — References preceded by a section mark (§) are to the Introduction; those beginning with a Roman numeral are to the Odes; those beginning with an Arabic numeral, to the Epodes; "in." refers to the introductory note of the commentary on the poem cited.

---

## I. INDEX TO THE POEMS.

# II. INDEX OF CITATIONS.

# III. GENERAL INDEX.

(The references are mostly to the Introduction and to the Notes, where cross-references may be further consulted.)

# COLLEGE SERIES OF LATIN AUTHORS

EDITED BY

CLEMENT LAWRENCE SMITH AND TRACY PECK

---

## SATIRES AND EPISTLES OF HORACE

GREENOUGH

*COLLEGE SERIES OF LATIN AUTHORS*

# THE

# SATIRES AND EPISTLES

OF

# HORACE

EDITED, WITH NOTES,

BY

J. B. GREENOUGH

GINN & COMPANY
BOSTON · NEW YORK · CHICAGO · LONDON

611.10

The Athenæum Press
GINN & COMPANY · PRO-
PRIETORS · BOSTON · U.S.A.

I would dedicate this book, such as it is, to Professor HENRY W. TORREY, but for whose suggestions in regard to the poet it could never have been written at all

J. B. GREENOUGH.

# PREFACE.

THIS book is intended for use in the class-room. There are therefore many things in the notes which the advanced Latin scholar may pass over. But the editor has derived so much advantage from editions of the Classics in which the notes reminded him in particular connections of things which in general he knew before, that he has not inquired so much whether a thing was likely to be known, as whether it was likely to be thought of in the connection. The notes are intended not so much to aid the student in the study of the Latin language as in the study of Horace, — what he meant, how he felt, and what prompted him to write as he did. In accordance with the plan of the "College Series," the notes are put at the bottom of the page to facilitate reference. The editor is persuaded that college students sufficiently advanced to undertake Horace, ought no longer to get and recite lessons, but to study the literature, and understand and enjoy it. If the editor's suggestions enable anybody to do this, his purpose will have been accomplished.

J. B. GREENOUGH.

Jan. 1, 1888.

# CONTENTS.

# INTRODUCTION.

HORACE says (*Sat.* I. 10. 74),—

> . . . *An tua demens*
> *Vilibus in ludis dictari carmina malis?*
> *Non ego.*

But his genius and fame very early brought upon him the fate which he deprecates, of having his works used as a literary text-book in all kinds of schools. And this use of his poetry has brought with it several important consequences. In the first place, it insured their preservation to our own times, while so many writers have been absolutely lost. Secondly, it has prevented any serious interpolation by imitators of later times. Thirdly, it has caused an arrangement of his works in manuscripts and in later printed editions which is not chronological but educational. The Satires and Epodes were his earliest poetical efforts, being written, for the most part, about the same time, between B.C. 40 and B.C. 30, though in manuscripts and editions, as well as in educational use, the Odes precede them. Fourthly, it has produced in the manuscripts a state of things that is perhaps unparalleled in those of any other author. Classical authors generally have come down to us in such a form, that by a careful study such as has been given to the subject by the scholars of the last fifty years, the manuscripts can be divided into families, and their genesis and trustworthiness determined with considerable accuracy and certainty. But with Horace, the number and late date of the manuscripts, — some two hundred and fifty, all probably of later date than the tenth century, — along with the uninterrupted cross correction of one by another, caused by the general familiarity with the poet, has made it next to impossible to establish any families, or any precedence of any one over others, or even of any dozen over the rest. So that what we have of Horace is a text very much altered by the tinkering of scholars according to their knowledge and whims, but at the same time checked off by reference to the constant stream of tradition. This process has apparently been going on from the poet's own time. So that very little can be done now in the way of improvement of the text, unless some manuscript should come to light that has lain unused for more than a thousand years. For a description of the manuscripts, the student is referred to Orelli and (less fully) Keller and Holder.

The Satires and the poems generally seem to have been first written for private reading and circulation, somewhat as single poems appear nowadays in ephemeral literature and are later collected into volumes, and not to have been properly published until some time after their composition. Exactly at what time this was done in the case of the Satires is unknown, but we may well suppose that the first book was published before B.C. 33, in which year Horace received from Mæcenas the gift of his Sabine farm, a gift which can hardly be looked upon otherwise than as a return for the compliment of the dedication to Mæcenas in I. 1. There is no clear indication that the two books of Satires were published separately, yet there is a slight difference of style between the two, and the scene with Trebatius in II. 1. seems to indicate a new undertaking, a conclusion which is also strengthened by the completeness of the first book and the evident incompleteness of the second.

The form of composition Horace himself calls *Sermones*, to distinguish it from the higher flights of poetry which he attempts in his lyrics. But the name *Satura* must also have been given to the work at the time (as in II. 1. 1), and has always been the prevailing title.

This kind of literature, which is almost entirely, if not entirely, Roman (*Satura quidem tota nostra est*, Quint. X. 1. 93), had not originally the same meaning that *satire* has at present. Its real meaning is "miscellany" (cf. *lanx satura*, *lex satura*), and it was first used, so far as we know, by Ennius (B.C. 239–169) to describe a collection of verse with mixed metres as well as mixed subjects. This meaning was also followed by Pacuvius, his nephew, and later by M. Terentius Varro, the great antiquarian, a contemporary of Cicero. Lucilius, in the time of Africanus the Younger, used the word to denote a series of pictures of life and manners in verse (generally hexameter), more nearly, though not entirely, in the style which we now call satirical. His satires, of which we have fragments, consist of scenes and character sketches from life, and are generally, though not always, aimed at the folly and wickedness of mankind, particularly as found in the party opposed to the clique of Scipio and his friends. The exact connection of Lucilius' efforts with Greek models is not clear. In Horace's time there seems to have been no idea that there was any immediate connection with anything Greek except a remote one with the Old Comedy. Some of the writings of Ennius may have suggested the development that Lucilius gave to satire. There was evidently also among the Romans a strong tendency towards dramatic composition of a lighter kind, as is indicated by the Fescennine and Atellane farces. There was also a strong tendency to "*convicia*," or personal abuse in conversational form, "chaffing," or "Billingsgate." There were also extant at that time some compositions in Greek called Σίλλοι, which seem to have been poetical semidramatic character sketches, something like the prose writings of Lucian. These *Silloi* may have given a suggestion to Ennius and Lucilius; and as the comedy which would naturally have sprung from all these seeds was crowded out by the translation of the more advanced Greek dramas, the Satire seems to have been the result of the comic tendency of the Romans turned by the want of Roman comedy and by the Greek character sketches in another direction. In this sense Satire is an abortive comedy.

The model of Lucilius was exactly followed by Horace, and the result is these two books of Satires, which for genial humor and amusing representation of the vices and follies of mankind, are unequalled in any literature. From the acute observation of human nature and social life that they show, and the felicity of expression that abounds on every page, they have always been among the most admired and most quoted works of ancient literature.

The style is always easy and graceful; never forced nor affected. They must have been written at a dash, however much Horace may have trimmed them and filed them afterwards. They are never labored, notwithstanding the care with which they must have been written, and if an idea attributed to Horace is far-fetched we may be almost sure it is wrong and not Horatian. The difficulties often found in following the thought are not caused, as in some authors, by a labored obscurity. They are the natural consequence of a quick seizing and setting forth of salient points to an audience that could readily supply the missing links.

The peculiar characteristic of Horace is his genial humor. He does not inveigh against the vices of mankind, but sets forth the laughable aspects of their vices, and constantly includes himself among the objects of his satire, being in this respect more like Thackeray than any other author before or since.

*Archaisms.*—The Satires, in accordance with their colloquial character, are full of expressions such as were used in common life, though they had become antiquated or had never appeared in literature.

*E.g.*, the passive infinitive in *-ier; quis* for *quibus;* the contracted forms of the perfect, like *erepsemus*, *surrexe*, *evasti;*

*caballus; quid agis; dulcissime rerum; unde mihi lapidem; licebit . . . celebret* (II. 2. 59); *mille ovium* (II. 3. 197); *nummo addicere* (II. 5. 109); *quid causae est; soldum; caldior; periclum; narrare* (for *dicere*), etc.

*Prosody.* — Horace allows himself several liberties in the composition of his verse: —

1. Short syllables lengthened before the caesura.
   *qui non defendit,* ‖ *alio* . . ., I. 4. 82.
   *confidens tumidus* ‖ *adeo* . . . (doubtful reading), I. 7. 7.
   *ne quis humasse velit* ‖ *Aiacem* . . ., II. 3. 187 (originally long).
   *Galloni praeconis erat* ‖ *acipensere* . . ., II. 2. 47 (originally long).
2. Consonantizing of *i*. *vindemyator*, I. 7. 30.
3. Frequent elisions, perhaps a colloquial usage.
   *nulla ne habes vitia, immo alio et fortasse minora*, I. 3. 20.
   *quam rem agis* (doubtful reading), II. 6. 29.
4. Shortening long vowels before another vowel.
   *si me amas*, I. 9. 38.
5. Synizesis, *cerea*, I. 8. 43, and Contraction, *deicere de saxo*.
6. Hypermetric verses, running over to the next verse (only two).
   . . . *convictore usus amicoque*
   *a puero* . . ., I. 4. 95.
   . . . *uti ne solus rusve peregreve*
   *exirem*. . ., I. 6. 102.
7. Hiatus, *nŭm adest* (doubtful reading), II. 2. 28.

# Q. HORATI FLACCI

# SERMONES

## LIBER PRIMVS

### I.

Qui fit, Maecenas, ut nemo, quam sibi sortem
seu ratio dederit seu fors obiecerit, illa
contentus vivat, laudet diversa sequentis?

Title, **Sermones.** Though this work of Horace is now universally called *Satires*, yet the ancient title seems to have been *Sermones* (*conversations*). See Introduction.

SATIRE I. The main theme is Horace's favorite one, of avarice. As usual, however, he does not at once attack the theme directly, but comes to it sidewise, under cover of a long preamble, which extends as far as v. 28.

VERSE I. **Maecenas**: this satire by being addressed to Mæcenas, serves as a sort of prologue to the work, and dedicates it to him. This address, as well as the interrogative form of the beginning, gives the conversational tone, of which Horace is fond. — **quam sortem**: notice that the Latin constantly puts the so-called antecedent noun in the relative clause, and puts that clause first in order. This is, no doubt, the earlier and more natural construction, according with the original interrogative character of the Latin relative. Translate by changing the order of the clauses: "*with that lot which*," etc. — **sibi**: the use of the reflexive is due to a feeling of indirect discourse, whereby the thought is put into the mind of the indefinite person spoken of, whose mental state **contentus** represents, and so implies a verb of saying.

2. **ratio**, *choice*, as deliberate or calculated (**ratus**). — **dederit**, *has assigned.* — **obiecerit**, *has thrown in his way.* The preposition **ob** is especially used of things happening by chance; cf. **obvenio**, **obtingo**. The subjunctives are occasioned by the dependence of the relative clauses on the **ut** clause.

3. **laudet**, *praises the lot of*, *i.e.* *calls happy*, or *envies.* The subject is an implied **quisque**, suggested by **nemo**. — **diversa**, *different pursuits* (from his own).

'O fortunati mercatores!' gravis annis
miles ait, multo iam fractus membra labore.
Contra mercator, navem iactantibus Austris,
'Militia est potior. Quid enim? Concurritur; horae
momento cita mors venit aut victoria laeta.'
Agricolam laudat iuris legumque peritus,
sub galli cantum consultor ubi ostia pulsat.
Ille, datis vadibus qui rure extractus in urbem est,
solos felices viventis clamat in urbe.

4. **O fortunati**, etc.: in accordance with the dramatic form which satire takes (perhaps on account of its origin, see Introduction), Horace gives the direct words of the persons referred to. — **fortunati**: as getting wealth without the toils to which the soldier is exposed. — **gravis annis**, *i.e.* he is getting old, but is not rich yet, while the toils are more grievous to him. Another reading, **armis**, is possible, but not so good.

5. **fractus**, *shattered*. — **membra**, *frame*. — **labore**: the battles of the Romans were won by the spade even more than by the sword, and in full marching order the soldier carried a weight of from forty to sixty pounds.

6. **mercator**: it must be remembered that the mercator is a *trader* who sails with his wares in his own ship; hence **iactantibus austris**. — **austris**: the south wind is an especially squally and rainy wind in the Mediterranean. Cf. *Il.* II. 145; Hor. *Od.* I. 7. 16. The word may be translated *souwesters*, or *southerly gales*.

7. **potior**: it is the long and tedious suffering that affects the trader, and he contrasts with it the short and sudden danger of battle. — **quid enim**, *of course* (lit. *why? in fact*). Cf. II. 3. 132, and **quid est** as an expression of assent. **enim** does not here have its explanatory force, but the earlier one of *in fact*, as in **quia enim, quippe enim, immo enim**. Cf. **quisnam**, etc. — **concurritur**, *the onset comes*.

8. **momento**, *short space*. — **laeta**: as enriching the soldier by booty. These occupations are all here looked upon as means of gain (cf. v. 28).

9. **iuris legumque peritus**, *the learned man of law and statute*, though of course **iuris**, etc., belong to **peritus**. The jurisconsult, or consulting lawyer, is referred to, who was not an advocate, but gave opinions for fees. — **agricolam**: because he does not have to get up at so early an hour.

10. **sub galli cantum**: as the proceedings of the Roman courts began at an early hour, the client must get advice at a still earlier one, but of course the statement here is hyperbolical.

11. **ille**, *the other*. — **datis vadibus**: the defendant, on answering to the first summons in a court of law, gave bail for his appearance at a subsequent day for the hearing. Cf. I. 9. 36. — **in urbem**: all the legal and other official business was transacted in the city itself, though many of the tribes lived many miles away. — **rure**, *i.e. from his farm*.

12. **in urbe**: naturally the countryman thinks those who live in the

Cetera de genere hoc, adeo sunt multa, loquacem
delassare valent Fabium. Ne te morer, audi
quo rem deducam. Si quis deus, 'En ego,' dicat,
'iam faciam quod voltis : eris tu, qui modo miles,
mercator ; tu, consultus modo, rusticus : hinc vos,
vos hinc mutatis discedite partibus. — Heia !
quid statis ?' — nolint. Atqui licet esse beatis.
Quid causae est, merito quin illis Iuppiter ambas
iratus buccas inflet, neque se fore posthac
tam facilem dicat, votis ut praebeat aurem ?

city would not have to get up so early. — **cetera de genere hoc,** *the other cases of this kind.* An old formula, borrowed by the poet from Lucretius.

13. **adeo,** *so,* to the degree indicated by the fact stated (not as a result, but directly) in **valent**. The same idea might be expressed as a result by **ut valeant,** but it would be more formal. This reference of demonstrative words to something not expressed but implied in the context is very common in Latin, and, indeed, in all languages, for that matter.

14. **delassare,** *i.e.* if he should undertake to enumerate them. — **valent,** *are enough to.* — **Fabium**: an old scholiast says the reference is to Q. Fabius Maximus of Narbo, who wrote on the Stoic philosophy in the wordy style of that sect. And, as this also agrees with the allusions in *Sat.* I. 2. 134, the two may well be the same person.

15. **quo rem deducam,** *the point I am coming to* (lit. *whither I am bringing the matter*), *i.e.* the insincerity of men in these wishes to change their lot. This insincerity he shows dramatically by introducing an imaginary scene of a god appearing and offering to grant their wishes. In such a case they would refuse. The reason why, which is their love of money, he begins to state in v. 28, which brings him to his main theme.

15. **en,** *look you.* — **ego**: the expression of **ego** by its emphasis gives a force something like "You want to have your lots changed; well, then, *I'll* do it for you."

17. **hinc,** *to that side;* lit. *from this side,* like **a parte dextra.** — **mutatis,** *changing.* The perf. part. is often best rendered by our present, which the Latin lacks.

18. **partibus,** *rôles,* the regular theatrical word. — **heia,** *halloo,* as if he said, "What does this mean? I thought you wanted to change."

19. **quid statis?** *why do you stand there? i.e.* instead of starting, as they are bidden in **discedite.** — **nolint,** *they wouldn't care to, would refuse,* the apodosis to **dicat,** v. 15. — **licet,** *they might.* One expects the subjunctive, but verbs of this kind take the indicative, in cases where there is a protasis expressed or implied.

21. **buccas inflet**: to show the extreme inconsistency of the behavior of these persons, the poet gives a comic picture of Jove's wrath. probably borrowed from the stage.

Praeterea, ne sic, ut qui iocularia, ridens
percurram, (quamquam ridentem dicere verum
quid vetat? ut pueris olim dant crustula blandi
doctores, elementa velint ut discere prima;
sed tamen amoto quaeramus seria ludo;)
ille gravem duro terram qui vertit aratro,
perfidus hic caupo miles nautaeque per omne
audaces mare qui currunt, hac mente laborem
sese ferre, senes ut in otia tuta recedant,
aiunt, cum sibi sint congesta cibaria: sicut
parvola (nam exemplo est) magni formica laboris

23. **praeterea,** *furthermore,* or *to continue.* — **qui**: supply the verb from **percurram.**

24. **ridentem,** *with laughter.* — **quamquam,** *though,* corrective to the preceding, not strictly opposed to **tamen.**

25. **quid vetat?** *what law forbids?* — **pueris,** *children,* the word being used often for both sexes. — **olim,** *now and then.* — **crustula,** *cookies, tarts, gingerbread,* evidently much like our own in modern times, though perhaps more elaborate. The name is from their being baked hard. — **blandi,** *coaxing.*

26. **elementa prima,** *their A-B-C's,* the proper meaning of the word.

27. **sed tamen,** *but still* (though we might with propriety go on in this vein). — **quaeramus,** *let us turn to.*

28. Here begins the real subject, but even here Horace attacks it carefully, beginning with the excuse of the money-getter. — **gravem duro**: these words are intended to heighten the color of the picture by indicating the hard labor which the farmer undergoes to gain wealth.

29. **perfidus caupo**: these words seem out of place, as the context would naturally have some word referring to the jurisconsult. But we may suppose that Horace abandons the lawyer because, though a good opposite to the farmer, yet he seeks honor more than money; and so in this place Horace substitutes the huckster. Certainly the epithet **perfidus** is more appropriate for the latter than the former. The rest of the satire does not follow the same line of thought, but presents another phase of the dissatisfaction of men, not with what they do, but with what they have; but this is only the other side of the same thing, and is the real reason why they would not change if they could.

30. **mente,** *idea, purpose.*

31. **senes,** *in their old age.* — **tuta,** *untroubled, i.e.* by the toils and dangers they have undergone before.

32. **cum sibi,** etc., *when they have heaped up a sufficient store.* — **cibaria,** lit. *rations* or *subsistence;* which Horace makes them say in allusion to the gathered store of the ant, referred to below.

33. **parvola**: inserted to set off the force of **magni**; not a merely ornamental epithet, for such are rare in this work, and are not to be

ore trahit quodcumque potest atque addit acervo,
quem struit, haud ignara ac non incauta futuri.
Quae, simul inversum contristat Aquarius annum,
non usquam prorepit et illis utitur ante
quaesitis sapiens; cum te neque fervidus aestus
demoveat lucro, neque hiemps, ignis, mare, ferrum,
nil obstet tibi, dum ne sit te ditior alter.
  Quid iuvat immensum te argenti pondus et auri
furtim defossa timidum deponere terra?
'Quod si comminuas, vilem redigatur ad assem.'
At ni id fit, quid habet pulchri constructus acervus?
Milia frumenti tua triverit area centum,

presumed. — **exemplo est**, *she is their pattern, i.e.* they justify themselves by her example, but, as Horace shows, their conduct is different from hers. See v. 36. — **laboris**: a qualitative genitive. That construction is unusual without a general word like **animal**, but this may be a conversational idiom.

36. **inversum**, *changing, closing;* lit. turned back to begin again. — **Aquarius**: the sun is in this constellation about the middle of January, at which time really begins the short Italian winter.

38. **sapiens**, *i.e.* she knows enough to gather provision in summer and stay at home in winter; another reading, **patiens**, which is very old, would mean *contented*, not greedy for more. Cf. II. 6. 91. — **cum te**, etc., *i.e.* though the searcher for gain makes the ant his pattern, yet he does not follow her in her use of what she gets but still accumulates, undeterred by any peril. — **aestus**, etc.: proverbial expressions for obstacles, just as we say "go through fire and water."

40. **dum ne**, *so long as . . . not, i.e.* provided you can outstrip your neighbor in getting gain (cf. Cic. de Off. 3. 21). — **alter**, *your neighbor*. **Alter** is used for any one of a class opposed to some particular person mentioned.

41. **quid iuvat?** *i.e.* what good does this acquisition of wealth do, which you don't use? — **immensum**, *enormous, countless.*

42. **furtim**, etc., *stealthily*. The picture is of a miser hiding his gold in the earth (the usual place in ancient times) while anxiously watching that no one shall see where.

43. **quod si**, etc.: the miser's reply. The moment you begin to take from the heap it all goes. "Change a ten-dollar bill, and it is all gone." — **assem**: the copper coin of account of the Romans, worth at this time about one cent.

44. **at ni**: Horace's reply. — **quid pulchri**: a colloquial form of expression for the abstract. — **acervus**: notice that, as the main idea is that of amassing wealth generally, the figure under which the wealth is represented constantly changes.

45. **triverit**, *suppose it yields;* the hortatory subj. used in a concession. — **area**, *threshing floor*. The ancients threshed their grain

non tuus hoc capiet venter plus ac meus : ut si
reticulum panis venalis inter onusto
forte vehas umero, nihilo plus accipias quam
qui nil portarit. Vel dic, quid referat intra
naturae finis viventi, iugera centum an
mille aret? 'At suave est ex magno tollere acervo.'
Dum ex parvo nobis tantundem haurire relinquas,
cur tua plus laudes cumeris granaria nostris?
ut tibi si sit opus liquidi non amplius urna,
vel cyatho, et dicas, 'Magno de flumine mallem
quam ex hoc fonticulo tantundem sumere.' Eo fit,
plenior ut si quos delectet copia iusto,
cum ripa simul avolsos ferat Aufidus acer;
at qui tantuli eget quanto est opus, is neque limo
turbatam haurit aquam, neque vitam amittit in undis.

by making a hard clay floor in the open air, and treading out the grain with cattle, — a method which is still used in Greece and Italy. — **milia**, *i.e.* **modium**, *pecks;* but we may translate *bushels.*

46. **ac**, *than*, an archaic use preserved in poetry and conversation. — **ut si**, *just as, if*, *i.e.* though you have the trouble of taking care of your great crop, you can't enjoy any more than the rest; just as the slave who happens to be carrying the rations in a train gets no more than his share, for all that.

47. **venalis**, *a gang of slaves.*

49. **referat**: notice the **rē**, from **refert**, not **refero**.

50. **finis**, the limits which nature sets to our wants. — **viventi**, the usual construction is genitive, but it may be that the colloquial or popular construction was dative.

51. **at suave est**, *but it is so sweet*, etc.; the miser's reply.

52. **relinquas nobis**, *let me draw.* Cf. Eng. *leave* in "leave me be."

53. **cumeris**, *baskets;* opposed to the greater store implied in **granaria**.

54. **urna**, a measure of three gallons, *a jar.* — **cyatho**, also a measure, of about a twelfth of a pint, *a spoonful.*

55. **mallem**: this reading is perhaps preferable to **malim**, inasmuch as **hoc** seems to indicate that the person supposed has the spring to draw from but not the river; hence the construction might naturally be contrary to fact.

56. **eo**, *in that way*, *i.e.* on account of this desire to take from a great quantity.

57. **si quos delectet**, *whoever takes pleasure in*, etc. The statement is a kind of parable continuing the case supposed in v. 54.

58. **Aufidus**: Horace as usual takes a particular river, the one near his birthplace, to represent any rapid stream.

60. **turbatam**, *turbid;* but also of life, *unquiet.* — **vitam**: implying that riches are likely to be one's ruin.

At bona pars hominum, decepta cupidine falso,
'Nil satis est,' inquit, 'quia tanti quantum habeas sis.'
Quid facias illi? Iubeas miserum esse, libenter
quatenus id facit; ut quidam memoratur Athenis
sordidus ac dives, populi contemnere voces
sic solitus: 'Populus me sibilat, at mihi plaudo
ipse domi, simul ac nummos contemplor in arca.'
Tantalus a labris sitiens fugientia captat
flumina. . . . Quid rides? Mutato nomine, de te
fabula narratur; congestis undique saccis
indormis inhians, et tamquam parcere sacris
cogeris, aut pictis tamquam gaudere tabellis.

61. **at**: the Ms. authority is perhaps in favor of **ut**, which would introduce another comparison like **ut** in v. 54. The sense, however, seems better with **at**, as if Horace said, "All this is true, yet men won't act accordingly, but justify their seeking of gain, by v. 62, which shows them to be incurable"; hence **quid facias**, etc. — **bona pars**, *the best part*, *i.e.* the greatest. — **falso**, *vain*, *i.e.* for which there is no real good as its object.

62. **tanti sis**, *you are rated at*, etc. The subjunctive is the regular one of the second person with indefinite subject. — **quantum**, *what.*

63. **quid facias illi?** *what can you do for a man like that? i.e.* one who is determined to go on in this way, as is indicated by **nil satis est**. — **miserum esse**, *enjoy his misery;* but the expression has the idea of an imprecation, like "go and be hanged." — **libenter**: *i.e.* with his eyes open, knowing the true state of the case.

64. **quatenus**, here *inasmuch as* (which is an expression of the same origin in English). — **ut quidam**, etc.: implying that he must get his consolation for his misery out of the wretched pleasure of avarice, as was the case with the Athenian.

65. **contemnere**, *scorn, saying to himself.* — **voces**, *cries*, of the populace as they hooted after him.

66. **at mihi plaudo**: *i.e.* I take my satisfaction for the hisses of the people in my approval of myself.

68. **Tantalus**, etc.: Horace begins as though he were going to warn the miser by the story of Tantalus in the world below, in the manner of a preacher of virtue, a class of men not held in much respect. See *Sat.* II. 3 and I. 1. 120.

69. **quid rides**: the miser, who has no longer any belief in the stories of Hades, or any care for this sort of preaching, laughs at Horace's attempt to convert him with the fables of the world below. But Horace turns upon him, and shows that Tantalus' fate is not a future terror, but *his* condition *now*. He then proceeds to prove the similarity of his condition with that of Tantalus, in sight of good things which he cannot enjoy.

71. **inhians**, *gloating*, *i.e.* with his mouth open, staring at them in admiration, as if he would like to eat them, and continuing his enjoy-

Nescis quo valeat nummus, quem praebeat usum?
Panis ematur, holus, vini sextarius, adde
quis humana sibi doleat natura negatis.
An vigilare metu exanimem, noctesque diesque
formidare malos fures, incendia, servos,
ne te compilent fugientes, hoc iuvat? Horum
semper ego optarem pauperrimus esse bonorum.
At si condoluit temptatum frigore corpus,
aut alius casus lecto te affixit, habes qui
assideat, fomenta paret, medicum roget, ut te
suscitet ac gnatis reddat carisque propinquis.
Non uxor salvum te volt, non filius; omnes
vicini oderunt, noti, pueri atque puellae.
Miraris, cum tu argento post omnia ponas,
si nemo praestet, quem non merearis, amorem?
At si cognatos, nullo natura labore

ment of them till he falls asleep. — **tanquam**, with **sacris**.

73. **nescis quo**, etc.: *i.e.* "Don't you know what can be done with all this money you have, that you keep it in this way untouched?" He begins as if he were going to state some grand object, but suddenly turning, he gives merely the absolute wants of humanity. He thereby implies that this, after all, is the only thing money can do. The turn is not strictly logical, but all the more effective for that.

75. **quis** = **quibus**. — **doleat . . . negatis**, *suffers from the want of*.

76. **an**, etc.: here used, as often, in a kind of *reductio ad absurdum*. Prosaically expressed, "Isn't money to be used to be a blessing, or do you enjoy, etc.," the other alternative, which is obviously absurd.

79. **optarem**: *i.e.* if the case were mine; hence imperfect. The reading **optarim** has a more general sense.

80. **at si**, etc., *but of course*, etc., an argument in favor of the miser, but with obvious irony. — **temptatum**, *attacked*, a regular word. — **frigore**, *a chill*, referring to the fevers so common in Italy.

82. **assideat**, *nurse*, an almost technical word. — **roget**, *call in*, also technical.

84. **non**, *no, not even*, etc., the word getting emphasis from its position. This is Horace's answer to his ironical defence of the miser's position.

85. **noti**, *acquaintances*. — **pueri atque puellae**, *boys and girls and all*, an almost proverbial expression for *without distinction of age or sex*. — **quem non merearis**, *which you do nothing to deserve*.

87. **praestet**: subjunctive on account of its connection with **miraris**, in a kind of indirect discourse.

88. **at si**, etc.: *i.e.* by devoting yourself to the pursuit of gain, you make it impossible to keep even

quos tibi dat, retinere velis servareque amicos,
infelix operam perdas, ut si quis asellum
in campo doceat parentem currere frenis.
Denique sit finis quaerendi, cumque habeas plus,
pauperiem metuas minus, et finire laborem
incipias, parto quod avebas, ne facias quod
Vmmidius quidam. Non longa est fabula: dives,
ut metiretur nummos, ita sordidus, ut se
non umquam servo melius vestiret, ad usque
supremum tempus, ne se penuria victus
opprimeret metuebat. At hunc liberta securi
divisit medium, fortissima Tyndaridarum.
'Quid mi igitur suades? ut vivam Maenius? aut sic
ut Nomentanus?' Pergis pugnantia secum

the love of your kindred which nature gives you at the start without your taking any trouble. The reading **an si** could mean, "Do you think it would be useless labor to attempt to win friends?" The first seems better. Notice Horace does not say *get*, but *keep*.

90. **asellum**, etc.: evidently proverbial. "By your conduct you have made yourself as incapable of friendship as an ass is of speed."

92. **cum**, *now that*.

93. **metuas**, *begin to fear*.— **finire**, *set a limit*. Notice that Horace does not advise him to stop suddenly, but begin, as it were, to think of an end.

94. **parto**: in early prose the antecedent of **quod** would be expressed in agreement with **parto**, but conversation and poetry allow the omission, which is common later.

95. **Vmmidius**: the story is not otherwise known, though the name occurs elsewhere.

98. **supremum tempus**, *the last day of his life*.

100. **divisit**: change the voice in translating. — **Tyndaridum**, *of Tyndareus' line*. The allusion is to Clytemnestra, who killed her lord in the same manner, as if it were "the most undaunted of husband-slayers." It is of course implied that the woman was a concubine, so that the case is an illustration of the idea in **non uxor**, etc., and the following.

101. **quid mi suades**, etc.: the miser thinks that the poet in condemning avarice approves extravagance, and asks if he wants him to be a **Maenius** (a spendthrift). A reading **Naevius** refers to a person said to have been a miser. This gives a passable sense, though not approved by the commentators; as if he said, "What do you advise me, then, to be a miser, or do you want me to be a spendthrift?" as if these were the only alternatives, and there could be no doubt which was the better. The reading retained gives two examples of spendthrifts.

102. **Nomentanus**: a noted spendthrift. — **pergis**, *do you persist, do you always? i.e.* "Do as

frontibus adversis componere? Non ego, avarum
cum veto te fieri, vappam iubeo ac nebulonem.
Est inter Tanain quiddam socerumque Viselli.
Est modus in rebus, sunt certi denique fines,
quos ultra citraque nequit consistere rectum.
Illuc, unde abii, redeo: nemon' ut avarus
se probet ac potius laudet diversa sequentis,
quodque aliena capella gerat distentius uber,
tabescat, neque se maiori pauperiorum

you always do?" — **secum**, *with* (*to*) *each other*, a very common use of the reflexive. — **pugnantia**, *opposed*, *at variance*. — **frontibus adversis**, *utterly*, *squarely*, *diametrically*. The figure is drawn from bulls and rams, but is hardly admissible in English.

103. **componere**: the technical sense of the word is *match*, *pair off*. If this is taken, the meaning is, "Why do you always match (in argument) things squarely opposed to each other, as if there were nothing between, setting only the two extremes against each other, and not, as you should, one extreme against the mean." It may also be taken in the sense of *put together*, *i.e.* identifying things utterly inconsistent and unlike, as *not being a miser* with *being a spendthrift*, and *not being a spendthrift* with *being a miser*, whereas Horace shows that there is a middle ground, and consequently these things supposed by the miser to be the same are really utterly opposed to each other.

105. **Tanain**: said to be a eunuch of whom, as of Visellius, nothing else is known. — **quiddam**, *a point*, that is, a mean, so that one isn't obliged to be either one or the other. — **socerum, etc.**: a man we are told who had the swelling of a hernia.

106. **modus in rebus**, *a just measure in everything*. — **fines**, *limits*. Horace's favorite ethical principle.

107. **ultra citraque**, *on either side of*.

108. **nemon' ut avarus**: a troublesome passage of which nobody can find the key. The meaning is obvious, being the same as the point in v. 1, the discontent of mankind. The difficulty is in the construction. No authenticated reading omits the **ne** (**n'**), nor would the hiatus seem very tolerable, though perhaps paralleled by *Od.* I. 28. 24. But the **ne** is apparently superfluous. If the **ut** clause is taken as the ordinary one denoting a state of things, the **ne** might be a colloquial usage like clauses of exclamation, **egone ut interpellam** (*the idea that*, etc.), or it is barely possible to treat **ut** as interrogative, *how*, in which case a pleonastic **ne** might be justified; cf. **utrum ne**. — **avarus**, *in his greed*, added as the true reason why no man is contented with his lot.

110. **quodque**, etc.: a different phase of discontent is here represented. At the outset, men appear as praising the lot of another on account of its supposed ease, but here, for its greater gain. Cf. note to v. 29. — **distentius**, etc.: simply to express greater prosperity.

turbae comparet, hunc atque hunc superare laboret.
Sic festinanti semper locupletior obstat,
ut, cum carceribus missos rapit ungula currus,
instat equis auriga suos vincentibus, illum
praeteritum temnens extremos inter euntem.
Inde fit, ut raro, qui se vixisse beatum
dicat, et, exacto contentus tempore, vita
cedat uti conviva satur, reperire queamus.
Iam satis est. Ne me Crispini scrinia lippi
compilasse putes, verbum non amplius addam.

## II.

Ambubaiarum conlegia, pharmacopolae,
mendici, mimae, balatrones, hoc genus omne

112. **hunc atque hunc**, *this man and this* (in succession, opposed to the crowd).

113. **obstat**, *stands in his path*, *i.e.* is before him in the race.

114. **ungula**, *the flying hoof*, to make the figure endurable in Eng. — **carceribus**, *the barriers*, special stalls in which the horses stood until the rope at the entrance was dropped, and they rushed forth (**emissos**) to the track (**spatium**).

115. **illum**, *that other*.

116. **euntem**, *as running*, *i.e.* as soon as he is passed, he belongs with all the rest in the rear, and is no better than the hindmost himself.

117. **inde**, *i.e.* from this rivalry.

118. **exacto tempore**, *when the term of his life is complete*.

119. **conviva satur**, *a well-fed guest*, a diner-out who has enjoyed his dinner, but has had enough. An idea common to several schools of philosophy, but more particularly the Epicurean (cf. Lucr. III. 951).

119. **iam satis est**: notice that the end as well as the beginning is informal. Horace breaks off abruptly for fear of being too verbose and tedious, which fear he jocularly expresses by his allusion to Crispinus. This person was a Stoic philosopher who preached the cant of that school, to the disgust of full-blooded, fastidious, and sincere natures like Horace. The high morality and rigid logic and precepts of the Stoics made it easy for them to fall into cant, and one could profess and teach the tenets of the school without much mental or moral effort, using the high-sounding sermons and glittering paradoxes of previous sermonizers. Horace, whose doctrine of the mean approaches the Peripatetic school, never loses a chance to gibe the Stoics. This does not prevent him however from often urging Stoic precepts. Cf. II. 3.

Satire 2. This satire is upon a particular form of excess, but the preamble (to the middle of v. 28), on extremes in general, is as usual, far from the main subject, and treats of the want of perception

maestum ac sollicitum est cantoris morte Tigelli:
quippe benignus erat. Contra hic, ne prodigus esse
dicatur metuens, inopi dare nolit amico
frigus quo duramque famem propellere possit.
Hunc si perconteris, avi cur atque parentis
praeclaram ingrata stringat malus ingluvie rem,
omnia conductis coemens obsonia nummis,
sordidus atque animi quod parvi nolit haberi,
respondet. Laudatur ab his, culpatur ab illis.
Fufidius vappae famam timet ac nebulonis,
[dives agris, dives positis in faenore nummis];
quinas hic capiti mercedes exsecat, atque

among mankind of the true course of virtue, which consists in keeping the golden mean.

1. **Ambubaiarum**, *music-girls*, or musicians from the East, not of the best reputation. — **conlegia**: humorously used to describe the troupes of these persons, as if they had an official corporate organization, like more respectable *guilds*, or *societies*, especially those of the religious musicians. — **pharmacopolae**, *quacks*, who sold their own medicines, or *sellers of perfumes*, in both which senses the word is used.

2. **mendici**, *beggars*, including many Eastern priests and fortune-tellers, as also jugglers. — **mimae**, *low players*. The lowest class of farces, the mimes, allowed women on the stage. *Actresses* is rather too respectable a word here. — **genus**: *i.e.* the classes that thrive on the vices (and virtues) of the prodigal, by catering to a life of luxury.

3. **Tigelli**: Marcus Hermogenes Tigellius was a skilful musician and remarkable singer, and a friend of Julius Cæsar, as well as later of Augustus, famous also, like many of that class of persons in later times, for his luxury and prodigality.

4. **quippe benignus erat**, *for he was a generous soul.* — **contra**, *on the other hand*, contrasting another (**hic**), who is a parsimonious creature.

5. **inopi**, *in want.*

6. **frigus**, etc.: *i.e.* to clothe and feed him. — **duram**, with both nouns.

7. **hunc**: a third, but also a prodigal, like Tigellius.

8. **ingrata**, *unsatisfying;* lit. that gives no pleasure and yields no return.

9. **conductis**, *borrowed*, *i.e.* at usurious interest. — **obsonia**, *dainties*, any food which is used to give relish to bread, the main staple of ancient diet.

10. **animi parvi**, *small-souled.*

11. **respondet**: *i.e.* **se stringere**, etc., **quod**, etc. — **his**, *this class;* **illis**, *the other.*

12. **Fufidius**, a usurer

13. Rejected by some editors.

14. **quinas**, *i.e.* fivefold. As the ordinary rate of interest was one per cent a month, this would be sixty per cent. — **exsecat**, *slices off*, *i.e.* in advance, as in bank discount.

quanto perditior quisque est, tanto acrius urget;
nomina sectatur modo sumpta veste virili
sub patribus duris tironum. 'Maxime' quis non
'Iuppiter!' exclamat, simul atque audivit? 'At in se
pro quaestu sumptum facit hic.' Vix credere possis
quam sibi non sit amicus, ita ut pater ille, Terenti
fabula quem miserum gnato vixisse fugato
inducit, non se peius cruciaverit atque hic.
Si quis nunc quaerat, 'Quo res haec pertinet?' illuc:
dum vitant stulti vitia, in contraria currunt.
Malthinus tunicis demissis ambulat; est qui

15. **quanto perditior**, *the nearer to ruin.* — **quisque**, *one.* This use of **quisque** is common in all kinds of comparisons to make the idea more individual, as if it said, "each man in proportion to," etc. We may use '*always*.'

16. **nomina**, *debts.* In the account-books of the Romans, the name at the head of the ledger was the evidence of debt; hence **nomen** comes to be used for the account (in all senses, as in English), and for the debt against one, where we should say notes or bills. — **sumpta**, etc., *just come to manhood*, when of course their desire for pleasure and their dependence would be greatest. The manly toga, or plain white robe, was put on at the pleasure of the father about the age of seventeen, and this (**dies tirocinii**) was an important occasion in the life of the young man as 'his coming out' as a man among men.

17. **duris**, *harsh*, as not indulging their sons in their pleasures, whence the young men had more need of money.

18. **in se . . . sumptum facit**, *he spends upon himself.*

19. **pro quaestu**, *in proportion to his gains.* — **vix**, etc.: notice that the connectives are constantly omitted to give the freedom of conversation; *on the contrary*, or *why!*

20. **quam non amicus**, *what an enemy*, as torturing himself with privation in the miser's fashion. — **pater ille**, *the father*, *i.e.* the well-known one.

21. **fabula**: the *Hautontimorumenos*, or Self-Tormentor, of Terence. — **miserum vixisse inducit**, *shows living in wretchedness.* The word **inducit** properly means *brings on to the stage*, but, as **vixisse** is past, it means here "shows to have lived."

22. **atque**, *than*, a meaning and use of **atque** often found in early Latin.

23. **quo . . . pertinet**, *whither . . . tends*, *i.e.* what is shown by these examples?

24. **dum vitant**, etc.: the general statement of the doctrine of the mean as held by the Peripatetic school.

25. **Malthinus**, etc.: examples of extremes in other matters. There is a supposed reference to Mæcenas, but it might be any one of a hundred others. — **est qui** (*sc.* **ambulat**), *another.*

inguen ad obscenum subductis usque facetus.
Pastillos Rufillus olet, Gargonius hircum.
Nil medium est. Sunt qui nolint tetigisse nisi illas,
quarum subsuta talos tegat instita veste:
contra alius nullam nisi olenti in fornice stantem.
Quidam notus homo cum exiret fornice 'Macte
virtute esto,' inquit sententia dia Catonis.
'Nam simul ac venas inflavit taetra libido,
huc iuvenes aequum est descendere, non alienas
permolere uxores.' 'Nolim laudarier,' inquit,
'sic me' mirator cunni Cupiennius albi.
Audire est operae pretium, procedere recte
qui moechos non vultis, ut omni parte laborent;
utque illis multo corrupta dolore voluptas

26. **obscenum**: translate as adv., *indecently;* properly, *indecent*, because not usually exposed. — **facetus**, *an exquisite.* The word is especially applied to persons who are over-refined by intercourse with society, in one age a dandy, in another a dude.

27. **pastillos**, *lozenges*, to perfume the person. As the ancients were unacquainted with distillation, perfumes were conveyed in various vehicles, especially in oils, or, as here, in little cakes. — **hircum**, *dirt and sweat.* The word is very often used of the smell of the body in confined places, like the armpits. One of the extremes is over-care of the body; the other, neglect of simple cleanliness, of both of which the poet complains.

28. **nil medium est**, *there is no middle course*, a repetition in other words of the principal theme.—**sunt qui**, etc.: instances of extremes in another direction. — **tetigisse**: the perf. inf. is apparently an archaic construction, which survived especially in conversational and legal usage.

29. **quarum**: *i.e.* matrons, as appears from **instita**. — **subsuta**, *trailing:* the **instita** was apparently a flounce sewed on to the bottom of the stola, or long tunic of married women.

30. **fornice**: the arches of the Circus Maximus were the special abodes of people of the kind referred to; cf. I. 6. 113. Hence the name.

31. **notus**, *of his acquaintance.*

32. **sententia dia**, etc.: an imitation of Lucilius (*Valeri sententia dia*), and Lucretius, 3. 371; cf. II. 1. 72.

36. **albi**: referring to women of respectability, who are not obliged to wear the dark-colored toga of the prostitute.

37. **audire est**, etc.: imitated for the comic effect from Ennius, who uses this line in regard to the Roman state, of course with **vultis** in the affirmative.

39. **corrupta**, *spoiled, marred.*

atque haec rara cadat dura inter saepe pericla.
Hic se praecipitem tecto dedit; ille flagellis
ad mortem caesus; fugiens hic decidit acrem
praedonum in turbam; dedit hic pro corpore nummos;
hunc perminxerunt calones; quin etiam illud
accidit, ut quidam testes caudamque salacem
demeteret ferro. 'Iure,' omnes; Galba negabat.
Tutior at quanto merx est in classe secunda,
libertinarum dico, Sallustius in quas
non minus insanit, quam qui moechatur. At hic si,
qua res, qua ratio suaderet quaque modeste
munifico esse licet, vellet bonus atque benignus
esse, daret quantum satis esset nec sibi damno
dedecorique foret. Verum hoc se amplectitur uno,
hoc amat et laudat 'Matronam nullam ego tango.'
Vt quondam Marsaeus, amator Originis ille,

40. **rara**: the pleasure is marred and rare at that.

41. **hic**, etc.: describing the **pericla**.

46. **iure omnes**, *served him right, say all.* — **Galba**: it is implied that he was one of the sufferers, who naturally can't see the justice of it. He is said by a scholiast to have been a jurisconsult; and if so, **negabat** is equivalent to **non placuit**, and refers in jest to his professional opinion, as if he had been formally consulted on the point. — **negabat**, *thought not.*

47. **secunda**: equally removed from the class of v. 30, and that of v. 29.

48. **Sallustius**, etc.: but even in this safer course there is a chance for an excess, which is ruinous. Probably the person referred to is an adopted son of the historian.

50. **qua**, *as* (really limiting, *only so far as*). — **res**, *his interest, i.e.* his pecuniary condition. — **ratio**, *reason, good sense.* — **suaderet**: changed from **suadeat**, an apodosis with omitted protasis (*would suggest*), on account of the tense of **vellet**; but as **licet** would be in the indicative on account of the meaning of the word ("verbs of necessity, propriety," etc.), the tense of **vellet** has no effect on it. — **modeste munifico**: a kind of oxymoron, *lavish in moderation.*

51. **bonus atque benignus**, *kindly and generous.* Notice that these words are much less strong than **munifico**, which has an idea of *princeliness*, but they represent what the man means to be. In his want of moderation, however, he oversteps his mark.

53. **hoc** (abl.): *i.e.* **matronam**, etc. Cf.

"Compound for sins they are inclined to
By damning those they have no mind to.'

55. **Originis**, a famous **mima**.

qui patrium mimae donat fundumque laremque,
'Nil fuerit mi,' inquit, 'cum uxoribus unquam alienis.'
Verum est cum mimis, est cum meretricibus, unde
fama malum gravius quam res trahit. An tibi abunde
personam satis est, non illud, quidquid ubique
officit, evitare? Bonam deperdere famam,
rem patris oblimare, malum est ubicunque. Quid interest in matrona, ancilla peccesne togata?
Villius in Fausta Sullae gener, hoc miser uno
nomine deceptus, poenas dedit usque superque
quam satis est, pugnis caesus ferroque petitus,
exclusus fore, cum Longarenus foret intus.
Huic si mutonis verbis mala tanta videntis
diceret haec animus 'Quid vis tibi? Numquid ego a te
magno prognatum deposco consule cunnum
velatumque stola, mea cum conferbuit ira?'
quid responderet? 'Magno patre nata puella est.'
At quanto meliora monet pugnantiaque istis
dives opis natura suae, tu si modo recte

57. **fuerit**: hortatory subjunctive.

59. **res**, *property*, really the same as in v. 50, but differently expressed in English.

60. **personam**, *the particular character* (here **matronarum**), as opposed to the ruinous vice in general, expressed in **illud**, etc.

62. **ubicumque**, *in any case*, in regard to any of the classes mentioned.

63. **togata**: the toga was the necessary dress of all such women, as the **stola** of the respectable matron (cf. v. 71).

64. **Villius**, probably Sextus Villius Annalis, a friend of Milo, cf. Cic. *ad Fam.* II. 6. 1. — **in**, *in the case of*, as often. — **Fausta**, wife of Milo and daughter of Sulla. — **gener**: so called in jest.

65. **nomine**: *i.e.* Fausta, by which her noble birth was indicated.

67. **fore**: abl. of **foris**. — **Longarenus**, another lover of the woman.

68. **verbis**, *on behalf of*, as the spokesman.—**videntis**, *i.e.* suffering.

69. **diceret**, *had said*, cf. note to I. 3. 5. — **animus**, *i.e.* his passions.

71. **stola**: worn only by respectable matrons, cf. v. 29, and **togata**, v. 63.

73. **at**: opposing the following to the thought contained in **magno**, etc. — **pugnantia**, *utterly at variance*, cf. I. 1. 102.— **istis**: the dative instead of **cum**, in accordance with the Greek (and perhaps also the popular) usage, cf. I. 4. 48.

74. **dives opis suae**, *rich in her own resources*, *i.e.* who can easily satisfy her wants. — **natura**, *i.e.*

dispensare velis ac non fugienda petendis
immiscere. Tuo vitio rerumne labores,
nil referre putas? Quare, ne paeniteat te,
desine matronas sectarier, unde laboris
plus haurire mali est quam ex re decerpere fructus.
Nec magis huic inter niveos viridisque lapillos,
sit licet hoc, Cerinthe, tuum, tenerum est femur aut crus
rectius, atque etiam melius persaepe togatae est.
Adde huc, quod mercem sine fucis gestat, aperte
quod venale habet ostendit, nec, si quid honesti est
iactat habetque palam, quaerit quo turpia celet.
Regibus hic mos est: ubi equos mercantur, opertos
inspiciunt, ne, si facies, ut saepe, decora
molli fulta pede est, emptorem inducat hiantem,
quod pulchrae clunes, breve quod caput, ardua cervix.
Hoc illi recte: ne corporis optima Lyncei
contemplere oculis, Hypsaea caecior illa,

unsophisticated, not perverted by refinements.

75. **dispensare,** *manage, i.e.* use one's means with discretion. — **fugienda,** etc., *i.e. confound right and wrong.* But the words are used in the sense of the Stoic philosophy in reference to things which nature would suggest to us to seek and to avoid respectively; cf. I. 3. 114.

76. **tuo**: in regard to his desires, which are in his own power to control, so that the trouble arising from want of control is really his own fault. — **rerum,** *circumstances,* which it is not in his power to prevent, as it is in the other case.

77. **nil referre,** *it makes no difference, i.e.* do you think it is all the same whether you bring your misfortunes on yourself, or suffer undeservedly? — **paeniteat,** *have reason to repent.*

79. **est,** *it is necessary, one is likely.* The construction, a favorite one with Horace, seems to be imitated from the Greek.

80. **huic,** *i.e.* **matronae.** — **lapillos**: pearls and emeralds which the women of quality wear.

81. **sit licet hoc ... tuum,** *though this may be your taste,* referring to the preceding line.

85. **quo,** *how she may, ways to.*

86. **regibus,** *princes, nabobs, rich men,* cf. II. 2. 45.

87. **facies,** *figure, shape.*

88. **molli,** *tender, weak.* — **inducat,** *take in;* a figure derived from the net or snare. — **hiantem,** *greedy.* Cf. I. 1. 71 and note.

90. **illi,** *they,* as opposed to the lover, who is less careful. — **ne,** *so do not,* lit. (I tell you this) that you may not, etc. — **Lyncei** (with **oculis**), one of the Argonauts, famous for his keen sight.

91. **Hypsaea,** unknown.

quae mala sunt, spectes. O crus! O brachia! Verum
depugis, nasuta, brevi latere ac pede longo est.
Matronae praeter faciem nil cernere possis,
cetera, ni Catia est, demissa veste tegentis.
Si interdicta petes, vallo circumdata, nam te
hoc facit insanum, multae tibi tum officient res,
custodes, lectica, ciniflones, parasitae,
ad talos stola demissa et circumdata palla,
plurima, quae invideant pure apparere tibi rem.
Altera, nil obstat: Cois tibi paene videre est
ut nudam, ne crure malo, ne sit pede turpi;
metiri possis oculo latus. An tibi mavis
insidias fieri pretiumque avellier ante
quam mercem ostendi? 'Leporem venator ut alta
in nive sectetur, positum sic tangere nolit,'
cantat et apponit: 'Meus est amor huic similis; nam
transvolat in medio posita et fugientia captat.'
Hiscine versiculis speras tibi posse dolores
atque aestus curasque gravis e pectore pelli?

92. **O crus**: the words of the blind admirer.

93. **brevi latere**, *short-waisted.*

95. **Catia**: one of Horace's favorite side hits.

96. **nam te**, etc.: the common and well-known longing for forbidden fruit.

98. **custodes**, etc.: *i.e.* all of this train surrounds, and so conceals her, thus exciting curiosity and desire. — **ciniflones**, *dressing-maids*, strictly servants who used the curling-tongs.

100. **plurima**, *a thousand things.* — **invideant**, *hinder.* — **apparere**, after the analogy of the infinitive with **impedio** and **prohibeo**. — **rem**, *i.e. things*, as they are.

101. **altera**: subject of **quin appareat**, or the like. Translate, *with the other*, and omit the verb as in Latin. — **Cois** (*sc.* **vestibus**): a transparent gauzy kind of silk garments made in Cos, and worn only by this sort of people. — **est**, *it is possible*, cf. v. 79, and II. 5. 103.

105. **ut**, *how*, with **cantat**.

106. **positum**, *set before him.* — **sic**, *just as he is*, without any trouble on the hunter's part. — **nolit**: cf. I. 1. 19.

107. **cantat**, *quotes;* the sentiment being from Callimachus, *Ep.* 31 (Meineke). — **amor**: abstract.

108. **in medio posita**, *what is set before it*, open to everybody. — **fugientia captat**, *chases flying game*, cf. I. 1. 68.

109. **versiculis**, *lines;* referring to the quotation, but treating it as a charm to conjure away the pangs of love.

110. **aestus**, *fever.* — **pelli**, *be exorcised, charmed.*

Nonne, cupidinibus statuat natura modum quem,
quid latura sibi, quid sit dolitura negatum,
quaerere plus prodest et inane abscindere soldo?
Num, tibi cum fauces urit sitis, aurea quaeris
pocula? Num esuriens fastidis omnia praeter
pavonem rhombumque? Tument tibi cum inguina, num, si
ancilla aut verna est praesto puer, impetus in quem
continuo fiat, malis tentigine rumpi?
Non ego: namque parabilem amo venerem facilemque.
Illam, 'Post paulo,' 'Sed pluris,' 'Si exierit vir,'
Gallis, hanc Philodemus ait sibi, quae neque magno
stet pretio neque cunctetur, cum est iussa venire.
Candida rectaque sit; munda hactenus, ut neque longa
nec magis alba velit, quam dat natura, videri.
Haec ubi supposuit dextro corpus mihi laevum,
Ilia et Egeria est: do nomen quodlibet illi,
nec vereor, ne, dum futuo, vir rure recurrat,
ianua frangatur, latret canis, undique magno
pulsa domus strepitu resonet, vepallida lecto
desiliat mulier, miseram se conscia clamet,

111. **natura**: *i.e.* natural wants, as opposed to perverted desires born of an artificial civilization.

112. **quid (latura)**, *what satisfaction* she *will give herself*. — **quid negatum**, *what privation*, etc.

113. **inane**, *the show*. — **soldo**, *the substance* (for form see Introd.).

114. **num**, *say*, or *tell me*.

120. **illam** (*sc.* **esse**): opposed to **hanc**, v. 121. — **sed pluris**, *but for more money*. These quotations are treated as descriptive adjectives, or epithets of the woman.

121. **Gallis**, the priests of Cybele. — **Philodemus**, an Epicurean philosopher, a contemporary of Cicero. Some lost epigram of his is no doubt quoted or alluded to.

123. **sit**, *should be*, *must be*. — **munda**, *adorned*. — **hactenus**: as a limitation, *only so far*. — **longa**: by means of any coiffure or high heels.

124. **dat**, *grants*, *i.e.* than nature has made her.

126. **Ilia**, etc.: *i.e.* of the noblest birth.

129. **pulsa**, *with his knocking*. — **vepallida**, *white as a sheet*, with **ve-** intensive (orig. *out?* cf. **ex**).

130. **miseram**, etc.: in English we should keep the direct discourse, *ah, wretched me!* — **conscia**, *her confidante*, a slave, the go-between.

cruribus haec metuat, doti deprensa, egomet mi.
Discincta tunica fugiendum est ac pede nudo,
ne nummi pereant aut puga aut denique fama.
Deprendi miserum est; Fabio vel iudice vincam.

## III.

Omnibus hoc vitium est cantoribus, inter amicos
ut numquam inducant animum cantare rogati,
iniussi numquam desistant. Sardus habebat
ille Tigellius hoc. Caesar, qui cogere posset,

131. **cruribus**: for heinous offences, such as this treachery to her master would be, slaves had their legs broken on an anvil. — **deprensa**: the woman, who in such a case lost a part of her marriage portion.

133. **denique**, *at any rate*, even if he escapes the other misfortunes.

134. **Fabio**, no doubt the same philosopher mentioned in I. 1. 14, according to whose doctrine, of course as a Stoic, nothing was **miserum** to the sage. Yet even he would have to admit that this was. The abrupt ending after the climax in **deprendi**, etc., is in Horace's favorite manner. However far he may go, he stops unexpectedly, doubtless on purpose to avoid the appearance of formal preaching.

SATIRE 3. This satire is directed against the fault of censoriousness and the habit of detraction and disparagement of one's friends. These vices had probably increased, as often happens, with the increase of refinement and the scarcity of other objects on which to exercise men's critical faculties. Horace evidently saw that they were fatal to the social intercourse of a court, and found them the more hurtful in that they were practised in a Pharisaic spirit under the pretence of virtue. Hence the precepts of this satire. Here again the poet advances, not directly, but by a flank attack, starting off with a diatribe against a member of the court circle now dead, as if he himself were one of the detractors. Presently, however, he shows that what he has said is only an example of the disparagement which he wishes to inveigh against.

1. The poet begins with a general charge, but the emphatic position of **omnibus** shows that the stricture is supposed to be intended for some particular person to be mentioned later.

3. **iniussi**, *unbidden, uninvited.* — **Sardus**: the word may well be supposed to have a disparaging tone, as the Sardinians were not much esteemed at Rome.

4. **Tigellius**: the same person who is mentioned in the second satire. — **Caesar**: Augustus. — **posset**, etc.: these subjunctives are not in the contrary-to-fact construction, but stand for present tenses transferred to past time. If we imagine them used of a case in the present, their true character is easily seen. **posset**, in any case, comes under the characteristic class. See A. & G. Gr. § 307. *f*.

si peteret per amicitiam patris atque suam, non
quicquam proficeret; si collibuisset, ab ovo
usque ad mala citaret 'Io Bacchae!' modo summa
voce, modo hac resonat quae chordis quattuor ima.
Nil aequale homini fuit illi; saepe velut qui
currebat fugiens hostem, persaepe velut qui
Iunonis sacra ferret; habebat saepe ducentos,
saepe decem servos; modo reges atque tetrarchas,
omnia magna loquens, modo, 'Sit mihi mensa tripes et
concha salis puri et toga, quae defendere frigus,
quamvis crassa, queat.' Deciens centena dedisses
huic parco, paucis contento, quinque diebus
nil erat in loculis. Noctis vigilabat ad ipsum

5. **patris**, *i.e.* Julius Cæsar, his adoptive father. — **non quicquam proficeret**, *he would not have the least effect.*

6. **si collibuisset**, *if he took a fancy.* — **ab ovo usque ad mala**: *i.e.* from the beginning to the end, since the *promulsis* or antepast consisted of eggs and the like, and the dessert came last, as with us. If we substitute *oysters* for *eggs*, and *dessert* for *apples*, the translation will be tolerably near.

7. **citaret**, *would shout.* — **Bacchae**: from some favorite song, probably from a Greek tragedy like the Bacchae of Euripides. — **summa**: as the lyre was held, the deepest note was above and the highest below. Hence we must invert the words in English, referring them to pitch and not position.

8. **resonat**, *accords.* — **chordis**: dative.

9. **aequale**, *uniform, regular, consistent.* — **homini illi**, *about the man.* — **qui**: *sc.* **curreret**.

10. **persaepe**: *sc.* **incedebat**. Notice the economy of words, where **curreret** is suggested by **currebat**, and its form by **ferret**. Again, some word of walking is indicated by the manner of proceeding described, but its form is determined by **currebat**.

11. **habebat**: *i.e.* in his train as he appeared abroad.

12. **decem**: a small number for the princely style of the Romans. Cf. I. 6. 116. — **reges**, *princes, rich men, i.e.* of his intercourse with them, and of matters in which they were concerned, indicating a life at courts.

13. **magna**, *on a grand scale.* — **modo**, *now saying.* — **tripes**, *three-legged*, as opposed to the finer tables with one support in the centre (*orbis*). — **concha salis puri**: suggesting simplicity with cleanliness and decency. There was a kind of sanctity about the saltcellar (**salinum**), which was in a manner dedicated to the household gods.

15. **deciens centena**: *sc.* **milia sestertium**, *a million.* — **dedisses**, *suppose you had given* or *gave*, a hortatory subjunctive transferred to past time.

16. **paucis**, *a little.*

17. **erat**, *there would be.* The

mane, diem totum stertebat. Nil fuit umquam
sic impar sibi. — Nunc aliquis dicat mihi: 'Quid tu,
nullane habes vitia?' Immo alia et fortasse minora.
Maenius absentem Novium cum carperet, 'Heus tu,'
quidam ait, 'ignoras te, an ut ignotum dare nobis
verba putas?' 'Egomet mi ignosco,' Maenius inquit.
Stultus et improbus hic amor est, dignusque notari.
Cum tua pervideas oculis mala lippus inunctis,

construction is similar to the general condition. In present time it would be, "Give him a million; in ten days there is nothing," etc., as a general character of the man. — **noctis vigilabat,** *he would watch the night through.*

18. **nil,** *no one.* The use of the neuter in this way is very common to make the statement more universal.

19. **impar,** *inconsistent.* — **nunc aliquis,** etc.: here the poet turns to the proper subject of the satire, representing some person who hears him as becoming indignant at this abuse of Tigellius, and asking if he himself is free from faults, that he is thus severe upon another. He thus shows that his abuse is an example of what he satirizes. — **quid tu**: *sc.* **agis**; but the expression has become idiomatic, and the verb is lost sight of. Trans. *How about yourself?*

20. **immo alia,** *oh, no* (I do not say that), *but different ones.* — **et fortasse minora**: best assigned with the two preceding words to Horace, though by some they are given to the interlocutor.

21. **Maenius,** etc.: Horace, as usual, illustrates his meaning by an example. — **heus tu,** *look here, my friend.*

22. **quidam,** *one, some one, a man.* Cf. **aliquis,** v. 19. The difference is that in the former no definite person is conceived of, while here a particular person is meant, though not described or identified. — **ut ignotum** (*sc.* **te**), *as a stranger to us,* or *as if we didn't know you, i.e.* "Is it ignorance of your own character, or the hope of deceiving us, that leads you to attack another man's faults, when you have so many of your own?" — **dare verba,** *deceive, impose upon,* a common colloquial expression.

23. **egomet,** etc.: the naïve answer of Mænius shows the disposition which Horace is attacking, and serves as a text for the following. — **improbus,** *conscienceless.*

24. **amor,** *self-love.* — **notari,** *to be censured.* The construction is poetic or colloquial, for which Ciceronian prose would require **ut** or **qui** with the subjunctive. The meaning of the word comes from the mark (*nota*) which the censor in making up the rolls affixed to the name of any person whom he wished to remove from his position for misconduct.

25. **lippus inunctis,** *with your blear eyes daubed with eye-salve.* One is tempted to make **in** negative in **inunctis**, as if the man had weak eyes and did not care to put on the usual remedy. But there seems to be no authority for this.

cur in amicorum vitiis tam cernis acutum
quam aut aquila aut serpens Epidaurius? At tibi contra
evenit, inquirant vitia ut tua rursus et illi.
Iracundior est paulo, minus aptus acutis
naribus horum hominum; rideri possit eo, quod
rusticius tonso toga defluit, et male laxus
in pede calceus haeret: at est bonus, ut melior vir
non alius quisquam, at tibi amicus, at ingenium ingens
inculto latet hoc sub corpore. Denique te ipsum
concute, num qua tibi vitiorum inseverit olim
natura, aut etiam consuetudo mala; namque

27. **Epidaurius:** the serpent was a special symbol of the worship of Æsculapius, and was often identified with the god himself. It was in this form that the god was supposed to have come from Epidaurus to Rome, where a temple was built to him on the island in the Tiber. The serpent was famous for keen vision (cf. the name δράκων), and was supposed to possess prophetic powers. The connection here is probably only from Horace's favorite way of giving an individual instead of a class, and there is no special reference to this particular Æsculapius serpent.

28. **rursus et illi**, *they too in turn*, *i.e.* those you criticise.

29. **iracundior**, *quick-tempered*, an example of a case where injustice is done by this criticism, inasmuch as the subject of it cannot, like most men, disregard it, but is angered by it. — **minus aptus**: *i.e.* he has a quick temper impatient of criticism. — **acutis naribus**, *the keen criticism*, the figure derived from the natural turning up of the nose in fastidious disgust. (Cf. I. 4. 8, and I. 6. 5.)

30. **horum**, *of our day*, when this fault is so common.

31. **rusticius tonso**: with his hair in rustic style. — **toga**: the Romans paid the utmost attention to the set of the toga, plaiting it in folds which were secured in a fixed position. This requirement of fashion the man neglects, letting his toga fall loosely and awry. — **male laxus**, *loose and ill-fitting*.

32. **at est bonus**, etc.: *i.e.* he has all these good qualities, which are lost sight of in this over-fastidious criticism.

34. **denique**, etc.: *i.e.* in short, learn tolerance of such minor faults by self-examination, through which you will very likely find that you have some as well.

35. **concute**: the figure derived from shaking out the loose garments of the ancients for purposes of search. We should say search your pockets or the like. — **olim**, *at any time*. — **inseverit**: by changing the voice the order of words and ideas may be kept in English.

36. **namque**: introducing the reason for saying **consuetudo** as well as **natura**. Even if one is free from bad habits by nature, it may happen that they have grown up unawares, like weeds in neglected ground.

neglectis urenda filix innascitur agris.
Illuc praevertamur, amatorem quod amicae
turpia decipiunt caecum vitia, aut etiam ipsa haec
delectant, veluti Balbinum polypus Hagnae.
Vellem in amicitia sic erraremus, et isti
errori nomen virtus posuisset honestum.
At pater ut gnati, sic nos debemus amici
si quod sit vitium non fastidire; strabonem
appellat *paetum* pater, et *pullum*, male parvus
si cui filius est, ut abortivus fuit olim
Sisyphus; hunc *varum* distortis cruribus; illum
balbutit *scaurum* pravis fultum male talis.

37. **urenda**, *to be burned with fire*.

38. **illuc**, *to this point*, referring, as often in Latin, to what follows. — **praevertamur**, *let us turn*, in preference to any other subject.

39. **decipiunt**, *escape the notice of*. Cf. **fallo**.

40. **Balbinum**: nothing is known of this case, but it explains itself.

41. **vellem**: notice that the wish is contrary to the actual fact.

42. **virtus**: *i.e.* philosophers in their discussions on virtue. The Stoics are particularly referred to, whose high ideal of virtue and tendency to puritanism apparently made them especially inclined to censoriousness, and against whom Horace never loses an opportunity to break a lance. Cf. v. 96 *et seq.* — **honestum**: the Stoic made "the becoming," *τὸ πρέπον*, *i.e.* what was in accordance with the nature of man and the universe, the criterion of virtue. Of this expression **honestum** is the Latin translation, and the word is here used with reference to this technical sense. Hence it means *virtuous*, but as **virtus** is best translated *virtue*, we may translate *honorable*. At any rate, the whole means, 'that Ethics had reckoned this among the virtues,' which of course in the Stoic school it could not do.

43. **gnati**, *with his son*, changing the construction to keep the emphasis and the order of the words.

44. **fastidire**, *be too critical*. — **strabonem**: the point of the passage lies in the fact that the descriptive words, most of which are real Roman names, are of two classes, the first denoting an excessive degree of the quality referred to, and the second a slight degree, with which latter class the fond father nicknames his son. — **strabonem**, *his "cock-eyed" son*. All the names should be given in Latin with the translation.

45. **appellat**: cf. Lucr. IV. 1160. — **paetum**, *Blinky*. — **pullum**, *Chicky*. — **male**, *wretchedly*.

47. **Sisyphus**: a famous dwarf, kept by Mark Antony. Such persons were very common in the suites of the Roman nobles, acting as jesters. — **varum**, *little Bandy-legs*.

48. **balbutit**, *calls in childish accents*. — **scaurum**, *little Stumpy*, properly with misshapen ankles. — **male**, *sadly* (with **pravis**).

Parcius hic vivit, *frugi* dicatur. Ineptus
et iactantior hic paulo est, *concinnus amicis*
postulat ut videatur. At est truculentior atque
plus aequo liber ; *simplex fortisque* habeatur.
Caldior est ; *acris* inter numeretur. Opinor,
haec res et iungit, iunctos et servat amicos.
At nos virtutes ipsas invertimus, atque
sincerum cupimus vas incrustare. Probus quis
nobiscum vivit, multum demissus homo ; illi
*tardo* cognomen *pingui* damus. Hic fugit omnis
insidias nullique malo latus obdit apertum,
cum genus hoc inter vitae versetur, ubi acris
invidia atque vigent ubi crimina ; pro bene sano
ac non incauto *fictum astutumque* vocamus.
Simplicior quis et est, qualem me saepe libenter

49. **parcius**: in the same way the moral qualities are expressed by two sets of epithets, one exaggerating, the other extenuating, the fault. — **frugi**, *thrifty*. — **ineptus**, *an ass;* strictly, wanting in the sense of propriety, and so putting himself forward in the manner which we speak of as "making an ass of one's self." (Cf. Cic. *de Or*. II. 4. 17.)

50. **iactantior**, *forward*. — **concinnus**, *agreeable*, *i.e.* making an effort to be prominent in amusing one's friends.

52. **liber**, *free-spoken*. — **simplex**, *frank*. — **fortis**, *fearless*, not afraid to speak his mind.

53. **acris**, *high-spirited*. — **opinor**, *I fancy*, *I take it*, with its cognates used of a mere notion not thoroughly thought out or well-founded, though of course it may be true.

55. **invertimus**, *distort;* lit. tip them upside down so as to make vices of them.

56. **sincerum**, etc.: the figure is derived from the tartar which forms on the inside of a wine-jar. — **cupimus**, *we are eager*, always a stronger word than **volo**, etc. — **probus quis**, *some good honest*, etc., as an honorable epithet, but with a suggestion of want of spirit. Cf. *silly* (originally *good*), *bonhomme*, *good-natured*, and New-England *clever*, as well as the translation suggested.

57. **multum**, modifying **demissus**, a colloquial use. Cf. Pl. Aulul. II. 1. 5. — **demissus**, *modest and unassuming*.

58. **tardo**, **pingui**, *stupid and dull*. The text authority for **illi**, and the parallelism of the following clauses, indicate that this is the true meaning, in spite of many objections that can be made.

59. **nulli malo**, *to no man's hostile thrust*. — **malo**, masculine.

60. **cum genus**, etc.: giving the reason and excuse for the caution.

61. **vigent**, *are rife*. — **sano**, *a level-headed man*.

63. **simplicior**, *thoughtless*, *outspoken*. — **et**, *again*.

obtulerim tibi, Maecenas, ut forte legentem
aut tacitum impellat quovis sermone; '*Molestus;*
*communi sensu plane caret*,' inquimus. Eheu,
quam temere in nosmet legem sancimus iniquam!
Nam vitiis nemo sine nascitur; optimus ille est
qui minimis urgetur. Amicus dulcis, ut aequum est,
cum mea compenset vitiis bona; pluribus hisce
(si modo plura mihi bona sunt) inclinet, amari
si volet; hac lege in trutina ponetur eadem.
Qui ne tuberibus propriis offendat amicum
postulat, ignoscet verrucis illius; aequum est
peccatis veniam poscentem reddere rursus.
   Denique, quatenus excidi penitus vitium irae,
cetera item nequeunt stultis haerentia, cur non
ponderibus modulisque suis ratio utitur, ac res
ut quaeque est, ita suppliciis delicta coercet?
Si quis eum servum, patinam qui tollere iussus

65. **tacitum,** *in silent thought.* — **quovis sermone**: taken with **impellat.** Probably **molestus** also belongs in the same clause, but it means the same thing taken with the following, *the bore, he is absolutely*, etc.

66. **communi sensu**: the universal feeling belonging to mankind of the fitness of things, *sense of propriety.*

67. **temere,** *thoughtlessly.* — **sancimus,** *set up.* — **iniquam,** *harsh and unkind.*

70. **cum mea,** etc.: *set off my good qualities against*, etc.

71. **amari si volet,** *if he wishes me to love him.*

72. **hac lege,** *on this condition, these terms.* — **in trutina,** etc., *weighed in the same balance.*

73. **tuberibus, verrucis,** *warts* (properly *wens*), *pimples,* reducing the scale somewhat, but keeping the proportion. The Romans seem to have been very subject to wens and similar excrescences of larger size to which we are not liable.

75. **poscentem,** *for one asking.* — **reddere** (*sc.* **veniam**) **rursus,** *to render the like again.*

76. **quatenus**: cf. I. 1. 64. — **irae**: perhaps this fault is chosen because it is regarded as not necessarily a vice, but possibly a virtue, by the Peripatetics.

77. **stultis**: here in its technical meaning, as opposed to **sapiens,** the ideal (and, as Horace would intimate, impossible) Stoic sage.

78. **ponderibus,** etc.: here first crops out plainly the opposition to the Stoic school, of which Horace is thinking doubtless throughout, though he has not till now clearly referred to it. Cf. v. 96.

79. **coercet suppliciis,** *visit with punishment.*

semesos piscis tepidumque ligurrierit ius
in cruce suffigat, Labeone insanior inter
sanos dicatur. Quanto hoc furiosius atque
maius peccatum est : paulum deliquit amicus,
quod nisi concedas, habeare insuavis, acerbus :
odisti, et fugis ut Rusonem debitor aeris,
qui nisi, cum tristes misero venere Kalendae,
mercedem aut nummos undeunde extricat, amaras
porrecto iugulo historias captivus ut audit.
Comminxit lectum potus, mensave catillum
Evandri manibus tritum deiecit : ob hanc rem,
aut positum ante mea quia pullum in parte catini
sustulit esuriens, minus hoc iucundus amicus
sit mihi ? Quid faciam si furtum fecerit, aut si

81. **ligurrierit**, *gobble up*, a very common offence of slaves everywhere. Cf. "Massa's nigger, Massa's meat," an old negro saying.

82. **in cruce**, the common way of punishing slaves with death. — **Labeone** : it is not known what Labeo is referred to, but it is enough to guess that either his was a well-known case of insanity, or that Horace, as often, gives him a thrust in passing in regard to some conduct which would bear the appearance of a craze.

85. **acerbus**, *embittered*, along with **insuavis** after **habeare**.

86. **ut Rusonem**, etc., *as the man that owes him money does Ruso*, evidently a usurer who had unsuccessful literary aspirations in the line of history. This is another of Horace's side thrusts.

87. **Kalendae** : the first of the month was the most common day for payment.

88. **mercedem**, *the interest*. — **nummos**, *the money*, *i.e.* the principal. — **extricat**, *scrapes together*. — **amaras**, *dreary*.

89. **porrecto**, etc. : the position for execution, as of a prisoner of war awaiting his doom, a situation which Horace no doubt has in his mind in his description of the poor man bored to death. It is, however, only a kind of passing thought of his, and not to be insisted on too strongly.

90. **potus**, *in his cups*.

91. **Evandri** : there are two possible explanations of this name, either as a famous potter, in which case the dish is valuable for its intrinsic excellence; or as the ancient king, in which case there is a humorous indication of its age. The second seems the better. Cf. II. 3. 21.

92. **mea in parte catini** : there is no indication that the Romans used plates as we do. They no doubt ate with their fingers from small dishes on the table which stood in the centre of the triclinium.

93. **esuriens**, *in his hunger*. — **minus hoc iucundus**, etc. : *i.e.* "Shall I renounce his friendship ?"

94. **furtum fecerit**, the technical phrase.

prodiderit commissa fide sponsumve negarit?
Quis paria esse fere placuit peccata, laborant
cum ventum ad verum est; sensus moresque repugnant
atque ipsa utilitas, iusti prope mater et aequi.
Cum prorepserunt primis animalia terris,
mutum et turpe pecus, glandem atque cubilia propter
unguibus et pugnis, dein fustibus, atque ita porro
pugnabant armis, quae post fabricaverat usus,
donec verba, quibus voces sensusque notarent,

95. **commissa fide** (dat.), *a trust.* The two classes of offences are of course made as different in enormity as possible, to bring out more fully the absurdity of the Stoic paradox in v. 96.

96. **quis**: the constant use of this old form in the satires is an indication of their colloquial character. — The connection of thought is: Such offences are recognized as of different magnitude by every one, and though the Stoic may preach in theory the paradox **paria**, etc., as an answer to Horace's view, yet when we come to real life (**ad verum**), he gets into trouble.

97. **sensus**, *our feelings*, our sense of right and wrong, almost equal to "instincts" or "conscience." — **mores**, *habits*, our customary mode of life. — **repugnant**, *rebel*, or *protest.*

98. **utilitas**, *utility* (as a technical philosophical term), or *selfish advantage*, *i.e.* the selfish interests of mankind, from which, he goes on to say, the ideas of right and wrong have risen through the making of laws to protect these interests.

99. **cum prorepserunt**, etc.: the doctrine of the development of society, in accordance generally with the notions of the ancients as to the origin of man, but especially of the Epicurean school. Cf. Lucretius, V. 780 *seq.* The chief point is, that the law of the strongest alone obtained at the outset, though the Stoic would perhaps not admit that right did not exist because the inhabitants of the earth were not able or inclined to practise it. The argument is, however, not the mere setting of one dogma against another, but an explanation of **utilitas iusti mater** in accordance with what was in the main the generally received opinion.

100. **mutum**, *dumb, speechless*, and so unable to defend his rights in any other way than by fighting. — **turpe**, *shapeless, unsightly*, in accord with the Epicurean notion of development from lower animals. — **glandem atque cubilia**: *i.e.* for food and lodging, to supply their natural wants from Nature's store in which there was as yet no individual property.

101. **unguibus**, etc.: not having learned to make better weapons. — **fustibus**: one step in advance, at least an acquired, not a natural, weapon. — **atque ita porro**, etc.: and so they went on, till experience taught them the manufacture of arms. But still there could be no society and no rights until they invented language, which made association possible.

103. **verba nominaque**, *words* (to express ideas) *and names* (to assign to things). — **voces sensusque**, almost equal to *ideas* and *sen-*

nominaque invenere; dehinc absistere bello,
oppida coeperunt munire et ponere leges,
ne quis fur esset, neu latro, neu quis adulter.
Nam fuit ante Helenam cunnus taeterrima belli
causa; sed ignotis perierunt mortibus illi,
quos venerem incertam rapientis more ferarum
viribus editior caedebat, ut in grege taurus.
Iura inventa metu iniusti fateare necesse est,
tempora si fastosque velis evolvere mundi.
Nec natura potest iusto secernere iniquum,
dividit ut bona diversis, fugienda petendis;
nec vincet ratio hoc, tantundem ut peccet idemque
qui teneros caules alieni fregerit horti,
et qui nocturnus sacra divom legerit. Adsit
regula, peccatis quae poenas inroget aequas,

*sations*, *i.e.* predications and conceptions.

104. **dehinc**, etc.: *i.e.* as soon as language made association possible, they exchanged a state of war for mutual rights and individual property, in order peaceably to satisfy their primal appetites, and protect themselves in the possession of the means for this satisfaction.

107. **nam fuit**, etc.: explanatory of **neu quis adulter**. For lust must have caused war long before the famous case of Helen, but as marriages were not established, no rights were violated, and the wars were never celebrated in song.

109. **venerem incertam rapientis**, *satisfying by violence unregulated passion.*

110. **editior**, *the superior.* — **caedebat**, *fell at the hands of*, or *were slain by.*

111. **iniusti**: neuter, cf. **iusto**, vv. 113 and 98.

112. **tempora**, *history* (in its chronological development). — **fastos**, *records* (in chronological order).

113. **natura**, *i.e. the natural instincts*, distinguishing by means of the senses.

114. **bona diversis**, *good things from their opposites*, speaking in reference to the natural instincts which are supposed to teach living creatures through the senses what is good for them. — **fugienda petendis**, *things to be shunned from objects of desire*, used in the same sense as the preceding, but more technical.

115. **vincet**, *can sustain*, with **hoc** as a cognate accusative. — **tantundem et idem**, *in the same degree and kind.*

117. **legerit**, *steals*, an old sense preserved in legal phrase, and also in **sacrilegus**.

118. **regula**, *a sliding scale*, properly a straight-edge. — **inroget**, *inflict*, the use of the word being derived from punishment inflicted by the vote of the people, to whom, by early Roman custom, was submitted (**rogare**) the bill for the punishment of offenders.

ne scutica dignum horribili sectere flagello.
Nam, ut ferula caedas meritum maiora subire
verbera, non vereor, cum dicas esse pares res
furta latrociniis, et magnis parva mineris
falce recisurum simili te, si tibi regnum
permittant homines. Si dives qui sapiens est,
et sutor bonus et solus formosus et est rex,
cur optas quod habes? 'Non nosti quid pater,' inquit,
'Chrysippus dicat: "Sapiens crepidas sibi numquam

119. **scutica**, *the whip*, an instrument of whipping more severe than the rod (**ferula**), and less so than the scourge (**flagellum**), which last had pieces of metal attached to its lashes.

120. **ut caedas**: the regular grammar requires **ne** (as the clause must be affirmative), and no explanation of the irregularity is satisfactory. Perhaps Horace allows himself a popular construction, *i.e.* a mistake in grammar. The meaning of course is, "I say the rule is needed to prevent too great severity, for there is no fear that the Stoic principle will lead to too great indulgence." A similar use of **ut** occurs in Livy, 28. 22, where, as here, the **ut** clause precedes.

122. **furta**, without violence.— **latrociniis**, accompanied by force. The same distinction exists between *theft* and *robbery*.— **magnis**, with **simili** (cf. "hair like the Graces").

123. **falce**, etc.: *i.e.* punishment, regarded as a pruning away of the vices of the State.— **tibi**: *i.e.* the Stoic, against whom the whole argument is aimed, and against whose follies and unfitness for social life the remainder of the satire is directed. The transition is afforded by the words which Horace quotes, as it were from the Stoic: "I would prune away, etc., if men would make me king," implying a wish to be so (hence **optas**, v. 126). Horace then replies, "According to your doctrine, you are a king already." To which the Stoic replies, "The Stoic doctrine is not that a *sapiens* is an actual king, but only a king *in posse*." Thus the Stoic shows the inapplicability of his own doctrines to actual life, which is the effect Horace wishes to produce, in order to nullify the excuse which the Stoic views give for censoriousness and harshness.

124. **si dives**, etc.: the Stoic paradox is, ὅτι μόνος ὁ σοφὸς πλούσιος, *solum sapientem esse divitem*. See Cic. *Paradox*, VI.

125. **sutor**: alluding to the perfection of the *sapiens* in all directions, but containing in itself a *reductio ad absurdum*.— **formosus**: of course the perfect man must possess perfect physical beauty among his other perfections.— **rex**: according to the Stoic doctrine, the *sapiens* is king, and all others are slaves. (Cf. Ep. I. 1. 106.)

126. **pater**, *the venerable*.

127. **Chrysippus**: the second great expounder of the Stoic views, so famous that it was said, εἰ μὴ γὰρ ἦν Χρύσιππος, οὐκ ἂν ἦν Στοά.— **sapiens**, etc.: the Stoic is represented as explaining the doctrine of the existence in perfection of all qualities in the *sapiens* by a ridicu-

nec soleas fecit, sutor tamen est sapiens."' Qui?
'Vt, quamvis tacet Hermogenes, cantor tamen atque
optimus est modulator; ut Alfenus vafer, omni
abiecto instrumento artis clausaque taberna,
sutor erat; sapiens operis sic optimus omnis
est opifex solus, sic rex.' Vellunt tibi barbam
lascivi pueri; quos tu nisi fuste coerces,
urgeris turba circum te stante, miserque
rumperis, et latras, magnorum maxime regum!
Ne longum faciam: dum tu quadrante lavatum
rex ibis, neque te quisquam stipator ineptum
praeter Crispinum sectabitur, et mihi dulces
ignoscent, si quid peccaro stultus, amici,
inque vicem illorum patiar delicta libenter,
privatusque magis vivam te rege beatus.

lous example, thus, of course, belittling the argument.

129. **Hermogenes,** probably the person referred to in 2. 3.

130. **Alfenus**: no doubt a side hit at a rich usurer, probably, who had once been a cobbler, said to be from Cremona, now dead.

133. **vellunt,** etc.: the meaning is, "Well, enjoy your imaginary royalty (*i.e.* your Stoic doctrine which makes you a king), and reject the elegances of social life; appear as a philosopher in the streets to be the butt of the street-boys, and howl at the vices of mankind till you burst. Meanwhile I, adopting a more accommodating doctrine, will enjoy the pleasures of social intercourse, indulging my friends with charity, and being indulged in return." — **barbam**: the long beard, no doubt from adherence to an old fashion, but favored also as indicating want of care of the person, was generally characteristic of philosophers, especially of the Cynics and Stoics.

134. **fuste**: the philosopher regularly carried a staff, probably following the old fashion.

135. **urgeris**: to the stately Roman nothing could be more insulting than to be hustled in the crowd, and the picture is intended to show the degrading contrast between his royalty and his actual life.

136. **rumperis,** *you burst with rage.* — **latras,** *howl, i.e.* at the crowd. There is a special reference to the Cynics, so called from κύων.

137. **quadrante,** *a farthing; i.e.* you go to the common bath instead of enjoying the luxuries of the rich.

138. **stipator,** *companion,* the regular word for a person belonging to an escort or suite, either as a friend or a satellite. — **ineptum**: with **Crispinum.**

139. **Crispinum**: cf. I. 120. — **et,** correlative with **-que,** v. 141. — **dulces,** *kindly.*

141. **patiar,** *put up with.*

142. **te**: in prose **quam tu.**

## IV.

Eupolis atque Cratinus Aristophanesque poetae,
atque alii, quorum comoedia prisca virorum est,
si quis erat dignus describi, quod malus ac fur,
quod moechus foret aut sicarius aut alioqui
famosus, multa cum libertate notabant.
Hinc omnis pendet Lucilius, hosce secutus
mutatis tantum pedibus numerisque, facetus,
emunctae naris, durus componere versus.
Nam fuit hoc vitiosus: in hora saepe ducentos,
ut magnum, versus dictabat stans pede in uno;
cum flueret lutulentus, erat quod tollere velles;
garrulus atque piger scribendi ferre laborem,
scribendi recte; nam ut multum, nil moror. — Ecce,

SATIRE 4. An answer to Horace's critics, and defence of his form of composition.

1. **Eupolis**, etc.: he begins with the origin of satire, connecting it with the Old Comedy of Athens, of which the three names mentioned are the greatest.

2. **prisca**: used technically of the Old Comedy, which introduced actual persons upon the stage in order to cast ridicule upon them.

5. **notabant**, *stigmatized*. See 3. 24.

6. **hinc** = **ab his**. — **pendet**, *springs, i.e.* he is an imitation of them, and so hangs on them, or is supported by them. (Cf. "On these two commandments hang all the law and the prophets.")

7. **pedibus**: using the hexameter instead of the iambic measure. — **numeris**, *measures*, the same idea in another form.

8. **emunctae naris**, *of keen sense*, lit. with his nose free from obstruction, so that his scent is keen. — **durus**, etc.: it would seem that his critics had compared him with Lucilius to his disadvantage, and he proceeds to state the defects of that poet.

10. **ut magnum**, *as a great feat, i.e.* he regarded easy and rapid composition as the great object to be attained in art, rather than elegance and polish. — **pede in uno**: proverbial, not changing his position (just as we say "at a stretch") from one foot to the other.

11. **flueret lutulentus**, *hurried on with turbid flow*. — **tollere**: the figure is of a freshet carrying all sorts of foreign matter in its course, much of which is worthless, and so ought to be removed. (But cf. Quintil. X. 1. 94.)

12. **garrulus**, *wordy*.

13. **ut multum**: *sc.* **scripserit**. — **nil moror**: a colloquial expression for "I don't care," "I don't mind." — **ecce**, etc.: to show his disregard of rapidity in writing,

Crispinus minimo me provocat: 'Accipe, si vis,
accipiam tabulas; detur nobis locus, hora,
custodes; videamus uter plus scribere possit.'
'Di bene fecerunt, inopis me quodque pusilli
finxerunt animi, raro et perpauca loquentis;
at tu conclusas hircinis follibus auras,
usque laborantis dum ferrum molliat ignis,
ut mavis, imitare.' Beatus Fannius, ultro
delatis capsis et imagine, cum mea nemo
scripta legat, volgo recitare timentis ob hanc rem,
quod sunt quos genus hoc minime iuvat, utpote pluris
culpari dignos. Quemvis media elige turba:

Horace represents a challenge to himself from the loquacious moralizer Crispinus (see I. 120) to show his skill in writing. At the same time he disparages this branch of skill by making a poetaster like Crispinus excel him in it.

14. **minimo**, *at great odds*, lit. with a very small wager on my part.

17. **di bene**, etc.: an expression of thankfulness, — Horace's answer to Crispinus' challenge. — **inopis, pusilli animi**, *with an unproductive* (opp. to **copiosi**) *and unaspiring* (opp. to **magni**) *intellect*. — **quodque**, etc.: the full construction would be **quod inopis, quodque pusilli**, etc. The expression of the second **quod** with **-que**, thus implying the first, is almost a mannerism with Horace. Cf. v. 115.

18. **raro**, in reference to **pusilli**, **perpauca**, in reference to **inopis**, *speaking rarely, and very little at that.*

20. **laborantis**, *puffing away*. — **dum ferrum**, etc.: only to complete the picture.

21. **imitare**, imperative. — **Fannius**, a poet of the clique opposed to Horace, but otherwise unknown. The sense is, "Happy the popular poet, like Fannius, whose admirers present him, etc." The poet now turns from the criticism of Lucilius to a discussion of the difference between himself and the popular poets of the day, and explains why he is not popular.

22. **delatis capsis et imagine**: *with his works and bust offered for sale without his asking*, *i.e.* he is so popular that the booksellers voluntarily put his books on the market as an advantageous speculation. The reference is certainly to sales of the books, but whether by Fannius himself or the booksellers is not quite so clear, more likely the latter.

22. **nemo**: opposed to the popularity of Fannius, as indicated by the preceding act of his admirers.

23. **legat**, *reads*, by himself. — **recitare**: the regular word for public reading, which was the common method at that time of bringing out an author's works. — **timentis**, agreeing with the genitive implied in **mea**.

24. **genus hoc**, *i.e.* satire. — **pluris**, *the greater part*. In English we must supply a verb, but the Latin construction is a kind of apposition.

aut ob avaritiam aut misera ambitione laborat;
hic nuptarum insanit amoribus, hic puerorum;
hunc capit argenti splendor; stupet Albius aere;
hic mutat merces surgente a sole ad eum quo
vespertina tepet regio, quin per mala praeceps
fertur, uti pulvis collectus turbine, ne quid
summa deperdat metuens aut ampliet ut rem.
omnes hi metuunt versus, odere poetas.
'Faenum habet in cornu, longe fuge; dummodo risum
excutiat sibi, non hic cuiquam parcet amico;
et quodcumque semel chartis illeverit, omnis
gestiet a furno redeuntis scire lacuque
et pueros et anus.' Agedum, pauca accipe contra.
Primum ego me illorum dederim quibus esse poetas
excerpam numero: neque enim concludere versum
dixeris esse satis; neque si quis scribat, uti nos,
sermoni propriora, putes hunc esse poetam.
Ingenium cui sit, cui mens divinior atque os

26. **laborat**, *is troubled with*, a regular word for diseases.

28. **hunc capit**, *is captivated* (as better English). — **stupet**, *is dazed by the beauty of*, *i.e.* has an admiration which amounts to a craze.

29. **hic mutat**, etc.: *i.e.* voyages as a trader to the farthest East and the farthest West.

30. **mala**, *dangers*, *sufferings*.

32. **ampliet ut**, here in the proper meaning of the construction, *that he may not*, etc.

33. **metuunt**: because they are conscious of being proper subjects of satire.

34. **faenum**, etc.: a mark of dangerous cattle. It may be translated literally, or, abandoning the details of the figure, by, *He's a vicious brute.* — **longe fuge**, *keep well away from him*, like "give him a wide berth."

37. **a furno redeuntis**, etc.: *i.e.* the common crowd in the street, as they went to get bread or water, things which the better classes would provide in their own houses. These errands were no doubt occasions for gossip.

39. **primum ego me**, etc.: *i.e.* first, Horace doesn't claim to be a poet, so that the rules of the art of poetry don't apply to him. He thus avoids criticism as to his style.

40. **concludere versum**, *round off verses*, *i.e.* make metrical lines by bringing them to a proper conclusion.

41. **dixeris**: an apodosis, but the indefinite second person singular regularly has the subjunctive.

42. **sermoni**, *conversation*.

43. **ingenium**, *talent*. — **mens divinior**, *an inspired genius*. — **os magna sonaturum**, *a grand and*

magna sonaturum, des nominis huius honorem.
Idcirco quidam comoedia necne poema
esset quaesivere, quod acer spiritus ac vis
nec verbis nec rebus inest, nisi quod pede certo
differt sermoni, sermo merus. 'At pater ardens
saevit, quod meretrice nepos insanus amica
filius uxorem grandi cum dote recuset,
ebrius et, magnum quod dedecus, ambulet ante
noctem cum facibus.' Numquid Pomponius istis
audiret leviora, pater si viveret? Ergo
non satis est puris versum perscribere verbis,
quem si dissolvas, quivis stomachetur eodem
quo personatus pacto pater. His, ego quae nunc,
olim quae scripsit Lucilius, eripias si
tempora certa modosque, et quod prius ordine verbum est
posterius facias, praeponens ultima primis,

*lofty style.* As all poetry was originally to be sung, the Latin retains figures in reference to its style derived from sound which we have lost.

45. **quidam**: the Alexandrine grammarians.

46. **acer spiritus**, *a lively inspiration.*

47. **verbis**, *in the diction.* — **rebus**, *in the matter.* — **pede certo**, *by its fixed measure.*

48. **sermo**, in apposition with **comoedia**. — **at pater**, etc.: the objection of one who maintains that comedy has passages of poëtry in it. A very common scene in comedy is that of the angry father under the circumstances here referred to.

49. **nepos**, *spendthrift*, used as an adjective.

51. **ambulet**: a common form of revelry was the *comissatio*, in which the drinkers after a supper paraded through the city with torches, committing all sorts of wild disorder. Here it is done even before night, the intoxicated youth doing it without shame in broad daylight.

52. **numquid Pomponius**, etc.: the reply is that any dissolute young man would be addressed in the same way in real life; but to express this Horace takes an actual case of a young man of this kind, thus satirizing him as well as making out his own point. These side thrusts are very characteristic of the poet.

53. **ergo**: the reasoning is, if comedy has only the language of real life, it cannot be called poetry though put into metrical form.

55. **dissolvas**, *i.e.* change the order so that the metre disappears. Cf. v. 60.

56. **his**, etc.: in the same way Lucilius and Horace use only the language of common conversation put into metre; whereas in the extract from Ennius in v. 60, there is a poetic diction, and the thoughts suggested are on a higher plane than the language of common life.

non, ut si solvas '*Postquam Discordia taetra*
*belli ferratos postis portasque refregit,*'
invenias etiam disiecti membra poetae.
Hactenus haec: alias iustum sit necne poema,
nunc illud tantum quaeram, meritone tibi sit
suspectum genus hoc scribendi. Sulcius acer
ambulat et Caprius, rauci male cumque libellis,
magnus uterque timor latronibus; at bene si quis
et vivat puris manibus, contemnat utrumque.
Vt sis tu similis Caeli Birrique latronum,
non ego sum Capri neque Sulci: cur metuas me?
Nulla taberna meos habeat neque pila libellos,
quis manus insudet volgi Hermogenisque Tigelli:
nec recito cuiquam nisi amicis, idque coactus,
non ubivis coramve quibuslibet. In medio qui
scripta foro recitent sunt multi, quique lavantes:
suave locus voci resonat conclusus. Inanis
hoc iuvat, haud illud quaerentis, num sine sensu,
tempore num faciant alieno. 'Laedere gaudes,'

62. **etiam**, *still.*

63. **hactenus haec**, *so much for that point.* — **iustum**, *properly*, *i.e.* according to the rights and laws of poetry.

64. **suspectum**, *viewed with suspicion*, an allusion to v. 24.

65. **Sulcius**, etc.: the idea is that those informers who plied a trade in bringing accusations are a terror only to evil-doers, and one would expect the argument to continue: if you are honest men, you have no reason to fear me; but instead of that the poet turns sharply, and says in v. 69, "Though you have all the vices of the worst men, still you need not fear me, for I am no informer."

66. **ambulat**, *walks abroad.* — **rauci**, *i.e.* with pleading. — **libellis**, *their indictments.*

71. **nulla taberna**, etc.: the distinction is that Horace does not publish his strictures. — **pila**: the manuscripts were hung or placed out by the pillars to be inspected. — **habeat**: a weak hortatory, only implying determination.

73. **nec recito**: *i.e.* he does not even read in public, but only for the amusement of friends, when urged.

75. **recitent**, etc.: others are fond of reading in public in the Forum and at the public baths, because they like to hear themselves in the enclosed space, which gives a resonance to their elocution, regardless of tact or time.

78. **laedere gaudes**: another point made by his enemies, that he is malicious in his satires, in answer

inquis, 'et hoc studio pravus facis.' Vnde petitum
hoc in me iacis? Est auctor quis denique eorum
vixi cum quibus? 'Absentem qui rodit amicum,
qui non defendit, alio culpante, solutos
qui captat risus hominum famamque dicacis,
fingere qui non visa potest, commissa tacere
qui nequit, hic niger est, hunc tu, Romane, caveto.'
Saepe tribus lectis videas cenare quaternos,
e quibus unus amet quavis aspergere cunctos
praeter eum qui praebet aquam; post hunc quoque potus,
condita cum verax aperit praecordia Liber.
Hic tibi comis et urbanus liberque videtur,
infesto nigris; ego si risi, quod ineptus
pastillos Rufillus olet, Gargonius hircum,
lividus et mordax videor tibi? Mentio si qua
de Capitolini furtis iniecta Petilli

to which he calls in the evidence of his friends, asking his detractors where they get that stone to throw at him, *i.e.* the authority for such an accusation (**auctor**).

81. **absentem**, etc.: the objector answers: "Your satire shows it; a man who satirizes is a malicious person, and should be shunned by every honest Roman."

85. **niger**, *the black-hearted slanderer.* — **Romane**, *honest Roman*, alluding to the supposed honorable character of the Romans, as opposed to other nations.

86. **saepe tribus**, etc.: as the usual number was nine a larger company is indicated, of whom no one is safe from the malice of the detractor.

87. **aspergere**, *to bespatter.*

88. **aquam**: of course the host is referred to. Water, to mix with wine and for the washing of hands, which was necessary in the Roman manner of eating, played a more prominent part at a Roman feast than with us.

89. **condita praecordia,** *the hidden secrets of the heart.*

90. **hic tibi**, etc.: *i.e.* such a fellow seems to you, pretending to be the enemy of slanderers in literature, only an agreeable companion, witty and outspoken; whereas my sportive jests upon the follies of men seem to you expressions of envy, hatred, and malice.

92. See 2. 27.

93. **mentio si qua, etc.**: a still more striking example of malicious slander in social intercourse under pretence of friendship is introduced to show what that vice really is, and by the contrast to show Horace's freedom from it. Cf. vv. 100 and 101.

94. **Capitolini**: Petillius is so called in derision on account of his stealing gold from the statue of Jupiter on the Capitol, for which crime he was tried, but escaped through the influence of Augustus.

te coram fuerit, defendas, ut tuus est mos:
'Me Capitolinus convictore usus amicoque
a puero est, causaque mea permulta rogatus
fecit, et incolumis laetor quod vivit in urbe;
sed tamen admiror, quo pacto iudicium illud
fugerit.' Hic nigrae sucus loliginis, haec est
aerugo mera. Quod vitium procul afore chartis,
atque animo prius, ut si quid promittere de me
possum aliud vere promitto. Liberius si
dixero quid, si forte iocosius, hoc mihi iuris
cum venia dabis: insuevit pater optimus hoc me,
ut fugerem exemplis vitiorum quaeque notando.
Cum me hortaretur, parce frugaliter atque
viverem uti contentus eo quod mi ipse parasset:
'Nonne vides Albi ut male vivat filius utque
Baius inops? Magnum documentum ne patriam rem

96. **convictore usus**, etc.: *has enjoyed my intimacy and friendship.* — **causa**, etc.: *i.e.* "I owe much to him."

98. **incolumis . . . in urbe**, instead of losing his citizenship and being exiled, as he would have been if convicted.

100. **nigrae sucus loliginis,** *i.e.* the essence of black malignity. The figure is from the excretion of the cuttlefish from which India ink is made. Cf. **hic niger est**, v. 85.

101. **aerugo mera,** *pure verdigris:* comparing slander to rust eating into bronze, etc., which rust appears to do. Cf. A. P. 330.

102. **animo,** *from my heart.* — **prius,** *to begin with:* not having it in his heart he could not put it down on paper. — **ut si quid**, etc., *as truly as I can*, etc., lit. I promise, as I promise, in case I can promise any thing (else) truly.

103. **liberius,** *with too much freedom.* — **iocosius,** *with too rough a jest.*

104. **hoc iuris,** *this privilege.*

105. **insuevit**, etc.: giving a reason why he should be indulged in his habit of satire, and at the same time showing that there is no malice in his strictures because it is for a moral purpose. — **hoc,** *i.e.* **ut fugerem.**

106. **exemplis notando,** *by censuring them through examples,* — the manner of **insuevit.**

107. **hortaretur**: the so-called subjunctive of repeated action. Cicero would have used the indicative.

108. **contentus eo**, etc.: *i.e.* with that style of living which was within the income that his father had left him; not living in the style of the spendthrifts mentioned below.

110. **magnum documentum,** *an urgent warning:* the words are in a kind of apposition with the preceding clauses. A. & G. 240, *g.*

perdere quis velit.' A turpi meretricis amore
cum deterreret: 'Scetani dissimilis sis.'
Ne sequerer moechas, concessa cum venere uti
possem: 'Deprensi non bella est fama Treboni,'
aiebat. 'Sapiens, vitatu quidque petitu
sit melius, causas reddet tibi; mi satis est, si
traditum ab antiquis morem servare tuamque,
dum custodis eges, vitam famamque tueri
incolumem possum; simul ac duraverit aetas
membra animumque tuum, nabis sine cortice.' Sic me
formabat puerum dictis; et sive iubebat
ut facerem quid: 'Habes auctorem, quo facias hoc,'
unum ex iudicibus selectis obiciebat;
sive vetabat: 'An hoc inhonestum et inutile factu
necne sit addubites, flagret rumore malo cum

111. **ne quis velit**: an expression of prohibition borrowed from the laws. Cf. the common *noli facere*. — **meretricis**: this seems a contradiction to what follows, but the kind of person here referred to is the mistress, corresponding to the Parisian woman of the *demi monde*, to whom a lasting attachment was disapproved.

113. **moechas**, *faithless wives*, married women.

114. **deprensi Treboni**: an example from real life.

115. **sapiens**, *the philosopher*, as opposed to the plain practical man. — **quidque**: the **-que**, implies an omitted **quid** before. Cf. v. 17. **quid**, depending on the ethical question implied though not expressed in **causas**, may be rendered, *as to what*.

116. **causas**, *the theory*, lit. the reasons, as a philosophical basis of ethics.

117. **morem**, *the mode of life*.

119. **duraverit**, *has matured*.

121. **dictis**, *by his precepts*.

122. **auctorem**, *an example*, properly a voucher for such a course of conduct. Cf. **auctor**, v. 80.

123. **iudicibus selectis**: the prætor urbanus made a list of the persons qualified to sit as judices (jurors) in criminal cases, in which selection they used their discretion, so that naturally the body would be supposed to be composed of respectable citizens, and for the most part of equites and senators, though in Horace's time other classes were also admitted. Cf. *Praetores urbani, qui iurati debent optimum quemque in selectos iudices referre*. Cic. *pro Cluent.* xliii. 121.

124. **an**, *what!* as often, introducing the real second member of a double question where the first is omitted, "Will you not decide this question or will you still doubt," etc. — **inutile**, *injurious*.

125. **flagret**, etc.: *ill-fame* runs like wild-fire, of this man and that.

hic atque ille?' Avidos vicinum funus ut aegros
exanimat, mortisque metu sibi parcere cogit,
sic teneros animos aliena opprobria saepe
absterrent vitiis. Ex hoc ego sanus ab illis
perniciem quaecumque ferunt mediocribus et quis
ignoscas vitiis teneor; fortassis et istinc
largiter abstulerit longa aetas, liber amicus,
consilium proprium: neque enim, cum lectulus aut me
porticus excepit, desum mihi. 'Rectius hoc est.'
'Hoc faciens vivam melius.' 'Sic dulcis amicis
occurram.' 'Hoc quidam non belle; numquid ego illi
imprudens olim faciam simile?' Haec ego mecum
compressis agito labris; ubi quid datur oti,
illudo chartis. Hoc est mediocribus illis
ex vitiis unum; cui si concedere nolis,
multa poetarum veniet manus auxilio quae
sit mihi (nam multo plures sumus), ac veluti te
Iudaei cogemus in hanc concedere turbam.

126. **avidos**, *greedy*, over-eating.

127. **sibi parcere**, *take care of themselves.*

128. **teneros**, *youthful* (and plastic). Cf. **duraverit**, v. 119.

130. **mediocribus**, *i.e.* and only by these.

131. **et istinc** = **ex istis**: the beginning of a statement of the reason why Horace continues the custom derived from his father.

133. **consilium**, *determination*, resulting from his own reflection. — **neque enim**, *for, you see . . . not.* — **lectulus** (for repose); **porticus** (for exercise), *i.e.* in his moments of leisure, — *my couch has received me, or the portico.*

134. **desum**, *do I neglect myself.* — **rectius**, *the truer course.*

136. **hoc quidam**, etc.: Horace thus connects his strictures with his own self-improvement. Of course this is not to be taken too literally, as appears by his jest in the following. — **numquid**, etc., *I hope I shall not, etc.*

138. **agito**, *I turn over.* — **datur**, *is allowed me.*

139. **inludo**, *I playfully jot down.* — **hoc est**, etc.: after representing this proceeding as an effort at self-culture, he jocosely says that this fault of writing down his meditations is a pardonable fault, one of those he has not been able to cure himself of.

141. **multa**, etc.: a droll form of vengeance, forcing his critic to join him in the same offence, the suggestion of which ends his satire with a jest, as usual, and removes all appearance of formal preaching.

142. **nam multo**, etc.: in the

## V.

Egressum magna me accepit Aricia Roma
hospitio modico ; rhetor comes Heliodorus,
Graecorum longe doctissimus ; inde Forum Appi,
differtum nautis cauponibus atque malignis.
Hoc iter ignavi divisimus, altius ac nos

dearth of public interests literature had become the fashionable employment of the day, and everybody wrote poetry that could write and spell. (Cf. Ep. II. 1. 108.)

143. **Iudaei**: the Jews were famous with the ancients for their energy in proselyting.

SATIRE 5. This satire describes a journey of the poet from Rome to Brundisium, and is imitated from a similar work of Lucilius. The occasion of the journey has been somewhat disputed. Horace went, as was usual in those times, as a companion in the suite of his noble patrons, on an embassy to arrange terms between Octavianus (Augustus) and Antonius. There were two such embassies. One was in 40 B.C., which met Antonius at Brundisium, and concluded the so-called Peace of Brundisium, by which Antonius received Octavia, the sister of Augustus, as his wife, and the domains of the state were divided between the two parties. The other was in B.C. 37, which actually went to Tarentum, but was originally intended for Brundisium. By this treaty Antonius lent assistance to Augustus against Sex. Pompey, who had renewed hostilities since the preceding peace. On both these occasions Mæcenas was present, and the journey described might be on either, but it is more probable that it was the latter. See Kirchner, *Quaest. Horat.* I. 54. The interest of the work is chiefly antiquarian, rather than literary, except so far as it gives some light upon Horace's person and character. But from the personal interest felt in the poet the Satire has always been a favorite ; and indeed, in the scarcity of unaffected personal narrative of ancient times, may well be so still.

1. **Aricia**, the first stopping-place for the night on the Appian Way, sixteen Roman miles (not quite fifteen of ours) south by east of Rome.

2. **hospitio**, *quarters*, no doubt a public house.

3. **doctissimus**: probably a friendly overestimate, as no account of him has come down to us with all his learning. — **Forum Appi**: twenty Roman miles on the same road, at the head of the canal through the Pomptine Marshes. Thus far Horace and his companion seem to have travelled on foot, while the other members of the party drove and met them, some at Appii Forum (cf. **comites**, v. 9), and some at Anxur.

4. **malignis**: as if their cheating was from enmity to the human race. Cf. Tony Weller's estimate of pike keepers.

5. **divisimus**, *i.e.* taking two days for it instead of one. — **altius praecinctis**: as the clothing of the ancients was long and flowing, "girding up the loins" was a symbol of activity and energy, as appears by the contrasted **ignavi** and **tardis**.

praecinctis unum ; minus est gravis Appia tardis.
Hic ego propter aquam, quod erat deterrima, ventri
indico bellum, cenantis haud animo aequo
exspectans comites. Iam nox inducere terris
umbras et caelo diffundere signa parabat ;
tum pueri nautis, pueris convicia nautae
ingerere : 'Huc appelle!' 'Trecentos inseris!' 'Ohe,
iam satis est!' Dum aes exigitur, dum mula ligatur,
tota abit hora. Mali culices ranaeque palustres
avertunt somnos, absentem ut cantat amicam
multa prolutus vappa nauta atque viator
certatim. Tandem fessus dormire viator
incipit, ac missae pastum retinacula mulae
nauta piger saxo religat stertitque supinus.
Iamque dies aderat, nil cum procedere lintrem
sentimus, donec cerebrosus prosilit unus
ac mulae nautaeque caput lumbosque saligno
fuste dolat ; quarta vix demum exponimur hora.

6. **gravis**, *severe*. The road was paved the whole length with large polygonal stones which were much worn and slippery, as they appear to this day.

7. **hic ego**, etc.: *i.e.* he took no dinner on account of the state of his bowels.

9. **iam nox**, etc.: an imitation of the Epic style for the burlesque effect. The canal journey was made by night, as formerly often on the Erie Canal, and nowadays in steamboats.

11. **pueri**: the slaves of the passengers.

12. **huc appelle**: the cry of persons who wish to get on board. — **trecentos inseris, ohe iam satis est**: the cry of the passengers, who are afraid of overloading the boat.

13. **aes exigitur**, *they are collecting the fare* (*naulum*). — **mula**: that towed the boat.

15. **absentem amicam**, his *absent sweetheart*, "The girl I left behind me." — **ut**, *while*, in the loose manner of using that conjunction in the comedy.

16. **viator**, *a passenger* on board (possibly *the passengers* collectively). The sleeping of the passengers is the occasion of the stopping of the boat. The word ordinarily means a passenger on foot, but here the supposition of a traveller on the tow-path seems unnatural.

18. **retinacula**, *the halter*. — **missae**, *turned out*.

20. **iamque dies**, etc.: *i.e.* the passengers wake up, and discover the trick.

21. **cerebrosus**, *hot-headed*, less patient than the rest.

23. **dolat**, *pounds*, lit. *hews*: a col-

Ora manusque tua lavimus, Feronia, lympha.
Milia tum pransi tria repimus, atque subimus
impositum saxis late candentibus Anxur.
Huc venturus erat Maecenas, optimus atque
Cocceius, missi magnis de rebus uterque
legati, aversos soliti componere amicos.
Hic oculis ego nigra meis collyria lippus
illinere. Interea Maecenas advenit atque
Cocceius, Capitoque simul Fonteius, ad unguem
factus homo, Antoni, non ut magis alter, amicus.
Fundos Aufidio Lusco praetore libenter

loquial expression. — **vix demum,** *at last and hardly then.* — **quarta hora**: about ten o'clock, though the distance was less than twenty miles.

24. **Feronia**: an old Italian divinity of uncertain attributes and functions. She had a sacred grove and fountain on the Appian Way, at the end of the canal, where Horace landed, made his morning toilet, and took his breakfast.

25. **subimus**: Tarracina (Anxur) was situated on a high rocky hill on the sea. Hence the use of **sub,** and of **impositum**, etc.

27. **huc,** etc.: apparently the dignitaries came by some rapid conveyance on the Appian Way, or they may have been already in the neighborhood, and were met by the poet at Tarracina, where the Appian turns eastward away from the coast.

28. **Cocceius,** L. Cocceius Nerva, the great-grandfather of the Emperor Nerva. He, as well as Mæcenas, was a friend of Octavian, and had in B.C. 40 assisted in arranging the Peace of Brundisium. (See Introduction to this Satire.) Hence **soliti,** v. 29.

30. **hic oculis,** etc.: a detail like that in v. 48. The poet consumes the time in medical treatment.

32. **Capito**: Fonteius Capito, who assisted in the embassy as a friend and partisan of Antonius. He remained with the latter and assisted him in the contest later. — **ad unguem**: a proverbial expression drawn from trying the surface of marble and wood with the nail; *perfect to a hair.*

33. **ut,** *sc. esset* or *est.*

34. **Fundos**: eleven miles east of Tarracina, traversed by the Appian Way. — **praetore**: the name of the man and his office are inserted in the form of a date, as if he were important enough to give his name to the year like the consuls. Originally **praetor** was the Italian name for the highest magistrate of an independent city; and some cities were allowed to retain the old name after their subjugation by the Romans, though generally such magistrates were called *duoviri.* The person here seems to have made himself ridiculous by putting on the airs of a consul, assuming the *honors* (**praemia**) of that office, — the *toga praetexta* with its crimson border, the broad crimson stripe on the front of the tunic, and further, what does not seem to have been used by the consul, a pan of charcoal

linquimus, insani ridentes praemia scribae,
praetextam et latum clavum prunaeque vatillum.
In Mamurrarum lassi deinde urbe manemus,
Murena praebente domum, Capitone culinam.
Postera lux oritur multo gratissima; namque
Plotius et Varius Sinuessae Vergiliusque
occurrunt, animae, qualis neque candidiores
terra tulit, neque quis me sit devinctior alter.
O qui complexus et gaudia quanta fuerunt!
Nil ego contulerim iucundo sanus amico.
Proxima Campano ponti quae villula tectum
praebuit, et parochi quae debent ligna salemque.

for burning incense before him. Whether this display was in honor of the distinguished visitors, as is very likely, does not appear. — **libenter,** *i.e.* we are glad not to stop there.

35. **insani,** *weak-headed: i.e.* his head was turned by his position. — **scribae**: *i.e.* a mere clerk who had risen to the office. These clerks might be of low origin, or even freedmen. Cf. v. 66.

37. **Mamurrarum urbe**: Formiæ, a town twelve miles further. The form of expression no doubt contains a bit of satire. Mamurra was a knight from Formiæ, whose other names even are not known, who rose through the favor of Julius Cæsar to wealth and some distinction, but spent his wealth in extravagant living, and never possessed a very noble reputation. Of his family (implied in the plural) nothing whatever is known. — **manemus,** *spend the night.* Cf. v. 87.

38. **Murena**: L. Licinius Terentius Varro Murena, the brother of Terentia, Mæcenas' wife, apparently had like many noble Romans a villa at Formiæ; as probably also Fonteius did, who entertained the travellers at dinner (**culinam**).

40. **Plotius**: Plotius Tucca, whom with **Varius**, both literary friends of Virgil, that poet made his literary executors. Cf. I. 10. 44 and 81, and I. 6. 55. — **Sinuessae**, eighteen miles from Formiæ, towards Campania.

41. **qualis**: we should expect **quibus** depending on **candidiores,** but the poet says, "of a kind of which kind the earth has produced none fairer than they."

42. **neque quis,** *and to whom no, etc.*

44. **sanus,** *in my senses.*

45. **Campano ponti,** a bridge (three miles from Sinuessa) over the *Savo*, a small river just north of the Volturnus. The word **Campano** seems to be used loosely, as the real boundary between Latium and Campania is a few miles farther north. — **villula**: apparently an inn especially for public officers, who regularly travelled at the public expense.

46. **parochi,** *the stewards;* apparently persons whose duty it was to furnish the entertainment which the cities were bound to supply to

Hinc muli Capuae clitellas tempore ponunt.
Lusum it Maecenas, dormitum ego Vergiliusque;
namque pila lippis inimicum et ludere crudis.
Hinc nos Coccei recipit plenissima villa,
quae super est Caudi cauponas. Nunc mihi paucis
Sarmenti scurrae pugnam Messique Cicirri,
Musa, velim memores, et quo patre natus uterque
contulerit litis. Messi clarum genus Osci;
Sarmenti domina exstat: ab his maioribus orti
ad pugnam venere. Prior Sarmentus: 'Equi te

state travellers. It may be that they were in this case bound to supply only certain articles, the travellers bringing the rest, or the words **ligna salemque**, may mean entertainment generally, with a hint at its meagreness. Cf. v. 50.

47. **hinc**, *from here; i.e.* starting the next morning. — **Capuae**, twenty-two miles farther on, the largest and most important city of Campania. — **muli**: the baggage only is mentioned, but the whole train is referred to.

48. **lusum**: *sc.* **pila** (cf. v. 49), for exercise before dinner as was the custom of the Romans, while the two poets took a nap instead, as was also not unusual.

49. **pila**: the Romans had several games of ball which consisted chiefly in throwing and catching, the use of the bat being a modern improvement. Cf. I. 6. 126. — **lippis**, *to sore eyes.* — **et crudis**, *and weak stomachs.* The word means properly undigested, but was regularly transferred to the dyspeptic himself.

50. **plenissima**, *well-stocked.* Cf. v. 46. — **villa**: many noble Romans had country-seats in various parts of Italy.

51. **Caudi**: Caudium, the scene of the great defeat of the Romans by the Samnites, was in the mountain region of the Hirpini, twenty-one miles from Capua, eastward towards the Apennines. — **super**, on the heights above the town. — **nunc mihi**, etc.: the poet again assumes the Epic style. The scene described was evidently of a kind very common among the rich Romans, who were particularly fond of these scurrilous encounters. Cf. the word **scurra**, and Plin. *Ep.* IX. 17.

52. **Sarmenti**: a buffoon (**scurra**) accompanying the expedition in the capacity of clerk. — **Messi Cicirri**: a person of the same kind belonging in the town, and so no doubt brought out by Cocceius, who was familiar with the region, to pit against the favorite from Rome. Cicirrus (*κίκιρρος, cock*) is a nickname.

53. **quo patre**; the genealogy of the hero is always a matter of interest in romance. The burlesque here is the more striking because Sarmentus as a slave was *filius nullius*, and Messius was a despised Oscan.

54. **Osci**: predicate of **est** to be supplied with **genus**, which is here equivalent to a plural, as meaning the man's ancestors.

56. **equi feri**: apparently the fabled unicorn, famous for its sup

esse feri similem dico.' Ridemus, et ipse
Messius 'Accipio,' caput et movet. 'O, tua cornu
ni foret exsecto frons,' inquit, 'quid faceres, cum
sic mutilus miniteris?' At illi foeda cicatrix
saetosam laevi frontem turpaverat oris.
Campanum in morbum, in faciem permulta iocatus,
pastorem saltaret uti Cyclopa rogabat;
nil illi larva aut tragicis opus esse cothurnis.
Multa Cicirrus ad haec: Donasset iamne catenam
ex voto Laribus, quaerebat; scriba quod esset,
nilo deterius dominae ius esse: rogabat
denique, cur umquam fugisset, cui satis una
farris libra foret, gracili sic tamque pusillo.

posed ferocity. The comparison was partly on account of his size and ugliness, partly on account of the scar referred to in v. 61.

58. **accipio**: as if he said, "So I am; you'd better look out for me!" shaking his head like the supposed animal. — **O tua**, etc.: the reply of Sarmentus: "How dangerous you would be if you hadn't had your horn cut off." Messius had had a great wen (Campanus morbus) removed from his forehead. — **cornu**, abl. of quality.

60. **sic**, *thus . . . as you are.* — **at**, *but*, introducing the explanatory words of Horace, 'it was a scar.'

61. **saetosam**: *i.e.* a hairy scar was left.

62. **Campanum**: diseases arising from loose living which disfigure the face or body are regularly assigned to some foreign country, as by the English to France, by the French to Italy.

63. **pastorem**: a cognate acc., like "to play Hamlet." The point is in the ugliness, huge size, and scarred forehead (representing a cyclops' eye) of the buffoon, all of which agreed with the character of Polyphemus, whose hopeless love for Galatea was a favorite theme with the ancients, somewhat like Beauty and the Beast. — **saltaret**: *i.e.* to act in pantomime.

65. **multa**: the chaffing of Cicirrus is aimed at the servile condition of Sarmentus as well as his diminutive size. Much of the fun to a Roman would lie in the contrast between the puny, dainty favorite from the city and the huge, overgrown countryman with his phenomenal ugliness; and it will be seen that their abuse of each other is directed at these peculiarities. Such cross-matches had a charm for the Romans, as we see by some of their gladiatorial contests. — **donasset**: the whole point is in the ironical suggestion that he was a runaway slave, as it was the custom for manumitted slaves to make an offering to the household gods, though probably not of a chain, an allusion which is inserted here in analogy to cases like *Od.* III. 26. 4, *Ep.* I. 1. 5.

68. **cui satis**, etc.: he might have saved enough from his rations, such a puny fellow as he, to buy his freedom.

Prorsus iucunde cenam producimus illam.
Tendimus hinc recta Beneventum, ubi sedulus hospes
paene macros arsit dum turdos versat in igni;
nam vaga per veterem dilapso flamma culinam
Volcano summum properabat lambere tectum.
Convivas avidos cenam servosque timentis
tum rapere, atque omnis restinguere velle videres.
Incipit ex illo montis Apulia notos
ostentare mihi, quos torret Atabulus, et quos
numquam erepsemus, nisi nos vicina Trivici
villa recepisset, lacrimoso non sine fumo,
udos cum foliis ramos urente camino.
Quattuor hinc rapimur viginti et milia raedis,
mansuri oppidulo quod versu dicere non est,
signis perfacile est: venit vilissima rerum
hic aqua; sed panis longe pulcherrimus, ultra

71. **tendimus**: the eighth day, twelve miles. — **sedulus**, *officious*.

72. **arsit**, *set himself* (*i.e.* his house) *afire*.

73. **dilapso**, *escaping*, of course from the *focus* or fireplace in the kitchen, and so spreading.

75. **convivas**, etc.: the picture of the efforts to save the dinner. — **avidos**: *in their hunger*. — **timentis**: *frightened*, as accords with their servile nature.

77. **Apulia**: close on the borders of which Horace passed his early childhood; hence **notos**.

78. **Atabulus**: a local name for a hot southern wind, the Sirocco.

79. **erepsemus**: the colloquial shortening for **erepsissemus**.—**Trivici**: an unimportant village where they passed the night. But for the rest afforded them, they never could have dragged on over the mountains.

81. **udos**: the cause of the smoke. — **camino**: properly the word for forge or furnace, but here no doubt some kind of a fireplace for warming. But no chimney like ours can be shown to have existed among the Romans.

86. **rapimur**: of the rapid pace; cf. **erepsemus**, v. 79. — **raedis**: a heavy travelling coach with four wheels. The exact shape is not known, but it must have been large and roomy, and was the ordinary public carriage.

87. **mansuri**, *stop*, pass the night. Cf. *Od.* I. 1. 25.—**oppidulo**: according to Porphyrion, Equos Tuticus (which could not easily be introduced in hexameter on account of the succession of longs and shorts, ∪ — — ∪ ∪); but this is extremely uncertain.

88. **venit**: *i.e.* water, elsewhere the cheapest of all things, is actually sold for money here.

89. **ultra**: the traveller supplies himself with bread in advance, for the next town farther on, Canusium, has gritty bread.

callidus ut soleat umeris portare viator:
nam Canusi lapidosus, aquae non ditior urna
qui locus a forti Diomede est conditus olim.
Flentibus hinc Varius discedit maestus amicis.
Inde Rubos fessi pervenimus, utpote longum
carpentes iter et factum corruptius imbri.
Postera tempestas melior, via peior ad usque
Bari moenia piscosi; dein Gnatia Lymphis
iratis exstructa dedit risusque iocosque,
dum flamma sine tura liquescere limine sacro
persuadere cupit. Credat Iudaeus Apella,
non ego: namque deos didici securum agere aevum,
nec, si quid miri faciat natura, deos id
tristis ex alto caeli demittere tecto.
Brundisium longae finis chartaeque viaeque est.

90. **soleat**: for prosody, see Introduction.

91. **ditior**: this construction seems odd to an English-speaking person, but an antecedent which would be in apposition with some preceding idea is, in Latin, embodied in the relative clause, *a place no richer*, etc., *which*, etc., as in **quae res**, *a thing which*, and the like. — **aquae**, genitive after **ditior**, as an adjective of plenty.

92. **Diomede**: the settlement of this Greek chief in Apulia was a common tradition. Cf. *Æn.* VIII. 9.

94. **Rubos**: the town Rubi, the next stopping-place. — **utpote**: more commonly found with relatives, but used by Horace several times with adjective expressions. Cf. I. 4. 24, and II. 4. 9.

97. **Bari**: Barium, on the coast; hence **piscosi**. — **Gnatia Lymphis iratis**: because the place has no water-springs, of which the Lymphæ — a Latin equivalent of Nymphæ — were the tutelary divinities.

99. **limine sacro**: *i.e.* the inhabitants claim a miraculous melting of incense without fire, probably some volcanic effect (cf. Plin. *H. N.* II. 111, *Reperitur in Salentino oppido Egnatia imposito ligno in saxum quoddam ibi sacrum protinus flammam exsistere*).

100. **Apella**: a name apparently Greek, but a common one of freedmen, and here assigned to a Jew, perhaps a converted Greek. The Jews were regarded as especially superstitious (cf. I. 9. 71 and II. 3. 281 *seq.*).

101. **securum**: the Epicurean doctrine that the gods paid no attention to human affairs, but lived at ease in the intermundane spaces. Cf. Lucr. V. 82.

102. **miri**: all strange occurrences were supposed by the ancients to be direct interpositions of the gods in human affairs to indicate their displeasure (**tristis**), a notion that the Epicureans combated, asserting that all such took place by the operations of nature.

104. **Brundisium**: either the

## VI.

Non quia, Maecenas, Lydorum quidquid Etruscos
incoluit finis, nemo generosior est te,
nec quod avus tibi maternus fuit atque paternus,
olim qui magnis legionibus imperitarent,
ut plerique solent, naso suspendis adunco
ignotos, ut me libertino patre natum.
Cum referre negas quali sit quisque parente
natus, dum ingenuus, persuades hoc tibi vere,

rest of the journey (if it continued any farther) was taken by sea to Tarentum, or Horace may have stopped here.

SATIRE **6**. There probably never was a nation in which family pride was stronger than it was among the Romans. And this pride had its natural accompaniment of mean servility and vulgar striving for social and political advancement. Horace, of low birth but recommended by his talents to the favor of the great, seems to have been a mark for all sorts of attacks from envious rivals and ignoble souls. But his whole life and writings show a remarkable freedom from all vulgar social ambitions, and a truly refined self-respect and independence. This Satire is an answer to the attacks of his enemies, and a statement of his creed in regard to social position.

1. **non quia**: *you do not Mæcenas, because, etc.;* this is not the common construction of **non quia** (*not because . . . but*), as the mood of **est** shows, *but* the negative belongs to **suspendis**, being placed in this emphatic position to show that the reason for which Mæcenas might have scorned humbler men did not cause him to do so. — **Maecenas**: the Satire is addressed to Mæcenas, both as a compliment to him and to give it additional weight from the authority of so great a man. — **Lydorum**: partitive genitive with **quidquid**, a colloquial and archaic form of speech, though common in all styles. — **quicquid** would have for its antecedent an **omnium** or the like, a partitive genitive after **nemo**. The Etrurians were supposed to have come originally from Lydia. Their origin is still a mystery, but the old tradition is as likely to be true as any other view.

2. **generosior**: Mæcenas was descended from the Cilnii, a noble family of Etruria.

4. **legionibus**: used loosely for bodies of troops in general.

5. **naso**, etc.: *i.e.* turn up your nose at.

7. **cum**, etc.: *when you say that it makes no difference*, etc., *you are convinced, and rightly so, that*, etc.

8. **ingenuus**: the inevitable taint of slavery was still regarded as a disqualification for social advancement, even by men as large-minded as Mæcenas and Horace; but the son of a freedman was free from that taint.

ante potestatem Tulli atque ignobile regnum
multos saepe viros nullis maioribus ortos
et vixisse probos, amplis et honoribus auctos;
contra Laevinum, Valeri genus, unde superbus
Tarquinius regno pulsus fugit, unius assis
non umquam pretio pluris licuisse, notante
iudice, quo nosti, populo, qui stultus honores
saepe dat indignis et famae servit ineptus,
qui stupet in titulis et imaginibus. Quid oportet
nos facere, a volgo longe longeque remotos?
Namque esto, populus Laevino mallet honorem

9. **Tulli**: Servius Tullius was supposed to have been a slave. The whole idea is, that the view of Mæcenas is correct, which makes virtue and not mere birth the criterion of nobility.

10. **multos**, etc.: *i.e.* that this has always been the case from the first, though the other cases have not come down to us.

11. **honoribus**, *i.e.* honors conferred by the people, offices.

12. **contra**: introducing the opposite case of a worthless noble. — **Laevinum**: the particular individual is unknown, but there were many famous members of this branch of the Valerian family. This one is no doubt one of the stock, who was a candidate for office, but failed to be elected on account of his worthless character, as sometimes happened even in Rome. — **Valeri**: Marcus Valerius Poplicola, the associate of Brutus in the expulsion of the Tarquins. The gens Valeria was one of the oldest and most distinguished of the great Roman families, and had many branches, all counting distinguished men among their number. — **genus**: cf. *Od.* I. 3. 27, and Virg. *Æn.* IV. 12. — **unde** = **a quo**.

13. **assis**: depending on **pretio**.

14. **licuisse**, *went for*, a jocose expression for *was worth*, as if he had been offered for what he would bring. — **notante**: alluding to the censorial *nota*, or mark set by the censor against any name on the list to exclude the person from the order or tribe.

15. **iudice**, etc., *i.e. in the critical estimation of the people.* — **quo**: for **quem**, attracted by **populo**. See Gr. § 200. *b.* — **qui stultus**: *i.e.* even the people, who are led astray by the glamour of rank, know better than to choose a Lævinus.

16. **famae**: *i.e.* of one's ancestors who were famous, though their descendant is worthless.

17. **titulis et imaginibus**: any person who had held a curule office left to his descendants the right to put up in their houses the wax mask of their ancestor, with an inscription bearing his name and honors. Such masks and lists of honor were therefore a sign of nobility. — **quid oportet**, etc.: *i.e.* if the foolish crowd have right ideas, how much more ought we to have right ideas who are far better educated.

19. **namque esto**, etc., *for after all suppose that*, etc.; *i.e.* even if the

quam Decio mandare novo, censorque moveret
Appius, ingenuo si non essem patre natus :
vel merito, quoniam in propria non pelle quiessem.
Sed fulgente trahit constrictos gloria curru
non minus ignotos generosis. Quo tibi, Tilli,
sumere depositum clavum fierique tribuno ?

people preferred a Lævinus to an obscure worthy man (which, as he has just said, they do not), it would be justified in doing so ; and the man of low birth would have no reason to complain, because he has no right to get out of his place. The logical connection is : "We ought to hold virtue higher and birth lower than they, for even if they did prefer the high-born to the worthy in this particular case (of political preferment), they would be justified ; hence, as they do not, their example is all the more forcible for us." It must be remembered that after all Horace is dealing with social relations, which fact he always keeps in mind underlying the whole. — **mallet** : a condition without **si**, *suppose they did prefer.*

20. **Decio** : P. Decius, a plebeian consul who devoted himself to death for the success of the Roman arms in the Latin War, B.C. 340 ; and his son, of the same name, imitated his father's example in B.C. 295. — **novo** : a person whose ancestors had held no curule office was a *novus homo.* — **moveret** : turn out of the senate, as Appius Claudius Pulcher in his censorship, 50 B.C., did all sons of freedmen. — **essem** : the general idea is represented by Horace's own case, though he had never been in the senate. As he was, however, the son of a freedman, his case would be like the one referred to if he had, and the mention of a special person makes the whole more vivid.

22. **vel merito** : *sc.* **moveret,** though both cases are really meant. — **in propria pelle,** *i.e.* his proper position. (An allusion to the fable of "The Ass in the Lion's Skin.")

23. **sed** : but though the people would be right in the case supposed, and such men have no claims, yet the ambition of the humble will not be quenched as it ought to be by that fact. — **trahit,** *i.e.* leads captive, the figure being drawn from the triumph, which the captives accompanied in chains, just before the conqueror's chariot, possibly originally chained to it. — **gloria,** *Ambition.*

24. **generosis,** *the nobly born* : in prose, **quam generosos.** — **quo,** *to what end?* hence, *of what use?* — **Tilli** : a Tillius said to have been removed from the senate, who, as was customary in such cases, began anew to seek the senatorial rank. He was doubtless a freedman.

25. **clavum** : the single broad stripe of red down the front of the tunic which was the sign of magisterial and senatorial dignity. — **tribuno** : apparently *tribunus militum,* since the tribune of the people appears not to have worn any insignia as such, though the office would entitle him to be enrolled in the senate, and so afterwards to receive the insignia mentioned. Some of the tribunes of the soldiers wore the laticlave, and were chosen into the senate, a custom introduced by Augustus.

Invidia accrevit, privato quae minor esset.
Nam ut quisque insanus nigris medium impediit crus
pellibus, et latum demisit pectore clavum,
audit continuo 'Quis homo hic est, quo patre natus?'
Vt, si qui aegrotet quo morbo Barrus, haberi
et cupiat formosus, eat quacumque, puellis
iniciat curam quaerendi singula, quali
sit facie, sura, quali pede, dente, capillo;
sic qui promittit **civis,** urbem sibi curae,
imperium fore et Italiam, delubra deorum,
quo patre sit natus, num ignota matre inhonestus,
omnis mortalis curare et quaerere cogit.
'Tune, Syri, Damae, aut Dionysi filius, audes
deicere e saxo civis aut tradere Cadmo?'
'At Novius collega gradu post me sedet uno;
namque est ille, pater quod erat meus.' 'Hoc tibi Paulus
et Messalla videris? At hic, si plaustra ducenta

27. **insanus**: *i.e.* with ambition. — **nigris**: the senatorial shoe was tied with four black thongs (*corrigiae*).

29. **homo,** *fellow*, implying a certain degree of contempt.

30. **morbo,** *i.e.* inordinate vanity.

32. **iniciat**: pretending to be a handsome man, he attracts attention and criticism of details which would otherwise pass unnoticed. The same is the case with the ambitious man.

34. **civis,** etc.: perhaps taken from the official oath of the magistrates generally without particular reference to any one.

38. **Syri,** etc.: common slaves' names, indicating that the man was the son of a freedman.

39. **deicere**: throwing from the Tarpeian Rock was the old punishment for many offences. The man's functions as magistrate would include the condemnation of citizens. — **Cadmo**: evidently an executioner.

40. **Novius**: perhaps chosen by Horace as formed from **novus** — **sedet**: in allusion to the graded seats of the theatre, where the senators sat in the orchestra and the equites in fourteen rows of seats behind them. The ambitious upstart claims that he is of better family than his colleague, for he is only a freedman, while the speaker was born free at any rate.

41. **hoc tibi**: The people answer, "Do you plume yourself so much on that, that you think you belong to one of the old families, the Æmilii (**Paulus**) or the Valerii (**Messala**)?" These are indicated by common family names in those clans.

42. **at hic**: Horace, with that double meaning which is character

concurrantque foro tria funera magna sonabit
cornua quod vincatque tubas ; saltem tenet hoc nos.'
  Nunc ad me redeo libertino patre natum,
quem rodunt omnes libertino patre natum,
nunc, quia sim tibi, Maecenas, convictor ; at olim,
quod mihi pareret legio Romana tribuno.
Dissimile hoc illi est ; quia non, ut forsit honorem
iure mihi invideat quivis, ita te quoque amicum,
praesertim cautum dignos assumere, prava

istic of him, justifies the advancement of the freedman colleague by stating a quality of his which weighs much in the minds of the people, but which you feel sure at the same time Horace himself despises. "The man is a blatant popular speaker, and has at least that claim to the favor of the people." — **plaustra**: the heavy carrying wagon of the Romans, noted, and probably named, for its creaking (*plaudo*).

43. **funera**: the funeral procession was accompanied with music. — **magna**: often taken with **funera**, as only a great funeral would be noisy; but as **magna sonare** is a standing phrase, it is better to take it so here (cf. I. 4. 44), making **magna** an adverb.

44. **quod**: the antecedent **id** would be a cognate accusative. — **cornua**, curved brass horns. — **tuba**, a straight trumpet.

45. **nunc ad me**, etc.: after showing the folly of *political* ambition, he now comes back to the main idea of *personal* and *social* dignity as independent of birth, defending himself against the slurs of his vulgar detractors.

46. **rodunt**, *disparage* (gnaw like rats). — **libertino**, etc.: the repetition indicates a direct quotation from his detractors, just as they keep repeating it.

47. **sim**, the subjunctive as usual puts the words into the mouth of the detractors. — **convictor**: notice that this indicates only a social advancement as the friend of Mæcenas, not a political preferment, which he claims no right to.

48. **tribuno**: see life of Horace. Sixteen (or twenty-four) tribunes were elected by the people, and were real magistrates, but others could be chosen by the generals, and were called *rufuli*. This advancement was a matter rather of favor than of merit, and was certainly so in Horace's case.

49. **dissimile**: here is brought out more fully the distinction which underlies the whole. The tribunate is an official honor, to which a lowborn man had perhaps no claim; but the friendship of Mæcenas nobody has a right to envy him, because that is a matter of personal worthiness. — **forsit**: only found here, but no doubt another of Horace's colloquialisms.

51. **cautum**: Mæcenas' reputation for selecting only the worthy, and those not from motives of ambition (*i.e.* to increase his political influence and gain supporters), makes his friendship still more a tribute to worth than the friendship of others might be.

ambitione procul. Felicem dicere non hoc
me possim, casu quod te sortitus amicum;
nulla etenim mihi te fors obtulit: optimus olim
Vergilius, post hunc Varius dixere quid essem.
Ut veni coram, singultim pauca locutus
(infans namque pudor prohibebat plura profari),
non ego me claro natum patre, non ego circum
me Satureiano vectari rura caballo,
sed, quod eram, narro. Respondes, ut tuus est mos,
pauca; abeo, et revocas nono post mense iubesque
esse in amicorum numero. Magnum hoc ego duco,
quod placui tibi, qui turpi secernis honestum,
non patre praeclaro, sed vita et pectore puro.
Atqui si vitiis mediocribus ac mea paucis
mendosa est natura, alioqui recta, — velut si

52. **ambitione**: referring to Mæcenas. Every means of adding to one's influence, and every attempt to get on in the political career, the object of both high and low, was among the Romans called **ambitio**. Especially so was any attempt to gain favor either by the powerful or the humble. — **felicem**: *i.e.* because that implies good luck, an idea which is repeated in **casu** and **sortitus** (*sc.* **sim**), and again in **fors**, etc.

55. **Vergilius**, the poet Virgil, who, like most of the writers of talent at the time, was an intimate friend of Mæcenas, whose generous patronage of literature has become a proverb. — **Varius**: see I. 5. 40. — **quid**: *i.e.* his character and talents.

56. **ut veni coram**: at his first introduction. — **singultim . . . locutus**, *stammering out*, or *speaking incoherently*.

57. **infans**: in its original sense of *speechless;* here, of course, applied to **pudor** as making a man so.

58. **non ego**: *i.e.* I did not pretend, as many do, to be a man of consequence from some provincial city, nor that my father had great estates at Tarentum.

59. **Satureiano**: said by a scholiast to be from Satureia, a name of Tarentum; at any rate it was in that vicinity, and indicates estates in Southern Italy. — **caballo**: apparently the popular word (cf. the Romance words).

60. **quod eram**: we should expect in Latin an indirect question (cf. v. 55), but here it is "the position, etc., that I held."

63. **turpi, honestum**: strictly the neuter forms; *turpe* and *honestum*, the technical Stoic names for virtue and vice, but here used to include persons (cf. I. 3. 42, note, and *Ep.* I. 9. 5).

65. **atqui**: *i.e.* though I claim no proud descent from my father, yet it is to him that I owe whatever I am. — **mediocribus**: *i.e.* only such. Cf. I. 4. 130.

egregio inspersos reprehendas corpore naevos, —
si neque avaritiam neque sordes ac mala lustra
obiciet vere quisquam mihi, purus et insons
(ut me collaudem) si et vivo carus amicis,
causa fuit pater his, qui, macro pauper agello,
noluit in Flavi ludum me mittere, magni
quo pueri magnis e centurionibus orti,
laevo suspensi loculos tabulamque lacerto,
ibant octonos referentes Idibus aeris,
sed puerum est ausus Romam portare, docendum
artis quas doceat quivis eques atque senator
semet prognatos. Vestem servosque sequentis,
in magno ut populo, si qui vidisset, avita
ex re praeberi sumptus mihi crederet illos.

67. **egregio**: in form generally, but slightly disfigured by insignificant moles, etc.

68. **sordes**: this word, connected by the conjunctions with what follows, and separated from **avaritiam**, must refer to vulgar tastes and habits. — **mala lustra**, *dens of vice*.

69. **purus et insons**: take with **carus** after **si**.

71. **his**: neuter, *i.e.* **his rebus**. — **macro**: opposed to **pinguis**.

72. **Flavi**, a local schoolmaster in Venusia, to whom the young natives went. — **magni, magnis**: both referring to size, but perhaps with a reference to their excess of muscle over brain. Horace himself was small of person.

73. **centurionibus**: as Venusia was a colony, the citizens would be retired soldiers. In the ancient method of fighting bodily strength counted for more than with us, and a centurion who had risen from the ranks would be one of the stoutest of his class.

74. **loculos**: (depending on **suspensi** taken in a middle sense, § 240. *c*, probably a Grecism), answering to the satchel of modern times. — **tabulam**: corresponding to the slate, the ordinary writing material of the Romans, a thin board covered with wax.

75. **octonos**, *sc.* **asses**, implied in **aeris**, a method of stating sums of money not uncommon with the Romans; about ten cents. A cheap school, of course, is intended. The distributive means every month. — **idibus**: apparently a common time for monthly payments. — **referentes**: their carrying the pay themselves also indicated a humble kind of persons.

76. **puerum**, *i.e.* while still a boy.

77. **artis**: Gr. § 239. *c*. Rem. — **eques atque senator**: *i.e.* this mode of education was much above his station.

78. **vestem servosque**: *i.e.* he dressed his son and gave him a style of appearance that would indicate inherited wealth.

79. **magno populo**, *i.e.* in the

Ipse mihi custos incorruptissimus omnis
circum doctores aderat. Quid multa? Pudicum,
qui primus virtutis honos, servavit ab omni
non solum facto, verum opprobrio quoque turpi;
nec timuit sibi ne vitio quis verteret, olim
si praeco parvas aut, ut fuit ipse, coactor
mercedes sequerer; neque ego essem questus: at hoc nunc
laus illi debetur et a me gratia maior.
Nil me paeniteat sanum patris huius, eoque
non, ut magna dolo factum negat esse suo pars,
quod non ingenuos habeat clarosque parentes,

crowd of a great city, as opposed to a little provincial town. Cf.

> Postremo in magno populo mulierem inclutam
> Amare oportet omnis qui quod dent habent.
> *Plaut. Truc.* I. 1. 55.—

**ut**: *as* is natural, or expected.—**vidisset . . . crederet**: § 308. ***a.***

81. **custos**: it was customary to send boys in charge of a trustworthy slave (*paedagogus*), as nowadays girls in charge of a nurse. This office the father performed himself.

82. **quid multa**: *sc.* **dicam,** ***i.e.*** why should I say more on a point that every one understands?

83. **honos,** *ornament;* purity of morals would be the first and highest virtue.

84. **facto . . . opprobrio**: *sc.* he not only committed no impropriety, but gave no handle for slander.

85. **nec timuit**: *i.e.* he did not refrain from giving me this education for fear any one should complain that he was educating his son above his station, even if the son rose no higher than he himself.—**vitio verteret,** *charge it as a fault;* § 233.

86. **praeco,** *a crier, an auctioneer,* a very common humble occupation.—**coactor,** *a collector,* of taxes and the like.

87. **mercedes,** the wages of a humble profession.—**essem questus**: *i.e.* if it had turned out so, I should not have found fault with him for unfitting me for that humble life. In this sentence the close connection between the 'future condition' and the 'contrary to fact construction' is very apparent, **sequerer** being a future condition in an indirect form changed to past time, but it also serves for the condition contrary to fact of **essem questus.**—**hoc,** *on this account, i.e.* because he did so educate me.—**nunc,** *now, as it is.*

89. **paeniteat,** etc., *could I regret having had such a father?* ***i.e.*** under any supposable circumstances, an apodosis with an indefinite protasis omitted. The whole idea is, that while others might be ashamed of their fathers if they were of low birth, he had no such feeling.

90. **negat,** etc.: *i.e.* most persons would apologize for such a father, saying that it was not their fault that that they had such, while admitting that it was a dishonor.

sic me defendam. Longe mea discrepat istis
et vox et ratio: nam si natura iuberet
a certis annis aevum remeare peractum,
atque alios legere ad fastum quoscumque parentes
optaret sibi quisque, meis contentus, honestos
fascibus et sellis nollem mihi sumere, demens
iudicio volgi, sanus fortasse tuo, quod
nollem onus haud umquam solitus portare molestum.
Nam mihi continuo maior quaerenda foret res,
atque salutandi plures; ducendus et unus
et comes alter, uti ne solus rusve peregreve
exirem; plures calones atque caballi
pascendi, ducenda petorrita. Nunc mihi curto
ire licet mulo vel si libet usque Tarentum,
mantica cui lumbos onere ulceret atque eques armos:

92. **istis**: masc. and dative.

93. **ratio**, *way of thinking*. — **si iuberet**: *i.e.* if it were the course of nature that a man after a certain age might choose his own father and expunge his previous life, Horace says he would not change.

94. **aevum**: acc. after **remeare**, like **navigare mare**, and the like.

95. **ad fastum**, *to suit his pride*.

97. **fascibus** (the means of **honestos**), namely, curule offices, of which the lictor's rods and the curule chair were the symbols.

98. **tuo**: Mæcenas had himself refused to be advanced in official station, no doubt for the reason Horace assigns, his dislike to the burdensome state and social duties required of the great.

100. **res**: a larger property would be necessary to support the dignity of his position.

101. **salutandi**: the *salutatio*, or morning visit of humbler persons to the great, was a prominent feature in Roman social life. — **ducendus**: such persons had to take with them a retinue of companions, like princes in modern times.

102. **uti ne**: apparently an expression more common in early Latin in purpose clauses, not different essentially from **ne**. The clause is here treated as a purpose, but in English we may translate *so as not to*, etc., or *so that I could not*, etc.

103. **calones**, etc.: all these would be necessary for the proper state of such a person.

104. **pascendi**, *must be kept*. — **ducenda**, *taken in my train*. — **petorrita** (a Gallic word), a four-wheeled travelling carriage, the exact form of which is not known, but it must have been more bulky and roomy than other forms. — **nunc**, etc. (cf. v. 87): the advantages of his present humble position. — **curto**, *sorry*, *little*, only referring to the size as suited to his dignity.

105. **Tarentum**: *i.e.* the whole length and breadth of Italy.

106. **mantica**: *i.e.* with no train

obiciet nemo sordes mihi quas tibi, Tilli,
cum Tiburte via praetorem quinque sequuntur
te pueri, lasanum portantes oenophorumque.
Hoc ego commodius quam tu, praeclare senator,
milibus atque aliis vivo. Quacumque libido est,
incedo solus; percontor quanti holus ac far;
fallacem circum vespertinumque pererro
saepe forum; adsisto divinis; inde domum me
ad porri et ciceris refero laganique catinum.
Cena ministratur pueris tribus, et lapis albus
pocula cum cyatho duo sustinet; adstat echinus

nor baggage except a pair of saddle-bags behind him on the same mule.

107. **obiciet**, etc.: *i.e.* such a proceeding would not in Horace indicate stinginess (**sordes**), as it would in the case of Tillius (probably the same mentioned in v. 24).

108. **Tiburte via**, a frequented road, and only a short distance, where one would expect him to appear properly. — **praetorem**: as a magistrate a man ought to keep up a still more brilliant state. — **quinque**: a small number even for an ordinary gentleman. Cf. 3. 11.

109. **lasanum**: his kettle for cooking his meals along the road, instead of stopping at a tavern, or receiving hospitality which he would not like to return. — **oenophorum**, *wine-basket*, carried in the same manner as the kettle.

110. **hoc** (neuter), *in this respect*. — **tu**: without special reference, but making the whole vivid by singling out some one person, as it were.

111. **milibus**: neuter.

112. **solus**: see notes on vs. 101 *seq.* An example of the thousand other things. — **percontor**: *i.e.* he strolls about the market, and acts as a humble citizen pricing his own provisions.

113. **fallacem circum**: the region of the Circus Maximus (the valley where was the early commercial forum) seems to have been the resort of all kinds of loose characters. Shops occupied the outer walls of the substructions of the building. Horace doubtless refers to sharpers, confidence men, and the like, who always ply their trade in the lower parts of a city.

113. **vespertinum**: *i.e.* when the refuse of the people were out, as in any great city.

114. **divinis**: fortune-tellers, astrologers, and the like. — **inde**: from his stroll.

115. **porri**, etc.: as a simple repast without dainties, but of course not to be taken too literally. — **laganum**, a sort of pancake.

116. **tribus**: of course a small number for the Romans. — **pueris**: the poetic (and colloquial?) use of the dative to express the agent. — **lapis albus**: only white marble, not the variegated and costly foreign sorts.

117. **pocula duo**: for wine and water, which the Romans generally mixed. — **cyatho**, the little ladle for measuring the quantities in mixing. — **echinus**, an unknown uten-

vilis, cum patera guttus, Campana supellex.
Deinde eo dormitum, non sollicitus, mihi quod cras
surgendum sit mane, obeundus Marsya, qui se
voltum ferre negat Noviorum posse minoris.
Ad quartam iaceo ; post hanc vagor ; aut ego, lecto
aut scripto quod me tacitum iuvet, unguor olivo,
non quo fraudatis immundus Natta lucernis.
Ast ubi me fessum sol acrior ire lavatum
admonuit, fugio campum lusumque trigonem.

sil in the shape of a sea-urchin. It seems as if it must be a salt-cellar, the most necessary utensil, and not elsewhere mentioned, and if so, it perhaps should not be taken as earthen like the **patera**. (Cf. *Od.* II. 16. 14.)

118. **cum patera guttus**: for libations, a platter, and a narrow-necked pitcher, of common earthenware (**Campana**), not necessarily mean, but not silver or gold or bronze.

120. **mane,** *i.e.* early. — **obeundus Marsya**: *i.e.* go to the forum. (See note on verse 122.) In the forum stood a statue of Marsyas. The precise action of the statue to which Horace refers is uncertain. Perhaps the agony in his face, or possibly the fact merely that his back was turned, is jocosely assumed by Horace to indicate his dislike of Novius, evidently a usurer who had his money-changer's table in the vicinity.

121. **minoris** shows that a definite person is meant, the younger of two of the same name. The whole reference is unnecessary, but Horace likes to give a side thrust wherever he can.

122. **ad quartam**: the privilege of lying abed till ten was not possessed by the great, who must receive the **salutatio** at sunrise, and be escorted to the forum. — **vagor**: *i.e.* he takes a stroll (cf. 9. 1), or stays at home, and reads or writes in solitude (**tacitum**) till the hour for exercise comes.

123. **unguor**: the ancients prepared themselves for exercise by stripping and anointing themselves with oil.

124. **Natta**: another side thrust, indicating the parsimony of the unknown person. — **immundus**: careless of his person, as a miser. — **lucernis**: of course only the poorest of oil was used for burning, and this Natta uses for his body.

125. **sol acrior**: about noon. — **lavatum**: next the bath, and then the European breakfast or lunch; the first meal (*ientaculum*) not being a formal meal, just as now in Europe, has not been mentioned at all.

126. **campum lusumque trigonem**: another reading is, **rabiosi tempora signi**. Both readings are so old that the passage would seem to have been altered by Horace himself, a thing which happens sometimes with modern poets. If so, one cannot help thinking he wrote the one in the text last. — **Campum**: the Campus Martius, where such exercises took place. — **trigonem**: used in apposition with the force of an adjective, a not uncommon construction. The ancients had several games of ball, but ap-

Pransus non avide, quantum interpellet inani
ventre diem durare, domesticus otior. Haec est
vita solutorum misera ambitione gravique;
his me consolor victurum suavius ac si
quaestor avus pater atque meus patruusque fuisset.

## VII.

Proscripti Regis Rupili pus atque venenum
hybrida quo pacto sit Persius ultus, opinor
omnibus et lippis notum et tonsoribus esse.
Persius hic permagna negotia dives habebat
Clazomenis, etiam litis cum Rege molestas,

parently without the use of the bat. In this particular game three persons threw to each other, but in what the skill consisted is uncertain. (See Becker's *Gallus* Exc. II.). — [**rabiosi**, etc.: put loosely for the extreme heat of midday, though it should mean the heat of the dog-days, when the sun is in the Dog, but there is Horace's favorite confusion of ideas, between the mad dog and the raging heat. Cf. *Ep.* I. 10. 16, *Od.* I. 17. 17.]

127. **pransus**, etc.: only a light breakfast, at about two, to stay his stomach till dinner, the hour of which was rather late with him. Cf. 113. The dinner hour varied, as with us, from say three o'clock till seven.

130. **his**: neuter, and depending as an ablative of manner on **victurum.**

131. **quaestor**: the lowest of the offices is put for them all. His reason for preferring the lowest is not clear. Perhaps it is one of his unexpected turns, coming in as a jest upon himself, as it were.

SATIRE 7. This Satire contains an account of a lawsuit before Brutus when acting as governor of Asia. Horace was probably present, and gives this account among the other trifles upon which he composed his satires. The point of the whole is in the pun in v. 35. The occurrence was in 43 B.C.

1. **proscripti**, Rupilius Rex, of Præneste (see v. 28), had served under Varus, an adherent of Pompey, in Africa, and had been proscribed by Augustus. — **pus atque venenum**, *gall and venom*.

2. **hybrida**, *half-breed*, son of a Greek father and Roman mother. — **Persius**: evidently a **negotiator,** or capitalist, doing business at Clazomenæ. See v. 5.

3. **lippis, tonsoribus**: the physicians' booths and the barbers' shops were frequented by loungers as well as customers, so that they were favorite places for gossip. Cf. Ter. *Phormio* 89, Plaut. *Amph.* 1013. The disease of sore eyes was very common at Rome, and was one that had constant treatment. See I. 5. 30.

5. **litis**: connected humorously in the same construction as **negotia.** — **molestas,** *i.e. bitter*.

durus homo, atque odio qui posset vincere Regem,
confidens tumidusque, adeo sermonis amari,
Sisennas, Barros ut equis praecurreret albis.
Ad Regem redeo. Postquam nihil inter utrumque
convenit (hoc etenim sunt omnes iure molesti,
quo fortes, quibus adversum bellum incidit; inter
Hectora Priamiden animosum atque inter Achillem
ira fuit capitalis, ut ultima divideret mors,
non aliam ob causam nisi quod virtus in utroque
summa fuit: duo si discordia vexet inertis,
aut si disparibus bellum incidat, ut Diomedi
cum Lycio Glauco, discedat pigrior, ultro

6. **durus homo**, *a tough customer*. — **odio**, *bitterness*, hateful conduct. — **vincere**: implying that Rupilius was not wanting in this respect.

7. **tumidus**, *i.e.* arrogant.

8. **Sisennas, Barros**, abusive persons, otherwise unknown, perhaps informers, and so famous for their abusive language in courts of justice. — **equis albis**: proverbial; white horses being supposed to possess superior swiftness, — *with race-horse speed*.

9. **postquam**, etc.: the main clause is below (**pugnat**, v. 19). — **utrumque**, *the two*, a meaning that this word often has without any distributive idea.

10. **nihil convenit**: *i.e.* they could come to no agreement. — **hoc**: correlative with **quo**, and used as if the adjectives were comparative. The parenthesis gives the reason why they couldn't agree. — **iure**, *naturally*, *regularly*.

11. **fortes**, *brave*, *i.e.* good fighters. — **quibus**, *when they fall into*, etc., or simply *who fall* (changing the construction), etc. — **adversum bellum**, *opposing strife*: tautological, but not out of place, as giving the idea of mutuality.

12. **Hectora**: an illustration of his general statement. — **inter**: sometimes unnecessarily repeated, as here.

13. **capitalis**, *mortal*, *deadly*, *i.e.* so that they sought each other's life. — **ultima**, *only . . . at last; i.e.* death at the end of their lives.

15. **duo**, etc.: a proof from the opposite, in case of two cowards or a brave warrior and a coward. — **vexet**: the condition is a future less vivid one, but is meant to be general.

16. **Diomedi**: see *Il.* VI. 119, where, however, Glaucus' cowardice does not appear. The heroes refuse to fight because of ancient friendship, but exchange armor, an act which amounted to a gift on Glaucus' part. Horace may have purposely put this construction on the acts, or it may have been already done through the belittling spirit of later times.

17. **ultro**, *to boot*: in addition to declining to fight, the coward goes so far as to give something to buy off his adversary.

muneribus missis): Bruto praetore tenente
ditem Asiam, Rupili et Persi par pugnat, uti non
compositum melius cum Bitho Bacchius. In ius
acres procurrunt, magnum spectaculum uterque.
Persius exponit causam; ridetur ab omni
conventu; laudat Brutum laudatque cohortem:
solem Asiae Brutum appellat, stellasque salubris
appellat comites, excepto Rege; canem illum,
invisum agricolis sidus, venisse. Ruebat,
flumen ut hibernum, fertur quo rara securis.
Tum Praenestinus salso multoque fluenti
expressa arbusto regerit convicia, durus
vindemiator et invictus, cui saepe viator
cessisset, magna compellans voce cuculum.

18. **praetore**: he is called *prætor* because he had held that office the year before, though his command in Asia was really a consular one. But the word is also used generically of a governor or judicial magistrate, and it may be so used here.

19. **par pugnat**: Rupilius and Persius *are matched as gladiators*, or *enter the arena;* **par** (neuter) is the technical word.

20. **compositum melius**, a *better matched pair.*—**Bacchius**: subject of **sit**, having for its predicate **par**, to be supplied with **compositum**. — **in ius**: the proceedings before a judge were said to be **in iure**, *within the bar*.

21. **procurrunt**: of course with the figure of a battle or gladiatorial contest.

22. **ridetur**, *raises a laugh*, by his presentation of the case.

23. **conventu**: a technical expression for the persons who met at any place in the provinces, at a term of court, to have justice administered (cf. **conventus agere**, used of the governor). — **cohortem** (**amicorum**), *the suite* of young men who constituted a kind of staff.

25. **canem**, *the dog-star* (cf. 6. 126).

26. **agricolis**: *i.e.* simply as suggesting drought, which is injurious to their interests. — **ruebat**, *poured forth a torrent*.

27. **rara securis**: *i.e.* in the depth of the woods where the torrent is fullest.

28. **Praenestinus**: see note v. 1. — **salso**, etc., *on him with his bitter torrent*. — **multo**, with **Persio**, adjective for adverb.

29. **expressa**, *wrung from*, in response to the taunts of the passer-by (see note on v. 30). — **re-gerit**, *hurls back*.

30. **vindemiator** (four syllables), *like a*, etc.: in many cases the Latin allows the figure to be identified with the object where we cannot go beyond a simile. — **invictus**, *not to be outdone*. — **viator**, *the passer-by*, on the road.

31. **cessisset**: characteristic subjunctive. — **cuculum**: it appears that the country people of Italy

At Graecus, postquam est Italo perfusus aceto,
Persius exclamat: ‘Per magnos, Brute, deos te
oro, qui reges consueris tollere, cur non
hunc Regem iugulas? Operum hoc, mihi crede, tuo-
rumst.’

## VIII.

Olim truncus eram ficulnus, inutile lignum,
cum faber, incertus scamnum faceretne Priapum,
maluit esse deum. Deus inde ego, furum aviumque
maxima formido; nam fures dextra coercet

were much given to coarse language and rude abuse of each other, a tendency that gave rise to two or three kinds of dramatic composition, and was not without influence on satire itself. Here the passer-by is supposed to call out to the belated vine-pruner, “Cuckoo,” meaning that the cuckoo had come. The billingsgate of Rupilius is likened to the rude torrent poured out by the vine-dresser in reply. As often, Rupilius is not merely likened to the rustic, but identified with him.

32. **at Graecus**: inserted to give the contrast of the Greek's fine wit, to the coarse vituperation of the Italian (**Italo aceto**).

34. **reges**: alluding to Junius Brutus, the expeller of the Tarquins. — **tollere**, *put out of the way*, like Shakespeare's “taking off.”

35. **Regem**: the pun is of course wholly lost in English, but the word is so familiar to English ears that the connection is suggestive. — **operum** (predicate gen., Gr. § 214, *c*), *a fitting task for you*: this **rex** is a worse nuisance than any you or your ancestors have removed.

Satire **8**. This Satire is supposed to be written in ridicule of the same Gratidia referred to in *Epodes* III., VIII. 5, (?) and XVII. It represents an incantation scene, in which the woman, by the aid of a sorceress, performs magic rites to recover the alienated affections of a lover. This main idea of the Satire is worked up with a number of details in Horace's manner, which present the scene in a still more ridiculous light. The eighth Eclogue of Virgil may be compared for the incantations, which were no doubt common enough at that time. As the fig-tree gives a very poor wood, it is very likely that the whole is founded upon a sudden cracking of some wooden image of Priapus in Mæcenas' garden.

2. **scamnum**, etc.: *i.e.* **utrum scamnum an Priapum** (see Gr. § 211. *a*). — **Priapum**: a not very highly esteemed divinity of the fertility of the earth, originally brought from Lampsacus, whose image was set up in gardens as half god and half scarecrow. It was customary for poets to put into his mouth any poetry too indecent for other sponsors, and here the abuse of the women is heightened by making him the spokesman.

4. **formido**, *a terror*, as in English. — **fures dextra**: a sickle or

obscenoque ruber porrectus ab inguine palus ;
ast importunas volucres in vertice harundo
terret fixa vetatque novis considere in hortis.
Huc prius angustis eiecta cadavera cellis
conservus vili portanda locabat in arca ;
hoc miserae plebi stabat commune sepulchrum,
Pantolabo scurrae Nomentanoque nepoti :
mille pedes in fronte, trecentos cippus in agrum
hic dabat, heredes monumentum ne sequeretur.

club was usually held in his right hand (cf. Virg. *Georg.* IV. 110).

5. **ruber**: the god was regularly painted red.

6. **harundo**: *i.e.* a reed waving in the wind and serving as a scarecrow.

7. **novis . . . hortis**: Mæcenas had laid out a magnificent garden on the Esquiline, on a spot occupied from very ancient times as a burial place. Tombs of very great antiquity and also common burial places have lately been excavated in that region. This particular spot seems to have been only a part of the burial place, devoted to the poorer classes.

8. **eiecta,** *hustled out:* simply heightening the picture of the misery of the slaves, and not probably referring to any special usage. The body of a respectable person would be **elatum**.

9. **conservus**: the slaves were often united into societies for the purposes of burial; and when they were not, doubtless they took care of the burial of their fellows. Many tombstones are found erected by fellow-slaves and fellow-freedmen. —**locabat**: *i.e.* the fellow-slaves paid the expenses of the burial, and contracted with the regular undertakers.

10. **hoc**: *i.e.* the public lot described in v. 12, but agreeing with **sepulchrum**. — **stabat sepulchrum**: the word **stabat** would seem to imply a real tomb, but as **sepulchrum** is used of any burial place, **stabat** goes with it naturally in the sense of *was*.

11. **Pantolabo,** etc. (*Get-what-you-can*): one of Horace's favorite side thrusts at two poor creatures whom he despises. — **scurrae**: many persons in antiquity literally lived by their wits, getting invitations to dinner in return for the amusement they afforded, acting somewhat like the court fools of later times. Naturally, being without visible means of support, they were despised by their more fortunate patrons.

12. **in fronte,** *i.e. on the street.* — **cippus**, a small square pillar with the inscription to mark the place and size of the lot. Such inscriptions are numerous. *E.g.*

D.M. FORTVNATO IVLI FRONTONIS
ACTORI
PATRATA CONIVƎ BENEMERENTI ET
FILI FECERVNT IN F P XX IN AGR P XXV
HMHNS.

(*Hoc Monumentum Heredes Ne Sequatur.*)

— **in agrum,** *in depth.*

13. **dabat,** *assigned* for a burial place for the people. — **heredes,** etc.: *i.e.* separating the lot from the property of the person who gave it. — **monumentum**: refer-

Nunc licet Esquiliis habitare salubribus atque
aggere in aprico spatiari, quo modo tristes
albis informem spectabant ossibus agrum;
cum mihi non tantum furesque feraeque, suetae
hunc vexare locum, curae sunt atque labori,
quantum carminibus quae versant atque venenis
humanos animos. Has nullo perdere possum
nec prohibere modo, simul ac vaga luna decorum
protulit os, quin ossa legant herbasque nocentis.
Vidi egomet nigra succinctam vadere palla

ring loosely to the place, but quoting the most common form of the provision, as above given. **locus**, which is often used, would be more exact. — **ne sequeretur**, *i.e. with the provision that*, etc., quoted indirectly from the language of the inscriptions. Horace's form implies a direct **sequatur**, which does not occur in full in inscriptions. The word, however, is very rarely written out in full, and the sense of **non sequitur**, which does occur, is really the same.

14. **nunc**, etc.: later, apparently, the burial place had been discontinued in part, though tombs farther out, perhaps beyond the *agger* of Servius, were still remaining (see v. 36). — **salutaribus**, *i.e. and find it wholesome;* in a predicate use.

15. **aggere**: the great earth-wall built on the east side of the city by Servius Tullius, part of which still exists. Probably the ground was appropriated to ordinary uses as far as this, still leaving tombs beyond. — **quo**, abl. = **ubi**: referring to the Esquiline in general, not to the **agger**. — **tristes**, *sadly*.

16. **informem**, *hideous*.

17. **cum**, *while:* the construction seems to be that of **cum** *inversum* (Gr. § 325, *b*). — **fures**: to steal the fruit, cf. v. 4. — **ferae**: possibly birds and beasts of prey prowling for the bones, etc., but more probably in search of the fruit, as in v. 4, **aves**. Cf. also **curae atque labori**, v. 18. — **suetae**: three syllables.

19. **carminibus atque venenis**, *spells and charms*, referring to the whole magical paraphernalia. — **quae**, *the women who*, *i.e.* who came to this old cemetery for magic. Everything connected with death has been an instrument of witchcraft in all ages.

20. **perdere**, *confound;* used loosely as the active of **pereant**, which would be his wish for them.

21. **vaga**: *i.e.* among the stars.

22. **protulit**: *i.e.* probably at the rising of the full moon, which was a favorite time for magic. — **ossa herbasque**: these were particularly efficacious. Cf. *Epode* V. 17 and note to v. 19.

23. **vidi**: here begins the special incident, and in a kind of epic style, to produce a pseudo-pathetic effect. — **nigra**: as the funereal color. Cf. the "black art." — **palla**: we can not be sure exactly what sort of a dress she wore, but it was no doubt different from the ordinary wear. The palla seems to have been a plain piece of cloth for drapery, but capable of adjustment to the body by a girdle and by clasps on the

Canidiam pedibus nudis passoque capillo,
cum Sagana maiore ululantem. Pallor utrasque
fecerat horrendas aspectu. Scalpere terram
unguibus et pullam divellere mordicus agnam
coeperunt; cruor in fossam confusus, ut inde
manis elicerent, animas responsa daturas.
Lanea et effigies erat, altera cerea: maior
lanea, quae poenis compesceret inferiorem;
cerea suppliciter stabat servilibus, ut quae
iam peritura, modis. Hecaten vocat altera, saevam
altera Tisiphonen; serpentis atque videres
infernas errare canes, Lunamque rubentem,
ne foret his testis, post magna latere sepulchra.
Mentior at si quid, merdis caput inquiner albis

shoulders. Probably it was also girded up shorter than usual, as is indicated by **succinctam** (see Rich, *Dictionary of Antiquities*).

25. **Sagana maiore**: there seems no reason why the natural meaning of "the elder of two Saganas," both sorceresses, should not be taken. The person is mentioned again in *Epode* V. 25. — **ululantem**: repeating the incantations in a tone suitable to the occasion; used regularly of women's cries. — **pallor**: naturally the officiating persons are frightened also (*Epode* V. 27).

26. **scalpere terram**, etc.: the regular rite in necromancy seems to have been to dig a ditch and sacrifice a black sheep into it. This process was to make the shades give prophetic answers, which are also referred to in v. 41, the nature of which, however, does not appear. Still we need not expect the story to be exact about such a matter. Cf. next note for a similar loose statement.

27. **mordicus**: to give the picture of furies, as it were.

30. **lanea**: the process here is often referred to. The two puppets represent the person seeking the enchantment and the one to be affected, one being subject to the action of heat, and the other not. In Virgil (*Ecl.* VIII. 80) they are of clay and wax respectively. The waxen one is to be melted in the fire of love, while the other remains unaffected. — **maior**: as indicating superior power and mastery. The whole implies that whatever the puppet suffers will be transferred by the magic art to the person represented. So the symbolism is carried as far as possible, even to **peritura** (**suppliciter stabat**).

32. **servilibus**, *i.e.* die in torment. Probably in all this two or three rites are confounded (cf. Virgil, *Ecl.* VIII. 80), as also in the following. — **serpentis atque canes**, attendants upon Hecate.

35. **rubentem**: the moon is comically represented as blushing, and hiding behind the great tombs in the neighborhood.

37. **mentior**, etc.: the adjuration

corvorum, atque in me veniat mictum atque cacatum
Iulius et fragilis Pediatia furque Voranus.
Singula quid memorem? quo pacto alterna loquentes
umbrae cum Sagana resonarent triste et acutum,
utque lupi barbam variae cum dente colubrae
abdiderint furtim terris, et imagine cerea
largior arserit ignis, et ut non testis inultus
horruerim voces Furiarum et facta duarum:
nam, displosa sonat quantum vesica, pepedi
diffissa nate ficus: at illae currere in urbem;
Canidiae dentes, altum Saganae caliendrum
excidere atque herbas atque incantata lacertis
vincula cum magno risuque iocoque videres.

gives a comic effect to the story, just as if one said, "You may not believe it, but it's a fact," at the end of a Munchausen tale. Of course his oath is suited to his nature.

39. **Iulius**, etc.: another side thrust. The first person is unknown, but he must be the same sort of person as the others who are described. — **fragilis**, *the weakling;* of effeminacy. — **Pediatia**: really a man, but spoken of thus on account of his effeminacy.

40. **alterna**, *i.e.* of questions and answers.

41. **resonarent**: the imperfect cannot be explained. Either the reading **resonarint** ought to be adopted, or we must suppose it a lapse on Horace's part. — **triste et acutum**: the feeble and piping voice regularly attributed to the shades. Cf. *Aen.* VI. 493.

42. **lupi barbam**: these seem to have been charms against opposing magic on the part of others.

43. **cerea**: dissyllabic by synizesis.

44. **arserit**: *i.e.* the wax melted and ran into the fire. This has not been mentioned before, but is understood as one of the regular accompaniments. Cf. note to v. 30. — **ut non**, etc., *how it was not as an unavenged spectator that*, etc.

45. **Furiarum**: cf. note to v. 27.

46. **quantum**: a kind of cogn. acc. with **sonat**.

48. **dentes**, *false teeth*, which were not uncommon among the ancients. — **caliendrum**, some sort of a headdress, the form of which is unknown. It was evidently, however, tall, and perhaps some Eastern cap, like the Persian tiara, for instance.

49. **herbas, vincula**: the machinery of their magic that they held in their arms. — **incantata**, equal to *enchanted*, *i.e.* arranged with spells, solemn formulæ to give magic power. The vincula would be love-knots to bind fast the person to be affected. The whole is probably not very exact.

50. **videres**, *you might have seen* (Gr. § 311, *a*).

## IX.

Ibam forte via Sacra, sicut meus est mos,
nescio quid meditans nugarum, totus in illis:
accurrit quidam notus mihi nomine tantum,
arreptaque manu, 'Quid agis, dulcissime rerum?'
'suaviter, ut nunc est,' inquam, 'et cupio omnia quae vis.'
Cum adsectaretur, 'Numquid vis?' occupo. At ille
'Noris nos' inquit; 'docti sumus.' Hic ego 'Pluris

SATIRE 9. This Satire, one of the most famous, treats of the efforts of a pushing aspirant to social recognition to attach himself to Horace from ambitious motives. In a society so aristocratic, and at the same time so unstable, as was the Roman at this period, social ambitions must have had a very active stimulation. Horace's own rise in life had been extraordinary, and mere vulgar aspirants and snobs could not but attribute it to the same selfish and pushing arts that they were in the habit of using, and endeavor to unite with him, and get his support for their own advancement.

1. **ibam**: cf. 6. 112 and 122. — **via sacra**: the Boulevards of Rome, the favorite lounging-place, alongside the forum, and where the most brilliant out-door life was carried on.

2. **nugarum**: probably some effort in verse.

3. **accurrit**: his manner of approach already suggests his effusiveness.

4. **arrepta**: this action is also excessive; a simple **salve** would have been enough. — **quid agis**: the common very familiar salutation, like *How are you?* or *How goes it?* — **dulcissime**, etc., *my dearest fellow;* still more familiar. — **rerum**: partitive genitive (equivalent to "in the world"), but the gender of the adjective is determined by the sense. The best translation is that given under the previous word.

5. **suaviter**, etc.: a polite but distant reception of the salute; especially is **cupio**, etc. (I wish you every success, I'm sure) only an expression of thanks for his interest. — **ut nunc est**, *i.e. as the times go.*

6. **adsectaretur**, *followed me up*, as Horace proceeds on his way. — **numquid vis**: the regular formula of leave-taking, *There's nothing I can do for you, is there?* — **occupo**, *I anticipate him with.*

7. **noris nos**, *yes, make my acquaintance.* It was not uncommon to reply to this formula in a sense contrary to its meaning, with a kind of pleasantry, as, *Yes, take care of yourself;* but here the snob will not be turned off, and so rudely tells the object of his address. The verb properly depends on **vis**. — **docti**, *an accomplished artist, i.e.* a trained literary man, and diner out, cf. v. 22. — **pluris**, etc.: like *O indeed! I shall think more of you, I'm sure,* a cool reply.

hoc' inquam 'mihi eris.' Misere discedere quaerens,
ire modo ocius, interdum consistere, in aurem
dicere nescio quid puero, cum sudor ad imos
manaret talos. 'O te, Bolane, cerebri
felicem!' aiebam tacitus; cum quidlibet ille
garriret, vicos, urbem laudaret. Vt illi
nil respondebam, 'Misere cupis' inquit 'abire;
iamdudum video; sed nil agis; usque tenebo;
persequar: hinc quo nunc iter est tibi?' 'Nil opus est te
circumagi; quendam volo visere non tibi notum;
trans Tiberim longe cubat is, prope Caesaris hortos.'
'Nil habeo quod agam, et non sum piger; usque sequar te.'
Demitto auriculas, ut iniquae mentis asellus,
cum gravius dorso subiit onus. Incipit ille:
'Si bene me novi, non Viscum pluris amicum,
non Varium facies; nam quis me scribere pluris

8. **hoc,** *i.e.* on account of your accomplishments. — **misere quaerens,** *wretchedly anxious.*

10. **puero**: pretending to have some business with his slave who was following him. — **sudor**: from desperation.

11. **Bolane,** an unknown person of a hot temper. — **cerebri**: governed by **felicem,** Gr. § 218. *c.*

12. **felicem,** that is, *blessed with,* because he would not be restrained by politeness from shaking off the intruder, as Horace was. — **tacitus,** *to myself.*

13. **vicos, urbem**: *i.e.* talking about the parts of the city as they went on, for the purpose of making conversation.

14. **misere,** etc.: the bore could not help seeing that his presence was unwelcome, and so resorts to the vulgar expedient of jesting about it in a way which would be almost rude even in the greatest intimacy.

15. **nil agis,** *it's of no use.* — **usque tenebo,** *I will stick fast to you.*

16. **persequar,** *I will follow you up.* — **quo**: interrogative, *whither? which way?* — **nil opus,** etc., *oh, there's no occasion for you to go out of your way.*

17. **quendam,** *a man.*

18. **cubat,** *lies sick.* — **hortos,** an estate on the Janiculum, left by Julius Cæsar to the Roman people.

20. **demitto auriculas**: as an indication of forced submission to a disagreeable necessity. — **iniquae mentis,** *of sullen temper.*

21. The bore now gradually leads up to his accomplishments to show what a useful friend he would be in society.

22. **Viscum**: Vilius Viscus Nervius; cf. I. 10. 83, II. 8. 20.

23. **Varium**: cf. I. 5. 40. — **nam quis,** etc.: for Horace's estimate of this accomplishment, see I. 4. 14.

aut citius possit versus? quis membra movere
mollius? invideat quod et Hermogenes ego canto.'
  Interpellandi locus hic erat: 'Est tibi mater,
cognati, quis te salvo est opus?'—'Haud mihi quisquam;
omnis composui.'—'Felices! Nunc ego resto.
Confice; namque instat fatum mihi triste, Sabella
quod puero cecinit divina mota anus urna:
"*Hunc neque dira venena, nec hosticus auferet ensis,*
*nec laterum dolor aut tussis, nec tarda podagra;*
*garrulus hunc quando consumet cumque; loquacis,*
*si sapiat, vitet, simul atque adoleverit aetas.*"'
  Ventum erat ad Vestae, quarta iam parte diei
praeterita, et casu tunc respondere vadato
debebat; quod ni fecisset, perdere litem.

24. **membra movere**, *dance*.

25. **mollius**, *more gracefully*. Dancing was a rather disreputable accomplishment among the Romans at this time (cf. Cic. *pro Mur*. VI. 13).—**quod**: the acc. of the thing after **invideat**. Its antecedent **id** or **tale** would be the object of **canto**.

26. **hic locus erat**, etc.: apparently the opportunity was his mention of his accomplishments, to which Horace replies, as if feeling that so accomplished a man was too valuable to expose to danger; "have you any friends dependent on you?" implying that there is danger in going to see the sick person. The answer destroys this hope of getting rid of him, and Horace's reply as far as v. 35 must be supposed to be made aside in his own thought. It is obvious that if Horace's good nature would allow him to speak in that tone to the fellow, he would have got rid of him long before.

29. **confice**: jocosely said, as if he had bored all his friends to death, and now was going to crown the whole by killing off Horace. Of course the allusion to his destiny is an invention.—**Sabella**: the Sabines and the mountain people generally were famous for superstitions and divination, acting, it would seem, as a sort of gipsies.

30. **divina**, *prophetic*.—**urna**, in which the lots (**sortes**) were cast (cf. *Od*. II. 3. 26), and shaken (**mota**), whereupon one came to the surface, which was drawn out.

32. **tussis**: *i.e.* consumption.—**tarda**, *crippling*: a transferred epithet; it was the patient that was slow.

33. **quando ... cumque**, *at some time or other*, whenever it is.

35. **Vestae** (Gr. § 214. *b*): in their ramble they had come to the south end of the Forum, near which was the temple of Vesta and the courts of justice.—**quarta**: *i.e.* it was past nine.

36. **vadato**, *a plaintiff in a lawsuit*, who had made him give bail to appear on this day.

37. **debebat**, *he was bound*.—**fecisset**: in informal indirect discourse for **fecerit** of the direct (cf.

'Si me amas,' inquit, 'paulum hic ades.' 'Inteream, si
aut valeo stare aut novi civilia iura;
et propero quo scis.' 'Dubius sum quid faciam,' inquit,
'tene relinquam an rem.' 'Me, sodes.' 'Non faciam,' ille,
et praecedere coepit. Ego, ut contendere durum est
cum victore, sequor. 'Maecenas quomodo tecum?'
hinc repetit; 'paucorum hominum et mentis bene sanae;
nemo dexterius fortuna est usus. Haberes
magnum adiutorem, posset qui ferre secundas,
hunc hominem velles si tradere; dispeream, ni
summosses omnis.' 'Non isto vivimus illic

**reddidisses**, *Od.* I. 10. 9), as it would appear in the terms of the contract of bail. — **perdere** (with **debebat**): *i.e.* the case would go against him by default.

38. **si me amas**, equal to *if you will be so kind.* Prosody, *sī mĕ ămās. e* shortened before *a*, as in Greek. — **ades**, *attend me;* as *advocatus*, not an advocate, but an adviser and friend to suggest the law and give him moral support. — **inteream**, *confound me.* The condition (**si valeo**, etc.) is of the kind where no opinion is expressed, and a wish takes the place of the indicative in apodosis.

39. **stare**: best taken literally, "bear the fatigue of the court." — **novi**, etc.: *i.e.* he would be of no use.

41. **rem**, his case. — **sodes** (**si audes**, if you please), *i.e. by all means.*

43. **victore**: *i.e.* he had beaten him so many times that Horace was now discouraged and let him have his own way. — **Maecenas**, etc.: the bore now comes to his real object. — **quomodo**, equal to *on what terms.*

44. **hinc repetit**, *he begins again* (his talk) *with that.* — **paucorum**, etc., *of few friends, and has a very level head, i.e.* has made a shrewd use of his luck. This is said as if Mæcenas' choice of friends had been prompted by such motives.

45. **haberes** (in the contrary to fact construction) implies, of course, that Horace has no desire of making his acquaintance, but thereby makes the request all the more importunate.

46. **secundas** (*sc.* **partes**), etc., *support you*, or with another figure, *play into your hands.*

47. **hunc hominem**, *your humble servant.* — **tradere**, *introduce*, a technical term, almost. — **dispeream**: the same construction as in v. 38; its protasis is the truth of the proposition **ni summosses**, which is itself conditioned on the preceding **si velles**.

48. **summosses**: the pluperfect seems to refer to the rapidity of the action; *you would shove them all aside in a twinkling.* Horace hereupon endeavors to persuade the bore that he misunderstands the situation; the coterie has no such relations among its members.

quo tu rere modo; domus hac nec purior ulla est
nec magis his aliena malis; nil mi officit,' inquam,
'ditior hic aut est quia doctior; est locus uni
cuique suus.' 'Magnum narras, vix credibile!' 'Atqui
sic habet.' 'Accendis, quare cupiam magis illi
proximus esse.' 'Velis tantummodo: quae tua virtus,
expugnabis; et est qui vinci possit, eoque
difficilis aditus primos habet.' 'Haud mihi deero:
muneribus servos corrumpam; non, hodie si
exclusus fuero, desistam; tempora quaeram,
occurram in triviis, deducam. Nil sine magno
vita labore dedit mortalibus.' Haec dum agit, ecce
Fuscus Aristius occurrit, mihi carus et illum
qui pulchre nosset. Consistimus. 'Vnde venis?' et
'Quo tendis?' rogat et respondet. Vellere coepi
et prensare manu lentissima brachia, nutans,

49. **domus**: of Mæcenas. — **purior**, *more free.*

50. **aliena**, *at variance with.*

52. **magnum**, etc.: the bore cannot believe in such a state of things; so he flatteringly says that it increases his eagerness to get into the set.

54. Horace now changes his tone, and says humorously that he has only to try and he will succeed, no doubt covertly alluding to the bore's prowess in his own case.

55. **est qui**, etc.: *i.e.* he has his weak spots, and so guards more carefully the first access to him.

56. Horace shows the worthless character of the fellow by the view which he takes of Horace's suggestion, and the means which he proposes to use.

58. **tempora**, *favorable opportunities.*

59. **triviis**, *at the street corners.* — **deducam**, *escort to the Forum*, a technical expression. — **nil**, etc.: the comic effect is heightened by the use of a proverb which in the mouth of a hero would be commendable. The kind of labor referred to, however, makes it contemptible here.

60. **haec dum agit**, *while he is talking in this way.*

61. **Fuscus Aristius**, one of the poet's best friends. Cf. I. 10. 83, *Ep.* I. 10, *Od.* I. 22.

62. **nosset**: a characteristic relative clause, showing clearly the nature of such clauses by its connection with an adjective, to which it is equivalent. — **unde venis**, etc.: ordinary familiar salutations.

63. **rogat**, etc., *is asked and answered*, on both sides. — **vellere**, etc.: the poet begins to nudge him (strictly, pull his toga), and make signs for Fuscus to relieve him by claiming an engagement with him, or the like.

64. **lentissima**, *unresponsive*, which did not resist enough to feel the pull.

distorquens oculos, ut me eriperet. Male salsus
ridens dissimulare; meum iecur urere bilis.
'Certe nescio quid secreto velle loqui te
aiebas mecum.' 'Memini bene, sed meliore
tempore dicam; hodie tricesima sabbata: vin' tu
curtis Iudaeis oppedere?' 'Nulla mihi,' inquam,
'religio est.' 'At mi; sum paulo infirmior, unus
multorum. Ignosces; alias loquar.' Huncine solem
tam nigrum surrexe mihi! Fugit improbus ac me
sub cultro linquit. Casu venit obvius illi
adversarius, et, 'Quo tu, turpissime?' magna
inclamat voce, et 'Licet antestari?' Ego vero
oppono auriculam. Rapit in ius; clamor utrimque,
undique concursus. Sic me servavit Apollo.

65. **male salsus,** *the wicked wag*, wishing to play a malicious joke on Horace.

66. **dissimulare,** pretended not to notice it. — **bilis**: the bile was anciently supposed to be the seat of the passions, here of anger.

67. **certe,** etc., *I'm sure you were saying*, etc., making up an engagement for the purpose.

69. **tricesima**: the Jews seem to have had a festival once a month, not strictly the thirtieth Sabbath, but so called because of the familiar weekly Sabbath. The mention of the Jews at all shows an extraordinary spread of their rites. — **vin'**, the colloquial form for **visne**, as in the comedy.

70. **curtis,** *circumcised*. — **oppedere**: a coarse term for *insult*, of course by doing business on their holy day.

71. **religio,** *religious scruple*. — **infirmior**: rather weak in those matters, not strong-minded enough to be free from superstition.

72. **huncine,** etc.: a construction especially common in the Comedy, equal to *to think that this*, etc.

73. **surrexe,** old form for **surrexisse**, cf. 5. 79.

74. **sub cultro**: a figure from the sacrifice.

75. **adversarius,** the same person referred to as **vadatus** in v. 36. — **quo** (*sc.* **is**), *i.e.* why don't you appear?

76. **licet antestari**: the formula used to appeal to a person, asking his permission to use him as a witness; here, of course, to establish the fact that the man was found breaking his bail, in which case the plaintiff could seize him.

77. **auriculam**: the party seems to have touched the ear, the seat of memory, to warn the witness to remember the circumstances. See *Ecl.* VI. 4, and Fig. 21, Greenough's Virgil.

78. **Apollo**: probably only as the president of the Muses, and patron of poetry and guardian of poets. The poet's usual guardian is Mercury (*Od.* II. 17. 29).

## X.

*Lucili, quam sis mendosus, teste Catone,*
*defensore tuo, pervincam, qui male factos*
*emendare parat versus; hoc lenius ille,*
*quo vir est melior, longe subtilior illo,*
*qui multum puer et loris et funibus udis*
*exhortatus, ut esset opem qui ferre poetis*
*antiquis posset contra fastidia nostra,*
*grammaticorum equitum doctissimus. Ut redeam illuc:*

Nempe incomposito dixi pede currere versus
Lucili. Quis tam Lucili fautor inepte est
ut non hoc fateatur? At idem, quod sale multo
urbem defricuit, charta laudatur eadem.

SATIRE 10. This satire contains a defence of Horace's criticisms on Lucilius in *Sat.* I. 4; and a general defence of his own style of composition.

1. The first eight lines, printed in italics, are found in some but not all of the Mss., and their authenticity is denied by most scholars. It does not seem likely from the internal evidence that they are Horace's work. It is barely possible that they may have been originally written by him, and afterwards left out upon a revision of the Satire. But even this is not likely. — **Catone,** Valerius Cato, a poet and grammarian, of Gaul, who, we may conclude, undertook to modernize Lucilius.

3. **hoc,** *so much,* correlative with **quo.**

4. **illo:** apparently refers to another emender of Lucilius, afterwards referred to as **equitum doctissimus.**

5. **qui:** referring to **illo.**

6. **exhortatus:** used passively like many participles of deponents. — **opem ferre,** *come to the rescue of, i.e.* by modernizing and emending, as English poets have sometimes done with Chaucer.

7. **fastidia,** *fastidious taste.*

8. **illuc:** must be taken as referring to the general subject of Lucilius, from which he has diverged in his talk about his emenders. But the whole eight lines are very obscure, and perhaps not worth understanding.

1. **nempe,** *yes,* or *true;* in answer to a criticism on his remark about Lucilius, in I. 4. 8 and 11, and opposed by **at** in v. 3. — **incomposito,** *careless* or *rough* measure.

2. **inepte:** modifying **fautor,** which is used in the sense of an adjective. In translating, it is better to make **fautor** a noun, and **inepte** an adjective.

3. **idem,** *he, at the same time.* — **sale:** used often of witty satire, but the figure is here made more vivid by **defricuit.** It may be imitated by *made the city smart, with caustic wit.*

4. **charta:** cf. I. 5. 104. — **laudatur:** see I. 4. 1–8, where he is spoken of in the highest terms.

Nec tamen, hoc tribuens, dederim quoque cetera; nam sic
et Laberi mimos ut pulchra poemata mirer.
Ergo non satis est risu diducere rictum
auditoris (et est quaedam tamen hic quoque virtus);
est brevitate opus, ut currat sententia neu se
impediat verbis lassas onerantibus auris;
et sermone opus est modo tristi, saepe iocoso,
defendente vicem modo rhetoris atque poetae,
interdum urbani, parcentis viribus atque
extenuantis eas consulto. Ridiculum acri
fortius et melius magnas plerumque secat res.
Illi, scripta quibus comoedia prisca viris est,
hoc stabant, hoc sunt imitandi; quos neque pulcher
Hermogenes umquam legit, neque simius iste

5. **tribuens**, *paying him this tribute.* — **dederim**: cf. I. 4. 39. — **quoque**, belonging to the whole clause. — **cetera**, the other qualities that make a poet. — **sic**, *on that principle*, by that rule.

6. **Laberi**, Decimus Laberius, a Roman knight of the end of the Republic, who wrote mimes, farcical dramatic poems of the lowest class, often obscene, and always representing common realistic scenes from low life. The argument is that if witty ridicule alone made poetry, these productions must be counted as such.

7. **ergo**: *i.e.* since the *reductio ad absurdum* above proves that wit alone is not sufficient. — **diducere rictum**, *raise a laugh:* lit. open wide the jaws as in laughter.

8. **hic**, *in this.*

9. **brevitate**: *i.e.* the common talk of the street is too wordy for art. — **currat**, *flow on freely.* — **sententia**, *the thought.*

11. **sermone**, etc.: *i.e.* farcical dialogue alone is not enough; there must be a serious vein as well, to give variety.

12. **defendente**, *support:* cf. **tueri**, the more common expression. — **vicem**, *the part.* — **rhetoris atque poetae**, the serious style of the orator and poet.

13. **urbani**, *of the wit.* — **parcentis**: *i.e.* treating a subject lightly, not speaking with as much moral fervor as the poet or orator.

14. **ridiculum**: the style of the **urbanus** just referred to. — **acri**: the style of the orator and poet.

15. **secat**, *decides* (cuts knots), cf. *Ep.* I. 16. 42.

16. **illi**: Aristophanes and the like, the writers of the old comedy (**prisca**). Cf. I. 4. 1.

17. **stabant**, kept their ground, a word borrowed from the stage, like "run" in English. — **pulcher**: a term of reproach, indicating effeminacy.

18. **Hermogenes**, etc.: referring, no doubt, to the clique of

nil praeter Calvum et doctus cantare Catullum.
'At magnum fecit, quod verbis Graeca Latinis
miscuit.' O seri studiorum! quine putetis
difficile et mirum, Rhodio quod Pitholeonti
contigit? 'At sermo lingua concinnus utraque
suavior, ut Chio nota si commixta Falerni est.'
Cum versus facias, te ipsum percontor, an et cum
dura tibi peragenda rei sit causa Petilli?

Horace's critics, who, he implies, are incapacitated for criticism in this matter because they never read Greek, and don't know what they are talking about. — **simius**: perhaps on account of his tricks which he used to amuse society. Cf. I. 9. 24 and v. 80. The reference is said to be to Demetrius. See v. 79.

19. **Calvum**, C. Licinius Calvus, a contemporary of Cicero, and friend of Catullus. The reproach here is aimed, no doubt, at the prettiness of their love songs. We can hardly tell about Calvus, but Catullus was certainly superior to Horace in the poetic gift.

20. **magnum fecit**: in the general admiration of Greek literature, no doubt there were men who actually thought the interlarding of Greek words was a merit. Their claim is introduced to be disallowed. — **Graeca**: Lucilius uses whole sentences of Greek.

21. **seri studiorum** (cf. **cerebri felicem**, I. 9. 11), *pedantic blockheads*, a translation of ὀψιμαθεῖς, late to learn, and so filled with the zeal of a new convert, putting in at all times what they have just learned. Cf. Gell. XI. 7. — **quine**: this difficult expression is the despair of grammarians. The **-ne** absolutely requires a question either in the clause itself or in the principal clause (cf. Plaut. *Truc.* II. 6. 53). But no question including the meaning of **qui** seems exactly right. It is best taken in the sense of "How can you think," etc., in which case the **-ne** would only be added to the interrogative as in **utrumne.** Possibly **qui** might be indefinite, as in **Hercle qui,** and the like, of the comedy. In this case it would mean, "Can you have any idea?" etc., and the expression would be a popular one not appearing elsewhere in literature.

22. **Pitholeonti**, an unknown poetaster. Possibly Pitholaus. Cf. Suet. *J. C.* 75.

23. **at**: introducing an argument of his adversaries; *but, you say.* — **lingua**: abl. of means. — **concinnus**, *neatly joined.*

24. **Chio**: the Greek wines were sweeter and less harsh than the Latin, and hence an agreeable mixture was made of the two. — **nota**: *the brand* put for the wine. The opponent uses this practice as an example to prove the advantage of mixing the two languages.

25. **cum**, etc.: Horace meets the argument by reducing it to an absurdity, asking if it is only in poetry, or will it hold good in oratory also. — **te ipsum**, etc.: implying that they themselves could see the folly of such a course in a plea in court.

26. **Petilli**: a famous law case (see I. 4. 94) is used as a sample of all.

scilicet oblitus patriaeque patrisque Latini
cum Pedius causas exsudet Publicola atque
Corvinus, patriis intermiscere petita
verba foris malis, Canusini more bilinguis?
atque ego cum Graecos facerem, natus mare citra,
versiculos, vetuit me tali voce Quirinus,
post mediam noctem visus, cum somnia vera:
'In silvam non ligna feras insanius, ac si
magnas Graecorum malis implere catervas.'
  Turgidus Alpinus iugulat dum Memnona, dumque
defingit Rheni luteum caput, haec ego ludo,

27. **scilicet**, etc.: *i.e.* to be consistent, of course, they must also ask the great orator to use Greek as well. — **oblitus**, etc.: that is, forgetting that you are a Roman.

28. **Pedius**: Q. Pedius Publicola was a brother of M. Valerius Messala Corvinus, but adopted into the gens Pedia. These two are types of great orators. — **exsudet**: a humorous expression for "work out" their difficult cases for their orations.

29. **patriis** (*sc.* **verbis** from **verba** below). — **intermiscere**: the regular grammar would require **eos** expressed, but it is readily supplied from the names which have just occurred.

30. **foris**: *i.e.* from Greece. — **Canusini**: at Canusium Greek and Oscan would both be spoken.

31. **atque ego**, etc.: the answer is supposed already to be given, and the absurdity shown, whereupon Horace makes the argument still stronger by showing that it isn't well for a Roman to write Greek poetry at all. This he enforces by a fable of his own case. It is probably true so far as the main idea is concerned.

32. **tali**, the words in vv. 34, 35.

33. **cum**, etc., an old superstition.

34. **in silvam**, etc., a common proverb, like coals to Newcastle, and *Γλαῦκ' εἰς 'Αθήνας*. The fable gives him a transition to his own style and his reason for adopting it.

36. **turgidus**: probably with a double meaning, as there is no reason to doubt the assertion of the scholiast that M. Furius Bibaculus is meant (cf. II. 5. 41). If he is, he was no doubt called Alpinus in mockery of his poem on the Alps. (see above citation). — **iugulat**: with a double meaning, of a poem in which Memnon, son of Tithonus and Aurora, was killed by Achilles. The poem is said by a scholiast to have been an Æthiopis.

37. **defingit**, *muddles*: *i.e.* by describing it badly, using no doubt the epithet **luteum**. — **caput**: probably the mouth, but it may mean the source. The former seems more likely on account of **luteum**. — **haec ego ludo**, *i.e.* "I, having been advised not to write Greek poetry, and not wishing to imitate the tasteless effusions of Alpinus in epic poetry, content myself with these trifles in a sportive strain, not to be recited for a prize, nor to appear on the stage. Others can do

quae neque in aede sonent certantia iudice Tarpa,
nec redeant iterum atque iterum spectanda theatris.
Arguta meretrice potes Davoque Chremeta
eludente senem comis garrire libellos
unus vivorum, Fundani; Pollio regum
facta canit pede ter percusso; forte epos acer,
ut nemo, Varius ducit; molle atque facetum

those things better." He then proceeds to assign the mastery in the different styles to others, — to Fundanius in comedy (cf. *Sat.* II. 8. 19); to C. Asinius Pollio, famed as a statesman, orator, and historian as well, in tragedy; in epic poetry, to Varius (cf. I. 5. 40); in rural scenes to Virgil, whose Æneid had not yet been written. He has not tried to rival these, but has chosen a branch in which he could excel.

38. **in aede**, etc.: a free allusion to recitation for prizes, though no definite occasion is known. — **Tarpa**: Sp. Mæcius Tarpa was a friend of Pompey, and chosen by him as a literary critic to select the play for his new theatre. He probably contrived to hold the same position, as a judge of literature under Augustus (cf. *A. P.* 387), though the reference may be to any judge.

40. **arguta**, etc.: the two methods of publication are referred to in chiastic order: first, comedy and tragedy for the theatre; second, epic and bucolic poetry for recitation. — **meretrice**: in the abl. absolute with **eludente**, giving the subject of the writing through the characters usually appearing in that form of composition. — **arguta**, *cunning*. — **meretrice**, one of the most common characters in the comedy. — **Davo**, a characteristic slave name. See Ter. *Andria*. — **Chremeta**, the old man of the comedy. See Ter. *Adelphi*.

41. **eludente**: the tricks of the slave, who assists his young master in deceiving the father, form the staple of the new comedy. The **meretrix** also assisted in these.

41. **comis** (with **libellos**), *witty and elegant*. — **garrire**, *rattle off*. The word is chosen on account of the light character of the dialogue. — **libellos**, *i.e.* works, a cognate acc. with **garrire**.

42. **Fundani**: mentioned also in II. 8. 19, as belonging to the Mæcenas coterie, but none of his works are known. — **regum**, *i.e.* chieftains like Agamemnon, etc., in tragedy. See next note.

43. **pede ter percussa**, *i.e.* in the iambic trimeter, the staple verse of tragedy. Though the verse has six feet, it has only three marked ictus. Cf. *A. P.* 252. — **forte**, *powerful*, on account of the stirring scenes depicted. — **acer**, *vigorous*, on account of the spirit which the author must have.

44. **Varius**: cf. I. 5. 40. — **ducit**: the figure is from spinning, but *weaving the web of*, etc., is perhaps better in English. — **ut nemo**, *sc.* **alius**. — **molle**: the gentleness of bucolic poetry, as opposed to the vigor of epic. — **facetum**, *i.e. elegant and polished.* Cf. Facetum quoque non tantum circa ridicula opinor consistere. . . . Decoris hanc magis et excultae cuiusdam elegantiae appellationem puto. Quintil. VI. 3. 20.

Vergilio adnuerunt gaudentes rure Camenae.
Hoc erat, experto frustra Varrone Atacino
atque quibusdam aliis, melius quod scribere possem,
inventore minor; neque ego illi detrahere ausim
haerentem capiti cum multa laude coronam.
At dixi fluere hunc lutulentum, saepe ferentem
plura quidem tollenda relinquendis. Age, quaeso,
tu nihil in magno doctus reprehendis Homero?
nil comis tragici mutat Lucilius Acci?
non ridet versus Enni gravitate minores,
cum de se loquitur non ut maiore reprensis?
Quid vetat et nosmet Lucili scripta legentis
quaerere, num illius, num rerum dura negarit

45. **adnuerunt,** *have granted, i.e.* given the power to write in that manner.

46. **hoc,** *i.e.* satire. — **erat**: referring to the time when Horace made his choice. — **experto**: *i.e.* had tried it unsuccessfully, not as those in the other branches in such a way as to forbid competition. — **Varrone**: P. Terentius Varro, called Atacinus from the river Atax in Narbonese Gaul, where he was born, was a very industrious and copious poet, who tried many styles of composition, but whose light was obscured by the more brilliant men who succeeded him. He was born 82 B.C.

47. **quibusdam**: such as M. Terentius Varro, L. Abbucius, Servius Nicanor. — **melius**: *i.e.* than they.

48. **inventore minor,** *i.e. though inferior* to Lucilius. — **neque ego,** etc.: the main point of the whole. Horace was charged with setting himself up as superior to Lucilius, and criticising arrogantly the work of his master. This he here expressly denies.

50. **at dixi,** *but I did say* (I admit), proceeding to show that such criticism is the natural thing in the improvement of literature from age to age, even in regard to so great a genius as Homer. The passage referred to is I. 4. 11, and the figure is that of a torrent.

51. **tollenda**: the part to be rejected is even more than that to be retained.

52. **doctus,** *learned critic,* an almost technical expression for a professional man in any art.

53. So also Lucilius improves on Accius, though in the line of tragedy. — **comis,** *genial and witty.*

54. **gravitate minores,** *inferior in dignity,* to the requirements of the subject.

55. At the same time Lucilius does not claim that he is superior to these earlier writers, though he criticises them.

56. Therefore there is no objection to Horace's following Lucilius' example, and criticising him in his turn.

57. **illius,** *his own, i.e.* the character of the poet's genius. — **re-**

versiculos natura magis factos et euntis
mollius, ac si quis, pedibus quid claudere senis,
hoc tantum contentus, amet scripsisse ducentos
ante cibum versus, totidem cenatus; Etrusci
quale fuit Cassi rapido ferventius amni
ingenium, capsis quem fama est esse librisque
ambustum propriis. Fuerit Lucilius, inquam,
comis et urbanus, fuerit limatior idem
quam rudis et Graecis intacti carminis auctor,
quamque poetarum seniorum turba; sed ille,
si foret hoc nostrum fato dilatus in aevum,
detereret sibi multa, recideret omne quod ultra

**rum**: the character of his subjects. — **dura,** rough and stiff, not flexible so as to yield to the elegances of poetry.

58. **versiculos,** etc.: *i.e.* smooth and flowing, and carefully finished verse.

59. **ac,** etc.: than would naturally be the case with one that wrote as he did, carelessly and copiously, in the manner of his age. — **pedibus senis,** *i.e.* hexameters. — **claudere,** *compose,* an almost technical expression for writing poetry, rounding off the lines.

60. **hoc**: *i.e.* merely making verse without regard to polish.

61. **Etrusci**: so called, probably, to distinguish him from the Cassius in *Ep.* I. 4. 3.

62. **Cassi,** an unknown poet. — **ferventius,** rolling on more swiftly.

63. **capsis,** etc.: *i.e.* he wrote enough to make his own funeral pile of his manuscripts and their cases. — **capsis**: these were cases for rolls in which they stood up on end.

64. **fuerit**: a concession, to which is opposed the sentence with **sed ille,** v. 67.

65. **limatior,** *more polished.* — **idem,** *at the same time,* a still greater concession.

66. **quam,** etc.: *i.e.* than the inventor of this kind of composition could be expected to be. — **rudis,** *untried* (with **carminis**). Satire was probably not in fact a really new form of literary art, but the Greeks had not brought it to perfection as they had other forms, and hence Lucilius had strictly no one to imitate; therefore the first attempts must necessarily be rough. — **intacti**: the Romans of Horace's time considered satire as entirely of Roman origin, which in some sense it was. Cf. Quintil. X. 1. 93.

67. **ille**: emphatic; *even he* would write with much more care and pains if he were alive now; an argument, of course, in favor of Horace's criticism, as well as for his style.

68. **dilatus**: another reading, **dilapsus,** gives no sense, and **delapsus** seems forced.

69. **detereret,** *smooth away;* referring to the use of the file, cf. **limatior.** — **recideret,** *prune away;* not merely polishing, as in **detereret,** but suppressing. — **ultra perfectum traheretur**: *i.e.* overdone, beyond the golden mean of perfection.

perfectum traheretur, et in versu faciendo
saepe caput scaberet, vivos et roderet unguis.
Saepe stilum vertas, iterum quae digna legi sint
scripturus, neque te ut miretur turba labores,
contentus paucis lectoribus. An tua demens
vilibus in ludis dictari carmina malis?
non ego; nam satis est equitem mihi plaudere, ut audax,
contemptis aliis, explosa Arbuscula dixit.
Men' moveat cimex Pantilius, aut cruciet quod
vellicet absentem Demetrius, aut quod ineptus
Fannius Hermogenis laedat conviva Tigelli?
Plotius et Varius, Maecenas Vergiliusque,

71. **saepe**, etc.: humorous expressions indicating greater pains in writing, as opposed to the careless style of Lucilius. This thought leads Horace to descant on the necessity of erasing and doing over again one's first effort.

72. **stilum vertas**: the ancient *stilus*, for writing on wax, was made with a sharp point at one end, and a flat piece at the other to smooth down (**inducere**) the wax and obliterate the previous writing.

73. **scripturus**, *if you mean to write*. — **labores**, *trouble yourself to have, try to have*.

74. **paucis**: only the better educated few could appreciate perfect work; it would be too refined to please the people, for whom a different style would be necessary. — **an**: a *reductio ad absurdum*, as often with **an**.

75. **vilibus**: cf. I. 6. 72. — **dictari**: *i.e.* to be used as exercises in teaching the ignorant to write. It is probable, however, that it was just this use of Horace's works and others that has, by the multiplication of copies, preserved them to us.

76. **equitem**, for the higher classes. — **audax**, *undaunted*, not abashed by the displeasure of the crowd.

77. **explosa**, hissed off the stage, whence comes our expression, an "exploded theory," though we have a different conception of it now. — **Arbuscula**, a famous actress in the mimes, the only class of plays in which women appeared. She is also mentioned by Cic. *ad Att.* VI. 15. Her acting was probably too tame and decent for the coarse Romans of the lower class.

78. The distinction between the two kinds of readers gives him an opportunity to hold up to scorn the opposing clique, by putting them among the populace, and to claim for himself the approval of the more refined. — **cimex**: as we might say *reptile*. — **Pantilius**, an unknown poet.

79. **Demetrius**, also unknown, but very likely the **simius** referred to in v. 18.

80. **Fannius**, a third of the clique, the garrulous coxcomb mentioned in I. 4. 21. — **Hermogenis**: cf. I. 4. 72, 9. 25, 3. 129 — **conviva**: probably to indicate that they are both parasites, worthless fellows who made a living by their wits.

81. **Plotius**: see I. 5. 40. — **Varius**: see v. 44.

Valgius, et probet haec Octavius, optimus atque
Fuscus, et haec utinam Viscorum laudet uterque!
Ambitione relegata te dicere possum,
Pollio, te, Messalla, tuo cum fratre, simulque
vos, Bibule et Servi, simul his te, candide Furni,
compluris alios, doctos ego quos et amicos
prudens praetereo; quibus haec, sunt qualiacumque,
arridere velim, doliturus si placeant spe
deterius nostra. Demetri, teque, Tigelli,
discipularum inter iubeo plorare cathedras.
I, puer, atque meo citus haec subscribe libello.

82. **Valgius,** C. Valgius Rufus, an elegiac and epigrammatic poet, a friend of Horace, to whom *Od.* II. 9 is addressed. His writings are now lost. — **Octavius,** a poet and historian. Virgil(?) speaks of him, *Catalecta* XIV., —

"Scripta quidem tua nos multum mirabimur et te
Raptum et Romanam flebimus historiam."

83. **Fuscus**: see I. 9. 61, *Od.* I. 22, *Ep.* I. 10. He was probably only a literary connoisseur, as no works of his are known to us. — **Viscorum,** one of them is mentioned in I. 9. 22, but they are otherwise unknown.

84. **ambitione**: as the others were of high rank in prominent positions, he might be accused of ambitious designs in mentioning them; therefore he declares that he has no such designs, and implies that their prominence is so great that he can mention them without suspicion.

85. **Pollio**: see v. 42. — **Messalla**: see v. 29. — **fratre,** Pedius.

86. **Bibule, Servi, Furni**: otherwise unknown. — **his**: dative following **simul** by an imitation of the Greek ἅμα and an extension of words of nearness and likeness.

87. **doctos,** *connoisseurs;* cf. v. 52 and I. 9. 7.

88. **prudens,** *purposely;* cf. **imprudens.** — **haec,** the Satires, to which this one is a kind of *envoi.* — **qualiacumque,** *such as they are.*

89. **arridere,** *give pleasure,* a meaning transferred from its proper meaning of smile upon. Cf. Cic. *ad Att.* XIII. 21. 3. — **doliturus**: a favorite construction with Horace, but better rendered in English by *and I should,* etc.

90. **deterius,** being applied to a good thing, is equivalent to **minus,** and is very likely colloquial.

91. **discipularum**: by this word Horace scoffs at these poets as effeminate women's darlings. — **iubeo**: the regular word, like our *bid,* here with a kind of double meaning. — **plorare,** *whine,* referring to the love-sick songs that these men sang (and perhaps taught also), to the delight of women, and also to the Greek οἰμώζειν (the opposite of χαίρειν). The whole only amounts to, "I leave you to whine among your petticoated pupils, bad luck to you."

92. **puer**: an amanuensis. — **citus**: adjective for adverb; "be quick and go." — **libello**: the first book of Satires.

# LIBER SECUNDUS.

## I.

*Horat.* Sunt quibus in satura videor nimis acer et ultra
legem tendere opus; sine nervis altera, quicquid
composui, pars esse putat, similisque meorum
mille die versus deduci posse. Trebati,
quid faciam praescribe. *Trebat.* Quiescas. *Horat.* Ne faciam, inquis,

BOOK II.

SATIRE 1. There is no distinct evidence that the two books of Satires were published separately so as to need an introduction to each, yet this Satire serves as a sort of introduction to the second book, as Satire I. 1. is an introduction to the whole. We have in this a defence of the poet's treatment of satire, in answer to the many charges which had been made by his enemies and critics, upon the reading of the various pieces in a rather large circle of friends. That the Satires must have been given to the world separately in this quasi-public way appears from I. 2. 27 and I. 4. 92. The conception of the piece is perfectly natural, and in the highest degree witty and humorous. Horace is supposed to take advice of an old lawyer as to his proper course, in view of the contradictory criticisms made upon his work; and in the conversation which ensues he treats the subject from all sides, while at the same time he keeps the person of the lawyer distinct from his own in a perfectly dramatic form. As a piece of composition it could hardly be excelled.

1. **satura**: here, for the first time in literature, this word seems to be used in the sense to which it has later been confined. — **videor**: the mood of the verb seems to imply that he has definite persons in mind, but it is always the privilege of a poet to speak as if he had, whether he has or not (cf. *Od.* I. 1. 3). — **acer**: *i.e.* in his criticism or invective.

2. **legem**, *i.e.* the proper limits of the style of composition (cf. *A. P.* 135). — **tendere**, *force*, a figure taken from the bow. — **sine nervis**, just the opposite fault to the first, *without force*, being mere inartistic prose.

4. **deduci**, *spun off;* keeping the same figure. — **Trebati**, C. Trebatius Testa, a *jurisconsult*, or consulting lawyer, in his youth a friend of Cicero; cf. Cic. *ad Fam.* VII. 6 and 22. The shortness and authoritative manner of his answers (cf. **quiescas**, v. 5, and **aio**, v. 6) indicate an old and experienced lawyer, though at that time he perhaps was not much above fifty, while Horace was about thirty.

5. **praescribe**: probably the technical term for giving directions

omnino versus? *Trebat.* Aio. *Horat.* Peream male, si non
optimum erat; verum nequeo dormire. *Trebat.* Ter uncti
transnanto Tiberim, somno quibus est opus alto,
irriguumque mero sub noctem corpus habento.
Aut, si tantus amor scribendi te rapit, aude
Caesaris invicti res dicere, multa laborum
praemia laturus. *Horat.* Cupidum, pater optime, vires
deficiunt; neque enim quivis horrentia pilis
agmina nec fracta pereuntis cuspide Gallos

which must be followed, as being in accordance with the law.

6. **aio**, *that's what I say.* — **peream male,** *confound me;* cf. I. 9. 47.

7. **erat**, *would be;* instead of the subjunctive, on account of the meaning of the phrase ("necessity, propriety," etc.). The expression is the apodosis contrary to fact of an omitted protasis, **si ita facerem**, or the like; but the whole conditional sentence, including both protasis and apodosis, is the protasis of **peream male** in the form where no opinion is expressed (cf. I. 9. 38 and 47). — **dormire**: this word at once indicates that it is Horace's nature to write so long as he is awake, thus making it an imperative necessity, and it also gives Horace a chance to allude to two of the foibles of Trebatius, swimming and wine. — **ter**, etc.: Trebatius, taking note of only the final expression, as if he did not know what it really meant, gives a prescription in the brief professional manner, for insomnia. There is an old superstition about this number. — **uncti**: the ancients in all their athletic exercises anointed themselves with oil, partly to render the skin soft, and partly to prevent the effect of cold.

8. **transnanto**: this form of the imperative is in the formal archaic style of laws and prescriptions.

9. **irriguum**: *i.e.* drink freely before going to bed.

10. **rapit**: *i.e.* with such force as to be irresistible. — **aude**: the daring would consist in trying so lofty a theme.

11. **Caesaris**, *i.e.* Augustus, though he did not receive this appellation till B.C. 27, a few years later. — **res**, *i.e.* his warlike exploits, in an epic.

12. **laturus**: we must break this into another sentence in English, as we are often obliged to do with this favorite construction of Horace. — **cupidum**: this also should be made a separate clause. — **pater**, *venerable sir*, a common form of address in Latin to older persons.

13. **deficiunt**: *i.e.* his powers are inadequate to the demands of epic poetry, a deficiency to which he often alludes (*Od.* I. 6. 9, etc.), but at the same time he contrives to give an indirect hint at what he would say if he tried such themes. — **horrentia**, etc.: descriptions which one must attempt who essays this form. — **pilis**: *i.e.* the Roman army.

14. **fracta cuspide**: sometimes taken as referring to the device by which the point of a spear was so

aut labentis equo describat volnera Parthi.
*Trebat.* Attamen et iustum poteras et scribere fortem,
Scipiadam ut sapiens Lucilius. *Horat.* Haud mihi deero,
cum res ipsa feret. Nisi dextro tempore, Flacci
verba per attentam non ibunt Caesaris aurem,
cui male si palpere, recalcitrat undique tutus.
*Trebat.* Quanto rectius hoc, quam tristi laedere versu
Pantolabum scurram Nomentanumque nepotem,
cum sibi quisque timet, quamquam est intactus, et odit!
*Horat.* Quid faciam? Saltat Milonius, ut semel icto
accessit fervor capiti numerusque lucernis;

arranged as to break or bend and become useless after being thrown. As this seems rather far-fetched, we may take it as representing the helpless condition of the enemy with their spears broken in the contest. — **Gallos**: Augustus conducted and sent several expeditions against the Gauls.

15. **equo**: the strength of the Parthians was in cavalry. — **Parthi**: these were at that time the most formidable enemies of the Romans, but what particular expedition is referred to is uncertain.

16. **iustum,** etc.: *i.e.* you might at least celebrate the *civic* virtues of Augustus. — **poteras**: a conclusion of a suppressed condition contrary to fact; something like "if you chose"; cf. **optimum erat,** v. 7. — **fortem,** *energetic,* as a ruler.

17. **Scipiadam,** the younger Africanus; cf. v. 72 *et seq.* The patronymic is chosen because **Scipionem** (— ◡ — —) could not be used in this verse. The form of the accusative is the more strictly Latin form, and agrees with the Doric dialect. — **sapiens**: *i.e.* he was wise enough to choose civil subjects for his praise of Scipio, and avoid warlike themes.

18. **res ipsa feret**: *i.e.* when the proper case shall arise. — **Flacci**: *i.e.* a humble man like me, as compared with the great Cæsar.

19. **ibunt per,** *find access to.*

20. **palpere**: the figure is of a horse; but, as often happens, the person and the figure are identified. In English the expression must be softened by saying "who is like a horse, if you stroke him the wrong way," etc. — **tutus,** *himself safe from attack.*

21. **quanto,** etc.: the reply of Trebatius. — **tristi,** *severe* or *abusive.*

22. **Pantolabum,** etc.: cf. I. 8. 11. — **Nomentanum**: mentioned in I. 1. 102, and elsewhere.

23. **cum sibi,** etc.: *i.e.* in this case the poet makes enemies of everybody, which is worse than running the risk of offending Cæsar.

24. **quid faciam**: the poet's answer: "Every man has his special weakness or hobby, and mine is like Lucilius', to write satire." — **saltat Milonius**: this unknown person had the habit of dancing at banquets, which among the Romans was considered disreputable (cf. Cic. *pro Mur.* VI. 13). — **icto,** etc., *the heat has flown to his head filled with the fumes of the wine.*

25. **numerus accessit**: the well-

Castor gaudet equis, ovo prognatus eodem
pugnis; quot capitum vivunt, totidem studiorum
milia: me pedibus delectat claudere verba
Lucili ritu, nostrum melioris utroque.
Ille velut fidis arcana sodalibus olim
credebat libris, neque, si male cesserat, usquam
decurrens alio, neque si bene; quo fit ut omnis
votiva pateat veluti descripta tabella
vita senis. Sequor hunc, Lucanus an Apulus anceps:
nam Venusinus arat finem sub utrumque colonus,
missus ad hoc, pulsis, vetus est ut fama, Sabellis,
quo ne per vacuum Romano incurreret hostis,
sive quod Apula gens seu quod Lucania bellum
incuteret violenta. Sed hic stilus haud petet ultro

known phenomenon of seeing double in intoxication.

26. **Castor**, etc.: even two twin brothers have different tastes, as in the case of the Dioscuri.

27. **pugnis**: *i.e.* as a boxer. — **capitum**: often used for persons. — **totidem**, etc., cf. **quot homines tot sententiae.** Ter. *Phorm.* II. 4. 14.

28. **pedibus**, etc.: a kind of light, depreciating way of speaking of his poetry.

29. **nostrum**, etc.: and so a safe example to follow.

30. **arcana**, *his secrets* (acts and thoughts), implying that he had no care to suppress anything from fear.

31. **si male cesserat** (impers.), *if he had fared ill: i.e.* he trusted to his books alike his good and evil fortune.

33. **votiva**: the ancients were accustomed to show their gratitude for escapes from peril by painting the scene on a tablet, usually in the most realistic manner, and hanging up the tablet in the temple of some divinity. Cf. *Od.* I. 5. 13. The same thank-offering is now paid to the saints.

34. **senis**, *the old poet* (not of age, but of antiquity). — **Lucanus an Apulus**: the mention of the nation seems to indicate that Horace comes of a warlike race, and so may be expected to be a fighting character, at least in poetry. — **anceps**: probably nom. masc., agreeing with the subject of **sequor.**

35. **Venusinus**, Venusia, the poet's birthplace, was on the boundary-line of the two races.

36. **missus**, etc.: this description indicates the warlike character of the two races. — **Sabellis**, *i.e.* the Samnites. The colony was planted B.C. 291, in the Third Samnite War.

37. **quo ne**: equivalent to **ut ne.** — **vacuum**, *an undefended point* in the line of defences.

39. **incuteret**: the subjunctive indicates, as usual, that it was the notion of some one else, here of the Romans. — **sed**: *i.e.* though I come of this warlike race, my weapon shall never be drawn except in defence. — **ultro**, *unprovoked*, prop-

quemquam animantem, et me veluti custodiet ensis
vagina tectus; quem cur destringere coner,
tutus ab infestis latronibus? O pater et rex
Iuppiter, ut pereat positum robigine telum,
nec quisquam noceat cupido mihi pacis! At ille
qui me commorit ('melius non tangere!' clamo),
flebit et insignis tota cantabitur urbe.
Cervius iratus leges minitatur et urnam,
Canidia Albuci quibus est inimica venenum,
grande malum Turius, si quid se iudice certes.
Vt quo quisque valet suspectos terreat, utque
imperet hoc natura potens, sic collige mecum:
dente lupus, cornu taurus petit: unde nisi intus
monstratum? Scaevae vivacem crede nepoti
matrem; nil faciet sceleris pia dextera: mirum,
ut neque calce lupus quemquam neque dente petit bos:
sed mala tollet anum vitiato melle cicuta.

Ne longum faciam: seu me tranquilla senectus

erly *beyond* what is called for by the occasion.

40. **animantem,** *living soul.*

41. **quem cur,** *and why . . . it?*

43. **ut**: used like **utinam.** — **positum,** *laid away.*

45. **commorit,** *stirs me up,* or *rouses me.* — **melius non tangere**: a common expression, *better let me be.* Inserted as a parenthesis, it gives a more popular form to the description.

46. **flebit,** *shall smart for it.* — **cantabitur,** *shall become a by-word.*

47. **Cervius,** etc.: Horace illustrates his use of satire as a weapon of defence, by a list of apparent examples, each of which, however, is a stinging characterization of some notable rascal. — **leges**: *i.e.* he is an informer, and uses this function as his weapon against his enemies.

48. **Albuci,** probably a seller of drugs.

49. **Turius,** a corrupt juror who will punish his enemy by deciding a case against him.

50. **ut**: indir. interrog. — **quo,** etc., *with the most powerful weapon which he has.*

51. **natura,** *a natural instinct.* — **sic,** *i.e.* by the following reasoning.

52. **intus monstratum,** *by an inward monition,* strictly **nisi hoc intus monstratum est.**

53. **vivacem**: *i.e.* too long-lived for him.

54. **nil . . . dextera**: *i.e.* no act of violence, as that would be contrary to his filial (**pia**) nature (of course ironical).

57. **longum,** *too long a story.*

exspectat seu Mors atris circumvolat alis,
dives, inops, Romae, seu fors ita iusserit, exul,
quisquis erit vitae, scribam, color. *Trebat.* O puer, ut sis
vitalis metuo, et maiorum ne quis amicus
frigore te feriat. *Horat.* Quid, cum est Lucilius ausus
primus in hunc operis componere carmina morem,
detrahere et pellem, nitidus qua quisque per ora
cederet, introrsum turpis, num Laelius aut qui
duxit ab oppressa meritum Carthagine nomen,
ingenio offensi, aut laeso doluere Metello
famosisque Lupo cooperto versibus? Atqui
primores populi arripuit populumque tributim,
scilicet uni aequus virtuti atque eius amicis.
Quin ubi se a volgo et scaena in secreta remorant
virtus Scipiadae et mitis sapientia Laeli,

59. **exul**: opposed to **Romae**, from which he might be banished on account of his satire.

60. **color**: *i.e.* as bright or dark with good or bad fortune.

61. **vitalis**, *long-lived* (on account of the danger in such a course). — **maiorum**, partitive genitive with **amicus**.

62. **frigore**, *with a chill* (by neglect).

64. **pellem**: probably a remote allusion to the fable of the ass in the lion's skin. Cf. *Ep.* I. 16. 45. — **nitidus**, *decked*, with a fair outside.

65. **turpis**, *foul*, not precisely in the full figurative use, but with a closer application of the figure than in English. — **Laelius**, etc.: in allusion to **amicus**, v. 61. — **qui**, etc., Scipio.

67. **Metello**, Q. Cæcilius Metellus Macedonicus, consul B.C. 143, a violent political opponent of Scipio, and hence the object of the satire of Lucilius.

68. **Lupo**, L. Cornelius Lentulus Lupus, consul B.C. 156, another prominent person satirized by Lucilius. The whole idea is, "if Lucilius' powerful friends were not alienated by his attacks on the vicious, why should Horace's be?" — **famosis**, *abusive*, that produce ill fame. — **atqui**, *and yet; i.e.* though they were not offended, yet they had as much reason to be, as Horace could give his friends.

69. **tributim**, *indiscriminately*, lit. a whole tribe at a time.

70. **scilicet**, *evidently; i.e.* his conduct shows that he spared only virtue.

71. **quin**, *why! i.e.* instead of being offended, the friends were only more intimate with him. — **scaena**, *the stage*, *i.e.* public life, where they were set up to the public gaze. — **in secreta**, *into retirement*.

72. **virtus**, etc.: an old Homeric usage (cf. βίη Ἡρακληίη) for *the brave Scipio*.

nugari cum illo et discincti ludere, donec
decoqueretur holus, soliti. Quicquid sum ego, quamvis
infra Lucili censum ingeniumque, tamen me
cum magnis vixisse invita fatebitur usque
invidia, et, fragili quaerens illidere dentem,
offendet solido, — nisi quid tu, docte Trebati,
dissentis. *Trebat.* Equidem nihil hinc diffindere possum.
Sed tamen ut monitus caveas, ne forte negoti
incutiat tibi quid sanctarum inscitia legum:
si mala condiderit in quem quis carmina, ius est
iudiciumque. *Horat.* Esto, si quis mala; sed bona si quis
iudice condiderit laudatus Caesare? si quis
opprobriis dignum latraverit, integer ipse?
*Trebat.* Solventur risu tabulae, tu missus abibis.

73. **discincti**: cf. "in dressing-gown and slippers." — **donec**, etc.: *i.e.* before dinner, while waiting for their simple country repast.

74. **quicquid**, etc., *such as I am; i.e.* though of humble station and abilities.

75. **censum**, *station*, as indicated by the census, according to which Lucilius was of Equestrian rank.

77. **fragili**, etc.: probably alluding to the fable of the Viper and the File.

78. **nisi quid**, etc.: *i.e.* "all this I submit with due deference to your learned opinion."

79. **equidem**, *I, I'm sure.* — **nihil hinc diffindere**, *take no exception to this*, lit. make no distinction, as the arguments in law consist in distinguishing the particular case from a general principle laid down.

80. **ut**, etc.: after a **moneo**, or the like, implied in the preceding. — **negoti**, *trouble*, as by a prosecution.

81. **incutiat**, *spring upon you*, or *catch you in*, with an idea of unexpectedness or surprise. — **sanctarum**, *sacred*, as sanctioned by antiquity and the divine character of the state.

82. **si mala**, etc.: a continuation of the same idea, quoting the law more exactly. — **mala**: a technical expression in the law, meaning *abusive*, which Horace, however, takes in the ordinary sense of *bad* artistically. — **ius**, *law*, *i.e.* a right of action.

83. **iudicium**, *a remedy*, the process for enforcing the rights of the person aggrieved. — **esto**, *oh, yes*, that's true.

84. **Caesare** (abl. abs. with **iudice**): *i.e.* approved even by the supreme source of justice.

85. **latraverit**, *assail*, as the figure is too strong for English ears.

86. **solventur tabulae**, *the indictment will be quashed.* — **missus**, *free* (discharged).

## II.

Quae virtus et quanta, boni, sit vivere parvo
(nec meus hic sermo est, sed quae praecepit Ofellus
rusticus, abnormis sapiens, crassaque Minerva),
discite, non inter lances mensasque nitentis,
cum stupet insanis acies fulgoribus et cum
acclinis falsis animus meliora recusat,
verum hic impransi mecum disquirite. 'Cur hoc?'
Dicam, si potero. Male verum examinat omnis
corruptus iudex. Leporem sectatus equove
lassus ab indomito, vel, si Romana fatigat
militia adsuetum graecari, seu pila velox,
molliter austerum studio fallente laborem,
seu te discus agit, pete cedentem aera disco;

SATIRE 2. This Satire is directed against luxurious living. The discourse is put into the mouth of a farmer, one of Horace's neighbors, named Ofellus.

1. **quae**, *i.e.* in its nature. — **quanta**, *i.e.* in degree.

3. **abnormis**, *outside the schools*, according to no particular pattern or sect. — **sapiens**: in its technical sense. — **crassa Minerva**, *plain homespun wit*, opposed to **subtilis**. The figure is derived from spinning, of which Minerva was patroness.

4. **non inter**, etc.: if one wants to study the subject of abstemiousness, a richly furnished table is not the best place for it.

5. **stupet**, *is dazed*. — **insanis**, *senseless*.

7. **hic**, *right here*, *i.e.* without the disturbing influences mentioned. — **impransi**, *on an empty stomach*. — **cur hoc**: a question of the hearer, which is answered in the next line.

9. **corruptus**: the mind of a man at a feast is compared to a judge who has been bribed. — **leporem**, etc.: to have an unbiassed mind one must be in the normal state of hunger, which is produced by exercise.

10. **Romana**: these rude sports are called Roman, as opposed to the more artistic athletic exercises of the Greeks.

11. **militia**: riding and hunting approach near to the exercises in military life.

12. **austerum**: the dry toil is relieved by the interest (**studio**) of the game.

13. **discus**: the quoit was a favorite means of exercise with the ancients, not thrown at a mark, as with us, but for long distances, like throwing the hammer or putting the stone. — **agit**, *attracts*, lit. spurs on. — **pete**: this parenthesis is strictly independent of the main construction, which is **si . . . fatigat**, etc., **sperne**, but the added clause, **seu discus agit**, suggests to the poet the apodosis, **pete cedentem**

cum labor extuderit fastidia, siccus, inanis
sperne cibum vilem; nisi Hymettia mella Falerno
ne biberis diluta. Foris est promus, et atrum
defendens piscis hiemat mare: cum sale panis
latrantem stomachum bene leniet. Vnde putas aut
qui partum? Non in caro nidore voluptas
summa, sed in te ipso est. Tu pulmentaria quaere
sudando; pinguem vitiis albumque neque ostrea
nec scarus aut poterit peregrina iuvare lagois.
Vix tamen eripiam, posito pavone, velis quin
hoc potius quam gallina tergere palatum,
corruptus vanis rerum, quia veneat auro
rara avis, et picta pandat spectacula cauda;
tamquam ad rem attineat quicquam. Num vesceris ista
quam laudas pluma? Cocto num adest honor idem?
Carne tamen quamvis distat nihil, hanc magis illa

**aera disco**, *hurl the discus through the yielding air*.

14. **cum labor**, *then when*, etc. — **extuderit**, *has knocked out of you*.

15. **sperne**, *i.e.* if you can.

16. **foris est promus**: a supposed extreme case, where the steward is out, so that no dainties can be got from the storeroom, and there is no fish to be had; in that case you will find even the simplest food grateful.

18. **latrantem**, etc., *the cravings of*, etc. — **unde . . . aut qui**, etc., *whence and how does this come? i.e.* that you find this food grateful. The answer is in the next sentence.

20. **tu**: repeating the emphasis in **te ipso**. — **pulmentaria**: probably an allusion to the story of Socrates, who, upon being discovered walking abroad before daylight, said, ὄψον συνάγω. The same idea is in the proverb, *fames est optimum condimentum*.

21. **vitiis**, *excesses*.

22. **iuvare**, *give pleasure*.

23. **tamen**: *i.e.* though the real pleasure depends upon the appetite and not the food, yet the epicure is beguiled by the empty show of the viand, even where there is no difference in taste.

24. **tergere**, *tickle*.

25. **vanis rerum**: a Greek construction for **vanis rebus**.

28. **cocto** (sc. **pavoni**), etc.: and furthermore, though the peacock is served with its plumage, the plumage loses much of its beauty when thus served.

29. **carne**, etc.: this passage has been a *crux grammaticorum* for more than a thousand years. The idea is obvious, but the construction difficult. If we take the reading in the text, the only difficulty is the position of **esto** after the infinitive clause. Otherwise the construction is precisely like **esto iam haec aeterno manere**, *Lucr.* II. 907, and

imparibus formis deceptum te petere esto,
unde datum sentis, lupus hic Tiberinus an alto
captus hiet, pontisne inter iactatus an amnis
ostia sub Tusci? Laudas, insane, trilibrem
mullum, in singula quem minuas pulmenta necesse est.
Ducit te species, video: quo pertinet ergo
proceros odisse lupos? Quia scilicet illis
maiorem natura modum dedit, his breve pondus.
Ieiunus raro stomachus volgaria temnit.
'Porrectum magno magnum spectare catino
vellem,' ait Harpyiis gula digna rapacibus. At vos
praesentes Austri, coquite horum obsonia! Quamquam
putet aper rhombusque recens, mala copia quando

*Ep.* I. 1. 81. The sense then is: "Allowing that you are deceived by appearances, so that you prefer (**magis petere**) this (bird or flesh) rather than the other (the fowl), yet how in the world can you tell the difference in the case of the **lupus**?" If we read **hac magis illa . . . te patet; esto,** we must take **illa** as nominative (with **caro** understood), and **hac** agreeing with **carne**; and take **distat** with **magis** in the sense of the Greek διαφέρω, *be superior*, "Though that flesh is no whit superior to this, yet it is plain you are taken in by the difference of appearance," etc.

31. **unde datum sentis,** *whence is it given you to tell* (by the taste), *i.e.* how can you possibly tell where the fish is caught — a thing which epicures make a great point of — whether in the Tiber or in the sea outside? — **lupus**: probably either bass or pike.

32. **hiet**: change the construction in English; *whether the lupus which yawns on the platter was caught*, etc.

33. **trilibrem**: these are points on which the epicures lay great stress, though they are really of no account, as the poet shows.

35. **quo pertinet ergo,** *what point is there then in*, etc.: *i.e.* if you like a big mullet, why despise a great lupus? The answer is, that the epicure demands something strange and unnatural.

36. **illis**: the **lupus**, as being more distant from the mind of the speaker.

38. **raro**: take with **ieiunus.**

39. **porrectum,** etc.: the idea suddenly changes, and a remark is interposed from a glutton, who cares for quantity rather than quality; "I wish I could see a big one, etc.," as if he said, "you can't have them too big for me." Thereupon the poet bursts out into an indignant exclamation directed both at the *gourmet* and the *gourmand*, calling on the hot south wind to come and spoil their dainties for them.

41. **quamquam**: corrective; though it is of no use to wish that, for the food, however fresh, is as good as spoiled when there is no appetite and the stomach craves sharp stimulants.

aegrum sollicitat stomachum, cum rapula plenus
atque acidas mavolt inulas. Necdum omnis abacta
pauperies epulis regum; nam vilibus ovis
nigrisque est oleis hodie locus. Haud ita pridem
Galloni praeconis erat acipensere mensa
infamis. Quid? tunc rhombos minus aequor alebat?
Tutus erat rhombus, tutoque ciconia nido,
donec vos auctor docuit praetorius. Ergo
si quis nunc mergos suavis edixerit assos,
parebit pravi docilis Romana iuventus.
Sordidus a tenui victu distabit, Ofello
iudice; nam frustra vitium vitaveris illud,
si te alio pravum detorseris. Avidienus,
cui Canis ex vero ductum cognomen adhaeret,
quinquennis oleas est et silvestria corna,
ac nisi mutatum parcit defundere vinum, et

44. **necdum**, etc.: the mention of the simple appetizers leads him to say that there are still simple viands served, implying that it might be so throughout, only it is a matter of fashion, and the dainties vary from time to time from mere caprice.

45. **regum**, *princes*, *i.e.* the rich. — **ovis**: cf. I. 3. 6.

46. **nigris oleis**: olives preserved after they are ripe, as they are still treated in Italy.

47. **Galloni**, a person satirized by Lucilius on account of his luxury, and especially on account of his serving the sturgeon (cf. Cic. *de Fin.* II. 8). — **praeconis**: he had been an auctioneer, or crier.

48. **rhombos minus**, etc.: *i.e.* was it because there were no turbots? No; but the fashion of turbots had not come in.

50. **praetorius**: Sempronius Rufus, who, as it appears, was defeated for the prætorship, hence so called in irony.

51. **mergos**, *sea-gulls*, a worthless bird for eating. But if some prætor (hence **edixerit**) like Rufus should set the fashion, all the *bons vivants* would begin to relish them.

53. **sordidus**, etc.: Horace, true to his principle of the golden mean, warns his readers as well against a mean and parsimonious living. "Nor yet did Ofellus fail to see the difference, etc."

54. **illud**: luxurious living.

55. **pravum**, *perversely*, but agreeing with **te**. — **Avidienus**, a noted miser.

56. **canis**: from his dirty habits. — **ex vero**, *from the fact*, *i.e.* justly.

57. **quinquennis**: *i.e.* kept so long as to have lost their flavor. — **est**: from **edo**. — **corna**: the tough berry of the cornel.

58. **mutatum**, *turned*, as we say — **defundere**, *serve*.

cuius odorem olei nequeas perferre (licebit
ille repotia, natalis, aliosve dierum
festos albatus celebret), cornu ipse bilibri
caulibus instillat, veteris non parcus aceti.
Quali igitur victu sapiens utetur, et horum
utrum imitabitur? Hac urget lupus, hac canis, aiunt.
Mundus erit, qua non offendat sordibus, atque
in neutram partem cultus miser. Hic neque servis,
Albuci senis exemplo, dum munia didit,
saevus erit, nec sic ut simplex Naevius unctam
convivis praebebit aquam: vitium hoc quoque magnum.
Accipe nunc victus tenuis quae quantaque secum
adferat. In primis valeas bene: nam variae res

59. **licebit,** *although*; a relic of a more general use of **licet,** only retained regularly in the present tense.

60. **repotia,** *the feast* the day after the wedding, at the house of the bridegroom. The miser serves no better fare than that mentioned, even on the highest festivals.— **natalis**: the Romans made great account of birthdays.

61. **albatus,** *in full dress,* in which the Romans appeared with their togas cleansed and whitened. — **cornu . . . bilibri**: opposed to the more elegant **gutta,** which was small, and served as a cruet, while the miser has a huge horn containing his whole stock, as it were.— **ipse**: *i.e.* he doles it out himself.

62. **non parcus**: he keeps his wine till it sours, and of course has plenty of vinegar, the only thing of which he is liberal.

63. **horum**: the two extremes. The answer to the question is contained in the following proverb: *i.e.* neither, for both are equally bad, there is danger on both sides. The true precept is given in v. 65.

65. **mundus erit** (sc. **sapiens**): will be decent so far as not to give offence by meanness.

66. **neutram**: neither too miserly nor too luxurious. — **cultus**: genitive of reference with **miser**; cf. **cerebri felicem,** I. 9. 11. — **miser,** *pitiable,* as he would be in case of excess in either direction. — **servis,** etc.: *i.e.* in giving directions to his slaves, he punishes them beforehand, to guard against any carelessness on their part, which is an indication of excessive fastidiousness about his table; whereas the other is so careless in this regard that he lets the slaves give the guests dirty water. The wise man will avoid both extremes.

68. **simplex,** *good-natured,* easily imposed upon by his slaves.

69. **vitium,** etc.: this particular matter, negligence in table service, the poet gives as an example of the other extreme. Then he changes the subject entirely to the advantages of a frugal life.

71. **valeas bene**: good health is the first advantage.

ut noceant homini credas, memor illius escae
quae simplex olim tibi sederit; at simul assis
miscueris elixa, simul conchylia turdis,
dulcia se in bilem vertent, stomachoque tumultum
lenta feret pituita. Vides ut pallidus omnis
cena desurgat dubia? Quin corpus onustum
hesternis vitiis animum quoque praegravat una,
atque affigit humo divinae particulam aurae.
Alter, ubi dicto citius curata sopori
membra dedit, vegetus praescripta ad munia surgit.
Hic tamen ad melius poterit transcurrere quondam,
sive diem festum rediens advexerit annus,
seu recreare volet tenuatum corpus, ubique
accedent anni et tractari mollius aetas
imbecilla volet; tibi quidnam accedet ad istam
quam puer et validus praesumis mollitiem, seu
dura valetudo inciderit seu tarda senectus?
Rancidum aprum antiqui laudabant, non quia nasus
illis nullus erat, sed, credo, hac mente, quod hospes

73. **olim tibi sederit,** *used to agree with you.*

75. **dulcia,** etc.: the ancient and popular modern idea of physiology.

76. **pituita**: referring to the "sluggish humors" of the body, which, according to ancient ideas, produced disease.

77. **dubia,** *puzzling;* where a man is puzzled what to take first, an allusion to Ter. *Phorm.* III. 1. 28, where the word is comically used in that sense. — **corpus,** etc.: *i.e.* and not only is the body unhealthy, but the soul, which ought to be like its divine original, is weighed down and deteriorated (cf. Cic. *Tusc.* V. 13 and *de Sen.* 77).

79. **aurae,** *ether,* the finer element of which the soul was formed.

80. **alter**: the abstemious man. — **curata,** etc.: like **curare corpus,** which is constantly used of refreshing the body by eating. — **sopori,** etc.: *i.e.* no indigestion keeps him awake.

82. **tamen**: *i.e.* though ordinarily abstemious, yet he can at times indulge more freely, on occasion either of a festival or of ill health or age.

86. **tibi,** etc.: *i.e.* but for the epicure no change in that direction is possible because he has indulged himself to the extreme before.

89. **rancidum,** etc.: the frugal man has also something on hand for an unexpected guest. This Horace expresses indirectly by the example of their ancestors who kept their boar till it was "high," a practice which he attributes to the desire to keep something in store. The superior-

tardius adveniens vitiatum commodius quam
integrum edax dominus consumeret. Hos utinam inter
heroas natum tellus me prima tulisset!
Das aliquid famae, quae carmine gratior aurem
occupat humanam, grandes rhombi patinaeque
grande ferunt una cum damno dedecus; adde
iratum patruum, vicinos, te tibi iniquum
et frustra mortis cupidum, cum deerit egenti
as, laquei pretium. 'Iure,' inquit, 'Trausius istis
iurgatur verbis; ego vectigalia magna
divitiasque habeo tribus amplas regibus.' Ergo
quod superat non est melius quo insumere possis?
Cur eget indignus quisquam te divite? Quare
templa ruunt antiqua deum? Cur, improbe, carae
non aliquid patriae tanto emetiris acervo?
Vni nimirum recte tibi semper erunt res,
o magnus posthac inimicis risus! Vterne
ad casus dubios fidet sibi certius, hic qui
pluribus adsuerit mentem corpusque superbum,
an qui contentus parvo metuensque futuri
in pace, ut sapiens, aptarit idonea bello?

ity of that fashion he indicates by the wish in v. 92.

94. **das aliquid**, etc.: then again, one's reputation is better for this frugality.

96. **damno**, ruin of one's fortunes.

97. **iniquum**, *hateful to*, despising yourself.

99. **iure**, etc.: the answer of a rich interlocutor, who excuses his prodigality by the extent of his fortune. — **Trausius**, some luxurious liver who had not the fortune to stand such expenses.

100. **vectigalia**: properly of public revenues, but here used purposely on account of the great estate.

102. **quod superat**, *the surplus*. — **non est**, etc.: *i.e.* suppose you have this great wealth, are there not more worthy objects to spend it on.

106. **uni**, etc.: *i.e.* and in any case this wealth is uncertain, expressed by the contrary ironically. If, then, a change of fortune occurs, the fall will be more conspicuous and ruinous than in case of a man who is frugal even in the midst of wealth.

111. **aptarit idonea bello**, *provides the needs of war*, *i.e.* a frugal and contented spirit, and habits of self-control and abstemiousness (a proverbial expression).

Quo magis his credas, puer hunc ego parvus Ofellum
integris opibus novi non latius usum
quam nunc accisis. Videas metato in agello
cum pecore et gnatis fortem mercede colonum,
'Non ego,' narrantem, 'temere edi luce profesta
quicquam praeter olus fumosae cum pede pernae.
Ac mihi seu longum post tempus venerat hospes,
sive operum vacuo gratus conviva per imbrem
vicinus, bene erat non piscibus urbe petitis,
sed pullo atque haedo; tum pensilis uva secundas
et nux ornabat mensas cum duplice ficu.
Post hoc ludus erat culpa potare magistra,
ac venerata Ceres, ita culmo surgeret alto,
explicuit vino contractae seria frontis.

112. **quo magis,** etc.: to enforce his doctrine Horace gives the example of Ofellus himself, who had lost his property, and now hires it of its new proprietor, but, as he himself says, he is just as well off, having never indulged himself amid his better fortune.

113. **latius**: cf. **anguste**.

114. **metato,** *confiscated,* measured out by the commissioners, who assigned lands to the veterans of the army.

115. **fortem mercede colonum,** *a sturdy farmer for hire on the land* he no longer owns.

116. **narrantem,** etc.: his words prove his content and indomitable spirit. The description of his mode of life indicates the frugal style which Horace recommends. — **non . . . temere,** *not without special reason, i.e.* not commonly.

118. **hospes**: the arrival of a guest gives occasion for some simple luxuries.

119. **vacuo**: social intercourse with his neighbors, at times when the labors of the field were stopped by the weather, was also frugally celebrated, not with foreign luxuries, but with the dainties such as the farm afforded.

121. **pensilis uva,** *raisins,* grapes hung up to dry. — **secundas,** *i.e. the dessert.*

122. **duplice ficu,** *split figs,* hence *dried.*

123. **ludus**: *i.e.* not the elaborate music, etc., of the cities. — **culpa . . . magistra**: with only their sense of shortcoming to regulate the drinking, instead of a symposiarch, who was appointed at city feasts for that purpose. Shirking in such cases would be a **culpa**.

124. **venerata Ceres**: *i.e.* the worship of Ceres, which consisted in a libation followed by drinking. — **ita**: the correlative would be, **ut hoc vinum tibi fundo,** or the like. — **surgeret**: the indirect representative of **surge** or **surgas** of the prayer. The goddess is here, as often, identified with the grain of which she was patroness.

125. **seria,** *the frowning.*

Saeviat atque novos moveat Fortuna tumultus,
quantum hinc imminuet? Quanto aut ego parcius aut vos,
o pueri, nituistis, ut huc novus incola venit?
Nam propriae telluris erum natura neque illum
nec me nec quemquam statuit: nos expulit ille,
illum aut nequities aut vafri inscitia iuris,
postremum expellet certe vivacior heres.
Nunc ager Vmbreni sub nomine, nuper Ofelli
dictus, erit nulli proprius, sed cedet in usum
nunc mihi, nunc alii. Quocirca vivite fortes,
fortiaque adversis opponite pectora rebus.'

## III.

*Damasippus.* Sic raro scribis, ut toto non quater anno
membranam poscas, scriptorum quaeque retexens,

127. **hinc,** *from this condition* in which we now are. It is implied in the whole that Ofellus could still enjoy the simple life he had led in his prosperity.

128. **pueri,** his sons who were working with him. Cf. v. 115.

129. **propriae,** *as his own.*

131. **nequities,** *his prodigality;* regularly opposed to **frugalitas**: cf. **nequam** and **frugi**. — **iuris**: *i.e.* he will lose it by the tricks of the law.

132. **postremum,** etc.: at any rate he won't live forever, and then the surviving heir will at last dispossess him.

133. **Vmbreni,** the veteran to whom the land had been assigned. Cf. *Ep.* II. 1. 171 ff.

134. **proprius,** *permanent.* — **cedet,** *will pass.* — **in usum,** *to the possession* temporarily for use, but not for permanent property; so that the tenant is after all as well off as the proprietor.

135. **vivite fortes,** *live undismayed.* With this exhortation, Horace breaks off abruptly, as is his custom, without a definite close.

SATIRE 3. This Satire has a peculiarly Horatian double edge. On the one hand, it ridicules the Stoic doctrine, πᾶς ἄφρων μαίνεται, *omnem stultum insanum esse,* that every man except the sage is insane. But at the same time Horace uses that doctrine in a half-serious way to assail the vices and follies of mankind, with the spirit of true humor, including himself with the rest. He puts the greater part of the discourse into the mouth of Damasippus, a merchant and speculator, who, having failed in business, is about to kill himself, but is dissuaded therefrom, and turns Stoic

iratus tibi, quod, vini somnique benignus,
nil dignum sermone canas. Quid fiet? At ipsis
Saturnalibus huc fugisti. Sobrius ergo
dic aliquid dignum promissis! Incipe! Nil est.
Culpantur frustra calami, immeritusque laborat
iratis natus paries dis atque poetis.
Atqui voltus erat multa et praeclara minantis,
si vacuum tepido cepisset villula tecto.
Quorsum pertinuit stipare Platona Menandro,
Eupolin, Archilochum, comites educere tantos?
Invidiam placare paras virtute relicta?
Contemnere, miser! Vitanda est improba Siren

preacher. The conversation is introduced abruptly by the Stoic, who assails Horace for his indolence. This diatribe Horace puts in a half-serious way, ridiculing the meddlesomeness and want of tact of the importunate Stoic, but at the same time satirizing himself, and no doubt justly.

2. **membranam poscas**: for engrossing a new finished composition. — **scriptorum**: neuter, with **quaeque**. — **retexens**: *i.e.* never finishing anything satisfactory, but always undoing and working over his old poems.

3. **vini somnique**: genitive after **benignus**; *indulging in* (cf. **cultus miser**, II. 2. 66).

4. **dignum sermone**, *worth talking about; i.e.* that would bring you any fame if you published it. — **quid fiet**, *What is going to be done? i.e.* What are you going to do? — **ipsis**: *i.e.* just at the time of the holidays, when festivity was at its height, indicating a set purpose to do something.

5. **Saturnalibus**: this festival was a time of universal freedom from restraint for all classes. — **huc**: to Horace's Sabine estate. — **sobrius**: as opposed to the festivity of the city.

6. **dic**, *write*. — **promissis**: given by his acts in coming away from the city — **nil est**, *it's of no use*, nothing comes of it.

7. **laborat**, *suffers*, being beaten by the poet in his vexation.

8. **iratis**: the usual way of expressing that a person is born to misfortune, but here varied by the humorous insertion of **poetis**.

9. **atqui**: *i.e.* though you do nothing, yet you had the expression of one who promised great feats.

10. **vacuum**, *at leisure*. — **cepisset**: an indirect quotation from the supposed threat expressed in his countenance.

11. **Platona**: on account of the philosophical tendency of his Satires. — **Menandro**: on account of the close connection of satire with comedy.

12. **Eupolin**: as representing the Old Comedy. — **Archilochum**: as the inventor of the Epode.

13. **virtute**: referring to his supposed abandonment of satire, and consequently of the cause of good morals, in order to avoid the jealousy and ill-will which his satire had

desidia, aut quicquid vita meliore parasti
ponendum aequo animo. *Hor.* Di te, Damasippe, deaeque
verum ob consilium donent tonsore. Sed unde
tam bene me nosti? *Dam.* Postquam omnis res mea Ianum
ad medium fracta est, aliena negotia curo,
excussus propriis. Olim nam quaerere amabam,
quo vafer ille pedes lavisset Sisyphus aere,
quid sculptum infabre, quid fusum durius esset;
callidus huic signo ponebam milia centum;
hortos egregiasque domos mercarier unus
cum lucro noram; unde frequentia Mercuriale
imposuere mihi cognomen compita. *Hor.* Novi,
et miror morbi purgatum te illius. *Dam.* Atqui

occasioned; *i.e.* do you expect to avoid ill-will by ceasing to write? On the contrary, you will only be despised for want of courage.

15. **quicquid**: *i.e.* his fame.

16. **ponendum aequo animo,** *you must be content to lay aside.* — **di te,** etc.: Horace replies, beginning as if he were going to wish Damasippus the greatest blessings, but ends with the thing he thinks the philosopher needs most, *a barber,* on account of the long beard affected by philosophers.

18. **postquam,** etc.: in answer to Horace's query, how Damasippus came to know him so well, the Stoic replies, that, having failed in his own business, he has taken up other people's, that is to say, has become a philosopher. — **Ianum**: one of the three arches near the Forum, at Rome, sacred to Janus, in or around which were the shops of the money lenders. Damasippus means that his fortune was lost by borrowing money, and making unprofitable investments.

20. **quaerere,** etc.: he used to buy up objects of art and bric-à-brac.

21. **quo . . . aere**: a humorous expression for antique bronze vessels of Corinth.

22. **quid sculptum infabre**: *i.e.* works of sculpture whose value depended on their antiquity, of which their rudeness was proof. — **fusum durius**: works in metal of the same kind.

23. **callidus,** *i.e.* a shrewd judge of values and works of art.

25. **frequentia . . . compita,** *the crowds at the "corners,"* where the auction sales took place. — **Mercuriale**: in apposition with **cognomen,** and made to agree with it in gender; *favorite of Mercury, Fortune's own child.*

27. **morbi**: in accordance with the Stoic way of thinking, Horace speaks of this devotion to gain as a disease (πάθος) or insanity. The genitive is in imitation of the Greek construction of separation, justified, however, by the Latin construction of relative adjectives. Cf. **plenus** and **vacuus.**

emovit veterem mire novus, ut solet, in cor
traiecto lateris miseri capitisve dolore,
ut lethargicus hic cum fit pugil et medicum urget.
*Hor.* Dum ne quid simile huic, esto ut libet. *Dam.* O bone, ne te
frustrere; insanis et tu stultique prope omnes,
si quid Stertinius veri crepat, unde ego mira
descripsi docilis praecepta haec, tempore quo me
solatus iussit sapientem pascere barbam
atque a Fabricio non tristem ponte reverti.
Nam, male re gesta, cum vellem mittere operto
me capite in flumen, dexter stetit et 'Cave faxis
te quicquam indignum! Pudor' inquit 'te malus angit,
insanos qui inter vereare insanus haberi.
Primum nam inquiram quid sit furere: hoc si erit in te

28. **mire,** *it is marvellous how,* etc. The whole idea is, that one disease has been cured by another.

30. **lethargicus,** etc.: the patient suffering under a lethargy suddenly has a paroxysm of violence and attacks his physician, this being an instance of one form of madness driving out another.

31. **dum,** etc.: Horace in his reply jocosely says, provided your madness does not take that violent form, you may have any craze you like. This of course implies that Damasippus has a craze, while Horace is sound, hence Damasippus in his answer proceeds to set him right on that subject, and so gives the long discussion of the Stoic paradox, πᾶς ἄφρων μαίνεται.

33. **Stertinius,** an unknown Stoic, probably a windy street-preacher like Crispinus. — **crepat,** *if there is any truth in the chatter of Stertinius.* The word seems to be carelessly used from Horace's standpoint instead of Damasippus'.

34. **descripsi,** *copied,* not literally, but as much as *adopted.*

35. **sapientem . . . barbam:** the philosophers allowed the beard to grow long, originally as a mark of neglect of their persons.

36. **Fabricio,** the bridge to the island in the Tiber, built B.C. 62, as appears from the inscription still extant.

38. **dexter,** *at my side;* but the side on which he appeared was a good omen also.

39. **te indignum,** *unbecoming to you,* or *shameful.* — **malus,** *false;* unfounded, and so bad under the circumstances. — **angit:** *i.e.* this is the reason why you are about to destroy yourself.

40. **insanos:** containing the gist of the whole matter. These people before whom you are ashamed of appearing to be insane on account of having lost your property in pursuit of a craze, are themselves insane, and hence you need have no shame about it.

41. **primum,** etc.: he begins in

solo, nil verbi pereas quin fortiter addam.
Quem mala stultitia et quemcumque inscitia veri
caecum agit, insanum Chrysippi porticus et grex
autumat. Haec populos, haec magnos formula reges,
excepto sapiente, tenet. Nunc accipe quare
desipiant omnes aeque ac tu, qui tibi nomen
insano posuere. Velut silvis, ubi passim
palantis error certo de tramite pellit,
ille sinistrorsum, hic dextrorsum abit: unus utrique
error, sed variis illudit partibus: hoc te
crede modo insanum, nihilo ut sapientior ille,
qui te deridet, caudam trahat. Est genus unum
stultitiae nihilum metuenda timentis, ut ignis,
ut rupis fluviosque in campo obstare queratur;
alterum et huic varum et nihilo sapientius ignis
per medios fluviosque ruentis: clamet amica
mater, honesta soror cum cognatis, pater, uxor,
'Hic fossa est ingens, hic rupes maxima, serva!'

the regular philosophical, and especially Stoic style, in which definitions played a prominent part. — **hoc si erit**, etc.: *i.e.* "if you are the only person who comes under the description, I will not say a word to hinder you."

43. **mala**, *perverse;* cf. **prava**, v. 220. — **stultitia**, *folly;* in the technical sense, as opposed to the **sapientia** of the sage.

44. **caecum agit**, *drives blindly on*, without the guidance of philosophical reason. — **Chrysippi**, the second great expounder of the Stoic doctrines, of whom it was said, Εἰ μὴ γὰρ ἦν Χρύσιππος, οὐκ ἂν ἦν Στοά. — **porticus**, the Στοὰ ποικίλη, a colonnade in which Zeno and his followers taught. — **grex**, *troupe;* a semi-comical expression for the school or sect.

45. **autumat**, *affirms to be;* a rather formal expression. — **populos**, *whole nations* together, without exception. — **formula**: *i.e.* the definition given above.

46. **tenet**, *embraces.*

50. **unus . . . error**: *i.e.* ignorance of the true path.

51. **partibus**, *directions.*

53. **caudam trahat**, *is made a fool of* (*i.e.* is as crazy as you); an allusion to the boys in the street who make fools of the half-witted by fastening some appendage to them behind. — **est genus**, etc.: the first class think there are dangers, etc., where there are none, *i.e.* have positive delusions.

56. **alterum**: the second class do not see things that really exist.

57. **amica**: with **mater**.

58. **honesta**: with **soror**. The

non magis audierit quam Fufius ebrius olim,
cum Ilionam edormit, Catienis mille ducentis
'*Mater, te appello!*' clamantibus. Huic ego volgus
errori similem cunctum insanire docebo.
Insanit veteres statuas Damasippus emendo:
integer est mentis Damasippi creditor? Esto!
'Accipe quod numquam reddas mihi' si tibi dicam,
tune insanus eris si acceperis? an magis excors
reiecta praeda, quam praesens Mercurius fert?
Scribe decem a Nerio; non est satis: adde Cicutae
nodosi tabulas centum, mille adde catenas:
effugiet tamen haec sceleratus vincula Proteus.

blindness of the madman is shown by these details. No warning can make him take care.

60. **Fufius**, etc.: it appears that this actor on one occasion playing Ilione, in Pacuvius' play of that name, really went to sleep, so that he did not hear the ghost of Deiphilus (the son of Ilione and Polymestor) when it rose and addressed to her the words, **mater te appello**. Catienus was playing the ghost.

61. **edormit**, *slept through the part of*: a humorous use of the construction in I. 5. 63, **saltare Cyclopa**. — **mille ducentis**: *a thousand*, with **clamantibus**, just double the usual number 600, continuing the supposition in **audierit**.

62. **huic . . . errori**: *i.e.* not seeing what is really the case. All who do not have right views of things of course have a similar delusion.

63. **similem**: *sc.* **errorem**; cog. acc. with **insanire**.

64. **insanit**, *has a craze;* because he does not set the right value on such things.

65. **creditor**: the one who would particularly regard Damasippus as insane. — **esto**, *well; i.e.* suppose he is for a moment, until it is shown by an example that he is not.

66. **accipe**, etc.: a supposed case which shows that Damasippus is the sounder man of the two, because he only takes money which he certainly can't pay back.

68. **praesens**, *propitious*.

69. **scribe**, etc.: addressed to the creditor. "Take all the securities you can, yet the debtor will after all escape you." The usual way of paying money was through a banker (**a Nerio**), and here the creditor is to draw ten drafts on Nerius, which would be stronger evidence of the payment. — **Cicutae**, a usurer, who would of course be skilful in securing his debts. Cf. v. 175.

70. **nodosi**: equivalent to crafty, shrewd in making knots to bind the debtor. — **mille**, etc.: another more general expression for the same idea of taking security, but with a reference to Proteus.

71. **Proteus**, the famous prophetic sea-divinity who only gave his answers when caught and bound, and who had the power of changing into all sorts of forms to avoid capture. The whole means simply, the debtor will be more difficult to catch

Cum rapies in ius malis ridentem alienis,
fiet aper, modo avis, modo saxum, et, cum volet, arbor.
Si male rem gerere insani est, contra bene sani,
putidius multo cerebrum est, mihi crede, Perelli
dictantis quod tu numquam rescribere possis.

Audire atque togam iubeo componere, quisquis
ambitione mala aut argenti pallet amore,
quisquis luxuria tristive superstitione
aut alio mentis morbo calet; huc propius me,
dum doceo insanire omnis, vos ordine adite.

Danda est ellebori multo pars maxima avaris;
nescio an Anticyram ratio illis destinet omnem.
Heredes Staberi summam incidere sepulchro,
ni sic fecissent, gladiatorum dare centum
damnati populo paria atque epulum arbitrio Arri,

than a Proteus (see Hom. *Od.* IV. 456, and cf. *Ep.* I. 1. 90).

72. **malis**, etc: *laughing at his creditor's expense;* the allusion is to Hom. *Od.* XX. 347, though the sense there is a forced laugh.

75. **putidius,** *less sound.* — **Perelli,** the creditor.

76. **dictantis,** *taking receipts for money,* literally dictating what the debtor shall write for the money which, etc. — **tu**: the debtor. — **rescribere,** *repay.*

77. **audire,** etc.: the Stoic takes up the other branches of the subject, and in a more formal manner, so he purposely bids his hearers arrange themselves for a long sermon.

78. **ambitione,** etc.: the four forms of insanity are *ambition, avarice, prodigality,* and *superstition.* Of these Stertinius takes up first avarice, as the most violent form. — **argenti,** here *money,* as in I. 1. 86, not, as often, silver ware.

81. **ordine,** one after the other.

82. **ellebori**: the usual medicine for insanity.

83. **nescio an,** *I don't know but,* as usual. — **Anticyram,** the city in Greece whence the best hellebore was brought. — **ratio,** *sound reason, i.e.* true philosophy, which regards this as the prevailing and most ruinous form of insanity.

84. **heredes,** etc.: the poet shows the insanity of avarice by the example of one Staberius, who ordered the amount of his estate to be carved on his tombstone, thinking that the best epitaph he could have.

85. **fecissent**: for the future perfect used in the will. — **dare**: the penalty that the heirs were to pay if they failed to perform.

86. **damnati**: the technical words were *heres damnas esto.* — **epulum**: a public banquet like a "barbecue," such as was often given at Rome for political purposes. — **arbitrio Arri**: *i.e.* a sumptuous one, such

frumenti quantum metit Africa. 'Sive ego prave
seu recte hoc volui, ne sis patruus mihi.' Credo
hoc Staberi prudentem animum vidisse. Quid ergo
sensit, cum summam patrimoni insculpere saxo
heredes voluit? Quoad vixit, credidit ingens
pauperiem vitium et cavit nihil acrius, ut, si
forte minus locuples uno quadrante perisset,
ipse videretur sibi nequior: omnis enim res,
virtus, fama, decus, divina humanaque pulchris
divitiis parent; quas qui construxerit, ille
clarus erit, fortis, iustus. Sapiensne? Etiam, et rex,
et quicquid volet. Hoc, veluti virtute paratum,
speravit magnae laudi fore. Quid simile isti
Graecus Aristippus? qui servos proicere aurum
in media iussit Libya, quia tardius irent
propter onus segnes. Vter est insanior horum?—
Nil agit exemplum, litem quod lite resolvit.

as Q. Arrius would prescribe, who gave a famous funeral banquet B.C. 59 to several thousand citizens. He is also referred to in v. 243.

87. **frumenti**, etc.: also a distribution of grain to the people. Perhaps **et** has fallen out after **frumenti**. — **quantum**, etc.: a proverbial expression. — **sive**, etc.: a quotation from the will.

88. **patruus**, *unkind*, as not an indulgent judge like a father, a proverbial expression.

89. **hoc**: *i.e.* that they would regard his fancy as absurd. — **quid . . . sensit**, *what was his idea?*

92. **acrius**: *sc.* **quam pauperiem**.

94. **nequior**, *a more thriftless person*.

96. **parent**, *are subject to*, as men think.

97. **sapiensne**: this short question is in the style of the Stoic argument, and is also a Stoic idea. — **rex**: following out the Stoic idea, that the **sapiens** is the only king, while all *stulti* are slaves.

98. **hoc**: the glory of being rich. — **paratum**, *won*, or *gained*, like glory in war, or any other noble attainment.

99. **simile**: *sc.* **fecit**; how unlike this was Aristippus' conduct, who represents the other extreme of wastefulness.

100. **Aristippus**, the disciple of Socrates, and founder of the Cyrenaic school. His principle was to enjoy the good things of life, but so as not to be a slave to them. Hence his wastefulness of the gold because it hindered his journey.

101. **Libya**: the country of gold, where any one else would have gathered all he could.

102. **uter**, etc.: *i.e.* since both go to extremes.

103. **nil agit**, etc.: *i.e.* his case

Si quis emat citharas, emptas comportet in unum,
nec studio citharae nec musae deditus ulli,
si scalpra et formas non sutor, nautica vela
aversus mercaturis, delirus et amens
undique dicatur merito. Qui discrepat istis
qui nummos aurumque recondit, nescius uti
compositis, metuensque velut contingere sacrum?
Si quis ad ingentem frumenti semper acervum
porrectus vigilet cum longo fuste, neque illinc
audeat esuriens dominus contingere granum,
ac potius foliis parcus vescatur amaris;
si positis intus Chii veterisque Falerni
mille cadis — nihil est, tercentum milibus — acre
potet acetum; age, si et stramentis incubet, unde-
octoginta annos natus, cui stragula vestis,
blattarum ac tinearum epulae, putrescat in arca:
nimirum insanus paucis videatur, eo quod
maxima pars hominum morbo iactatur eodem.
Filius aut etiam haec libertus ut ebibat heres,
dis inimice senex, custodis? Ne tibi desit?
Quantulum enim summae curtabit quisque dierum,

proves nothing, because one question (**litem**) is not solved by introducing another; namely, whether he was not insane also. Still Horace has gained the opportunity to criticise the other extreme, which was what he wanted. He now turns to an example about which there can be no doubt, of a man collecting things which he can't use, which is really the miser's case.

105. **musae,** *branch of music.*

106. **non sutor,** *not being a shoemaker.*

108. **qui discrepat**: *how, i.e.* not at all, for the miser is just like the cases supposed.

110. **sacrum**: which it would be sacrilege to use. Cf. I. 1. 71.

113. **esuriens dominus,** *though starving, and the owner.*

120. **nimirum,** etc.: the preceding has prepared us to expect the natural conclusion, "He would seem insane to everybody," but this is changed to the idea in the text, to show more clearly that this insanity is an almost universal one.

121. **iactatur,** *is suffering,* properly of a fever.

123. **dis inimice,** *God-forsaken.* The poet changes to a direct appeal to the miser himself, and shows the folly of his course.

unguere si caulis oleo meliore caputque
coeperis impexa foedum porrigine? Quare,
si quidvis satis est, periuras, surripis, aufers
undique? Tun' sanus? Populum si caedere saxis
incipias servosve tuos quos aere pararis,
insanum te omnes pueri clamentque puellae:
cum laqueo uxorem interimis matremque veneno,
incolumi capite es? Quid enim? Neque tu hoc facis Argis,
nec ferro ut demens genetricem occidis Orestes.
An tu reris eum occisa insanisse parente,
ac non ante malis dementem actum Furiis quam
in matris iugulo ferrum tepefecit acutum?
Quin, ex quo est habitus male tutae mentis Orestes,
nil sane fecit quod tu reprehendere possis:
non Pyladen ferro violare aususve sororem
Electram, tantum maledicit utrique, vocando
hanc Furiam, hunc aliud, iussit quod splendida bilis.
Pauper Opimius argenti positi intus et auri,

127. **quidvis**, *i.e.* so little as you use.

128. **populum**, etc.: *i.e.* the crimes he commits for the sake of money are as much marks of insanity as the conduct described would be.

130. **pueri, puellae**: proverbial; *i.e.* everybody.

132. **quid enim**? *why yes* (cf. I. 1. 7), adopting the miser's view ironically. — **neque tu**, etc.: the miser would argue that he was not insane, because in their ignorance of the true essence of human conduct men take the accidents of place, time, and circumstance, for the real characteristics of those actions which are held to be insane, as in the case of Orestes. Because the deed is not done at Argos, nor with the sword, it is not insane like that of Orestes.

134. **an tu reris**, etc.: *i.e.* (am I not right in my interpretation of the matter?) or do you suppose that Orestes went mad only after killing his mother? The Stoic doctrine makes all criminal conduct evidence of insanity in itself. In fact, after his crime, Orestes did nothing that could be called insane at all. All this goes to prove the Stoic doctrine, that all misconduct is insane.

142. **pauper**, etc.: another example to show the insanity of avarice. Opimius is called poor, because, with all his wealth, he acts like a poor man. — **argenti**: Horace's favorite genitive with adjectives; **cf.** Gr. 218, c.

qui Veientanum festis potare diebus
Campana solitus trulla vappamque profestis,
quondam lethargo grandi est oppressus, ut heres
iam circum loculos et clavis laetus ovansque
curreret. Hunc medicus multum celer atque fidelis
excitat hoc pacto: mensam poni iubet atque
effundi saccos nummorum, accedere pluris
ad numerandum; hominem sic erigit. Addit et illud,
'Ni tua custodis, avidus iam haec auferet heres.'
'Men' vivo?' 'Vt vivas, igitur, vigila, hoc age.' 'Quid
vis?'
'Deficient inopem venae te, ni cibus atque
ingens accedit stomacho fultura ruenti.
Tu cessas? Agedum, sume hoc ptisanarium oryzae.'
'Quanti emptae?' 'Parvo.' 'Quanti, ergo?' 'Octus-
sibus.' 'Eheu!
quid refert, morbo an furtis peream que rapinis?'

Quisnam igitur sanus? Qui non stultus. Quid avarus?
Stultus et insanus. Quid, si quis non sit avarus,
continuo sanus? Minime. Cur, Stoice? Dicam.

143. **Veientanum**, a cheap wine.

144. **Campana**, common earthenware. Cf. I. 6. 118.

145. **heres**, etc.: *i.e.* expecting the man to die at once.

146. **loculos**, *coffers*.

148. **hoc pacto**: *in the following manner*, *i.e.* by means of his ruling passion.

150. **ad numerandum**: as if to divide the estate, considering him already dead.

152. **hoc age**, *look alive now*.

157. **furtis pereamque rapinis**: *i.e.* the enormously expensive medicine required to cure him.

158. **quisnam sanus**: Horace represents Damasippus as if persuaded by these examples, asking, "Who, then, is sane?" but he is really speaking himself, and is not careful of the dramatic form. — **qui non stultus**: the natural Stoic answer, for according to that doctrine, the *sapiens* is the only perfect man, and all others are alike *stulti*. — **quid avarus** (*sc.* **est**): a recapitulation of the preceding exposition in a formal shape, to prepare for the turn in **si quis non**, etc. The whole of this discussion in disjointed questions is in the Stoic style of argument.

160. **continuo**, *at once; i.e.* does

Non est cardiacus (Craterum dixisse putato)
hic aeger: recte est igitur surgetque? Negabit,
quod latus aut renes morbo temptentur acuto.
Non est periurus neque sordidus: immolet aequis
hic porcum Laribus; verum ambitiosus et audax:
naviget Anticyram. Quid enim differt, barathrone
dones quicquid habes, an numquam utare paratis?
Servius Oppidius Canusi duo praedia, dives
antiquo censu, gnatis divisse duobus
fertur, et hoc moriens pueris dixisse vocatis
ad lectum: 'Postquam te talos, Aule, nucesque
ferre sinu laxo, donare et ludere vidi,
te, Tiberi, numerare, cavis abscondere tristem,
extimui ne vos ageret vesania discors,

it at once follow if the man is free from avarice that he is sound? The Stoic replies, no; and illustrates by the case of disorders of the body, to which the Stoics were fond of likening the failings of the soul (πάθη).

161. **cardiacus**, *troubled with heartburn.* — **Craterum**, a distinguished physician, Cic. *Att.* XII. 13 and 14.

163. **quod**, etc.: *i.e.* though he has no disorder of the stomach, yet his lungs or his kidneys are affected, so that he is none the less a sick man.

164. **periurus neque sordidus**: vices characteristic of the avaricious man. — **immolet**: *i.e.* let him be thankful for that; lit. let him make a sacrifice of purification to the household gods, as it would seem from this passage to have been customary upon recovery from disease.

165. **ambitiosus**, etc.: vices the opposite of avarice, because the course of ambition was attended with enormous expense, and accompanied by luxurious living intended to gain popularity. Hence the comparison in the next verse, **quid enim**, etc. — **audax**, *reckless.*

166. **naviget**, etc.: *i.e.* that is equally a mark of insanity with the other. — **barathro**: *i.e.* recklessly spend in the pursuit of ambition.

168. **Servius**, etc.: he illustrates by the case of a father who saw his two sons affected by opposite evil tendencies (**insania discors**), one devoted to avarice, and the other to reckless extravagance. He exhorts them accordingly, but particularly against the recklessness of expenditure for ambition (v. 179), to which the latter would be especially liable.

169. **antiquo censu**, *according to the old rating* (cf. "before the war"), when fortunes were less gigantic. — **divisse** (= **divisisse**), for **dividse**, like **faxe**.

171. **talos, nucesque**: his playthings. The Roman boys apparently used nuts for marbles.

172. **sinu laxo**: *i.e.* carelessly. — **ludere**, gambling with them.

173. **tristem**, *i.e.* anxiously, for fear of losing them.

174. **discors**, *in contrary direc-*

tu Nomentanum, tu ne sequerere Cicutam.
Quare per divos oratus uterque Penatis,
tu cave ne minuas, tu ne maius facias id
quod satis esse putat pater et natura coercet.
Praeterea ne vos titillet gloria, iure
iurando obstringam ambo: uter aedilis fueritve
vestrum praetor, is intestabilis et sacer esto.
In cicere atque faba bona tu perdasque lupinis,
latus ut in Circo spatiere et aeneus ut stes,
nudus agris, nudus nummis, insane, paternis?
Scilicet ut plausus, quos fert Agrippa, feras tu,
astuta ingenuum volpes imitata leonem!' —
'Ne quis humasse velit Aiacem, Atrida, vetas cur?'
'Rex sum.' 'Nil ultra quaero plebeius.' 'Et aequam
rem imperito; ac si cui videor non iustus, inulto

*tions;* one a spendthrift, and the other a miser.

175. **Nomentanum**: cf. II. 1. 22. — **Cicutam**: cf. v. 69.

176. **oratus**, *be entreated;* but agreeing with **uterque**, which is appositive with **tu . . . tu.**

178. **quod coercet**: *to which nature sets a limit, i.e.* the requirements of nature; cf. I. 1. 50.

179. **vos titillet**, *tickle your fancy.*

181. **intestabilis**, *incapable of inheriting*, with other legal disabilities. The oath consisted in the young men assenting to the curse.

182. **in cicere**: distribution of food to the lower classes, for the sake of popularity, especially on the part of the ædile at the Floralia.

183. **latus spatiere**, *make a spread;* referring to the *state* in which he would appear at the games as an official. The whole is a jocose description of the advantages of prominent position. — **aeneus**: in a statue.

184. **nudus**, etc.: cf. note to v. 165.

185. **Agrippa**, a really great man, whom the ambitious aspirant could only feebly imitate by his popular arts.

187. **ne quis**: with a very sudden transition, the Stoic illustrates the insanity of ambition by a supposed dialogue between Agamemnon and a common soldier in his army, by which it is shown that the ambitious king of kings is quite as insane as Ajax, to whose body he refuses burial. — **humasse**: the infinitive perfect in this use is archaic, and imitated from legal language.

188. **rex sum**: *i.e.* I have the right to do as I will without criticism from my subjects. — **nil ultra**, etc.: *i.e.* if you put it on that ground, I have nothing more to say, being only a humble common soldier. — **et aequam**, etc.: the king, as if conscious of the weakness of his position, comes down from his arrogance, and tries to justify himself.

189. **ac si cui**, etc.: a still further concession, as the king gradually weakens.

dicere quod sentit permitto.' 'Maxime regum,
di tibi dent capta classem reducere Troia!
Ergo consulere et mox respondere licebit?'
'Consule.' 'Cur Aiax, heros ab Achille secundus,
putescit, totiens servatis clarus Achivis?
Gaudeat ut populus Priami Priamusque inhumato,
per quem tot iuvenes patrio caruere sepulchro?'
'Mille ovium insanus morti dedit, inclutum Ulixen
et Menelaum una mecum se occidere clamans.'
'Tu, cum pro vitula statuis dulcem Aulide natam
ante aras, spargisque mola caput, improbe, salsa,
rectum animi servas?' 'Quorsum?' 'Insanus quid enim Aiax
fecit, cum stravit ferro pecus? Abstinuit vim
uxore et gnato; mala multa precatus Atridis,

191. **di tibi dent,** etc.: imitation of *Il.* I. 18; a polite response to the graciously given permission.

192. **consulere, respondere**: technical words of submitting questions to be decided by a jurisconsult. The latter word must refer to the king, who is here the person consulted. The attitude of a client accords with the assumed humility of the soldier playing Stoic.

193. **ab Achille secundus**: cf. *Il.* II. 768.

194. **putescit,** *i.e.* unburied.

195. **gaudeat,** etc.: an imitation of *Il.* I. 255. The disgrace of their enemy would be a joy to Priam and his people.

197. **mille**: here treated as a substantive, like **milia**. — **insanus**: the main point in the whole. After the award of the arms of Achilles to Ulysses, Ajax went mad and slew a flock of sheep, thinking them to be the Greek heroes, in which delusion consisted his insanity.

199. **tu cum pro vitula,** etc.: the treating of Iphigenia as a victim, instead of a heifer was, the soldier argues, no less a mark of insanity than the delusion of Ajax.

200. **improbe,** *unnatural father,* or *monster.* — **mola,** a regular accompaniment of a sacrifice. Probably because meal and salt were the necessaries of life.

201. **rectum animi**: *i.e.* **rectum animum,** or **rectum statum animi,** as opposed to its overthrow in insanity. — **quorsum**: *sc.* **tendis,** or **haec pertinet,** *what do you mean by that?* what does that prove? — **insanus**: *i.e.* when you consider him insane, or regard these as marks of his insanity. — **quid enim,** *why! what,* etc.; where **enim** is explanatory of the implied statement that Agamemnon is himself insane.

202. **abstinuit vim,** *he kept his violent hands.*

203. **mala multa**: angry words were not considered proof of madness (cf. v. 140).

non ille aut Teucrum aut ipsum violavit Vlixen.'
'Verum ego, ut haerentis adverso litore navis
eriperem, prudens placavi sanguine divos.'
'Nempe tuo, furiose.' 'Meo, sed non furiosus.'
Qui species alias veris scelerisque tumultu
permixtas capiet, commotus habebitur, atque
stultitiane erret nihilum distabit an ira.
Aiax immeritos cum occidit desipit agnos:
cum prudens scelus ob titulos admittis inanis,
stas animo, et purum est vitio tibi, cum tumidum est, cor?
Si quis lectica nitidam gestare amet agnam,
huic vestem, ut gnatae, paret, ancillas paret, aurum,
Rufam aut Pusillam appellet, fortique marito
destinet uxorem, interdicto huic omne adimat ius
praetor, et ad sanos abeat tutela propinquos.

204. **non ille**: cf. **multum ille,** Virg. *Æn.* I. 3. — **ipsum**: as opposed to the sheep.

205. **adverso,** *opposite* to where he then was.

206. **prudens**: as opposed to **insanus**; *in my wise counsel.*

207. **tuo**: a natural mark of insanity, and hence the man adds **furiose,** indicating the most violent form of madness.

208. **qui,** etc.: in answer to the protest of Agamemnon, the Stoic proceeds to give a definition of insanity, as consisting in delusion, which he afterwards applies in v. 211. — **species,** *conceptions,* ideas of objects, etc. — **veris**: the ablative on account of the comparative force of **alias.** The ablative after comparatives is originally an ablative of separation. — **tumultu,** *the craze,* the disturbed state of the mind from criminal desires, in which it is incapable of calm reasoning.

209. **commotus,** *unsound,* of shaken intellect.

210. **stultitia**: like Agamemnon from ambition, to which passion the Stoic refers the Trojan expedition; cf. v. 212. — **ira**: as Ajax; cf. v. 211.

212. **prudens**; cf. v. 206. — **titulos,** *honors;* strictly the inscriptions containing the dignities attained by a Roman, and hung up in the atrium of his descendants, by his wax mask; cf. I. 6. 17. — **inanis**: as having no real value to the philosophic mind.

213. **stas animo**; cf. **commotus,** v. 209. — **cor**: including the intellect as well as the moral powers.

214. **si quis,** etc.: the Stoic makes his meaning plain by an example that cannot be mistaken, the converse of the treatment of Iphigenia. — **nitidam,** *cossetted,* well kept and fed.

216. **Rufam, Pusillam,** names of girls, the second a diminutive of affection. — **forti,** *sturdy;* merely as a masculine epithet.

217. **interdicto,** etc.: **a madman**

Quid? si quis gnatam pro muta devovet agna,
integer est animi? Ne dixeris. Ergo ubi prava
stultitia, hic summa est insania; qui sceleratus,
et furiosus erit; quem cepit vitrea fama,
hunc circumtonuit gaudens Bellona cruentis.

Nunc age, luxuriam et Nomentanum arripe mecum;
vincet enim stultos ratio insanire nepotes.
Hic simul accepit patrimoni mille talenta,
edicit, piscator uti, pomarius, auceps,
unguentarius, ac Tusci turba impia vici,
cum scurris fartor, cum Velabro omne macellum,
mane domum veniant. Quid tum? Venere frequentes.
Verba facit leno: 'Quicquid mihi, quicquid et horum

could be deprived of the custody and care of his estate by means of a proceeding before the prætor.

221. **stultitia**: folly consisting in a wrong estimate of the value of things. — **sceleratus**: inasmuch as crime proceeds from wrong conceptions; cf. v. 208.

222. **vitrea**, *glittering*. — **fama**, etc.: the thing to be proved, as implied in v. 165. But the words refer immediately to Agamemnon, whose example has been last referred to.

223. **hunc**, etc.: *i.e.* he is crazed, like the priests of Bellona, who performed an orgiastic worship of the goddess, in which they raved and cut themselves with knives. — **circumtonuit**: like **attonitus**, of the loss of the senses produced by lightning.

224. **nunc**, etc.: the third head, luxurious living. — **Nomentanum**: cf. v. 175. — **arripe**: cf. II. 1. 69.

225. **vincet ratio**: cf. I. 3. 115.

226. **hic simul**, etc.: the conduct of the spendthrift is essentially the same as if he actually did what he is described as doing; hence this description is inserted immediately without explanation, as if it were literally true.

227. **edicit**, *makes proclamation;* a formal word of official action. — **piscator**, etc.: suppliers of dainties for the table.

228. **unguentarius**: the dealer in perfumes. — **Tusci**: the Vicus Tuscus, the street leading from the Forum between the Basilica Julia and the Temple of Castor, to the low ground between the Forum and the river, was the haunt of strumpets, pimps, and worthless characters generally.

229. **scurris**: the parasites who afforded amusement by their buffoonery to the gay young men about town, and were in consequence entertained by them. — **fartor**, *the sausage-maker*. — **Velabro**, in the same region as the Forum Boarium near the river, mentioned here as a market place for viands.

230. **veniant**: depending on **edicit**.

231. **verba facit**: *i.e.* is the

cuique domi est, id crede tuum, et vel nunc pete vel cras.'
Accipe quid contra iuvenis responderit aequus:
'In nive Lucana dormis ocreatus, ut aprum
cenem ego; tu piscis hiberno ex aequore verris;
segnis ego, indignus qui tantum possideam: aufer!
sume tibi deciens; tibi tantundem; tibi triplex,
unde uxor media currit de nocte vocata.'
Filius Aesopi detractam ex aure Metellae,
scilicet ut deciens solidum absorberet, aceto
diluit insignem bacam: qui sanior ac si
illud idem in rapidum flumen iaceretve cloacam?
Quinti progenies Arri, par nobile fratrum,
nequitia et nugis pravorum et amore gemellum,
luscinias soliti impenso prandere coemptas,
quorsum abeant? Sanin' creta, an carbone notandi?

spokesman for all the crowd who minister to the wants of the spendthrift. All they have is at his service, either at once or whenever he likes.

233. **aequus**, *honest*, not wishing to take without payment, nor without appreciation of their services.

234. **nive . . . ocreatus**: to indicate the difficulties of the pursuit. — **Lucana**, the mountains of Lucania, the haunts of the wild boar. — **ocreatus**, *in hunting boots;* properly leather leggings, an important part of the huntsman's costume, and naturally uncomfortable to sleep in.

235. **tu**: another of the caterers, the fishmonger. — **hiberno**: and hence stormy and dangerous. — **verris**, *scour*, as with a net.

236. **segnis**, *a lazy fellow*, who incur none of these hardships.

237. **tibi**: the hunter.—**deciens**: *sc.* **centena milia**, *a million* sesterces, forty to fifty thousand dollars. — **tibi**: the fisherman.

238. **unde**, *whose*, lit. from whom, equal **a quo**, the obliging husband.

239. **Aesopi**, a famous actor of Cicero's time. — **Metellae**, doubtless his paramour, perhaps the wife of Cornelius Lentulus Spinther.

240. **solidum**, *at a draught*, lit. in a lump.

241. **ac si**, *than if*, as often.

242. **in rapidum**, etc.: which would be a sign of insanity. — **cloacam**: cf. **barathro**, v. 166.

243. **Arri**, probably the same one mentioned in v. 86.

245. **impenso**, at an enormous price.

246. **quorsum**, *in which group*, *i.e.* to the sane or the insane. — **creta, an carbone**, as good or bad, a figure derived from notation in the calendar of lucky and unlucky days, but possibly also connected with some commercial custom. — **carbone**: *i.e.* **ut insani**.

Aedificare casas, plostello adiungere mures,
ludere par impar, equitare in harundine longa,
si quem delectet barbatum, amentia verset.
Si puerilius his ratio esse evincet amare,
nec quicquam differre utrumne in pulvere, trimus
quale prius, ludas opus, an meretricis amore
sollicitus plores, quaero, faciasne quod olim
mutatus Polemon, ponas insignia morbi,
fasciolas, cubital, focalia, potus ut ille
dicitur ex collo furtim carpsisse coronas,
postquam est impransi correptus voce magistri?
Porrigis irato puero cum poma, recusat:
'Sume, catelle!' negat; si non des, optet: amator
exclusus qui distat, agit ubi secum eat an non,

247. **casas,** *card houses.* — **plostello,** *a toy cart.*

248. **par impar,** *odd and even;* a boy's game, as with us. — **equitare,** *ride a cockhorse.*

249. **barbatum,** *a bearded man,* full-grown. — **verset**: *i.e. he would be a victim of;* such conduct would be a sure sign of insanity.

250. **puerilius his,** etc.: *i.e.* the conduct of a lover is more childish than the acts mentioned. — **amare**: in a bad sense, *intrigue.*

251. **pulvere**: *i.e.* making mud pies.

252. **opus**: cog. acc. with **ludas,** *waste your time;* lit. make serious work of play, almost equal to *play at work.*

253. **plores**: as the especial mark of childishness. — **faciasne,** *wouldn't you do* like Polemo, *i.e.* feel that you had reason to reform, thus admitting your former insanity, as he did when shown the better way by the voice of philosophy.

254. **mutatus,** *the converted.* — **Polemo,** a fast young man of Athens, who happening in, when returning from a drinking-bout with his garland on, to a discourse of Xenocrates, leader of the Academic school, became ashamed of his condition (**furtim carpsisse,** etc.), reformed, and succeeded Xenocrates as the leader of the school. — **insignia,** *symptoms.* — **morbi**: as a form of insanity.

255. **fasciolas,** *leg-wrappings:* these and the following are the coddling apparel of an effeminate voluptuary. — **cubital,** *armlets.* — **focalia,** *neckcloths.* — **potus,** *reveller,* one who has well drunken.

257. **impransi**: *i.e.* sober; opposed to **potus.**

258. **porrigis,** etc.: the childishness of the lover is still further illustrated by showing that the lover desires when he cannot obtain, and refuses when he is invited, as in the case in Terence's *Eunuchus,* when Phædria uses the words quoted in v. 262, in reference to his mistress, who has sent for him.

259. **catelle,** *little rat.*

260. **qui**: adverb. — **agit**: with ī, an unexplained irregularity, per-

quo rediturus erat non arcessitus, et haeret
invisis foribus? 'Nec nunc, cum me vocat ultro,
accedam, an potius mediter finire dolores?
Exclusit; revocat: redeam? Non, si obsecret.' Ecce
servus, non paulo sapientior: 'O ere, quae res
nec modum habet neque consilium, ratione modoque
tractari non volt. In amore haec sunt mala, bellum,
pax rursum: haec si quis tempestatis prope ritu
mobilia et caeca fluitantia sorte laboret
reddere certa sibi, nihilo plus explicet ac si
insanire paret certa ratione modoque.'
Quid? cum, Picenis excerpens semina pomis,
gaudes si cameram percusti forte, penes te es?
Quid? cum balba feris annoso verba palato,
aedificante casas qui sanior? Adde cruorem
stultitiae, atque ignem gladio scrutare. Modo, inquam,
Hellade percussa Marius cum praecipitat se,
cerritus fuit? An commotae crimine mentis
absolves hominem, et sceleris damnabis eundem,
ex more imponens cognata vocabula rebus?

haps a mistaken extension of cases like **condiderit**, II. 1. 82.

261. **non arcessitus**: cf. **si non des optet**, v. 259.

265. **servus**, Parmeno, Phædria's slave. — **quae res**: *i.e.* love; the whole showing the irrationality and consequent insanity of the passion.

268. **tempestatis**, etc.: *i.e.* almost as changeable as the weather.

269. **fluitantia**, *drifting*.

272. **cum Picenis**, etc.: another childish act, snapping apple-seeds, a process by which lovers sought omens in regard to their love. — **Picenis**: cf. II. 4. 70.

274. **cum balba**, etc.: the lisping accents of love are compared to the baby-talk of childhood.

275. **cruorem**: in reference to the acts of violence often inspired by love; *i.e.* suppose these to exist also, and the insanity is still more obvious.

276. **ignem**, etc.: the same idea, but alluding to a dictum of Pythagoras, πῦρ μαχαίρᾳ μὴ σκαλεύειν, the meaning of which is not clear, perhaps, "excite not the wrathful to violence," which dictum Horace twists into this meaning. — **modo**: *i.e.* take, I say, an example that happened only just now, of the kind referred to.

277. **Hellade**, a woman otherwise unknown.

280. **cognata**, *kindred; i.e.* not the true philosophical ones.

Libertinus erat, qui circum compita siccus
lautis mane senex manibus currebat et 'Vnum'
('Quid tam magnum?' addens), 'unum me surpite morti,
dis etenim facile est!' orabat; sanus utrisque
auribus atque oculis; mentem, nisi litigiosus,
exciperet dominus cum venderet. Hoc quoque volgus
Chrysippus ponit fecunda in gente Meneni.
'Iuppiter, ingentis qui das adimisque dolores,'
mater ait pueri mensis iam quinque cubantis,
'frigida si puerum quartana reliquerit, illo
mane die, quo tu indicis ieiunia, nudus
in Tiberi stabit.' Casus medicusve levarit
aegrum ex praecipiti: mater delira necabit
in gelida fixum ripa febrimque reducet,
quone malo mentem concussa? Timore deorum.

281. **libertinus**, etc.: an example of superstition, the fourth subject. — **compita**: where were the shrines of the Lares. — **siccus**, *fasting*.

282. **lautis manibus**: a custom of the Jews, as well as many other nations, in religious observance. — **senex**, *in his old age*, when the fear of death would most affect him. — **unum**, *me, just one man*.

283. **surpite**: for **surripite**. — **quid tam magnum**: a common suggestion in prayers (cf. Theognis, XIV., and *Odys.* V. 25), as again in **dis**, etc.

284. **sanus**: in possession of all his senses, but disordered in intellect.

285. **nisi litigiosus**, *unless he wanted a lawsuit*, which would be brought against him by the purchaser of the slave, for breach of warranty of soundness. Cf. *Ep.* II. 2. 18.

286. **exciperet**, *would have specially stated* (if he had wanted to sell him), which was necessary to avoid liability. — **dominus**, his master, inasmuch as he was once a slave. — **volgus**: in allusion to their great number.

287. **Chrysippus**: as leader of the Stoics (cf. I. 3. 127, and II. 3. 44). — **Meneni**, an unknown madman.

288. **Iuppiter**: used as a name of the Supreme Being, in association with Thursday, by the woman, perhaps a Jewess, or one who had adopted the rites of that nation referred to. The fast and the placing in the Tiber (baptism?) are both Oriental.

291. **die**, Thursday, *dies Iovis*. — **ieiunia**: the Jews fasted on Thursday, as well as Monday.

292. **casus medicusve**: expressly excluding the god from any share in it. — **levarit**: hortatory; *suppose*, etc.

293. **necabit**: by performing the vow.

295. **quone**: cf. **uterne**, II. 2. 107; **quine**, I. 10. 21; so **utrumne**, v. 251; **quantane**, v. 317.

Haec mihi Stertinius, sapientum octavus, amico
arma dedit, posthac ne compellarer inultus.
Dixerit insanum qui me, totidem audiet, atque
respicere ignoto discet pendentia tergo.

*Hor.* Stoice, post damnum sic vendas omnia pluris,
qua me stultitia, quoniam non est genus unum,
insanire putas? Ego nam videor mihi sanus.
*Dam.* Quid? caput abscissum manibus cum portat Agave
gnati infelicis, sibi tum furiosa videtur?
*Horat.* Stultum me fateor (liceat concedere veris),
atque etiam insanum; tantum hoc edissere, quo me
aegrotare putes animi vitio? *Dam.* Accipe: primum
aedificas, hoc est, longos imitaris, ab imo
ad summum totus moduli bipedalis; et idem
corpore maiorem rides Turbonis in armis
spiritum et incessum: qui ridiculus minus illo?
An quodcumque facit Maecenas, te quoque verum est,

296. **amico,** *as a friend.*

297. **arma,** *weapons* to defend myself with, *i.e.* these precepts. — **compellarer,** *i.e.* called madman.

299. **pendentia**: alluding to the fable of the two sacks, one containing the faults of others, and hanging in front, the other containing one's own and hanging behind.

300. **Stoice,** etc.: to give a more humorous close, and to include himself in the persons satirized, Horace appeals to the Stoic to give his diagnosis. — **sic**: the regular formula in adjurations; *so*, as you grant my request, *i.e.* on condition that. Cf. "So may each airy moon-elf and fairy," etc. T. Moore. "Tell me, kind seer." — **pluris**: *i.e.* than before, so as to recover from his embarrassments.

303. **quid,** etc.: in answer to Horace's statement, that he is not conscious of any insanity, Damasippus refers to the case of Agave, mother of Pentheus, familiar doubtless on the stage (hence **videtur**), implying that a raving maniac even has no knowledge of his condition.

305. Horace jocosely assents to the Stoic's statement. — **liceat**: *i.e.* let it be no shame to be convinced.

306. **edissere,** *state fully,* discourse at large.

307. **aegrotare**: in the Stoic manner, as **morbus** and the like.

308. **longos,** *the great,* but with reference to Horace's small stature.

309. **idem,** *at the same time;* showing his inconsistency.

310. **corpore maiorem,** *too great for,* etc. — **Turbonis,** a gladiator of small size.

312. **verum,** *right.*

tantum dissimilem, et tanto certare minorem?
Absentis ranae pullis vituli pede pressis,
unus ubi effugit, matri denarrat, ut ingens
belua cognatos eliserit. Illa rogare:
'Quantane, num tantum,' sufflans se, 'magna fuisset?'
'Maior dimidio.' 'Num tantum?' Cum magis atque
se magis inflaret, 'Non, si te ruperis,' inquit,
'par eris.' Haec a te non multum abludit imago.
Adde poemata nunc, hoc est, oleum adde camino;
quae si quis sanus fecit, sanus facis et tu.
Non dico horrendam rabiem — *Hor.* Iam desine!
*Dam.* Cultum
maiorem censu — *Hor.* Teneas, Damasippe, tuis te.
*Dam.* Mille puellarum, puerorum mille furores —
*Hor.* O maior tandem parcas, insane, minori!

## IV.

*Hor.* Vnde et quo Catius? *Cat.* Non est mihi tempus aventi

314. **absentis,** etc.: the fable of the frog and the ox.

317. **quantane:** cf. **quone,** v. 295.

320. **non multum abludit,** *hits not very far;* a metaphor probably derived from fencing; cf. **eludo.**

321. **poemata:** doubtless epodes or odes. — **oleum,** etc.: a proverbial expression, doubtless meaning that the ebullition of insanity in poetry (cf. next verse) makes it worse.

322. **si quis,** etc.: according to the idea of the ancients that the poet was inspired, and so frenzied; cf. **vates.**

323. **rabiem:** a stricture which, as probably did the others, came very near the truth, plainly in accordance with the spirit of Horace's satire, including the poet himself among the rest. — **iam desine:** Horace represents himself as angry at the closeness of the Stoic's hits. — **cultum,** *style of living.*

326. **maior . . . insane:** Horace's impatience rises to its height, and he closes with an outburst which includes even the preaching Stoic in the category of the crazy fools.

SATIRE 4. In this Satire Horace ridicules the epicures, who attach so much importance to trifling matters in everything that pertains to the table. He puts the Satire into the form of a dialogue between himself and a certain epicure, Catius, who has just heard a discourse on these matters from some noted master in the art, who is not named, and who now gives them second-hand to Horace, with all the form and importance of philosophical dogmas.

1. **unde et quo Catius:** a com-

ponere signa novis praeceptis, qualia vincant
Pythagoran Anytique reum doctumque Platona.
*Hor.* Peccatum fateor, cum te sic tempore laevo
interpellarim; sed des veniam bonus, oro.
Quod si interciderit tibi nunc aliquid, repetes mox,
sive est naturae hoc sive artis, mirus utroque.
*Cat.* Quin id erat curae, quo pacto cuncta tenerem,
utpote res tenuis, tenui sermone peractas.
*Hor.* Ede hominis nomen, simul et Romanus an hospes.
*Cat.* Ipsa memor praecepta canam, celabitur auctor.

'Longa quibus facies ovis erit, illa memento,
ut suci melioris et ut magis alba rotundis,
ponere; namque marem cohibent callosa vitellum.
Cole suburbano qui siccis crevit in agris
dulcior; irriguo nihil est elutius horto.

mon form of salutation; cf. I. 9. 62 and 63. — **tempus**: *i.e.* to stop and talk.

2. **ponere signa**: a formal expression for **consignare literis**, *commit to writing, set down, record.* There is no certain reference to the mnemonic art, though such a reference is possible. — **praeceptis**: the regular word for philosophical doctrines.

3. **Anyti**, the accuser of Socrates.

4. **laevo**, *unfavorable;* from the language of augury.

5. **bonus**, *kindly.*

6. **quod si**, *and* (as to that) *if.* — **repetes**, *will recall.*

7. **sive**, etc.: *i.e.* so good is your memory, either naturally, or from practice in the art.

8. **quin id**, etc.: *why, that was my anxiety*, etc.; in allusion to Horace's supposition of his forgetting something, especially as the matters are so subtle and so subtly expressed. The doctrines are treated like the profoundest discoveries in philosophy.

10. **hominis**: the author.

11. **ipsa**: the name is purposely concealed, most probably because he is a man of too much consequence to be ridiculed. — **memor**: *i.e.* exactly, with a good memory.

12. **longa**, etc.: the precious doctrines begin at once without further preamble, and in a rambling style, as they happen to come up in his mind.

13. **suci**, *taste.*

14. **ponere**, *to serve;* the regular word. Cf. **posito**, II. 2. 23. — **namque**: the reason of the better taste. — **callosa**, *of firm texture.*

15. **cole**: the popular form of **caule**. — **suburbano**: *i.e.* grown in the well-watered market-gardens around the city. — **siccis**: the farms in the country.

16. **elutius**, *more insipid;* of course referring to the productions of the garden, but with an allusion to the constant watering.

Si vespertinus subito te oppresserit hospes,
ne gallina malum responset dura palato,
doctus eris vivam mixto mersare Falerno;
hoc teneram faciet. Pratensibus optima fungis
natura est; aliis male creditur. Ille salubris
aestates peraget, qui nigris prandia moris
finiet, ante gravem quae legerit arbore solem.
Aufidius forti miscebat mella Falerno,
mendose, quoniam vacuis committere venis
nil nisi lene decet; leni praecordia mulso
prolueris melius. Si dura morabitur alvus,
mitulus et viles pellent obstantia conchae
et lapathi brevis herba, sed albo non sine Coo.
Lubrica nascentes implent conchylia lunae;
sed non omne mare est generosae fertile testae;
murice Baiano melior Lucrina peloris,
ostrea Circeiis, Miseno oriuntur echini,
pectinibus patulis iactat se molle Tarentum.

17. **si vespertinus**, etc.: *i.e.* in case it is necessary to serve a fowl freshly killed, on account of the sudden arrival of an unexpected guest.

18. **malum**: the neuter adverbial accusative.— **responset**, *suit*, as answering the demands of the palate. — **dura**, *tough*.

19. **doctus eris**, *you will be wise to*, etc.; lit. you will be taught to. — **mixto**: with water, *diluted*.

20. **pratensibus**, *of the meadows*, as opposed to the woods.

21. **male creditur**, *are not to be trusted*, as likely to be poisonous.

22. **prandia**, *déjeuner*, or *lunch*, the first real meal of the day, taken about noon.

24. **Aufidius**, an unknown epicure. — **miscebat**: *i.e.* for *mulsum*, which was taken at the beginning of a meal for an appetizer, hence **vacuis**.

29. **brevis**, *small-leaved*. — **alba . . . Coo**, wine of Cos mixed with sea water (λευκόκωον), in which apparently the shell-fish and sorrel were boiled.

30. **lubrica**: on account of their slipping down the throat easily. — **nascentes**, etc.: the new moon is the best time for taking shell-fish, and the different localities vary in the excellence of the fish.

31. **generosae**, *the choicest;* used regularly of fine breeds of animals.

32. **murice**, a turbinate shell-fish or cockle, of which many kinds are eaten in Italy. — **peloris**, a bivalve.

33. **Miseno**, on the promontory of Misenum; cf. Virg. *Æ*. VI. 234.

34. **pectinibus**, the long comb-

'Nec sibi cenarum quivis temere arroget artem,
non prius exacta tenui ratione saporum;
nec satis est cara piscis averrere mensa
ignarum quibus est ius aptius et quibus assis
languidus in cubitum iam se conviva reponet.
Vmber et iligna nutritus glande rotundas
curvat aper lances carnem vitantis inertem;
nam Laurens malus est, ulvis et harundine pinguis.
Vinea submittit capreas non semper edulis.
Fecundae leporis sapiens sectabitur armos.
Piscibus atque avibus quae natura et foret aetas,
ante meum nulli patuit quaesita palatum.
Sunt quorum ingenium nova tantum crustula promit.
Nequaquam satis in re una consumere curam,

like bivalve, "razor-blade(?)." — **patulis**, *gaping*, *i.e.* bivalve.

35. **quivis**, *everybody*. — **temere**, *ignorantly*, without a thorough understanding of the nicer points of cookery. — **artem**: *i.e.* of preparing; used of the cook.

36. **non prius**, etc., *without having*, etc. — **exacta**, *weighed;* cf. **examen**. — **tenui**, *subtle*, as in v. 9. — **saporum**, *of flavoring and sauces*. — **ratione**, *art*. The mere choice of viands such as he has described is not enough, without the art of preparing them.

37. **cara**, *costly*. — **averrere**, *sweep off*, *i.e.* monopolize the whole stock of dainties. — **mensa**: in the market.

38. **ignarum**: taking the place of the indefinite subject of **averrere**. — **ius**: *i.e.* in which they are boiled. — **assis**, *roasted*.

39. **in cubitum**: in reference to the reclining position in which the ancients took their meals, meaning, of course, to beguile the guest to begin again.

41. **curvat**, *bends* (with its weight). — **aper**: cf. II. 8. 6. — **vitantis**, *i.e.* if one wishes to avoid, or prefers the opposite. — **inertem**, *tasteless*, *insipid*.

42. **malus**, *poor*, *worthless*.

43. **submittit**, *supplies*. — **non semper**: *i.e.* those in the woods are to be preferred.

44. **fecundae**: the main idea, these in preference to any others. — **armos**: specified merely because that is the part eaten. — **sapiens**, *the connoisseur*.

45. **natura**: *i.e.* what kind in each case was best for the table. — **aetas**: the age at which they should be served.

46. **meum**: to be referred to the unknown epicure. — **patuit**, *has been fully known*. — **quaesita**: *i.e.* though much studied.

47. **crustula**, *sweets*, cakes and the like. — **promit**, *invents;* *i.e.* they content themselves with inventing dainties for dessert.

48. **nequaquam satis**: *i.e.* this is a very narrow scope for the true artist, to devote himself to one branch alone.

ut si quis solum hoc, mala ne sint vina, laboret,
quali perfundat piscis securus olivo.
Massica si caelo supponas vina sereno,
nocturna, si quid crassi est, tenuabitur aura,
et decedet odor nervis inimicus; at illa
integrum perdunt lino vitiata saporem.
Surrentina vafer qui miscet faece Falerna
vina, columbino limum bene colligit ovo,
quatenus ima petit volvens aliena vitellus.
Tostis marcentem squillis recreabis et Afra
potorem cochlea: nam lactuca innatat acri
post vinum stomacho; perna magis ac magis hillis
flagitat immorsus refici; quin omnia malit,
quaecumque immundis fervent allata popinis.
Est operae pretium duplicis pernoscere iuris
naturam. Simplex e dulci constat olivo,
quod pingui miscere mero muriaque decebit,
non alia quam qua Byzantia putuit orca.

50. **securus,** *careless, not caring.*

51. **supponas**: *i.e.* expose to the night air under a clear sky.

52. **si quid crassi,** *if it is at all thick* or *muddy.* — **tenuabitur,** *will be refined.*

53. **odor,** *the bouquet.*

54. **integrum,** *pure;* opposed to **perdunt.** — **lino**: *i.e.* they are spoiled by straining or filtering.

55. **faece**: the deposit, or lees, of wine was burnt, and used to flavor wine, and for other flavors; cf. II. 8. 9.

56. **limum colligit,** *i.e.* clarifies the wine.

57. **quatenus,** *since;* cf. I. 1. 64. — **volvens,** *gathering.* — **aliena,** *all foreign matters.*

58. **marcentem,** *i.e.* who has lost his appetite from excess of wine. — **squillis,** probably a shell-fish. — **Afra**: these seem to have been famous as the best.

59. **innatat,** *does not digest,* swims in the full stomach.

60. **perna**: means of **immorsus.** — **magis,** *rather.*

61. **immorsus,** *stimulated,* properly *gnawed.* — **omnia**: *i.e.* rather than lettuce.

62. **popinis,** the low taverns or restaurants. — **allata,** *served; i.e.* the rich strong food of the common people in their low resorts.

63. **est operae pretium**: a purposely chosen epic phrase from Ennius, to give pomposity to the style. — **duplicis**: a technical name, no doubt, for this sauce made of the ordinary sauce treated as described.

65. **muria,** *fish-brine,* or the pickle in which fish has been preserved, was a favorite ingredient in the sauces or relishes of the ancients.

66. **Byzantia**: referring to the tunny fish of Byzantium, which was

Hoc ubi confusum sectis inferbuit herbis
Corycioque croco sparsum stetit, insuper addes
pressa Venafranae quod baca remisit olivae.
Picenis cedunt pomis Tiburtia suco;
nam facie praestant. Venucula convenit ollis;
rectius Albanam fumo duraveris uvam.
Hanc ego cum malis, ego faecem primus et allec,
primus et invenior piper album cum sale nigro
incretum puris circumposuisse catillis.
Immane est vitium dare milia terna macello
angustoque vagos piscis urgere catino.
Magna movet stomacho fastidia, seu puer unctis
tractavit calicem manibus, dum furta ligurrit,
sive gravis veteri craterae limus adhaesit.

a great article of export; see Plin. *H. N.* IX. 20. — **putuit**: a not unnatural expression for the raw material, whatever the product.

67. **hoc**: the **ius simplex**. — **inferbuit**, *has been boiled.*

68. **stetit**, has been left to cool.

69. **pressa**, etc., *i.e.* oil of Venafrum, which was considered the best. He here imitates the Epic style.

71. **nam**, *i.e.* I say this, because, etc. — **venucula**: *sc.* **uva**. — **convenit ollis**, *is suitable for packing*, storing away to eat fresh, as opposed to the raisins mentioned in the next verse. Cf. Plin. *H. N.* XIV. 16.

73. **hanc**: *i.e.* grapes; the discovery consists in the combination, like "nuts and raisins." — **ego faecem**, etc.: the novelty apparently consisted in serving these relishes in a separate dish, and in precisely this mixture. — **faecem**: cf. II. 8. 9. — **allec**, a sauce prepared from various marine animals, like anchovy sauce, or caviare.

74. **invenior**: a poetic extension of the construction of **dicor** and the like. — **piper**, etc.: another combination of condiments. — **sale nigro**: made of wood ashes, like "pearlash."

75. **puris**: *i.e.* in separate clean plates, without any other viands.

76. **immane**, etc.: the mention of the setting things on the table suggests to the man the importance of the style of service, etc. — **dare**, etc.: *i.e.* spend an enormous sum for the fish, and then spoil the effect in the serving.

77. **angustoque**, etc.: the fault consists in having too small a plate. This, however, the connoisseur speaks of as confining the fish, which are accustomed to freedom, in too narrow limits.

78. **magna**, etc.: other details of the service.

79. **furta**, *stolen dainties;* the slave is represented as hastily snatching something from the dish with his fingers, and greasing the cups while handing them, in consequence.

80. **gravis**, etc.: the sediment re-

Vilibus in scopis, in mappis, in scobe quantus
consistit sumptus? Neglectis, flagitium ingens.
Ten' lapides varios lutulenta radere palma
et Tyrias dare circum inluta toralia vestis,
oblitum, quanto curam sumptumque minorem
haec habeant, tanto reprehendi iustius illis
quae nisi divitibus nequeant contingere mensis?'

*Horat.* Docte Cati, per amicitiam divosque rogatus,
ducere me auditum, perges quocumque, memento.
Nam quamvis memori referas mihi pectore cuncta,
non tamen interpres tantundem iuveris. Adde
voltum habitumque hominis, quem tu vidisse beatus
non magni pendis, quia contigit; at mihi cura
non mediocris inest, fontis ut adire remotos
atque haurire queam vitae praecepta beatae.

maining in the mixing-jar from long use and neglect in cleansing.

81. **vilibus**, etc.: *i.e.* what a fault is uncleanliness, when the means of cleansing are so cheap.

83. **ten'**: the short colloquial form for **te-ne**. — **varios**, *variegated*, and so costly. — **lutulenta**: indicating carelessness in attending to the costly pavement so that the effect is lost. — **radere**: with **ten** in the infinitive of exclamation, *the idea that, to think that.*

84. **Tyrias**: the most costly coverings of the couches. —**toralia**, the "valance," around the feet of the couch. — **vestis**, after **circum**.

86. **haec**: these details of service, depending merely on cleanliness. — **illis**: the splendid pavements and couch-coverings.

87. **divitibus**, *i.e.* of the rich.

88. **docte**, etc.: Horace, as if impressed with the importance of the doctrines, begs Catius to take him with him whenever he goes to hear such valuable truths.

91. **interpres**, *a reporter*, giving the things at second hand. — **adde**, *consider also*, *i.e.* think what an advantage there would be to me in seeing the man's face and bearing when giving these great truths.

95. **vitae praecepta beatae**: *i.e.* in a double sense: on the one hand, of moral precepts such as secured a happy life, the aim of all the later philosophies: and on the other, of the advantages that come from attention to the rules of good living in the epicure's sense. The whole close is probably parodied from Lucr. I. 927, *iuvat integros accedere fontis, atque haurire*, etc.

## V.

*Vlixes.* Hoc quoque, Tiresia, praeter narrata petenti
responde, quibus amissas reparare queam res
artibus atque modis. Quid rides? *Tir.* Iamne doloso
non satis est Ithacam revehi patriosque penatis
aspicere? *Vlix.* O nulli quicquam mentite, vides ut
nudus inopsque domum redeam, te vate; neque illic
aut apotheca procis intacta est aut pecus; atqui
et genus et virtus, nisi cum re, vilior alga est.

*Tir.* Quando pauperiem, missis ambagibus, horres,
accipe qua ratione queas ditescere. Turdus

SATIRE 5. There was at Rome at the beginning of the Empire, in consequence of the disorganization of society and the ease with which fortunes had been acquired in the civil war, a large number of rich men and women for whom family ties did not exist or were held in little esteem. To ingratiate themselves into the favor of persons of this class, and secure a rich inheritance, became almost a profession followed by many adventurers. It is against this practice that Horace directs this satire, in which he describes ironically the methods to be pursued by the legacy hunter, apparently as if they were perfectly legitimate, and thus shows their contemptible meanness. The directions are put into the mouth of Tiresias and addressed to Ulysses at the end of the interview in the world below (Hom. *Odys.* XI. 148), in which Ulysses is assured by the seer of a safe return, but only after losing all his possessions. The satire has thus the form of a travesty.

1. **narrata**: the statements of the seer related in *Od.* XI. 90.

3. **rides**: the seer smiles at the greed of mankind as shown by Ulysses, who is not satisfied with escaping with his life, but being assured of that, at once wishes to get rich again. — **iam**, *already*, when he is assured of his life. — **doloso**: representing the standing epithets of Ulysses (πολύτροπος, etc.), but at the same time suggesting his character as illustrated by his conduct here.

6. **te vate**, *according to your prophecy.*

7. **apotheca**: containing his stores of grain, wine, and oil. — **procis**: the suitors of Penelope, who lived as her guests in the house of her husband while awaiting her decision. (See Hom. *Odys.* I. 106 *et seq.*). — **pecus**: both as means of subsistence, and as constituting a great part of the wealth of a barbaric chief. — **atqui**: the adversative turn in the thought depends on an idea not expressed; "I have birth and worth, to be sure; yet they are worthless without money."

9. **ambagibus**: *i.e.* the excuse he makes in **et genus et virtus**, etc.

10. **turdus**: a delicacy for the table.

sive aliud privum dabitur tibi, devolet illuc
res ubi magna nitet domino sene ; dulcia poma
et quoscumque feret cultus tibi fundus honores,
ante larem gustet venerabilior lare dives ;
qui quamvis periurus erit, sine gente, cruentus
sanguine fraterno, fugitivus, ne tamen illi
tu comes exterior, si postulet, ire recuses.
*Vlix.* Vtne tegam spurco Damae latus ? Haud ita Troiae
me gessi, certans semper melioribus. *Tir.* Ergo
pauper eris. *Vlix.* Fortem hoc animum tolerare iubebo ;
et quondam maiora tuli. Tu protinus, unde
divitias aerisque ruam dic, augur, acervos.
*Tir.* Dixi equidem et dico : captes astutus ubique

11. **privum,** *rare,* not possessed by everybody. — **devolet**: chosen on account of the thrush.

12. **nitet,** *flourishes ;* the figure no doubt derived from animals and lands which are well kept.

13. **honores**: cf. *ruris honorum*, *Carm.* I. 17. 16.

14. **ante larem**: the first fruits were offered to the household god. Cf.

pomiferi laribus consuevimus horti
Mittere primitias.
Calp. *Ecl.* II. 64.

15. **sine gente**: a freedman, as once having been a slave, and so *filius nullius.*

17. **comes**: one of the principal functions of a humble dependent was to escort his superior wherever he appeared abroad. Cf. I. 6. 101 and 112. — **exterior,** *on the left hand,* where the more humble companion would go. Cf. Suet. *Claud.* 24; Eutrop. VII. 13; see also **tegam latus,** meaning the same thing.

18. **utne tegam,** *the idea of,* etc. — **Damae**: a common slave's name. The little struggle of the hero gives the more force to his very speedy submission.

19. **melioribus**: dative, as in Greek. — **ergo pauper eris,** *then you'll have to be,* etc., in a Laconic style, showing the necessity of this degradation. To which Ulysses replies as it were, "Oh well, if I must, I will."

20. **fortem hoc,** etc.: the point of this lies in the fact that his other sufferings had contained no abasement, while here the degradation is self-imposed, though the words are imitated from his expressions of heroic fortitude. Cf. *Odys.* XX. 18, and V. 224. — **hoc**: of course the degradation, not the poverty.

22. **ruam,** *dig up* (like **eruam**), as the earth is the source of the precious metals.

23. **dixi,** etc.: with a little impatience, as if he said, I told you before, that is the only way. Cf. the abruptness of **pauper eris.**

testamenta senum, neu, si vafer unus et alter
insidiatorem praeroso fugerit hamo,
aut spem deponas aut artem illusus omittas.
Magna minorve foro si res certabitur olim,
vivet uter locuples sine gnatis, improbus, ultro
qui meliorem audax vocet in ius, illius esto
defensor; fama civem causaque priorem
sperne, domi si gnatus erit fecundave coniunx.
'Quinte,' puta, aut 'Publi' (gaudent praenomine molles
auriculae) 'tibi me virtus tua fecit amicum;
ius anceps novi, causas defendere possum;
eripiet quivis oculos citius mihi, quam te
contemptum cassa nuce pauperet; haec mea cura est,
ne quid tu perdas, neu sis iocus.' Ire domum atque
pelliculam curare iube; fi cognitor ipse.
Persta atque obdura, seu *rubra Canicula findet*

24. **si vafer,** etc.: *i.e.* don't be discouraged by any want of success.

25. **praeroso,** etc.: the figure of course is of a fish stealing the bait, and escaping uncaught.

27. **magna,** etc.: the Romans went into court accompanied by one or more friends (**advocati**), who assisted them with advice and services. Cf. I. 9. 38. This is one of the services by which the will-hunter can ingratiate himself with the rich. — **res**: *case.* Cf. **reus** (orig. *party*).

28. **ultro,** etc.: *i.e.* take no account of the justice of the cause, but be guided by the position of the parties.

32. **Quinte,** etc.: the use of the prænomen denotes familiarity and affection, in which the sensitive nature, looked upon by the Romans as a weakness, of these men delight. As childless old men they feel the want of affection. — **puta,** with *ă*, as often in this sense, following the popular prosody as in comedy.

34. **ius anceps,** *the doubtful points of law.*

36. **contemptum,** *cast contempt upon,* treating it as another verb. The contempt would consist in getting the better of him in a lawsuit, showing that he can be attacked with impunity. Cf. **sis iocus,** v. 37.

38. **pelliculam,** *his precious health;* a variation on **cutis** (cf. *Ep.* I. 2. 29), in the sense of coddling one's self. No doubt the expression is derived from the bathing and anointing which the Romans made great use of. — **cognitor,** *his attorney;* the person who appeared to represent the party in court. The advocate proper would be *patronus.*

39. **rubra,** etc.: no doubt a quotation made in jest from the poet Furius. The whole is a comic expression for the extremes of hot and cold weather. — **Canicula**: this ought properly to be the constellation of the Little Dog, προκύων (cf. *Od.* III. 29. 18), but it prob-

*infantis statuas*, seu pingui tentus omaso
Furius *hibernas cana nive conspuet Alpis*.
'Nonne vides,' aliquis cubito stantem prope tangens
inquit, 'ut patiens! ut amicis aptus! ut acer!'
plures adnabunt thynni et cetaria crescent.

Si cui praeterea validus male filius in re
praeclara sublatus aletur, ne manifestum
caelibis obsequium nudet te, leniter in spem
adrepe officiosus, ut et scribare secundus
heres, et, si quis casus puerum egerit Orco,
in vacuum venias: perraro haec alea fallit.
Qui testamentum tradet tibi cumque legendum,

ably refers to or is confused with Sirius, whose rising in earlier times in Greece was the mark of the hot season.

40. **infantis**: literally, *dumb*. — **statuas**: they are cracked by the excessive drought, being of wood. — **pingui**: doubtless alluding to the poetaster's personal appearance. — **Furius**: cf. *Sat.* I. 10. 36. M. Furius Bibaculus, whose nickname Alpinus appears to have been derived from this passage or a similar one. He was a ridiculous poet of Cremona.

42. **stantem prope**, *his neighbor*.

43. **aptus**, *accommodating*, strictly, adapted, *i.e.* adapting himself to his needs. Cf. Cic. *ad Fam.* XII. 30, *O hominem semper illum quidem mihi aptum*.

44. **thynni**: cf. v. 25. — **cetaria**, *fish ponds*, probably arrangements like modern weirs, but in which fish were kept awaiting a demand, and taken out as wanted, as is sometimes done nowadays with fish sold for bait.

45. **si cui**, etc.: *i.e.* occasionally as a blind the will-hunter should be content with the second chance, and pay court to a man who is not absolutely childless, but has a son, in case the son's health is poor.

46. **sublatus**, *born*, strictly, in allusion to the custom of laying a new-born child on the ground to be taken up by the father (**tollere**) if he wished it to be reared as his, instead of being exposed and abandoned.

47. **leniter**, *slyly*; *i.e.* by gentle means, so as not to be caught at it.

48. **secundus**: *i.e. in the second place*, failing the first disposition of the estate to the child, through his death.

49. **Orco**: the common poetic construction of the dative as end of motion is more justifiable from the fact that Orcus is properly a person. Cf. Ἄϊδι προϊάπτειν.

51. **qui**: with **cumque**. — **legendum**: *i.e.* he either wishes, as a mark of his confidence, to assure his friend that he is remembered in his will, or else to show that he is not deceived by his friend's pretended devotion.

abnuere et tabulas a te removere memento,
sic tamen, ut limis rapias, quid prima secundo
cera velit versu; solus multisne coheres,
veloci percurre oculo. Plerumque recoctus
scriba ex quinqueviro corvum deludet hiantem,
captatorque dabit risus Nasica Corano.
*Vlix.* Num furis? an prudens ludis me obscura canendo?
*Tir.* O Laertiade, quicquid dicam aut erit aut non:
divinare etenim magnus mihi donat Apollo.
*Vlix.* Quid tamen ista velit sibi fabula, si licet, ede.
*Tir.* Tempore quo iuvenis Parthis horrendus, ab alto
demissum genus Aenea, tellure marique

52. **abnuere,** etc.: to show the disinterestedness of his devotion.

53. **sic tamen,** etc.: *i.e.* but do not fail to assure yourself that you are not taken in yourself. — **prima . . . cera**: the first of the two tablets on which such documents were written. Cf. note on I. 6. 74. — **secundo . . . versu**: the first line would have the testator's name; the second, the heir's.

55. **plerumque,** etc.: *i.e.* it very often happens that the testator sees through the wiles of the will-hunter and finally eludes him. This idea, however, is jocosely expressed by reference to a single instance where such a thing has happened. As the incident has happened since the time of Ulysses, the whole is put in the form of a prophecy, keeping up the form of the travesty, and producing a most comic effect. — **recoctus,** *boiled down;* an allusion to the story of Medea, which had become almost proverbial. Cf. Cic. *de Sen.* XXIII. 83.

56. **scriba**: cf. II. 6. 36. — **quinqueviro**: apparently a kind of policeman. Cf. Cic. *Acad.* II. 44. 136, though boards of five men for several other purposes are mentioned. At any rate, the office is that of some humble magistrate. — **corvum**: an allusion to the fable of the fox and the crow.

58. **num furis**: the use of the proper names, unknown of course to Ulysses, makes him doubt the sanity of the seer. — **prudens,** *purposely,* as opposed to **furis.**

59. **O Laertiade**: the seer replies in effect that the allusion is a prophetic one. — **aut erit aut non**: this would naturally mean, will or will not according as I say it will or will not, but no doubt there is a double meaning, with a jest at divination.

60. **divinare**: a poetic use of the infinitive probably influenced by the Greek. — **donat**: present because the gift is a continued one.

61. **tamen**: as if he said, "yes, but still I wish you would explain what the story means."

62. **tempore,** etc.: purposely put in the heroic style. The time referred to is the establishment of Augustus' power after the battle of Actium.

63. **demissum**: cf. Virg. *Æn.* I. 288. — **genus,** *a scion,* in apposition with **iuvenis.** Cf. I. 6. 12.

magnus erit, forti nubet procera Corano
filia Nasicae, metuentis reddere soldum.
Tum gener hoc faciet: tabulas socero dabit atque
ut legat orabit; multum Nasica negatas
accipiet tandem et tacitus leget, invenietque
nil sibi legatum praeter plorare suisque.

Illud ad haec iubeo: mulier si forte dolosa
libertusve senem delirum temperet, illis
accedas socius; laudes, lauderis ut absens;
adiuvat hoc quoque, sed vincit longe prius ipsum
expugnare caput. Scribet mala carmina vecors:
laudato. Scortator erit: cave te roget; ultro
Penelopam facilis potiori trade. *Vlix.* Putasne?

64. **forti**: cf. II. 1. 16, 3. 216. — **procera**: corresponding to **forti** and suggesting a fine figure. Both are no doubt stock epithets for a newly married pair, like "gallant bridegroom" and "fair bride."

65. **Nasicae**, etc.: the father-in-law being indebted to the son-in-law, has given him his daughter to secure his favor. — **metuentis**: simply a strong form for **nolentis**. — **soldum**: *i.e.* **solidum**, the principal of the debt.

66. **tabulas**: as in v. 52.

69. **legatum**: a technical word. Under the Roman law of wills it was necessary that one or more persons should be *heredes* or direct legatees who represented the estate or succession, and any sum that they were directed to pay was said to be *legatum ab eis*. Here, however, Horace probably does not use the word technically, but only in a general sense, as English *left*. — **plorare**: treated like a noun governed by **praeter**. It is used as in I. 10. 91, equivalent to a curse. The whole story shows comically how "the biter" may sometimes be "bit."

70. **illud**, etc.: other less direct means of gaining favor. — **mulier**: doubtless a freedwoman mistress.

72. **socius**: implying that they are engaged in the same enterprise.

73. **hoc**: *i.e.* the scheme referred to. — **vincit**, *carries off the palm*, as compared with the indirect means. — **longe prius**, *by far the better course*.

74. **caput**, *the main stronghold*, the old man himself. — **scribet**: with the force of a condition. — **mala**, *worthless* (cf. II. 1. 83). — **vecors**: in Latin **cor** included the intellectual as well as the moral powers, to which last we have limited the heart later.

75. **laudato**: the second form of the imperative used as often in a general command. — **roget**: the **ne** is omitted here as frequently elsewhere.

76. **potiori**, *your superior*, more worthy than you. — **putasne**: in response to the idea implied in the

perduci poterit tam frugi tamque pudica,
quam nequiere proci recto depellere cursu?
*Tir.* Venit enim magnum donandi parca iuventus
nec tantum Veneris, quantum studiosa culinae.
Sic tibi Penelope frugi est, quae si semel uno
de sene gustarit tecum partita lucellum,
ut canis a corio numquam absterrebitur uncto.

Me sene quod dicam factum est: anus improba Thebis
ex testamento sic est elata: cadaver
unctum oleo largo nudis umeris tulit heres,
scilicet elabi si posset mortua; credo,
quod nimium institerat viventi. Cautus adito,
neu desis operae, neve immoderatus abundes.
Difficilem et morosum offendet garrulus ultro;

preceding, and repeated in the following words.

77. **frugi**, *virtuous*, properly referring to her housewifely qualities as opposed to luxury and wantonness (cf. I. 3. 49 and 4. 107).

78. **proci**: cf. Hom. *Odys.* I. 106.

79. **enim**, *oh yes, for*.— **donandi**: cf. *parcus aceti*, II. 2. 62; and *cupidus te audiendi*, Cic. *de Or.* II. 4. For the idea, cf.

Αὐτοὶ τοί γ' ἀπάγουσι βόας καὶ ἴφια μῆλα
Κούρης δαῖτα φίλοισι, καὶ ἀγλαὰ δῶρα διδοῦσιν·
Ἀλλ' οὐκ ἀλλότριον βίοτον νήποινον ἔδουσιν. — *Hom. Odys.* XVIII. 277.

81. **sic**, *that's why*, referring to the circumstances just mentioned. — **uno**: opposed to the number of the suitors.

83. **canis**, etc.: proverbial, cf. χαλεπὸν χορίω κύνα γεῦσαι. Here is the usual identification of the figure with the object. Cf. II. 1. 20.

84. **me sene**: a jocose expression in accordance with the dramatic setting varied from **me iuvene**, and the like. The anecdote shows the necessity of caution in the pursuit of this profession. — **improba**, *malicious*.

85. **sic**, *in this fashion*, as follows. — **elata**: the technical word for carrying to the grave.

86. **tulit**: the statement implies (cf. **ex testamento**) that these were the conditions of the will, which is the real fact to be stated though it is not directly set down.

87. **scilicet**, *to see, no doubt*. — **posset**: the so-called indirect question with **si**. — **mortua**: *i.e.* since she never had been able to get away from him while alive, which is stated indirectly in the next line.

88. **cautus adito**: as a kind of conclusion from the preceding, followed by further amplification of the same theme. — **abundes**: *sc.* **opera** supplied from **operae**.

90. **difficilem et morosum**: the common characteristics of old men. Cf. *at sunt morosi et anxii et iracundi et difficiles senes.* Cic. *de*

non etiam sileas; Davus sis comicus, atque
stes capite obstipo, multum similis metuenti.
Obsequio grassare; mone, si increbuit aura,
cautus uti velet carum caput; extrahe turba
oppositis umeris; aurem substringe loquaci.
Importunus amat laudari; donec 'Ohe iam!'
ad caelum manibus sublatis dixerit, urge,
crescentem tumidis infla sermonibus utrem.

Cum te servitio longo curaque levarit,
et certum vigilans, QVARTAE SIT PARTIS VLIXES
audieris HERES: 'Ergo nunc Dama sodalis
nusquam est? Vnde mihi tam fortem tamque fidelem?'

*Sen.* XVIII. 65. Evidently this was thought to be their ordinary character, though Cicero maintains that this is not the fault of age. — **garrulus**: an example of one **qui immoderatus abundat**. — **ultro**, *rather*, *i.e.* instead of pleasing, which he hopes to do, he will fail to please, and will offend the old man besides.

91. **non**: here not different from **ne**, though doubtless the construction is of different origin, coming from the potential use of the subjunctive. Cf. *Ep.* I. 18. 72. — **etiam**, *either*, properly *too*. — **Davus**: a stock name for slaves in the comedy. Cf. *e.g.* Ter. *Andria*.

92. **obstipo**, *humbly bowed*, properly, slanting, bowed and turned to one side. Cf. λοξός, Theognis, 548. — **multum**: apparently colloquial in this sense. Cf. I. 3. 57, where its connection with a participle is more regular.

95. **substringe**, *prick up*, properly, *tie up*.

96. **importunus**, *spoiled* or *exacting*, in so far as he is inconsiderate of the claims of others, and so is troublesome.

96. **ohe iam**: cf. I. 5. 12.

97. **ad caelum**, etc.: properly a gesture of supplication to be delivered from the excess of flattery, impliedly, however, in this case half affected.

98. **crescentem . . . utrem**, *the swelling wind-bag.* — **tumidis**: active, *puffing* (?). Cf. *tumidus Auster*, Virg. *Æn.* III. 357.

100. **certum**: *sharply*, so as to be perfectly sure of your aim. Cf. **certum scire**, etc.

101. **Dama**: cf. v. 18.

102. **fortem**, *noble*. Cf. v. 64, and II. 1. 16, where, however, the conception is somewhat different. The word, expressing courage, spirit, and the stalwart virtues generally, is very widely used to express the highest ideal of a Roman worthy. So **bonus et fortis**, the stock Roman expression for a gentleman. Cf. *Ep.* I. 9. 13; Cic. *Brut.* 2. 6. For the construction, supply **quaeram**, or the like, which is regularly omitted, cf. II. 7. 116.

sparge subinde, et, si paulum potes, illacrimare: est
gaudia prodentem voltum celare. Sepulchrum
permissum arbitrio sine sordibus exstrue; funus
egregie factum laudet vicinia. Si quis
forte coheredum senior male tussiet, huic tu
dic, ex parte tua seu fundi sive domus sit
emptor, gaudentem nummo te addicere. — Sed me
imperiosa trahit Proserpina: vive valeque!

## VI.

Hoc erat in votis: modus agri non ita magnus,
hortus ubi et tecto vicinus iugis aquae fons
et paulum silvae super his foret. Auctius atque
di melius fecere. Bene est. Nil amplius oro,

103. **est,** *'tis well,* properly like ἔξεστιν, *it is allowable, one may* (well).

104. **celare**: *i.e.* with tears.

105. **arbitrio**: cf. II. 3. 86. — **sordibus**: cf. I. 6. 107.

108. **fundi,** *land.* — **domus**: buildings in the city.

109. **emptor,** *disposed to buy.* — **nummo,** *for a song,* or nominal price. Cf. Plaut. *Most.* 115.

110. **imperiosa** (cf. ἐπαινὴ Περσεφόνεια, Hom. *Il.* IX. 457), *all-powerful,* whose **imperia** cannot be disobeyed. To Hecate, identified with Proserpine, was assigned the control of the shades, and to her were addressed the prayers intended to summon them. Cf. I. 8. 33, and *Odys.* XI. 225 (ὤτρυνεν γὰρ ἀγαυὴ Περσεφόνεια). — **vive valeque**: a common form of parting salutation. Cf. *Ep.* I. 6. 67, and *Hospes vive vale,* Inscript. in *Bull. Ist. Arch.* 1872, p. 30.

SATIRE **6**. This Satire combines a cry of the heart against the worries of the city and praises of the delights of country life, with a delicate expression of thanks to Mæcenas for his gift of the Sabine farm, which has enabled Horace to satisfy his craving. The fable of the city and the country mouse ingeniously introduced gracefully repeats the same general theme.

1. **hoc**: referring to the following. For the spirit of the expression of satisfaction, cf. *Od.* II. 18. 14, III. 16. 29; *Ep.* I. 16. 5–16 and I. 18. 104. — **in votis,** *among my prayers.* Cf. *in optatis,* Cic. *ad Fam.* II. 13. 2. — **modus**: *i.e.* a moderate amount. — **ita**: cf. II. 2. 46.

2. **iugis**: either with **aquae** or **fons.** The latter would follow the favorite interlocked order, but cf. *Ep.* I. 15. 16.

3. **super his,** *in addition to this;* in prose it would be accusative. —

Maia nate, nisi ut propria haec mihi munera faxis.
Si neque maiorem feci ratione mala rem,
nec sum facturus vitio culpave minorem;
si veneror stultus nihil horum: 'O si angulus ille
proximus accedat, qui nunc denormat agellum!
O si urnam argenti fors quae mihi monstret, ut illi,
thesauro invento qui mercennarius agrum
illum ipsum mercatus aravit, dives amico
Hercule!' si quod adest gratum iuvat, hac prece te oro:
pingue pecus domino facias et cetera praeter
ingenium, utque soles, custos mihi maximus adsis!

**auctius**: *more generously*, a rare adverb, but in accordance with the meaning of **auctus**, *abundant.*

5. **Maia nate**: Mercury, as the god of gain, cf. II. 3. 68; but cf. also v. 15 with *Od.* II. 17. 29, and II. 7. 13. — **propria**: cf. II. 2. 129, and *Ep.* II. 2. 172. — **faxis**: this use of the perfect for the present seems to be colloquial and archaic, as certainly the use of the short form is.

6. **si**: introducing the protasis of **oro**, v. 13, a common form of supplication in ancient times. Cf. "as we forgive those," etc., *Od.* III. 18. 5; Σμινθεῦ! εἴποτέ τοι χαρίεντ' ἐπὶ νηὸν ἔρεψα, Hom. *Il.* I. 39. — **maiorem**, etc.: cf. I. 4. 108. — **ratione mala**, *any base means* prompted by avarice. This is spoken of in the past because the poet takes the present condition of his estate as the starting point.

7. **sum facturus**, etc.: *i.e.* have no bad habits of luxury (**vitio**) to waste, nor idleness (**culpa**) to neglect, and so lose my property. These are spoken of as to their future results. The whole claims the favor of the god on account of past virtues and present character.

8. **veneror**: *i.e.* pray for in my worship of the gods. Cf. II. 2. 124; and *qui multa deos venerati sunt contra eius salutem*, Cic. *ad Fam.* VI. 7. — **stultus**: *i.e.* as covetous, and so not a *sapiens*, who would have no vain desires. — **nihil horum**, *nothing like this.*

9. **denormat**, *breaks the line of*, a technical word of surveying.

10. **urnam argenti**: the ancients on account of the insecure state of society were often wont to bury their treasure, and at times to lose it. Cf. Plaut. *Aulularia* and *nec vero quemquam senem audivi oblitum quo loco thesaurum obruisset*, Cic. *de Sen.* 21.

11. **qui mercennarius**: a shorthand way of saying *qui agrum, quem mercennarius araverat, mercatus* (and so the owner) *aravit.* This compendious form seems colloquial like so many other expressions in the Satires.

13. **Hercule**: regarded as a giver of gain (πλουτοδότης), especially from hidden treasures. — **gratum**, *my grateful soul*, *i.e.* if I am satisfied and thankful.

14. **pingue**, *heavy* (to render the punning force of the word as applied to **ingenium**), *dull, thick.* — **cetera**, *all the rest.*

15. **ut soles**: cf. *Od.* II. 17. 29, and *Od.* II. 7. 13. Mercury being

Ergo ubi me in montis et in arcem ex urbe removi,
quid prius illustrem saturis Musaque pedestri ?
Nec mala me ambitio perdit nec plumbeus Auster
autumnusque gravis, Libitinae quaestus acerbae.
Matutine pater, seu Iane libentius audis,
unde homines operum primos vitaeque labores
instituunt (sic dis placitum), tu carminis esto

the god of eloquence is regarded by Horace as his tutelary divinity.

16. **ergo**: *i.e.* since I am thus contented and thankful. — **arcem**, *my stronghold*, with a reference at once to the heights and the secure retreat from cares. Cf. *Ep.* I. 10. 8.

17. **prius**, *rather*, *i.e.* than the pleasures of my country home (cf. note to **ergo**, v. 16). — **saturis**: *i.e.* in a composition which reflects the whole life of the author, and is an indiscriminate collection of thoughts, facts, and feelings (cf. II. 1. 30), and so may well begin with what is nearest the poet's heart. — **pedestris**: cf. *Ep.* II. 1. 250.

18. **mala ambitio**, etc.: *i.e.* in this retreat I secure at the same time health of mind and of body.— **plumbeus**, *leaden*, as weighing down the body, making one feel lifeless and inert. — **Auster**: *i.e.* the sirocco, an especially oppressive and deadening wind.

19. **gravis**, *fatal*, inducing fevers. — **Libitinae**: in the temple of Venus Libitina were found the undertakers and all the paraphernalia of interment. The connection of this temple with death was probably merely accidental, but in course of time the name of the goddess came to be associated with funerals. Cf. *Od.* III. 30. 7. — **quaestus**: a fee was paid at the registration of burials, and hence the autumn as causing death was a gain to the goddess. Trans. *profitable to.* The poet means to say that this country abode is salutary for soul and body too.

20. **matutine pater**, *god of the morning*, apparently a half humorous invocation used merely to express the morning itself. — **Iane**: following the custom of the ancients in addressing their gods (cf. *Carm. Saec.* 14 *seq.*, *Ilithyia . . . Sive tu Lucina probas vocari, Seu Genitalis*) he identifies his supposed divinity with Janus, the god of beginnings generally. The vocative is used as the actual form that the god would hear. Cf. Ep. I. 7. 38. — **audis**, *art called*, perhaps originally an imitation of ἀκούειν but afterwards thoroughly Latinized (cf. *Ep.* I. 7. 38, and *erat surdaster M. Crassus, sed aliud molestius quod male audiebat*, Cic. *Tusc.* V. 40).

21. **unde . . . instituunt** (= **a quo incipiunt**), *with whom* (as the god invoked) *men begin*, etc. — **operum vitaeque**: a case of what is called hendiadys, where a particular idea is mentioned first, and a general one including the first is added. But the same form is also used in English, and really has no claim to be called a figure at all. — **operum** refers to the thing to be done, **labores** to the effort to do it.

22. **sic dis**, etc.: *i.e.* in the arrangement of the world this god has this particular function of presiding over beginnings (cf. Januarius, and the temple of Janus in relation to war).

principium. Romae sponsorem me rapis. 'Heia,
ne prior officio quisquam respondeat, urge!'
Sive Aquilo radit terras seu bruma nivalem
interiore diem gyro trahit, ire necesse est.
Postmodo quod mi obsit clare certumque locuto,
luctandum in turba et facienda iniuria tardis.
'Quid vis, insane, et quas res agis?' improbus urget
iratis precibus; 'tu pulses omne quod obstat,
ad Maecenatem memori si mente recurras?'
Hoc iuvat et melli est, non mentiar. At simul atras

23. **Romae**: as opposed to the undisturbed quiet of country life. — **sponsorem**, *as a bondsman*. In the Roman legal proceedings there were many cases in which bail was necessary, so that it seems to have been a common friendly *officium* to act as security. Cf. I. 1. 11 and *Ep.* II. 2. 67. The trials began about nine (cf. I. 9. 35); and probably the preliminary proceedings (**in iùre**) were earlier. — **Heia**, etc.: the poet's own reflection is put into the mouth of the god.

24. **prior**, *before you*. — **officio**: cf. note to v. 23, and **officiosus**, II. 5. 48, *Ep.* I. 7. 8.

24. **respondeat**: answer to the call of duty, *i.e. perform* the duty itself.

25. **Aquilo**, etc.: notwithstanding the raw wind or freezing cold, the *Tramontana*. — **radit**, *rasps*.

26. **interiore**: *i.e.* at the winter solstice, when the short day seems to make a circle of small diameter, as the sun does in the heaven. — **trahit**: as if the day came unwillingly to an end.

27. **postmodo**: with **obsit**. — **obsit**, *cause loss*, when by and by he has to pay the amount of his surety. — **clare**: *i.e.* without shrinking. — **certum**: in the exact form prescribed, as otherwise the act would be invalid.

28. **luctandum**, etc.: *i.e.* he has at once to hurry away to the next duty, his morning call (**salutatio**) on Mæcenas. — **facienda**, etc.: indicating his hurry in a more lively way by its effects.

29. **quid vis**, etc.: the remonstrance of the persons he runs against. — **improbus**, *impudently*.

30. **precibus**, *imprecations*. — **pulses**, *do you think you must knock down*. Subjunctive of indignant question.

31. **ad Maecenatem**, etc.: implying that his relation to Mæcenas is known and envied. — **memori mente**, *thinking of nothing but him*. There seems to be an implied taunt.

32. **melli est**, *is sweet as honey to me*. — **non mentiar**, *I will not deny*, *i.e.* to tell the truth, though the statement is contrary to my argument. The words contain also of course a compliment to Mæcenas. — **at**: *i.e.* but when I arrive it is no better, as it might be, if it were only on the way that he was subject to these annoyances, which after all have their compensations as he has just said. — **atras**: cf. I. 8. 10.

ventum est Esquilias, aliena negotia centum
per caput et circa saliunt latus. 'Ante secundam
Roscius orabat sibi adesses ad Puteal cras.'
'De re communi scribae magna atque nova te
orabant hodie meminisses, Quinte, reverti.'
'Imprimat his cura Maecenas signa tabellis.'
Dixeris, 'Experiar:' 'Si vis, potes,' addit et instat.

Septimus octavo propior iam fugerit annus,
ex quo Maecenas me coepit habere suorum
in numero; dumtaxat ad hoc, quem tollere raeda
vellet iter faciens, et cui concredere nugas
hoc genus: 'Hora quota est?' — 'Thraex est Gallina Syro par?' —

33. **Esquilias**: on the Esquiline was Mæcenas's house and a fine garden. — **negotia**, *affairs*.

34. **saliunt**, *assail;* the figure is too strong to be literally rendered, though it was originally in our English word as well. — **ante**, etc.: the words of a messenger of Roscius who had some claim or other upon the poet. — **ante secundam**: *i.e.* in the first twelfth of the day.

35. **orabat**: like the epistolary imperfect, which is written with reference to the time of the reading. Very likely the messages are conceived as written and quoted verbatim. — **Puteal**: the Puteal Libonis, a kind of well curb in the Forum (cf. *Ep.* I. 19. 8) around a place once struck by lightning. As it was near the tribunal of the prætor, the matter was probably a judicial one in which Horace would appear as *advocatus*. Cf. I. 9. 38.

36. **de re communi**, etc., *a new matter of great importance to our body*. Horace had once been a regular clerk of the treasury. The expressions **aliena negotia, reverti**, and **re communi** seem to indicate that he was a clerk still, but only a nominal one. Cf. the case of Sarmentus, I. 5. 66.

37. **meminisses**, *you will not forget*. — **Quinte**, *friend Horace* (cf. II. 5. 32), as the prænomen indicates intimacy. — **reverti**, *come in*, probably to the office of the quæstors, which he would not always do if he was a mere nominal clerk.

38. **imprimat**, etc.: the words of some one who wished to get a favor from Mæcenas through Horace's influence.

39. **dixeris**, *if you* (*i.e.* Horace) *say;* hortatory subjunctive. — **si vis**, etc.: this statement Horace ingeniously uses as a transition to his relations with Mæcenas.

40. **septimus**, etc.: this would give as the date of the Satire B.C. 31, as that of his introduction was about B.C. 38. Cf. **Dacis**, v. 53.

42. **dumtaxat ad hoc**, *merely to this extent; i.e.* not in a close intimacy as a confidential friend.

43. **nugas**: *i.e.* only the merest trifles of conversation.

44. **hoc genus**, *of this sort*, prop-

'Matutina parum cautos iam frigora mordent;'—
et quae rimosa bene deponuntur in aure.
Per totum hoc tempus subiectior in diem et horam
invidiae noster. Ludos spectaverat una,
luserat in Campo: 'Fortunae filius!' omnes.
Frigidus a Rostris manat per compita rumor:
quicumque obvius est, me consulit: 'O bone (nam te
scire, deos quoniam propius contingis, oportet),
numquid de Dacis audisti?' 'Nil equidem.' 'Vt tu

erly in apposition with **nugas.** — **Threax,** *the Thracian, i.e.* a gladiator in Thracian arms, a round shield and curved sword. The Romans were fond of fights in which gladiators of different and outlandish arms were matched against each other, and they talked about their favorites much as our sporting men talk about oarsmen and ball-players. — **Gallina,** *the Chicken,* a nickname. — **Syro**: a gladiator's name, probably of a *mirmillo* (the kind that usually fought against the **Thraeces,** cf. Cic. *Phil.* III. 12, Suet. *Dom.* 10) armed in the Gallic fashion, with a large, strong shield, and heavy armor.

45. **matutina,** etc.: mere remarks about the weather.

46. **rimosa, deponuntur**: the figure of a deposit is not uncommon in reference to secrets, cf. *Od.* I. 27. 18; and *mihi quod credideris sumes ubi posiveris,* Pl. *Trin.* 145. Cf. also Ter. *Eun.* 105, *plenus rimarum sum hac atque illac perfluo.* The whole means that Horace was only trusted with things that would do no harm if betrayed, though people outside thought otherwise, as appears from the following.

48. **noster,** *our friend,* Horace. — **una**: *i.e.* with Mæcenas.

49. **omnes**: *sc.* **inquiunt.**

50. **frigidus,** *chilling,* as being bad news. — **a Rostris**: *i.e.* from the rostra, where news would be announced to the crowd in the Forum; or if not publicly announced first made known there. — **per compita,** *by the street corners,* where the next largest assemblies of men would be collected.

51. **quicumque,** etc.: further explaining the **invidia,** but at the same time showing that the real state of the case was different from that supposed by the envious crowd. — **O bone,** *my good friend,* but apparently with a touch of depreciation.

52. **deos**: trans. literally, but referring to the leading statesman with whom Horace was supposed to be in contact from his intimacy with Mæcenas.

53. **num quid,** etc.: *you haven't,* etc., *have you?* The question formally but not really expects a negative answer, as often the corresponding form in other languages. — **Dacis**: in B.C. 31, after the battle of Actium, an invasion of Italy was feared from the Dacians who had been on the side of Antony (cf. v. 41). — **nil equidem,** *not a thing.* — **ut tu,** etc., *what a wag,* etc., the answer of the incredulous interlocutor.

semper eris derisor!' 'At omnes di exagitent me,
si quicquam.' 'Quid, militibus promissa Triquetra
praedia Caesar, an est Itala tellure daturus?'
Iurantem me scire nihil mirantur, ut unum
scilicet egregii mortalem altique silenti.

Perditur haec inter misero lux non sine votis:
O rus, quando ego te aspiciam? quandoque licebit
nunc veterum libris, nunc somno et inertibus horis
ducere sollicitae iucunda oblivia vitae?
O quando faba Pythagorae cognata simulque
uncta satis pingui ponentur holuscula lardo?
O noctes cenaeque deum! quibus ipse meique
ante larem proprium vescor vernasque procacis
pasco libatis dapibus. Prout cuique libido est,
siccat inaequalis calices conviva, solutus

54. **at omnes**, etc.: Horace's asseveration in reply.

55. **quid**, etc.: another similar inquiry. — **promissa**, etc.: *i.e.* the allotments of land to the veterans, which had been promised by Augustus.

57. **unum**: not merely *a*, but *the one* of all men.

59. **perditur**: instead of **perit**, which is the usual substitute for the passive.— **haec**: this envy and worry which are unavoidable in the city.

61. **veterum**: cf. II. 3. 11. — **libris**: abl. of means with **ducere**.

63. **faba**, etc.: the simple viands of the country. — **Pythagorae**: beans were forbidden as food by Pythagoras, because, as was said by some, they contain the souls of the dead. Hence Horace jocosely calls them the kinsfolk of that philosopher. — **simulque**, *and with them*.

64. **satis**, *well* (with **uncta**). — **holuscula**, *humble greens*.

65. **deum**: *i.e.* as enjoyable as theirs. — **mei**: *i.e.* friends.

66. **ante larem**: *i.e.* the hearth, which, according to the simple custom of the early Romans, stood at the back of the atrium, where also was the place for the household god, the *lar familiaris*. Cf. *Epod.* 2. 66; Serv. to *Æn.* I. 730. — **vernas**, *household servants;* this also points to the simple habits of early times retained in country life, according to which the slaves also ate in the atrium. — **procacis**, *saucy*, a characteristic of the slaves brought up in the house along with the children.

67. **libatis dapibus**: the remnant of the feast. Properly the words refer to a rich feast, of which part was offered to the gods (**libare**). — **libido**, *fancy*.

68. **inaequalis**: not (as was usual at formal dinners) prescribed by regulation (**legibus**) as to the

legibus insanis, seu quis capit acria fortis
pocula, seu modicis uvescit laetius. Ergo
sermo oritur, non de villis domibusve alienis,
nec male necne Lepos saltet; sed quod magis ad nos
pertinet et nescire malum est agitamus: utrumne
divitiis homines an sint virtute beati;
quidve ad amicitias, usus rectumne, trahat nos;
et quae sit natura boni, summumque quid eius.

Cervius haec inter vicinus garrit anilis
ex re fabellas. Si quis nam laudat Arelli
sollicitas ignarus opes, sic incipit: 'Olim

amount of wine and water. Cf. II. 2. 123.

69. **insanis,** *absurd, crazy,* as being irrational, merely freaks of fashion. — **capit**: *i.e.* is able to stand. — **acria,** *strong.*

70. **laetius,** etc., *delights rather to,* etc. — **ergo**: *i.e.* in accordance with the frugal character of the meal. Cf. II. 2. 4 *seq.*

71. **alienis**: which would indicate envy or rivalry in display, whereas their conversation is directed to their own ethical improvement.

72. **Lepos** (a pantomime dancer): as a sample of trivial themes.

73. **utrumne**: cf. II. 3. 295 with note.

74. **divitiis,** etc.: one of the favorite ethical questions of the ancients was whether men could be perfectly happy (**beatissimi**) through virtue alone, the Stoic school holding that it was possible, against the Peripatetics. Cf. Cic. *Tusc. Disp.* V. *passim.*

75. **usus rectumne,** *advantage* (cf. I. 1. 73), or *virtue* (*honestum,* τὸ πρέπον, cf. I. 1. 107), the former being the Epicurean, and the latter the Stoic view. — **trahat**: *i.e.* the origin of friendship.

76. **boni,** *the good;* the technical name for that which being in itself desirable may be used as the criterion of human action, answering in ancient philosophy to "the chief end of man." — **summum eius**: the *summum bonum,* called also *finis bonorum,* and *extremum bonum,* the ultimate foundation of all ethical systems. Cf. Cicero *de Finibus, passim,* which is a treatise on that subject.

77. **Cervius**: doubtless a neighbor (cf. **mei,** v. 65) dining with the poet. — **haec inter,** *in the talk.* — **garrit,** *tells in lively strain.* — **anilis fabellas,** *nursery tales,* like "old wives' fables," but without the contempt implied in that phrase.

78. **ex re,** *in point,* arising from the subject, and illustrating it. — **Arelli**: a rich neighbor, — so that after all, human nature was too much for them, and they did talk "de villis domibusve alienis."

79. **sollicitas,** *care-haunted.* — **ignarus,** *foolishly,* not knowing the true nature of happiness. — **olim,** *once upon a time.*

rusticus urbanum murem mus paupere fertur
accepisse cavo, veterem vetus hospes amicum,
asper et attentus quaesitis, ut tamen artum
solveret hospitiis animum. Quid multa? neque ille
sepositi ciceris nec longae invidit avenae,
aridum et ore ferens acinum semesaque lardi
frusta dedit, cupiens varia fastidia cena
vincere tangentis male singula dente superbo;
cum pater ipse domus palea porrectus in horna
esset ador loliumque, dapis meliora relinquens.
Tandem urbanus ad hunc: 'Quid te iuvat,' inquit, 'amice,
praerupti nemoris patientem vivere dorso?
Vis tu homines urbemque feris praeponere silvis?
Carpe viam, mihi crede, comes, terrestria quando
mortalis animas vivunt sortita, neque ulla est
aut magno aut parvo leti fuga: quo, bone, circa,
dum licet, in rebus iucundis vive beatus,
vive memor quam sis aevi brevis.' Haec ubi dicta
agrestem pepulere, domo levis exsilit; inde

81. **veterem vetus**: *two old friends, guest and host.* Notice the general Epic flavor of the story.

82. **asper**, *ascetic*, not self-indulgent. — **ut**: *i.e.* **talis** or **ita ut**. — **artum**, *careful*, properly not allowed to expand in genial relaxation.

83. **quid multa**: a common form of transition, like "to make a long story short."

84. **ciceris**: genitive after **invidit**, apparently an imitation of the Greek; for the usual construction, see I. 6. 50.

86. **fastidia**, *want of appetite*, disdaining common food. The viands are what the host regards as delicacies.

87. **male**, *hardly*. — **superbo**, *disdainful*.

88. **pater domus**: a variation on **paterfamilias**.

91. **patientem**, *contented*, patient of the privations which your life brings with it. — **dorso**, etc.: the rocky wooded ridge.

92. **vis**, an informal exhortation, like our *will you?* or *won't you?*

93. **mihi crede**, *take my advice*, a common form of encouragement and exhortation. — **terrestria**, etc.: *i.e.* since life is so short, enjoy it while it lasts.

94. **sortita**, *with the destiny of;* lit. having got by lot.

95. **quo . . . circa**: separated for the sake of the metre.

ambo propositum peragunt iter, urbis aventes
moenia nocturni subrepere. Iamque tenebat
nox medium caeli spatium, cum ponit uterque
in locuplete domo vestigia, rubro ubi cocco
tincta super lectos canderet vestis eburnos,
multaque de magna superessent fercula cena,
quae procul exstructis inerant hesterna canistris.
Ergo, ubi purpurea porrectum in veste locavit
agrestem, veluti succinctus cursitat hospes
continuatque dapes, nec non verniliter ipsis
fungitur officiis, praelambens omne quod affert.
Ille cubans gaudet mutata sorte bonisque
rebus agit laetum convivam, cum subito ingens
valvarum strepitus lectis excussit utrumque.
Currere per totum pavidi conclave, magisque
exanimes trepidare, simul domus alta Molossis
personuit canibus. Tum rusticus 'Haud mihi vita
est opus hac,' ait, 'et valeas; me silva cavusque
tutus ab insidiis tenui solabitur ervo.'

98. **levis**: *i.e.* gladly.

104. **fercula**, *courses;* properly the trays on which the courses were served at a Roman banquet.

105. **procul**, *at one side*, not necessarily at a distance; derived from **pro**, cf. **Proculus** and **proximus**. — **exstructis**, *well filled, heaped high*, with the plenteous food.

107. **succinctus**, *a waiter;* cf. II. 8. 10.

108. **verniliter**, *like a pampered house-servant*, tasting everything with the greed of that class. — **ipsis**: *i.e.* he not only bustles about as busy as a waiter, which he might do even as a host, but he also performs the servile offices like a slave and with the greedy taste of one as well.

111. **agit**, *plays the part of.*

112. **valvarum**, etc.: *i.e.* when the work of the day begins. — **Molossis**: cf. Virg. *Georg.* III. 405.

114. **simul**: *i.e.* **simul ac**.

115. **haud mihi est opus**, *I have no occasion for*, with the same spirit as in "no, I thank you."

117. **ervo**: abl. of means. The meaning of course is that the security of his home even with his humble fare will console him for the loss of the dainties which it does not afford.

## VII.

*Davus.* Iamdudum ausculto, et cupiens tibi dicere servus
pauca, reformido. *Horat.* Davusne? *D.* Ita, Davus, amicum
mancipium domino et frugi, quod sit satis, hoc est,
ut vitale putes. *H.* Age, libertate Decembri,
quando ita maiores voluerunt, utere; narra.

*D.* Pars hominum vitiis gaudet constanter et urget
propositum; pars multa natat, modo recta capessens,
interdum pravis obnoxia. Saepe notatus
cum tribus anellis, modo laeva Priscus inani,
vixit inaequalis, clavum ut mutaret in horas,

SATIRE 7. Horace here makes sport of the Stoic paradox, "*Solum sapientem esse liberum et omnem stultum servum*" (cf. I. 3 and II. 3). In this, however, as in the other cases, the poet uses the truth underlying the paradox to ridicule the follies of mankind, including himself. The argument is put into the mouth of his slave, who represents himself as having got his teachings through the doorkeeper of the Stoic preacher, Crispinus (cf. I. 1. 120). To give probability to the license of the slave, he sets the scene at the Saturnalia, during which, in memory of the Golden Age, the equality of all men was in a manner recognized.

1. **ausculto**, etc.: as the master is busy, apparently writing or thinking, he does not see the slave, who, after listening by the door to see whether his master is engaged with anybody, finally ventures to make his presence known. The master still does not look up, but recognizes him by his voice.

2. **Davusne**, *is it you, Davus?* For the name, cf. II. 5. 91.

3. **frugi**, *an honest fellow* (cf. II. 5. 77), referring to the virtues of industry, sobriety, and the like.

4. **ut vitale**, etc., *not too good to live;* cf. "the good die young," a familiar notion with the ancients (cf. Plaut. *Bacch.* 816; Ov. *Am.* II. 6. 39). — **libertate Decembri**: *i.e.* of the Saturnalia.

6. **pars**, etc.: the slave in Horace's regular manner approaches the subject gradually (cf. v. 21), beginning with a philosophical division of the vicious into those who follow vice with vigor, and those who weakly show their feebleness of purpose even in vicious courses.

7. **natat**, *drift.*

8. **notatus**, *conspicuous*, but with a shade of blame in it, on account of the display of luxury and effeminacy.

9. **Priscus**: a man of senatorial rank, an example of this inconsistency, and want of constant purpose.

10. **inaequalis**: cf. I. 3. 9. — **clavum mutaret**: *i.e.* from broad to narrow, now appearing with pride as a senator, now as a simple *eques.*

aedibus ex magnis subito se conderet, unde
mundior exiret vix libertinus honeste;
iam moechus Romae, iam mallet doctus Athenis
vivere, Vertumnis quotquot sunt natus iniquis.
Scurra Volanerius, postquam illi iusta cheragra
contudit articulos, qui pro se tolleret atque
mitteret in phimum talos, mercede diurna
conductum pavit; quanto constantior isdem
in vitiis, tanto levius miser ac prior illo,
qui iam contento, iam laxo fune laborat.
*H.* Non dices hodie quorsum haec tam putida tendant,
furcifer? *D.* Ad te, inquam. *H.* Quo pacto, pessime?
*D.* Laudas
fortunam et mores antiquae plebis, et idem,
si quis ad illa deus subito te agat, usque recuses,

12. **mundior,** *respectable; i.e.* of the better class. — **honeste,** *with decency.*

13. **doctus,** *a philosopher.*

14. **Vertumnis**: there was properly only one god of this name, the god of the changing seasons. The poet, however, jocosely multiplies the number, and represents them as having given him at his birth all their fickleness to his injury.

15. **Volanerius**: an example of persistence. — **iusta,** *well earned,* by excesses at the table, which he frequented as *scurra,* or professional diner-out.

16. **contudit**: *i.e.* so that he could no longer do the service for himself. — **se**: the reflexive allowed because the clause is a purpose of the man.

17. **talos,** *the knuckle-bones,* used by the ancients as well as dice for gaming.

18. **conductum,** etc.: indicating his devotion to the game. — **pavit,** *kept.*

19. **levius miser**: the slave makes the consistently vicious man the better off of the two.

20. **contento,** etc.: the figure probably derived from leading an animal, whose attempts to get free only trouble it the more.

21. **hodie**: not in the literal sense, but as in the comedy in its weakest use, *now.* — **quorsum . . . tendunt,** *what . . . is driving at,* the regular expression (often with **tendere** omitted) for asking the meaning of an argument. — **putida,** *silly stuff.*

22. **ad te,** *at you,* the slave taking the **quorsum** in a different sense, and so bringing the argument home in Horace's usual manner, as he proceeds to explain in the next verse. — **laudas**: cf. II. 6. 60. It is characteristic of Horace that this reproach should be selected, which is in the main true (cf. *Ep.* I. 8. 12).

23. **fortunam,** *condition,* in regard to their mode of life.

24. **usque,** "*every time.*"

aut quia non sentis, quod clamas, rectius esse,
aut quia non firmus rectum defendis, et haeres
nequiquam caeno cupiens evellere plantam.
Romae rus optas; absentem rusticus urbem
tollis ad astra levis. Si nusquam es forte vocatus
ad cenam, laudas securum holus, ac, velut usquam
vinctus eas, ita te felicem dicis amasque
quod nusquam tibi sit potandum. Iusserit ad se
Maecenas serum sub lumina prima venire
convivam: 'Nemon' oleum fert ocius? Ecquis
audit?' cum magno blateras clamore fugisque.
Mulvius et scurrae, tibi non referenda precati,
discedunt. 'Etenim fateor me,' dixerit ille,
'duci ventre levem, nasum nidore supinor,
imbecillus, iners, si quid vis, adde, popino.
Tu, cum sis quod ego et fortassis nequior, ultro
insectere velut melior, verbisque decoris

25. **sentis**, *really think; i.e.* it is pure affectation on Horace's part.

26. **firmus**, etc.: *i.e.* or else it is on account of infirmity of purpose, in which case Horace is in the position of those referred to in v. 7.

30. **securum**, *quiet*, as free from the cares and worries of intercourse with the great. Cf. **sollicitae opes**, II. 6. 79. — **velut (ita)**, *just as if.* — **usquam**, *anywhere*, used on account of the negative implied. Equivalent to "as if you were obliged to go, like a slave to the country, in case you were invited."

31. **ita**, referring to **velut**. — **amas**, *hug yourself* (cf. I. 2. 54).

32. **iusserit**: hortatory subjunctive, expressing a condition.

33. **serum**, etc.: *i.e.* he is only invited at the last moment, when it is already getting dark.

34. **oleum**: for the lantern to conduct him. — **fert**: the ordinary colloquial use of present for future as in the comedy.

35. **fugis**: *are off like a shot.*

36. **Mulvius et scurrae**: guests who hoped to dine with Horace; hence their wrath. — **non referenda**, *unmentionable things.*

37. **etenim**: explaining his disappointment. — **dixerit**, *he might say*, if you asked him. — **ille**: Mulvius, who makes no pretensions to be a philosopher.

38. **levem**, *weakly.* — **nasum**, etc., *I enjoy the delightful fragrance*, *i.e.* of well-cooked viands.

39. **si quid vis**, *if you like.*

40. **ultro**, *arrogantly*, having no excuse for so doing, as a better man might have; referring to Horace's habit of hitting such persons.

41. **insectere**: question of indignation. — **decoris**, *specious; i.e.* his duty to Mæcenas and the like.

obvolvas vitium?' Quid, si me stultior ipso
quingentis empto drachmis deprenderis? Aufer
me voltu terrere; manum stomachumque teneto,
dum quae Crispini docuit me ianitor edo.

Te coniunx aliena capit, meretricula Davum.
Peccat uter nostrum cruce dignius? Acris ubi me
natura intendit, sub clara nuda lucerna
quaecumque excepit turgentis verbera caudae,
clunibus aut agitavit equum lasciva supinum,
dimittet neque famosum neque sollicitum ne
ditior aut formae melioris meiat eodem.
Tu cum proiectis insignibus, anulo equestri
Romanoque habitu, prodis ex iudice Dama
turpis, odoratum caput obscurante lacerna,
non es quod simulas? Metuens induceris, atque
altercante libidinibus tremis ossa pavore.

42. **quid si**, etc.: the slave takes up the reproach of Mulvius. — **me**, etc.: the qualities here mentioned were especially ascribed to slaves. Cf. vv. 102, 109; II. 6. 109; I. 3. 81.

43. **quingentis drachmis**: *i.e.* five hundred denarii, less than $100.00, a low price for a slave of any worth. — **deprenderis**: not merely found to be, but *found out to be*, or detected in being, as if caught in his pretence of virtue. — **aufer**, *don't try.* Horace represents himself as angered by the reproach, thus indicating that the blow has struck home. Whereupon the slave replies, as it were, "Oh, you needn't try to frighten me with your frowns; wait till I show you why."

44. **terrere**: with **aufer**, as a complementary infinitive, in accordance with Horace's fondness for the infinitive with any word whose meaning is akin to the verbs which take that construction regularly. The charges are of course overdrawn, and Horace does not have reference to himself alone, but he includes himself along with others. Cf. v. 111. and *Ep.* I. 1. 97, etc.

53. **tu**: referring to any respectable person, not necessarily Horace, of whom we do not know that he was an *eques.* Still his military tribuneship makes it possible.

54. **Romano**, etc.: *i.e.* the toga. — **ex iudice**, etc.: *i.e.* you change your station from an *eques* to a slave, and in fact are what you pretend to be, which is in accordance with the Stoic dogma, *omnem stultum esse servum.*

55. **lacerna**: a coarse, rough cloak, often with a capuchin or hood, as is intimated here.

57. **libidinibus**: dative after verbs of contending, as in Greek.

Quid refert, uri virgis ferroque necari
auctoratus eas, an turpi clausus in arca,
quo te demisit peccati conscia erilis,
contractum genibus tangas caput? Estne marito
matronae peccantis in ambo iusta potestas?
In corruptorem vel iustior. Illa tamen se
non habitu mutatve loco peccatve superne,
cum te formidet mulier neque credat amanti.
Ibis sub furcam prudens, dominoque furenti
committes rem omnem et vitam et cum corpore famam.
Evasti: credo metues doctusque cavebis:
quaeres quando iterum paveas, iterumque perire
possis, o totiens servus! Quae belua ruptis,
cum semel effugit, reddit se prava catenis?
'Non sum moechus,' ais. Neque ego, hercule, fur, ubi vasa
praetereo sapiens argentea. Tolle periclum,
iam vaga prosiliet frenis natura remotis.
Tune mihi dominus, rerum imperiis hominumque

59. **auctoratus**, *bound;* the technical expression for the contract of one who sold himself as a gladiator. Cf. *illius turpissimi auctoramenti verba sunt: uri vinciri ferroque necari*. Sen. *Ep.* 37. Of course another proof that such a man is a slave.

60. **conscia**: cf. I. 2. 130.

61. **contractum**, etc.: cf. Falstaff in the buck-basket, *Merry Wives of Windsor*. — **estne marito**, *hasn't the husband*. Therefore the gallant is a slave.

63. **illa**, etc.: she is the less guilty one of the two.

64. **mutat**, etc.: cf. vv. 53–55. — **loco**, *in position*.

65. **cum**, etc.: the reason why she is an unwilling partner.

66. **sub furcam**: a common punishment of slaves. Cf. **furcifer**, v. 22.

68. **evasti** (old and colloquial form for **evasisti**), *you have got off*, *i.e.* we will suppose so. — **credo**: ironical, with the following.

69. **quaeres**, etc.: *i.e.* instead of that, you will only look for another opportunity to be a slave.

72. **non sum**, etc.: *i.e.* that is not my character; this argument does not apply to me. The answer is, "you want to be, only you don't dare," and this according to the Stoic doctrine was just as bad. Cf. *Ep.* I. 16. 53.

74. **vaga**, *and run wild*.

75. **imperiis**, *to the dictates* (ablative).

tot tantisque minor, quem ter vindicta quaterque
imposita haud umquam misera formidine privet?
Adde super, dictis quod non levius valeat: nam,
sive vicarius est qui servo paret, uti mos
vester ait, seu conservus, tibi quid sum ego? Nempe
tu, mihi qui imperitas, alii servis miser, atque
duceris, ut nervis alienis mobile lignum.

Quisnam igitur liber? Sapiens, sibi qui imperiosus,
quem neque pauperies, neque mors, neque vincula terrent,
responsare cupidinibus, contemnere honores
fortis, et in se ipso totus, teres, atque rotundus,
externi ne quid valeat per leve morari,
in quem manca ruit semper fortuna. Potesne
ex his ut proprium quid noscere? Quinque talenta

76. **minor,** *subject.* Cf. *Od.* I. 12. 57. — **vindicta**: in the process of manumission *per vindictam*, a formal claimant asserted a right to the slave by striking him with a rod; the master abandoned his claim, and the prætor then declared him free. In the case of a slave to passion, such a process would be tried in vain; hence how much more a slave is he.

78. **super**: cf. *Ep.* II. 2. 33.

79. **vicarius**: a slave bought by another out of his *peculium* to take his place.

80. **tibi,** etc.: *i.e.* I am only a *vicarius* or *conservus*, and yet you pretend to be my master.

81. **alii,** *i.e.* to your passions.

82. **alienis,** *in the hands of another.* — **mobile lignum,** *like a dancing puppet.* Such automata were very familiar to the ancients.

83. **quisnam,** etc.: the argument follows the ordinary Stoic form. Cf. II. 3. 158; Cic. *Parad.* V. 1. 34, and I. 1. 19. — **sapiens**: of course in the technical sense *the sage*, the ideal perfect man of the Stoics. — **sibi imperiosus**: *i.e.* over whom no one but himself has an *imperium*.

84. **pauperies,** etc.: these evils being mere accidents independent of virtue, the *solum bonum*, of course have no effect on the truly wise man.

85. **responsare,** *defy*, depending on **fortis.**

86. **totus,** etc.: *i.e.* independent of all external influence; a familiar idea with the Stoics. Cf. Cic. *Parad.* II.; *Tusc. Disp.* V. 12. 36. — **teres atque rotundus,** etc.: the figure is of a smooth cylinder or globe, on which nothing can gain a foothold, as it offers no place of lodgement, as it were, for external accidents.

88. **manca,** *powerless*, crippled so as to do him no harm.

89. **quinque,** etc.: Davus answers his own question in the nega-

poscit te mulier, vexat foribusque repulsum
perfundit gelida, rursus vocat: eripe turpi
colla iugo. 'Liber, liber sum,' dic age! Non quis;
urget enim dominus mentem non lenis, et acris
subiectat lasso stimulos, versatque negantem.
Vel cum Pausiaca torpes, insane, tabella,
qui peccas minus atque ego, cum Fulvi Rutubaeque
aut Pacideiani contento poplite miror
proelia rubrica picta aut carbone, velut si
re vera pugnent, feriant, vitentque moventes
arma viri? Nequam et cessator Davus; at ipse
subtilis veterum iudex et callidus audis.
Nil ego, si ducor libo fumante: tibi ingens

tive by showing that Horace is the slave of passion. The point is in **rursus vocat**, wherein the lover is assumed to be so vexed with his mistress as to desire to break off the connection, but is not sufficiently master of himself to assert his freedom when she summons him again.

94. **subiectat**, etc., *plies the spur; i.e.* like spurs. — **versat**: the same figure of a restive horse.

95. **Pausiaca**, *of Pausias*, a painter of Sicyon, remarkable for his skill in foreshortening. There was a famous painting of his in the portico of Pompey. See Plin. *N. H.* XXXV. 123 *seq.* — **torpes**, *stand dazed before*, indicating a craze for painting (cf. *Ep.* I. 6. 14, and **stupet**, *Sat.* I. 4. 28). The point of the reproach is that such a passion is regarded by the Stoics as inconsistent with the serious purpose of the Sage (cf. Cic. *Parad.* 5. 2). — **tabella**, *a bit of a picture*, with depreciation. Cf. the vivid description in v. 99.

96. **peccas**: *i.e.* when Davus stops to look at the advertisements of gladiatorial shows (cf. circus posters) he is regarded (see v. 100) as a worthless loiterer (cf. the modern errand boy), of course a slavish vice; why should not then Horace's admiration in a similar case be regarded as a slavish fault. — **Fulvi**, etc.: gladiators.

97. **contento**, etc., *standing on tiptoe*, as he looks at the pictures.

98. **rubrica**: such posters were drawn on the walls. Some are found in Pompeii, scratched in the plaster (cf. Plin. *N. H.* XXXV. 52).

99. **vitent**, *parry*, though the corresponding process with the ancients was one of dodging (cf. **eludere**).

100. **Davus**, *sc.* **audit**, from **audis**, v. 101.

101. **veterum**, *the old masters.* — **callidus**, *a connoisseur.* — **audis**, cf. II. 6. 20.

102. **nil**: *i.e.* **nequam**, *a good-for-nothing*, referring to the slavery of the appetite. — **libo**: such dainties were apparently for sale in full view on the street, as at chestnut stands or fruit stalls. — **tibi ingens**, etc.: *i.e.* "are not you equally greedy?"

virtus atque animus cenis responsat opimis?
Obsequium ventris mihi perniciosius est cur?
Tergo plector enim. Qui tu impunitior illa,
quae parvo sumi nequeunt, obsonia captas?
Nempe inamarescunt epulae sine fine petitae,
illusique pedes vitiosum ferre recusant
corpus. An hic peccat, sub noctem qui puer uvam
furtiva mutat strigili; qui praedia vendit,
nil servile, gulae parens, habet? Adde, quod idem
non horam tecum esse potes, non otia recte
ponere, teque ipsum vitas, fugitivus et erro,
iam vino quaerens, iam somno fallere curam:
frustra: nam comes atra premit sequiturque fugacem.

*H.* Vnde mihi lapidem? *D.* Quorsum est opus?
*H.* Vnde sagittas?
*D.* Aut insanit homo, aut versus facit. *H.* Ocius hinc te
ni rapis, accedes opera agro nona Sabino!

104. **perniciosius est cur**: *i.e.* how, in fact, do I suffer for it more than you?

105. **enim**, *to be sure*; cf. **quid enim**, note to I. 1. 7.

107. **nempe**, *why!*

108. **illusi**, *failing you*; properly, being deceived themselves as to their powers. — **vitiosum**, *unhealthy*, from eating too much.

109. **qui**, etc.: another servile vice, where the slave is led astray by his appetite.

113. **ponere**, *dispose of*; *i.e.* employ to advantage. — **fugitivus et erro**: another allusion to the faults of slaves.

115. **comes**: cf. *Od.* III. 1. 40.

116. **unde mihi**, etc.: Horace, to close the satire without forcing, represents himself as enraged (cf. II. 3. 323), and stopping the diatribe by a threat of punishment, which is of course an admission of its truth. — **lapidem**: cf. II. 5. 102.

117. **insanit**: the allusion is to the other Stoic paradox, as in II. 3. The suggestion of insanity is in the similarity of Horace's cry to that of some insane person on the stage, so that Horace is either crazy himself or writing a tragedy to represent Ajax or some similar person, which is just as bad. Cf. II. 3. 322.

118. **accedes**, etc.: *i.e.* you shall be sent into the country to work on the farm, a common punishment of city slaves. Cf. Plaut. *Mostell.* I. 1. 18, and many other cases in Plautus and Terence. — **opera**, *laborer*. — **nona**: hence it would seem Horace had eight, a very moderate number of farm hands.

## VIII.

*Horat.* Vt Nasidieni iuvit te cena beati?
Nam mihi quaerenti convivam dictus heri illic
de medio potare die. *Fundan.* Sic, ut mihi numquam
in vita fuerit melius. *H.* Da, si grave non est,
quae prima iratum ventrem placaverit esca.
*F.* In primis Lucanus aper; leni fuit Austro
captus, ut aiebat cenae pater; acria circum
rapula, lactucae, radices, qualia lassum
pervellunt stomachum, siser, allec, faecula Coa.
His ubi sublatis puer alte cinctus acernam
gausape purpureo mensam pertersit, et alter

SATIRE 8. This satire is a report made by Fundanius, one of Horace's friends, of a dinner given by a millionaire of the time to Mæcenas and some of his friends. Although the host evidently is depicted as having more money than brains, yet it is not merely the ostentation of the *parvenu* that is satirized, but the misplaced diligence of the epicure (cf. II. 2. and 4). Nor must we suppose that every fact stated is to be taken as ludicrous any more than in *Sat.* II. 5. The piece is only a narrative, of which parts are satirical, parts are humorous incident, and parts again merely the necessary detail to make a picture.

1. **Nasidieni** (four syllables): otherwise unknown, and perhaps only a fictitious name. — **beati**, *the millionaire.*

2. **nam**: *i.e.* I ask, for I learned you were there when I went to invite you myself.

3. **de medio**: indulgence in the pleasures of the table was indicated by sitting down early rather than by staying late as in modern times; cf. **tempestiva convivia**. — **potare**, *to have been*, etc. (Gr. 276. *a*).

4. **fuerit melius**, cf. **bene erat** II. 2. 120.

5. **prima**: *i.e.* in the first course (**ferculum**) exclusive of the **gustatio**. — **iratum**, cf. **latrantem**, II. 2. 18.

6. **leni**, etc.: *i.e.* the excellence of the viand depended on the weather. This detail suggests an excessive particularity in these matters.

7. **cenae pater**, (probably a jocose variation on *pater familias*), *our respected host.* — **circum**: *i.e.* as a garnish. Cf. II. 4. 75.

8. **allec**: cf. II. 4. 73. Such stimulating condiments are especially grateful in sluggish and bilious climates, and were much used by the Roman epicures.

10. **puer**, etc.: these statements seem to indicate a special elegance of service. — **alte cinctus**: apparently only a neatly dressed slave (cf. v. 70). — **acernam**: the fine tables of the ancients were made either of choice specimens of wood or of colored marble. Of course there was here no table-cloth.

11. **purpureo**: a useless elegance. — **alter**: a special slave, called *analecta.*

sublegit quodcumque iaceret inutile quodque
posset cenantis offendere, ut Attica virgo
cum sacris Cereris procedit fuscus Hydaspes,
Caecuba vina ferens, Alcon Chium maris expers.
Hic erus: 'Albanum, Maecenas, sive Falernum
te magis appositis delectat, habemus utrumque.'
*H.* Divitias miseras! Sed quis cenantibus una,
Fundani, pulchre fuerit tibi, nosse laboro.
*F.* Summus ego, et prope me Viscus Thurinus, et infra,

13. **Attica virgo**: *i.e.* a Κανηφόρος (cf. I. 3. 10), indicating a solemnity and dignity of demeanor suited to his august mission.

14. **Hydaspes**: *i.e.* an East Indian, a rare luxury.

15. **Caecuba**: one of the finer wines, but not necessarily indicating any vulgar display (cf. *Od.* II. 14. 25). — **Alcon**: the mention of the name seems to indicate another rare slave, but whence brought is not known, perhaps from Greece. But a Greek slave would be no rarity (cf. **Alcis**, a German divinity). — **Chium**: the Greek wines were milder and sweeter than the Italian, and thus formed a contrast and gave variety. — **maris expers**, *without sea-water*, which was usually added to all but the very best Greek wines, as men drink Apollinaris with their wine nowadays. *In summa gloria . . . fuere Thasium Chiumque . . . Nunc gratia ante omnia est Clazomenio postquam parcius mari condiunt. Lesbium sponte suae naturae mare sapit.* Plin. *H. N.* XIV. 7 (73). There is not necessarily anything of bad taste in the things served. The host gives his guests a choice between the hot but rich Italian wines and the sweet and mild but equally choice Chian, serving the last in its full strength and at the same time without the *tang* which the sea-water would have given it. If there is anything wrong in the whole matter, it is only the overstrained and anxious nicety of selection and service.

16. **Albanum**, etc.: here is apparently an overwrought anxiety to please the distinguished guest, but not necessarily intended as an ostentatious display, notwithstanding Horace's exclamation. He may merely mean that such resources cause a host to worry over the matter.

19. **Fundani**, cf. I. 10. 42. — **laboro nosse**, *I am dying to know.*

20. **summus**, etc.: the triclinium was arranged round three sides of a square, within wnich was the table, and the guests reclined three on a couch, thus:

| | |
|---|---|
| 1. Fundanius. | 5. Vibidius. |
| 2. Viscus. | 6. Mæcenas. |
| 3. Varius. | 7. Nomentanus. |
| 4. Servilius. | 8. Host. |

9. Porcius.

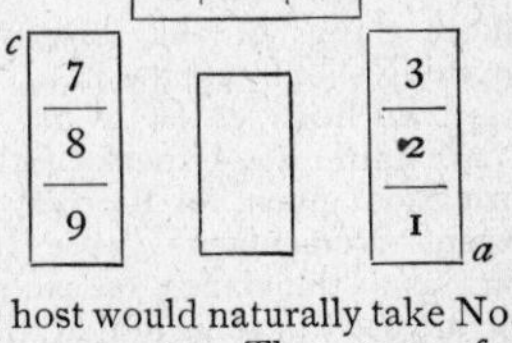

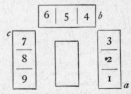

The host would naturally take No. 7; but see v. 25. The arms of the

si memini, Varius; cum Servilio Balatrone
Vibidius, quas Maecenas adduxerat umbras;
Nomentanus erat super ipsum, Porcius infra,
ridiculus totas simul absorbere placentas;
Nomentanus ad hoc, qui, si quid forte lateret,
indice monstraret digito: nam cetera turba,
nos, inquam, cenamus avis, conchylia, piscis,
longe dissimilem noto celantia sucum;
ut vel continuo patuit, cum passeris atque
ingustata mihi porrexerat ilia rhombi.
Post hoc me docuit melimela rubere minorem
ad lunam delecta. Quid hoc intersit, ab ipso
audieris melius. Tum Vibidius Balatroni,
'Nos nisi damnose bibimus, moriemur inulti;'
et calices poscit maiores. Vertere pallor
tum parochi faciem, nil sic metuentis ut acris
potores, vel quod male dicunt liberius vel

couches were at *a*, *b*, *c*, the other places having only cushions.— **Thurinus**, *of Thurii*, and so probably not either of those in I. 10. 83.

21. **Varius**, cf. I. 10. 44. — **Servilio, Vibidius**: unknown.

22. **umbras**: uninvited persons brought as parasites by the distinguished guest. Cf. *Ep.* I. 5. 28.

23. **Nomentanus** was (as also Porcius) a parasite of the host. Here he takes the chief place partly because of the dulness of the host himself and partly to point out the choice things of the feast in case anything should escape notice.

25. **ad hoc**: cf. II. 1. 36.

26. **nam**: *i.e.* I speak of this information given, for the rest of us, except Nomentanus, were in the dark as to the viands, on account of the art used in their preparation.

29. **ut**, etc.: *i.e.* as I soon found out when he (the host) handed me something which, if not informed, I never should have recognized as the fishes mentioned, never having tasted the like before.

31. **melimela rubere**, etc., *that the bright red apples were picked*, etc.

32. **quid hoc**: probably originally **quid** was the subject in such cases, but idiomatically **hoc** must be regarded as the subject here, and **quid** as a kind of accusative adverb.

34. **damnose**, *to his ruin*, by their potations of his costly wine. — **moriemur**, etc.: *i.e.* being nauseated by the talk about eating, the guests humorously resolve to avenge themselves in the manner indicated.

36. **parochi**, *our provider*, jocosely for host.

37. **maledicunt**: *i.e.* produce free-spoken chaffing. Cf. I. 4. 89.

fervida quod subtile exsurdant vina palatum.
Invertunt Allifanis vinaria tota
Vibidius Balatroque, secutis omnibus; imi
convivae lecti nihilum nocuere lagenis.

Affertur squillas inter murena natantis
in patina porrecta. Sub hoc erus 'Haec gravida,' inquit,
'capta est, deterior post partum carne futura.
His mixtum ius est: oleo quod prima Venafri
pressit cella; garo de sucis piscis Hiberi;
vino quinquenni, verum citra mare nato,
dum coquitur — cocto Chium sic convenit, ut non
hoc magis ullum aliud; — pipere albo, non sine aceto,
quod Methymnaeam vitio mutaverit uvam.
Erucas viridis, inulas ego primus amaras
monstravi incoquere; inlutos Curtillus echinos,
ut melius muria quod testa marina remittat.'
Interea suspensa gravis aulaea ruinas
in patinam fecere, trahentia pulveris atri
quantum non Aquilo Campanis excitat agris.

38. **fervida**, etc.: *i.e.* the wines would prevent the culinary skill from being appreciated.

39. **Allifanis**: a large style of goblet from Allifae in Samnium.

40. **imi lecti**: *i.e.* the parasites who refrain on account of obsequiousness.

44. **futura**, *it would be*, etc., making a separate sentence in English.

45. **prima**: *i.e.* the oil first pressed, which would be the choicest. — **Venafri**: cf. II. 4. 69.

46. **Hiberi**: *i.e.* the *scomber*, or *mackerel*.

48. **dum coquitur**, *while cooking*. — **cocto**, *after it is cooked*, a different wine must be added. All these niceties are of the same kind as those in II. 4.

49. **hoc**: ablative after **magis**.

50. **quod**: lit. the vinegar, but properly the acid which turned the wine and spoiled it (**vitio**) by making it vinegar.

51. **ego primus**: cf. II. 4. 74. — **incoquere**, *stew in* the mixture. — **inlutos**: *i.e.* the sea-urchins soaked give a better juice than the ordinary fish brine. — **Curtillus**, another *gourmet*.

53. **melius**: a forced apposition to **echinos**, agreeing with (**id**) antecedent of **quod**. — **testa**: *i.e.* the echinus.

54. **aulaea**: apparently a canopy over the table. Cf. *Od.* III. 29. 15; Virg. *Æn.* I. 697.

Nos maius veriti, postquam nihil esse pericli
sensimus, erigimur: Rufus posito capite, ut si
filius immaturus obisset, flere. Quis esset
finis, ni sapiens sic Nomentanus amicum
tolleret: 'Heu, Fortuna, quis est crudelior in nos
te deus? Vt semper gaudes illudere rebus
humanis!' Varius mappa compescere risum
vix poterat. Balatro suspendens omnia naso,
'Haec est condicio vivendi,' aiebat, 'eoque
responsura tuo numquam est par fama labori.
Tene, ut ego accipiar laute, torquerier omni
sollicitudine districtum, ne panis adustus,
ne male conditum ius apponatur, ut omnes
praecincti recte pueri comptique ministrent!
Adde hos praeterea casus, aulaea ruant si,
ut modo; si patinam pede lapsus frangat agaso.
Sed convivatoris, uti ducis, ingenium res
adversae nudare solent, celare secundae.'
Nasidienus ad haec: 'Tibi di quaecumque preceris
commoda dent! Ita vir bonus es convivaque comis:'
et soleas poscit. Tum in lecto quoque videres

57. **maius**: *i.e.* a real danger, as of the fall of the ceiling or house.

58. **erigimur**, *rally.* — **Rufus**: cognomen of Nasidienus. — **posito capite**: *i.e.* in despair, in a manner opposed to **erigimur**.

59. **esset**: imperfect, referring to past time instead of the ordinary pluperfect (Gr. § 308. *a*). This is an extreme case of the usage, and hardly to be paralleled, and it may be therefore colloquial.

60. **sapiens**, *like a philosopher*, perhaps with a shade of irony. The absurdity consisted in the parasite's treating the matter as an overwhelming calamity.

64. **suspendens**, etc., *always a scornful cynic*, which agrees with his contemptuous irony. Cf. I. 6. 5.

67. **tene**, etc.: cf. Ter. *Phorm.* II. 2. 25, a passage which Balatro must have had in his mind.

72. **agaso**: *i.e.* a clumsy slave, fit only for the stable.

74. **nudare**: *i.e.* only serve to reveal the genius which in success might be undiscovered.

75. **tibi di**, etc.: the host evidently takes the jest in earnest.

77. **soleas poscit**: *i.e.* to go and order the continuance of the banquet. The shoes were taken off upon reclining.

stridere secreta divisos aure susurros.

*H.* Nullos his mallem ludos spectasse; sed illa
redde, age, quae deinceps risisti. *F.* Vibidius dum
quaerit de pueris, num sit quoque fracta lagena,
quod sibi poscenti non dantur pocula, dumque
ridetur fictis rerum Balatrone secundo,
Nasidiene, redis mutatae frontis, ut arte
emendaturus fortunam; deinde secuti
mazonomo pueri magno discerpta ferentes
membra gruis sparsi sale multo, non sine farre,
pinguibus et ficis pastum iecur anseris albae,
et leporum avolsos, ut multo suavius, armos,
quam si cum lumbis quis edit. Tum pectore adusto
vidimus et merulas poni et sine clune palumbes,
suavis res, si non causas narraret earum et

78. **divisos**, *exchanged*, uttered now to this side, now to that (cf. *Od.* I. 15. 15). — **secreta aure**: privately in the ear of one's neighbor, *i.e.* they put their heads together and whisper.

79. **ludos**: referring as well to the sport on this occasion as to public amusements in general. Cf. the English, "as good as a play." — **mallem**: Gr. § 311. *b.* — **spectasse**: Gr. § 288. *d.* Rem.

80. **deinceps**, *next.*

81. **quoque**: *i.e.* as well as whatever the hangings fell on.

83. **ridetur**: of course impersonal. — **fictis rerum** (cf. II. 2. 25), *pretended jests*, invented to cover their laughter at Nasidienus.

84. **Nasidiene**: in a style of apostrophe suggestive of Epic poetry. — **mutatae frontis**, *with a changed bearing;* recovered from his despair, and resolved to triumph over fortune by resolute endeavor. — **ut arte**, etc.: apparently proverbial. Cf. Ter. *Adelph.* IV. 7. 21 *seq.*

88. **iecur**: cf. the modern *pâté de foie gras.* — **anseris albae**: a female and white, both details made much of by the host, as of course these would not appear in the liver.

89. **armos**: cf. II. 4. 44.

90. **edit**: probably subjunctive. — **adusto**: apparently broiled. There is no reason to think of any want of excellence in the cooking.

91. **sine clune**: doubtless a fine touch. Cf., for a different fashion, *Gell.* 15. 8.

92. **suavis res**, *choice viands enough.* In strict grammar we should have *quae suaves res essent si*, but here the **res** is put in apposition without a verb, and the sentence proceeds as if the verb had been used.

92. **causas**, etc.: *i.e.* the dinner is spoiled by the details, because

naturas dominus ; quem nos sic fugimus ulti,
ut nihil omnino gustaremus, velut illis
Canidia afflasset peior serpentibus Afris.

minutiæ of the art of the cuisine are disgusting to the guests.

93. **ulti**: *i.e.* when the host is so devoted to the culinary art, and so proud of his dinners, the worst they can do to him is to refuse to enjoy his viands.

95. **Canidia**: the sorceress mentioned in *Epod.* V., XVII. and *Sat.* I. 8. — **Afris**: cf. *Od.* III. 10. 18.

# THE EPISTLES.

# INTRODUCTION.

The Epistles belong, as well as the Satires, to Horace's *Musa pedestris*. They are, like them, conversational moral or literary essays (*Sermones;* cf. II. 1. 250), of which the topics are suggested by current events or occasional moods and relations. They were not, however, called *Sermones* by the ancients, nor do they have that title in the manuscripts, but have always been called *Epistulae*. They differ from the Satires in being connected in some manner with some particular person to whom each is addressed. They are not, to be sure, letters like those of Cicero and Pliny, originally intended for private reading and afterwards collected and published. They were from the first intended for the public. But it must be remembered that publication in ancient times was a different matter from what it is nowadays. The author sent his manuscript to be read and copied, and it would be put on sale if it was found to be popular. The only difference between these letters and other compositions was probably that these were first sent to the person addressed and afterwards copied by his permission. They were written after Horace's fame became established, so that any person was honored by being associated with one of his compositions. But the association is not merely one of dedication. Each one seems to have been suggested by some condition of mind, trait of character, or temporary situation of the person addressed. So that there is something personal and intimate in the tone and matter of each of them. The date of their composition is not exactly fixed except in a few cases, but they belong to the latter part of the poet's life (see I. 3; I. 20), about B.C. 20–12, later than any other of his works, except some occasional Odes and the *Carmen Saeculare*. They consequently have a less acrid tone, giving evidence of a mellower and more philosophical way of thinking, and dwell particularly upon ethical subjects, treating them more in the style of common-places and with less personal attack than in the Satires.

The second book is entirely devoted to the discussion of literary topics, and is probably the last of the poet's works. It seems to have been begun at the request of Augustus, and lacks something of the spontaneity of the other works. It is chiefly interesting as giving Horace's personal views on poetic composition, and has always been looked upon as containing the ultimate canons of poetic art.

Q. HORATI FLACCI

# EPISTVLAE

## LIBER PRIMVS

### I.

Prima dicte mihi, summa dicende Camena,
spectatum satis et donatum iam rude quaeris,
Maecenas, iterum antiquo me includere ludo.
Non eadem est aetas, non mens. Veianius, armis
Herculis ad postem fixis, latet abditus agro,

EPISTLE 1. Addressed to Mæcenas in answer to a request of his to try again the lyric poetry, which no doubt to Horace's contemporaries seemed his best form of composition. Horace explains the motives of his refusal by extolling the pursuit of philosophy in which he is now engaged.

VERSE 1. **prima**, etc.: a form of expression first found in Homer, *Il.* IX. 97, and imitated with variations by many writers after him. Cf. Virg. *Ecl.* VIII. 11, and Hor. *Od.* III. 6. 6. — **Camena**: the proper Latin name of the goddesses of inspired song, the Greek Μοῦσαι. The construction is a loose one of *means.*

2. **spectatum**, etc.: as is often done in Latin and Greek, instead of using a figure or simile, the poet identifies the real object with that to which it is compared. Here Horace compares himself to a gladiator of approved (**spectatum**) valor who, by the favor of the people, has been relieved from the necessity of appearing again. To force such a one into the arena anew would be rather unjust. — **rude**, *wooden sword.* With this emblem, as a symbol of bloodless exercise, the gladiator was presented when discharged.

3. **ludo**, *quarters*, the **ludus gladiatorius**, but with a play, no doubt, on the word, referring to the lighter and more frivolous poetry of his youth.

4. **Veianius**: a retired gladiator of the kind mentioned.

5. **Herculis**: the patron god of athletes and gladiators. — **ad postem**, etc.: the arms had been dedicated to the god upon the abandonment of the profession, as was customary with the ancients. Cf. *Od.* III. 26. 4. — **latet**, *buries himself*, *i.e.* retires to a country life.

ne populum extrema totiens exoret harena.
Est mihi purgatam crebro qui personet aurem:
'Solve senescentem mature sanus equum, ne
peccet ad extremum ridendus et ilia ducat!'
Nunc itaque et versus et cetera ludicra pono;
quid verum atque decens curo et rogo et omnis in hoc sum;
condo et compono quae mox depromere possim.
Ac ne forte roges quo me duce, quo lare tuter:
nullius addictus iurare in verba magistri,
quo me cumque rapit tempestas, deferor hospes.

6. **ne . . . exoret,** *that he may not have to appeal,* etc., as he would, if he voluntarily continued to fight (cf. Quint. *Decl.* 302). This, no doubt, many did to win glory and the favor of the people. — **extrema . . . harena:** *i.e.* near the spectators. — **totiens,** *so many times again, i.e.* as he had before, in order to win the privilege of retirement.

7. **est . . . qui,** *there is a voice which.* — **purgatam,** *listening,* lit. freed from all impediments to hearing, such as in a figurative sense ambition and vanity would be.

8. **solve,** *turn out,* lit. unharness (from the racing chariot). — **mature,** *betimes.* — **ridendus,** *ridiculously.* — **ilia ducat,** *pant with broken wind.* Cf. *ilia tendunt,* Virg. *Georg.* III. 507; *ilia pulsare, Æn.* IX. 413; *anhelitum ducere,* Ovid. *Met.* VII. 555; and the common *spiritum ducere.*

10. **itaque:** *i.e.* in consequence of the voice of wisdom just referred to. — **ludicra,** *youthful follies,* among which Horace includes poetry.

11. **verum:** *i.e.* sound in philosophy, true as a guide of life. Cf. II. 2. 144. — **decens, honestum:** τὸ πρέπον, the Stoic equivalent for virtue. — **curo,** *study* (by himself). — **rogo,** *inquire* (of philosophers in their writings or discourses). — **omnis:** cf. *Sat.* I. 9. 2.

12. **condo:** of storing up. — **compono:** of arranging so as to have no difficulty in finding by and by. — **depromere:** the regular word for taking out of the storehouse for use. Cf. **condus promus,** *a steward,* Plaut. *Pseud.* II. 2. 14.

13. **ne,** etc.: the purpose not of anything which is said, but of saying it (as of a "let me tell you," or the like implied), a common form of speech in many languages. Cf. "to be brief," "to say no more," and the like. The connection is, as you might naturally inquire when I say I am devoted to philosophy, to what school I belong, I forestall the inquiry by saying "to none." — **lare:** *i.e.* to what family I belong. Cf. *familia Peripateticorum,* Cic. *Div.* II. 1.

14. **addictus:** properly of a debtor assigned to his creditor as a slave (the ancient form of imprisonment for debt), but here in a mixed metaphor transferred to the relation of the gladiator or soldier who swears an oath dictated by his master or commander.

15. **tempestas,** *the weather, i.e.* he drifts without any definite aim,

Nunc agilis fio et mersor civilibus undis,
virtutis verae custos rigidusque satelles;
nunc in Aristippi furtim praecepta relabor,
et mihi res, non me rebus, subiungere conor.
Vt nox longa quibus mentitur amica, diesque
longa videtur opus debentibus, ut piger annus
pupillis quos dura premit custodia matrum,

making himself a guest or sojourner, not a permanent citizen, in whatever school he happens to find himself (Cic. *Tusc.* IV. 47). — **deferor**: the technical word for being driven to port or to land. Cf. Cic. *Acad.* II. 3. 8.

16. **nunc**, etc.: in the regular Horatian manner he gives an example of his course of conduct. — **agilis**: it was a special principle of the Stoics, in opposition to the Epicureans, to engage in active civil life as members of the body politic. Cf. Cic. *de Off.* I. 7. 22, and *de Fin.* III. 20. 67. — **civilibus undis**, *the tide of civil life.*

17. **verae**: as the only true guide of life, the highest and only good. — **custos**, *a champion.* — **rigidus**, *strict*, in accordance with the unbending character of the Stoic doctrines. The whole means, "now I become a conscientious Stoic," and sacrifice myself to my public duties.

18. **Aristippi**: *i.e.* now I fall into the opposite extreme of self-indulgence, and endeavor to harmonize philosophy and inclination. Aristippus of Cyrene (380 B.C.) was the most worldly of the followers of Socrates, and originated the Hedonic school, whose ethical principles were afterwards adopted by the Epicureans. He is put here as the opposite extreme from the Stoics, inasmuch as he made the enjoyment of the senses the summum bonum or ultimate motive to action ("the chief end of man"). — **furtim**, *imperceptibly.* — **relabor**: the passage from the altruism of the Stoics to the egotism of Aristippus is regarded as a falling back.

19. **et mihi res**, etc.: this is opposed directly to **agilis**, etc., in so far as the conscientious citizen is hampered by his duties (**me rebus subiungere**) as much as the thoughtless man by his desires. But the verse contains also a summary of the doctrine of Aristippus, whose principle was to enjoy everything in life without becoming a slave to any desire or duty. Thus the poet represents himself (probably with truth) as insensibly relaxing his zeal in the performance of civil duties, and giving himself up to enjoyment and self-culture. Cf. *Ep.* I. 16 and 17.

21. **ut . . . videtur sic . . . fluunt**: *i.e.* as philosophy is my chief concern, I am impatient of everything that hinders me in the pursuit of it. This is at the same time an expression of unwillingness to be diverted by poetry, and of discontent at the obstacles to becoming a real philosopher. — **opus debentibus**: *i.e.* the hireling by the day. — **piger annus**: because he is in haste to become of age, and be free from restraint.

22. **pupillis**: indicating that they are orphans and under age. — **custodia matrum**: not as wards, but merely under control on account of their age.

sic mihi tarda fluunt ingrataque tempora, quae spem
consiliumque morantur agendi gnaviter id quod
aeque pauperibus prodest, locupletibus aeque,
aeque neglectum pueris senibusque nocebit.

Restat ut his ego me ipse regam solerque elementis.
Non possis oculo quantum contendere Lynceus,
non tamen idcirco contemnas lippus inungi;
nec, quia desperes invicti membra Glyconis,
nodosa corpus nolis prohibere cheragra.
Est quadam prodire tenus, si non datur ultra.
Fervet avaritia miseroque cupidine pectus:
sunt verba et voces, quibus hunc lenire dolorem
possis et magnam morbi deponere partem.
Laudis amore tumes: sunt certa piacula, quae te

23. **spem**: *i.e.* the fulfilment of his hope. — **consilium**: *i.e.* the accomplishment of his purpose.

27. **restat**: *i.e.* not being able to become a real philosopher (cf. v. 20 *seq.*), the poet can only do the best he can with the slight acquisitions that he can make (cf. v. 12). — **his**: *i.e.* these few that I can get. — **me regam**, *direct my life.* — **soler**, *solace its ills*, the main object of philosophy since the third century B.C.

28. **non possis**, *though you may not be able*, concessive (or possibly conditional). — **quantum contendere**, *see as far as*, lit. reach, with the accusative of extent of space. — **Lynceus**: cf. *Sat.* I. 2. 90.

29. **lippus**, *for weak eyes*, lit. having weak eyes. — **inungi**, *to use eye-salve.*

30. **desperes**: a subjunctive of condition, such as is usual with the indefinite second person, the whole being a supposed case. — **Glyconis**: evidently an athlete.

31. **corpus prohibere cheragra** (cf. *Sat.* II. 7. 15): with verbs of repelling, removing, and the like, either the thing kept off or that from which it is kept may take the prominent position and be in the accusative, with the other in the ablative (cf. I. 8. 10).

32. **est quadam**, etc.: *i.e.* improvement to a certain extent is possible, even if perfection as a sage is unattainable.

33. **fervet**, *is in a fever*, an instance of the preceding; a condition without the conditional form, as in English. — **cupidine**, *covetousness.*

34. **verba**, *magic words*, alluding to formulæ used for medical purposes in ancient times (cf. *Odys.* XIX. 457, and Cato *R. R.* 160), but referring to the precepts of philosophy. — **voces**, *accents*, alluding to the tones and manner in which such magical formulæ were recited, but not different in real meaning from **verba**.

35. **morbi**: vices are here, as usual, regarded as diseases.

36. **laudis amore**: *i.e.* ambition. — **piacula**: as philosophy is before

ter pure lecto poterunt recreare libello.
Invidus, iracundus, iners, vinosus, amator,
nemo adeo ferus est ut non mitescere possit,
si modo culturae patientem commodet aurem.
Virtus est vitium fugere, et sapientia prima
stultitia caruisse. Vides quae maxima credis
esse mala, exiguum censum turpemque repulsam,
quanto devites animi capitisque labore;
impiger extremos curris mercator ad Indos,
per mare pauperiem fugiens, per saxa, per ignis:
ne cures ea, quae stulte miraris et optas,
discere, et audire, et meliori credere non vis?

compared to the healing art, so it is here compared to the expiations through which disease, especially madness, as proceeding from divine displeasure could be cured. Cf. the example of Orestes.

37. **ter**: the element of magic (in the number three) was present even in religion (cf. *Tib.* I. 2. 54). — **pure**: alluding to the religious cleansing necessary in ancient observances, but referring, of course, to moral purpose, the cleansing of the soul. — **libello**: indicating a religious ritual, to which the moral precepts are compared.

38. **invidus**, etc.: in a kind of partitive apposition with **nemo**.

39. **ferus**, etc.: the figure here varies between a wild animal and a rough farm, though both figures are so common as hardly to be considered as figures at all.

41. **virtus est**, etc.: a continuation of the same general argument that a beginning in the practice of philosophy is worth an effort even though one may not be a finished philosopher. This is, of course, contrary to the Stoic dogmas, but fits well with less strict doctrines.

42. **caruisse**: the perfect is probably chosen for the metre, but it differs from the present, meaning to have refrained from some act of folly by some special effort such as is referred to in the following.

43. **censum**: cf. *Sat.* II. 1. 75. — **repulsam**, *rejection* by the citizens at the polls, of course the greatest misfortune to the ambitious Roman, whose success in life depended upon the *cursus honorum*.

44. **animi**: *i.e.* anxiety of mind. — **capitis**: *i.e.* peril of life. Cf. v. 45.

45. **impiger**, *tireless*, an example of activity in the race for wealth.

46. **fugiens**: really pursuing wealth, but made more vivid by being put in the form of a flight from poverty. — **per saxa**, etc.: proverbial expressions for danger, as we say, "through fire and water."

47. **ne cures**, etc.: if you are willing to undergo such trials in the pursuit of wealth, how much rather should you be willing to take a little trouble in gaining the same end by extinguishing desire. And this is effected by philosophy, whereby a far nobler prize is won.

48. **meliori**, *a wiser teacher* (than yourself), *i.e.* the philosopher.

Quis circum pagos et circum compita pugnax
magna coronari contemnat Olympia, cui spes,
cui sit condicio dulcis sine pulvere palmae?
Vilius argentum est auro, virtutibus aurum.

'O cives, cives, quaerenda pecunia primum est,
virtus post nummos.' Haec Ianus summus ab imo
prodocet, haec recinunt iuvenes dictata senesque,
laevo suspensi loculos tabulamque lacerto.
Est animus tibi, sunt mores et lingua fidesque,
sed quadringentis sex septem milia desunt:
plebs eris. At pueri ludentes, 'Rex eris,' aiunt,

49. **circum pagos**, etc.: the person indicated is some local champion, who fights at the insignificant festivals in the country. Such a one would of course wish to gain the prize at the great Olympic games as champion of the world if he could do so without the trouble of working for it. In the same measure is freedom from desire superior to worldly success (cf. v. 53), and this freedom can be got without the toil of worldly ambition.

52. **vilius**, etc.: *i.e.* as gold is more precious than silver, so is virtue than gold.

53. **O cives**, etc.: *i.e.* but the world thinks differently, and is bent on securing money first, wherein it shows its folly, as the poet proceeds to demonstrate.

54. **Ianus**, etc.: there seem to have been three arches in the Forum, around which the most important money affairs were transacted, so that the expression is equivalent to the whole Stock Exchange, or all Wall Street in modern times. We may translate, "*the whole Forum from the upper to the lower Janus.*"

55. **prodocet**, *preaches*, *i.e.* propagates the doctrine. — **dictata**: *i.e.* given them as a lesson which they thus learn and repeat, a method of instruction very common, as it would seem, in ancient times. Cf. *Sat.* I. 10. 75. — **senesque**: *i.e.* young and old go alike to that school.

56. **laevo**, etc.: this line is doubtful, and seems to have crept in from the margin, where some scholar had put it as a parallel passage from *Sat.* I. 6. 74. Still it is possible that Horace meant to emphasize the idea that all ages are scholars alike to learn this all-important lesson.

57. **est animus**, etc.: an illustration of the degree to which the supremacy of wealth is recognized, being embodied even in the constitution of the state. — **tibi**: a supposed case. — **mores**, *character*, for good character, just as we use that word. — **lingua**, *eloquence*, one of the highest recommendations among the Romans.

58. **quadringentis**: the 400,000 sesterces ($20,000) required for the equestrian census.

59. **plebs**: *i.e.* not an eques. — **ludentes**, *at their play*. — **rex eris**, etc.: the rest of the trochaic verse here quoted is given by Isidore (*Origg.* IX. 3, 4), *si non faciet non*

'si recte facies.' Hic murus aeneus esto,
nil conscire sibi, nulla pallescere culpa.
Roscia, dic sodes, melior lex, an puerorum est
nenia, quae regnum recte facientibus offert,
et maribus Curiis et decantata Camillis?
Isne tibi melius suadet qui rem facias, rem,
si possis, recte, si non, quocumque modo rem,
ut propius spectes lacrimosa poemata Pupi,
an qui fortunae te responsare superbae
liberum et erectum praesens hortatur et aptat?
Quod si me populus Romanus forte roget, cur

*erit.* The whole may have had originally a serious meaning, though fallen in time to a mere singsong of children at play. The precise game in which it was used is not certain, but see Plato *Theaet.* 146. A.

60. **hic murus**, etc.: the tone of this sentiment is so different from the preceding, that many editors have rejected it as an interpolation; and, in fact, it is almost impossible to justify the connection. Still the two parts may have belonged to the same song in Horace's time, though originating at different times. It is also difficult to reconstruct v. 60 without the suspected words. Perhaps Horace gives the words as his own interpretation of the supposed deeper meaning of the song. The whole of the last part belongs among the commonplaces of philosophy. Cf. Sen. *Ep.* IX. 3. 19; Cic. *Parad.* IV. 1.

62. **Roscia**: cf. *Sat.* I. 6. 40.—**melior**: *i.e.* sounder, for the law has a lower standard than the song, as making precedence depend on wealth.

63. **nenia**, *old song*, a word used of any often-repeated or rude song, perhaps originally spinning song (?), as it was especially sung by women.

64. **maribus**, *sturdy*, free from the effeminating influences of later times. — **Curiis**, etc.: *i.e.* such as the old worthies used to repeat, implying that the heroes were brought up on it and acted accordingly.

67. **propius**: see v. 62. — **lacrimosa**: used disparagingly of tragedy, as we might say, "the mournful play of Kotzebue," or "the tearful Stranger." — **Pupi**: a tragedian, (perhaps deservedly) unknown.

68. **fortunae**: cf. *Sat.* II. 7. 88. — **responsare**: cf. *Sat.* II. 7. 85 and 103. — **superbae**, *arrogant*, as lording it over mankind, and expecting them to yield to her power. Hence the resistance of the wise man is more praiseworthy.

69. **hortatur**: by his precepts. — **aptat**: by the strength gained by following the precepts.

70. **quod si**, etc.: an answer to an imaginary objector who asks the poet why he does not follow the principles of his neighbors and countrymen among whom he lives. As he does not withdraw himself from their society, why should he refuse to agree with them? The answer is contained in allegorical form in v. 74 *seq.*, and continued in v. 76 *seq.*

non, ut porticibus, sic iudiciis fruar isdem,
nec sequar aut fugiam quae diligit ipse vel odit,
olim quod volpes aegroto cauta leoni
respondit referam: 'Quia me vestigia terrent,
omnia te adversum spectantia, nulla retrorsum.'
Belua multorum es capitum. Nam quid sequar aut quem?
Pars hominum gestit conducere publica; sunt qui
crustis et pomis viduas venentur avaras,
excipiantque senes quos in vivaria mittant;
multis occulto crescit res faenore. Verum
esto aliis alios rebus studiisque teneri:
idem eadem possunt horam durare probantes?
'Nullus in orbe sinus Baiis praelucet amoenis'

71. **porticibus**: the common lounging-places of the Romans, and the most frequent place for meeting one's friends and acquaintances.

72. **sequar et fugiam**: almost technical words in regard to the objects of desire and avoidance.

73. **volpes**: cf. Lucilius (*Müller*) XXX. 84 *seq.*: —

Deducta tunc voce leo, cur tu ipsa venire
Non vis huc . . . ?
Quid sibi volt, quare fit, ut introvorsus et ad te
Spectent atque ferant vestigia se omnia prosus?

The fable is a famous one of Æsop. Of course the poet means that all are swallowed up by this greed of gain, and no one is ever found to return to a natural life.

76. **belua**, etc.: *i.e.* and then again, you are so diverse and inconsistent with yourselves. This seems really only a quibble, for he might easily follow the principles of the crowd, and select his own method of carrying them out. But the moral lesson loses nothing by that. The figure in **multorum capitum** is an old and familiar one. Cf. Plato *Rep.* IX. 12.

77. **pars**, etc.: examples of the ruling passion of different men in the pursuit of wealth. — **publica**: the most extensive use of money in Rome, analogous to our great railroad enterprises, was in the purchase of government contracts, either for the collection of the revenue, or for jobs of various kinds for the state.

78. **crustis**, etc.: cf. *Sat.* II. 5. 12. — **vivaria**: cf. *Sat.* II. 5. 44.

80. **occulto**: because usury was prohibited at Rome.

81. **esto**, etc.: *i.e.* to waive that point, allow different persons to adopt different means of making a fortune, if you will.

82. **idem eadem**: *i.e.* they have no fixed purposes that can last an hour at a time; they are too vacillating to follow as guides.

83. **Baiis**: this was the favorite watering-place of Rome, and filled with fine villas of the nabobs of the time.

si dixit dives, lacus et mare sentit amorem
festinantis eri; cui si vitiosa libido
fecerit auspicium, 'Cras ferramenta Teanum
tolletis, fabri.' Lectus genialis in aula est:
nil ait esse prius, melius nil caelibe vita:
si non est, iurat bene solis esse maritis.
Quo teneam voltus mutantem Protea nodo?
Quid pauper? Ride: mutat cenacula, lectos,
balnea, tonsores, conducto navigio aeque
nauseat ac locuples quem ducit priva triremis.
Si curatus inaequali tonsore capillos
occurri, rides; si forte subucula pexae
trita subest tunicae vel si toga dissidet impar,
rides: quid, mea cum pugnat sententia secum,
quod petiit spernit, repetit quod nuper omisit,

84. **lacus et mare**: the edifices were built far out into the Lucrine Lake and the sea. Cf. *Od.* II. 15. 3.

85. **vitiosa**: *morbid*, as having no sound reason. — **libido**, *caprice*, mere fancy.

86. **fecerit auspicium**, *give the word*, as if the dictates of a morbid fancy were a divine command. — **Teanum**: another favorite place for villas, an inland city of Campania, whither in his caprice the nabob suddenly changes the site of his proposed country seat.

87. **lectus genialis**, the symbolic marriage couch, retained in the atrium long after the private apartments had been withdrawn to the back of the house.

91. **pauper**, etc.: nor is this indulgence of whims confined to the rich; the poor man also changes his lodgings, furniture, and barber, and, if yachting is in fashion, hires a craft, and can be as seasick as ever a lord is in his sea-going yacht. — **cenacula**: from meaning dining-rooms, this word came to be used of all the upper parts of a house, which were usually let for lodgings.

93. **triremis**: properly a war-galley, but used here of the rich man's yacht on account of its size (*three-decker?*).

94. **si curatus**, etc.: to show the universality of this want of settled purpose, the poet says that the indications of it excite no remark even from your friends who are interested in your welfare, whereas the slightest disorder in your apparel would raise a laugh at once. — **inaequali**: *i.e.* irregularly, the description being transferred to the barber himself. — — **tonsore**: treated as a kind of means, not as an agent with **ab**.

95. **subucula**: an under-tunic, worn next the skin.

96. **impar**, *uneven* on the two sides. The toga, though a loose robe, was put on with the greatest care.

97. **mea**, etc.: *i.e.* moral incongruity does not excite even a laugh.

aestuat et vitae disconvenit ordine toto,
diruit, aedificat, mutat quadrata rotundis?
Insanire putas sollemnia me neque rides,
nec medici credis nec curatoris egere
a praetore dati, rerum tutela mearum
cum sis et prave sectum stomacheris ob unguem
de te pendentis, te respicientis amici.
Ad summam: sapiens uno minor est Iove, dives,
liber, honoratus, pulcher, rex denique regum,
praecipue sanus, nisi cum pituita molesta est.

99. **aestuat**, *vacillates*, like the ebb and flow of the tide. — **ordine**, *course*, the ablative of respect.

100. **quadrata**, etc.: *i.e.* in his buildings he substitutes round for square forms.

101. **sollemnia**: cf. **Olympia**, v. 50.

102. **nec medici**, etc.: still less do you (as you ought, if you had the true view of wisdom) regard all this caprice as an evidence of madness. — **medici**: see A. & G. § 243 f. — **curatoris**: as is done in modern times, insane persons had a guardian appointed by the court. Cf. *Sat.* II. 3. 218.

103. **tutela**: equivalent to **tutor**, the abstract for the concrete.

104. **prave sectum**, etc.: these words repeat in a brief and pungent form the same idea which is expressed in v. 84.

105. **respicientis**: *i.e.* looking to you for counsel and direction. Thus it would be the duty of Mæcenas, if he were wise, to warn Horace, a thing he would not fail to do in case of any error in apparel.

106. **ad summam**, etc.: the poet sums up the advantages of philosophy half jestingly in Stoic phrase (cf. *Sat.* I. 3. 125). Cf. Cic. *de Fin.* III. 22. 76: —

> Quod si ita est ut neque quisquam nisi bonus vir et omnes boni beati sint quid philosophia magis colendum aut quid est virtute divinius?

108. **nisi cum pituita**, etc.: Horace cannot forbear deriding the Stoic dogma even while using it, and so he closes in his customary manner with a jest, a play upon **sanus**. This is naturally to be taken in a moral sense, but it is followed by an exception of a mere physical annoyance, just as we might speak of the toothache. It is as if he said, a philosopher is superior to all the ills of life, unless he happens to have the hay fever (the kind of malady to which **pituita** refers). We have in one of the *graffiti* at Pompeii a complaint of such a sufferer: *pituita me tenet*, a cry of the heart preserved for all time in a scratch on plaster.

## II.

Troiani belli scriptorem, maxime Lolli,
dum tu declamas Romae, Praeneste relegi;
qui quid sit pulchrum, quid turpe, quid utile, quid non,
plenius ac melius Chrysippo et Crantore dicit.
Cur ita crediderim, nisi quid te distinet, audi.
Fabula, qua Paridis propter narratur amorem
Graecia barbariae lento collisa duello,
stultorum regum et populorum continet aestus.
Antenor censet belli praecidere causam:

EPISTLE 2. This epistle, again, is an exhortation to the study of philosophy, but of philosophy as drawn from the practical examples given in the *Iliad* and *Odyssey*. It is apparently addressed to a young man not yet devoted to philosophy, and seeks to win him to that pursuit by showing what moral lessons can be got from literature apart from the abstruse discussions of the sages. Which of several Lollii, of whom we have accounts, this one was, and even whether he is the same who is addressed in I. 18, is uncertain. A Lollius also appears in *Od.* IV. 9.

1. **maxime**: probably half in jest in allusion to his aspirations and promise (*flower of the house of Lollius*, or the like).

2. **declamas**: the technical word for the exercises practised in the study of oratory. — **Praeneste**: one of the favorite retiring places or country resorts of the Romans.

3. **pulchrum**: *τὸ καλὸν, τὸ πρέπον*, in a technical sense for virtuous conduct. — **turpe**: *τὸ αἰσχρὸν*, the opposite. — **utile**: *χρηστὸν, advantageous*, a worthy object of desire from a moral point of view. — **quid non**: *ἄχρηστον, injurious.* The whole contains the sum and substance of the fundamental question of ethics. Cf. Aristotle *Nicomach, Eth.* II. 2.

4. **plenius**: in reference to the range of topics. — **melius**: in reference to clearness and convincing power. — **Chrysippo**: cf. *Sat.* I. 3. 127 and note. — **Crantore**: the head of the Academic school, contemporary with Chrysippus. The use of these distinguished examples gives the meaning, "than any philosopher."

5. **distinet**: properly, "distracts your attention," meaning, keeps you busy, and prevents you from giving attention to philosophy.

7. **barbariae**: *i.e.* Asia, as a foreign country to the Greeks.

8. **stultorum**: and hence examples of the opposite of **sapientia**. — **aestus**, *disordered passions*, with an allusion to the philosophical idea of fever or other unsoundness in the passions.

9. **Antenor**: an example of a philosopher to whom Paris refuses to listen. — **praecidere**: depending on **censet** used in the sense of a verb of commanding. For the reference, cf. *Il.* VII. 347 *seq.* Livy also refers to the same story, I. 1.

quid Paris? Vt salvus regnet vivatque beatus
cogi posse negat. Nestor componere litis
inter Peliden festinat et inter Atriden;
hunc amor, ira quidem communiter urit utrumque.
Quicquid delirant reges, plectuntur Achivi.
Seditione, dolis, scelere, atque libidine et ira,
Iliacos intra muros peccatur et extra.
Rursus, quid virtus et quid sapientia possit,
utile proposuit nobis exemplar Vlixen;
qui, domitor Troiae, multorum providus urbes
et mores hominum inspexit, latumque per aequor,
dum sibi, dum sociis reditum parat, aspera multa
pertulit, adversis rerum immersabilis undis.
Sirenum voces et Circae pocula nosti;
quae si cum sociis stultus cupidusque bibisset,
sub domina meretrice fuisset turpis et excors
vixisset canis immundus vel amica luto sus.
Nos numerus sumus et fruges consumere nati,

10. **quid Paris**: originally no doubt **agit** or **facit** was to be supplied, but the expression becomes idiomatic, like "*How was it with Paris?*" or "*But Paris?*"

11. **componere**, etc.: cf. *Il.* I. 247.

13. **hunc**: better taken as referring to Agamemnon, as if Horace were going to say **illum ira**, but corrected it (as is indicated by **quidem**) into **utrumque**. The love of Agamemnon for Chryseis is the original cause of the quarrel.

14. **quidquid**, etc.: *i.e.* there are plenty of examples of the consequences of folly to serve as lessons.

19. **domitor**: as called πτολίπορθος, since it was his craft and not the prowess of Agamemnon that took the city. Cf. *Odys.* I. 2, and Cic. *ad Fam.* X. 13. — **multorum**: with **hominum**. — **providus**: a general representative of the epithets πολύμητις and πολύτροπος, but expressing his character as well.

20. **inspexit**: referring to *Odys.* I. 3, but here representing the hero as improving his opportunities by studying human nature and institutions.

21. **dum . . . parat**: a common form of translation of the Greek participle. Cf. ἀρνύμενος, *Odys.* I. 5.

22. **pertulit**, etc.: thus showing the power of wisdom under the trying circumstances of life.

23. **Sirenum**: *Odys.* XII. 39 *seqq.* — **Circae**: *Odys.* X. 1. 36 *seq.*

25. **turpis**, *unshapely*, as a beast.

26. **canis**: the dog was proverbial for uncleanness as the pig is with us. Hence came part of the reproach to the Cynic philosophy.

27. **nos**, etc.: *i.e.* an example that comes nearer home to us is

sponsi Penelopae, nebulones, Alcinoique
in cute curanda plus aequo operata iuventus,
cui pulchrum fuit in medios dormire dies et
ad strepitum citharae cessantem ducere somnum.
Vt iugulent hominem, surgunt de nocte latrones;
ut te ipsum serves, non expergisceris? Atqui
si noles sanus, curres hydropicus; et ni
posces ante diem librum cum lumine, si non
intendes animum studiis et rebus honestis,
invidia vel amore vigil torquebere. Nam cur
quae laedunt oculum festinas demere; si quid
est animum, differs curandi tempus in annum?
Dimidium facti qui coepit habet: sapere aude:

found in the self-indulgent Phæacians (*Odys.* VIII. 11), or in the riotous suitors of Penelope (*Odys.* II. 74 *et al.*) — **numerus** (as ἄριθμος in Greek), *mere ciphers*, persons of no significance except to swell the number of mankind. — **fruges**, etc.: doubtless proverbial of persons good for nothing else. — **consumere**: poetic (and colloquial?) for **ad consumendas**.

29. **cute curanda**: see *Sat.* II. 5. 38.

30. **pulchrum**: *i.e.* their only ambition. Cf. **pulchrum**, v. 3.

31. **ad strepitum**: cf. *Od.* III. 1. 20. — **cessantem**, *reluctant*, that does not come when desired on account of the want of natural fatigue. Cf. *Sat.* II. 2. 80. (Another reading, **cessatum . . . curam**, is approved by many editors.)

32. **ut iugulent**, etc.: the description of a self-indulgent life naturally leads to an exhortation to end it, and devote one's self to the study of philosophy as a defence against it. — **surgunt**: *i.e.* if cut-throats are willing to rise early to take life, how much more should one rise early to save his own, and this rising early is a beginning of strenuous resistance to self-indulgence.

33. **expergisceris**: present for future, as in the language of comedy. — **atqui**: as if the answer had been in the negative, the poet proceeds to argue the point, hence the adversative.

34. **noles sanus**: *i.e.* if you won't take exercise (another effort against self-indulgence) while in good health, you will be obliged to do so under the advice of your physician when you have become dropsical through your sloth. Cf. *Multum ambulandum, currendum aliquid*, Celsus, III. 21.

35. **posces**, etc.: if you won't wake and fortify yourself against passion by the study of philosophy, your passions will keep you awake all night by and by.

37. **nam cur**, etc.: *i.e.* you take instant measures against bodily ills; why do you postpone the cure of moral affections?

40. **dimidium, etc.**: an old proverb. ἀρχὴ γὰρ λέγεται μὲν ἥμισυ παντὸς, κτλ. Plato *de Legg.* VI. (cf. the sentiment of *Ep.* I. 1. 28). — **aude**: *have the courage, i.e.* to

incipe. Qui recte vivendi prorogat horam,
rusticus exspectat dum defluat amnis; at ille
labitur et labetur in omne volubilis aevum.
Quaeritur argentum puerisque beata creandis
uxor et incultae pacantur vomere silvae.
Quod satis est cui contingit, nihil amplius optet.
Non domus et fundus non aeris acervus et auri
aegroto domini deduxit corpore febris,
non animo curas. Valeat possessor oportet,
si comportatis rebus bene cogitat uti.
Qui cupit aut metuit, iuvat illum sic domus et res,
ut lippum pictae tabulae, fomenta podagram,
auriculas citharae collecta sorde dolentes.
Sincerum est nisi vas, quodcumque infundis acescit.

withstand temptation, not in reference to any risk, but merely to the pain of self-denial.

42. **rusticus**, *is like the countrymen who* (cf. I. 1. 2, note), referring to some well-known story.

44. **quaeritur**, etc.: we keep on seeking to get more of the good things of life without paying attention to our moral state, whereas true philosophy would teach us that moral health is the first thing which would make all our desired good things unnecessary and without which we cannot enjoy them at all. — **argentum**: put for wealth generally. — **pueris creandis**: *i.e.* to found a family to preserve our estates and our memory after death, an object of ambition not sanctioned by philosophy. — **beata**, *rich*, to increase our wealth by her dowry, and by uniting families to establish an illustrious house.

45. **pacantur**, etc.: *i.e.* we enlarge our landed estates. All these things are the objects of worldly ambition which become nought in the eyes of the contented (**quod satis est**, etc.) sage.

47. **non domus**, etc.: a familiar idea with Horace, cf. *Od.* III. 1. 41 *seqq.* The real force, however, is in the **non animo curas**, "they will not do the one any more than the other." Cf. *neque . . . nec*, *Od.* III. 5. 27.

48. **deduxit**: the so-called gnomic aoristic perfect, "they never did, and so presumably they never will."

49. **valeat**: in reference to both the bodily and the mental ills just spoken of, but of course particularly to the latter. The same comparison, almost confusion, of bodily and moral unsoundness is continued in the next verses.

50. **cogitat**, *expects*, like the dialectic "calculates."

51. **cupit aut metuit**: referring to moral diseases, *πάθη*, passions.

52. **fomenta**: hot water applications used by the ancients for pleasurable indulgence, but in this case the deep-seated disease prevents any enjoyment.

54. **sincerum**, etc.: *i.e.* pleasure offered to a soul disturbed by passion is spoiled.

Sperne voluptates; nocet empta dolore voluptas.
Semper avarus eget; certum voto pete finem.
Invidus alterius macrescit rebus opimis;
invidia Siculi non invenere tyranni
maius tormentum. Qui non moderabitur irae,
infectum volet esse dolor quod suaserit et mens,
dum poenas odio per vim festinat inulto.
Ira furor brevis est: animum rege, qui nisi paret,
imperat; hunc frenis, hunc tu compesce catena.
Fingit equum tenera docilem cervice magister
ire viam qua monstret eques; venaticus ex quo
tempore cervinam pellem latravit in aula,
militat in silvis catulus. Nunc adbibe puro
pectore verba puer, nunc te melioribus offer.
Quo semel est imbuta recens servabit odorem
testa diu. Quodsi cessas aut strenuus anteis,
nec tardum opperior nec praecedentibus insto.

55. **sperne**, etc.: here follows a string of general moral precepts in regard to sensual pleasure, covetousness, envy, and anger.

58. **Siculi**: the cruelty of Dionysius and Phalaris, Sicilian tyrants, passed into a proverb.

60. **dolor et mens**, *angry heart*, of the momentary purpose inspired by **dolor**.

63. **hunc frenis**, etc.: the peculiar Horatian connection of thought is very well illustrated by this passage. The idea contained in **paret, imperat, frenis**, suggests the figure of the horse trained when a colt, and so obedient, but in the mean time the object compared has changed in Horace's mind, and becomes not the passions to be controlled, but the boy himself who is to be trained by himself while he is still young and docile.

66. **cervinam pellem**, etc.: it would seem that dogs were taught to hunt by showing them the hide of a deer, and teaching them to recognize that animal as the object of their pursuit. The moral is, that men learn their habits while young, and follow them ever after. — **in aula**, *in the courtyard*, where the lesson is given, as in a school, before the real hunting in the forest, which presents difficulties comparable to those of actual life.

67. **puro**, *unsullied*, *i.e.* before bad habits are formed.

68. **melioribus**: cf. I. 1. 48.

70. **quodsi**, etc.: in closing, Horace half-jestingly reasserts his doctrine of the golden mean; if his pupil lingers, he himself will pursue his even way without him, or, if in the enthusiasm of youth, the pupil presses on, he himself will not be thrown out of his calm philosophic spirit even in pursuit of philosophy itself.

## III.

Iuli Flore, quibus terrarum militet oris
Claudius, Augusti privignus, scire laboro.
Thracane vos Hebrusque nivali compede vinctus,
an freta vicinas inter currentia turris,
an pingues Asiae campi collesque morantur?
Quid studiosa cohors operum struit? Hoc quoque curo.
Quis sibi res gestas Augusti scribere sumit?
Bella quis et paces longum diffundit in aevum?
Quid Titius, Romana brevi venturus in ora,
Pindarici fontis qui non expalluit haustus,
fastidire lacus et rivos ausus apertos?
Vt valet? Vt meminit nostri? Fidibusne Latinis

EPISTLE 3. This epistle, of a less general character than the two preceding, is only a familiar letter addressed to a friend, Julius Florus. He was at the time one of the suite (**cohors amicorum**) of Tiberius (cf. notes to *Sat.* I. 5.), who was then (B.C. 20) in Armenia with an army threatening Parthia.

1. **Iuli Flore**: the full name is a little formal and serious. He appears also in II. 2.

2. **Claudius**: Tiberius Claudius Nero. — **privignus**: this description is meant as a compliment, and the gentile name alone is respectful in the case of a dignitary. — **laboro**: cf. *Sat.* II. 8. 19.

3. **Thracane**, etc.: the route of an army would be through Thrace, across the Hellespont over through Asia Minor into Armenia. The question is only a formal way of asking how far along he is on his march. — **vinctus**: not at the time, but proverbially so as being in a cold region.

4. **turris**: Sestos and Abydos.

6. **studiosa**, etc.: all the young nobles were litterateurs to some extent. In fact, such had been often taken in the suite of a commander ever since Ennius went into Ætolia with Fulvius.

8. **diffundit**: *i.e.* preserves the memory of them in literature. Cf. II. 3. 346, and *Od.* IV. 14. 3.

9. **Titius**: unknown, except from the allusion here. — **venturus**: *i.e.* about to become famous, a prophecy apparently not fulfilled.

10. **Pindarici**: he seems to have attempted the Pindaric ode, for the difficulty of which, cf. *Od.* IV. 2.

11. **lacus et rivos apertos**: alluding to the quieter style of ordinary poets, as opposed to the mountain torrent of Pindar. — **apertos**: in the open plain, not in woods or mountains.

12. **fidibusne**, etc. (cf. *Od.* III. 30. 13): *i.e.* does he still attempt the ode, and with success, or has he abandoned it for the turgid eloquence of the drama?

Thebanos aptare modos studet auspice Musa,
an tragica desaevit et ampullatur in arte?
Quid mihi Celsus agit? Monitus multumque monendus,
privatas ut quaerat opes et tangere vitet
scripta, Palatinus quaecumque recepit Apollo;
ne si forte suas repetitum venerit olim
grex avium plumas moveat cornicula risum
furtivis nudata coloribus. Ipse quid audes?
Quae circumvolitas agilis thyma? Non tibi parvum
ingenium, non incultum est ac turpiter hirtum:
seu linguam causis acuis seu civica iura
respondere paras seu condis amabile carmen,
prima feres hederae victricis praemia. Quodsi
frigida curarum fomenta relinquere posses,
quo te caelestis sapientia duceret, ires.
Hoc opus, hoc studium parvi properemus et ampli,
si patriae volumus, si nobis vivere cari.

13. **auspice Musa**, *with favoring Muse, i.e.* does he succeed in his venturesome attempt?

14. **desaevit**, *rave,* referring to the intensity of passion. — **ampullatur**, *bluster*, referring to the diction. Without supposing any direct ridicule on Horace's part of his young friend's efforts, one can hardly help feeling a tone of raillery in the whole allusion. For the word, cf. II. 3. 97, and ληκύθους, Cic. *ad Att.* I. 14.

15. **mihi**, *my friend, tell me,* or *I should like to know*, ethical dative. — **Celsus**: perhaps the same to whom *Ep.* I. 8 is addressed, wh. see.

16. **privatas**, etc.: *i.e.* to write something of his own, and not borrow from the ancients. Of course all Romans borrowed, but this man must have copied without making the ideas his own.

17. **Palatinus**, etc.: Augustus, in B.C. 28, established a library in connection with the temple of Apollo on the Palatine.

20. **audes**, *venture on.*

22. **hirtum**, *rough*, like land foul with weeds and bushes.

23. **linguam**, etc.: the three literary professions, so to speak, of orator, jurisconsult, and poet.

24. **amabile**, *charming*, lyric poetry, neither tragic nor epic.

25. **hederae**: cf. *Od.* I. 1. 29.

26. **frigida**, *chill* (*clammy*), *comfortless*, as not giving the warmth and comfort they were intended to. — **curarum** (objective), *anxious cares*, the worries of worldly life. — **fomenta**, *solace, relief, i.e.* the ambitious pursuits with which (as in I. 2. 44 *seq.*) he seeks to satisfy the cravings of his soul, and solace the anxieties of a worldly life. — **relinquere**: if he could but abandon

Debes hoc etiam rescribere, sit tibi curae
quantae conveniat Munatius? An male sarta
gratia nequicquam coit et rescinditur? At vos
seu calidus sanguis seu rerum inscitia vexat
indomita cervice feros, ubicumque locorum
vivitis indigni fraternum rumpere foedus,
pascitur in vestrum reditum votiva iuvenca.

## IV.

Albi, nostrorum sermonum candide iudex,
quid nunc te dicam facere in regione Pedana?
Scribere quod Cassi Parmensis opuscula vincat,

the pursuit of ambition and take up philosophy, then his talent would carry him far on in the road to wisdom.

31. **Munatius**: probably the son of Lucius Munatius Plancus, for whom see *Od.* I. 7. With him Florus had, it seems, fallen out, and had been reconciled (perhaps by Horace himself).

32. **at vos**, etc.: in either case, whether you remain friends, or otherwise, I shall be ready to greet you both on your return, for which I have made a vow. The evidence of his friendship for both and his words in reference to their quarrel indicate a strong desire to reconcile them — a desire which may be the kernel of this letter.

33. **calidus sanguis**, etc.: implying that there is no real cause for persons of such a character (**indigni**, etc.) to quarrel, but that their difference comes either from the fiery temper of youth or from want of experience.

EPISTLE 4. Addressed to the poet Tibullus.

1. **Albi**: Cf. *Od.* I. 33. 1. The poet's prænomen is unknown. — **sermonum**: the word includes the satires, and possibly some of the epistles. The mention of these, excluding the odes, would seem to indicate that such fair-minded judges were rare, and that Horace's *musa pedestris* was very generally disapproved, while his odes met no such disapproval. This agrees with what is implied in *Sat.* I. 4, I. 10, and II. 1. — **candide**, etc.: an expression of thanks for Tibullus' approval.

2. **quid te dicam**, etc.: a colloquial form of expression, common in comedy. — **Pedana**: Pedum, a hill-city in the vicinity of Rome, was one of the many favorite country resorts of the Romans. Every available spot of high land near Rome seems to have been occupied by their villas. Tibullus must have had a villa near Pedum.

3. **scribere**, etc.: *i.e.* are you engaged in poetry or philosophy? — **Cassi**: a fellow-soldier of Horace in the army of Brutus and Cassius (Longinus). He seems to have tried many styles of composition, but here only elegies seem to be referred to (**opuscula**), in which he

an tacitum silvas inter reptare salubris,
curantem quicquid dignum sapiente bonoque est?
Non tu corpus eras sine pectore: di tibi formam,
di tibi divitias dederunt artemque fruendi.
Quid voveat dulci nutricula maius alumno,
qui sapere et fari possit quae sentiat, et cui
gratia, fama, valetudo contingat abunde,
et mundus victus non deficiente crumena?
Inter spem curamque, timores inter et iras
omnem crede diem tibi diluxisse supremum:
grata superveniet quae non sperabitur hora.
Me pinguem et nitidum bene curata cute vises,
cum ridere voles Epicuri de grege porcum.

was successful, though only insignificant fragments of his work remain.

4. **tacitum**, *musing*. Cf. *Sat.* I. 3. 65. — **reptare**, *are strolling*. Cf. *repimus*, *Sat.* I. 5. 25.

5. **curantem**, *absorbed in*, *i.e.* meditating thoughtfully upon. — **quicquid**, etc.: *i.e.* ethics, as the guide to a noble life.

6. **eras**: *i.e.* the last time I saw you, and so are not likely to be now; hence I expect something good of you. — **pectore**, *a soul*, *i.e.* a fine intellect and good heart. — **di tibi**, etc.: *i.e.* you have all these blessings that ought to make you a happy man, and give you a contented spirit (the aim of philosophy) if you take the right view of human life. The melancholy tone of Tibullus' poetry makes it probable that he had a morbid disposition, or, at least, a vein of melancholy, to which Horace alludes. Cf. *Od.* I. 33.

8. **nutricula**, *fond nurse*, a diminutive of affection. Cf. **matercula**, I. 7. 7.

9. **fari**, etc.: *i.e.* sufficient eloquence.

10. **gratia**, *friends*, substituting in translation the concrete for the abstract.

11. **mundus victus**, *a life of elegance*.

12. **inter spem**, etc.: *i.e.* amid all human experiences, the chance and change of life, which the wise man can meet with serenity if he regards each day as his last.

15. **vises**: equivalent to an imperative, *come and find me*, etc.

16. **Epicuri**, etc.: referring apparently to one of Horace's periods of backsliding (cf. I. 1. 18), though he has just exhorted his friend to moral effort. — **porcum**, etc.: apparently a common reproach upon the Epicureans, on account of their making the pleasure of the senses the summum bonum. Cf. Cic. *in Pis.* 16. 37; Cic. *ad Fam.* IX. 20. 1; *de Off.* III. 33. 117.

## V.

Si potes Archiacis conviva recumbere lectis
nec modica cenare times holus omne patella,
supremo te sole domi, Torquate, manebo.
Vina bibes iterum Tauro diffusa palustris
inter Minturnas Sinuessanumque Petrinum.
Si melius quid habes, arcesse, vel imperium fer.
Iamdudum splendet focus et tibi munda supellex
Mitte leves spes et certamina divitiarum
et Moschi causam: cras nato Caesare festus

EPISTLE 5. An invitation to dinner, addressed to Torquatus, probably the same to whom *Od.* IV. 7 is written. It is as if a jovial friend should say to his busy and less self-indulgent companion, "Come, let's have a dinner; it will do you good. I will invite you, or, if you are not content with my bill of fare, then you invite me." Which of the many Torquati this is, is uncertain.

1. **potes**, *can bear*, to dine in such humble guise. — **Archiacis**: probably the well-known name of a cheap wooden triclinium made by a carpenter, Archias. Cf. "Windsor chairs." — **lectis**: cf. *Sat.* II. 8. 20 and note.

2. **modica**: not sumptuous, such as the great man would be accustomed to. — **holus omne**: *any kind of vegetables*, lit. all kinds, not excluding the poorer. — **patella**, *dinner service*, the characteristic plate offered to the Lares being put for the whole. Cf. *patera*, *Sat.* I. 6. 118.

3. **supremo**: cf. *primo sole*, *prima luce*. The dinner hour varied from early afternoon to evening. Cf. *Sat.* I. 6. 114. — **manebo**, *I shall expect*.

4. **iterum Tauro** (*sc.* **consule**): the date is B.C. 26, and the wine would be about five or six years old, respectable but not choice. — **palustris**, etc.: a region of good wines, among which was the Massic. — **diffusa**, *bottled*, drawn off from the great jars, in which it was first made, into the amphora.

6. **si melius**, etc.: Torquatus is bidden to come, unless he himself has something better to offer in the way of an entertainment, in which case he is to invite Horace instead. Cf. St. Jerome, *Ep.* 48 (Migne, Vol. I. p. 509), *Aut profer meliores epulas et me conviva utere aut qualicumque nostra cenula contentus esto*, where the Father is evidently thinking of this passage. — **arcesse**, *send for me, invite me*. — **imperium fer**, *submit to my orders*, as host or master of the feast.

7. **focus**: the sacred symbolic hearth, dedicated to the Lares, to whom every meal was in a manner a sacrifice. This had been polished in anticipation of the occasion. Cf. *Epod.* 2. 66. — **supellex**: the table service, which also had been put in order.

8. **mitte**: *i.e.* dismiss all cares of business and ambition.

9. **Moschi causam**, a *cause célè*

dat veniam somnumque dies; impune licebit
aestivam sermone benigno tendere noctem.
Quo mihi fortunam, si non conceditur uti?
Parcus ob heredis curam nimiumque severus
adsidet insano: potare et spargere flores
incipiam, patiarque vel inconsultus haberi.
Quid non ebrietas designat? Operta recludit,
spes iubet esse ratas, ad proelia trudit inertem,
sollicitis animis onus eximit, addocet artes.
Fecundi calices quem non fecere disertum,
contracta quem non in paupertate solutum?
Haec ego procurare et idoneus imperor et non
invitus: ne turpe toral, ne sordida mappa
corruget nares; ne non et cantharus et lanx
ostendat tibi te; ne fidos inter amicos
sit qui dicta foras eliminet; ut coeat par
iungaturque pari. Butram tibi Septiciumque

*bre* of the time in which Torquatus was engaged. — **Caesare**: apparently Julius, whose birthday, July 12th, agrees better than Sept. 23, the day of Augustus' birth, with **aestivam noctem.** — **festus**: the next day being a holiday gives excuse for festivity, and at the same time allows a later hour of rising after the indulgence.

11. **tendere**, *while away*, lit. extend the night with, etc., for extend through the night.

12. **quo mihi**, etc.: the strenuous and sober Torquatus seems to have been thought to need some apology from Horace, or an exhortation, as it were, to indulgence. — **fortunam**: cf. *quo sumere? Sat.* I. 6. 24, and *unde mihi lapidem? Sat.* II. 7. 116.

14. **adsidet**, *is next neighbor to.* Cf. "next door to a fool."

16. **designat**, *contrive*, *i.e.* stimulate the mind to activity so as to make any undertaking seem possible. Cf. *Od.* III. 21. 13; Ter. *Ad.* 87. — **operta recludit**: *reveals mysteries*, *i.e.* discovers things not understood in more sluggish moments. The divulging of secrets is out of place here.

17. Cf. *Od.* III. 21. 18, and I. 7. 31.

18. **addocet**, etc.: *teaches new arts.*

19. **fecundi**: as producing a *copia loquendi*, suggesting ideas.

20. **solutum**, *free*, *i.e.* from the benumbing influence of poverty.

21. **haec**: referring to the following, the duties of host, and opposed to the idea of v. 30. — **imperor**: *make it my duty*, a rare middle use.

26. **Butram**, etc.: persons unknown.

et nisi cena prior potiorque puella Sabinum
detinet adsumam. Locus est et pluribus umbris;
sed nimis arta premunt olidae convivia caprae.
Tu quotus esse velis rescribe et rebus omissis
atria servantem postico falle clientem.

## VI.

Nil admirari prope res est una, Numici,
solaque, quae possit facere et servare beatum.
Hunc solem et stellas et decedentia certis
tempora momentis sunt qui formidine nulla
imbuti spectent. Quid censes munera terrae,

28. **umbris**: cf. *Sat.* II. 8. 22.

29. **sed nimis**, etc.: but not too many, lest if they recline too close to each other, they should be mutually disagreeable.

30. **tu**: opposed to **ego**, *i.e.* all you have to do is to say how many we shall be, and dodge a waiting client, and come. — **atria**: the great hall was the common reception room in which the visitors of a great man waited for his appearance from the more private parts of his house. Here Torquatus is to slip out by a back door, and so avoid the importunities which might hinder him from coming.

Epistle 6. The Numicius here addressed is otherwise unknown. There is nothing personal, however, in the epistle except the possible indication in v. 31, that Numicius was a disbeliever in virtue. It is a philosophical lecture which might be addressed to anybody.

1. **nil admirari**, *to be disturbed by nothing*, including all sensations which would disturb the even serenity (εὐθυμία) of the sage, whether of desire, fear, superstition, or envy. This state of mind corresponds to the ἀθαμβία and ἀθαυμαστία of the Greeks. This principle belongs to many philosophers, but is differently worked out by them in detail. Cf. Diog. Laert. VII. 123. Synonymous with **admirari** in this sense are **stupere, torpere**.

3. **hunc solem**, etc.: *i.e.* there are men so free from superstition that they can observe all the great phenomena of nature without alarm. — **hunc**: with a gesture implying the grandeur of the visible heavens. — **decedentia**, *moving on*.

4. **tempora**, *the seasons*. — **momentis**, *times*, properly the degrees or steps by which the seasons seem to proceed. The whole indicates the grandeur of the machinery of the universe, which excites the awe of the unphilosophical and leads them to tremble at the power of the gods.

5. **quid censes**, etc.: *i.e.* if the sage can look unmoved at the grandest phenomena of the heavens, how much less should a man be moved by the paltry things of earth! — **munera**: *i.e.* what earth has to bestow, such as gold and silver, etc.

quid maris extremos Arabas ditantis et Indos,
ludicra quid plausus et amici dona Quiritis,
quo spectanda modo, quo sensu credis et ore?
Qui timet his adversa, fere miratur eodem
quo cupiens pacto; pavor est utrobique molestus;
improvisa simul species exterret utrumque.
Gaudeat an doleat, cupiat metuatne, quid ad rem,
si quidquid vidit melius peiusque sua spe
defixis oculis animoque et corpore torpet?
Insani nomen sapiens ferat, aequus iniqui,
ultra quam satis est virtutem si petat ipsam.
I nunc, argentum et marmor vetus aeraque et artes
suspice, cum gemmis Tyrios mirare colores;
gaude quod spectant oculi te mille loquentem;
gnavus mane forum et vespertinus pete tectum,

6. **maris**: *i.e.* pearls from the Red Sea and the Persian Gulf.

7. **ludicra**, *trifles, playthings*, in apposition with **plausus et dona**. This verse refers to the objects of ambition as the preceding do to wealth. — **dona**: *i.e.* office.

8. **quo spectanda modo**, etc.: *i.e.* they (*a fortiori*) are not to be looked upon with awe (**admiranda**), but scorned (**contemnenda**) as worthless. This attitude of mind as well as freedom from fear is included in **nil admirari** (cf. v. 9).

9. **his adversa**: *i.e.* poverty or disgrace in the eyes of the people. — **miratur**, *is in awe*.

10. **pavor**, *awe*, referring to the excited state of mind which is common both to desire and fear; cf. "all in a quiver," "all in a flutter." — **molestus**: *i.e.* and hence prevents one from being **beatus**, the point to be proved.

11. **species**, *apparition*, *i.e.* the sight either of the object of desire, or of anything that threatens to take it away.

14. **defixis oculis**: cf. **ore**, v. 8. — **torpet**, *is dazed*, the state of mind and body referred to in **admirari** (v. 1) and **mirari** (v. 9).

15. **insani**: the opposite of **sapiens**, and equal to **stultus**. — **aequus**, *just*, in the sense of rendering everything its due.

16. **ultra quam**, etc.: *i.e.* even virtue itself may become the object of this **admiratio**, so that the sage (as with the Stoics) may become a fool by pursuing virtue to excess.

17. **i nunc**: if what has been said is true, then go (if you can) and admire the objects of men's desire and ambition. — **argentum**, etc.: *i.e.* all the paraphernalia of a luxurious life of splendor and wealth. — **artes**, *works of art*.

18. **suspice**, *gaze upon* with awe.

19. **gaude quod**, etc.: the marks of a life of successful ambition.

20. **forum**, etc.: as a statesman or lawyer to win fortune, and perhaps also by marrying a rich woman (cf. **dotalibus**, v. 21) to found a distinguished family; cf. I. 2. 44.

ne plus frumenti dotalibus emetat agris
Mutus et — indignum, quod sit peioribus ortus, —
hic tibi sit potius quam tu mirabilis illi.
Quicquid sub terra est in apricum proferet aetas,
defodiet condetque nitentia. Cum bene notum
porticus Agrippae et via te conspexerit Appi,
ire tamen restat Numa quo devenit et Ancus.

Si latus aut renes morbo tentantur acuto,
quaere fugam morbi. Vis recte vivere? Quis non?
Si virtus hoc una potest dare, fortis omissis
hoc age deliciis. Virtutem verba putas et

21. **dotalibus**: if this is taken as referring to Mutus also, it means that he has only that sort of wealth. It may, however, be used of both; cf. preceding note.

22. **Mutus**: an unknown parvenu. — **peioribus ortus**: at Rome high birth was regarded as a sort of claim to political distinction.

23. **mirabilis**, *an object of envy*.

24. **quicquid sub terra**, etc.: *i.e.* these objects of splendor are only temporary and will perish; they came from the earth (cf. **proferet**) and will return to it again (cf. **munera terrae**, v. 5).

25. **bene notum**, etc.: however great you may be in the eyes of the people, still death awaits you.

26. **porticus Agrippae**: a colonnade near the Pantheon built by Marcus Agrippa, a favorite lounging-place of the Romans. — **via Appi**: the favorite place for driving and riding. Here the great Roman would be seen in his carriage, as he would be seen on foot in the **porticus Agrippae**.

27. **ire**: poetical and colloquial instead of **ut eas**. — **Numa**, etc.: *i.e.* nobody could be greater or more esteemed than the ancient kings. Yet they are dead, and so will you soon be, and then your fame will be of no avail.

28. **si latus**, etc.: the beginning of the personal application (as it were) of the sermon. "If what I have said is true, then it behooves you to set about securing happiness, just as, if you had a bodily disease, you would at once set about curing it. Then the question comes up: but how? Horace then proceeds to give several proposed remedies, on the one hand the pursuit of virtue, and on the other the pursuit of wealth, distinction, and pleasure.

29. **quaere**, etc.: *i.e.* do so, as you would of course. — **vis recte vivere**: *i.e.* of course you do, and if so, you should adopt the right means.

30. **si virtus**, etc.: *i.e.* virtue carried to the extreme in the Stoic method. If this be the only way to happiness, the natural conclusion is that you should devote yourself wholly to it, abandoning all enjoyment. This course the poet has already disapproved in v. 16. Perhaps however the next verse is to be taken literally, representing Numicius as a disbeliever in virtue, in which case he of course can't pursue it.

31. **virtutem**, etc.: if, on the

lucum ligna: cave ne portus occupet alter,
ne Cibyratica, ne Bithyna negotia perdas;
mille talenta rotundentur, totidem altera, porro et
tertia succedant, et quae pars quadret acervum.
Scilicet uxorem cum dote fidemque et amicos
et genus et formam regina Pecunia donat,
ac bene nummatum decorat Suadela Venusque.
Mancipiis locuples eget aeris Cappadocum rex.
Ne fueris hic tu. Chlamydes Lucullus, ut aiunt,
si posset centum scaenae praebere rogatus,
'Qui possum tot?' ait, 'Tamen et quaeram et quot habebo
mittam.' Post paullo scribit sibi milia quinque
esse domi chlamydum; partem vel tolleret omnes.

other hand, you go to the other extreme, and think that virtue is the mere fustian of philosophers, then the natural conclusion is that you should devote yourself to the objects of human desire with insatiable greed. This strenuousness he illustrates in detail in the following. — **et**, *and* (as you naturally would).

32. **lucum ligna**: *i.e.* a sacred grove is nothing but firewood, the sanctity being a mere pretence or notion. — **portus occupet**, *gain the harbor before you*, to get higher prices for his wares by bringing them in early. Cf. the races of the first tea-ships in our own times.

33. **Cibyratica**: from Cibyra, a commercial city of Phrygia. The whole region of the Black Sea and of Asia Minor was the seat of the most lucrative commerce of the times. Here the capitalist or speculator is referred to, as the humbler **mercator** is in the preceding.

35. **quadrat**: *i.e.* makes it four times as much, referring to rolling up wealth in arithmetic ratio.

36. **scilicet**, *for of course*, an ironical statement of the advantages of wealth as giving the sources of happiness. — **uxorem cum dote**: cf. I. 2. 44. — **fidem**, *credit*, both in a business sense, and also almost equivalent to **auctoritas**.

38. **decorat**: *i.e.* each with her own peculiar gift. — **Suadela**: the goddess of persuasion or eloquence. — **Venus**: as the goddess of grace and favor.

39. **mancipiis**, etc.: *i.e.* don't be satisfied with wealth in one direction; be not content even with regal position without enormous riches. — **Cappadocum rex**: the allusion is doubtless to Ariobarzanes, mentioned several times by Cicero as in an embarrassed condition. Cf. *ad Att.* VI. 1. 3, and VI. 3. 5. From Cappadocia came a favorite breed of slaves. Cf. Plut. *Luc.* 39.

40. **fueris**: with long ī, preserving the ancient quantity. — **Lucullus**, etc.: be rather like Lucullus, who didn't know how much he did have, as is illustrated by the anecdote.

41. **scaenae**: *i.e.* for the stage on some festive occasion. — **rogatus**: *i.e.* by the aedile.

44. **chlamydum**: with the ancients these were objects of wealth.

Exilis domus est ubi non et multa supersunt
et dominum fallunt et prosunt furibus! Ergo
si res sola potest facere et servare beatum,
hoc primus repetas opus, hoc postremus omittas.
Si fortunatum species et gratia praestat,
mercemur servum qui dictet nomina, laevum
qui fodicet latus et cogat trans pondera dextram
porrigere. 'Hic multum in Fabia valet, ille Velina,
cui libet hic fasces dabit, eripietque curule
cui volet importunus ebur.' Frater, Pater adde;
ut cuique est aetas, ita quemque facetus adopta.
Si, bene qui cenat, bene vivit; lucet, eamus
quo ducet gula: piscemur, venemur, ut olim
Gargilius, qui mane plagas, venabula, servos,
differtum transire forum populumque iubebat,
unus ut e multis populo spectante referret

He didn't know that he had a hundred, and found he had five thousand. — **tolleret**: indirect quotation from the imperative of his letter.

46. **dominum fallunt**: as in the case of Lucullus. — **furibus**: *i.e.* ready to be stolen and never missed.

47. **si res**, etc.: a repetition of the idea begun in v. 31, but not formulated until now.

49. **species et gratia**, *distinction and popularity*, in the political world.

50. **servum**: a person called *nomenclator* whose business it was to find out the names of humble persons and inform his master, so that he could greet them by name. — **laevum**: cf. *Sat.* II. 5. 17.

51. **trans pondera**, *over the counter*, of the little shops, on which the balances of the shopkeeper stood, and behind which stood the keeper himself. Cf. the shops at Pompeii in Museo Borbonico X.

52. **hic multum**, etc.: like our ward politicians.

53. **curule . . . ebur**, *the curule chair* of the magistrates.

54. **pater**, *uncle*, our corresponding word. — **adde**: *i.e.* to the handshake implied in the preceding.

55. **facetus**, *with graceful courtesy*. — **adopta**, *take him into your family*.

56. **si bene**, etc.: a third object of men's desire, thought to produce happiness.

57. **ut olim Gargilius**, etc.: *i.e.* with all the eagerness of Gargilius, the anecdote only illustrating the devotion to the pursuit shown by that unknown personage. The poet, however, cannot forbear depicting the ludicrous side of Gargilius' behavior, even though that has nothing to do with the case.

60. **unus e multis**: *i.e.* only one boar, and that one bought of some country hunter, after all the preparation for hunting.

emptum mulus aprum; crudi tumidique lavemur,
quid deceat, quid non, obliti, Caerite cera
digni, remigium vitiosum Ithacensis Vlixi,
cui potior patria fuit interdicta voluptas.
Si, Mimnermus uti censet, sine amore iocisque
nil est iucundum, vivas in amore iocisque.
Vive, vale: si quid novisti rectius istis,
candidus imperti; si non, his utere mecum.

61. **crudi**, etc.: *i.e.* let us devote ourselves to the pleasures of the palate, taking the luxurious bath without waiting for the last excessive meal to digest. Cf. Persius, III. 98; Juvenal, I. 142.

62. **quid deceat**, etc.: *i.e.* the proprieties of life, which would forbid such indulgence.

62. **Caerite cera**, etc.: *i.e.* good for nothing as citizens, and so deserving to be deprived of citizenship. This process was performed by removing a man's name from the list of his tribe, and enrolling him among the citizens of Caere, who at a very early period were taken into the state without the right of suffrage. Cf. Aul. *Gel.* XVI. 13.

63. **remigium**, *the crew;* cf. Hom. *Odys.* XII. 313 *seq.*

64. **voluptas**: the feasting on the cattle of the Sun.

65. **si Mimnermus**, etc.: a fourth object of desire. — **Mimnermus**: an elegiac poet of Colophon. — **censet**: cf. a fragment of his, preserved to us; *τίς δὲ βίος, τί δὲ τερπνὸν ἄτερ χρυσέης Ἀφροδίτης;*

67. **vive, vale**: cf. *Sat.* II. 5. 110. — **rectius**, *better*, *i.e.* as a mode of life. Cf. **recte**, v. 29. — **istis**: *than all that*, which the poet has set forth as the rule of conduct to be reached by any one who adopts any of the views beginning with v. 30.

68. **candidus**: almost equal to "*be generous and.*" — **si non**: *i.e.* if you have nothing better to offer as a scheme of life than the obviously absurd ideas that I have set forth (from v. 30) on that side. — **his**, *this view of mine*, referring to the doctrine of **nil admirari** set forth from vv. 1 to 27.

## VII.

Quinque dies tibi pollicitus me rure futurum
Sextilem totum mendax desideror. Atqui
si me vivere vis sanum recteque valentem,
quam mihi das aegro, dabis aegrotare timenti,
Maecenas, veniam, dum ficus prima calorque
dissignatorem decorat lictoribus atris;
dum pueris omnis pater et matercula pallet,
officiosaque sedulitas et opella forensis
adducit febris et testamenta resignat.

EPISTLE 7. Though Horace was a man of humble extraction and position, brought by his genius and education into companionship with the great, yet he seems to have been entirely free from servility of nature, and accordingly to have preserved his independence even in the difficult relation of client and patron. For his self-respect we may compare *Sat.* I. 6, and for his views of the relation of clientship, *Ep.* I. 18. This epistle was evidently written to Mæcenas to justify himself for preferring considerations of health to the claims of his patron. He had apparently retired from the city to the country (perhaps to Tibur. Cf. vv. 45 and 10) for a few days, and had continued away for a month, and now had it in mind to remain away the whole winter. While excusing himself on the plea of ill health, he also asserts (v. 34 *seq.*) his liberty of action within the limits of friendship.

1. **quinque**: often loosely used of a short indefinite time. — **rure**: probably at Tibur.

2. **Sextilem**: the month of August was not so named until 8 B.C. — **desideror**, *I allow myself to be missed.* — **atqui**, *and yet* (though I fail to keep my promise).

3. **sanum recteque valentem**: without essential difference of meaning, like *well and strong*, *in good health and vigor*.

4. **aegrotare**: here equivalent to the regular construction with **ne**, though properly used with a different meaning.

5. **dum ficus**, etc.: a poetical description of the unhealthy season of autumn.

6. **dissignatorem**, *the undertaker*, who managed funerals, much as in modern times. — **decorat**: of course the presence of the lictors, as "assistant marshals," would indicate a splendid funeral, and so they are said to be the undertaker's adornments. — **atris**: clothed in black, as in modern times.

7. **matercula**, *fond mother*, the diminutive of affection, reversed as it were.

8. **officiosa**: *i.e.* in the performance of duties, especially social (**officia**), as the attendance upon the great and the like. — **opella forensis**: in reference to the services of the *patronus*, which at this season would be petty and insignificant.

9. **testamenta resignat**: naturally, by killing off the testator.

10. **quodsi bruma**, etc.: *i.e.* if the winter becomes too cold there.

Quodsi bruma nives Albanis illinet agris,
ad mare descendet vates tuus et sibi parcet
contractusque leget; te, dulcis amice, reviset
cum Zephyris, si concedes, et hirundine prima.
Non quo more piris vesci Calaber iubet hospes,
tu me fecisti locupletem. 'Vescere sodes!'
'Iam satis est.' 'At tu quantum vis tolle.' 'Benigne.'
'Non invisa feres pueris munuscula parvis.'
'Tam teneor dono quam si dimittar onustus.'
'Vt libet; haec porcis hodie comedenda relinques.'
Prodigus et stultus donat quae spernit et odit;
haec seges ingratos tulit et feret omnibus annis.
Vir bonus et sapiens dignis ait esse paratus;

11. **descendet**: merely of the descent from the hills to some southern resort (cf. v. 45). — **sibi parcet,** *take care of himself* by avoiding the cold.

12. **contractus,** *in a cosy corner,* referring merely to the poet's "cuddling himself up" to keep warm. Cf. *Gravissimo frigore solus atque contractus Dormitantius vigilabit in lecto.* St. Jerome, *in Vig.* § 15.

Inque manus venit tritus de more libellus,
Nescio quid nugarum contractusque legebam.
Nam rore Auctumni matutinisque pruinis
Frigidula intrabat male sartas aura fenestras.

Q. SECTANI (L. Sergardi, A.D. 1650), *Satyrae*, 4. 6.

13. **Zephyris**: cf. Lucr. V. 738.

14. **non quo more,** etc.: the transition is abrupt, but is founded on the relations of the parties. Mæcenas had been such a munificent patron to Horace that he might seem to have a right to the society of his friend under any and all circumstances. But Horace puts their friendship upon a basis which excludes ingratitude in the receiver as well as selfish arrogance in the giver. The anecdote of the Calabrian host (no doubt a story current at the time, and localized as such stories usually are) gives an instance of thoughtless giving merely of that which is superfluous, without thought of the character or merit of the receiver, and without any personal regard. Such has not been Mæcenas' generosity to the poet.

16. **tolle**: *i.e.* take away with you. — **benigne,** *no, thank you,* like *merci* in French.

19. **haec porcis,** etc.: representing the worthlessness of the gift to the host himself.

20. **prodigus et stultus**: *i.e.* it is the prodigal and fool who, etc. — **spernit et odit**: *i.e.* cares nothing for, and in fact wants to be rid of.

21. **ingratos,** etc.: for naturally where there is no personal regard nor sacrifice, no gratitude is likely to be felt.

22. **dignis**: *i.e.* the wise man makes a distinction in the objects of his bounty, so that the gift is a mark of esteem, and is prized as such. — **ait esse**: a familiar Greek construction borrowed by the Latin poets for brevity.

nec tamen ignorat quid distent aera lupinis.
Dignum praestabo me etiam pro laude merentis.
Quodsi me noles usquam discedere, reddes
forte latus, nigros angusta fronte capillos;
reddes dulce loqui; reddes ridere decorum et
inter vina fugam Cinarae maerere protervae.
Forte per angustam tenuis volpecula rimam
repserat in cumeram frumenti, pastaque rursus
ire foras pleno tendebat corpore frustra.
Cui mustela procul: 'Si vis,' ait, 'effugere istinc,
macra cavum repetes artum, quem macra subisti.'
Hac ego si compellor imagine, cuncta resigno;
nec somnum plebis laudo satur altilium, nec
otia divitiis Arabum liberrima muto.
Saepe verecundum laudasti, rexque paterque
audisti coram, nec verbo parcius absens;

23. **nec tamen**, etc.: and yet the giver knows the value of the gift; though he gives freely, he makes something like a sacrifice. — **lupinis**: the regular stage money, used as children count with beans.

24. **dignum**, etc.: *i.e.* Horace also recognizes the value of the gift, and will show gratitude in proportion.

25. **quodsi**, etc.: *i.e.* yet if the gift is to constitute a claim to incessant attendance, the poet must have back his lost youth, whose vigor made such attendance possible. This, of course, cannot be, and he proceeds by the use of a fable to assert delicately that he cannot by any munificence be bound to lose his independence, and would rather resign all than be fattened as a humble dependent, or be forced to activity against his will.

27. **dulce loqui**: cf. *Od.* I. 22. 23. The inf. as a noun is colloquial.

28. **Cinarae**: cf. *Od.* IV. 1. 3; IV. 13. 22; *Epist.* I. 14. 32.

29. **volpecula**: the substitution of **nitedula** (Bentley) is unnecessary, inasmuch as old fables are often regardless of natural history. Cf. The Fox and the Grapes.

34. **si compeller**, etc.: *i.e.* if your demands are to be understood in the sense of the remark of the weasel, I give up all your gifts.

35. **somnum**: *i.e.* the idleness of a mere pampered dependent.

36. **otia**, etc.: *i.e.* the freedom to pursue my own vocations uninterrupted.

37. **saepe verecundum**, etc.: *i.e.* yet from my former conduct you can see how much it would cost me to give up this relation; but I value my independence more, and would abandon the gift if it brings obligations for which I am unfitted, and so becomes an unsuitable gift, like horses to Telemachus. — **verecundum**: *modest and respectful*, showing that his present attitude is not a mere wilful impertinence, or the arrogance of a spoilt favorite.

inspice si possum donata reponere laetus.
Haud male Telemachus, proles patientis Vlixi:
'Non est aptus equis Ithace locus, ut neque planis
porrectus spatiis nec multae prodigus herbae;
Atride, magis apta tibi tua dona relinquam.'
Parvum parva decent: mihi iam non regia Roma,
sed vacuum Tibur placet aut imbelle Tarentum.
Strenuus et fortis causisque Philippus agendis
clarus, ab officiis octavam circiter horam
dum redit atque foro nimium distare Carinas
iam grandis natu queritur, conspexit, ut aiunt,
adrasum quendam vacua tonsoris in umbra
cultello proprios purgantem leniter ungues.
'Demetri' (puer hic non laeve iussa Philippi
accipiebat), 'abi; quaere et refer, unde domo, quis,
cuius fortunae, quo sit patre quove patrono.'
It redit et narrat Volteium nomine Menam,

40. **Telemachus**: cf. *Odys.* IV. 601. — **patientis**: cf. πολύτλας, πολυτλήμων, *laboriosus* (*Epod.* XVII. 16).

44. **parvum**, etc.: cf. I. 3. 28. — **parva decent**: *i.e.* the humble life of the country remote from courts, as opposed to the splendor to be enjoyed in the society of Mæcenas at Rome, fit the poet better, as a man of humble aspirations.

45. **vacuum**, *deserted*, as opposed to the populous city. — **imbelle**: *peaceful*, in reference to its luxurious idleness.

46. **strenuus**, etc.: the anecdote illustrates the readiness with which Horace would abandon his claims to the munificence of Mæcenas if it is to be bought by the sacrifice of his valued freedom from care. — **Philippus**: L. Marcius, cos. B.C. 91, famous as an orator. Cicero says of him, *multae facetiae* (in his orations); and, *erat . . . in altercando cum aliquo aculeo et maledicto facetus*. Cic. *Brut.* 47. 173.

47. **ab officiis**: pleading causes in the Forum or the like.

48. **Carinas**: the narrow ridge on which now stands the church of S. Pietro in Vincoli. It was not far from the Forum, and was occupied like other heights around the Forum by the houses of wealthy citizens. The seeming distance is only the effect of Philippus' age and the steep ascent.

50. **tonsoris**, etc.: all such trades were carried on in little open booths (**tabernae**).

51. **leniter**, etc.: the magistrate is doubtless attracted by the careless ease and contentment of this humble man of the people, and wishes to see what stuff he is made of.

54. **quo patre quove patrono**: *i.e.* if born free, who his father was,

praeconem, tenui censu, sine crimine, notum
et properare loco et cessare, et quaerere et uti,
gaudentem parvisque sodalibus et lare certo
et ludis et post decisa negotia campo.
'Scitari libet ex ipso quodcumque refers ; dic
ad cenam veniat.' Non sane credere Mena ;
mirari secum tacitus. Quid multa ? 'Benigne,'
respondet. 'Neget ille mihi ?' 'Negat improbus, et te
neglegit aut horret.' Volteium mane Philippus
vilia vendentem tunicato scruta popello
occupat et salvere iubet prior. Ille Philippo
excusare laborem et mercennaria vincla,
quod non mane domum venisset, denique quod non
providisset eum. 'Sic ignovisse putato
me tibi, si cenas hodie mecum.' 'Vt libet.' 'Ergo
post nonam venies : nunc i, rem strenuus auge.'
Vt ventum ad cenam est, dicenda tacenda locutus

or, if a freedman (in which case he would be *filius nullius*), by whom he had been enfranchised.

56. **praeconem**: an auctioneer. Cf. v. 65. — **loco**: *i.e.* at proper times.

58. **lare certo**: *i.e.* he had a house of his own.

59. **ludis**, etc.: devoted to the ordinary amusements of the people. — **campo**: the Campus Martius, the field where athletic exercises took place, which were attended by a crowd of spectators. Cf. I. 18. 53.

62. **mirari**, etc.: doubtless suspecting some trick in so incredible an invitation. The magnate must want something of him. Hence his refusal. — **benigne**: cf. v. 16.

64. **neglegit**, *doesn't care for.* — **horret**, *is afraid of.* — **mane**: the next day Philippus goes himself to get the explanation of such a strange refusal.

65. **tunicato**: men of social standing wore the toga abroad, much as we wear a coat. — **popello**: diminutive of disparagement, "the common people in their shirt-sleeves."

66. **occupat**, *surprises*, *i.e.* he speaks to him first without waiting for a natural respectful salutation, which would be in accordance with their positions in society.

67. **laborem**: the natural etymological construction of **excusare**, (*make an excuse of something*). — **mercennaria**, *of his trade.*

68. **mane**: *i.e.* for the morning call, or *salutatio.*

69. **providisset**: *i.e.* instead of being spoken to first. — **sic**, *on this condition* (so, and so only).

72. **dicenda tacenda locutus**: the fellow warmed with wine puts no restraint upon his tongue.

tandem dormitum dimittitur. Hic ubi saepe
occultum visus decurrere piscis ad hamum,
mane cliens et iam certus conviva, iubetur
rura suburbana indictis comes ire Latinis.
Impositus mannis arvum caelumque Sabinum
non cessat laudare. Videt ridetque Philippus,
et sibi dum requiem, dum risus undique quaerit,
dum septem donat sestertia, mutua septem
promittit, persuadet uti mercetur agellum.
Mercatur. Ne te longis ambagibus, ultra
quam satis est, morer, ex nitido fit rusticus atque
sulcos et vineta crepat mera, praeparat ulmos,
immoritur studiis et amore senescit habendi.
Verum ubi oves furto, morbo periere capellae,
spem mentita seges, bos est enectus arando,
offensus damnis media de nocte caballum
arripit iratusque Philippi tendit ad aedes.
Quem simul adspexit scabrum intonsumque Philippus,
'durus,' ait, 'Voltei, nimis attentusque videris
esse mihi.' 'Pol, me miserum, patrone, vocares,
si velles, inquit, verum mihi ponere nomen.

75. **mane cliens**: at the *salutatio*. — **certus**, *never failing*.

76. **indictis . . . Latinis**: at the great festivals all public business was stopped, and the dignitaries generally sought the opportunity to retire into the country for rest. — **comes**, etc.: the fellow is now transformed from the careless, independent citizen to a regular humble companion.

77. **impositus**, etc.: in the *raeda*, or travelling-carriage.

78. **videt**, etc.: *i.e.* Philippus sees the change in the character of his companion, his growing ambition and discontent.

79. **requiem**: *diversion*, in seeing how he would behave in his new condition. — **risus**: *i.e.* he knew that the fellow's behavior would be ridiculous, and wished to enjoy the spectacle. — **dum, . . . quaerit**: equivalent to a present participle, as often.

83. **nitido**: *i.e.* well fed, and well cared for, as even the poorer classes would be in the city. — **rusticus**: *i.e.* in the rough garb and with the coarse fare of the country.

84. **mera**, *nothing but*. — **ulmos**: on which to train his vines.

85. **immoritur studiis**, *he works himself to death*.

92. **miserum**: instead of **durus**

Quod te per genium dextramque deosque Penates
obsecro et obtestor, vitae me redde priori.'
Qui semel adspexit, quantum dimissa petitis
praestent, mature redeat repetatque relicta.
Metiri se quemque suo modulo ac pede verum est.

## VIII.

Celso gaudere et bene rem gerere Albinovano
Musa rogata refer, comiti scribaeque Neronis.
Si quaeret quid agam, dic multa et pulchra minantem
vivere nec recte nec suaviter; haud quia grando
contuderit vitis oleamque momorderit aestus,
nec quia longinquis armentum aegrotet in agris;
sed quia mente minus validus quam corpore toto
nil audire velim, nil discere, quod levet aegrum;
fidis offendar medicis, irascar amicis,
cur me funesto properent arcere veterno;
quae nocuere sequar, fugiam quae profore credam;
Romae Tibur amem ventosus, Tibure Romam.
Post haec ut valeat, quo pacto rem gerat et se,
ut placeat iuveni percontare utque cohorti.
Si dicet 'recte,' primum gaudere, subinde

96. **qui semel,** etc.: the moral of the anecdote as given by Horace.

98. **metiri,** etc.: *i.e.* and not get himself into a place which is not fitted for him.

EPISTLE 8. A friendly epistle to a literary friend of Horace, otherwise unknown, in which he complains of his own dissatisfied and restless spirit.

2. **rogata**: *i.e.* in answer to his supposed inquiries. — **comiti**: cf. notes to *Sat.* I. 5. — **Neronis**: Tiberius; cf. I. 3. 2.

3. **multa,** etc.: cf. *Sat.* II. 3. 9.

4. **haud quia,** etc.: *i.e.* not on account of the ills to which the wealthy man is exposed.

6. **longinquis,** etc.: the wealthy Romans pastured great herds of cattle on the public lands throughout Italy, paying a small hire to the state (*scriptura*).

7. **mente minus validus**: cf. I. 6. 29, I. 2. 33 *seq.*, I. 1. 102, and many other passages where diseases of the soul are referred to.

12. **ventosus,** *fickle as the wind.*

14. **iuveni**: Tiberius. — **cohorti**: *i.e.* **amicorum,** his *fellows.*

15. **gaudere,** *say you are glad to hear it,* as Horace himself would say **gaudeo.**

praeceptum auriculis hoc instillare memento:
'ut tu fortunam, sic nos te, Celse, feremus.'

## IX.

Septimius, Claudi, nimirum intellegit unus,
quanti me facias: nam cum rogat et prece cogit,
scilicet ut tibi se laudare et tradere coner,
dignum mente domoque legentis honesta Neronis;
munere cum fungi propioris censet amici,
quid possim videt ac novit me valdius ipso.
Multa quidem dixi, cur excusatus abirem;
sed timui, mea ne finxisse minora putarer,
dissimulator opis propriae, mihi commodus uni.
Sic ego maioris fugiens opprobria culpae
frontis ad urbanae descendi praemia. Quodsi
depositum laudas ob amici iussa pudorem,
scribe tui gregis hunc et fortem crede bonumque.

17. **fortunam**: here of good fortune, in reference to his acceptability to his patron and his companions.

EPISTLE 9. A letter of recommendation of a friend Septimius, to Tiberius, such as were very common among the Romans (see Cic. *ad Fam.* II. 14; Plin. IV. 4).

4. **legentis,** *selecting.*—**honesta,** *honorable friends,* but made more general by the use of the neuter.

5. **munere,** etc.: the poet while asking what can properly be asked only by an intimate friend, delicately waives any claim of such intimacy. The tone certainly implies a want of confidence in the generosity of Tiberius. One can hardly imagine a Mæcenas addressed with such caution.

8. **finxisse,** etc.: *i.e.* he feared he should be charged with refusing because he wanted all the good things himself, and to have made an excuse of his want of intimacy.

9. **dissimulator,** *disparaging.*—**commodus,** etc.: *i.e.* using his influence in his own behalf alone.

11. **frontis**: cf. the slang "cheek." —**urbanae,** *of the astute man of the world* (who is free from the modesty of the simple countryman). —**descendi,** *have descended,* as one may be said to descend when having recourse to a less worthy action.—**praemia,** *privileges,* that which the impudence of the man of the world allows him to seek to gain.

13. **gregis**: *i.e.* **cohortis amicorum.** The construction is that of the predicate genitive. —**fortem bonumque**: cf. *Sat.* II. 5. 64 and note; and *Od.* IV. 4. 29.

## X.

Vrbis amatorem Fuscum salvere iubemus
ruris amatores, hac in re scilicet una
multum dissimiles, at cetera paene gemelli:
fraternis animis quicquid negat alter, et alter;
adnuimus pariter vetuli notique columbi.
Tu nidum servas; ego laudo ruris amoeni
rivos et musco circumlita saxa nemusque.
Quid quaeris? Vivo et regno, simul ista reliqui,
quae vos ad caelum effertis rumore secundo,
utque sacerdotis fugitivus liba recuso;
pane egeo iam mellitis potiore placentis.
Vivere naturae si convenienter oportet
ponendaeque domo quaerenda est area primum,
novistine locum potiorem rure beato?
Est ubi plus tepeant hiemes, ubi gratior aura

EPISTLE **10.** This epistle, addressed to the poet's friend Aristius Fuscus (cf. *Od.* I. 22; *Sat.* I. 9. 61, I. 10. 83), is in praise of the country as superior to the city as an abode of content and moral health.

2. **amatores**: the plural of one person, as usual with the pronoun of the first person in Latin.

4. **negat**: the construction is ungrammatical, throwing in the third person as a parenthesis where the first person plural would be either untrue or else clumsy.

8. **quid quaeris**: like **quid multa**, etc., transferring, however, the person from the speaker to the one addressed: "Why do you ask more," instead of "Why should I say more." — **vivo**: *i.e.* I enjoy true life. — **regno**: *i.e.* have the freedom of a king.

9. **rumore secundo**, *with shouts of applause.*

10. **fugitivus**, etc.: in the usual manner, the figure is identified with the object. — **liba**: the favorite offerings of the common people, of which in the house of the priest the slave, now a runaway, has had his fill. Like him, Horace has enjoyed the luxuries of the city to his satisfaction, and is glad to be rid of them.

11. **pane**: *i.e.* some more solid food. — **iam**: *i.e.* now that he has had enough of the delights of the city.

12. **vivere**, etc.: the Stoic rule of life, ὁμολογουμένως τῇ φύσει ζῆν, is here used more or less jocosely by Horace in a double sense, to include also material as well as spiritual life.

leniat et rabiem Canis et momenta Leonis,
cum semel accepit Solem furibundus acutum?
Est ubi divellat somnos minus invida cura?
Deterius Libycis olet aut nitet herba lapillis?
Purior in vicis aqua tendit rumpere plumbum,
quam quae per pronum trepidat cum murmure rivum?
Nempe inter varias nutritur silva columnas,
laudaturque domus longos quae prospicit agros.
Naturam expellas furca, tamen usque recurret
et mala perrumpet furtim fastidia victrix.
Non, qui Sidonio contendere callidus ostro
nescit Aquinatem potantia vellera fucum,
certius accipiet damnum propiusve medullis,
quam qui non poterit vero distinguere falsum.
Quem res plus nimio delectavere secundae,
mutatae quatient. Si quid mirabere, pones

16. **rabiem canis**: *Sat.* I. 7. 25; *Od.* I. 17. 17; and *Sat.* II. 5. 39. — **momenta leonis**, *the fury of the ramping lion*, as if the lion were roused to fierce activity by the arrival of the sun.

19. **Libycis**: *i.e.* of marble from Numidia. — **lapillis**: referring to the mosaic pavements of the great Roman houses.

21. **trepidat**: of the broken course of the brook as it seems to bustle over the stones.

22. **nempe**, *why!* — **nutritur**, etc.: *i.e.* even amid the splendor of the city, the rich endeavor to imitate rural beauties, thus admitting the superiority of the country.

24. **naturam**: *i.e.* the natural instinct of preference for the country. — **expellas**, etc.: proverbial. — **recurret**: as indicated by the words beginning with **nempe**.

25. **mala fastidia**, *annoying disdain*.

26. **non qui**, etc.: the material aspect of the subject is here connected with the spiritual, through the false and unnatural preference for artificial life shown by the lover of city splendor. Such a person is deceived by glare, and has no true estimate of the relative value of things, and he is here compared to a dealer in stuffs who is no judge of his merchandise.

26. **Sidonio ostro**: the real Tyrian purple which was of the most value. — **contendere**, *compare*, so as to decide on their value.

27. **Aquinatem fucum**: a lichen which made an imitation of the real purple.

28. **propius medullis**, *coming closer home*.

29. **vero falsum**: in a moral sense, the true goods of life from the false; hence the statement in v. 30.

31. **mirabere**: cf. **nil admirari**, I. 6. 1.

invitus. Fuge magna; licet sub paupere tecto
reges et regum vita praecurrere amicos.
Cervus equum pugna melior communibus herbis
pellebat, donec minor in certamine longo
imploravit opes hominis frenumque recepit.
Sed postquam victor violens discessit ab hoste,
non equitem dorso, non frenum depulit ore.
Sic qui pauperiem veritus potiore metallis
libertate caret, dominum vehet improbus atque
serviet aeternum, quia parvo nesciet uti.
Cui non conveniet sua res, ut calceus olim,
si pede maior erit, subvertet, si minor, uret.
Laetus sorte tua vives sapienter, Aristi,
nec me dimittes incastigatum, ubi plura
cogere quam satis est, ac non cessare videbor.
Imperat aut servit collecta pecunia cuique,
tortum digna sequi potius quam ducere funem.
Haec tibi dictabam post fanum putre Vacunae,
excepto quod non simul esses, cetera laetus.

33. **amicos**: *i.e.* courtiers, favorites.

34. **cervus**, etc.: this fable of Æsop (cf. Phædrus IV. 4; Aristot. *Rhet.* II. 20) continues the moral application of the discourse, as explained in v. 39.

34. **communibus herbis**, *from their common pasture.*

37. **violens**: like **ferox**, of confident, exultant strength.

40. **dominum**: *i.e.* the attachment to luxury in which riches become a necessity.

42. **non conveniet**: *i.e.* being either too great for his condition, or too meagre.

43. **uret**, *will gall.*

44. **laetus**: including both happiness and contentment.

45. **nec me, etc.**: in return for Horace's advice, Aristius is requested to do the like for him in turn.

47. **imperat aut servit**: *i.e.* it rules unless it is enslaved; cf. I. 1. 62.

48. **tortum**: simply *strained;* the natural composition of the rope, as it is held by the leader, makes the epithet a really descriptive one, though it is often used merely for ornament. — **digna**: *i.e.* it ought to be led rather than the leader. The figure is, of course, derived from leading an animal.

49. **haec tibi**, etc.: the poet humorously shows by the date of his letter the perfect repose which he is himself enjoying. — **dictabam** (epistolary imperfect): *i.e.* not even writing with his own hand. — **putre**, *mouldering.* The temple

## XI.

Quid tibi visa Chios, Bullati, notaque Lesbos,
quid concinna Samos, quid Croesi regia Sardis,
Smyrna quid et Colophon? Maiora minorane fama?
Cunctane prae campo et Tiberino flumine sordent?
An venit in votum Attalicis ex urbibus una?
An Lebedum laudas odio maris atque viarum?
Scis Lebedus quid sit; Gabiis desertior atque
Fidenis vicus: tamen illic vivere vellem,
oblitusque meorum obliviscendus et illis
Neptunum procul e terra spectare furentem.

itself is unoccupied and in decay, and so presents a picture of inactivity.—**Vacunae**: a Sabine deity, either really a god of vacations (*vaco*), or mistakenly supposed to be such. For the form, cf. *Fortuna*, *Portunus*. The character of the goddess heightens the picture of idleness.

50. **laetus**: no doubt with an allusion to the contentment which he recommends to Fuscus in v. 44.

Epistle xi. The Bullatius to whom this epistle is addressed is not otherwise known. He appears to have been for some reason travelling perhaps as an exile. Cf. **incolumis.** Horace takes occasion to express as a contrast to the love of foreign lands his own impatience of the evils of the transit and his preference for home.

1. **quid tibi**, etc.: amounting merely to "how did you like?" For the use of **quid**, cf. *Sat.* I. 6. 55.—**nota**, *famous.*

2. **concinna**, *well built*, probably alluding to the regularity of its buildings, such as is often admired in the newer Paris.—**regia**, *royal abode.*—**Sardīs**: Σάρδεις.

3. **maiora**: for the gender, cf. **quid**, v. 3.

4. **prae campo**, etc.: *i.e.* in comparison with the scenes of home.—**sordent**, etc.: the three questions are: "Do you prefer your native home, or would you desire to live in one of these famous and wealthy cities, or, finally, do you find the meanest place attractive after the discomforts of travel?" As for himself, Horace goes on to say, he would rather live in the most wretched old town than cross the sea even to get home. The poet's dislike of the sea appears also in *Od.* I. 3 and II. 6. 7.

7. **Gabiis, Fidenis**: these towns, once famous, fell into decay after being captured by the Romans, and became almost proverbial for desolation. Cf. Juv. VI. 56 and X. 100.

8. **vellem**: the contrary-to-fact condition implied is, 'if it were my case,' or 'I were there,' or the like.

9. **obliviscendus**: apparently in the sense of a present passive participle, a signification which this form must earlier have had (Gr. § 296, note).

10. **Neptunum**, etc.: the kernel is in the **procul e terra**. He would live there forever, and look

Sed neque qui Capua Romam petit, imbre lutoque
adspersus volet in caupona vivere; nec qui
frigus collegit, furnos et balnea laudat
ut fortunatam plene praestantia vitam;
nec, si te validus iactaverit Auster in alto,
idcirco navem trans Aegaeum mare vendas.
Incolumi Rhodos et Mitylene pulchra facit, quod
paenula solstitio, campestre nivalibus auris,
per brumam Tiberis, Sextili mense caminus.
Dum licet ac vultum servat Fortuna benignum,
Romae laudetur Samos et Chios et Rhodos absens.
Tu quamcumque deus tibi fortunaverit horam
grata sume manu, neu dulcia differ in annum,

at the sea from a safe distance. Cf. Lucr. II. 1.

11. **sed neque qui**, etc.: *i.e.* the following six lines are connected in thought with the third branch of the question (v. 6). The parenthesis vs. 7–10 expresses only Horace's own feelings about sea-voyages, and he continues his advice in another strain. "Even Lebedus may seem agreeable to you after a voyage, but that ought not to warp your judgment of these places as a permanent residence, just as in the three cases mentioned in vs. 11–16, one ought not to conclude that the momentary relief insures permanent happiness." To the sound philosopher (cf. v. 17 *seq.*), the beauties of foreign cities are mere incumbrances, only a nuisance and hindrance.

12. **volet . . . vivere**: *i.e.* even though the inn affords him a temporary relief, he would not wish to pass his life there.

13. **frigus collegit**, *has become stiff with cold*, not of catching cold, or of a chill as a morbid condition.

15. **iactaverit**, etc.: of the *mercator's* outward voyage.

16. **navem**, etc.: he wouldn't sell his ship and stay abroad forever.

18. **paenula**, etc.: each of these four things is directly the opposite of what one would want under the supposed circumstances. The paenula (*overcoat?*) was a heavy cloak for rough weather. — **campestre**: a mere clout worn during exercise, "circus trunks."

19. **Tiberis**: *i.e.* a bath therein. — **caminus**: cf. *Sat.* I. 5. 81.

20. **dum licet**, etc.: *i.e.* as long as I can help it, I will not travel, but I will enjoy these cities at a distance.

22. **tu**, etc.: "Do you, wherever you are, and whatever enjoyments you may have, seize the pleasure of the moment with gratitude, without losing the present by constantly expecting enjoyment in the future. Thus you will be able to be happy in any place." For, as the poet goes on, happiness is not to be found in change of place, nor in effort to attain it, but it is in our state of mind. It is at Rome or in the meanest village if you know how to find happiness.

ut quocumque loco fueris vixisse libenter
te dicas. Nam si ratio et prudentia curas,
non locus effusi late maris arbiter aufert,
caelum, non animum, mutant qui trans mare currunt.
strenua nos exercet inertia; navibus atque
quadrigis petimus bene vivere; quod petis, hic est,
est Vlubris, animus si te non deficit aequus.

## XII.

Fructibus Agrippae Siculis, quos colligis, Icci,
si recte frueris, non est ut copia maior
ab Iove donari possit tibi. Tolle querellas;
pauper enim non est, cui rerum suppetit usus.
Si ventri bene, si lateri est pedibusque tuis, nil
divitiae poterunt regales addere maius.

25. **ratio**, *a settled plan of life*.

26. **arbiter**, *commanding;* but the word is really here used in its old sense of *witness*. — **aufert**: *i.e.* visiting such places to enjoy the beauty of the landscape does not relieve the troubles of mind.

27. **caelum**, etc.: for a diluted version of this line, see Sen. *Ep.* 28.

28. **strenua**: referring to the strenuous efforts of the idle to amuse themselves. The connection is: though hurrying from place to place does not give us distraction, yet we continue to run after it with bustling activity. — **navibus**: *i.e.* by voyaging by sea.

29. **quadrigis**: *i.e.* by travel on land. — **hic**, *at home*, without going away for it.

30. **Vlubris**: *i.e.* in the meanest deserted village, without going to famous cities. — **animus . . . aequus**: the even temper (ἀπαθία) of the philosopher.

EPISTLE 12. This epistle is evidently an answer to one of Iccius, in which he had complained of the position which he held in Sicily as manager of the estates of Marcus Agrippa, and of his fortunes generally. For Iccius' character, cf. *Od.* I. 29, also addressed to him. His service under Ælius Gallus there referred to must have failed of yielding the desired wealth, as in fact we know that the expedition on which he went met with disaster. The two compositions addressed to Iccius give us a hint at the careers open to a young man trying to get on in life at Rome, and the success with which they were pursued.

2. **si recte**, etc.: there are two reasons given why Iccius should not complain. First, if he knows how to enjoy the material advantages of his position, living well and keeping good health, riches could give him no more. Second, if, on the other hand, he lives simply and frugally though abundance is accessible to him, he would desire no

Si forte in medio positorum abstemius herbis
vivis et urtica, sic vives protinus, ut te
confestim liquidus Fortunae rivus inauret;
vel quia naturam mutare pecunia nescit,
vel quia cuncta putas una virtute minora.
Miramur, si Democriti pecus edit agellos
cultaque, dum peregre est animus sine corpore velox,
cum tu inter scabiem tantam et contagia lucri
nil parvum sapias et adhuc sublimia cures:
quae mare compescant causae; quid temperet annum;
stellae sponte sua iussaene vagentur et errent;
quid premat obscurum lunae, quid proferat orbem;
quid velit et possit rerum concordia discors;

more even in the midst of wealth, in which case a fortune would do him no good.

7. **in medio positorum**, *what is ready at hand*, *i.e.* the abundance of Agrippa's house.

8. **urtica**, cf. Plin. *H. N.* XXI. 15. 93. — **ut**: concessive.

10. **vel quia**, etc.: *i.e.* your nature is such that money wouldn't spoil it, and besides, your philosophical studies have given you true views of virtue and all other goods.

12. **miramur**, etc.: an indirect proof of the philosophical enthusiasm of Iccius, and so still more indirectly of the truth of v. 11. — **Democriti**: the great atomist of Abdera, the Laughing Philosopher, of whom the story was told alluded to in v. 12. Cf. *Democritus ut quam minime animus a cogitationibus abduceretur patrimonium neglexit, agros deseruit incultos*, Cic. *de Fin.* V. 29. 87.

14. **inter scabiem**, etc.: *i.e.* the times of Democritus were less worldly than our own, and hence it is a stronger proof of devotion to philosophy when you study such themes amid the present race for wealth than when Democritus did so.

15. **nil parvum**, etc., *study no petty wisdom*, *i.e.* are not drawn away from lofty themes to the petty interests of the day. — **sublimia**, *celestial themes* (τὰ μετέωρα), *i.e.* the study of the heavens, pure science, the questions enumerated below.

16. **mare compescant**: *i.e.* control the waves.

17. **iussaene**: whether there is any law in their movement as natural bodies, or whether they are directed by mechanical forces, untrammelled by law.

18. **obscurum**: a kind of predicate adjective belonging only with **premat**.

19. **quid velit**: *i.e.* what it means, or aims at. — **possit**: *i.e.* what are the limits of its power, as the question is spoken of in Lucretius, *quid fieri possit et quid non*, particularly, no doubt, in reference to the influence of celestial phenomena on human affairs. — **concordia discors**, *the dissentient harmony*, *i.e.* various in manifestation, but joined in a common plan; cf. v. 20.

Empedocles an Stertinium deliret acumen.
Verum seu piscis seu porrum et caepe trucidas,
utere Pompeio Grospho et si quid petet ultro
defer: nil Grosphus nisi verum orabit et aequum.
Vilis amicorum est annona, bonis ubi quid deest.
Ne tamen ignores, quo sit Romana loco res:
Cantaber Agrippae, Claudi virtute Neronis
Armenius cecidit; ius imperiumque Phraates

20. **Empedocles** (444 B.C.): the first great natural philosopher who referred all things to natural causes, excluding intelligence from any share in natural events. — **Stertinium**: taken jocosely as a type of the Stoic philosopher, who assigned an intelligent will (λόγος) to the universe. Cf. *Sat.* II. 3. 33. — **acumen**: cf. *virtus Scipiadae*, *Sat.* II. 1. 72.

21. **verum seu**, etc.: returning to the idea in vv. 5–8. — **piscis**: as a type of good living, fish being bought in the market, and so regarded as a luxury. — **porrum et caepe**: as examples of frugal fare, cf. **herbis et urtica**, vs. 7, 8. — **trucidas**: a jocose use of an inappropriate word.

22. **utere**, etc.: *i.e.* whichever course of life you take, either of enjoying the good things, or of suppressing the desire for them like a philosopher, don't forget to cultivate my friend Grosphus, etc. — **Grospho**: a friend of the poet having estates in Sicily. Cf. *Od.* II. 16. — **petet**: Iccius would probably have favors to grant as manager of the estates of Agrippa. The two estates were probably contiguous. — **ultro**, *freely*, *i.e.* go beyond his request.

23. **verum**: cf. *Sat.* II. 3. 312, note.

24. **vilis**: *i.e.* only costing the outlay of a small favor. — **amicorum**: objective genitive. — **annona**, *the price*, properly the year's crop. Here the idea is that friends are to be bought at a cheap rate when good men need anything, — a little with grateful people goes a great way. Cf. νῦν διὰ τὰ πράγματα εὐωνοτάτους ἔστι φίλους ἀγαθοὺς κτήσασθαι, Xen. *Mem.* II. 40. 4.

25. **tamen**: *i.e.* though my letter has been taken up with other matters than news, the usual theme of letters, yet, etc. — **quo loco**: an almost proverbial expression (hence without the **in**), doubtless derived from military usage. Cf. Virg. *Æn.* II. 322. — **Romana res**, *affairs at Rome*, but with a different idea underlying it, inasmuch as all the interests and circumstances of the state as a whole are summed up in this one expression.

26. **Cantaber**, etc.: the Cantabrians were conquered by an expedition under Agrippa, B.C. 20. In the same year the expedition of Tiberius referred to in *Ep.* I. 3, conquered and caused the death of Artaxias, who was hostile to the Romans, and set Tigranes on the throne of Armenia. Cf. Tac. *Ann.* II. 3.

27. **Phraates**: in the same year, B.C. 20, the king of the Parthians, apparently alarmed by the progress of the Roman arms, sought peace of the Romans and restored the standards taken in the great defeats of Crassus and Antonius (B.C. 53 and 36).

Caesaris accepit genibus minor ; aurea fruges
Italiae pleno defundit Copia cornu.

## XIII.

Vt proficiscentem docui te saepe diuque,
Augusto reddes signata volumina, Vini,
si validus, si laetus erit, si denique poscet ;
ne studio nostri pecces, odiumque libellis
sedulus importes opera vehemente minister.
Si te forte meae gravis uret sarcina chartae,
abicito potius quam, quo perferre iuberis,
clitellas ferus impingas Asinaeque paternum
cognomen vertas in risum et fabula fias.
Viribus uteris per clivos, flumina, lamas ;
victor propositi simul ac perveneris illuc,
sic positum servabis onus, ne forte sub ala

28. **genibus minor,** *suppliant on his knees;* the construction is that of the degree of difference. — **aurea,** etc.: merely telling of a bountiful harvest.

EPISTLE 13. This epistle was undoubtedly intended to accompany some production of the poet sent to Augustus, though it is in form addressed to the messenger. There is in the tone an extreme diffidence and fear of boring the foremost man of the world, which gives a hint at the reason why Horace so long declined to address any of his works to the emperor. Cf. *Ep.* II. 1. Introd.

1. **proficiscentem:** probably from some country resort, where Horace was at the time.

2. **signata:** merely made into a packet. — **Vini:** Vinius Asella (Porphyrio), or C. Vinius Fronto (Acron), otherwise unknown, some humble friend of the poet.

3. **si validus,** etc.: *i.e.* the bearer is to consider the health, spirits, and even the desire of the great man.

4. **studio nostri,** *from zeal in my behalf.* — **pecces:** *i.e.* by importunity. Cf. **opera, vehemente,** and **sedulus** (*over-earnest*).

6. **si te forte,** etc.: the poet, with a jocose allusion to the name of the messenger, warns him against too great haste in performing his task.

9. **fabula:** cf. *Epod.* 11. 8.

10. **viribus,** etc.: *i.e.* hasten as much as you like on the way, but upon arriving show your grace, and avoid clumsy behavior which might offend the fastidious court.

12. **sic:** correlative with **ne.** — **ne:** instead of **ut non,** as often with **ita,** where the clause which is a result may also be regarded as a purpose. Probably the construction is to be explained as a paratactic description of the **sic** given in the

fasciculum portes librorum ut rusticus agnum,
ut vinosa glomus furtivae Pyrria lanae,
ut cum pileolo soleas conviva tribulis.
Ne vulgo narres te sudavisse ferendo
carmina, quae possint oculos aurisque morari
Caesaris; oratus multa prece, nitere porro.
Vade, vale; cave ne titubes mandataque frangas.

## XIV.

Vilice silvarum et mihi me reddentis agelli,
quem tu fastidis habitatum quinque focis et
quinque bonos solitum Variam dimittere patres,
certemus, spinas animone ego fortius an tu

form of a command. "In this way, namely, don't carry, etc." — **sub ala**, etc.: the three ways of carrying the packet under his arm, which he is to avoid, are (*a*) the awkward vigor of the rustic who fears his burden may escape; (*b*) the timid concealment of the slave who fears discovery; and (*c*) the tight grip of the humble guest on his hat and sandals, who is dazed by the unaccustomed splendor.

14. **Pyrria**: said to be a slave in a comedy of Titinius.

15. **pilleolo, soleas**: the humble guest, having no slave, would carry his own out-door costume.

16. **ne volgo**, etc.: the messenger is also warned against babbling on the way and boasting of the value and importance of his mission.

18. **oratus**: *i.e.* with questions as to his mission.

19. **cave**: retaining the short final syllable of comedy, and doubtless also of conversation; *cf.* **cauneas (cave ne eas)**. — **frangas**: returning to the play upon the name of the messenger. As his wares are not fragile, the meaning must be general.

EPISTLE 14. This epistle is in form addressed to the poet's steward, but is really a kind of apologue of which the moral is an exhortation to contentment and to a life suited to one's nature. It is doubtless founded on some actual complaints of the steward.

2. **fastidis**: probably on account of its small proportions and its dulness. — **habitatum**: *i.e.* though it is not so small, after all. — **quinque focis**, etc.: *i.e.* families, tenants of the poet.

3. **Variam**: the market town of the neighborhood. — **dimittere**: probably to the meetings of the *pagani* for civil or religious purposes. Each *pagus* or territorial division formed a commune with corporate privileges and common religious rites.

4. **certemus**, *let us try*, *i.e.* in a kind of wager, to decide which of us does his duty best in his domain, Horace in self-improvement, or the steward in husbandry.

evellas agro, et melior sit Horatius an res.
Me quamvis Lamiae pietas et cura moratur,
fratrem maerentis, rapto de fratre dolentis
insolabiliter, tamen istuc mens animusque
fert et amat spatiis obstantia rumpere claustra.
Rure ego viventem, tu dicis in urbe beatum;
cui placet alterius, sua nimirum est odio sors.
Stultus uterque locum immeritum causatur inique;
in culpa est animus, qui se non effugit umquam.
Tu mediastinus tacita prece rura petebas,
nunc urbem et ludos et balnea vilicus optas;
me constare mihi scis et discedere tristem,
quandocumque trahunt invisa negotia Romam.
Non eadem miramur; eo disconvenit inter

5. **res**: *i.e.* the farm.

6. **me,** etc.: a confession of the poet's own weakness, opposed to the **tu** in v. 14. At the same time Horace justifies himself as consistent in his desire for a quiet life in the country; cf. v. 16. — **quamvis,** etc.: *i.e.* though I am detained in the city, yet my heart is there in the country. — **Lamiae**: possessive genitive. — **pietas**: the fraternal affection which causes Lamia to mourn for his brother. — **cura**: *i.e.* his trouble or sorrow. — **moratur**: on account of Horace's duty to console him. The person referred to is the same friend of the poet, L. Ælius Lamia, mentioned in *Od.* I. 26 and addressed in III. 17.

7. **maerentis**: of external mourning. — **dolentis**: of inward sorrow. Cf. Cic. *ad Att.* XII. 28 *maerorem minui, dolorem nec potui nec si possem vellem.*

8. **mens animusque,** *my mind and heart,* thoughts and desires.

9. **amat,** *longs;* cf. *Od.* III. 9. 24. — **spatiis,** *the open field,* properly the race course, shut off by the barriers (**claustra**) in front of the *carceres,* or stalls in which the horses were confined till the word was given. — **obstantia,** *which bar,* by a change of point of view governing **spatiis**, instead of that which is really barred.

12. **causatur,** *finds fault with;* properly, assigns as the cause.

14. **tu,** etc.: *i.e.* you also are discontented, and with less consistency than I, for you were equally unsatisfied in the city. — **mediastinus,** *a man of all work,* in the city house. — **tacita**: *i.e.* you looked upon it as such a boon that you hardly dared express the wish aloud.

15. **ludos et balnea**: delights of the city.

16. **me,** etc.: but I am consistent with myself.

18. **non eadem,** etc.: *i.e.* while I should be glad to be always in the country, you are dissatisfied as soon as you get there; and the cause of this difference is that we have different views of the pleasures of life. You have no care for rural beauties,

meque et te. Nam quae deserta et inhospita tesqua
credis, amoena vocat mecum qui sentit, et odit
quae tu pulchra putas. Fornix tibi et uncta popina
incutiunt urbis desiderium, video, et quod
angulus iste feret piper et tus ocius uva,
nec vicina subest vinum praebere taberna
quae possit tibi, nec meretrix tibicina, cuius
ad strepitum salias terrae gravis. Et tamen urgues
iampridem non tacta ligonibus arva, bovemque
disiunctum curas et strictis frondibus exples.
Addit opus pigro rivus, si decidit imber,
multa mole docendus aprico parcere prato.
  Nunc age, quid nostrum concentum dividat, audi.
Quem tenues decuere togae nitidique capilli,
quem scis immunem Cinarae placuisse rapaci,
quem bibulum liquidi media de luce Falerni,
cena brevis iuvat et prope rivum somnus in herba.
Nec lusisse pudet, sed non incidere ludum.
Non istic obliquo oculo mea commoda quisquam

but prize only the pleasures of appetite.

23. **piper et tus**: which of course cannot be grown in Italy, but only in tropical climates.

25. **nec meretrix**, etc.: *i.e.* you complain that you have no relaxation, though your labor is of the hardest.

26. **urgues**, *you contend with*, implying the difficulty of the task.

27. **non tacta**, etc.: and so requiring more labor on account of previous neglect. — **bovem**, etc.: *i.e.* and have the cattle to care for besides.

28. **frondibus**: anciently used for fodder. Cf. Virg. *Ecl.* IX. 61.

31. **nunc age**, etc.: *i.e.* now look more deeply to see precisely why we differ.

32. **quem tenues**, etc.: *i.e.* the fact is I am getting old, and the pleasures I once enjoyed I care for no more. — **tenues**, *fine-spun*, as opposed to the coarse cloth that satisfies him now. He was sufficiently handsome then to justify personal adornment.

33. **immunem**, *with empty hands*, by his own personal charms. — **rapaci**: *i.e.* not usually thus pleased.

34. **media de luce**: cf. *Od.* I. 1. 20.

35. **cena brevis**: *i.e.* without many courses.

36. **nec lusisse pudet**: *i.e.* he is not ashamed of these indulgences, because they were suited to his age.

37. **istic**, *there*, in the country, where you are. — **obliquo**: of the glance of envy, which was anciently

limat, non odio obscuro morsuque venenat;
rident vicini glebas et saxa moventem.
Cum servis urbana diaria rodere mavis,
horum tu in numerum voto ruis; invidet usum
lignorum et pecoris tibi calo argutus et horti.
Optat ephippia bos piger optat arare caballus.
Quam scit uterque libens censebo exerceat artem.

## XV.

Quae sit hiems Veliae, quod caelum, Vala, Salerni,
quorum hominum regio et qualis via (nam mihi Baias

supposed to have a magic influence, to the injury of the object.

38. **morsu**: alluding to slander, under the figure of the serpent's tooth.

39. **rident,** etc.: *i.e.* instead of envy, I only excite a smile at my efforts at husbandry.

40. **cum servis**, etc.: here Horace returns to the tastes of his steward, and so closes with the theme of discontent and an exhortation against it. — **diaria**, *the measured rations*, instead of the unlimited food of the country; cf. v. 42.

41. **usum**, etc.: which, to the steward of the farm, would be free, not measured out like the city rations.

42. **argutus**, *shrewd*, knowing well which was the better condition.

43. **optat . . . bos**, etc., *so the lazy ox desires*, etc.

44. **quam scit**, etc.: *but let each, I should say*, etc.; alluding to the common proverb, *Quam quisque norit artem in hac se exerceat* (Cic. *Tusc.* I. 18. 41. For the Greek, see Aristoph. *Wasps*, 1431), which he here applies to the ox and the horse, and through them to the country and city slave, particularly the former.

EPISTLE 15. To a letter of inquiry, addressed to a friend, Numonius Vala, in regard to the climate and accommodations of Velia and Salernum as sanitary resorts, the poet attaches a humorous sketch of himself as a self-indulgent Epicurean. The moral hidden beneath is perhaps none the less obvious from the fact that the jesting moralist makes an example of himself.

1. **quae sit**, etc.: the main clause is postponed by two parentheses to v. 25. — **Veliae**: a coast town of Lucania, about twenty-five miles southeast of Pæstum. It was famous as the seat of the Eleatic school of philosophy. — **caelum**: *i.e.* the weather. — **Salerni**: *Salerno*, still a considerable town on the bay of Salerno, just south of the promontory of Sorrento.

2. **quorum**, etc.: *i.e.* what sort of people are there in the region? still an important question for travellers in that country. — **via**: *i.e.* the means of getting there, as the places were off the main lines of travel. — **nam mihi**, etc.: the poet's reason for inquiring, extending through v. 13. — **Baias**: the favorite watering-place in the Bay of

Musa supervacuas Antonius, et tamen illis
me facit invisum, gelida cum perluor unda
per medium frigus. Sane murteta relinqui,
dictaque cessantem nervis elidere morbum
sulfura contemni vicus gemit, invidus aegris
qui caput et stomachum supponere fontibus audent
Clusinis Gabiosque petunt et frigida rura.
Mutandus locus est, et deversoria nota
praeteragendus equus. 'Quo tendis? Non mihi Cumas
est iter aut Baias,' laeva stomachosus habena
dicet eques; sed equis frenato est auris in ore);

Naples, famous for its warm and mineral baths, here opposed to the cold bathing prescribed by Horace's physician.

3. **Musa**: Antonius Musa, on account of a cure of Augustus, B.C. 23, by a cold-water treatment, became the fashionable physician of the times in much the same manner in which such reputations are made nowadays. — **supervacuas**, *useless*, *i.e.* in the advice which he gives. — **tamen**: *i.e.* though the people of Baiæ have no reason to find fault, inasmuch as I follow a prescription in avoiding their baths.

4. **invisum**: *i.e.* because Horace neglects their baths, as explained in **cum perluor**, etc.

5. **per medium frigus,**: cf. **hiems**, v. 1. — **sane**, *at any rate; i.e.* the following is true, whether the inference (**me facit invisum**) is true or not. — **murteta**: in a myrtle grove near Baiæ were Russian (or Turkish?) baths. Cf. *maximeque utiles naturales et siccae sudationes sunt, quales super Baias habemus in murtetis*, Celsus III. 21.

6. **dicta**, *said to*, *i.e.* so reputed until the new cure was invented. Compare modern vagaries in medicine. — **cessantem**, *lingering*, *chronic*. — **nervis**: dative with **elidere**.

7. **sulfura**: *i.e.* in the sulphur baths. — **vicus**, *the town*, of Baiæ. — **invidus**: *i.e.* on account of their abandoning the old remedies and seeking new ones which Baiæ does not furnish.

8. **caput et stomachum**, etc.: probably to be taken literally of a douche. — **audent**, *have the presumption*, *i.e.* to venture on a new cure.

9. **Clusinis**: *i.e.* cold baths such as were at Clusium and Gabii, as opposed to the hot ones of Baiæ.

10. **mutandus**, etc.: continuing the idea of v. 2 (**nam mihi**, etc.). — **deversoria**: *i.e.* at Baiæ, or Cumæ.

11. **praeteragendus**: because the road to Salernum, etc., leads further on down the coast. — **quo tendis**: addressed to the horse, which, as we all know by experience, turns in habitual directions; here towards Cumæ and Baiæ.

12. **laeva**: because the road to Cumæ turns to the right. — **habena**: the means by which the rider speaks to the horse; cf. **in ore**, v. 13. He speaks with the bit and is heard by the mouth.

maior utrum populum frumenti copia pascat,
collectosne bibant imbres puteosne perennes
iugis aquae; (nam vina nihil moror illius orae.
Rure meo possum quidvis perferre patique;
ad mare cum veni, generosum et lene requiro,
quod curas abigat, quod cum spe divite manet
in venas animumque meum, quod verba ministret,
quod me Lucanae iuvenem commendet amicae);
tractus uter plures lepores, uter educet apros;
utra magis pisces et echinos aequora celent
pinguis ut inde domum possim Phaeaxque reverti,
scribere te nobis, tibi nos adcredere par est.
Maenius, ut rebus maternis atque paternis
fortiter absumptis urbanus coepit haberi,
scurra vagus, non qui certum praesepe teneret,

14. **maior,** etc.: continuing the question in vv. 1 and 2. Inquiries as to the bread and water of the region.

15. **collectos**: *i.e.* in cisterns, rain water being less agreeable than that of wells.

16. **nam vina,** etc.: *i.e.* I ask about the water, for I don't care for the wine there.

17. **rure meo,** etc.: the poet explains his fastidiousness in regard to the wine; *i.e.* at home in retirement he doesn't mind what he has. — **perferre,** *get along with;* cf. I. 16. 74.

18. **ad mare,** etc.: *i.e.* in the social life of a watering-place to which he goes for relaxation. — **generosum et lene,** *fine and mellow,* as more stimulating.

19. **curas, spe.**: cf. I. 5. 17, and *Od.* I. 18. 4, a very common idea with the poet.

21. **Lucanae**: *i.e.* at Velia.

22. **tractus,** etc.: continuing the questions in reference to the food.

24. **Phaeax**: cf. I. 2. 28 and I. 4. 15.

25. **par est**: cf. the common **aequum est,** as in *Sat.* I. 3. 74.

26. **Maenius,** etc.: the poet, in order to explain the Epicurean tone of his questions, goes on to illustrate his double character by the story of a ruined *bon vivant,* who retained his appetite, but could adjust himself to circumstances. This account, though humorously exaggerated, is in perfect accord with Horace's statement of his lapses into Aristippean philosophy. Cf. I. 1. 18, 19.

27. **fortiter**: a humorous misapplication of a noble quality to an unworthy action. The fearlessness would consist in his disregard of consequences. — **urbanus,** *a hanger on,* who lives by his wits. — **haberi,** *to act as,* lit. to be considered such by the patrons who invited him.

28. **vagus**: *i.e.* not dining at his own house, but wherever he could get an invitation, as explained in the following.

impransus non qui civem dinosceret hoste,
quaelibet in quemvis opprobria fingere saevus,
pernicies et tempestas barathrumque macelli,
quidquid quaesierat, ventri donabat avaro.
Hic ubi nequitiae fautoribus et timidis nil
aut paullum abstulerat, patinas cenabat omasi
vilis et agninae, tribus ursis quod satis esset;
scilicet ut ventres lamna candente nepotum
diceret urendos corrector Bestius. Idem
quicquid erat nactus praedae maioris, ubi omne
verterat in fumum et cinerem, 'Non Hercule miror,'
aiebat, 'si qui comedunt bona, cum sit obeso
nil melius turdo, nil volva pulchrius ampla.'

29. **civem dinosceret hoste**: apparently proverbial, ready to accept an invitation from either.

30. **opprobria**, etc.: *i.e.* in his quality as **scurra**, abusing anybody to make himself agreeable. Cf. *Sat.* I. 4. 86–90, and *Ep.* I. 18. 11, as well as the English word *scurrilous* with its developed meaning.

33. **nequitiae fautoribus**: such as Hermogenes Tigellius, *Sat.* I. 2. 1–4. — **timidis**: *i.e.* those who were afraid of his abuse.

34. **abstulerat**: *i.e.* had failed to secure any gifts sufficient to enable him to indulge his appetite for dainties. — **patinas**, *whole platters*, indicating his greediness even when he had less inviting food than the luxuries to which he was ordinarily invited. He did not disdain this humble food, but enjoyed what he had to repletion.

36. **scilicet ut**, etc.: in this lies the kernel of the whole anecdote. In time of scarcity he consoled himself by becoming a reformer, and venting his abuse upon spendthrifts who, it must be remembered, were the very **nequitiae fautores** who fed him. It is this tone of abuse that Horace represents as corresponding to his own preaching against the vices of mankind. — **ventres**: in allusion to the punishment of slaves, which was made to fit the crime by branding the offending member. — **lamna**: cf. *ignes candentesque laminae ceterique cruciatus*, Cic. *Verr.* V. 63.

37. **corrector**: better than the Ms. **correctus** as making a more exact parallel with Horace. — **Bestius** (in apposition with subject of **diceret**): a contemporary or earlier inveigher against luxury; cf. temperance reformers in modern times.

38. **praedae**: Horace treats the parasite's drafts on his patrons as plunder. — **maioris**: cf. **paullum**, v. 34. His plunder in this case was sufficient to gratify his old tastes, and accordingly he lives in luxury while it lasts.

39. **non Hercule miror**, etc.: this remark emphasizes the fact that his preaching against extravagance is only a temporary phase, lasting only so long as he had nothing.

41. **volva**: considered a great delicacy by the Romans.

Nimirum hic ego sum; nam tuta et parvula laudo,
cum res deficiunt, satis inter vilia fortis;
verum ubi quid melius contingit et unctius, idem
vos sapere et solos aio bene vivere, quorum
conspicitur nitidis fundata pecunia villis.

## XVI.

Ne perconteris fundus meus, optime Quincti,
arvo pascat erum an bacis opulentet olivae,
pomisne an pratis an amicta vitibus ulmo,
scribetur tibi forma loquaciter et situs agri.
Continui montes, ni dissocientur opaca

42. **nimirum,** *you see,* humorously putting a construction upon his behavior which it might apparently bear, but which is not the true one. — **hic**: cf. I. 6. 40. — **tuta et parvula,** *humble circumstances* and *careless ease,* as opposed to the dangers attending dignity and riches.

43. **fortis,** *unmoved,* strong to resist the temptations of appetite. — **vilia**: *coarse fare.*

44. **unctius,** *more toothsome and rich,* as opposed to dry and humble diet. — **idem,** *none the less;* lit. the same man who was so content with humble circumstances.

45. **vos**: this would imply that Numonius had a villa in the neighborhood of Velia.

46. **nitidis**: implying that they were well stocked. — **fundata,** *invested.*

EPISTLE 16. This description of Horace's villa, united with some moral precepts as to the true source of happiness in accordance with his philosophy, is evidently addressed to a young and successful politician. But who he was beyond his gentile name is entirely unknown, though the name agrees with the person addressed in *Od.* II. 11.

1. **ne perconteris,** etc.: *i.e.* for fear you should suppose that my farm is a productive source of income, I hasten to tell you that it is chiefly a charming and salutary resort for hours of retirement. We need not necessarily suppose that the estate was not a source of income at all, cf. I. 14. 2 and 26. Horace is only answering some exaggerated suppositions of his young friend.

2. **arvo,** etc.: the five most profitable products of husbandry in ancient times, grain, oil, fruit, cattle (cf. **pratis**), and wine.

4. **forma et situs**: these apparently show at once that none of the great products mentioned thrive there. Wine would not seem to be excluded necessarily; but as Horace expressly says it cannot be produced (cf. I. 14. 23), we may suppose the exposure indicated is unfavorable. — **loquaciter**: indicating that it was a theme he loved to dwell on.

5. **continui montes**: *sc.* **ager**

valle, sed ut veniens dextrum latus adspiciat sol,
laevum discedens curru fugiente vaporet.
Temperiem laudes. Quid, si rubicunda benigni
corna vepres et pruna ferant, si quercus et ilex
multa fruge pecus, multa dominum iuvet umbra?
Dicas adductum propius frondere Tarentum.
Fons etiam rivo dare nomen idoneus, ut nec
frigidior Thracam nec purior ambiat Hebrus,
infirmo capiti fluit utilis, utilis alvo.
Hae latebrae dulces, etiam, si credis, amoenae,
incolumem tibi me praestant Septembribus horis.
Tu recte vivis, si curas esse quod audis.
Iactamus iam pridem omnis te Roma beatum;
sed vereor, ne cui de te plus quam tibi credas,

**est.** — **ni dissocientur**: an early and colloquial use of present for imperfect subjunctive. The apodosis is implied in **continui**, to which the protasis is a kind of correction, — "they would be if they were not."

6. **veniens**, etc.: *i.e.* the valley opens to the south; being however only a little lateral valley, it was probably shaded by a high mountain directly in front. — **dextrum**: *i.e.* as you look down.

8. **quid si**, etc.: *i.e.* you would admire the climate, I am sure, but what would you say if in addition to this delightful climate, the underbrush bears berries to make the woods beautiful and perhaps also to feed flocks, the chief branch of industry. Cf. *Od.* I. 17.

11. **Tarentum**: famous for its flocks, as well as for its beauty.

12. **fons**: cf. *Ep.* I. 18. 104, and *Od.* III. 13. — **dare**: poetic and colloquial for **qui det**. — **idoneus**: *i.e.* large enough. — **ut**, *such that.*

14. **infirmo**, etc.: probably for bathing in the one case, and for drinking in the other; but cf. I. 15. 8. The emphatic repetition of **utilis** points to a twofold use.

15. **latebrae**, *retreat*, pointing to the chief use of the estate. — **dulces**, *dear to me.* — **amoenae**: *i.e.* really charming for anybody.

16. **Septembribus**: cf. I. 7. 5.; *Sat.* II. 6. 19.

17. **tu**, etc.: *i.e.* so much for my happy condition on my estate (a happiness which is rather implied than expressed); as for you, your life must be a happy one if you endeavor to be all that you are reputed. — **recte**: cf. I. 6. 29; II. 2. 213; and *Od.* II. 10. 1. — **audis**: cf. *Sat.* II. 6. 20; *Ep.* I. 7. 38.

18. **iactamus iam**, etc.: an explanation of the preceding line. — **Roma**: by including himself among the people of Rome, the poet makes the verb first person plural, as if it were 'we at Rome.'

19. **sed vereor**, etc.: whether this antithesis to v. 18 is or is not intended to refer to anything actually existing in Quinctius' character, we cannot be sure. The probability is that the words have some foundation. Yet

neve putes alium sapiente bonoque beatum,
neu, si te populus sanum recteque valentem
dictitet, occultam febrem sub tempus edendi
dissimules, donec manibus tremor incidat unctis.
Stultorum incurata pudor malus ulcera celat.
Si quis bella tibi terra pugnata marique
dicat, et his verbis vacuas permulceat auris:
'Tene magis salvum populus velit an populum tu,
servet in ambiguo, qui consulit et tibi et urbi,
Iuppiter,' Augusti laudes agnoscere possis:
cum pateris sapiens emendatusque vocari,
respondesne tuo, dic sodes, nomine? 'Nempe
vir bonus et prudens dici delector ego ac tu.'
Qui dedit hoc hodie, cras, si volet, auferet, ut si

we need not conclude that the man was really spoiled, but only that Horace saw in him a tendency to substitute reputation for character, and made that fact a text for a more general sermon.

20. **alium sapiente**: an extension of the construction of comparatives, probably imitated from the Greek. Cf. *Ep.* II. 1. 240, and Cic. *ad Fam.* XI. 2.

21. **neu si te**, etc.: an illustration drawn from a man's physical condition. Here, as usual, the simile is incorporated in the thought itself.

22. **sub tempus edendi**: the time when a sick man ought to think of his condition and abstain. Not doing this, he is attacked while at the table.

24. **stultorum**: the emphatic position gives it the force, "It is only fools who," etc. — **pudor malus**: cf. *Sat.* II. 3. 39.

25. **si quis bella**, etc.: an example of a tribute which Quinctius would at once recognize as not justly paid to him. Why not, then, recognize any other undeserved compliment as such?

26. **vacuas**, *listening*, unoccupied by anything else.

27. **tene magis**, etc.: this sounds like a quotation, and is in fact said by the scholiasts to be taken from a poem of Varius.

28. **servet**: a wish that no circumstance may arise to decide the question through any misfortune that may happen to either.

30. **cum pateris**, etc.: *i.e.* do you in like manner recognize this praise as undeserved, as you ought unless you are truly wise and blameless?

31. **tuo . . . nomine**, *in your own name*, as if the description were applicable to you. — **nempe vir bonus**, etc.: *i.e.* "I like to be spoken well of, and so do you"; an imaginary objection to Horace's course of reasoning, which he meets in the next verse.

33. **qui dedit**, etc.: *i.e.* but if the praise is false, being only in reputation, the people who give it can take it away again with equally arbitrary caprice.

detulerit fascis indigno, detrahet idem.
'Pone, meum est,' inquit: pono tristisque recedo.
Idem si clamet furem, neget esse pudicum,
contendat laqueo collum pressisse paternum;
mordear opprobriis falsis mutemque colores?
Falsus honor iuvat et mendax infamia terret
quem nisi mendosum et medicandum? Vir bonus est quis?
Qui consulta patrum, qui leges iuraque servat;
quo multae magnaeque secantur iudice lites;
quo res sponsore et quo causae teste tenentur.
Sed videt hunc omnis domus et vicinia tota
introrsum turpem, speciosum pelle decora.
'Nec furtum feci nec fugi' si mihi dicat
servus, 'Habes pretium, loris non ureris' aio.
'Non hominem occidi.' 'Non pasces in cruce corvos.'
'Sum bonus et frugi.' Renuit negitatque Sabellus.

34. **fascis**: *i.e.* a curule office.

36. **idem si clamet**, etc.: an example of undeserved calumny to offset that of undeserved honor.

37. **laqueo collum**, etc.: as a type of monstrous crime. Cf. *Od.* II. 13. 5, and *Epod.* 3. 1.

39. **falsus honor**, etc.: to be affected by mere reputation is a mark of an unsound nature, needing the healing power of good morals.

40. **vir bonus**, etc.: this question introduces the erroneous standards of the people, who estimate the **vir bonus** only from his external conduct, which may not proceed at all from a virtuous soul, but from selfish motives.

41. **qui consulta**, etc.: the answer of the people to the question in the preceding verse. — **consulta patrum**, etc.: the whole description applies to the prominent statesman, and refers to the maintenance of good government as well as obedience to the laws.

42. **secantur**: cf. *Sat.* I. 10. 15. — **iudice**: cf. *Sat.* I. 4. 123.

43. **quo**: in the ablative absolute construction. — **sponsore**, etc.: *i.e.* his faithfulness as a surety makes property secure. — **teste**, etc.: his honesty as a witness makes a case certain to win. — **tenentur**, *are not lost.*

44. **sed videt**, etc.: his true character, as known by his household and near neighbors.

45. **introrsum turpem**: cf. *Sat.* II. 1. 64.

46. **nec furtum**, etc.: *i.e.* such a man is like a slave who refrains from wrong-doing only from fear of punishment.

49. **Sabellus**: *i.e.* a strict judge, who looks at the motive. The Sabines had a reputation for preserving the old-fashioned country virtues. Cf. *Epod.* 2. 41; *Od.* III. 6. 37

Cautus enim metuit foveam lupus accipiterque
suspectos laqueos et opertum miluus hamum.
Oderunt peccare boni virtutis amore;
tu nihil admittes in te formidine poenae:
sit spes fallendi, miscebis sacra profanis;
nam de mille fabae modiis cum surripis unum,
damnum est, non facinus, mihi pacto lenius isto.
Vir bonus, omne forum quem spectat et omne tribunal,
quandocumque deos vel porco vel bove placat,
'Iane pater,' clare, clare cum dixit 'Apollo';
labra movet metuens audiri: 'Pulchra Laverna,
da mihi fallere! Da iusto sanctoque videri:
Noctem peccatis et fraudibus obice nubem!'
Qui melior servo, qui liberior sit avarus,
in triviis fixum cum se demittit ob assem,
non video; nam qui cupiet, metuet quoque; porro
qui metuens vivet, liber mihi non erit umquam.
Perdidit arma, locum virtutis deseruit, qui

50. **cautus**, etc.: *i.e.* refraining from evil-doing for fear of punishment is no more a virtue than avoiding the snare is in a brute.

55. **nam de mille**, etc.: *i.e.* one can see that you would break all laws if there were a chance of concealment, because a slight peccadillo, which is not noticed by the people, is in the eye of philosophy a crime which shows that you are not **bonus et sapiens**. In this passage, and down to v. 69, the poet falls into the Stoic line of argument, from which sect he doubtless draws much of his philosophy, though he often ridicules its extremes.

56. **pacto isto**, *in that case, i.e.* of the supposed trifling delinquency. — **lenius**: *i.e.* than when **misces sacra profanis**.

57. **vir bonus**, etc.: an example of the secret conduct of a man such as he has described. — **forum**: in his political character, cf. v. 41. — **tribunal**: in his judicial functions, cf. v. 42.

59. **clare**: opposed to **labra movens**.

60. **Laverna**: the goddess of thieves.

61. **iusto**: attracted to the case of **mihi**; cf. *mediocribus esse poetis*, II. 3. 372.

63. **qui melior servo**: and so of course not **vir bonus**; cf. note on v. 55. Here begins a new point; avarice also is fatal to the character of a *vir bonus* which is claimed.

64. **in triviis fixum**: doubtless proverbial as a test of cupidity; cf. Persius, V. 111.

67. **perdidit arma**, etc.: proverbially the deepest disgrace to a

semper in augenda festinat et obruitur re.
Vendere cum possis captivum, occidere noli;
serviet utiliter: sine pascat durus aretque,
naviget ac mediis hiemet mercator in undis,
annonae prosit, portet frumenta penusque.
Vir bonus et sapiens audebit dicere: 'Pentheu,
rector Thebarum, quid me perferre patique
indignum coges?' 'Adimam bona.' 'Nempe pecus, rem,
lectos, argentum: tollas licet!' 'In manicis et
compedibus saevo te sub custode tenebo.'
'Ipse deus, simul atque volam, me solvet.' Opinor,
hoc sentit: moriar. Mors ultima linea rerum est.

Roman, as it would deprive him of his citizenship and as good as make a slave of him. — **locum**, *the ranks*, in the technical sense, as a figure.

69. **vendere cum possis**, etc.: *i.e.* to be sure such a man is not wholly useless; he may be tolerated in society for the service he renders, but he is only a slave after all.

70. **pascat**, etc.: these are all employments of money-getting, but they benefit society. — **durus**: cf. I. 7. 91.

72. **annonae prosit**, *relieve the market*, by importing grain so as to make it cheap.

73. **vir bonus**, etc.: *i.e.* the true **vir bonus** will look with contempt upon all earthly good and evil, since his *summum* and *solum bonum* is a virtuous soul. This thought is presented in the form of a free paraphrase of the interview in which Dionysus in disguise defies the power of Pentheus of Thebes, (see Eur. *Bacchae*, 450 *seq.*). The only direct imitation is from v. 487, λύσει μ' ὁ δαίμων αὐτὸς ὅταν ἐγὼ θέλω, which Horace interprets as referring to suicide. This is not intended in the original, but is introduced here in accordance with the general doctrine of the ancients.

76. **lectos**: cf. *neque ego unquam bona perdidisse dicam, si quis pecus aut supellectilem amiserit*, Cic. *Parad.* 1. 8.

79. **linea**: referring to the chalk-line which served as the goal in the circus.

## XVII.

Quamvis, Scaeva, satis per te tibi consulis, et scis
quo tandem pacto deceat maioribus uti,
disce docendus adhuc quae censet amiculus, ut si
caecus iter monstrare velit; tamen adspice si quid
et nos quod cures proprium fecisse loquamur.
Si te grata quies et primam somnus in horam
delectat, si te pulvis strepitusque rotarum,
si laedit caupona, Ferentinum ire iubebo.
Nam neque divitibus contingunt gaudia solis,
nec vixit male qui natus moriensque fefellit.
Si prodesse tuis paulloque benignius ipsum

EPISTLE 17. In a social state in which so much depended upon patronage and favor as was the case in Rome at all times, and especially after the destruction of the Republic, it was of the utmost importance for young men to know how to conduct themselves with the great, so as to gain advancement in life and at the same time preserve their self-respect. Both these objects had been attained by Horace, and in this epistle he gives instructions to a young friend on this subject with his customary delicacy and wisdom. Scæva is otherwise unknown.

1. **quamvis**, etc.: a modest introduction to avoid the appearance of preaching in an arrogant tone.

2. **quo tandem pacto**, *just how.* The direct question asked by the intended inquirer would be, "How *shall* I conduct myself in consorting with my superiors?" Hence the emphatic **tandem**.

3. **docendus adhuc**: opposed sharply to **disce**; *i.e.* submit to learn from one who has still much to learn himself, at least his views, which you may take or leave, as you feel inclined. — **amiculus**, *your humble* (*i.e. modest*) *friend.*

6. **si te**, etc.: *i.e.* in the first place, it is not at all indispensable to consort with the great, but a life of obscurity, ease, and independence has its attractions, as well as a life of worldly success. — **somnus**: as opposed to the early rising necessary for a client, who must make the early *salutatio*.

7. **pulvis**, etc.: necessary discomforts of life in the city, where one must live to attend upon the great.

8. **caupona**: *i.e.* the noisy taverns full of brawling roisterers.

10. **fefellit**: cf. λάθε βιώσας, the maxim of Epicurus.

11. **si prodesse**, etc.: *i.e.* if, on the other hand, you wish to help your friends by your advancement, and enjoy the luxuries that the rich alone possess, then you must consort with them, being yourself poor. These two conditions are humorously expressed by words which relate only to the food enjoyed by each.

te tractare voles, accedes siccus ad unctum.
'Si pranderet holus patienter, regibus uti
nollet Aristippus.' 'Si sciret regibus uti,
fastidiret holus qui me notat.' Vtrius horum
verba probes et facta, doce, vel iunior audi
cur sit Aristippi potior sententia. Namque
mordacem Cynicum sic eludebat, ut aiunt:
'Scurror ego ipse mihi, populo tu; rectius hoc et
splendidius multo est. Equus ut me portet, alat rex,
officium facio: tu poscis vilia rerum
dante minor, quamvis fers te nullius egentem.'

12. **tractare**: cf. *Sat.* II. 2. 85.

13. **si pranderet**, etc.: the arguments for the two modes of life are put into the mouths of Diogenes the Cynic and Aristippus the Hedonist (cf. I. 1. 18). The anecdote from which the interview is paraphrased is told by Diog. Laert. II. 68. — **regibus**: in the original *τύραννος*, but here used in reference to magnates generally.

14. **si sciret**, etc.: in accordance with the general views of Aristippus, cf. I. 1. 19.

15. **qui me notat**, *i.e. my censor*, the term being derived from the action of the Censor at Rome. — **utrius horum**, etc.: the poet puts the alternative directly, whether a man should scorn the advantages of intercourse with the great, like the Cynic, or make the most of them, like the versatile Aristippus.

16. **doce**, etc.: *i.e.* either convince me, or else, being younger, listen to my decision of the point.

17. **namque**, etc.: *i.e.* I say Aristippus' view is better, for he had a valid reply to the reproach of Diogenes.

18. **mordacem**: in allusion to the etymology of Cynic from *κύων*. — **eludebat**, *parried*. The imperfect represents that his answer was a possible regular reply to such an argument.

19. **scurror**, *I play the parasite*, implying that Diogenes had in effect taunted him with being a **scurra**. The reply is, "We both are that; but I am so for my own benefit, you for the crowd; and my way is much happier and more noble." — **hoc**: referring to his own way, which is nearer in fact, though farther away on the page. See A. & G. § 102. — **rectius**: cf. **recte**, I. 12. 2.

20. **equus**, etc.: translation of a Greek proverb, *ἵππος με φέρει, βασιλεύς με τρέφει*, doubtless used in reference to courtiers.

21. **officium facio**, *I do service*, as a dependent. — **poscis vilia rerum**: *i.e.* you also beg, and only for a paltry reward. — **vilia rerum**: cf. *vanis rerum*, *Sat.* II. 2. 25, and *fictis rerum*, *Sat.* II. 8. 83.

22. **dante minor**: *i.e.* you recognize your inferiority to the poor wretches from whom you get your sustenance. "I at least serve a worthy person for a worthy reward; you serve the crowd for a wretched fare." Diogenes and such persons supported themselves by begging

Omnis Aristippum decuit color et status et res,
temptantem maiora, fere praesentibus aequum.
Contra, quem duplici panno patientia velat,
mirabor vitae via si conversa decebit.
Alter purpureum non exspectabit amictum,
quidlibet indutus celeberrima per loca vadet
personamque feret non inconcinnus utramque;
alter Mileti textam cane peius et angui
vitabit chlamydem, morietur frigore, si non
rettuleris pannum: refer, et sine vivat ineptus!
Res gerere et captos ostendere civibus hostis,
attingit solium Iovis et caelestia temptat:
principibus placuisse viris non ultima laus est.

See his life in Diogenes Laertius. — **fers te**, *you pose as.*

23. **omnis**, etc.; *i.e.* and then again the man of the world can adapt himself to any circumstances, while the Cynic cannot live without his rags. — **color**, *vicissitude*, as good or evil fortune, agreeable or disagreeable incidents; cf. *Sat.* II. 1. 60. — **status**, *position*, as high or low. — **res**, *circumstances*, as riches or poverty.

24. **temptantem**: alluding to a motto of Aristippus, *τὰ μὲν παρόντα στέργειν, τὰ δὲ βελτίω ζητεῖν.* — **fere**, *generally.* — **aequum**, *satisfied;* cf. **aequus animus**, and *Od.* III. 29. 33.

25. **duplici panno**, *the double cloak of rags*, a humorous translation of *διπλοῒς*, but with a reference to the quality of the garment as well. The rough cloak of the ascetic philosophers served a double purpose as tunic and cloak (shirt and coat). Antisthenes, the founder of the Cynic school, was said to have been the first who *doubled* his blanket. The reference here is to the cloak thus doubled, which became the symbolic garb of philosophers; cf. *Anth. Pal.* VII. 65, 66, 67, 68, and Diog. Laert. VI. 1. (13), 2. (3). The purpose of the doubling is seen in the anecdote of Antisthenes (ibid. 1. 16), *Διογένει χιτῶνα αἰτοῦντι πτύξαι προσέταξε θοἰμάτιον.* An example of the *διπλοῒς* or *τρίβων* may be found in Baumeister, Denkmäler, etc., under Aristotle (from Visconti, *Iconographie Grecque*, Vol. I. p. 230).

27. **non exspectabit**, etc.: *i.e.* he will go out without it, in such raiment as he has.

29. **personam utramque**, *the part of either*, the courtier or the ascetic. Cf. (*φασι*) *Στράτωνα, οἱ δὲ Πλάτωνα πρὸς αὐτὸν εἰπεῖν, Σοὶ μόνῳ δέδοται καὶ χλανίδα φορεῖν* **καὶ ῥάκος,** Diod. II. 8. (67).

30. **Mileti**: cf. Virg. *Georg.* III. 306; here used as a type of costly clothing.

33. **res gerere**, etc.: an argument to show that the humble friend's career is an honorable one. As the most glorious career is that of a leader, so it is not an inglorious one to be the confidential friend of a leader. *Je ne suis pas la rose, mais j'ai vecu avec elle.*

Non cuivis homini contingit adire Corinthum.
Sedit qui timuit ne non succederet. Esto.
Quid, qui pervenit, fecitne viriliter? Atqui
hic est aut nusquam quod quaerimus. Hic onus horret,
ut parvis animis et parvo corpore maius;
hic subit et perfert. Aut virtus nomen inane est,
aut decus et pretium recte petit experiens vir.

36. **non cuivis**, etc.: *i.e.* the nobleness of the career is shown by the fact that everybody cannot succeed in it. This thought is put in the form of the Greek proverb, *οὐ παντὸς ἀνδρὸς ἐς Κόρινθον ἔσθ' ὁ πλοῦς.* The origin of the proverb is unknown, but its form suggests a quotation from some play. The explanation of Gellius (I. 8) referring it to the famous courtesan Lais sounds like a later invention. But at any rate the proverb came to be used of anything which everybody could not attain.

37. **sedit qui timuit**, etc.: this verse, which has the style of the sententious single-line colloquies of the Greek tragedy, is either purposely imitated by Horace from that style, or it may possibly be actually quoted from the same play as the proverb. Although the connection is difficult, and has been much debated, it seems best to take the statement as a reply to the preceding, assented to by Horace in **esto**, and afterwards turned to his own purpose in the next verse. The sense would be then: not every man can be the friend of princes. To which the other side of Horace's mind, as it were, replies (yes, for) he sits inactive, who fears he may not succeed. "Well, then," says Horace, "he who has tried and succeeded has shown a manly spirit in doing what another has feared to attempt, which is the very point in question, whether it is a manly thing to do or not." — **sedit** (gnomic perfect), *he sits inactive.* — **succederet** (impers.): *sc.* **sibi**.

38. **pervenit**: keeping up the figure in v. 36. — **fecitne**, *has he not*, etc.: the conclusion drawn from the preceding, if the fear of failure prevents men from trying to become the friends of the great, then *per contra* it shows courage and manliness to try and succeed. — **atqui**: *i.e.* you must answer, *yes, and yet* that gives away the whole case, for that is just the point, whether the service of the great is a **virile officium**, and so praiseworthy, or is a kind of slavery, and so unworthy the true philosopher, as the Cynic would hold.

39. **quod quaerimus**, *the point at issue*, here not the object of search, but the object of inquiry. — **hic**: *i.e.* the one who sits inactive. — **onus horret**: and thereby shows a pusillanimity and weakness that is foreign to the philosopher.

41. **hic subit**: the one who makes the attempt. He takes up the burden, and carries it through instead of shrinking from it. This of course is an act of **virtus**, if there is any such thing at all. — **virtus**: apparently in this passage the Roman meaning (cf. **virtus**, sturdy manhood, and courage to do, dare, and suffer) shines through the philosophical sense in which Horace professes to use it.

42. **decus et pretium**: which are attained in the service of the great

Coram rege sua de paupertate tacentes
plus poscente ferent. Distat sumasne pudenter
an rapias. Atqui rerum caput hoc erat, hic fons.
'Indotata mihi soror est, paupercula mater,
et fundus nec vendibilis nec pascere firmus,'
qui dicit, clamat 'victum date'; succinit alter
'et mihi': dividuo findetur munere quadra.
Sed tacitus pasci si posset corvus, haberet
plus dapis et rixae multo minus invidiaeque.
Brundisium comes aut Surrentum ductus amoenum
qui queritur salebras et acerbum frigus et imbres,
aut cistam effractam et subducta viatica plorat,

as well as in the active conduct of affairs. Cf. v. 33 *seq.* The two words belong together, but **decus** refers more to the honor, **pretium** to the material advantages, wealth, etc. — **recte**: in the adverb lies the significant part of the expression, *does well to*, etc. — **experiens vir**, *the man of enterprise*, who makes the effort instead of shrinking from it.

43. **coram**, etc.: in view of the fact that the worthiness of such a career depends much upon the manner in which the dependent advances himself, the poet suddenly without warning proceeds to a caution as to the manner of conducting one's self in regard to gifts. — **rege**, *his patron*, used in reference doubtless to the ancient relations of philosophers to kings (as of Plato with Dionysius). Cf. **regibus**, v. 14, which is translated directly from the Greek.

44. **distat**: *i.e.* it makes a difference in the worthiness of the relation.

44. **sumas**: *i.e.* what is given with free will, which a *vir bonus* might honorably accept, cf. I. 11. 23.

45. **rapias**: as a persistent beggar does in effect, and which is unworthy the man of honor. — **atqui**: in the same loose adversative relation as in v. 38. — **rerum caput et fons**: *i.e.* this was the main point, the end and aim of your friendship with the great, namely, to be enriched by gifts. — **erat**: probably only used instead of **est** for metrical reasons, but justified by the reference to the original object of the dependent, cf. **fuerat**, Juvenal, V. 76.

48. **clamat, victum date**: *i.e.* such conduct is simply begging. — **succinit**, *chimes in*, *i.e.* one who begs thus will find a rival ready to divide with him.

49. **et mihi**, *so have I*, *i.e.* a sister, etc. — **dividuo munere**: a loose ablative of manner. — **quadra**, *the loaf*, used generally for a gift to provide subsistence. It is so called from being cut across the top into four sectors of a circle.

50. **sed tacitus**, etc.: alluding to the fable of the fox and the crow.

52. **Brundisium**: *i.e.* on an errand of business; cf. *Sat.* I. 5. — **comes**: cf. *Sat.* II. 6. 42. — **Surrentum amoenum**: *i.e.* on a pleasure journey, cf. I. 7. 76.

nota refert meretricis acumina, saepe catellam,
saepe periscelidem raptam sibi flentis, uti mox
nulla fides damnis verisque doloribus adsit.
Nec semel irrisus triviis attollere curat
fracto crure planum, licet illi plurima manet
lacrima, per sanctum iuratus dicat Osirim:
'Credite, non ludo; crudeles, tollite claudum!'
'Quaere peregrinum' vicinia rauca reclamat.

## XVIII.

Si bene te novi, metues, liberrime Lolli,
scurrantis speciem praebere, professus amicum.
Vt matrona meretrici dispar erit atque
discolor, infido scurrae distabit amicus.
Est huic diversum vitio vitium prope maius,

55. **nota refert**, etc.: *i.e.* repeats the well-known tricks of the courtesan, whose rapacity was proverbial.

58. **nec semel**, etc.: *i.e.* the patron having been once deceived, becomes incredulous, like a man often deceived by a vagabond in the street who pretends to have fallen and broken his leg. — **triviis**: *i.e.* at the places where are the most passers by.

60. **Osirim**: intimating that such persons were usually foreigners, Egyptians, or the like.

62. **quaere peregrinum**, *try it on a stranger*, as all the town knows the trick too well; cf. "tell that to the marines." — **rauca**, *till it is hoarse*, being made so by crying thus so often.

Epistle 18. This epistle, upon the same general subject as the last, is addressed to one of the Lollii mentioned in I. 2. It differs, however, from the other in that it gives directions as to the manner of conducting one's self in intercourse with the great. It shows the same self-respect and refinement of feeling which we see in Horace's other utterances on this subject.

1. **liberrime**, *most independent of men*, a quality at once fatal to the relation spoken of, if carried to excess, and fitted to yield the best results if wisely managed.

3. **ut matrona**, etc.: *i.e.* the friend will be as far from the toady as the matron from the harlot. — **dispar**, etc.: the difference is indicated in vv. 10–14.

4. **scurrae**: an extension of the construction of words of nearness and likeness. Cf. **differt sermoni**, *Sat.* I. 4. 48.

5. **huic vitio**: *i.e.* the fault implied in **scurra**, and described in vv. 10–14.

asperitas agrestis et inconcinna gravisque,
quae se commendat tonsa cute, dentibus atris,
dum vult libertas dici mera veraque virtus.
Virtus est medium vitiorum et utrimque reductum.
Alter in obsequium plus aequo pronus et imi
derisor lecti sic nutum divitis horret,
sic iterat voces et verba cadentia tollit,
ut puerum saevo credas dictata magistro
reddere vel partes mimum tractare secundas.
Alter rixatur de lana saepe caprina,
propugnat nugis armatus: 'Scilicet ut non
sit mihi prima fides et vere quod placet ut non

6. **inconcinna**, *uncongenial.* — **gravis**: cf. *molestus*, *Sat.* I. 3. 65.

7. **commendat**, *recommends; i.e.* tries to make the great man prize him by a show of excessive simplicity, honesty, and frankness, which becomes ill-mannered and disagreeable. — **tonsa cute**, *hair cut close to the skin*, as opposed to the prevailing fashion of hair carefully trimmed, but allowed to grow to some length; see next note. — **dentibus atris**: such affected neglect of one's personal appearance was intended to give the impression of an artless, unsophisticated nature with the old republican simplicity.

8. **libertas**: *i.e.* a frank outspokenness which conceals no opinions, and hence is mistaken for uncompromising virtue.

9. **virtus est**, etc.: Horace's decision between the two styles of intercourse is given in the formula of the Peripatetic philosophy, and in accordance with his well-known views. Cf. Ἔστιν ἄρα ἡ ἀρετὴ ἕξις προαιρετική, ἐν μεσότητι οὖσα τῇ πρὸς ἡμᾶς ὡρισμένῃ λόγῳ, καὶ ὡς ἂν φρόνιμος ὁρίσειε· μεσότης δὲ δύο κακιῶν τῆς μὲν καθ' ὑπερβολὴν τῆς δὲ κατ' ἔλλειψιν, Aristot. *Nicomach. Eth.* II. 6. It is from this point of view that Horace so often criticises the Stoics.

10. **alter**: *i.e.* the **scurra**. Horace proceeds to describe in detail the two kinds of conduct. — **obsequium**: cf. Cic. *de Am.* 24. 89 *seq.* — **imi**: cf. *Sat.* II. 8. 23 and note.

11. **derisor**, *the buffoon*, such persons being introduced to make sport for the company. Cf. the scene at table, in *Sat.* I. 5. 51 *seq.*

12. **verba cadentia**, etc.: as we see them picked up and preserved by Boswell, in his *Life of Johnson.*

14. **partes**, etc.: cf. the imitations of performers and ringmaster given by the circus clown. These are no doubt survivals of the action in the mimes. For the relation of the second actor to the first, cf. *Sat.* I. 9. 46 and note.

15. **alter**: the affectedly independent friend. — **rixatur**: *i.e.* in order to show that he is no *scurra*, he contests every point, no matter how unimportant. This class is still found, at any rate across the Atlantic. — **lana caprina**: proverbial for a mere nothing.

16. **armatus**: indicating the

acriter elatrem? Pretium aetas altera sordet.'
Ambigitur quid enim? Castor sciat an Dolichos plus;
Brundisium Minuci melius via ducat an Appi.
Quem damnosa Venus, quem praeceps alea nudat,
gloria quem supra vires et vestit et unguit,
quem tenet argenti sitis importuna famesque,
quem paupertatis pudor et fuga, dives amicus
saepe decem vitiis instructior odit et horret,
aut, si non odit, regit ac veluti pia mater
plus quam se sapere et virtutibus esse priorem
vult et ait prope vera: 'Meae, contendere noli,
stultitiam patiuntur opes; tibi parvula res est:
arta decet sanum comitem toga; desine mecum
certare.' Eutrapelus cuicumque nocere volebat

man's vehement obstinacy. — **scilicet**, etc.: *Why! the idea that*, etc.; a remark of the ill-mannered fellow in his defence, showing his misapprehension of the real case; he mistakes impertinence for honesty. For **scilicet**, cf. *Sat.* II. 1. 70; *Ep.* I. 9. 3, I. 10. 2.

18. **elatrem**: the word is purposely chosen to hint at the brusqueness of his conduct. — **pretium**, *to buy me*. — **aetas altera**: *another life*, *i.e.* if it could be given as a bribe. — **sordet**, *is too poor a gift*.

19. **enim**, *well!* or *why!* The connection really is, this vehemence is of course justifiable, for the question is, etc. — **Castor, Dolichos**: gladiators. — **sciat plus**: *has more skill*.

21. **quem damnosa**, etc.: instructions as to certain special relations, beginning with the advice not to imitate the patron in vices, particularly in expensive ones; for though he have a dozen more vices, he likes to have a friend more virtuous than himself.

22. **gloria**: *vanity*. — **vires**, *his means*. — **vestit et unguit**: of the care of his person.

23. **argenti**: *i.e.* money. — **importuna**, *insatiable*.

24. **fuga**: *horror*. — **dives**: this word seems to hint at the real reason of the dislike; the vices are expensive.

25. **instructior**: a humorous application of the word.

26. **regit**, *wishes to direct*. — **pia**, *devoted*, the word being used both of filial and paternal relations.

28. **prope vera**, *not so far from the truth*, but cf. *Sat.* II. 2. 100.

30. **arta**: the full and flowing toga, though beginning now to be common, was still considered luxurious, and belonged only to high life.

31. **Eutrapelus**, etc.: an anecdote to show the folly of vying with the rich patron. The person mentioned was P. Volumnius, who received this nickname on account of his wit (εὐτραπελία, cf. Cic. *ad Fam.* VII. 32 and 33). It will be noticed that the action here is a practical joke, like that of Philippus, I. 7. 46.

vestimenta dabat pretiosa: beatus enim iam
cum pulchris tunicis sumet nova consilia et spes,
dormiet in lucem, scorto postponet honestum
officium, nummos alienos pascet, ad imum
Thraex erit aut holitoris aget mercede caballum.
  Arcanum neque tu scrutaberis illius umquam,
commissumque teges et vino tortus et ira.
Nec tua laudabis studia aut aliena reprendes;
nec, cum venari volet ille, poemata panges.
Gratia sic fratrum geminorum, Amphionis atque
Zethi, dissiluit donec suspecta severo
conticuit lyra. Fraternis cessisse putatur
moribus Amphion: tu cede potentis amici
lenibus imperiis, quotiesque educet in agros
Aetolis onerata plagis iumenta canesque,

32. **beatus iam**, *now become a rich man*, *i.e.* in his tastes and feelings.

33. **sumet**: the thought of Eutrapelus, *he will, said he*, etc. — **consilia**, *plan of life*.

35. **pascet**, *will cultivate*.

36. **Thraex**: cf. *Sat.* II. 6. 44. — **holitoris**, *a huckster*, who carried about vegetables on a horse or donkey through the streets for sale. This custom is still common in Italy, while the corresponding business is done with us in a wagon. Of course the employment of a driver of such an animal would be of the lowest kind. We should say, dig ditches, or carry mortar.

37. **arcanum**, etc.: *i.e.* be not too inquisitive as to his secrets, nor garrulous as to his confidences.

38. **tortus**: cf. II. 3. 435, a common idea with the ancients, derived from evidence under torture. — **ira**, *i.e.* from some offence taken at the patron.

39. **nec tua laudabis**, etc.: *i.e.* do not exalt your tastes above his, but gracefully conform to his favorite pursuits. — **aliena**, *i.e.* such as the patron's.

40. **venari**, etc.: this advice, accompanied by the details which follow, seems not to be merely general, but to have reference to the pursuits of the unknown patron, and the literary leanings of Lollius.

41. **gratia**, etc.: an anecdote showing the separating force of uncongenial tastes. — **Amphionis**: cf. *Od.* III. 11. 2.

42. **suspecta**: the ancients, with all their devotion to the Muses, were inclined to look upon literature and music as more or less effeminate and frivolous. — **severo**: the character of Zethus is represented as somewhat savage, or at least serious and warlike.

45. **lenibus**: *i.e.* only expressed in gentle invitation.

46. **Aetolis**: probably in allusion to the chase of the Calydonian boar. — **onerata**: cf. I. 6. 58.

surge et inhumanae senium depone Camenae,
cenes ut pariter pulmenta laboribus empta:
Romanis sollemne viris opus, utile famae
vitaeque et membris, praesertim cum valeas et
vel cursu superare canem vel viribus aprum
possis. Adde virilia quod speciosius arma
non est qui tractet. Scis quo clamore coronae
proelia sustineas campestria; denique saevam
militiam puer et Cantabrica bella tulisti
sub duce, qui templis Parthorum signa refigit
nunc et si quid abest Italis adiudicat armis.
Ac ne te retrahas et inexcusabilis absis,
quamvis nil extra numerum fecisse modumque

47. **inhumanae**, *unsocial*, as exacting, and intolerant of distractions. — **senium**, *churlishness*, the ill-humor which is characteristic of literary pursuits.

49. **sollemne**, *habitual*, and so all the more appropriate for a Roman. — **opus**: in apposition with the whole previous exhortation. Such words expressing the result of the action of a verb are regularly in the accusative; cf. the cognate accusative. Cf. Tac. *Ann.* I. 74.

50. **valeas**, etc.: a further reason for engaging in hunting, drawn from Lollius' personal characteristics.

51. **cursu**, *speed*. — **viribus**, *endurance*.

52. **adde**, etc.: *i.e.* furthermore it is an exercise in which Lollius appears to advantage.

53. **coronae**, *the crowd*, of spectators witnessing the exercises on the Campus Martius. Cf. **campo**, I. 7. 59.

54. **proelia**: *i.e.* javelin throwing, and perhaps foil practice; possibly mimic cavalry battles: cf. the Game of Troy, Virg. *Aen.* V. 545 *seq.*

55. **Cantabrica bella**: in B.C. 25 Augustus undertook an expedition into Spain to subdue the Cantabri and Astures (cf. *Od.* III. 14 and IV. 14. 41). Lollius must have served in this expedition.

56. **templis**, etc.: alluding to the army sent by Augustus against the Parthians so often referred to. Cf. *Od.* IV. 15. 6 and III. 5. 4; *Ep.* I. 12. 27. — **signa refigit**: as the standards captured from Crassus and Antonius had been presumably dedicated in Roman fashion on the columns of the Parthian temples, so they are now being unhung to be restored to the Romans. The epistle must therefore have been written in B.C. 20.

57. **si quid abest**, etc.: *i.e.* he is completing the conquest of the world. This action is spoken of as a decision of a judge who maintains the right of the Romans to universal empire and gives them possession of their domain.

58. **ne te retrahas**, etc.: not the purpose of what is said, but the purpose of saying it (cf. I. 1. 13), as of "I may say," or the like.

59. **nil extra numerum, etc.:**

curas, interdum nugaris rure paterno.
Partitur lintres exercitus; Actia pugna
te duce per pueros hostili more refertur:
adversarius est frater, lacus Hadria, donec
alterutrum velox victoria fronde coronet.
Consentire suis studiis qui crediderit te,
fautor utroque tuum laudabit pollice ludum.
  Protinus ut moneam, si quid monitoris eges tu,
quid de quoque viro et cui dicas saepe videto.
Percontatorem fugito; nam garrulus idem est,
nec retinent patulae commissa fideliter aures,
et semel emissum volat irrevocabile verbum.
  Non ancilla tuum iecur ulceret ulla puerve
intra marmoreum venerandi limen amici,
ne dominus pueri pulchri caraeve puellae

*i.e.* you would do nothing frivolous or trifling; you are not above representing a mimic battle, a fact which shows that you have no excuse for absenting yourself from active sports. — **extra numerum modumque**: *i.e.* unbecoming, out of character, or contrary to propriety; a regular expression drawn from the art of music; lit. out of time and tune.

60. **rure paterno**: *i.e.* in the retirement of the country, so often referred to; cf. *Sat.* II. 1. 73.

62. **pueros**: either slaves or boys, either of which classes might engage in the sport.

64. **velox**, *winged.*

65. **consentire**, etc.: a return to the main idea after the long parenthesis.

66. **utroque**: as we might say, vote with both hands. — **pollice**: the allusion must be to the amphitheatre, at which approval was shown by turning down the thumb (**premere**), but warmer approval is here expressed by turning both thumbs. The opposite to this is **pollicem vertere**, holding up the thumb. The origin of the custom is uncertain; perhaps it was like "pointing the finger of scorn," and from that the opposite came to signify approval. — **ludum**: the regular word for gladiatorial exercise; here figuratively of the action of the client, who is approved for joining in his patron's favorite pursuits.

67. **protinus ut moneam**, etc.: a warning against indiscreet comment on others' characters, and too much indulgence shown to the inquisitive "interviewer." Cf. *Sat.* II. 5. 51, although there the subject is a different one.

70. **patulae**: with a double reference. The ears are wide open to catch, but they for the same reason readily let go what they have heard.

72. **non**: cf. *Sat.* II. 5. 91. — **ancilla**, etc.: cf. *Od.* II. 4; Virg. *Ecl.* II. — **iecur**: the seat of the

munere te parvo beet, aut incommodus angat.
  Qualem commendes etiam atque etiam adspice, ne mox
incutiant aliena tibi peccata pudorem.
Fallimur et quondam non dignum tradimus: ergo
quem sua culpa premet, deceptus omitte tueri;
ut penitus notum, si temptent crimina, serves
tuterisque tuo fidentem praesidio; qui
dente Theonino cum circumroditur, ecquid
ad te post paullo ventura pericula sentis?
Nam tua res agitur, paries cum proximus ardet,
et neglecta solent incendia sumere vires.
  Dulcis inexpertis cultura potentis amici;
expertus metuit. Tu dum tua navis in alto est
hoc age, ne mutata retrorsum te ferat aura.
  Oderunt hilarem tristes tristemque iocosi,
sedatum celeres, agilem gnavumque remissi;
[potores bibuli media de nocte Falerni]
oderunt porrecta negantem pocula, quamvis
nocturnos iures te formidare tepores.
Deme supercilio nubem; plerumque modestus

passions, according to the ancients; cf. *Od.* IV. 1. 12.

75. **parvo**: *i.e.* for fear his generosity may be cooled from jealousy, even if actual enmity does not ensue (**incommodus**, etc.). — **beet**, *enrich* (cf. **beatus**), purposely used with **parvo** (*too small*) for the contrast.

76. **qualem commendes**, etc.: *i.e.* be careful for whom you make yourself responsible by introduction. — **commendes**: an almost technical word used as well as **tradere** in this sense.

77. **aliena**: *i.e.* of the friend introduced.

78. **fallimur**: *i.e.* if such a thing does happen, as it sometimes will, recognize your error and abandon the unworthy person, so that your defence may have weight in the case of one unjustly accused.

81. **qui**, etc.: *i.e.* if another is slandered, you may be sure your turn will come by and by.

82. **Theonino**: from Theon, an unknown calumniator, whose name passed into a proverb.

86. **dulcis**, etc.: a general warning of the dangers of the career to the inexperienced, and a recommendation not to be thrown off one's guard by success.

89. **oderunt hilarem**, etc.: a recommendation to a certain conformity (**obsequium**) of one's tastes and moods to those of one's

occupat obscuri speciem, taciturnus acerbi.
Inter cuncta leges et percontabere doctos,
qua ratione queas traducere leniter aevum;
num te semper inops agitet vexetque cupido,
num pavor et rerum mediocriter utilium spes;
virtutem doctrina paret naturane donet;
quid minuat curas, quid te tibi reddat amicum;
quid pure tranquillet, honos, an dulce lucellum,
an secretum iter et fallentis semita vitae.
Me quotiens reficit gelidus Digentia rivus,
quem Mandela bibit, rugosus frigore pagus,
quid sentire putas, quid credis, amice, precari?
Sit mihi quod nunc est, etiam minus, et mihi vivam
quod superest aevi, si quid superesse volunt di.
Sit bona librorum et provisae frugis in annum
copia, neu fluitem dubiae spe pendulus horae.
Sed satis est orare Iovem quae donat et aufert;
det vitam, det opes, aequum mi animum ipse parabo.

friend, and an exhortation to a genial and cheerful demeanor.

95. **obscuri**, *disingenuous*, concealing his real feelings, and wanting in frankness. — **acerbi**, *a harsh critic*, in that silence seems to cover disapproval.

96. **inter cuncta**, etc.: a general direction as to self-culture aside from all relations with others: amid all your endeavors to please, do not forget to acquire a well-ordered soul by the study of philosophy, — a suggestion which might well perhaps have taken precedence of all the other precepts. The questions mentioned are the commonplaces of ethics.

104. **me quotiens**, etc.: the poet closes with a picture of his own contented life upon his little estate, perhaps as an example of the proper aim in such a career and the proper way of attaining it. He himself, by his friendship with Mæcenas, had acquired the estate, no doubt having followed his own precepts, and by the study of philosophy, recommended in vv. 96–103, had preserved his independence of worldly advancement, and the *aequus animus* which is the chief end of philosophy and of life. He is thus a pattern for his young friend to follow.

111. **sed satis est**, etc.: a correction of **neu fluitem**, etc., inasmuch as that condition is the result of an *aequus animus* which is of course in the philosopher's own power.

## XIX.

Prisco si credis, Maecenas docte, Cratino,
nulla placere diu nec vivere carmina possunt,
quae scribuntur aquae potoribus. Vt male sanos
adscripsit Liber Satyris Faunisque poetas,
vina fere dulces oluerunt mane Camenae.

EPISTLE **19.** This epistle, addressed to Mæcenas, gives vent to the poet's scorn, on the one hand, of imitators, and on the other, of envious critics. Underneath the expressions of scorn lies a defence of Horace's own writings. The line of connection between the underwarp and the two-threaded woof is found in the implication that his imitating admirers, as well as his critics, suppose him also to be an imitator of the same calibre as themselves; but some of them are angry because he does not seek to conciliate their favor, and so they decry him in public while they admire his works in secret. Hence he attacks the imitators, shows that he is not one of them, and declares his independence of the suffrages of the throng who have no guide in art but the fashion set by the work of the imitators of the day.

1. **prisco si credis**, etc.: with the same humorous turn as in Sat. I. 3. 1–19, Horace begins his attack on the imitators by dwelling upon an accidental peculiarity of many men of genius, as if he were discussing the character of genius in sober earnest. Nor does he make clear what use he intends to make of his text until v. 17. — **prisco**: probably with reference to the *Old Comedy* to the writers of which Cratinus belonged. Cf. *Sat.* I. 4. 1. — **docte**: implying that, therefore, he is a judge of literature, and will understand the scope of the epistle. — **Cratino**: no extant fragment of his contains the sentiment here expressed, but he seems to have had a notoriety as a winebibber, and an epigram has been preserved alluding to this failing.

Οἶνός τοι χαρίεντι πέλει ταχὺς ἵππος ἀοιδῷ
ὕδωρ δὲ πίνων οὐδὲν ἂν τέκοι σοφόν.
Τοῦτ' ἔλεγεν, Διόνυσε, καὶ ἔπνεεν οὐχ ἑνὸς ἀσκοῦ
Κρατῖνος, ἀλλὰ παντὸς ὠδώδει πίθου.
Τοιγὰρ ὑπὸ στεφάνοις μέγαρ' ἔβρυεν εἶχε δὲ κισσῷ
μέτωπον ὥσπέρ καὶ σὺ κεκροκωμένον.

*Anthol. Palat.* XIII. 29.

Cf. also Aristoph. *Pax*, 701 *seq.* The idea was very familiar to the ancients and became almost a proverb. Cf. Dem. *de Fals. Leg.* 46.

3. **ut**, *ever since*. — **male sanos**: alluding to the inspired bard (**vates**), supposed to be filled with a frenzy which raised him above ordinary mortals in intellectual power. But the source of Horace's statement is unknown.

4. **adscripsit**, *enrolled*, as his regular followers. The idea is, ever since the remotest antiquity, the votaries of the Muses have been drinkers of wine. — **Satyris Faunisque**: these deities are really the same, the latter being the less gross Italian representatives of the former. The latter also had a prophetic power which makes them still more appropriate here. Cf. Ennius, V. 221.

5. **oluerunt mane**: cf. **putere diurno**, v. 11. — **Camenae**: the character of the poets is ascribed to the Muses themselves.

Laudibus arguitur vini vinosus Homerus;
Ennius ipse pater nunquam nisi potus ad arma
prosiluit dicenda. 'Forum Putealque Libonis
mandabo siccis, adimam cantare severis.'
Hoc simul edixi, non cessavere poetae
nocturno certare mero, putere diurno.
Quid si quis vultu torvo ferus et pede nudo
exiguaeque togae simulet textore Catonem,
virtutemne repraesentet moresque Catonis?
Rupit Iarbitam Timagenis aemula lingua,
dum studet urbanus tenditque disertus haberi.
Decipit exemplar vitiis imitabile. Quodsi

6. **laudibus**: cf., among other passages, *Il.* VI. 260. — **vinosus**, *a wine-drinker*, producing his poetry under that stimulus.

7. **Ennius**, etc.: the chief evidence of the statement is the fact that Ennius suffered from the gout.

8. **prosiluit**: as if he himself were the warrior he describes. — **Forum**, etc.: *i.e.* the sober business of life to the exclusion of poetry. — **Puteal**: a famous locality in the Forum, frequented by the money-lenders. Cf. *Sat.* II. 6. 35.

10. **hoc simul edixi**, *as soon as I have laid down this law*, like a prætor administering justice. — **non cessavere**: the poet gradually approaches the turn which he means to make. (As soon as I have thus maintained that poets are given to wine-drinking, all those who desire to be poets adopt the practice of wine-bibbing.)

12. **quid si quis**, etc.: *i.e.* but is it sufficient to copy external habits or garb in order to reproduce an inward nature? Obviously not, and this brings the poet to the point he is aiming at. This point he brings out by an example where an unknown Iarbitas was ruined by imitating the caustic wit of a man of genius, thinking thereby to be like his model. — **ferus**, *rough*, as not polished by culture. — **pede nudo**: *i.e.* in the old rough style of early republican times.

13. **exiguae**: the early republican Romans wore the toga in scanty folds and closely bound around the body (cf. I. 18. 30), while the imperial style became more and more flowing. — **textore**: an ablative of means in the same construction as **vultu**. The weaver is treated as one of the means. — **Catonem**: probably the Elder.

15. **Timagenis** (genitive with **aemula**): a historian from Alexandria who acted as a teacher in the house of Augustus. He was famous for his unbridled tongue. Cf. Sen. *de Ira*, III. 23.

16. **urbanus**, *a wit;* cf. *Sat.* I. 10. 65. — **disertus**, *a master of style*.

17. **decipit**: *i.e.* in that we mistake the faults of a great man for the real causes of his greatness, and so proceed to imitate them. — **vitiis**: ablative of respect.

pallerem casu, biberent exsangue cuminum.
O imitatores, servum pecus, ut mihi saepe
bilem, saepe iocum vestri movere tumultus!
Libera per vacuum posui vestigia princeps,
non aliena meo pressi pede. Qui sibi fidet,
dux reget examen. Parios ego primus iambos
ostendi Latio, numeros animosque secutus
Archilochi, non res et agentia verba Lycamben.
Ac ne me foliis ideo brevioribus ornes
quod timui mutare modos et carminis artem,
temperat Archilochi Musam pede mascula Sappho,
temperat Alcaeus, sed rebus et ordine dispar,

18. **pallerem**, etc.: *i.e.* this tendency proceeds so far that men will imitate the accidents of the moment (cf. **casu**). — **exsangue**: as producing that effect.

19. **O imitatores**, etc.: here the poet fully unmasks his battery, and tells plainly what he has been driving at.

20. **tumultus**, *worrying and fussing*, as opposed to the steady pursuit of some definite object.

21. **libera**: opposed to **servum**. Horace here begins to distinguish his own action from that of the imitators, in that he has followed worthy examples, to be sure, but in an independent spirit, and with such changes as, confident in his own powers, he had thought best to make, acting therein in the same manner as his great predecessors. — **per vacuum**, *through an unoccupied field*, as the Epodes certainly were. — **posui vestigia**, *I have traced a course*. — **princeps**, *a pioneer*.

22. **non aliena**, etc., *I have not placed my feet in another's track*.

23. **dux reget examen**, *will be the queen of the hive*. — **Parios**: *i.e.* of Archilochus of Paros. — **iambos**: referring to the Epodes, which are modelled after the caustic productions of Archilochus. Cf. *Od.* I. 16. 24.

25. **non res**: *i.e.* his subjects and his terms of expression are his own, and not borrowed from his original. — **agentia**, *which pursued*. — **Lycamben**: one of the objects of the elder poet's satire. This person, having refused Archilochus as a son-in-law, was attacked by him with such virulence that he is said to have hanged herself along with his daughter Neobule.

26. **ac ne me**, etc.: he here justifies the imitation that he has allowed himself, by the examples of Sappho and Alcæus, who did the same. — **foliis brevioribus**, *scantier laurels*.

27. **timui**, *have not ventured*. — **modos**, *the measures*, *i.e.* the metre. — **carminis artem**, *the structure of the song*, *i.e.* the form of the strophe.

28. **temperat**, *models*, lit. regulates. — **Archilochi**: depending on **pede**. — **pede**, *on the measure*, following his metre. Examples of Archilochian metres are *Od.* I. 4, IV. 7; *Epod.* 11. 13.

29. **ordine**, *manner*, properly,

nec socerum quaerit quem versibus oblinat atris,
nec sponsae laqueum famoso carmine nectit.
Hunc ego non alio dictum prius ore Latinus
vulgavi fidicen ; iuvat immemorata ferentem
ingenuis oculisque legi manibusque teneri.
Scire velis mea cur ingratus opuscula lector
laudet ametque domi, premat extra limen iniquus ?
Non ego ventosae plebis suffragia venor
impensis cenarum et tritae munere vestis ;
non ego, nobilium scriptorum auditor et ultor,
grammaticas ambire tribus et pulpita dignor.
Hinc illae lacrimae. ' Spissis indigna theatris
scripta pudet recitare et nugis addere pondus '

arrangement of ideas, but apparently including course of treatment, so that his poetry is not satirical.

30. **nec socerum**, etc.: *i.e.* his poetry is not abusive like that of Archilochus. Cf. v. 25 and note. — **atris**: as blackening the character.

31. **famoso**, *abusive*, as making the person attacked **famosus**. Cf. v. 25 and note.

32. **Latinus**: as opposed to the Greek Alcæus. Cf. *Od.* IV. 3. 23.

33. **iuvat**: *i.e.* I am proud to do so. — **immemorata**, *words before unheard*. Cf. II. 2. 117.

34. **ingenuis**: alluding to the class of readers for whom he writes. Cf. v. 37, and also *Sat.* I. 10. 81–87.

35. **scire velis**, etc.: *i.e.* that being the case, if you are surprised that I am disparaged by the critics in public, I will say it is precisely for the reason that I do not toady to the crowd, nor to the pedantic critics.

37. **ventosae**, *fickle*, in matters of art, just as in politics, from which last sphere the whole figure is drawn.

38. **impensis**, etc.: not literally, but continuing the figure of political canvassing. These are the means used by the political aspirant to whom Horace compares himself.

39. **nobilium scriptorum**, etc.: *i.e.* Horace does not seek the favor of the lower orders of literary workers, but hears only the works of the great, and repays in kind. He consorts only with the choice spirits of the Augustan circle.

40. **grammaticas**, *of the critics*. — **ambire tribus**: continuing the figure. — **pulpita**: the readers' desk, which Horace does not frequent, as do others, to recite his works. Cf. *Sat.* I. 4. 73.

41. **hinc illae lacrimae**: a proverbial expression derived from Ter. *And.* 126, for "there's where the trouble is." He means, it is because I refuse to recite my works, and submit them to the approval of the crowd, that they disparage me. —**spissis indigna**, etc.: the excuse of Horace for not reciting. — **theatris**: not necessarily the theatre proper, though such recitations may have taken place in these, but *public halls*. Cf. *Sat.* I. 10. 38. — **spissis**, *crowded*.

42. **addere pondus**: *i.e.* by giv-

si dixi, 'Rides,' ait, 'et Iovis auribus ista
servas; fidis enim manare poetica mella
te solum, tibi pulcher.' Ad haec ego naribus uti
formido, et luctantis acuto ne secer ungui,
'Displicet iste locus,' clamo, et diludia posco.
Ludus enim genuit trepidum certamen et iram,
ira truces inimicitias et funebre bellum.

## XX.

Vertumnum Ianumque, liber, spectare videris,
scilicet ut prostes Sosiorum pumice mundus.

ing them such publicity, and making so much of them.

43. **rides, ait,** etc.: *i.e.* when I excuse myself thus, these men won't believe me, but ascribe it to arrogance, and to scorn of other literary men.

44. **manare**: in a rare active sense.

45. **naribus uti,** *turn up my nose.*

46. **formido**: *i.e.* he is afraid of offending them on account of their slanderous tongues, and so he simply refers his disinclination to the place of recitation, and refuses to argue the case further.

47. **diludia,** *a truce in the contest;* the allusion is to the off-days or intervals between gladiatorial fights (**ludi**), to which he compares his argument with his opponent.

48. **ludus,** *such sport,* properly the fighting of gladiators, but with a side reference to the original meaning of the word, *sport.* — **genuit**: gnomic perfect. — **trepidum certamen,** *hot rivalry.*

49. **funebre bellum,** *bloody warfare,* as the climax of the contest of words between Horace and the critics.

EPISTLE 20. This epistle forms the epilogue to the first book of Epistles, and is addressed to the book itself, personified as a young slave brought up in the house, but now tired of restraint, and wishing to seek his fortune in the world outside. The characteristics of book and slave are confused in a manner that is puzzling and incongruous to us, but to the less fastidious imagination of the ancients, who constantly confounded the figure with the thing signified, was not objectionable.

1. **Vertumnum**: at the corner of the Forum between the Palatine and Capitoline stood a statue of Vertumnus (cf. *Sat.* II. 3. 228) near which were the book shops in the Vicus Tuscus, which led from the Forum through the low ground towards the Tiber. The word stands here as indicating one of the prominent objects of the booksellers' quarter. — **Ianum**: apparently the arch over the Vicus Tuscus, where it led out from the Forum.

2. **scilicet,** *forsooth,* in a mocking vein, implying the folly of the purpose. — **prostes**: figuratively applied to the exposure for sale at the

Odisti clavis et grata sigilla pudico;
paucis ostendi gemis et communia laudas,
non ita nutritus. Fuge quo descendere gestis.
Non erit emisso reditus tibi. 'Quid miser egi?
Quid volui?' dices, ubi quis te laeserit; et scis
in breve te cogi, cum plenus languet amator.
Quodsi non odio peccantis desipit augur,
carus eris Romae donec te deseret aetas;
contrectatus ubi manibus sordescere vulgi
coeperis, aut tineas pasces taciturnus inertis
aut fugies Vticam aut vinctus mitteris Ilerdam.
Ridebit monitor non exauditus, ut ille,
qui male parentem in rupes protrusit asellum
iratus: quis enim invitum servare laboret?
Hoc quoque te manet, ut pueros elementa docentem

front of the book-stall, but literally referring to the exposure of the slave. — **Sosiorum**: a famous firm of booksellers. Cf. II. 3. 345. — **pumice**: used for polishing the ends of the rolls. — **mundus**, *beautified*, referring alike to the roll and the slave.

3. **clavis, sigilla**: with a double meaning as with the other words, the keys of the bookcase and the chamber as well.

4. **gemis**: *i.e.* from love of admiration, here ascribed to the book in its personified character. — **communia**: like **publicum**, the public streets accessible to all.

5. **non ita**, etc.: *i.e.* the slave had been brought up to shun admiration as a modest young person. — **fuge**: *i.e.* since you will have it so, go your way. — **descendere**: cf. *Od.* III. 1. 11, and *Ep.* I. 7. 48 with note.

6. **quid miser**, etc.: the words of regret of the slave (book) when he sees the consequences of his wilfulness.

7. **quid volui**, *what was I thinking of?* — **laeserit**: alluding to the abuse of critics.

8. **in breve**, etc., *reduced to straits.* — **languet**: *i.e.* when readers are tired of you.

10. **aetas**, *youth* (as often), the figure being kept up throughout.

11. **contrectatus**, etc.: of the wearing out of youth and beauty. — **ubi**: opposed to **donec te**, etc.

12. **taciturnus**: *i.e.* unread.

13. **fugies**, etc.: *i.e.* you will be packed off to the provinces as unsalable merchandise.

14. **monitor**: *i.e.* Horace himself, who impliedly has endeavored to dissuade him from his purpose. — **non exauditus**, *unheeded.*

15. **qui male parentem**, etc.: *i.e.* the driver tried to prevent the ass from going over a precipice, but not succeeding, shoved him over, bidding him go to destruction, since he was determined to go. Of course the loss would be the driver's after all.

17. **pueros elementa**, etc.: *i.e.*

occupet extremis in vicis balba senectus.
Cum tibi sol tepidus pluris admoverit auris,
me libertino natum patre et in tenui re
maiores pennas nido extendisse loqueris,
ut quantum generi demas virtutibus addas;
me primis urbis belli placuisse domique;
corporis exigui praecanum solibus aptum
irasci celerem, tamen ut placabilis essem.
Forte meum si quis te percontabitur aevum,
me quater undenos sciat implevisse Decembris,
collegam Lepidum quo duxit Lollius anno.

the book would be used to teach boys their letters. For this purpose, slaves acted as schoolmasters.

18. **extremis**, etc.: *i.e.* in out-of-the-way places, "hedge schools."

19. **cum tibi sol**, etc.: here Horace skilfully inserts an account of the author of the book, which he puts into the mouth of the supposed slave. If the words are taken in immediate connection with the preceding verse, they must be supposed to refer to the words of the schoolmaster to his pupils. But it is much better to connect them with the general subject, and so refer them to the book as it is exposed for sale in the Vicus Tuscus. — **sol tepidus**: *i.e.* the declining sun of afternoon, when it was cool enough for people to be about the streets and visit the book-stalls. Thus he would have a larger audience.

20. **libertino**: cf. *Sat.* I. 6. 45.

21. **maiores**, etc.: *i.e.* for a higher flight, a rise in life.

22. **quantum**, etc.: *i.e.* the lower his origin, the greater his merit in achieving distinction.

23. **primis**, etc.: cf. I. 17. 35 and *Sat.* II. 1. 76.—**belli domique**: limiting **primis**, *i.e.* warriors and statesmen.

24. **corporis exigui**: cf. *Sat.* II. 3. 309. — **praecanum**: *early gray*. — **solibus aptum**: *fond of the sun*, *i.e.* of sunning himself for warmth, as was the habit of the Romans, perhaps with a hint at a fondness for lounging. Cf. I. 7. 10 *seq.*

25. **irasci celerem**: cf. *Sat.* II. 3. 323.

27. **Decembris**: as the month of his birth. — **undenos**: notice that the Latin regularly uses the distributives in multiplication (**bis bina**, twice two).

28. **collegam**, etc.: in the year B.C. 21. Lollius was first elected consul, and afterwards Lepidus was chosen as his colleague; hence **duxit**.

# LIBER SECVNDVS

## I.

Cum tot sustineas et tanta negotia solus,
res Italas armis tuteris, moribus ornes,
legibus emendes, in publica commoda peccem,
si longo sermone morer tua tempora, Caesar.

EPISTLE 1. In the life of Horace ascribed to Suetonius it is said: [Augustus] scripta eius usque adeo probavit ut . . . post sermones lectos nullam sui mentionem habitam ita sit questus: "Irasci me tibi scito quod non in plerisque eiusmodi scriptis mecum potissimum loquaris. An vereris ne apud posteros tibi infame sit, quod videaris familiaris nobis esse?" expressitque eclogam cuius initium est: Cum tot sustineas, etc.

At any rate the poet's personal relations with Augustus seem to have been of the most formal character. He may well without hypocrisy have joined in the praise addressed to the restorer of peace and good order, and he doubtless appreciated his patron's many good qualities; but in all his allusions to Augustus, there seems to be something perfunctory: "If Alexander wishes to be a god, let him be a god." The tone of Epistle I. 13 is entirely inconsistent with any unaffected personal relations between Horace and Augustus. In fact, Augustus was one of the class of men that Horace was engaged all his life in ridiculing and unmasking, an actor, a *poseur*, a sham. It is entirely in harmony with this view that Horace, being requested to address an epistle to the monarch, should have attached such an address to this poetical treatise on literary taste at Rome, a subject in which Augustus was thought (perhaps even by himself) to be interested. Nor was Horace so unskilful an artist as not to be able to dovetail the treatise to its address with a smooth joint. The binding pin is the wise acquiescence of the Romans in their present form of government, taken in connection with their dissatisfaction with the present tendencies of literary art, and its present representatives. This was a subject in which Horace did have an interest, and he makes it carry the load of a tribute to his patron, as poets are often bound to do whether that patron is a crowned head, or a semi-cultivated Demos.

2. **moribus ornes**, etc.: Augustus took it upon himself to reform the morals of the state. Cf. Suet. *Oct. passim.*, also *Od.* IV. 15. 9.

4. **morer tua tempora**, *waste your time*, though the Latin has a much more picturesque implication. It represents Augustus' time as fully employed in the great duties of state, each moment (hence the plural) devoted to some particular duty from which he would be detained

Romulus et Liber pater et cum Castore Pollux,
post ingentia facta deorum in templa recepti,
dum terras hominumque colunt genus, aspera bella
componunt, agros adsignant, oppida condunt,
ploravere suis non respondere favorem
speratum meritis. Diram qui contudit hydram
notaque fatali portenta labore subegit,
comperit invidiam supremo fine domari.
Vrit enim fulgore suo qui praegravat artis
infra se positas, exstinctus amabitur idem.
Praesenti tibi maturos largimur honores
iurandasque tuum per numen ponimus aras,
nil oriturum alias, nil ortum tale fatentes.
Sed tuus hic populus sapiens et iustus in uno,
te nostris ducibus, te Graiis anteferendo,
cetera nequaquam simili ratione modoque

by the necessity of reading the poet's trivial discourse, if it should be made too long. The reader will notice that the excuse, as usual with Horace, is made far more complimentary than any performance could be. Cf. *Sat.* II. 1. 12.

5. **Romulus,** etc.: *i.e.* all the great benefactors of the race before you have failed of recognition in their lifetime, and only attained divine honors after their death.

9. **ploravere,** *had to mourn.* — **favorem,** *applause.*

12. **invidiam,** etc.: *i.e.* only by his death did he finally overcome jealousy and hatred. — **domari**: as if that too were a monster like the others.

13. **urit**: *i.e.* and so excites the animosity of lesser minds whom his greatness throws in the shade. — **artis,** etc., *the virtues that lie below him, i.e.* inferior minds.

14. **exstinctus,** etc.: *i.e.* as a dead man he ceases to be a rival, and is then appreciated.

15. **praesenti,** *among us, i.e.* while still alive we give you the honors for which the others had to wait till their death. — **maturos,** *timely*, as not too late for you to enjoy.

16. **iurandas,** *to witness oaths,* used transitively, as often, perhaps following Greek usage. With this construction, however, is combined the more common one with **per.** As to the fact, cf. *Claudius natus est Lugduni eo ipso die* (B.C. 10) *quo primum ara ibi Augusto dedicata est* (Suet. *Claud.* 2); and *Templa, quamvis sciret etiam proconsulibus decerni solere, in nulla tamen provincia nisi communi suo Romaeque nomine recepit, nam in urbe quidem pertinacissime abstinuit hoc honore* (Suet. *Octav.* 52).

18. **sed tuus,** etc.: in this line begins the neatly wrought joint. In

aestimat, et nisi quae terris semota suisque
temporibus defuncta videt, fastidit et odit,
sic fautor veterum, ut tabulas peccare vetantes,
quas bis quinque viri sanxerunt, foedera regum
vel Gabiis vel cum rigidis aequata Sabinis,
pontificum libros, annosa volumina vatum,
dictitet Albano Musas in monte locutas.
Si, quia Graiorum sunt antiquissima quaeque
scripta vel optima, Romani pensantur eadem
scriptores trutina, non est quod multa loquamur:

this one thing the people are sound, but not so in literary matters, in which they affect to prefer the old to the new.

21. **nisi quae**, *except those who*, applying, in translation, the statement to the authors instead of their works, as in fact Horace does. — **terris semota**, *passed from the earth.* — **suisque temporibus defuncta**, *finished their allotted existence.*

23. **sic fautor**, *such a partisan.* The nouns in **-tor** are so adjectival in their nature, that they can take an adverb, as here. In fact, almost any noun can be restored to its original adjective meaning, if it has not been specialized too much. Cf. **late regem**, Virg. *Æn.* I. 21. — **veterum**, *of antiquity*, neuter. — **tabulas**: the Twelve Tables, which constituted the oldest collection of laws at Rome.

25. **Gabiis**: with **cum**, belonging to both nouns. For the allusion, see Livy I. 54 *seq.;* Dionys. Hal. IV. 58. — **rigidis**: cf. **Sabellus** I. 16. 49 and note. — **aequata**, *made on equal terms.* — **Sabinis**: cf. Livy I. 13.

26. **pontificum libros**: books of ritual and religious law kept by the *pontifices* from the earliest use of writing. Cf. *provocationem autem etiam a regibus fuisse declarant pontificii libri, significant nostri etiam augurales, itemque ab omni iudicio poenaque provocari licere indicant XII tabulae compluribus legibus*, Cic. *de Rep.* II. 31. 54, where it will be noticed that they are cited as authority along with the Twelve Tables. — **volumina vatum**: the most ancient works of this description are the Sibylline books; but as these were in Greek, Horace could hardly have referred to them except by a careless use of language. As oracles and prophecies were kept with great care, we must suppose there were collections of these preserved, which may be referred to here. Cf. *Religio deinde* (B.C. 212) *nova obiecta est ex carminibus Marcianis. Vates hic Marcius illustris fuerat, et cum conquisitio priore anno ex senatus consulto talium librorum fieret, in M. Aemili praetoris urbani qui eam rem agebat manus venerant.* — Livy XXV. 12. 3.

27. **Albano in monte**: *i.e.* like another Parnassus, a seat of the Latin Muses. — **Musas**, etc.: *i.e.* that these antiquated writings, without any literary merit, were uttered directly by the goddesses of song, simply because they were ancient.

28. **si quia Graiorum**, etc.:

nil intra est olea, nil extra est in nuce duri ;
venimus ad summum fortunae: pingimus atque
psallimus et luctamur Achivis doctius unctis.
Si meliora dies, ut vina, poemata reddit,
scire velim chartis pretium quotus adroget annus.
Scriptor abhinc annos centum qui decidit, inter
perfectos veteresque referri debet an inter
viles atque novos ? Excludat iurgia finis.
'Est vetus atque probus centum qui perficit annos.'
Quid, qui deperiit minor uno mense vel anno,
inter quos referendus erit ? Veteresne poetas,
an quos et praesens et postera respuat aetas ?
'Iste quidem veteres inter ponetur honeste,
qui vel mense brevi vel toto est iunior anno.'
Vtor permisso, caudaeque pilos ut equinae
paullatim vello et demo unum, demo etiam unum,
dum cadat elusus ratione ruentis acervi,

*i.e.* if, because the Greek authors are better in proportion to their age, we must hold the same of the Romans, there is nothing more to be said; it is like applying the same rule to the olive and the walnut, an extension of an analogy to a case of exactly the opposite nature, which shows utter folly and misapprehension.

31. **nil intra est**, etc.: apparently proverbial for an analogy between two things utterly unlike, as in the olive the soft part is outside and in the nut inside.

32. **venimus**, etc. : *i.e.* we have conquered the Greeks in arms, therefore (according to the false analogy) we must be better than they in all the arts as well.

34. **si meliora dies**: an example of the argument called Sorites, which proceeds as by the gradual diminution (or increase) of a pile of sand, asking how many grains one must take away (or add) to make it cease (or begin) to be a pile. So the poet calls upon the admirer of antiquity to set a limit of age at which an author shall be admirable, and then proceeds by the method of the Sorites to show the impossibility of setting up age as a criterion of merit.

35. **quotus annus**, *how many years;* properly, which year in order of succession, first, second, etc.

37. **referri**, *to be reckoned*, a mercantile (book-keeping) word. Cf. **referre acceptum**.

39. **probus**, *classic*, originally first class, A 1, of wares, cf. **proba merx**.

43. **iste**, etc.: the reply of the opponent.

45. **utor permisso**, *I take advantage of the concession.*—**caudae**, etc.: a mixed allusion to the old fable of Sertorius (Val. Max. VII. 3. 6) and to the φαλακρός, a sophism like the Sorites, cf. v. 34 note.

47. **cadat**, *fails, loses his case.*—

qui redit ad fastos et virtutem aestimat annis
miraturque nihil nisi quod Libitina sacravit.
Ennius et sapiens et fortis et alter Homerus,
ut critici dicunt, leviter curare videtur
quo promissa cadant et somnia Pythagorea.
Naevius in manibus non est et mentibus haeret
paene recens? Adeo sanctum est vetus omne poema.
Ambigitur quotiens uter utro sit prior, aufert
Pacuvius docti famam senis, Accius alti;
dicitur Afrani toga convenisse Menandro,
Plautus ad exemplar Siculi properare Epicharmi,
vincere Caecilius gravitate, Terentius arte.
Hos ediscit et hos arto stipata theatro
spectat Roma potens; habet hos numeratque poetas

**elusus**, *baffled*, a fencing word; cf. I. 17. 18. — **ratione**, *by the argument*, *i.e.* the Sorites. — **acervi**: a translation of σωρός, from which the name of the argument is derived.

48. **fastos**, *the calendar*, *i.e.* reckoning the years.

49. **Libitina**: cf. *Sat.* II. 6. 19.

51. **leviter curare**, *to heed little*, *i.e.* have no cause to be anxious, inasmuch as his fame is assured. The allusion is to his epitaph, ascribed to himself:

Nemo me dacrumis decoret nec funera fletu
Faxit. Cur? Volito vivus per ora virum; —

or some similar expression of the poet. See also *Cum somniavit* [Ennius] *ita narravit: Visus Homerus adesse poeta.* Cic. *Acad. Pr.* II. 16. 51.

52. **quo cadant**, *what becomes of.* — **promissa**: see note v. 51. — **Pythagorea**: the allusion is to the doctrine of Metempsychosis held by Pythagoras, in accordance with which doctrine Ennius appears to have dreamed that he was inhabited by the soul of Homer. Cf. Pers. VI. 10, 11. See also *sic enim ait Ennius in Annalium suorum principio ubi se dicit vidisse in somnis Homerum dicentem fuisse se quondam pavonem et ex eo translatam esse animam in se. Schol.* in Persium.

53. **Naevius**, etc.: another instance to prove the popularity of the ancient poets.

54. **paene recens**: *i.e.* in spite of his age, he is known almost as if he had written but yesterday.

55. **ambigitur**, etc.: another way of expressing that these authors are held in repute.

56. **docti**, *skilful.* — **senis**, *old worthy*, in reference to their antiquity. — **alti**, *inspired*, in reference to his lofty style.

57. **toga**: an allusion to the *fabula togata*, or play on a Roman subject, of which Afranius was a distinguished author. — **convenisse**, *would have fitted; i.e.* his style is such as the Greek comedian would have written if he had treated Roman subjects.

58. **properare**, *to bustle*, in refer-

ad nostrum tempus Livi scriptoris ab aevo.
interdum vulgus rectum videt, est ubi peccat.
Si veteres ita miratur laudatque poetas
ut nihil anteferat, nihil illis comparet, errat.
Si quaedam nimis antique, si pleraque dure
dicere credit eos, ignave multa fatetur,
et sapit et mecum facit et Iove iudicat aequo.
Non equidem insector delendave carmina Livi
esse reor, memini quae plagosum mihi parvo
Orbilium dictare, sed emendata videri
pulchraque et exactis minimum distantia miror.
Inter quae verbum emicuit si forte decorum et
si versus paullo concinnior unus et alter,
iniuste totum ducit venditque poema.
Indignor quicquam reprehendi, non quia crasse
compositum illepideve putetur, sed quia nuper,
nec veniam antiquis, sed honorem et praemia posci.
Recte necne crocum floresque perambulet Attae

ence to the rapid and drastic action of the plays of Plautus.

63. **interdum vulgus**, etc.: *i.e.* in the indiscriminate admiration for these ancients, the Roman public is in many respects right, but not so when it praises only these, and sees nothing equal or superior in modern times.

67. **ignave**, *carelessly*, of the cases where the ancient poets disregard the labored perfection which in Horace's view should be the aim of art, cf. *Sat.* I. 10. — **multa**: *sc.* **dicere**.

68. **Iove aequo**, *with the favor of Jove*, as securing him a sound head.

71. **Orbilium**: evidently Horace's early instructor. Cf. *Sat.* I. 6. 76, and Suet. *de Gramm.* 9. — **dictare**: apparently the education of Roman youth consisted chiefly in learning by heart (cf. v. 60) from dictation (cf. *Sat.* I. 10. 75) the Greek and Roman poets. — **sed emendata**, etc.: *i.e.* while Horace does not despise the old poets, he wonders that their faults are not seen by their admirers.

72. **exactis**, *perfection*.

75. **totum ducit**, *takes the whole with it*, making all alike seem fine.

76. **indignor**, etc.: *i.e.* he finds fault with the fact that excellence is not made the criterion, but antiquity.

79. **recte necne**, etc.: *i.e.* when I inquire whether the old plays ought to keep the stage, they think I have lost all shame to doubt that what was good enough for the famous old actors must be the best possible. — **crocum**: the stage was perfumed with saffron water. Cf.

Et cum scaena croco Cilici perfusa recens est. — Lucr. II. 416.

— **flores**: there is no other allusion

fabula si dubitem, clament periisse pudorem
cuncti paene patres, ea cum reprehendere coner,
quae gravis Aesopus, quae doctus Roscius egit;
vel quia nil rectum nisi quod placuit sibi ducunt,
vel quia turpe putant parere minoribus et quae
imberbi didicere senes perdenda fateri.
Iam Saliare Numae carmen qui laudat, et illud,
quod mecum ignorat, solus volt scire videri,
ingeniis non ille favet plauditque sepultis,
nostra sed impugnat, nos nostraque lividus odit.
Quodsi tam Graecis novitas invisa fuisset
quam nobis, quid nunc esset vetus? Aut quid haberet,
quod legeret tereretque viritim publicus usus?

to flowers on the stage; but as a scenic representation was always a festival, such a scattering of flowers is not improbable. — **Attae**: a writer of plays, T. Quinctius Atta is mentioned by several ancient authors. He seems to have died B.C. 78.

81. **patres,** *elders,* intimating that their conservatism belongs to their age.

82. **gravis**: as especially great in (heavy) tragedy. — **Aesopus**: a tragic actor, a friend of Cicero, and the father of the spendthrift mentioned in *Sat.* II. 3. 239. Cf. *Vidi . . . in Aesopo familiari tuo tantum ardorem voltuum atque motuum ut eum vis quaedam abstraxisse a sensu mentis videretur.* Cic. *de Div.* I. 37. 80. — **Roscius**: cf. Cic. *pro Arch.* VIII. 17. Both these actors had for some time been dead, but could be remembered by the older men.

83. **nil rectum,** etc.: *i.e.* because they are so opinionated that they make their own taste the criterion.

84. **turpe putant,** etc.: *i.e.* because they are too proud to admit that their juniors can be wiser than they, or that anything new has been learned since they were young.

86. **iam Saliare,** etc.: a still more emphatic statement of the same general idea. Such admirers of antiquity wish to be thought the only critics of sound taste, and praise the ancients not from real admiration for them, but from envious hatred of the moderns. — **iam,** *now* (the fact is). — **Saliare**: cf. *Salios item Marti Gradivo* (*Numa*) *legit . . . et per urbem ire canentes carmina cum tripudiis sollemnique saltatu iussit,* Livy I. 20; and *Saliorum carmina vix sacerdotibus satis intellecta,* Quint. I. 6. 40. The hymns are here mentioned as a type of the antiquity referred to. The words must not be taken literally, but only as a kind of reductio ad absurdum of the principle of these critics.

92. **legeret,** etc., *for the universal public to read and wear out by indiscriminate use.* — **viritim**: used of anything which is done to or by every man indiscriminately. — **usus**: properly belonging only to **tereret,** but by a fusion of ideas put for the people themselves.

Vt primum positis nugari Graecia bellis
coepit et in vitium fortuna labier aequa,
nunc athletarum studiis nunc arsit equorum,
marmoris aut eboris fabros aut aeris amavit,
suspendit picta vultum mentemque tabella,
nunc tibicinibus nunc est gavisa tragoedis;
sub nutrice puella velut si luderet infans,
quod cupide petiit, mature plena reliquit.
Quid placet aut odio est, quod non mutabile credas?
Hoc paces habuere bonae ventique secundi.
Romae dulce diu fuit et sollemne reclusa
mane domo vigilare, clienti promere iura,
cautos nominibus rectis expendere nummos,
maiores audire, minori dicere per quae

93. **ut primum,** etc.: the poet here describes the rise of art in Greece and Rome, showing that it was the passion for novelty, and the recognition of new artists, which made the Greeks superior in their works of art. With this is coupled a statement of the practical spirit of the earlier Romans which prevented them from attaining the excellence that among the Greeks bloomed of a sudden on account of the leisure afforded by prosperity. — **nugari,** *to divert itself,* as compared with the serious business of the earlier wars.

94. **vitium**: in the true Roman spirit, Horace calls all such frivolities faulty, and so impliedly puts the Roman practical serious pursuits above the Greek trifling, while at the same time he asserts the Greek superiority in these trifles.

96. **fabros,** *workers in,* etc.

99. **sub nutrice,** etc.: *i.e.* they were like children in their inconstancy, captivated by one object and, soon satiated, leaving it for another. All this refers to the **novitas** of v. 90.

101. **quid placet,** etc.: *i.e.* and naturally, for that is the law of taste, that variety should be attractive.

102. **paces,** *times of peace;* see Gr. A. & G. 75, 3 *c*.

103. **Romae,** etc.: *i.e.* at Rome, on the other hand, the people were devoted to political and economic pursuits and moral culture (cf. II. 3. 323 *seq.*); hence they could not be expected to practise the frivolous arts; but cf. v. 108 for the change which took place under Augustus. — **reclusa,** *with open doors,* expecting a throng of clients, who came to make the morning call and get advice (cf. **promere iura**). This receiving of visits was a necessary duty of a politician.

104. **mane**: cf. *Sat.* I. 1. 10; *Ep.* I. 7. 75. — **vigilare,** *be up early.*

105. **cautos,** *secured.* — **rectis,** *good,* in a commercial sense.

106. **maiores,** etc.: to listen to, and in turn to dispense, worldly wisdom. Upon receiving the **toga virilis,** the young Roman was put in charge of some statesman or warrior, to learn his duties as a citizen

crescere res posset, minui damnosa libido.
Mutavit mentem populus levis et calet uno
scribendi studio; puerique patresque severi
fronde comas vincti cenant et carmina dictant.
Ipse ego, qui nullos me adfirmo scribere versus,
invenior Parthis mendacior, et prius orto
sole vigil calamum et chartas et scrinia posco.
Navem agere ignarus navis timet; habrotonum aegro
non audet nisi qui didicit dare; quod medicorum est
promittunt medici; tractant fabrilia fabri:
scribimus indocti doctique poemata passim.
  Hic error tamen et levis haec insania quantas
virtutes habeat, sic collige. Vatis avarus
non temere est animus, versus amat, hoc studet unum;
detrimenta, fugas servorum, incendia ridet;

and a politician. Cf. Cic. *de Am.* I. 1.

107. **minui**, etc.: cf. the elder Horace's instructions to his son, *Sat.* I. 4. 105.

108. **mutavit**, etc.: *i.e.* but now we have changed all that, and have suddenly become frivolous like the Greeks, and the natural consequence is that everybody writes, whether well or ill. This is apparently inserted to account for the poor quality of much that is written. The mistake made by the critics is in classing all alike, — a side glance at the main theme again. — **calet**, *is fired.*

109. **severi**: *i.e.* who should be devoted to more serious pursuits.

110. **fronde**, etc.: *i.e.* as devotees of the Muses. — **dictant**, *improvise*, dictating them on the spot to a slave to take down.

111. **ipse ego**: Horace, with his usual humor, includes himself among the objects of his satire.

112. **Parthis**: proverbial; cf. *perfide Albion*, and the British idea of French disingenuousness.

113. **vigil**: cf. **vigilare**, v. 104. — **scrinia**, *books;* the article itself is not distinguishable from the **capsa** or book-holder; it evidently contained rolls, intended here perhaps to be translated or imitated, as that was the way in which the poetry he is speaking of was written.

114. **navem**, etc.: *i.e.* all other professions are recognized as requiring preparation, but anybody can write, they think. — **habrotonum**: a bitter herb, used as a remedy for several diseases. Cf. Pliny, *H. N.* XXI. 92 (160). It is doubtless chosen here as a common and innocuous remedy.

118. **hic error**, etc.: the poet jocosely enumerates the advantages that after all flow from this craze.

119. **sic collige**: cf. *Sat.* II. 1. 51. — **vatis avarus**, etc.: *i.e.* this passion keeps the poet from covetousness.

121. **detrimenta**, etc.: *i.e.* in

non fraudem socio puerove incogitat ullam
pupillo; vivit siliquis et pane secundo;
militiae quamquam piger et malus, utilis urbi,
si das hoc, parvis quoque rebus magna iuvari.
Os tenerum pueri balbumque poeta figurat,
torquet ab obscenis iam nunc sermonibus aurem;
mox etiam pectus praeceptis format amicis,
asperitatis et invidiae corrector et irae,
recte facta refert, orientia tempora notis
instruit exemplis, inopem solatur et aegrum.
Castis cum pueris ignara puella mariti
disceret unde preces, vatem ni Musa dedisset?
Poscit opem chorus et praesentia numina sentit;
caelestis implorat aquas docta prece blandus,
avertit morbos, metuenda pericula pellit;

consequence of his freedom from greed of gain, the poet is undisturbed by losses, and does not commit crime for money.

123. **vivit siliquis**, etc.: *i.e.* he is free from luxury. — **siliquis**: properly pods, but put here for all kinds of leguminous vegetables, as cheap food. — **secundo**: *i.e.* of the poorer quality.

124. **militiae**: may be construed either as dative or locative. — **urbi**: *i.e.* though he is of no use in war, he does perform a useful function as a teacher of morals.

125. **si das**, etc.: *i.e.* if you admit that even the great object of the well-being of the state is aided also by slight influences in favor of good morals. Of course the condition is really an implied assurance of the fact.

127. **torquet**, etc.: *i.e.* by familiarizing the youth with elegant diction from his earliest age, the poet keeps him pure and clean in language. — **iam nunc**, *even then; i.e.* from his infancy, before his mind and heart can yet be affected.

128. **mox etiam**, etc.: *i.e.* later the moral precepts can take effect.

130. **recte facta**, *virtuous deeds;* in the past to serve as examples for the future. — **tempora**, *generation.* — **notis**, *famous, i.e.* he gives currency among the next generation to the well-known examples of virtue.

131. **solatur**: *i.e.* by the examples and precepts which he presents. — **aegrum**, *sick at heart.*

132. **pueris, puella**: cf. *Carmen Saeculare*, esp. v. 6; also *Decrevere pontifices ut virgines ter novenae per urbem euntes carmen canerent. Id cum in Iovis Statoris aede discerent conditum ab Livio poeta carmen*, etc.; the narrative continues in reference to another rite: *Tum septem et viginti virgines longam indutae vestem carmen in Iunonem reginam canentes ibant*, Livy, XXVII. 37. Similar rites must have been very ancient in Italy. Cf. Dionys. Hal. I. 21.

impetrat et pacem et locupletem frugibus annum.
Carmine di superi placantur, carmine Manes.
Agricolae prisci, fortes parvoque beati,
condita post frumenta, levantes tempore festo
corpus et ipsum animum spe finis dura ferentem,
cum sociis operum, pueris et coniuge fida,
Tellurem porco, Silvanum lacte piabant,

138. **Manes**: *i.e.* Di Manes, *the gods below.*

139. **agricolae prisci**, etc.: the mention of the employment of poetry in sacred rituals affords a natural transition to a description of the rise of literature from festal rites in Rome independent of Greek influence, and the later fuller development of literary taste and activity under that influence, and further to a statement of the present hindrances and discouragements with which the poet has to contend. — **agricolae**, etc.: Horace refers, no doubt correctly, the origin of Latin poetry, so far as there was any, to primitive harvest festivals, at which songs were sung of a merry kind, accompanied with good-natured chaffing and raillery.

141. **spe finis**, etc.: *i.e.* as the festivity marks the end of the year's labor, so its expectation, confirmed by the recurring festival, has sustained the laborer through the year.

142. **cum sociis operum**: the numerous allusions to the union of slaves and freemen in these festivals, make it almost necessary to take **sociis** as referring to slaves, the two groups being put together without a connective; cf. *Od.* III. 17. 16; *Epod.* 2. 65, and Marquardt, *Privatleben*, p. 172. Probably Horace's picture does not go very far back.

143. **Tellurem porco**, etc.: in the general inosculation of all Roman cults with each other, there is no known festival that exactly corresponds to this description. After harvest, on the 25th of August, a sacrifice called Opeconsiva was made, and Ops can hardly be distinguished from Tellus, but details of this sacrifice are wanting. Later in the year, about Dec. 15, after the sowing of the new crop, there was a festival, the Feriae Sementivae; later still came the Saturnalia, and in January the Paganalia, a rustic festival to Tellus and Ceres (hardly distinguishable divinities); cf. Ov. *Fast.* I. 663 *seq.* Horace may refer to any of these, or his words may be a confused allusion to all of them. — **porco**: for some reason or other the pig was the special sacrifice to Ceres, and all other Chthonic deities. Cf.

> Placentur matres frugum, Tellusque Ceresque
> Farre suo gravidae visceribusque suis.
> — Ov. *Fast.* I. 671.

It is to be noticed that this animal especially belongs to settled life, and so to the life of husbandry, as opposed to a nomadic life, in which the herds accompanied their owners in their wanderings. It formed also the special food of the countryman throughout Italy, the only animal that was not too valuable to kill. — **Silvanum**: here as the god of pasturage, which was one of his provinces, as opposed to agriculture represented in Tellus. — **lacte**: cf. *silvicolam tepido lacte precare Palen* (another pastoral divinity), Ov. *Fast.* IV. 746. — **piabant**, *appeased*

floribus et vino Genium, memorem brevis aevi.
Fescennina per hunc inventa licentia morem
versibus alternis opprobria rustica fudit,
libertasque recurrentis accepta per annos
lusit amabiliter, donec iam saevus apertam
in rabiem coepit verti iocus et per honestas
ire domos impune minax. Doluere cruento
dente lacessiti, fuit intactis quoque cura
condicione super communi; quin etiam lex
poenaque lata, malo quae nollet carmine quemquam
describi: vertere modum formidine fustis
ad bene dicendum delectandumque redacti.
Graecia capta ferum victorem cepit et artis

lit. made **pius**, a word which is applied to gods in their relation to men, as well as *vice versa;* cf. *pia mater*, *Ep.* I. 18. 26 and note.

144. **Genium**: this word, from the same root as **gigno**, expressed to the Romans a very vague and ill-defined conception, as were all their religious conceptions. It evidently at first meant a divinity that presided over the birth of the individual. Cf. *lectus genialis*, *Ep.* I. 1. 87, and *Genium appellant Deum, qui vim obtineret rerum omnium generandarum*, Paul. Diac. p. 71. This divinity would seem to have been supposed to be an attendant spirit, and to fix in some manner the person's destiny through life. (Cf. *Ep.* II. 2. 187.) Either originally or later it was identified with the soul of the person. (Cf. **genio indulgere, genium curare, placare,** and *Od.* III. 17. 14.) Slaves were wont to entreat their master by this genius, and it was especially worshipped on birthdays. Here it is identified with the worshippers (hence **memorem**).

145. **Fescennina,** etc.: the allusion is to the Fescennine verses, so called from their origin in Fescennium, a town of Etruria. The fullest description of them is found here. But there are many allusions to them in other authors. Cf. Livy, VII. 2; Sen. *Medea*, 107 and 112. They were in the chaffing, abusive tone that the Italians seem to have loved. They survived chiefly in wedding ceremonies.

151. **intactis**, etc.: cf. *Sat.* II. 1. 23.

152. **lex**: in the Twelve Tables. This provision has not been preserved, except as quoted by St. Augustine, but the verb used was **occentassit.** Cf. *Sat.* II. 1. 82. Another provision which has been partially preserved, **qui malum carmen incantassit,** refers to incantations.

155. **ad bene dicendum**, etc.: *i.e.* poetry was improved, and made to praise and please. Horace may have in his mind here the songs sung in the triumphal processions, which were a curious mixture of mocking and eulogy.

156. **Graecia**, etc.: Livius Andronicus, the earliest poet of Rome

intulit agresti Latio; sic horridus ille
defluxit numerus Saturnius et grave virus
munditiae pepulere, sed in longum tamen aevum
manserunt hodieque manent vestigia ruris.
Serus enim Graecis admovit acumina chartis,
et post Punica bella quietus quaerere coepit,
quid Sophocles et Thespis et Aeschylus utile ferrent.
Temptavit quoque rem si digne vertere posset,
et placuit sibi natura sublimis et acer,
nam spirat tragicum satis et feliciter audet,

in so far as he produced a continuous work, was a native of Tarentum, and was brought to Rome as a slave by M. Livius Salinator. All his works were translations from the Greek. His first play was presented B.C. 240. Cf. Livy VII. 2; Cic. *Brut.* 72; *de Sen.* 50. Naevius (B.C. 235) was a citizen of Campania, but mostly followed Greek originals. Plautus (born B.C. 254) was an Umbrian, but only adapted Greek plays. Ennius (born B.C. 239) was a Calabrian, and followed Greek models with close imitation. Cf. *Antiquissimi doctorum, qui idem et poetae et semigraeci erant, Livium et Ennium dico, quos utraque lingua domi forisque docuisse adnotatum est, nihil amplius quam Graecos interpretabantur aut si quid ipsi Latine composuissent praelegebant*, Suet. *de Gramm.* I.

158. **numerus Saturnius**: the old Roman metre, which was supplanted by the hexameter. It was a rude kind of iambic catalectic septenarius, with occasional omission of the arsis (which alone to Horace's ear would make it *horridus*), and occasional accented short theses. Cf. Naevius' epitaph attributed to himself:

Immórtalés mortáles sí forét fas flére, etc.;

and his epigram on the Metelli:

Fató Metélli Rómaí fíunt cónsules;

also:

Terrá pestém tenéto sálus hic manéto.
—Varro, *R. R.* I. 2. 27.

and others in Allen's *Remnants of Early Latin*, p. 95. — **virus**: *i.e.* the venom of the old rustic poetry.

159. **munditiae**, *decency*, improvement in elegant manners.

161. **serus**, *only late* (its usual meaning), agreeing with a **Romanus** implied in **victorem**.

162. **post Punica**, etc.: *i.e.* not till then. Cf. the dates given above. — **quietus**: *i.e.* it was at the close of the Punic wars that he found the repose necessary for study.

163. **Thespis**: loosely used of the supposed earliest playwright.

164. **temptavit**, etc.: *i.e.* he began to study (v. 161) and then tried also to imitate. — **rem**, *the matter*, *i.e.* disregarding the style; another reason for v. 160. — **vertere**, *reproduce*, a little more than translate.

165. **placuit sibi**: *i.e.* he was satisfied with his efforts, and did well enough, saving the exception in v. 167. — **natura**, etc.: *i.e.* the Roman, from his serious nature, was well fitted for forms of composition requiring strength and intensity.

166. **spirat tragicum** (cognate accusative), *he breathes the tragic style.* Cf. *spirantes bellum*, Lucr. V.

sed turpem putat inscite metuitque lituram.
Creditur, ex medio quia res arcessit, habere
sudoris minimum, sed habet comoedia tanto
plus oneris, quanto veniae minus. Adspice Plautus
quo pacto partes tutetur amantis ephebi,
ut patris attenti, lenonis ut insidiosi,
quantus sit Dossennus edacibus in parasitis,
quam non adstricto percurrat pulpita socco.
Gestit enim nummum in loculos demittere, post hoc
securus cadat an recto stet fabula talo.
Quem tulit ad scaenam ventoso gloria curru,
exanimat lentus spectator, sedulus inflat.
Sic leve, sic parvum est, animum quod laudis avarum
subruit aut reficit. Valeat res ludicra, si me
palma negata macrum, donata reducit opimum.

392; *i.e.* the same idea as **sublimis,** etc., but here applied to the stage as the preceding refers to character generally. — **audet**: *i.e.* is successful in these higher flights.

167. **turpem,** etc.: *i.e.* but he thinks it a shame to correct his first rough inspired effort, and hence his work lacks elegance.

168. **creditur,** etc.: *i.e.* the common idea is that comedy is easier, as not requiring the higher flights on account of the every-day nature of the subject; but what he has said of tragedy is even more true of comedy.

170. **adspice,** etc.: *i.e.* see how carelessly Plautus, for instance, sustains the parts which he attempts. The form is ironical.

171. **partes**: regularly in the plural of a single character. — **tutetur**: cf. **defendente,** *Sat.* I. 10. 12. — **amantis,** etc.: the stock characters of the comedy.

173. **quantus**: cf. note to **adspice,** v. 170. — **Dossennus**: a regular character in the Atellane farces, and put for a rude clown such as are found in those farces. The name is also said to be that of a writer of Mimes; at any rate he must be an example of careless writing: cf. v. 174.

174. **non adstricto,** *down at the heel;* the carelessness of the writer is transferred to the character on the stage.

175. **gestit,** etc.: *i.e.* he does not care for art, but only for money. — **post hoc**: *i.e.* having got that.

176. **cadat**: *i.e.* fails. — **recto talo,** *square on its feet.*

177. **quem tulit,** etc.: *i.e.* if a poet, as nowadays is the case, is led to write comedies for glory instead of for money, he is easily affected by the attitude of the spectator. It is implied that the uncertainty of pleasing keeps men from writing for the stage; cf. v. 180. — **ventoso,** *wind-wafted,* as uncertain and changeable on account of the inconstancy of the popular taste.

178. **lentus,** *unmoved.*

180. **valeat,** etc.: *i.e.* I am sure

Saepe etiam audacem fugat hoc terretque poetam,
quod numero plures, virtute et honore minores,
indocti stolidique et depugnare parati,
si discordet eques, media inter carmina poscunt
aut ursum aut pugiles, his nam plebecula gaudet.
Verum equitis quoque iam migravit ab aure voluptas
omnis ad incertos oculos et gaudia vana.
Quattuor aut plures aulaea premuntur in horas,
dum fugiunt equitum turmae peditumque catervae ;
mox trahitur manibus regum fortuna retortis,
esseda festinant, pilenta, petorrita, naves,

that would be my case; I bid good by to the comic stage if my happiness depends on the uncertain favor of the spectator.

182. **saepe etiam**, etc.: another reason why men do not write for the stage. — **audacem**, *the boldest; i.e.* one who ventures to try it once, as it were, and meets with this discouragement.

183. **plures**: *i.e.* the **plebecula** of v. 186.

184. **depugnare**, etc.: *i.e.* they are unwilling to yield to the better taste of the higher class (**eques**), but are ready to fight it out and have their way by main force.

185. **carmina**: *i.e.* the verses of the play.

186. **ursum**: *i.e.* a bear-baiting.

187. **verum equitis**, etc.: *i.e.* but the fact is, that the taste of the higher classes, too, has deteriorated, and even they take more pleasure in spectacular plays with "live horses" and "real water" than in the true dramatic art.

188. **incertos**, *restless; i.e.* the various spectacle draws their eyes now this way and now that, while they do not look upon any one thing long enough to take any thought of the meaning of the whole (hence **vana**). — **vana**, *idle*, mere pleasures of sense which have no thought or even emotion behind them.

189. **quattuor**, etc.: *i.e.* a real battle is presented (cf. the modern realistic drama), lasting four or five hours. — **premuntur**: it must be remembered that the ancient curtain rolled down, instead of up, as with us.

191. **mox trahitur**, etc.: *i.e.* after the battle, the triumph is represented. Cf. *Sat.* I. 6. 23, and note. — **regum fortuna**: a common poetical figure by which the fortunes of the kings are put for the kings themselves. Translate, *kings of fallen fortune.* The case of Perseus is perhaps the most pathetic.

192. **esseda**: the war chariot of the Gauls. — **pilenta**: a covered two-wheeled carriage, the regular conveyance of matrons, and also of vestal virgins and priestesses; as these latter accompanied the triumphal procession, the reference here may be to them. — **petorrita**: a covered carriage differing from the *pilentum* in having four wheels (whence its name). It hardly appears who rode in it in a triumph. — **naves**: all sorts of representa-

captivum portatur ebur, captiva Corinthus.
Si foret in terris, rideret Democritus, seu
diversum confusa genus panthera camelo,
sive elephas albus volgi converteret ora;
spectaret populum ludis attentius ipsis
ut sibi praebentem mimo spectacula plura;
scriptores autem narrare putaret asello
fabellam surdo. Nam quae pervincere voces
evaluere sonum, referunt quem nostra theatra?
Garganum mugire putes nemus aut mare Tuscum:
tanto cum strepitu ludi spectantur et artes
divitiaeque peregrinae! Quibus oblitus actor
cum stetit in scaena, concurrit dextera laevae.

tions of towns, rivers, and the like, were borne in procession, and it may be that models of ships were also carried.

193. **ebur**: cf. *tulit* (*L. Scipio*) *in triumpho eburneos dentes mille ducentos triginta unum.* Liv. XXXVII. 59—**captiva Corinthus**, *all the spoils of Corinth*, *i.e.* as much Corinthian bronze as ever came from Corinth, when captured by Mummius.

194. **rideret Democritus**: there was a popular notion that this philosopher was constantly laughing at the vicissitudes as well as follies of mankind, to such a degree that his fellow-citizens thought him crazy. The origin of this notion it is impossible to trace, but there is found among the writings of Hippocrates a spurious letter to Damagetus (No. 17), written probably as early as the first century B.C., describing this condition of the philosopher. This must have been founded on some previously existing notion of the kind, and probably served to crystallize it. Cf. Juv. X. 28–53. See also Burton's *Anatomy of Melancholy*, Introduction.

195. **diversum**, etc., *the hybrid creature panther confused with camel*, *i.e.* the camelopard, or giraffe, brought to Rome by Julius Cæsar, B.C. 46, to grace the Ludi Circenses held at his triumph.—**genus**: apposition; but cf. **suspensi loculos**, *Sat.* I. 6. 74.

196. **elephas albus**: then as now a rarity.

198. **ut sibi**, etc.: *i.e.* he, in accordance with his reputed habit, would be more amused by the folly of the spectators than by the player.

199. **scriptores**, etc.: the statement of the point he is aiming at, that authors have little encouragement to write for such a public.—**asello**, etc.: a curious combination of two proverbs, *surdo narrare fabulam* and *ὄνῳ τις ἔλεγε μῦθον, ὁ δὲ τὰ ὦτα ἐκίνει.* Zenobius, V. 42.

200. **pervincere**, *overpower.*

201. **evaluere**: cf. the gnomic perfect.

202. **Garganum**: cf. *Od.* II. 9. 7.

203. **artes**, *works of art* (as often), such as statues and vases, which were carried in the triumphal processions referred to in v. 191 *seq.*

'Dixit adhuc aliquid?' 'Nil sane.' 'Quid placet ergo?'
'Lana Tarentino violas imitata veneno.'
Ac ne forte putes me quae facere ipse recusem,
cum recte tractent alii, laudare maligne;
ille per extentum funem mihi posse videtur
ire poeta, meum qui pectus inaniter angit,
irritat, mulcet, falsis terroribus implet,
ut magus et modo me Thebis modo ponit Athenis.
Verum age, et his qui se lectori credere malunt
quam spectatoris fastidia ferre superbi
curam redde brevem, si munus Apolline dignum
vis complere libris et vatibus addere calcar,
ut studio maiore petant Helicona virentem.

207. **lana**, etc.: *i.e.* the magnificent dress of the actor. The same effect is often produced by the modern actress' wardrobe.—**Tarentino**: cf. *Nepos Cornelius qui divi Augusti principatu obiit: Me, inquit, iuvene violacea purpura vigebat, cuius libra denariis centum venibat, nec multo post rubra Tarentina. Huic successit dibapha Tyria, quae in libras denariis mille non poterat emi.* Plin. *Nat. Hist.* IX. 39 (63). The ancient *purpura*, made from the shellfish of the Mediterranean, had a very wide range, including reds (on the crimson side) almost to black, browns, oranges, lilacs, mauves, as well as what we should now call purple, all the colors seen in the modern pansy.—**veneno**, *drug*, perhaps a translation of *φάρμακον*.

208. **ac ne forte**, etc.: *i.e.* for fear you should think I damn with faint praise the works of poets in a line which I do not attempt myself, and so you should distrust my opinion on the state of the art, I assure you that I think the dramatic art is the most difficult, and merits the highest praise when it is well done, in that its effect is so powerful upon the spectator.

209. **maligne**, *grudgingly*, *meagrely*, the opposite of **benigne**, *generously;* cf. *Od.* I. 9. 6.

210. **per extentum**, etc.: apparently proverbial for difficulty.

212. **irritat**, etc.: by the vividness of dramatic presentation.

213. **Thebis, Athenis**: the usual scenes of the heroic tragedy.

214. **verum age**, etc.: the poet now turns from the stage to published works. This is a branch worthy of consideration if Augustus wishes to encourage literature, so as to fill the Palatine library with worthy productions.

216. **Apolline**: the Palatine library was attached to the temple of Apollo, dedicated to him as the leader of the Muses. Cf. I. 3. 17 and note.

217. **addere calcar**, *to apply an additional spur*.

218. **Helicona**, etc.: *i.e.* as the seat of the Muses, to which their votaries would resort.

Multa quidem nobis facimus mala saepe poetae,
ut vineta egomet caedam mea, cum tibi librum
sollicito damus aut fesso; cum laedimur, unum
si quis amicorum est ausus reprendere versum,
cum loca iam recitata revolvimus irrevocati,
cum lamentamur non apparere labores
nostros et tenui deducta poemata filo,
cum speramus eo rem venturam, ut simul atque
carmina rescieris nos fingere, commodus ultro
arcessas et egere vetes et scribere cogas.

219. **multa quidem,** etc.: *i.e.* we ourselves are partly to blame in several respects, first, when we are not cautious in presenting our productions to you at proper times. We thereby produce an unfavorable impression. Cf. the tone of I. 13, and *Sat.* II. 1. 18. — **quidem**: concessive, opposed to **sed tamen,** v. 229. — **mala,** *harm.*

220. **vineta,** etc.: proverbial, like "cut one's own nose off," of doing one's self an injury. It is implied that Horace himself had thus offended. Cf. citations under v. 219, as well as *Sat.* I. 3. 63. — **caedam,** *cut down*, not merely prune.

221. **cum laedimur,** etc.: *i.e.* or second, when we are too sensitive to criticism, and are offended by it.

223. **cum loca,** etc.: or third, when in our conceit we repeat, without being asked, what we consider a fine passage. — **recitata**: of course in this case the poem is supposed to be presented by the author in person, and read to the patron, as was done by Virgil in the case of the Marcellus passage, *Æn.* VI. 860 *seq.* — **revolvimus**: notice the form of the ancient book, a roll unwound on one side, and rewound after being read on the other. — **irrevocati**: the regular word for *recall, ask to repeat,* is **revocare,** derived from the stage; cf. Cic. *pro Arch.* 18.

224. **cum lamentamur**: *i.e.* or fourth, when we complain that our work is not appreciated in proportion to the labor we expend on it, and the subtlety (**tenui**) of the art which is in it.

225. **deducta**: a regular word for poetical effort, derived from spinning. Cf. *Sat.* II. 1. 4; I. 10. 44 note. — **filo**: also a common word in reference to style. Cf. Cic. *de Am.* 25.

226. **cum speramus,** etc.: or when we hope for an instantaneous result in patronage even before we have accomplished anything. — **eo rem venturam,** *that the result will be, i.e.* that we shall have the good luck to get a commission at once to write. These things, he would say, are to be earned by worthy production, not voluntarily given in advance.

227. **fingere**: *i.e.* are engaged in composition. — **commodus**: *i.e.* obligingly. — **ultro**: *i.e.* going out of your way to invite us in.

228. **egere vetes**: *i.e.* put us out of danger of want by presents. The erroneous idea in these cases

Sed tamen est operae pretium cognoscere, quales
aedituos habeat belli spectata domique
virtus, indigno non committenda poetae.
Gratus Alexandro regi magno fuit ille
Choerilus, incultis qui versibus et male natis
rettulit acceptos regale nomisma Philippos.
Sed veluti tractata notam labemque remittunt
atramenta, fere scriptores carmine foedo
splendida facta linunt. Idem rex ille, poema
qui tam ridiculum tam care prodigus emit,
edicto vetuit ne quis se praeter Apellen
pingeret aut alius Lysippo duceret aera

is that poems are to be paid for in advance.

229. **sed tamen**, etc.: *i.e.* though we often injure our prospects by the faults enumerated, still it is well worth while for the patron to take an active part in looking out for a worthy herald of his praises. — **cognoscere**, *to consider well*, examine into the case and determine; an almost judicial word in this sense.

230. **aedituos** (μυσταγωγοί), *temple guides*, *ciceroni*, the guardians of a temple who, like the sacristan in modern times, showed visitors about, and dilated upon the beauties of statues and pictures. Cf. Cic. *in Verr.* II. iv. 59. 132. The figure has too much local color to be at once appreciated in English. The virtue is set up in a temple as an object of veneration, and the poet is the *cicerone* who points out its beauty or sanctity, or what not. Only a great poet is worthy to perform such service.

232. **gratus**, etc.: *i.e.* to be sure, Alexander allowed Chœrilus with his wretched verses to win solid coin, but this is only an exception, and usually a poor writer dims the praises of the hero he sings.

233. **Choerilus**: a wretched poet who was in favor with Alexander, and wrote his exploits. — **incultis**, *uncouth*. — **male natis**, *ill-fated*, *i.e.* doomed to failure from their birth, the opposite of **felix**. — **versibus**, *for*, etc., but in the Latin, dative (*to their credit*).

234. **rettulit acceptos**, *pocketed*, a mercantile term, meaning to put to the credit side of an account. The poems are the *nomen* to which the credit is made. — **regale nomisma**, *good royal coin*, implying that it was a regal reward.

235. **tractata notam**, etc.: cf. the English proverb of touching pitch. — **remittunt**, *leave*, properly *give off*.

236. **foedo**: almost like the British "nasty," but with the figure sustained as in **splendida, linunt** (*besmirch*, and so dim the brightness).

237. **idem rex ille**, etc.: *i.e.* that was the only case in which he was so unwise.

240. **alius Lysippo**: cf. I. 16. 20 and note. — **duceret**: cf. Plin. *H. N.* VII. 37 (125).

fortis Alexandri voltum simulantia. Quodsi
iudicium subtile videndis artibus illud
ad libros et ad haec Musarum dona vocares,
Boeotum in crasso iurares aere natum.
At neque dedecorant tua de se iudicia atque
munera, quae multa dantis cum laude tulerunt,
dilecti tibi Vergilius Variusque poetae:
nec magis expressi vultus per aenea signa
quam per vatis opus mores animique virorum
clarorum apparent. Nec sermones ego mallem
repentis per humum quam res componere gestas,
terrarumque situs et flumina dicere et arces
montibus impositas et barbara regna, tuisque
auspiciis totum confecta duella per orbem,
claustraque custodem pacis cohibentia Ianum,
et formidatam Parthis te principe Romam,

242. **artibus,** *works of art* (abl. of respect), alluding to Alexander's taste in selecting these great artists, as opposed to his foolish approval of Chœrilus.

243. **vocares**: *i.e.* if you had called in his judgment to decide on books, etc., you would have sworn he was a dull Bœotian, if we are to judge by the choice he made of a poet. As to the tense, cf. *Sat.* I. 3. 4. The nature of the use of tenses is best seen by supposing Horace to speak, say, of Mæcenas, in which case he would say **voces** and **iures**.

244. **Boeotum,** etc.: cf. Cic. *de Fato*, 4, *Athenis tenue caelum, ex quo acutiores etiam putantur Attici, crassum Thebis, itaque pingues Thebani.* This estimate of the Bœotians was proverbial in antiquity. It no doubt began at Athens.

245. **at neque,** etc.: *i.e.* but in your case your poets justify your choice, nor is there less expressiveness in the poet's art than in the sculptors to whom Alexander gave so much praise. The implication is that Augustus is superior to Alexander in this respect.

250. **nec sermones,** etc.: the poet, from the mention of Varius and Virgil, naturally comes to say why he himself is not to be reckoned with them, and so he gracefully ends his epistle with a compliment. — **sermones**: cf. *Sat.* I. 1. 1 and note; *Ep.* II. 3. 95; *Sat.* II. 6. 17.

251. **repentis,** etc.: as opposed to the flight of poetry. — **res gestas**: cf. I. 17. 33.

252. **terrarum,** etc.: *i.e.* the description of the countries conquered.

255. **claustra,** etc.: alluding to the closing of the temple of Janus by Augustus in B.C. 29, B.C. 25, and again, perhaps, B.C. 10.

256. **Parthis**: cf. I. 12. 27; *Sat.* II. 5. 62. Doubtless the reason why these are so often mentioned is to

si quantum cuperem possem quoque: sed neque parvum
carmen maiestas recipit tua, nec meus audet
rem temptare pudor, quam vires ferre recusent.
Sedulitas autem stulte quem diligit urget,
praecipue cum se numeris commendat et arte;
discit enim citius meminitque libentius illud,
quod quis deridet quam quod probat et veneratur.
Nil moror officium quod me gravat, ac neque ficto
in peius voltu proponi cereus usquam,
nec prave factis decorari versibus opto,
ne rubeam pingui donatus munere et una
cum scriptore meo capsa porrectus operta
deferar in vicum vendentem tus et odores
et piper et quicquid chartis amicitur ineptis.

be found in the fact that they had been so long the most dreaded enemies of Rome, though the actual events of their subjection were not very memorable.

258. **recipit**, *admit, i.e. is too great for*, so that you would not be justified in receiving it; and, on the other hand, my modesty is too great to allow me to try.

260. **sedulitas**, *officious devotion*. — **stulte**: with emphasis, *i.e.* it is foolish for one to do so. — **urget**, *depreciate*, as a man of inferior talent would do in attempting to exalt the object of his praise.

261. **praecipue**, etc.: *i.e.* especially in an ambitious work like poetry, in which art and grace count for so much. For the good is forgotten, but the faults are remembered.

264. **officium**, *dutiful service, i.e.* a tribute of respect such as a poem would be. — **gravat**, *lowers my dignity*. — **ac**, *and consequently*. — **neque**: *i.e.* neither to be represented in portraiture (a truism, with which the other is compared), nor to be praised in ill-wrought verse (any more than the first). Cf. *Od.* I. 6. 5.

267. **pingui**: cf. Cic. *de Fato*, cited under v. 244, and *Sat.* II. 6. 14. — **munere**, *tribute*, the poem referred to.

268. **cum scriptore**, etc.: *i.e.* that we should both be consigned to oblivion. The figure treats only of the poem, which is supposed to be carried off packed up in a waste-paper basket, to be used for wrapping-paper. Into this oblivion (regardless of the figure, except in **porrectus**, stretched out as on a bier), the eulogized is to accompany his eulogist.

269. **vicum**: *i.e.* the Vicus Tuscus. With this jest the letter closes in Horace's usual manner.

## II.

Flore, bono claroque fidelis amice Neroni,
si quis forte velit puerum tibi vendere natum
Tibure vel Gabiis et tecum sic agat: 'Hic et
candidus et talos a vertice pulcher ad imos
fiet eritque tuus nummorum milibus octo,
verna ministeriis ad nutus aptus eriles,
litterulis Graecis imbutus, idoneus arti
cuilibet; argilla quidvis imitaberis uda;
quin etiam canet indoctum sed dulce bibenti.
Multa fidem promissa levant, ubi plenius aequo
laudat venales qui volt extrudere merces.

EPISTLE 2. Horace's friend, Florus, the same to whom *Ep.* I. 3 is addressed, being absent with Tiberius on some expedition, had complained of the poet's silence, and had demanded the ode which had been promised him. Horace, half in jest and half in earnest, gives excuses both for not writing (vs. 1–24) and for not sending the ode. The excuses for the last are (*a*) that the stimulus of the ambition of his earlier career is withdrawn by his success (24–54); (*b*) that advancing years are beginning to extinguish his powers (55–57); (*c*) that tastes are so different that it is useless to try to satisfy anybody (58–64); (*d*) that writing at Rome amid so many hindrances is impossible (65–86); (*e*) that the guild of poets is a mutual admiration society, and if he writes himself he will be obliged to listen to their works as well. This last excuse leads him to the true attitude of the poet, and the true spirit of poetry itself, the difficulty of the art, and finally to his favorite topic of ethical culture, and to a discussion of his own moral condition.

1. **Neroni**: Tiberius; cf. I. 3. 2.

3. **Tibure vel Gabiis**: *i.e.* as opposed to foreign slaves, a *verna* sold at private sale. Cf.

> Civis non Syriaeve Parthiaeve.
> Nec de Cappadocis eques catastis
> Sed de plebe Remi Numaeque verna.
> Mart. X. 76. 2 *seq.*

4. **candidus**: of his complexion. — **pulcher**: of his form.

5. **fiet eritque**: a double expression, as often in legal forms. — **nummorum**: *i.e.* sesterces. — **milibus octo**: about $350 or $400, a common price for a choice slave. Cf. Dig. XXI. 1. 57.

7. **imbutus**: *i.e.* with just a smattering of. — **idoneus**, etc.: *i.e.* he has capacity for being educated in any art.

8. **argilla**, etc.: *i.e.* he is young and docile, and you can make what you will of him.

9. **indoctum**: *i.e.* he has not been trained yet, but has a voice that already is pleasing at a symposium, where not much is demanded.

10. **multa**, etc.: *i.e.* I will say

Res urget me nulla, meo sum pauper in aere.
Nemo hoc mangonum faceret tibi, non temere a me
quivis ferret idem. Semel hic cessavit et, ut fit,
in scalis latuit metuens pendentis habenae:'
des nummos, excepta nihil te si fuga laedit;
ille ferat pretium poenae securus, opinor.
Prudens emisti vitiosum, dicta tibi est lex;
insequeris tamen hunc et lite moraris iniqua.
Dixi me pigrum proficiscenti tibi, dixi
talibus officiis prope mancum, ne mea saevus
iurgares ad te quod epistula nulla rediret.
Quid tum profeci, mecum facientia iura

no more, for too many promises make men suspicious when a man wants to get rid of any article.

12. **res,** *necessity.* — **meo . . . aere,** *but out of debt,* opposed to *aes alienum.* — **pauper,** *in humble circumstances.*

13. **mangonum**: the regular slave-dealers. — **faceret**: *i.e.* would give you such a bargain. — **temere . . . quivis,** *any chance person;* properly, without some special reason; here, the desire to oblige a friend.

14. **cessavit,** *loitered, i.e.* when sent on an errand. Cf. *Sat.* II. 7. 100.

15. **in scalis,** etc.: a mild case of running away. Cf. **fuga,** v. 16. — **metuens**: with the genitive properly indicating the slave's disposition, but in fact hardly to be distinguished from the use of the accusative. — **pendentis**: *i.e.* hung up *in terrorem.* — **habenae**: the *lorum,* or strap, from which one or more of the slaves was called *lorarius.*

16. **des**: apodosis to **velit,** v. 2. — **excepta**: the technical term for any express provision, mention, or exception in a document or bargain. Here it is used of the exception of the one fault from the general warranty which was implied in the sale of a slave. Cf. Aul. Gel. IV. 2 and VI. 4.

17. **securus,** *without fear.*

18. **prudens**: cf. **imprudens,** the opposite. — **vitiosum**: the slave would be *erro,* or *fugitivus,* either of which tendencies would be a **vitium.** But this fault having been mentioned in the contract, no action would arise on account of it. — **lex**: *i.e.* the conditions of the sale.

19. **insequeris,** etc.: another of the cases in which the simile is confused with the object. Florus' action in regard to Horace amounts to the same thing as the proceeding mentioned. — **moraris,** *try to hold him,* opposed to letting him go free from damages.

20. **dixi,** *I told you,* with emphasis.

21. **mancum,** *incapacitated,* properly, crippled in the hands.

22. **rediret**: cf. **reddere,** used of delivering a letter, to which verb **redire** forms a sort of passive. Cf. **perdo, pereo.**

23. **mecum facientia**: *i.e.* that are on my side. Cf. II. 1. 68. — **iura,** *the law, i.e.* the courts.

si tamen attemptas? Quereris super hoc etiam, quod
exspectata tibi non mittam carmina mendax.
Luculli miles collecta viatica multis
aerumnis, lassus dum noctu stertit, ad assem
perdiderat; post hoc vehemens lupus et sibi et hosti
iratus pariter, ieiunis dentibus acer,
praesidium regale loco deiecit, ut aiunt,
summe munito et multarum divite rerum.
Clarus ob id factum donis ornatur opimis,
accipit et bis dena super sestertia nummum.
Forte sub hoc tempus castellum evertere praetor
nescio quod cupiens hortari coepit eundem
verbis, quae timido quoque possent addere mentem:
'I bone quo virtus tua te vocat, i pede fausto,
grandia laturus meritorum praemia. Quid stas?'
Post haec ille catus quantumvis rusticus: 'Ibit,
ibit eo, quo vis, qui zonam perdidit,' inquit.

24. **hoc**: referring to what goes before.

26. **Luculli,** etc.: Horace answers this complaint also by an anecdote, extending to v. 41, but the application is made in vv. 53, 54. — **viatica,** *his store*, gained in service from pay and booty.

29. **dentibus**: continuing the figure of **lupus**.

30. **regale**: probably of King Mithridates. — **loco deiecit,** *dislodged*, a technical military phrase. Cf. *loco motus est*, Cic. *Cat.* II. 1. — **ut aiunt,** *as the story goes*. Cf. I. 7. 49.

31. **munito**: *i.e.* so that it could with difficulty be taken by storm (best translated with **praesidium**). — **divite,** etc.: *i.e.* so that it could with difficulty be taken by siege. The whole indicates the desperate valor of the soldier.

32. **donis**: such as crowns, chains, arms, or bosses (*phalerae*), which were the "medals" and "crosses" of ancient times.

33. **dena**: the regular distributive used in multiplication.

34. **praetor,** *the commander*, the original meaning of the word. Cf. *Sat.* I. 5. 34 and note.

35. **nescio quod**: the words disparage the difficulty of the undertaking in comparison with the preceding. — **eundem,** *the man*.

36. **verbis,** *in language*. — **timido quoque**: *i.e.* and still more a valiant veteran like him.

37. **bone,** *my good friend*. — **i pede fausto**: both a good wish and an assurance.

38. **laturus**: cf. *Sat.* II. 1. 12. — **quid stas**: cf. *Sat.* I. 1. 19.

39. **rusticus,** *unlearned*, as a countryman. He had, however, a native shrewdness.

40. **zonam,** *his wallet*, a belt with

Romae nutriri mihi contigit atque doceri
iratus Grais quantum nocuisset Achilles.
Adiecere bonae paullo plus artis Athenae,
scilicet ut possem curvo dinoscere rectum,
atque inter silvas Academi quaerere verum.
Dura sed emovere loco me tempora grato,
civilisque rudem belli tulit aestus in arma
Caesaris Augusti non responsura lacertis.
Vnde simul primum me dimisere Philippi,
decisis humilem pennis inopemque paterni
et laris et fundi paupertas impulit audax,
ut versus facerem. Sed quod non desit habentem

pockets in it, in which, in the absence of modern pockets, the ancients carried their valuables. The whole, of course, means that such courage comes only of desperation. The man who is well off will run no such risk.

41. **Romae**, etc.: the poet proceeds to show how his case is parallel with that of the soldier. — **mihi contigit**, *I had the luck*. In these advantages he corresponds to the soldier with his original competence.

42. **iratus**, etc.: *i.e.* he learned the *Iliad*. Cf. II. 1. 71 and note.

43. **bonae artis**, *liberal education*. — **Athenae**: cf. *Athenis iam diu doctrina ipsorum Atheniensium interiit; domicilium tantum in illa urbe remanet studiorum quibus vacant cives, peregrini fruuntur*, Cic. *de Orat.* III. 11. 43. The better class of Roman young men seem to have gone to Athens to complete their education, as our young men go to Europe.

44. **scilicet**, *that is to say*. — **possem**: others read **vellem** with about equal authority. — **curvo**: jocosely put for **pravo**, representing the line of vice as opposed to the straight course of virtue; imitated by Persius, 4. 12.

45. **inter silvas**, etc.: the Academic school is put for philosophy in general. — **quaerere**: no doubt with reference to the sceptical turn of the later Academy.

46. **dura sed emovere**, etc.: the parallel to the soldier's misfortunes. — **tempora**: *i.e.* of the war between Octavius and the party of Brutus and Cassius. — **loco**: cf. v. 30 and note.

47. **civilis . . . aestus**, *the tide of civil war*. — **rudem belli**, *a raw recruit*. — **in arma**, *among the forces*, *i.e.* the side of Brutus and Cassius. Cf. *Od.* II. 7. 10, and *Sat.* I. 6. 48.

48. **non responsura**, *doomed not to cope with*. Cf. Cic. *Cat.* II. 11. — **lacertis**, *the strong arm*.

49. **dimisere**, *discharged*, a technical word.

50. **decisis**, *clipped*. — **inopem**, etc.: a shorthand way of saying in poverty deprived of, etc.

51. **audax**, *barefaced*.

52. **ut versus**, etc.: neither this nor any of the statements here are to be taken too literally. Horace had no doubt written before, and

quae poterunt umquam satis expurgare cicutae,
ni melius dormire putem quam scribere versus?
Singula de nobis anni praedantur euntes:
eripuere iocos, venerem, convivia, ludum;
tendunt extorquere poemata: quid faciam vis?
Denique non omnes eadem mirantur amantque:
carmine tu gaudes, hic delectatur iambis,
ille Bioneis sermonibus et sale nigro.
Tres mihi convivae prope dissentire videntur,
poscentes vario multum diversa palato.
Quid dem? Quid non dem? Renuis tu quod iubet alter;
quod petis, id sane est invisum acidumque duobus.

there is no reason to believe that he ever wrote for money. But disappointed in his first hopes of advancement, and having had a taste of life with the great, he must seek a career, and was forced to this one. His success in this is *his* desperate storming of the royal fortress. — **sed quod,** etc.: *i.e.* he has now won his decorations and booty, and, like the rustic soldier, fights no more. — **quod**: equivalent to **tantum ut** with the verb impersonal, *wherewith to keep from want.*

53. **quae poterunt**, etc.: *i.e.* his fever must be incurable, if he does not give over writing. — **cicutae**: apparently used as a remedy, like many poisonous plants. Cf. *fit ex eo* (*semine cicutae*) *et ad refrigerandum stomachum malagma*, Pliny, *N. H.* XXV. 153 (95).

55. **singula de nobis**, etc.: another reason why Horace does not write. — **singula praedantur**, *take each its prey.*

56. **eripuere**: these they have already stolen. — **ludum**: used generally of all amusements which require youthful spirits for their enjoyment, but especially poetry.

57. **tendunt**: *i.e.* having destroyed other capacities, they have begun to attack his creative power in poetry. — **extorquere**: apparently indicating that this capacity dies hard, but still it is doomed. — **quid faciam vis**: *que voulez-vous?* a submission to the inevitable.

58. **denique,** etc.: another excuse (rather than reason) is that he cannot satisfy all tastes, and so does nothing.

59. **carmine**: *i.e.* odes. — **iambis**: *i.e.* epodes.

60. **ille,** etc.: *i.e.* satires. — **Bioneis**: Bion was a Scythian philosopher of caustic wit and cynical disposition, who lived about B.C. 250. Cf. *Ἦν δὲ καὶ θεατρικὸς καὶ πολὺς ἐν τῷ γελοίῳ διαφορῆσαι, φορτικοῖς ὀνόμασιν κατὰ τῶν πραγμάτων χρώμενος*, Diog. Lært. IV. 7. 5. — **sale nigro**: as wit is *common salt* (cf. *Sat.* I. 10. 3), this kind is *caustic potash* (cf. *Sat.* II. 4. 74).

61. **prope**, *almost like*, the figure and the object being identified as usual.

63. **quid dem,** etc.: keeping up the figure to the end; 'whatever I serve will be distasteful to two out of three.'

Praeter cetera, me Romaene poemata censes
scribere posse inter tot curas totque labores?
Hic sponsum vocat, hic auditum scripta relictis
omnibus officiis, cubat hic in colle Quirini,
hic extremo in Aventino, visendus uterque;
intervalla vides humane commoda. Verum
purae sunt plateae, nihil ut meditantibus obstet.
Festinat calidus mulis gerulisque redemptor,
torquet nunc lapidem nunc ingens machina tignum,
tristia robustis luctantur funera plaustris,
hac rabiosa fugit canis, hac lutulenta ruit sus:
i nunc, et versus tecum meditare canoros!
Scriptorum chorus omnis amat nemus et fugit urbes,

65. **praeter cetera**, etc.: another excuse (though the excuses gradually become serious reasons) is found in the occupations and disturbances of the great city.

66. **curas**: *i.e.* things to think of. — **labores**: *i.e.* things to do.

67. **sponsum** (supine): cf. *Sat.* II. 6. 23. — **auditum**: cf. *Sat.* I. 4. 23 and 73; *Ep.* I. 19. 42. For a picture of the same thing later, cf. Pliny, *Ep.* III. 18. — **relictis**, etc.: indicating the urgency of the invitation.

68. **cubat**: cf. *Sat.* I. 9. 18.

69. **visendus**: such visits seem to have been regarded as a duty then, more even than nowadays.

70. **intervalla**: about a mile each way (hence the plural), and up and down two rather steep hills. His whole walk to visit the two would be about four miles. — **humane**, *for a poor mortal.* — **commoda**: ironical. — **verum**, etc.: Horace ironically says in answer to his own objection, "but one can study on the way"; cf. *Sat.* I. 9. 2.

71. **purae**, *clear.* — **meditantibus**, *the work of the poet*, an almost technical word of persons engaged in literary composition. Cf. v. 76, and *Phoebo meditante*, Virg. *Ecl.* VI. 82.

72. **festinat**: with emphasis, *on the contrary* (or *why!*) *the contractor*, etc. — **calidus**, *in hot haste;* cf. *fervet opus*, Virg. *Æn.* I. 436. — **mulis**, etc.: referring to the loads drawn or carried through the streets. The streets, though closed to wagons except at night, were open to public contractors for transportation at all hours. For the crowded streets later, cf. Juv. III. 243 *seq.* — **redemptor**: cf. *Od.* III. 1. 35.

73. **machina**: *i.e.* a derrick hoisting the materials for building, poetically regarded as hurling them through the air.

74. **funera**: the same state of things is alluded to as being noisy in *Sat.* I. 6. 43.

76. **i nunc**, etc.: *i.e.* if you can, after what I've told you. Cf. I. 6. 17.

77. **scriptorum**, etc.: *i.e.* poetry requires a freedom from distractions, and a harmonious environment suited to the inspired condi-

rite cliens Bacchi, somno gaudentis et umbra;
tu me inter strepitus nocturnos atque diurnos
vis canere et contracta sequi vestigia vatum?
Ingenium, sibi quod vacuas desumpsit Athenas
et studiis annos septem dedit insenuitque
libris et curis, statua taciturnius exit
plerumque et risu populum quatit; hic ego rerum
fluctibus in mediis et tempestatibus urbis
verba lyrae motura sonum conectere digner?
  Frater erat Romae consulti rhetor, ut alter

tion of mind in which the poet worships Bacchus and the Muses. These words refer to the din, as the preceding refer to the obstructions, of the streets.

78. **rite**: *i.e.* as he has always been; cf. I. 19. 4.—**cliens Bacchi**: cf. *Od.* III. 25, esp. v. 19.

80. **contracta**: *i.e.* the narrow path which needs repose of mind and close application to follow it.

81. **ingenium sibi**, etc.: *i.e.* a man under the most favorable condition for study often comes out as dumb as a graven image, and is only laughed at. How then should Horace expect or desire to try poetry in the storm and stress of actual affairs at Rome? He would be more ridiculous in the eyes of the world than the other. In other words, the pursuit of literature in the right spirit doesn't pay nowadays among these scribblers that plaster each other with praise. — **ingenium**, *a man of talent*, as often. The tone of these words suggests that some notable example is meant. — **vacuas**, *deserted*, *i.e.* by all actual life, the home of quiet study.

82. **studiis**: *i.e.* chiefly philosophy and rhetoric.

83. **libris**: dative; cf. I. 7. 85. The idea is of becoming a bookworm.—**curis**, *meditation;* cf. *quo tandem gaudio adfici necesse est sapientis animum cum his habitantem pernoctantemque curis* (Natural Philosophy, Ethics, and Dialectics). Cic. *Tusc.* V. 24. 69. — **statua**: proverbial. — **taciturnius**, etc.: *i.e.* a mere day-dreamer.

84. **hic ego**, etc.: *i.e.* when such is the result of a liberal education in the academic stillness of Athens, should I undertake to write poetry in the very whirl of affairs, and make myself a laughing-stock for the public who do not understand the necessary conditions of success in so difficult a branch of art?

85. **tempestatibus**, *the stormy life.*

86. **motura**, *to wake*, *i.e.* to be sung to the accompaniment of the lyre. — **conectere**, *to weave the web of*, etc.

87. **frater erat Romae**, etc.: *i.e.* another reason is that one by writing poetry becomes a member of the mutual admiration society, and must flatter the other members of the guild and so expose himself to hearing their writings. It is implied that this guild is composed of persons who have no real knowledge of what the profession really is, and how much application it demands; cf. v. 109. The instance is no doubt drawn from life. —

alterius sermone meros audiret honores,
Gracchus ut hic illi, foret huic ut Mucius ille.
Qui minus argutos vexat furor iste poetas?
Carmina compono, hic elegos. 'Mirabile visu
caelatumque novem Musis opus!' Adspice primum,
quanto cum fastu, quanto molimine circumspectemus vacuam Romanis vatibus aedem;
mox etiam, si forte vacas, sequere et procul audi,
quid ferat et quare sibi nectat uterque coronam.
Caedimur et totidem plagis consumimus hostem

**frater**: apparently equivalent to an adjective, or to **talis frater**. It has been suggested that a line has been lost, *uterque Alterius laudum sic admirator*, etc.; but it is dangerous to rewrite Horace even to avoid a harsh construction.

88. **meros honores**, *nothing but tributes of praise*.

89. **Gracchus**: both Tiberius and Gaius were famed as orators. — **Mucius**: the Mucius Scævola family was famous for its lawyers.

90. **qui minus argutos**, etc.: *i.e.* the same craze of mutual admiration possesses the poets. For the phrase, cf. *Sat.* II. 3. 311. — **argutos**, *tuneful*. Cf. *Od.* III. 14. 21; IV. 6. 25. An epithet almost ornamental, but referring to the poets as opposed to the practical men of the two political professions in which puffing might be excused. Cf. the references to the poetical clique in *Sat.* I. 10.

91. **carmina**: cf. v. 99. — **elegos**: cf. v. 100.

92. **caelatum**, *wrought*, as if the work were in silver. — **adspice**: *i.e.* first notice our important air, opposed to **sequere**, etc., v. 95.

93. **fastu . . . molimine**, *a proud and pompous air*.—**circumspectemus**: in Homer, who dates back to a time when the prepositions were still adverbs, and had not yet become attached to the verbs at all, they are frequently found separated even by several words. In later times this usage was thought to be a poetical figure, and was imitated or allowed as such, so that in Latin, in which the prepositions had long been firmly attached, they are sometimes found divided as here. Cf. the *cere — comminuit — brum* of Ennius. The word refers to the air of the poets as they survey the temple in which they are to recite for each other's delectation.

94. **vacuam**, *opened*, left vacant for them to recite in.

95. **mox**: *i.e.* when they are under way in their poetic compliments. — **procul**: cf. *Sat.* II. 6. 105 and note.

96. **quid ferat**, etc., *what each has to offer*, *i.e.* what tribute of praise each brings. For an example, though of a later time, cf.

> Dum centum studet auribus virorum
> hoc quod saecula posterique possint
> Arpinis quoque comparare chartis.
> — Mart. X. 19. 15
> (addressed to Pliny).

96. **nectat**, etc.: cf. *Od.* I. 26. 8.

97. **caedimur**, etc.: *we belabor each other in turn blow for blow with strokes of compliment, like Samnites in a hard-fought bout*

lento Samnites ad lumina prima duello.
Discedo Alcaeus puncto illius, ille meo quis?
Quis nisi Callimachus? Si plus adposcere visus,
fit Mimnermus, et optivo cognomine crescit.
Multa fero, ut placem genus irritabile vatum,
cum scribo et supplex populi suffragia capto;
idem, finitis studiis et mente recepta,
obturem patulas impune legentibus auris.
  Ridentur mala qui componunt carmina, verum
gaudent scribentes et se venerantur, et ultro,
si taceas, laudant quicquid scripsere beati.
At qui legitimum cupiet fecisse poema,
cum tabulis animum censoris sumet honesti,
audebit quaecumque parum splendoris habebunt

etc. The give and take of compliment is compared to the alternate assaults of gladiators. Cf. *Sat.* II. 6. 44.

98. **lento**, etc.: *i.e.* the lingering bout between two well-matched combatants, lasting till dark.

99. **discedo**, *come off*, used with reference to the supposed encounter. — **Alcaeus**: whom Horace follows as his model; cf. v. 91. — **puncto**: cf. the manner of voting at the Roman elections.

100. **Callimachus**: an Alexandrine poet, chiefly famous for his elegies; cf. v. 91. Propertius claimed to be the Roman Callimachus, and may be alluded to here, but it may be anybody else. — **si plus**, etc.: *i.e.* if this does not satisfy his vanity, I will go higher and call him a Mimnermus (B.C. 632), the first and greatest of elegiac poets.

101. **crescit**, *grows in greatness*.

102. **multa fero**, etc.: *i.e.* I bear a great deal, from the vanity of my fellows, when I undertake to write, which I am relieved from by my own silence. — **irritabile**, *sensitive*, so that I am obliged to praise them in order not to anger them.

104. **mente recepta**: as if poetry were a craze; cf. *Sat.* II. 7. 117.

105. **impune**: with **obturem**; *i.e.* he can then refuse to hear bad verses, without fear of suffering from the poet's revengeful criticism.

106. **ridentur**, etc.: a concession, the real statement being contained in **gaudent**, etc.

107. **ultro laudant**, *begin themselves to praise*.

108. **beati**, *in blissful self-conceit*.

109. **at qui**, etc.: *i.e.* but the mental attitude of the real poet is far different; he is the most rigid censor of his own work. — **fecisse**: not different from the present infinitive.

110. **tabulis**, *book*, with a double meaning, at once the Censor's list and the poet's tablets. — **honesti**, *conscientious*.

111. **splendoris**, etc.: Horace has in mind throughout the action of the Censor in detail, but does not feel bound to keep to it consistently.

et sine pondere erunt et honore indigna ferentur,
verba movere loco, quamvis invita recedant
et versentur adhuc intra penetralia Vestae.
Obscurata diu populo bonus eruet atque
proferet in lucem speciosa vocabula rerum,
quae priscis memorata Catonibus atque Cethegis
nunc situs informis premit et deserta vetustas;
adsciscet nova, quae genitor produxerit usus.
Vehemens et liquidus puroque simillimus amni
fundet opes Latiumque beabit divite lingua;
luxuriantia compescet, nimis aspera sano

112. **honore**: cf. **splendoris** and note.

113. **movere loco,** *turn out* (*i.e.* of his poetical vocabulary), a technical expression of the act of the Censor in degrading an unworthy person. — **invita,** etc.: *i.e.* though they have a strong hold on the language.

114. **et versentur,** etc.: *i.e.* and still linger at Rome in the common use of the people. But why **Vestae**? Servius (to *Aen.* vii. 153) says: *ad Atrium Vestae conveniebat* (*senatus*). If this statement can be relied on, no doubt Horace, keeping up the figure, makes the words linger, like an expelled Senator about his meeting place. Other views have been suggested. One possible view refers to the domestic expressions of the fireside. Every one knows how many colloquial expressions are retained in the family circle. But Vesta is not certainly shown in Latin to represent the household hearth. The best way seems to be to take the phrase as referring to the 'heart' of the Roman people, *i.e.* in common use.

115. **obscurata,** etc.: *i.e.* the poet in his search for a fresh and vigorous diction will restore to use good old words that were picturesque but have slipped out of use. The figure of the Censor is half preserved here also. — **populo**: *i.e.* in common use. — **bonus**: as opposed to his severity towards the unworthy. — **eruet,** *will unearth.*

116. **speciosa**: *i.e.* vivid and picturesque.

117. **quae priscis,** etc.: cf. II. 3. 50.

118. **situs,** *neglect,* originally of things left to lie and gather rust from want of care and use (hence **informis**). — **informis,** *uncomely,* as producing that effect. — **premit,** *obscures,* keeps out of use. — **deserta,** *forsaken, i.e.* their age has caused the words to be abandoned.

119. **genitor,** *creative;* cf. II. 3. 71.

120. **vehemens** (two syllables), *strong.* The whole idea is taken from a river.

"Though deep yet clear . . .
Strong without rage; without overflowing, full."
— Sir John Denham.

The style is to be rich and strong, but still clear.

121. **opes,** *a stream of wealth.*

122. **luxuriantia**: *i.e.* excess of ornament. — **compescet,** *prune,* as a too luxuriant growth of vegetation, of which the word is often used. — **aspera,** *roughness,* as of a

levabit cultu, virtute carentia tollet,
ludentis speciem dabit et torquebitur ut qui
nunc Satyrum, nunc agrestem Cyclopa movetur.
Praetulerim scriptor delirus inersque videri,
dum mea delectent mala me vel denique fallant,
quam sapere et ringi. Fuit haud ignobilis Argis,
qui se credebat miros audire tragoedos,
in vacuo laetus sessor plausorque theatro,
cetera qui vitae servaret munia recto
more, bonus sane vicinus, amabilis hospes,
comis in uxorem, posset qui ignoscere servis
et signo laeso non insanire lagenae,
posset qui rupem et puteum vitare patentem.

statue or the like. — **sano**, *i.e.* with moderation, not so as to produce a namby-pamby polish.

123. **virtute carentia**: cf. **parum splendoris** and **sine pondere**. — **tollet**, *elevate*, *i.e.* by a little forcing, so as to give a loftier tone to common things. Cf. Quint. X. 4. 1; VIII. 6. 11; Cic. *de Orat.* III. 26. 104; but cf. *Sat.* I. 4. 11.

124. **ludentis**, etc.: *i.e.* the result will be apparently an easy style and a light touch, which, however, the writer can gain only by a serious effort.

125. **Satyrum**, etc.: *i.e.* a pantomimic actor performing a part which seems comic to the spectators, but is to him a very serious and difficult business. Cf. *Ὅλως δὲ τὸν ὀρχηστὴν δεῖ πανταχόθεν ἀπηκριβῶσθαι, ὡς εἶναι τὸ πᾶν εὔρυθμον, εὔμορφον, σύμμετρον, αὐτὸ αὑτῷ ἐοικὸς ἀσυκοφάντητον, ἀνεπίληπτον, μηδαμῶς ἐλλιπὲς, ἐκ τῶν ἀρίστων κεκραμένον*, Lucian, *de Salt.* Cf. also Athenæus, XIV. 28. — **movetur**: cf. *saltaret*, *Sat.* I. 5. 63 and note.

126. **praetulerim**, etc.: *i.e.* as if Horace would say that after all it might on the whole be better to be self-deceived like the vain poets of the day than to have sound ideas and suffer the consequent worry. — **delirus**: *i.e.* foolish in his ignorance of what has just been laid down as rules. — **iners**: *i.e.* clumsy in his efforts to write. — **scriptor**, *as an author*, *i.e.* if I should write.

127. **delectent**, etc.: cf. *Sat.* I. 3. 39, where, however, the two ideas are put, naturally, in the opposite order.

128. **ringi**, *be in agony*, on account of his own imperfections. — **fuit**, etc.: an anecdote showing that sometimes a delusion is more comfortable than a sound mind.

129. **credebat**, etc.: in this consisted the man's monomania.

131. **cetera**, etc.: showing his sanity in all other respects. — **servaret**: a quality of the man, whereas **credebat** only states a fact about him.

134. **signo**: cf. *Od.* III. 8. 10. — **laeso**: *i.e.* when a slave has broken the seal of a jar, and drunk the wine.

135. **rupem**, *a precipice;* cf. *Sat.* II. 3. 56 *seq.*

Hic ubi cognatorum opibus curisque refectus
expulit elleboro morbum bilemque meraco,
et redit ad sese 'Pol, me occidistis, amici,
non servastis,' ait, 'cui sic extorta voluptas
et demptus per vim mentis gratissimus error.'
Nimirum sapere est abiectis utile nugis
et tempestivum pueris concedere ludum,
ac non verba sequi fidibus modulanda Latinis,
sed verae numerosque modosque ediscere vitae.
Quocirca mecum loquor haec tacitusque recordor:
'Si tibi nulla sitim finiret copia lymphae,
narrares medicis: quod quanto plura parasti,
tanto plura cupis, nulline faterier audes?
Si volnus tibi monstrata radice vel herba
non fieret levius, fugeres radice vel herba

136. **cognatorum**: cf. the case of illness described in *Sat.* I. 1. 80, and *ibid.* v. 88.

137. **elleboro**: cf. *Sat.* II. 3. 82. — **bilem**: as the cause of madness. — **meraco**: *i.e.* as if Horace said, "by the free use of strong draughts of the medicine," like "by a thorough course of."

138. **redit ad sese**: cf. *non sum apud me*, Ter. *Phorm.* 204, and *ad te redi, Adelphi*, 794. — **occidistis**: cf. II. 3. 467. — **pol**: the introduction of this word gives a comic turn to the whole, showing that the man himself is not serious.

139. **sic**, *in this way*, *i.e.* as they had done.

141. **nimirum**: introducing the final reason for his literary inactivity, the same as given in I. 1. The connection is loose, and seems to hang merely upon the word **sapere** used in v. 128. As if Horace said, "speaking of wisdom, doubtless the most serviceable wisdom is to let such things alone, and study philosophy." — **nugis**: cf. *nugarum*, *Sat.* I. 9. 2, and *ludicra*, I. 1. 10.

142. **pueris**: belonging both to **tempestivum** and **concedere**, as often in Latin. — **ludum**: cf. I. 18. 66; 14. 36; I. 1. 3 and note; *Sat.* I. 10. 37; Virg. *Ecl.* VII. 17.

143. **ac non verba**, etc.: cf. v. 86; *Od.* IV. 3. 23; *Ep.* I. 3. 12.

144. **numerosque modosque**: a common mode of expression, here used with conscious reference to v. 143. Cf. I. 18. 59.

145. **quocirca**, etc.: *i.e.* therefore, having given up verse-making, I devote myself silently to moral improvement.

146. **si tibi**, etc.: *i.e.* if you had the symptoms of dropsy (to himself).

147. **quod quanto**, etc.: *i.e.* if you have symptoms of the moral dropsy of avarice, do you refrain from seeking advice? Cf. *Od.* II. 2. 13.

149. **si volnus**, etc.: *i.e.* you would avoid a remedy if you found it did no good; and will you still

proficiente nihil curarier : audieras, cui
rem di donarent, illi decedere pravam
stultitiam, et cum sis nihilo sapientior, ex quo
plenior es, tamen uteris monitoribus isdem ?
At si divitiae prudentem reddere possent,
si cupidum timidumque minus te, nempe ruberes,
viveret in terris te si quis avarior uno.
Si proprium est quod quis libra mercatus et aere est,
quaedam, si credis consultis, mancipat usus ;
qui te pascit ager tuus est, et vilicus Orbi,
cum segetes occat tibi mox frumenta daturas,
te dominum sentit ; das nummos, accipis uvam,
pullos, ova, cadum temeti : nempe modo isto
paullatim mercaris agrum, fortasse trecentis

seek wealth as a cure for folly when you have found by experience that it is useless?

151. **audieras**, etc.: the application of the parallel.

155. **at si**, etc.: an indirect proof that riches do not give wisdom.

158. **si proprium**, etc.: an examination into the nature of property, in which Horace shows that in both of the two ways in which property is acquired all the wealth which serves your purposes is really yours. — **libra et aere**: the conventional form of conveyance at Rome (*per aes et libram*). This process, a relic of the earlier payment of money by weight, required five Roman citizens as witnesses and a weigher (*libripens*), before whom the parties appeared. With a set form of words the buyer claimed the property (*manu capere*) and pretended to weigh a piece of money which he handed over to the seller. This worked a *mancipatio*, hence **mancipat**.

159. **consultis**, *the learned lawyers*. — **mancipat**: *i.e.* passes the property, or makes a title.

160. **pascit**: *i.e.* for this constitutes the **usus** in the sense in which Horace takes that word, though the preceding verse is only true in the other, the technical, sense, *i.e.* of adverse possession, prescription (*usu capio*). Cf. Cic. *ad Fam.* VII. 30. — **usus**: here used in the sense of **usucapio**. Cf. the two preceding notes. — **vilicus Orbi**, etc.: here the poet proceeds to show that the enjoyer practically owns the property even by the first method, for he buys it by degrees. — **Orbi**: an unknown person, probably a famous nabob of the time, or a rich neighbor of the poet. — **vilicus**: cf. I. 14. 1.

161. **segetes**, *field*, properly the growing crop. — **occat**: put for all the operations of husbandry. — **tibi**: because you will buy it.

162. **te dominum sentit**, *recognizes*, etc.; in so far as he knows that he works for your advantage.

164. **fortasse trecentis**, etc.:

aut etiam supra nummorum milibus emptum.
Quid refert vivas numerato nuper an olim?
Emptor Aricini quondam Veientis et arvi
emptum cenat holus, quamvis aliter putat; emptis
sub noctem gelidam lignis calefactat aenum.
Sed vocat usque suum qua populus adsita certis
limitibus vicina refugit iurgia, tamquam
sit proprium quidquam, puncto quod mobilis horae
nunc prece, nunc pretio, nunc vi, nunc morte suprema
permutet dominos et cedat in altera iura.
Sic, quia perpetuus nulli datur usus, et heres
heredem alterius velut unda supervenit undam,
quid vici prosunt aut horrea? Quidve Calabris

*i.e.* which cost a very much larger sum.

166. **numerato**, etc.: *i.e.* whether with money paid from day to day for provisions, or paid earlier as the price of the estate.

167. **emptor quondam**, *the sometime purchaser;* see Gr. § 207, note. Here begins the converse of the argument. "The lord of the acres is in the same condition as you, for he has simply bought his dinner like you."

168. **putat**: see Gr. § 313 *g*.

170. **sed vocat**: *i.e.* his property rests only on an erroneous notion; he calls it his, but it is not.—**usque**: *i.e.* this is the extent of his claim, "all the way to where, etc."—**populus**: the beginner will notice the quantity. The line of poplars forms the boundary.

171. **limitibus**: means or manner of **refugit**. — **vicina**, *with the neighbors*.—**refugit**: this word has been questioned, and seems a little out of place. But to avoid lawsuits by the marked limits of a man's property is certainly not very different from preventing them. This idea may then very well be ascribed to that which marks the bounds instead of to the proprietor. — **tamquam**, *as if forsooth;* introducing the facts which show the folly of the proprietor's idea.

172. **puncto**: cf. *Sat.* I. 1. 8.

173. **morte suprema**: cf. *supremo fine*, II. 1. 12.—**prece**, etc.: *i.e.* it is liable to be given away, sold, stolen, or resigned at death.

174. **in altera iura**: cf. *Sat.* II. 2. 134.

175. **perpetuus nulli**, etc.: cf. *nulli proprius*, *Sat.* II. 2. 134.

176. **alterius**: *i.e.* the first possessor, himself the heir of another, is followed by his own heir.— **undam**: the construction is rare, but the accusative is governed by the preposition in composition, perhaps a colloquial irregularity.

177. **vici**: apparently used for the group of buildings on a farm. Cf. Cic. *ad Fam.* XIV. 1. 5. As it only occurs in this sense in Cicero's letters, it may be colloquial. — **horrea**: as representing great crops. — **Calabris, Lucani**: representing great flocks in pastures. Cf. *Epod.* I. 27.

saltibus adiecti Lucani, si metit Orcus
grandia cum parvis, non exorabilis auro?
Gemmas, marmor, ebur, Tyrrhena sigilla, tabellas,
argentum, vestes Gaetulo murice tinctas,
sunt qui non habeant, est qui non curat habere.
Cur alter fratrum cessare et ludere et ungi
praeferat Herodis palmetis pinguibus, alter
dives et importunus ad umbram lucis ab ortu
silvestrem flammis et ferro mitiget agrum,
scit Genius, natale comes qui temperat astrum,
naturae deus humanae, mortalis in unum
quodque caput, voltu mutabilis, albus et ater.

180. **sigilla**, *statuettes*.

181. **Gaetulo**: cf. *Tyri praecipuus hic* (sucus muricis) *Asiae, in Meninge Africae et Gaetulo litore Oceani, in Laconia Europae*, Pliny, *N. H.* IX. 127 (60).

182. **sunt qui**, etc.: *i.e.* that the objects of wealth are not indispensable is shown by the fact that many do without them, and there is now and then one who has no desire for them. — **est qui**: probably (not necessarily) the poet himself.

183. **cur alter**, etc.: the suggestion of the difference of tastes leads Horace to ascribe it with a kind of wonder to an inexplicable inborn difference of temperament existing even in the case of own brothers. It is as if Horace said: "Why men differ, the Lord who made them only knows, but they do." Cf. *Sat.* II. 1. 26. — **cessare**, etc.: *i.e.* contented idleness as opposed to hardly won wealth represented in **palmetis**. — **ungi**: as the making of alcohol was unknown to the ancients, their only vehicle for perfumes was oils; here put as a mark of luxury.

184. **Herodis**: Herod the Great. Cf. *regnum* (*Iudaeorum*) *ab Antonio Herodi datum victor Augustus auxit*, Tac. *Hist.* V. 9. The wealth and fertility of the region were proverbial. — **palmetis**: cf. *primus Idumaeas referam tibi, Mantua, palmas*, Virg. *Georg.* III. 12, and *Iudaea vero incluta est vel magis palmis*, Pliny, *H. N.* XIII. 26 (6). The income of the palm groves must have been very large.

185. **importunus**, *insatiable*, instant in season and *out of season*.

186. **mitiget**: cf. *pacantur*, I. 2. 45; *urges*, I. 14. 26; *rastris terram domare*, Virg. *Æn.* IX. 608. The idea is, bring new lands under cultivation.

187. **Genius**: cf. II. 1. 144 and note. — **comes**: *attendant*, as an adjective with **Genius**. — **temperat**, *regulates*, mixing in due proportion the good and evil influences of the planets at one's birth. — **astrum** (**natale**), *the horoscope*.

188. **deus**: here treated as a single divinity. — **mortalis**, etc.: here again regarded as manifest and mortal in each man's life. Such contradictions were not at all troublesome to the ancients. Cf. Our Lady of Lourdes, or this, that, and the other in modern times.

189. **voltu mutabilis**, etc.: in

Vtar et ex modico quantum res poscet acervo
tollam, nec metuam quid de me iudicet heres
quod non plura datis invenerit; et tamen idem
scire volam, quantum simplex hilarisque nepoti
discrepet et quantum discordet parcus avaro.
Distat enim, spargas tua prodigus, an neque sumptum
invitus facias, neque plura parare labores,
ac potius, puer ut festis Quinquatribus olim,
exiguo gratoque fruaris tempore raptim.
Pauperies immunda domus procul absit, ego utrum
nave ferar magna an parva, ferar unus et idem.
Non agimur tumidis velis Aquilone secundo,

so far as it is manifest in various characters of individuals. — **albus et ater**: vaguely used as well for character as destiny.

190. **utar,** etc.: the mention of the two extremes of self-indulgence and avarice leads Horace as usual to proclaim his doctrine of the middle course between prodigality and hoarding. There is an emphasis on **utar** (*enjoy*, instead of *hoarding*). — **modico**: *i.e.* which I do not care to increase. Cf. *Sat.* I. 1. 51.

192. **plura datis,** *more left him*, literally, more than what is left. Cf. I. 5. 13.

193. **scire volam**: *i.e.* to realize, and act accordingly. — **simplex,** *guileless*, *i.e.* not **duplex,** with no undercurrent of selfishness, according to which the man would be after the main chance through all his actions. — **hilaris,** *the cheerful spirit*, as opposed to the prodigal.

195. **spargas,** etc.: like the **nepos.** — **neque sumptum,** etc.: like the free-handed and unavaricious **hilaris** and **simplex.**

197. **puer,** etc.: *i.e.* act like a boy in the holidays, enjoying to the full the brief time allotted to enjoyment. This is opposed to **parare,** and is a part of the alternative with **an.** — **raptim**: *i.e.* making haste to enjoy, on account of the brevity of the time.

199. **pauperies,** etc.: *i.e.* if only I am free from want, the amount of my possessions is immaterial. — **domus procul**: a genitive of separation after the manner of the Greek. But the reading is doubtful. Some editors simplify matters by omitting **domus** and inserting **modo.** — **pauperies**: not absolute want, but straitened circumstances, such as to deprive the poet of the elegancies (**munditiae**) of a refined life. — **immunda,** *squalid* or *unrefined.* — **utrum nave,** etc.: a shorthand expression, where, as in so many cases, the figure is confused with the object. "I care not whether I am rich or poor, but shall live my life in either case, just as I should not care whether I went in a big ship or a little one, for I should finish my journey essentially the same." The idea on which the double question depends is implied **in ferar unus et idem.**

201. **non agimur,** etc.: keeping up the figure of the voyage. — **tumidis,** etc.: *i.e.* in prosperity I cannot

non tamen adversis aetatem ducimus Austris,
viribus, ingenio, specie, virtute, loco, re
extremi primorum, extremis usque priores.
Non es avarus, abi. Quid, cetera iam simul isto
cum vitio fugere? Caret tibi pectus inani
ambitione? Caret mortis formidine et ira?
Somnia, terrores magicos, miracula, sagas,
nocturnos lemures portentaque Thessala rides?
Natalis grate numeras? Ignoscis amicis?
Lenior et melior fis accedente senecta?
Quid te exempta levat spinis de pluribus una?
Vivere si recte nescis, decede peritis.
Lusisti satis, edisti satis atque bibisti;
Tempus abire tibi est, ne potum largius aequo
rideat et pulset lasciva decentius aetas.'

carry so much sail. — **non tamen,** etc.: *i.e.* but then, on the other hand, I am not so much exposed to the storms of adversity.

203. **specie,** *display,* "style." Cf. I. 6. 49; or perhaps, *beauty.*

204. **extremis,** etc.: the figure is derived from a race.

205. **non es avarus**: *i.e.* but thus far only one vice has been treated, and there are others to be regarded also. Cf. *Sat.* II. 3. 159. — **abi,** *pass on then; i.e.* so far there is no fault to be found.

208. **somnia,** etc.: cases of superstition. Cf. *Sat.* II. 3. 281 *seq.*

209. **Thessala**: the Thessalians were famous for magic. Cf. *Od.* I. 27. 21; *Epod.* V. 45.

210. **natalis,** etc.: *i.e.* do you thankfully rejoice in the years as they pass, without repining at increasing age? Cf. I. 11. 22; I. 4. 13. — **ignoscis amicis**: *i.e.* have you a good temper? Cf. *Sat.* I. 3. 84.

212. **quid te levat,** *what relief do you get?* a medical expression. Here the Stoic doctrine of the unity of virtue crops out. — **spinis**: cf. I. 14. 4.

215. **tempus abire,** etc.: not necessarily here a recommendation to suicide, though such an idea would be quite in accord with ancient philosophy. Cf. Lucr. III. 938.

216. **decentius**: *i.e.* in which wanton behavior is more becoming. — **aetas**: *i.e.* youth, to which the old man would become a laughing-stock if he indulges too freely in the follies of youth.

## III.

Humano capiti cervicem pictor equinam
iungere si velit et varias inducere plumas
undique collatis membris, ut turpiter atrum
desinat in piscem mulier formosa superne,
spectatum admissi risum teneatis, amici?
Credite, Pisones, isti tabulae fore librum
persimilem, cuius velut aegri somnia vanae
fingentur species, ut nec pes nec caput uni
reddatur formae. 'Pictoribus atque poetis
quidlibet audendi semper fuit aequa potestas.'
Scimus et hanc veniam petimusque damusque vicissim,
sed non ut placidis coeant immitia, non ut
serpentes avibus geminentur, tigribus agni.
Inceptis gravibus plerumque et magna professis
purpureus, late qui splendeat, unus et alter

EPISTLE 3. The best information we have on this epistle is given by Porphyrio: *Hunc librum qui inscribitur De arte poetica ad L. Pisonem qui postea urbis custos fuit misit. Nam et ipse Piso poeta fuit et studiorum liberalium antistes.* It is a rambling treatise on the art of poetic composition, touching on this and that point as it is suggested by prevalent faults and fashions. For the title, cf. Quint. VIII. 3. 60.

1. **humano,** etc.: the first canon is that a work should be consistent with itself. This point Horace approaches in his usual indirect way. It would seem that some one had claimed a like freedom of the imagination from the trammels of realism in poetry as was allowed in pictorial art. Hence he begins to answer this claim by giving absurd cases of the use of imagination in painting. Then he introduces the point made by the *unrealist,* applying it to both painting and poetry, and then proceeds to show its limitations. The whole means, "as you say, a poet is not tied down to absolute facts any more than a painter, but a painter must not attempt to represent the impossible, no more must the poet."

3. **undique**: *i.e.* from all sorts of animals. — **ut**: introducing the result of **collatis**. — **turpiter**: of appearance, its proper meaning. Cf. αἰσχρός.

9. **reddatur**: *i.e.* to correspond.

10. **aequa**: *i.e.* alike to both.

12. **placidis**: see examples in next verse.

13. **geminentur,** *united,* so as to make one creature.

14. **inceptis,** etc.: an example of the disregard of the canon. The poem starts out with a lofty design,

adsuitur pannus, cum lucus et ara Dianae
et properantis aquae per amoenos ambitus agros
aut flumen Rhenum aut pluvius describitur arcus.
Sed nunc non erat his locus. Et fortasse cupressum
scis simulare: quid hoc, si fractis enatat exspes
navibus aere dato qui pingitur? Amphora coepit
institui, currente rota cur urceus exit?
Denique sit quod vis simplex dumtaxat et unum.
Maxima pars vatum, pater et iuvenes patre digni,
decipimur specie recti: brevis esse laboro,
obscurus fio; sectantem levia nervi
deficiunt animique; professus grandia turget;
serpit humi tutus nimium timidusque procellae.
Qui variare cupit rem prodigialiter unam,
delphinum silvis appingit, fluctibus aprum.
In vitium ducit culpae fuga, si caret arte.
Aemilium circa ludum faber imus et ungues

but it is spoiled by incongruity of details.

19. **sed**: opposed to an implied concession, "very fine, but," etc. — **erat**: imperfect for present time in the contrary-to-fact construction, of that which is not done. Cf. *tempus erat, Od.* I. 37. 4; see *Gr.*, §§ 311 *c* and 308 *c*. — **et**, *and so*, continuing the same principle applied to painting.

20. **scis**, etc.: *i.e.* you may be skilful in painting trees; but if you want to paint a sea-piece, it would only spoil it to put them in. — **fractis**, etc.: the ancients were accustomed to hang up in temples votive tablets, representing in a very realistic fashion any narrow escape from death. Italian churches are full of pictures made in the same spirit. Cf. *Sat.* II. 1. 33 and note.

21. **amphora**, etc.: *i.e.* why, when you have a purpose, do you change it on the way, bringing out something else by the use of incongruous details?

24. **maxima**, etc.: *i.e.* this, like many other faults, comes from a desire for excellence carried too far.

29. **prodigialiter**: *i.e.* with an ornament of marvels to make it interesting.

31. **in vitium**, etc.: the formal statement of the idea in vv. 24–30.

32. **Aemilium circa ludum**, etc.: another aspect of the same idea. It is the want of skill in making the whole (implied in **arte**) that produces the unfortunate result. The most ordinary worker will excel in some details but will fail for want of skill in some other detail which is equally necessary. — **Aemilium ludum**: doubtless a gladiatorial establishment, but otherwise unknown. The brass founders must have worked near by.

exprimet et mollis imitabitur aere capillos,
infelix operis summa, quia ponere totum
nesciet. Hunc ego me, si quid componere curem,
non magis esse velim, quam pravo vivere naso,
spectandum nigris oculis nigroque capillo.
Sumite materiam vestris, qui scribitis, aequam
viribus, et versate diu quid ferre recusent,
quid valeant umeri: cui lecta potenter erit res,
nec facundia deseret hunc nec lucidus ordo.
Ordinis haec virtus erit et venus, aut ego fallor,
ut iam nunc dicat iam nunc debentia dici,
pleraque differat et praesens in tempus omittat,
hoc amet, hoc spernat promissi carminis auctor.
In verbis etiam tenuis cautusque serendis
dixeris egregie, notum si callida verbum

34. **ponere**: apparently technical. Cf. *Od.* IV. 8. 8, and the Greek ἱστάναι, drawn from the sculptor's art.

35. **hunc**, etc.: cf. *ne fueris hic tu*, I. 6. 40.

37. **spectandum**, etc.: *i.e.* with some beauties, marred, however, by flagrant defects.

38. **sumite**, etc.: the second canon, to choose a suitable subject. This division loosely corresponds to the rhetorical *inventio.*

40. **potenter**: *according to his power*, apparently. — **res**: cf. *rem tene, verba sequentur*, Cato.

41. **facundia**: power of expression; technically, *elocutio* (φράσις). Cf. *elocutio est idoneorum verborum et sententiarum ad inventionem accommodatio*, Cic. *de Inv.* I. 7. 9. — **ordo**, *arrangement.* Cf. *dispositio est rerum inventarum in ordinem distributio*, ibid.

42. **ordinis**, etc.: the excellences of arrangement are so simple that Horace dismisses the subject with a few words.

45. **hoc amet**, etc.: *i.e.* at any given time, each in its turn.

46. **in verbis**, etc.: a discussion of the *elocutio.* Cf. *ornatus autem verborum duplex, unus simplicium alter conlocatorum*, Cic. *Orator*, 24. 80. — **tenuis**, *simple*, as opposed to a florid and turgid style. Cf. *ac primum informandus est ille nobis quem solum quidam vocant Atticum; summissus est et humilis, consuetudinem imitans, ab indisertis re plus quam opinione differens* (Cic. *Orator*, 23. 75); *ergo ille tenuis* [*orator*] *modo sit elegans*, etc. (ibid. 24. 81). So farther on *hic subtilis; hic acutus; haec tenuitas; summissus orator, magnus tamen et germanus Atticus.* This style is opposed to *uberius aliud aliquantoque robustius quam hoc humile*; and *tertius ille amplus copiosus gravis ornatus in quo profecto vis maxima est* (ibid. 28. 97). The whole passage is nearly parallel with Horace's canons. — **serendis**: cf. **sermo**.

47. **callida iunctura**: a clever combination by which a familiar

reddiderit iunctura novum. Si forte necesse est
indiciis monstrare recentibus abdita rerum,
fingere cinctutis non exaudita Cethegis
continget, dabiturque licentia sumpta pudenter.
Et nova fictaque nuper habebunt verba fidem, si
Graeco fonte cadent, parce detorta: quid autem
Caecilio Plautoque dabit Romanus, ademptum
Vergilio Varioque? Ego cur acquirere pauca
si possum invideor, cum lingua Catonis et Enni
sermonem patrium ditaverit et nova rerum
nomina protulerit? Licuit semperque licebit

word is made to seem new, perhaps such expressions as **rubente dextera**, **Attalicis condicionibus**, **pronos annos** (v. 60); though Horace has in mind doubtless a less lofty flight than is generally found in his odes. Cf. Persius V. 14.

48. **si forte**, etc.: *i.e.* though in accordance with Horace's description, the author will rely upon ordinary words made fresh by combination, yet if occasion arises, he may coin new ones in moderation.

49. **indiciis monstrare recentibus**, etc., *reveal by new signs thoughts hitherto unknown.* The figure is from the investigation of crime, or the like. — **abdita rerum**: cf. *Sat.* II. 8. 83.

50. **cinctutis**, *half naked*, or *kilted*, clad in the *cinctus*, a kind of kilt covering the middle of the body, used before the more civilized tunic. — **non exaudita**: cf. II. 2. 117. — **Cethegis**: M. Cornelius Cethegus (cons. B.C. 204) was the first Roman orator (Cic. *Brut.* 15). A time far back is taken to make plain the necessity of new words on account of the great development of ideas since that time. Apparently such words are meant as new formations in **-tas**, **-alis**, or the like.

51. **continget**, *occasion will arise.* — **sumpta pudenter**: *i.e.* if so used.

52. **et**: these too as well as new Latin formations. — **fidem**: *i.e. acceptance;* properly, the words will gain confidence, and not be looked upon with suspicion. — **si Graeco fonte cadent**: apparently new translations from the Greek like the old *mundus*, *qualitas*, *exhibere negotium.* Horace's own exclusion of Greek words proper, and his objection to Lucilius (*Sat.* I. 10. 20) seem to preclude the idea of such words as **malacissare** (μαλακίζειν), taken bodily into the language.

53. **parce detorta**: *i.e.* slightly varied in their use from their originals. Some editors take this to mean a slight variation in the inflexions. — **quid autem**, etc.: *i.e.* this was allowed the earlier poets, and why not to the later as well?

55. **ego**, etc.: simply another example of the same kind as the preceding, only here is considered the effect on the language rather than the right of the poet.

56. **invideor**: probably a colloquial use instead of **invidetur mihi**, a popular corruption of grammar. Cf. *imperor*, I. 5. 21. — **lingua**: *i.e.* their writings.

signatum praesente nota producere nomen.
Vt silvae foliis pronos mutantur in annos,
prima cadunt, ita verborum vetus interit aetas,
et iuvenum ritu florent modo nata vigentque.
Debemur morti nos nostraque, sive receptus
terra Neptunus classis Aquilonibus arcet,
regis opus, sterilisve diu palus aptaque remis
vicinas urbes alit et grave sentit aratrum;
seu cursum mutavit iniquum frugibus amnis,
doctus iter melius: mortalia facta peribunt,
nedum sermonum stet honos et gratia vivax.
Multa renascentur, quae iam cecidere, cadentque
quae nunc sunt in honore vocabula, si volet usus,
quem penes arbitrium est et ius et norma loquendi.
  Res gestae regumque ducumque et tristia bella
quo scribi possent numero monstravit Homerus.
Versibus impariter iunctis querimonia primum,

59. **signatum**: the figure drawn from money. A new coinage is always in order; as in coins, so in words. — **praesente nota**, *the modern stamp.* — **producere**: cf. *produxerit*, II. 2. 119.

60. **ut silvae**, etc.: *i.e.* for everything earthly passes away, words as well as things. — **in annos**: cf. *in dies*, *in horas* (v. 160).

61. **prima cadunt**: a co-ordinate clause with **mutantur**, but containing a subordinate idea, "while, etc." — **vetus aetas**, *the aging life.*

63. **receptus**, etc.: the allusion is apparently (*a*) to the Portus Iulius made by the union of the Lucrine Lake with the sea (Suet. *Oct.* 16); (*b*) the attempted draining of the Pomptine Marshes (Schol. *ad locum*); (*c*) improvements in the course of the Tiber (Suet. *Oct.* 30).

64. **classis**, etc.: for construction, cf. I. 1. 31 and note.

65. **palus**: with *ŭ* contrary to the usual prosody.

67. **iniquum frugibus**: *i.e.* on account of inundations.

68. **facta**: repeating **nostra**, but with emphasis on works as opposed to words (**sermonum**).

69. **honos**, *dignity*, the respect in which they are held. — **stet vivax**, *continues to live.*

71. **usus**: cf. II. 2. 119.

73. **res gestae**, etc.: Horace, having finished the matter of diction, comes to the choice of metre. One can hardly see why this topic was inserted unless it was intended to be learned by heart by one of Pisos. Those enumerated are the Hexameter (vv. 73, 74), Elegiac (vv. 75–78), the Iambic metres (vv. 79–82), Lyric metres (vv. 83–85).

75. **impariter**: only found here. Cf. "unequally yoked together." — **querimonia**, etc.: *i.e.* the elegy was originally the lament of hapless

post etiam inclusa est voti sententia compos.
Quis tamen exiguos elegos emiserit auctor,
grammatici certant et adhuc sub iudice lis est.
Archilochum proprio rabies armavit iambo;
hunc socci cepere pedem grandesque cothurni,
alternis aptum sermonibus, et populares
vincentem strepitus et natum rebus agendis.
Musa dedit fidibus divos puerosque deorum
et pugilem victorem et equum certamine primum
et iuvenum curas et libera vina referre.
Descriptas servare vices operumque colores
cur ego si nequeo ignoroque poeta salutor?
Cur nescire pudens prave quam discere malo?
Versibus exponi tragicis res comica non volt.
Indignatur item privatis ac prope socco

love, but afterwards used also for other amatory strains.

77. **quis tamen**, etc.: accounts vary between Archilochus, Mimnermus, and Callinus. — **exiguos**, *light*, in matter, as opposed to the heroic strain.

79. **proprio**: *i.e.* his own invention, as it was supposed.

80. **hunc**, etc.: *i.e.* it was afterwards adopted by the drama, in Comedy (**socci**) and Tragedy (**cothurni**).

81. **alternis**, etc.: cf. *qui* [*Aristoteles*] *indicat heroum numerum grandiorem quam desideret soluta oratio, iambum autem nimis e volgari esse sermone*, Cic. *Orator*, 57. 192; and *at comicorum senarii propter similitudinem sermonis sic saepe sunt abiecti, ut non numquam vix in eis numerus et versus intellegi possit*, ibid. 55. 184.

82. **rebus agendis**: *i.e.* the imitated actual life of the stage.

83. **fidibus**: *i.e.* the lyric measures. — **divos puerosque**, *i.e.* in hymns.

84. **pugilem**, etc.: *i.e.* odes such as Pindar's, in honor of victors at the games.

85. **iuvenum curas**: *i.e.* love-songs. — **libera**: *i.e.* freeing from cares, as we should say, "the merry bowl." — **vina**: *i.e.* drinking-songs.

86. **descriptas**, etc.: the fourth requisite is a style in harmony with the subject. — **vices**, *line*, properly the part or function which the work has to perform. — **colores**, *tone*, as in *vitae color*, *Sat.* II. 1. 60.

87. **salutor**: *i.e.* claim the name of, expect to be addressed as such.

88. **cur nescire**, etc.: *i.e.* one at least ought to admit the rule, and try to learn, not perversely ignore it.

89. **versibus**, etc.: just what is meant is seen best in the cases where the rule may be broken, given in vv. 93 *seq.* and 95 *seq.*

90. **privatis**: *i.e.* words of ordinary life. — **socco**: cf. v. 80.

dignis carminibus narrari cena Thyestae.
Singula quaeque locum teneant sortita decentem.
Interdum tamen et vocem comoedia tollit,
iratusque Chremes tumido delitigat ore;
et tragicus plerumque dolet sermone pedestri
Telephus et Peleus, cum pauper et exsul uterque
proicit ampullas et sesquipedalia verba,
si curat cor spectantis tetigisse querella.
Non satis est pulchra esse poemata; dulcia sunto,
et, quocumque volent, animum auditoris agunto.
Vt ridentibus arrident, ita flentibus adsunt
humani voltus: si vis me flere, dolendum est
primum ipsi tibi; tunc tua me infortunia laedent,
Telephe vel Peleu; male si mandata loqueris,
aut dormitabo aut ridebo. Tristia maestum
voltum verba decent, iratum plena minarum,
ludentem lasciva, severum seria dictu.
Format enim natura prius nos intus ad omnem

91. **cena Thyestae**: a proverbial expression, but here only used as an example of a tragic theme.

92. **singula quaeque**, *each particular style*. — **locum sortita**: *i.e.* the place allotted to it.

93. **interdum**, etc.: cf. *Sat.* I. 4. 48 and note.

94. **Chremes**: cf. Ter. *Heaut.* 1035 *seq.*

96. **Telephus et Peleus**: examples of heroes in reduced circumstances, entreating favors, in which case they are made to adopt the simple language of pathos in order to touch the heart of the spectator.

97. **ampullas**: cf. I. 3. 14, and Greek **λήκυθος**. No doubt the Greek word became proverbial from the jest in Aristoph. *Frogs*, 1200 *seq.* — **sesquipedalia verba**: *i.e.* the sounding style which belongs to kings and heroes.

98. **tetigisse**: not different from the present.

99. **pulchra**, *fine*, merely commanding admiration for the art. — **dulcia**: *i.e.* pathetic, which the language of common life only can be.

100. **animum agunto**: the idea is that it is only by sympathy, which does not respond to language too far removed from common life, that the audience can be moved.

102. **voltus**: of course the feelings are meant under the guise of their expression in the face.

104. **male mandata**, *words ill-assigned*, *i.e.* language not adapted to their situation.

106. **voltum**: again the face put for the feelings.

108. **format**, etc.: *i.e.* we are so made as to have a capacity for feel-

Ars Poetica



fortunarum habitum; iuvat aut impellit ad iram,
aut ad humum maerore gravi deducit et angit;
post effert animi motus interprete lingua.
Si dicentis erunt fortunis absona dicta,
Romani tollent equites peditesque cachinnum.
Intererit multum divusne loquatur an heros,
maturusne senex an adhuc florente iuventa
fervidus, an matrona potens, an sedula nutrix,
mercatorne vagus, cultorne virentis agelli,
Colchus an Assyrius, Thebis nutritus an Argis.
Aut famam sequere, aut sibi convenientia finge.
Scriptor honoratum si forte reponis Achillem,
impiger, iracundus, inexorabilis, acer
iura neget sibi nata, nihil non arroget armis.
Sit Medea ferox invictaque, flebilis Ino,
perfidus Ixion, Io vaga, tristis Orestes.
Si quid inexpertum scaenae committis et audes
personam formare novam, servetur ad imum
qualis ab incepto processerit et sibi constet.
Difficile est proprie communia dicere, tuque
rectius Iliacum carmen deducis in actus,

ing every aspect of fortune in actual experience, and afterwards by sympathy we are brought to the same state of mind through language which is associated with these experiences. Mimic life produces the same sensations as real life.

113. **equites peditesque**: *i.e.* high and low in station.

114. **intererit**, etc.: besides the difference of situation, there is also the difference of character to be considered. The drawing of character is one of the most important parts of the art, and the shades mentioned are especially delicate.

119. **aut famam**, etc.: *i.e.* in characterization, one must follow conventional models, or in case one invents a new character he must make it consistent.

120. **honoratum**: probably only *illustrious.* — **reponis**: cf. **ponere**, v. 34.

121. **impiger**, etc.: because these are his conventional characteristics, and so with the others.

125. **si quid**, etc.: a development of **sibi convenientia**, v. 119.

128. **proprie**, *with originality*, *i.e.* so as to make them one's own, as opposed to mere imitation.

129. **Iliacum**, etc.: *i.e.* it is better for you to keep to the conventional types than attempt anything unheard of. The precept has a

quam si proferres ignota indictaque primus.
Publica materies privati iuris erit, si
non circa vilem patulumque moraberis orbem;
nec verbum verbo curabis reddere fidus
interpres, nec desilies imitator in artum,
unde pedem proferre pudor vetet aut operis lex.
Nec sic incipies, ut scriptor cyclicus olim:
'Fortunam Priami cantabo et nobile bellum.'
Quid dignum tanto feret hic promissor hiatu?
Parturient montes, nascetur ridiculus mus.
Quanto rectius hic, qui nil molitur inepte:
'Dic mihi Musa virum, captae post tempora Troiae
qui mores hominum multorum vidit et urbes.'
Non fumum ex fulgore, sed ex fumo dare lucem
cogitat, ut speciosa dehinc miracula promat,
Antiphaten Scyllamque et cum Cyclope Charybdim;
nec reditum Diomedis ab interitu Meleagri,
nec gemino bellum Troianum orditur ab ovo.
Semper ad eventum festinat et in medias res,

personal air, as if one of the young men had composed plays on Homeric themes. Cf. the contrary-to-fact construction in v. 130.

131. **publica**, etc.: here, as elsewhere, the middle course is recommended, not to be a mere imitator through keeping strictly to the conventional. To the material, which belongs to all, you will have a right if you do not servilely follow your models.

133. **curabis**: best taken as a continuation of the protasis.

134. **desilies**: *i.e.* plunge without reflexion into a place where you will be hampered by your respect for your model, or by the laws of the composition.

136. **incipies**: in an imperative sense as a recommendation. Here begins a new canon, namely, that the plan of the work should have a modest beginning, and rise in interest to the end.—**cyclicus**: one of the cycle of poets who imitated and tried to complete or enlarge upon the Iliad and Odyssey. Tradition says Antimachus is meant.

138. **hiatu**: of the opening the mouth to speak.

141. **dic**, etc.: *Od.* I. 1.

146. **nec reditum**, etc.: *i.e.* he does not begin his subject with irrelevant details, so that the hearer would be tired out before he comes to the important point.—**Meleagri**: he was the uncle of Diomedes, so that the stories would be remotely connected, but not forming one whole so as to be treated together.

147. **ovo**: *i.e.* from the birth of

non secus ac notas, auditorem rapit, et quae
desperat tractata nitescere posse, relinquit;
atque ita mentitur, sic veris falsa remiscet,
primo ne medium, medio ne discrepet imum.

Tu, quid ego et populus mecum desideret, audi.
Si plausoris eges aulaea manentis et usque
sessuri donec cantor 'Vos plaudite' dicat,
aetatis cuiusque notandi sunt tibi mores,
mobilibusque decor naturis dandus et annis.
Reddere qui voces iam scit puer et pede certo
signat humum, gestit paribus colludere, et iram
colligit ac ponit temere et mutatur in horas.
Imberbus iuvenis, tandem custode remoto,
gaudet equis canibusque et aprici gramine campi,
cereus in vitium flecti, monitoribus asper,
utilium tardus provisor, prodigus aeris,
sublimis cupidusque et amata relinquere pernix.

Helen, though she was the cause of the war.

151. **ita mentitur**: *i.e.* the fictions which the poet introduces are so united with the rest, that there is no want of harmony in the treatment.

153. **tu quid ego**, etc.: a recommendation to the study of life, and careful attention to the treatment of character. This is closely connected with v. 114 *seq.*, but there the poet speaks first of diction as connected with character, and afterwards of conventional character, while here he is treating of naturalness as drawn from the study of real life.

155. **cantor**: in the manuscripts of the plays, the final words or "tag" are assigned to a separate character marked ω. Hence it is supposed that the person here referred to was the vocalist who sang the *arias* or **cantica**; but cf. Cic. *pro Sest.* 55. 118, and *de Sen.* 19. 70.

157. **mobilibus**, etc.: *i.e.* the fitting charm must be given to each character as it changes with changing years, by observing carefully those changes in real life.

158. **scit, signat**: marking the age merely.

159. **gestit**, etc.: Horace now gives the appropriate conduct for each age.

161. **tandem**: *i.e.* he has long been impatient for this moment. — **custode**: cf. *Sat.* I. 4. 118, and I. 6. 81.

162. **equis canibusque**: cf. Ter. *Andria*, 56, 57. — **campi**: cf. I. 18. 53 and note.

164. **utilium**: *i.e.* of what is good for him.

165. **pernix**: a *callida iunctura.* Cf. Virg. *Æn.* IV. 180. For the thought, cf. II. 1. 100.

Conversis studiis aetas animusque virilis
quaerit opes et amicitias, inservit honori,
commisisse cavet quod mox mutare laboret.
Multa senem circumveniunt incommoda, vel quod
quaerit et inventis miser abstinet ac timet uti,
vel quod res omnis timide gelideque ministrat,
dilator, spe longus, iners, avidusque futuri,
difficilis, querulus, laudator temporis acti
se puero, castigator censorque minorum.
Multa ferunt anni venientes commoda secum;
multa recedentes adimunt. Ne forte seniles
mandentur iuveni partes pueroque viriles,
semper in adiunctis aevoque morabimur aptis.
  Aut agitur res in scaenis, aut acta refertur.
Segnius irritant animos demissa per aurem
quam quae sunt oculis subiecta fidelibus et quae
ipse sibi tradit spectator. Non tamen intus

166. **studiis**, *tastes*. Cf. Cic. *de Am*. 20. 74.

167. **honori**, *ambition*, *i.e.* the pursuit of office.

169. **incommoda**: *i.e.* unlovely features, *désagréments*, disagreeable to other people as well as himself.

170. **inventis**, etc.: cf. *Sat.* II. 3. 110.

171. **gelide**: *i.e.* without enthusiasm. — **ministrat**: a livelier term for **agit**.

172. **spe longus**: *i.e.* he looks far into the future, as opposed to the youth, who lives in the present. Cf. **avidus futuri** (*i.e.* eager for a long life in which to realize the hope whose fulfilment he does not, like the youth, expect at once).

173. **difficilis**: cf. Cic. *de Sen.* 18. 65.

174. **castigator**, etc.: cf. II. 1. 84.

175. **venientes**: the years up to the prime of life, the *bona aetas*, are regarded as coming, because there is an increase of pleasing characteristics, while the later years (*mala aetas*) are regarded as going because of a corresponding decrease. Cf. II. 2. 55.

176. **ne forte**, etc.: a summing up of the same general idea.

177. **partes**: *i.e.* the characteristic actions as expressed in a drama.

178. **aevoque**: cf. **quidque**, *Sat.* I. 4. 115 and note. — **morabimur**: equivalent to a hortatory subjunctive.

179. **aut agitur**, etc.: a precept as to what is to be actually put on the stage, and what merely to be described. Here again a middle course is recommended.

182. **tradit**: as the narrator would communicate the action to the persons on the stage, so here the spectator is said to communicate it to himself, be his own witness.

digna geri promes in scaenam, multaque tolles
ex oculis quae mox narret facundia praesens,
ne pueros coram populo Medea trucidet,
aut humana palam coquat exta nefarius Atreus,
aut in avem Procne vertatur, Cadmus in anguem.
Quodcumque ostendis mihi sic, incredulus odi.
  Neve minor neu sit quinto productior actu
fabula, quae posci volt et spectata reponi.
Nec deus intersit, nisi dignus vindice nodus
inciderit: nec quarta loqui persona laboret.
Actoris partes chorus officiumque virile
defendat, neu quid medios intercinat actus

184. **praesens**: *i.e.* of a person on the stage, as opposed to the action behind the scene.

185. **pueros**, etc.: favorite subjects for dramatic treatment, but in which the action is too painful or too preposterous to be represented.

188. **odi**: merely *dislike;* the imagination refuses to credit the acts when brought face to face with them, and so we find them disagreeable.

189. **minor**, etc.: a precept as to the received length of a play. The division of a play into acts seems to have been the work of the Alexandrine critics. It undoubtedly grew out of the Prologue, three Episodes, and Exodus of the Greek Play.

191. **deus**: in the Greek Tragedy not infrequently supernatural personages were introduced. We may suppose that this became more common, so that they were employed to work the *dénouement* in cases where it was unnecessary, in order to save working out a plot by natural means. Hence the *dictum* of Horace. Cf. Eur. *Andromache*, v. 1227 *seq.;* Soph. *Electra*, v. 1233. — **vindice**, *such interference*, properly, *champion*, one to whom a person has recourse in time of trouble. Here the difficulty in which the hero is (**nodus**) must be one which seems naturally to require divine interposition. Cf. *ut tragici poetae cum explicare argumenti exitum non potestis* (Stoic philosophers) *confugitis ad deum* Cic. *N. D.* I. 20. 53.

192. **quarta**, etc.: the actors appearing on the Greek stage at one time, originally only one, were gradually increased to two (Æschylus) and three (Sophocles). If a fourth appeared, he was almost always a mere silent person. The Comedy was a little less strict, but yet this was the rule.

193. **actoris**, etc.: *i.e.* the chorus should have a distinct character as a group of persons with a definite part in the action, and not be an excrescence coming in to amuse the audience between the acts, with something unconnected with the plot. Cf. the piper between the first and second act of the *Pseudolus* of Plautus. — **officiumque virile**, *its independent part* (see above). — **chorus**: for the presence of the chorus on the Latin stage, see Ribbeck, *Römische Tragödie*, p. 637.

194. **defendat**: cf. *Sat.* I. 10. 12.

quod non proposito conducat et haereat apte.
Ille bonis faveatque et consilietur amice,
et regat iratos et amet peccare timentes;
ille dapes laudet mensae brevis, ille salubrem
iustitiam legesque et apertis otia portis;
ille tegat commissa, deosque precetur et oret
ut redeat miseris, abeat fortuna superbis.
Tibia non, ut nunc, orichalco vincta, tubaeque
aemula, sed tenuis simplexque foramine pauco
adspirare et adesse choris erat utilis, atque
nondum spissa nimis complere sedilia flatu,
quo sane populus numerabilis, utpote parvus,
et frugi castusque verecundusque coibat.
Postquam coepit agros extendere victor et urbes

196. **ille bonis**, etc.: *i.e.* let the chorus (as is usual in the Greek Tragedy) be the spokesman of the moral views and precepts of the poet.

198. **brevis**: cf. I. 14. 35.

200. **tegat commissa**: as the chorus is present during the action, it would be the depositary of secrets, and by keeping them faithfully it should enforce the duty of this form of good faith. Cf. I. 18. 38; *Sat.* I. 3. 95; *Od.* III. 2. 25.

202. **tibia**, etc.: the poet in his rambling way proceeds to give an account of the development of the musical part of the drama. — **orichalco vincta**: the wood of the **tibia** was reinforced with metal to increase its resonance, but Horace here evidently is thinking of the double pipe and possibly only of the binding of the two reeds. The particular metal only indicates luxury.

203. **tenuis**: *i.e.* of feeble tone. — **simplex**: *i.e.* not blown in pairs, as it was later. — **foramine pauco**: three or four holes only, from which the ancient scales were made out by the use of harmonics.

204. **adspirare**, etc., *accompany and support.* — **utilis**, *suitable*, impliedly for the purpose mentioned, and no other.

205. **nondum spissa nimis**: of the small audience, the smallness of which is explained by the next line.

206. **sane**: this word in such connections gives a light tone, like our *rather*, *pretty*, *not very* (with **haud**), and the like. — **numerabilis**: Ritter compares εὐαρίθμητος, making this an example of the choice of words mentioned in v. 53. — **parvus**: indicating the reason for **numerabilis**.

207. **frugi**, etc.: the reason why the people were contented with the simple music; they were not prone to luxurious gratification of the senses.

208. **postquam**, etc.: *i.e.* when the population became greater, and at the same time luxury and wantonness increased, the taste for more complicated virtuoso music

latior amplecti murus vinoque diurno
placari Genius festis impune diebus,
accessit numerisque modisque licentia maior.
Indoctus quid enim saperet liberque laborum
rusticus, urbano confusus, turpis honesto?
Sic priscae motumque et luxuriam addidit arti
tibicen traxitque vagus per pulpita vestem;
sic etiam fidibus voces crevere severis,
et tulit eloquium insolitum facundia praeceps,
utiliumque sagax rerum et divina futuri
sortilegis non discrepuit sententia Delphis.
Carmine qui tragico vilem certavit ob hircum,

grew, and instead of being merely a support for the chorus, the music became a pleasure in itself.

209. **diurno**: cf. *solido de die*, *Od.* I. 1. 20. The whole gives a picture of license and festivity as opposed to the (supposed) earlier religious simplicity of the Greek Tragedy.

210. **Genius**: cf. II. 1. 144. — **impune**: *i.e.* without restraint.

211. **numeris modisque**: cf. II. 2. 144.

212. **saperet**: *i.e.* have just ideas and good taste to hold in check the extravagant growth of sensuous music. — **liber laborum**: the recoil from hard work would increase the wildness of dissipation.

213. **confusus**: the mingling of country and city would increase the evil tendencies; so also would the confusion of classes (**turpis honesto**).

214. **sic**: *i.e.* from these causes. — **motum**, etc.: *i.e.* to the stately measures of the old music greater liveliness and more florid ornament were added.

215. **traxit**: alluding to the long tunic which the piper wore on the stage. — **vagus**: *i.e.* he had full possession of the stage, instead of being merely a supporter of the voices.

216. **fidibus**: *i.e.* the lyre also went through the same development. — **voces crevere**: alluding to the gradual increase of the number of strings of the lyre, but expressing also the more free development of the music. — **severis**, *earnest*, or serious in the simplicity of its strains.

217. **et tulit**, etc.: *i.e.* the same change took place in the style of the choral song. This forms in a manner the connection of v. 202 *seq.* with v. 93 *seq.* — **tulit**, *brought in.* — **facundia praeceps**, *fervid eloquence*, as a quality of the writer, while **eloquium** refers to the result produced.

218. **utilium rerum**: *i.e.* moral precepts and wise saws, such as abound in Euripides.

219. **non discrepuit**, etc.: *i.e.* it did not differ much from the style of the inspired oracles, doubtless in obscurity as well as wildness.

220. **qui**, etc.: *i.e.* the earliest tragedian. Cf. II. 1. 163. — **hircum**: cf. the commonly received derivation of τραγῳδός, from τρά-

mox etiam agrestis Satyros nudavit, et asper
incolumi gravitate iocum tentavit eo, quod
illecebris erat et grata novitate morandus
spectator, functusque sacris et potus et exlex.
Verum ita risores, ita commendare dicacis
conveniet Satyros, ita vertere seria ludo,
ne quicumque deus, quicumque adhibebitur heros,
regali conspectus in auro nuper et ostro,
migret in obscuras humili sermone tabernas,
aut, dum vitat humum, nubes et inania captet.
Effutire levis indigna tragoedia versus,

*γος*, considered as the prize of the rivalry in song. This view assumes that there were contests in the earlier times, as there were later.

221. **mox etiam**: *i.e.* the Satyr drama followed very early the invention of Tragedy. — **agrestis Satyros**: it would appear from the directions given that the Satyric drama was also cultivated at Rome, at least by authors. Whether such plays were ever acted is uncertain. — **nudavit**: the Satyrs as wild creatures naturally appeared with the upper and lower part of their bodies really or apparently naked. — **asper**: *i.e.* rude and simple in art.

222. **gravitate**: *i.e.* the dignity of the occasion as one of worship, and one in which gods and heroes appeared.

223. **morandus**: *i.e.* after the tragedies and the completion of the serious part of the festival.

224. **sacris**: the festival of Dionysus, in whose honor the tragedy was performed. — **exlex**: freed from restraint by the festival character of the day. The picture does not differ much from that in v. 210, though Horace assigns the two to different times. It would seem that Horace conceived the Satyric drama as an outlet for the merriment of the spectator, designed to keep him out of mischief in his riotous condition.

225. **verum**, etc.: but even in this riotous performance a middle course is recommended as the law of the work, so that the dignity of the higher characters should still be preserved, though the humorous aspects of the situation are to be brought out. — **risores**: in accordance with their nature the Satyrs were a merry crew. — **dicacis**: *i.e.* making sport of the humors of the situation, sarcastic and abusive.

226. **seria**: the Satyr drama was far removed from Comedy. In the only one preserved, the *Cyclops* of Euripides, the characters are Ulysses, Silenus, the Cyclops, and a Chorus of Satyrs. The plot is treated as seriously as in a tragedy, only a comic myth is used instead of a tragic one, and the humorous aspects of the situation are brought out.

228. **conspectus nuper**: *i.e.* in the tragedy which had preceded.

230. **nubes**, etc.: *i.e.* the style should not, on the other hand, be too grandiloquent for the situation.

231. **effutire**, etc.: the caution

ut festis matrona moveri iussa diebus,
intererit Satyris paullum pudibunda protervis.
Non ego inornata et dominantia nomina solum
verbaque, Pisones, Satyrorum scriptor amabo;
nec sic enitar tragico differre colori,
ut nihil intersit, Davusne loquatur et audax
Pythias, emuncto lucrata Simone talentum,
an custos famulusque dei Silenus alumni.
Ex noto fictum carmen sequar, ut sibi quivis
speret idem, sudet multum frustraque laboret
ausus idem: tantum series iuncturaque pollet,
tantum de medio sumptis accedit honoris.
Silvis deducti caveant, me iudice, Fauni,
ne velut innati triviis ac paene forenses
aut nimium teneris iuvenentur versibus umquam,
aut immunda crepent ignominiosaque dicta.

against too undignified a style is further developed as far as v. 239. — **indigna**, *not deigning*, too dignified for such dialogue.

232. **matrona**: *i.e.* as a respectable matron, though dancing at a festival, will still preserve a proper decorum.

233. **pudibunda**, *with modesty*, so as not to drop to a level with the Satyric characters proper.

234. **dominantia**, *literal*, a translation (probably in a wrong sense) of κύριος, opposed to figurative expressions. — **nomina verbaque**: cf. *Sat.* I. 3. 103.

236. **differre**: *i.e.* in order to avoid the majestic style of Tragedy, one must not descend to the level of Comedy.

237. **Davus**, etc.: three characters of Comedy.

238. **emuncto**: a word borrowed from Comedy.

239. **Silenus**: cf. note to v. 226. — **alumni**: *i.e.* Bacchus.

240. **noto**: *i.e.* familiar words. — **quivis**: cf. quotations from Cicero under v. 46.

243. **accedit**, *is gained by; i.e.* comes from the appropriate use.

244. **Fauni**: *i.e.* Satyrs.

245. **innati triviis**, etc.: like the sharp fellows of the city. — **paene forenses**: almost like the rude *gamins* of the street.

246. **teneris**, *effeminate, dissolute*, as opposed to the healthy vigor of the rustic. Though these are merry rioters, yet they are to have the unspoiled virility of the country. They should be coarse, but not vicious. Cf. *teneri saltatores*, Cic. *in Pis.* XXXVI. 89, and the use of **mollis, fluens, fluxus**. — **iuvenentur**: cf. νεανιεύομαι, *frolic, wanton*.

247. **immunda**, *obscenities*. — **crepent**, *roll out*. — **ignominiosa**, *shameful* (to the speaker, or possi-

Offenduntur enim, quibus est equus et pater et res,
nec si quid fricti ciceris probat et nucis emptor,
aequis accipiunt animis donantve corona.
Syllaba longa brevi subiecta vocatur iambus,
pes citus; unde etiam trimetris accrescere iussit
nomen iambeis, cum senos redderet ictus,
primus ad extremum similis sibi: non ita pridem,
tardior ut paullo graviorque veniret ad aures,
spondeos stabilis in iura paterna recepit
commodus et patiens, non ut de sede secunda
cederet aut quarta socialiter. Hic et in Acci
nobilibus trimetris apparet rarus, et Enni

bly to the person addressed, like *billingsgate*).

248. **equus**: the allusion is to the *equus publicus* originally assigned to the *equites*.

249. **ciceris, nucis**: the food of the poorer classes; cf. *Sat.* II. 3. 182. These viands were sold in booths around the theatre; hence **emptor**.

250. **aequis animis**, *with favor*, or *approval*. — **corona**: the idea is derived from Greek contests, and is here only figuratively used.

251. **syllaba**, etc.: apparently an unnecessary explanation. But as Horace is going to discuss the strict metre of the Greeks as opposed to the license of the early Roman dramatists, it is not so unnatural for him to begin with a definition, especially as it is precisely the **syllaba brevis** that makes the difference.

252. **pes citus**: the same general idea is expressed in, *Sed sunt insignes percussiones eorum numerorum* (Iambic and Trochaic) *et minuti pedes*, Cic. *de Orat.* III. 47, 182. — **unde**: *i.e.* from the rapidity of the feet, and frequent occurrence of the ictus (cf. **percussiones**, above). — **trimetris**: cf. *nomen mihi Mercuriost.* — **accrescere**: *become attached.* — **iussit**: *i.e.* **pes citus**.

254. **iambeis**: as a noun, after **accrescere**. — **senos**: *i.e.* six feet with only three principal ictus, like music in $\frac{6}{8}$ time as opposed to $\frac{3}{8}$.

254. **primus**, etc.: *i.e.* pure iambs, as in the alternate lines of *Epode* XVI. — **non ita pridem**, etc.: Horace conceives the pure iambic as the original form of the verse, made more sonorous by the occasional spondee (so called) after the time of Archilochus; cf. v. 80.

256. **stabilis**, *stately*, steady-going.

257. **non ut**, *but not so as to*.

258. **socialiter**: only here, and of uncertain meaning; (probably), *as full allies, in equal partnership*, inasmuch as spondees are not *socii aequo iure*, but are excluded from certain places. — **hic**: the iambus. — **Acci**: cf. *Accius isdem aedilibus* (B.C. 140) *ait se et Pacuvium docuisse fabulam cum ille octoginta, ipse triginta annos natus esset*, Cic. *Brut.* LXIV. 229. Horace probably refers to him as the most learned of the early dramatists.

259. **Enni**, etc.: *i.e.* his power

in scaenam missos cum magno pondere versus
aut operae celeris nimium curaque carentis
aut ignoratae premit artis crimine turpi.
Non quivis videt immodulata poemata iudex,
et data Romanis venia est indigna poetis.
Idcircone vager scribamque licenter, an omnes
visuros peccata putem mea, tutus et intra
spem veniae cautus? Vitavi denique culpam,
non laudem merui. Vos exemplaria Graeca
nocturna versate manu, versate diurna.
  At vestri proavi Plautinos et numeros et
laudavere sales, nimium patienter utrumque,
ne dicam stulte, mirati, si modo ego et vos
scimus inurbanum lepido seponere dicto,
legitimumque sonum digitis callemus et aure.
Ignotum tragicae genus invenisse Camenae
dicitur et plaustris vexisse poemata Thespis,

ful lines are marred by carelessness or want of knowledge of art.

260. **cum magno pondere**: cf. **sine pondere**, II. 2. 112.

262. **premit**: *i.e.* the iambus, from its omission.

263. **non quivis**, etc.: *i.e.* but the Romans are not good judges of rhythm, and so the metrical faults of these early poets are pardoned.

264. **indigna**, *undeserved*, that ought not to have been granted.

265. **idcircone**: *i.e.* because others have been pardoned. — **vager**, *take liberties*. — **an**, *or rather*, the second alternative being preferred as usual.

267. **vitavi**, etc.: *i.e.* if I do exercise this care, I have after all deserved no credit, but only avoided blame, implying that it would be a disgrace to him not to do so.

268. **vos**, etc.: *i.e.* I recommend you to study the true models, and aim at something higher than merely escaping censure.

270. **at vestri**, etc.: a loose chapter in which the poet, being reminded by the mention of careless metre of the faults of Plautus in that regard, criticises the taste of the ancients on account of their admiration of the careless writing of Plautus. This admiration extended both to the verse and the wit of Plautus, and on both these points Horace finds him unworthy as a model. Giving a brief account of the rise of the drama, Horace comes to his ever-present idea that careful composition is the one indispensable virtue.

271. **patienter**, *with indulgence*.

273. **inurbanum**: *i.e.* coarse, unpolished, the characteristic of Plautus.

276. **Thespis**: cf. II. 1. 163. — **plaustris**: apparently an erroneous notion, to which Horace's words here have given currency.

quae canerent agerentque peruncti faecibus ora.
Post hunc, personae pallaeque repertor honestae,
Aeschylus et modicis instravit pulpita tignis
et docuit magnumque loqui nitique cothurno.
Successit vetus his comoedia, non sine multa
laude, sed in vitium libertas excidit et vim
dignam lege regi: lex est accepta chorusque
turpiter obticuit sublato iure nocendi.
Nil intentatum nostri liquere poetae;
nec minimum meruere decus vestigia Graeca
ausi deserere et celebrare domestica facta,
vel qui praetextas vel qui docuere togatas.
Nec virtute foret clarisve potentius armis
quam lingua Latium, si non offenderet unum-

277. **peruncti,** etc.: doubtless for the same purpose as the later masks, to prevent the recognition of the identity of the actor from destroying the illusion.

278. **personae,** etc.: Æschylus was supposed to be the inventor of the mask and other theatrical paraphernalia. The earlier performance was doubtless a mere merry-making, without special costume. Cf. Καὶ Αἰσχύλος δὲ οὐ μόνον ἔξευρε τὴν τῆς στολῆς εὐπρέπειαν, καὶ σεμνότητα, ἣν ζηλώσαντες (ζηλώσας ἣν) ἱεροφάνται καὶ δᾳδοῦχοι ἀμφιέννυνται. Athenæus I. 21.

279. **modicis**: as in a small theatre. — **pulpita**: *i.e.* the raised stage, as opposed to the earlier *θυμέλη*, or table of the single reciter. — **tignis**: *i.e.* the first stage was a temporary structure of wood. Cf. Müller, *Bühnenalterthümer*, p. 128 *seq.*

280. **magnum,** etc.: *i.e.* he introduced the dignity and solemnity of Tragedy.

281. **vetus**: cf. *Sat.* I. 4. 1.

282. **libertas**: cf. *Sat.* I. 4. 5; 3. 52, note.

283. **lex,** etc.: *i.e.* the law was passed and obeyed.

285. **nil,** etc.: a brief statement, of the adoption of the Greek drama by the Romans, and its attempted development.

287. **domestica facta**: *i.e.* the choice of Roman subjects.

288. **praetextas**: *i.e.* plays answering to Tragedy, as representing the acts of consuls and the like, clothed in the *toga praetexta.* Titles preserved are *Romulus* (Nævius), *Sabinae* (Ennius), *Aeneadae* (Accius), and others. — **docuere**: the regular word for producing a play. — **togatas**: plays on themes from common life (of persons clad in the ordinary toga). They correspond to the Greek Comedy as represented in the *palliatae* of Plautus and Terence, but there are traces of a chorus, or at least of a number of persons speaking in concert. Titles are *Augur, Libertus, Psaltria, Simulans, Brundisinae.*

290. **si non offenderet,** etc.: this brings Horace to the kernel of the whole, the want of care in writing

quemque poetarum limae labor et mora. Vos, o
Pompilius sanguis, carmen reprehendite, quod non
multa dies et multa litura coercuit atque
perfectum decies non castigavit ad unguem.
 Ingenium misera quia fortunatius arte
credit et excludit sanos Helicone poetas
Democritus, bona pars non unguis ponere curat,
non barbam; secreta petit loca, balnea vitat.
Nanciscetur enim pretium nomenque poetae,
si tribus Anticyris caput insanabile nunquam
tonsori Licino commiserit. O ego laevus,
qui purgor bilem sub verni temporis horam!
Non alius faceret meliora poemata. Verum
nil tanti est: ergo fungar vice cotis, acutum
reddere quae ferrum valet, exsors ipsa secandi:
munus et officium, nil scribens ipse, docebo,

which has prevented the Romans from excelling in art.

291. **limae**: cf. *limatior*, *Sat.* I. 10. 65.

293. **coercuit, castigavit**: the figure is from pruning.

294. **ad unguem**: cf. *Sat.* I. 5. 32. — **perfectum**: cf. v. 346. A reading **praesectum** has some authority, but seems to be ingeniously made out of **unguem**.

295. **ingenium misera**, etc.: a humorous development of v. 290. — **ingenium**, *genius*, as inborn and not cultivable by art. — **fortunatius**, *more successful*, as succeeding in literature better than study can.

296. **excludit**, etc.: cf. ὃς δ' ἂν ἄνευ μανίας Μουσῶν ἐπὶ ποιητικὰς θύρας ἀφίκηται . . . ἀτελὴς αὐτὸς, κτλ. Plato, *Phædr.* p. 245, and *saepe enim audivi poetam bonum neminem, id quod a Democrito et Platone in scriptis relictum esse dicunt, sine inflammatione animorum existere posse et sine quodam adflatu quasi furoris.* Cic. *de Or.* 46. 194; *de Div.* I. 37. Also *Sat.* I. 4. 34.

297. **bona pars**, etc.: *i.e.* poets put on the outward signs of madness, such as the neglect of their personal appearance, and the avoidance of society.

299. **nanciscetur**, etc.: as the poets think. — **pretium**: *i.e.* the honor.

300. **Anticyris**: cf. *Sat.* II. 3. 83.

301. **O ego**, etc.: the poet jocosely shows the folly of the idea in words which give an easy transition to his proposed theme, the requirements of poetry.

302. **bilem**: see Gr. § 240 c, note; cf. II. 2. 137. — **verni**: cf. Cels. II. 13.

303. **faceret**: *i.e.* if I omitted to take the anti-bilious treatment. — **verum**, etc.: *i.e.* but there is nothing I think so much of as guarding against insanity.

304. **ergo fungar**, etc.: *i.e.* being obliged by this prejudice to forego being a poet, I will content myself with showing others how to write.

306. **munus**, *function*, what is

unde parentur opes, quid alat formetque poetam,
quid deceat, quid non, quo virtus, quo ferat error.
Scribendi recte sapere est et principium et fons.
Rem tibi Socraticae poterunt ostendere chartae,
verbaque provisam rem non invita sequentur.
Qui didicit, patriae quid debeat et quid amicis,
quo sit amore parens, quo frater amandus et hospes,
quod sit conscripti, quod iudicis officium, quae
partes in bellum missi ducis, ille profecto
reddere personae scit convenientia cuique.
Respicere exemplar vitae morumque iubebo
doctum imitatorem et vivas hinc ducere voces.
Interdum speciosa locis morataque recte
fabula nullius veneris, sine pondere et arte,
valdius oblectat populum meliusque moratur
quam versus inopes rerum nugaeque canorae.
Graiis ingenium, Graiis dedit ore rotundo

necessary to give satisfaction to the hearer. — **officium,** *profession*, what the work itself demands, emphasizing the responsibility of the author. These ideas are not different, but, as often, the two phases of the same idea.

307. **unde parentur,** etc.: cf. vv. 309–322. — **quid alat,** etc.: cf. vv. 323–332.

308. **quid deceat,** etc.: cf. vv. 333–365. — **quo virtus,** etc.: cf. vv. 366–452. — **quo error**: cf. vv. 453–476.

309. **sapere**: with reference to v. 296.

310. **rem**: *material*, such as is described in v. 312 *seq.* — **Socraticae**: *i.e. philosophic*, but chiefly with reference to Ethics (cf. v. 312 *seq.*); see *Od.* I. 29. 14; III. 21. 9.

311. **verba**: etc.: cf. Cato's *rem tene, verba sequentur.*

315. **partes**: cf. I. 18. 14.

316. **reddere,** *assign*. The reference here, as for the most part throughout the epistle, is to dramatic poetry, in which characterization is of course the most important thing.

317. **exemplar,** etc.: in addition to philosophy the poet should study real life.

318. **imitatorem**: *delineator; i.e.* imitator of real life.

319. **speciosa locis**: *i.e.* with noble and pleasing sentiments (*communes loci*). — **morata recte**: *i.e.* with sound moral precepts suited to each character.

320. **sine pondere,** *without power; i.e.* to move the feelings, tame in the action, dull.

321. **moratur,** *holds*.

322. **rerum**: *i.e.* **sententiarum,** the same as the **loci** above, thoughts, sentiments, moral truths. — **nugae**: *i.e.* in so far as they have no moral purpose.

323. **Graiis,** etc.: the mention of **sententiae** leads Horace to account

Musa loqui, praeter laudem nullius avaris.
Romani pueri longis rationibus assem
discunt in partes centum diducere. 'Dicat
filius Albini: Si de quincunce remota est
uncia, quid superat? Poteras dixisse.' '*Triens.*' 'Eu!
rem poteris servare tuam! Redit uncia, quid fit?'
'*Semis.*' At haec animos aerugo et cura peculi
cum semel imbuerit, speramus carmina fingi
posse linenda cedro et levi servanda cupresso?
  Aut prodesse volunt, aut delectare poetae,
aut simul et iucunda et idonea dicere vitae.
Quicquid praecipies, esto brevis, ut cito dicta
percipiant animi dociles teneantque fideles.

for the superiority of the Greeks in genius. For it is their devotion to liberal arts, more especially philosophy, as opposed to the more commercial education of the Romans, that has caused this difference.

324. **avaris**: an anticipation of what Horace has in his mind from the first, that is, the sordid character he is going to assign to the Romans in the next verse. Of this the Greeks had nothing, except in regard to fame.

325. **longis**, etc.: *i.e.* what we call Vulgar Fractions, which would be learned at a very early age; hence the simplicity of the example.

326. **dicat**, etc.: an example of the principal teaching at Rome.

327. **Albini**: as the name is not a common one, it is probably that of a usurer, as Acron says. — **quincunce**: the calculation is in the complicated duodecimal system of of the Romans.

328. **poteras dixisse**, *come; you can tell.* The teacher encourages the pupil who hesitates for a moment. This hesitation accounts for the use of the imperfect **poteras**, *you could tell* (if you chose, or the like). Cf. *tempus erat*, *Od.* I. 37. 4. — **dixisse**: the perfect only for metrical reasons. — **triens**: one-third, *i.e.* four-twelfths. — **eu! rem**, etc.: the approval of the teacher, induced by the correct answer of the pupil. But there is also a moral approval; for if the boy understands fully that taking away a twelfth actually reduces the sum to a third, he is likely to look sharply after his fractional c[illegible]

329. **redit**: *is added*, a kind of passive of **reddo**. Cf. for red, also **redigo**, used of moneys.

330. **aerugo**, *gangrene*, properly *rust;* cf. *Sat.* I. 4. 101.

332. **linenda cedro**: *i.e.* to be preserved. The oil of cedar was used to keep off moths. — **cupresso**: the elegant bookcase suggests the value of the work.

333. **aut prodesse**, etc.: the beginning of the topic **quid deceat** (v. 308). This Horace treats under two heads, as to instruction and as to amusement.

335. **quicquid**, etc.: in reference to the **prodesse** and **idonea**.

Omne supervacuum pleno de pectore manat.
Ficta voluptatis causa sint proxima veris,
ne quodcumque velit poscat sibi fabula credi,
neu pransae Lamiae vivum puerum extrahat alvo.
Centuriae seniorum agitant expertia frugis;
celsi praetereunt austera poemata Ramnes:
omne tulit punctum qui miscuit utile dulci
lectorem delectando pariterque monendo.
Hic meret aera liber Sosiis, hic et mare transit
et longum noto scriptori prorogat aevum.
Sunt delicta tamen quibus ignovisse velimus.
Nam neque chorda sonum reddit, quem volt manus et
mens,

337. **omne supervacuum,** etc.: *i.e.* as everything additional overflows after a vessel is full, so if precepts are too long, they "go in at one ear and out at the other."

338. **ficta,** etc.: in reference to the **delectare** and **iucunda.** — **proxima veris**: an exhortation to realism in art.

339. **ne quodcumque,** etc.: *i.e.* too wild an imagination must not be indulged. — **fabula,** *a play,* which Horace has always in mind throughout, though not exclusively.

340. **Lamiae,** *an ogress,* a monster of Libya supposed to feed on children, and used as a bugbear. She was probably introduced on the stage in the Atellane farces, and perhaps in this very situation. Cf. Aristoph. *Wasps,* 1177. See Diod. Sic. XX. 41.

341. **centuriae seniorum,** etc.: a reason for combining the profitable and pleasing. — **seniorum,** *veterans,* in allusion to the divisions of the Servian constitution, cf. II. 1. 81, 85. — **agitant**: *i.e.* reject, cf. 456. — **expertia frugis**: *i.e.* a play that has no edification in it.

342. **celsi,** *high-spirited,* as disdaining instruction with the arrogant spirit of youth. — **austera**: *i.e.* containing only instruction. — **Ramnes,** *young nobles,* as bent on pleasure only. The word is used in allusion to the earliest *equites,* who consisted of the juniors of the first families. One branch of these *equites* were Ramnes. See Lange, *Röm. Alterth.* I. 353. Also Livy, I. 13.

343. **omne,** etc.: *i.e.* by combining the two excellences, an author carries all the votes of both the parties mentioned. — **tulit**: see Harpers' Dictionary, *s.v.* II. B. 4. — **punctum**: cf. II. 2. 99 and note.

345. **meret,** etc.: *i.e.* it sells well. — **Sosiis**: cf. I. 20. 2 and note. — **mare transit**: cf. I. 20. 13, but here the same idea has a different turn.

347. **sunt delicta,** etc.: as in Horace's mind every rule of conduct has its opposite phase, so here he warns against drawing the line of propriety too closely. *Vitiis nemo sine nascitur,* either in conduct or in art. Cf. *Sat.* I. 3. 68.

348. **chorda,** etc.: a figure drawn from the lyre.

poscentique gravem persaepe remittit acutum,
nec semper feriet, quodcumque minabitur arcus.
Verum ubi plura nitent in carmine, non ego paucis
offendar maculis, quas aut incuria fudit,
aut humana parum cavit natura. Quid ergo est?
Vt scriptor si peccat idem librarius usque,
quamvis est monitus, venia caret, et citharoedus
ridetur chorda qui semper oberrat eadem,
sic mihi, qui multum cessat, fit Choerilus ille,
quem bis terve bonum cum risu miror; et idem
indignor quandoque bonus dormitat Homerus.
Verum operi longo fas est obrepere somnum.
Vt pictura, poesis; erit quae, si propius stes,
te capiat magis, et quaedam, si longius abstes.
Haec amat obscurum; volet haec sub luce videri,
iudicis argutum quae non formidat acumen;
haec placuit semel, haec deciens repetita placebit.

350. **minabitur**: *sc.* **ferire**.

351. **plura**, etc.: cf. *si modo plura mihi bona sunt, Sat.* I. 3. 71.

353. **humana**: with emphasis; the necessary failings of human nature.—**quid ergo est**: *what shall we say then?* (cf. *Romans* VI. 1), a correction of the inference which might be drawn from the above leniency.

357. **multum cessat**: *i.e.* is ever negligent.—**Choerilus**: cf. II. 1. 233.

358. **bis terve bonum**: *i.e.* it is a matter of proportion.—**miror**: *i.e.* I marvel that he should happen to succeed once or twice, and laugh at the odd accident.

359. **indignor**, *feel pained*, because I should have expected better of him. The two feelings thus contrasted show Horace's general estimate of the two poets; a good thing in Chœrilus makes him laugh, it is so unexpected, and for the same reason a bad thing in Homer makes him indignant.

360. **verum operi longo**: *i.e.* there is an excuse for Homer in the length of his work.—**somnum**, *a sleepy moment.*

361. **ut pictura**, etc.: *i.e.* a work of art should be judged like a picture, not by an immutable criterion, but in reference to its character and scope. Tintoretto and Holbein are not expected to have the same touch. All this applies also to poetry.

363. **amat obscurum**: *i.e.* ***needs** a dim light.*

365. **semel, deciens**: *i.e.* a picture, for instance, to be seen once at some festival would need a different treatment from a permanent work of art.

O maior iuvenum, quamvis et voce paterna
fingeris ad rectum et per te sapis, hoc tibi dictum
tolle memor, certis medium et tolerabile rebus
recte concedi: consultus iuris et actor
causarum mediocris abest virtute diserti
Messalae, nec scit quantum Cascellius Aulus,
sed tamen in pretio est; mediocribus esse poetis
non homines, non di, non concessere columnae.
Vt gratas inter mensas symphonia discors
et crassum unguentum et Sardo cum melle papaver
offendunt, poterat duci quia cena sine istis:
sic animis natum inventumque poema iuvandis,
si paullum summo decessit, vergit ad imum.
Ludere qui nescit, campestribus abstinet armis,
indoctusque pilae discive trochive quiescit,
ne spissae risum tollant impune coronae;

366. **O maior iuvenum**, etc.: a development of **quo virtus, quo ferat error** (308). First, a natural gift is necessary. We know too little of the persons addressed to say why the elder son is selected here, but one might almost suppose that Horace thought his vocation doubtful. It is possible, however, that the boy had only come to the age when it was necessary to determine his ability. This last supposition would account for **quamvis et voce**, etc., as well as for v. 385.

368. **certis rebus**: *i.e.* such as he enumerates in the next three verses. Cf. Cic. *de Orat.* I. 26. 118.

370. **abest**: *i.e.* may be, etc., a simple statement, as often in suppositions.

371. **Messalae**: cf. *Sat.* I. 10. 29; *Od.* III. 21. — **scit**: *i.e.* as a lawyer. — **Cascellius**: a famous jurisconsult; cf. Val. Max. VI. 2. 12.

372. **mediocribus**: cf. *tribuno*, *Sat.* I. 6. 25.

373. **di**: cf. *dis hominibusque invitis*, Cic. *ad Q. Frat.* III. 2, evidently a proverbial expression. — **columnae**: *i.e.* the booksellers, whose wares were exposed for sale on pillars in front of their booths. Cf. *pila*, *Sat.* I. 4. 71.

374. **symphonia**, *music*, not a necessity, but a luxury.

375. **crassum**, *coarse*, and so not well prepared. — **Sardo**: the honey of Sardinia was said to be bitter; cf. *melle Corsico quod asperrimum habetur*, Plin. *H.N.* XXX. 28. (10). — **papaver**: cf. (*Papaveris*) *semen tostum in secunda mensa cum melle apud antiquos dabatur*, Plin. *H.N.* XIX. 168. (53).

376. **duci**: cf. *producimus*, *Sat.* I. 5. 70.

379. **campestribus**: cf. I. 18. 54.

380. **pilae**: cf. *Sat.* I. 5. 48 *seq.* — **disci**, etc.: cf. *Sat.* II. 2. 13. — **trochi**: cf. *Od.* III. 24. 57.

381. **spissae**: cf. v. 205. and I. 19. 41. — **impune**, *without re-*

qui nescit versus, tamen audet fingere. 'Quidni?
Liber et ingenuus, praesertim census equestrem
summam nummorum, vitioque remotus ab omni.'
Tu nihil invita dices faciesve Minerva;
id tibi iudicium est, ea mens: si quid tamen olim
scripseris, in Maeci descendat iudicis auris
et patris et nostras, nonumque prematur in annum,
membranis intus positis. Delere licebit
quod non edideris; nescit vox missa reverti.
Silvestris homines sacer interpresque deorum
caedibus et victu foedo deterruit Orpheus,
dictus ob hoc lenire tigris rabidosque leones.
Dictus et Amphion Thebanae conditor urbis

*straint,* which nobody would have a right to hinder. — **coronae**: cf. I. 18. 53.

382. **quidni**, etc.: an ironical suggestion that any free citizen with a competence and a good moral character can write.

383. **ingenuus**, *a gentleman; i.e.* not only a free citizen, but the son of a free father. — **census**, *with a fortune of,* or *assessed for.* — **equestrem**: cf. I. 1. 58 and note.

384. **summam**: governed by **census**, used after the analogy of verbs taking a double accusative.

385. **invita**: cf. **di**, v. 373, and *quia nihil decet invita (ut aiunt) Minerva, id est adversante et repugnante natura,* Cic. *Off.* I. 31. 110.

386. **iudicium**: cf. v. 367. — **mens**, *purpose; i.e.* you have the good judgment and (at present) a fixed purpose, etc.

387. **Maeci**: cf. *Sat.* I. 10. 38. — **in aures**, etc.: *i.e.* seek the most rigid criticism.

388. **nonum**: not to be taken too literally, but there is perhaps an allusion to the *Smyrna* of Helvius Cinna, which was nine years in the making. See Catull. 95. 1. Wieland takes the words as intended to dissuade the young man from publishing. But this Horace would be likely to do privately, rather than in an open letter.

391. **silvestris**, etc.: a defence of the dignity of poetry. It must be remembered that the practical Roman regarded everything but war, statesmanship, and money-making as idle and unmanly employments, and hence even Cicero has to defend his interest in these *leviores artes* (as in *pro Arch.* 12 *seq.*). — **sacer**: the early poets were regarded as inspired (cf. Virg. *Æn.* VI. 662 and 645), and had in all literature a kind of superhuman character; cf. *vate sacro, Od.* IV. 9. 28.

392. **victu foedo**: *i.e.* the rude subsistence consisting of the natural growth of trees. Cf. *Sat.* I. 3. 100. — **Orpheus**: cf. Virg. *Æn.* VI. 645; Aristoph. *Frogs,* 1032.

393. **ob hoc**, etc.: *i.e.* Horace explains the myths about Orpheus as referring to his taming the savage hearts of men.

394. **Amphion**: cf. I. 18. 41.

saxa movere sono testudinis et prece blanda
ducere quo vellet. Fuit haec sapientia quondam,
publica privatis secernere, sacra profanis,
concubitu prohibere vago, dare iura maritis,
oppida moliri, leges incidere ligno.
Sic honor et nomen divinis vatibus atque
carminibus venit. Post hos insignis Homerus
Tyrtaeusque mares animos in Martia bella
versibus exacuit; dictae per carmina sortes,
et vitae monstrata via est; et gratia regum
Pieriis tentata modis, ludusque repertus
et longorum operum finis: ne forte pudori
sit tibi Musa lyrae sollers et cantor Apollo.
  Natura fieret laudabile carmen an arte
quaesitum est: ego nec studium sine divite vena,
nec rude quid possit video ingenium; alterius sic
altera poscit opem res, et coniurat amice.
Qui studet optatam cursu contingere metam,
multa tulit fecitque puer, sudavit et alsit;

395. **testudinis**: cf. *Od.* I. 32. 14. — **prece blanda**: *i.e.* the persuasive accents of his song; cf. *Od.* I. 24. 13.

396. **fuit haec sapientia**: *i.e.* such acts as those of Orpheus and Amphion were regarded as wisdom, inasmuch as they gave civilization to mankind. Cf. Cic. *de Am.* 2. 6 and 7.

397. **publica**, etc.: cf. Horace's account of the origin of society. *Sat.* I. 3. 99.

399. **ligno**: alluding to the ἄξονες, the wooden tablets of the laws at Athens. Cf. Plut. *Solon*, 25.

400. **sic**, etc.: *i.e.* inasmuch as the poets performed these services, they were regarded with reverence.

402. **post hos**, etc.: *i.e.* the next service to mankind was that of Homer and Tyrtæus in inspiring men to warlike deeds by their poems.

403. **sortes**: *i.e.* oracles were in poetical form.

404. **vitae via**, etc.: referring to the didactic and gnomic poets, Hesiod and the like. — **gratia regum**: alluding to lyric poets, who flourished at the courts of monarchs.

405. **Pieriis**: cf. *Od.* IV. 3. 18. — **ludus**: *i.e.* dramatic poetry; cf. II. 1. 140.

406. **finis**: cf. II. 1. 141. — **ne forte**: cf. I. 1. 13, note.

408. **natura**, etc.: cf. v. 295.

409. **nec studium**, etc.: cf. Cicero's view, in *pro Archia*, 15, so also *Od.* IV. 4. 33. — **vena**: cf. *Od.* II. 18. 10.

410. **rude**, *raw.*

412. **qui studet**, etc.: a confirmatory parallel from gymnastic art.

abstinuit venere et vino. Qui Pythia cantat
tibicen, didicit prius extimuitque magistrum.
Nunc satis est dixisse: 'Ego mira poemata pango;
occupet extremum scabies; mihi turpe relinqui est
et quod non didici sane nescire fateri.'
  Vt praeco ad merces turbam qui cogit emendas,
adsentatores iubet ad lucrum ire poeta
dives agris, dives positis in faenore nummis.
Si vero est unctum qui recte ponere possit,
et spondere levi pro paupere, et eripere atris
litibus implicitum, mirabor, si sciet inter-
noscere mendacem verumque beatus amicum.
Tu seu donaris, seu quid donare voles cui,
nolito ad versus tibi factos ducere plenum

414. **qui . . . cantat**, etc.: another parallel from music. — **Pythia**: referring to the musical contests at the Greek games; cf. *Olympia*, I. 1. 50.

416. **nunc**, etc.: *i.e.* but now we have changed all that, and everybody enters the race and is ashamed to be left behind. — **ego mira**, etc.: *i.e.* go to, I'll rhyme it with the best, and the Devil take the hindmost.

417. **occupet**, etc.: evidently a children's challenge in a game: cf. "Last in bed put out the light."

418. **sane**, *at all*, cf. I. 7. 61. The whole is a repetition of the theme in v. 382 *seq.*

419. **ut praeco**, etc.: a warning against flattery; cf. v. 387 *seq.*

420. **ad lucrum ire**: *i.e.* the auctioneer bids the people come and make their fortune by great bargains, and so the rich author tacitly says to his flattering hearers that it will be their gain.

421. **dives agris**, etc.: repeated from *Sat.* I. 2. 13.

422. **si vero est**: opposed to **tu**, etc.; *i.e.* such a man can hardly tell the difference between the true friend and the flatterer, so it isn't much use to warn him; but *you* must be on your guard. Cf. Cicero's picture of the *assentator*, *de Am.* 25. 94 *seq.* — **unctum**: cf. *Sat.* II. 6. 64, and *Ep.* I. 14. 21, I. 15. 44. — **recte**, *in style*. — **ponere**: cf. *Sat.* II. 2. 23. — **possit**: it is implied also that he can descend to such means.

423. **spondere**: *i.e.* become his security on one of the numerous occasions where that service was required; cf. II. 2. 67. — **levi**: *i.e.* *humble, irresponsible;* cf. *gravis auctor* and the like. — **atris**, *dismal;* *i.e.* harassing, worrying; cf. **atra cura**.

425. **beatus**, *tickled with men's praise*, but cf. II. 2. 108.

426. **donaris** (fut. perf.): *i.e.* if you have already a *protégé*.

427. **nolito**, etc.: *i.e.* amid the pleasures of the table, when the poet is made happy by your entertainment.

laetitiae; clamabit enim 'pulchre! bene! recte!'
pallescet super his; etiam stillabit amicis
ex oculis rorem, saliet, tundet pede terram.
Vt qui conducti plorant in funere, dicunt
et faciunt prope plura dolentibus ex animo, sic
derisor vero plus laudatore movetur.
Reges dicuntur multis urgere culullis
et torquere mero quem perspexisse laborant,
an sit amicitia dignus: si carmina condes,
nunquam te fallant animi sub volpe latentes.
Quintilio si quid recitares, 'Corrige sodes
hoc,' aiebat, 'et hoc:' melius te posse negares
bis terque expertum frustra, delere iubebat
et male tornatos incudi reddere versus.
Si defendere delictum quam vertere malles,
nullum ultra verbum aut operam insumebat inanem,
quin sine rivali teque et tua solus amares.
Vir bonus et prudens versus reprehendet inertes,
culpabit duros, incomptis adlinet atrum

429. **pallescet**: *i.e.* with interest in the poem. — **super his**, *besides;* see *Sat.* II. 6. 3 (but cf. II. 1. 152).

430. **saliet**, etc.: of the guest's extreme enthusiasm over the work.

433. **derisor**: *i.e.* the parasite who makes sport by excessive flattery. Cf. *Sat.* II. 8. 65 *seq.*

434. **reges**, etc.: *i.e.* instead of using your wine and dainties to extract insincere praise, do as kings are wont, use the bowl to discover whether admirers are honest; cf. *laetitiae*, v. 428.

435. **torquere**: cf. I. 18. 38; *Sat.* I. 4. 89. — **laborant**: cf. I. 3. 2.

437. **fallant**: hortatory.

438. **Quintilio**: Quintilius Varus (cf. *Od.* I. 24. 5), an example of a sincere friend and critic, such as one ought to choose. — **recitares**: general condition in the second person singular, thrown into past time.

439. **negares**: hortatory subjunctive used as a condition, thrown into past time.

440. **bis terque**, etc.: *i.e.* after trying several times.

441. **incudi reddere**: *i.e.* to forge them all over anew.

442. **malles**: cf. note to **negares**.

444. **quin**: on account of the idea of hindrance in the preceding verse. — **sine rivali**: *i.e.* as Cicero says of Pompey, "in love with himself without a rival," *ad Q. Frat.* III. 8. 4.

445. **vir bonus et prudens**: *i.e.* a friend who is both honest and wise when applied to as a critic.

transverso calamo signum, ambitiosa recidet
ornamenta, parum claris lucem dare coget,
arguet ambigue dictum, mutanda notabit,
fiet Aristarchus, nec dicet, 'Cur ego amicum
offendam in nugis?' Hae nugae seria ducent
in mala derisum semel exceptumque sinistre.
Vt mala quem scabies aut morbus regius urget,
aut fanaticus error et iracunda Diana,
vesanum tetigisse timent fugiuntque poetam
qui sapiunt, agitant pueri incautique sequuntur.
Hic, dum sublimis versus ructatur et errat,
si veluti merulis intentus decidit auceps
in puteum foveamve; licet 'Succurrite' longum
clamet 'io cives,' non sit qui tollere curet.
Si curet quis opem ferre et demittere funem,
'Qui scis an prudens huc se proiecerit atque

447. **transverso**: *i.e.* crossing out. — **calamo**: the reference here is to writing with a pen, as above in **delere** to writing with a *stilus*. — **ambitiosa**: not merely *ambitious* in our sense, but with the figure still alive, courting admiration by the use of forced expressions, *ostentatious*.

450. **Aristarchus**: the great Alexandrine critic of Homer, whose name had become proverbial. Cf. Cic. *ad Att.* I. 14. 3.

451. **nugis**: *i.e.* slight faults.

452. **derisum semel**, etc.: *i.e.* in his public appearance, inasmuch as these faults will hazard the poet's reputation.

453. **ut mala**, etc.: *i.e.* the faults will make men avoid the poet as if he had a contagious disease or a frenzy. — **morbus regius**: *i.e.* the jaundice, regarded as contagious.

454. **Diana**: the Thracian Brauronia, identified with Artemis, and so with Diana, was supposed to cause madness in those who offended her; cf. Soph. *Ajax*, 172.

456. **agitant**, etc.: cf. *Sat.* II. 3. 130, and I. 3. 134. The worrying of a crazy man by the street Arabs seems to have been a common joke in all ages.

459. **longum**: *i.e.* so as to be heard afar. Cf. the Scotch "a far cry."

460. **clamet**: cf. I. 17. 60. — **non sit**: amounting to an imperative, whether it is directly hortatory (as in I. 18. 72) or in the "potential" construction in accordance with **timent**, v. 455, implying "no wise man," etc.

461. **si curet**, etc.: *i.e.* the fellow is so foolish, the presumption is that he wished to destroy himself like Empedocles.

462. **qui scis an**, *how do you know but?* with the affirmative idea contained in **nescio an**, etc.

servari nolit?' dicam, Siculique poetae
narrabo interitum. 'Deus immortalis haberi
dum cupit Empedocles, ardentem frigidus Aetnam
insiluit. Sit ius liceatque perire poetis.
Invitum qui servat, idem facit occidenti.
Nec semel hoc fecit, nec, si retractus erit, iam
fiet homo et ponet famosae mortis amorem.
Nec satis apparet, cur versus factitet; utrum
minxerit in patrios cineres, an triste bidental
moverit incestus: certe furit, ac velut ursus
obiectos caveae valuit si frangere clatros,
indoctum doctumque fugat recitator acerbus;
quem vero arripuit, tenet occiditque legendo,
non missura cutem, nisi plena cruoris, hirudo.'

463. **Siculique poetae**: Empedocles who, according to the story which Horace gives, threw himself into the crater of Ætna in order to disappear miraculously.

465. **dum cupit**, etc.: cf. I. 2. 21 and note. — **frigidus**: a grim joke. Empedocles is called cold as opposed to the fire of Ætna, implying that his act was done without excitement, in cold blood; cf. the uses of *calidus*.

467. **idem**: *i.e.* just as much, an equal outrage. — **occidenti**, governed by **idem**, in imitation of a Greek construction. This is the only spondaic verse in Horace.

468. **nec semel**, etc.: *i.e.* this isn't the first time, and in a confirmed case there is no hope of his recovery; 'he is joined to his idols, let him alone.'

470. **nec satis**, etc.: *i.e.* we cannot account for his madness, it is true, but he is certainly raving, and is avoided by everybody just as if he were a wild animal. If, however, he catches anybody, he sticks to him like a leech. So with this jocose view of the poetic craze Horace closes the epistle.

ANNOUNCEMENTS

# COLLEGE SERIES OF LATIN AUTHORS

Edited under the Supervision of CLEMENT LAWRENCE SMITH, recently Professor of Latin in Harvard University, and TRACY PECK, Emeritus Professor of the Latin Language and Literature in Yale University

---

CATULLUS, Edited by Professor Elmer T. Merrill of The University of Chicago. l + 273 pages . . . . . . . . . . . . . . . . . . . . $1.40

CICERO, BRUTUS OF. Edited by Martin Kellogg, late of the University of California. xxix + 196 pages . . . . . . . . . . . . . . . . 1.25

CICERO, SELECTED LETTERS. Edited by Professor Frank F. Abbott of Princeton University. lxxvi + 315 pages . . . . . . . . . . . 1.25

CICERO, TUSCULAN DISPUTATIONS (BOOK I), AND THE SOMNIUM SCIPIONIS. Edited by Professor Frank Ernest Rockwood of Bucknell University. xliv + 109 + xiii + 22 pages . . . . . . . . . . 1.00

HORACE, ODES AND EPODES (REVISED EDITION). Edited by Professor Clement L. Smith, late of Harvard University. lxxxvii + 443 pages . . . . . . . . . . . . . . . . . . . . . . . . . . . 1.50

HORACE, ODES AND EPODES, SATIRES AND EPISTLES. Professor Smith's Edition of "Odes and Epodes" and Professor Greenough's Edition of "Satires and Epistles," in One Volume. lxxvii + 404 + 306 pages . . . . . . . . . . . . . . . . . . . . . . . . . 2.00

HORACE, SATIRES AND EPISTLES. Edited by the late Professor J. B. Greenough of Harvard University. ix + 306 pages . . . . . . . . 1.25

JUVENAL, SATIRES. Edited by Professor Henry P. Wright of Yale University. xliv + 240 pages . . . . . . . . . . . . . . . . . . 1.25

LIVY, BOOKS I AND II. Edited by the late Professor J. B. Greenough of Harvard University. xvii + 270 pages . . . . . . . . . . . . . 1.25

LIVY, BOOKS XXI AND XXII. Edited by the late Professor J. B. Greenough of Harvard University, and Emeritus Professor Tracy Peck of Yale University. xiv + 232 pages . . . . . . . . . . . . . . . 1.25

LIVY, BOOKS I, XXI, AND XXII. Edited by the late Professor J. B. Greenough of Harvard University, and Emeritus Professor Tracy Peck of Yale University. xvii + 379 pages . . . . . . . . . . . 1.35

LIVY, BOOKS I, II, XXI, AND XXII. Professor Greenough's Edition of Books I and II, and Professor Greenough and Professor Peck's Edition of Books XXI and XXII, in One Volume. xvii + 270 + xiv + 232 pages 1.50

MARTIAL, SELECTED EPIGRAMS. Edited by Professor Edwin Post of De Pauw University. li + 402 pages . . . . . . . . . . . . . 1.50

PLAUTUS, CAPTIVES AND TRINUMMUS. Edited by Professor E. P. Morris of Yale University. xxxviii + 185 pages . . . . . . . . . . . . 1.25

TACITUS, ANNALS, BOOKS I–VI. Edited by the late Professor W. F. Allen of the University of Wisconsin. xlii + 444 pages . . . . . . . . . 1.50

TACITUS, DIALOGUS DE ORATORIBUS. Edited by Professor Charles E. Bennett of Cornell University. xxviii + 87 pages . . . . . . . . .75

# ALLEN AND GREENOUGH'S

# CAESAR: GALLIC WAR

*REVISED EDITION*

Edited by JAMES B. GREENOUGH, late Professor of Latin in Harvard University B. L. D'OOGE, Professor of Latin and Greek in Michigan State Normal College, Ypsilanti, and M. GRANT DANIELL, late Principal of Chauncy-Hall School, Boston

BOOKS I–V. 12mo, half leather, lix + 268 + 162 pages, illustrated, $1.00
BOOKS I–VII. 12mo, half leather, lx + 616 pages, illustrated, $1.25

THIS new edition of Caesar's "Gallic War" keeps prominently in view the needs of the beginner, on the ground that a large majority of those who read Caesar take it up immediately after finishing their first lessons. It is believed that all this class of students' needs have been fully met in the present edition.

Professor Greenough has specially qualified himself for editing this edition by traveling and making recent investigations in France. Not only the Notes but the illustrations have profited greatly. A considerable number of the pictures in this edition are from photographs made especially for it. In other cases, pictures not previously seen in this country have been obtained. The museums have been visited and many new illustrations drawn from them. At the same time all the standard and essential illustrations are used. It is believed that this part of the editing will be found of signal excellence and practical value.

Several reading courses are suggested, each one of which, while embracing an amount of text equal to the first four books, contains choice selections of narrative and adventure from the various books. It is believed that this feature will be especially acceptable to teachers who have found the monotony of Caesar irksome but have seen no way to vary the course.

Except in amount of Latin text, the four-book edition is practically identical with the new edition of the complete Caesar's "Gallic War." It contains the Introduction, with the exception of two irrelevant pages, the groups of related words, and the full Vocabulary. Many of the illustrations of Books V, VI, and VII are inserted at the close, in order to explain graphically a number of the references in the Introduction and in the Notes. Quantities of long vowels are marked.



GINN & COMPANY PUBLISHERS